Southern Living®

ANNUAL RECIPES
MASTER INDEX

1979-2005

Oxmoor House®

ISBN: 0-8487-3113-1
ISSN: 0272-2003

Printed in the United States of America
First printing 2006

To order additional publications, call 1-800-765-6400.

For more books to enrich your life, visit **oxmoorhouse.com**

Oxmoor House, Inc.
Editor in Chief: Nancy Fitzpatrick Wyatt
Executive Editor: Susan Carlisle Payne
Copy Chief: Allison Long Lowery

Southern Living®
Executive Editor: Susan Dosier

Southern Living® Annual Recipes Master Index 1979-2005
Editor: Susan Ray
Copy Editor: Donna Baldone
Designer: Donna Sophronia-Sims
Director of Production: Laura Lockhart
Production Manager: Amorice K. Nall
Production Assistant: Faye Porter Bonner

Contributor
Indexer: Mary Ann Laurens

INTRODUCTION

Thousands of kitchen-tested recipes have appeared in *Southern Living* magazine over the years. When readers call us asking for help finding recipes, this *Annual Recipes Master Index* is what we use to find the answer.

We've cross-referenced every recipe in the *Southern Living® Annual Recipes* collection by the type of dish and by one or more of its main ingredients. The handy step-by-step reference on the following page gives simple instructions on how to find the recipe you want—quickly and easily.

This volume puts your favorite recipes and food columns—and new ones to treasure—at your fingertips.

Occasionally, you'll find that the same recipe appears in different volumes of *Southern Living® Annual Recipes*. There's a simple reason: A recipe may appear in the magazine edition for one state before it appears in the edition for another state. This index gives all of the page references to those bonus recipes that have appeared in more than one edition of the magazine. It also lists those recipes featured in our *Southern Living® Favorites, Southern Living® Cooking School,* and *Southern Living® Cook-Off* bonus sections.

You can also find favorite recipes under the headings of our monthly food columns, past and present. Under "From Our Kitchen," you'll find a handy reference to helpful hints and Test Kitchens secrets. Recipes under the headings "Quick & Easy" and "What's for Supper?" will help you get dinner on the table in a hurry. If you're searching for true regional fare, look no further than "Taste of the South." The name of our light section has changed over time, but now you can find recipes from past "On the Light Side," "Cooking Light," and "Living Light" columns under "Healthy & Light."

We hope you'll be pleased with this cumulative index of our recipes. Use this cook's companion to find the perfect recipe for any occasion in just seconds.

Susan Dosier

Susan Dosier
Executive Editor, *Southern Living*

HOW TO FIND A RECIPE—FAST

Look for the main ingredient in the recipe you want or even the basic type of dish it is (appetizer, cookie, etc.). You can find it either way in this cross-referenced index. Use the step-by-step guide below to help you find a recipe in record time.

1. *As you turn through the index, "continued" lines in the upper left corner remind you of the current category.*

2. *Main categories help you cross-reference each recipe by the type of dish and one or more of its main ingredients.*

3. *Boldfaced subcategories help you scan for a recipe through long main categories.*

POTATOES, Stuffed
(continued)

    Vegetable-Topped Stuffed Potatoes, **'85** 235
    Yogurt-Stuffed Potatoes, **'88** 24
    Zesty Stuffed Potatoes, **'94** M46
Tacos, Breakfast, **'91** 316
Tortilla Campesina, **'89** 85
Tortilla Española, **'92** 175
Vinaigrette, Potato-Broccoli, **'85** 84
Wedges, Lemon Potato, **'88** 21
Wedges, Lemony Potato, **'90** M61

PRALINE. *See also* **CANDIES/Pralines.**
Almonds, Praline, **'97** 285
Bananas, Praline, **'84** 313
Brownies, Praline, **'93** 243
Buns, Praline, **'90** 195
Buttercream, Praline, **'95** 243
Cake, Praline, **'81** 162
Cake, Praline Ice Cream, **'80** 84
Cake, Praline Pound, **'82** 88
Cheesecake, Praline, **'83** 270; **'89** 93
Coffee, Praline, **'97** 17
Coffee, Praline-Flavored, **'87** 69
Compote, Warm Praline Fruit, **'85** 260
Cookies, Praline, **'91** 271
Cookies, Praline Shortbread, **'88** 242
Cookies, Praline Thumbprint, **'89** 328
Filling, Praline, **'89** 328
Freeze, Praline, **'89** 60; **'90** 48
Glaze, Apple-Stuffed Tenderloin with
    Praline-Mustard, **'97** 216
Glaze, Praline, **'82** 196
Ham, Praline, **'85** 302; **'96** 303
Horns, Praline, **'96** 316
Ice Cream, Praline, **'89** 318
Ice Cream, Pralines and Cream, **'82** 184; **'83** 159
Pastries, Praline, **'89** 318
Pecans, Praline, **'97** 285
Pie, Chocolate-Praline, **'86** 259
Pie, Frosty Pumpkin-Praline, **'91** M234
Pie, Peach Praline, **'89** 136
Pie, Pear-Praline, **'97** 192
Pie, Pumpkin Praline, **'80** 244
Powder, Praline, **'95** 243
Sauce, Bourbon Praline, **'81** 170
Sauce, Chocolate-Praline, **'85** M295
Sauce, Peach-Praline, **'85** 161
Sauce, Praline, **'83** 25; **'84** 143; **'89** 95; **'92** 282;
    '93 214; **'94** 206, 312; **'96** 285
Sauce, Praline Ice Cream, **'85** 189
Sauce, Southern Praline Ice Cream, **'86** M227
Toast, Orange Praline, **'79** 36
Torte, Chocolate Praline, **'84** 165
Torte, Lucy's Apricot Praline, **'95** 243

PRETZELS
Brownies, Saucepan Pretzel, **'85** 171
Chocolate-Covered Pretzels, **'82** 295
Dressing, Pretzel, **'86** 280
Frosted Pretzels, **'92** 280
Garlands, Pretzel, **'93** 286
Herb Pretzels with Lower Sodium
    Horseradish Mustard, **'86** 325
Homemade Pretzels, **'84** 159; **'91** 185
Popcorn, Pretzel, **'84** 30
Soft Pretzels, **'83** 18
Soft Pretzels, Chewy, **'87** 159
Whole Wheat Pretzels, **'89** 20

PRUNES
Bavarian, Prune, **'86** 223
Bread, Prune-Nut, **'87** 255; **'91** 55
Butter, Prune-Orange, **'92** 49
Cake and Sauce, Prune, **'85** 118
Cake, Prune, **'85** 223
Cake, Spicy Prune, **'79** 136
Chicken with Prunes, Saffron, **'97** 264
Compote, Baked Prune, **'94** 50
Muffins, Miniature Prune, **'85** 223
Muffins, Spicy Prune, **'97** 271
Muffins, Wheat Germ-Prune, **'81** 106
Pork Chops Stuffed with Prunes, **'84** 7
Pork Loin Roast, Prune-Stuffed, **'80** 29
Raspberry Prunes, **'82** 124
Relish, Peppy Prune, **'90** 227
Spiced Prunes, Orange-, **'85** 224
Stuffed Prunes, **'85** 47
Tarts, Brandied Prune, **'85** 223
Tzimmes, **'95** 102

PUDDINGS. *See also* **CUSTARDS, MOUSSES.**
Apple-Nut Pudding with Hot Rum Sauce, **'79** 86
Applesauce-Graham Cracker Pudding, **'81** 34
Banana
    Almost Banana Pudding, **'88** 174
    Banana Pudding, **'82** 53; **'84** 94; **'85** 255;
        '88 16, 32
    Basic Banana Pudding, **'81** 59
    Creamy Banana Pudding, **'89** M130
    Delicious Banana Pudding, **'80** 9
    Fudge-Banana Pudding, **'97** 331
    Mallow Pudding, Banana-, **'86** 139
    No-Bake Banana Pudding, **'91** 172
    Old-Fashioned Banana Pudding, **'92** 94
    Peanut Butter-Banana Pudding, **'93** 340
    Pops, Banana Pudding Parfait, **'96** 180
    Surprise Banana Pudding, **'86** 7
Beach, The, **'95** 168
Blackberry Pudding Tarts, **'93** 200
Blueberry-Raspberry Pudding, Russian,
    '97 128
Bread
    Amish Bread Pudding, **'80** 8

4. *Frequently, we'll direct you to other categories to help you find similar recipes.*

5. *Each recipe title is alphabetized by its most descriptive word. We've boldfaced the year in which it appeared in* Southern Living® Annual Recipes; *its page number follows.*

6. *An "M" precedes the page numbers of all microwave recipes. It refers to recipes cooked totally or partially in the microwave.*

7. *An alphabetical guide word at the bottom of each page helps you quickly locate main reference categories.*

MASTER INDEX

This index lists all recipes by their complete titles under a specific food category and ingredient. The volume is indicated in bold, followed by the page number. Microwave recipe page numbers are preceded by an "M." For information about how to use this index, see facing page.

ALMONDS

Appetizers

Ball, Easy Chut-Nut, '00 280
Cheese, Almond, '88 173
Cheese Ball, Fruit-and-Nut, '91 251
Cheese Ball, Pinecone, '93 288
Chicken Almondette Fingers, '93 12
Chicken Nut Puffs, '81 260
Crostini, Almond-Bacon-Cheese, '94 318
Curried Almonds, '82 297
Dip, Almond Delight, '90 226
Dip with Strawberries, Almond Cream, '92 164
Mix, Jalapeño Nut, '96 27
Nippy Nuts, '93 301
Olives, Almond-Stuffed, '88 95
Pastry Cups, Mushroom-Almond, '88 210
Pesto-Spiced Nuts, '95 173
Quick Party Nuts, '04 197
Rollups, Almond-Ham, '89 284
Spread, Curry-Almond Cheese, '01 238
Spread, Date-Orange-Nut, '02 59
Toasts, Cheddar-Almond, '97 30
Tuna Amandine, '02 165
Braid, Almond, '89 86
Bread, Cocoa-Nut Swirl, '80 257
Bread, Lemon-Almond Tea, '04 209
Bread, Saffron, '96 50
Bread, Tipsy Peach, '02 21
Breakfast Ring, Almond-Vanilla, '04 M249
Butter, Almond-Raisin, '02 258
Caramelized Almonds, '92 303
Coffee Cake, Almond-Blueberry, '85 152
Coffee Cake, Apricot-Almond, '93 26; '04 193
Coffee Cake Twist, Almond, '91 22
Coffee, Chocolate-Almond, '84 54
Coffee Delight, Almond-, '84 115
Coleslaw with Grapes and Almonds, '83 59
Couscous with Raisins, Almonds, and Lemon, '00 295
Cream, Peaches 'n' Almond, '86 229
Danish, Almond, '87 301

Desserts

Apricot-Almond Squares, '95 272
Bake, Apple-Almond, '02 M209
Balls, Coconut-Almond, '84 256
Balls, Toasted Almond Chip, '84 240
Bars, Almond-Chocolate, '83 304
Bars, Swedish Almond, '97 322
Biscotti, Almond, '91 108
Biscotti, Almond-Anise, '93 266
Biscotti, Cocoa-Almond, '96 280
Biscuits, Raspberry-Almond, '93 160
Bonbons, Dark Chocolate, '02 297
Bread, Mandel, '97 220

Bread Pudding with Amaretto Cream Sauce, Layered Almond-Cream Cheese, '03 330
Brickle Treats, Almond, '95 321
Brie, Almond-Raspberry, '94 M89
Brittle, Almond, '03 281
Brownies, Date-and-Almond, '88 217
Butter-Nut Strips, '82 167
Cake, Almond-Butter, '86 107
Cake, Almond-Butter Wedding, '86 106
Cake, Almond Legend, '82 8
Cake, Almond Whipping Cream, '80 295
Cake, Apricot-Almond Upside-Down, '97 204
Cake, Chocolate-Almond, '91 248
Cake, Heaven, '04 193
Cake, Peach-Almond Pound, '89 86
Cake, Peachy Almond-Butter, '90 107
Cake Squares, Almond, '79 111
Cake, Sullivan's Lemon-Almond Pound, '04 278
Cake, Toasted Almond-Butter, '99 315
Cake, White Chocolate-Almond, '03 M287
Cake with Cherry Filling, Chocolate-Almond, '84 225
Candied Nuts, '81 261
Candy, Almond Brittle, '80 255
Cheesecake, Amaretto, '99 273
Cheesecake, Black-and-White, '99 334
Cheesecake, Chocolate-Almond, '93 53
Cheesecake, Coconut-Chocolate-Almond, '98 322
Cheesecake, Island Breeze, '03 144
Chocolate-Almond Dessert, '82 306
Chocolate-Almond Hearts, '03 42
Chocolate Almond Velvet, '81 148
Cinnamon Stars, Swiss, '87 293
Cobbler, Blackberry-Almond, '81 132
Combs, Almond, '84 136
Confections, Almond Cream, '87 198; '90 310
Cookies, Almond, '83 22, 181; '91 51; '92 176; '97 288; '99 49
Cookies, Almond Butter, '79 52
Cookies, Almond Lace, '98 336
Cookies, Almond Sand Dollar, '05 130
Cookies, Almond Spritz, '82 306
Cookies, Almond-Toffee Chocolate Chip, '05 87
Cookies, Amaretti, '02 270
Cookies, Chewy Almond, '02 258
Cookies, Chocolate-Almond, '98 293
Cookies, Chocolate-Almond Surprise, '88 M45
Cookies, Chocolate-Brickle, '99 127
Cookies, Cranberry-Almond, '98 26
Cookies, Double Chocolate Chunk-Almond, '95 178
Cookies, Lemon-Almond, '02 293
Cookies, Light Almond, '83 151
Cookies, Skillet Almond, '97 288

Cookies, Snow, '99 167
Cookies, Swedish Almond, '85 312
Cookies, Texan-Size Almond Crunch, '91 236
Cookies with Ice Cream Balls, Almond Brittle, '96 202
Cream, Almond, '00 27
Cream, Chocolate-Almond, '91 108
Cream, Peach Almond, '82 108
Cream with Fresh Strawberries, Almond, '87 93
Crème Brûlée, Almond, '95 323
Crêpes Gelée Amandine, '83 126
Crescents, Almond, '97 273
Crisps, Dark Chocolate-Almond, '05 M30
Crunch, Almond Butter, '80 301
Crunch, Vanilla Almond, '93 243
Crust, Vanilla Wafer, '98 216
Custard with Raspberries, Almond Crème, '88 174
Drops, Cherry-Almond, '81 20
Drops, Chocolate-Coconut Almond, '87 223
Filling, Almond, '87 301; '96 316
Filling, Almond Cream, '85 320; '91 248
Filling, Ground Almond, '87 14
Filling, Nut, '91 35
Flan, Almond-Orange, '04 241
Float, Nutmeg-Almond, '84 106
Frosting, Almond-Butter, '86 107
Frosting, Almond Buttercream, '97 61; '99 155
Frosting, Chocolate-Almond, '83 241
Frozen Almond Crunch, '94 283
Fudge, Creamy Almond, '95 51
Glaze, Honey-Nut, '87 15
Ice Cream, Almond, '98 221
Ice Cream, Almond-Fudge, '93 205
Ice Cream Balls, Almond, '86 315
Ice Cream Dessert, Rocky Road, '00 332
Ice Cream, No-Cook Chocolate-Almond, '04 179
Ice Cream, Peach-Almond, '89 156
Ice-Cream Sandwiches, Mocha-Almond-Fudge, '05 62
Leaves, Almond Holly, '86 319
Mandelbrot, Rhoda's, '98 243
Marzipan Bees, '98 100
Meringue Fingers, Chocolate-Almond, '84 158
Mocha-Almond Dessert, '80 289; '81 62
Mousse, Chocolate-Almond, '93 316
Nutcracker Sweets, '02 293
Pastry, Almond, '85 177; '89 317; '92 30
Pears, Almond-Stuffed, '83 207
Petits Fours, Chocolate-Almond, '93 255; '00 72
Pie Amandine, Chocolate, '83 300
Pie, Apple-Amandine, '89 215
Pie, Cinnamon-Almond-Pecan, '98 89
Pie, Creamy Chocolate-Almond, '85 102

Pie, Toasted Almond, '86 163
Pineapple-Almond Delight, '85 96
Polvorones, '00 123
Praline Sauce, '93 214
Pudding, Chocolate-Almond, '82 142; '88 24
Pudding, Chocolate-Almond Silk, '96 266
Pudding, Mandarin-Almond, '85 M12
Roca, Almond, '86 49
Romanoff, Strawberry-Almond, '98 99
Sauce, Almond-Vanilla Custard, '88 M177
Sauce, Angel Food Cake with Amaretto-Almond,
    '90 199
Shortbread, Apricot-Almond, '99 29
Shortbread Thumbelinas, '05 307
Snaps, Almond, '92 273
Sorbet, Apricot-Almond, '98 126
Sour Cream-Almond Dessert, '92 120
Spread, Almond Cheese, '87 292
Squares, Cream Cheese-Almond, '85 68
Strudel, Pear, '98 253
Tart, Almond, '89 232
Tart, Almond-Apple, '01 253
Tart, Almond-Pear, '01 253
Tart, Apricot-Almond, '97 99
Tart, Bakewell, '97 110
Tart, Raspberry-Almond Pear, '05 230
Tarts, Almond Tea, '85 120
Tarts, Raspberry-Almond, '99 280
Tart with Brandy Sauce, Peach, '98 119
Tassies, Lucky Almond, '91 13
Toffee, '01 218
Toffee, Almond, '04 235
Toffee Crunch, Almond-, '88 285
Topping, Almond, '85 152; '86 200
Topping, Ginger-Almond, '01 215
Torte, Chocolate-Almond, '96 M253; '98 273
Tortoni, Coffee-Almond, '81 30
Truffles, Almond, '83 298
Wafers, Almond-Filled, '88 120
French Toast, Almond, '88 62
French Toast, Amaretto, '98 280
Fruit, Almond-Curried, '83 261
Glazed Almonds, '96 64
Liqueur, Almond-Flavored, '81 287
Main Dishes
Casserole, Chicken-Almond, '94 199
Catfish Amandine, Mandarin, '84 183
Catfish Amandine, Spicy, '89 52
Chicken, Almond, '01 26
Chicken and Vegetables, Almond, '86 21
Chicken, Creamy Almond, '89 281
Chicken in Orange-Almond Sauce, '79 219; '80 13
Chicken, Spicy Almond, '88 150
Fish, Almond Baked, '88 270; '89 203
Fish Amandine, '85 179
Fish Amandine, Fillet of, '80 M54
Flounder Amandine, '89 M196
Orange Lake Amandine, '80 99
Pollo Almendrado, '81 193
Quiche, Almond-Topped Crab, '79 127
Salmon with Almonds and Parsley, '05 68
Salmon with Almonds and Tomato-Lemon Sauce,
    '04 23
Trout Amandine, '99 53
Trout Amandine, Classic, '96 202; '01 110
Trout Amandine, Gaston's, '96 232
Muffins, Almond, '90 87
Muffins, Banana-Honey-Nut, '88 62
Muffins, Peachy-Almond, '86 301
Phyllo Nests, Nutty, '87 277

Pilaf, Persian Rice, '02 167
Popcorn, Spicy Nut, '02 287; '03 272
Praline Almonds, '97 285
Rice, Almond, '81 195; '85 M112; '89 100; '91 291
Rice, Almond Wild, '86 50
Rice, Indian, '96 202
Rice, Orphan's, '03 32
Rice with Almonds, Curried, '83 M285
Rolls, Almond Crescent, '90 283
Rolls, Cherry-Almond, '84 M198
Salad, Almond-Citrus, '96 274; '01 42
Salad Amandine, Chicken, '81 37
Salad, Cheesy Fruit-'n'-Nut, '87 56
Salad, Chicken-Almond, '81 133
Salad, Crunchy Tuna-and-Almond, '04 72
Salad, Cucumber-Almond, '86 147
Salad Dressing, Almond, '81 37
Salad, Orange-Almond, '99 107
Salad Oriental, Mandarin, '02 175
Salad, Sesame-Almond, '89 123
Salad Shanghai, Almond-Chicken, '90 160
Sandwiches, Chicken-Almond Pocket, '81 240; '83 69
Sauce, Grilled Snapper with Orange-Almond, '01 158
Sauce, Mandarin-Almond Cream, '84 183
Sauce, Shrimp-and-Almond, '87 282
Seasoned Almonds, '03 101
Slaw, Asian, '99 108
Slaw, Crunchy Cabbage, '02 95
Slaw, Pineapple-Almond, '92 171
Snack Balls, Orange-Almond, '95 214
Snack Mix, Sweet 'n' Savory, '03 199
Soup, Almond, '79 48
Soup, Chicken-Almond Cream, '92 21
Spoons, Dipped Chocolate-Almond, '95 M277
Streusel, Almond-Garlic, '95 159
Stuffing, Apple-Almond, '01 184
Sugared Almonds, '04 105
Sunburst, Almond, '94 245
Sweet-and-Spicy Almonds, '96 274; '01 42
Syrup, Almond, '82 47
Tea, Almond, '85 43; '86 329; '89 212; '97 226;
    '01 93
Tea, Almond-Lemonade, '86 229; '99 207
Tea, Ginger-Almond, '94 131
Toast Amandine, Baked, '82 47
Vegetables
Asparagus, Almond, '83 86; '02 64
Asparagus Amandine, '03 295
Asparagus with Almond Butter, '84 85
Asparagus with Almond Sauce, '91 117
Broccoli Casserole, Almond-, '88 62
Broccoli in Sherry Sauce, Almond, '02 45
Broccoli with Almonds, Glazed, '80 12
Brussels Sprouts Amandine, '79 213
Cabbage with Almonds, Creamed, '79 4
Cauliflower and Peas with Curried Almonds,
    '79 221; '80 82
Cauliflower with Almond Sauce, '82 270
Celery Almondine, '85 116
Celery Amandine, Buttered, '82 98
Eggplant with Almonds, '79 179
Green Beans, Almond, '79 276; '82 M20; '97 238
Green Beans, Dill-and-Almond, '05 81
Green Beans, Lemon-Almond, '05 218
Green Beans with Almonds, '84 253
Green Beans with Almonds, Italian, '81 207
Green Beans with Smoked Almonds, Thyme-
    Scented, '01 57
Leeks with Brussels Sprouts and Almonds, '00 222
Peas with Almonds, Curried, '88 M294
Potatoes, Almond-Fried, '82 25
Potatoes, Broccoli-and-Almond-Topped, '83 3
Stir-Fry, Almond-Vegetable, '86 222
Wild Rice, Cranberry-Almond, '04 204

AMBROSIA
Ambrosia, '00 325; '04 233
Anytime Ambrosia, '86 182
Baked Ambrosia, '83 303
Bowl, Ambrosia, '80 138; '84 313
Brunch, Ambrosia, '83 57
Cake, Ambrosia, '79 229
Cake, Cranberry-Ambrosia, '01 271
Cake Royale, Ambrosia, '89 335
Carrot-Marshmallow Ambrosia, '80 5
Cheesecake, Ambrosia, '02 296
Chicken Salad Ambrosia, '85 216
Citrus Ambrosia, '82 287
Cookies, Ambrosia, '81 301; '82 110; '86 313
Cranberry Ambrosia, Glazed, '00 269
Cups, Sherbet Ambrosia, '82 159
Custard Sauce Ambrosia, '84 256
Easy Ambrosia, '92 45
Fantastic Ambrosia, '91 277
Filling, Cranberry-Ambrosia, '01 271
Fruit Ambrosia, Fresh, '88 184
Fruit Ambrosia, Mixed, '83 10
Ginger Ale Ambrosia, '99 125
Gingered Ambrosia, '02 245
Grandma's Ambrosia, '90 254
Honey Bee Ambrosia, '83 267
Kitchen Express Ambrosia, '04 233
Layered Ambrosia, '88 304
Mold, Ambrosia, '79 241
Mold, Ambrosia Cream Cheese, '79 249
Old-Fashioned Ambrosia, '80 5
Orange Ambrosia Supreme, '79 37
Pancakes with Orange Syrup, Ambrosia, '89 254
Peach Ambrosia, '83 53
Pie, Ambrosia, '79 284
Pie, Orange Ambrosia, '80 237
Pineapple-Orange Ambrosia, '88 252
Rhubarb Ambrosia, '88 93
Salad, Ambrosia, '83 231; '94 271
Salad, Carrot-Ambrosia, '81 252
Sauce, Hot Ambrosia, '89 335
Sherried Ambrosia, '84 324; '86 317
Sorbet, Ambrosia, '04 317
Spread, Ambrosia, '92 50
Sprinkles, Ambrosia with, '01 250
Tropical Ambrosia, '79 74
ANCHOVIES
Antipasto, Grandpa's, '98 183
Appetizers, Zesty Anchovy, '83 93
Butter, Lemon-Anchovy, '97 307
Mayonnaise, Anchovy, '86 179
Rémoulade, Criolla, '97 227
Salad, Caesar, '99 265; '00 19; '02 269
Salad, Dawn's World-Famous Greek, '98 276
Sauce Niçoise, '96 190
Tapenade, '92 194; '00 135
APPETIZERS. *See also* **CRACKERS, FONDUE, PÂTÉS.**
Almond-Ham Rollups, '89 284
Almonds, Curried, '82 297
Anchovy Appetizers, Zesty, '83 93
Antipasto, Easy, '92 24
Antipasto, Grandpa's, '98 183
Antipasto, Lemon-Vinaigrette Marinated, '04 256
Antipasto Relish, '86 327
Antipasto Squares, '03 292
Apple-Phyllo Rolls, '88 213
Apple Quarters, Honey-Baked, '86 93
Artichoke-and-Shrimp Appetizer, '93 271
Artichoke Appetizer Frittata, '92 58
Artichoke Appetizer, Zesty, '80 146
Artichoke-Caviar Mold, '87 239
Artichoke-Cheese Bottoms, Baked, '94 61
Artichoke Oysters, '96 154
Artichoke-Parmesan Phyllo Bites, '87 54

Artichokes, Marinated, '87 250
Artichokes, Spring, '86 62
Asparagus Croquettes, '85 265
Asparagus, Prosciutto-Wrapped, '91 98
Asparagus Rolls, '79 296; '80 31
Asparagus Rolls, Hot, '93 329
Asparagus Rollups, '79 63; '01 239
Asparagus Roll-Ups, '84 270
Asparagus with Dill Sauce, '97 59
Asparagus with Garlic Cream, '95 83; '00 71
Avocado-Crabmeat Cocktail, Sherried, '87 95
Bacon Appetizers, Hot, '80 248
Bacon, Black Pepper-Brown Sugar, '04 70
Bacon, Brown Sugar, '04 70
Bacon-Chestnut Wraps, '84 M216
Bacon-Jalapeño-Tomato Quesadillas, '95 240
Bacon-Onion Appetizers, '94 290
Bacon Rolls, '84 270; '93 330
Bacon Rollups, '79 34
Bacon Swirls, '89 214; '98 26
Bacon-Wrapped Crackers, '93 280
Bacon-Wrapped Pineapple Chunks, '84 25
Bacon-Wrapped Water Chestnuts, '79 63
Bagel Chips, '91 138
Bagel Chips, Cinnamon-and-Sugar, '91 139
Bagel Chips, Garlic, '91 139
Bagel Chips, Lemon-and-Herb, '91 139
Bagel Chips, Parmesan Cheese, '91 138
Bagel Crisps, '86 278
Basil-Pepper Appetizers, '98 133
Bean Burrito Appetizers, '94 226
Beef on a Stick, '99 336
Beef on a Stick, Marinated, '85 234
Beef Sticks, '93 331
Beef Tenderloin, Holiday, '01 238
Beefy Party Snacks, '80 249
Beets, Blue Cheese-Stuffed, '88 211
Beggar's Purses with Smoked Salmon, '04 244
Biscuits, Cornmeal, '04 257
Biscuits, Miniature Buttermilk, '02 103
Biscuits, Quick Whipping Cream, '03 238
Biscuits with Beef and Horseradish-Chive Cream, Blue
    Cheese, '02 313
Biscuits with Ham, Ranch, '97 59
Biscuits with Olive-Parsley Spread, Cream Cheese-and-
    Olive, '04 238
Black Bean Appetizer, '83 50
Black Bean Cakes with Greens and Apple Dressing,
    '92 216
Black-Eyed Pea Cakes, '01 32
Black-Eyed Pea Pinwheels, '85 300; '86 18
Bread Ring, Braided, '96 322
Breadstick Haystacks, '99 246
Broccoli-Cheese Appetizer, '92 265
Broccoli, Cocktail, '80 192
Broccoli Soup, Mock Cream of, '85 288
Bruschetta. *See also* **APPETIZERS/Canapés,**
    Crostini.
    Black Truffle Bruschetta, '99 323
    Caper-and-Olive Bruschetta, '00 276
    Prosciutto Bruschetta and Cantaloupe Chutney,
        '00 108
    Red-and-Green Bruschetta, '01 62
    Roasted Pepper-Tomato Bruschetta, '02 213
    Roasted Red Pepper Bruschetta, '00 278
Brussels Sprouts, Marinated, '88 265
Burgers, Saucy Cocktail, '83 217
Burrito Rollups, '90 119
Burritos, Chinese, '87 181
Buzzard's Nests, '93 244
Cakes, Little Bitty, '98 154
Canapés. *See also* **APPETIZERS/Bruschetta,**
    Crostini.
    Bread, Canapé, '89 292

Bread, Rye Canapé, '89 293
Bread, Whole Wheat Canapé, '89 293
Chicken-Cucumber Canapés, '98 154
Crab Canapés, '93 130
Crab Canapés, Cheesy, '86 262
Crab Canapés, Hot, '86 70; '87 239
Crabmeat Canapés, '88 150
Cucumber Canapés, '95 88
Fruit-Topped Canapés, '85 80
Green Onion Canapés, '84 M216
Lemon-Cheese, Canapés, '87 93
Mushroom Canapés, '80 285; '97 23
Party Canapés, '86 128
Roasted Garlic Canapés, '96 95
Salmon Canapés, Smoked, '99 140
Shrimp-and-Cucumber Canapés, '93 164
Shrimp Canapés, '84 116
Swiss Canapés, Hot, '83 259
Vegetable Canapés, '91 252
Caponata, '87 166
Caponata alla Siciliana, '02 269
Caramel Corn, Oven-Made, '91 233
Caramel Good Stuff, Baked, '80 284
Caraway Wafers, '81 261
Carrots, Dilled Baby, '84 80
Carrots, Dill-Spiced, '87 200
Carrots, Pickled, '93 12
Catfish Appetizer, Layered, '92 209
Cauliflower, Crispy Fried, '80 220
Cauliflower, Dilled, '83 93
Cauliflower, French-Fried, '86 211
Cauliflower, Golden Fried, '82 78
Cauliflower, Pickled, '94 183
Cauliflower with Cheese Sauce, Fried, '87 231
Caviar Crown, '83 78
Caviar, Eggplant, '88 262; '99 217
Caviar, Mexican, '98 135
Caviar Pie, '79 154
Caviar Potatoes, '84 80
Caviar Potatoes, Appetizer, '86 223
Caviar, Texas, '86 218; '99 84; '01 160, 257
Caviar Tomatoes, '91 12
Celery, Creamy Stuffed, '82 102
Celery, Jalapeño Stuffed, '79 70
Celery, Stuffed, '82 98
Celery Trunks, Stuffed, '85 115
Cereal Bites, Buttery, '89 97
Cereal Nibblers, Great, '82 297
Cereal Snack, Toasted, '85 215
Ceviche (Marinated Raw Fish), '80 194
Ceviche, Mexican-Style, '88 115
Cheese. *See also* **APPETIZERS/Dips, Spreads and**
    Fillings.
    Bacon-and-Cheese Melts, '04 324
    Bacon-Cheese Fingers, '00 133
    Bacon Puffs, Cheesy, '02 145
    Bagel Chips, Parmesan Cheese, '91 138
    Bake, Appetizer Cheese, '92 209
    Baked Brie with Blueberry-Ginger Topping, '05 179
    Baked Honey-Raisin Brie, '05 M258
    Ball, Apple Cheese, '98 250
    Ball, Blue Cheese, '80 259; '84 221
    Ball, Blue Cheese-Olive, '82 248
    Ball, Bourbon Cheese, '81 57
    Ball, Brandied Blue Cheese, '85 283
    Ball, Carrot-Cheese, '86 325
    Ball, Cheese, '82 161; '91 200
    Ball, Cheese and Chutney, '87 247
    Ball, Cheese 'n' Beef, '83 230
    Ball, Chicken-Cheese, '93 216
    Ball, Chicken-Curry Cheese, '85 118
    Ball, Cocktail Cheese, '83 174
    Ball, Curried Shrimp Cheese, '86 135
    Ball, Deviled Pecan, '80 258

Ball, Easy Chut-Nut, '00 280
Ball, Festive Cheese, '79 44; '94 279
Ball, Fruit-and-Nut Cheese, '91 251
Ball, Herbed Cheese, '89 246
Ball, Holiday Cheese, '79 285
Ball, Mediterranean Cheese, '05 143
Ball, Olive Cheese, '80 258
Ball, Parmesan-Cream Cheese, '89 246
Ball, Party Cheese, '84 258
Ball, Party Pecan Cheese, '81 235
Ball, Peanut Butter-Cheese, '86 136
Ball, Pecan Cheese, '83 127
Ball, Peppered Cheese, '79 100; '94 118
Ball, Pimiento Cheese, '80 258
Ball, Pineapple Cheese, '81 160
Ball, Pineapple-Cheese, '84 26
Ball, Pinecone Cheese, '93 288; '98 265; '05 300
Ball, Pumpkin Cheese, '02 222
Balls, Bite-Size Cheese, '92 321
Balls, Cheese and Mushroom, '79 63
Ball, Shrimp-Cheese, '85 208
Ball, Smoky Salmon Cheese, '82 247
Balls, Olive-Cheese, '84 206
Balls, Pumpkin Patch Cheese, '99 245
Balls with Sun-Dried Tomatoes, Cheese, '94 317
Ball, Tangy Cheese, '81 263, 287
Bar, Savory Cheese, '91 98
Bars, Bacon-Cheese Toast, '79 36
Bars, Camembert, '86 58
Bear Claws, '81 161
Biscuits, Cheese, '79 296; '80 31
Biscuits, Cheesy Sausage, '80 78
Biscuits, Mixer Cheese, '96 22
Biscuits, Petite Ham and Cheese, '79 193
Biscuits, Spicy Cheese Cocktail, '05 173
Biscuits, Tiny Cheese, '80 192
Biscuits with Sun-Dried Tomato Spread and Bacon,
    Cream Cheese-and-Olive, '02 313
Biscuits with Tapenade, Cream Cheese-and-Olive,
    '02 313
Bites, Benne Cheese, '80 121
Bites, Cheese, '93 329
Bites, Cheesy Pecan, '82 248
Bites, Crispy Cheese, '03 179
Bites, Curried Swiss, '85 220
Bites, Lemon-Cheese Party, '95 160
Bites, Parmesan Cheese, '99 221; '00 20; '01 123;
    '02 108
Bites, Starlight Cheese, '95 329
Bit-of-Brie Appetizer, '88 M8
Bonbons, Cheese, '87 93
Box, Cranberry-Cheese, '03 238
Brick, Cheese, '99 170
Brie, Chutney-Bacon, '90 M292
Brie en Croûte, Stuffed, '97 162
Brie, Honey-Mustard, '91 252
Brie in Braided Bread Ring, '96 322
Brie in Rye, Raspberry, '93 252
Brie, Kahlúa-Pecan, '92 289
Brie, Parmesan-Coated, '95 286
Brie, Tropical Breeze, '94 M18
Brie, Warmed Cranberry, '01 245
Brie with Brown Sugar and Nuts, '03 282
Brie with Fresh Fruit, Caramel, '90 266
Brie, Wrapped, '92 126
Brie Wrapped in Phyllo, '93 173
Calzones, Surprise, '00 282
Camembert Cremes, '03 248
Caraway Cheese, '89 246
Caraway-Cheese Crisps, '95 284
Cheesecake, Cheddar-Chili, '02 251
Cheesecake, Ham-and-Asparagus, '02 103
Cheesecake, Roasted Vegetable, '99 140
Cheesecake, Salsa, '98 33

APPETIZERS, Cheese
(continued)

Cheesecake, Savory Spinach Appetizer, '02 M207
Cheesecakes, Herbed, '99 182
Cheesecake, Smoked Salmon, '99 92
Cheesecake, Southwest, '04 293; '05 249
Cheesecake, Spinach-Herb, '99 139
Cheesecake, Taco, '00 56
Cheesecake, Three-Layer, '99 140
Chiles-Rellenos Squares, '91 161
Chutney Appetizer, Fiery Cheese-and-, '04 177
Cookie Snacks, Cheese, '01 231
Cracker Nibbles, Cheese, '84 328
Crackers, Cheddar, '84 236
Crackers, Tomato-Blue Cheese, '02 213
Cream Cheese Appetizer, Baked, '92 58
Cream Cheese Round, Pesto-and-, '90 242
Crème Brûlée, Roquefort-and-Black Pepper, '95 324
Crispies, Cheese-Bacon, '84 270
Crispies, Pecan-Cheese, '87 168
Crisps, Blue Cheese, '98 285; '01 235
Crisps, Parmesan, '01 197
Crisps, Spicy Jack Cheese, '02 135
Croquettes, Hot Cheese, '89 182
Crostini, Almond-Bacon-Cheese, '94 318
Crostini, Cheesy, '03 223
Crostini, Mozzarella, '94 319
Crostini, Roasted Peppers-Feta Cheese, '96 87
Crostini, Swiss-Blue Cheese, '94 318; '96 215
Crostini, Zippy Cheese, '97 90
Cucumber Slices, Cheesy, '84 80
Cups, Cottage Cheese-Spinach, '87 190
Cutouts, Sesame-Cheese, '82 296
Feta Cheesecakes, Little, '86 277
Fiesta Cheesecake, '93 273
Flaming Cheese, '84 187
Fondue, Cheese, '81 40
Fondue, Nacho, '94 332; '95 35
Fondue, Party Cheese, '92 20
Fondue, Pub, '94 332; '95 35
Fondue, Swiss Cheese, '91 48
Fried Cheddar Cheese, '89 182
Fried Cheese Balls, '89 181
Fried Cheese Bites, '82 77
Fried Cheese, Italian-Style, '83 250; '89 182
Garnished Cheese, '91 98
Goat Cheese, Dried Tomato Mock, '97 105
Goat Cheese, Endive with Herbed, '04 244
Goat Cheese, Mock, '97 105
Goat Cheese, Peppered, '94 128
Goat Cheese Rosemary, '89 270
Goat Cheese with Sun-Dried Tomatoes and
    Rosemary, '93 175
Grapes, Blue Cheese-Pecan, '95 48
Green Chile-Cheddar Cheese with Avocado-Mango
    Salsa, Smoky, '00 328
Grits, Garlic-Cheese, '97 58
Herb Cheese, Pot-of-, '85 210
Herbed Cheese, '88 152
Herb-Pepper Cheese, '97 90
Horseshoe, Strawberry-Cheese, '00 106
Kebabs, Peppered Cheese, '91 279
Little Bits, '79 196
Loaf, Four-Layer Cheese, '99 222
Log, Black Pepper-Goat Cheese, '98 285
Log, Cheesy Surprise, '82 247
Log, Garlic Cheese, '85 21
Log, Hawaiian Cheese, '89 246
Log, Roquefort Pecan, '89 247
Logs, Black Pepper Cheese, '90 61
Logs, Blue Cheese, '04 53
Logs, Candy Cane-Cheese, '03 298

Logs, Chile-Cheese, '05 64
Logs, East Indian Cheese, '88 173
Logs, Port Wine Cheese, '02 279
Logs, Spicy Monterey Jack Cheese, '02 279
Log, Toasted Pecan Cheese, '86 M288
Marinade, Cheese, '04 238
Marinated Cheese, '90 244; '95 21
Marinated Cheese, Olives, and Peppers, '04 238
Meat-and-Cheese Appetizers, '87 7
Melt, Brie-and-Cranberry Chutney, '98 M318
Mexicali Appetizer, Cheesy, '82 108
Mold, Blue Cheese, '85 210
Mold, Cheese-and-Wine, '84 197
Mold, Cream Cheese-Crabmeat, '90 71
Mold, Garlic-Chive Cheese, '85 210
Mousse, Roquefort, '82 71
Nachos, Smoked, '01 146
Nuggets, Cheesy Ham, '81 290
Olive Appetizers, Cheesy, '85 113
Olive Appetizers, Cheesy-, '87 246
Olive Snack, Open-Faced Cheese-and-, '89 97
Pasta Bites, Pesto-Cheese, '87 251
Pastries, Cream Cheese, '80 250
Pastries, Date-Filled Cheese, '83 259
Pastry, Brie Wrapped in, '80 241
Pastry, Sausage Balls in Cheese, '80 248
Pastry Shells, Miniature Cream Cheese, '87 190
Patty, Lemon-Pepper Cheese, '84 117
Patty Shells, Cream Cheese, '82 249
Peachy Cream Cheese, '92 289
Pepper-Cheese Stacks, '87 80
Peppers, Cheesy Jalapeño, '80 195
Phyllo-Cheese Triangles, '87 246
Phyllo Cheese Triangles, '93 329
Phyllo, Goat Cheese Wrapped in, '99 43
Phyllo Triangles, Cheese-Filled, '83 259
Pie, Cheesy Hors d'Oeuvre, '88 91
Pinwheels, Mexican, '95 21
Pinwheels, Santa's, '91 275
Pita Crisps, Cheesy, '97 45
Potato Skins, Cheesy, '82 78
Puffs, Bavarian Cheese, '80 191
Puffs, Blue Cheese, '04 18
Puffs, Blue Cheese-and-Bacon, '97 98; '01 236
Puffs, Cheese, '79 110; '97 240; '02 69; '03 269;
    '04 107
Puffs, Cheese-and-Spinach, '87 246
Puffs, Cream Cheese, '84 151
Puffs, Gouda-Shrimp, '79 234
Puffs, Ham-and-Cheese, '86 277
Puffs, Mexican Cheese, '87 8
Puffs, Oregano Cheese, '95 21
Puffs, Surprise Cheese, '79 295; '80 31
Quesadillas, Green Chile, '90 121
Quesadillas, Quick, '02 143
Queso Blanco, '93 322
Queso, Chunky Cheese, '99 279
Quiches, Miniature Bacon-Cheese, '83 93
Quiches, Miniature Cheese, '80 150
Quick Cheese Snack, '89 98
Ring, Cheese, '81 261; '05 33
Ring, Strawberry-Cheese, '86 14
Roll, Chili-Cheese, '84 114
Roll, Ham-and-Cheese, '79 234
Rollups, Cream Cheese, '98 134
Rollups, Ham-and-Swiss, '95 113
Rollups, Mexican, '98 134
Rollups, Southwestern, '01 135
Round, Brie Appetizer, '82 41
Round, Herbed Cheese, '84 300
Rounds, Cheese, '86 262
Rounds, Parmesan, '85 131
Rounds, Parmesan Party, '82 248
Salami-Cheese Snacks, '88 96

Salsa Parmesan, Broiled, '98 33
Sandwiches, Checkerboard Cheese, '05 18
Sandwiches, Cheese Tea, '92 276
Sandwiches, Cheshire Claret Cheese-and-Ham
    Striped Tea, '94 16
Sandwiches, Duck Party, '02 48
Sandwiches, Easter Bunny Party, '02 48
Sandwiches, Easter Egg Party, '02 48
Sandwiches, Flower Party, '02 48
Sandwiches, Nutty Cream Cheese Party, '00 119
Sandwiches, Pimiento Cheese Finger, '99 86
Sesame Cheese Bites, '89 24
Shrimp-and-Cheese Appetizer, '01 134
Soufflé, Blue Cheese, '91 244
Sour Cream Appetizer, Cheesy, '84 51
Southwestern Cheese Appetizer, '01 232
Spinach-Cheese Bites, '94 23
Squares, Cream Cheese-Almond, '85 68
Squares, Cream Cheese-Vegetable, '04 293
Squares, Feta, '02 59
Squares, Green Chile-Cottage Cheese, '86 85
Squares, Jalapeño Cheese, '80 195
Squares, Quick Cheese, '84 191
Sticks, Parmesan, '82 297
Sticks, Parmesan-Bacon, '99 65
Sticks, Parmesan Sesame, '81 39
Sticks, Peppery Cheese, '81 M289
Straws, Brie Cheese, '94 216
Straws, Cheese, '80 150; '82 137; '88 77
Straws, Chili-Cheese, '94 216
Straws, Easy-as-Pie Cheese, '94 216
Straws, Italian Cheese, '94 217
Straws, Parmesan Cheese, '94 216
Straws, Sally's Cheese, '97 121
Tartlets, Cheese, '88 211
Tarts, Blue Cheese Appetizer, '85 300; '86 18
Terrine, Basil-Cheese, '96 322
Terrine, Chèvre-and-Avocado, '00 276
Terrine, Italian Cheese, '93 64
Terrine with Tomato-Basil Vinaigrette, Blue Cheese,
    '99 288
Three-Cheese Appetizer, '80 174
Toasts, Cheddar-Almond, '97 30
Toast Treats, Cheese, '83 100
Torta, Basil-Cheese, '01 100
Torta, Three-Layer Cheese, '04 323
Torte, Pesto, '02 278
Torte, Showstopping Appetizer, '98 319
Torte, Tomato-Cheese, '97 49
Tortillas, Jumpin' Jack, '02 54
Truffles, Herb-and-Garlic Goat Cheese, '05 143
Turnovers, Cheesy Sesame Seed, '91 252
Twists, Double Cheese, '85 131
Twists, Parmesan, '99 323
Vegetable Cheesecake, '96 110
Wafers, Blue Cheese-Walnut, '00 56
Wafers, Cheese, '80 151; '95 174; '99 279; '00 164;
    '05 97
Wafers, Hope Farm Cheese, '93 282
Wafers, Pam's Cheese, '98 268
Wafers, Pecan-Cheese, '81 119
Wafers, Sage-Pecan Cheese, '93 12
Wafers, Spicy Cheese-Walnut, '03 61
Wedges, Cheesy Party, '84 84
Wonton Chips, Parmesan Cheese, '91 138
Wonton Envelopes, Fried, '95 96
Wontons with Hot Sauce, Cheese, '83 74
Yogurt Cheese Appetizer, '04 217
Cherries, Stuffed, '85 81
Cherry Pepper Appetizers, Fiery Stuffed, '97 269
Chicken. See also **APPETIZERS/Dips, Spreads and
    Fillings.**
    Balls, Coconut Curried Chicken, '91 165
    Balls, Curried Chicken, '91 98

Bites, Curried Chicken, '85 40
Bites, French-Fried Chicken, '85 160
Bites, Savory Chicken, '92 209
Bites with Sweet-Hot Tomato Chutney, Chicken,
  '00 309
B'steeya with Chicken, '98 210
Cakes with Avocado Cream, Southwestern Chicken-
  and-Corn, '97 M311
Deep-Fried Walnut Chicken, '87 175
Drummettes, Down-Home Chicken, '93 157
Drummettes, Ginger-Garlic Appetizer, '93 157
Drummettes, Orange-Pecan Chicken, '93 158
Drummettes, Southwestern Chicken, '93 158
Empanadas, '04 135
Fingers, Chicken Almondette, '93 12
Fingers, Chicken Little, '80 249
Fingers with Come Back Sauce, Fried Chicken,
  '00 211
Fingers with Honey-Mustard Sauce, Chicken,
  '05 300
Firecrackers, Texas, '95 96; '99 94
Jamaican Jerk Raspberry Chicken, '00 88
Liver and Bacon Roll-Ups, Chicken, '80 200; '81 57
Livers, Garlic Chicken, '96 105
Livers, Party Chicken, '83 242
Liver Turnovers, Chicken, '79 141
Log, Chicken-Pecan, '81 290
Mushroom Appetizers, Chicken-, '88 210
Nuggets, Baked Chicken, '81 149
Nuggets, Chicken-Bacon, '03 292; '04 146
Nuggets, Lemon-Chicken, '87 283
Nuggets Supreme, Chicken, '85 160
Nuggets with Pineapple Sauce, Chicken, '84 236
Puffs, Appetizer Chicken, '85 72
Puffs, Chicken Nut, '81 260
Quesadillas, Spicy Chicken, '95 42
Quesadillas with Chipotle Salsa, Chicken-and-Brie,
  '99 311
Rollups, Southwestern, '01 135
Salad, Old-Fashioned Chicken, '83 79
Salad Spirals, Southwestern Chicken, '02 58
Sandwiches, Curried Chicken Tea, '97 23
Sesame Chicken, '97 256
Sesame Chicken Appetizers, '89 61
Skewers, Taco-Chicken, '99 119
Sticks, Italian Chicken, '98 25
Sticky Chicken, '97 239
Strips, Sesame Chicken, '98 250
Strips with "Come Back" Dipping Sauce, Miss
  Mary's Chicken, '96 213
Tarts, Chicken Salad, '84 257
Tarts, Deviled Chicken, '94 14
Tempura Delight, Chicken, '85 66
Terrine, Vegetable-Chicken, '83 224
Wings, Broiled Chicken, '80 149
Wings, Buffalo, '00 203; '05 64
Wings, Buffalo Hot, '03 184
Wings, Chinese Chicken, '96 111
Wings, Curried Chicken, '96 110
Wings, Grilled Honey Chicken, '96 111
Wings, Honey Chicken, '00 15
Wings, Honey-Glazed Chicken, '91 251
Wings, Hot Buffalo, '87 176
Wings, Maple-Glazed Chicken, '99 110
Wings, Satan's, '87 214
Wings, Sesame-Maple Chicken, '00 57
Wings, Spicy Buffalo, '95 239
Wings, Spicy Oriental-Style, '96 215
Wings, Sweet-and-Hot Citrus, '00 202
Wings, Sweet-and-Sour Chicken, '90 206;
  '96 110
Wings, Tandoori Chicken, '96 110
Wings, Teriyaki Chicken, '85 300; '86 18
Wings with Spanish Rice, Chicken, '00 202

Wontons with Hoisin Peanut Dipping Sauce,
  Chicken, '99 14
Wraps, Chicken Lettuce, '02 65
Chile-Sausage Squares, '86 297
Chiles Rellenos, Bite-Size, '87 246
Chiles Rellenos, Roasted, '95 64
Chili in Pastry Cups, '90 68
Chips
  Bagel Chips, '91 138
  Bagel Chips, Cinnamon-and-Sugar, '91 139
  Bagel Chips, Garlic, '91 139
  Bagel Chips, Lemon-and-Herb, '91 139
  Bagel Chips, Parmesan Cheese, '91 138
  Beet Chips, '97 229
  Cumin Crisps, '02 205
  Homemade Texas Chips with Guacamole Spread,
    '90 119
  Pita Chips, '89 19; '91 138
  Pita Chips, Baked, '99 138
  Plantain Chips, '95 M203
  (Plantain Chips), Tostones de Plátano, '92 158
  Sweet Potato Chips, '91 138; '93 332; '95 M203
  Sweet Potato Chips with Blue Cheese, '93 290
  Tortilla Chips, '91 137
  Tortilla Chips, Corn, '91 17
  Tortilla Chips, Light, '91 257
  Wonton Chips, Baked, '91 138; '99 138
  Wonton Chips, Cinnamon-and-Sugar, '91 138
  Wonton Chips, Garlic, '91 138
  Wonton Chips, Lemon-and-Herb, '91 138
  Wonton Chips, Parmesan Cheese, '91 138
Chocolate-Almond Cream, '91 108
Chocolate Bites, Snowy, '90 47
Chocolate Clusters, Triple, '01 242
Chocolate-Dipped Horns, '93 197
Chocolate-Peanut Butter Snacks, '90 226
Chocolate-Sesame Sticks, '91 316
Chutney, Cranberry, '96 275
Chutney Roll, '83 259
Chutney, Texas Cranberry, '04 257
Chutney with Cream Cheese, Cranberry-Amaretto,
  '87 244
Cinnamon Sticks, '95 244
Cinnamon Wafers, '84 324
Clam Crisps, '80 151
Clam Puffs, '90 60
Clams Casino, '81 125
Clams Oreganata, '85 104
Clams with Cilantro-Black Walnut Pesto, Littleneck,
  '97 164
Cocktail Puffs, '91 106
Confetti Appetizers, '84 191
Corn Salsa, Spicy, '93 322
Crab. See also APPETIZERS/Dips, Spreads and
  Fillings.
  Balls, Crabmeat, '88 150
  Ball, Spicy Crab, '01 332
  Bites, Crabmeat, '97 98
  Bites, Crab-Zucchini, '84 M216
  Bites, Spicy Crab, '91 165
  Broiled Crab Meltaways, '93 287
  Cakes and Dijon Sauce, Mini Crab, '03 92
  Cakes, Crab, '99 267; '01 245
  Cakes, Crab-and-Scallop, '02 165
  Cakes, Miniature Crab, '96 306
  Cakes with Cress Sauce, Baked Crab, '96 176
  Cakes with Maui Sauce, Crab, '99 310
  Casserole, Easy Crab, '93 270
  Chafing Dish Crabmeat, '89 284
  Crisps, Crab, '79 63
  Deviled Crab, Devilish, '85 264
  Hors d'Oeuvre, Crabmeat, '94 236
  Imperial, Crab, '02 103
  Mold, Crab, '85 318

  Oysters, Crabmeat Stuffed, '94 328
  Polenta, Crab, '00 277
  Pot Stickers, Hoisin Crab, '96 92
  Puffs, Crab, '80 20; '84 269
  Puffs, Crabmeat, '99 335
  Rémoulade, Crabmeat, '93 280
  Salsa with Sesame Wontons, Spicy Crab-and-Ginger,
    '01 283
  Sandwiches, Miniature Crab Cake, '96 306
  Snacks, Crab, '83 93
  Topping, Crabmeat, '91 64
Crackers, Bone, '01 204
Cranberry-Nut Triangles, '04 273
Crawfish on Eggplant, Soft-Shell, '88 222
Crème Brûlée, Onion, '95 324
Crème Brûlée, Roasted Garlic, '95 324
Crème Brûlées, Savory, '95 324
Crêpes, Basic, '04 245
Crostini. See also APPETIZERS/Bruschetta,
  Canapés.
  Almond-Bacon-Cheese Crostini, '94 318
  Artichoke Crostini, Hot, '94 319
  Cheese Crostini, Zippy, '97 90
  Cheesy Crostini, '03 223
  Christmas Crostini, '94 318
  Festive Crostini, '98 183; '99 325
  Green Onion Crostini, '96 93
  Grilled Crostini with Olive Tapenade, '05 172
  Mexican Crostini, '95 142
  Mozzarella Crostini, '94 319
  Olive Crostini, '02 205
  Parmesan-Artichoke Crostini, '98 285
  Pear-and-Gorgonzola Crostini, '02 314
  Roasted Peppers-Feta Cheese Crostini, '96 87
  Roasted Red Pepper-Feta Crostini, '04 69
  Spinach Crostini, '01 283
  Spinach-Red Pepper Crostini, '03 34
  Swiss-Blue Cheese Crostini, '94 318; '96 215
  Tomato-and-Goat Cheese Crostini, '04 168
  Tomato Crostini, '99 230
  Walnut-Blue Cheese, Crostini with, '01 321
Crunch, Oriental, '96 215
Crunchy Munchies, '94 196
Cucumber Delights, '84 117
Cucumber-Dill Rounds, '05 96
Cucumber Fingers, Fried, '86 146
Cucumber Rounds, '88 78
Cucumber Sandwiches, '90 81; '94 14; '97 99
Cucumber Soup with Dill Cream, '00 130
Cucumber Vichyssoise, '94 90
Date-Nut Ball, '92 326
Dates, Apricot-Stuffed, '80 250
Dips. See also APPETIZERS/Caviar, Salsas.
  Almond Cream Dip with Strawberries, '92 164
  Almond Delight Dip, '90 226
  Antipasto Dip, '93 313
  Apple Dip, '93 205; '96 M190
  Apricot Dip, '86 178
  Artichoke-Chile Dip, '98 234
  Artichoke Dip, Baked, '95 239; '03 294
  Artichoke Dip, Deluxe, '80 87
  Artichoke Dip, Florentine, '96 274
  Artichoke Dip, Greek, '97 315
  Artichoke Dip in a Bread Basket, '93 13
  Artichoke Dip, Italian, '97 315
  Artichoke Dip, Mexican, '90 292
  Artichoke Dip, Quick, '02 69; '03 270; '04 107
  Artichoke Dip, Seasoned Mayonnaise, '80 87
  Artichoke-Seafood Dip, Hot, '80 241
  Artichoke Seafood Dip, Hot, '85 M212
  Avocado Dip, '80 285; '81 57, 306
  Avocado Dip, "Bring-Home-the-Bacon," '92 80
  Avocado Dip, Zippy, '82 9; '83 69
  Bacon-and-Tomato Dip, '90 147

Bacon-Cheese Dip, '01 194
Bacon Dip, '82 197
Bacon Dip, Zesty, '92 156
Bacon-Guacamole Dip, '85 25
Basket, Dips and Dippers in a, '83 171
Bean Dip, '89 97
Bean Dip, Barbecue, '03 138
Bean Dip, Hot, '04 323
Bean Dip, Hotshot, '87 195
Bean Dip, Prairie Fire, '80 195
Beau Monde Dip in Rye Bread, Party, '83 127
Beef-and-Pasta Sauce Dip, Creamy, '01 108
Beef-and-Spinach Dip, '99 65
Beef Dip, Chipped, '88 M8
Beef Dip, Hot Cheesy, '80 85
Beef Dip, Spicy Cheese-, '02 58
Black Bean Dip, '95 93
Black-Eyed Pea con Queso, '96 274
Black-Eyed Pea Dip, '81 8; '04 M18
Black-Eyed Pea Dip, Bill D's, '97 M89
Blue Cheese-Bacon Dip, '04 287
Blue Cheese Dip, '80 285; '83 169; '93 313; '01 194
Braunschweiger-and-Beer Dip, '85 69
Broccoli Dip, Cheesy, '83 92
Broccoli-Garlic Dip, '82 59
Brown Sugar Dip with Fruit, Buttery, '90 243
Cabbage, Dock Dip in, '86 179
Catfish Dip, Layered, '03 185; '05 55
Cheddar-Bacon Dip, '89 M119
Cheese-and-Chile Dip, '83 31
Cheese and Crab Dip, Hot, '81 261
Cheese-Bean Dip, '85 208
Cheese-Crab Dip, '91 200
Cheese Dip, Hot, '91 171
Cheese Dip, Meaty, '82 59; '92 160
Cheese Dip, Seaside, '85 284
Cheese Dunk, Deviled, '80 265
Cheese-Garlic Dip, '80 192
Cheese-Herb Dip, '89 20
Chicken Dip, Hot, '80 86
Chickpea-and-Red Pepper Dip, '99 138
Chile-Beef Dip, Hot, '83 218
Chile-Cheese Dip, '87 173
Chile con Queso, '80 194; '81 195
Chile Con Queso, Roasted Poblano, '01 186
Chile con Queso Supreme, '80 265
Chile Dip, Hot, '82 248
Chile Sauce, Hot, '92 156
Chili-and-Black-Eyed Pea Dip, '92 155
Chili-and-Cheese Dip, '89 328
Chili-Cheese Dip, '90 225
Chili Con Queso, '04 69
Chili con Queso Dip, '86 81
Chili Dip, '82 161; '88 218; '89 47; '91 143
Chili Dip, Cheesy, '80 150
Chipotle-Black Bean Dip, Creamy, '05 247
Chive-Cheese Dip, '94 62
Christmas Confetti Dip, '92 279
Cilantro Dip, '00 248
Clam Dip, '79 151; '80 265; '01 194
Clam Dip, Hot, '82 59; '89 48
Clam Dip, Zesty, '92 25
Confetti Snack Dip, '79 107
Corn-and-Avocado Dip, Roasted, '91 279
Corn-and-Field Pea Dip, '01 177
Cottage Cheese Sun-Dried Tomato Dip, '93 13
Crab-and-Cheese Dip, Hot, '94 282
Crab Dip, Creamy, '80 M135
Crab Dip, Festive, '92 285
Crab Dip, Hot, '93 269; '97 89; '05 124

Crab Dip, Oven-Baked, '82 59
Crab Dip, Tangy, '83 5
Crab Dip, Trawler, '93 238
Crabmeat Dip, Hot, '95 154
Cranberry Fruit Dip, '89 60
Cranberry-Horseradish Dip, '85 65
Cream Cheese Dip, Fruited, '88 261
Cream Cheese-Onion Dip, '79 236
Creamy Texas Dip, '94 161
Crudité Dip, '86 105
Crudité Platter with Dip, '84 139
Cucumber-and-Yogurt Dipping Sauce, '02 172
Cucumber Dipping Sauce, '94 47
Cucumber-Yogurt Dip, '99 93
Curried Dip, '81 262
Curry Dip, '80 84; '81 9; '85 132; '86 184; '87 25; '99 138
Curry Dip and Vegetable Platter, '89 327
Curry Dip, Creamy, '84 206
Curry-Onion Dip, '93 313
Delight, Dipper's, '98 93
Devil, Dipsy, '00 132
Deviled Dip, '87 25
Dill Dip, '80 265; '93 330
Dill Dip, Refreshing, '99 324
Dilled Garden Dip, '84 324
Dried Beef Dip, '01 90
Dried Beef Dip, Extra-Creamy, '03 240
Egg Dip, Festive, '79 285
Eggplant Dip, '96 275
Feta Dip, Zesty, '04 71
Fiesta Dip, '81 206; '92 263; '96 212; '03 284
Fiesta Dip, Quick, '99 M197
Fish Dip, Smoked, '84 46
Fondue, Beer-and-Cheddar, '03 223
Fondue, Cheese, '81 40
Fondue, Fruitcake, '84 258
Fondue, Nacho, '94 332; '95 35
Fondue, Party Cheese, '92 20
Fondue, Peppermint, '94 332; '95 35
Fondue, Pub, '94 332; '95 35
Fondue, Swiss Cheese, '91 48
Fruit Dip, Coconut-Honey, '84 171
Fruit Dip, Creamy, '84 51
Fruit Dip, Fresh, '80 265; '95 94
Fruit Dip, Ginger, '96 110
Fruit Dip, Heavenly, '81 160
Fruit Dip, Marshmallow, '84 171
Fruit Dip, Quick, '90 110
Fruit Dips, Fun, '01 109
Fruit Dip, Sweet, '89 328
Garbanzo Dip, '93 94
Gazpacho Dip, '95 243
Ginger Dip, '94 12, 19; '99 139
Goblin Dip with Bone Crackers, '01 204
Grand Marnier Dip, '86 142
Green Goddess Dip, '84 159
Guacamole, '79 185; '80 74; '83 179; '91 161; '96 170; '03 95
Guacamole, Black Bean, '94 277
Guacamole, Creamy, '79 91; '83 174; '99 119; '02 168
Guacamole Dip, '86 4; '95 96
Guacamole Dip, Bacon, '85 25
Guacamole, Easy, '95 94
Guacamole in Shells, '86 74
Guacamole, Margarita, '97 167
Guacamole, Roasted Onion, '00 334
"Guacamole" with Cumin Crisps, Green Goddess, '02 205
Guac, Baine's, '98 88
Ham Dip, Creamy, '93 125
Herbal Dip, '86 14
Herb Dip, Creamy, '04 54

Holiday Dip, '83 321; '84 289
Honey-Herb Dip, Creamy, '98 135
Horseradish Dip, Creamy, '94 122
Hummas, '92 155
Hummus, '96 158
Hummus, Black-Eyed Pea, '94 123
Hummus, Creamy Dried Tomato, '95 284
Hummus Dip, Quick, '05 206
Hummus, Low-Fat, '99 137
Hummus, Quick, '95 93
Hummus, Red Pepper, '00 132; '02 31; '05 97
Hummus, White Bean, '01 32
Indonesian Dip, '96 190
Kahlúa Dip, '99 139
Leek Dip, Creamy, '86 77
Lime-Dill Dip, '92 65
Lime Dressing, Creamy, '04 46
Marmalade Dip, '99 324
Mexican Appetizer, Chilled, '87 197
Mexican Fiesta Dip, '98 234
Mint Dip with Fresh Fruit, '87 146
Monster Mash Dip, '93 244
Mushroom Dip, Hot, '89 48
Mustard Dip, Sweet-and-Spicy, '96 M274
Nacho Dip, '83 239; '93 M330
Nacho Dip, Layered, '81 261; '03 207
Nacho Dip, Quick, '90 168
Niçoise, Sauce, '96 190
Olive-Relish Dip, '84 205
Onion Dip, '94 21
Onion Dip, Cheesy, '83 145
Onion Dip, Chunky, '84 257
Orange Cream, '90 126
Orange Dip, Creamy, '84 117; '87 247
Orange Dip, Spicy, '85 230
Orange Fruit Dip, '96 190
Orange-Lime Dip, '96 248
Orange Sour Cream Dip, '79 208
Oyster Dip, Smoked, '79 233
Parsley-Dill Dip with Fresh Vegetables, '85 79
Peach Dip, Creole, '80 142
Peachy Dip, '92 179
Peanut Butter Dip, '86 135; '01 109
Peanut Butter-Honey Dip, '85 19
Peanut Butter Lovers' Dip, '93 162
Peas, Passion, '89 17
Pepperoncini-Cream Cheese Dip, '91 252
Pesto Dip, '95 93; '97 226
Pesto-Garbanzo Dip, '03 299
Pico de Gallo, '02 168, 306
Pineapple Dip, Cheesy, '80 249
Pineapple-Ginger Dip, '86 104
Pine Nut-Spinach Dip, '99 138
Pink Lemonade-Lime Dip, '04 133
Pizza Dip, '99 65
Pizza Dip, Quick, '00 M168
Plantain Dip, '92 158
Pumpkin Pie Dip, '01 242
Quick Fiesta Dip, '95 M237
Ranch Dip, Skinny, '93 96
Ranch-Style Dip, '90 138; '92 148
Salsa-Bean Dip, '98 285
Salsa, Chunky, '86 130; '90 206
Salsa Cruda, '87 180; '88 148
Salsa Dip, Southwestern, '05 212
Salsa, Fresh Summer, '87 89
Salsa, Greek Vegetable, '98 32
Salsa, Olive, '00 277
Salsa Picante, '84 108; '04 41
Salsa, Quick Party, '03 292; '04 146
Salsa with Cinnamon Crisps, Fruit, '01 108
Sauce, Citrus Dipping, '97 208
Sauce, Hoisin Peanut Dipping, '99 14
Seafood Dip, '79 3

Seafood Dip, Hot Cheesy, '84 221
Seafood Dip, Super, '90 292
Shrimp Dip, '86 84; '88 M261; '98 67; '01 194
Shrimp Dip, Chunky, '96 214
Shrimp Dip, Hot, '87 190
Shrimp Dip, Monterey, '99 M65
Shrimp Dip, Quick, '79 153
Shrimp Dip, Zesty, '80 150
Six-Layer Dip, '81 160
Skinny Dip, Santa Fe, '94 137
Smoked Salmon Dip, Extra-Creamy, '03 240
Sour Cream Dip, '86 278
Sour Cream Dip, Cilantro-Lime, '05 247
Sour Cream Dip, "Salsafied," '05 247
South-of-the-Border Dip, '81 235
Spinach-Artichoke Dip, '00 26
Spinach-Cheese Dip, Hot, '89 48
Spinach con Queso, Easy, '88 101
Spinach Dip, '80 86; '86 159; '87 25, 214; '93 324
Spinach Dip, Cheesy, '82 59
Spinach Dip, Creamy, '88 132
Spinach Dip, Hot, '80 249
Spinach Dip in Cabbage, '82 155
Spinach Dip in Sourdough Round, '98 173
Strawberry Dip, '01 109
Sugar Snap Dip, '88 91
Summer Dip, '94 157
Swiss-Onion Dip, '95 93
Taco Dip, Hot, '93 238
Tarragon Dip, '83 78
Tennessee Sin, '95 218; '96 204
Tequila Dip, '91 166
Thick-and-Creamy Dip, '90 271
Tofu Dip, '86 109
Tomato-Basil Dip, '05 219
Tomato-Basil Dip, Steamed Asparagus with, '00 69
Tomato Pesto Dip with Tortellini, Creamy, '00 196
Tostada Dip, '84 206
Tropical Dip for Fruit, '91 252
Tuna-Curry Dip, '84 31
Tuna Dip, Low-Cal, '87 25
Tuna Dip, Tasty, '96 190
Turnip Green Dip, '91 13
Turnip Green Dip with Jalapeño-Corn Muffins, Hot,
   '93 164
Vegetable Dip, '79 52; '82 161; '02 18
Vegetable Dip, Creamy, '82 132; '83 99, 180;
   '03 25
Vegetable Dip, Cucumber-Cheese, '83 128
Vegetable Dip, Fresh, '80 249
Vegetable Dip, Herb, '89 269
Vegetable Dip, Quick Creamy, '00 34; '05 20
Vegetable Dip, Starburst, '82 248
Vegetable Dip, Tangy, '87 196
Vegetable Dip, Zippy, '84 256
Vegetable Garden Dip, '85 215
Vidalia Onion Dip, Baked, '02 88
Water Chestnut Dip, '80 86; '86 183
Yellow Squash-Zucchini Dip, '89 48
Yogurt Dip, '94 21
Yogurt Dip, Fruited, '84 171
Yogurt Herring Dip, '80 232
Zesty Party Dip, '83 259
Dumplings, Steamed Sesame, '97 208
Eggplant Appetizer, '83 187
Eggplant Appetizer, Grilled, '95 198
Eggplant Caviar, '88 262; '99 217
Eggplant, Cheesy Fried, '90 75
Eggplant, Fried Parmesan, '87 166
Eggplant Sticks, Ned's, '95 309
Egg Rolls, '86 81; '05 50
Egg Rolls, Chiles Rellenos, '86 296
Egg Rolls, Golden Sausage, '03 284
Eggrolls, Shrimp and Pork, '82 240; '83 18

Egg Rolls, Tex-Mex, '01 328
Egg Rolls, Vegetarian, '86 148
Egg Rolls with Creamy Cilantro Dipping Sauce, Tex-
   Mex, '03 327
Eggs and Ham, Green, '96 90
Eggs, Armadillo, '05 139
Eggs, Bacon-Stuffed, '04 290
Eggs, Black-and-Blue, '96 90
Eggs, Deviled Green Goblin, '02 222
Eggs, Double Stuffed Spinach-and-Bacon, '00 M333
Eggs, Marbleized Garlic-Cheese-Stuffed, '96 91
Elephant Ears, Garlic-and-Herb Baby, '00 87
Elephant Ears, Mushroom-and-Brie Petite, '00 87
Elephant Ears, Parmesan-Pepper Baby, '00 87
Elephant Ears Provençale, Baby, '00 87
Elephant Ears, Southwestern Baby, '00 87
Empanadas, '92 156
Empanadas, Pork Picadillo, '03 60
Endive Boats, '84 80
Endive with Arugula Tabbouleh Appetizers, '98 67
Endive with Caviar, '93 118
Escargots Provençal, '82 238; '83 156
Eye-of-Round, Burgundy, '90 243
Fast Goodies, '84 206
Fig Bites, Baked, '02 160
Figs with Prosciutto, Walnuts, and Cream, '96 194
Filet Mignon, Cajun Blackened, '95 85
Fish Taco Appetizers, '04 324
Flank Steak, Marinated, '83 258; '88 262
Flank Steak, Red Wine-Marinated, '95 283
Flank Steak Skewers, Lemon, '02 134
Frankfurter Appetizers, Bourbon, '85 207
Franks, Pickled Party, '83 174
Franks, Saucy Appetizer, '84 M12
Franks, Tipsy, '85 52
Frog Legs, Crispy, '80 99
Fruit and Cheese Tray, '83 171
Fruit Bowl, Sparkling Fresh, '80 146
Fruit Cascade, '86 104
Fruit Cup, Appetizer, '86 131
Fruit Kebabs, '86 181
Fruit Kebabs with Coconut Dressing, '87 251
Fruit with Curried Rum Sauce, Tropical, '91 164
Fruit with Dressing, Chilled, '85 222
Fruit with Honey-Sour Cream Dip, Fresh, '90 180
Gingerbread Bites with Orange-Cream Cheese Frosting,
   '04 258
Granola, '93 197
Granola, Fabulous, '92 213
Granola Gorp, '89 59
Granola, Nutty, '90 95
Granola, Pecan-Coconut, '02 70
Green Beans and Carrots, Sweet 'n' Hot, '00 211
Green Onion Teasers, '82 42
Griddle Cakes, Levee Camp, '03 29
Grouper Fingers, '00 167
Guacamole. See also APPETIZERS/Dips, Spreads
   and Fillings.
   Crisps, Guacamole, '98 173
   Mold, Guacamole, '86 184
   Spread, Guacamole, '90 119
Ham-and-Cheese Balls, Fried, '84 221
Ham Appetillas, '93 63
Ham Balls, '03 299
Ham-Filled Party Puffs, '84 116
Ham-Pineapple Nibbles, '95 283
Ham Rolls, '79 153
Ham Rolls, Party, '85 318
Ham Stack-Ups, '96 109
Ham Tapas, Garlic-, '92 175
Ham Turnovers, Chile-, '88 64
Ham Turnovers, Party, '82 39
Ham Twists, Deviled, '82 86
Hawaiian Dream Boats, '86 151

Hazelnuts, Curried, '93 301
Honey-and-Spice Crunch, '94 290
Horseradish Squares, Baked, '92 24
Hot Browns, Baby, '03 238
Hot Munch, Oriental, '87 8
Jalapeño Peppers, Fried Stuffed, '95 22
Jalapeño Peppers, Stuffed, '96 215
Jalapeños, Fiery Fried Stuffed, '90 118
Jalapeños, Fried, '96 292
Jalapeños, Shrimp-Stuffed, '88 115
Jalapeños, Stuffed, '98 234
Jezebel Sauce, '93 331
June Bugs, '85 11
Lamb Chops, Easy Baked, '02 66
Lamb Chops, Fried, '02 66
Lamb Chops, Glazed, '02 66
Lettuce Folds, Thai, '94 47
Links, Cocktail Smoky, '90 168
Liver, Mock Chopped, '00 281
Lobster-and-Roasted Corn Beignets, '00 51
Lobster Scallion Shooters, '00 197
Mango Chutney Torta, '96 322
Meatballs
   Bacon-Wrapped Meatballs, '79 81
   Baked Meatballs, '02 25
   Bourbon Meatballs, '00 252
   Brandied Meatballs, '83 78
   Burgundy-Bacon Meatballs, '80 283
   Chafing Dish Meatballs, '81 260
   Chestnut Meatballs, '79 110
   Chipotle-Barbecue Meatballs, Spicy, '05 305
   Cocktail Meatballs, '79 63, 207
   Cranberry Meatballs, '05 310
   Flavorful Meatballs, '84 206
   German Meatballs, Crisp, '92 326
   Glazed Meatballs, Bourbon-Mustard, '05 305
   Ham Balls, '86 256
   Ham Balls, Appetizer, '82 39
   Polynesian Meatballs, '80 207
   Quesadillas, Meatball, '00 242
   Saucy Party Meatballs, '80 149
   Sauerkraut Meatballs, '86 257
   Spiced Meatballs, '79 284
   Spicy Holiday Meatballs, '01 238
   Spicy Party Meatballs, '00 242
   Sweet-and-Sour Meatballs, '82 247; '99 325; '05 305
   Sweet-and-Sour Meatballs, Spicy, '03 186
   Sweet-and-Sour Party Meatballs, '79 233
   Tamale Meatballs, '80 194
   Venison Sausage Balls, '80 42
   Zesty Meatballs, '80 250
Melon Balls, Minted, '87 162
Melon, Berry-Filled, '86 93
Mints, Cream Cheese, '93 79; '00 41
Mints, Party, '81 119
Mints, Special, '99 323
Mirliton Balls, '90 217
Mixes, Snack
   Apple Spice-Raisin Snack Mix, '05 222
   Asian Snack Mix, '05 306
   Bunny Trail Mix, '95 101
   Buried Treasure Snack Mix, '04 162
   Cereal Snack Mix, '93 129
   Creole Snack Mix, '91 171
   Crunchy Snack Mix, '93 94
   Dried Fruit Mix, '92 22
   Gorp, Elf, '90 270
   Gorp, Fancy, '89 253
   Granola Snack Mix, '86 229
   Honey-Nut Snack Mix, '02 187
   Jalapeño Nut Mix, '96 27
   Make-Ahead Snack Mix, '04 M92
   Mexicali Snack Mix, '86 230
   Nutty Snack Mix, '92 22

Party Mix, '87 257; '96 306; '97 108, 322; '98 234
Quick Party Mix, '83 92
Raisin-Nut Party Mix, '83 60
Rice Mix, Crunchy, '85 327
Sea-and-Ski Cocktail Mix, '90 319
Sherry Snack Mix, '00 329
Snack-Attack Party Mix, '84 328
Snack Mix, '89 19
Spicy Party Mix, '81 M138
Starry Snack Mix, '00 329
Sweet 'n' Savory Snack Mix, '03 199
Trash Mix, '01 204
Monster Eyes, '02 222
Monster Mouths, '95 274
Moroccan Triangles, Crispy, '03 60
Mousses
Catfish Mousse, '92 327
Caviar Mousse, '82 71; '83 258; '85 86
Chicken Mousse, Curried, '95 328
Crabmeat Mousse, '90 190; '91 244
Crab Mousse, '79 117; '95 327
Ham Mousse Pitas, '95 328
Horseradish Mousse, '84 126
Mustard Mousse, '84 127; '86 184; '95 328
Oyster Mousse, '81 245
Oyster Mousse, Smoked, '84 320; '99 162
Salmon Dill Mousse, '81 21
Salmon Mousse, '83 79
Salmon Mousse, Irresistible, '79 284
Shrimp Mousse, '87 196, 251
Tuna Mousse, '80 275
Munchies, Reindeer, '91 276
Mushrooms. *See also* **APPETIZERS/Canapés.**
Drunk Mushrooms, '83 174
French-Fried Mushrooms, '82 78
French-Fried Mushrooms with Tartar Sauce, '86 233
Logs, Mushroom, '84 206
Marinated Herb Mushrooms, '86 327
Marinated Mushroom Caps, '83 128
Marinated Mushrooms, '80 82, 270; '86 135;
'91 306; '92 328
Marinated Mushrooms, Easy, '86 217
Pastry Cups, Mushroom-Almond, '88 210
Rollups, Mushroom, '85 318
Samurai 'shrooms, '93 258
Sour Cream, Mushrooms in, '00 106
Stems, Mushrooms with, '86 258
Stuffed Mushroom Appetizers, '88 210
Stuffed Mushroom Caps, Crab-, '84 160
Stuffed Mushroom Delight, '87 281
Stuffed Mushrooms, '79 212; '81 239; '83 13, 66,
126, 136; '93 172
Stuffed Mushrooms, Artichoke-, '01 239
Stuffed Mushrooms, Beef-, '00 278
Stuffed Mushrooms, Black Olive-, '86 258
Stuffed Mushrooms, Cheese 'n' Bacon-, '86 258
Stuffed Mushrooms, Crab-, '81 190; '97 102
Stuffed Mushrooms, Crawfish-, '86 258
Stuffed Mushrooms, Elegant Cheese-, '81 57
Stuffed Mushrooms, Flavor-, '85 288
Stuffed Mushrooms, Herbed Cheese-, '96 171
Stuffed Mushrooms, Italian Sausage-, '83 127
Stuffed Mushrooms, Parmesan, '83 115
Stuffed Mushrooms, Pâté-, '85 118
Stuffed Mushrooms, Pecan-, '84 261
Stuffed Mushrooms, Pesto-, '86 150
Stuffed Mushrooms, Pistachio-, '86 141
Stuffed Mushrooms, Ricotta-, '85 20
Stuffed Mushrooms, Sausage-, '80 248; '91 164;
'05 300

Stuffed Mushrooms, Seasoned, '84 206
Stuffed Mushrooms, Shrimp-, '80 M135; '99 324
Stuffed Mushrooms, Spinach-, '86 81; '88 131,
M261; '89 M133
Stuffed Shiitakes Parmigiana, '98 25
Stuffed with Crab, Mushrooms, '82 249
Stuffed with Ham, Mushrooms, '97 237
Tapas, Majorcan Mushroom, '95 159
Tarts, Hot Sherried Mushroom, '83 78
Tarts, Mushroom, '88 161
Tipsy Mushrooms, '84 M216
Turnovers, Hot Mushroom, '97 102
Turnovers, Mushroom, '05 310
Vegetable Mushroom Caps, '81 246
Nachos
Barbecue Nachos, Commissary, '91 171
Best-Ever Nachos, '79 91
Chicken Nachos, '84 244
Easy Nachos, '84 30
Make-Ahead Nachos, '80 M135
South Texas Nachos, '93 321
Southwestern Nachos, '96 170
Supreme, Nachos, '81 306
Texas Oyster Nachos, '87 39
Tex-Mex Nachos, '89 97
Tuna Nachos, '95 127; '96 201
Turkey Nachos, '90 118
Nectarine Cocktail, '85 107
New Potatoes, Ham-Stuffed, '88 211
Nibbles, Party, '90 249
Nuts. *See also* **APPETIZERS/Pecans.**
Cashews, Caribbean, '04 196
Cashews, Spicy, '01 134
Chesapeake Nuts, '93 269
Curried Nuts, Spicy, '82 250
Deviled Nuts, '93 118
Hot Chili Nuts, '81 254
Nippy Nuts, '93 301
Party Nuts, Chesapeake Bay, '03 179
Peanuts, Hot, '00 278
Peanuts, Sugar-and-Spice, '04 197
Peanuts, Sugared, '82 249
Pesto-Spiced Nuts, '95 173
Pistachios, Spicy, '04 197
Quick Party Nuts, '04 197
Sherry-Orange Nuts, '86 M289
Soup Nuts, '96 106
Spiced Nuts, '84 257; '91 M316
Spicy Nuts, '82 161
Walnuts, Chinese Fried, '81 254
Okra Rellenos, '97 156
Olive Cups, Greek, '99 221
Olive Quiche Appetizers, '86 159
Olives, Balsamic Marinated, '02 135
Olives, Caliente Marinated, '95 177
Olives, Herb-Marinated, '92 176
Olives, Lemon-Garlic, '94 118
Onion Blossom, '94 226
Onion Crescent Crunch Sticks, '90 206
Onions, Rosemary Roasted, '98 16
Onion Toasties, '97 225
Orange-Almond Snack Balls, '95 214
Orange-Berry Appetizer, '85 81
Orange Halves, Broiled, '85 288
Oyster Nachos, Texas, '87 39
Oysters à la Casino, '80 296
Oysters Annapolis, '89 195
Oysters, Barbecued, '82 247
Oysters Bienville, Baked, '90 27
Oysters Buccaneer, '87 40
Oysters Chesapeake, '92 254
Oysters, Creamed, '92 254
Oysters, Fried Bacon-Wrapped, '02 103
Oysters in Patty Shells, '85 257

Oysters Italiano, Baked, '89 97
Oysters with Paul's Cocktail Sauce, Grilled, '05 244
Pasta Bites, Pesto-Cheese, '87 251
Pears, Pineapple-Honey, '86 94
Pecans
Barbecued Pecans, '83 222
Christmas Eve Pecans, '91 276
Christmas Pecans, '03 300
Citrusy Pecans, '03 292; '04 146
Coffee 'n' Spice Pecans, '88 256
Curried Pecans, '91 208
Hot-and-Spicy Pecans, '89 161
Hot Pepper Pecans, '85 4
Hot Smoky Pecans, '98 173
Mexico Nuts, '01 27
Orange-Glazed Pecans, '97 225
Orange Pecans, '87 292
Party Nuts, Chesapeake Bay, '03 179
Pear-Pecan Appetizers, '96 262
Pepper Pecans, '87 137; '93 79
Roasted Bacon Pecans, '96 262
Roasted Pecans, Creole, '01 241
Salted Pecans, Southern, '80 285
Savory Southern Pecans, '95 240
Smoky Pecans, '01 168
Spiced Pecans, '79 296; '80 31
Spicy Pecans, '93 279
Sticks, Pecan, '01 242
Sugar-and-Spice Nuts, '05 274
Sugar and Spice Pecans, '82 297
Sugar-and-Spice Pecans, '86 121
Sweet-and-Spicy Pecans, '92 321; '00 334; '01 20
Sweet-and-Spicy Texas Pecans, '02 306
Toasted Chili Pecans, '85 154
Toasted Pecans, '84 321; '86 229; '03 300
Toasted Pecans, Buttery, '88 77
Pepper Feet, '93 258
Pepperoni Pie Hors d'Oeuvres, '98 251
Pepperoni Rolls, Ground-, '83 244
Peppers, Marinated Roasted, '92 176
Peppers, Stuffed Hungarian Yellow Banana, '00 132
Peppers with Balsamic Vinaigrette, Roasted, '94 128
Pesto Rounds, Toasted, '94 289
Pickles, French-Fried, '82 77
Pickles, Fried Dill, '84 206
Pineapple and Strawberries, Skewered, '84 251
Pineapple Delight, Fresh, '79 111
Pineapple Spritz, '86 94
Piroshki, '92 84
Pistachio Twists, '02 164
Pita Bread Triangles, '88 211
Pita Chips, '89 19; '91 138
Pita Pizza Snack, '94 193
Pita Triangles, Benne Seed, '05 97
Pita Wedges, Garlic, '93 98
Pizza Bites, '95 244
Pizza-Burger Snacks, '84 30
Pizza, Ham-and-Pineapple, '96 169
Pizza Horns, '89 214
Pizza, Mexican, '99 119
Pizza Party Snacks, '86 262
Pizza Pumpkins, '98 255
Pizzas, Appetizer, '89 M118
Pizzas, Cocktail, '79 110
Pizza Slices, '84 269
Pizza Snacks, '01 231
Pizza Snacks, Tasty Little, '79 248
Pizzas, Pita, '89 19
Pizza Squares, '87 168
Pizzas, Quick Little, '88 227
Pizza Turnovers, Little, '85 327
Pizzettes, Party, '80 192
Plantain Chips, '95 M203
(Plantain Chips), Tostones de Plátano, '92 158

Pop Graham Munchies, '96 28
Pork Rounds, Sesame, '89 122
Pork Strips, Marinated, '92 219
Pork Tenderloin on Cornmeal Biscuits, '04 257
Pork Tenderloin with Miniature Buttermilk Biscuits,
    Honey-Mustard, '02 103
Pork Tenderloin with Mustard Sauce, '03 238
Potato-Pea Soup, '94 90
Potato Shell Appetizers, '89 M119
Potato Skins, Baked, '86 81
Potato Skin Snack, '91 18
Power Munch, '96 180
Puff Nibbles, '84 191
Puffs, Cajun Hot, '94 277
Pull-Apart Ring, Southwestern, '03 298
Quesadillas, Poblano-and-Corn, '01 333
Quesadilla Torta, '97 325
Quiche, South-of-the-Border, '93 321
Quiche Squares, '84 222
Quiches, Tarragon Cocktail, '84 127
Raisin-Granola Treats, '92 22
Raspberry Party Puffs, '90 170
Ravioli, St. Louis Toasted, '95 117
Ravioli, Sweet, '91 107
Relish Tree, Christmas, '84 257
Reuben Rolls, Snappy, '02 58
Reubens, Golden-Baked Mini, '01 62
Reubens, Party, '90 61
Riblets, Sweet-and-Sour, '85 276
Rice Balls, '81 51
Rice with Spring Vegetables, '96 132
Risotto with Greens, '96 132
Risotto with Shellfish and Peas, '96 131
Roasted Red Pepper Rollups, '98 285
Rolls, Blue Cheese, '00 210
Rolls with Thai Dipping Sauce, Summer, '97 236
Rollups, Mediterranean, '00 277
Rosettes, Savory, '91 107
Rumaki, '80 136
Rumaki, Scallop, '98 M173
Rye Appetizers, Party, '86 262
Salami Rollups, '90 226
Salmon Ball, '80 149; '86 262
Salmon, Drizzled Smoked, '88 91
Salmon Log, '81 22
Salmon Party Log, '98 154
Salmon Party Roll, '83 127
Samosas, '89 266; '96 239
Samurai 'shrooms, '93 258
Sandwiches, Apple Party, '92 234
Sandwiches, Asparagus Spear, '84 165
Sandwiches, Bacon-Olive Party, '04 196
Sandwiches, Bread Basket of, '86 126
Sandwiches, Calla Lily, '91 106
Sandwiches, Chicken-Mandarin Orange Spread, '04 259
Sandwiches, Cucumber, '90 81; '94 14; '97 99
Sandwiches, Cucumber-Salmon-Watercress, '03 111
Sandwiches, Curried Tea, '91 314
Sandwiches, Dainty Cucumber, '81 119
Sandwiches, Double-Filled Party, '93 159
Sandwiches, Goat Cheese-Olive, '04 272
Sandwiches, Mini Muffuletta Bacon-Olive Party,
    '04 196
Sandwiches, Olive-Nut Spread, '04 259
Sandwiches, Party Ham, '97 240
Sandwiches, Rolled Olive, '01 241
Sandwiches, Stacking, '86 127
Sandwiches, Tiny Ham-and-Cheese, '99 87
Sandwiches, Turkey Tea, '99 86
Sandwiches, Victoria, '94 16
Sandwiches, Watercress, '90 82
Sandwiches, Watercress-Cucumber, '97 108
Sandwiches with Cranberry-Coriander Conserve, Pork
    Tenderloin, '04 286

Sandwiches with Dill, Cucumber-Salmon, '02 131
Sandwich Wreath, Festive, '86 333
Saté Mixed Grill with Spicy Peanut Sauce, '04 134
Sauce, Paul's Cocktail, '05 244
Sausage-Apple Balls, '90 85
Sausage-Bacon Rollups, '88 51
Sausage Balls, '98 93
Sausage Bites, Bourbon-Mustard Glazed, '05 305
Sausage Bites, Spicy Chipotle-Barbecue, '05 305
Sausage Bites, Sweet-and-Sour, '05 305
Sausage-Mushroom-Phyllo Bites, '89 284
Sausage Party Ryes, '89 315
Sausage Pinwheels, '80 209; '93 238
Sausage Quesadillas, '90 118
Sausage, Sweet-and-Sour, '88 296
Sausages with Mustard Sauce, Smoked, '81 56
Scallop Appetizer, '86 155
Scallop Appetizers, Flaky, '86 327
Scallops, Bacon-Wrapped, '87 94
Scallops in Vermouth-Cream Sauce, '96 49
Scallops with Orange-Honey Sauce, Bacon-Wrapped,
    '97 236
Seafood Appetizer, Layered, '88 2
Seafood Mold, Chilled, '86 70
Seafood Tartlets, '87 247
Sea Scallops with Tomato Puree, Seared, '97 201
Seeds, Santa Fe, '02 145
Seviche Cocktail, '83 258
Shortbread, Blue Cheese-Walnut, '03 108
Shortbread, Cajun-Benne Seed, '97 95
Shortbread, Herbed-Feta Cheese, '03 109
Shortbread, Jalapeño-Pecan, '03 108
Shortbread, Pesto, '03 108
Shrimp. *See also* **APPETIZERS/Canapés, Dips,
    Spreads and Fillings.**
Afterburners, '03 159
Bacon-Shrimp Bites, '98 234; '99 213
Bacon, Shrimp 'n', '98 222
Balls, Curried Shrimp, '94 180
Barbecue Shrimp, '96 210; '97 58; '00 30
Bayou, Shrimp, '88 261
Biscuits, Shrimp-and-Grits, '02 313
Boiled Shrimp, Spicy, '84 289
Boiled Shrimp with Cocktail Sauce, '79 151
Braised Shrimp with Garlic Rémoulade, '98 133
Bundles with Chive Butter Sauce, Crispy Shrimp,
    '03 91
Butter on Crostini, Shrimp, '04 259
Cheese Appetizer, Shrimp-and-, '01 134
Chilled Shrimp with Rémoulade Sauce, '02 134
Cocktail, Cinco de Mayo Shrimp, '05 138
Cocktail, Mexican Shrimp, '00 249
Cocktail Shrimp, '87 173
Cocktail, Shrimp, '96 174
Coconut-Beer Shrimp, '85 230
Coconut Fried Shrimp, '96 248
Coconut Shrimp with Mustard Sauce, '02 245
Croustades, Shrimp, '97 23
Dilled Shrimp, '88 150
Dippers, Shrimp, '84 324
Double-Dip Shrimp, '99 112
Garlic-and-Rosemary Shrimp, '01 101; '04 52
Grilled Jerk Shrimp with Creamy Tomatillo Sauce,
    '01 332
Herbed Jalapeño Cheese, Shrimp with, '87 112
Kebabs, Appetizer Shrimp, '91 251
Kebabs, Shrimp, '80 150
Key West Shrimp, '94 278
Manale, Shrimp, '86 268
Marinated Shrimp and Artichokes, '97 89; '98 335
Marinated Shrimp and Cucumber, '91 166
Marinated Shrimp, Icy, '84 215
Marinated Shrimp with Capers, '00 279

Marinated Shrimp, Zesty, '87 173
Miniquiches, Shrimp, '87 146
Mold, Shrimp, '87 94
Mold with Asparagus, Shrimp, '93 214
Mushrooms, Shrimp-Stuffed, '80 M135; '99 324
Oven-Fried Shrimp with Marmalade Dip, '99 324
Pickled Shrimp, '94 182
Pickle, Shrimp-in-a-, '86 326
Pineapple Appetizer, Shrimp-, '85 80
Pizza Wedges, Shrimp, '89 158
Puffs, Shrimp, '96 211; '98 316
Rémoulade, Galatoire's Shrimp, '04 103
Rémoulade, Shrimp, '83 173
Rock Shrimp Conga, '80 2
Rolls with Sweet Soy Sauce, Jumbo Shrimp, '03 248
Rounds, Shrimp, '98 167
Salsa Picante with Shrimp, '92 210
Sandwiches, Open-Faced Shrimp-Cornbread, '02 141
Sesame Shrimp, '95 92
Sherried Garlic Shrimp, '92 175
Skewers with Vegetable Salsa, Shrimp, '98 32
Smoked Shrimp, Citrus-Marinated, '95 114
Smoked Shrimp, Stove-Top, '01 168
Steamed Shrimp, '03 206
Tangy Shrimp, '04 18
Tartlets, Shrimp, '00 71
Toast, Shrimp, '86 91; '00 109
Tortilla Bites, '95 42
Tostadas, Shrimp-and-Black Bean, '93 204
Tree, Shrimp, '83 320; '84 288; '85 318
Vegetable Appetizer, Shrimp-and-, '97 161
Snackwiches, '88 172
Snow Peas and Dip, Crunchy, '86 62
Snow Peas, Crab-Stuffed, '85 288
Snow Peas, Stuffed, '84 80
Spanakopita, '96 233
Spinach and Artichokes in Puff Pastry, '00 277
Spinach-and-Cheese Pastries, Greek, '96 76
Spinach-Artichoke-Tomato Puffs, '95 284
Spinach-Filled Phyllo Triangles, '84 52
Spinach Madeleine in Chafing Dish, '85 319
Spinach-Mushroom Cheesecake, '92 326
Spinach Puffs, '95 316
Spinach Quichelets, '87 67
Spinach Quiches, '01 241
Spinach Quiches, Miniature, '82 38
Spinach-Ricotta Phyllo Triangles, '88 212
Spinach Rollups, '98 251
Spinach Squares, '88 131
Spinach Strudels, '93 249
Spinach Supreme, Layered, '82 38
Spinach Tarts, '82 249
Spinach Triangles, Phyllo-, '87 53
Spreads and Fillings
Aloha Spread, '83 93
Antipasto Spread, '81 25
Apple-Date Spread, '91 231; '92 67
Apricot Brie Spread, '86 275
Apricot-Cream Cheese Spread, '82 161; '87 158
Artichoke-Cheese Spread, '04 294
Artichoke-Crab Spread, Hot, '85 81
Artichoke Hearts with Caviar, '79 142
Artichoke-Parmesan Spread, '92 95
Artichoke Spread, Chunky, '89 98
Artichoke Spread, Hot, '79 110
Avocado-Cheese Spread, Herbed, '98 335
Beef Spread, Hot, '83 50; '84 M216
Beef Spread in Puff Pastry, Chipped, '98 M335
Beer Cheese, '98 82
Beer Cheese Spread, '81 160; '94 123
Beer-Cheese Spread, '85 69
Black-Eyed Pea Spread, '86 77
Blue Cheese Spread, '90 215; '95 92; '97 240
Blue Cheese Spread with Walnuts, Buttery, '00 329

APPETIZERS, Spreads and Fillings
(continued)

Boursin Cheese Spread, Buttery, '94 301; '96 318
Boursin Cheese Spread, Garlic, '94 301
Braunschweiger-Onion Spread, '79 82
Broccamoli Curry Spread, '88 55
Caraway Spread, '85 276
Carrot-Pecan Spread, '96 108
Carrot Spread, Nutty, '94 123
Catfish Spread, Best-Ever, '98 60
Caviar-Artichoke Mound, '91 244
Caviar-Cream Cheese Spread, '84 256
Caviar Spread, Creamy, '92 58
Cheese-and-Orange Filling, '93 159
Cheese-Horseradish Spread, '84 222
Cheese-Olive Spread, '79 82
Cheese, Peppered Pimiento, '01 137
Cheese Spread, '86 135
Cheese Spread, Almond, '87 292
Cheese Spread, Confetti, '84 256
Cheese Spread, Creamy Sweet, '79 264
Cheese Spread, Fresh Basil-, '97 108
Cheese Spread, German, '79 82
Cheese Spread, Hawaiian, '87 158
Cheese Spread, Make-Ahead, '93 324
Cheese Spread, Mexican, '90 119
Cheese Spread, Peppered, '01 123
Cheese Spread, Tipsy, '80 150
Cheese Spread, Zippy, '85 4
Cheesy Beer Spread, '87 196
Chicken-Artichoke-Cheese Spread Gift Box, '00 328
Chicken Salad Party Spread, '88 M8
Chicken Salad Spread, Curried, '00 68
Chicken Spread, Festive, '87 158
Chicken Spread, Tasty, '84 193
Chickpea Spread, Creamy, '03 293; '04 146
Chile-Cheese Spread, '02 205
Chili Cheese Spread, '93 242
Chili-Cheese Spread, '99 336
Chive-Mustard Spread, '91 12
Chocolate Chip Cheese Loaves, '91 299
Chutney-Onion Cheese Spread, '01 94
Chutney Spread, Curried, '89 283
Clam Spread, Creamy, '91 274
Coconut-Cranberry Cheese Spread, '92 328
Corn-and-Walnut Spread, '96 26
Corned Beef Spread, '87 196
Crabmeat-Horseradish Spread, '90 292
Crabmeat Spread, '79 81
Crabmeat Spread, Layered, '83 127; '04 69
Crab Soufflé Spread, '85 4
Crab Spread, '93 167
Crab Spread, Baked, '80 86
Crab Spread, Best-Ever, '98 60
Crab Spread, Superb, '81 235
Cranberry Ambrosia-Cream Cheese Spread, '00 308
Cream Cheese Filling, '90 170
Cream Cheese Spread, Deviled, '81 235
Cream Cheese Spread, Fruited, '91 306; '93 79
Cream Cheese Spread, Nutty, '89 327
Cream Cheese Spread, Tri-Flavored, '98 134
Cucumber Spread, '79 295; '80 31
Curry-Almond Cheese Spread, '01 238
Curry Spread, '93 159
Date-Orange-Nut Spread, '02 59
Date-Walnut-Cheese Spread, '96 322
Dried Tomato-Cheese Spread, '90 204
Edam-Sherry Spread, '84 257
Egg Mound, Frosted, '79 33
Eggplant-Mushroom Spread, '92 156
Egg, Sour Cream, and Caviar Spread, '85 279
Feta Cheese Spread, '96 265

Fruit and Cheese Spread, '81 245
Fruit-and-Cheese Spread, Nutty, '87 246; '02 164
Fruit Spread, '85 135
Garbanzo Bean Spread, Herbed, '99 160
Garden Spread, '86 135
Garlic Spread, '85 111
Goat Cheese Spread, '02 198
Gouda Cheese Spread, '90 36
Green Onion-Cheese Spread, '92 24
Gruyère-Apple Spread, '81 160
Guacamole Spread, '90 119
Ham and Pimiento Spread, '80 285; '81 56
Ham Spread, Buttery, '95 93; '97 98
Ham Spread, Cold, '82 248
Ham Spread, Country, '87 8
Hearts of Palm Spread, '90 293
Herb-Cheese Spread, '91 124
Herb-Cream Cheese Spread, '83 24
Honey-Nut Spread, '87 157
Horseradish-Chive Cream, '02 313
Horseradish Spread, '90 243
Hummus, '96 158; '03 60
Hummus, Black-Eyed Pea, '03 60
Italian Spread, '85 135
Jalapeño-Cheese Spread, '82 248
Lemon-Raisin Spread, '01 48
Lentil Spread, '99 288
Liver Spread, '89 161
Liver Spread, Sherried, '80 86
Mayonnaise, Tex-Mex, '01 134
Mullet Spread, '94 159
Mushroom Spread, Hot, '81 190
Olive Spread, Creamy, '81 290; '05 311
Olive Spread, Tomatoes with, '85 114
Oyster Spread, Smoked, '91 64
Party Bread Spread, '82 161
Party Spread, Spicy, '97 240
Peanut Butter Spread, '92 21
Pear-Cream Cheese Spread, '93 80
Pepper Spread, Roasted, '94 123
Pesto Goat Cheese, '03 110
Pesto, Lucinda's Garden, '01 100
Pimiento Cheese, Baked, '04 291
Pimiento Cheese, Hot, '87 173
Potato-Garlic Spread, Creamy, '02 35
Radish Spread, Fresh, '84 166
Raisin Spread, Creamy, '90 36
Roasted Red Bell Pepper Spread, '97 217
Salmon-and-Horseradish Spread, '87 146
Salmon Spread, '81 149
Salmon Spread, Smoked, '84 324; '98 285
Salmon Spread with Capers, Smoked, '98 49
Seafood Spread, '86 M58; '87 146
Seafood Spread, Grandma Reed's, '98 268
Shrimp Paste, '05 98
Shrimp Spread, '81 306; '85 135; '87 111; '93 205
Shrimp Spread, Chunky, '85 300; '86 18
Shrimp Spread, Curried, '87 158
Shrimp Spread, Tempting, '79 57
Shrimp Spread, Zippy, '90 36
Smoked Fish Spread, '92 305
Smoked Whitefish Spread, '92 58
Sombrero Spread, '87 111
Spinach-Bacon Spread, '92 M310
Spinach Spread, '88 132
Spinach Spread, Savory, '82 180
Sun-dried-Tomato-and-Basil Spread, Layered,
'05 275
Sweet 'n' Sour Spread, '86 184
Swiss Cheese Spread, '90 60
Tomato-Cheese Spread, '81 157
Tomato-Cheese Spread, Fiery, '87 196
Tomato-Cheese Torte, '00 72
Tomato Spread, '94 123

Tuna Spread, '91 305
Tuna Spread, Chunky, '89 147
Tuna Tapenade, '95 127; '96 201
Turkey Party Spread, '83 282
Turkey Spread, Curried, '92 16
Vegetable Party Spread, '84 166
Vegetable Sandwich Spread, '85 135
Vegetable Spread, '90 144
Vegetable Spread, Garden, '93 184
Watercress Spread, '88 103
White Bean Spread, '95 279
Spring Rolls, '99 238
Spring Rolls with Sweet Chili Sauce, Shanghai, '01 236
Squash Nosh, '90 147
Squash, Spinach-Stuffed, '02 165
Stalks, Splendid, '93 258
Steak-and-Chestnut Appetizers, Marinated, '84 323
Strawberries, Spiked, '97 58
Strawberries, Stuffed, '98 155
Strawberries with Chocolate Cream, '85 81
Strawberries with Lemon Cream, '90 170
Strawberries with Walnuts, Stuffed, '85 122
Sugar Peas with Dip, '86 170
Sugar Plums, '92 281
Sugar Snap Pea Appetizers, '86 115
Swamp Sticks, '95 274
Sweet Potato Chips, '91 138; '93 332; '95 M203
Sweet Potato Chips with Blue Cheese, '93 290
Tabbouleh, '88 211
Taco Appetizer, Layered, '84 206
Taco Teasers, '01 134
Tamale Balls, Tangy, '89 60
Tamales, Miniature, '85 154
Tapas with Spicy Ranch Dip, Tortellini, '98 318
Tapenade, '01 70
Tartlets, Country Ham-and-Asparagus, '98 82
Tartlets, Creamy Citrus, '02 136
Tartlets, Raspberry-Brie, '04 287
Tarts, Party, '95 90
Texas Rockets, '05 175
Toasted Appetizers, '94 167
Toast Points, '93 270
Toast Strips, Seasoned, '93 98
Tomato Appetizers, Oven-Baked, '95 172
Tomato Bites, '84 80
Tomatoes, Cucumber-Stuffed Cherry, '88 262
Tomatoes, Honey-Baked, '02 166
Tomatoes Rockefeller, '97 169
Tomatoes, Stuffed Cherry, '84 160; '88 95, 212; '92 25
Tomatoes, Tuna-Stuffed Cherry, '89 214
Tomato Soup, Appetizer, '86 258
Tomato Soup, Savory, '94 91
Tomato Tapas, Two-, '00 308
Tortilla Appetizers, Tex-Mex, '86 297
Tortilla Bites with Sesame-Soy Dipping Sauce, '02 145
Tortilla Chips, '91 137
Tortilla Chips, Corn, '91 17
Tortilla Chips, Light, '91 257
Tortilla Dippers, Rolled, '86 4
Tortilla Espanola, '92 175
Tortilla Snacks, Pesto, '89 19
Tortilla Snack, Two-Cheese, '90 119
Tostadas, Party, '98 M33
Tostados, Hot Chile Salsa with Homemade, '88 115
Tuna Amandine, '02 165
Tuna Mound, '80 276
Tuna Nachos, '95 127; '96 201
Tuna-Pecan Ball, '87 94
Turkey Appetizers, '91 314
Turkey, Country-Fried Wild, '94 306
Turkey Sausage Turnovers, '95 239
Turkey-Spinach Rollups, '00 178
Turnovers, Meat, '86 326
Vegetable Appetizer, Tarragon, '83 277

Vegetable Juice Appetizer, Hot, '93 324
Vegetable Nachos, '91 17
Vegetable Party Tray, Fresh, '82 122
Vegetable Platter with Creamy Honey-Herb Dip, '98 135
Vegetable Rollups, '98 134
Vegetables Italian, Marinated, '90 242
Vegetables, Marinated, '94 183; '96 213
Vegewiches, '99 86
Veggie Bites, '91 171
Veggie Rollup, '01 109
Veggies, Fried, '96 19
Venison Tenderloin Appetizers, '88 249
Watermelon and Prosciutto, '98 164
Wienie Rollups, '02 186
Wings and Ribs, Thai, '97 M225
Wonton Chips, Baked, '91 138; '99 138
Wonton Chips, Cinnamon-and-Sugar, '91 138
Wonton Chips, Garlic, '91 138
Wonton Chips, Lemon-and-Herb, '91 138
Wonton Nibbles, '85 287
Zucchini Bites, Scalloped, '91 165
Zucchini Caviar, '88 212
Zucchini French Fries, '82 78
Zucchini Fries, '90 147
Zucchini Hors d'Oeuvres, '80 151
Zucchini Pizzas, '88 212
Zucchini-Shrimp Appetizers, '89 311
Zucchini with Cocktail Sauce, French Fried, '86 146

APPLES
Acorn Squash, Apple-Stuffed, '83 296; '84 285
Bacon, Sweet Apple, '03 305
Baked. *See also* **APPLES/Desserts.**
 à l'Orange, Baked Apples, '90 280
 Apples, Baked, '79 276; '86 40
 Carrot-Apple Bake, '98 232
 Carrot Bake, Apple-, '93 304
 Cheese Bake, Apple-, '92 225
 Easy Baked Apples, '82 22, 238
 Ham and Apples, Baked, '82 M237
 Honey-Baked Apple Quarters, '86 93
 Honey-Baked Apples, '83 234; '84 244
 Honey-Baked Apples and Pear, '97 303
 Imperial Baked Apples, '82 273
 Maple Baked Apples, '85 232
 Mincemeat-Filled Apples, Baked, '80 276
 Orange-Pecan Baked Apples, '85 45
 Orange Sauce, Baked Apples with, '84 314
 Sharpe Baked Apples, '99 83
 Squash and Apple Bake, '79 210
 Stuffed Baked Apples, '89 217
 Sweet Potato-Apple Bake, '83 25; '86 282
Balls, Sausage-Apple, '90 85
Beets and Apples, '80 137; '88 155
Beverages
 Appleade, Hot Spiced Lemon-, '05 23
 Aztec Gold, '99 160
 Berry Sparkler, Apple-, '93 104
 Berry Sparkler, Apple, '94 100
 Cider, Apple, '95 198
 Cider, Apple-Orange, '92 20
 Cider, December, '91 260
 Cider, Holiday, '82 264
 Cider, Hot Apple, '90 21, 225
 Cider, Hot Burgundy, '96 306
 Cider, Hot Mexican, '87 213
 Cider, Hot Molasses, '98 242
 Cider, Hot Mulled, '79 205; '84 323
 Cider, Hot Mulled Apple-Orange, '97 301
 Cider, Hot Spiced, '99 248
 Cider, Hot Spiced Apple, '84 318
 Cider Ice, '83 162
 Cider, Mulled, '91 209; '94 227
 Cider, Mulled Apple, '92 208

Cider, Mulled Cranberry, '99 278
Cider Nog, Hot, '98 241
Cider Nog, Hot Apple, '84 42
Cider, Red Apple, '80 259
Cider Sipper, Apple, '02 220
Cider Sipper, Apricot-Apple, '02 220
Cider Sipper, Citrus, '05 23
Cider Sour, Bourbon, '98 242
Cider, Sparkling Apple, '88 276
Cider, Spirited Apple, '96 214
Cider Tea, '98 241; '99 335
Cooler, Apple, '90 14
Cooler, Minted Apple, '88 169
Hot Apple Pie, '99 321
Juice, Hot Apple, '86 270
Juice, Perky Cinnamon-Apple, '90 22
Juice, Sparkling Apple, '95 141
Julep, Apple, '86 103, 215
Lemonade, Apple, '89 212; '03 169
Limeade, Pink Apple, '89 46
Mint Juleps, Apple, '97 120
Punch, Apple Bobbing, '99 246
Punch, Apple-Tea, '85 82
Punch, Honey-Apple, '05 23
Punch, Hot Apple, '84 324
Punch, Hot Spiced, '80 250
Punch, Party Apple, '00 271
Punch, Spicy Sparkling, '05 24
Shrub, Shenandoah Apple Juice, '79 282
Sparkler, Cranberry-Apple, '05 61
Tea, Apple, '05 24
Tea, Cranberry-Apple, '88 169
Tea, Hot Apple-Cinnamon, '87 57
Tea, Iced Apple, '98 84
Tea, Johnny Appleseed, '85 23
Braised Carrots, Apples, and Celery, '96 107
Breads
 Apple Bread, '79 205; '80 226; '05 210
 Banana-Apple Bread, '85 250
 Biscuit Braid, Apple-Pecan, '02 326
 Blue Cheese-Apple Sunburst, '94 245
 Buns, Cinnamon-Apple Breakfast, '00 M198
 Butter Bread, Apple, '84 49; '86 69
 Cheddar-Apple Bread, '96 83
 Danish, Deep-Dish Apple, '96 161
 Date-Nut Ring, Apple-, '90 212
 French Toast, Baked Apple, '03 M283
 Loaf, Fresh Apple, '82 206
 Loaf, Spiced Apple, '79 215
 Muffins, Apple, '83 96; '84 193; '87 23; '99 234
 Muffins, Apple-Bran, '85 M89
 Muffins, Apple-Carrot, '91 213
 Muffins, Apple-Cinnamon Oat Bran, '89 106
 Muffins, Caramel-Apple, '05 210
 Muffins, Fresh Apple, '84 264
 Muffins, Pumpkin-Apple, '96 242
 Muffins, Spiced Apple, '79 60
 Muffins, Spicy Apple-Oat, '86 45
 Nut Bread, Apple-, '79 12; '85 281
 Nut Bread, Fresh Apple-, '87 256
 Pinwheel, Quick Apple, '85 42
 Pull-Apart Bread, Apple, '86 330
 Swirl Bread, Apple, '85 4
 Zucchini-Apple Bread, '87 255
Breakfast Apples, Spiced, '00 193
Breakfast Delight, '93 195
Brussels Sprouts with Apples, '02 243
Burgers, Apple, '86 137
Burgers, Apple-Bacon, '99 202
Butter, Apple, '79 200; '81 217; '92 311
Butter, Half-Hour Apple, '81 203
Butter, Oven Apple, '00 237
Butter, Slow Cooker Apple, '97 235

Butter, Spiced Oven Apple, '00 237
Cabbage with Apples and Franks, '87 42
Casserole, Apple-Cheese, '84 287
Casserole, Apple-Egg, '85 44
Casserole, Apple Ham, '79 213
Casserole, Cranberry-Apple, '83 311
Casserole, Squash and Apple, '79 209
Casserole, Sweet Potato-and-Apple, '94 280
Casserole, Sweet Potatoes-and-Apple, '90 228
Chard with Onion and Apple, Sautéed, '98 48
Cheese Delight, Apple-and-, '98 97
Chicken, Apple, '85 57
Chicken Breasts, Apple-Bacon Stuffed, '99 313
Chutney, Apple, '92 309
Chutney, Pear-Apple, '89 141
Chutney, Quick Cranberry-Apple, '05 231
Chutney, Sweet-'n'-Hot Apple, '96 14
Chutney, Sweet Potato, '99 45
Chutney, Tomato-Apple, '84 180
Cider Sauce, '87 224
Cider Sauce, Cheddar-, '98 242
Cinnamon Apples, Rosy, '87 M37
Coffee Cake, Apple, '81 249; '97 326
Coffee Cake, Apple-Pecan, '84 242
Coffee Cake, Fresh Apple, '92 32
Coffee Cakes, Caramel-Apple, '05 210
Collards with Apples, '98 250
Conserve, Apple-Cranberry, '82 308
Cooked Apples, '93 338
Cornbread-Sausage-Apple Pie, '87 171
Crêpes, Apple Breakfast, '97 331
Curried Apples, '93 252
Desserts. *See also* **APPLES/Pies and Tarts.**
 Bake, Apple-Almond, '02 M209
 Bake, Cherry-Apple, '04 29
 Bake, Cinnamon-Apple, '04 29
 Baked Alaska, Apple, '80 226
 Baked Apples, Pecan-and-Dried Fruit, '03 269
 Baked Apples with Cookie Crumbs, Orange, '95 271
 Bars, Apple Butter, '84 153
 Betty, Apple Brown, '83 213; '05 232
 Betty, Pineapple-Apple, '85 46
 Brandied Apples, '81 248
 Brandied Apples and Cream, '82 M237
 Brownies, Frosted Apple, '86 216
 Bundles, Quick Apple, '04 242
 Cake, Apple, '83 312; '84 262
 Cake, Apple Cider Pound, '84 10
 Cake, Apple Coconut, '80 226
 Cake, Apple-Ginger Upside-Down, '94 180
 Cake, Apple-Nut, '87 76; '96 268
 Cake, Apple-Pecan, '92 167
 Cake, Apple Pie, '82 226; '86 301
 Cake, Apple Pudding, '01 47
 Cake, Apple Slice, '85 93
 Cake, Apple Spice, '92 225
 Cake, Apple Stack, '05 108
 Cake, Apple-Walnut, '94 242
 Cake, Covered Apple, '89 317
 Cake, Dried-Apple, '79 13
 Cake, Dried Apple Stack, '85 242
 Cake, Fresh Apple-Date, '83 300
 Cake, Fresh Apple Upside-Down, '05 231
 Cake, Golden Apple-Oatmeal, '86 301
 Cake, Honey-Apple, '99 210
 Cake Squares, Apple-Date Dream, '85 10
 Cake Squares, Apple-Orange, '84 150
 Cake with Cream Cheese Frosting, Chunky Apple, '01 185
 Candied Red Apples, '81 217
 Candy Apple Creations, '94 256
 Candy Apples, '84 243; '01 M205
 Caramel Apples, '79 220; '89 M231; '03 M216
 Caramel Apples, Black-and-White, '03 M216

APPLES, Desserts
(continued)

Caramel Apples, Calypso, '03 M216
Caramel Apples, Old English, '85 231
Caramel-Peanut Apples, '93 M244
Charlotte, Apple, '99 84
Cheesecake, Dieter's Apple, '86 318
Chimichangas, Apple, '95 43
Chocolate Apples on a Stick, '96 255
Cinnamon Apples with Brandied Date Conserve, '85 315
Cobbler à la Mode, Apple, '97 16
Cobbler, Apple-Berry, '04 330
Cobbler, Apple Dumpling, '04 29
Cobbler, Apple-Gingerbread, '03 21; '04 219
Cobbler, Apple-Pecan, '84 M198
Cobbler, Apple-Pecan Pie, '04 200
Cobbler, Apple-Vinegar Biscuit, '01 215
Cobbler, Apple Walnut, '79 154
Cobbler, Apple-Walnut, '81 248
Cobbler, Country Apple, '99 255
Cobbler, Cranberry-and-Apple, '84 306; '90 294
Cobbler, Easy Apple, '83 174
Cobbler for Two, Apple, '85 261
Cobbler, New-Fashioned Apple, '91 221
Cobbler, Sweet Potato-Apple, '04 M232
Cobbler with Cinnamon Biscuits, Cranberry-Apple, '99 256
Cobbler with Oatmeal Muffin Crust, Caramel Apple-Pear, '04 201
Compote, Apple-Cranberry, '04 237
Compote, Apricot-Apple, '98 17
Cookies, Apple Butter Spice, '79 291
Cookies, Apple-Filled, '92 311
Cookies, Apple-Nut, '80 228
Cookies, Apple-Oatmeal, '85 215; '90 218
Cookies, Fresh Apple, '84 36
Cranberry Apple Dessert, '80 253
Cranberry Apples, '99 246
Crescent Roll Apples, '05 231
Crisp, Apple, '84 122; '98 215
Crisp, Apple-Cheese, '92 235
Crisp, Delicious Apple, '82 303
Crisp, Granola Apple, '85 78
Crisp, Oatmeal Cherry-Apple, '90 M16
Crisp, Orange-Apple, '80 295
Crisp, Tart Apple, '92 226
Crumble, Whole Wheat-Apple, '90 M213
Crunch, Apple-Blueberry, '02 128
Crunch, Apple-Cranberry, '86 300; '87 178
Crunch, Apple-Nut, '82 M238
Cupcakes, Apple-Nut, '82 279
Delight, Apple, '80 109
Dumplings, Apple, '82 273; '00 96
Dumplings, Apple-Cranberry, '00 16
Dumplings, Cinnamon Apple, '97 M330
Dumplings, Old-Fashioned Apple, '84 226
Dumplings, Quick Apple, '01 185
Dumplings with Maple-Cider Sauce, Apple, '95 288
Dumplings with Orange Hard Sauce, Apple, '88 224
Dutch Apple Dessert, Creamy, '91 19
Enchiladas, Apple, '99 63
Filling, Apple-Date, '83 301
Filling, Dried Apple, '85 242; '87 229; '05 108
Flambé, Hot Apples and Rum, '92 88
Flan, Apple, '81 309
Foldovers, Apple, '84 136
Fritter Rings, Apple, '88 44
Fritters, Apple, '81 105; '82 273; '85 14; '97 153
Fritters, Apple Holiday, '86 314
Fritters with Lemon Sauce, Apple, '01 184
Goblins, Apple, '94 256

Grahams, Caramel-Apple, '04 M183
Grahams, Peanut Butter-Apple, '04 M183
Honey-Baked Apple Dessert, '90 M213
Ice, Cranberry-Apple, '82 290
Kuchen, Apple, '79 24
Melting Apples, '88 19
Mousse, Cran-Apple, '93 255
Napoleon, Giant Apple, '99 282
Napoleons, Caramel-Apple, '01 M313
Pears, Saucy Apples 'n', '96 72
Pecan Apples, Taffy, '99 247
Pizza, Apple-Pineapple Dessert, '00 313
Poached Apples, Spicy, '90 M141
Pudding, Apple-Raisin Bread, '88 175
Pudding, Apple Rice, '91 217
Pudding with Bourbon Sauce, Pineapple-Apple Bread, '05 119
Pudding with Hot Rum Sauce, Apple-Nut, '79 86
Pudding with Vanilla-Nutmeg Sauce, Pineapple-Apple Bread, '02 208
Quesadillas, Apple, '99 248
Quesadillas, Caramel-Apple, '05 223
Quesadillas, Dessert, '02 54
Rings, Apple, '85 232
Roasted Apples, Orange-Ginger, '01 184
Roll, Apple, '82 178
Rolls, Cinnamon-Apple, '02 215
Rolls, Luscious Apple, '88 225
Rugelach, Apple, '97 220
Sauce, Apple Ambrosia, '89 95
Sauce, Apple-Cinnamon, '93 42
Sauce, Apple Dessert, '87 M165
Sauce, Spicy Apple Dessert, '82 177
Shortcake, Quick Apple, '93 42
Shortcakes, Caramel-Apple, '03 194
Snack Squares, Apple-Oat, '00 332
Sorbet, Cran-Apple Spice, '93 153
Squares, Apple, '92 311
Squares, Apple-Gingerbread, '03 297
Squares, Sour Cream Apple, '82 262
Strudel, Apple, '85 259; '89 267; '92 269; '97 238
Strudel, Autumn-Apple, '98 253
Stuffed Apples, '99 247
Sugar-Crusted Apples in Walnut-Phyllo Baskets, '93 210
Sundae, Hot Apple Spice, '92 239
Sundaes, Spicy Apple Ice Cream, '86 M195
Topping, Apple-Nut, '93 162
Topping, Spicy Apple, '87 125
Torte, Huguenot, '05 98
Turnovers, Baked Apple, '93 338
Turnovers, Delicious Apple, '86 25
Turnovers, Fried Apple, '81 161
Turnovers, Orange-Apple, '99 294
Turnovers, Puffy Apple, '87 276
Waffles with Apples and Caramel, Gingerbread, '98 M237
Dip, Apple, '93 205; '96 M190
Dressing, Andouille Sausage, Apple, and Pecan, '02 249
Dressing, Apple, '92 216
Dressing, Sausage-Apple, '93 305; '94 296
Dried Apple Side Dish, '92 226
Dried Lady Apple Slices, '95 263
Fillets, Apple-Carrot Stuffed, '88 M192
Filling, Apple, '85 5; '96 53; '97 239
French Toast, Apple, '98 55
Fried Apples, '05 109
Glazed Apples, '99 233
Glazed Apples, Honey-, '90 125
Glazed Apples, Orange-, '82 51
Golden Apples, '82 254
Grilled Ham and Apples, '96 M303
Honey-Yogurt Apples, '92 46
Jelly, Apple, '82 149

Jelly, Apple-Mint, '87 134
Jelly, Crabapple, '79 120; '81 217
Jelly, Spiced Apple, '95 251
Juice, Nectarines in Apple, '83 183
Marmalade, Apple, '79 120
Minted Apples, '99 231; '00 21
Minted Apples, Lamb Chops with, '00 20
Minted Apples, Pork Chops with, '00 21
Monster Mouths, '95 274
Muesli, '89 208
Omelet Stack, Apple, '94 50
Pancake, Apple-Filled, '86 96
Pancakes, Apple, '01 24
Pancakes, Apple-Topped, '93 339
Pancakes with Caramel Sauce, Baked Apple, '04 249
Pancakes with Cider Sauce, Spicy Apple, '87 224
Pasta with Apple, Curried, '02 68

Pies and Tarts
Almond-Apple Tart, '01 253
Amandine Pie, Apple-, '89 215
Apple Pie, American, '91 197
Applesauce Pie, '98 259; '99 26; '01 213
Apricot-Apple Crumb Tart, '94 60
Autumn Apple Pie, '79 205
aux Pommes, La Tarte, '80 125
Berry-Apple Pie, '88 251
Blackberry-Apple Pie, '87 130
Bourbon Pie, Apple-, '95 302
Brandied Apple Tarts, '96 284; '99 28
Brandy-Apple Pie, '86 301
Brandy Raisin-Apple Pie, '83 192
Bumbleberry Pie, '97 163
Caramel-Pecan Apple Pie, '85 247
Cheese Pastry, Apple Tart with, '88 225
Cheese Pie, Apple-, '85 284
Cider Pie, Apple, '84 227
Cinnamon Crème, Apple Pie with Warm, '99 337
Cinnamon Sauce, Apple Pie with Hot, '88 210
Cran-Apple Pie, '92 304
Cranberry-Apple Holiday Pie, '81 M269
Cranberry-Apple Pie, '79 264
Cranberry-Apple-Raisin Pie, '98 270
Cranberry-Apple Tart, '97 M316
Cranberry Pie, Apple-, '97 276; '99 M269
Cranberry Tart, Rustic Apple-, '01 M314
Cream Cheese Pie, Apple-, '81 247
Cream Cheese Tart, Apple-, '96 228
Creamed Apple Tart, '94 17
Cream Tart, Apple, '84 207
Custard Pie, Apple, '88 236
Custard Pie, Warm Apple-Buttermilk, '99 98
Deluxe Apple Tart, '84 227
Dutch Apple Pie, '81 105; '82 273
Easy-Crust Apple Pie, '87 11
Filling in a Jar, Apple Pie, '95 251
Fresh Apple Pie, '84 178
Fried Apple Pies, '81 217; '86 302; '88 112, 225; '94 61
Fried Pies, Delicious, '83 84
Georgie's Apple Pie, '02 325
Grandmother's Apple Pie, '87 212
Granny Smith Apple Pie, '01 143
Grated Apple Pie, '83 304
Holiday Apple Pie, '87 260
Honey Apple Pie, '00 331
Honeyed Apple-Cranberry Fried Pies, '02 214
Lemon-Apple Pie, Tart, '80 100
Lemon Chess Pie, Apple-, '86 220
Maple Pie, Apple-, '97 276
Mexican Apple Pie, '94 97
Mincemeat Pie, Apple-, '85 316
No-Crust Apple Pie, '88 204
Old-Fashioned Apple Pie, '82 M299; '88 94
Pear-Apple Pie, Natural, '88 226

Pear Pie, Apple-, '83 249
Pear Pull-Up Pie, Apple-, '98 259
Pecan Tarts, Apple-, '80 282
Pineapple Pie, Apple-, '97 276
Praline-Apple Pie, '99 331; '05 251
Raisin Brandy Pie, Apple-, '89 58
Red Apple Pie, '79 282
Upside-Down Apple Tart, '98 35
Upside-Down Southern Apple Pie, '88 226
Piggy Apple, '94 194
Poached Lemon Apples, Chilled, '86 182
Pockets, Toasted Cream Cheese-and-Apple, '01 200
Pork and Vegetables, Apple Cider, '97 210
Pork Chops, An Apple-a-Day, '01 35
Pork Chops and Apples, Baked, '81 10
Pork Chops, Apple, '91 198
Pork Chops, Apple-Crumb Stuffed, '81 234; '82 26
Pork Chops, Apple-Glazed, '84 212; '87 35
Pork Chops, Apple-Kraut, '84 50
Pork Chops, Apple-Sage Stuffed, '04 250
Pork Chops, Apple-Stuffed, '79 125
Pork Chops, Cider, '02 307; '03 271
Pork Chops, Glazed Apple, '86 300
Pork Chops, Rosemary, '98 329
Pork Chops, Sherry-Apple, '88 40
Pork Chops, Spicy Apple, '87 230
Pork Chops, Stuffed, '02 204
Pork Chops with Apples, Balsamic, '03 204
Pork Chops with Apples, Parmesan, '93 338
Pork Chops with Cornbread-Apple Stuffing, '99 14
Pork Chops with Crabapple Peaches, Broiled, '81 83
Pork Chops with Mustard-Glazed Apple and Onion,
    '01 47
Pork Chops with Pecans and Apples, Commune's
    Maple-Glazed, '04 102
Pork Cutlets, Apple-Glazed, '92 181
Pork Loin with Apples and Mushrooms, Roast, '92 218
Pork Tenderloin, Apple-Ginger, '86 75
Pork Tenderloin, Apple-Mushroom, '95 53
Pork Tenderloin with Apples, Celery, and Potatoes,
    Grilled, '95 161
Pot Roast, Spicy Apple, '83 7
Praline Sweet Potatoes and Apples, '03 260
Quail, Sage-Smoked Champagne, '97 164
Quesadillas, Apple Pie 'n' Cheddar, '03 61
Quiche, Crustless Sausage-Apple, '87 70
Red Cabbage, '96 272
Red Cabbage and Apples, '85 32
Red Cabbage, Braised, '01 193; '02 277
Red Cabbage, German-Style, '98 279
Relish, Apple, '96 323; '97 27
Relish, Apple-Celery, '89 141
Relish, Apple-Raisin, '03 83
Relish, Cran-Apple, '84 300
Relish, Cranberry, '98 310
Relish, Spicy Apple, '84 M323
Ribs, Apple Barbecued, '80 111
Rice, Apple-Cinnamon, '86 249
Rice, Curried, '04 21
Rings, Cinnamon Apple, '82 M237; '90 250
Rings, Cinnamon-Apple, '85 107
Rings, Fried Apple, '81 209
Rings, Honey Apple, '80 243
Rolls, Apple-Phyllo, '88 213
Salads
    Apple Salad, '87 233; '00 176
    Apricot Salad, Apple-, '88 121
    Aspic, Sunshine Apple-, '81 73
    Avocado-Apple Salad with Maple-Walnut
        Vinaigrette, '04 45
    Beet, Apple, and Walnut Salad, '98 269
    Beet Salad, Apple-, '91 237
    Blue Cheese Dressing, Apple Salad with, '87 103
    Blue Cheese-Pear-Apple Salad, '81 224

Cabbage-Apple Salad with Sugared Pecans, '05 91
Carrot Salad, Apple-, '85 22
Cheesy Apple Salad, '86 301
Cherry-Apple Salad, '86 31
Chicken-Apple Salad, '90 216
Cider Salad, Apple, '83 123
Coleslaw, Apple, '89 315
Coleslaw, Apple-Bacon, '04 181
Coleslaw, Lemon-Apple, '05 44
Congealed Apple Salad, '85 252
Cranberry-Apple Salad, '02 255; '05 65
Crunch Salad, Apple, '84 232; '86 331
Crunchy Apple Salad, '80 138
Curried Apple-Raisin Salad, '80 24
Double Apple Salad, '84 227
English Pea-and-Apple Salad, '87 24
Fennel-and-Apple Salad, '00 321
Fresh Apple Salad, '81 207
Frozen Apple-Cream Salad, '82 80
Grapefruit-Apple Salad, '89 41
Greens with Apple and Brie Salad, '93 241
Greens with Seasoned Almonds and Tangy
    Balsamic Vinaigrette, Mixed, '03 101
Ham-and-Apple Salad, '88 139
Lemony Apple-Bran Salad, '86 223
Lemony Apple Salad, '80 226
Marinated Potato-Apple Salad, '05 41
Mold, Apple Cider Salad, '85 54
Mold, Cranberry-Apple, '89 277
Nut Salad, Apple-, '80 226
Peanut-Apple Salad, '80 5
Poppyseed Dressing, Apple Wedges with, '86 131
Rudolph's Apple Salad, '02 277
Sesame-Apple Toss, '88 21
Slaw, Apple-Carrot, '92 243
Slaw, Apple-Pineapple, '79 241
Slaw, Fresh Apple, '81 63
Slaw, Nutty Apple, '88 216
Slaw, Red Cabbage-and-Apple, '87 31; '91 309
Snow Salad, Apple, '81 224
Spicy Apple Salad, '85 215
Spinach-and-Apple Salad with Cinnamon
    Vinaigrette, Fresh, '05 44
Spinach-Apple Salad, '90 89; '92 13; '97 308
Spinach Salad, Apple-, '97 14; '99 222; '02 230
Stuffed Apple Ring Salad, '91 198
Stuffed Apple Salad, '92 266
Summer Apple Salad, '80 149
Sweet Potato-Apple Salad, '96 240
Swiss-Apple Salad, '84 81
Thai Green Apple Salad, '99 111
Triple Apple Salad, '88 122
Turkey-Apple Salad, '88 123; '90 181
Waldorf, Pineapple, '97 86
Waldorf Salad, '89 278; '97 204
Waldorf Salad, Congealed, '82 80
Waldorf Salad, Creamy, '87 311
Waldorf Salad, Deluxe, '83 81
Waldorf Salad, Frozen, '79 126; '82 145
Waldorf Salad, Jiffy, '88 100
Waldorf Salad, New Wave, '92 36
Waldorf Salad, Old-Fashioned, '81 295
Waldorf Salad, Pineapple, '92 97
Waldorf Salad, Southern Classic, '92 36
Waldorf Salad, Tropical, '89 12
Waldorf Salad, Winter, '04 245
Wild Rice-Green Apple Salad, '92 90
Zucchini Salad, Apple-and-, '97 216
Sandwiches, Apple, '79 164; '80 130
Sandwiches, Apple Breakfast, '92 332
Sandwiches, Apple-Cinnamon Breakfast, '85 298
Sandwiches, Apple Party, '92 234
Sandwiches, Curried Tuna-Apple, '00 247
Sandwiches, Sweet Smoky, '97 219

Sauce, Apple Barbecue, '99 173
Sauce, Apple-Bourbon, '99 142
Sauce, Apple-Horseradish, '82 229
Sauce, Apple-Pear, '97 M272
Sauce, Cranberry-Apple, '92 203
Sauce, Double Cranberry-Apple, '03 231
Sausage-Apple Kraut Dinner, '02 234
Sausage-Apple Pie, Cornbread-, '87 171
Sausage Patties, Apples on, '82 120
Sauté, Chicken-Apple, '97 48
Sautéed Apples, Onions, and Pears over Spinach,
    '94 212
Scalloped Apples, '84 70; '87 156
Scalloped Sweet Potatoes with Apples, '00 253
Scallop, Yam-and-Apple, '91 199
Shells, Sweet Potatoes in Apple, '85 206
Shrunken Heads (Halloween Decor), '01 204
Snack Mix, Apple Spice-Raisin, '05 222
Soup, Chestnut, '02 272
Soup, Creamed Butternut-and-Apple, '88 228
Soup, Curried Acorn Squash-and-Apple, '03 221
Spareribs, Apple-Barbecue, '90 160
Spiced Apples, '93 123; '03 36
Spiced Apple Slices, '83 289
Spiced Apples, Skillet, '83 234; '84 244
Spread, Apple-Date, '91 231; '92 67
Spread, Feta-and-Apple, '99 106
Spread, Gruyère-Apple, '81 160
Squash, Apple-and-Pecan-Filled, '88 228
Squash, Apple-Stuffed, '85 206
Stir-Fry, Apple-Sesame-Chicken, '92 226
Stuffed Apples, Peanutty, '85 25
Stuffed Apples, Sweet Potato-, '97 216; '00 232
Stuffing, Apple-Almond, '01 184
Stuffing, Apple-Crumb, '81 234; '82 26; '83 39
Stuffing, Apple-Walnut, '95 289
Sweet-and-Sour Red Cabbage and Apples, '00 62
Sweet Potatoes and Apples, '97 249
Sweet Potatoes, Apple-Glazed, '82 303
Sweet Potatoes, Apple-Stuffed, '88 207
Sweet Potatoes, Cinnamon-Apple, '95 M23
Sweet Potatoes Stuffed with Apples, '82 228
Syrup, Spiced Apple, '79 114
Tenderloin with Praline-Mustard Glaze, Apple-Stuffed,
    '97 216
Toast, Apple, '81 278
Topping, Apple, '89 107
Turkey, Apple Brandy, '03 230
Turkey, Apple-Rosemary Roasted, '99 252
Turkey Breast, Apple-Rosemary, '99 253
Veal Chops, Apple, '87 220
Vinaigrette, Apple Cider, '98 284; '01 306; '05 201
Vinaigrette, Apple-Ginger, '05 230
Vinaigrette, Spinach Salad with Apple-Onion, '94 276
APPLESAUCE
Applesauce, '90 255; '97 252; '00 256
Bread, Applesauce-Honey Nut, '87 300
Bread, Applesauce Nut, '81 305
Bread, Applesauce-Pecan, '90 66
Bread, Bran-Applesauce, '84 229
Butter, Half-Hour Apple, '81 203
Cake, Applesauce, '80 270; '96 67
Cake, Applesauce Carrot, '81 202
Cake, Applesauce-Oatmeal, '92 119
Cake, Applesauce-Spice, '83 42
Cake, Applesauce Spice, '89 296
Cake, My Favorite Applesauce, '87 263
Cakes, Applesauce Snack, '88 215; '89 20
Cake Squares, Applesauce, '86 8
Cake with Bourbon Frosting, Applesauce, '88 236
Cobbler with Bourbon-Pecan Ice Cream, Caramel-
    Applesauce, '00 260
Dip, Apple-Berry, '01 109
Doughnuts, Applesauce, '81 203

APPLES, Applesauce
(continued)

Doughnuts, Applesauce Drop, '90 70
Dressing, Apple, '83 181
Fluff, Applesauce, '91 173
Fruitcake, Applesauce, '83 258
Gingerbread, Applesauce, '94 179; '05 231
Homemade Applesauce, '05 231
Hot Spiced Applesauce, '01 60
Loaf, Brandy Applesauce, '81 263
Muffins, Applesauce, '84 284; '91 141
Muffins, Applesauce Spice, '88 236
Muffins, Bite-Size Applesauce, '82 104
Oatmeal, Applesauce, '89 108
Onion Applesauce, Sweet, '02 319
Pancakes, Applesauce, '79 114
Pie, Applesauce, '98 259; '99 26; '01 213
Pudding, Applesauce-Graham Cracker, '81 34
Ribs, Apple Barbecued, '80 111
Salad Dressing, Honey-Applesauce, '99 210
Savory Applesauce, '01 47
Spiced Applesauce, '05 231
Spicy Applesauce, '82 296
Squares, Applesauce-Spice, '86 248
Sweet Potatoes, Applesauce, '91 292; '92 256
Turnovers, Applesauce, '05 231
APRICOTS
Bake, Sweet Potato-Apricot, '85 206
Beverages
Bellinis, Apricot, '99 145; '05 96
Cooler, Apricot, '81 100
Cooler, Apricot Mint, '90 165
Cooler, Apricot-Orange-Carrot, '96 108
Coolers, Apricot, '99 29
Fruit Flip, Apricot, '91 18
Nectar, Hot Apricot, '81 265
Nectar, Mulled Apricot, '86 229
Punch, Apricot Spiced, '80 269
Shake, Apricot, '84 115
Sipper, Apricot-Apple Cider, '02 220
Slush, Apricot, '93 205
Slush, Apricot Brandy, '91 278
Slush, Apricot-Citrus, '88 82
Tea, Hot Spiced Apricot, '88 248
Wassail, Pineapple-Apricot, '83 275
Bread, Apricot-Nut, '79 24
Bread, Apricot-Orange, '92 285
Bread, Apricot-Pecan, '97 266
Bread, Pineapple-Apricot, '84 7
Bread, Tangy Apricot, '81 249
Butter, Apricot, '82 308; '99 212
Carrots, Apricot, '84 6
Carrots, Apricot Glazed, '80 89
Carrots, Apricot-Glazed, '98 231; '01 212
Chutney, Cranberry-and-Apricot, '02 286
Coffee Cake, Apricot-Almond, '93 26; '04 193
Coffee Cake, Apricot Lattice, '94 48
Crescents, Apricot-Cheese, '99 284
Croissants, Strawberry or Apricot, '96 303
Curried Apricots, '91 315
Dates, Apricot-Stuffed, '80 250
Delight, Apricot, '81 42
Desserts
Almond Squares, Apricot-, '95 272
Baked Apricots, Delicious, '82 10
Balls, Apricot, '79 274
Balls, Crunchy Apricot, '89 307
Bars, Apricot, '81 247
Bars, Apricot-Oatmeal, '86 216; '04 331
Bars, Apricot-Raisin, '87 32
Bars, Layered Apricot, '01 161
Cake, Apricot-Almond Upside-Down, '97 204

Cake, Apricot Brandy Pound, '83 267
Cobbler, Peach-Apricot, '99 255
Cobbler with Custard Sauce, Apricot, '97 16
Cobble Up, Apricot, '82 138
Compote, Apricot-Apple, '98 17
Cookie Rolls, Apricot, '80 282
Cookies, Apricot, '95 322
Cookies, Frosted Apricot, '81 192
Cream, Peachy-Apricot, '86 163
Crescents, Apricot, '90 181
Divinity, Apricot, '83 297
Filling, Apricot, '83 84; '86 107; '93 316; '01 330
Filling, Lemon-Apricot, '90 105
Flan, Apricot, '99 146
Freeze, Apricot, '82 10
Frosting, Apricot, '81 192
Frozen Apricot Fluff, '86 242
Glaze, Apricot, '82 8; '97 60; '98 260
Glaze, Apricot-Kirsch, '87 14
Glaze, Sweet Apricot, '82 304
Ice, Apricot Yogurt, '81 177
Ice Cream, Apricot, '99 146
Kolaches, Apricot, '83 84; '94 291
Mousse, Apricot, '82 72; '91 297
Noodle Kugel, Apricot, '92 251
Pastries, Apricot, '83 297
Pastries, Apricot-Cream Cheese, '03 245
Pie, Apricot Surprise, '88 99
Pie, Dried Fruit, '83 249
Pies, Apricot Cream Fried, '00 212
Pies, Apricot Fried, '86 269
Pies, Dried Apricot Hand, '98 259
Pies, Fried Apricot, '95 215
Pies, Special Apricot, '94 60
Pie, Yogurt-Apricot, '85 132
Pinwheels, Apricot, '87 276
Pudding, Apricot Bread, '85 24
Sauce, Apricot, '82 212
Sauce, Apricot Ice Cream, '91 57
Sauce, Apricot-Walnut Hard, '88 153
Sherbet, Apricot, '81 177; '92 164
Shortbread, Apricot-Almond, '99 29
Sorbet, Apricot-Almond, '98 126
Soufflé, Baked Apricot, '88 267
Tart, Apricot-Almond, '97 99
Tart, Apricot-Apple Crumb, '94 60
Tart, Apricot-Nut, '99 249
Tarts, Apricot, '79 282; '88 281
Tarts, Apricot-Pecan-Brie, '97 236
Tea Cakes, Brandied Apricot, '91 241
Torte, Apricot, '02 220
Torte, Apricot-Filled Chocolate, '90 107
Torte, Apricot Sponge, '90 59
Torte, Lucy's Apricot Praline, '95 243
Tortoni, Apricot-Yogurt, '95 124
Turnovers, Fried Apricot, '86 24
Wonders, Apricot, '93 316
Dip, Apricot, '86 178
Dressing, Apricot, '99 245
Dressing, Honeydew Salad with Apricot Cream, '84 191
Dried Apricot Spiders, '96 255
French Toast, Stuffed, '96 52
Glaze, Apricot, '80 280; '82 8; '86 197
Glaze for Ham, Apricot, '85 256
Glaze, Sweet Potatoes with Apricot, '89 331
Granola, '99 212
Granola, Superhero, '98 206
Jam, Golden Apricot, '80 31
Jam, Quick-Cooked Apricot, '99 146
Loaf, Apricot-Cranberry, '79 235
Loaf, Apricot-Nut, '81 8
Loaf, Tasty Apricot-Nut, '82 10

Main Dishes
Brisket, Spicy Apricot, '04 247
Chicken, Apricot, '92 12
Chicken Breasts, Apricot, '88 301
Chicken with Apricot Salsa, '98 126
Chicken with Roasted Potato Thins, Apricot, '02 23
Chicken with Tangy Apricot Glaze, '98 275
Cornish Hens, Apricot-Glazed, '80 84; '87 306
Cornish Hens, Apricot-Stuffed, '84 6
Ham and Apricots, '90 53
Ham, Apricot Baked, '84 160
Ham Slice, Apricot-Glazed, '93 252
Lamb Kebabs, Apricot-Grilled, '98 102
Pork Chops, Apricot-Mushroom Stuffed, '95 287
Pork Chops, Apricot-Sauced, '85 22
Pork Chops, Apricot-Stuffed, '86 76; '92 219; '03 49
Pork Loin, Apricot-Glazed-and-Spiced, '05 259
Pork Chops, Curried Apricot, '89 191
Pork Chops, Mustard-Apricot, '89 225
Pork Chops with Apricot Glaze, Stuffed, '89 M36
Pork Loin, Apricot-Glazed-and-Spiced, '05 259
Pork Loin, Apricot-Pecan Stuffed, '94 274
Pork Tenderloin with Apricot Sauce, '99 44
Sausage-Apricot Breakfast Dish, '82 10
Mayonnaise, Apricot, '97 320
Rice Pilaf, Apricot, '99 146
Rolls, Apricot-Orange Sweet, '03 235
Rolls, Cheese-Apricot Sweet, '90 195
Salad, Apple-Apricot, '88 121
Salad, Apricot, '81 251; '83 123
Salad, Apricot-Chicken, '99 163
Salad, Apricot Congealed, '02 256
Salad, Apricot Fruit, '82 132
Salad, Apricot Nectar, '83 218; '87 236
Salad, Creamy Apricot, '85 263
Salad, Frosted Apricot, '80 248
Salad, Spinach-Apricot, '94 63
Salad with Cider Vinaigrette, Harvest, '99 322
Salsa, Apricot, '98 126
Sauce, Apricot, '82 212; '87 172
Sauce, Fresh Cranberry-Apricot, '87 243
Sauce, Holiday Cranberry, '02 M311
Spread, Apricot Brie, '86 275
Spread, Apricot-Cream Cheese, '82 161; '87 158
Sweet Potatoes, Apricot, '82 228
Sweet Potatoes, Apricot-Glazed, '81 295
Syrup, Apricot Fruit, '82 10
Topping, Apricot Flambé, '98 127
Vinaigrette, Apricot, '02 120; '05 M312
ARTICHOKES
Appetizers
Baked Artichoke-Cheese Bottoms, '94 61
Caviar, Artichoke Hearts with, '79 142
Crostini, Hot Artichoke, '94 319
Crostini, Parmesan-Artichoke, '98 285
Dip, Artichoke-Chile, '98 234
Dip, Baked Artichoke, '95 239; '03 294
Dip, Deluxe Artichoke, '80 87
Dip, Florentine Artichoke, '96 274
Dip, Greek Artichoke, '97 315
Dip, Hot Artichoke-Seafood, '80 241
Dip, Hot Artichoke Seafood, '85 M212
Dip in a Bread Basket, Artichoke, '93 13
Dip, Italian Artichoke, '97 315
Dip, Mexican Artichoke, '90 292
Dip, Quick Artichoke, '02 69; '03 270; '04 107
Dip, Seasoned Mayonnaise Artichoke, '80 87
Dip, Spinach-Artichoke, '00 26
Frittata, Artichoke Appetizer, '92 58
Marinated Artichoke Hearts, '88 95
Marinated Artichokes, '87 250
Marinated Shrimp and Artichokes, '97 89; '98 335
Mold, Artichoke-Caviar, '87 239

Mound, Caviar-Artichoke, '91 244
Mushrooms, Artichoke-Stuffed, '01 239
Oysters, Artichoke, '96 154
Phyllo Bites, Artichoke-Parmesan, '87 54
Puff Pastry, Spinach and Artichokes in, '00 277
Puffs, Spinach-Artichoke-Tomato, '95 284
Shrimp Appetizer, Artichoke-and-, '93 271
Spread, Antipasto, '81 25
Spread, Artichoke-Cheese, '04 294
Spread, Artichoke-Parmesan, '92 95
Spread, Chunky Artichoke, '89 98
Spread Gift Box, Chicken-Artichoke-Cheese,
    '00 328
Spread, Hot Artichoke, '79 110
Spread, Hot Artichoke-Crab, '85 81
Zesty Artichoke Appetizer, '80 146
Artichokes, '92 107
au Gratin, Crab, Shrimp, and Artichoke, '90 240
Bake, Spinach-Artichoke, '95 48
Bake, Tomato-and-Artichoke Heart, '85 81
Beef with Tomatoes and Artichokes, '92 282
Bread, Artichoke, '93 140
Casserole, Alii Artichoke, '93 294
Casserole, Asparagus-Artichoke, '86 279
Casserole, Brussels Sprouts-and-Artichoke, '94 279
Casserole, Chicken-and-Artichoke, '96 133
Casserole, Italian Green Bean-and-Artichoke, '85 81
Casserole, Mushroom-Artichoke, '87 241
Casserole, Spicy Spinach-Artichoke, '01 49
Casserole, Spinach and Artichoke, '81 103
Casserole, Spinach-Artichoke, '88 252; '93 44; '00 254;
    '01 49
Chicken and Artichoke Hearts, Baked, '82 260
Chicken-and-Artichoke Olé, '05 59
Chicken and Artichokes, '03 26
Chicken and Artichokes, Italian, '95 68; '00 219
Chicken, Artichoke, '81 97
Chicken, Dijon, '99 21
Chicken Pasta with Artichokes and Capers, '04 129
Chicken, Sanibel Island, '97 66
Chicken Sauté with Artichokes and Mushrooms,
    '03 57
Chicken with Artichoke Hearts, '88 54
Chicken with Artichokes, '02 314
Chicken with Artichokes and Mushrooms, '90 35
Chicken with Artichokes, Sherried, '87 143
Chilled Artichokes with Lemon-Pepper Dressing, '87 55
Chowder, Artichoke-Shrimp, '03 91
Cooked Artichokes, Whole, '04 53
Crabmeat with Artichoke Hearts, Creamed, '93 26
Dressing, Artichoke, '84 126
Dried Beef with Artichokes, Creamed, '85 81
Eggs Sardou, '92 93
Flan, Artichoke, '96 22
Flatbread, Sicilian Artichoke, '98 136
Herb-Mayonnaise Dip, Artichokes with, '84 67
Lemon, Artichoke Hearts with, '90 98
Linguine, Artichoke and Shrimp, '95 210
Marinated Artichoke Hearts, '95 66
Marinated Artichokes, '87 250; '88 41
Marinated Cucumbers and Artichokes, '82 111
Marinated Mirlitons, Artichokes, and Peppers,
    '00 246
Pasta with Artichoke Hearts, '86 209
Pasta with Catfish and Artichokes, '90 123
Pasta with Rosemary, Chicken-Artichoke, '98 15
Pie, Artichoke, '79 25
Pizza, Grilled, '97 190
Pizza with Artichoke and Prosciutto, '87 182
Quiche, Artichoke, '91 71
Quiche, Shrimp-and-Artichoke, '03 196
Quick 'n' Easy Whole Cooked Artichokes, '96 M132
Ragoût, Veal-and-Artichoke, '94 43
Relish, Jerusalem Artichoke, '89 197

Salads
Artichoke Salad, '86 333
Asparagus-Artichoke Salad, '85 162
Aspic, Tomato-Artichoke, '84 320; '86 92
Avocado Acapulco, '83 2
Chicken-Rice Salad, Artichoke-, '94 132
Chicken-Rice Salad, Mediterranean Artichoke-,
    '97 321
Chicken Salad with Artichokes, '86 186
Couscous Salad, Mediterranean, '03 127
Goat Cheese Salad, Artichoke-, '98 118
Italian House Salad, '02 300
Italian Salad, '87 145
Marinated Artichoke Salad, '83 241; '95 66
Marinated Cucumbers and Artichokes, '82 111
Orzo Salad, Artichokes with, '88 M193
Pasta Salad, Artichoke-, '94 180
Rice Salad, Artichoke-, '80 178; '81 41; '85 81;
    '01 144
Rice Salad with Artichoke Hearts, '80 232
Shrimp-and-Artichoke Salad, '04 50
Stuffed Tomato Salad, Artichoke-, '82 101
Tomato Salad, Artichoke-, '82 239
Tortellini Salad, '02 186
Zucchini-Artichoke Salad, '91 229
Salsa, Artichoke-Tomato, '96 182
Sandwich, Beef-and-Artichoke Open-Faced Italian,
    '98 22
Sandwich, Italian Stuffed, '99 15
Sauce, Chicken Breasts with Artichoke-Pepper, '05 139
Sauce, Creamy Mushroom-Artichoke, '05 312
Sauté, Herbed Artichoke, '96 133
Shrimp Platter with Béarnaise Sauce, Artichoke and,
    '96 132
Soup, Artichoke, '89 269
Soup, Artichoke Cream, '94 62
Soup, Chicken, Artichoke, and Mushroom, '92 324
Soup, Cream of Artichoke, '82 232
Soup, Louisiana Oyster-and-Artichoke, '92 81
Soup, Oyster-and-Artichoke, '97 21
Spring Artichokes, '86 62
Steamed Artichokes, '81 59
Strata, Artichoke-Cheese, '90 236
Stuffed Artichokes, '79 76; '82 92; '91 117; '99 64
Stuffed Artichokes, Ham-Mushroom-, '95 228
Stuffed Artichokes, Shrimp-, '84 67; '87 55
Stuffed Artichokes, Shrimp, '94 62
Stuffed with Shrimp and Scallops, Artichokes, '84 174
Tetrazzini with Artichokes and Red Bell Peppers,
    Smoked Turkey, '05 97
Tomatoes with Curry Sauce, Stuffed, '97 170
Tortellini Alfredo with Prosciutto and Artichoke Hearts,
    '02 322
Turkey Scaloppine with Angel Hair Pasta, '02 44
Veal with Artichoke Hearts, Lemon, '87 219
Vinaigrette, Artichokes, '88 101
Whole Cooked Artichokes, '94 61

ASPARAGUS
Almond Asparagus, '83 86; '02 64
Almond Butter, Asparagus with, '84 85
Almond Sauce, Asparagus with, '91 117
Amandine, Asparagus, '03 295
Balsamic-Browned Butter Asparagus, '05 260
Basil Butter, Asparagus with, '85 40
Basil Sauce, Asparagus with, '86 33
Bean Sprouts, Asparagus and, '96 95
Beef with Asparagus, '90 100
Bundles, Grilled Chile-Rubbed Rib Eyes with Herb
    Cheese and Asparagus, '03 326
Caesar, Asparagus, '88 133
Carrots and Asparagus, Sunshine, '99 277
Cashew Butter, Asparagus with, '87 56

Casseroles
Artichoke Casserole, Asparagus-, '86 279

Asparagus Casserole, '98 310
Cheesy Asparagus Casserole, '82 281; '83 32
Chicken-Asparagus Casserole, '83 76; '84 71
Creamy Asparagus Casserole, '82 76
Easy Asparagus Casserole, '83 255
English Pea Casserole, Asparagus-and-, '86 324
Pea Casserole, Asparagus-, '88 M294
Peas Casserole, Asparagus and, '80 152
Spaghetti Casserole, Asparagus-, '80 77
Turkey-Asparagus Casserole, '86 284
Cheesecake, Ham-and-Asparagus, '90 174; '02 103
Chicken, Asparagus, and Mushrooms with Penne Pasta,
    '98 212
Chicken, Szechuan, '98 155
Chilled Asparagus with Garlic Dipping Sauce, '98 136
Company Asparagus, '85 82
Creamed Asparagus on Toast, '95 61
Cream Sauce, Asparagus with, '90 291
Croquettes, Asparagus, '85 265
Curry Sauce, Asparagus with, '90 17
Cutlets, Asparagus, '80 147
Delight, Asparagus, '82 269
Delight, Ham-Asparagus, '86 48
Dill Sauce, Asparagus with, '97 59
Dilly Asparagus, '88 180
Dressing, Asparagus with Warm Citrus, '96 M86
Eggs à la Asparagus, Creamed, '81 201
en Papillote, Shrimp with Asparagus, '86 145
Fettuccine, Ham-and-Asparagus, '94 84
Fish-Asparagus Divan, '87 128
French-Fried Asparagus, '79 66; '83 46
Frittata, Bacon-and-Asparagus, '88 136
Garlic Cream, Asparagus with, '95 83; '00 71
Ginger, Asparagus with, '04 237
Goat Cheese Sauce, Asparagus with, '93 116
Goldenrod, Asparagus, '79 66
Grilled Asparagus, '00 165; '05 197
Grilled Portobello Mushrooms and Asparagus, '02 122
Guacamole, Mock, '93 36
"Guacamole" with Cumin Crisps, Green Goddess,
    '02 205
Ham-Asparagus Dinner, '80 M10
Ham Rolls, Asparagus, '91 117
Holiday Asparagus, '85 260
Jeweled Asparagus, '80 42
Lemon, Asparagus with, '98 103
Lemon Butter, Asparagus in, '80 M123
Lemon Butter, Asparagus with, '87 M151; '98 168
Lemon-Marinated Asparagus, '03 119
Lemon Sauce, Asparagus with, '86 62
Lemon-Sesame Asparagus, '91 31
Loaf, Asparagus-Pimiento, '84 86
Marinated Asparagus, '81 108; '83 46; '84 67, 86;
    '86 92; '87 74; '02 243; '05 105
Marinated Asparagus, Easy, '81 148
Marinated Asparagus Spears, '88 130
Marinated Asparagus with Prosciutto, '95 83
Mayonnaise, Asparagus with Hot Wine, '81 83
Meringue, Asparagus, '88 131
Mornay, Asparagus, '99 102
Mushrooms, Asparagus and, '85 108
Orange Butter Sauce, Asparagus with, '85 43
Orange Sauce, Asparagus with, '83 46
Oven-Roasted Asparagus, '05 55
Pasta with Asparagus, Tomatoes, and Shrimp, Garlicky,
    '95 82
Pasta with Shrimp and Asparagus, Angel Hair, '92 100
Pasta with Toasted Pecans, Asparagus, '04 90
Pickled Asparagus, '83 46; '04 161
Pie, Cheesy Asparagus, '01 103
Pilaf, Turkey-Asparagus, '88 200
Pimientos, Asparagus with, '98 286
Pork Arlo, '87 229
Prosciutto-Wrapped Asparagus, '91 98

ASPARAGUS

(continued)

Quiche, Asparagus-Tomato, '88 198
Quiche, Springtime, '83 122
Rarebit, Uptown Welsh, '87 279
Rice and Asparagus, '93 324
Risotto, Asparagus, '03 68
Risotto with Shrimp and Asparagus, '03 86
Roasted Asparagus, '05 298
Roasted Asparagus-and-Hazelnut Couscous, '04 60
Roasted Asparagus, Simple, '00 103
Roasted Asparagus with Red Pepper Sauce, '98 322
Roasted Shallot Asparagus, '02 64
Rolls, Asparagus, '79 296; '80 31
Rolls, Chicken-Asparagus, '86 M211
Rolls, Ham-Asparagus, '79 41
Rolls, Hot Asparagus, '93 329
Rollups, Asparagus, '79 63; '01 239
Roll-Ups, Asparagus, '84 270
Roulade, Asparagus, '86 102
Salads
   Artichoke Salad, Asparagus-, '85 162
   Asparagus Salad, '88 121; '94 67
   Aspic, Asparagus, '96 65
   Avocado-Asparagus Salad, '00 331
   Blue Crab Salad with Asian Vinaigrette, '98 142
   Bluegrass Salad, '02 255
   Chicken Salad, Asparagus-, '89 83
   Chicken Salad with Asparagus, Curried, '81 36
   Congealed Asparagus Salad, '83 260
   Crab-and-Asparagus Salad, '92 141
   Crabmeat-and-Asparagus, Congealed Salad with, '84 86
   Cups, Asparagus Salad, '83 47
   Easy Asparagus Salad, '88 131
   Egg Salad, Asparagus-and-, '86 305
   Fresh Asparagus Salad, '01 159
   Ginger Asparagus, Chilled, '02 64
   Grilled Asparagus Salad with Orange Vinaigrette, '99 102
   Grilled Mushroom-Asparagus Salad, '02 122
   Horseradish Salad, Asparagus-, '87 80
   Lemon-Asparagus Salad, Creamy, '93 116
   Marinated Asparagus, '83 46; '84 67, 86; '86 92
   Marinated Asparagus and Hearts of Palm, '90 91
   Marinated Asparagus Medley, '91 105
   Marinated Asparagus Salad, '79 20
   Marinated Asparagus with Prosciutto, '95 83
   Mold, Asparagus, '80 104
   Mold, Asparagus-Cucumber, '85 252
   Mousse Salad, Asparagus, '86 252
   Mustard Sauce, Chilled Asparagus in, '88 130
   New Potato Salad, Asparagus-and-, '86 69
   Papaya Salsa, Asparagus Salad with, '97 144
   Peas-and-Asparagus Salad, '83 141
   Roasted-Beet, and Goat Cheese Salad, Asparagus, '02 96
   Roasted Beet, and Goat Cheese Salad, Asparagus, '03 98
   Tarragon Marinade, Asparagus with, '83 47
   Tart Asparagus Salad, '81 203
   Tomato-Asparagus Salad, '92 79
   Tomatoes with Herb Vinaigrette, Asparagus and, '99 56
   Vinaigrette, Asparagus, '80 77; '90 82, 138; '93 174
   Vinaigrette, Asparagus Salad, '88 56
   Vinaigrette, Light Asparagus, '82 50
   White Bean-and-Asparagus Salad, '05 100
   Yogurt Dressing, Asparagus with, '79 66
Sandwiches, Asparagus-and-Ham Melt, '88 M96
Sandwiches, Asparagus Grill, '79 164; '80 130
Sandwiches, Asparagus Spear, '84 165

Sandwiches, Ham-and-Asparagus, '01 307
Sandwiches, Ham-Swiss-and-Asparagus, '01 52
Sandwiches, Turkey-Asparagus, '96 74
Sandwich, Warm Asparagus, '99 102
Sauce, Asparagus White, '80 147
Sauté, Asparagus, '01 275
Sauté, Asparagus-and-Mushroom, '93 115
Sautéed Asparagus, '79 66
Sesame Asparagus, '96 154; '00 282; '02 64
Sesame Asparagus, Chilled, '03 67
Shrimp Mold with Asparagus, '93 214
Soufflé, Asparagus, '79 66; '83 265; '89 89
Soup, Asparagus, '84 67; '98 290; '00 84
Soup, Asparagus-Potato, '85 23
Soup, Cream of Asparagus, '84 111
Soup, Creamy Asparagus, '94 225
Soup, Creamy Asparagus-and-Chicken, '95 82
Sour Cream, Asparagus with, '83 46
Spears, Buttered Asparagus, '97 282
Squares, Asparagus, '79 161; '02 183
Squash Rings, Asparagus in, '87 68
Steamed Asparagus, '92 211
Steamed Asparagus with Tomato-Basil Dip, '00 69; '04 53
Stir-Fried Asparagus, '87 52
Stir-fried Asparagus with Garlic, '05 86
Stir-Fry, Asparagus, '95 83
Stir-Fry Beef and Asparagus, '91 124
Stir-Fry, Sweet Onion-Asparagus, '98 135
Supreme, Asparagus, '80 77; '89 245
Supreme, Cauliflower and Asparagus, '79 287; '80 35
Sweet-and-Sour Asparagus, '89 159
Tangy Asparagus, '84 86
Tartlets, Country Ham-and-Asparagus, '98 82
Terrine with Dill Sauce, Asparagus-Seafood, '98 157
Tomatoes, Fresh Asparagus and, '94 162
Tomato Sauce, Asparagus with, '83 46
Toss, Asparagus-Carrot-Squash, '91 45
Toss, Asparagus-Vermicelli, '00 102
Tostadas with Goat Cheese, Asparagus-and-Mushroom, '03 242
Vinaigrette, Asparagus, '80 77; '90 82, 138; '93 174

ASPIC
Apple Aspic, Sunshine, '81 73
Asparagus Aspic, '96 65
Basic Aspic for Garnishing, '84 189
Beet Aspic, '90 123
Blue Cheese Aspic, '96 66
Chicken Salad, Aspic-Topped, '88 88
Coating, White Aspic, '85 151
Cucumber-Curry Dressing, Aspic with, '89 178
Fish Aspic, '84 190
Fish 'n Aspic, '84 190
Gazpacho Aspic, '89 179; '96 65
Grapefruit Aspic, '80 297; '82 112; '83 153
Madeira Aspic, '86 65
Orange-and-Carrot Aspic, '86 199
Rosemary Aspic, Spicy, '99 183
Shrimp-Coleslaw Aspic, '79 88
Shrimp-Cucumber Aspic, '83 108
Sunshine Aspic, '80 103
Three-Layer Aspic, '88 120
Tomato
   Artichoke Aspic, Tomato-, '84 320; '86 92
   Bloody Mary-Tomato Aspic, '81 77
   Chicken in Tomato Aspic, '84 190
   Chili Sauce Tomato Aspic, '85 252
   Classic Tomato Aspic, '91 229
   Crab Aspic, Tomato-, '85 287
   Herbed Tomato Aspic, '81 73
   Layered Tomato Aspic, '90 99
   Light Tomato Aspic, '85 83
   Ranch Tomato Aspic, '83 218
   Raspberry-Tomato Aspic, '05 65

   Shrimp, Tomato Aspic with, '79 241
   Spicy Tomato Aspic, '81 40; '89 288
   Tangy Tomato Aspic, '83 124
   Two, Aspic for, '83 209
   Vegetable Aspic, Cheesy, '81 73
   Vegetable Aspic with Horseradish Dressing, Crisp, '87 152

AVOCADOS
Baked Avocado-and-Crabmeat, '84 119
Broiled Crab and Avocado, '79 116
Butter, Avocado, '05 159
Chicken, Orange-Avocado, '80 38
Cocktail, Sherried Avocado-Crabmeat, '87 95
Crabmeat, Avocado with, '86 119
Cream, Avocado, '92 158
Dagwoods, Chicken-Avocado, '96 200; '99 337
Dip, Avocado, '80 285; '81 57, 306
Dip, "Bring-Home-the-Bacon" Avocado, '92 80
Dip, Gazpacho, '95 243
Dip, Roasted Corn-and-Avocado, '91 279
Dip, Six-Layer, '81 160
Dip, Zippy Avocado, '82 9; '83 69
Dressing, Avocado, '80 15; '92 321; '96 138
Dressing, Avocado Fruit Salad, '82 93
Eggs and Ham, Green, '96 90
Filled Avocados, Shrimp-, '83 2
Frittata, Avocado-and-Black Bean, '02 212
Gazpacho, Tomato-Avocado-Corn, '97 182
Guacamole
   Baine's Guac, '98 88
   Coleslaw, Guacamole Mexican, '82 302
   Creamy Guacamole, '79 91; '83 174; '99 119; '02 168
   Crisps, Guacamole, '98 173
   Dip, Bacon-Guacamole, '85 25
   Dip, Guacamole, '86 4; '95 96
   Dressing, Guacamole, '92 64
   Easy Guacamole, '95 94; '01 17
   Guacamole, '79 185; '80 74; '83 179; '89 226; '90 205; '91 161; '94 116; '96 160, 170; '99 84; '02 118; '03 95
   Margarita Guacamole, '97 167
   Mold, Guacamole, '86 184
   Po'Boys, Guacamole-Topped Ham, '04 170
   Roasted Onion Guacamole, '00 334
   Salad, Guacamole, '80 14; '87 181
   Salad, Guacamole-Tomato, '81 302
   Sandwiches, Guacamole, '82 9; '83 68
   Shells, Guacamole in, '86 74
   Spicy Guacamole, '93 218
   Spread, Guacamole, '90 119
   Subs, Guacamole, '84 293
Ice, Avocado, '83 179
Kebabs, Chicken-Avocado, '82 9; '83 68
Lasagna, Avocado-Vegetable, '01 310
Mayonnaise, Avocado, '00 335
Mayonnaise, Spicy Salmon Fillets with Avocado, '02 327
Mousse with Shrimp Salad, Avocado, '98 333
Omelet, Yogurt-Avocado, '81 33
Pie, Mexican Cheese, '83 69
Potatoes, Avocado-Topped, '83 3
Relish, Avocado, '87 120
Salads
   Acapulco, Avocado, '83 2
   Apple Salad with Maple-Walnut Vinaigrette, Avocado-, '04 45
   Asparagus Salad, Avocado-, '00 331
   Avocado Salad, '81 195; '82 9; '83 69; '92 246; '97 250; '02 99
   Bread Salad, Avocado-, '02 210
   Chicken-Avocado Salad, '80 139
   Chicken-Avocado Salad, Fruited, '82 101
   Chicken-Avocado Salad Platter, '83 2

Chicken-Avocado Salad, Tossed, '80 4
Chicken Salad, Avocado-, '87 107
Chicken Salad in Avocados, '85 216
Chicken Salad in Avocados, Fruited, '87 41
Citrus-and-Avocado Salad, '99 26
Citrus-Avocado Salad, '82 265
Citrus Salad, Avocado, '01 133
Congealed Avocado Crunch Salad, '85 26
Congealed Avocado Salad, '84 266
Congealed Avocado Salads, '87 42
Corn-Poblano Salad, Avocado-, '01 320
Crab-Avocado Salad, '81 114
Dude Ranch Salad, '80 15
Endive Salad, Avocado-, '94 88
Fruit Salad, Avocado, '87 41
Fruit Salad with Honey-Yogurt Dressing,
 Avocado-, '93 172
Garbanzo Salad, Avocado-, '81 33
Grapefruit-Avocado Salad, '83 316; '84 16; '89 41
Grapefruit Salad, Avocado-, '85 26; '93 282
Melon Salad, Avocado-, '82 164
Mexican Salad Supper, '82 9; '83 68
Orange-Avocado Salad, '99 331
Orange Salad, Avocado-, '91 44
Pita, Avocado Salad-Hummus, '02 99
Potato Salad with Avocado, '98 332
Potato Salad with Horseradish Dressing,
 Avocado-, '96 200
Rice-and-Avocado Salad, '89 146
Romaine Salad, Tangy, '80 155
Salad, Mozzarella, Avocado, and Tomato, '05 41
Shrimp and Avocado Salad, '80 266
Shrimp Salad, Avocado Stuffed with, '82 207
Shrimp Salad on the Half Shell, '86 73
Southwestern Spiral Salad, '98 66
Spanish Avocado Salad, '87 41
Spinach Salad, Green, '79 142
Tomato-Avocado Salad, '86 74
Tomatoes, Avocado-Stuffed, '82 101
Zucchini Salad, Creamy Avocado and, '79 208
Salsa, Avocado, '91 182
Salsa, Avocado-Corn, '94 201; '99 335
Salsa, Avocado-Feta, '96 15; '05 298
Salsa, Avocado-Mango, '00 328
Salsa, Avocado-Peach, '02 159
Salsa, Fresh Avocado, '02 247
Salsa, Sweet, '98 174
Salsa, Tomato-Avocado, '94 83
Sandwiches, Avocado, Bacon, and Cheese, '87 279
Sandwiches, Avocado-Crabmeat, '83 2
Sandwiches, Avocado Deluxe, '99 72
Sandwich with Tomato, Avocado, and Bacon, Grilled
 Four-Cheese, '00 199
Sauce, Avocado, '80 198; '83 200
Sauce, Avocado Béarnaise, '01 317
Sauce, Avocado-Lime, '03 90
Sauce, Avocado-Tomatillo, '95 206
Sauce, Chunky Avocado, '03 128
Sauce, Grilled Swordfish with Avocado-Lime, '97 127
Shells, Ceviche in Avocado, '81 33
Sherbet, Avocado, '83 162
Sherbet, Mexican, '79 155
Sorbet, Avocado, '88 117
Soup, Avocado, '88 160; '05 159, 200
Soup, Avocado-Banana-Yogurt, '80 78
Soup, Chilled Avocado, '81 34; '87 37; '93 108
Soup, Creamy Avocado, '79 107; '01 176
Soup, Creamy Avocado-Mushroom, '85 25
Soup, Sherried Avocado, '84 181
Spread, Herbed Avocado-Cheese, '98 335
Stuffed Avocados, Crab-, '86 73
Stuffed Avocados, Salmon-, '86 74
Stuffed Broiled Avocados, '88 246
Terrine, Chèvre-and-Avocado, '00 276

Tomatoes, Crab-and-Avocado Stuffed, '94 141
Topping, Avocado, '93 309; '94 96
Tostadas, Crispy, '83 2
Whip, Avocado, '79 107
Wraps, Thai Chicken-Avocado, '02 206

Bacon

Appetizers
Biscuits with Sun-Dried Tomato Spread and Bacon,
 Cream Cheese-and-Olive, '02 313
Bites, Bacon-Shrimp, '98 234; '99 213
Blue Cheese-and-Bacon Puffs, '97 98
Brie, Chutney-Bacon, '90 M292
Cheese-Bacon Crispies, '84 270
Chestnut Wraps, Bacon-, '84 M216
Crackers, Bacon-Wrapped, '93 280
Crostini, Almond-Bacon-Cheese, '94 318
Crostini, Green Onion, '96 93
Crostini, Pear-and-Gorgonzola, '02 314
Dip, Bacon, '82 197
Dip, Bacon-and-Tomato, '90 147
Dip, Bacon-Cheese, '01 194
Dip, Bacon-Guacamole, '85 25
Dip, Blue Cheese-Bacon, '04 287
Dip, "Bring-Home-the-Bacon" Avocado, '92 80
Dip, Cheddar-Bacon, '89 M119
Dip, Zesty Bacon, '92 156
Eggs, Bacon-Stuffed, '97 52; '00 70; '04 290
Eggs, Double Stuffed Spinach-and-Bacon, '00 M333
Fingers, Bacon-Cheese, '00 123
Hot Bacon Appetizers, '80 248
Meatballs, Burgundy-Bacon, '80 283
Mushrooms, Cheese 'n' Bacon-Stuffed, '86 258
Onion Appetizers, Bacon-, '94 290
Oysters, Fried Bacon-Wrapped, '02 103
Oysters in Bacon, '83 211
Pineapple Chunks, Bacon-Wrapped, '84 25
Popcorn, Bacon-Cheese, '86 74
Puffs, Blue Cheese-and-Bacon, '01 236
Puffs, Cheesy Bacon, '02 145
Quesadillas, Bacon-Jalapeño-Tomato, '95 240
Quiches, Miniature Bacon-Cheese, '83 93
Rolls, Bacon, '84 270; '93 330
Rollups, Bacon, '79 34
Roll-Ups, Chicken Liver and Bacon, '80 200;
 '81 57
Rollups, Sausage-Bacon, '88 51
Rumaki, '80 M136
Rumaki, Scallop, '98 M173
Scallops, Bacon-Wrapped, '87 94
Scallops with Orange-Honey Sauce, Bacon-Wrapped,
 '97 236
Shrimp 'n' Bacon, '98 222
Spread, Bacon-Cheese, '83 241
Sticks, Parmesan-Bacon, '99 65
Swirls, Bacon, '89 214; '98 26
Water Chestnuts, Bacon-Wrapped, '79 63
Apple Bacon, Sweet, '03 305
Bagels, Meal-in-One, '88 159
Bake, Bacon, Zucchini, and Cornbread, '99 123
Bake, Lima-Bacon, '86 9
Banana Peppers, Stuffed, '02 55
Bars, Bacon-Cheese Toast, '79 36
Beans, Barbecue, '02 167
Beans, Frolickers Baked, '03 92
Beans, Lowcountry Baked, '98 332
Beef-and-Bacon Twirls, '91 163
Biscuit Bites, Savory Tomato-Bacon, '03 196
Biscuit Cups, Bacon, '99 214
Biscuits, Bacon-Cheese, '88 84
Biscuits, Potato-Bacon, '94 214
Black Pepper-Brown Sugar Bacon, '04 70
Bread, Bacon-and-Cheese, '83 255

Bread, Bacon-Cheddar Grits, '05 83
Bread, Bacon-Cheese French, '92 54
Bread, Bacon Monkey, '94 283; '97 154
Breakfast Bake, '85 45
Breakfast Eye-Openers, '82 231
Breakfast, Farmer's, '81 44
Broccoli Bakers, '99 308
Broccoli with Bacon, '92 302
Brown Sugar Bacon, '04 70
Brown Sugar Bacon, Crispy, '05 283
Bundles, Bean, '80 246
Burgers, Apple-Bacon, '99 202
Burgers, Cheesy Bacon, '81 29
Butterbeans, Bacon, and Tomatoes, '96 36; '00 184
Butterbeans with Bacon and Green Onions, '96 267
Butternut and Bacon, Skillet, '85 9
Cabbage, Creole, '00 105
Cabbage, Fried, '02 272
Canadian Bacon-and-Brie Quiche, '04 248
Canadian Bacon, Lima Beans with, '83 219; '84 245
Canadian Bacon Squares, Sunrise, '99 103
Canadian-Style Bacon, Glazed, '82 197
Carrots with Bacon and Onion, Glazed, '87 200;
 '02 283
Casserole, Bacon and Egg, '81 225
Casserole, Bacon-and-Egg, '03 166
Casserole, Campfire, '00 173
Casserole, Cheesy Bacon-and-Ham, '01 256
Casserole, Egg-and-Bacon, '85 248
Casseroles, Hot Brown Pasta, '96 290
Casserole with Creole Sauce, Brunch, '98 98
Cauliflower with Parmesan and Bacon, '96 137
Champignons au Vin, '79 47
Chicken-Bacon Nuggets, '03 292
Chicken Breasts, Apple-Bacon Stuffed, '99 313
Chicken Bundles with Bacon Ribbons, '87 68
Chowder, Fresh Corn and Bacon, '93 203
Chowder, Southern Corn-and-Bacon, '96 166
Coleslaw, Apple-Bacon, '04 181
Coleslaw, Bacon, '83 58
Collard Greens, Esau's, '03 17
Cookies, Breakfast, '97 52
Cookies, Take-Along Breakfast, '84 59
Cornbread, Bacon-Cheddar Hot-Water, '01 29; '02 107;
 '04 25
Cornbread, Cowboy, '81 188
Cornbread, Loaded, '99 214
Corn, Creamy Fried Confetti, '02 160
Corn, Skillet Creamed, '02 204
Corn with Bacon and Caramelized Onion, '99 94
Cream Cheese, Bacon-Olive, '04 196
Cups, Bacon-Cheese, '02 219
Delight, Bacon-and-Egg, '85 143
Dressing, Green Beans with Bacon, '85 147
Dressing, Hot Bacon, '84 12
Dressing, Jeweled Hot Bacon, '97 196
Dressing, Potatoes with Hot Bacon, '88 M294
Dressing, Sweet Bacon, '93 108
Egg Salad, Bacon-Horseradish, '94 181
Eggs, and Hominy, Bacon, '85 143
Eggs, Bacon Deviled, '86 136
Eggs Benedict, '98 55
Eggs Benedict, Bacon-and-Tomato, '87 195
Eggs Benedict, Traditional, '03 52
Eggs, Brunch, '98 93
Eggs Oso Grande, '98 279
Flank Steak, Bacon-Wrapped, '85 59
Franks, Bacon-Wrapped, '81 202
Frittata, Bacon-and-Asparagus, '98 136
Frittata, Potato-Bacon, '95 269; '98 330
Green Beans, Bacon-Topped, '80 M123
Green Beans, Mushroom-Bacon, '91 291; '92 255
Green Beans, Southern Smothered, '02 55
Green Beans with Bacon and Mushrooms, '92 13

BACON
(continued)

Green Beans with Zucchini, '02 251
Greens and Bacon, Shelly, '96 290
Grits, Nassau, '99 214
Hash Browns, Sweet Potato, '02 248
Hush Puppies, Bacon, '91 201
Kebabs, Scallop-Bacon, '81 111
Kale, Homestyle, '00 91
Lettuce Wedges with Blue Cheese Dressing,
    Iceberg, '00 217
Linguine Carbonara, '87 108
Meatballs, Bacon-Wrapped, '79 81
Meat Loaf, Sweet Ketchup-and-Bacon-Topped, '03 203
Muffins, Bacon-and-Cheese, '89 205
Muffins, Bacon-Cheese, '96 280
Mushrooms with Bacon, Stir-Fried, '80 123
Nuggets, Chicken-Bacon, '04 146
Okra Pilau, '99 184
Omelet, Open-Faced Bacon-and-Potato, '02 246
Omelet, Spinach, Cheddar, and Bacon, '03 204
Oysters, Bacon-Baked, '86 132
Oysters Rockefeller, '98 222
Pancake, Maple-Bacon Oven, '89 255
Pasta, Bacon, '97 52; '05 224
Pears, Field Greens with Roasted Bacon-Wrapped,
    '05 230
Peas and Bacon, Sautéed, '89 331
Peas with Crispy Bacon, Green, '04 60
Pecans, Roasted Bacon, '96 262
Pie, Country Breakfast, '93 M328
Pimiento Cheese, Bacon-, '05 142
Pinto Beans, Mexican, '00 241
Pizza, Breakfast, '97 172; '00 193
Pizza, Tex-Mex Chicken-and-Bacon, '05 325
Pizza, The King Henry, '95 267
Pork Chops, Stuffed, '02 204
Pork Tenderloin, Peppered Bacon-Wrapped, '02 55
Pork Tenderloin, Spinach-and-Bacon Stuffed, '94 81
Potatoes, Bacon-Stuffed, '86 193
Potatoes, Bacon-Topped Blue Cheese, '79 46
Potatoes, Baked Sweet-and-Savory Mashed, '02 244
Potatoes, Cheesy Bacon-Stuffed, '81 M61
Potatoes, Green Onion-and-Bacon Mashed, '02 110
Potatoes, Phyllo, '02 219
Potatoes, Stuffed, '01 48
Quail, Bacon-Wrapped, '02 238
Quesadillas, Bacon-and-Egg, '05 88
Quiche, Bacon, '85 60
Quiche Lorraine, '80 M108; '99 M218; '01 88
Quiche Lorraine, Classic, '81 131
Quiche Lorraine, Mushroom-, '86 242
Quiche Lorraine, Peppery, '81 228
Quiche, Spinach-and-Bacon, '00 240
Rice, Bacon-Chive, '83 129
Rice, Bacon Fried, '80 115
Rice, Spicy, '99 214
Rolls, Onion-Bacon, '99 47
Rouladen, '99 242
Rutabaga with Bacon, '83 243
Salad, Bacon-Lettuce-Mozzarella-and-Tomato, '98 209
Salad, Bacon-Mandarin, '02 87
Salad, Bacon 'n' Onion Potato, '05 188
Salad, Bacon Potato, '05 171
Salad, Bacon-Topped Potato, '85 59
Salad, BLT Chicken, '87 144
Salad, BLT Potato, '05 213
Salad, Eight-Layer, '99 107
Salad, Endive, Bacon, and Pecan, '89 12
Salad, Escarole-and-Bacon, '84 85
Salad, Hot Bacon and Black-Eyed, '85 7
Salad, Italian BLT Bread, '03 90

Salad, Layered BLT, '01 96
Salad, Roasted Potato-and-Bacon, '05 289
Salad, Spinach, '03 246
Salad, Spinach and Bacon, '81 143
Salad, Wilted Bacon-and-Lettuce, '85 69
Salad with Bacon, Rice, '79 52
Salad with Sweet Parsley Dressing, Spinach, '02 120
Sandwiches
    Avocado, Bacon, and Cheese Sandwiches, '87 279
    Bagel, Breakfast on a, '94 66
    Beef, Bacon, and Blue Cheese Sandwiches, '96 23
    BLT, Caramelized Onion, '03 90
    BLT Sandwiches, Italian, '02 230
    Breakfast Sandwiches, '82 M123; '89 M230
    Breakfast Sandwiches, BLT, '04 171
    Breakfast Sandwiches, Open-Faced, '92 140
    Cheese, and Tomato Sandwiches, Bacon, '84 14
    Cheesy BLT's, '85 92
    Croissants, BLT, '93 158
    Curried BLT Sandwiches, '93 158
    Empanadas, Bacon 'n' Egg Breakfast, '02 324
    Good-Start Sandwiches, '99 134
    Grilled Bacon, Cheese, and Tomato Sandwiches,
        '97 170
    Grilled Bacon-Cheese Sandwiches, '83 242
    Grilled Four-Cheese Sandwich with Tomato,
        Avocado, and Bacon, '00 199
    Hoagies, Bacon, Pimiento, and Cheese, '90 144
    Hot Browns, Baby, '00 107
    Melts, Bacon-and-Cheese, '04 324
    Melts, Tomato-Cheese-Bacon, '99 72
    Muffuletta Bacon-Olive Party Sandwiches, Mini,
        '04 196
    Olive Party Sandwiches, Bacon-, '04 196
    Open-Faced Cheesy Bacon Sandwiches, '80 78
    Open-Faced Sandwiches, Super, '97 52
    Pita Pockets, BLT in, '93 158
    Poor Boys, Oyster-and-Bacon, '87 40
    Stuffed Sandwich, Italian, '99 15
    Tomato, Swiss, and Bacon Sandwiches, '04 140
    Turkey, Bacon, and Havarti Sandwich, '05 92
    Welsh Rarebit with Tomatoes and Bacon, '92 M159
    Wrap, BLT, '04 298
    Wraps, BLT, '05 224
    Wrap, Southwest BLT, '03 90
    Wraps, Western, '99 194
Sauté, Orange-Watercress, '98 83
Scallops, Maple, '99 176
Scramble, Bacon-and-Eggs, '80 M267
Slaw, Blue Cheese-Bacon, '05 91
Slaw, German Cabbage, '00 105
Soufflés, Parmesan, '97 280
Soup, Bacon-Beer Cheese, '87 M7
Soup, Bacon, Lettuce, and Tomato, '91 207
Soup, Bacon-Topped Cheese, '80 M224
Soup, Bean and Bacon, '83 26
Soup, Potato-Bacon, '84 M38
Spaghetti, Bacon, '86 213; '87 82
Spaghetti Carbonara, '03 123
Spoonbread, Corn and Bacon, '81 129
Spread, Spinach-Bacon, '92 M310
Squash, Bacon-Flavored, '82 158
Squash, Creole, '01 180
Strata, Tomato-Bacon, '03 100
Supper Supreme, Sunday, '79 76
Sweet Potatoes, Bacon-Stuffed, '86 224
Tart, Tomato-Leek-Bacon, '03 325
Taters, Bacon-Fried, '02 55
Tomatoes, Bacon-and-Egg-Stuffed, '80 162
Tomatoes, Cornbread-Stuffed, '02 213
Tomatoes with Bacon, Saucy Fried, '81 210
Tortellini Carbonara, Creamy, '99 171
Trout Stuffed with Crawfish, Bacon-Wrapped, '99 54
Trout, Sweet Onion-Stuffed, '99 52

Turnovers, Turnip-Bacon, '04 213
Vegetable-Bacon Bowl, Marinated, '79 191
Vegetable Skillet, Summer, '00 138
BAKING POWDER
Single-Acting Baking Powder, '96 142
BANANAS
Alaskas, Banana Split, '87 10
Baked Bananas, '79 103; '96 163
Baked Bananas, Coffee-Kissed, '98 279
Baked Bananas, Honey-, '81 268
Baked Bananas with Orange Sauce, '79 115
Bars, Banana Breakfast, '79 124
Beverages
    Berry Flip, Banana-, '88 215; '89 20
    "Concrete," All Shook Up, '94 114
    Coolers, Banana, '91 308
    Crush, Banana, '80 88; '83 142
    Flip, Banana, '83 303
    Float, Strawberry-Banana, '87 160
    Frostee, Banana, '91 66
    Funky Monkey, '99 161
    Kabana, Banana, '86 316
    Malt, Banana-Chocolate, '89 170
    Milkshake, Banana, '85 47; '90 179
    Milk Shake, Banana-Pineapple, '84 59
    Milk Shake, Chocolate-Banana, '94 113
    Nog, Banana, '82 290
    Orange-Banana Flip, '82 48
    Orange-Banana Whip, '95 244
    Orange Slush, Banana-, '80 48; '81 155
    Pineapple-Banana Slush, '90 14
    Punch, Banana, '99 161; '01 93
    Purple Cow, '98 206
    Shake, Banana, '97 172
    Shake, Banana-Mocha, '05 45
    Shake, Double Strawberry-Banana, '01 173
    Shake, Light Double Strawberry-Banana, '01 173
    Shake, Peanut Butter-Banana, '97 172
    Shake, Pineapple-Banana, '85 215
    Shake, Pineapple-Orange-Banana, '97 172
    Shake, Raspberry-and-Banana, '89 183
    Shake, Strawberry-Banana, '89 35; '97 172
    Slush, Banana, '83 56
    Smoothie, Banana, '87 160; '93 95
    Smoothie, Banana-Berry, '05 24
    Smoothie, Banana-Blueberry, '90 104
    Smoothie, Banana Breakfast, '03 46
    Smoothie, Banana-Peach Buttermilk, '04 22
    Smoothie, Berry-Banana Buttermilk, '00 49
    Smoothie, Honey-Banana, '89 144
    Smoothie, Orange-Banana, '97 173
    Smoothie, Quick Banana-Pineapple, '93 195
    Smoothies, Sunshine, '98 330
    Smoothie, Strawberry-Banana, '81 59
    Smoothie, Tropical, '81 50
    Strawberry Frost, Banana-, '87 199
    Tropical Delight, '89 182
Bisque, Banana-Raspberry, '93 161
Boats, Banana, '82 50; '00 173
Breads
    Apple Bread, Banana-, '85 250
    Banana Bread, '87 72
    Blueberry Bread, Banana-, '81 163
    Butterscotch Bread, Banana, '79 116
    Chocolate Chip-Banana Bread, '90 267
    Chocolate Chip-Banana Loaf, '85 115
    Cranberry-Banana Bread, '80 281; '90 294
    Cream Cheese-Banana-Nut Bread, '05 27
    Cream Cheese-Banana-Nut Bread, Cinnamon Crisp-
        Topped, '05 27
    Cream Cheese-Banana-Nut Bread, Orange-Pecan-
        Topped, '05 27
    Cream Cheese-Banana-Nut Bread, Peanut Butter
        Streusel-Topped, '05 27

Cream Cheese-Banana-Nut Bread, Toasted Coconut-Topped, '05 27
Cream Cheese-Banana-Nut Bread, Toffee-Topped, '05 27
Date-Banana Loaves, Tropical, '95 143
Easy Banana Bread, '96 97
Fruity Banana Bread, '95 78
Hawaiian Loaf, '80 225
Honey-Banana Bread, '91 68
Jam Bread, Banana-, '84 73
Muffins, Banana, '80 88; '84 75
Muffins, Banana Bran, '83 48
Muffins, Banana-Chocolate, '94 197
Muffins, Banana-Honey-Nut, '88 62
Muffins, Banana-Nut, '93 140
Muffins, Banana-Oat, '87 188
Muffins, Banana Oat Bran, '89 106
Muffins, Banana-Oatmeal, '84 20
Muffins, Banana-Orange, '84 148
Muffins, Banana-Poppyseed, '89 205
Muffins, Banana-Praline, '04 21
Muffins, Banana-Raisin, '89 218
Muffins, Banana Surprise, '82 105
Muffins, Cream Cheese-Banana-Nut, '05 27
Muffins, Jumbo Banana-Chocolate Chip, '93 339
Muffins, Oat Bran-Banana, '91 18
Muffins, Peanut Butter-Banana, '03 195
Nut Bread, Banana-, '86 8, 70; '01 239; '04 259
Nut Bread, Hawaiian Banana, '79 235
Nut-Raisin Bread, Banana-, '81 59
Oat Tea Loaf, Banana-, '87 256
Roll, Banana-Nut, '85 112
Sour Cream-Banana Bread, '79 190
Wheat Bread, Banana, '81 14
Whole Wheat Banana Bread, '80 88
Whole Wheat-Banana Nut Bread, '84 50
Zucchini Bread, Banana-, '85 326
Breakfast-in-a-Bowl, '89 87
Broiled Bananas with Honey, '84 175
Brownies, Banana-Split, '03 M43
Brownies, Chocolate-Banana, '80 160
Brown Sugar Bananas, '05 45
Cake, Banana, '84 151
Cake, Banana-Blueberry, '86 247
Cake, Banana-Coconut, '93 154
Cake, Banana-Nut, '92 120
Cake, Banana Pound, '96 60; '98 195
Cake, Bananas Foster Crunch, '93 339
Cake, Banana Split, '99 48
Cake, Banana Waldorf, '85 118
Cake, Chocolate-Banana, '86 138
Cake, Deluxe Light Banana, '84 314
Cake, Hummingbird, '03 315
Cake, Lightened Hummingbird, '01 34
Cake, Marvelous Banana, '79 115
Cake, Peanut Butter-Banana, '80 87
Cake, Triple-Layered Banana, '00 244
Cake with Coconut-Cream Cheese Frosting, Decadent Banana, '05 317
Cake with Coconut Custard, Supreme Banana, '97 131
Candied Bananas, '83 179
Caramelized Bananas, '99 49
Casserole, Sweet Potato-Banana, '86 276
Cheesecake, Chocolate-Wrapped Banana, '99 M48
Chicken with Black Bean Sauce, Banana, '96 156
Cinnamon Toasty Fruity Delight, '00 193
Coffee Cake, Banana, '81 288
Coffee Cake, Banana Cream, '85 46
Coffee Cake, Banana-Sour Cream, '80 186; '97 231; '04 194
Coffee Cakes, Banana-Toffee, '02 M324
Cookies, Banana Oatmeal, '79 217
Crêpes Flambé, Banana, '84 262
Cupcakes, Banana-Chocolate, '02 187

Cupcakes, Banana-Cocoa, '80 130
Cupcakes, Banana Pudding Ice-Cream, '01 173
Curried Bananas, Fillets with Horseradish Sauce and, '85 230
Delights, Choco-Peanut, '99 197
Dessert, Banana Cream, '81 180
Dessert in a Nutshell, '96 318
Doughnuts, Banana, '86 137
Dressing, Banana-Poppy Seed, '98 184
Éclairs, Banana-Chocolate, '01 45
Fish, Caribbean Banana, '95 202
Flambé, Banana-Peach, '85 316
Foster, Bananas, '79 18; '83 M114; '86 139; '96 99
Foster, Elegant Bananas, '81 59
Foster for Two, Bananas, '80 115
Foster, Orange-Glazed Bananas, '91 91
Foster, Tropical Bananas, '79 231
Fritters, Banana, '79 213
Frosting, Banana-Nut, '79 115
Glace, Bananas, '96 46
Green Bananas Escabeche (Pickled Green Bananas), '92 169
Hawaiian, Bananas, '89 94
Ice Cream, Banana-Coconut, '02 164
Ice Cream, Banana-Graham, '91 56
Ice Cream, Banana-Nut, '00 143
Ice Cream, Banana Split, '80 176
Ice Cream, Straw-Ba-Nut, '80 177
Ice Cream, Strawberry-Banana-Nut, '88 203
Ice Milk, Banana Yogurt, '89 199
Jam, Banana, '82 296
Jam, Rosy Peach-Banana, '80 142
Napoleons, Banana, '00 50
Nutty Bananas, '79 251
Pancakes, Banana, '03 305
Pancakes, Banana-Nut, '98 160
Pancakes, Best, '99 194
Pancakes, Island, '87 225
Pancakes, Wheat Germ-Banana, '79 114
Pancakes with Peanut Butter and Jelly Syrups, Banana, '01 24
Pie, Banana Cream, '84 48; '87 207
Pie, Blueberry-Banana, '93 115
Pie, Caramel-Banana, '86 M165
Pie, Chocolate-Banana-Pecan Cream, '94 210
Pie, Creamy Coco-Nana, '00 95
Pie, Hawaiian Banana Cream, '90 105
Pie, Layered Banana Split, '83 189
Pie, Luscious Caramel Banana, '79 115
Pie, Peanut Butter-Banana, '01 315
Pie, Strawberry-Banana Glazed, '81 181
Pie, White Chocolate-Banana Cream, '94 314
Pie with Hot Buttered Rum Sauce, Banana, '88 204
Pizza, Banana Split-Brownie, '96 M164
Pops, Banana, '83 60; '84 44
Pops, Orange-Banana, '82 129
Pops, Yummy Banana, '01 231
Praline Bananas, '84 313
Pudding, Almost Banana, '88 174
Pudding, Banana, '82 53; '84 94; '85 255; '88 16, 32; '03 24
Pudding, Banana-Mallow, '86 139
Pudding, Bananas Foster Bread, '04 235
Pudding, Basic Banana, '81 59
Pudding, Best-Ever Banana, '00 332
Pudding, Creamy Banana, '89 M130
Pudding, Delicious Banana, '80 9
Pudding, Fudge-Banana, '97 331
Pudding, Graham Banana, '02 62
Pudding, No-Bake Banana, '91 172; '99 197
Pudding, Old-Fashioned Banana, '92 94
Pudding, Over-the-Moon Banana, '03 140
Pudding Parfait Pops, Banana, '96 180
Pudding, Peanut Butter-Banana, '93 340; '05 44

Pudding, Sour Cream Banana, '98 90
Pudding, Surprise Banana, '86 7
Pudding with Caramel Syrup, The Ultimate No-Bake Cheesecake Banana, '05 326
Pudding with Sugar Biscuits, Banana, '04 72
Regal Bananas, '85 46
Salad, Banana, '87 80
Salad, Banana-Mixed Fruit, '79 270
Salad, Banana Split, '91 58
Salad, Frozen Banana, '82 80, 132
Salad with Celery Seed Dressing, Grapefruit-Banana, '91 237
Salsa, Banana, '96 85
Salsa, Banana Rum, '94 97
Salsa, Caribbean, '96 70
Sauce, Banana-Pineapple, '83 48
Sauce, Bananas Foster, '03 94
Sauce, Banana Sundae, '84 275
Sauce, Buttered Rum Pound Cake with Bananas Foster, '03 94
Sauce, Strawberry-Banana, '81 41
Sherbet, Banana-Orange, '83 162
Shortcake, Banana-Pecan, '93 43
Slaw, Banana-Nut, '86 250
Sorbet, Banana-Orange, '88 117
Soufflé, Banana Daiquiri, '84 317
Soup, Avocado-Banana-Yogurt, '80 78
Soup, Strawberry-Banana, '86 181
Spiced Bananas with Rum Sauce, '99 247
Split, Banana-Berry, '05 193
Splits, Cottage Cheese-Banana, '87 56
Splits, French Toast Banana, '96 M164
Sticky Fingers, '03 M168
Sundae, Breakfast, '98 206
Supreme, Banana-Berry, '81 205
Supreme, Bananas, '84 256
Syrup, Maple-Banana, '03 47
Syrup, Rum, '05 279
Terrine, Banana Split, '96 164
Topping, Pound Cake with Strawberry-Banana, '89 200
Topping, Strawberry-Banana, '87 125
Trifle, Banana Pudding, '98 273
Tropical Bananas, Easy, '00 141
Waffles, Banana-Ginger, '86 96
Waffles, Banana-Oatmeal, '94 206
Waffles, Banana Split, '89 205
BARBECUE. *See also* **GRILLED.**
Bean Dip, Barbecue, '03 138
Beans, Barbecue, '02 167
Beans, Barbecued, '94 248
Beans, Barbecued Green, '86 252
Beans, Barbecued Lima, '82 2
Beans, Barbecued Pork and, '79 100
Beans, Commissary Barbecue, '90 120
Beans, Skillet Barbecued, '93 217
Beans, Slow Cooker Barbecue, '05 M180
Beef. *See also* **BARBECUE/Ribs.**
Barbecued Beef, '81 18
Beach Barbecue, Trish's, '03 206
Bourbon Barbecue, '88 129
Brisket, Barbecued, '86 154; '88 218
Brisket, Barbecued Beef, '83 11
Brisket, Denton, Texas, Barbecued Beef, '81 55
Brisket, Oven Barbecue, '01 259
Brisket, Smoky Barbecue, '03 160
Brisket with Sauce, Barbecued Beef, '86 153
Burgers, Barbecued, '82 168; '89 164
Chuck Roast Barbecue, '96 71
Corned Beef Sandwiches, Barbecued, '83 130
Cups, Barbecue, '79 129
Flank Steak with Molasses Barbecue Glaze, Grilled, '00 59
Four-Hour Barbecue, '00 18
Kebabs, Barbecued Steak, '79 89

BARBECUE, Beef
(continued)

Liver, Barbecued, '85 219
Loaves, Individual Barbecued Beef, '95 242
Meatballs, Oven Barbecued, '82 233
Meat Loaf, Barbecued, '80 60; '81 275; '87 216
Pot Roast, Barbecued, '79 17; '83 319
Rib Roast, Barbecued, '86 152
Roast, Barbecue, '98 245
Roast Barbecue, Beef, '79 159
Roast, Barbecued Beef, '82 96; '83 103
Sandwiches, Barbecue Beef, '99 327; '01 136
Sandwiches, Barbecued Beef, '81 25; '82 31; '83 34
Sandwiches, Debate Barbecue, '97 234
Sandwiches, Slow-Cooker Barbecue Beef, '05 64
Saucy Barbecued Beef, '82 156
Slow-Cooker Beef Barbecue, '02 299
Steak, Barbecued Flank, '79 89
Steak, Marinated Barbecued Chuck, '80 156
Steak, Saucy Oven-Barbecued, '83 10
Supper, Barbecue Hobo, '99 108
Tenderloin, Barbecued Beef, '94 26
Bread, Barbecue, '99 105
Cabrito, Barbecued, '86 153
Chicken
Bake, Barbecued Chicken, '81 97
Barbecue Chicken, '86 122
Barbecued Chicken, '82 97, 106; '83 103; '85 144; '86 153; '89 167
Braised and Barbecued Chicken, Melt-in-Your-Mouth, '03 326
Carambola-Glazed Barbecued Chicken, '92 246
Chili-Barbecued Chicken, '98 170
Cranberry Chicken, Barbecued, '83 178
Fingers, Barbecue-Battered Chicken, '04 139
Foil, Barbecued Chicken in, '04 222
Golden Barbecued Chicken, '83 136
Grilled Barbecued Chicken, '81 154
Honey Barbecue Chicken, '04 197
Legs and Thighs, Barbecued Chicken, '94 94
Lemon Barbecued Chicken, '93 215
Marinated Barbecued Chicken, '79 90
Old South Barbecued Chicken, '82 97; '83 103
Orange Barbecued Chicken, '88 123
Oven-Baked Barbecue Chicken, '03 160
Oven-Barbecued Chicken, Kentucky-Style, '96 328
Oven-Barbecued Cranberry Chicken, '93 332
Pizza, Barbecue Chicken, '03 49
Pizza, Quick 'n' Easy Chicken Barbecue, '04 139
Pizza, Southwestern BBQ Chicken, '05 33
Raspberry-Barbecue Chicken, '05 203
Salad, Warm Barbecue Chicken, '99 124
Sauce, Chicken with White Barbecue, '89 M84; '97 322; '01 168
Saucy Barbecued Chicken, '83 11
South-of-the-Border Barbecued Chicken, '97 311
Sweet-and-Spicy Barbecued Chicken, '01 316
Tangy Barbecued Chicken, '86 186; '98 170
Zesty Barbecued Chicken, '80 M76
Zippy Barbecued Chicken, '83 213
Coleslaw, Barbecue, '97 139
Coleslaw, Best Barbecue, '97 214; '04 100
Corn on the Cob, Barbecued, '81 128
Deviled Eggs, Barbecue, '05 167
Dressing, Barbecue, '99 124
Dressing, Barbecue Salad, '80 74
Eggplant, Barbecue, '02 180
Fish. *See also* **BARBECUE/Seafood.**
Catfish, Barbecue Baked, '02 51
Catfish, Barbecued, '80 157
Catfish, Lemon Barbecued, '89 202
Fillets, Barbecued Fish, '86 182

Salmon, Barbecued, '81 181
Tacos, Barbecued Fish, '95 339
Tuna, Barbecued, '80 275
Frank Barbecue, Tangy, '79 63
Frankfurters, Barbecued, '83 144
Frankfurters, Oven-Barbecued, '83 11
Franks, Barbecued, '85 192
Lamb, Barbecued, '79 58
Lamb Chops, Barbecued, '79 89
Lamb Shanks, Barbecued, '92 128; '93 113
Meatballs, Spicy Chipotle-Barbecue, '05 305
Meat Loaf Sandwiches, Barbecue, '04 188
Muffins, Barbecue, '96 246
Outdoor Cooking, '82 109
Popcorn, Cheesy Barbecue, '95 239
Pork. *See also* **BARBECUE/Ribs.**
Bannister's Barbecue, '92 166
Barbecued Pork, '80 72
Chops, Barbecue-Battered Pork, '04 139
Chops, Barbecued Pork, '81 10
Chops, Marinated Barbecued Pork, '79 90
Chops, Oven-Barbecued Pork, '81 234; '82 26; '83 40
Ham Slices, Barbecued, '81 110
Home-Style Barbecue, '88 145
Nachos, Commissary Barbecue, '91 171
Pot Pie with Cheese Grits Crust, Barbecue, '03 21
Pot Pie with Mashed Potato Crust, Barbecue, '03 21
Quesadillas, Barbecue, '02 121
Quesadillas, Barbecued Pork, '04 187
Roast, Barbecued Pork, '03 147
Roast, Barbecued Pork Loin, '93 34
Roast Barbecue, Pork, '82 97; '83 104
Roast, Berry Barbecued Pork, '80 288
Sandwiches, Barbecue Pork, '00 23
Sausage, Barbecued, '86 153
Sausage Bites, Spicy Chipotle-Barbecue, '05 305
Shoulder, Barbecued Pork, '81 111; '82 11
Shoulder, Barbecue Pork, '00 274
Spaghetti, Barbecue, '02 121
Spicy Barbecued Pork, '84 296
Sundae, Barbecue, '02 121
Tabb's Barbecue Pork, '05 166
Tenderloin, Barbecued Pork, '05 245
Potatoes, Barbecued, '91 311; '92 26
Potatoes, Barbecue Scalloped, '04 139
Potatoes, Double-Stuffed Barbecue, '05 162
Rabbit, Hickory Barbecued, '82 216
Ribs
Apple Barbecued Ribs, '80 111
Apple-Barbecue Spareribs, '90 160
Baby Back Ribs, Barbecued, '97 234
Barbecued Ribs, '80 111; '85 159; '91 205
Barbecued Spareribs, '81 112; '82 12; '86 232; '95 236
Barbecue Ribs, '99 68
Beef Short Ribs, Barbecued, '83 178
Country-Style Barbecued Ribs, '79 42
Country-Style Ribs, Barbecued, '95 237
Country-Style Spareribs, Barbecued, '80 73
Easy Barbecued Spareribs, '82 97; '83 104
Herbed Barbecued Ribs, '86 185
Oven-Barbecued Pork Ribs, '88 132
Saucy Barbecued Spareribs, '79 14
Short Ribs, Barbecued, '90 148
Slow-Cooker Barbecue Ribs, '03 160
Smoky Barbecued Ribs, '80 111
Southern Barbecued Spareribs, '79 90
Spicy Barbecued Spareribs, '84 93
Tangy Barbecued Ribs, '83 160
Tangy Barbecued Spareribs, '82 106
Rub, All-Purpose Barbecue, '03 130; '04 104

Rub, Barbecue, '03 130; '04 104; '05 166
Rub, Master Class Barbecue, '98 244
Salad, Barbecue Macaroni, '82 276
Sauces
Apple Barbecue Sauce, '99 173
Bannister's Barbecue Sauce, '92 166
Barbecue Sauce, '84 172; '86 153; '88 218; '91 16, 205; '93 129; '94 27
Barbecue Sauce, Baked Fish with, '84 92
Basting Sauce, '90 120; '01 106
Basting Sauce, Grill, '00 177
Beef Marinade, Tangy, '86 113
Beer Barbecue Sauce, '84 173
Blender Barbecue Sauce, Ribs with, '90 12
Bourbon Barbecue Sauce, '85 90
Brisket with Barbecue Sauce, Smoked, '85 144
Cider Vinegar Barbecue Sauce, '01 148
Cola Barbecue Sauce, '03 130; '04 104
Crickhollow Barbecue Sauce, '99 200
Dressed-Up Barbecue Sauce, '84 173
Drunken Sauce, '03 33
Eastern-Style Barbecue Sauce, '88 145
Easy Barbecue Sauce, '79 90; '82 178
Green Barbecue Sauce, '02 183
Handcrafted Barbecue Sauce, '98 45
Honey Barbecue Sauce, '04 197
Honey-Mustard Barbecue Sauce, '05 167
John Wills's Barbecue Sauce, '92 255
Lemon Barbecue Sauce, Herbed, '94 154; '98 334
Lemony Barbecue Sauce, '88 M177; '95 31
Maple Syrup Barbecue Sauce, '94 154
Mustard Barbecue Sauce, '84 173
Orange Barbecue Sauce, Spareribs with, '83 11
Oven Barbecue Sauce, '82 233
Paprika Barbecue Sauce, '79 90
Paul's Barbecue Sauce, '05 175
Peanut Butter Barbecue Sauce, '81 233
Peppery Barbecue Sauce, '00 255
Piquant Barbecue Sauce, '79 159
Ranch-Barbecue Sauce, '05 163
Raspberry-Barbecue Sauce, '05 203
Savory Barbecue Sauce, '86 153
Smoky Chipotle 'Cue Sauce, '04 87
Special Barbecue Sauce, '82 177
Spicy Southwest Barbecue Sauce, '94 154
Sweet-and-Sour 'Cue Sauce, '04 87
Sweet-and-Sour Marinade, '86 113
Sweet-and-Tangy Barbecue Sauce, '00 119
Sweet Sauce, '90 120; '01 106
Tangy Barbecue Sauce, '97 323; '99 104; '00 230
Teriyaki Marinade, '86 114
Texas Barbecue Sauce, '99 210
Texas Barbecue Sauce, LBJ's, '97 42
The Sauce, '00 177
Thick and Robust Barbecue Sauce, '94 95
Thick and Sweet Barbecue Sauce, '94 95
Thin and Tasty Barbecue Sauce, '94 95
Tomato Barbecue Sauce, Fresh, '84 172
Vinegar Sauce, Peppery, '01 148
Western-Style Barbecue Sauce, '88 145
White Barbecue Sauce, '94 95; '05 196
White Barbecue Sauce, Chicken with, '89 M84; '97 322; '01 168
Zippy Barbecue Sauce, '92 166
Seafood. *See also* **BARBECUE/Fish.**
Oysters, Barbecued, '82 247
Shrimp and Cornbread-Stuffed Peppers, Barbecued, '97 261
Shrimp, Barbecue, '96 210; '97 58; '00 30
Shrimp, Barbecued, '82 74; '84 93; '90 28
Shrimp, Cajun Barbecued, '87 95
Shrimp, Hickory-Smoked Barbecue, '00 89
Shrimp, New Orleans Barbecue, '02 201
Turkey Barbecue, '90 158

BARLEY

Baked Barley, '91 133
Casserole, Barley, '84 281
Medley, Barley, Vegetable, and Fruit, '05 127
Pilaf, Barley-Vegetable, '91 33
Rolls, Wine-Sauced Beef-and-Barley, '87 269
Salad, Barley, '92 212
Salad, Barley-Broccoli, '90 135
Salad, Barley-Pine Nut, '05 126
Salad, Black Bean-and-Barley, '94 174
Soup, Hearty Bean-and-Barley, '86 304
Soup, Turkey-Barley, '91 312
Stuffing, Cornish Hens with Barley-Mushroom, '97 242
Vegetables, Barley and, '91 81

BEANS. *See also* LENTILS.

Anasazi Beans with Mushrooms, Stewed, '95 226
Bake, Cheesy Beef-and-Bean, '82 89
Baked
Baked Beans, '01 127, 334
Barbecue Beans, '02 167
Barbecued Beans, '94 248
Barbecued Pork and Beans, '79 100
Barbecue Sundae, '02 121
Beefy Baked Beans, '80 136; '84 149; '85 142
Bourbon Baked Beans, '95 182
Chuckwagon Beans, '81 188
Crowd-Pleasing Baked Beans, '82 127
Easy Baked Beans, '85 141
Favorite Baked Beans, '86 210
Five-Bean Bake, '03 139
Franks, Beans and, '85 142
Franks, Beany Kraut and, '79 64
Franks, Hawaiian Baked Beans and, '80 136
Frolickers Baked Beans, '03 92
Genuine Baked Beans, '83 26
Ham, Baked Beans and, '05 45
Ham, Baked Beans with, '80 136
Hamburger-Bean Bake, '95 121
Hawaiian-Style Baked Beans, '86 210
Hearty Baked Beans, '01 259
Home-Style Baked Beans, '00 172
K.C. Baked Beans, '98 244; '03 107
Lowcountry Baked Beans, '98 332
Maple Heights Baked Beans, '91 223
Meat Baked Beans, Three-, '86 210
Medley, Baked Bean, '80 100
Mixed Baked Beans, '87 92
Molasses Baked Beans, '82 139; '84 327; '86 20; '99 105
More Beans, Baked Beans and, '92 173
Old-Fashioned Baked Beans, '84 25
Picnic Baked Beans, '83 143; '85 142
Polynesian Beans-and-Franks, '84 M11
Pork Chops with Baked Beans, '93 18
Quick Baked Beans, '80 136
Quintet, Baked Beans, '93 105; '94 100
Root Beer Baked Beans, '04 212
Rum-Laced Bean Bake, '82 283; '83 72
Slow Cooker Bean Bake, '99 88
Smoked Baked Beans, '79 150
Sorghum Baked Beans, '03 106
Spiced Baked Beans, '85 142
Spicy Baked Beans, '05 328
Three-Bean Bake, '81 155; '99 88; '03 106
White Bean Bake, Turnip Greens and, '94 246
Barbecue Beans, Commissary, '90 120
Barbecue Beans, Slow Cooker, '05 M180
Barbecued Beans, Skillet, '93 217
Beefy Beans, '82 59
Black. *See also* BEANS/Salads, Soups.
Appetizer, Black Bean, '83 50
Black Beans, '93 28
Bow Ties, Black Beans, and Key Limes, '96 291

Broth with Black Beans and Cilantro, Southwestern Scallop, '87 123
Burgers, Black Bean, '98 144
Cakes with Greens and Apple Dressing, Black Bean, '92 216
Cakes with Smoked Salmon Salsa, Corn-and-Black Bean, '96 272
Casserole, Easy Enchilada, '02 143
Casserole of Black Beans, '95 27
Chicken Cobbler, Spicy Tex-Mex, '03 324
Chicken with Black Beans and Oranges, '00 94
Chicken with Black Beans and Salsa, Poached, '87 217
Chili, Black Bean, '02 20
Chili Goes Southwest, Basic, '93 326
Chili Marsala, Black Bean, '95 16
Cuban Black Beans, '88 196; '99 56; '05 295
Cuban Black Beans, Traditional, '98 21
Dip, Black Bean, '95 93
Dip, Creamy Chipotle-Black Bean, '05 247
Dip, Southwestern Salsa, '05 212
Egg Rolls, Tex-Mex, '01 328
Egg Rolls with Creamy Cilantro Dipping Sauce, Tex-Mex, '03 327
Enchiladas, Black Bean-Chicken-Spinach, '05 95
Enchiladas, Black Bean 'n' Spinach, '05 95
Frijoles con Cerveza (Beans with Beer), '81 66
Frittata, Avocado-and-Black Bean, '02 212
Garbanzo-Black Bean Medley, '99 236
Guacamole, Black Bean, '94 277
Lasagna, Easy Mexican, '03 22
Lasagna, Spinach-Black Bean, '02 44
Marinated Black Beans, '93 131
Mexicorn, Black Bean, '96 189
Pancakes with Gazpacho Butter, Black Bean, '92 86
Pizza, Fiesta, '00 85
Puree, Spicy Chicken with Black Bean, '97 48
Quesadillas, Chicken-and-Black Bean, '96 288
Quesadillas, Chorizo, Black Bean, and Corn, '00 148
Relish, Black Bean-Tomatillo, '87 121
Relish, Cranberry-Black Bean, '03 243
Rice, Black Beans and, '80 222; '89 178; '91 82; '95 309; '05 214
Rollups, Southwestern, '01 135
Salsa, Black Bean, '93 155; '94 161; '97 226; '00 122; '03 146, 323; '04 25
Salsa, Black Bean-and-Corn, '94 80; '05 297
Salsa, Black Bean-and-Mango, '05 297
Salsa, Black Bean-Corn, '96 126; '04 322
Salsa, Chunky Black Bean, '03 25
Salsa, Corn-Black Bean, '96 15
Salsa, Fruity Black Bean, '05 16
Salsa, Hill Country, '97 123
Salsa, Orange-Black Bean, '98 231
Salsa Pork Chops, Black Bean-and-Corn, '01 320
Salsa with Black Beans and Corn, Southwestern, '96 275
Salsa with Citrus Dressing, Black Bean, '01 60
Sandwiches, Caribbean Seafood, '98 105
Sauce, Banana Chicken with Black Bean, '96 156
Sauce, Black Bean, '93 59; '98 46
Sauce, Southwest Pork in Black Bean, '05 139
Sauce, Spicy Beef Fillets with Black Bean, '97 184
Spaghetti, Black Bean, '92 217
Spaghetti, Salsa, '00 58
Spanish Black Beans, '84 327
Spicy Beef and Black Beans, '99 331
Spicy Black Beans, '04 119
Stew, Baja Pork, '98 283
Strudel, Meatless Mexican, '98 29
Terrine with Fresh Tomato Coulis and Jalapeño Sauce, Black Bean, '93 230
Terrine with Goat Cheese, Black Bean, '87 120

Tony's Black Beans, '96 289
Tostadas, Rice-and-Black Bean, '97 65
Tostadas, Shrimp-and-Black Bean, '93 204
Wraps, Black Bean, '00 211
Wraps, Western, '99 194
Yellow Rice, Black Beans and, '95 126
Yellow Rice, Black Beans with, '82 2
Yellow Rice, Easy Black Beans and, '92 308
Burgers, Spicy Bean, '00 84
Burgers with Adobo Mayonnaise, Bean, '02 202
Burrito Appetizers, Bean, '94 226
Burritos, Chicken, '01 55
Burritos, Meat-and-Bean, '81 194
Butterbeans, '90 166
Butterbeans, Bacon, and Tomatoes, '96 36; '00 184
Butterbeans, Smoky Speckled, '04 167
Butterbeans with Bacon and Green Onions, '96 267
Cabbage Rolls, Southwestern, '97 214
Cannellini Beans, Rosemary, '95 213
Casserole, Bean-and-Cornbread, '92 243
Casserole, Chuck Wagon Bean, '93 198
Casserole, Fajita, '97 96
Casserole, Mexican, '00 280
Casserole, Spicy Mexican Bean, '84 114
Casserole, Three-Bean, '88 56
Cassoulet, '96 328
Cassoulet, Easy Chicken, '00 43; '04 325
Cassoulet, Easy Herb Crust, '01 311
Cassoulet, Vegetarian, '96 329
Chickpea-Chipotle Tostadas, '03 181
Chickpea Spread, Creamy, '03 293; '04 146
Chickpea Stew, Chicken, Kale, and, '98 47
Chili, '98 95
Chili and Beans, Ranch, '79 270; '80 11
Chili Bean Roast, '87 268; '88 102
Chili, Big-Batch, '04 242
Chili, Chilly Night, '99 317
Chili, Easy, '02 299
Chili, Game-Day, '00 238
Chili in a Biscuit Bowl, '98 224
Chili, Mom's, '93 292
Chili, Red Bean, '02 20
Chili, Slow-Cooker Red Bean, '02 20
Chili, Spicy 3-Bean, '03 291
Chili Supper, Hot, '99 279
Chili Surprise, '82 229
Chili, Three-Bean, '00 34
Chili, Turkey-Bean, '88 M213
Chili, White, '91 284
Chili, White Bean, '02 20
Chili, White Christmas, '98 266; '02 260
Chili with Beans, Easy, '92 262
Chili with Beans, Meaty, '85 250
Chimichangas, Baked Spicy Beef, '97 319
Chimichangas, Bean-and-Cheese, '01 16
Creole Beans and Rice, '80 223
Crostini, Mexican, '95 142
Crostini, Roasted Red Pepper-Feta, '04 69
Dinner, Quick Mexican, '98 224
Dip, Barbecue Bean, '03 138
Dip, Bean, '89 97
Dip, Cheese-Bean, '85 208
Dip, Chickpea-and-Red Pepper, '99 138
Dip, Fiesta, '96 212; '03 284
Dip, Garbanzo, '93 94
Dip, Hotshot Bean, '87 195
Dip, Layered Nacho, '81 261; '03 207
Dip, Mexican Fiesta, '98 234
Dip, Prairie Fire Bean, '80 195
Dip, Salsa-Bean, '98 285
Dip, South-of-the-Border, '81 235
Dip with Bone Crackers, Goblin, '01 204
Dogs, Taco, '02 M57
Enchiladas, Three-Bean, '91 133

BEANS
(continued)

Farmer's Beans and Rice with Rosemary Biscuits, '99 16
Franks, Jiffy Beans and, '91 M172
Franks 'n' Beans, Stove-Top, '88 201
Garbanzo Bean Spread, Herbed, '99 160
Garbanzo Dinner, Beef-and-, '84 31
Garbanzo Dip, Pesto-, '03 299
Garbanzo Stew, Greek, '02 43
Garbanzo-Vegetable Pitas, '00 58
Gorditas with Turkey Mole, '03 18
Great Northern Beans with Tomatoes, '05 23
Green. *See also* **BEANS/Salads, Soups.**
  Alfredo with Cheese Ravioli, Green Bean, '01 180
  Almonds, Green Beans with, '84 253
  Amandine, Green Beans, '79 276; '82 M20; '85 156; '97 238
  Appalachian Green Beans, '81 215
  Asian Green Beans, '01 237
  au Gratin, Green Beans, '80 116
  Bacon and Mushrooms, Green Beans with, '92 13
  Bacon Dressing, Green Beans with, '85 147
  Bacon-Topped Green Beans, '80 M123
  Baked Green Beans, '91 159
  Bake, Green Bean, '99 112
  Barbecued Green Beans, '86 252
  Basil Beans and Tomatoes, '83 172
  Basil, Green Beans with, '82 96
  Basil Vinaigrette, Green Beans with, '02 172
  Blue Cheese, Green Beans with, '88 57; '05 177
  Bow-Tie Green Beans, '94 320
  Buffet Green Beans, '93 325
  Bundles, Bean, '80 246; '83 67
  Bundles, Green Bean, '83 180; '87 118
  Buttered Green Beans, '92 54
  Buttery Green Beans, '02 307
  Caramelized Onion, Green Beans with, '00 33
  Caramelized Onions, Green Beans with, '95 288
  Cashews, Green Beans with, '89 202
  Casserole, Chicken-Green Bean, '85 296
  Casserole, Corn-and-Bean, '90 208
  Casserole, Creamy-and-Crunchy Green Bean, '05 245
  Casserole, Creamy Chicken-Green Bean, '97 158
  Casserole, Easy Green Bean, '87 284
  Casserole, Green Bean, '79 106; '84 145; '02 197
  Casserole, Green Bean-and-Corn, '88 123; '99 36
  Casserole, Italian Green Bean-and-Artichoke, '85 81
  Celery, Green Beans and Braised, '84 254
  Cheese-Topped Green Beans, '79 100
  Cheesy Green Beans, '80 157
  Chinese Green Beans, '96 330
  Creamed Green Beans, French-Style, '88 252
  Cumin Green Beans, '82 90
  Dill-and-Almond Green Beans, '05 81
  Dilled Carrots and Green Beans, '99 223
  Dilled Green Beans, '82 106; '86 157; '88 101; '89 203; '93 279; '96 172; '99 170
  Dill Green Beans, '93 136
  Dilly Green Beans, '80 116
  Excellent, Green Beans, '94 321
  French Green Beans, '90 208
  French Quarter Green Beans, '80 298; '81 26
  Fresh Green Beans, '79 122
  Garlic Green Beans, '91 159; '94 273; '00 260; '01 111
  Garlic-Herb Butter, Green Beans with, '02 61
  Garlic-Tarragon Green Beans, '04 246
  Gingered Green Beans, '02 283; '05 290
  Goldenrod Beans, '83 111
  Grape Tomatoes, Green Beans with, '03 231

Gratin, Gourmet Green Bean, '99 M334
Greek Green Beans, '94 165
Green Beans, '80 126; '87 M151; '97 263
Ham and Potatoes, Green Beans with, '01 223
Herbed Green Beans, '83 M147, 177; '88 M190
Herb Green Beans, '89 321
Herbs, Green Beans with, '82 90
Indian-Style Green Beans, '88 265
Italian Green Beans, '85 147; '90 164; '92 183
Italian, Green Beans, '87 10
Italian Green Beans, Sesame, '82 174
Italian Green Beans with Almonds, '81 207
Italian Green Beans with Onion and Basil, '03 241
Italiano, Green Bean, '94 248
Italiano, Green Beans, '86 144
Lemon-Almond Green Beans, '05 218
Lemon-and-Dill Green Beans, '05 17
Lemon-Dill Butter, Green Beans with, '99 141
Lemon-Dill Green Beans, '01 181
Lemon-Dill Sauce, Potatoes and Green Beans with, '01 89
Lemon Green Beans, '89 275
Lemon, Green Beans with, '03 66
Lemon-Pecan Green Beans, '04 285
Lemon-Walnut Green Beans, '93 304
Lemony Green Beans, '85 190; '99 259
Linguine with Green Beans and Walnut Sauce, '04 128
Lorraine's Green Beans, '99 319
Marinated Beets, Green Beans, and Carrots, '88 162
Marinated Green Beans, '83 145
Marinated Green Beans with Tomatoes, Olives, and Feta, '03 163
Marinated Italian Beans, '86 M226
Marinated Vegetables, '81 239
Marjoram, Fresh Green Beans with, '91 159
Mediterranean-Style Green Beans, '79 100
Medley, Green Bean, '85 108
Medley, Peppery Green Bean, '93 181
Minted Green Beans, '84 104
Mushroom-Bacon Green Beans, '91 291; '92 255
Mushrooms and Sage, Green Beans with, '02 314
Mushroom Sauce, Green Beans in Sherried, '93 206
Mushrooms, Green Beans with, '82 21; '93 89
Mustard, Green Beans and Tomatoes with, '87 83
New Potatoes, Green Beans with, '87 164
Nutty Green Beans, '88 M187
Oregano, Green Beans with, '97 218
Oriental Green Beans, '88 43
Oriental, Green Beans, '91 158
Parmesan Green Beans, '04 327
Pecans, Green Beans with Buttered, '92 61
Pepper Strips, Green Beans and, '86 170
Pesto Green Beans, '01 181; '03 185
Pickled Beans, Dressed-Up, '86 251
Pimiento, Tangy Green Beans with, '00 170
Pole Beans, Old-Fashioned, '80 100
Potatoes, Down-Home Beans and, '85 254
Potatoes, Green Beans and, '91 221
Potatoes, Snap Beans and, '98 177
Provençal, Green Beans, '81 182; '91 158
Red Peppers and Pearl Onions, Green Beans with Roasted, '93 260
Red Potatoes, Green Beans and, '03 158
Risotto, Green Bean, '03 68
Roasted Green Beans, Ginger-, '01 180
Roasted Green Beans, Potatoes, and Fennel, '00 322
Roasted Green Beans with Mushrooms, '04 182
Roquefort Cheese and Walnuts, Green Beans with, '02 255
Rosemary Green Beans, Speedy, '05 241
Saucy Green Beans, '83 206
Sautéed Green Beans, '05 206

Sautéed Green Beans, Lemon-Garlic Roast Chicken with, '05 43
Sautéed Green Beans with Bacon, '05 M160
Savory Green Beans, '89 70, 235
Seasoned Green Beans, '88 304
Shallots and Red Bell Pepper, Green Beans with, '97 251
Shallots, Green Beans with, '00 315; '04 248
Shuck Beans, '81 216
Simple Green Beans, '92 100
Smothered Green Beans, Southern, '02 55
Snap Beans, '86 218
Snap Beans, Simple, '85 148
Snap, or Wax Beans, Green, '85 105
Sour Cream, Green Beans in, '80 116
Sour Cream, Green Beans with, '82 90
Southern-Style Green Beans, '79 283
Spaghettini with Green Beans and Walnut Brown Butter, '03 170
Spanish Green Beans, '80 116
Spanish-Style Green Beans, '84 128
Special Green Beans, '90 268
Spicy Green Beans with Purple Onion, '98 286
Squash, Beans, and Tomatoes, '83 148
Steamed Green Beans, Basic, '01 180
Stir-Fried Green Beans, '85 148; '86 305
Sugared Green Beans, '04 223
Surprise, Green Bean, '86 9
Sweet-and-Sour Beans, '87 197
Sweet-and-Sour Green Beans, '79 184; '81 158; '82 90; '91 250
Sweet-and-Sour Green Beans and Carrots, '83 6
Sweet-and-Sour Snap Beans, '89 173
Sweet 'n' Hot Green Beans and Carrots, '00 211
Tangy Green Beans, '85 M142; '89 314, 332
Tangy Green Beans with Pimiento, '01 21
Tarragon Dressing, Green Beans with Creamy, '93 191
Tarragon, Green Beans, '98 328
Thyme-Scented Green Beans with Smoked Almonds, '01 57
Tomatoes, Bean-Stuffed, '84 34
Tomatoes, Green Beans with, '85 137
Tomatoes, Green Beans with Cherry, '86 177
Tomato-Feta Green Beans, '99 59
Tomato Sauce, Green Beans in, '01 84
Tomato Skillet, Bean-and-, '90 316
Vegetable-Herb Trio, '83 172
Vinaigrette, Green Beans, '83 25; '93 120; '94 90; '96 177
Vinaigrette, Kentucky Wonder Green Beans, '94 158
Walnut Dressing, Green Beans with, '94 279
Zesty Green Beans, '05 204
Zucchini, Green Beans with, '84 128; '02 251
Hot Dogs, Beany, '82 190
Hummas, '92 155
Hummus, '96 158; '02 99
Hummus, Creamy Dried Tomato, '95 284
Hummus, Low-Fat, '99 137
Hummus, Quick, '95 93
Hummus, Red Pepper, '00 132; '02 31; '05 97
Hummus, White Bean, '01 32
Kidney Bean Casserole, '90 136
Kidney Beans and Rice, Smoky, '03 290
Kidney Beans, Mexican, '90 205
Kielbasa with Beans, Easy Cheesy, '01 28
Lasagna, Mexican, '01 282
Lasagna, Spinach-Bean, '92 96
Legumes, Marinated, '90 197
Lemon-Mint Beans, '88 22
Lima. *See also* **BEANS/Salads, Soups.**
  Baked Lima Beans, '96 217
  Bake, Lima-Bacon, '86 9
  Barbecued Lima Beans, '82 2

Beans, Lima, '80 127
Beef-and-Lima Bean Dinner, '84 292
Canadian Bacon, Lima Beans with, '83 219; '84 245
Casserole, Ham and Lima, '79 192
Casserole, Lima Bean, '79 189; '83 313; '86 225; '87 284; '95 132
Casserole, Lima Bean Garden, '83 218; '84 246
Casserole, Spicy Lima Bean, '79 189
Casserole, Swiss Lima Bean, '80 191
Cheese and Limas in Onion Shells, '81 86
Cheese Limas, Spanish, '86 225
Chilly Lima Beans, '81 206
Combo, Hot Lima and Tomato, '83 219
Creole, Lima Beans, '80 191; '85 137
Deluxe, Lima Beans, '79 289; '80 26
Fresh Lima Beans and Scallions, '82 133
Gratin with Lima Beans and Egg, New Potato, '01 71
Marinated Limas, '86 225
Medley, Carrot-Lima-Squash, '80 123
Minted Lima Beans, '98 86
Pâté, Lima Bean-and-Fresh Herb, '04 70
Rancho Lima Beans, '80 191
Savory Lima Beans, '83 219; '84 246
Savory Sauce, Lima Beans and Carrots with, '84 196
Sour Cream, Lima Beans in, '79 189; '88 41
Spanish-Style Lima Beans, '83 25
Stew, Brunswick, '97 315
Succotash, '98 177; '02 16
Succotash, Easy, '80 165
Succotash, Garden, '04 160
Succotash, Quick, '97 302
Succotash, Savory, '96 63
Super Lima Beans, '79 189
Supper, Sausage-Bean, '86 52
Toss, Succotash Rice, '05 218
Mogumbo, '93 32
Nachos, Best-Ever, '79 91
Nachos, Easy, '84 30
Nachos, Make-Ahead, '80 M135
Nachos, Southwestern, '96 170
Navy Beans, Curried, '00 201
Pasta, Beans and, '99 35
Pasta with Beans, '99 236
Pasta with Beans and Greens, '02 202
Pie, Tortilla, '96 135
Pigs in a Blanket, Mexican, '00 199
Pinto
  Beef-and-Bean Supper, '82 2
  Best Pinto Beans, '03 159
  Burgers, Pinto, '98 51
  Burritos, Hot Phyllo, '98 312
  Casserole, Beef, Bean, and Cornbread, '99 215
  Chalupa, Bean, '80 223
  Chalupas, Bean, '83 313
  Chalupas, Pork, '83 160
  Chili, Tex-Mex, '83 26
  Chili, Vegetable, '97 179
  Cow Camp Pinto Beans, '94 28
  Dip, Hot Bean, '04 323
  Enchiladas, Spicy Bean, '88 18
  Frijoles, '02 119
  Frijoles Rancheros, '88 148
  Ham Hocks, and Rice, Pinto Beans, '05 46
  Ham, Pinto Beans with, '97 210
  Lasagna, Texas, '98 52
  Mexican Pinto Beans, '93 69; '94 30; '00 241
  Pie, Pinto Bean, '80 40
  Pinto Beans, '87 303
  Potatoes, Chili-Topped, '98 M289
  Ranch Beans, Laredo, '81 75
  Ranch Beans, Texas, '90 198
  Razorback Beans, '84 328
  Refried Beans, '79 185
  Rice, South Texas Beans and, '85 252

Salsa, Warm Pinto Bean-and-Bacon, '03 331
Sandwiches, Bean Salad, '81 243
Sausage, Hearty Pintos and, '88 296
Smashed Pinto Beans, '03 129
Souper Pintos, Texas, '98 51
Southwestern Beans, '89 16
Spicy-Hot Beans, '89 17
Spicy Hot Pintos, '83 26
Sweet-Hot Pinto Beans, '86 114
Texas Beans, '97 139
Texas Pinto Beans, '01 65
Trailride Pinto Beans, '85 154
Wraps, Chicken-and-Bean Slaw, '04 163
Pitas, Fajita, '99 239
Pizza, Cheesy Mexican, '00 314
Pizza, Mexican, '99 119
Pizza, Red Pepper Hummus, '01 56
Pole Beans, Home-Cooked, '96 46
Pork Chops, Mexican, '99 108
Pork Loin, Braised Tuscan, '04 202
Pot of Beans, Buzz's, '03 19
Quesadillas, Easy, '98 M205
Quesadilla Torta, '97 325
Ragoût with Cilantro-Cornmeal Dumplings, Bean, '97 209
Ranch-Style Beans, '00 43
Red Bean Salsa, '97 227
Red Beans and Couscous, '99 22
Red Beans and Rice, '80 58; '83 89; '84 37; '87 45; '90 27; '96 218; '02 35
Red Beans and Rice, Cajun, '83 26
Red Beans and Rice, Delta, '98 146
Red Beans and Rice, Easy, '90 220; '99 M219
Red Beans and Rice, New Orleans, '97 235
Red Beans and Rice, Spicy, '02 56
Red Beans and Rice with Sausage, '05 125
Red Beans, Wilted Greens and, '05 21
Refried Beans, '79 185; '96 160
Refried Beans, Easy, '99 57
Ribs and Beans, Spicy-Sweet, '02 299; '03 314
Rice, Caribbean Beans and, '99 121
Rollups, Mediterranean, '00 277
Salads
  Black Bean-and-Barley Salad, '94 174
  Black Bean and Black-Eyed Pea Salad, '03 54
  Black Bean-and-Cheese Salad, '92 217
  Black Bean-and-Rice Salad, '00 327
  Black Bean Salad, '89 217; '97 196; '98 208; '01 198
  Black Bean Salad, Caribbean Shrimp-and-, '93 143
  Black Bean Salad, Mandarin-, '05 319
  Black Bean Salad, Roasted Corn-and-, '05 209
  Cannellini Bean Salad, Tuna-and-, '86 143
  Chicken-Black Bean Salad, '99 124
  Chickpea Salad, '01 55
  Chilled Bean Salad, '80 178
  Confetti Bean Salad, '01 198
  Cornbread Salad, Dianne's Southwestern, '04 133
  Corn Salad, Confetti, '96 168
  Cucumber-Bean Salad, '83 81
  Dill-Icious Green Beans, '98 53
  Fennel-Salad, Bean-and-, '01 198
  Five-Bean Salad, Hot, '81 149
  Four-Bean Salad, '79 20; '84 82
  Full o' Beans Salad, '81 38
  Garbanzo Salad, '82 2
  Garbanzo Salad, Avocado-, '81 33
  Garbanzo Salad, Couscous-and-, '02 65
  Garden Medley Salad, '80 122
  Green Bean-and-Okra Salad with Feta, Marinated, '00 131
  Green Bean-and-Tomato Salad, '86 180
  Green Bean-Peanut Salad, '86 117
  Green Bean-Potato Salad, '83 80; '01 181; '04 142
  Green Bean-Red Potato Salad, '96 175

Green Bean-Red Potato Salad, Layered, '05 146
Green Bean Salad, '87 90
Green Bean Salad, Cold, '84 106
Green Bean Salad, Crispy, '82 239
Green Bean Salad, German, '92 169
Green Bean Salad, Hot, '86 298; '87 176
Green Bean Salad in Tomatoes, '01 181
Green Bean Salad, Lettuce and, '80 79
Green Bean Salad, Molded, '85 252
Green Bean Salad, Paprika-, '86 191
Green Bean Salad, Pickled, '82 239
Green Bean Salad, Potato-and-, '00 162
Green Bean Salad, Roasted Red Pepper-and-, '99 322
Green Bean Salad, Speedy, '84 283
Green Bean Salad, Tomato-and-, '97 162
Green Bean Salad with Feta, '04 169
Green Beans-and-Cheese Salad, '91 159
Green Bean Slaw, '95 108
Green Beans, Marinated Dill, '05 129
Green Beans Vinaigrette, '83 25; '93 120; '94 90; '96 177
Green Bean, Walnut, and Feta Salad, '96 273; '00 321
Hominy-Bean Salad, '88 266
Hot German-Style Bean Salad, '91 314
Kidney Bean-Salami Pasta Toss, '85 165
Layered Salad, '86 35
Layered Salad, Mexican, '02 65
Layered Salad, Tex-Mex, '03 201
Layered Southwestern Salad, '01 97
Lima Bean-Tomato Salad, '85 137
Lima Salad), You Lima My Life (Paprika, '96 159
Marinated Bean-and-Rice Salad, '87 152
Marinated Bean-Pasta Salad, '94 167; '97 328
Marinated Bean Salad, '85 137, 296; '89 314; '93 312; '94 167; '98 331
Marinated Bean Salad, Crunchy, '84 197
Marinated Combo Salad, '82 267
Marinated Corn-Bean Salad, '87 9
Meal in a Bowl, '96 138
Mexican Dinner Salad, '98 330
Mexican Salad, '94 202
Mexican Tossed Salad, '81 280
Mexicorn-Bean Salad, '96 184
Mixed Bean Salad, '83 217
Niçoise, Salad, '86 35; '03 35
One-Bean Salad with Lime-Mustard Dressing, '00 202
Overnight Fiesta Salad, '83 80
Pinto Salad, '86 169
Pole Bean-Potato Salad, Hot, '79 74
Pork-'n'-Bean Salad, '87 83
Potato-Bean Salad, '82 301
Quick Bean Salad, '89 128
Red Bean Slaw, '79 247
Rice-and-Bean Salad, '85 22
Rice-and-Bean Salad, Zesty, '02 84
Rice Salad, Beans-and-, '91 44
Saucy Bean Salad, '84 18
Sausage Salad, Bean-and-, '91 313
Six-Bean Salad, Colorful, '87 82
Southwest Salad, '81 113; '03 280
Spicy Bean Salad, '96 46
Sprout Salad, Bean, '82 113
Supreme Bean Salad, '91 202
Sweet-and-Sour Bean Salad, '85 198; '86 147
Sweet-and-Sour Beans with Sprouts, '86 32
Sweet-and-Sour Vegetable Salad, '81 25
Sweet Bean Salad, '01 46
Tabbouleh Salad, Southwestern, '01 216
Tangy Bean Salad, '05 158
Two-Bean Salad, Garlic-Herb, '05 209
Veggie-Bean Salad, '04 328
Veggie Salad, Sweet-and-Hot Bean-and-, '04 184

BEANS, Salads
(continued)

Veggies, Marinated, '01 127
White Bean-and-Asparagus Salad, '05 100
White Bean-and-Tuna Salad, '01 35
White Bean-and-Tuna Salad Sandwiches, '02 31
White Bean Salad, Tuna-and-, '98 209
White Bean-Tuna Salad, '98 208
Wild Rice-and-Kidney Bean Salad, '01 175
Salsa, Pork Chops with Black-and-White, '97 200
Salsa, Smoky Three-Bean, '02 202
Sandwiches, Falafel, '96 23
Sauce, Picante-Bean, '96 220
Sauce, Pork-and-Onions with Bean, '85 76
Sausage-and-Bean Dinner, '95 108
Sausage-and-Bean Supper, '02 233
Sausage, Beans, and Rice, Texas, '84 296
Sauté, Vegetarian, '95 69
Shuck Beans, '81 216; '05 109
Soups
Bacon Soup, Bean and, '83 26
Barley Soup, Hearty Bean-and-, '86 304
Bean-Chicken Soup, '99 283
"Bean Counter" Soup, '92 80
Beanolla Soup, '94 248
Bean Soup, '80 25
Black Bean Soup, '88 30, 266; '89 28; '93 231;
    '98 291; '02 121; '03 219; '05 120
Black Bean Soup, Carolina, '92 139
Black Bean Soup, Marge Clyde's, '96 29
Black Bean Soup, Pork-and-, '05 32
Cabbage-Bean Soup, '97 301
Capitol Hill Bean Soup, '80 222
Chicken-and-Black Bean Soup, '05 102
Chicken Soup, Fiesta, '04 323
Chicken Soup, Mexican, '00 336; '03 63
Chicken Soup, Witches' Brew, '01 205
Chili Bean Soup, '96 71
Chill-Chaser Soup, '87 282
Drunken Bean Soup, '87 283
Fiesta Chowder, '02 305
French Market Soup, '92 49; '94 317
French Market Soup Mix, '94 317
Green Bean, Mushroom, and Ham Chowder,
    Creamy, '99 M336
Green Bean Soup, Cream of, '84 111
Guadalajara Soup, '88 30
Ham-and-Bean Soup, '84 4; '05 45
Ham-and-Bean Soup, Spicy, '94 322
Ham Soup, Bean-and-, '04 325
Hominy Soup, Bean-and-, '95 23
Italian Soup, Chunky, '99 20
Leafy Bean Soup, '86 223
Minestra, '97 246
Minestrone, Cheesy, '99 17
Minestrone, Mama's Mexican, '05 254
Minestrone, Meatball, '00 242
Minestrone Soup, '91 258
Minestrone Soup Mix, '91 258
Mix, Bean Soup, '99 283
Navy Bean Soup, '84 280; '96 19
Navy Bean Soup, Chunky, '83 291
Navy Bean Soup, Savory, '87 282
Pasta Soup, Bean and, '94 220
Polish Sausage Soup, '99 317
Quick Bean Soup, '99 97
Red Bean Soup with Walnuts,
    '96 243
Refried Bean Soup, '96 136
Sausage-Bean Chowder, '83 20
Sausage-Bean Soup, '85 88
Sausage-Bean Soup, Spicy, '83 229

Sausage, Spinach, and Bean Soup,
    '99 311
Taco Soup, '99 36
Three-Bean Soup, '89 17
Three-Bean Soup, Spicy, '91 28
Tortellini Soup, '98 68
Tortilla Soup, '04 26
Turkey Soup, Bean-and-, '93 319
Vegetable-Bean Soup, '83 317
White Bean Chowder with Sage Pesto,
    '97 22
White Bean Soup, '83 229; '90 201
White Bean Soup, Spicy, '94 225
White Bean Soup with Gremolata, '05 319
Spicy Beans with Coconut Milk, '03 175
Stew, Brunswick, '01 148, 219
Stew, Santa Fe Chicken, '97 193
Taco Bake, '97 326
Tacos, Chicken-and-Bean, '93 293
Taco Stacks, Soft, '02 54
Tomatoes, Stuffed, '96 82
Tortas, Grilled Chicken, '01 M187
Tostadas, Chickpea-Chipotle, '01 54
Tostadas, Party, '98 M33
Turkey Strips with Roasted Peppers and Beans, Herbed,
    '04 282
White Bean Chili, '02 20
White Bean Pot, '86 194
White Bean Puree, Pork Chops with, '96 226
White Bean Puree, Stuffed Chicken Breasts with,
    '98 270; '02 200
White Bean Ragoût, '96 232
White Bean Relish, '93 229
White Beans, Caesar Salad with, '93 30
White Bean Spread, '93 30; '95 279; '96 122
White Bean Spread with Creamy Cucumber Sauce,
    '00 178
BEEF. *See also* **BEEF, GROUND; CASSEROLES/**
    Meat; GRILLED/ Beef; LIVER;
    SANDWICHES.
Appetizers, Meat-and-Cheese, '87 7
Asparagus, Beef with, '90 100
Ball, Cheese 'n' Beef, '83 230
Barbecue, Bourbon, '88 129
Barbecued Beef, Saucy, '82 156
Barbecue, Slow-Cooker Beef, '02 299
Baria, '97 91
Bouilli, '80 58
Bourguignon, Beef, '79 104; '82 288
Bourguignon, Royal Beef, '80 106
Brisket
Apricot Brisket, Spicy, '04 247
au Jus, Baked Brisket, '00 281
Baked Brisket, Polly's, '00 194
Barbecue Brisket, Oven, '01 259
Barbecue Brisket, Smoky, '03 160
Barbecued Beef Brisket, '83 11
Barbecued Beef Brisket, Denton, Texas, '81 55
Barbecued Beef Brisket with Sauce, '86 153
Barbecued Brisket, '86 154; '88 218
Beer, Beef Brisket in, '93 63
Brisket, '96 228; '01 273
GG's Brisket, '97 251
Home-Style Brisket, '87 303
Marinated Brisket, '86 129
Passover Brisket, '95 102
Pot Roast, '00 65
Pot Roast, Beef Brisket, '93 20
Roast, Peppery Brisket, '83 319
Saucy Brisket, '00 83
Smoke-at-Home Brisket, '93 192
Smoked Brisket, '89 168; '01 169
Smoked Brisket, Heavenly, '95 114
Smoked Brisket, Texas-, '98 89

Smoked Brisket with Barbecue Sauce, '85 144
Suzi's Brisket, Aunt, '02 321
Traditional Brisket, '03 188
Vegetables, Beef Brisket with Fall, '02 237
Broccoli, Quick Beef and, '91 123
Broccoli with Chive Gravy, Beef and, '88 214
Burgoo, Five-Meat, '87 3
Burgoo, Kentucky, '88 235; '97 138
Burgoo, Old-Fashioned, '87 3
Burgundy, Beef, '82 259; '83 125, 281; '88 25; '95 69
Burgundy, Simple Beef, '90 234
Burgundy with Pearl Onions, Beef, '81 108
Burritos, Carne Guisada, '95 43
Burritos, Cheesy Beef, '85 193
Burritos, Meat-and-Bean, '81 194
Caldo de Rez (Mexican Beef Stew), '89 276
Carne Guisada, '93 68
Chalupa, Bean, '80 223
Chili
Black Bean Chili Marsala, '95 16
Bodacious Chili, '95 14
Chuck Wagon Chili, '81 282; '82 57
Chunky Beef Chili, '05 235
Chunky Chili, '82 M282; '86 3
con Carne, Chili, '82 310; '83 30; '86 2
Cowboy Chili, '86 2
Firestarter Chili, '93 34
Out West Chili, '95 15
Red Chili, '93 108
Red Chili, North Texas, '87 303
South-of-the-Border Chili, '83 283; '91 283
Texas Championship Chili, '81 54
Verde, Chili, '95 14
Zippy Chili, '87 110
Chimichangas (Fried Burritos), '85 244; '86 114
Chimichangas, Oven-Fried Beef, '92 124
Chinese-Style Beef, '87 50
Chipped Beef and Toast, Creamy, '79 180
Chipped Beef Spread in Puff Pastry, '98 M335
Corned Beef
Birming "Ham," '94 229
Brunch Bake, Corned Beef, '82 44
Cabbage au Gratin, Corned Beef and, '83 16
Cabbage, Corned Beef and, '83 104; '93 64; '96 328
Cabbage, Corned Beef Squares and, '82 86
Cabbage, Quick Corned Beef and, '79 54
Dijon Glaze, Corned Beef with, '87 54
Dinner, Corned Beef, '87 54
Hash, Corned Beef, '95 262
Hash, Red Flannel, '79 191
Reuben Buns, '88 298
Reuben Casserole, '90 240
Reuben Casserole, Chicken, '03 69
Reuben Cheesecake, '90 175
Reuben Loaf, '95 338
Reuben Meat Pie, '80 189
Reuben Pizza, '03 69
Reuben Puffs, '98 231
Reuben Quesadillas, '05 131
Reuben Rolls, Snappy, '02 58
Reuben Sandwiches, '80 M201
Reuben Sandwiches, Broiled, '81 240
Reuben Sandwiches, Crispy, '85 299
Reuben Sandwiches, Grilled, '81 206
Reuben Sandwiches, Open-Face, '91 199
Reuben Sandwich, Rolled, '99 219
Reubens, Golden-Baked Mini, '01 62
Reubens, Open-Faced Coleslaw, '03 169
Reuben Soup, Cream of, '97 26
Reubens, Oven-Grilled, '97 304
Reubens, Party, '90 61
Reubens, Spicy Coleslaw, '04 63
Reubens, Summer, '00 134
Reuben Strudel, '98 28

Reuben Turnovers, '94 253
Roll, Corned Beef, '85 66
Salad, Corned Beef, '80 104
Salad, Corned Beef-Cauliflower, '83 16
Salad, Corned Beef-Potato, '85 213
Salad, Molded Corned Beef, '82 86
Salad, Potato-Corned Beef, '81 36
Salad, Vegetable-Corned Beef, '80 148
Sandwich, Corned Beef and Cheese, '79 214
Sandwiches, Barbecued Corned Beef, '83 130
Sandwiches, Corned Beef, '83 291; '85 242; '92 23
Sandwiches, Grilled Corned Beef, '87 54
Sandwiches, Meal-in-One, '80 218
Soup, Corned Beef, '83 16
Soup, French Onion-Beef, '87 54
Spread, Corned Beef, '87 196
Creamed Beef and Chicken-Topped Potatoes, '83 210
Creamed Chipped Beef, '92 42
Creamed Dried Beef with Artichokes, '85 81
Cubes in Wine Sauce, Beef, '79 264
Curried Beef Dinner, '83 4
Dip, Chipped Beef, '88 M8
Dip, Dried Beef, '01 90
Dip, Hot Cheesy Beef, '80 85
Dried Beef Dip, Extra-Creamy, '03 240
Elégante, Beef, '80 125
en Daube, Beef, '79 163
Fajitas, Beef, '88 233
Fajitas, Favorite, '86 114
Filet Mignon, Cajun Blackened, '95 85
Filet of Beef, Marinated Stuffed, '99 165
Fillet of Beef with Blue Cheese Sauce, Pan-Roasted, '94 320
Fillet of Beef with Red Pepper Butter, '96 32
Flautas, Rancho Ramillete, '96 M125
Ginger Beef with Bok Choy, '96 99
Goulash, Beef, '83 231
Goulash, Hungarian, '81 227; '92 227
Green Peppers, Beef and, '79 104
Grillades and Grits, '89 47; '93 62
Grilled Beef with Mashed Potatoes and Chipotle Cream, '02 M320
Gumbo, Texas Ranch-Style, '82 226
Gumbo z'Herbes, '94 239
Hash, Beef, '95 24; '99 62
Hash with Cabbage Salad, Austrian, '95 262
Jerky, Beef, '80 269; '81 26

Kebabs
Barbecued Steak Kebabs, '79 89
Beef Kebabs, '85 110
Beef on a Stick, '99 336
Chile-Beef Kebabs, '94 251
Deluxe, Beef Kebabs, '82 182
Hot-and-Spicy Kebabs, '87 193
Liver Kebabs, '80 185
Marinated Beef Kebabs, '82 105; '85 159
Marinated Beef Kebabs with Rice, '84 32
Marinated Beef Kebabs with Vegetables, '99 292
Marinated Beef on a Stick, '85 234
Marinated Sirloin Kebabs, '82 162
Marinated Steak Kebabs, '80 184
Pineapple-Beef Kebabs, '83 212
Saucy Beef Kebabs, '83 109
Shrimp Kebabs, Steak-and-, '80 184
Spicy Grilled Kebabs, '98 158
Spirited Beef Kebabs, '87 142
Steak Kebabs, '82 4; '93 95
Steak on a Stick, '83 109
Steak with Vegetables, Skewered, '81 124
Teriyaki Beef Kebabs, '80 207
Vegetable Kebabs, Beef-and-, '91 148
Vegetables, Beef Kebabs with, '90 148

Liver
Balsamic Vinegar, Beef Liver with, '98 130

Creamy Liver and Noodle Dinner, '80 11
Creole Liver, '96 236
Creole Sauce, Liver in, '87 33
French-Style Liver, '80 10
Gravy, Liver and, '80 10
Herbs, Liver with, '81 277
Kebabs, Liver, '80 185
Patties, Beef Liver, '81 277
Saucy Liver, '81 277
Sauté, Liver, '81 277
Spanish-Style Liver, '80 11
Stroganoff, Liver, '79 54
Sweet-and-Sour Liver, '81 277
Tasty Liver, '83 29
Mango-Beef and Rice, '88 138
Meatballs, Quick Processor, '87 111
Medaillons, Italian Beef, '87 305
Medaillons of Beef with Ancho Chile Sauce, '87 122
Medaillons of Beef with Horseradish Cream, '90 96
Mongolian Beef, '85 2, 75; '01 94
Mushrooms, Beef-Stuffed, '00 278
Oriental, Beef and Cauliflower, '80 220
Oriental Beef and Snow Peas, '79 105
Oriental Beef with Pea Pods, '86 M328
Pastichio, '85 194
Peppered Beef in a Blanket, Bourbon, '00 109
Philly Firecrackers, '01 142
Pies, Carry-Along Beef, '80 224; '81 56
Pie, Sensational Beef, '03 M284
Pie, Shepherd's, '92 168
Pot Pie, Oriental Beef, '92 253
Pot Pies with Yorkshire Pudding Topping, Beef, '93 45
Ravioli in Basil-Cream Sauce, Beef, '05 293

Ribs
Baby Loin Back Ribs, '01 106
Barbecued Beef Short Ribs, '83 178
Barbecued Short Ribs, '90 148
Beans, Spicy Black, '04 119
Braised Short Ribs, '98 44; '01 193
Grilled Ribs, Sweet-and-Sour, '98 331
Hearty Beef Shortribs, '79 14
Supreme, Beef Shortribs, '79 14
Rice, Beef and Cauliflower over, '93 94

Roasts
à la Beer, Beef, '98 64
à la Mode, Beef, '98 122
Barbecue, Beef Roast, '79 159
Barbecued Beef Roast, '82 96; '83 103
Barbecue, Four-Hour, '00 18
Barbecue Roast, '98 245
Barbecue, Trish's Beach, '03 206
Beer-and-Onion Sauce, Roast in, '80 124
Brisket Roast, Peppery, '83 319
Burgundy Gravy, Beef Roast with, '95 263
Burgundy Roast, Beef, '85 291
Burritos, Easy, '04 32
Chili Bean Roast, '87 268; '88 102; '89 68
Chuck Roast Barbecue, '96 71
Chuck Roast, Fruited, '91 289
Chuck Roast in Sauce, '91 47
Chuck Roast, Marinated, '80 59
Chuck Roast, Orange Marinated, '85 179
Chuck Roast, Savory, '00 18
Chuck Roast, Slow Cooker, '98 32
Classic Roast Beef, '03 296
Cola Roast, '81 298
Deli-Style Roast Beef, '93 15
Diablo, Beef, '79 17
Easy Banquet Roast, '99 291
Easy Beef Roast, '89 M65
Easy Oven Roast, '93 64
Eye-of-Round, Burgundy, '90 243
Eye of Round, Grilled Beef, '82 91
Eye of Round Roast, '99 60

Eye-of-Round Roast with Fruited Onion Marmalade, '96 323
Eye of Round Roast with Marmalade, '97 27
Eye-of-Round Roast with Rice Gravy, Seasoned, '89 118
Eye of Round, Slow Cooker Spicy Marinated, '99 291
Eye of Round, Spicy Marinated, '99 291
Eye Round Roast, Mexican, '89 190
Flautas, '00 293
French-Style Beef Roast, '89 32
Grillades and Grits, '88 126
Grilled Marinated Beef Roast, '93 141
Grilled Pepper Roast, '81 110
Herbed Roast, '91 288
Herbed Roast Beef, '05 297
Java Roast, '83 319
Marengo, Beef, '82 284; '83 14
Marinated Roast, '85 3
Marinated Roast Beef, '97 14
Marinated Roast, Dijon Wine-, '91 289
Mary's Roast Beef, '01 86
Mix, Mexican Meat, '00 292
New York Strip Roast, Spicy, '93 131
Onion-and-Mushroom Gravy, Roast with, '00 293
Patio Steak, '87 141
Pizza, Taco, '00 293
Potatoes, Stuffed Baked, '00 293
Pot Pie, Beef Roast, '88 296
Pot Roast, '00 65
Pot Roast, All-Seasons, '86 89
Pot Roast and Gravy, '89 234
Pot Roast and Gravy, Country-Style, '94 308
Pot Roast, Aunt Mary's, '04 47
Pot Roast, Autumn Gold, '83 7
Pot Roast, Barbecued, '79 17; '83 319
Pot Roast, Basic, '81 M208
Pot Roast, Bavarian-Style, '79 17
Pot Roast, Beef Brisket, '93 20
Pot Roast, Bloody Mary, '86 47
Pot Roast, Cardamom, '79 12
Pot Roast, Company, '79 162; '88 M14
Pot Roast, Country, '87 216
Pot Roast, Cowboy, '05 35
Pot Roast, Dillicious, '81 187
Pot Roast, Easy Oven, '86 52
Pot Roast, Favorite, '89 118
Pot Roast, Fruited, '90 211
Pot Roast, Gee's Italian, '96 18
Pot Roast, Hawaiian, '81 298
Pot Roast, Indian, '87 215
Pot Roast in Red Sauce, '87 215
Pot Roast in Sour Cream, '89 117
Pot Roast in White Wine Gravy, '81 299
Pot Roast, Italian, '81 299; '87 95; '02 88; '05 34
Pot Roast, Marinated, '85 21
Pot Roast Medley, Vegetable-, '83 319
Pot Roast, Mexican, '98 64
Pot Roast, Mushroom, '79 17; '96 250
Pot Roast of Beef with Vegetables, '98 65
Pot Roast, Old-Fashioned, '98 64
Pot Roast, Peppered, '87 215
Pot Roast, Perfect, '83 7
Pot Roast, Polynesian, '80 59
Pot Roast, Regal, '79 17
Pot Roast, Root Beer, '04 212
Pot Roast, Spicy Apple, '83 7
Pot Roast, Swedish, '80 59
Pot Roast, Sweet-and-Sour, '83 8; '99 291
Pot Roast with Dumplings, '98 245
Pot Roast with Gravy, '81 298
Pot Roast with Herbed Red Sauce, '88 29
Pot Roast with Mushroom Gravy, '02 90
Pot Roast with Sour Cream Gravy, '79 17

BEEF, Roasts
(continued)

Pot Roast with Spaghetti, '80 59
Pot Roast with Vegetables, '80 59; '81 M208; '00 18
Pot Roast with Vegetables, Marinated, '88 M52
Pot Roast, Zesty, '81 206
Pressure-Cooker Roast, '91 289
Pressure Cooker Roast Beef, '01 86
Prime Rib, Perfect, '96 197
Prime Ribs and Yorkshire Puddings, Mini, '01 283
Prime Rib, Smoked, '97 161; '02 177
Prime Rib with Spicy Horseradish Sauce, '02 235
Pumpernickel Roast, '97 234
Rib-Eye Beef, Spicy, '84 259
Rib-Eye Roast, Marinated, '90 318
Rib-Eye Roast, Peppered, '01 122
Rib Roast, Barbecued, '86 152
Rib Roast, Rosemary, '03 294
Rib Roast, Rosemary-Thyme, '05 248
Rib Roast, Standing, '80 246; '84 187; '95 28
Rib Roast with Yorkshire Pudding, Standing,
    '80 252; '98 86
Rump Roast, Easy, '93 217
Sandwiches, French Dip, '97 211
Sandwiches, Grilled Roast Beef-and-Brie, '03 296
Sauerbraten, '98 278
Sauerbraten Beef, Marinated, '93 16
Sauerbraten, Quick, '80 139
Simple Roast, '81 298
Sirloin Roast, Canary, '89 117
Sirloin Tip Roast with Mustard Cream Sauce,
    Herbed, '88 61
Sirloin Tips, Braised, '98 45
Slices, Roast Beef, '02 246
Slow Cooker Roast Beef, '01 86
Sunday Roast Beef, '99 327
Supreme, Roast Beef, '83 8
Vegetables, Beef and, '01 86
Vegetables, Company Beef and, '88 234
Wellington, Beef, '83 319
Rolls, Stuffed Sherried Beef, '79 105
Rolls, Wine-Sauced Beef-and-Barley, '87 269
Rolls with Mustard-Horseradish Cream, Beef, '02 53
Roll-Ups, Mexican Beef, '90 176
Roll-Ups, Savory Beef and Cheese, '96 235
Rollups with Rice, Royal Beef, '79 105
Roulades, Beef, '83 47; '85 234
Roulades, Roquefort Beef, '88 215
Salads. *See also* **BEEF/Corned Beef.**
Broccoli Salad, Beef-and-, '87 187
Cilantro, Beef Salad with, '97 202
Cucumber-Roast Beef Salad, '89 162
Fajita Salad, Beef, '91 70
Gingered Beef Salad, '88 61
Greek Steak Salad, '92 107
Niçoise, Beef Salad, '99 159
Peking Beef Salad, '88 60
Pepper Steak Salad Cups, '86 206
Roast Beef Salad, '80 223; '81 56; '90 318
Sirloin Salad, Grilled, '94 129
Spicy Beef-Pasta Salad, '01 311
Spicy Beef Salad, '02 174
Steak-and-Spinach Salad with Hot Pan Dressing,
    '05 19
Steak Salad Niçoise, Grilled, '98 148
Steak Salad with Peach Salsa, '97 183
Stir-Fry Beef Salad, '96 129
Tangy Beef Salad, '87 M218
Vinaigrette Salad, Beef, '95 177
Western-Style Beef Salad, '93 321
Zesty Beef Salad, '79 56
Sandwich, Beef-and-Kraut, '91 167

Sandwiches
Barbecue Beef Sandwiches, Slow-Cooker, '05 64
Flank Steak Mini-Sandwiches, Shredded, '05 158
Panini Sandwiches, Roast Beef-Cheddar, '05 223
Philly Sandwiches, Open-Faced, '05 32
Wraps, Tangy-and-Sweet Roast Beef, '05 92
Sandwiches, Beef and Pork Tenderloin, '80 175
Sandwiches, Beef, Bacon, and Blue Cheese, '96 23
Sandwiches, Beef Salad Pocket, '83 267
Sandwiches, Beef Tenderloin Picnic, '90 91
Sandwiches, Dilly Beef, '98 288
Sandwiches, Dried Beef Pita, '86 160
Sandwiches, Hot Beef, '00 98
Sandwiches, Wake-Up, '84 58
Sandwiches with Yogurt-Cucumber Sauce, London
    Broil, '01 162
Sandwich, Roast Beef Hero, '91 167
Sandwich, Saucy Beef Pocket, '80 92
Seasoning Blend, Meat, '88 29
Shredded Beef over Rice Noodles, '85 74
Sirloin, Sweet Skillet, '04 20
Sirloin with Cherry-Merlot Sauce and Gorgonzola,
    Peppered, '02 320
Soup, Beefy Lentil, '87 282
Soup, Beefy Vidalia Onion, '97 212
Soup, Chunky Italian, '99 20
Soup, Hearty Vegetable-Beef, '84 102
Soup, Steak, '99 260
Soup, Tomato-Beef-Wild Rice, '04 42
Soup, Vegetable-Beef, '88 296
Spaghetti, Meaty, '82 19
Spicy Beef and Black Beans, '99 331
Spread, Hot Beef, '83 50; '84 M216
Steaks. *See also* **BEEF/Kebabs, Salads.**
American Steakhouse Beef, '93 15
Appetizers, Marinated Steak-and-Chestnut,
    '84 323
au Poivre, Steak, '88 232
Bacon Twirls, Beef-and-, '91 163
Bake, Asian Noodle Beef, '98 31
Barbecued Beef, '81 18
Barbecued Steak, Saucy Oven-, '83 10
Bean Sprouts, Beef and, '82 281; '83 42
Benedict for Two, Steaks, '85 295
Biscuits with Beef and Horseradish-Chive Cream,
    Blue Cheese, '02 313
Bistecca, '02 170
Blackened 'n' Peppered Steak, '95 174
Blue Cheese Steaks, '84 171
Blue Cheese-Walnut Stuffed Fillets, '95 327
Blue, Elegant Beef, '97 97
Bourbon Steak, '90 148
Braised Steaks, Beer-, '87 96
Broiled Oriental Steaks, '83 110
Broiled Steaks, '96 172
Caramel-Brandy Sauce, Steaks with, '03 56
Carne Guisada, '94 219
Carpetbagger Steak, '84 87
Cheesesteaks, Chimichurri, '04 312
Chicken-Fried Steak, '92 214; '97 307; '01 47;
    '03 72, 311; '05 67
Chicken-Fried Steak and Cream Gravy, Threadgill's,
    '98 62
Chicken-Fried Steak Fingers with Creole Mustard
    Sauce, '99 142
Chicken-Fried Steak, Matt's, '97 25
Chicken-Fried Steaks, '88 110
Chili, Black Bean, '02 20
Chuck Steak, Marinated Barbecued, '80 156
Coconut-Beef Stir-Fry, '97 18
Continental, Steak, '83 178
Country-Fried Steak and Cream Gravy, '84 8
Country-Fried Steak, Cajun-Style, '01 318
Country-Fried Steak in Paradise, '98 62

Country-Fried Steak, Mock, '87 163
Country-Fried Steak with Creamy Salsa Gravy,
    '05 67
Crêpes, Special Steak, '91 24
Curried Beef Steak, '88 60
Cutlets, Lemon-Flavored, '79 105
de Burgo, Steak, '84 117
Diane Flambé, Steak, '79 103
Diane, Steak, '82 275; '92 306
Dianne, Steak, '83 47
Fajita Casserole, '97 96
Fajita Crêpes, '94 116
Fajitas, '84 233
Fajitas, Beef and Chicken, '02 119
Fajitas (Bo Nuong Xa), Vietnamese, '05 117
Fajitas, Java, '96 227
Fajitas, Plum Good, '94 115
Fajitas, Slow Cooker, '02 43
Fajitas, Tex-Mex, '01 188
Fajitas with Pico de Gallo, '98 87; '04 61
Fiery Steak with Pimiento Cheese Salsa, '99 331
Filet Mignon, Marinated, '84 171
Filet Mignons with Shiitake Madeira Sauce, '95 265
Filet Mignon Tarragon, '94 46
Filet Mignon with Horseradish Gravy, '92 262
Filet Mignon with Mushroom Sauce, '94 250
Filets Mignons, Skillet, '03 258
Filets, Spicy Beef, '00 121
Filets with Green Peppercorn Sauce, Beef Tender-
    loin, '00 309
Filets with Stilton-Portobello Sauce, Beef, '00 309
Fillet, Acapulco, '98 174
Fillets au Vin, Beef, '79 137
Fillets with Black Bean Sauce, Spicy Beef, '97 184
Fillets with Green Peppercorn Sauce, Beef, '02 285
Fillets with Horseradish Sauce and Curried Bananas,
    '85 230
Fillets with Orange Cream, Beef, '97 66
Fillets with Stilton-Portobello Sauce, Beef, '02 310
Fillets with Wine Sauce, Beef, '01 317
Fingers, Golden Steak, '85 110
Flank Steak and Dried Tomato-Basil Pesto Linguine,
    '04 101
Flank Steak and Mushrooms, '87 61
Flank Steak-and-Spinach Pinwheels, '95 56
Flank Steak, Bacon-Wrapped, '85 59
Flank Steak, Barbecued, '79 89
Flank Steak, Beer-Marinated, '87 35
Flank Steak, Cheese-Stuffed, '98 182
Flank Steak, East-West, '04 90
Flank Steak, Easy Greek, '05 207
Flank Steak, Flavorful, '96 32
Flank Steak, Ginger-Marinated, '89 25; '05 216
Flank Steak, Grilled, '80 152; '89 168; '91 80;
    '92 166; '03 146
Flank Steak, Grilled Marinated, '97 182
Flank Steak, Herbed, '92 127
Flank Steak, Herb-Marinated, '85 275
Flank Steak in Mexican Marinade, '98 128
Flank Steak, Lemon-Lime, '95 55
Flank Steak, Marinated, '82 162; '83 35, 258; '85 86;
    '88 262; '95 237; '04 118
Flank Steak, Mashed Potato-Stuffed, '01 25
Flank Steak, Mediterranean, '00 145
Flank Steak, Oriental, '83 178
Flank Steak, Peppery Grilled, '99 157
Flank Steak Pinwheels, '87 141
Flank Steak, Red Wine-Marinated, '95 283
Flank Steak, Rosemary Grilled, '03 125
Flank Steak Sandwiches with Apple Barbecue Sauce,
    '99 173
Flank Steaks, Delicious Marinated, '83 110
Flank Steak Skewers, Lemon, '02 134
Flank Steak, Soy-Ginger, '02 90

Flank Steak Sukiyaki, '88 233
Flank Steaks with Mushrooms, '00 121
Flank Steak, Tangy, '86 184
Flank Steak, Tenderized, '82 105
Flank Steak Teriyaki, '81 110
Flank Steak, Texas, '86 185
Flank Steak, Tomato-Stuffed, '97 49
Flank Steak with Apple-Bourbon Sauce and Roasted
    Vegetables, Grilled, '99 142
Flank Steak with Black Bean-and-Corn Salsa,
    Grilled, '94 80
Flank Steak with Chili Butter, '00 177
Flank Steak with Horseradish Sauce, Grilled, '02 19
Flank Steak with Molasses Barbecue Glaze, Grilled,
    '00 59
Flank Steak with Noodles, Stuffed, '90 101
Flank Steak with Salsa, Southwest, '03 95
Flank Steak with Sweet Peppers, Grilled, '90 138
Flank Steak with Tomato-Olive Relish, '03 210
French Quarter Steak, '81 17
Garlic-Herb Steaks, '98 169; '99 175
Garlic Steak, '84 8
Ginger, Beef with, '03 64
Glazed Balsamic Steaks with Blue Pecan Confetti,
    Maple-Mustard-, '05 330
Greek Pocket Steaks, '81 262
Grillades and Baked Cheese Grits, '94 240
Grilled Black Pepper Steak, '86 184
Grilled Steaks, '96 172
Grilled Steaks Balsamico, '05 84
Grilled Steaks, Mesquite-, '85 154
Grilled Steak, Spicy, '97 211
Grilled Steaks with Green Chiles, '85 144
Grilled Steaks with Spicy Herb Sauce, Asian,
    '03 280
Grill, Steak Brunch, '82 44
Ham-and-Mushroom Sauce, Steak with, '83 109
Horseradish Steak, '88 39
Italian Steak, '03 180
Kebabs, Spicy Grilled, '98 158
Kebabs, Steak-and-Shrimp, '00 124
Kebabs, Steak-and-Vegetable, '04 218
Korean Steak, '89 190
Lemon-Butter Steak with Brandy Sauce, '85 78
lo Mein, Steak, '90 100
London Broil, Grilled, '92 59
London Broil, Marinated, '87 32; '05 84
London Broil, Peppercorn, '88 60
London Broil, Teriyaki, '92 282
Marinated Bourbon Steak, '95 91
Marinated Steak, '88 233
Marinated Steak, Mexican, '88 148
Mediterranean Steak, '03 180
Mesquite-Ginger Beef with Fresh Fruit Relish,
    '95 158
Mexican Steak, '84 76
Minute Steak with Mushroom Gravy, '05 67
Mushroom Sauce, Steak with, '83 212
Mush, Steak and Gravy with, '81 215
New York Steaks, Grilled, '05 123
Oriental Beef, '85 20
Pan-Grilled Steaks, '96 172
Parmesan, Steak, '93 41
Parmigiana, Beef, '84 8; '85 234
Pasta and Sesame-Ginger Butter, Steak with, '99 142
Pasta, Red Wine-Tomato-and-Steak, '05 140
Pepper-Beef Steak, '85 21
Pepper-Cheese Steaks, Mexican, '97 190
Pepper Cream, Steak in, '94 117
Pepper Steak, '81 273; '85 57; '88 113
Pepper Steak and Rice, '81 17
Pepper Steak and Rice, Skillet, '04 326
Pepper Steak, Chinese, '82 236
Pepper Steak, Cold, '91 208

Pepper Steak, Cracked, '83 109
Pepper Steak, Festive Cajun, '03 23
Pepper Steak, Simple, '01 82
Pepper Stir-Fry Steak, '81 240
Pies, Cornish Meat, '84 23
Pirate Steak, '79 89
Quesadillas with Mango Salsa, Beefy Crab, '00 124
Red Wine Marinade, Beef with, '91 46
Rib-Eye Grill, '02 306
Rib Eyes, Grecian Skillet, '96 234
Rib-Eyes, Italian, '98 215
Rib-Eye Steaks, Molasses-Grilled, '05 218
Rib-Eye Steaks, Peppered, '97 46; '00 146; '02 110
Rib-Eye Steaks with Roquefort Glaze, '89 310
Rib Eyes with Herb Cheese and Asparagus Bundles,
    Grilled Chile-Rubbed, '03 326
Rib Eyes with Red Pepper-Polenta Fries and Chile
    Corn Jus, '00 196
Ropa Vieja, '93 28; '98 20
Rouladen, '99 242
Round Steak, Braised, '87 35
Round Steak over Rice, Burgundy, '90 M33
Round Steak, Parmesan, '80 106
Round Steak, Red Pepper, '88 214
Round Steak, Savory Stuffed, '81 18
Round Steak, Skillet, '83 29
Round Steak, Tangy, '82 284; '83 14
Round Steak, Tender Grilled, '85 3
Saltillo, Beef (Beef with Tomatillos), '82 219
Sandwich, Beef-and-Artichoke Open-Faced Italian,
    '98 22
Sandwiches, Steak, '96 136
Sandwiches, Steak-and-Onion, '02 126
Sandwiches, Steak Bagel, '96 249
Shish Kebabs, Beef Tenderloin, '00 200
Shrimp, Steak and, '88 123
Sirloin in Vodka Sauce, '03 96
Sirloin, Mustard Marinated, '94 41
Sirloin, Peppery Grilled, '02 212
Sirloin Steak, Secret, '81 110
Sirloin Steaks, Italian, '04 61
Sirloin Steaks with Thyme Pesto, '97 182
Sirloin Supreme, Shrimp and, '81 131
Sirloin with Zesty Corn Salsa, Cilantro-Garlic,
    '02 193
Skillet Steak in Red Wine Sauce, '85 21
Skillet Steak 'n Potatoes, '81 18
Smothered Beef and Onions, '85 293
Smothered Steak, '79 212
Smothered Steak, Onion-, '87 M189
Soup, Steak, '99 260
Stately Steaks, '00 121
Stir-Fried Beef, '84 26
Stir-Fried Steak, Fast-and-Easy, '87 50
Stir-Fry, Beef-and-Carrot, '98 335
Stir-Fry, Beef-and-Vegetable, '87 22; '99 204
Stir-Fry Beef-and-Vegetables, '84 141
Stir-Fry, Curried Beef, '01 162
Stir-Fry, Italian Beef, '99 35
Stir-Fry, Pepper Steak, '89 191
Stir-Fry, Steak-and-Vegetable, '84 8
Strip Steaks, Coffee-Rubbed, '03 282
Stroganoff, Creamy Beef, '02 124
Stuffed Steak, Italian-, '88 232
Stuffed Steak Rolls, '82 135
Stuffed Steaks, Cheese-, '81 17
Sweet-and-Sour Marinated Steaks, '83 110
Swiss Steak Cheese Skillet, '80 106
Swiss Steak, Deviled, '80 107
Swiss Steak, Easy, '00 90
Swiss Steak Monterey, '99 23
Swiss Steak, Oven, '85 234
Swiss Steak, Pizza, '02 36
Swiss Steak, Smothered, '04 321

Swiss Steak Surprise, '81 17
Swiss Steak with Vegetables, '81 273
Tabasco Steak, '95 207
Tacos, Jerk Steak, '01 170
Tartare, Steak, '83 78
Tenderloin Steak, Gingered, '96 154
Tenderloin Steaks with Balsamic Sauce, Beef,
    '98 319
Tenderloin Steaks with Peperonata, Beef, '97 291
Tenderloin with Horseradish Cream, Beef, '05 309
Teriyaki Beef Broil, '92 56
Teriyaki, Marinated Steak, '84 50
Thai Beef, Spicy Lemon, '97 320
Thai Lemon Beef, '97 292
Tomatoes and Artichokes, Beef with, '92 282
Vegetables, Beef with Chinese, '81 211
Vegetables, Beef with Oriental, '84 140
Wellingtons, Individual Beef, '82 259
Wellingtons, Mini Beef, '01 252
Wraps, Cheese-Steak, '00 M335
Zippy Steak and Gravy, '90 35

Stews
Beef Stew, '86 51; '90 230; '96 16
Brown Stew, '85 239
Brunswick Stew, Bama, '87 4
Brunswick Stew, Easy, '92 280
Brunswick Stew, Georgian, '92 35
Brunswick Stew, Virginia Ramsey's Favorite, '91 16
Burgundy Beef Stew, '88 234
Burgundy Stew with Drop Dumplings, '83 125
Celery Root Stew, Beef-and-, '98 292
Company Beef Stew, '83 85; '97 198
Dumplings, Beef Stew with, '84 3
Dumplings, Beef Stew with Parsley, '81 76; '82 13;
    '85 M246
Emerald Isle Stew, '95 71
Hungarian Beef Stew, '03 35
Hungarian Stew with Noodles, '80 263
Irish Stew, '90 64
Mexican Stew, '82 231
Mexican Stew Olé, '86 296
Onion Stew, Beef-and-, '87 18
Oven Beef Stew, '79 222; '80 64
Quick Beef Stew, '92 71
Red Chili Stew, '95 226
Slow-Cooker Beef Stew, '05 235
Spicy Beef Stew, '86 228
Sweet-and-Sour Beef and Vegetable Stew, '85 87
Texas Stew, '97 211
Vegetable-Beef Stew, '94 323
Vegetable-Beef Stew, Shortcut, '89 218
White Wine Stew, '82 228
Stir-Fried Beef and Vegetables, '88 301
Stir-Fry Beef and Asparagus, '91 124
Stir-Fry Beef and Broccoli, '79 47
Stir-Fry, Beef-and-Broccoli, '91 46
Stir-Fry Beef and Pea Pods, '80 19
Stir-Fry, Beef-and-Shrimp, '93 32
Stir-Fry, Beef and Snow Pea, '82 98
Stir-Fry Beef and Snow Peas, '83 22
Stir-Fry, Beef-and-Vegetable, '81 211
Stir-Fry Broccoli and Beef, '83 110
Stir-Fry, Chinese Beef, '83 151
Stir-Fry, Hungarian, '93 64
Stir-Fry, Indian, '92 126
Stir-Fry, Lime-Ginger Beef, '92 65
Stir-Fry, Mongolian Beef, '89 25
Stir-Fry, Peanutty Beef, '95 157
Stir-Fry, Teriyaki, '83 110
Stock, Beef, '95 17
Stock, Brown Meat, '90 31
Stroganoff, Beef, '79 163; '81 179; '91 134; '93 18;
    '03 23
Stroganoff, Beef Burgundy, '85 31

Beef   **31**

BEEF

(continued)

Stroganoff, Light Beef, '86 36
Stroganoff, Liver, '79 54
Stroganoff, Quick Beef, '92 20; '99 327
Stroganoff Sandwiches, Steak, '85 110
Stroganoff, Sirloin, '81 297
Stroganoff with Parslied Noodles, Steak, '85 31
Tacos al Carbón, '86 19
Tacos al Carbón, Tailgate, '79 185
Tamales, '80 195
Tempting Twosome, '81 240
Tenderloin, Barbecued Beef, '94 26
Tenderloin Bundles, Peppered Beef, '89 272
Tenderloin, Chutneyed Beef, '94 270
Tenderloin Deluxe, Beef, '85 109
Tenderloin, Easy Beef, '90 268
Tenderloin, Elegant Beef, '88 244
Tenderloin for Two, Beef, '90 295
Tenderloin, Garlic-and-Rosemary Beef, '02 255
Tenderloin, Grilled, '91 166
Tenderloin, Hampton Place Beef, '04 272
Tenderloin, Herb Marinated, '83 109
Tenderloin, Holiday Beef, '01 238
Tenderloin in Wine Sauce, Beef, '02 136
Tenderloin, Lobster-Stuffed Beef, '87 248
Tenderloin, Marinated, '80 146
Tenderloin, Marinated Beef, '81 246; '85 302; '93 215;
    '03 241
Tenderloin, Mustard Greens-Stuffed, '96 324
Tenderloin Picnic Sandwiches, Beef, '90 91
Tenderloin, Spicy Beef, '88 29
Tenderloin, Spicy Marinated Beef, '83 262
Tenderloin, Spinach-Stuffed, '89 311
Tenderloin, Stuffed, '86 323; '88 50
Tenderloin, Stuffed Beef, '00 124
Tenderloin, Stuffed Tuscany, '99 269
Tenderloin with Avocado Béarnaise Sauce, Beef,
    '01 317
Tenderloin with Five-Onion Sauce, Beef, '98 272
Tenderloin with Henry Bain Sauce, Beef, '00 107;
    '01 20; '04 52
Tenderloin with Horseradish Cream Sauce, Pepper-
    Seared Beef, '01 280
Tenderloin with Mushroom Sauce, Beef, '88 3
Tenderloin with Mushrooms, Beef, '87 115
Tenderloin with Mushroom-Sherry Sauce, Beef, '87 306
Tenderloin with Pan-Roasted Pears, Beef, '02 197
Tenderloin with Peppercorns, Beef, '91 246
Tenderloin with Portobello-Marsala Sauce, Peppered
    Beef, '05 280
Tips and Noodles, Beef, '86 293
Tips on Rice, Beef, '85 87
Tournedos Diables, '87 60
Tournedos Mouton, '83 262
Turnovers, Roast Beef, '88 273; '89 180
Tzimmes, Sweet Potato-Beef, '92 234
Tzimmes with Brisket, Mixed Fruit, '93 114
Vegetables in a Noodle Ring, Beef and, '85 285
Vegetables, Savory Beef and, '79 163
Wellington, Beef, '93 288

BEEF, GROUND

Acorn Squash, Stuffed, '83 15
Appetizer, Cheesy Mexicali, '82 108
Barbecue Cups, '79 129
Bean Bake, Cheesy Beef-and-, '82 89
Bean Medley, Baked, '80 100
Beans, Beefy, '82 59
Beans, Beefy Baked, '80 136; '84 149; '85 142
Beans, Rancho Lima, '80 191
Beans, Three-Meat Baked, '86 210
Brunswick Stew, Breeden Liles's, '91 14

Burger Boat, '95 70
Burgoo, Harry Young's, '87 3
Burritos, Chinese, '87 181
Burritos, Fiesta, '86 114
Cabbage-and-Beef Rolls, Easy, '88 49
Cabbage, Italian Stuffed, '84 294
Cabbage Leaves, Stuffed, '00 270
Cabbage Rolls, '83 104
Cabbage Rolls, Beef Stuffed, '81 87; '82 7
Cabbage Rolls, Fried, '95 270
Cabbage Rolls, Hungarian, '94 47
Cabbage Rolls, Spicy, '84 2
Cabbage Rolls, Stuffed, '84 217
Cabbage Rollups, Beef-and-, '80 63
Cabbage, Stuffed, '84 282
Calzones, Beef-and-Pepperoni, '03 202
Calzones, Easy, '99 133
Calzones, Ground Beef, '97 95
Calzones with Italian Tomato Sauce, '03 202
Casseroles. *See also* **BEEF, GROUND/Lasagna.**
    Bean, and Cornbread Casserole, Beef, '99 215
    Bean Bake, Hamburger-, '95 121
    Bean Bake, Three-, '03 106
    Beef Casserole, '01 199
    Biscuit Casserole, Beef-and-, '83 75
    Cabbage Beef Bake, Zesty, '80 300
    Cavatini, '94 214
    Cheese, and Noodle Casserole, Beef, '99 58
    Cheeseburger Casserole, '95 255
    Cheesy Ground Beef Casserole, '79 44
    Cheesy Mexican Casserole, '82 224
    Chiles Rellenos Casserole, '98 48
    Chili-Rice Casserole, '79 54
    Cornbread Casserole, '81 91
    Cornbread Skillet Casserole, '83 243; '84 101
    County Fair Casserole, '79 130
    Creamy Ground Beef Casserole, '81 142
    Crusty Beef Casserole, '82 88
    Easy Beef Casserole, '86 M58; '00 208
    El Dorado Casserole, '81 140
    Enchilada Casserole, '87 287
    Enchilada Casserole, Firecracker, '80 260
    Enchilada Casserole, Lightened Texas-Style, '05 247
    Enchilada Casserole, Sour Cream, '82 113
    Enchilada Casserole, Texas-Style, '05 247
    Enchiladas, American, '81 170
    Enchiladas, Chili and, '00 55
    Enchiladas, Enticing, '99 57
    Enchiladas, Quicker, '96 103
    Enchiladas, Smothered, '05 59
    Enchiladas, Sour Cream, '87 37
    Enchiladas, Weeknight, '93 63
    Five-Layer Meal, '81 140
    Grits Italiano, '92 43
    Hamburger Casserole, '95 210
    Hamburger-Corn Bake, '99 58
    Italian Cabbage Casserole, '87 42
    Italian Casserole, '80 81
    Italian Casserole, Light, '03 198
    Layered Beef Casserole, '82 M203
    Layered Grecian Bake, '82 119
    Linguine with Meat Sauce, Baked, '01 41
    Linguine with Meat Sauce Casserole, '03 22
    Lombardi, Beef, '03 214
    Macaroni Bake, Beef-, '94 255
    Macaroni-Cheese-Beef Casserole, '95 125
    Macaroni Combo, Beef-, '79 194
    Manicotti, Ground Beef-and-Tomato, '03 257
    Manicotti, Meaty Cheese, '05 34
    Manicotti, Meaty Stuffed, '00 19
    Matador Mania, '86 19
    Mexican Casserole, '92 M22; '00 280
    Mexican Casserole, Cabin, '97 95
    Mexican Casserole, Microwave, '90 M231

    Mexi Casserole, '83 M87
    Moussaka, '97 94
    Moussaka Casserole, '79 179
    Noodle Bake, Hamburger-, '81 140
    Noodles Casserole, Beef-and-, '84 72
    Pasta Bake, Layered, '04 326
    Pasta Italiano, '01 41
    Pastitsio, '87 12; '88 11; '99 167
    Pizza Bake, Upside-Down, '98 224
    Pizza Casserole, '88 273; '89 181
    Pizza Casserole, Beefy, '05 217
    Pizza Casserole, Microwave, '89 M248
    Pizza Casserole, Quick, '83 266
    Potato Casserole, Beefy, '03 218
    Rotini, Baked, '01 185
    Sausage Casserole, Ground Beef and, '80 260
    Seashell-Provolone Casserole, '80 189
    Shells, Spinach-Stuffed, '99 64
    Sour Cream-Noodle Bake, '79 55
    Spaghetti and Beef Casserole, '79 129
    Spaghetti-and-Spinach Casserole, '02 199
    Spaghetti, Casserole, '95 132
    Spinach and Beef Casserole, '79 192
    Spinach-Beef-Macaroni Casserole, '83 313
    Stroganoff Casserole, '98 48
    Taco Bake, '97 326
    Taco Beef-Noodle Bake, '81 141
    Taco Casserole, '80 33
    Taco Squares, Deep-Dish, '91 88
    Tamale, Mozzarella, '95 70
    Tortilla Bake, Texas, '94 285
    Vegetable Casserole, Beefy, '79 248
    Vegetable Chow Mein Casserole, Beef-and-, '83 313
    Ziti, Baked, '05 214
    Zucchini-Beef Bake, '86 146
Chiles Rellenos Egg Rolls, '86 296

Chili

Basic Chili, '82 M11; '93 326
Basic Chili Embellished, '93 327
Basic Chili Goes Southwest, '93 326
Bean Chili, Spicy 3-, '03 291
Bean Chili, Three-, '00 34
Before-and-After Burner, Roy's, '89 316
Big-Batch Chili, '04 242
Biscuit Bowl, Chili in a, '98 224
Cheese-Topped Chili, '82 M11
Cheesy Chili, '82 310
Chili, '87 17; '89 143; '93 89; '98 95
Chilly Night Chili, '99 317
Choo-Choo Chili, '89 316
Cincinnati Chili, '96 18
Cincinnati-Style Chili, '00 34
Company Chili, '82 311; '83 30
con Carne, Beef and Sausage Chili, '83 284
con Carne, Chili, '84 72
Con Carne, Chili, '03 19
con Carne, Favorite Chili, '86 293
con Carne, Quick-and-Easy Chili, '86 2
Dip, Chili, '89 47
Double-Meat Chili, '79 269; '80 12
Easy Chili, '82 310; '83 30; '02 299
Easy Texas Chili, '90 201
Five-Ingredient Chili, '95 212
Friday Night Chili, '86 228
Game-Day Chili, '00 238
Greek Chili, '95 16
Hominy Bake, Chili, '81 282; '82 58
Hot Dog Chili, '04 199
Hot Texas Chili, '80 222; '81 77
Hotto Lotto Chili, '89 316
I-Cious, Chili-, '89 315
"In-the-Red Chili over "Rolling-in-Dough" Biscuits,
    '92 80
Kielbasa Chili, Hearty, '91 28

Lolly's Pop Chili, '89 316
Lunchtime Chili, '81 230
Meaty Chili, '81 282; '82 58
Meaty Chili with Beans, '85 250
Mexican Chili, '89 18
Noodles, Chili with, '81 282; '82 57
Now, Thatsa Chili, '95 16
Pastry Cups, Chili in, '90 68
Potato Chili, Savory, '83 284
Potatoes, Chili-Topped, '83 3; '98 M289
Quick-and-Easy Chili, '92 20
Quick and Simple Chili, '81 282; '82 58
Quick Chili, '83 283
Ranch Chili and Beans, '79 270; '80 11
Red Bean Chili, '02 20
Red Bean Chili, Slow-Cooker, '02 20
Rice, Chili with, '82 M11
Roundup Chili, '79 269; '80 12
Sauce, Chili Meat, '83 4
Sausage-Beef Chili, '86 232
Sausage Chili, Beefy, '82 M11
Simple Chili, '79 269; '80 11
Slow Cooker Cincinnati-Style Chili, '00 34
Speedy Chili, '92 66
Spiced Chili, Hot, '83 214
Spicy Chili, Old-Fashioned, '79 269; '80 11
Supper, Hot Chili, '99 279
Texas-Style Chili, '82 311; '83 30
Tex-Mex Chili, '83 26
Tomato Chili, Chunky Beef 'n', '05 20
Tree-Hunt Chili, '87 292
Chimichangas, Baked Spicy Beef, '97 319
Chimichangas, Traditional Spicy Beef, '97 319
Cornbread, Beefy Jalapeño, '82 142
Cornbread, Cheesy Beef, '81 242
Cornbread Tamale Bake, '79 163
Crêpes, Italian, '90 157
Crêpes, Sherried Beef, '85 M29
Crêpes, Southwestern Cornbread, '98 42
Curried Beef and Rice, '88 164
Dinner, Beef-and-Garbanzo, '84 31
Dinner, Beef-and-Lima Bean, '84 292
Dinner, Beef-Cabbage, '81 179
Dinner, Beefy Sausage, '80 M9
Dinner, Black-Eyed Pea Skillet, '86 6
Dinner, Fiesta, '85 110
Dinner, Ground Beef Skillet, '82 60
Dinner, Mexican Beef-and-Rice, '88 199
Dip, Beef-and-Spinach, '99 65
Dip, Creamy Beef-and-Pasta Sauce, '01 108
Dip, Hot Chile-Beef, '83 218
Dip, Meaty Cheese, '82 59; '92 160
Dip, Quick Nacho, '90 168
Dip, Spicy Cheese-Beef, '02 58
Dip, Tostada, '84 206
Dumplings, Steamed Sesame, '97 208
Eggplant, Baked Stuffed, '81 133
Eggplant, Beefy Stuffed, '81 204
Eggplant, Cheesy Stuffed, '79 188
Empanadas, '92 156
Empanadas, Meaty, '05 138
Enchiladas. See also BEEF, GROUND/Casseroles.
  Green Chile Enchiladas, '02 188
  Hot and Saucy Enchiladas, '81 141; '82 6
  Skillet Enchiladas, '82 89
Fiesta, '87 180
Filet Mignon, Mock, '80 81
Filet Mignon Patties, Mock, '82 M68
Fillets, Poor Boy, '82 106
Filling, Beef, '80 81
Filling, Blue-Corn Crêpes with Beef,
  '97 197
Flips, Pea, '80 7
Gumbo, Carolina, '95 70

Gumbo, Ground Beef, '87 283
Gumbo Joes, '88 158
Hamburgers
  Apple-Bacon Burgers, '99 202
  Apple Burgers, '86 137
  au Poivre Blanc, Burgers, '87 186
  Bacon Burgers, Cheesy, '81 29
  Barbecued Burgers, '82 168; '89 164
  Beefburger on Buns, '84 71
  Beerburgers, '79 129
  Big Juicy Burgers, Barbara's, '03 M138; '04 M178
  Blue Cheese Burgers, '89 M66
  Brie-Mushroom Burgers, '95 128
  Burgundy Burgers, '80 156
  Caramelized Onions, Beef Burgers with, '98 143
  Cheeseburger Biscuits, '79 194
  Cheeseburger Loaves, '86 19
  Cheese Burgers, Beef-and-, '96 139
  Cheeseburgers, Fried Green Tomato, '94 138
  Cheeseburgers, Inside Out, '99 202
  Cheeseburgers, Mini-, '97 203
  Cheesy Beef Burgers, '83 217
  Chili Burgers, Open-Face, '81 24; '82 31; '83 33
  Cocktail Burgers, Saucy, '83 217
  Cracked Pepper Patties, '89 M131
  Deluxe, Burgers, '84 125
  Dill Pickle Rémoulade, Beef Burgers with, '04 310
  Favorite Burgers, '89 165
  Garden Herb Burgers, '01 136
  Glorified Hamburgers, '81 73
  Grilled Hamburgers, '93 198
  Grilled Hamburgers, Flavorful, '81 110
  Grilled Hamburgers, Spicy, '98 158
  Gyro Burgers with Tahini Sauce, '03 183
  Hawaiian, Beefburgers, '86 137
  Italian Burgers, '00 326
  Italian-Style Burgers, '05 180
  Jalapeño-Stuffed Burgers with Roasted Bell Pepper
    Ketchup, '97 318
  Marmalade-Glazed Beef Patties, '01 136
  Mexicali Beef Patties, '86 137
  Mexicali, Hamburgers, '93 217
  Mushroom Burgers, '89 164
  Nutty Burgers, '87 185
  Old-Fashioned Hamburgers, '79 149
  Oven Burgers, '83 130
  Party Burgers, '83 164; '84 39
  Patties, Deviled-Beef, '87 22
  Patties, Hamburger, '82 M172
  Pepper Burgers with Caramelized Onions, '00 218
  Pineapple Burgers, '82 169
  Pizza Burger, '87 185
  Pizza Burgers, '80 M201; '81 73
  Pizza Burgers, All-American, '92 148
  Pizza Burgers, Easy, '82 190
  Sauce, Hamburgers with Tomato, '81 73
  Saucy Burgers, '80 93
  Saucy Hamburgers, Quick, '82 60
  Sausage Burgers, '83 212
  Seasoned Burgers, '85 158
  Seasoned Hamburgers, '84 230
  Seasoned Stuffed Burgers, '86 136
  Sour Cream Burgers, Grilled, '87 287
  Spinach Burgers, '00 26
  Spirals, Burger, '94 139
  Sprouts, Burgers with, '89 164
  Steak, Hamburger, '99 45
  Steak-House Burgers, '87 186
  Steaks, Company Hamburger, '82 169
  Steaks, Smothered Hamburger, '00 289
  Steaks with Mustard Sauce, Hamburger, '84 230
  Stuffed Border Burgers, '04 127
  Stuffed Burgers, '85 159
  Stuffed Burgers, Spicy Cheddar-, '05 163

  Stuffed Hamburger Steaks, Mushroom-, '99 202
  Stuffed Southwestern-Style Burgers, '99 201
  Superburgers, '79 89
  Super Hamburgers, '79 129
  Super Supper Burgers, '82 110
  Surprise Burgers, '82 169
  Sweet-and-Savory Burgers, '03 163
  Sweet-and-Sour Burgers, '90 128
  Taco Burgers, '98 224
  Tahiti Burgers, '85 179
  Teriyaki Burgers, '81 72
  Teriyaki, Hamburgers, '89 309; '99 332
  Teriyaki Hamburgers, '94 138
  Tortilla Burgers, '94 138
  Triple-Layer Burgers, '89 165
  Vegetable Burgers, '89 164
  Vegetable Burgers, Beef-and-, '84 125
  Vegetable Burgers, Beefy, '98 143
  Venison Burgers, '87 304
Italian-Style Meat and Potatoes, '03 97
Kheema, Indian, '81 226
Kielbasa, '92 242
Lasagna
  Beefy Lasagna, '80 81
  Bun, Lasagna in a, '90 176
  Cheesy Lasagna, '82 224; '88 299
  Cups, Lasagna, '04 293
  Easy Lasagna, '92 M197; '93 M24
  Egg-Noodle Lasagna, '04 219
  Ellie's Lasagna, '02 186
  Extra-Easy Lasagna, '00 326
  Ground Sirloin Lasagna, '03 143
  Lasagna, '82 119; '83 M6; '98 95
  Light Lasagna, '95 212
  Mexican Lasagna, '89 63; '01 282
  Microwave Lasagna, '96 M225
  Noodles Lasagna, Lots of, '91 M127
  Quick Lasagna, '84 220
  Quick 'n Easy Lasagna, '80 M10
  Simple Lasagna, '81 188
  South-of-the-Border Lasagna, '84 31
  Spinach Lasagna, Cheesy, '83 204
  Supreme, Lasagna, '92 198; '93 24
  Taco Lasagna, Fiesta, '05 140
  Tex-Mex Lasagna, '05 58
  Two, Lasagna for, '81 91
  Vintage Lasagna, '79 194
  White Lasagna, Gourmet, '96 225
Log, Stuffed Beef, '79 71
Macaroni, Cheeseburger, '02 119
Macaroni, Easy Beef and, '02 188
Macaroni, Ground Beef and, '85 218
Macaroni, Skillet Beef and, '82 130
Madras, Beef, '87 284
Manicotti, Quick, '79 6
Manicotti, Saucy Stuffed, '83 288
Manicotti, Special, '88 50
Meatballs
  Bacon-Wrapped Meatballs, '79 81
  Baked Meatballs, '02 25
  Barbecued Meatballs, Oven, '82 233
  Brandied Meatballs, '83 78
  Burgundy-Bacon Meatballs, '80 283
  Chafing Dish Meatballs, '81 260
  Charleston Press Club Meatballs, '93 129
  Chestnut Meatballs, '79 110
  Chinese Meatballs, '83 116; '87 194
  Cocktail Meatballs, '79 63, 207
  Cranberry Meatballs, '05 310
  Creole, Meatball-Okra, '83 156
  Creole, Meatballs, '82 233
  Espanol, Meatballs, '82 110
  Flavorful Meatballs, '84 206
  Golden Nugget Meatballs, '82 233

BEEF, GROUND, Meatballs
(continued)

Gravy, Meatballs in, '79 136
Hawaiian Meatballs, '85 86
Hawaiian Meatballs, Tangy, '79 129
Heidelberg, Beef Balls, '83 164; '84 39
Horseradish Dressing, Meatballs and Vegetables
   with, '91 32
Kebabs, Meatball, '95 192
Marmalade-Glazed Meatballs, '01 136
Meatballs, '89 237
Paprikash with Rice, Meatballs, '85 31
Pineapple and Peppers, Meatballs with, '90 145
Pizza Meatballs, '85 86
Polynesian Meatballs, '80 207
Red Delicious Meatballs, '85 85
Red Sauce and Meatballs, '04 17
Royal Meatballs, '87 268; '88 102; '89 67
Sandwiches, Open-Faced Meatball, '99 239
Sandwich, Giant Meatball, '92 196
Saucy Meatballs, '85 68; '90 122
Saucy Party Meatballs, '80 149
Sauerbraten Meatballs, '85 85
Soup, Mexican Meatball, '98 315
Spaghetti-and-Herb Meatballs, '84 75
Spaghetti with Meatballs, '81 38
Spiced Meatballs, '79 284
Spicy Holiday Meatballs, '01 238
Spicy Meatballs and Sausage, '79 163
Stew, Meatball, '79 198
Stroganoff, Meatball, '81 297; '02 50
Stroganoff, Mushroom-Meatball, '85 85
Swedish Meatballs, '80 80; '86 256
Sweet-and-Sour Meatballs, '82 233; '86 240; '99 325
Sweet-and-Sour Party Meatballs, '79 233
Tamale Balls, Tangy, '89 60
Tamale Meatballs, '80 194
Zesty Meatballs, '80 250

Meat Loaf
Alabama Meat Loaf, '04 188
All-American Meat Loaf, '92 341; '93 46
Barbecued Beef Loaves, Individual, '95 242
Barbecued Meat Loaf, '80 60; '81 275; '84 50;
   '87 216
Basic Meat Loaf, '88 M14
Blue Cheese Meat Loaf Roll, '93 247
Cheeseburger Loaf, '81 236, 276
Cheeseburger Meat Loaf, '03 204
Cheesy Meat Roll, '82 136
Chili Meat Loaf, '81 275
Corny Meat Loaf, '86 68
Crunchy Meat Loaf Oriental, '79 212
Curried Meat Loaf, '86 43
Easy Meat Loaf, '88 M214; '95 125; '97 24
Elegant Meat Loaf, '89 243
Family-Style Meat Loaf, '93 18
Fennel Meat Loaf, '88 46
French Market Meat Loaf, '02 33
German Meat Loaf, '87 216
Glazed Beef Loaf, '86 19
Gonzales Meat Loaf, '04 206
Green Chile-Tomato Gravy, Meat Loaf with, '05 42
Herb-and-Veggie Meat Loaf, '05 161
Hurry-Up Meat Loaf, '82 21
Hurry-Up Meat Loaves, '88 15
Individual Meat Loaves, '81 279; '82 24; '83 154;
   '92 229; '00 214
Italian Meat Loaf, '79 187
Ketchup-and-Bacon-Topped Meat Loaf, Sweet,
   '03 203
Meat Loaf, '81 170; '89 109
Mexicali Meat Loaf, '81 275

Mexican Meat Loaf, '87 217
Mexican Meat Loaves, Mini, '02 90
Mini Alabama Meat Loaves, '04 188
Miniature Meat Loaves, '85 24
Moist-and-Saucy Meat Loaf, '99 270
Mozzarella-Layered Meat Loaf, '79 71
My-Ami's Meat Loaf, '94 229
Old-Fashioned Meat Loaf, '05 95
Oriental Meat Loaf, '81 M122; '83 M194
Parsleyed Meat Loaf, '83 35
Parsley Meat Loaf, '87 22
Pineapple Loaves, Individual, '81 M121
Pizza Meat Loaf, Cheesy, '81 M121
Roll, Meat Loaf, '79 129
Sandwich, Meat Loaf, '01 210
Saucy Meat Loaves, '79 186
Savory Meat Loaf, '87 216
Southwestern Meat Loaf, '93 248
Southwestern Roll with Cilantro Hollandaise Sauce,
   '99 16
Spaghetti Sauce, Meat Loaves with, '03 204
Special Meat Loaf, '89 70
Spicy Meat Loaf, '79 71
Spinach Meat Loaf, '96 131
Sprout Meat Loaf, '85 51
Stuffed Beef Log, '79 71
Stuffed Meat Loaf, '79 187
Stuffed Meat Loaf, Rolled, '80 80
Summer Meat Loaf, '01 162
Sun-Dried Tomatoes and Herbs, Meat Loaf with,
   '92 192
Supreme, Meat Loaf, '92 33
Swedish Meat Loaf, '81 M121
Sweet 'n' Saucy Meat Loaf, '01 210
Tasty Meat Loaf, '83 213
Teriyaki Loaves, Mini, '98 224
Teriyaki Meat Loaf, '98 224; '03 172
Teriyaki Meat Loaf, Mini-, '90 69
Tex-Mex Meat Loaf for Two, '90 234
Tomato Gravy, Meat Loaf with, '00 330
Tomato Sauce, Meat Loaf with Chunky, '95 264
Triple Meat Loaf, '79 186
Vegetable Loaf, Beef-, '79 164
Vegetable Meat Loaf, '85 M29
Wellington, Meat Loaf, '79 186; '87 284
Wrap, Meat Loaf in a, '89 122
Mexican Dinner, Quick, '98 224
Mexican Stack-Up, '95 69
Mexicorn Main Dish, '96 189
Mix, Ground Beef, '84 71
Mix, Ground Meat, '89 143
Moussaka, '87 166; '90 68
Moussaka, Corn, '87 190
Muffins, Barbecue, '96 246
Mushrooms, Stuffed, '83 13
Noodle Dinner, Beefy, '81 179
Noodles, Easy Beef and, '83 288
Omelet, Beefy Vegetable, '83 188
Omelet con Carne, Tex-Mex, '81 209
Pasta, Easy Skillet Beef 'n', '02 63
Pasta, One-Pot, '05 202
Patties, Foo Yong, '80 223
Peppers, Beefed-Up, '82 186
Peppers, Beef-Stuffed, '84 154; '85 146;
   '91 M127
Peppers, Beefy Stuffed Green, '81 86
Peppers for Two, Stuffed, '80 84
Peppers, Mexican Green, '80 65
Peppers, Stuffed, '81 239; '83 66
Peppers, Stuffed Green, '03 62
Peppers Stuffed with Beef, '84 72
Picadillo II, '93 72
Picadillo, Lettuce-Wrapped, '03 193
Picadillo (Spanish Hash), '91 87

Picadillo (Spicy Beef over Rice), '80 193; '84 118; '85 57
Picadillo Tarts, '91 279
Pies
Broccoli-Beef Pie, '83 196
Burrito Pie, Mexican, '87 287
Cheese-Beef Pie, '85 33
Cheeseburger Pie, '89 121
Cheeseburger Pie, Jack-O'-Lantern, '00 234
Continental Meat Pie, '95 256; '96 75
Cornbread Pie, Beef-and-Onion, '01 298
Corn Burger Pie, '83 156
Country Pie, '83 155
Enchilada Pie, '83 155
Fried Beef Pies, '96 108
Hamburger Pie, '81 92; '84 13
Hamburger Pie, Deep-Dish, '00 334
Italian Meat Pie, '01 297
Mexicali Meat Pie, '81 194
Natchitoches Meat Pies, '84 21; '91 241
Old-Fashioned Meat Pie, '82 110
Potato Pie, Meat-and-, '84 23
Savory Beef Pies, '01 230
Shepherd Pie, '83 116
Shepherd's Pie, '00 55
Shepherd's Pie, Shortcut Greek, '05 238
Sombrero Pie, '81 140
Spaghetti Pie, '81 32
Spaghetti Pie, Weeknight, '95 312
Taco Pie, '88 256
Taco Pie, Crescent, '80 80
Taco Pie, Double-Crust, '88 272; '89 180
Taco Pies, Individual, '82 M282
Vegetable-Beef Pies, '80 286
Pintos, Texas Souper, '98 51
Pitas, Curried Beef, '85 220
Pizza, Best Ever Homemade, '80 233
Pizza-Burger Snacks, '84 30
Pizza, Cheeseburger, '97 318
Pizza, Cheesy Ground Beef, '03 62
Pizza Cups, '81 215
Pizza, Double Cheesy Beef-and-Sausage, '86 77
Pizza Horns, '89 214
Pizza, Quick Hamburger, '85 243
Pizzas, Five-Ring, '96 180
Pizza Supreme, '81 214
Pizza, Taco, '98 176
Pizza, Tostada, '81 16; '82 13
Pizza, Upside-Down, '91 185
Potatoes, Taco-Topped, '93 M18
Quiche, Green Chile, '83 31
Ravioli, Homemade, '87 230
Rice, Arabic, '94 200
Rice, Dirty, '03 147
Rice, Picadillo, '98 237
Rice, Spanish, '81 51
Rice, Spiced Beef and, '84 285
Rice, Spicy Beef and, '83 231
Rolls, Italian Meat, '86 137
Rolls, Spicy Beef, '85 110
Roulades, Beef, '80 80
Salad, Beef-and-Lime Rice, '03 172
Salad, Beefy Taco, '03 128
Salad Cups, Taco, '85 M29
Salad, Dude Ranch, '80 15
Salad in a Shell, Mexican, '86 4
Salad, Mexican, '81 36
Salad, Mexican Chef, '85 84; '92 64
Salad, Mexican Dinner, '98 330
Salad, Mexican Olive, '85 84
Salad, Mexi-Pea, '81 7
Salad, Party Taco, '97 19
Salad, Spicy Chili, '86 71
Salad, Spicy Taco, '87 287
Salad Supper, Mexican, '82 9; '83 68

Salad, Taco, '79 56; '83 145; '84 221; '85 84; '90 20
Salisbury Steak Deluxe, '81 170
Salisbury Steak, Tex-Mex, '05 204
Salisbury Steak with Mushroom Gravy, '03 202
Sandwiches, Barbecue Beef, '01 136
Sandwiches, Barbecued Beef, '81 25; '82 31; '83 34
Sandwiches, Bavarian Pita, '83 31
Sandwiches, Beef-Eater, '86 72
Sandwiches, Hearty Pocket, '80 93
Sandwiches, Hot Pita, '83 217; '87 M6
Sandwiches, Open-Face Pizza, '82 3
Sauce, Ground Beef-Tomato, '05 290
Sauce, Italian, '90 67
Sauce, Italian Meat, '83 193; '01 160
Sauce, Szechuan Noodles with Spicy Beef, '97 95
Sausage, Summer, '99 85
Shells, Cheesy Beef-Stuffed, '83 217
Shells, Mexican Stuffed, '91 55
Skillet, Hamburger-Rice, '00 236
Skillet, Vegetable-Beef, '86 172
Slice, French Beef, '79 125
Sloppy Joe Cups, '98 204
Sloppy Joe Dogs, '85 192
Sloppy Joe Pocket Sandwiches, '81 200
Sloppy Joes, '81 279; '82 24; '83 153; '89 143; '91 172; '02 188
Sloppy Joes, Easy, '82 31, 278; '83 34
Sloppy Joes, Pocket, '85 M328
Sloppy Joe Squares, '97 95
Sloppy Joes, Simple, '82 130
Sloppy Joes, Super, '83 130
Sloppy José Sandwiches with Cilantro Slaw, '05 324
Snacks, Beefy Party, '80 249
Soup, Beef-and-Barley Vegetable, '89 31
Soup, Beefy Black-Eyed, '85 6
Soup, Beefy Vegetable, '79 113; '84 M38
Soup, Cheeseburger, '04 298
Soup, Chunky Italian, '99 20
Soup, Hamburger, '80 263
Soup, Italian-Style Beef-and-Pepperoni, '00 316
Soup, Mexican Meatball, '98 315
Soup, Quick Beefy Vegetable, '80 25
Soup, Quick Italian Beef and Vegetable, '96 235
Soup, Spicy Vegetable-Beef, '88 11
Soup, Taco, '94 225; '99 36
Soup, Tamale, '95 213
Soup, Vegetable-Beef, '99 219
Soup, Vegetable-Burger, '82 6

Spaghetti. *See also* BEEF, GROUND/Casseroles, Meatballs, Pies.
All-in-One Spaghetti, '98 295
Black-Eyed Pea Spaghetti, '81 7
Easy Spaghetti, '83 M317; '84 72; '92 66
Italian Spaghetti, Real, '81 233
Marzetti's Spaghetti, '99 85
Meaty Spaghetti, '82 19
Mushrooms, Spicy Spaghetti with, '85 2
One-Pot Spaghetti, '00 58
Pepperoni Spaghetti, Quick, '88 40
Pizzazz, Spaghetti with, '80 85
Sauce, Beer Spaghetti, '85 13
Sauce for 4, Easy Spaghetti Meat, '92 244
Sauce for Spaghetti, Meat, '00 256
Sauce for 25, Easy Spaghetti Meat, '92 245
Sauce, Herbed Spaghetti, '85 13
Sauce, Quick Spaghetti and Meat, '94 64
Sauce, Sicilian Spaghetti, '03 62
Sauce, Spaghetti with Meat, '02 188
Sauce, Thick Spaghetti, '84 118
Thick-and-Spicy Spaghetti, '83 287
Zucchini Spaghetti, '83 160
Squash, Beef-Stuffed, '83 134
Steak, Matt's Chicken-Fried, '97 25
Steak, Spanish, '80 80

Stew, Camp, '02 42
Stew, Campeche Bay Rib-Tickling, '89 317
Stew, Hamburger Oven, '84 4
Stew, Mixed Vegetable, '84 13
Stew, Quick Beef, '86 302
Sticks, Beef, '93 331
Stroganoff, Easy Hamburger, '79 208
Stroganoff, Ground Beef, '84 71
Stroganoff, Hamburger, '82 108, 110
Stroganoff, Quickie, '81 200
Stromboli, '87 283
Supper, Beef-and-Bean, '82 2
Supper, Beef-and-Eggplant, '84 291
Supper, Beef-and-Vegetable, '03 219
Supper, Oriental Beef, '79 192
Supper, Quick Skillet, '84 69
Supreme, Beef, '83 196
Taco Dinner Mac and Cheese, '05 208
Taco Joes, '91 167
Tacoritos, '90 133
Taco Rolls, Chinese, '95 339
Tacos, '80 196
Tacos, Basic, '83 199
Tacos, Corn Chip, '81 67
Tacos, Easy, '96 159
Tacos, Easy Skillet, '04 180
Tacos, Jiffy, '83 M318
Tacos, Microwave, '88 M213
Tacos, Soft Beef, '91 88
Tacos Wrapidos, '03 172
Taco Tassies, '95 339
Taco Teasers, '01 134
Texas Straw Hat, '85 293
Torta Mexican Style, '89 122
Tostada Compuestas, '81 194
Tostadas, Crispy, '83 2
Tostadas, Super, '83 199
Turnovers, Meat, '86 326
Wontons, Tex-Mex, '87 196
Zucchini, Beef-Stuffed, '86 M139

BEETS
Apples, Beets and, '80 137; '88 155
Asparagus, Roasted-Beet, and Goat Cheese Salad, '02 96
Aspic, Beet, '90 123
Borscht, Crawfish, '92 84
Borscht, Ruby Red, '83 176
Cake, Chocolate Beet, '80 40
Cake with Almond Topping, Beet, '86 200
Chilled Beets and Cauliflower, '80 137
Chips, Beet, '97 229
Creamy Beets, '80 136
Deviled Beets, '84 217; '86 252
Eggs, Marbleized Garlic-Cheese-Stuffed, '96 91
Fritters, Beet, '96 36
Fruited Beets, '97 28
Glazed Beets, Ginger-Marmalade, '93 35
Glazed Beets, Orange-, '81 167; '85 289; '86 187; '99 24
Glazed Beets, Strawberry-, '83 234
Glazed Fresh Beets, '81 167
Glazed Orange Beets, '02 138
Greens, Beets 'n', '95 179
Harvard Beets, '83 M195
Ivy League Beets, '84 122
Marinated Beets, Green Beans, and Carrots, '88 162
Orange Beets, '91 219
Orange Beets, Spicy, '94 280
Orange-Ginger Beets, '80 137
Pickled Beets, '79 276; '81 216; '87 163; '97 229; '02 138
Pickled Beets, Easy, '80 137
Pickles, Beet, '81 210
Pineapple, Beets with, '79 249; '82 204

Relish, Beet, '84 179
Relish, Colorful Beet, '85 136
Relish, Horseradish, '01 60
Rice Ring with Beets, '79 225
Salad, Apple-Beet, '91 237
Salad, Asparagus, Roasted Beet, and Goat Cheese, '03 98
Salad, Beet, Apple, and Walnut, '98 269
Salad, Beet-Nut, '79 74
Salad, Fresh Beet, '02 236
Salad, Marinated Beet, '83 216
Salad Mold, Beet, '82 267
Salad, Orange-and-Beet, '88 43
Salad, Pickled Beet, '83 234
Salad, Red-and-Green, '90 55
Salad, Tangy Beet, '86 199
Salad with Orange Vinaigrette, Roasted Beet-and-Sugared Walnut, '97 229
Slaw, "Think Pink," '94 247
Soup, Potato-Beet, '88 156
Sour Cream Dressing, Beets with, '88 M295
Spiced Beets, '79 22
Spread, Beet-and-Pecan Sandwich, '99 274
Stuffed Beets, '88 155
Stuffed Beets, Blue Cheese-, '88 211
Stuffed Beets, Potato-, '83 234
Sweet-and-Sour Beets, '81 167; '82 22; '89 314
Vinaigrette, Beet, '97 229
Winter Beets, '02 283

BEVERAGES. *See also* **COFFEE, EGGNOG, TEA.**
Alcoholic
Almond-Flavored Liqueur, '81 287
Amaretto, '90 272
Amaretto Breeze, '83 172
Amaretto Slush, '90 322; '95 90
Apricot Brandy Slush, '91 278
Apricot Slush, '93 205
Aztec Gold, '99 160
Banana Flip, '83 303
Banana Kabana, '86 316
Batida, Citrus, '02 274
Bay Bloodies, '93 268
Bellini, '01 89
Bellinis, '88 77
Bellinis, Apricot, '99 145; '05 96
Bellinis, Frosted, '97 122
Bellinis, Mint, '02 136
Bloody Mary, '80 221
Bloody Mary Bowl, '99 268
Bloody Mary, Easy, '84 115
Bloody Marys, '79 33, 38; '80 51; '04 68
Bloody Marys, Eye-Opener, '82 48
Bloody Marys, Overnight, '81 270
Bloody Marys, Pitcher, '81 198
Bloody Marys, Spicy, '87 173; '90 207
Blueberry Cordial, '95 142
Blue Woo-Woo, '94 226
Bole, '97 245
Bourbon Blizzard, '92 287
Bourbon, Hot Buttered, '97 17
Bourbon Slush, '84 58
Bourbon Slush, Summertime, '81 101
Brandy Alexander, '92 283
Brandy Cream, '84 312; '00 271
Brandy Slush, '89 110
Brandy Velvet, '89 170
Burgundy Bowl, Sparkling, '83 276
Champagne Delight, '83 304
Champagne Fruit Slush, '90 322
Champagne Shooters, '02 280
Champagne with Orange Juice, '91 71
Chimayo Cocktails, '02 118
Chocolate, Flaming Brandied, '80 M290
Chocolate, Hot Laced Marshmallow, '93 53

Christmas Blossom, '99 321
Cider, Cinnamon Winter, '95 337
Cider, December, '91 260
Cider, Hot Burgundy, '96 306
Cider, Hot Mexican, '87 213
Cider, Hot Mulled, '84 323
Cider Nog, Hot, '98 241
Cider, Red Apple, '80 259
Cider Sour, Bourbon, '98 242
Cider, Spirited Apple, '96 214
Clam Diggers, '91 63
Cocktails, Sea Breeze, '97 161
Coconut Frost, Pink, '79 174; '80 128
Coconut-Pineapple Drink, '83 172
Cranapple Glogg, Hot, '90 22
Cranapple Wine, '90 272
Cranberry Cooler, '86 229; '01 93
Cranberry-Rum Slush, '84 259
Cranberry-Vodka Refresher, '91 210
Cranberry Wine Cup, '85 23
Cricket, '89 289
Cruising Drink, '00 167
Daiquiris, Cranberry, '81 245
Daiquiris, Creamy Strawberry, '91 66
Daiquiris, Freezer Lime, '79 141
Daiquiris, Mint, '89 157
Daiquiris, Peach, '90 322
Daiquiris, Strawberry, '90 125; '98 99
Daiquiri, Strawberry, '81 156
Daiquiritas, '82 160
Daiquiri, Watermelon, '95 143; '98 165; '04 172
Dessert, After Dinner-Drink, '82 100
Dessert Drink, Creamy, '86 131
Dessert Drink, Simply Super, '83 303
"French 75," Wayne's, '05 282
Frosty Sours, '81 156
Fruit 'ritas, '94 157
Funky Monkey, '99 161
Fuzz Buzz, '82 160
Game-Cocktails, '93 214
Gin Cooler, Sparkling, '90 272
Ginger Beer, '84 159
Golden Dream, '82 100
Grapefruit Drink, '95 238
Hot Apple Pie, '99 321
Hot Chocolate Deluxe, '90 272; '00 33
Hot Chocolate, Tennessee, '96 214
Kahlúa Beverage Sipper, '99 27
Kahlúa Hummer, '91 176
Kahlúa Smoothie, '87 242
Kahlúa Velvet Frosty, '82 244
King Alfonso, '80 259
Lemonade, Claret, '93 72
Lemonade, Hot Buttered, '88 208
Lemonade, Loaded, '01 93
Lemon Cooler, '82 48
Limeade, Pineapple, '01 235
Limeade, Rio Grande, '01 186
Lime Fizz, '81 172
Liqueur Sampler, Miniature, '95 332
Magnolia Blossoms, '87 72
Magnolias, '82 196
Margarita Granita, '02 49
Margaritas, '92 210; '93 273
Margaritas, Blue, '02 143
Margaritas, Frances's, '02 118
Margaritas, Frosted, '84 115
Margaritas, Frosty, '83 172
Margaritas, Frozen Blueberry, '05 179
Margaritas, Lemon-Lime, '94 227

Margaritas, Mango, '96 126
Margaritas, Merry, '04 275
Margaritas, Orange-Lime, '97 140
Margaritas, Pitcher, '83 175
Margaritas Supreme, Frozen, '80 160
Margaritas, Tangy, '01 93
Margaritas, Tart, '85 153
Margarita, Strawberry, '04 107
Margaritas, Watermelon, '02 185
Martini, Individual Chocolate, '02 88
Martini, Mint Julep, '04 106
Martinis, Chocolate, '02 88
Melon Ball Cooler, '86 131
Mimosa, '04 106
Mimosa Hawaiian, '85 44
Mimosas, '86 91
Minted Delight, '87 107
Mint Julep, '97 120; '02 49
Mint Julep, Classic, '03 129
Mint Juleps, '81 155; '82 41; '85 40; '90 81; '04 94
Mint Juleps, Apple, '97 120
Mix, Bloody Mary, '89 110
Mix, Hot Wine, '81 287
Mix, Mulled Wine Spice, '85 266
Mocha Chocolate Fluff, '89 170
Mocha Deluxe Hot Drink, '82 289
Mocha Polka, '89 171
Mocha, Spirited Hot, '91 M260
Mojito, '05 295
Mojito, A Ritzy, '03 171
New Orleans, Mr. Funk of, '95 57
Oklahoma Sunrise, '87 67
Old-Fashioneds, '86 270
Old-Fashioned Slush, '93 340
Orange Blossom Flips, '80 51
Orange Brandy Smash, '99 30
Orange-Champagne Cocktail, '79 39
Orange Liqueur, '81 287
Orange Milk Shake, '84 166
Orange Thing, '04 290
Peach Frosty, '81 156
Peach Petals, '90 104
Peach Smash, '88 161
Peppermint Flip, Hot, '86 329
Peppermint Patti, The Peabody, '99 321
Pimm's Cup, '96 214
Piña Coladas, '95 203; '96 127
Piña Coladas, Frosty, '83 176
Piña Coladas, Luscious, '81 134
Piña Colada Slush, '95 90
Pineapple-Strawberry Slush, '94 227
Pink Palace, '93 293
Pirate's Painkiller, '99 161
Plum Slush, '84 139
Pomegranate-Champagne Cocktail, '05 282
Punch, Amaretto, '91 277
Punch, Anytime Wine, '79 232
Punch, Autumn Harvest, '96 277
Punch, Berry-Colada, '96 277
Punch, Bloody Mary, '04 106
Punch, Bourbon, '92 208
Punch, Bourbon-Citrus, '94 227
Punch, Bourbon-Tea, '87 57
Punch, Brandy Milk, '85 44; '88 83
Punch, Brandy Slush, '87 72
Punch, Caribbean, '95 173
Punch, Champagne, '85 153, 257; '86 101; '96 277;
    '98 310; '99 30; '03 118, 141
Punch, Champagne Blossom, '81 50; '99 290
Punch, Chatham Artillery, '80 121
Punch, Chilly Coffee, '01 64
Punch, Citrus-Wine, '98 197
Punch, Cranapple-Vodka, '87 72
Punch, Cranberry, '85 90

Punch, Cranberry Percolator, '88 248
Punch, Cranberry-Wine, '01 242
Punch, Extra-Kick, '91 209
Punch, Festive, '94 289
Punch, Frozen Margarita, '95 91
Punch, Fruit, '83 52; '02 162
Punch, Fruit Juice-and-Vodka, '96 214
Punch, Fruit Juicy Rum, '91 175
Punch, Gin, '80 160
Punch, Golden Gin, '79 233
Punch, Golden Spiked, '79 285
Punch, Health-Kick, '80 174
Punch, Hot Cranberry, '84 41
Punch, Hot Molasses-Milk, '86 329
Punch, Hot Pineapple, '82 264
Punch, Hot Spiced Rum, '96 214
Punch, Hot Wine, '85 265
Punch, Hurricane, '00 61
Punch, Irish Coffee-Eggnog, '95 314
Punch, Jefferson County, '86 267
Punch, Lemonade-Bourbon, '95 287
Punch, Lemon Champagne, '94 176
Punch, Lime, '84 58
Punch, Margarita, '05 212
Punch, Milk, '79 38; '02 298
Punch, Mixed Fruit, '95 239
Punch, Mulled Wine, '95 337
Punch, New Orleans Milk, '81 50
Punch, Orange-Lime, '82 160
Punch, Party, '81 265
Punch, Perky Rum, '85 116
Punch, Pimms, '92 167
Punch, Piña Colada, '89 212
Punch, Pineapple, '79 174; '80 128
Punch, Pineapple-Gin, '95 140
Punch, Pink, '96 190
Punch, Poinsettia, '02 251
Punch, Raspberry-Rosé, '87 242
Punch, Red Velvet, '84 289
Punch, Refreshing Champagne, '84 259
Punch, Rum, '85 265
Punch, Southern Fruit, '95 238
Punch, Sparkling Champagne, '84 58
Punch, Sparkling Holiday, '81 290
Punch, Sparkling Orange, '05 170
Punch, Spiced Rum, '86 179
Punch, Spiked Tea, '86 101
Punch, Spirited Fruit, '81 100
Punch, Stormy Petrel Rum Thunder, '93 269
Punch, Strawberry Champagne, '90 315
Punch, Streetcar Champagne, '88 82
Punch, Tropical Fruit, '83 176
Punch, Vodka, '85 265
Punch, Wedding, '86 107
Punch, Whiskey, '90 64; '91 175; '05 276
Punch, Whiskey Sour, '91 209
Punch, Wine, '93 331
Punch, Yacht Club Milk, '89 86
Raspberry Kir, '86 183
Red Roosters, '87 147
Red Ruby, '92 209
Rum, Hot Buttered, '80 259; '82 244; '88 247;
    '96 213
Rum Slush, Easy, '79 174; '80 129
Sangría, '79 186; '81 67, 196; '82 121; '86 214;
    '98 178; '00 122
Sangría, Cranberry, '95 238
Sangría, Easy Citrus, '80 218
Sangría, Easy Frozen, '92 208
Sangría, Garden, '01 100
Sangría, Grapefruit, '89 92
Sangría, Orange, '81 237
Sangría, Pineapple, '91 176
Sangría, Punchy, '80 160

Sangría, Quick, '81 156
Sangría Slush, White, '90 322
Sangría, Spanish, '83 81
Sangría, Teaberry, '87 147
Sangríaa, Texas White, '02 86
Sangría, Three-Fruit, '89 212
Sangría, White, '83 180; '94 289
Sazerac, '04 106
Screwdrivers, '79 33
Sea Mist, '93 167
Sherry Sour, '87 74
Sipper, Creamy Coconut, '02 298
Sipper, Sunset Vodka-Orange, '05 122
Sipper, Sunshine, '86 179
Slush, Lemon-Rum, '00 271; '04 240
Slush, Mexican, '83 176
Slush, Strawberry, '02 185
Slush with a Punch, '90 322
Spritzer, Cranberry, '91 66; '92 265
Spritzer, Fruit, '01 174
Spritzer, Lemon-Mint, '99 175
Spritzer, Pineapple-Grapefruit, '04 143
Spritzers, Bellini, '90 110
Spritzers, Citrus, '91 231; '92 67
Spritzers, Cranberry, '89 213
Spritzers, Grapefruit-White Wine, '96 56; '01 319
Spritzers, Spiced, '86 229
Spritzers, Wine, '81 94
Strawberry-Banana Smoothie, '81 59
Strawberry Mimosa, Sparkling, '88 169
Strawberry Slush, '98 178
Strawberry Sparkler, '99 49
Sunny Morning, '93 295
Sunrise, Bourbon, '01 326
Sunrise, St. Pete, '94 227
Swamp Breeze, '01 146
Syllabub, '81 265; '84 319
Syrup, Bourbon, '03 233
Tangerine Sparkler, '98 54
Tart Caribbean Cooler, '81 134
Tea Juleps, '99 90
Tequila Slush, '83 176
Tequila Sunrise, '83 175
Toddy, Molasses Rum, '91 36
Tomato Bouillon, New Year's, '94 24
Tomato-Orange Juice Cocktail, '83 169
Tomato Sipper, Peppy, '94 227
Vanilla Cream, '97 272
Vodka, Frozen Pink, '89 170
Vodka-Orange Slush, '89 92
Vodka Slush, '88 82
Wassail, '83 311
Wassail, Bourbon, '86 270
Wassail, Four-Fruit, '90 22
Whiskey Sour, '04 107
Whiskey Sours, '03 258
Whiskey Sours, Frozen, '93 176
Whiskey Sours, Frozen Orange-, '92 67
Whiskey Sour Slushies, '04 106
Whiskey Sours, Slushy, '03 258
Whisky Sour Slush, '86 183
Whispers, '86 317
Wine, Christmas Dreams in, '91 260
Wine Cocktail, Citrus, '99 93
Wine Cooler, '82 41
Wine Cooler, Fruited, '86 176
Wine, Hot Mulled, '83 251
Wine, Hot Spiced, '84 41; '03 210
Wine, Mulled, '03 233
Wine Tasting, '95 332
Wine Welcomer, '81 100
Yellow Birds, '90 103
Appleade, Hot Spiced Lemon-, '05 23
Apple-Berry Sparkler, '93 104

Apple Berry Sparkler, '94 100
Apple Cooler, '90 14
Apple Cooler, Minted, '88 169
Apple Juice, Hot, '86 270
Apple Juice, Perky Cinnamon-, '90 22
Apple Juice Shrub, Shenandoah, '79 282
Apple Juice, Sparkling, '95 141
Apple Julep, '86 103, 215
Apricot Bellinis, '99 145
Apricot-Citrus Slush, '88 82
Apricot Cooler, '81 100
Apricot Coolers, '99 29
Apricot Fruit Flip, '91 18
Apricot Mint Cooler, '90 165
Apricot Nectar, Hot, '81 265
Apricot Nectar, Mulled, '86 229
Apricot-Orange-Carrot Cooler, '96 108
Aztec Gold, '99 160
Banana-Berry Flip, '88 215; '89 20
Banana-Chocolate Malt, '89 170
Banana Coolers, '91 308
Banana Crush, '80 88; '83 142
Banana Frostee, '91 66
Banana Nog, '82 290
Banana-Orange Slush, '80 48; '81 155
Banana Slush, '83 56
Banana-Strawberry Frost, '87 199
Berry Shrub, '95 29
Blackberry Breeze, '98 179
Black Russian, Mock, '92 322
Bloodless Mary, '80 146
Breakfast Drink, Yummy, '01 133
Breakfast Eye-Opener, '87 199
Brew, Beach, '91 177
Brew, Holiday, '90 272
Brew, Quilter's, '85 43
Brew, Witch's, '93 244
Bullshots, '86 91
Cantaloupe-Lime Refresher, '01 332
Carambola-Yogurt Calypso, '90 169
Caribbean Cooler, '95 203
Carrot Cooler, '89 35
Champagne, Mock Pink, '89 46
Champions' Cooler, '96 M181
Chiller, Royal Cup, '98 218
Chocolate Malt, '86 183
Chocolate, Mexican-Style, '81 187
Chocolate Milk, French, '79 38
Chocolate Sipper, '88 83
Cider, Apple, '95 198
Cider, Apple-Orange, '92 20
Cider, Cherry, '94 288
Cider, Holiday, '82 264
Cider, Hot Apple, '90 21, 225
Cider, Hot Molasses, '98 242
Cider, Hot Mulled, '79 205
Cider, Hot Mulled Apple-Orange, '97 301
Cider, Hot Spiced, '82 290; '99 248
Cider, Hot Spiced Apple, '84 318
Cider, Hot Spicy, '84 265
Cider, Mulled, '91 209; '94 227
Cider, Mulled Apple, '92 208
Cider, Mulled Pomegranate, '05 309
Cider Nog, Hot, '98 241
Cider Nog, Hot Apple, '84 42
Cider Sipper, Apple, '02 220
Cider Sipper, Apricot-Apple, '02 220
Cider, Sparkling Apple, '88 276
Cider, Spiced Apple, '85 256
Cider, Spiced Cranberry, '84 261; '98 278
Cider, Warm Citrus, '01 46
Citrus Blush, '98 197
Citrus Cooler, '82 160; '93 105
Citrus Float, '89 171

Citrus Slush, '93 198
Cocoa, Mocha, '83 318
Coco-Berry Calypso, '89 171
Coffee Soda, '97 272
Cooler, Caribbean, '98 333
Cooler, Speedy Spring, '02 58
Cooler, Spring, '86 214
Cooler, White Grape-and-Orange, '05 61
Cranberry Cocktail, Hot, '89 310
Cranberry Drink, Mulled, '92 12; '03 36
Cranberry Frappé, '82 263
Cranberry Juice, Sparkling, '88 275
Cranberry-Orange Soda, '79 148
Cranberry-Raspberry Drink, '97 154
Cranberry Shimmer, '98 168
Cubes, Berry-Good, '95 201
Cubes, Cranberry, '95 201
Cubes, Florida, '95 201
Cubes, Lemonade, '95 201
Cubes, Lemon-Mint, '95 201
Currant Warmer, '00 271
Fizz, Berry Blue, '03 M164
Float, Classic Cola, '04 107
Float, Frosty Fruit, '87 159
Float, Nutmeg-Almond, '84 106
Float, Pineapple Sherbet, '79 148
Float, Root Beer, '04 211
Floats, Maple-Coffee, '86 195
Float, Sparkling Cranberry, '86 195
Float, Strawberry-Banana, '87 160
Frappé, Hootenanny, '89 110
Freeze, Berry, '05 220
Fruit Beverage, Blender, '83 318
Fruit Cooler, Four-, '86 101
Fruit Coolers, '98 197
Fruit Drink, Three-, '79 38; '80 50; '87 199
Fruit Drink, Tropical, '85 43
Fruit Juice Cooler, '92 67
Fruit Juicy, Breakfast, '86 176
Fruit Refresher, '91 203
Fruit Refresher, Four-, '79 174; '80 129
Fruit Slush, '96 157
Fruit Slush, Refreshing, '82 35
Fruit Slushy, '80 146
Fruit Whisper, Tropical, '89 212
Funshine Fizz, '91 66
Ginger Beer, '01 292
Ginger-Mint Cooler, '89 92
Grapefruit Cooler, '88 81
Grapefruit Drink, '90 84; '95 238
Grapefruit-Orange Refresher, '82 174
Grapefruit Refresher, '88 85
Grape Juice, Mulled, '90 21
Grape Juice, Spiced White, '92 320
Grape-Lime Cooler, '94 227
Hawaiian Crush, '91 66
Hot Chocolate, '94 290; '04 209
Hot Chocolate, Cherry Cordial, '02 220
Hot Chocolate, Creole, '80 M290
Hot Chocolate, Favorite, '83 55
Hot Chocolate, French, '86 328
Hot Chocolate, Mexican, '98 313; '04 210, 299
Hot Chocolate, Old-Fashioned, '85 23
Hot Chocolate, Special, '82 5
Hot Chocolate, Spiced, '80 50
Hot Chocolate, Spicy, '85 278
Hot Chocolate, Sugar-and-Spice, '95 34
Hot Cocoa, Fudgy, '00 235
Hot Cocoa, Quick, '82 5
Ice Bowl, '83 152
Ice Cream Ginger Fizz, '83 303
Ice Cubes, Lemonade, '02 48
Ice Mold, Strawberry, '91 278
Ice Ring, '95 140; '03 141

Ice Ring, Easy, '03 141
Ice Ring, Strawberry, '94 176
Jogger's Sunrise, '93 213
Kid's Cooler, '90 95
Kiwi-Peach Slushy, '00 201
Kona Luscious, '84 54
Latte, White Chocolate, '04 210
Lemonade, Apple, '89 212; '03 169
Lemonade, Berry Delicious, '93 205
Lemonade, Blackberry, '99 130; '03 89
Lemonade, Blueberry, '98 179
Lemonade by the Glass, '96 161
Lemonade, Cayenne, '03 169
Lemonade, Cherry-Berry, '03 89
Lemonade Concentrate, '89 110
Lemonade Cooler, Watermelon-, '04 172
Lemonade, Cranberry, '05 205
Lemonade, Dazzling, '97 99
Lemonade, Fizzy Raspberry, '05 61
Lemonade, Fizzy Strawberry, '05 61
Lemonade, Fresh, '00 139
Lemonade, Fresh Squeezed, '81 172
Lemonade, Fresh-Squeezed, '99 220
Lemonade, Front Porch, '90 156
Lemonade, Homemade, '01 143
Lemonade, Hot Buttered, '94 18
Lemonade, Pineapple, '93 194
Lemonade, Raspberry, '03 89
Lemonade Slush, Pink, '80 151
Lemonade, Strawberry, '80 160
Lemonade, Sunny Spring, '00 70
Lemonade, Sweet-Tart, '96 161; '02 160
Lemonade, Watermelon, '98 165
Lemonade with Frozen Tea Cubes, '85 161
Lemon Frappé, '92 44
Lemon Slush, '00 271
Lemon Velvet, '90 15
Limeade, '01 143
Limeade, Fresh, '00 139
Limeade, Pineapple, '01 235
Limeade, Pink Apple, '89 46
Lime Cooler, '87 160
Lime Fizz, Frosty, '90 104
Malt, Chocolate-Yogurt, '01 173
Malt Special, '85 198
Mango Frappé, '86 216
Margaritas, Mock, '88 209; '99 120
Melon Julep, Rainbow, '80 183
Milk, Santa Claus, '92 281
Milk Shakes. *See* **BEVERAGES/Shakes.**
Mint Juleps, Apple, '97 120
Mix, Beetle Cider, '82 308
Mix, Bloody Mary, '89 110
Mix, Cappuccino, '90 87
Mix, Deluxe Hot Chocolate, '80 M290
Mix, Hot Chocolate, '04 209
Mix, Hot Cocoa, '81 287
Mix, Hot Mocha-Cocoa, '82 296
Mix, Hot Spiced Cider, '84 42
Mix, Instant Cocoa, '86 332
Mix, Mexican Mocha Spice, '00 334
Mix, Minted Hot Cocoa, '91 316
Mix, Mocha-Flavored Hot Cocoa, '91 316
Mix, Spiced Cider, '03 289
Mix, Spiced Mocha, '01 64
Mix, Spicy-Hot Chocolate, '85 278
Mocha Espresso, Italian, '82 254
Mocha Frosty, '92 44
Mocha, Hot, '84 60
Mocha Latte Beverage, '03 46

Mocha Melt, Spiced, '01 240
Mocha, Mexican, '93 M341
Mocha, Quick Viennese, '79 232
Mocha, Swiss-Style, '82 253
Mocha Warmer, '97 272
Nicely Iced, '03 164
Orange-Banana Flip, '82 48
Orange-Banana Whip, '95 244
Orange Blush, '80 51
Orange-Cranberry Cocktail, '01 103
Orange Frosty, '86 101
Orange Jubilee, '03 305
Orange Juicy, '90 178
Orange-Lemon Mist, '79 288; '80 35
Orange Pick-Me-Up, '80 232
Orange-Pineapple Drink, '89 35
Orange Slush, '82 49
Patio Blush, '92 43; '99 93
Peach Cooler, '85 198
Peaches 'n' Almond Cream, '86 229
Peach Frost, '89 155
Peach Frosty, '83 318
Peach Pick-Me-Up, '89 183
Peach Refresher, '86 103
Peanut Butter Cooler, '84 115
Piña Colada, Mock, '92 322
Piña Colada, Parson's, '89 46
Pineapple-Banana Slush, '90 14
Pineapple Cooler, '90 207
Pineapple Drink, Hot Buttered, '91 260
Pineapple Nectar, Hot, '90 21
Pineapple Slush, '88 82
Pineapple Soda, '90 179
Pineapple Sparkle, Spiced, '92 322
Pineapple-Yogurt Whirl, '91 132
Pink Soda, Blushing, '90 104
Punch. *See also* **BEVERAGES/Alcoholic.**
Apple Bobbing Punch, '99 246
Apple Punch, Hot, '84 324
Apple Punch, Party, '00 271
Apple-Tea Punch, '85 82
Apricot Spiced Punch, '80 269
Autumn Punch, '88 209
Banana Punch, '99 161; '01 93
Berry-Colada Punch, '96 277
Berry Punch, '92 67
Brew-Ha-Ha Punch, '98 255
Brunch Punch, '04 281; '05 335
Bubbling Jade Punch, '79 174; '80 129
Bunch, Punch for a, '95 90
Cantaloupe Punch, '81 147; '00 140
Caribbean Punch, '95 173
Champagne Punch, '99 30
Children's Punch, '85 322
Christmas Eve Punch, '86 314
Christmas Punch, '84 259; '89 330
Cider Punch, Hot, '95 238
Cider Punch, Spiced, '84 258
Citrus Party Punch, '83 141; '92 289
Citrus Punch, '85 319; '93 99
Citrus Punch, Budget, '82 121
Citrus Punch, Fresh, '85 154
Citrus Punch, Party, '84 117
Citrus Punch, Sparkling, '95 337
Coffee-Ice Cream Punch, '05 136
Cola Punch, '91 144
Cottontail Punch, '02 48
Cranapple Punch, '83 142
Cranberry-Cherry Punch, '91 176
Cranberry-Cinnamon Punch, '86 270
Cranberry-Pineapple Punch, '00 284
Cranberry Punch, '83 275; '99 290
Cranberry Punch, Holiday, '85 265
Cranberry Punch, Hot, '80 288; '84 319; '85 265

Cranberry Punch, Sparkling, '85 277; '95 101
Cranberry Punch, Spiced, '89 290
Cranberry Punch, Tart, '83 318
Cran-Grape-Tea Punch, '92 209
Emerald Sea Punch, '04 163
False-Kick Punch, '82 121
Frozen Punch Ring, '83 152
Fruited Ice-Cube Punch, '98 197
Fruit Juice Punch, '96 214
Fruit Punch, '01 106
Fruit Punch, Can-Can, '94 122
Fruit Punch, Florida, '92 247
Fruit Punch, Fresh, '98 155
Fruit Punch, Golden, '80 299; '83 56; '96 278
Fruit Punch, Holiday, '79 232
Fruit Punch, Holiday Hot, '92 286
Fruit Punch, Hot, '83 33
Fruit Punch, Mixed, '90 207; '95 239
Fruit Punch, Party, '82 137
Fruit Punch, Passion, '90 169
Fruit Punch, Slushy, '98 92
Fruit Punch, Southern Fresh, '99 70
Fruit Punch, Spiced, '88 2
Fruit Punch, Summertime, '80 160
Fruit Punch, Tropical, '80 51; '90 169
Fruit Slush Punch, '91 278
Fruit Sparkle, '99 289
Fruity Witches' Brew, '95 273
Ginger Ale-Nectar Punch, '92 171
Goblin Punch, '88 228
Golden Punch, '85 207
Grape Punch, Sparkling, '82 48
Happy New Year Punch, '98 26
Holiday Punch, '87 252
Honey-Apple Punch, '05 23
Hot Cider Punch, '03 233
Hot Spiced Punch, '96 214
Irish Coffee-Eggnog Punch, '95 314
Lemonade Punch, Sparkling, '88 276
Lemon Balm Punch, '80 42
Lime-Pineapple Punch, '83 142
Lime Punch, Calypso Presbyterian Church Women's, '95 141
Lime Punch, Foamy, '82 264
Lime Slush Punch, '90 273
Margarita Punch, '98 88
Merry Christmas Punch, '79 285
Mocha Punch, '84 58, 166; '86 270; '95 141
Mock Champagne Punch, '93 340
Morning Punch, '88 82
Nectar Punch, '93 283
Nog Punch, Creamy, '01 240
Orange Blossom Punch, '83 142
Orange-Mint Punch, '82 121
Orange Punch, Refreshing, '81 39
Orange Sherbet Party Punch, '83 142
Orange Soda Punch, '87 214
Parsonage Punch, '79 148
Party Punch, '91 106, 278
Party Punch in a Pail, '94 289
Party Punch, Special, '81 119
Peppermint-Eggnog Punch, '90 273
Peppermint Punch, Cupid's Creamy, '04 253
Percolator Punch, '91 306
Percolator Punch, Hot, '81 288
Pineapple-Citrus Punch, '96 134
Pineapple Fruit Punch, '02 49
Pineapple-Mint Punch, '88 209
Pineapple-Orange Punch, '85 236
Pineapple Punch, '79 174
Pineapple Punch, Frosty, '91 66
Pineapple Punch, Spiced, '83 33; '92 66
Pineapple Sherbet Punch, '95 141
Pink Lady Punch, '81 100

Polka Dot Punch, '95 178
Ponche de Piña, '84 58
Raspberry Sherbet Punch, '95 141
Raspberry Sparkle Punch, '84 57
Sherbet Punch, Double, '79 232
Spiced Punch, Hot, '80 250
Spicy Sparkling Punch, '05 24
Strawberry-Lemonade Punch, '85 116; '91 175
Strawberry Punch, '90 273
Strawberry Punch, Creamy, '86 195
Sunset Punch, '96 278
Tangy Punch, '83 142
Tea Party Punch, '87 147
Tea Punch, '90 143, 207
Tea Punch, Citrus-, '85 116
Tea Punch, Mint, '04 63
Tea Punch, Minted, '00 164
Traders' Punch, '87 94
Tropical Punch, '90 207
Vegetable Punch, Hot, '93 12
Watermelon Punch, '89 204; '92 190; '00 140
White Grape Punch, '90 15
White Grape Punch, Spiced, '96 170
Purple Cow, '98 206
Raspberry Cooler, '89 171
Raspberry Fizz, Rosy, '90 179
Raspberry Shrub, Red, '97 132
Refresher, Peach Yogurt, '03 166
Rice-and-Cinnamon Cooler, '00 139
Sangría, Mock Tea, '99 336
Sangría, Southern, '88 170
Sangría, Virgin, '89 46
Scarlet Sipper, '90 198
Scuppernong Juice, '98 221
Shakes
    Apricot Shake, '84 115
    Banana Milkshake, '85 47; '90 179
    Banana-Mocha Shake, '05 45
    Banana-Pineapple Milk Shake, '84 59
    Banana Shake, '97 172
    Berry Blue Shake, '01 200
    Berry Milk Shake, Double-, '00 81
    Chocolate-Banana Milk Shake, '94 113
    Chocolate Milk Shake, '05 193
    Chocolate Mint Shake, '89 170
    "Concrete," Abaco Mocha, '94 114
    "Concrete," All Shook Up, '94 114
    "Concrete," Cardinal Sin, '94 113
    "Concrete," Foxtreat, '94 113
    Cranberry Shake, '83 171
    Date Shake, '92 44
    Fruit Shake, Frosty, '87 23
    Fruit Shake, Tangy, '95 129
    Fruit Yogurt Shake, Three-, '01 173
    Get-Up-and-Go Shake, '00 179
    Mocha Milkshake, '89 35
    Mocha-Mint Shake, '02 297
    Orange Milk Shake, '84 166
    Orange Shake, Peachy, '81 156
    Papaya Shake, '90 169
    PBJ Shake, '93 292
    Peach Melba Shake, '02 158
    Peach Melba Sundae Shake, '93 134
    Peanut Butter-Banana Shake, '97 172
    Peanut Butter Milkshakes, '85 198
    Peanut Butter Shake, '82 48
    Pep Shake, '79 38
    Pineapple-Banana Shake, '85 215
    Pineapple-Buttermilk Shake, '01 173
    Pineapple-Buttermilk Shake, Light, '01 173
    Pineapple Milkshake, '87 199
    Pineapple Milk Shake, '94 113
    Pineapple-Orange-Banana Shake, '97 172
    Raisin Shake, Amazin', '86 195

Raspberry-and-Banana Shake, '89 183
Raspberry Milk Shakes, '95 238
Strawberry-Banana Shake, '89 35; '97 172
Strawberry-Banana Shake, Double, '01 173
Strawberry-Banana Shake, Light Double, '01 173
Strawberry-Cheesecake Shake, '92 44
Strawberry Milk Shake, '94 113
Strawberry Milkshake, Fresh, '82 113
Strawberry-Orange Breakfast Shake, '87 186
Strawberry-Pear Shake, '92 139
Strawberry-Pineapple Shake, '84 166
Strawberry Shake, '97 172
Strawberry Shake, Double, '00 179
Strawberry-Yogurt Shake, '87 199
Summer Shake, '82 161
Sunshine Shake, '79 53
Tropical Shake, '87 200; '93 212; '00 179; '04 21
Sipper by the Glass, Fresh Mint-Citrus, '03 89
Sipper, Citrus Cider, '05 23
Sipper, Fresh Mint-Citrus, '03 89
Slush, Peach, '04 141
Slush, Santa's, '90 271
Slush, Strawberry-Lemonade, '03 169
Slush, Strawberry Tea, '04 63
Slushy, Fruit Parfait, '02 185
Smoothies
    Banana-Berry Smoothie, '05 24
    Banana-Blueberry Smoothie, '90 104
    Banana Breakfast Smoothie, '03 46
    Banana-Peach Buttermilk Smoothie, '04 22
    Banana-Pineapple Smoothie, Quick, '93 195
    Banana Smoothie, '87 160; '93 95
    Berry-Banana Buttermilk Smoothie, '00 49
    Berry Smoothie, Four-, '97 173
    Blackberry Smoothies, '04 141
    Chocoholic Smoothie, '97 173
    Chocolate-Mint Smoothie, '84 166
    Citrus Smoothie, '98 17; '99 196
    Cranberry Smoothie, '86 183; '91 307
    Fruit Smoothie, '89 87
    Fruit Smoothie, Two-, '89 182
    Honey-Banana Smoothie, '89 144
    Honey-Yogurt Smoothie, '97 326
    Honey-Yogurt Smoothie, Fruited, '88 231; '89 23
    Kahlúa Smoothie, '87 242
    Mango-Orange Smoothie, '86 216
    Mango Smoothie, '03 122
    Orange-Banana Smoothie, '97 173
    Peachy-Pineapple Smoothie, '97 173
    Pineapple Smoothie, '97 172
    Pineapple Smoothie, Easy, '00 199
    Strawberry-Banana Smoothie, '81 59
    Strawberry-Peach Smoothie, '89 182
    Strawberry Smoothie, '86 183; '97 173
    Sunrise Smoothie, '93 139
    Sunshine Smoothies, '98 330
    Tropical Smoothie, '81 50; '90 169
    Yogurt-Fruit Smoothie, '03 25
Soda, Homemade Orange, '03 141
Southern Breeze, '02 185
Sparkler, Cherry, '00 329
Sparkler, Cranberry-Apple, '05 61
Spiced Brew, Hot, '91 36
Spices, Barclay House Mulling, '86 289
Spritzers. See also BEVERAGES/Alcoholic.
    Fruit Spritzer, '01 174
    Kiwi-Lemonade Spritzer, '03 89
    Lemon-Mint Spritzer, '99 175
    Raspberry Spritzers, '99 207
    Strawberry-Kiwi-Lemonade Spritzer, '03 89
    Strawberry Spritzer, '90 14; '97 272
Strawberry Cooler, '83 56; '84 51
Strawberry Coolers, '92 67
Strawberry-Mint Cooler, '84 57

Strawberry-Orange Slush, '83 172
Strawberry Refresher, Frozen, '93 213
Strawberry Slurp, '81 96
Strawberry Soda, '84 115
Strawberry Soda, Old-Fashioned, '79 49
Strawberry Sparkler, '99 49
Sunshine Fizz, '92 44
Syllabub, Plantation, '79 233
Syrup, Berry, '96 161
Syrup, Ginger, '96 161
Syrup, Mint, '90 89; '96 161; '97 120
Syrup, Mint Simple, '03 129
Syrup, Orange, '96 161
Syrup, Simple, '99 161; '05 135
Syrup, Sugar, '96 161; '03 224
Tahitian Flower, '87 159
Toddy, Jolly, '86 229
Toddy, Tasty, '88 82
Tofruitti Breakfast Drink, '88 26
Tomato Bouillon, '83 8
Tomato-Clam Cocktail, '87 252
Tomato Cocktail, '83 M203
Tomato Juice Cocktail, '79 212; '83 230; '90 12
Tomato Juice Cocktail, Zesty, '83 289
Tomato Juice, Homemade, '81 50
Tomato Juice, Spicy, '85 189
Tomato Refresher, '83 318
Tomato Sipper, Peppy, '94 227
Tomato Sipper, Spicy, '86 229
Tomato Warm-Up, Spicy, '95 328
Tropical Cooler, '84 120
Tropical Delight, '89 182
Tropical Ice, '79 174; '80 129
Tropical Refresher, '85 198; '96 157
Vanilla Cream, '97 272
Vanilla Frosty, French, '79 148
Vegetable Cocktail, Fresh, '82 165
Vegetable Juice Delight, '84 58
Virgin Mary, Spicy, '92 323
Wassail, '84 259, 318; '88 248; '90 273; '97 240;
    '99 268
Wassail, Christmas, '93 295
Wassail, Cranberry, '88 289
Wassail, Golden, '96 278
Wassail, Holiday, '89 289; '91 260
Wassail, Pineapple, '01 240
Wassail, Pineapple-Apricot, '83 275
Wassail, Winter, '03 295
Watermelon-Berry Slush, '90 137
Watermelon-Strawberry Cooler, '98 178
Zippy Red Eye, '91 209
BISCUITS
Angel Biscuits, '80 49; '90 28; '93 270
Angel Biscuits, Ham-Filled, '80 159
Anise Biscuits with Balsamic Strawberries, '02 170
Bacon Biscuit Cups, '99 214
Baking Powder Biscuits, '82 195; '89 144
Basic Buttery Biscuits, '04 280; '05 335
Basil Biscuits, '93 160
Beaten Biscuits, '86 54
Benne Seed Biscuits, '79 38
Biscuits, '92 31
Blueberry Biscuits, '00 286
Blueberry Buttermilk Biscuits, '89 210
Blue Cheese-and-Ham Cornmeal Biscuits, '98 136
Bowl, Chili in a Biscuit, '98 224
Bowls, Biscuit, '03 222
Bowls, Chicken Pot Pie in Biscuit, '03 222
Bowls, Creamed Chicken in Biscuit, '03 222
Bran Biscuits, '85 228
Bread, Biscuit, '84 284
Bread, Brown Sugar Biscuit, '02 M224
Buttermilk Biscuits, '83 208; '85 255, 321; '99 32;
    '03 24

BISCUITS
(continued)

Buttermilk Biscuits, Basic, '94 214; '00 48
Buttermilk Biscuits, Deluxe, '82 130
Buttermilk Biscuits, Favorite, '81 191
Buttermilk Biscuits, Fluffy, '84 102
Buttermilk Biscuits, Old-Fashioned, '80 77
Buttermilk Biscuits, Quick, '83 311; '88 15; '92 269;
    '03 314
Buttermilk Biscuits with Virginia Ham, '96 142
Buttermilk-Raisin Biscuits, '92 338
Caramel Dessert Biscuits, '95 36
Casserole, Beef-and-Biscuit, '83 75
Casserole, Biscuit-Topped Tuna, '79 113
Cheese
    Angel Biscuits, Cheese, '89 211
    Bacon-Cheese Biscuits, '88 84
    Beer-and-Cheese Biscuits, '94 215
    Blue Cheese Biscuits, '88 83; '05 309
    Blue Cheese Biscuits with Beef and Horseradish-
        Chive Cream, '02 313
    Butter Cheese Dips, '80 46
    Cheddar Biscuits, Easy, '01 103
    Cheese Biscuits, '79 296; '80 31; '81 288; '83 253;
        '85 32; '87 78
    Cheeseburger Biscuits, '79 194
    Chipotle Butter, Cheese Biscuits with, '01 234
    Chive Biscuits, Cheese-, '94 324
    Cocktail Biscuits, Spicy Cheese, '05 173
    Cream Cheese-and-Olive Biscuits With Olive-Parsley
        Spread, '04 238
    Cream Cheese-and-Olive Biscuits with Sun-Dried
        Tomato Spread and Bacon, '02 313
    Cream Cheese-and-Olive Biscuits with Tapenade,
        '02 313
    Easy Cheese Biscuits, '81 99
    Garlic Biscuits, Cheese-, '02 260
    Garlic Biscuits, Cheese, '03 185
    Ham and Cheese Biscuits, Petite, '79 193
    Ham-and-Swiss Cheese Biscuits, '04 209
    Hot Cheesy Biscuits, '80 186
    Lightnin' Cheese Biscuits, '90 283
    Mixer Cheese Biscuits, '96 22
    Onion Biscuits, Cheesy, '95 98; '01 330
    Pepper-Cheese Biscuit Fingers, '88 283
    Refrigerator Biscuits, '96 17
    Roquefort Biscuits, Herbed, '84 95
    Rosemary Biscuits, '99 17
    Sausage Biscuits, Cheesy, '80 78
    Tiny Cheese Biscuits, '80 192
Chicken in a Biscuit, '79 263
Cinnamon Biscuits, Cranberry-Apple Cobbler with,
    '99 256
Cinnamon-Pecan Biscuits with Cinnamon Butter,
    '01 309
Cinnamon-Raisin Breakfast Biscuits, '93 159
Cloud Biscuits, '87 15
Coconut Biscuits, Yummy, '95 99
Cornmeal Biscuits, '85 228; '95 98; '04 257
Cornmeal-Jalapeño Biscuits, '94 214
Country Ham Biscuits, '94 215
Country Ham, Biscuits with, '90 93
Cranberry-Orange-Glazed Biscuits, '04 280; '05 335
Daisy Biscuits, '90 86
Dressing, Cornbread-Biscuit, '79 296
Dumplings and Chicken, Biscuit, '99 326
Easy-Bake Biscuits, '96 157
Elf Biscuits, '99 309
Elgin Biscuits, '93 281
Elsie's Biscuits, '97 129
Feather Biscuits, '80 78
Feather Light Biscuits, '80 246

Flaky Biscuits, '84 228
Grapefruit Juice Biscuits, '83 10
Green Chile Biscuits, '04 233
Green Elf Biscuits and Ham, '02 277
Ham and Biscuits, Southern, '91 12
Ham Biscuits, '99 233
Ham 'n' Angel Biscuits, Kentucky, '90 83
Heart Biscuits, Country Ham in, '86 105
Heart Biscuits with Sausage, Angel, '87 156
Hearty Biscuits, '83 121
Herb Biscuits, Easy, '90 283
Herbed Biscuit Ring, '95 161
Herbed Biscuits, '85 228; '93 67
Homemade Biscuits, '04 209
Honey Angel Biscuits, '95 138; '03 111
Hot Biscuits, '86 269
Hot Browns, Biscuit, '02 94
Lemon Drop Biscuits, '97 332
Light Biscuits, '89 53
Marmalade Biscuits, Carolina, '85 42
Marmalade Biscuit Squares, '79 193
Mile-High Biscuits, '85 41
Miniature Buttermilk Biscuits, '02 103
Muffins, Biscuit, '98 136
Nannie's Biscuits, '82 156
Nutty Tea Biscuits, '89 210
Oatmeal Biscuits, '89 108
Omelet Biscuits, Deluxe, '98 101
One-Step Biscuits, '82 173
Orange Biscuits, '88 85
Orange Puffs, Upside-Down, '83 57
Pan Biscuits, Easy, '05 26
Pandy's Biscuits, '99 277
Parker House-Style Biscuits, '79 162
Pecan Biscuits, Peppered Pork with, '01 33
Pepperoni Biscuits, '84 95
Potato-Bacon Biscuits, '94 214
Processor Biscuits, Easy, '84 218
Pudding, Biscuit, '79 86; '93 51
Pudding, Chocolate Biscuit Bread, '94 215
Pull-Apart Biscuits, Surprise, '95 46
Quick Biscuits, '89 30
Raised Biscuits, Southern, '82 94
Raisin Biscuits, Glazed, '89 210
Ranch Biscuits with Ham, '97 59
Raspberry-Almond Biscuits, '93 160
Rise-and-Shine Biscuits, '89 211
"Rolling-in-Dough" Biscuits, '92 80
Rosemary Biscuits, '95 91; '99 17
Rye Biscuits, '84 96
Sausage and Biscuits, Southern, '82 43
Sausage, Best Biscuits with, '99 103
Sausage Biscuit Bites, '84 95
Sausage Gravy, Biscuits and, '92 270; '94 20
Shrimp-and-Grits Biscuits, '02 313
Snowflake Biscuits, '90 158
Sour Cream Biscuits, '79 128; '04 209
Sour Cream Biscuits, Soft-as-a-Cloud, '86 138
Sourdough Biscuits, '82 201
Southern Biscuits, Old, '02 218
Spicy Kickin' Biscuits, '03 207
Spoon Biscuits, Mexican Fiesta, '95 161
Sugar Biscuits, '03 85; '04 72
Sweetened Biscuits, '80 42
Sweet Little Biscuits, '85 305
Sweet Potato Angel Biscuits, '93 312; '01 42
Sweet Potato Biscuits, '80 287; '84 140; '89 210;
    '98 222; '00 232; '01 250; '05 22
Taco Biscuit Bites, '91 89
Three-Step Biscuits, '98 97
Tomato-Bacon Biscuit Bites, Savory, '03 196
Tomato Biscuits, '86 72
Tomato Biscuits, Fresh, '04 138
Tomato-Eggplant Biscuit Cakes, '95 170

Tomato-Herb Biscuits, '94 215
Topping, Biscuit, '86 157, 265
Up-and-Down Biscuits, '88 263
Velvet Cream Biscuits, '92 303
Wheat Bran Biscuits, '81 49
Wheat Germ Biscuits, '86 261
Wheat Quick Biscuits, '85 278
Whipping Cream Biscuits, '80 77
Whipping Cream Biscuits, Quick, '02 27; '03 238
Whole Wheat Biscuits, '83 18; '84 60, 268; '85 227;
    '88 83; '91 222
Yeast Biscuits, '87 71, 301
Yeast Biscuits, Refrigerator, '85 48

BISQUES. *See* SOUPS/Bisques.

BLACKBERRIES

Bars, Blackberry, '87 130
Bars, Blackberry-Filled, '79 124
Bars, Blackberry Jam, '82 M185
Berry Shrub, '95 29
Breeze, Blackberry, '98 179
Butter, Blackberry, '97 306; '03 27
Cake, Blackberry-Raspberry Truffle, '03 245
Cake, Blackberry Upside-Down, '01 314
Cake, Fresh Blackberry, '81 132
Cake, Tennessee Jam, '04 55
Cake, Triple-Layer Tennessee Jam, '04 55
Chantilly, Blackberries, '99 130
Cobbler, Blackberry, '82 139; '83 175; '99 131; '02 17
Cobbler, Blackberry-Almond, '81 132
Cobbler, Deep-Dish Blackberry, '80 186
Cobbler, Deluxe Blackberry, '81 132
Cobbler, Juicy Blackberry, '89 137
Cobbler, New-Fashioned Blackberry, '87 164
Cobbler, Southern Blackberry, '81 132
Crème Brûlée, Berry, '95 323
Crisp, Lemon-Blackberry, '98 171
Custard, Blackberry, '99 132
Dumplings, Blackberries and, '86 196
Dumplings, Blackberry, '97 253
Filling, Blackberry Curd, '05 182
Flan, Blackberry, '79 182
Gazpacho, Berry, '97 181
Jam, Berry Refrigerator, '89 139
Jam, Blackberry, '82 149; '89 138; '99 M131
Jam, Freezer Blackberry, '84 M181
Jelly, Blackberry, '82 149
Juice, Blackberry, '05 182
Lemonade, Blackberry, '99 130; '03 89
Napoleons, Berry, '94 120
Parfait, Blackberries-and-Cream, '87 129
Pie, Berry-Apple, '88 251
Pie, Blackberry, '84 141; '86 152
Pie, Blackberry-Apple, '87 130
Pie, Blackberry Cream, '81 132
Pie, Creamy Blackberry, '88 179
Pie, Fresh Blackberry, '03 164
Pie, Peach-and-Blackberry, '89 136
Roll, Blackberry, '82 178
Sandwiches, Smoked Turkey, Mozzarella, and
    Blackberry, '99 220
Sauce, Berry, '94 130
Sauce, Blackberry, '86 152; '94 232
Sauce, Ducklings with Blackberry, '82 251
Sauce, Grilled Quail with Red Wine-Blackberry,
    '98 319
Sauce, Pork Medaillons with Blackberry, '02 136
Sherbet, Blackberry-Buttermilk, '05 133
Sherbet, 1-2-3 Blackberry, '99 130; '00 21
Sherbet, Three-Ingredient Blackberry, '01 105
Smoothies, Blackberry, '04 141
Sorbet, Blackberry-Lemon, '02 85
Supremes, Blackberry, '99 179
Syrup, Blackberry, '99 131
Tamales, Blackberry Dessert, '94 190

Tart, Cherry and Blackberry, '83 225
Tart, Pick-a-Berry, '91 118
Tarts, Berry Good Lemon, '91 119
Tarts, Blackberry Pudding, '93 200; '00 147
Tea, Blackberry Iced, '04 158
Vinaigrette, Blackberry-Basil, '04 97

BLUEBERRIES
à la Frederick, Blueberries, '93 123
Appetizer, Orange-Berry, '85 81
Basket, Summer Berry, '84 158
Berry Tartlets, Fresh, '91 98
Bordeaux, Beauberries, '98 18
Breads
    Banana-Blueberry Bread, '81 163
    Biscuits, Blueberry, '00 286
    Biscuits, Blueberry Buttermilk, '89 210
    Buns, Deluxe Blueberry, '81 164
    Hot Blueberry Bread, '81 164
    Lemon Bread, Blueberry-, '85 190
    Muffin Batter, Blueberry, '04 200
    Muffins, Berry-and-Spice Whole-Wheat, '05 25
    Muffins, Blueberry, '80 143; '91 140, 203; '99 234;
       '04 200, 209
    Muffins, Blueberry-Bran, '89 23
    Muffins, Blueberry Buttermilk, '80 16
    Muffins, Blueberry-Cinnamon, '02 177
    Muffins, Blueberry-Cream Cheese, '86 14
    Muffins, Blueberry Ice Cream, '82 143
    Muffins, Blueberry-Lemon, '79 7
    Muffins, Blueberry-Oat, '92 119
    Muffins, Blueberry Oat Bran, '89 106
    Muffins, Blueberry-Oatmeal, '87 24
    Muffins, Blueberry Streusel, '80 46
    Muffins, Blueberry-Streusel, '96 146; '01 131
    Muffins, Blueberry Sweet, '00 210
    Muffins, Easy Blueberry, '81 197
    Muffins, Golden Blueberry, '79 235
    Muffins, Lemon-Blueberry, '03 26
    Muffins, Old-Fashioned Blueberry, '86 161
    Muffins, Speedy Blueberry, '95 135
    Muffins with Streusel Topping, Blueberry, '88 129
    Oatmeal Bread, Blueberry-, '83 139
    Orange Bread, Blueberry-, '87 140; '02 21
    Orange Nut Bread Blueberry-, '84 141
    Pancakes With Wild Blueberry-and-Peach Topping,
       Sour Cream-Blueberry Morning, '05 326
    Pinwheels, Blueberry, '82 205
    Tea Bread, Blueberry, '96 146
Buckle, Blueberry, '85 30
Buckle Blueberry, Huckle-, '86 151
Cake, Banana-Blueberry, '86 247
Cake, Blueberry Brunch, '83 183
Cake, Blueberry-Sour Cream, '90 140
Cake, Blueberry Streusel, '92 144
Cheesecake, Blueberries 'n' Cream, '87 140
Cheesecake, Blueberry, '00 153; '03 182
Cheesecake, Blueberry Chiffon, '87 76
Cheesecake, Reduced-fat Blueberry, '00 153
Chutney, Blueberry, '95 190; '00 154
Cobbler, Blueberry, '83 175
Cobbler, Blueberry-Pecan, '00 154; '03 106
Cobbler, Blueberry Pinwheel, '87 140
Cobbler, Blueberry Upside-Down, '96 146
Cobbler, Cran-Blueberry, '04 28
Cobbler, Easy Blueberry, '83 183
Cobbler, Fresh Blueberry, '80 144
Cobbler, No-Dough Blueberry-Peach, '86 177
Cobbler, Peachy Blueberry, '80 143
Cobbler, Warm Blueberry, '98 153
Coffee Cake, Almond-Blueberry, '85 152
Coffee Cake, Blueberry, '82 206; '85 326;
    '88 263
Coffee Cake, Blueberry Streusel, '88 154
Coffee Cake, Fresh Blueberry, '81 164

Coffee Cake, Sour Cream-Blueberry, '00 154
Cointreau, Blueberries and, '82 100
Compote, Berry-Peach, '82 133
Compote, Peach-Berry, '89 112
Conserve, Blueberry, '82 149
Cordial, Blueberry, '95 142
Cream, Lemon-Blueberry, '92 153
Crisp, Blueberry, '84 177
Crumble, Blueberry, '81 84
Crunch, Apple-Blueberry, '02 128
Crunch, Blueberry, '96 146
Crunch, Fresh Blueberry, '82 143
Cupcakes, Lemon-Blueberry Ice-Cream, '01 172
Delight, Blueberry, '96 17
Dessert, Easy Blueberry, '89 M130
Dessert, Lemon-Blueberry Layered, '05 206
Dessert, Peach-Blueberry, '92 184
Dessert Squares, Chocolate-Blueberry, '87 299
Dream, Blueberry, '88 94
Fritters, Blueberry, '85 152
Gazpacho, Berry, '97 181
Glaze, Blueberry, '83 143
Ice Cream, Blueberry, '88 203
Ice Cream, Blueberry-Peach, '00 153
Jam, Blueberry, '79 120; '85 130
Jam, Blueberry Refrigerator, '89 139
Jam, Green Tomato-Blueberry, '01 140
Kuchen, Blueberry, '80 143
Lemonade, Blueberry, '98 179
Lemon Curd with Berries, '90 102
Margaritas, Frozen Blueberry, '05 179
Marmalade, Blueberry, '96 145
Marmalade, Spicy Blueberry-Citrus, '03 135
Napoleons, Blueberry, '96 147
Napoleons, Blueberry-Lemon, '94 122
Pancake, Brunch Popover, '96 28
Pancakes, Blueberry, '85 152; '89 138
Pancakes, Blueberry Buttermilk, '79 114
Pancakes, Blue Cornmeal-Blueberry, '94 115
Pancakes, Lemon-Blueberry, '04 148
Pancakes, Sour Cream Blueberry, '81 164
Pie, Blueberry-Banana, '93 115
Pie, Blueberry Cream, '84 142
Pie, Blueberry-Cream Cheese, '88 154
Pie, Blueberry-Peach, '94 158
Pie, Blueberry-Sour Cream, '83 183
Pie, Bumbleberry, '97 163
Pie, Chilled Blueberry, '89 136
Pie, Fresh Blueberry, '83 183; '85 152
Pie, Fresh Blueberry Cream, '80 144
Pie, Fresh Blueberry Streusel, '89 137
Pie, Old-Fashioned Blueberry, '89 136
Pie, Red, White, and Blueberry, '98 162
Pie, Spicy Blueberry, '96 147
Pizza, Blueberry, '96 147
Pork Tenderloin, Blueberry-Rum Marinated, '05 178
Pudding, Blueberry Bread, '88 154; '03 119
Pudding, Russian Blueberry-Raspberry, '97 128
Puree, Grapefruit with Pear-Berry, '89 213
Quick Blueberry Slump, '91 20
Raspberry Custard Sauce, Fresh Berries with, '88 163
Salad, Berry Delicious Summer, '05 179
Salad, Chicken-Blueberry, '02 177
Salad, Layered Berry, '79 173
Salad, Melon-Berry, '90 180
Salad, Watercress, '97 249
Salsa, Blueberry, '05 179
Sauce, Berry, '94 130; '95 103
Sauce, Blueberry, '80 144; '86 248; '88 155; '89 M130;
    '94 122; '95 135
Sauce, Blueberry-Lemon, '01 117
Sauce, Cinnamon-Blueberry, '86 11
Sauce, Melon Wedges with Berry, '86 178
Sauce, Peach-Berry, '87 M165

Sauce, Peach-Blueberry, '81 170
Sauce, Peach-Blueberry Pancake, '82 177
Shake, Berry Blue, '01 200
Sherbet, Blueberry, '04 283
Sherbet, Blueberry-Buttermilk, '05 133
Shortcakes, Southern Peach-and-Blueberry, '05 318
Shortcake, Warm Blueberry-Nectarine, '97 205
Smoothie, Banana-Blueberry, '90 104
Smoothie, Banana Breakfast, '03 46
Smoothie, Four-Berry, '97 173
Snow, Berries on, '82 227
Sorbet, Blueberry-Kirsch, '83 120
Soup, Chilled Blueberry, '05 178
Squares, Blueberry-Amaretto, '83 220
Tart, Pick-a-Berry, '91 118
Tarts, Berry Good Lemon, '91 119
Topping, Baked Brie with Blueberry-Ginger, '05 179
Topping, Blueberry, '87 125
Topping, Wild Blueberry-and-Peach, '05 326
Trifle, Lemon-Blueberry, '88 210
Vinaigrette, Blueberry, '00 154
Yum Yum, Blueberry, '98 91

BOK CHOY
Beef with Bok Choy, Ginger, '96 99
Greens, Super-Charged, '01 211
Pork on Mixed Greens, Hot Sesame, '97 19
Salad, Bok Choy, '01 129
Salad, Ramen Noodle, '97 18
Stir-Fried Bok Choy, '97 105
Stir-Fry, Bok Choy-Broccoli, '84 2

BOYSENBERRIES
Cobbler, Boysenberry, '82 133
Compote, Berry-Peach, '82 133
Cream Mold, Peachy Berry, '83 130
Cream Supreme, Boysenberries and, '82 133
Crisp, Berry, '83 130
Pie, Boysenberry, '82 133

BRAN
Biscuits, Bran, '85 228
Biscuits, Wheat Bran, '81 49
Bread, Bran-Applesauce, '84 229
Bread, Honey-Oat, '93 232
Bread, Wheat-and-Oat Bran, '92 102
Bread, Whole Wheat Bran, '79 58
Chocolate-Bran Raisin Jumbos, '91 142
Crêpes, Bran, '83 70; '86 44
Cupcakes, Carrot-Bran, '82 16
Eggplant, Ratatouille-Bran Stuffed, '86 44
Muesli, Bran-and-Fruit, '91 134
Muffins
    All-Bran Oat Bran Muffins, '91 134
    Apple-Bran Muffins, '85 M89
    Apple-Cinnamon Oat Bran Muffins, '89 106
    Banana Bran Muffins, '83 48
    Banana Oat Bran Muffins, '89 106
    Big Batch Moist Bran Muffins, '95 214
    Blueberry-Bran Muffins, '89 23
    Blueberry Oat Bran Muffins, '89 106
    Bran Muffins, '84 53
    Buttermilk Muffins, Bran-, '85 7
    Cranberry Oat Bran Muffins, '89 107
    Easy Bran Muffins, '83 55
    Ever-Ready Bran Muffins, '81 106
    Freezer Bran Muffins, '91 141
    Fruit-and-Bran Muffins, '04 22
    High-Fiber Muffins, '85 250
    Honey Bran Muffins, '88 171
    Honey-Bran Muffins, '89 250
    Made of Bran Muffins, '86 103
    Maple-Bran Muffins, '90 66
    Oat Bran-Banana Muffins, '91 18
    Oat Bran Muffins, '89 106
    Oatmeal Bran Muffins, '81 236
    Oatmeal-Bran Muffins, '91 83

BRAN, Muffins
(continued)

Quick Bran Muffins, '86 85
Raisin Oat Bran Muffins, '89 106
Refrigerator Bran Muffins, '79 6
Sour Cream-Bran Muffins, '87 98
Spiced Bran Muffins, '84 229
Two, Bran Muffins for, '84 211
Whole Wheat Bran Muffins, '88 M274
Pancakes with Cinnamon Syrup, Bran, '91 315
Rolls, Bran, '85 145
Rolls, Bran Yeast, '87 116
Salad, Lemony Apple-Bran, '86 223
Waffles, Oat Bran, '92 139
BREADS. *See also* **APPETIZERS/Crostini; BISCUITS;**
CAKES/Coffee Cakes; CORNBREADS;
CRACKERS; CRÊPES; CROUTONS;
FRENCH TOAST; MUFFINS; PANCAKES;
PIES, PUFFS, AND PASTRIES/Pastries;
ROLLS AND BUNS; WAFFLES.
Apple Bread, '79 205; '80 226; '05 210
Apple Butter Bread, '84 49; '86 69
Apple Loaf, Fresh, '82 206
Apple Loaf, Spiced, '79 215
Apple-Nut Bread, '79 12; '85 281
Apple-Nut Bread, Fresh, '87 256
Applesauce-Honey Nut Bread, '87 300
Applesauce Loaf, Brandy, '81 263
Applesauce Nut Bread, '81 305
Applesauce-Pecan Bread, '90 66
Apple Toast, '81 278
Apricot Bread, Tangy, '81 249
Apricot-Cranberry Loaf, '79 235
Apricot-Nut Bread, '79 24
Apricot-Nut Loaf, '81 8
Apricot-Nut Loaf, Tasty, '82 10
Apricot-Orange Bread, '92 285
Apricot-Pecan Bread, '97 266
Artichoke Bread, '93 140
Asparagus Squares, '79 161
Bacon-and-Cheese Bread, '83 255
Bacon-Cheese Cups, '02 219
Bacon-Cheese Toast Bars, '79 36
Banana-Apple Bread, '85 250
Banana-Blueberry Bread, '81 163
Banana Bread, '87 72
Banana Bread, Easy, '96 97
Banana Bread, Fruity, '95 78
Banana Bread, Sour Cream-, '79 190
Banana Bread, Whole Wheat, '80 88
Banana Butterscotch Bread, '79 116
Banana-Jam Bread, '84 73
Banana-Nut Bread, '86 8, 70; '01 239; '04 259
Banana-Nut Bread, Cream Cheese-, '05 27
Banana Nut Bread, Hawaiian, '79 235
Banana Nut Bread, Whole Wheat-, '84 50
Banana-Nut-Raisin Bread, '81 59
Banana-Nut Roll, '85 112
Banana-Oat Tea Loaf, '87 256
Banana Wheat Bread, '81 14
Banana-Zucchini Bread, '85 326
Barbecue Bread, '99 105
Basil-Garlic Bread, '05 202
Basket, Bread Dough, '04 64
Batter Bread, Soft, '84 253
Batter, Primary, '89 192
Beer Bread, '00 238
Beer Bread, Easy, '79 213; '84 160
Beer Bread, Sweet, '03 207
Biscuit Bread, '84 284
Black-Eyed Pea Bread, '02 224
Blueberry Bread, Hot, '81 164

Blueberry-Lemon Bread, '85 190
Blueberry-Oatmeal Bread, '83 139
Blueberry-Orange Bread, '87 140; '02 21
Blueberry-Orange Nut Bread, '84 141
Blueberry Tea Bread, '96 146
Blue Cheese-Apple Sunburst, '94 245
Blue Cheese Bread, '03 54
Bourbon-Pecan Bread, '93 308; '96 27
Bowls, Toasted Bread, '98 30
Bowl, Veggie Bread, '01 132
Braided Bread Ring, '96 322
Bran-Applesauce Bread, '84 229
Breadstick Haystacks, '99 246
Breadsticks, Easy, '04 298
Breadsticks, Italian Herb, '04 35
Breadsticks, Quick, '00 317
Breakfast Bread, Crunchy, '93 327
Breakfast Bread, Easy, '83 289
Brie Bread, '87 143
Brie Cheese Bake, '87 117
Brown Bread, '84 242; '88 63
Brown Bread, Eighteenth-Century, '79 72
Brown Bread, Steamed Buttermilk, '86 261
Brown Sugar Biscuit Bread, '02 M224
Bruschetta and Cantaloupe Chutney, Prosciutto, '00 108
Bruschetta, Black Truffle, '99 323
Bruschetta, Red-and-Green, '01 62
Bruschetta, Roasted Red Pepper, '00 278
Buschetta, Caper-and-Olive, '00 276
Buttermilk-Cheese Loaf, '91 52
Butternut-Raisin Bread, '79 25
Butternut Spice Loaf, '92 235
Calas, Easy, '92 89
Calas, Quick, '96 64
Carrot Bread, '89 143
Carrot Bread, Tasty, '84 328
Carrot-Nut Loaf, '83 117
Carrot-Pineapple Bread, '82 210
Carrot Puffs, '87 200
Carrot-Walnut Bread, '88 284
Cheddar-Apple Bread, '96 83
Cheddar Cheese Loaf, '00 317
Cheddar Cheese-Pepper Bread, '98 25
Cheddar-Chive Beer Bread, '03 207
Cheddar-Nut Bread, '85 41; '03 42
Cheese Bread, '82 174
Cheese Bread, Dilly, '83 5
Cheese Bread, Easy, '82 74; '86 17
Cheese Bread, Peppery, '04 295
Cheese Bread, Quick, '83 9
Cheese Breadsticks, Italian, '95 126
Cheese Delights, Toasted, '79 37
Cheese-Herb Bread, '85 283
Cheese Loaf, '87 92; '90 93
Cheese Loaves, Little, '86 213
Cheese-Olive Bread, Spicy, '84 150
Cheese Puffs, '03 269
Cheese Puffs, Bavarian, '80 191
Cheesy Twists, '84 284
Cheesy Witches' Brooms, '01 205
Cherry Nut Bread, '81 306; '82 36
Cherry Nut Bread, Maraschino, '79 234
Cherry-Nut Bread, Quick, '85 55
Chocolate Chip-Banana Bread, '90 267
Chocolate Date-Nut Bread, '81 284
Chocolate-Zucchini Bread, '93 308
Cinnamon Loaves, '99 260
Cinnamon Loaves, Miniature, '99 260
Cinnamon Logs, '98 325
Cinnamon Puffs, '81 209
Cinnamon Sticks, '95 244
Cinnamon Toast, Buttery Skillet, '79 36
Citrus-Nut Bread, '83 294
Cocoa Bread with Stewed Yard Peaches, '05 23

Coconut Bread, '83 140
Cracklin' Cakes, Grannie's, '98 252
Cranberry-Banana Bread, '80 281; '90 294
Cranberry Bread, '79 242
Cranberry Fruit-Nut Bread, '79 275
Cranberry-Orange Bread, '87 244
Cranberry-Orange Nut Bread, '80 288
Cream Cheese-Banana-Nut Bread, Cinnamon Crisp-
Topped, '05 27
Cream Cheese-Banana-Nut Bread, Orange-Pecan-
Topped, '05 27
Cream Cheese-Banana-Nut Bread, Peanut Butter
Streusel-Topped, '05 27
Cream Cheese-Banana-Nut Bread, Toasted Coconut-
Topped, '05 27
Cream Cheese-Banana-Nut Bread, Toffee-Topped,
'05 27
Cream Cheese-Pumpkin Bread, '05 251
Crescent Twists, Pecan, '99 47
Crostini with Walnut-Blue Cheese, '01 321
Damper, '97 22
Date-Banana Loaves, Tropical, '95 143
Date-Nut Bread, '85 306
Date-Nut Loaf, '85 10
Date-Walnut Loaf, Blue Ribbon, '80 15
Easy Bread, '87 168
Egg Bread, '95 121
Eggnog Bread, '83 294
Feta Cheese-Spinach Roll, '91 22
Flatbread, Mexican, '80 197
Flatbread, Quick, '00 119
Flatbread, Sicilian Artichoke, '98 136
Focaccia, Basil Pesto, '00 195
Focaccia, Easy Herb, '02 201
Focaccia, Fast Rosemary-Dried Tomato, '98 53
Focaccia, Herb, '97 31
Focaccia, Mustard-and-Onion, '90 321; '92 97
Focaccia, Rosemary-Red Pepper, '01 307
Focaccia with Roasted Pepper Vinaigrette, Stuffed,
'00 134; '04 142
Fou-Fou, '96 325
French Baguettes, Rosemary, '97 165
French Bread, Bacon-Cheese, '92 54
French Bread Bowls, '95 58
French Bread, Cheesy, '88 172; '95 218; '96 205;
'97 325
French Bread, Chive-Garlic, '89 29
French Bread, Garlic, '05 57
French Bread, Herbed, '82 174; '93 283; '99 47
French Bread, Herb-Seasoned, '83 198
French Bread, Hot Garlic, '81 83
French Bread, Lemony, '97 147
French Bread, Onion-Cheese, '89 29
French Bread, Tangy, '98 166
French Loaf, Herbed, '87 243
Frozen Roll Dough, '03 224
Fruit-Nut Bread, Kahlúa, '79 235
Fruit-Nut Twists, '82 253
Fry Bread, '84 140; '85 155
Fry Bread, Indian, '81 56
Garlic Bread, '82 19; '89 282; '91 204; '95 218;
'96 204; '04 288; '05 215
Garlic Bread, Buttery, '02 25, 110
Garlic Bread, Cheesy, '84 150
Garlic Bread, Dilly, '95 218; '96 205
Garlic Bread, Quick, '90 283
Garlic Breadsticks, '79 70
Garlic-Stuffed Bread, Cheesy, '95 176
Gingerbread, '05 219
Gingerbread, Applesauce, '05 231
Gingerbread, Gingery, '96 100
Gingerbread Loaf, '82 14
Gingerbread, Mocha, '81 207; '82 14
Gingerbread, Molasses, '88 203

Gingerbread, Old English, '79 265
Gingerbread, Old-Fashioned, '81 157, 207; '82 14; '91 240
Gingerbread, Refrigerator, '80 52
Gingerbread, Spicy, '84 263
Gingerbread Squares, '84 16
Gingerbread Squares, Apple-, '03 297
Gingerbread, Very Moist, '86 261
Gingerbread with Key Lime Curd, Kahlúa, '96 126
Gorditas with Turkey Mole, '03 18
Greek Bread, '89 200
Greek Sunburst, '94 245
Grilled Bread, '00 88
Ham-and-Cheese Bread, '86 213
Hawaiian Loaf, '80 225
Herb-and-Cheese Pull Aparts, '87 143
Herb Bread, '86 17
Herb Loaf, Toasted, '84 150
Herbs-and-Cheese Bread, '93 56
Herb Sticks, '83 252
Herb-Vegetable-Cheese Bread, '88 172
Hobo Bread, '86 86
Honey-Banana Bread, '91 68
Ice-Cream Bread, '05 252
Irish Bread, '02 67
Irish Soda Bread, '90 214; '95 71
Italian Bread, Easy, '03 48
Jam-and-Cheese Loaf, '89 246
Koulourakia, '90 193
Lahvosh Cracker Bread Bowls, '95 58
Lemon-Almond Tea Bread, '04 209
Lemon Bread, '79 275; '87 256
Lemon-Cream Tea Loaf, '84 50
Lemon-Nut Bread, '79 24
Lemon-Pecan Bread, '83 54
Lemon Tea Bread, '92 268; '93 183; '04 209
Lemon-Walnut Tea Bread, '05 59
Mandel Bread, '97 220
Mandelbread, Chocolate Chip, '00 282
Mango Bread, '96 205
Marbled Loaves with Orange Glaze, '99 293
Mayonnaise Bread, '89 29
Mix, Quick Bread, '81 90; '86 8
Molasses-Nut Bread, '84 24
Monkey Bread, Bacon, '94 283; '97 154
Monkey Bread Bites, '04 333
Monkey Bread, Cheese-Filled, '91 21
Monkey Bread, Quick, '81 306; '82 36
Mustard Bread, '01 146
Mustard-Rye Ovals, '84 149
Nautical Knots, '93 168
Nut Bread, '04 281
Oatmeal Bread, '81 236, 300
Oatmeal Raisin Bread, '81 14
Onion Bread, Easy, '81 162
Onion-Cheese Bread, '79 180; '81 8
Onion-Cheese Supper Bread, '83 112
Onion-Herb Bread, Toasted, '83 266
Onion-Parmesan Bread, '84 284
Orange, Baba au, '86 138
Orange-Cranberry Bread, '85 266
Orange-Cream Cheese Bread, '82 210
Orange-Nut Bread, '82 75
Orange Nut Loaf, '80 226
Orange-Pecan Bread, '79 148
Orange-Pecan Bread, Glazed, '81 250
Orange-Pecan Loaves, '79 215
Orange Praline Toast, '79 36
Orange Puffs, Upside-Down, '83 57
Orange-Pumpkin Bread, '87 300
Orange Tea Bread, '79 234
Pane Cunsado (Fixed Bread), '95 218
Pane Cunsado (Sicilian for "Fixed Bread"), '96 205

Papaya Bread, '88 138
Parmesan Cheese Bread, '99 61
Parmesan Cheese Breadsticks, '05 20
Parmesan-Garlic Breadsticks, '99 46
Parmesan Herb Bread, '82 235; '83 41
Parmesan-Pepper Toasts, '98 242
Parmesan Puffs, '98 235
Parmesan Rounds, '79 170
Parmesan Sesame Sticks, '81 39
Parmesan Twists, '83 239; '99 323
Parmesan-Wine Bread, '97 31
Peach Bread, '82 170
Peach Bread, Georgia, '79 161
Peach Bread, Tipsy, '02 21
Peanut Bread, '87 184
Peanut Butter Bread, '88 64; '99 111
Pear Bread, '80 218
Pecan-Cornmeal Rounds, '95 99
Pepper Bread, '85 156
Persimmon Bread, '80 228
Persimmon Date-Nut Bread, '82 218
Pig-in-a-Blanket Bread, '99 134
Pineapple-Apricot Bread, '84 7
Pineapple Bread, '83 139
Pineapple Breakfast Puffs, '98 326
Pineapple-Carrot Bread, '79 106
Pineapple-Nut Bread, '79 215
Pineapple-Pecan Loaf Bread, '87 256
Pita Bread Salad, '95 86
Pita Triangles, Cheesy, '93 70
Pizza Sticks, '98 255
Pizza Sunburst, '94 245
Popovers
    Blender Popovers, Perfect, '79 53
    Cheddar Cheese Popovers, '85 41
    Cheddar Popovers, '00 64
    Cheese Popover Puffs, '85 6
    Cinnamon Popovers, '90 66
    Good Old Southern Popovers, '79 138
    Herbed Popovers, '00 64
    Jumbo Popovers, '83 225
    Muffin Tin Popovers, '79 138
    Parmesan Popovers, '90 66; '00 64
    Pecan Popovers, '01 206
    Pecan Popovers, Giant, '83 208
    Pimiento Popovers, '79 138
    Popovers, '94 43; '00 64
    Ring, Cheesy Popover, '80 45
    Seasoned Popovers, '86 86
    Two, Popovers for, '81 304
    Whole Wheat Popovers, '90 66; '05 195
    Yorkshire Popovers, '00 65
Poppy-Onion Loaf, '04 35
Poppy Seed Bread, '83 140
Poppy Seed Bread, Orange-Scented, '04 300
Poppy Seed Loaf, Quick, '82 75
Poppy Seed-Swiss Cheese Bread, '91 52
Potato Bites, Mashed, '98 249
Prune-Nut Bread, '87 255; '91 55
Puddings
    Almond-Cream Cheese Bread Pudding with Amaretto Cream Sauce, Layered, '03 330
    Amish Bread Pudding, '80 8
    Apple-Raisin Bread Pudding, '88 175
    Apricot Bread Pudding, '85 24
    Bananas Foster Bread Pudding, '04 235
    Berry Bread Pudding with Vanilla Cream Sauce, '05 260
    Blueberry Bread Pudding, '88 154; '03 119
    Blueberry-Lemon Sauce, Bread Pudding with, '01 117
    Bread Pudding, '89 M130; '90 219
    Brown Sugar Bread Pudding with Crème Anglaise, '05 239

Buttermilk Bread Pudding with Butter-Rum Sauce, '95 134
Cheesy Bread Pudding, '83 68
Chocolate Bread Pudding, '80 8
Chocolate Bread Pudding with Custard Sauce, '03 244
Chocolate Bread Pudding with Whiskey Sauce, '99 277
Cinnamon-Raisin Bread Pudding, '01 315
Cinnamon Toast Pudding with Caramel Sauce, '96 284
Cranberry-Raisin Bread Pudding, Stuffed Pumpkin with, '02 231
Croissant Bread Pudding, '03 66
Custard Sauce, Bread Pudding with, '97 313
Durfee's Bread Pudding, '96 48
Fig-Walnut Pudding, '03 244
French Bread Pudding, '85 231
Lemon Bread Pudding, Old-Fashioned, '88 95
Mushroom Bread Pudding, '99 58
Old-Fashioned Bread Pudding, '83 213; '88 175; '00 105; '01 223
Old-Fashioned Bread Pudding with Bourbon Custard Sauce, '95 271
Old-Fashioned Bread Pudding with Rum Sauce, '88 32
Peachy Bread Pudding, '88 175
Piña Colada Bread Pudding, '98 34
Pineapple-Apple Bread Pudding with Bourbon Sauce, '05 119
Pineapple-Apple Bread Pudding with Vanilla-Nutmeg Sauce, '02 208
Plum Bread Pudding, Refrigerator, '97 177
Pumpkin Bread Pudding, '98 240
Raisin Bread Pudding, '94 215
Raisin Bread Pudding with Bourbon Sauce, '98 336
Rosemary-Tasso Bread Pudding, '00 104
Sauce, Bread Pudding, '04 235
Soufflé, Creole Bread Pudding, '92 87
Spiced Bread Pudding, '93 52
Sweet Potato Bread Pudding, '94 241
Sweet Roll Pudding, '96 283
Tennessee Bread Pudding with Bourbon Sauce, '93 51
Vanilla Sauce, Bread Pudding with, '97 M15
Whiskey Sauce, Bread Pudding with, '80 58; '90 230; '92 93
White Chocolate Bread Pudding, '00 M104
Pull-Apart Ring, Southwestern, '03 298
Pull-Apart Ring, Veggie Southwestern, '03 299
Pull-Away Bread, '98 137
Pull-Away Bread, Cinnamon, '98 137
Pumpkin Bread, '81 8; '05 232
Pumpkin Bread, Brother Boniface's, '98 26
Pumpkin Bread, Harvest, '90 M215
Pumpkin Bread, Holiday, '03 281
Pumpkin Bread, Moist, '80 245
Pumpkin Bread, Spiced, '91 233
Pumpkin Bread with Cream Cheese and Preserves, '84 264
Pumpkin-Coconut Bread, '87 255
Pumpkin Loaf, Harvest, '85 232
Pumpkin-Nut Bread, '83 294
Pumpkin-Oatmeal Loaf, '81 49
Pumpkin-Pecan Bread, '87 221; '02 224
Raisin-Cranberry Bread, '81 305; '82 36
Roasted Garlic-Rosemary Bread, '04 16
Rollups, Pizza Bread, '04 M35
Saffron Tea Bread, '85 26
Salad, Avocado-Bread, '02 210
Salad, Italian BLT Bread, '03 90
Salad, Italian Bread, '99 259; '03 54
Sally Lunn, Quick, '87 16
Salt-Rising Bread, '79 145

BREADS

(continued)

Santa Gertrudis Pan de Campo, '94 27
Sausage-Onion Squares, '83 112
Scones
  Breakfast Scones, '88 231; '89 22
  Cheddar Cheese Scones, Golden, '99 82
  Cherry-and-Cream Scones, '99 49
  Cranberry-Nut Yeast Scones, Merry, '99 274
  Cranberry-Orange Scones, '97 45
  Cranberry Scones, '95 283
  Cream Scones, '97 44
  Cream Scones, Classic, '02 41
  Currant Scones, '84 117; '92 332
  Drop Scones, '00 239
  Drop Scones, Breakfast, '88 83
  Hazelnut Scones, '94 16
  Lemon-Poppy Seed Scones, '97 44
  Lemon-Raisin Scones, '87 69
  Mocha-Pecan Scones, '97 45
  Orange-Pecan Scones, '94 215; '01 72
  Orange Scones with Orange Butter, Double-, '97 44
  Pizza Scones, '03 207
  Scottish Scones, '97 44
Seasoned Breadsticks, '81 84; '96 46
Sesame Bread Twists, '84 283
Sesame-Cheddar Sticks, '81 150
Sesame-Cheese Breadsticks, '97 31
Sesame Sticks, '83 9
Sesame Wheat Crisps, '81 106
Shrimp Toast, '86 91
Sourdough Dill Bread, '89 192
Sourdough Starter, '89 192
Sourdough Wedges, '90 199
Spinach Bread, '83 121; '87 144
Spoonbreads
  Barbara Sue's Spoonbread, '99 83
  Cheddar Spoonbread, '82 196
  Cheese Spoonbread, '86 261
  Chorizo, Spoonbread with Simple, '04 207
  Corn and Bacon Spoonbread, '81 129
  Corn-Cheese Spoonbread, '88 9
  Corn Spoonbread, '97 301
  Dressing, Southwestern-Style Spoonbread, '94 273
  Garlic Spoonbread, '79 269; '80 14
  Golden Spoonbread, '83 286; '84 17
  Grits Spoonbread, '79 38
  Grits with Savory Mushroom Sauce, Spoonbread, '96 236
  Memmie's Spoonbread, '95 27; '04 57; '05 105
  Old Virginia Spoonbread, '84 102
  Spoonbread, '80 43; '81 138; '90 200; '95 156; '04 58
Squash Bread, '79 210
Squash Bread, Spicy, '83 121
Stars, Bread, '93 286
Starter Food, '94 324; '95 77
Sticks, Crispy, '03 211
Stollen, '86 291
Strawberry Bread, '81 250; '83 140; '84 49
Strawberry Jam Bread, '79 216
Strawberry-Nut Bread, '79 24
Sun-dried Tomato-Herb Bread, '05 252
Tacos, Navajo, '84 246
Tennessee Sin, '95 218; '96 204
Three-C Bread, '81 284
Toast, Basil Pesto, '01 17
Toast Points, '93 270
Toast Points, Parmesan, '00 316
Toasts, Crispy Parmesan, '01 307
Toasts, Tomato-Basil, '01 254
Toast Strips, Seasoned, '93 98

Tomato-Cheese Bread, '98 172; '99 M157
Tomato-Cheese Bread, Herbed, '88 143
Tortillas, Flour, '81 303
Tortillas, Never-Fail Flour, '80 198
Vegetable Bread, Breakaway, '82 74
Wampus Bread, '81 305
Wheat Loaf, Nutty, '90 65
Whole Wheat Cardamom Bread, '86 223
Whole Wheat Coffee Can Bread, Molasses, '85 111
Whole Wheat Date-Nut Bread, '04 208
Whole Wheat Nut Bread, '04 208
Whole Wheat Orange Bread, '85 5
Whole Wheat Quick Bread, '82 65; '00 49
Whole Wheat Raisin-Nut Bread, '04 208
Wine-Date Nut Bread, '82 253
Yeast
  Almond Braid, '89 86
  Almond Danish, '87 301
  Anillos, '02 82
  Anise-Orange Bread, '83 295
  Apple Danish, Deep-Dish, '86 161
  Apple-Date-Nut Ring, '90 212
  Apple-Pecan Biscuit Braid, '02 326
  Apple Pull-Apart Bread, '86 330
  Apple Swirl Bread, '85 4
  Armenian Thin Bread, '94 108
  Austrian Sweet Bread, '83 294
  Austrian Twists, '80 45
  Bagels, '89 266
  Bagels, Whole Wheat, '84 20
  Baguettes, '85 70
  Baguettes and Rolls, '98 168
  Beer Bread, Best-Ever, '82 129
  Beer Bread, Hearty, '87 226; '88 133
  Beignets, '84 56; '01 59
  Beignets, French Market, '92 88; '93 219; '94 319; '95 80
  Beignets, Lobster-and-Roasted Corn, '00 51
  Binning Bread, '80 68
  Bowls, Irish Tater Bread, '96 111
  Bowls, Italian Bread, '98 292
  Braided Bread, '88 76
  Braided Loaf, '82 17
  Braids, Festive, '87 297
  Braids, Holiday, '83 295
  Braid, Sweet Yeast, '90 46
  Break-Away Bread, '86 56
  Brioche, '81 122; '89 90
  Brioche Chicken Curry, '88 124
  Brioche Loaves, Vienna, '87 300
  Brioche, Morrison House, '96 53
  Brown Bread, Light-, '84 268
  Bubble Bread, '81 107
  Bunny Bread, Glazed, '92 102
  Butter-Egg Bread, '85 269
  Butterhorns, '84 267
  Buttermilk-Oatmeal Bread, '97 212
  Cake Bread, Golden, '84 269
  Canapé Bread, '89 292
  Caramel Bread, '82 75
  Caramel-Orange Coffee Ring, '80 45
  Caraway Breadsticks, '89 239
  Caraway Puffs, '82 174
  Caraway Seed Bread, Dark, '80 256
  Challah, '92 62
  Cheddar Cheese Bread, '84 268
  Cheese Bread, '83 208; '87 11
  Cheese Bread, Crusty, '86 233
  Cheese-Caraway Batter Bread, '85 33
  Cheese Crescents, '82 18
  Cheese-Herb Bread, '84 M144
  Cheese Loaf, Jalapeño-, '84 76
  Cheese-Wine Bread, '87 254
  Chocolate Loaf Bread, '88 M188

Chocolate Pinwheel Loaf, '80 256
Christmas Bread, '87 296; '88 288
Christmas Bread, Norwegian, '79 234
Christmas Wreath, '80 280
Cinnamon Loaf, '82 18; '85 55
Cinnamon-Nut Bubble Bread, '80 22
Cinnamon-Oat Bread, '90 135
Cinnamon Raisin Bread, '80 22
Cinnamon Swirl Loaf, '79 23
Cinnamon Twists, '83 53
Cocoa-Nut Swirl Bread, '80 257
Coffee Ring, Filled, '82 18
Coffee Ring, Sugarplum, '83 M37
Cornmeal Yeast Bread, '89 54
Cottage Cheese-Dill Bread, '83 154
Country Ham Bread with Herb Butter, '99 18
Cracker Bread, Sesame, '87 2
Cream Cheese Braids, '82 243; '97 287
Cream Cheese Loaves, Processor, '85 48
Crescents, Festive, '80 281
Croissants, '83 54; '84 188; '96 303
Croissants, Chocolate-Filled, '96 303
Croissants, Cinnamon-Sugar, '96 303
Croissants, Flaky Butter, '85 42
Croissants, Strawberry or Apricot, '96 303
Crust Bread, Country, '80 225
Cuernitos, '02 82
Dill-Oat Bread, '91 95
Dough, Basic Yeast, '88 74
Easter Bread, Golden, '91 54
Easter Egg Bread, '84 94; '96 88
Easy Yeast Bread, '79 147
Egg Bread, Braided, '03 M234
Egg Bread, County Fair, '87 68
Elephant Ears, '84 18
English Muffin Bread, '95 M79
English Muffin Loaf, '82 96
English Muffin Loaves, '85 42
Figure-8 Bread, '79 171
Flatbread, '98 106
Flat Bread, Italian-Style, '82 235; '83 41
Flatbread, Parmesan-Onion, '98 65
Focaccia, Dried Tomato, '94 65
Focaccia, Herbed, '04 208
Focaccia, Onion, '93 77
Focaccia, Roquefort-and-Onion, '98 54
Focaccia, Rosemary, '95 190
Focaccia with Rosemary, '96 84
French Bread, '79 158; '87 227; '89 54; '96 191
French Bread, Easy, '88 299
French Bread, Glazed, '88 75
French Bread, Herbed, '85 222; '86 166
French Bread, Mom's, '98 281
French Bread, New Orleans, '80 212
French Bread, Whole Wheat, '88 63
French Loaves, Crusty, '85 37
French Onion Bread, '91 90
French Pistou Bread, Crusty, '97 68
Fruit-and-Cheese Braid, '86 214
Gingerbread Men, Yeast, '92 312
Golden Bread, '90 47
Gouda Bread, '91 52
Grits Bread, Bacon-Cheddar, '05 83
Grits Bread, Basil Pesto-Cheese, '05 83
Grits Bread, Cheesy, '05 83
Grits Bread, Tomato-Black Olive, '05 83
Grittibanz (Swiss Bread Figure), '93 265
Ham Bread with Herb Butter, Country, '86 255
Heartland Loaves, '89 287
Herb Bread, '84 268
Herb Bread, No-Knead, '81 217
Herb-Cheese Bread, '85 70
Herbed Bread, '89 34

Herb Loaf, Butterflake, '86 261
Herb-Sour Cream Bread, '85 268
Herman Food, '82 200
Holiday Wreath, '81 284
Honey-Cinnamon Swirl Bread, '88 287
Honey-Curry Bread, '89 250
Honey Graham Bread, '99 211
Honey-Granola Bread, '86 56
Honey Loaves, Hint o', '81 104
Honey-Oat Bread, '89 107; '93 232; '98 27
Honey Oatmeal Bread, '80 60
Honey Puffs, '96 153
Honey Twist, '79 80
Honey-Walnut Swirl, '80 21
Honey Wheat Bread, '85 18, 268
Honey-Wheat Bread, '91 223
Italian Bread, '82 297; '04 208
Knots, Two-Seed Bread, '02 292
Kolecz (Polish Bread), '80 29
Kulich, '01 87
Lightbread, Coffee Can, '79 59
Light Yeast Bread, '81 299
Loaf Bread, Hospitality, '86 299
Loaf Bread, Old-Fashioned, '88 75
Loaves, Sweet-Filled Yeast, '90 46
Mandelkrantz, '92 32
Marble Loaf, '80 230
Monkey Bread, '82 243; '95 174
Monkey Bread, Easy, '90 214
Multi-Grain Bread, '86 236
Oat Bread, Caraway-Raisin, '86 44
Oatmeal Bread, '81 300; '92 212; '97 130
Oatmeal Bread, Round, '84 20
Oatmeal-Molasses Bread, '97 194
Oatmeal Pan Bread, Herbed, '97 243
Oatmeal-Raisin Bread, '83 59
Oat-Molasses Bread, '82 139
Old-Fashioned Yeast Bread, '79 284
Olive Bread, '93 78
Olive-Dill Casserole Bread, '92 16
Onion-Dill Bread, Easy, '85 5
Onion-Herb Bread, '90 165
Onion-Poppy Seed Twist, '97 242
Onion-Rye Bread, '99 55
Onion Twist Loaves, '84 300
Pandoro, '93 267
Panettone, '93 266
Parmesan Bread, '92 19; '93 231; '00 54
Party Bread, '86 218
Peanut Butter Bread, '86 171
Peanut Lover's Bread, '93 211
Pimiento-Cheese Bread, '85 223; '86 166
Pitas, Puffy, '97 69
Pizza Batter Bread, '85 56
Pizza Crust, '04 208
Pizza Dough, '04 58
Pocket Bread, '79 58
Poppy Seed Loaf, '83 254
Portuguese Round Bread, '83 295
Potato Bread, '85 56
Potato Bread, Old-Fashioned, '86 57
Potato Lightbread, '80 225
Potato Loaves, '86 162
Pull-Apart Yeast Bread, '94 132
Pumpernickel Boule, Walnut-Raisin, '02 259
Pumpernickel Bread, '02 259
Pumpernickel Bread, Sour-Rye, '02 259
Raisin Batter Bread, Salt-Free, '86 33
Raisin Bread, Curried Chicken Salad on '85 96
Raisin Bread, Homemade, '87 300
Raisin Bread, Round, '89 230
Raisin-Whole Wheat Bread, '93 77
Refrigerator Bread, No-Knead, '83 155

Roasted Red Bell Pepper Bread, '95 241
Rounds, Individual Bread, '83 159
Rye Bread, '84 21
Rye Bread, Swedish Orange-, '85 111
Rye Canapé Bread, '89 293
Rye Loaves, Swedish, '97 68
Rye Sandwich Bread, '82 65
Saffron Bread, '96 50
Sally Lunn, '81 157; '88 163; '94 233
Sally Lunn Bread, '03 27
Sandwiches, Stacking, '86 127
Savarin, Holiday, '80 280
Scones, Merry Cranberry-Nut Yeast, '99 274
Sesame-Wheat Breadsticks, '93 114
Soft Breadsticks, '83 115
Sopaipillas, '80 197
Sour Cream Bread, '79 59
Sour Cream-Cheese Bread, '85 33
Sourdough Bread, '82 201
Sourdough Bread Dough, Potato, '94 324; '95 77
Sourdough Bread, Potato, '94 325; '95 77
Sourdough Starter, Herman, '82 200
Sourdough Starter, Potato, '94 324; '95 77
Sour Starter, '02 259
"Sponge," '93 267
Squares, Yeast Bread, '83 155
Starter Food, '94 324
Sugar Plum Bread, '80 256
Sweet Bread Wreath, Glazed, '90 192
Sweet Christmas Loaf, '84 278
Swiss Cheese Bread, '79 60
Swiss Cheese Loaves, Mini, '95 80
Techniques of Breadmaking, '82 17
Trinity Feast Bread, '82 92; '83 83
Walnut Bread, '93 77
Wheat-and-Oat Bran Bread, '92 102
Wheat Bread, Buttermilk, '86 236
Wheat Bread, Pull-Apart Maple, '85 222; '86 166
White Bread, '79 275
White Bread, Cardamom, '82 236; '83 41
White Bread, Old-Fashioned, '81 285
White Bread, Special, '86 57
Whole Wheat Bran Bread, '79 58
Whole Wheat Bread, '83 17
Whole Wheat Bread, Anchorage Country Store, '00 272
Whole Wheat Bread and Rolls, Hearty, '79 92
Whole Wheat Bread, Anise-, '93 36
Whole Wheat Bread, Quick, '92 25
Whole Wheat Breadsticks, '84 228
Whole Wheat Canapé Bread, '89 293
Whole Wheat Honey Bread, '82 65; '83 106
Whole Wheat-Oatmeal Bread, '87 85
Whole Wheat-Rye Bread, '83 M37
Whole Wheat-White Bread, '82 130
Wreaths, Holiday Coffee Cake, '00 307
Yogurt Bread, '97 130
Yellow Squash Bread, '84 140
Zucchini-Apple Bread, '87 255
Zucchini Bread, '85 111; '86 93
Zucchini Bread, Spiced, '79 161; '86 162
Zucchini Bread, Spicy, '81 305; '82 36
Zucchini-Carrot Bread, '83 190
Zucchini-Honey Bread, '89 143
Zucchini Loaves, '96 130

BROCCOLI
Almond Broccoli in Sherry Sauce, '02 45
Almond-Lemon Dip, Broccoli with, '05 292
Appetizer, Broccoli-Cheese, '92 265
au Gratin, Broccoli, '82 M20
Bacon, Broccoli with, '92 302
Bake, Broccoli, '81 246; '89 279
Bakers, Broccoli, '99 308
Beef and Broccoli, Quick, '91 123

Beef and Broccoli with Chive Gravy, '88 214
Burritos, Broccoli, '83 200
Carnival Broccoli, '81 2
Casseroles
Almond-Broccoli Casserole, '88 62
au Gratin, Broccoli-and-Eggs, '85 289
au Gratin, Broccoli-Ham, '90 239
Bake, Broccoli, '89 279
Blue Cheese Casserole, Broccoli-, '85 260
Breakfast Casserole, Broccoli-Cheese, '99 233
Broccoli Casserole, '87 284; '88 M146, 265; '05 M276
Cheese Casserole, Broccoli-, '82 269; '84 9; '94 132
Cheesy Broccoli Bake, '83 255
Cheesy Broccoli Casserole, '84 293; '92 342; '95 M191
Cheesy Italian Broccoli Bake, '83 5
Chicken, Broccoli, and Cauliflower Casserole, '00 337
Chicken-Broccoli Casserole, '79 48; '91 315
Chicken Casserole, Broccoli-, '82 33
Company Broccoli Bake, '83 279
Corn Casserole, Broccoli-, '83 313
Crabmeat-Broccoli Casserole, '84 232
Divan Casserole, Chicken, '82 M203
Divan, Chicken, '80 10; '87 M218
Divan, Creamy Turkey, '90 M34
Divan, Curried Chicken, '80 83
Divan, Easy Chicken, '94 310
Divan, Gourmet Chicken, '82 83
Divan, Overnight Chicken, '83 198
Divan Quiche, Chicken, '88 M125
Divan, Quick Turkey, '89 178
Divan, Sherried Chicken, '80 38
Divan, Turkey, '82 268
Easy Broccoli Casserole, '03 M49
Egg Casserole, Broccoli-and-, '86 324
English Walnut Broccoli, '89 68
Garden Surprise, '83 112
Gratin, Broccoli-and-Cauliflower, '01 43
Ham and Broccoli Casserole, '81 133
Ham and Broccoli Strata, '80 261
Ham-Broccoli Casserole, Quick, '82 40
Italian Broccoli Casserole, '82 6, 280; '83 32
Macaroni and Cheese, Broccoli, '02 36
Onion Deluxe, Broccoli-, '81 75
Pimiento Cheese Sauce, Broccoli with, '02 291
Potato-Broccoli-Cheese Bake, '80 114
Rice Casserole, Broccoli-, '81 101
Sausage and Broccoli Casserole, '80 33
Squash Casserole, Broccoli-and-, '01 175
Strata, Turkey-Cheddar-Broccoli, '03 100
Stuffing, Broccoli with, '95 341
Supreme, Broccoli, '85 68; '02 312
Swiss Cheese Casserole, Broccoli-, '83 322; '85 M211
Tuna-Broccoli Casserole, Tangy, '83 75
Turkey-and-Broccoli Casserole, '86 332
Winter Broccoli Casserole, '94 280
Cheese Sauce, Broccoli with, '82 107
Chicken with Broccoli, Spicy Ginger-and-Orange, '02 309
Chinese Broccoli, '85 M12
Chowder, Broccoli, '79 16
Chowder, Swiss-Broccoli, '80 73
Cocktail Broccoli, '80 192
Crêpes, Royal Brunch, '81 44
Cups, Broccoli, '00 53
Dip, Broccoli-Garlic, '82 59
Dip, Cheesy Broccoli, '83 92
Dip, Santa Fe Skinny, '94 137
Eggs, Broccoli and Creamed, '83 84
Elegant, Broccoli, '81 267
Fettuccine, Broccoli-Parmesan, '93 55

BROCCOLI
(continued)

Fettuccine with Broccoli, '90 97
Filling, Broccoli, '81 44
French Sauce, Broccoli with, '81 295
Frittata, Broccoli-Cheese, '81 243
Frittata, Ham-and-Broccoli, '98 101
Fritters, Broccoli-Cauliflower, '02 45
Fritters, Cheesy Broccoli, '79 53
Garlic Broccoli, '93 35; '95 54; '99 46
Glazed Broccoli with Almonds, '80 12
Herbed Broccoli, '88 101
Herbed Broccoli, Lemony, '02 45
Hollandaise Sauce, Broccoli with, '79 244, 276
Hollandaise Sauce, Broccoli with Mock, '82 272
Horseradish Sauce, Broccoli with, '81 2; '83 206; '84 33
Horseradish Sauce, Carrots and Broccoli with, '91 246
Italian-Style Broccoli, '88 41
Italienne, Broccoli, '82 300
Jade-Green Broccoli, '80 12
Lemon Broccoli, '88 119; '95 53
Lemon-Broccoli Goldenrod, '84 M89
Lemon Cream, Broccoli with, '89 245
Lemon Dressing, Chilled Broccoli with, '88 270
Lemon Sauce and Pecans, Broccoli with, '86 71
Lemon Sauce, Broccoli with, '91 292; '92 256
Linguine, Broccoli, '98 30
Linguine, Chicken-Broccoli, '98 30
Lo Mein Noodles and Broccoli, '97 18
Mac 'n' Cheese, Broccoli, '00 53
Marinated Broccoli, '80 79; '81 40; '85 207; '86 157; '88 255
Marinated Fresh Broccoli, '81 M139
Medley, Buttery Broccoli, '03 259
Medley, Cauliflower-Broccoli, '81 69
Muffins, Broccoli-Chicken, '96 27
Muffins, Broccoli Cornbread, '03 81
Olive-Butter Sauce, Broccoli with, '83 118
Omelet, Broccoli-Mushroom, '85 45
Onions, Broccoli-Stuffed, '84 154
Orange Broccoli, Easy, '85 267
Orange Sauce, Broccoli with, '80 243; '04 285
Parmesan, Broccoli, '97 302
Parsnips with Horseradish, Broccoli and, '02 235
Pasta, Broccoli, '84 176
Pasta, Chicken-and-Broccoli, '87 286
Pasta with Broccoli and Sausage, '87 109; '97 266
Pasta with Peppers and Broccoli, '91 69
Pecan Broccoli, '05 257
Pickled Broccoli, '81 308
Pie, Broccoli-and-Turkey Pasta, '88 269
Pie, Broccoli-Beef, '83 196
Pie, Broccoli-Cheese, '84 235
Pimiento Broccoli, '86 268
Pimiento Cheese Sauce, Broccoli with, '05 333
Pizza, Broccoli Supreme, '02 312
Polonaise, Broccoli, '86 55
Potatoes and Broccoli, Creamy, '92 61
Potatoes, Breakfast-Stuffed, '00 179
Potatoes, Broccoli-and-Almond-Topped, '83 3
Potatoes, Broccoli-Shrimp Stuffed, '92 M228
Potatoes, Broccoli-Topped Baked, '86 17
Potatoes, Cheddar, Broccoli, and Ham Stuffed, '04 26
Potatoes, Stuffed Mashed, '98 328
Pot Pie, Ham-Broccoli, '03 83
Puff, Broccoli, '81 94; '82 95
Quiche, Broccoli-Rice, '81 228
Quiche, Easy Broccoli, '82 34
Quiche, Italian Broccoli, '85 45
Quick-and-Easy Broccoli, '86 55
Rice, Holiday Broccoli with, '87 252

Risotto with Parmesan, Broccoli, '99 120
Roasted Broccoli and Cauliflower, '01 132
Rolls, Broccoli-Cheddar, '91 21
Rolls, Ham-and-Broccoli, '86 212; '87 82
Salads
Barley-Broccoli Salad, '90 135
Beef-and-Broccoli Salad, '87 187
Broccoli Salad, '82 24; '85 249; '90 292; '95 95; '99 84; '00 213; '01 58
Carrot-Broccoli Salad, '99 26
Cauliflower, and Carrot Salad, Broccoli, '04 140
Cauliflower-Broccoli Crunch, '88 216
Cauliflower-Broccoli Salad, '79 20
Cauliflower-Broccoli Toss, '82 54
Cauliflower Salad, Broccoli-, '92 97; '00 90
Cauliflower Salad, Broccoli and, '81 280
Cauliflower Salad, Broccoli 'n', '90 32
Cauliflower Salad, Creamy Broccoli and, '81 23
Cauliflower Toss, Crunchy Broccoli, '83 25
Chicken Salad, Broccoli-, '90 129; '00 53
Congealed Broccoli Salad, '84 124
Corn Salad, Broccoli-, '87 24
Creamy Broccoli Salad, '79 143
Crunchy Broccoli Salad, '83 39
Curried Broccoli Salad, '86 225
Fresh Broccoli Salad, '82 34; '87 103
Grape Salad, Broccoli-, '01 163
Mandarin Salad, Broccoli-, '93 325
Marinated Broccoli, '80 79
Marinated Broccoli Salad, '83 240
Marinated Broccoli, Tangy, '80 284
Medley, Broccoli, '81 206
Orange Salad, Broccoli-, '94 281
Pasta Salad, Broccoli-Cauliflower, '88 269
Pasta Salad, Broccoli-Cheese-, '96 184
Peanut Salad, Broccoli-, '92 35
Pepperoni-and-Broccoli Salad, '83 216
Potato Salad, Hot Broccoli-, '85 23
Raisin Salad, Classic Broccoli-, '02 24
Raisin Salad, Creamy Broccoli-, '92 106
Ramen Noodle Salad, '02 24
Red Pepper Salad, Broccoli and, '83 224
Red, White, and Green Salad, '90 18
Slaw, Broccoli, '01 49; '05 278
Slaw, Broccoli-Squash, '05 170
Slaw, Cilantro, '05 324
Slaw Salad, Sweet Broccoli, '05 91
Slaw, Sweet Broccoli, '96 20; '98 332
Slaw, Zesty Broccoli, '93 246
Supreme, Broccoli Salad, '83 260
Toss, Broccoli, '86 294
Toss, Crunchy Romaine, '00 30
Toss, Italian Cauliflower-Broccoli, '88 269
Warm Broccoli Salad, '92 35
Sauce, Broccoli, '91 85
Sauté, Broccoli and Walnut, '95 52
Sautéed Broccoli, '79 246
Savory Broccoli, '79 268; '80 14
Sesame Broccoli, '84 69; '85 8; '03 67
Sesame, Broccoli with, '80 13
Sesame Seeds, Broccoli with, '82 34; '02 45
Shrimp Sauce, Broccoli and Cauliflower with, '84 248
Skillet, Quick Broccoli, '05 86
Soufflé, Broccoli, '81 24
Soufflé, Golden Broccoli, '84 283
Soufflés, Broccoli, '96 218
Soup, Broccoli, '86 161, M194; '87 288
Soup, Broccoli-and-Chicken, '90 202
Soup, Broccoli-Swiss, '86 6
Soup, Cheese-and-Broccoli, '89 276
Soup, Cheesy-Broccoli, '86 258
Soup, Creamed Broccoli, '85 24
Soup, Cream of Broccoli, '79 130; '80 188, M225; '82 314; '83 66; '86 259

Soup, Cream-of-Broccoli, '88 56
Soup, Creamy Broccoli, '81 75; '82 13; '83 99; '91 307
Soup, Easy Broccoli, '81 307
Soup, Fresh Broccoli, '91 86
Soup, Hot Broccoli, '81 235; '83 44
Soup, Light Cream of Broccoli, '93 17
Soup, Mock Cream of Broccoli, '85 288
Sour Cream Sauce, Broccoli with, '87 127
Spears, Saucy Broccoli, '84 35
Spears, Zesty Broccoli, '79 152
Spread, Broccamoli Curry, '88 55
Stack-Ups, Jiffy Tomato, '80 161
Steamed Broccoli, '80 122
Steamed Broccoli, Lemon Pepper, '02 215
Steamed Broccoli with Tangy Chive Sauce, '83 101
Stew, Oyster-Broccoli, '89 242
Stir-Fried Broccoli, '83 227; '00 99
Stir-Fry Beef and Broccoli, '79 47
Stir-Fry, Beef-and-Broccoli, '91 46
Stir-Fry, Bok Choy-Broccoli, '84 2
Stir-Fry Broccoli, '80 19
Stir-Fry Broccoli and Beef, '83 110
Stir-Fry, Chicken-Broccoli, '82 33
Stir-Fry, Turkey-Broccoli, '91 62
Stroganoff, Chicken-and-Broccoli, '89 M248
Sunshine Sauce, Broccoli with, '84 248
Supreme, Broccoli, '82 34; '85 68
Supreme, Broccoli-Carrot, '89 331
Supreme, Creamy Broccoli, '82 287
Tomatoes, Broccoli-Stuffed, '83 136; '93 216
Vinaigrette, Potato-Broccoli, '85 84
White Wine, Broccoli with, '80 12
Wine Sauce, Broccoli with, '84 187
Ziti with Sausage and Broccoli, '95 340
BROWNIES. *See also* **COOKIES/Bars and Squares.**
Alaskas, Brownie, '83 299
Amaretto Brownies, '86 246
Amaretto-Walnut Brownies, '99 311; '04 142
Angel Fluff Brownies, '99 221
Apple Brownies, Frosted, '86 216
Banana-Split Brownies, '03 M43
Basic Brownies, '97 M34
Birthday Party Brownie Cakes, '00 199
Biscuit Mix Brownies, '94 M51
Bittersweet Brownies, Fudgy, '05 253
Blonde Brownies, Nutty, '81 64
Blonde Brownies with Chocolate Chunks, '91 271
Broadway Brownie Bars, '97 M35
Buttermilk Brownies, '85 249
Buttermilk Cake Brownies, '87 198
Butterscotch Brownies, '85 248
Butterscotch-Chocolate Brownies, '03 47
Cake, Brownie-Carrot, '92 120
Candy Bar Brownies, '92 204; '01 63
Caramel-Coconut-Pecan Brownies, '05 M288
Caramel-Pecan Filled Brownies, '03 M43
Cheesecake Brownies, '85 249
Chocolate-Banana Brownies, '80 160
Chocolate Brownies, '02 M207
Chocolate Brownies, Chunky, '04 248
Chocolate Brownies, Double-, '01 63; '04 100
Chocolate Brownies, Double, '04 M220
Chocolate Brownies with Caramel Frosting, Double, '04 M220
Chocolate Chip Brownies, '81 162
Chocolate Chip-Peanut Butter Brownies, '84 73
Chocolate-Coconut Brownies, '97 35
Chocolate Fudge Brownies, '05 M288
Chocolate-Glazed Brownies, '01 143
Chocolate Ice Cream Brownies, '89 124
Chocolate-Kahlúa Brownies, '93 99
Chocolate-Marshmallow Brownies, '01 246
Chocolate-Mint Brownies, '85 M294; '88 80
Chocolate-Mint Brownies, Southern, '93 216

Chocolate-Nut Brownies, '81 129
Chocolate-Peanut Butter Chip Brownies, '91 306
Chocolate-Pecan Brownies, '81 64
Chocolate-Peppermint Brownies, '88 262
Chocolate Tea Brownies, '83 79
Chocolate-Walnut Brownies, '89 325
Choco-Mallow Brownies, '87 198; '90 309
Cinnamon Brownie Bars, '81 230
Cocoa Brownies, Nutty, '81 64
Coconut-Pecan-Frosted Brownies, '97 99
Cookies, Brownie Chip, '90 320
Cookies, Brownie Waffle, '86 245
Cream Cheese Brownies, '04 M330
Cream Cheese Brownies à la Mode, Magnolias,
    '97 M178
Cream Cheese Brownies, Magnolia, '01 M63
Cream Cheese Swirl Brownies, '79 51
Crème de Menthe Brownies, '83 244
Crunch-Crust Brownies, '87 198
Dark Chocolate Brownies, '00 M211
Date-and-Almond Brownies, '88 217
Deluxe, Brownies, '03 330
Derby Brownies, Special, '90 94
Easy Brownies, '83 245
Elephant Stomp Brownies, '03 43
Favorite Brownies, '86 158
Frosted Brownies, '97 M87
Fudge Brownies, Nutty, '80 M171
Fudge Cake Brownies, '03 223
German Cream Cheese Brownies, '80 269
Glaze, Brownie, '02 M252
Gooey Brownies, '97 133
Heavenly Hash Brownies, '83 245
Honey Brownies, Heavenly, '79 83
Layered Brownies, '02 M252
Macadamia-Fudge Designer Brownies, '94 51
Marshmallow Brownies, Chewy, '83 306
Mint Dessert, Brownie-, '82 227
Mint Julep Brownies, '93 165
Mississippi Mud Brownies, '89 M25
Mississippi Mud Dessert Brownies, '01 M314
Mix, Blond Brownie, '01 247
Mix, Brownie, '82 6
Mocha Brownies, '87 93
Mocha Frosting, Brownies with, '94 292
Mother's Brownies, '93 239
Muffins, Fudge Brownie, '95 M50
No-Bake Brownies, '94 330
Oat Brownies, '89 59
Oatmeal Brownies, '87 199
Oat 'n' Crunch Brownies, '91 233
Passover Brownies, '98 M104
Passover, Brownies for, '99 56
Peanut Butter Brownies, '87 199
Peanut Butter Brownies, Frosted, '92 272;
    '00 M155
Pistachio-Mint Brownies, '94 50
Pizza, Banana Split-Brownie, '96 M164
Praline Brownies, '93 243
Praline-Pecan Brownies, '05 M288
Pretzel Brownies, Saucepan, '85 171
Quick and Easy Brownies, '82 6
Quick Brownies, '87 M302
Raspberry Brownies, '92 274; '97 M35
Rich Brownies, '95 84
Rocky Road Brownies, '86 320
Sundaes, Cream Cheese Brownie, '03 223
Tarts, Peppermint Brownie, '05 M288
Trifle, Brownie, '03 85
Trifle, Peanut Butter-Brownie, '03 200
Triple Decker Brownies, '92 319
Truffle Brownie Squares, Mint, '05 M254
Walnut-Cream Cheese Brownies, '84 240
White Chocolate Brownies, '89 169; '97 36

BRUSSELS SPROUTS
Amandine, Brussels Sprouts, '79 213
Apples, Brussels Sprouts with, '02 243
Beer, Brussels Sprouts in, '85 69
Brussels Sprouts, '89 278
Caramelized Onion-and-Pecan Brussels Sprouts,
    '99 254
Carrots and Brussels Sprouts, '82 300
Cashews, Brussels Sprouts with, '81 2
Casserole, Brussels Sprouts-and-Artichoke, '94 279
Casserole of Brussels Sprouts, '86 294
Celery, Brussels Sprouts and, '79 21
Cheese Sauce, Brussels Sprouts with, '79 246
Citrus Brussels Sprouts, Calico, '85 303
Creamed Brussels Sprouts and Celery, '83 322
Creamy Brussels Sprouts, '79 212
Deviled Brussels Sprouts, '84 248
Dijon, Brussels Sprouts, '96 91
Dilled Brussels Sprouts, '88 180
Fried Brussels Sprouts, '81 308
Glazed Brussels Sprouts and Baby Carrots, '97 302
Glorified Brussels Sprouts, '86 282
Leeks with Brussels Sprouts and Almonds, '00 222
Lemon Sauce, Brussels Sprouts in, '82 269
Lemon Sprouts, '85 288
Lemony Brussels Sprouts with Celery, '85 25
Marinated Brussels Sprouts, '88 265; '96 252; '97 29
Medley, Brussels Sprouts, '79 212; '85 267
Mustard Sauce, Brussels Sprouts in, '87 253; '90 228
Onion Sauce, Brussels Sprouts in, '81 308
Orange Brussels Sprouts, '84 34
Orange Sauce, Brussels Sprouts in, '86 55
Pierre, Brussels Sprouts, '84 248
Polonaise, Brussels Sprouts, '85 79
Rice, Brussels Sprouts and, '79 288; '80 26
Salad, Brussels Sprouts, '87 233
Salad, Cauliflower-Brussels Sprouts, '83 240
Sautéed Brussels Sprouts with Parmesan Soufflés,
    '97 280
Sesame Brussels Sprouts, '86 55
Shallots and Mustard, Brussels Sprouts with, '85 258
Spicy Brussels Sprouts, '02 307
Stir-Fry, Brussels Sprouts, '81 308
Tangy Brussels Sprouts, '88 40
Tarragon Brussels Sprouts, '83 291
Wine Butter, Brussels Sprouts in, '86 327

BULGUR
Burgers with Cucumber Sauce, Lamb, '98 102
Lentils, Tex-Mex, '99 288
Pilaf, Mixed Fruit, '05 205
Salad, Cracked Wheat-Fruit, '96 240
Salad, Layered Lebanese, '05 148
Salad with Citrus and Mint, Wheat, '99 163
Tabbouleh, '93 70; '99 175
Tabbouleh Pitas, '98 105
Tabbouleh Salad, '92 212; '94 174; '01 57
(Tabbouleh Salad), Boot Scoot Tabbouli, '96 159
Wild Rice Bulgur, '91 83

BUNS. *See* **ROLLS AND BUNS.**
BURRITOS
Bean Burrito Appetizers, '94 226
Beef Burritos, Cheesy, '85 193
Breakfast Burritos, '84 57; '90 192; '97 172; '99 103;
    '05 204
Broccoli Burritos, '83 200
Brunch Burritos, '91 77
Burritos, '80 196
Carne Guisada Burritos, '95 43
Chicken Burritos, '01 55
Chimichangas (Fried Burritos), '81 196; '85 244;
    '86 114
Chinese Burritos, '87 181
Easy Burritos, '04 32
Egg Burritos, Tex-Mex, '95 34

Fiesta Burritos, '86 114
Lentil Burritos, '99 287
Meat-and-Bean Burritos, '81 194
Monterey Burritos, '84 292
Phyllo Burritos, Hot, '98 312
Pie, Mexican Burrito, '87 287
Pork Burritos with Pico de Gallo, '97 140
Potato-and-Egg Burritos, '02 72
Rollups, Burrito, '90 119
Vegetable Burritos, '80 197; '90 134; '92 138
Vegetable Burritos with Avocado Sauce, '83 200
Vegetarian Burritos, '93 319
Veggie Burritos, Tony's, '96 289
BUTTER
Acorn Squash-and-Bourbon Butter, '94 266
Almond-Raisin Butter, '02 258
Ancho Chile Butter, '99 93
Apple Butter, '79 200; '81 217; '92 311
Apple Butter, Half-Hour, '81 203
Apple Butter, Oven, '00 237
Apple Butter, Slow Cooker, '97 235
Apple Butter, Spiced Oven, '00 237
Apricot Butter, '82 308; '99 212
Avocado Butter, '05 159
Balls, Butter, '82 189; '89 90
Basil Butter, '87 171; '99 274
Basil Butter, Asparagus with, '85 40
Basil-Garlic Butter, '03 208
Beehive Butter, '00 68
Beurre Blanc, '01 281
Blackberry Butter, '97 306; '03 27
Blue Cheese Butter, '97 306
Bourbon Butter, '97 306
Cashew Butter, Asparagus with, '87 56
Cheese Butter, '84 114
Chervil Butter, '83 129
Chervil Butter, Swordfish Steak with, '91 147
Chili Butter, '82 219; '97 306; '00 177
Chipotle Butter, '01 234
Chipotle Pepper Butter, '97 307
Chive-Mustard Butter, '98 156
Cilantro Butter, '98 182
Cilantro-Lime Butter, '98 156; '01 24; '02 109
Cinnamon Butter, '92 319; '01 M309
Cinnamon-Honey Butter, '89 281
Citrus Butter, '97 307
Clarified Butter, '81 59
Clarifying Butter, '82 189
Cranberry Butter, '97 307
Curls, Butter, '82 51, 189; '89 90
Flavored Butters, '97 306
Frosting, Browned Butter, '97 247
Garlic-Basil Butter, '98 156
Garlic Butter, '83 193; '84 108; '95 89; '00 90
Garlic-Chive Butter, Corn on the Cob with, '01 331
Garlic-Herb Butter, Green Beans with, '02 61
Garlic-Lemon Butter, '04 54
Gazpacho Butter, '92 86
Ginger Butter, '91 26
Green Peppercorn Butter, '88 60; '90 117
Herb Butter, '86 128, 255, 261, 306; '96 309; '97 306;
    '99 19
Herb Butter, Cauliflower with, '81 2
Herb Butter, Corn-on-the-Cob with, '84 160
Herb Butter, Holiday, '05 284
Herbed Caper Butter, '94 62
Herbed Unsalted Butter, '82 67
Herb-Garlic Butter, '96 173
Herb-Pesto Butter, '04 255
Honey Butter, '93 309; '94 206; '95 139; '97 307;
    '03 111
Honey-Lemon Butter, '04 231
Honey-Orange Butter, '79 36; '85 19
Honey-Spice Butter, '05 274

BUTTER

(continued)

Horseradish-Chive Butter, '86 277
Horseradish-Parsley Butter, '98 156
Jalapeño Butter, '97 306
Jalapeño-Chili Butter, '98 156
Jalapeño-Lime Butter, Grilled Corn with, '01 158;
    '04 178
Jalapeño-Pecan-Mustard Butter, '03 205
Lemon-Anchovy Butter, '97 307
Lemon Butter, '95 32; '96 124; '02 141
Lemon Butter, Asparagus with, '87 M151; '98 168
Lemon-Dill Butter, Green Beans with, '99 141
Lemon Pepper Butter, '97 307
Lemon-Thyme-Pecan Butter, Catfish Pecan with, '04 68
Lime Butter, Chicken with, '84 68
Maple-Flavored Butter, Whipped, '79 36
Marjoram Butter, Zesty, '00 145
Mediterranean Butter, '97 307
Molds, Butter, '89 90
Nectarine Butter, '79 175
Olive Butter, '91 295
Onion Butter, '86 253
Onion Butter, Sweet, '93 124
Orange Butter, '81 8, 42; '90 323; '92 319; '94 115;
    '97 44
Orange-Pecan Butter, '84 75; '97 15
Peach Butter, '82 308
Peach Butter, Golden, '91 178
Pear Butter, '85 130
Pear Butter, Spiced, '80 218
Pecan Butter, '97 307
Pecan-Honey Butter, '05 137
Pesto Butter, '97 307
Plum Butter, '88 152
Prune-Orange Butter, '92 49
Radish-and-Chive Butter, '01 101
Radish Butter, '01 101
Raisin Butter, '81 272
Red Pepper Butter, Fillet of Beef with, '96 32
Roasted-Garlic Beurre Blanc, '03 324
Roasted Garlic Butter, '97 46
Roasted Red Bell Pepper Butter, '95 242
Sage Butter, '96 269
Sauce, Brown Butter, '91 65
Sauce, Butter, '05 124
Sauce, Butter-Rum, '95 134
Sauce, Chive Butter, '03 91
Sauce, Cinnamon-Butter, '00 254
Sauce, Garlic Beurre Blanc, '88 222
Sauce, Garlic-Butter, '95 327
Sauce, Garlic Butter, '05 M253
Sauce, Garlic-Ginger Butter, '94 89
Sauce, Honey-Butter, '98 45
Sauce, Lemon-Butter, '99 198
Sauce, New Potatoes with Lemon-Butter, '00 103
Sauce, Pecan-Butter, '91 65
Sauce, Red Wine-Butter, '96 173
Sauce, Strawberry-Butter, '96 87
Sauce, White Butter, '92 107
Seafood Butter, '97 306
Sesame Butter, '97 307
Sesame-Ginger Butter, '99 142
Shrimp Butter, '92 91
Southwestern Butter, '92 320; '01 194
Spread, Cranberry-Butter, '99 86
Spread, Garlic-Butter, '96 199
Spread, Honey Mustard-Butter, '99 86
Strawberry Butter, '79 36; '81 286; '91 71;
    '99 44, 234
Sweet Potato Butter, '95 M290
Thyme-Lemon Butter, '96 121

Tomato Butter, '86 128
Tomato-Curry-Orange Butter, '93 159
Walnut Brown Butter, Spaghettini with Green Beans
    and, '03 170

BUTTERSCOTCH

Bars, Butterscotch, '82 209; '83 297
Bars, Chocolate-Butterscotch, '81 197
Bread, Banana Butterscotch, '79 116
Brownies, Butterscotch, '85 248
Brownies, Butterscotch-Chocolate, '03 47
Cake, Butterscotch, '91 270
Cake, Butterscotch-Pecan Pound, '92 153
Cheesecake, Butterscotch, '86 188
Cookies, Butterscotch, '87 58
Cookies, Butterscotch-Pecan, '84 36
Drops, Butterscotch, '01 33
Fantastic, Butterscotch, '83 76
Filling, Butterscotch, '91 271; '02 323
Fudge, Butterscotch-Peanut, '98 M282
Fudge, Butterscotch Rum, '88 256
Fudge, Four Chips, '92 318
Fudge Scotch Ring, '79 273
Mousse, Butterscotch, '93 254
Pie, Butterscotch, '97 212
Pie, Butterscotch Cream, '84 48; '87 207
Pie, Butterscotch Meringue, '83 158
Pinwheels, Butterscotch, '90 49
Pralines, Butterscotch, '81 253
Sauce, Butterscotch-Pecan, '82 212
Sticky Buns, Christmas Morning, '97 245
Trail Mix, Bunny, '95 101

CABBAGE. *See also* SAUERKRAUT, SLAWS.

Apples and Franks, Cabbage with, '87 42
au Gratin, Cabbage, '83 279
Bake, Zesty Cabbage Beef, '80 300
Beef-Cabbage Dinner, '81 179
Bubbling Cabbage, '84 2
Caraway Cabbage, '85 32, 289
Caraway, Cabbage with, '93 181
Casserole, Cabbage, '97 88
Casserole, Cheesy Cabbage, '79 4
Casserole, Creamy Cabbage, '80 63
Casserole, Italian Cabbage, '87 42
Casserole, Savory Cabbage, '82 168
Chop Suey, Cabbage, '81 101
Chow-Chow, Cabbage, '87 150
Chowchow, '87 150
Chowder, Hearty Cabbage, '80 25
Colcannon, '90 64
Corned Beef and Cabbage, '83 104; '93 64; '96 328
Corned Beef and Cabbage au Gratin, '83 16
Corned Beef and Cabbage, Quick, '79 54
Corned Beef Squares and Cabbage, '82 86
Country-Style Cabbage, '81 271
Creamed Cabbage, '01 49
Creamed Cabbage with Almonds, '79 4
Creole Cabbage, '87 189; '00 105
Duck Breast, Tender, '97 215
Dumplings, Steamed Sesame, '97 208
Egg Rolls, Scrumptious, '96 101
Fiesta Cabbage, '05 236
Frankfurter-Cabbage Skillet, '80 166
Fried Cabbage, '02 272
Garlic, Cabbage with, '04 62
Hot Cabbage Creole, '87 42
Kielbasa and Cabbage, '85 67; '89 M196
Kielbasa, Cabbage, '87 42
Lemon-Butter Cabbage, '88 156
Medley, Cabbage, '80 64; '83 104
Medley, Cabbage-Onion-Sweet Pepper, '96 252; '97 28
Orange Juice, Cabbage Cooked in, '97 129
Pasta with Cabbage and Cheese Sauce, '00 105

Peppers, Carrot-and-Cabbage Stuffed, '99 63
Piccalilli, Kentucky, '81 216
Pork Chops, Chinese, '97 320
Quick Cooked Cabbage, '95 270
Red Cabbage, '96 272
Red Cabbage and Apples, '85 32
Red Cabbage and Apples, Sweet-and-Sour, '00 62
Red Cabbage and Pears, Braised, '01 298
Red Cabbage, Braised, '95 343; '99 243; '01 193;
    '02 277; '05 236
Red Cabbage, Cooked, '97 28
Red Cabbage, German, '94 254
Red Cabbage, German-Style, '84 2; '98 279
Red Cabbage, Pickled, '81 271
Red Cabbage, Sweet-Sour, '79 5
Red Cabbage with Pineapple, '97 215
Relish, Cabbage, '83 260
Relish, Spanish Cabbage, '95 270
Reuben Strudel, '98 28
Rolls, Beef Stuffed Cabbage, '81 87; '82 7
Rolls, Cabbage, '83 104
Rolls, Crunchy Cabbage-Rice, '85 32
Rolls, Easy Cabbage-and-Beef, '88 49
Rolls, Fried Cabbage, '95 270
Rolls, Hot-and-Spicy Cabbage, '84 249
Rolls, Hungarian Cabbage, '94 47
Rolls, Southwestern Cabbage, '97 214
Rolls, Spicy Cabbage, '84 2
Rolls, Stuffed Cabbage, '84 217; '88 18; '92 251
Rolls, Vegetarian Cabbage, '91 86
Rollups, Beef-and-Cabbage, '80 63
Salad, Austrian Hash with Cabbage, '95 262
Salad, Cabbage, '87 120, 233
Salad, Cabbage and Fruit, '79 286
Salad, Chinese Cabbage, '81 271; '05 142
Salad, Chinese Green, '88 48
Salad, Garden Cabbage, '81 210
Salad, Nutty Cabbage, '87 42
Salad, Overnight Cabbage, '79 83
Salad, Red Cabbage Citrus, '94 72
Salad, Tangy Cabbage, '82 55; '05 162
Salad, Turkish, '96 137
Salad, Wilted Cabbage, '94 281
Salad, Winter Cabbage, '98 284
Salad with Cabbage Wraps, Spicy Chicken, '04 62
Salad with Dijon Vinaigrette, '03 237
Salad with Honey-Dijon Vinaigrette, Rice-Cabbage, '04 321
Salad with Pecan Vinaigrette, Ranch House, '00 162
Salad with Sugared Pecans, Cabbage-Apple, '05 91
Salad, Zesty Shredded, '04 324
Sausage and Cabbage, Skillet, '01 28
Sausage, Cabbage with Polish, '83 104
Sausage-Sauced Cabbage, '81 271
Sausage Surprise, '83 245; '84 42
Scalloped Cabbage, '82 269; '01 43; '05 236
Scalloped Cabbage, Cheese, '81 87; '82 7
Shrimp and Cabbage, Asian, '00 105
Skillet Cabbage, '89 314; '90 229
Skillet, Cabbage-and-Tomato, '86 110
Skillet, Rutabaga-Cabbage, '99 285
Soup, Cabbage, '83 291
Soup, Cabbage-Bean, '97 301
Soup, Sweet-and-Sour Cabbage, '89 314
Spinach Dip in Cabbage, '82 155
Stir-fried Cabbage, '81 75, 271; '85 109; '05 86
Stir-Fry, Cabbage, '04 62
Stir-Fry, Spicy Cabbage, '04 62
Stuffed Cabbage, '84 282
Stuffed Cabbage, Italian, '84 294
Stuffed Cabbage Leaves, '00 270
Supper, Cabbage, '89 314
Supreme, Cabbage, '79 4; '83 206
Sweet-and-Sour Cabbage, '86 295; '87 189
Tex-Mex Cabbage, '80 63

Tomatoes, Cabbage and, '83 104
Tomatoes, Tasty Cabbage and, '86 72
Wedges, Saucy Cabbage, '83 86
Wedges, Smothered Cabbage, '81 87; '82 7
Wilted Cabbage, '80 64; '88 229
CAKES. *See also* **BREADS, CHEESECAKES.**
Acorn Squash Cake, '96 216
Almond-Butter Cake, '86 107
Almond-Butter Cake, Peachy, '90 107
Almond-Butter Cake, Toasted, '99 315
Almond-Butter Wedding Cake, '86 106
Almond Legend Cake, '82 8
Almond Whipping Cream Cake, '80 295
Amaretto Cake, Easy, '85 79
Ambrosia Cake, '79 229
Ambrosia Cake Royale, '89 335
Angel Food
  Amaretto-Almond Sauce, Angel Food Cake with, '90 199
  Blue Ribbon Angel Food Cake, '01 35
  Cappuccino Mousse Cake, '99 154
  Chocolate Angel Cake, '88 128
  Chocolate Angel Food Cake, '87 21; '90 111; '91 55
  Chocolate Angel Food Cake with Custard Sauce, '88 259
  Coconut Angel Cake, Spiked, '85 279
  Deluxe Angel Food Cake, '86 121
  Ice Cream Angel Cake, '83 23
  Ice-Cream Angel Dessert, Triple Mint, '93 86
  Lemon Angel Cake, '80 147; '97 163
  No-Bake Ice-Cream Angel Food Cake, '05 107
  Orange Angel Food Cake, '96 246
  Orange-Coconut Angel Food Cake, '94 294
  Pineapple-Orange Sauce, Angel Cake with, '84 14
  Surprise, Angel Cake, '93 86
  Trifle, Pineapple Angel Food, '93 86
  White Chocolate Mousse Cake, Strawberry-Studded, '99 154
Apple-Blueberry Crunch, '02 128
Apple Cake, '83 312; '84 262
Apple Cake, Dried-, '79 13
Apple Cake with Cream Cheese Frosting, Chunky, '01 185
Apple-Date Cake, Fresh, '83 300
Apple-Ginger Upside-Down Cake, '94 180
Apple-Nut Cake, '87 76; '96 268
Apple-Oatmeal Cake, Golden, '86 301
Apple-Pecan Cake, '92 167
Apple Pie Cake, '86 301
Apple Pudding Cake, '01 47
Applesauce Cake, '80 270; '96 67
Applesauce Cake, My Favorite, '87 263
Applesauce Cake with Bourbon Frosting, '88 236
Applesauce Carrot Cake, '81 202
Applesauce-Oatmeal Cake, '92 119
Applesauce Snack Cakes, '88 215; '89 20
Applesauce-Spice Cake, '83 42
Applesauce Spice Cake, '89 296
Apple Shortcake, Quick, '93 42
Apple Slice Cake, '85 93
Apple Spice Cake, '92 225
Apple Stack Cake, '05 108
Apple Stack Cake, Dried, '85 242
Apple Upside-Down Cake, Fresh, '05 231
Apricot-Almond Upside-Down Cake, '97 204
Banana-Blueberry Cake, '86 247
Banana Cake, '84 151
Banana Cake, Deluxe Light, '84 314
Banana Cake, Marvelous, '79 115
Banana Cake, Triple-Layered, '00 244
Banana Cake with Coconut-Cream Cheese Frosting, Decadent, '05 317
Banana Cake with Coconut Custard, Supreme, '97 131

Banana-Coconut Cake, '93 154
Banana-Nut Cake, '92 120
Banana-Pecan Shortcake, '93 43
Bananas Foster Crunch Cake, '93 339
Banana Split Cake, '99 48
Banana Waldorf Cake, '85 118
Bars and Squares
  Almond Cake Squares, '79 111
  Angel Squares, Mocha, '98 61
  Apple-Date Dream Cake Squares, '85 10
  Apple-Gingerbread Squares, '03 297
  Apple-Orange Cake Squares, '84 150
  Applesauce Cake Squares, '86 8
  Applesauce-Spice Squares, '86 248
  Buttermilk Fudge Squares, '99 99
  Carrot-Lemon Squares, Golden, '80 40
  Carrot Snack Cake, Easy, '82 235
  Carrot Squares, '79 256
  Cherry Cheesecake Bars, '97 330
  Cinnamon Cake Squares, '87 222
  Cream Cheese Cake Squares, '84 321
  Crumb Cake, Calico, '87 261
  Gingerbread, Gingery, '96 100
  Gingerbread Squares, '84 16
  Ginger Cake, '87 222
  Honey Cake Squares, '89 250
  Honey-Oatmeal Cake, '87 222
  Jam Squares, '81 M289
  Orange Cake Squares, '81 34
  Orange-Pumpkin Cake Squares, '83 242
  Pecan Squares, Easy, '81 230
  Pumpkin Cake Bars, '80 245
  Rhubarb Squares, '92 129
  Strawberry Shortcake Squares, '85 122; '86 124
  Zucchini-Carrot Cake, '93 20
Beerquick Sugar Cake, '96 112
Beet Cake with Almond Topping, '86 200
Birdhouse Cake, '93 284
Birthday Cake, Clowning Around, '94 52
Blackberry Cake, Fresh, '81 132
Blackberry Flan, '79 182
Black Walnut Cake, '80 253; '84 316; '90 308
Black Walnut Cake, Maryland, '05 106
Blueberry-Sour Cream Cake, '90 140
Blueberry Streusel Cake, '92 144
Boston Cream Pie, '83 220
Bourbon Cake, '98 277
Bourbon-Pecan Cake, '84 25
Brown Mountain Cake, '84 39
Brown Sugar Meringue Cake, '81 70
Brown Sugar Snack Cake, '98 195
Bûche de Noël, '84 304; '87 241
Bûche de Noël, '82 262
Bunny Cake, '94 98
Butter Brickle Cake, '85 118
Butter Brickle Loaf Cakes, '98 137
Butter Cake, Old-Fashioned, '97 60
Butter Cake, Ooey-Gooey, '00 86
Buttermilk Layer Cake, '00 48
Butter Pecan Cake, '88 229
Butter Pecan Cake, Caramel-Filled, '88 278
Butterscotch Cake, '91 270
Cajun Cake, '87 138
Candy Bar Cake, '92 204; '98 90
Candy Bar Cake, Heavenly, '04 211
Caramel Cake, '89 55; '90 307
Caramel Layer Cake, Creamy, '81 71
Carolina Dream Cake, '88 278
Carrot
  Applesauce Carrot Cake, '81 202
  Best Carrot Cake, '97 230
  Blue Ribbon Carrot Cake, '81 70
  Brownie Carrot Cake, '92 120
  Carrot Cake, '79 45; '82 137; '84 315; '98 275

Cheater's Carrot Cake, '96 20
Coconut-Carrot Cake, Fresh, '80 299
Coconut-Pecan Carrot Cake, '84 322
Easy Carrot Cake, '83 215
Easy Carrot Snack Cake, '82 235
Frosted Carrot Cake, '92 19
Fruited Carrot Cake, Spicy, '85 117
German Carrot-Hazelnut Cake, '97 230
Madeira Syrup and Vanilla Ice Cream, Carrot Cakes with, '98 247
Mama Dip's Carrot Cake, '05 299
Miniature Carrot Cakes, '90 94
Old-Fashioned Carrot Cake, '83 M232; '97 330
Old-Fashioned Carrot Sheet Cake, '97 330
Old-South Carrot Cake, '80 120
Pecan-Carrot Cake, '99 223
Pound Cake, Carrot, '87 41
Praline-Filled Carrot Cake, '03 332
Pudding Cake, Carrot, '83 24
Quick-and-Easy Carrot Cake, '84 150
Raisin Cake, Carrot-, '01 58
Sheet Cake, Best Carrot, '03 55
Shortcut Carrot Cake, '02 83
Spiced Carrot Cake, '87 296
Zucchini-Carrot Cake, '93 20
Chart, Cake Failure, '81 72
Cherry Bourbon Cake, '82 287
Cherry Cake, '79 165
Cherry Cake, Dried, '97 33
Cherry Cake, Quick, '81 238
Cherry-Pineapple Dump Cake, '02 128
Cherry Upside-Down Cake, '82 56
Chocolate. *See also* **CAKES/Angel Food, Pound, Tortes.**
  Almond Cake, Chocolate-, '91 248
  Almond Cake with Cherry Filling, Chocolate-, '84 225
  Banana Cake, Chocolate-, '86 138
  Banana Loaf, Chocolate Chip-, '85 115
  Basket Cake, Chocolate-Strawberry, '98 100
  Batter, Chocolate Velvet Cake, '03 M286
  Beet Cake, Chocolate, '80 40
  Birthday Cake, Fishin'-for-Fun, '93 194
  Blackberry-Raspberry Truffle Cake, '03 245
  Black Forest Cake, '81 126; '92 174
  Black Forest Cake, Six-Layer, '85 125
  Black Forest Cherry Cake, '83 302
  Black Forest Crisp, '02 128
  Black Forest Dump Cake, '85 13
  Black Forest Pudding Cake, '02 210
  Bourbon-Pecan Cake, Chocolate-, '03 287
  Breakfast Cake, Chocolate-Swirl, '04 M41
  Brownie Baked Alaska, '80 66
  Brownie Delight, Chocolate, '87 224
  Buttercream Cake, Chocolate, '90 108
  Buttermilk Cake, Chocolate-, '00 48
  Buttermilk Chocolate Cake, '79 13
  Buttermilk Fudge Squares, '99 99
  Cameo Cake, '94 58
  Candy Cake, Chocolate, '81 238
  Candy Corn Chocolate Cakes, '00 235
  Caramel-Nut Cake, Chocolate-, '83 23
  Carrot Cake, Brownie, '92 120
  Cherry Cake, Choco-, '96 229
  Cherry Cake, Chocolate-, '84 200; '86 239
  Cherry Fudge Cake, '98 214
  Chiffon Cake with Coffee Buttercream, Chocolate, '95 277
  Chocolate Cake, '97 283
  Chocolate Cake, IV '05 322
  Cinnamon Cake, Chocolate-, '93 154
  Cocoa Crown Cake, '90 107
  Coconut Cake, Chocolate-, '83 23
  Coconut-Fudge Cake, '99 206

Cola Cake, '81 238
Cola Cake, Quick, '00 120
Cola Cake, Quick Chocolate, '95 56
Cookies-and-Cream Cake, '92 163
Custard Cake, Chocolate, '88 175
Decadence, Chocolate, '03 319
Decadent Chocolate Cake, '86 142
Easy Chocolate Cake, '80 140
Easy Perfect Chocolate Cake, '99 307
Éclair Cake, Chocolate, '03 206
Extra-Rich Chocolate Cake, '99 271
Father's Day Cake, '92 134
Frosting, Chocolate Cake with Double, '86 314
Fudge Cake, '94 M293; '98 110; '99 176
Fudge Cake, Best, '83 301
Fudge Cake, Brown Sugar, '86 316
Fudge Cake, Chocolate, '80 279
Fudge Cake, Coconut-, '99 206
Fudge Cake for Two, '81 205
Fudge Cake, Hot, '99 105
Fudge Cake, One-Foot-in-the-Fire, '90 252
Fudge Frosting, Chocolate Cake with, '89 56
German Chocolate Cake, '81 296; '83 M233;
  '05 107
German Chocolate Chip Cake, '86 247
German Chocolate Sheet Cake, '03 147
German Chocolate Snack Cake, '02 128
Grandma's Chocolate Cake, '94 133
Heart, Chocolate-Amaretto, '98 56
Italian Cake, Chocolate, '02 256
Kahlúa Cake, Chocolate, '91 298
Kahlúa Chocolate Cake, '81 303
Layers, Chocolate Cake, '96 229
Loaf Cakes, Chocolate Chip, '98 137
Macadamia-Fudge Cake, '01 278
Marbled Cake, Cocoa, '82 265
Marshmallow Cake, No-Egg Chocolate, '87 M97
Mayonnaise Cake, Chocolate, '83 99
Milk Chocolate Bar Cake, '00 86
Mint Cake, Chocolate-, '03 286
Mississippi Mud Cake, '03 288; '04 136
Mocha Cake, '02 87
Mocha Cake, Belgian, '84 316
Mocha Cake, Double, '84 311
Mocha Chiffon Cake, Delta, '00 286
Mocha-Chocolate Cake, Dark, '84 311
Mousse Cake, Chocolate, '87 264; '98 270; '03 320
Nut Cake, Rich Chocolate-, '86 8
Pastry Cake, Chocolate, '91 196
Peanut Butter Cake, Chocolate-, '84 240
Peanut Butter Cake, Fudgy, '85 91
Peanut Butter-Fudge Cake, '96 254; '01 59
Peanut Butter Mousse Cake, Chocolate-, '98 71
Peanut Cluster Cake, Chocolate-, '87 184
Perfect Chocolate Cake, '82 244; '90 307; '03 318
Praline Cake, Chocolate-, '01 235
Praline Pecan Cake, Chocolate-, '03 288
Pudding Cake, Hot Fudge, '88 255
Pudding, Chocolate Cake, '81 99
Pudding, Hot Fudge Sundae Cake, '88 167
Pumpkin, Chocolate, '96 254
Queen's Chocolate Cake, '89 271
Raspberry Cake, Chocolate-, '92 173; '01 M319
Raspberry-Fudge Cake, '97 34
Red Velvet Cake Batter, Chocolate-, '05 286
Red Velvet Cakes, Fluted Chocolate-, '05 287
Red Velvet Layer Cake, Chocolate-, '05 287
Rich Chocolate Cake, '89 43
Rocky Road Cake, '81 178
Roll, Chocolate, '04 85

Roll, Chocolate Cream, '85 317
Roll, Chocolate-Frosted Ice Cream, '84 200
Roll, Chocolate-Mocha Cream, '84 304
Roll, Chocolate Mousse, '83 290; '88 280
Roll, Chocolate-Orange, '87 21
Roll, Make-Ahead Chocolate-Mint Cake, '95 220
Rolls, Chocolate Cake, '94 312
Root Beer Float Cake, '04 211
Roulade, Kahlúa-and-Cream, '97 199
Royal, Chocolate Cake, '86 239
Rum Cake, Chocolate, '79 67
Sachertorte, '84 253
Sachertorte, Shortcut, '99 M243
Sheet Cake, Chocolate-Caramel, '05 210
Sheet Cake, Texas, '03 19
Shortbread Fudge Cake, '03 M331
Shortcake, Chocolate-Raspberry, '95 99
Snack Cake, Black Widow, '93 245
Snack Cake, Frosted Chocolate, '90 194
Sour Cream Cake, Chocolate-, '87 222
Sour Cream Cake, Chocolate Chip-, '85 115
Sour Cream Chocolate Cake, '79 282
Spice Potato Cake, Chocolate-, '96 111
Strawberry Shortcake, Chocolate-, '89 216
Swiss Chocolate Chip Cake, '87 85
Texas Cake, '01 59
Tic-Tac-Toe Cake, '94 52
Tiered Cameo Cake, '94 125
Toffee Cake, Chocolate-, '89 335
Tree Cakes, Miniature Chocolate Truffle, '97 M285
Triangle Cake, Chocolate, '85 126
Triple-Chocolate Cake, '05 221
Truffle Angel Cake, Chocolate, '97 283
Truffle Cake, Chocolate, '89 43
Truffle Cake, Rudolph's Chocolate, '04 M253
Turtle Cake, '03 287
Turtle Cake Squares, '05 M211
Velvet Cake with Coconut-Pecan Frosting,
  Chocolate, '03 289
Velvet Cake with Cream Cheese-Butter Pecan Frost-
  ing, Chocolate, '03 288
Velvet Cake with Vanilla Buttercream Frosting,
  Chocolate, '03 287
Wedding Cake, Cameo, '94 124
Wedding Cake, Double Chocolate, '91 100
Whipped Cream Cake, Chocolate-Mint, '90 265
White Chocolate-Almond Cake, '03 M287
White Chocolate-Cherry Cake, '88 268
White Chocolate Mousse Cake, '89 160
White Chocolate Mousse Cake, Strawberry-Studded,
  '99 154
White Chocolate-Raspberry Cake, '98 323
Yule Log, '79 281; '82 289
Zucchini Cake, Chocolate, '85 156
Zucchini Cake, Chocolate-, '02 181
Chocolate-Raspberry Cake, '01 M319
Cinderella Fantasy Cake, '98 70
Cinnamon Crumb Cake, '85 290
Cinnamon-Pecan Crumb Cakes, '05 288
Cinnamon Streusel Cake, '84 151
Cinnamon Swirl Cake, '01 255
Coca-Cola Cake, '02 181

Coconut
Anniversary Cake, '00 117
Apple Coconut Cake, '80 226
Carrot Cake, Coconut-Pecan, '84 322
Carrot Cake, Fresh Coconut-, '80 299
Chocolate-Coconut Cake, '83 23
Christmas Coconut Cake, '82 262
Coconut Cake, '03 278; '92 120; '05 335
Cream Cake, Coconut, '81 179; '91 269
Creamy Coconut Cake, '84 43
Four-Layer Coconut Cake, '00 117
Fresh Coconut Cake, '80 289; '82 52; '85 281

Fudge Cake, Coconut-, '99 206
Hibiscus-Nectar Cake, '96 248
Holiday Coconut Cake, '90 308
Layer Cake, Coconut, '05 M246
Layer Cake, Coconut-Pineapple, '80 140
Layer Cake, Stately Coconut, '81 70
Lemon Cake, Coconut-, '95 319
Lemon-Coconut Cream Cake, '81 179
Lemon-Coconut Sheet Cake, '85 117
MaMa's Coconut Cake, '97 71
Party Cake, Gathering of Stars, '00 307
Piña Colada Cake, '99 117
Pineapple Cake, Coconut-, '89 56
Pineapple Cake, Nanny's Famous Coconut-, '97 277
Pineapple Cake, Quick Coconut-, '05 106
Pineapple Cake Roll, Coconut-, '84 304
Pineapple-Coconut Cake, '00 86
Regal Coconut Cake, '83 299
Rum-Orange Coconut Cake, '88 224
Sheet Cake, Coconut, '04 136
Spice Cake, Coconut-, '84 255; '87 296
Star Cake, Twinkling, '00 306
Toasted Coconut Cake, '86 60
Unforgettable Coconut Cake, '90 104; '01 330
White Chocolate-Coconut Cake, '87 263

Coffee Cakes
Almond-Blueberry Coffee Cake, '85 152
Almond Coffee Cake Twist, '91 22
Almond Sunburst, '94 245
Almond-Vanilla Breakfast Ring, '04 M249
Apple Coffee Cake, '81 249; '97 326
Apple Coffee Cake, Fresh, '92 32
Apple Loaf, Spiced, '79 215
Apple-Pecan Coffee Cake, '84 242
Apricot-Almond Coffee Cake, '93 26; '04 193
Apricot Lattice Coffee Cake, '94 48
Banana Coffee Cake, '81 288
Banana Cream Coffee Cake, '85 46
Banana-Sour Cream Coffee Cake, '80 186; '97 231;
  '04 194
Banana-Toffee Coffee Cakes, '02 M324
Blueberry Brunch Cake, '83 183
Blueberry Coffee Cake, '82 206; '85 326; '88 263
Blueberry Coffee Cake, Fresh, '81 164
Blueberry Streusel Coffee Cake, '88 154
Braid Coffee Cake, Daisy, '82 197
Breakfast Pullapart, '81 278
Butterflake Coffee Ring, '79 216
Buttermilk Coffee Cake, '89 50
Buttermilk Crumb Cake, '79 72
Caramel-Apple Coffee Cakes, '05 210
Caramel Bread, '82 75
Caramel Breakfast Rolls, '79 193
Caramel-Orange Coffee Ring, '80 45
Caramel Ring, Easy, '85 M89
Cardamom Coffee Cake, '83 246; '84 17
Cheesecake Coffee Cake, Deep-Dish, '90 50
Cherry Blossom Coffee Cake, '80 21
Cherry Coffee Cake, '94 49
Chocolate-Chip Coffee Cake, '79 249
Chocolate Chip Coffee Cake, '83 231; '97 232;
  '04 194
Chocolate Coffee Cake, Triple-, '04 M299
Chocolate-Cream Cheese Coffee Cake, '03 288
Christmas-Tree Coffee Cakes, '87 298
Christmas Wreath, '80 280
Cinnamon-Buttermilk Coffee Cake, '80 45
Cinnamon-Cherry Coffee Cake, '98 330
Cinnamon Coffee Cake, '83 M203
Cinnamon Crisps, '81 113
Cinnamon-Nut Bubble Bread, '80 22
Cinnamon-Pecan Coffee Cake, '87 69
Cinnamon-Raisin Coffee Cake, '93 180
Cinnamon Twist Coffee Cake, '84 322

Cinnamon Upside-Down Coffee Cake, '85 256
Coffee Cake, '94 167
Cora's Coffee Cake, '91 186
Cowboy Coffee Cake, '95 84
Cranberry-Coconut Coffee Cake, '93 332
Cranberry Coffee Cake, '81 14; '90 159
Cranberry Crunch Coffee Cake, '97 231
Cranberry-Nut Coffee Cake, '81 250
Cranberry-Orange Coffee Cake, '82 283
Cream Cheese Coffee Cake, '86 290
Crescent Coffee Cake, '81 229
Danish Coffee Ring, '80 20
Fig Coffee Cake, Easy, '80 116
Heaven Cake, '04 193
Holiday Coffee Cake, '84 284
Holiday Wreath, '81 284
Honey Twist, '79 80
Lemon Coffee Cake, Lightly, '81 14
Macadamia Ring Coffee Cake, '85 326
Maple-Nut Coffee Twist, '86 290
Marbled Coffee Cake, '86 9
Mix, Quick, '94 167
Muffins, Coffee Cake, '79 7
Oatmeal-Coconut Coffee Cake, '83 312
Orange Breakfast Ring, '81 229
Orange Butter Coffee Cake, '89 229
Orange Coffee Cake, '85 M88
Orange Coffee Cake, Nutty, '95 160
Orange Marmalade Swirl Coffee Cake, '81 107
Orange-Pecan Coffee Cake, '86 86
Overnight Coffee Cake, '80 52; '92 213
Peach Flip, '79 217
Pecan-Topped Coffee Cake, '81 41
Pineapple-Coconut Coffee Cake, '94 49; '03 198
Plum Preserves Coffee Cake, '02 211
Raisin Coffee Cake, Spicy, '88 63
Raspberry-Cheese Coffee Cake, '97 231
Raspberry Coffee Cake, '83 112
Raspberry Tea Cake, '91 271
Ring, Coffee Cake, '85 M89
Savarin, Holiday, '80 280
Snack Cake, Coffee, '86 247
Sour Cream-Blueberry Coffee Cake, '00 154
Sour Cream Coffee Cake, '81 270; '93 154; '03 126;
    '04 333
Sour Cream Coffee Cakes, '05 212
Sour Cream Coffee Cakes, Mini, '05 212
Sour Cream-Walnut Coffee Cake, '79 209
Special Coffee Cake, Mama Cle's, '94 287
Strawberry Coffee Cake, '85 46
St. Timothy's Coffee Cake, '91 54
Sugar Cake, Moravian, '87 228
Sugar Cake, Polish, '89 267
Sugarplum Coffee Ring, '79 235; '83 M37
Sweet Roll Dough, '79 80
Tropical Coffee Cake, '80 232; '90 323
Walnut Coffee Cake, '93 124
Whole Wheat Coffee Cake, Crunchy-Topped, '79 93
Cola Cake, '81 238; '00 120
Cola Cake, Quick, '00 120
Compromise Cake, The, '90 253
Cranberry-Ambrosia Cake, '01 271
Cranberry-Pecan Cake Batter, '05 287
Cranberry Upside-Down Cake, '87 8
Cream Cheese Cake, Regal, '80 140
Cream Cheese Loaf Cake, '84 151
Crème de Menthe Cake, '81 178
Crêpe Cake, Southern Custard, '99 166
Cupcakes
    Angel Cakes with Almond Sugar, Mixed-Berry,
        '02 175
    Apple-Nut Cupcakes, '82 279
    A Tisket, a Tasket, '92 15
    Banana-Chocolate Cupcakes, '02 187

Banana-Cocoa Cupcakes, '80 130
Birthday Balloon Cakes, '92 15
Black Bottom Cups, '82 279
Brownie Cupcakes, '82 280
Brown Sugar-Frosted Cupcakes, '01 201
Candy Bar Cupcakes, Heavenly, '04 210
Carrot-Bran Cupcakes, '82 16
Choco Cupcakes, '03 200
Chocolate-Chip Chewies, '01 320
Chocolate Chip Cupcakes, '97 108
Chocolate Chip Cupcakes, Marble, '81 239
Chocolate-Cream Cheese Cupcakes, '03 169
Chocolate Cupcakes, '92 14
Chocolate Cupcakes, Chewy, '01 334
Chocolate-Peppermint Candy Cupcakes, '03 M287
Chocolate Surprise Cupcakes, '85 91
Cinnamon-Chocolate Cupcakes, '81 M139
Confetti Cupcakes, New Year's, '92 15
Cream Cheese Party Cupcakes, '82 279
Date Cupcakes, '84 7
Graveyard Grumblings, '92 15
Happy Day Cupcakes, '80 129
Hot Fudge Sundae Cakes, '00 333
Ice-Cream Cone Cakes, Fourth-of-July, '92 15
Ice-Cream Cupcakes, Banana Pudding, '01 173
Ice-Cream Cupcakes, Chocolate-Brickle, '01 M172
Ice-Cream Cupcakes, Lemon-Blueberry, '01 172
Ice-Cream Cupcakes, Mint-Chocolate Chip, '01 172
Lemonade Cupcakes, '04 163
Lemon Moist Cupcakes, '82 112; '83 153
Mocha Cupcakes, '85 250
Orange Cupcakes, '97 32
Piglets, '98 203
Pumpkin Cupcakes, '85 121
Red Velvet Cupcakes, '03 94
Self-Filled Cupcakes, '80 129
Surprises, Cupcake, '01 299
Sweetheart Cupcakes, '92 15
Tannenbaum Temptations, '92 14
Turkey Talk, '92 15
Vanilla Cupcakes, '92 14
Vanilla Cupcakes, Golden, '85 121
Yellow Cupcakes, Easy, '83 241
Daffodil Cake, '84 161
Date Nut Cake, '79 176; '80 5
Date-Nut Cake Roll, '89 94
Decorating Techniques, Cake, '83 72, 240; '84 224
Divinity Cake, '01 270
Dump Cake, Tropical, '02 128
Easter Egg Cake, '94 98
Easter Rabbit Cake, '94 99
Éclair Cake, '93 42
Fig Cake, '79 32; '99 314; '02 166
Fig Preserve Cake, '79 140; '84 316
Fig Preserves Cake, '89 335
Friendship Cake, '82 250
Fruit-and-Cereal Brunch Cake, '88 263
Fruit-and-Nut Cake, Stately, '84 226
Fruitcakes
    Applesauce Fruitcake, '83 258
    Aronowitz Fruitcake, '86 285
    Black Cake (A Kwanzaa Fruitcake), '01 292
    Bourbon Fruitcake, '85 315
    Brandy Fruitcake, '82 261
    Burgundy Fruitcake, '85 292
    Cake Mix Fruit Cake, '95 248
    Chocolate Fruitcakes, '95 250
    Classic Fruitcake, '91 258
    Favorite Fruitcake, Family, '88 284
    Fondue, Fruitcake, '84 258
    Grandmother's Fruitcake, '95 248
    Japanese Fruitcake, '83 268; '90 252
    Jeweled Fruitcake, '88 260
    Jill's Fruitcake, '95 249

Kentucky Fruitcake, '86 266
Layered Fruitcake, '87 265
Lemon Fruitcake, '83 258
Light Fruitcake, '90 309
Loaf, Fruitcake, '96 286
Mom's Fruitcake, '85 321
No-Bake Fruitcake, '95 249
Old-South Fruitcake, '79 289
Regal Fruitcake, '83 257
Sherry-Nut Fruitcake, '84 266; '00 299
Spice Cake, Fruit and, '87 M97
White Fruitcake, '80 280; '85 316; '00 299; '03 248
Zucchini Fruitcake, '88 284
Funnel Cakes, '83 250
Funnel Cakes, Nutty, '91 233
Gift Box Cake, '96 319
Gingerbread, '01 313
Gingerbread, Applesauce, '94 179
Gingerbread Cake Roll, '89 214
Gingerbread Mix, '92 312
Gingerbread, No-Molasses, '92 313
Gingerbread, Old English, '79 265
Gingerbread, Old-Fashioned, '91 240
Gingerbread, Refrigerator, '80 52
Gingerbread, Spicy, '84 263
Gingerbread with Caramel Sauce, Pumpkin, '93 235
Gingerbread with Key Lime Curd, Kahlúa, '96 126
Ginger Cake with Candied Cream, Spiced, '04 300
Ginger-Pear Upside-Down Cake, '97 205
Ginger Shortcakes, '94 179
Graham Cracker Cake, '79 13
Grapefruit Cake, Fresh, '89 308
Holiday Cake, Favorite, '81 264
Honey-Apple Cake, '99 210
Honey Bun Cake, '91 214
Honey Cake, '92 250
Honey Cake, Southern, '89 251
Hummingbird Cake, '82 244; '90 305; '03 315
Hummingbird Cake, Lightened, '01 34
Ice Cream Cake, '86 321; '89 71
Ice Cream Cake for Grown-Ups, '88 M192
Ice Cream Cake, Fruity, '87 110
Ice Cream Yule Log, '83 253
Irish Cream Cake, '02 323
Italian Cream Cake, '96 262
Italian Cream Cake, Fresh Orange, '02 294
Italian Cream Cake, Quick, '99 307
Jam Cake, Spicy, '89 236
Jellyroll, Easy, '82 176
Jellyroll Layer Cake, '85 125
Jellyroll, Spiced, '82 176
Journey Cakes, '04 99
Journey Cakes, Rosemary-Garlic, '04 99
Journey Cakes, Tomato, Parmesan, and Kalamata Olive,
    '04 99
Key Lime Cake, '91 214
King Cake, '90 20; '00 61
Lady Baltimore Cake, '90 45
Lane Cake, '80 121; '83 269; '96 144
Lane Cake, Holiday, '99 306
Lane Cake, Nanny's, '89 55
Lemon Cake, Easy, '83 24
Lemon Cake, Glazed, '86 70
Lemon Cake, Luscious, '93 81
Lemon Cake Pudding, '92 96; '98 35
Lemon Cake Roll, '89 312
Lemon Cake Roll, Elegant, '80 70
Lemon-Cheese Cake, Tart, '88 7; '03 317
Lemon Gold Cake, '83 301
Lemon Layer Cake, Luscious, '86 61
Lemon Layer Cake, Old-Fashioned, '85 191
Lemon Meringue Cake, '89 296; '99 118
Lemon-Pineapple Cake, '86 60, 239
Lemon-Poppy Seed Cake, '93 154

Lemon-Poppy Seed Cake Batter, '05 287
Lemon Pudding Cake, '83 106
Lemon-Raspberry Cake, '91 247
Lemon Roll, Snow-Capped, '79 68
Lemon Sponge Cups, '83 10
Light Cake, Basic, '90 107
Lime Cakes, Creamy, '04 89
Lime Icebox Pie Cake, '03 104
Lime Layer Loaf, '85 96
Little Bitty Cakes, '98 154
Little Cakes, Spring's, '01 M91
Lord Baltimore Cake, '90 45
Mandarin-Rum Cake, '84 150
Mango Cake, '83 150
Maple Nut Cake, '96 17
Maraschino Nut Cake, '83 268
Mincemeat Spice Cake, '79 246
Molasses Snack Cake, '86 20
Moravian Sugar Cake, '95 304
Neapolitan Cake, '88 168
Nutmeg Feather Cake, '81 238
Nutty Cakes, '89 50
Oatmeal Cake, '01 58
Oatmeal Cake, Dutch, '83 95
Orange Blossom Cake, '96 162
Orange Butter Cake, '95 46
Orange Cake, '86 61; '95 320
Orange Cake, Fresh, '83 300
Orange Cake, Mandarin, '83 24
Orange Cake, Williamsburg, '81 120; '82 23
Orange Chiffon Cake, '91 56
Orange Chiffon Cake, Fresh, '88 179
Orange Chiffon Cake with Orange Icebox Pie Filling,
    '03 105
Orange-Cranberry Cake, '85 314
Orange Cream Cake, '99 118
Orange-Date Cake, '94 60
Orange Date-Nut Cake, '01 285
Orange-Lemon Cake, General Robert E. Lee, '88 92
Orange Liqueur Cake, '87 84
Orange Marmalade Cake, '85 53
Orange Meringue Cake, '86 336; '87 84
Orange-Nut Butter Cake, '80 254
Orange Nut Cake, '80 70
Orange-Pecan Crunch Cake, '83 10
Orange Rum Cake, '79 2
Orange-Slice Cake, '81 264
Orange Streusel Cake, '88 10
Peach Cake, Fresh, '85 178
Peaches and Cream Cake, '80 142
Peaches-and-Cream Cake, '96 118
Peach Shortcakes, Spicy, '89 154
Peach Upside-Down Cake, '87 8
Peachy Picnic Cake, '79 178
Peanut Butter-and-Jelly Cake, '85 34
Peanut Butter-Banana Cake, '80 87
Peanut Butter Cake, '79 51; '83 M233
Peanut Butter Swirl Cake, '86 109
Peanutty Layer Cake, Super, '83 222
Pear Cake, Caramel-Glazed, '02 196
Pear Cakes with Praline Sauce, '96 284
Pear Cake with Caramel Drizzle, '86 247
Pear Preserve Cake, '85 52
Pear Preserves Cake, '00 139
Pecan Cake, '97 256
Pecan Cake, Kentucky, '84 263
Pecan Cake with Praline Glaze, '82 196
Pecan-Carrot Cake, '99 223
Pecan-Cornmeal Rounds, '95 99
Pecan Pie Cake, '98 254; '03 316

Pecan Roulade, '87 183
Peppermint Cake, Red Velvet, '98 308
Peppermint Candy Cake, '89 254
Persimmon Cake, '79 205
Petit Fours, Simple, '92 277
Petits Fours, '79 117; '96 282
Petits Fours, Chocolate-Almond, '93 255; '00 72
Petits Fours, From-the-Heart, '03 110
Petits Fours, Teatime, '85 119
Pig Pickin' Cake, '04 112; '05 63
Pineapple Cake, Heavenly, '83 303
Pineapple-Cherry Dump Cake, '04 91
Pineapple-Coconut Cake, '00 86
Pineapple-Pecan Upside-Down Cake, '84 25
Pineapple Right-Side-Up Snack Cake, '99 28
Pineapple Upside-Down Cake, '80 102; '88 10
Pineapple Upside-Down Cake, Express, '03 65
Pineapple Upside-Down Cake, Fresh, '97 204
Pineapple Upside-Down Cake Roll, '96 162
Pineapple Upside-Down Cake, Skillet, '85 242; '03 65
Pineapple Upside-Down Cake, Spiced, '02 214
Pineapple Upside-Down Cake, Stacked, '86 239
Plum Cake, '97 177
Popcorn-Gumdrop Cake, '87 262
Poppy Seed Cake, '92 174; '95 63
Poppy Seed Cake, Lemon-, '93 154
Poppy Seed Cake, Plantation, '79 13
Poppy Seed Loaf Cake, '81 63
Poppy Seed Loaf, Quick, '82 75
Pound
    Apple Cider Pound Cake, '84 10
    Apricot Brandy Pound Cake, '83 267
    Aztec Pound Cake, '96 61
    Banana Pound Cake, '96 60; '98 195
    Batter, Pound Cake, '04 84
    Black Pepper Pound Cake, '96 61
    Black Walnut Pound Cake, '92 16
    Bourbon-Pecan Pound Cake, '91 270
    Brandied Pound Cake, '89 292
    Brown Sugar Pound Cake, '82 135; '04 278
    Brown Sugar Pound Cake with Creamy Holiday
        Glaze, '03 281
    Brown Sugar-Rum Pound Cake, '96 60
    Buttered Rum Pound Cake with Bananas Foster
        Sauce, '03 94
    Buttermilk Pound Cake, '79 285; '85 255; '99 98
    Buttermilk Pound Cake, Old-Fashioned, '82 52;
        '88 16
    Buttermilk Pound Cake, Spiced, '84 73
    Butter-Nut Pound Cake, '86 235
    Butternut Pound Cake with Caramel Sauce, Betty's,
        '95 308
    Butterscotch-Pecan Pound Cake, '92 153
    Caramel Frosting, Pound Cake with, '87 39
    Caramel Pound Cake, '98 194
    Carrot Pound Cake, '87 41
    Cheesy Pound Cake, '96 62
    Cherry Pound Cake, Cute-as-a-Button, '95 139
    Chocolate Chip Pound Cake, '86 178; '93 105;
        '94 100
    Chocolate Marble Pound Cake, '88 16
    Chocolate-Orange Pound Cake, '89 94
    Chocolate Pound Cake, '82 88; '84 10; '89 325;
        '94 288; '98 336
    Chocolate Pound Cake with Frosting, '90 284
    Chocolate Pound Cake with Fudge Frosting, '87 296
    Chocolate-Sour Cream Pound Cake, '83 239; '92 153
    Chocolate-Swirled Pound Cake, '97 329
    Chocolate Velvet "Pound" Cake, '03 286
    Coconut-Cream Cheese Pound Cake, '85 297;
        '90 305
    Coconut Cream Pound Cake, '84 10
    Coconut Pound Cake, '82 87; '91 224
    Cream Cheese-Bourbon-Pecan Pound Cake, '04 280

Cream Cheese-Coconut-Pecan Pound Cake, '04 280
Cream Cheese Pound Cake, '81 290; '86 287;
    '95 304; '01 244; '03 312
Cream Cheese Pound Cake, Crusty, '89 124
Cream Cheese Pound Cake with Strawberries and
    Cream, '02 104
Croutons, Cinnamon Pound Cake, '93 161
Daiquiri Pound Cake, '93 83
Eggnog-Pecan Pound Cake, '95 313
Eggnog Pound Cake, '90 253
Favorite Pound Cake, '81 132; '92 171
Five-Flavor Pound Cake, '87 264
Four-Flavor Pound Cake, '91 136
French Toast, Pound Cake, '04 33
Fruited Pound Cake, '81 265
Gentleman's Pound Cake, '00 287
German Chocolate Pound Cake, '97 M254
Ginger Pound Cake, '02 97; '03 99
Ginger Pound Cake with Glazed Cranberry
    Ambrosia, '00 269
Glazed Pound Cake, '89 207
Golden Pound Cake, '90 284
Granny's Pound Cake, '05 269
I Remember Pound Cake, '86 180
Irish Cream-and-Coffee Pound Cake, '92 287
Lemon-Almond Pound Cake, Sullivan's, '04 278
Lemon Curd Pound Cake, '04 278
Lemon Geranium Pound Cake, '01 131
Lemon Pound Cake, '82 88; '03 94
Lemon Pound Cake with Mint Berries and Cream,
    '99 183
Lemon-Sour Cream Pound Cake, '87 38
Lemon Sour Cream Pound Cake, '01 117
Lemony Pound Cake, '96 60
Loaf, Noel Pound Cake, '04 279
Loaf, Pound Cake, '85 306
Loaf, Pretty and Pink Pound Cake, '96 60
Mahogany Pound Cake, '89 207
Marbled Pecan Pound Cake, '93 313
Marble Pound Cake, '95 29
Milk Chocolate Pound Cake, '90 306
Million Dollar Pound Cake, '90 306; '02 239;
    '03 270
Mini Pound Cakes, '86 148
Mocha Marble Pound Cake, '99 23
Old-Fashioned Pound Cake, '80 279; '82 88; '93 120
Orange-Pecan Pound Cake, '93 13
Orange-Pecan-Spice Pound Cake, '02 295
Orange Pound Cake, '87 84, 221; '92 69
Pastel Cake, '97 173
Peach-Almond Pound Cake, '89 86
Pecan Pound Cake, '01 253
Pineapple Pound Cake, '79 148
Pound Cake, '92 94
Praline Pound Cake, '82 88
Problems to Avoid Chart, '84 319
Pumpkin Pound Cake, '92 235
Rose-Geranium Pound Cake, Mrs. Willoughby's,
    '84 318
Rum Pound Cake, Buttered, '83 220
Sandwich, Grilled Pound Cake Dessert, '94 171
S'mores, Grilled Pound Cake, '98 179
Sour Cream-Orange Pecan Pound Cake, '89 207
Sour Cream Pound Cake, '89 56; '92 153
Sour Cream Pound Cake, Cinnamon-Topped, '82 43
Sour Cream Pound Cake, Elegant, '83 79
Sour Cream Pound Cake with Raspberry Sauce,
    '99 259
Southern Pound Cake, Smoothest, '93 237
Stick, Colorful Cakes on a, '04 84
Strawberry-Banana Topping, Pound Cake with,
    '89 200
Sweet Potato Pound Cake, '83 85
Teapot Cake, '04 83

Tea Pound Cake, '99 90
Two-Step Pound Cake, '00 36
Whipping Cream Pound Cake, '90 284
White Chocolate Pound Cake, '91 101
Wine Jelly, Pound Cake with, '98 125
Yogurt Pound Cake, '84 10
Praline Cake, '81 162
Praline Cream Cake, '01 272
Praline Ice Cream Cake, '80 84
Praline-Pecan Cakes, '05 286
Prune Cake, '85 223
Prune Cake and Sauce, '85 118
Prune Cake, Spicy, '79 136
Pudding Cake, Danish, '91 269
Pudding Cake, Saucy, '98 196
Pudding Cake with Blueberry Sauce, Buttermilk-
    Lemon, '95 135
Pumpkin Cake, '81 272; '93 303; '98 241
Pumpkin Cake with Little Ghosts, '03 212
Pumpkin Date Cake, '79 251
Pumpkin Kahlúa Cake, '86 292
Pumpkin Layer Cake, '80 245
Pumpkin Roll, '79 206; '91 297; '04 297
Pumpkin Spice Cake, '05 232
Queen Bee Cake, '81 237
Raisin Layer Cake, Spicy, '79 230
Red Velvet Cake, '93 318; '96 282; '01 244
Rhubarb Upside-Down Cake, '00 87
Root Beer Float Cake, '99 196
Rum Cake, '05 279
Satin Ribbon Cake, '92 68
Sauerkraut Cake, '94 254
Savarin, '79 171
Shortcakes
    Blueberry-Nectarine Shortcake, Warm, '97 205
    Caramel-Apple Shortcakes, '03 194
    Chicken Shortcakes, Cheesy, '95 98
    Chocolate-Raspberry Shortcake, '95 99
    Cinnamon-Crunch Shortcakes, '03 194
    Cinnamon-Crunch Shortcakes with Fruit Compote,
        '03 194
    Ginger-Pear Shortcakes, '03 194
    Orange Shortcake, Fresh, '80 100
    Orange-Strawberry Shortcake, '95 100
    Peach-and-Blueberry Shortcakes, Southern, '05 318
    Round Shortcakes, '02 105
    Shortcut, Shortcake, '02 105
    Strawberry-Brown Sugar Shortcake, '00 82
    Strawberry Crispy Shortcakes, '93 42
    Strawberry Pinwheel Shortcake, '89 112
    Strawberry Shortcake, '81 96; '83 122; '92 184;
        '94 162
    Strawberry Shortcake, A Favorite, '88 136
    Strawberry Shortcake, Elegant, '88 37
    Strawberry Shortcake Jubilee, '88 209
    Strawberry Shortcake Shells, '88 196
    Strawberry Shortcakes, Party-Perfect, '02 105
    Strawberry Shortcakes with Mint Cream, '97 144
Sorghum Cake, '85 239
Sorghum Tea Cakes, '85 239
Sour Cream Cake Batter, '05 286
Sour Cream Cake Layers, '01 270
Sour Cream-Pecan Cake Batter, '05 286
Spice Cake, '81 162
Spice Cake, Buttermilk, '81 211
Spice Cake, Dark, '82 314; '83 43
Spice Cake, Old South, '84 263
Spice Cake, Sugar 'n, '84 226
Spice Cake with Caramel Frosting, '82 314; '83 42
Spice Cake with Chocolate-Coffee Frosting, '88 268
Spice Cake with Cream Cheese Frosting, Harvest,
    '02 209
Spice Cake, Yule Log, '85 314
Spice Layer Cake with Coffee Frosting, '94 86

Sponge
    Burnt Sugar Sponge Cake with Berry Sauce, '95 103
    Chocolaty Sponge Cake, '86 60
    Coffee Sponge Cake, '83 229; '91 55
    Coffee Sponge Cake, Two-Day, '86 75
    Daffodil Sponge Cake, '79 175; '80 6; '84 315
    Passover Sponge Cake, '90 106
    Strawberries 'n Cream Sponge Cake Roll, '81 95
    Yellow Sponge Cake, '80 250
Squash Cake, '86 200
Stack Cake, Favorite, '87 228
Stack Cake, Old-Fashioned, '81 216
Strawberry Cake, Layered, '00 82
Strawberry Cake Roll, '79 49; '83 129; '84 305; '85 172
Strawberry Cake, Triple-Decker, '04 55
Strawberry Cream Cake, '86 61
Strawberry Crunch Cake, '79 288; '80 35
Strawberry Delight Cake, '85 30
Strawberry Ice Cream Roll, '84 105
Strawberry-Lemon Sheet Cake, '04 137
Strawberry Meringue Cake, '86 240
Strawberry Roll, '82 120
Strawberry Roll, Heavenly, '82 176
Strawberry Yogurt Layer Cake, '94 85
Sweet Potato Cake, '79 207; '89 295
Sweet Potato Cakes, '01 105
Sweet Potato Cake with Citrus Filling, '02 221
Sweet Potato Cake with Coconut Filling and Caramel
    Frosting, '03 329
Sweet Potato Loaf Cake, '81 224
Sweet Potato Log Roll, '82 227
Sweet Potato Surprise Cake, '80 287
Tea Cake, Lemon, '82 169
Tea Cakes and Fresh Strawberries, Telia's, '98 110
Teddy Bear Cakes, '92 278
Tennessee Jam Cake, '04 55
Tennessee Jam Cake, Triple-Layer, '04 55
Tilden Cake with Cherry-Wine Sauce, '97 132
Tipsy Squire, '85 41
Tortes
    Almond Torte, Chocolate-, '96 M253
    Amaretto Torte, '82 303
    Apricot Praline Torte, Lucy's, '95 243
    Apricot Sponge Torte, '90 59
    Apricot Torte, '02 220
    Black Forest Torte, '88 209
    Black Forest Cherry Torte, '88 178
    Blitz Torte, '01 65
    Bourbon-Chocolate Torte, '98 M84
    Caramel-Sweet Potato Torte, '96 312
    Carob-Pecan Torte, '85 218
    Chocolate-Almond Torte, '98 273
    Chocolate Mint Torte, '94 86
    Chocolate-Pecan Torte, '89 42
    Chocolate Praline Torte, '84 165
    Chocolate-Strawberry Ice Cream Torte, '79 7
    Chocolate Torte, Apricot-Filled, '90 107
    Chocolate Torte, Double-, '79 67
    Chocolate Torte, Flourless, '05 81
    Chocolate Torte Royale, '82 263
    Chocolate Torte, Triple, '96 58
    Chocolate Torte with Firewater Cream, '00 161
    Chocolate-Vanilla Holiday Torte, '01 252
    Chocolate Velvet Torte, '86 316
    Graham Cracker-Nut Torte, '97 275; '98 35
    Hazelnut Torte, '91 248
    Huguenot Torte, '05 98
    Lemon Meringue Torte with Raspberry Sauce,
        '93 82
    Mocha Brownie Torte, '85 102
    Mocha-Pecan Torte, '86 26
    Mocha Torte, '99 66
    Mocha Velvet Torte, '92 318
    Passover Linzer Torte, '90 106

Pecan Torte, Ground, '04 273
Pecan Torte, Heavenly, '81 266
Praline-Pumpkin Torte, '01 285
Spring Torte, '91 57
Strawberry Meringue Torte, '88 136
Sugar Cookie Torte, '79 68
Toffee Meringue Torte, '87 118
White Chocolate Mousse Torte, '99 154
Twelfth Night Cake, '93 337
Upside-Down Cake, Blackberry, '01 314
Upside-Down Cake, Mango, '05 120
Upside Down Cake, Quick, '90 219
Upside-Down Sunburst Cake, '87 9
Vanilla Chiffon Cake, '79 266
Vanilla-Jasmine-Sour Cream Tea Cake, '05 135
Walnut Cream Roll, '84 192
Wedding Cake, Rose Garden, '97 60
Whipped Cream Cake, '96 96
White Cake Batter, Basic, '99 117
White Cake, Buttermilk, '86 235
White Cake with Strawberries and Chocolate Glaze,
    '87 76
White Cake with Strawberry Frosting, Rich, '89 184
Winter Squash-Spice Bundt Cake, '99 248
Yogurt-Lemon-Nut Cake, '89 169
Zucchini Cake, '79 24
Zucchini-Pineapple Cake, '95 160
Zuppa Inglese, '85 229
CANDIES
Almond Brittle, '03 281
Almond Brittle Candy, '80 255
Almond Butter Crunch, '80 301
Almond Roca, '86 49
Almond-Toffee Crunch, '88 285
Apples, Candied Red, '81 217
Apples, Candy, '84 243
Apricot Balls, '79 274
Balls, Buckeye, '00 M280; '01 M322
Balls, No-Cook Candy, '85 14
Bourbon Balls, '81 254; '83 315; '90 83; '02 30
Bourbon Balls, Chocolate, '84 298
Bow, Candy, '99 M306
Box, White Candy, '97 M54
Brandy Balls, '86 319
Brittle, Cooktop, '02 223
Brittle, Microwave Pecan, '97 M245
Brittle with Crushed Peanuts, '87 184
Buckeyes, '85 321
Butter Creams, '80 302
Buttermilk Candy, '80 302
Candy Cane Swizzle Sticks, '02 298
Caramel Corn Candy, '84 243
Caramel Good Stuff, Baked, '80 284
Caramel O's, '99 M196
Caramel-Peanut Squares, '85 247
Caramels, Chocolate-Dipped, '02 30
Caramels, Coconut-Macadamia, '98 305
Caramels, Soft-and-Chewy, '03 297
Cherries, Cordial, '02 30
Cherry-Pistachio Bark, '00 M41
Chocolate-Almond Hearts, '03 42
Chocolate Bonbons, Dark, '02 297
Chocolate Brittle, '83 315
Chocolate Brittle, Quick, '82 114
Chocolate Caramels, '91 35
Chocolate-Coconut Almond Drops, '87 223
Chocolate-Covered Cherries, '81 286; '84 298; '97 M55
Chocolate-Covered Pecan Fritters, '79 205
Chocolate-Covered Pretzels, '82 295
Chocolate Drops, '84 111
Chocolate Greeting Card, '83 40
Chocolate-Lemon Creams, '98 M235
Chocolate-Marshmallow Squares, '92 M50
Chocolate-Nut Log Candy, '86 335

CANDIES

(continued)

Chocolate Nut Teasers, '91 35
Chocolate-Peanut Butter Balls, '80 87
Chocolate-Peanut Butter Bites, '92 M317
Chocolate-Peanut Butter Drops, '92 322
Chocolate-Peanut Clusters, '81 16
Chocolate Peanutty Swirls, '94 M330
Chocolate Rudolph Reindeer, '04 M254
Chocolate Rum Balls, '80 302
Chocolate-Rum Balls, '88 285
Chocolates, Liqueur Cream-Filled, '87 258
Chocolate Spiders, '85 236
Chocolates, Spirited, '86 278
Chocolate, Tempered, '91 35
Chocolate Velvets, '84 298
Coconut-Almond Balls, '84 256
Coconut-Black Walnut Bonbons, '82 307
Coconut Candy, '79 272; '80 250
Coconut Joys, '98 282
Coconut Joys, Chocolate-Covered, '98 M282
Coffee Buttons, '99 66
Cola Candy, '02 298
Corn Brittle, Crunchy, '85 208
Cracker Candy, '02 30
Crème de Cacao Balls, '86 266
Crème de Menthe Chocolates, '91 36
Crystal Candy, '84 299
Date Candy, '89 308
Date Loaf Candy, '80 302
Date Logs, '79 274
Divinity, Apricot, '83 297
Divinity Candy, '01 271
Divinity Candy with Sugared Maraschino Cherries,
   '01 271
Divinity, Cherry, '97 316
Divinity, Christmas, '81 286
Divinity Ghosts, '95 273
Divinity, Lemon, '97 316
Divinity, Mrs. Floyd's, '00 315
Divinity, Peanut, '85 233; '87 M278
Divinity, Pink, '86 49
Divinity, Strawberry, '91 272
Easter Egg Kaleidoscopes, '02 48
Frosting, Chocolate Candy, '81 238
Fruit Balls, '82 296; '84 299
Fudge. *See* FUDGE.
Kentucky Colonels, '79 273
Lollipops, Colorful Molded, '81 218
Marzipan, '83 306
Millionaires, '79 M262; '97 M55
Millionaires, Texas, '00 291
Mints, Butter, '03 300
Mints, Cream Cheese, '93 79; '00 41
Mints, Dinner, '88 66
Mints, Easy Holiday, '84 299
Mints, Party, '79 273; '81 119
Mints, Special, '99 323
Mint Twists, '86 106
Molded Candies, '84 40
Nests, Robin's Egg, '02 M48
Nut Clusters, '81 254
Nuts, Candied, '81 261
Orange Balls, '94 331
Orange-Nut Balls, '02 297
Orange Peel, Candied, '81 286
Peanut Brittle, '79 M263; '80 87; '84 298; '92 240
Peanut Brittle, Classic, '02 M223
Peanut Brittle, Golden, '83 223
Peanut Brittle, Never-Fail, '79 273
Peanut Brittle, Orange, '80 302
Peanut Brittle, Popcorn, '02 M223

Peanut Butter Candy, '93 166
Peanut Butter-Chocolate Balls, '80 269
Peanut Butter-Chocolate Candy Squares, '82 56
Peanut Butter Creams, '79 273
Peanut Butter Easter Eggs, '87 86
Peanut Butter Temptations, '84 29
Peanut Butter Yummies, '83 223
Peanut Clusters, '87 184; '92 288; '98 M282
Peanutty Clusters, '83 143
Pecan Brittle, '91 272; '02 M223
Pecan Clusters, '81 266; '98 305
Pecan Clusters, Roasted, '85 233; '90 310; '03 315
Pecan Clusters, Toasted, '00 M14
Pecan-Coconut Clusters, '86 M251
Pecan Rolls, '79 285
Pecans, Brown Sugar, '81 266
Pecans, Glazed, '81 254
Pecans, Honeycomb, '84 300
Pecans, Orange, '84 299
Pecans, Spiced, '79 296; '81 286
Pecans, Spicy, '81 289
Pecans, Sugar-and-Honey, '86 319
Penuche, Coffee, '98 305
Peppermint Patties, '86 278
Potato Candy, '79 273
Pralines

After-the-Dance Pralines, '03 251
Basic Pralines, '92 313; '93 50
Bourbon Pralines, '92 313; '93 51
Buttermilk Pralines, '99 99; '00 49
Butterscotch Pralines, '81 253
Café au Lait Pralines, '92 313; '93 51
Chocolate-Mint Pralines, '92 313; '93 51
Chocolate-Peanut Butter Pralines, '92 313; '93 51
Chocolate Pralines, '92 313; '93 51
Cinnamon Pralines, '97 317
Coffee Pralines, Plantation, '86 241
Creamy Pralines, '80 198; '92 289
Dark Praline Clusters, '86 313
Dark Pralines, '83 52
Hot Spicy Pralines, '92 313; '93 51
Maple-Pecan Pralines, '83 222
Mocha Pralines, '92 313; '93 51
New Orleans-Style Pralines, '86 335
Old-Fashioned Pralines, '89 318
Orange Pralines, '92 313; '93 51
Peanut Butter Pralines, '92 313; '93 51
Pecan Pralines, Original, '81 11
Pralines, '79 272; '86 M288; '89 60; '90 48; '99 295;
   '01 90, 201
Southern Pralines, '79 M263
Spicy Praline Delights, '84 299
Texas-Size Pralines, '79 186
Vanilla Pralines, '92 313; '93 51
Quemada (Burnt-Sugar Candy), '87 38
Raisin Candy, Mixed, '84 111
Raspberry Cream Chocolates, '91 36
Red Rock Candy, '92 240
Rocky Road, '84 298
Rocky Road-Peanut Butter Candy Cups, '04 M330
Rum Balls, '93 314
Strawberries, Christmas, '94 331
Sugared Rabbits, '04 94
Taffy, Old-Fashioned, '80 302
Toffee, '01 218
Toffee, Almond, '04 235
Toffee, Bourbon-Pecan, '04 235
Toffee, English, '79 273
Toffee, Hawaiian, '04 235
Toffee, Microwave, '92 M317
Toffee, Microwave Peanut, '04 M234
Toffee, Mildred's, '04 235
Toffee, Nutty, '79 M263
Toffee, Pecan, '00 42

Truffles

Almond Truffles, '83 298
Amaretto Dessert Truffles, '86 319
Bittersweet Truffles, '94 330
Chocolate-Cherry Cordial Truffles, '99 127
Chocolate-Kahlúa Truffles, '92 285
Chocolate Marble Truffles, '97 284
Chocolate-Praline Truffles, '97 284
Chocolate Truffles, '85 114; '89 43; '91 108
Hazelnut-Chocolate Truffles, '03 243
Hazelnut Truffles, '97 M54
Orange-Pecan Truffles, '95 92
Raspberry-Fudge Truffles, '00 M41
White Chocolate-Praline Truffles, '97 284
White Chocolate Truffles, '87 45
Yule Street Truffles, '90 242
Turtle Candies, '93 M41
White Chocolate-Peanut Butter Crunch, '02 M296
White Chocolate Salties, '92 50
White Chocolate Surprises, '91 36
CANNING AND PRESERVING
Apple Rings, Cinnamon, '85 107
Asparagus, Pickled, '83 46
Beets, Pickled, '81 216
Berries (except Strawberries), '80 128
Black-Eyed, Field, and Crowder Peas, '80 126
Cantaloupe, Pickled, '99 171
Carrot Marmalemon, '96 107
Catsup, Homemade, '85 188
Catsup, Spicy Tomato, '83 182
Chiles Medley, Fiery Pickled, '01 333
Chili Sauce, '81 175
Chili Sauce, Chunky, '85 188
Chow-Chow, '82 196
Chowchow, '00 158
Chutney, Pear, '98 243
Confit, Roasted Shallot-Garlic, '94 303
Corn, Cold-Pack, '81 216
Corn, Cream-Style, '80 127; '85 106
Corn, Whole Kernel, '85 106
Cranberry Conserve, '83 279
Fruit Juices, '85 107
Fruit, Unsweetened Mixed, '83 182
Grapes, Spiced, '98 220
Green Beans, '80 126
Green Bean Salad, Pickled, '82 239
Green Beans, Appalachian, '81 215
Green Beans, Dill, '93 136
Green Beans, Dilled, '99 170
Green, Snap, or Wax Beans, '85 105
Green Tomatoes, Pickled, '99 143
Lemons, Fresh Preserved, '00 17
Lima Beans, '80 127
Mincemeat, Homemade, '79 245
Nectarines in Apple Juice, '83 183
Okra, '80 127
Okra, Pickled, '98 177
Oranges, Brandied Cranberry, '98 309
Peaches, '80 128
Peaches and Pears, '85 106
Peaches, Honey-Sweet, '85 107
Pear Mincemeat, '79 196
Piccalilli, Kentucky, '81 216
Plums, Brandied, '97 176
Pomegranate Syrup, '96 241
Relish, Green Tomato, '98 124
Sauerkraut, Homemade, '81 216
Squash Pickles, '97 119
Squash, Summer, '80 127; '85 105
Succotash, '85 106
Sugar Snap Peas, Pickled, '01 112
Tomatoes, '80 128; '85 106
Tomatoes, Canned Flavored, '95 217
Tomatoes, Stewed, '83 182

Tomatoes with Okra, '85 106
Tomato Juice, Spicy, '85 189
Tomato Puree, Seasoned, '83 182
Vegetable Soup, '80 128; '85 106
Vegetables, Pickled Confetti, '00 133
CANTALOUPE. *See* MELONS.
CARAMEL
Apples, Black-and-White Caramel, '03 M216
Apples, Calypso Caramel, '03 M216
Apples, Caramel, '79 220; '89 M231; '03 M216
Apples, Caramel-Peanut, '93 M244
Apples, Old English Caramel, '85 231
Baked Caramel Good Stuff, '80 284
Bars, Caramel-Pecan Cheesecake, '05 210
Bars, Cranberry-Caramel, '98 277
Bars, Gooey Turtle, '96 M189
Bars, Oatmeal-Caramel, '85 247
Bars, Turtle, '00 334
Bars, Yummy, '92 171
Biscuits, Caramel Dessert, '95 36
Bombe, Caramel-Toffee, '93 214; '00 112
Bread, Caramel, '82 75
Brie with Fresh Fruit, Caramel, '90 266
Brownies, Caramel-Coconut-Pecan, '05 M288
Brownies, Caramel-Pecan Filled, '03 M43
Buns, Caramel Sticky, '00 52
Buns, Overnight Caramel Sticky, '00 52
Cake, Caramel, '89 55; '90 307
Cake, Caramel-Filled Butter Pecan, '88 278
Cake, Caramel-Glazed Pear, '02 196
Cake, Caramel Pound, '98 194
Cake, Chocolate-Caramel-Nut, '83 23
Cake, Chocolate-Caramel Sheet, '05 210
Cake, Creamy Caramel Layer, '81 71
Cake Squares, Turtle, '05 M211
Cake, Turtle, '03 287
Cheesecake, Chocolate-Caramel-Pecan, '91 197
Cheesecake, Peach-Caramel, '02 M158
Chocolate Caramels, '91 35
Chocolate-Dipped Caramels, '02 30
Cobbler, Peach-Caramel, '86 300; '87 178
Cobbler with Bourbon-Pecan Ice Cream, Caramel-
    Applesauce, '00 260
Cobbler with Oatmeal Muffin Crust, Caramel Apple-
    Pear, '04 201
Coconut-Macadamia Caramels, '98 305
Coffee Cakes, Caramel-Apple, '05 210
Cookies, Caramel-Filled Chocolate, '92 319;
    '02 53
Cookies, Peanut Butter-Toffee Turtle, '02 M325
Corn, Baked Caramel, '81 218
Corn Candy, Caramel, '84 243
Corn, Caramel, '88 64
Corn, Crispy Caramel, '04 112
Corn, Nutty Caramel, '92 317
Corn, Oven-Made Caramel, '91 233
Crème d'Ange, '83 91
Crunch, Caramel, '95 165
Custard, Caramel, '01 237
Dessert, Coconut-Caramel, '92 44
Dessert, Turtle, '04 127
Dip, Apple, '96 M190
Drizzle, Caramel, '86 247
Filling, Caramel, '88 278; '03 287
Filling, Caramel Whipped Cream, '96 312
Flans, Caramel-Crowned, '90 227
Flan with Caramel, Baked, '92 231
Fondue, Caramel, '94 331; '95 35
French Toast, Caramel-Pecan, '03 328
French Toast, Caramel-Soaked, '03 307
Frosting, Caramel, '81 278, M289; '82 314; '83 43;
    '84 39, 263; '86 239; '87 265; '89 55, 236;
    '90 307; '98 195; '00 52; '03 329
Frosting, Creamy Caramel, '81 71

Frosting, Double Chocolate Brownies with Caramel,
    '04 M220
Frosting, Easy Caramel, '87 39
Frosting, Favorite Caramel, '83 106
Frosting, Quick Caramel, '04 55; '05 211
Frosting, Quick Caramel-Coconut-Pecan,
    '05 211
Frosting, Quick Caramel-Pecan, '05 211
Fudge, Caramel, '91 273
Glaze, Caramel, '98 195; '02 196
Helado, Caramel-Vanilla (Caramel-Vanilla Ice Cream),
    '81 67
Ice Cream Dessert, Caramel, '95 36
Ice Cream, No-Cook Turtle, '04 M179
Ice Cream, Pecan-Caramel Crunch, '02 322
Millionaires, '79 M262; '97 M55
Millionaires, Texas, '00 291
Muffins, Caramel-Apple, '05 210
Napoleons, Caramel-Apple, '01 M313
O's, Caramel, '99 M196
Peaches, Caramel, '93 134
Pecan Triangles, Caramel-, '99 281
Pie, Burnt Caramel, '82 53
Pie, Caramel, '96 72
Pie, Caramel-Banana, '86 M165
Pie, Caramel Ice Cream, '82 181
Pie, Caramel Meringue, '97 109
Pie, Caramel-Nut Crunch, '94 244
Pie, Caramel-Peanut, '86 259
Pie, Caramel-Pecan, '88 282; '05 269
Pie, Caramel-Pecan Apple, '85 247
Pie, Cracked Caramel-Pumpkin, '99 254
Pie, Luscious Caramel Banana, '79 115
Pie, Maverick Lunar, '98 111
Pies, Coconut-Caramel, '87 260
Popcorn, Caramel, '79 219; '86 M212
Popcorn, Caramel Crunch, '96 255
Popcorn Clusters, Caramel-Nut, '00 M223
Popcorn, Crispy Caramel, '85 247
Quesadillas, Caramel-Apple, '05 223
Ring, Caramel-Orange Coffee, '80 45
Ring, Easy Caramel, '85 M89
Rolls, Caramel Breakfast, '79 193
Rolls, Caramel-Nut, '86 312
Rolls, Easy Caramel, '90 195
Sauce, Caramel, '79 79; '91 56, 180; '93 210, 235, 296;
    '94 234; '95 308; '96 284, 310; '97 178; '00 52,
    256; '01 313; '03 194; '04 249
Sauce, Caramel-Raisin, '88 127
Sauce, Easy Caramel, '87 38
Sauce, Pears with Orange-Caramel, '95 281
Sauce, Steaks with Caramel-Brandy, '03 56
Sauce, The Best Ever Caramel, '03 216
Sauce, Toffee-Fudge, '89 95
Sauce, White Caramel, '92 195; '99 28
Shortcakes, Caramel-Apple, '03 194
Soft-and-Chewy Caramels, '03 297
Squares, Caramel-Peanut, '85 247
Squares, Chocolate-Caramel Layer, '79 83
Sticky Buns, Easy Caramel-Chocolate, '95 36
Surprise, Caramel, '88 202
Syrup, Caramel, '82 43
Syrup, Citrus Compote with Caramel, '98 313
Syrup, The Ultimate No-Bake Cheesecake Banana
    Pudding with Caramel, '05 326
Tart, Caramel Turtle Truffle, '93 M131
Tarts, Caramel, '82 43
Tarts, Tiny Caramel, '99 179
Torte, Caramel-Sweet Potato, '96 312
Torte, Peanut Butter Turtle, '04 316
Torte, X-Treme Chocolate Double Nut Caramel
    Ladyfinger, '04 M315
Waffles with Apples and Caramel, Gingerbread,
    '98 M237

CARROTS
Aloha Carrots, '85 261
Ambrosia, Carrot-Marshmallow, '80 5
Apricot Carrots, '84 6
Asparagus, Sunshine Carrots and, '99 277
Aspic, Orange-and-Carrot, '86 199
Baby Carrots, Balsamic, '02 43
Baby Carrots, Zucchini with, '88 24
Bake, Apple-Carrot, '93 304
Bake, Carrot-Apple, '98 232
Bake, Creamy Carrot, '85 67
Ball, Carrot-Cheese, '86 325
Balls, Carrot, '79 178
Beef à la Mode, '98 122
Bourbon Carrots, '03 295
Bourbonnaise, Baby Carrots, '85 89
Braised Carrots and Celery, '86 327
Braised Carrots, Apples, and Celery, '96 107
Braised Red Cabbage, '99 243
Brandied Carrots, '87 253
Brandy Sauce, Carrots in, '83 86
Breads
    Carrot Bread, '89 143
    Cornbread, Carrot, '80 89; '81 163
    Muffins, Apple-Carrot, '91 213
    Muffins, Carrot-and-Raisin, '87 24
    Muffins, Carrot-Date-Nut, '86 262
    Muffins, Carrot-Pineapple, '81 6
    Muffins, Carrot-Wheat, '88 9
    Muffins, Carrot-Zucchini, '01 200
    Muffins, Morning Glory, '93 327
    Pineapple Bread, Carrot-, '82 210
    Pineapple-Carrot Bread, '79 106
    Tasty Carrot Bread, '84 328
    Three-C Bread, '81 284
    Walnut Bread, Carrot-, '88 284
    Zucchini-Carrot Bread, '83 190
Brisket, Aunt Suzi's, '02 321
Brussels Sprouts, Carrots and, '82 300
Buttered Carrots and Celery, '89 44
Cake. *See* CARROTS/Desserts.
Caprice, Carrots, '84 6
Cardamom Carrots, '89 271
Casserole, Carrot, '86 279; '87 285
Casserole, Carrot and Zucchini, '83 256
Casserole, Carrot-Pecan, '93 44; '98 231; '02 282
Casserole, Cauliflower-and-Carrot, '83 280
Casserole, Scrumptious Carrot, '84 328
Casserole, Squash-Carrot, '81 157
Casserole, Zucchini-Carrot, '99 61
Celeriac and Carrots, '91 219
Chicken, Sweet-and-Sour, '97 325
Chowchow, Carrot, '93 218
Classy Carrots, '94 36
Coleslaw, Best Barbecue, '97 214
Coleslaw, Memphis-Style, '98 104
Combo, Carrot, '79 45
Cooler, Apricot-Orange-Carrot, '96 108
Cooler, Carrot, '89 35
Curried Carrots and Pineapple, '90 228
Desserts
    Cake, Applesauce Carrot, '81 202
    Cake, Best Carrot, '97 230
    Cake, Best Carrot Sheet, '03 55
    Cake, Blue Ribbon Carrot, '81 70
    Cake, Brownie Carrot, '92 120
    Cake, Carrot, '79 45; '82 137; '84 315; '98 275
    Cake, Carrot Pound, '87 41
    Cake, Carrot Pudding, '83 24
    Cake, Carrot-Raisin, '01 58
    Cake, Cheater's Carrot, '96 20
    Cake, Coconut-Pecan Carrot, '84 322
    Cake, Easy Carrot, '83 215
    Cake, Easy Carrot Snack, '82 235

Cake, Fresh Coconut-Carrot, '80 299
Cake, Frosted Carrot, '92 19
Cake, German Carrot-Hazelnut, '97 230
Cake, Mama Dip's Carrot, '05 299
Cake, Old-Fashioned Carrot, '83 M232; '97 330
Cake, Old-Fashioned Carrot Sheet, '97 330
Cake, Old-South Carrot, '80 120
Cake, Pecan-Carrot, '99 223
Cake, Praline-Filled Carrot, '03 332
Cake, Quick-and-Easy Carrot, '84 150
Cake, Shortcut Carrot, '02 83
Cakes, Miniature Carrot, '90 94
Cake, Spiced Carrot, '87 296
Cake, Spicy Fruited Carrot, '85 117
Cakes with Madeira Syrup and Vanilla Ice Cream,
    Carrot, '98 247
Cake with Candied Cream, Spiced Ginger, '04 300
Cake, Zucchini-Carrot, '93 20
Cookies, Carrot, '82 137
Cookies, Carrot-Orange, '83 149
Cookies, Frosted Carrot, '81 7
Cupcakes, Carrot-Bran, '82 16
Loaf, Carrot-Nut, '83 117
Pie, Carrot, '83 117
Pie, Carrot Custard, '79 45
Pie, Carrot Ice Cream, '86 200
Squares, Carrot, '79 256
Squares, Golden Carrot-Lemon, '80 40
Deviled Carrots, '83 322
Dilled Baby Carrots, '84 80; '92 145
Dilled Carrots, '85 24; '90 17
Dilled Carrots and Green Beans, '99 223
Dill-Spiced Carrots, '87 200
Dilly Carrots, '85 85
Fillets, Apple-Carrot Stuffed, '88 M192
Fried Carrot Balls, '82 16
Fried Carrots, Crispy, '94 36
Garden Surprise, '83 112
Ginger Carrots, '83 9; '85 139
Gingered Carrots, '85 95; '92 302
Glazed
    Apricot Glazed Carrots, '80 89
    Apricot-Glazed Carrots, '98 231; '01 212
    Baby Carrots, Glazed, '91 291; '92 256
    Baby Carrots, Mint-Glazed, '89 102
    Bacon and Onion, Glazed Carrots with, '87 200;
        '02 283
    Brown Sugar-Glazed Carrots, '99 24
    Brussels Sprouts and Baby Carrots, Glazed, '97 302
    Candied Carrots, '82 269; '83 225
    Ginger Carrots, '83 9
    Ginger-Cinnamon Carrots, '93 168
    Gingered Carrots, '85 95
    Ginger-Glazed Carrots, '87 68
    Glazed Carrots, '81 304; '83 117; '85 258; '88 304;
        '89 106, 235
    Golden Carrots, '85 267
    Grapes, Glazed Carrots with, '82 287
    Harvard Carrots, '83 117
    Honey-Glazed Carrots, '80 115; '84 121; '85 18;
        '92 229; '99 63
    Honey-Kissed Carrots, '84 122
    Horseradish Glaze, Carrots with, '85 66
    Lemon-Glazed Carrots, '84 16
    Light Glazed Carrots, '92 227
    Mint-Glazed Carrots and Peas, '90 291
    Onions, Glazed Carrots and, '83 25; '87 128
    Orange-Glazed Carrots, '79 12; '81 M165; '90 M98
    Orange-Raisin Carrots, '80 24
    Parsnips, Glazed Carrots and, '02 129

Peach-Glazed Carrots, '90 13
Pepper Jelly-Glazed Carrots, '02 291; '05 334
Pineapple Carrots, '83 198
Rutabaga, Lemon-Glazed Carrots and, '97 46
Spiced-Glazed Carrots, '05 274
Spice-Glazed Carrots, '83 M58
Sunshine Carrots, '82 16
Hash Browns, Carrot, '96 107
Herbed Carrots and Onions, '87 31
Honey, Carrots with, '02 59
Horseradish Sauce, Carrots and Broccoli with, '91 246
Julienne Carrots, How to Prepare, '84 120
Julienne Carrots, Sautéed, '82 91
Julienne Carrots with Walnuts, '84 188
Julienne, Tarragon Carrots, '84 329
Julienne, Turnips and Carrots, '86 295
Julienne Zucchini and Carrots, '90 14
Lemon-Carrot Bundles, '91 80
Lemon Carrots, '82 300; '83 111
Madeira, Carrots, '80 125; '83 281
Marinated Beets, Green Beans, and Carrots, '88 162
Marinated Carrots, '86 108, 111; '91 103
Marinated Carrots, Creamy, '87 200
Marinated Carrots, Crispy, '81 7
Marinated Carrots, Crunchy, '02 197
Marinated Carrot Strips, '88 176
Marmalade, Carrot-Citrus, '81 148
Marmalade, Carrot-Orange, '03 134
Marmalemon, Carrot, '96 107
Marsala, Carrots, '83 56
Mash, Rutabaga-Carrot, '02 275
Medley, Carrot-and-Leek, '88 102
Medley, Carrot-Lima-Squash, '80 123
Medley, Parsnip-Carrot, '96 36
Minted Carrots, '81 101
Minted Carrots, Saucy, '82 252
Orange Carrots and Turnips, Sunset, '94 213
Orange Carrots, Julienned, '04 297
Orange-Fennel Carrots, '92 133
Orange Sauce, Carrots in, '82 107
Orange-Spiced Carrots, '88 18
Orangy Carrot Strips, '89 312
Parsleyed Turnips and Carrots, '79 253
Patties, Carrot, '80 89
Pecans, Carrots and Celery with, '84 254
Peppers, Carrot-and-Cabbage Stuffed, '99 63
Pickled Carrots, '93 12
Pie, Cauliflower-Carrot, '82 191
Polynesian, Carrots, '79 45
Pudding, Carrot-Potato, '94 279
Puff, Carrot, '84 328; '89 89
Puffs, Carrot, '87 200
Puree, Carrot-and-Sweet Potato, '94 56
Puree, Carrot-Sweet Potato, '92 90; '00 M32; '02 M285
Relish, Carrot, '03 67
Rice, Sweet Carrots and, '05 203
Ring, Festive Carrot, '82 16
Ring, Rice-Carrot, '79 246
Roasted Carrots, '92 340
Roasted Celery Root, Carrots, and Onions, '98 293
Roasted Potatoes, Carrots, and Leeks, '94 276
Rosemary Carrots, '91 219
Salad, Apple-Carrot, '85 22
Salad, Broccoli, Cauliflower, and Carrot, '04 140
Salad, Carrot, '82 137
Salad, Carrot-Ambrosia, '81 252
Salad, Carrot-and-Dill, '02 129; '03 99
Salad, Carrot-and-Zucchini, '83 240
Salad, Carrot-Broccoli, '99 26
Salad, Carrot-Caraway, '89 105
Salad, Carrot-Pineapple, '91 83
Salad, Carrot-Raisin, '83 117; '84 174; '87 10
Salad, Carrot-Tangerine, '83 316; '84 16
Salad, Creamy Carrot-Nut, '86 331

Salad, Favorite Carrot, '80 33
Salad, Fruity Carrot-and-Seed, '86 223
Salad, Harvest Carrot, '89 128
Salad, Honey-Sweet Carrot, '89 161
Salad, Lime-Carrot, '92 65
Salad, Orange-Carrot, '80 89; '84 325
Salad, Shredded Carrot, '80 178
Salad, Simple Carrot, '82 101; '84 152
Salad, Sunny Day, '96 90
Salad, Sunshine Carrot, '82 132
Salad, Sweet-and-Sour Carrot, '98 211
Salad, Turkey-Carrot, '86 283
Salad, Turnip-and-Carrot, '91 212
Salad with Orange-Nutmeg Dressing, Carrot-Raisin,
    '97 305; '98 19
Salsa, Zucchini-Carrot, '05 298
Saucy Carrots, '87 41
Sauté, Carrot-Turnip, '93 241
Sautéed Squash and Carrots, '05 42
Sautéed Zucchini and Carrots, '92 62, 99
Savory Sauce, Lima Beans and Carrots with, '84 196
Scalloped Carrots, '81 6; '96 107; '02 129; '03 99
Scalloped Carrots-and-Celery, '84 M112
Scalloped Carrots, Cheese, '94 36
Slaw, Apple-Carrot, '92 243
Slaw, Shredded Celery Root-and-Carrot, '98 293
Soufflé, Carrot, '79 73; '98 231; '99 25; '01 84, 284;
    '05 66
Soufflé, Carrots, '83 265
Soufflés, Carrot, '96 309
Soup, Carrot, '80 88; '89 146; '98 123
Soup, Carrot-and-Leek, '02 260
Soup, Carrot Cream, '90 210
Soup, Carrot-Leek, '86 34
Soup, Carrot-Orange, '79 172
Soup, Cheesy Carrot, '81 262
Soup, Chilled Carrot-Mint, '90 M168
Soup, Cream of Carrot, '81 307; '88 46; '91 69
Soup, Cream of Carrot-and-Tomato, '94 176
Soup, Creamy Carrot, '92 218
Soup, Curried Carrot, '82 157
Soup, Gingered Carrot-and-Parsnip, '03 221
Soup, Potato-Carrot, '88 297
Soup, Savory Carrot, '84 107
Soup with Parslied Croutons, Carrot-and-Butternut
    Squash, '97 217
Special Carrots, '81 108; '84 6
Spiced Carrots Polynesian, '88 85
Spread, Carrot-Pecan, '96 108
Spread, Feta-and-Apple, '99 106
Spread, Nutty Carrot, '94 123
Squash, Stuffed, '98 177
Steamed Carrots, Lemon-Dill, '93 180
Sticks, Carrot, '89 106
Stir-Fry, Beef-and-Carrot, '98 335
Stir-Fry, Turnip-and-Carrot, '96 36
Stuffed Carrots, '86 324; '87 40
Sugar Snaps and Carrots, Creamed, '93 139
Sunshine Carrots, '82 16; '83 25
Supreme, Broccoli-Carrot, '89 331
Swamp Sticks, '95 274
Sweet-and-Sour Carrots, '82 137
Sweet-and-Sour Green Beans and Carrots, '83 6
Sweet 'n' Hot Green Beans and Carrots,
    '00 211
Tarragon Carrots, '83 173
Tipsy Carrots, '87 40
Toss, Asparagus-Carrot-Squash, '91 45
Toss, Carrot-Fruit, '82 235
Tropical Carrots, '84 34
Veal and Carrots, Company, '85 22
Veal and Carrots in Wine Sauce, '81 31; '86 M139
White Wine, Carrots in, '81 109
Wine Sauce, Carrots in, '80 88

Zesty Carrots, '84 5
Zucchini and Carrots, Buttered, '83 252
Zucchini, Carrots and, '84 262
CASSEROLES. *See also* **LASAGNA.**
Apple-Cheese Casserole, '84 287
Barley, Baked, '91 133
Barley Casserole, '84 281
Bean
  Baked Bean Medley, '80 100
  Baked Beans, Hawaiian-Style, '86 210
  Baked Beans, Maple Heights, '91 223
  Baked Beans Quintet, '94 100
  Baked Beans, Three-Meat, '86 210
  Baked Beans with Ham, '80 136
  Beef-and-Bean Bake, Cheesy, '82 89
  Beef, Bean, and Cornbread Casserole, '99 215
  Black Beans, Casserole of, '95 27
  Chuck Wagon Bean Casserole, '93 198
  Cornbread Casserole, Bean-and-, '92 243
  Five-Bean Bake, '03 139
  Green Bean and Artichoke Casserole, Italian, '85 81
  Green Bean-and-Corn Casserole, '88 123; '99 36
  Green Bean Casserole, '79 106; '84 145; '02 197
  Green Bean Casserole, Creamy-and-Crunchy,
    '05 245
  Green Bean Casserole, Easy, '87 284
  Green Bean Italiano, '94 248
  Green Bean Salad, Hot, '86 298
  Green Beans au Gratin, '80 116
  Green Beans, Baked, '91 159
  Green Beans, French Quarter, '80 298; '81 26
  Green Beans, Herbed, '83 M147
  Green Beans in Sour Cream, '80 116
  Green Beans, Italian, '85 147
  Green Beans Italian, '87 10
  Green Bean Surprise, '86 9
  Green Beans with Sour Cream, '82 90
  Kidney Bean Casserole, '90 136
  Lentils with Cheese, Baked, '84 113
  Lima-Bacon Bake, '86 9
  Lima Bean Casserole, '79 189; '83 313; '86 225;
    '87 284; '95 132
  Lima Bean Casserole, Spicy, '79 189
  Lima Bean Casserole, Swiss, '80 191
  Lima Bean Garden Casserole, '83 218; '84 246
  Lima Beans Deluxe, '79 289; '80 26
  Lima Beans, Savory, '83 219; '84 246
  Lima Beans, Super, '79 189
  Lima Beans with Canadian Bacon, '83 219; '84 245
  Lima Casserole, Ham and, '79 192
  Limas, Spanish Cheese, '86 225
  Mexican Bean Casserole, Spicy, '84 114
  Three-Bean Bake, '81 155; '03 106
  Three-Bean Casserole, '88 56
  White Bean Bake, Turnip Greens and, '94 246
Breakfast and Brunch
  Apple-Egg Casserole, '85 44
  Bacon and Egg Casserole, '81 225
  Bacon-and-Egg Casserole, '03 166
  Bacon-and-Eggs Scramble, '80 M267
  Bacon-and-Ham Casserole, Cheesy, '01 256
  Breakfast Casserole, '91 285; '99 273; '01 130, 243
  Breakfast, Mexican, '00 194
  Brie-and-Sausage Breakfast Casserole, '00 284;
    '03 36
  Broccoli-Cheese Breakfast Casserole, '99 233
  Brunch Casserole, '82 124
  Bunch, Brunch for a, '88 57
  Campfire Casserole, '00 173
  Cheese-and-Egg Casserole, '99 268
  Cheese Blintz Casserole, '92 251
  Cheesy Breakfast Casserole, '85 247
  Cheesy Brunch Casserole, Easy, '92 91
  Chile-Hominy Casserole, '81 29

Chile 'n' Cheese Breakfast Casserole, '88 57
Christmas Morning Strata, '95 282
Corned Beef Brunch Bake, '82 44
Cornmeal Puff, '82 42
Cranberry-Apple Casserole, '83 311
Creole Sauce, Brunch Casserole with, '98 98
Egg-and-Bacon Casserole, '85 248
Egg-and-Cheese Casserole, '84 293
Egg-and-Cheese Puff, '85 45
Egg Casserole, '83 311; '98 98
Egg Casserole, Brunch, '86 329
Egg Casserole, Cheesy, '81 244; '86 15
Egg Casserole, Saucy Scrambled, '89 213
Egg Casserole, Scrambled, '80 51; '86 241
Egg Casserole, Sunday, '95 100
Egg-Mushroom Casserole, '83 49
Eggs Bel-Mar, '90 92
Eggs, Brunch, '98 93
Eggs, Bruncheon, '83 83
Eggs, Chile, '88 80
Eggs, Creole, '82 42
Eggs, Layered, '96 97
Egg Soufflé Casserole, '83 55
Enchiladas, Breakfast, '04 281; '05 333
English Muffin Breakfast Strata, '03 100
Fruit Bake, Hot, '81 270
Grits, Baked Cheese-and-Garlic, '83 292
Grits, Baked Garlic-and-Herb, '01 326
Grits Bake, Santa Fe, '00 123
Grits Casserole, Cheddar Cheese, '05 283
Grits Casserole, Cheesy, '81 270
Grits Casserole, Garlic, '81 47
Grits, Chili-Cheese, '01 86
Grits, Garlic, '00 194
Grits, Garlic-Cheese, '86 180; '99 270; '00 215
Grits, Jalapeño-Cheese, '00 239; '01 328
Grits, Mexican Cheese, '02 34
Grits, Orange, '81 47
Grits-Sausage Casserole, '84 75; '86 241
Grits, Swiss-and-Cheddar Baked, '91 71
Ham and Egg Casserole, Breakfast, '79 253
Hash Brown Breakfast Casserole, '03 306
Hash Brown Cheese Bake, '82 50
Hash Brown-Ham-Cheese Bake, '97 323
Hash Brown Potato Casserole, '81 40
Hearty Healthy Breakfast Casserole, '05 325
Hominy, Gold Coast, '83 52
Huevos Rancheros, '82 197
Italian Brunch Casserole, '03 29
Mexican Breakfast, '00 194
Omelet Casserole, Confetti, '05 169
Potato Breakfast Casserole, '80 52
Sausage-and-Egg Casserole, '94 284
Sausage Breakfast Casserole, '81 270
Sausage Brunch, Italian, '88 57
Sausage Casserole, Hawaiian, '85 42
Sausage Casserole, Swiss, '80 209
Sausage-Cheese Bake, '88 58
Sausage, Country Grits and, '83 54
Sausage Egg Bake, '81 225
Sausage-Egg Bake, Smoked, '85 248
Sausage-Egg Casserole, '86 M12
Sausage-Ham Breakfast Casserole, '01 54; '04 332
Sausage-Hash Brown Breakfast Casserole, '03 218
Sausage-Mushroom Breakfast Casserole, '86 95
Sausage-Spud Bake, Sunday Night Spicy Cheesy,
  '03 331
Sausage Strata, '83 243
Southwest Breakfast Strata, '05 136
Southwestern Brunch Casserole, '03 197
Broccoli-Ham au Gratin, '90 239
Brown Rice Casserole, '87 118
Cajun Casserole, Ragin', '02 199
Cannelloni, '92 17

Cheese Bake, Continental, '81 89
Cheese Casserole, Feather-Light, '79 84
Cheese Casserole, Four, '92 170
Chile-Cheese Casserole, '82 90
Chiles Rellenos Casserole, '79 84; '92 18
Chili Casserole, '90 176
Chili-Rice Casserole, '79 54
Chili-Tamale Pie, '83 68
Cornbread-Chili Strata, '03 100
Egg and Rice Bake, '83 119
Eggplant-and-Oyster Louisiane, '95 196
Eggplant-Sausage-Pasta Casserole, Freezer, '95 197
Enchilada Casserole, '87 287
Enchilada Casserole, Easy, '02 143
Enchilada Casserole, Green, '79 76
Enchiladas, Black Bean-Chicken-Spinach, '05 95
Enchiladas, Black Bean 'n' Spinach, '05 95
Enchiladas, Smothered, '05 59
Franks, Mexican, '93 78
Fruit Casserole, Sherried, '80 284
Fruit, Gingered Baked, '81 232
Grits, Garlicky Ham-and-Spinach, '94 177
Grits Italiano, '92 43
Grits with Green Chiles, Cheese, '95 208
Hominy-and-Corn Casserole, '97 291
Hominy Casserole, Cheesy, '83 170
Hominy Casserole), Four-Part Hominy (Cheesy, '96 158
Hominy-Chili Casserole, '86 255
Hominy, Hot Cheese, '84 77
Hominy, Jalapeño, '82 51
Hominy with Chiles and Cheese, '86 78
Italian Casserole, '90 238
Kale, Scalloped, '86 224
Lentils-and-Rice Casserole, '93 301
Mac and Texas Cheeses with Roasted Chiles, '04 207
Macaroni and Blue Cheese, '93 248
Macaroni and Cheese, '00 273
Macaroni-and-Cheese Bake, '01 41
Macaroni and Cheese, Baked, '00 271; '02 26; '03 184
Macaroni and Cheese, Caramelized Onion, '04 231
Macaroni and Cheese, Creamy, '93 249; '02 26
Macaroni and Cheese, Divine, '99 314
Macaroni and Cheese, Eleanor's, '97 253
Macaroni and Cheese, Golden, '04 24
Macaroni and Cheese, Italian, '04 327
Macaroni and Cheese, Old-Fashioned, '92 215
Macaroni and Cheese, Quick-and-Easy, '00 15
Macaroni and Cheese, Souper, '00 92
Macaroni and Cheese, Spicy Tomato, '03 68
Macaroni and Cheese, Tex-Mex, '00 92
Macaroni and Cheese, Thick-and-Rich, '84 329
Macaroni Bake, Jack-in-the-, '93 249
Macaroni Casserole, '84 220; '87 154
Macaroni, Extra Cheesy, '00 92
Macaroni, Glorious, '84 76
Macaroni, Gorgonzola, '97 28
Macaroni, Mexican, '96 73
Macaroni Mousse, '96 73
Macaroni-Mushroom Bake, '97 96
Macaroni-Mushroom Bake, Cheesy, '81 243
Macaroni, Three-Cheese, '00 M92
Macaroni with Blue Cheese and Walnuts, '02 M208
Manicotti, Make-Ahead, '98 68
Meat. *See also* **CASSEROLES/Breakfast and**
    Brunch, Pork.
  Beef-and-Bean Bake, Cheesy, '82 89
  Beef-and-Biscuit Casserole, '83 75
  Beef-and-Noodles Casserole, '84 72
  Beef-and-Vegetable Chow Mein Casserole, '83 313
  Beef Bake, Zesty Cabbage, '80 300
  Beef Bake, Zucchini, '86 146
  Beef, Bean, and Cornbread Casserole, '99 215
  Beef Casserole, '01 199
  Beef Casserole, Crusty, '82 88

CASSEROLES, Meat
(continued)

Beef Casserole, Easy, '00 208
Beef Casserole, Macaroni-Cheese-, '95 125
Beef Casserole, Spinach and, '79 192
Beef, Cheese, and Noodle Casserole, '99 58
Beef Lombardi, '03 214
Beef-Macaroni Bake, '94 255
Beef-Macaroni Combo, '79 194
Beef-Noodle Bake, Taco, '81 141
Beef Supreme, '83 196
Beefy Sausage Dinner, '80 M9
Beefy Vegetable Casserole, '79 248
Cavatini, '94 214
Cheeseburger Casserole, '95 255
Cheesy Mexican Casserole, '82 224
Chiles Rellenos Casserole, '79 84; '84 31, 234;
'92 18; '98 48
Chili and Enchiladas, '00 55
Chili Casserole, Ultimate, '99 239
Chili Hominy Bake, '81 282; '82 58
Chili Manicotti, '99 239
Cornbread Casserole, '81 91
Cornbread Skillet Casserole, '83 243; '84 101
Cornbread Tamale Bake, '79 163
Corned Beef and Cabbage au Gratin, '83 16
County Fair Casserole, '79 130
El Dorado Casserole, '81 140
Enchilada Casserole, Firecracker, '80 260
Enchilada Casserole, Lightened Texas-Style, '05 247
Enchilada Casserole, Sour Cream, '82 113
Enchilada Casserole, Texas-Style, '05 247
Fajita Casserole, '97 96
Five-Layer Meal, '81 140
Frankaroni Potluck Dish, '88 201
Franks 'n' Beans, Stove-Top, '88 201
Ground Beef and Sausage Casserole, '80 260
Ground Beef-and-Tomato Manicotti, '03 257
Ground Beef Casserole, Cheesy, '79 44
Ground Beef Casserole, Creamy, '81 142
Hamburger-Bean Bake, '95 121
Hamburger Casserole, '95 210
Hamburger-Corn Bake, '99 58
Hamburger-Noodle Bake, '81 140
Hamburger Pie, '81 92
Hot Doggie Casserole, '88 200
Italian Casserole, '80 81
Italian Casserole, Light, '03 198
Italian-Style Meat and Potatoes, '03 97
Layered Grecian Bake, '82 119
Linguine with Meat Sauce, Baked, '01 41
Linguine with Meat Sauce Casserole, '03 22
Manicotti, Meaty Cheese, '05 34
Manicotti, Meaty Stuffed, '00 19
Matador Mania, '86 19
Mexican Casserole, '00 280
Mexican Casserole, Cabin, '97 95
Moussaka, '87 166; '90 68; '97 94
Moussaka Casserole, '79 179
Moussaka, Corn, '87 190
Pasta Florentine, Layered, '00 56
Pastichio, '85 194
Pastitsio, '87 12; '88 11; '99 167
Pizza Bake, Upside-Down, '98 224
Pizza Casserole, '88 273; '89 181
Pizza Casserole, Beefy, '05 217
Pizza Casserole, Quick, '83 266
Rotini, Baked, '01 185
Shells, Spinach-Stuffed, '99 64
Sloppy Joe Squares, '97 95
Sour Cream-Noodle Bake, '79 55
Spaghetti and Beef Casserole, '79 129

Spaghetti Casserole, '84 241
Spaghetti, Casserole, '95 132
Spinach and Beef Casserole, '79 192
Spinach-Beef-Macaroni Casserole, '83 313
Stroganoff Casserole, '98 48
Swiss Steak, Pizza, '02 36
Taco Bake, '97 326
Taco Beef-Noodle Bake, '81 141
Taco Casserole, '80 33
Taco Squares, Deep-Dish, '91 88
Tamale, Mozzarella, '95 70
Tortilla Bake, Texas, '94 285
Veal and Wild Rice Casserole, '79 180
Veal Cutlet Casserole, '79 109
Venison-Vegetable Bake, '87 304
Ziti, Baked, '94 65
Microwave
Asparagus-Pea Casserole, '88 M294
Beans-and-Franks, Polynesian, '84 M11
Beef Casserole, Easy, '86 M58
Beef Casserole, Layered, '82 M203
Beefy Sausage Dinner, '80 M9
Broccoli Casserole, '88 M146; '05 M276
Broccoli-Swiss Cheese Casserole, '85 M211
Carrots-and-Celery, Scalloped, '84 M112
Chicken Divan, '80 M10
Chicken Divan Casserole, '82 M203
Chicken Mexicana, '91 M127
Chicken Tetrazzini, Cheesy, '83 M87
Green Beans, Herbed, '83 M147
Ham-and-Potato Casserole, '83 M87
Ham-Asparagus Dinner, '80 M10
Ham Roll Casserole, '91 M127
Macaroni-Ham Casserole, '81 M177
Macaroni with Blue Cheese and Walnuts, '02 M208
Mexican Casserole, '92 M22
Mexican Casserole, Microwave, '90 M231
Mexi Casserole, '83 M87
Okra and Tomatoes, Fresh, '81 M165
Onion-Potato Bake, '83 M195
Pineapple, Scalloped, '84 M323
Pizza Casserole, Microwave, '89 M248
Pork Casserole, Cheesy, '81 M74
Potato Casserole, Creamy, '84 M113
Potatoes, Parmesan, '90 M62
Sausage and Rice Casserole, Oriental, '82 M123
Sausage Casserole, Easy, '87 M189
Sausage-Egg Casserole, '86 M12
Sausage Jambalaya Casserole, '82 M203
Spinach Delight, '84 M144
Squash Bake, Cheddar-, '84 M113
Squash Casserole, Cheesy, '82 M21
Squash Casserole, Jiffy, '81 M144
Squash Medley, Fresh, '81 M165
Tuna Casserole, Easy, '82 M203
Turkey Casserole, Crunchy, '89 M282
Zucchini-Egg Casserole, '84 M113
Zucchini, Italian, '83 M147
Mostaccioli Casserole, '04 316
Noodle Casserole, Sweet, '02 238
Orzo, Mozzarella-and-Olive, '97 249
Paella Casserole, '95 254
Pasta Bake, Cheesy, '02 161
Pasta Bake, Layered, '04 326
Pasta Bake, Three-Cheese, '05 54
Pasta Casseroles, Hot Brown, '96 290
Pasta Italiano, '01 41
Pasta Shells Florentine, '00 326
Pineapple Bake, '79 251; '96 84
Pineapple, Baked, '84 287; '05 160
Pineapple, Scalloped, '79 106
Pork
Bacon-and-Ham Casserole, Cheesy, '01 256
Casserole, Pork, '83 116

Chop Casserole, Peppered Pork, '81 235; '82 25;
'83 39
Chop Casserole, Pork, '94 255
Chops and Potato Scallop, Pork, '82 114
Chops Italiano, Pork, '80 72
Chop-Vegetable Casserole, Pork, '90 208
Fiesta Pork Bake, '79 265
Frankfurter Casserole, Layered, '79 64
Franks, Family-Style, '79 54
Ham and Broccoli Casserole, '81 133
Ham and Broccoli Strata, '80 261
Ham-and-Cheese Casserole, '87 78
Ham-and-Cheese Layered Casserole, '98 160
Ham and Lima Casserole, '79 192
Ham and Noodle Casserole, '80 300
Ham-and-Potato Casserole, '96 103
Ham-and-Potato Casserole, Cheesy, '84 326
Ham-and-Rice Casserole, '84 75
Ham-and-Swiss Casserole, Savory, '01 308
Ham and Turkey Bake, Layered, '79 252
Ham Bake, Harvest, '79 210
Ham-Broccoli Casserole, Quick, '82 40
Ham Casserole, '96 302; '98 314
Ham Casserole, Apple, '79 213
Ham Casserole, Creamy, '03 83
Ham Casserole, Golden, '82 119
Ham Casserole, Macaroni-, '83 283
Ham Casseroles, Creamy, '01 55
Ham Casserole, Vegetable-and-, '84 91
Ham Medley, Creamy, '84 90
Ham Pie, Golden, '87 78
Ham-Rice-Tomato Bake, '87 78
Ham Strata, '95 308
Ham Strata, Baked, '83 283
Ham Tetrazzini, '84 241; '03 174
Pizza Casserole, Upside-Down, '03 284
Salami-Corn Casserole, '80 209
Sausage and Broccoli Casserole, '80 33
Sausage and Noodle Casserole, '82 123
Sausage-and-Noodle Casserole, '95 255
Sausage-and-Rice Bake, Creole, '88 58
Sausage and Rice Casserole, Oriental, '82 M123
Sausage-and-Tomato Manicotti, Cheesy, '03 257
Sausage and Wild Rice Casserole, '83 196
Sausage Bake, Eggplant, '85 221
Sausage Bake, Hominy-, '88 51
Sausage-Bean Supper, '86 52
Sausage Casserole, '81 112; '82 12
Sausage Casserole, Cheesy, '82 124
Sausage Casserole, Country, '79 192
Sausage Casserole, Crunchy, '81 288
Sausage Casserole, Easy, '87 M189
Sausage Casserole, Eggplant-, '84 215
Sausage Casserole, Ground Beef and, '80 260
Sausage Casserole, Skillet, '99 123
Sausage-Chile Rellenos Casserole, '88 52
Sausage-Egg Casserole, '86 M12
Sausage Grits, '86 92
Sausage Jambalaya Casserole, '82 M203
Sausage-Lasagna Rollups, '80 236
Sausage-Noodle Bake, '81 92
Sausage-Potato Casserole, '86 217
Sausage-Rice Casserole, '82 50; '83 75
Sausages, Baked Zucchini and, '80 300
Sausage-Stuffed Shells, '96 102
Sausage, Wild Rice and, '86 268
Sausage-Wild Rice Casserole, '84 250
Sausage Wild Rice Casserole, Turkey-and-,
'03 239
Spaghetti Bake, Pork, '81 11
Spaghetti Casserole, Low-Fat, '99 215
Strata, Christmas Morning, '95 282
Supper Supreme, Sunday, '79 76
Vegetable-Pork Combo, '85 113

Poultry

Chicken à la Russell, '95 175
Chicken-Almond Casserole, '94 199
Chicken-and-Artichoke Casserole, '96 133
Chicken and Artichokes, '03 26
Chicken-and-Cheese Enchiladas, Baked,
   '03 332
Chicken-and-Chiles Casserole, '93 107
Chicken-and-Dressing Casserole, '81 263
Chicken and Dressing, Santa Fe, '03 48
Chicken and Green Noodle Casserole, '80 32
Chicken and Grits, '95 263
Chicken-and-Pasta Casserole, '97 192
Chicken and Rice, '95 54
Chicken and Rice Casserole, '80 260
Chicken-and-Rice Casserole, Creamy, '02 309
Chicken-and-Rice Casserole, Crispy, '03 203
Chicken-and-Rice Casseroles, '01 52
Chicken-and-Shrimp Florentine, '89 64
Chicken-and-Spinach Enchiladas, '91 222
Chicken and Wild Rice, '79 248
Chicken-and-Wild Rice Casserole, '97 192; '00 257
Chicken-and-Wild Rice Casserole, Leslie's Favorite,
   '00 209; '03 107
Chicken-Asparagus Casserole, '83 76; '84 71
Chicken Bake, Company, '80 301
Chicken Bake, Spicy, '85 251
Chicken Bake with Sweet Bacon Dressing, Veg-
   etable-, '93 108
Chicken, Broccoli, and Cauliflower Casserole,
   '00 337
Chicken-Broccoli Casserole, '79 48; '91 315
Chicken-Brown Rice Bake, '91 314
Chicken Cannelloni with Roasted Red Bell Pepper
   Sauce, '02 287
Chicken Casserole, '96 103, 302
Chicken Casserole, Broccoli-, '82 33
Chicken Casserole, Cheesy, '85 34
Chicken Casserole, Chow Mein, '96 276
Chicken Casserole D'Iberville, '04 182
Chicken Casserole, Hearty Tex-Mex Squash-,
   '99 312; '03 107
Chicken Casserole, Jalapeño, '02 50
Chicken Casserole, King Ranch, '00 280
Chicken Casserole, Light King Ranch, '04 57
Chicken Casserole, Macaroni and, '80 260
Chicken Casserole, Make-Ahead, '84 241
Chicken Casserole, Mexi-, '93 69; '94 30
Chicken Casserole, Mexican, '82 143
Chicken Casserole, Oyster-and-, '99 320
Chicken Casserole, Pesto-, '94 231
Chicken Casserole, Quick, '81 91
Chicken Casserole, Rice-and-, '87 154
Chicken Casserole, Simply Good, '95 255
Chicken Casserole, Sunday, '83 290
Chicken Casserole, Swiss, '90 67
Chicken Casserole, Unforgettable, '04 294
Chicken Cassoulet, Easy, '00 43; '04 325
Chicken, Cheesy Mexican, '01 199
Chicken Chili Bake, '93 302
Chicken Chimichangas, '93 68
Chicken Curry Casserole, Cheesy, '05 311
Chicken Dinner, Hot-and-Spicy, '94 M94
Chicken Divan, '80 M10
Chicken Divan Casserole, '82 M203
Chicken Divan, Curried, '80 83
Chicken Divan, Easy, '94 310
Chicken Divan, Gourmet, '82 83
Chicken Divan, Overnight, '83 198
Chicken Divan, Sherried, '80 38
Chicken-Eggplant Parmigiana, '82 212
Chicken Enchiladas, '80 301; '00 45; '03 214
Chicken Enchiladas, Creamy, '97 250; '01 M94
Chicken Enchiladas, Easy, '82 89

Chicken Enchiladas, Three-Cheese, '99 330
Chicken Florentine, '93 107
Chicken, Fontina-Baked, '90 64
Chicken, French Herbed, '86 89
Chicken, Garlic-Spinach, '92 56
Chicken-Green Bean Casserole, '85 296
Chicken-Green Bean Casserole, Creamy, '97 158
Chicken, King Ranch, '95 193; '99 330; '03 313
Chicken Lasagna Bake, '95 55
Chicken, Lemony Pecan, '96 82
Chicken Linguine, '01 128
Chicken-Macaroni Casserole, '85 219
Chicken Mexicana, '91 M127
Chicken-Noodle Casserole, '94 286
Chicken Noodle Casserole, '01 308
Chicken, Orzo, and Spinach Casserole, '02 124
Chicken Parmesan, '04 42
Chicken Parmigiana, '80 190
Chicken Parmigiana, Zesty, '00 19
Chicken, Poppy Seed, '99 195
Chicken Reuben Casserole, '03 69
Chicken-Rice Casserole, '86 52; '99 215
Chicken-Rice Casserole, Creamy, '99 21
Chicken Salad, Baked, '86 297
Chicken Sausage and Shiitake Mushrooms, Cheese
   Grits with, '03 254
Chicken, Scarborough, '80 38
Chicken Skillet Casserole, Spaghetti Squash and,
   '94 134
Chicken-Sour Cream Enchiladas, '04 274
Chicken-Spaghetti Casserole, '84 15
Chicken Spaghetti, Spicy, '02 327
Chicken, Spicy Mexican, '82 89
Chicken-Squash Casserole, '95 121
Chicken, Stuffed Alfredo, '04 56
Chicken Superb Casserole, '89 83
Chicken Supreme Casserole, '84 219
Chicken Supreme, Hot, '81 76
Chicken, Swiss, '95 54
Chicken Tetrazzini, '79 268; '80 M75; '99 61;
   '00 45; '02 171; '04 221
Chicken Tetrazzini, Cheesy, '83 M87
Chicken Thighs, Swiss, '94 282
Chicken Tortilla Bake, '82 89
Chicken Tortilla Casserole, '81 166
Chicken-Wild Rice Casserole, '84 241; '85 65
Chicken-Wild Rice Supreme, '79 77
Chicken with Spinach Fettuccine, Creamy Basil,
   '97 328
Cornish Hens-and-Rice Casserole, '92 267
Crêpes Divan, Elegant, '81 91
Day-After-the-Holiday Casserole, '96 276
Duck and Wild Rice Casserole, '79 224
King Ranch Casserole, '02 210
Leftovers Casserole, Holiday, '04 232
Pollo, Chilaquiles con (Tortillas with Chicken),
   '81 66
Rice Casserole, Mexican, '83 31
Shells, Southwestern Stuffed, '99 238
Southwestern Casserole, '99 216
Turkey-and-Broccoli Casserole, '86 332
Turkey-and-Sausage Wild Rice Casserole, '03 239
Turkey-and-Shrimp Florentine Casserole, '92 122
Turkey-Asparagus Casserole, '86 284
Turkey Bake, Layered Ham and, '79 252
Turkey Casserole, '84 327; '96 302
Turkey Casserole, Crunchy, '89 M282
Turkey Casserole, Golden, '80 271
Turkey Casserole, Stuffed, '88 246
Turkey-Cheddar-Broccoli Strata, '03 100
Turkey Dinner Bake, Next-Day, '05 246
Turkey Florentine, '88 264
Turkey Noodle Bake, '93 243
Turkey-Noodle-Poppyseed Casserole, '90 239

Turkey-Olive Casserole, '87 268
Turkey Parmigiana, '87 193
Turkey Salad Bake, '79 253
Turkey Salad, Hot, '86 297
Turkey-Spinach Casserole, '84 71
Turkey-Swiss Casserole, '86 283
Turkey Tetrazzini, '00 318
Turkey Tetrazzini, Herbed, '86 47
Turkey Tetrazzini, Smoked, '02 286; '05 96
Turkey Tetrazzini with Artichokes and Red Bell
   Peppers, Smoked, '05 97
Wraps, Southwestern, '99 238
Provolone Casserole, Seashell-, '80 189
Quiche Casserole, '95 33
Ravioli, Mediterranean, '93 301
Reuben Casserole, '90 240
Rice-and-Cheese con Chiles, '89 99
Rice and Green Chiles, '83 152
Rice au Gratin Supreme, '86 78
Rice, Baked, '94 270
Rice, Baked Spicy, '96 125
Rice Bake, Green, '79 43
Rice Casserole, '87 45
Rice Casserole, Chili-, '79 54
Rice Casserole, Colorful, '82 199
Rice Casserole, Green, '95 181
Rice Casserole, Jalapeño, '81 66
Rice Casserole, Spanish, '79 192
Rice Chantilly, '86 82
Rice, Easy Mushroom, '89 286
Rice, Fiesta, '84 76
Rice, Hot Pepper, '92 310
Rice Mélange, '87 240
Rice, Mexican, '85 147
Rice Pilaf, '86 82
Rice, Savannah Red, '95 27
Rice, Spanish, '81 51; '90 183
Rice, Spicy, '85 256
Rotini Romano, '87 193

Seafood

Crab-and-Mushroom Casserole, '89 96
Crab-and-Shrimp Casserole, '84 71
Crab and Spinach Casserole, Creamy, '80 3
Crab Bake, Quick, '87 192
Crab Casserole, '79 228
Crab Casserole, Deviled, '91 238; '92 27
Crab Casserole, Easy, '93 270
Crab, Dressed, '82 276
Crab-Egg Casserole, '80 260
Crab Imperial, '79 82, 116
Crab Imperial, Elegant, '83 245
Crabmeat-Broccoli Casserole, '84 232
Crabmeat Imperial, '82 311
Crabmeat with Artichoke Hearts, Creamed, '93 26
Crab Puff, '79 116
Crab, Shrimp, and Artichoke au Gratin, '90 240
Crawfish Lasagna, '91 89
Crawfish Pasta Casserole, '97 106
Fish and Potato Bake, Herbed, '79 287; '80 34
Fish Casserole, Green Chile-and-, '84 32
Miss Hannah's Casserole, '92 236
Oyster-and-Chicken Casserole, '99 320
Oyster-and-Corn Bake, '83 34; '84 44
Oyster-and-Spinach Casserole, '83 34; '84 44
Oyster-and-Wild Rice Casserole, '83 34; '84 44
Oyster Casserole, '79 228
Oyster Casserole, Wild Rice-, '86 256
Oysters Johnny Reb, '82 42
Oysters, Scalloped, '79 225; '84 213; '86 132;
   '95 318; '99 321; '05 47
Parmesan, Savannah Seafood, '99 312
Salmon Casserole, '81 22
Salmon Florentine, '83 43
Scallop Casserole, '79 228

CASSEROLES, Seafood
(continued)

Seafood Casserole, '87 109; '89 63
Shrimp-and-Chicken Casserole, '91 102
Shrimp-and-Grits Casserole, Cheesy, '03 28
Shrimp-and-Noodle Casserole, '90 240
Shrimp and Rice Casserole, '79 228
Shrimp-and-Rice Casserole, '94 328
Shrimp-and-Scallops Casserole, Creamy, '01 256
Shrimp au Gratin, '85 79
Shrimp Casserole, '85 240
Shrimp Casserole, Cajun, '05 237
Shrimp Casserole, Chayotes and, '80 230
Shrimp Casserole, Spicy, '96 62
Shrimp-Crab Puff, '79 57
Shrimp Delight, '79 192
Shrimp Enchiladas, '01 104
Shrimp Fettuccine, '96 210
Shrimp Florentine Casserole, Turkey-and-, '92 122
Shrimp Manicotti, '97 96
Tuna and Peas in Wine Sauce, Baked, '83 196
Tuna-Broccoli Casserole, Tangy, '83 75
Tuna Casserole, '82 119; '96 103
Tuna Casserole, Biscuit-Topped, '79 113
Tuna Casserole, Easy, '83 255
Tuna Casserole, Nippy, '84 241
Tuna Casserole with Cheese Swirls, '88 256
Tuna Chopsticks, '94 255
Tuna-Macaroni Treat, '82 131
Tuna-Noodle Casserole, Fabulous, '02 63
Tuna Vegetable Casserole, '81 135
Shells and Cheese, Creamy, '01 216
Shells, Southwestern Stuffed, '93 234
Spaghetti-and-Spinach Casserole, '02 199
Spaghetti, Casserole, '95 132
Tamale Casserole, Quick, '94 255
Vegetable. *See also* **CASSEROLES/Bean.**
Artichoke Casserole, Alii, '93 294
Asparagus-and-English Pea Casserole, '86 324
Asparagus and Peas Casserole, '80 152
Asparagus-Artichoke Casserole, '86 279
Asparagus Casserole, '98 310
Asparagus Casserole, Cheesy, '82 281; '83 32
Asparagus Casserole, Creamy, '80 76
Asparagus Casserole, Easy, '83 255
Asparagus Delight, '82 269
Asparagus, Holiday, '85 260
Asparagus-Pea Casserole, '88 M294
Asparagus-Pimiento Loaf, '84 86
Asparagus-Spaghetti Casserole, '80 77
Asparagus Supreme, '89 245
Beets, Fruited, '97 28
Black-Eyed Peas with Rice, '83 12
Broccoli-and-Cauliflower Gratin, '01 43
Broccoli-and-Egg Casserole, '86 324
Broccoli-and-Eggs au Gratin, '85 289
Broccoli-and-Squash Casserole, '01 175
Broccoli Bake, '81 246; '89 279
Broccoli Bake, Cheesy, '83 255
Broccoli Bake, Cheesy Italian, '83 5
Broccoli Bake, Company, '83 279
Broccoli-Blue Cheese Casserole, '85 260
Broccoli Casserole, '87 284; '88 M146, 265;
    '05 M276
Broccoli Casserole, Almond-, '88 62
Broccoli Casserole, Cheesy, '84 293; '92 342;
    '95 M191
Broccoli Casserole, Easy, '03 M49
Broccoli Casserole, Italian, '82 6, 280; '83 32
Broccoli Casserole, Winter, '94 280
Broccoli-Cheese Casserole, '82 269; '84 9; '94 132
Broccoli-Corn Casserole, '83 313

Broccoli Elegant, '81 267
Broccoli, English Walnut, '89 68
Broccoli Macaroni and Cheese, '02 36
Broccoli-Onion Deluxe, '81 75
Broccoli Puff, '82 95
Broccoli-Rice Casserole, '81 101
Broccoli Supreme, '82 34; '85 68; '02 312
Broccoli-Swiss Cheese Casserole, '83 322; '85 M211
Broccoli with Lemon Cream, '89 245
Broccoli with Pimiento Cheese Sauce, '02 291
Broccoli with Rice, Holiday, '87 252
Broccoli with Stuffing, '95 341
Brussels Sprouts-and-Artichoke Casserole, '94 279
Brussels Sprouts, Casserole of, '86 294
Butternut Casserole, '83 280
Butternut Casserole, Sweet, '83 256
Butternut Squash Bake, '05 234
Butternut Squash Casserole, '79 210; '96 216;
    '01 293
Butternut Squash Puff, '85 205
Cabbage au Gratin, '83 279
Cabbage, Caraway, '85 32, 289
Cabbage Casserole, '97 88
Cabbage Casserole, Cheesy, '79 4
Cabbage Casserole, Creamy, '80 63
Cabbage Casserole, Italian, '87 42
Cabbage Casserole, Savory, '82 168
Cabbage, Cheese Scalloped, '81 87; '82 7
Cabbage, Scalloped, '82 269; '01 43
Cabbage Wedges, Smothered, '81 87; '82 7
Cabbage with Apples and Franks, '87 42
Calabaza Mexicano (Mexican Squash), '81 196
Carrot and Zucchini Casserole, '83 256
Carrot-Apple Bake, '98 232
Carrot Bake, Creamy, '85 67
Carrot Casserole, '86 279; '87 285
Carrot Casserole, Scrumptious, '84 328
Carrot-Pecan Casserole, '93 44; '98 231; '02 282
Carrot Puff, '84 328
Carrots, Scalloped, '81 6; '96 107; '02 129; '03 99
Carrots, Zesty, '84 5
Cashew Casserole, '95 166
Cauliflower and Asparagus Supreme, '79 287; '80 35
Cauliflower-and-Carrot Casserole, '83 280
Cauliflower and Peas with Curried Almonds, '80 82
Cauliflower au Gratin, '99 59
Cauliflower Bake, '95 342
Cauliflower Bake, Curried, '01 49
Cauliflower Casserole, '86 10, 279
Cauliflower Casserole, Easy, '82 204
Cauliflower Casserole, Festive, '87 232
Cauliflower Casserole, Herbed, '79 221
Cauliflower, Cheddar, '99 318
Cauliflower, Curried, '91 315
Cauliflower Italiano, Cheesy, '82 300
Cauliflower, Main-Dish, '79 221; '80 83
Cauliflower Medley, '80 220
Cauliflower 'n' Chiles Casserole, '87 285
Cauliflower-Pea Casserole, '85 260
Cauliflower Scallop, '88 270
Cauliflower, Spanish-Style, '79 21
Cauliflower Surprise, Crunchy, '99 318
Celery and Cheese Casserole, '79 178
Celery au Gratin, '83 38
Celery, Baked, '82 98
Celery Casserole, '80 246; '96 92
Celery Casserole, Creamy, '82 98; '83 255
Celery, Creamed, '79 247
Celery, Exotic, '83 280
Celery Oriental, '83 206; '85 116
Celery, Saucy, '83 39
Chayote-Cheese Bake, '80 230
Cheesy Vegetable Casserole, '81 103
Chilaquiles, '82 220

Chipotle Manicotti, Creamy, '03 96
Collards Casserole, Parmesan-, '95 233
Corn-and-Bean Casserole, '90 208
Corn and Cheese Casserole, '81 128
Corn-and-Green Chile Casserole, '89 68
Corn and Tomato Casserole, '81 127
Corn-and-Tomato Casserole, '84 145
Corn Bake, Cheesy, '98 244
Corn, Baked Jack, '97 86
Corn, Baked Scalloped, '85 290
Corn Casserole, '79 247; '89 126; '93 141
Corn Casserole, Chili-, '88 266
Corn Casserole, Fresh, '80 165
Corn Casserole, Jalapeño-, '83 256
Corn, Creamy Baked, '90 60; '02 234
Corn, Elegant Scalloped, '86 268
Corn Pudding, '86 192
Corn-Rice Casserole, '01 46
Corn, Scalloped, '80 164; '81 128; '86 111; '88 218
Corn with Sour Cream, Baked, '86 170
Corn-Zucchini Bake, '79 178
Creamy Vegetable Casserole, '98 96
Curry Casserole, Vegetable-, '91 286; '92 27
Eggplant and Noodle Casserole, '82 230
Eggplant and Squash, '83 187
Eggplant-and-Tomato Casserole, '83 187
Eggplant and Zucchini, Italian-Style, '79 289; '80 26
Eggplant Bake, '80 82
Eggplant Cakes, '95 196
Eggplant Casserole, '81 205; '84 217; '93 44;
    '94 214
Eggplant Casserole, Easy, '80 202
Eggplant Casserole, Elegant, '82 168
Eggplant Casserole, Flavorful, '79 92
Eggplant Casserole, Spicy Hot, '93 92
Eggplant Casserole, Super, '80 202
Eggplant Chiles Rellenos, '91 86
Eggplant Creole, '86 110
Eggplant Crêpes with Marinara Sauce, Mini, '99 266
Eggplant, Heavenly, '93 293
Eggplant, Italian, '84 216
Eggplant Italiano, '91 212
Eggplant, Lebanese, '81 24
Eggplant, Mexican, '83 187
Eggplant Parmesan, '83 186; '84 215; '92 18; '95 84;
    '01 53
Eggplant Parmesan with Feta, '03 174
Eggplant Parmigiana, '81 19; '95 197; '01 310
Eggplant, Rolled Stuffed, '80 63
Eggplant, Scalloped, '91 223
Eggplant, Spinach-and-Basil Stuffed, '02 147
Eggplant-Spinach Casserole, '99 217
Eggplant Supreme, '79 188; '86 170
English Pea Casserole, Cheesy, '83 216
English Pea Casserole, Quick Fresh, '84 145
English Pea-Pimiento Casserole, '83 207
Fennel, Creamy Pan-Braised, '02 43
Fresh Vegetable Casserole, '82 225
Garden Casserole, '82 168; '88 122
Garden Medley, '98 236
Garden Surprise, '83 112
Green-and-Gold Scallop, '81 159
Greens Dinner Bake, Grits 'n, '84 281
Green Vegetable Medley, '79 287; '80 34
Hash Brown Casserole, Cheesy, '03 218
Hash Brown Casserole, Creamy, '03 193
Hash Brown Cheese Bake, '82 50
Hash Brown-Cheese Bake, '97 323
Hominy, Mexican, '91 133, 162
Hominy Olé, '01 17
Hubbard Squash, Tart, '80 214
Lasagna Casserole, Vegetable, '92 198; '93 25
Layered Vegetable Casserole, '91 286; '92 27
Lentils with Cheese, Baked, '84 113

Mac-and-Cheese, Veggie, '01 111
Macaroni Primavera, '96 73
Medley, Baked Vegetable, '81 75
Medley Bake, Vegetable, '81 268
Medley, Vegetable-Cheese, '99 M287
Mexican Vegetarian Casserole, '96 276
Mixed Vegetable Casserole, '83 208, 256; '86 327
Mixed-Vegetable Casserole, '87 154
Mixed Vegetables, Scalloped, '83 5
Mushroom-Artichoke Casserole, '87 241
Mushroom Bake, Windsor, '88 132
Mushroom Casserole, '95 211; '96 47
Mushroom-Cheese Casserole, '83 216
Mushroom Deluxe Casserole, '96 20
Mushroom-Macaroni Casserole, '95 180
Mushrooms Supreme, '80 214
New Potatoes, Cheesy, '85 156
New Potatoes, Cheesy Jalapeño, '01 89
New Potato Gratin, Creamy, '01 M320
Noodle Casserole, Vegetable, '91 30
Okra Casserole, '79 160
Okra-Tomato Bake, '80 298; '81 26
Onion Bake, Four, '93 304
Onion Casserole, Cheesy, '79 101
Onion Casserole, French, '95 26
Onion Casserole, Sweet, '00 103
Onions, Baked Sweet, '91 79
Pea Casserole, Curry, '87 154
Pea Casserole, Reunion, '87 11
Pea Casserole Supreme, '82 281; '83 32
Peas and Rice, '88 97
Peas, Cajun, '88 3
Peas, Chinese-Style Baked, '86 305
Peas, Mexi-, '88 3
Peas, Party, '79 102
Peas, Sweet-and-Sour, '88 3
Poblano-and-Cheese Casserole, Zesty, '05 311
Potato-and-Gruyère Casserole, '05 248
Potato-and-Rutabaga Gratin, '96 237
Potato Bake, '83 209
Potato Bake, Creamy, '82 201
Potato Bake, Smoky Mashed, '00 214; '01 21
Potato Bake, Swirled Mashed-, '02 98
Potato Bake, Thyme-, '96 121
Potato-Broccoli-Cheese Bake, '80 114
Potato-Butternut Squash-and-Gruyère Gratin, '01 43
Potato Casserole, '87 190; '99 274
Potato Casserole, Au Gratin, '05 250
Potato Casserole, Beefy, '03 218
Potato Casserole, Cheesy, '80 244; '83 53; '92 229
Potato Casserole, Easy, '80 114
Potato Casserole, Fluffy, '80 268
Potato Casserole, Hash Brown, '81 40
Potato Casserole, Holiday, '92 302
Potato Casserole, Irish, '81 263
Potato Casserole, Mashed, '85 296; '99 223
Potato Casserole, Mushroom-, '84 5
Potato Casserole, Pepper Jack-, '03 218
Potato Casserole, Peppery, '95 182
Potato Casserole, Processor, '86 159
Potato Casserole, Saucy, '81 276
Potato Casserole, Three-Cheese Mashed, '03 72
Potato Casserole with Caramelized Onions, '03 231
Potato-Cheese Casserole, '79 101
Potato-Egg Casserole, Cheesy, '84 5
Potato-Eggplant Casserole, '87 166
Potatoes and Eggs au Gratin, '79 107
Potatoes and Onions, Cheesy, '00 275
Potatoes and Turnips, Scalloped, '85 235
Potatoes-and-Zucchini au Gratin, '84 5
Potatoes au Gratin, '02 197
Potatoes au Gratin, Shredded, '89 69
Potatoes, Baked Sweet-and-Savory Mashed, '02 244
Potatoes, Barbecue Scalloped, '04 139

Potatoes, Buffet, '98 92
Potatoes, Caramelized Onion-and-Gorgonzola
    Mashed, '01 256
Potatoes, Cheesy Scalloped, '83 82
Potatoes, Christmas, '88 252
Potatoes, Cottage, '89 69
Potatoes, Cream Cheese Mashed, '02 35
Potatoes, Double Cheddar Cheese, '00 331
Potatoes, Double-Cheese, '86 6
Potatoes, Easy Oven-Baked, '82 202
Potatoes, Escalloped, '01 239
Potatoes, Fix-Ahead Mashed, '89 70
Potatoes, Fluffy, '84 296; '85 196
Potatoes for Company, Saucy, '82 202
Potatoes, Garlic, '84 296; '85 196
Potatoes Gourmet, '80 114
Potatoes, Gruyère, '83 193
Potatoes, Hot Deviled, '84 296; '85 196
Potatoes, Italian-Style, '89 69
Potatoes, Jalapeño, '84 39
Potatoes, Jazzy Mashed, '87 192
Potatoes, Lemon and Nutmeg, '80 36
Potatoes, Light Scalloped, '89 311
Potatoes Lorraine, '87 190
Potatoes, Mexican-Style, '91 78
Potatoes, Missy, '85 259
Potatoes Moussaka, '93 44
Potatoes, Mushroom Scalloped, '87 191
Potatoes, Olive, '80 114
Potatoes, Out-of-This-World Scalloped, '04 296
Potatoes, Parmesan, '82 270; '90 M62
Potatoes, Party Scalloped, '87 191
Potatoes, Rosemary's, '98 53
Potatoes, Russian, '03 255
Potatoes, Scalloped, '82 300; '83 211; '92 48
Potatoes, Sour Cream, '84 39
Potatoes, Special Scalloped, '88 162
Potatoes, Three-Cheese Mashed, '00 112
Potatoes, Two-Cheese, '80 114
Potatoes, Wayside Scalloped, '79 283
Potatoes, Winter Herb Garden Scalloped, '99 289
Potatoes with Feta Cheese, '84 295; '85 196
Potatoes with Ham Bits, Creamy, '87 191
Potatoes with Sweet Marjoram and Parmesan
    Cheese, Scalloped, '91 246
Potato Gratin, Smoky, '00 233
Potato-Horseradish Gratin with Caramelized Onions,
    '99 314
Potato-Leek Gratin, '05 281
Potato-Tomato Bake, '86 17
Potato-Tomato Casserole, Saucy, '79 46
Potato Tuna Bake, Shoestring, '82 211
Pumpkin, Baked, '82 217
Spinach and Artichoke Casserole, '81 103
Spinach-and-Celery Casserole, '84 294
Spinach and Egg Casserole, '82 270
Spinach-Artichoke Bake, '95 48
Spinach-Artichoke Casserole, '88 252; '93 44;
    '00 254; '01 49
Spinach-Artichoke Casserole, Spicy, '01 49
Spinach Bake, Creamy, '89 68
Spinach, Baked Macaroni with, '99 244
Spinach Casserole, '79 265; '91 31; '99 271
Spinach Casserole, Cheesy, '81 263
Spinach Casserole, Cottage Cheese-and-, '84 77
Spinach Casserole, Creamy, '86 111
Spinach-Cheese Bake, '88 10
Spinach-Cheese Casserole, '83 216; '89 64
Spinach-Cheese Puff, '84 96
Spinach, Cheesy Topped, '84 85
Spinach, Company, '89 280
Spinach, Creamy Lemon, '82 302
Spinach Fantastic, '93 173
Spinach-Gorgonzola Custards, Savory, '99 313

Spinach, Gourmet Baked, '82 180
Spinach Parmesan, '93 72
Spinach-Parmesan Casserole, '82 281; '83 32
Spinach Rice, '85 146
Spinach Shells, '97 50
Spinach Supreme, '84 77
Spinach Surprise, '82 42
Spinach with Cheese, Scalloped, '79 8
Squares, Checkerboard Vegetable, '96 178
Squash, Amarillo, '99 M218
Squash and Apple Casserole, '79 209
Squash-and-Corn Casserole, Easy, '03 69
Squash and Egg Casserole, '80 146
Squash and Tomato Bake, '95 180
Squash, Bacon-Flavored, '82 158
Squash Bake, '82 107
Squash Bake, Cheddar-, '84 128
Squash Bake, Cheesy, '80 183
Squash-Carrot Casserole, '81 157
Squash Casserole, '87 163; '89 159; '90 161;
    '92 342; '96 247, 252; '97 29; '04 126; '05 277
Squash Casserole, Baked, '83 149
Squash Casserole, Blender, '81 212
Squash Casserole, Calico, '90 290
Squash Casserole, Cheesy, '79 123
Squash Casserole, Company, '81 183
Squash Casserole, Creamy Rice and, '95 26
Squash Casserole, Crunchy, '84 293
Squash Casserole, Fresh, '82 204
Squash Casserole, Jiffy, '81 M144
Squash Casserole, Southwestern, '05 M217
Squash Casserole, Summer, '81 102, 184
Squash Casserole, Two-, '79 101
Squash Casserole, Two-Cheese, '04 126
Squash Casserole, Yellow, '79 179; '85 135; '88 166
Squash Casserole, Zippy, '80 183
Squash, Country Club, '88 M16
Squash, Greek-Style, '91 285; '92 26
Squash, Mexican, '83 31
Squash Nicholas, '94 236
Squash, Posh, '81 159
Squash, Savory, '99 111
Squash, South-of-the-Border, '89 148; '96 178;
    '00 137
Strata, Vegetable-Cheese, '98 98
Summer Vegetable Gratin, '03 159
Sweet Potato-and-Apple Casserole, '94 280
Sweet Potato-Apple Bake, '83 25
Sweet Potato-Apricot Bake, '85 206
Sweet Potato Bake, '80 287
Sweet Potato Bake, Holiday, '90 291
Sweet Potato-Banana Casserole, '86 276
Sweet Potato Casserole, '79 289; '80 26; '85 256;
    '89 279; '02 309; '03 M24
Sweet Potato Casserole, Bell's, '04 271
Sweet Potato Casserole, Glazed, '90 250
Sweet Potato Casserole, Maple-, '05 245
Sweet Potato Cassserole, Pear-, '86 280
Sweet Potato Delight, '86 335
Sweet Potato-Eggnog Casserole, '95 291
Sweet Potatoes-and-Apple Casserole, '90 228
Sweet Potatoes-and-Berries Casserole, '84 231
Sweet Potatoes, Bourbon, '86 324; '87 280
Sweet Potatoes, Candied, '86 111; '88 207
Sweet Potatoes, Mashed, '98 269
Sweet Potatoes, Orange-Spice Mashed, '02 34
Sweet Potatoes, Praline-Topped, '98 96
Sweet Potatoes Royale, '91 250
Sweet Potatoes with Sherry and Walnuts, '86 286
Sweet Potato-Rum Casserole, '84 231
Sweet Potato Supreme, '94 196
Sweet Potato Surprise, '81 267
Swiss Vegetable Medley, '95 26
Tomato-and-Artichoke Heart Bake, '85 81

CASSEROLES, Vegetable
(continued)

Tomato-Bacon Strata, '03 100
Tomato Casserole, '05 22
Tomato Casserole, Scalloped, '88 144
Tomato Casserole, Stuffed Fried Green, '04 145
Tomatoes, Herbed, '81 102
Tomatoes, Italian-Sauced Green, '85 214
Tomatoes, Scalloped, '84 142
Torta, Mexican, '88 149
Turnip Casserole, '83 242; '84 229; '04 213
Turnip Casserole, Baked, '82 274
Turnip Puff, Whipped, '00 254
Turnips au Gratin, '84 229
Turnips, Scalloped, '79 254
Vegetarian Casserole, '96 302
Veggies Casserole, '88 123
Vidalia Deep Dish, '89 120
Vidalia Onions, Cheesy Baked, '01 145
Vidalia Onion Soufflé, '04 167
Wine Sauce Casserole, Vegetables in, '95 133
Winter Root Vegetable Casserole, '98 265
Yam-and-Apple Scallop, '91 199
Yams, Brandied, '94 273
Zucchini, and Cornbread Bake, Bacon, '99 123
Zucchini and Tomato Bake, '82 158
Zucchini-and-Tomato Casserole, '88 265
Zucchini, Baked, '83 209
Zucchini-Carrot Casserole, '99 61
Zucchini Casserole, '79 157; '87 154
Zucchini Casserole, Cheese-Egg-, '84 114
Zucchini Casserole, Cheesy, '82 168; '84 145
Zucchini Casserole, Italian, '85 59
Zucchini-Jack Casserole, '85 296
Zucchini-Rice Casserole Italiano, '89 146
Zucchini with Pasta, Stuffed, '97 101
Wild Rice Casserole, '82 199; '95 176
Ziti, Baked, '05 214

CAULIFLOWER
Almond Sauce, Cauliflower with, '82 270
au Gratin, Cauliflower, '82 204; '99 59
Bake, Cauliflower, '95 342
Bake, Curried Cauliflower, '01 49
Baked Swiss Cauliflower, '79 100
Beef and Cauliflower Oriental, '80 220
Beef and Cauliflower over Rice, '93 94
Beets and Cauliflower, Chilled, '80 137
Browned Butter, Cauliflower in, '02 45
Casserole, Cauliflower, '86 10, 279
Casserole, Cauliflower-and-Carrot, '83 280
Casserole, Cauliflower 'n' Chiles, '87 285
Casserole, Cauliflower-Pea, '85 260
Casserole, Chicken, Broccoli, and Cauliflower, '00 337
Casserole, Easy Cauliflower, '82 204
Casserole, Festive Cauliflower, '87 232
Casserole, Herbed Cauliflower, '79 221
Cheddar Cauliflower, '99 318
Cheese-Frosted Cauliflower, '85 68
Cheese Sauce, Cauliflower with, '81 101
Cheesy Cauliflower Italiano, '82 300
Crunchy Cauliflower Surprise, '99 318
Curried Cauliflower, '91 315
Dilled Cauliflower, '83 93
Festive Cauliflower, '84 34
French-Fried Cauliflower, '86 211
French-Fried Cauliflower au Gratin, '79 221; '80 82
Fried Cauliflower, '83 5; '84 248; '90 18
Fried Cauliflower, Crispy, '80 220
Fried Cauliflower, Golden, '82 78
Fried Cauliflower, Oven-, '99 318
Fried Cauliflower with Cheese Sauce, '87 231
Fritters, Broccoli-Cauliflower, '02 45

Fritters, Cauliflower-Cheddar, '98 25
Frosted Cauliflower, '97 105
Garden Surprise, '83 112
Goldenrod, Cauliflower, '79 21
Gratin, Broccoli-and-Cauliflower, '01 43
Gratin, Cauliflower with Chinese Mustard, '94 45
Herb Butter, Cauliflower with, '81 2
Italian-Style Cauliflower, '92 36
Lemon Cauliflower, Easy, '83 322
Main-Dish Cauliflower, '79 221; '80 83
Medley, Cauliflower, '80 220
Medley, Cauliflower-Broccoli, '81 69
Medley, Cauliflower-Snow Pea, '87 305
Oriental Cauliflower, '81 75
Peas and Cauliflower, '82 288
Peas with Curried Almonds, Cauliflower and, '79 221; '80 82
Pickled Cauliflower, '94 183
Pie, Cauliflower-Carrot, '82 191
Pimiento Sauce, Cauliflower with, '87 232
Quiche, Cauliflower, '83 86
Roasted Broccoli and Cauliflower, '01 132
Salads
  Broccoli and Cauliflower Salad, '81 280
  Broccoli and Cauliflower Salad, Creamy, '81 23
  Broccoli and Cauliflower Toss, Crunchy, '83 25
  Broccoli, Cauliflower, and Carrot Salad, '04 140
  Broccoli-Cauliflower Pasta Salad, '88 269
  Broccoli-Cauliflower Salad, '92 97; '00 90
  Broccoli Crunch, Cauliflower-, '88 216
  Broccoli 'n' Cauliflower Salad, '90 32
  Broccoli Salad, Cauliflower-, '79 20
  Broccoli Toss, Cauliflower-, '82 54
  Broccoli Toss, Italian Cauliflower-, '88 269
  Brussels Sprouts Salad, Cauliflower-, '83 240
  Cauliflower Salad, '79 221; '80 83; '81 225; '84 291; '85 240, 279; '92 36
  Celery-and-Cauliflower Salad, '83 39
  Corned Beef-Cauliflower Salad, '83 16
  Creamy Cauliflower Salad, '82 102; '04 36
  Crunchy Cauliflower Salad, '80 4; '82 75
  English Pea Salad, Cauliflower-, '95 66
  Green Salad, Crunchy, '89 321
  Layered Cauliflower Salad, '83 240
  Lemon Salad, Cauliflower-, '81 23
  Marinated Cauliflower Salad, '82 303; '84 232
  Olive Toss, Cauliflower-, '85 198; '86 147
  Orange-Cauliflower Salad, '82 266
  Parmesan and Bacon, Cauliflower with, '96 137
  Pea Salad, Cauliflower-, '87 231
  Pea Salad, Savory Cauliflower and, '81 280
  Red, White, and Green Salad, '90 18
  Slaw, Cauliflower, '92 167
  Sweet-and-Sour Cauliflower Salad, '81 2
  Vegetable Salad, Cauliflower-, '85 158
Sauté, Cauliflower, '94 67
Scallop, Cauliflower, '88 270
Shrimp Sauce, Broccoli and Cauliflower with, '84 248
Soufflé, Cauliflower, '82 76; '89 279; '90 17
Soup, Cauliflower, '90 211; '99 318
Soup, Cauliflower and Caraway, '82 264
Soup, Cream of Cauliflower, '87 M7; '88 12; '96 277
Soup, Cream of Cauliflower and Watercress, '83 126
Soup, Creamy Cauliflower, '82 76
Soup, Fresh Cauliflower, '84 279
Spanish-Style Cauliflower, '79 21
Supreme, Cauliflower and Asparagus, '79 287; '80 35
Toss, Cauliflower, '85 289

CAVIAR
Artichoke Hearts with Caviar, '79 142
Crown, Caviar, '83 78
Eggplant Caviar, '88 262; '99 217
Eggplant Caviar with Tapenade, '92 194
Eggs, Black-and-Blue, '96 90

Endive with Caviar, '93 118
Homemade Cowboy Caviar, '94 64
Mexican Caviar, '98 135
Mold, Artichoke-Caviar, '87 239
Mound, Caviar-Artichoke, '91 244
Mousse, Caviar, '82 71; '83 258; '85 86; '92 83
Pie, Caviar, '79 154
Potato Blini with Sour Cream and Caviar, '01 274
Potatoes, Appetizer Caviar, '86 223
Potatoes, Caviar, '84 80
Spread, Caviar-Cream Cheese, '84 256
Spread, Creamy Caviar, '92 58
Spread, Egg, Sour Cream, and Caviar, '85 279
Texas Caviar, '86 218; '99 84; '01 160, 257
Tomatoes, Caviar, '91 12
Zucchini Caviar, '88 212

CELERY
Almondine, Celery, '85 116
Amandine, Buttered Celery, '82 98
Ants on a Float, '91 177
au Gratin, Celery, '83 38
Baked Celery, '82 98
Braised Carrots and Celery, '86 327
Braised Carrots, Apples, and Celery, '96 107
Braised Celery, Green Beans and, '84 254
Brussels Sprouts and Celery, '79 21
Brussels Sprouts with Celery, Lemony, '85 25
Buttered Carrots and Celery, '89 44
Carrots and Celery with Pecans, '84 254
Casserole, Celery, '80 246; '96 92
Casserole, Celery and Cheese, '79 178
Casserole, Creamy Celery, '82 98; '83 255
Casserole, Spinach-and-Celery, '84 294
Chicken-and-Celery Skillet, '88 6
Coleslaw, Cumin-Celery-Scented, '02 51
Creamed Brussels Sprouts and Celery, '83 322
Creamed Celery, '79 247
Croutons, Celery, '79 16
Curried Corn and Celery, '86 192
Dressing, Celery-Honey, '80 42
Dressing, Watermelon Salad with Celery-Nut, '80 182
Exotic Celery, '83 280
Olives Scaciati, '99 266
Orange Sauce, Celery in, '79 70
Oriental, Celery, '83 206; '85 116
Peas and Celery, '93 289
Peas and Celery, Deluxe, '81 267
Pork Tenderloin with Apples, Celery, and Potatoes, Grilled, '95 161
Potatoes, Whipped Celery, '94 305; '99 45; '01 212
Potato Puffs, Celeried, '89 279
Relish, Apple-Celery, '89 141
Rice, Holiday, '98 289
Rice, Island, '98 276
Salad, Celery, '79 70
Salad, Celery-and-Cauliflower, '83 39
Salad, Chicken-Celery, '81 187
Salad, Overnight Alfalfa-Celery, '82 97
Salad, Pear-and-Celery, '87 56
Salad, Pineapple-Celery, '85 95
Sauce, Baked Fillets in Lemon-Celery, '84 91
Saucy Celery, '83 39
Scalloped Carrots-and-Celery, '84 M112
Snow Peas with Celery, Skillet, '84 123
Soup, Burnet-Celery, '84 107
Soup, Celery-and-Potato, '84 279
Soup, Cream of Celery, '79 71; '90 210
Soup, Light Cream-of-Celery, '82 279
Soup, Tomato-Celery, '83 M58
Splendid Stalks, '93 258
Stuffed Celery, '82 98; '86 324
Stuffed Celery, Creamy, '82 102
Stuffed Celery, Jalapeño, '79 70

Stuffed Celery, Light Pimiento Cheese-, '05 161
Stuffed Celery, Nutty, '03 184
Stuffed Celery Trunks, '85 115
Toss, Celery-Parmesan, '84 34

CELERY ROOT
Carrots, Celeriac and, '91 219
Mashed Potatoes, Celery Root, '98 293
Roasted Celery Root, Carrots, and Onions, '98 293
Slaw, Shredded Celery Root-and-Carrot, '98 293
Stew, Beef-and-Celery Root, '98 292

CHAYOTES
Bake, Chayote-Cheese, '80 230
Casserole, Chayotes and Shrimp, '80 230
Fried Chayotes, '80 230
Mirliton-Corn Chowder, '00 246
Mirlitons, Artichokes, and Peppers, Marinated, '00 246
Mirlitons, Stuffed, '97 263; '00 246
Mirliton Stew, '02 57
Pickles, Chayote Squash, '89 197
Sautéed Chayote Squash with Cilantro, '95 227
Stuffed Chayote, '92 247

CHEESE. *See also* **APPETIZERS/Cheese;**
CHEESECAKES.
Almond Cheese, '88 173
Apple-Cheese Bake, '92 225
Bake, Brie Cheese, '87 117
Bake, Chicken, Ham, and Cheese, '87 217
Baked Brie, Walnut-, '93 241
Bake, Pineapple-Cheese, '79 106
Bake, Spinach-Ricotta, '88 97
Batter, Cheese Grits Crust, '03 21
Beef and Black Beans, Spicy, '99 331
Beef Blue, Elegant, '97 97
Beef 'n' Pasta, Easy Skillet, '02 63
Beef Parmigiana, '85 234
Beef Roulades, Roquefort, '88 215
Blintzes, Cheese, '82 146; '83 71; '92 84
Blue Cheese, Creamy, '88 173
Breads
Apple Bread, Cheddar-, '96 83
Bacon-and-Cheese Bread, '83 255
Bacon-Cheese Toast Bars, '79 36
Batter Bread, Cheese-Caraway, '85 33
Biscuit Cups, Bacon, '99 214
Biscuit Fingers, Pepper-Cheese, '88 283
Biscuits, Bacon-Cheese, '88 84
Biscuits, Beer-and-Cheese, '94 215
Biscuits, Blue Cheese, '88 83; '05 309
Biscuits, Blue Cheese-and-Ham Cornmeal, '98 136
Biscuits, Cheese, '81 288; '83 253; '85 32; '87 78
Biscuits, Cheese Angel, '89 211
Biscuits, Cheeseburger, '79 194
Biscuits, Cheese-Chive, '94 324
Biscuits, Cheese-Garlic, '02 260
Biscuits, Cheese Garlic, '03 185
Biscuits, Cheesy Onion, '95 98; '01 330
Biscuits, Deluxe Omelet, '98 101
Biscuits, Easy Cheddar, '01 103
Biscuits, Easy Cheese, '81 99
Biscuits, Ham-and-Swiss Cheese, '04 209
Biscuits, Herbed Roquefort, '84 95
Biscuits, Hot Cheesy, '80 186
Biscuits, Lightnin' Cheese, '90 283
Biscuits, Mexican Fiesta Spoon, '95 161
Biscuits, Mixer Cheese, '96 22
Biscuits, Petite Ham and Cheese, '79 193
Biscuits, Refrigerator, '96 17
Biscuits, Rosemary, '99 17
Biscuits, Spicy Kickin', '03 207
Biscuits, Surprise Pull-Apart, '95 46
Biscuits, Tiny Cheese, '80 192
Biscuits with Beef and Horseradish-Chive Cream, Blue Cheese, '02 313
Biscuits with Chipotle Butter, Cheese, '01 234

Biscuits with Olive-Parsley Spread, Cream Cheese-and-Olive, '04 238
Biscuits with Sun-Dried Tomato Spread and Bacon, Cream Cheese-and-Olive, '02 313
Biscuits with Tapenade, Cream Cheese-and-Olive, '02 313
Black-Eyed Pea Bread, '02 224
Blue Cheese-Apple Sunburst, '94 245
Blue Cheese Bread, '03 54
Bobolis, Easy Cheesy, '92 278
Bowls, Toasted Bread, '98 30
Breadsticks, Italian Cheese, '95 126
Breadsticks, Italian Herb, '04 35
Breadsticks, Parmesan-Garlic, '99 46
Breadsticks, Sesame-Cheese, '97 31
Brie Bread, '87 143
Buns, Cheesy Onion, '85 5
Buns, Hurry-Up Cheese, '81 300
Buns, Onion-Cheese, '88 218
Butter Cheese Dips, '80 46
Buttermilk-Cheese Loaf, '91 52
Cheddar Cheese Bread, '84 268
Cheddar Cheese Loaf, '00 317
Cheddar Cheese-Pepper Bread, '98 25
Cheddar-Chive Beer Bread, '03 207
Cheddar-Nut Bread, '85 41
Cheese Bread, '82 174; '83 208; '87 11
Cinnamon Logs, '98 325
Cornbread, Bacon-Cheddar Hot-Water, '01 29; '02 107; '04 25
Cornbread, Cheddar, '83 285; '84 17
Cornbread, Cheddar-Jalapeño, '85 3
Cornbread, Cheese-and-Onion, '05 35
Cornbread, Cheesy Beef, '81 242
Cornbread, Chile-Cheese, '87 171
Cornbread, Cottage Cheese, '80 90
Cornbread, Jalapeño, '98 178
Cornbread, Loaded, '99 214
Cornbread, Southwestern Hot-Water, '01 29; '02 107; '04 25
Cornbread, Sweet Onion, '98 252
Cornbread, Swiss Cheese, '79 60
Cornbread, Vicksburg, '96 35
Corn Sticks, Pimiento-Cheese, '03 20
Cottage Cheese-Dill Bread, '83 154
Cream Cheese-Banana-Nut Bread, '05 27
Cream Cheese-Banana-Nut Bread, Cinnamon Crisp-Topped, '05 27
Cream Cheese-Banana-Nut Bread, Orange-Pecan-Topped, '05 27
Cream Cheese-Banana-Nut Bread, Peanut Butter Streusel-Topped, '05 27
Cream Cheese-Banana-Nut Bread, Toasted Coconut-Topped, '05 27
Cream Cheese-Banana-Nut Bread, Toffee-Topped, '05 27
Cream Cheese Braids, '82 243; '97 287
Cream Cheese Loaves, Processor, '85 48
Cream Cheese Pinches, '87 85
Crescents, Apricot-Cheese, '99 284
Crescents, Cheddar, '05 70
Crescents, Cheese, '82 18
Croissants, Cream Cheese, '92 159
Crusty Cheese Bread, '86 233
Cups, Bacon-Cheese, '02 219
Danish, Cheese, '97 31
Danish, Cream Cheese, '98 325
Dilly Cheese Bread, '83 5
Easy Cheese Bread, '82 74; '86 17
Elephant Ears, Mushroom-and-Brie Petite, '00 87
Elephant Ears, Parmesan-Pepper Baby, '00 87
English Cheese Muffins, '02 41
Flatbread, Parmesan-Onion, '98 65
Flatbread, Quick, '00 119

Flatbread, Sicilian Artichoke, '98 136
Focaccia, Roquefort-and-Onion, '98 54
French Bread, Bacon-Cheese, '92 54
French Bread, Cheesy, '88 172; '95 218; '96 205; '97 325
French Bread, Herbed, '99 47
French Bread, Onion-Cheese, '89 29
French Bread, Tangy, '98 166
French Toast au Fromage, '88 288
French Toast, Cottage-Topped, '85 49
French Toast, Stuffed, '96 52; '98 55, 313; '02 105
French Toast, Three Cheese Stuffed, '93 122
French Toast with Strawberry Sauce, Make-Ahead, '02 131
Fruit-and-Cheese Braid, '86 214
Garlic Bread, Cheesy, '84 150
Garlic-Stuffed Bread, Cheesy, '95 176
Gouda Bread, '91 52
Grilled Bread, '00 88
Grits Bread, Cheesy, '05 83
Ham-and-Cheese Bread, '86 213
Herb-and-Cheese Pull Aparts, '87 143
Herb Bread, Cheese-, '84 M144; '85 283
Herb-Cheese Bread, '85 70
Herbs-and-Cheese Bread, '93 56
Herb-Vegetable-Cheese Bread, '88 172
Jalapeño-Cheese Loaf, '84 76
Jam-and-Cheese Loaf, '89 246
Lemon-Cream Tea Loaf, '84 50
Little Cheese Loaves, '86 213
Loaf, Cheese, '90 93
Mashed Potato Bites, '98 249
Monkey Bread, Cheese-Filled, '91 21
Muffin Mix, Cheese-and-Pepper, '89 330
Muffins, Bacon-and-Cheese, '89 205
Muffins, Bacon-Cheese, '96 280
Muffins, Blueberry-Cream Cheese, '86 14
Muffins, Breakfast, '04 209
Muffins, Broccoli Cornbread, '03 81
Muffins, Buttery Herb-Cheese, '03 232
Muffins, Caraway-Cheese, '91 213
Muffins, Cheddar, '89 15
Muffins, Cheddar-Raisin, '91 51
Muffins, Cheese, '96 54; '97 287
Muffins, Cheese-and-Pepper, '84 139
Muffins, Cheesy Cornbread, '88 M275
Muffins, Cheesy Sausage, '92 252; '93 144
Muffins, Chive-and-Cheese, '04 332
Muffins, Cream Cheese-Banana-Nut, '05 27
Muffins, Dilly Cheese, '95 245; '96 55
Muffins, Green Onion-and-Cream Cheese, '01 289
Muffins, Ham-and-Cheddar, '03 81
Muffins, Ham-and-Cheese, '92 252; '93 144
Muffins, Ham-and-Swiss, '03 81
Muffins, Marvelous Cheese, '83 96
Muffins, Parmesan Cheese, '04 209
Muffins, Parmesan Corn, '01 255
Muffins, Pepper-Cheese, '96 280
Muffins, Peppered Cheddar, '99 234
Muffins, Reduced-Fat Ham-and-Cheddar, '03 81
Muffins, Sausage-and-Cheese, '03 81
Muffins, Sausage-Cheese, '86 213
Muffins, Sesame-Cheese, '86 16; '03 81
Muffins, Southwestern Corn, '02 212
Nut Bread, Cheddar-, '03 42
Olive Bread, Spicy Cheese-, '84 150
Onion-Cheese Bread, '79 180; '81 8
Onion-Cheese Supper Bread, '83 112
Onion-Parmesan Bread, '84 284
Orange-Cream Cheese Bread, '82 210
Pane Cunsado (Fixed Bread), '95 218
Pane Cunsado (Sicilian for "Fixed Bread"), '96 205
Parmesan Bread, '92 19; '93 231; '00 54
Parmesan Cheese Bread, '99 61

CHEESE, Breads
(continued)

Parmesan Herb Bread, '82 235; '83 41
Parmesan Puffs, '98 235
Parmesan Sesame Sticks, '81 39
Parmesan Twists, '83 239; '99 323
Peppery Cheese Bread, '04 295
Pig-in-a-Blanket Bread, '99 134
Pimiento-Cheese Bread, '85 223; '86 166
Pita Triangles, Cheesy, '93 70
Pizza Bread Rollups, '04 M35
Pizza Crust Wedges, Toasted, '03 280
Popover Puffs, Cheese, '85 6
Popover Ring, Cheesy, '80 45
Popovers, Cheddar, '00 64
Popovers, Cheddar Cheese, '85 41
Popovers, Parmesan, '90 66; '00 64
Poppy Seed-Swiss Cheese Bread, '91 52
Pull-Apart Ring, Southwestern, '03 298
Pull-Apart Ring, Veggie Southwestern, '03 299
Pull-Away Bread, '98 137
Pumpkin Bread, Cream Cheese-, '05 251
Quick Cheese Bread, '83 9
Roll, Feta Cheese-Spinach, '91 22
Rolls, Beer-Parmesan, '03 259
Rolls, Broccoli-Cheddar, '91 21
Rolls, Cheese, '80 286
Rolls, Cheese-Apricot Sweet, '90 195
Rolls, Cottage Cheese, '81 78
Rolls, Cream Cheese-Filled Cinnamon, '02 327
Rolls, Crunchy, '97 160
Rolls, Ham-and-Cheese, '82 3
Rolls, Italian Parker House, '99 47
Rolls, Parmesan, '79 181
Rolls, Romano Sesame, '87 144
Rolls, Whole Wheat, '96 50
Scones, Golden Cheddar Cheese, '99 82
Scones, Pizza, '03 207
Sour Cream-Cheese Bread, '85 33
Spinach Bread, '87 144
Spoonbread, Cheddar, '82 196
Spoonbread, Cheese, '86 261
Spoonbread, Corn-Cheese, '88 9
Sticks, Crispy, '03 211
Sticks, Sesame-Cheddar, '81 150
Swiss Cheese Bread, '79 60
Swiss Cheese Bread, Poppy Seed-, '91 52
Swiss Cheese Loaves, Mini, '95 80
Tennessee Sin, '96 204
Toasted Cheese Delights, '79 37
Toast Points, Parmesan, '00 316
Toasts, Crispy Parmesan, '01 307
Toasts, Parmesan-Pepper, '98 242
Tomato-Cheese Bread, '98 172; '99 M157
Tomato-Cheese Bread, Herbed, '88 143
Triangles, Savory, '02 54
Twists, Cheesy, '84 284
Wine Bread, Cheese-, '87 254
Wine Bread, Parmesan-, '97 31
Witches' Brooms, Cheesy, '01 205
Bugs in a Rug, '95 178
Burgers, Beef-and-Cheese, '96 139
Burgers, Blue Cheese, '89 M66
Burgers, Brie-Mushroom, '95 128
Burgers, Cheesy Bacon, '81 29
Burgers, Cheesy Beef, '83 217
Burgers, Spicy Cheddar-Stuffed, '05 163
Burgers, Spinach-Feta, '99 135
Burgers, Stuffed Southwestern-Style, '99 201
Burritos, Breakfast, '90 192; '97 172
Burritos, Cheesy Beef, '85 193
Burritos, Easy, '04 32

Burritos, Lentil, '99 287
Butter, Cheese, '84 114
Calzones, Spinach-and-Cheese, '95 310
Canadian Bacon Squares, Sunrise, '99 103
Casseroles
Apple-Cheese Casserole, '84 287
Asparagus Casserole, Cheesy, '82 281; '83 32
Bacon-and-Ham Casserole, Cheesy, '01 256
Beef-and-Bean Bake, Cheesy, '82 89
Beef Casserole, '01 199
Beef, Cheese, and Noodle Casserole, '99 58
Beef Lombardi, '03 214
Blintz Casserole, Cheese, '92 251
Breakfast Casserole, '91 285; '99 273; '01 130, 243
Breakfast Casserole, Brie-and-Sausage, '03 36
Breakfast Casserole, Cheesy, '85 247
Breakfast, Mexican, '00 194
Breakfast Strata, English Muffin, '03 100
Brie-and-Sausage Breakfast Casserole, '00 284
Broccoli-and-Squash Casserole, '01 175
Broccoli Bake, Cheesy, '83 255
Broccoli-Blue Cheese Casserole, '85 260
Broccoli Casserole, Cheesy, '84 293; '92 342; '95 M191
Broccoli-Cheese Breakfast Casserole, '99 233
Broccoli-Cheese Casserole, '82 269; '84 9; '94 132
Broccoli-Ham au Gratin, '90 239
Broccoli Supreme, '02 312
Broccoli-Swiss Cheese Casserole, '83 322; '85 M211
Broccoli with Pimiento Cheese Sauce, '02 291
Brunch Casserole, '82 124
Brunch Casserole, Easy Cheesy, '92 91
Brunch Casserole, Italian, '83 29
Brunch Casserole, Southwestern, '03 197
Brunch Casserole with Creole Sauce, '98 98
Brunch for a Bunch, '88 57
Cabbage au Gratin, '83 279
Cabbage Casserole, Cheesy, '79 4
Campfire Casserole, '00 173
Caramelized Onion Macaroni and Cheese, '04 231
Carrots, Cheese Scalloped, '94 36
Carrots, Scalloped, '02 129; '03 99
Cauliflower Surprise, Crunchy, '99 318
Celery and Cheese Casserole, '79 178
Celery au Gratin, '83 38
Chayote-Cheese Bake, '80 230
Cheeseburger Casserole, '95 255
Chicken and Dressing, Santa Fe, '03 48
Chicken-and-Wild Rice Casserole, Leslie's Favorite, '03 107
Chicken Cannelloni with Roasted Red Bell Pepper Sauce, '02 287
Chicken Casserole, Cheesy, '85 34
Chicken Casserole, Jalapeño, '02 50
Chicken Casserole, King Ranch, '00 280
Chicken Casserole, Swiss, '90 67
Chicken, Cheesy Mexican, '01 199
Chicken Enchiladas, '03 214
Chicken Enchiladas, Creamy, '97 250
Chicken Enchiladas, Quicker, '97 312
Chicken, Fontina-Baked, '90 64
Chicken, King Ranch, '99 330; '03 313
Chicken Parmesan, '04 42
Chicken, Poppy Seed, '99 195
Chicken Salad, Hot, '98 290
Chicken, Swiss, '95 54
Chicken Tetrazzini, '02 171
Chicken Tetrazzini, Cheesy, '83 M87
Chicken Thighs, Swiss, '94 282
Chilaquiles, '82 220
Chile-Cheese Casserole, '82 90
Chile 'n' Cheese Breakfast Casserole, '88 57
Chiles Rellenos Casserole, '79 84; '84 31, 234; '92 18; '98 48

Chili Casserole, Ultimate, '99 239
Collards Casserole, Parmesan-, '95 233
Continental Cheese Bake, '81 89
Corn and Cheese Casserole, '81 128
Corn Bake, Cheesy, '98 244
Corn, Baked Jack, '97 86
Cornbread-Chili Strata, '03 100
Corned Beef and Cabbage au Gratin, '83 16
Corn-Rice Casserole, '01 46
Crab, Shrimp, and Artichoke au Gratin, '90 240
Egg-and-Cheese Casserole, '84 293
Egg Casserole, '98 98
Egg Casserole, Cheese-and-, '99 268
Egg Casserole, Cheesy, '81 244; '86 15
Eggplant Crêpes with Marinara Sauce, Mini, '99 266
Eggplant Parmesan, '83 186; '84 215; '86 53; '95 84; '01 53
Eggplant Parmesan with Feta, '03 174
Eggplant Parmigiana, '81 19; '01 310
Eggplant, Spinach-and-Basil Stuffed, '02 147
Eggplant-Spinach Casserole, '99 217
Eggs, Brunch, '98 93
Enchilada Casserole, Easy, '02 143
Enchiladas, Baked Chicken-and-Cheese, '03 332
Enchiladas, Chicken, '00 45
Enchiladas, Chicken-Cheese, '02 236
Enchiladas, Quicker, '96 103
Enchiladas, Three-Cheese Chicken, '99 330
Enchiladas Verde, Chicken, '00 M240
English Pea Casserole, Cheesy, '83 216
Feather-Light Cheese Casserole, '79 84
Florentine Bake, Cheesy, '95 131
Four Cheese Casserole, '92 170
Garden Medley, '98 236
Green Bean Bake, '99 112
Green Bean Gratin, Gourmet, '99 M334
Grits, Baked Cheese, '80 49, 99; '83 311; '85 41; '01 289
Grits, Baked Cheese-and-Garlic, '83 292; '84 78
Grits, Baked Garlic-and-Herb, '01 326
Grits Bake, Santa Fe, '00 123
Grits Casserole, Cheddar Cheese, '05 283
Grits Casserole, Cheesy, '81 270
Grits, Cheese, '86 242
Grits, Chile-Blue Cheese, '04 240
Grits, Chili-Cheese, '01 86
Grits, Garlic-Cheese, '80 47; '81 197; '86 180; '00 215
Grits, Jalapeño-Cheese, '00 239; '01 328
Grits, Mexican Cheese, '02 34
Grits, Swiss-and-Cheddar Baked, '91 71
Grits with Chicken Sausage and Shiitake Mushrooms, Cheese, '03 254
Ground Beef Casserole, Cheesy, '79 44
Ham-and-Cheese Casserole, '87 78
Ham-and-Cheese Layered Casserole, '98 160
Ham-and-Swiss Casserole, Savory, '01 308
Ham Casserole, Creamy, '03 83
Ham Casseroles, Creamy, '01 55
Ham Tetrazzini, '03 174
Hash Brown Casserole, Cheesy, '03 218
Hash Brown Casserole, Creamy, '03 193
Hash Brown-Cheese Bake, '97 323
Hash Brown-Ham-Cheese Bake, '97 323
Hominy Casserole, Cheesy, '83 170
Hominy Casserole), Four-Part Hominy (Cheesy, '96 158
Hominy Olé, '01 17
Hominy with Chiles and Cheese, '86 78
Italian Casserole, Light, '03 198
King Ranch Casserole, '02 210
Lasagna, '98 95
Lasagna, Cheesy, '82 224; '88 299

Lasagna, Cheesy Spinach, '80 32; '83 204; '01 196
Lasagna, Cheesy Vegetable, '79 84
Lasagna, Crabmeat, '96 290
Lasagna, Easy Mexican, '03 22
Lasagna, Ellie's, '02 186
Lasagna, Extra-Easy, '00 326
Lasagna, Gourmet White, '96 225
Lasagna, Ground Sirloin, '03 143
Lasagna, Italian Sausage, '96 225
Lasagna Maria, '90 191
Lasagna, Meatball, '00 243; '03 142
Lasagna, Mexican, '98 283
Lasagna, Roasted Vegetable-Meat, '99 M332
Lasagna, Saucy Cheese-Vegetable, '01 306
Lasagna, Southwestern Chicken, '03 173
Lasagna, Spinach-Black Bean, '02 44
Lasagna, Texas, '98 52
Lasagna, Vegetable, '99 97
Leftovers Casserole, Holiday, '04 232
Lentils and Rice, Spanish-Style, '03 201
Lentils with Cheese, Baked, '84 113
Lima Bean Casserole, Swiss, '80 191
Limas, Spanish Cheese, '86 225
Linguine with Meat Sauce, Baked, '01 41
Linguine with Meat Sauce Casserole, '03 22
Mac-and-Cheese, Veggie, '01 111
Mac and Texas Cheeses with Roasted Chiles, '04 207
Macaroni and Blue Cheese, '93 248; '94 44
Macaroni and Cheese, '83 M7; '88 M147, M190; '90 30; '00 273
Macaroni-and-Cheese Bake, '01 41
Macaroni and Cheese, Baked, '82 199; '00 271; '02 26; '03 184
Macaroni and Cheese, Broccoli, '02 36
Macaroni and Cheese, Creamy, '93 249; '94 45; '02 26
Macaroni-and-Cheese Deluxe, '79 84
Macaroni and Cheese Deluxe, '80 236
Macaroni and Cheese, Divine, '99 314
Macaroni and Cheese, Eleanor's, '97 253
Macaroni and Cheese, Golden, '04 24
Macaroni and Cheese, Italian, '04 327
Macaroni and Cheese, Old-Fashioned, '92 215
Macaroni and Cheese, Quick-and-Easy, '00 15
Macaroni and Cheese, Souper, '00 92
Macaroni and Cheese, Tasty, '83 288
Macaroni and Cheese, Tex-Mex, '00 92
Macaroni and Cheese, Thick-and-Rich, '84 329
Macaroni-and-Cheese with Wine, '86 78
Macaroni Bake, Jack-in-the-, '93 249; '94 45
Macaroni, Cheese, and Tomatoes, '95 213
Macaroni-Cheese-Beef Casserole, '95 125
Macaroni, Double Cheese, '82 224
Macaroni, Extra Cheesy, '00 92
Macaroni, Gorgonzola, '97 28
Macaroni, Mexican, '96 73
Macaroni Mousse, '96 73
Macaroni-Mushroom Bake, Cheesy, '81 243
Macaroni Primavera, '96 73
Macaroni, Three-Cheese, '00 M92
Macaroni with Blue Cheese and Walnuts, '02 M208
Macaroni with Spinach, Baked, '99 244
Manicotti, Cheesy, '83 216
Manicotti, Cheesy Sausage-and-Tomato, '03 257
Manicotti, Creamy Chipotle, '03 96
Manicotti, Ground Beef-and-Tomato, '03 257
Manicotti, Make-Ahead, '98 68
Manicotti, Meaty Cheese, '05 34
Manicotti, Meaty Stuffed, '00 19
Manicotti, Special, '88 50
Manicotti, Stuffed, '83 M6
Mashed Potato Casserole, Three-Cheese, '03 72
Meat and Potatoes, Italian-Style, '03 97
Mexican Casserole, Cabin, '97 95

Mexican Casserole, Cheesy, '82 224
Mexican Casserole, Microwave, '90 M231
Mushroom-Cheese Casserole, '83 216
Mushroom Deluxe Casserole, '96 20
Mushrooms au Gratin, '81 108
New Potato Gratin, Creamy, '01 M320
Onion Casserole, Cheesy, '79 101
Onions, Cheesy Baked Vidalia, '01 145
Orzo, Mozzarella-and-Olive, '97 249
Parmigiana, Eggplant, '95 197
Pasta Bake, Cheesy, '02 161
Pasta Bake, Layered, '04 326
Pasta Bake, Three-Cheese, '05 54
Pasta Shells Florentine, '00 326
Pepper Jack-Potato Casserole, '03 218
Pineapple Bake, '96 84
Pineapple-Cheese Bake, '79 106
Pizza Bake, Upside-Down, '98 224
Pizza Casserole, Upside-Down, '03 284
Pork Casserole, Cheesy, '81 M74
Pork Parmigiana, Easy, '94 57
Potato Bake, Smoky Mashed, '01 21
Potato-Butternut Squash-and-Gruyère Gratin, '01 43
Potato Casserole, Au Gratin, '05 250
Potato Casserole, Beefy, '03 218
Potato Casserole, Cheesy, '80 244; '83 53; '92 229
Potato Casserole, Mashed, '99 223
Potato-Cheese Casserole, '79 101
Potato-Cheese Dream, '91 307
Potato-Egg Casserole, Cheesy, '84 5
Potatoes and Eggs au Gratin, '79 107
Potatoes and Onions, Cheesy, '00 275
Potatoes au Gratin, '02 197
Potatoes au Gratin, Shredded, '89 69
Potatoes, Baked Sweet-and-Savory Mashed, '02 244
Potatoes, Barbecue Scalloped, '04 139
Potatoes, Buffet, '98 92
Potatoes, Caramelized Onion-and-Gorgonzola Mashed, '01 256
Potatoes, Cheesy Scalloped, '83 82
Potatoes, Cottage, '89 69
Potatoes, Cream Cheese Mashed, '02 35
Potatoes, Double Cheddar Cheese, '00 331
Potatoes, Double-Cheese, '86 6
Potatoes, Escalloped, '01 239
Potatoes Gourmet, '80 114
Potatoes, Gruyère, '83 193
Potatoes, Mushroom Scalloped, '87 191
Potatoes, Out-of-This-World Scalloped, '04 296
Potatoes, Rosemary's, '98 53
Potatoes, Russian, '03 255
Potatoes, Scalloped, '83 211
Potatoes, Special Scalloped, '88 162
Potatoes, Three-Cheese Mashed, '00 112
Potatoes, Winter Herb Garden Scalloped, '99 289
Reuben Casserole, '90 240
Rice-and-Cheese con Chiles, '89 99
Rice au Gratin, '83 129
Rice au Gratin Supreme, '86 78
Rice, Cheese-Parslied, '89 99
Rice Strata, Cheese-, '81 176
Rotini, Baked, '01 185
Sausage Brunch, Italian, '88 57
Sausage Casserole, Cheesy, '82 124
Sausage Casserole, Swiss, '80 209
Sausage-Cheese Bake, '88 58
Sausage-Chile Rellenos Casserole, '88 52
Sausage-Spud Bake, Sunday Night Spicy Cheesy, '03 331
Seafood Parmesan, Savannah, '99 312
Seashell-Provolone Casserole, '80 189
Shells and Cheese, Creamy, '01 216
Shrimp-and-Grits Casserole, Cheesy, '03 28
Shrimp-and-Scallops Casserole, Creamy, '01 256

Shrimp Enchiladas, '01 104
Spaghetti-and-Spinach Casserole, '02 199
Spinach Casserole, '99 271
Spinach Casserole, Cheesy, '81 263
Spinach Casserole, Cottage Cheese-and-, '84 77
Spinach-Cheese Bake, '88 10
Spinach-Cheese Casserole, '83 216; '89 64
Spinach-Gorgonzola Custards, Savory, '99 313
Spinach-Parmesan Casserole, '82 281; '83 32
Spinach Ring au Fromage, '79 8
Spinach Shells, '97 50
Squash-and-Corn Casserole, Easy, '03 69
Squash Bake, Cheddar-, '84 M113, 128
Squash Casserole, Cheesy, '79 123; '82 M21
Squash Casserole, Two-Cheese, '04 126
Squash-Chicken Casserole, Hearty Tex-Mex, '03 107
Squash, Savory, '99 111
Squash, South-of-the-Border, '96 178; '00 137
Strata, Vegetable-Cheese, '98 98
Stroganoff Casserole, '98 48
Tamale, Mozzarella, '95 70
Tomato-and-Okra Bake, '03 158
Tomato Macaroni and Cheese, Spicy, '03 68
Tuna Casserole with Cheese Swirls, '88 256
Turkey-Cheddar-Broccoli Strata, '03 100
Turkey Parmigiana, '87 193
Turkey-Swiss Casserole, '86 283
Turkey Tetrazzini, '03 257
Turnip Casserole, '04 213
Vegetable Casserole, Cheesy, '81 103
Vegetable-Cheese Medley, '99 M287
Vegetable Medley, Swiss, '95 26
Vegetable Squares, Checkerboard, '96 178
Wraps, Southwestern, '99 238
Zucchini Casserole, Cheese-Egg-, '84 114
Zucchini Casserole, Cheesy, '82 168; '84 145
Zucchini-Jack Casserole, '85 296
Catfish Parmesan, '79 184; '86 210; '99 91
Catfish, Parmesan, '92 309
Cheeseburgers, Inside Out, '99 202
Cheeseburgers, Mini-, '97 203
Chicken Alouette, '91 295
Chicken, Baked Parmesan, '83 320
Chicken Breasts, Celebrity, '95 60
Chicken Breasts, Cream Cheese, '90 234
Chicken Breasts Gruyère, '80 189
Chicken Breasts over Angel Hair, Goat Cheese-Stuffed, '97 144
Chicken Breasts Romano, '79 218
Chicken Breasts Saltimbocca, '98 19
Chicken Breasts with White Bean Puree, Stuffed, '02 200
Chicken Bundles, Southwestern, '02 215
Chicken Caprese with Tomato-Basil Cream, '99 240
Chicken, Cheesy Mexican, '02 91
Chicken Cobbler, Spicy Tex-Mex, '03 324
Chicken Cordon Bleu, '81 304; '82 83; '86 37
Chicken, Crispy Parmesan, '80 M76
Chicken Fiesta, Breast-of-, '88 151
Chicken in Phyllo, Cheese-Stuffed, '01 251
Chicken in Phyllo, Cheesy, '02 308
Chicken Macaroni and Cheese, Spicy, '02 63
Chicken Monterey, '82 275
Chicken-Mozzarella Melt, Italian, '95 153
Chicken, Oven-Fried, '99 212
Chicken, Oven-Fried Parmesan, '81 97; '82 148
Chicken Packets, '96 104
Chicken Parmesan, '83 184; '95 210; '00 219
Chicken Parmesan, Baked, '83 137
Chicken Penne, Cheesy, '00 289
Chicken Penne, Spicy Cheesy, '00 289
Chicken Presents, Holiday, '01 251
Chicken Provolone, '93 323
Chicken Rollups, Cheesy, '82 44

Chicken, Roquefort, '89 320
Chicken, Seasoned, '99 316
Chicken Shortcakes, Cheesy, '95 98
Chicken Skillet, Cheesy, '80 115
Chicken, Stuffed Alfredo, '04 56
Chiles Rellenos, '88 116; '89 226
Chiles Rellenos, Roasted, '95 64
Chiles Rellenos with Walnut Cream Sauce, Havarti-and-
     Corn-Stuffed, '93 M275
Chili-Cheese Dogs, '81 M176
Chili, Cheese-Topped, '82 M11
Chili, Cheesy, '82 310
Chimichangas, Baked Spicy Beef, '97 319
Chimichangas, Bean-and-Cheese, '01 16
Chimichangas, Chicken, '98 95
Chunky Cream Cheese, '85 306
Chutney with Cream Cheese, Cranberry-Amaretto,
     '87 244
Coffee Cake, Chocolate-Cream Cheese, '03 288
Coffee Cake, Cream Cheese, '86 290
Coffee Cake, Deep-Dish Cheesecake, '90 50
Coffee Cake, Raspberry-Cheese, '97 231
con Queso, Chile, '97 25
Cookie Snacks, Cheese, '01 231
Corn on the Cob, Parmesan, '88 M187
Cottage Cheese, Italian, '01 124
Country Ham Puff, Cheesy, '90 88
Couscous, Quick Parmesan, '05 203
Couscous with Peas and Feta, '01 158
Crab Bake, Quick, '87 192
Crabmeat au Gratin, '86 154
Crackers, Hot Nut, '90 206
Crackers, Taco-Cheese Animal, '94 197
Cream Puffs with Chicken Salad, Cheesy, '86 260
Cream-Style Cheese, '85 209
Crème Brûlée, Roquefort-and-Black Pepper, '95 324
Crêpe Cups, Florentine, '89 44
Crêpes, Cheese and Mushroom, '81 88
Crêpes, Cheesy Sausage, '82 240; '83 71
Crêpes con Queso, '96 48
Crêpes, Goat Cheese-Filled Cornbread, '98 43
Crêpes, Mushroom-Cheese, '87 289; '88 135
Crêpes, Sausage-Filled, '98 266; '99 25
Crêpes, Spinach-Ricotta, '81 52
Crispies, Pecan-Cheese, '87 168
Crisps, Blue Cheese, '96 106
Crisps, Peppered Cheese, '98 107
Crostini, Feta-Tomato, '92 159
Croutons, Goat Cheese-and-Chive, '01 312
Croutons, Prosciutto, '99 89
Crust, Cheese, '80 286; '86 264
Crust, Cheesy Crumb, '88 86
Crust, Chicken Pot Pie with Cheese, '86 264
Crust, Parmesan, '94 304
Crust, Parmesan Pizza, '93 58
Desserts
     Almond-Raspberry Brie, '94 M89
     Apple-and-Cheese Delight, '98 97
     Bars, Caramel-Pecan Cheesecake, '05 210
     Bites, Starlight Cheese, '95 329
     Blackberry Supremes, '99 179
     Blintzes, Cheese, '82 146
     Blueberry Yum Yum, '98 91
     Bread Pudding with Amaretto Cream Sauce, Layered
          Almond-Cream Cheese, '03 330
     Brownie Bars, Broadway, '97 M35
     Brownies à la Mode, Magnolias Cream Cheese,
          '97 M178
     Brownies, Cream Cheese, '04 M330
     Brownies, Cream Cheese Swirl, '79 51

Brownies, German Cream Cheese, '80 269
Brownies, Magnolia Cream Cheese, '01 M63
Brownies, Walnut-Cream Cheese, '84 240
Cake, Cheesy Pound, '96 62
Cake, Coconut-Cream Cheese Pound, '85 297;
     '90 305
Cake, Cream Cheese-Bourbon-Pecan Pound, '04 280
Cake, Cream Cheese-Coconut-Pecan Pound, '04 280
Cake, Cream Cheese Loaf, '84 151
Cake, Cream Cheese Pound, '81 290; '86 287;
     '95 304; '01 244; '03 312
Cake, Crusty Cream Cheese Pound, '89 124
Cake, Ooey-Gooey Butter, '00 86
Cake, Poppy Seed, '95 63
Cake, Regal Cream Cheese, '80 140
Cake Squares, Cream Cheese, '84 321
Cake, Tart Lemon-Cheese, '88 7
Cake, Twinkling Star, '00 306
Cake with Strawberries and Cream, Cream Cheese
     Pound, '02 104
Cake with Wine Jelly, Pound, '98 125
Cannoli, '91 20
Chocolate-Cheese Cups, '91 142
Chocolate Heaven, '98 323
Cobbler, Country Apple, '99 255
Cobbler, Double-Cherry Cheesecake, '03 21
Cookies, Breakfast, '97 52
Cookies, Cream Cheese, '80 282; '02 229; '03 131
Cookies, Cream Cheese-Chocolate Chip, '02 229;
     '03 131
Cottage Cheese Dessert, Creamy, '87 191
Cream Cheese Eggs, '99 118
Cream Cheese Frills, '79 291
Cream Cheese Ladybugs, '05 211
Cream, Molded French, '99 72
Crisp, Apple-Cheese, '92 235
Cupcakes, Chocolate-Cream Cheese, '03 169
Cupcakes, Cream Cheese Party, '82 279
Cupcakes, Lemonade, '04 163
Cupcake Surprises, '01 299
Custard, Goat Cheese, '96 285
Date-Cream Cheese Rollups, '83 298
Date Dessert Cheese, Nutty, '87 299
Dip, Citrus-Cream Cheese, '03 93
Dip, Orange-Flavored Cream Cheese, '03 93
Dip, Orange Marmalade-Cream Cheese, '03 93
Dip, Strawberries with Fluffy Cream Cheese, '03 93
Éclairs, Mini Tiramisù, '03 M41
Filling, Cream Cheese, '04 273
Filling, Mascarpone, '02 146
Flan, Cream Cheese, '03 328
Frosting, Cherry-Nut Cream Cheese, '96 249
Frosting, Chocolate-Cream Cheese, '02 256
Frosting, Cinnamon-Cream Cheese, '03 332
Frosting, Citrus Cream Cheese, '99 223
Frosting, Coconut Cream Cheese, '86 60
Frosting, Coconut-Cream Cheese, '04 137; '05 317
Frosting, Cream Cheese, '79 45; '80 140, 253, 299;
     '82 135, 244; '83 105, 215, M233; '84 201, 255,
     315, 316; '85 118, 121; '86 217, 337; '87 58;
     '90 305, 308; '92 120; '93 20; '94 254; '95 139;
     '96 282; '97 230, 277, 330; '98 275; '99 307, 315;
     '01 34, 185, 244, 271; '02 83, 209, 323; '03 55,
     315; '05 232, 287, 299
Frosting, Cream Cheese-Butter Pecan, '03 288
Frosting, Deluxe Cream Cheese, '80 120
Frosting, Fluffy Cream Cheese, '80 245
Frosting, Lemon-Cream Cheese, '81 157
Frosting, Nutty Cream Cheese, '85 117; '96 263
Frosting, Orange Cream, '82 14
Frosting, Orange-Cream Cheese, '81 70; '82 16;
     '92 19; '04 258
Frosting, Pecan-Cream Cheese, '02 294
Frosting, Peppermint Cream Cheese, '98 308

Frosting, Pineapple-Cream Cheese, '95 160
Frosting, White Chocolate-Cream Cheese, '94 58;
     '98 323
Frosting, White Chocolate-Cream Cheese Tiered
     Cake, '94 125
Fruit, Cheese, and Nuts, '93 324
Fruited Cream Cheese, '85 306
Fruit with Cheese, Luscious Fresh, '79 153
Fudge, Cream Cheese, '84 111
Ginger Cheese, '92 163
Glaze, Cream Cheese, '84 150; '94 242
Icing, Chunky Cherry, '03 94
Jamwiches, Sweetheart, '03 M41
Kuchen, Cheese, '86 84
Lemon-Cream Cheese Dessert, '84 95
Loaves, Chocolate Chip Cheese, '91 299;
     '92 264
Mints, Butter, '03 300
Mints, Cream Cheese, '93 79; '00 41
Molds, Heavenly Dessert Cheese, '85 209
Noodle Casserole, Sweet, '02 238
Pastries, Apricot-Cream Cheese, '03 245
Pastries, Cream Cheese, '80 250
Pastries, German, '86 78
Pastry, Apple Tart with Cheese, '88 225
Pastry, Cheddar, '86 206
Pastry, Cheddar Cheese, '80 219; '82 194
Pastry, Cream Cheese, '86 78; '89 136; '96 228, 264
Pastry Mini Shells, Cream Cheese, '99 180
Pastry Shell, Cheese, '85 284
Pastry Shells, Cream Cheese, '86 13
Patty Shells, Cream Cheese, '81 266
Pear-Blue Cheese Gratin, '93 328
Pears Blue, '99 246
Pie, Apple-Cheese, '85 284
Pie, Apple-Cream Cheese, '81 247
Pie, Black-and-White Fudge, '99 249
Pie, Blueberry-Cream Cheese, '88 154
Pie, Cheddar-Pear, '02 197
Pie, Chocolate-Cream Cheese, '80 69
Pie, Chocolate Cream Cheese, '92 240
Pie, Coconut Cream, '02 92; '03 106
Pie, Cottage Cheese, '82 85
Pie, Fruited Cheese, '92 228
Pie, Lemon-Blueberry Cream, '02 92
Pie, Lemon Cream, '81 136; '82 146
Pie, Lemon-Cottage Cheese, '79 44
Pie, Lemon Cottage Cheese, '81 143
Pie, Mascarpone Pecan, '05 299
Pie, Mystery Pecan, '02 249
Pie, Tiramisù Toffee Trifle, '04 195
Pie with Berry Glaze, Mascarpone Cream, '00 312
Pie, Yogurt-Cheese, '82 121
Pizza Dolce (Italian Sweet Pies), '00 283
Quad, Chocolate, '02 272
Quesadillas, Apple, '99 248
Quesadillas, Apple Pie 'n' Cheddar, '03 61
Quesadillas, Dessert, '02 54
Soufflé, Blintz, '88 155
Soufflé, Cream Cheese, '88 11
Spread, Chocolate Cheese, '87 292
Spread, Orange Cheese, '87 292
Squares, Lemony Cream Cheese, '82 159
Strawberry Cheese Delight, '79 50
Strawberry-Cream Cheese Dessert, '83 123
Strudel, Fig, '98 253
Sundaes, Cream Cheese Brownie, '03 223
Tart, Apple-Cream Cheese, '96 228
Tart, Cream Cheese-Peach, '99 169
Tart, Pine Nut, '97 86
Tarts, Cranberry-Cream Cheese, '80 154
Tarts, Cream Cheese, '84 74; '90 312
Tarts, Lemon-Cheese, '79 2
Tart, Strawberry-Mascarpone, '02 146

Tiramisù, '91 21; '94 295; '98 280; '00 288; '02 285
Tiramisù, Easy, '00 167
Torte, Chocolate-Vanilla Holiday, '01 252
Trifle, Brownie, '03 85
Truffles, Raspberry-Fudge, '00 M41
Devonshire Cream, Mock, '99 275
Dogs, Taco, '02 M57
Dressing, Blue Cheese, '79 69; '82 166; '86 233;
   '90 286; '97 98; '98 248; '99 244; '00 217
Dressing, Blue Cheese-Buttermilk, '01 112
Dressing, Blue Cheese Salad, '82 94
Dressing, Cheese Fluff, '91 256
Dressing, Cheesy Barbecue Salad, '92 255
Dressing, Creamy, '95 66
Dressing, Creamy Blue Cheese, '81 150; '91 307
Dressing, Creamy Blue Cheese Salad, '86 123
Dressing, Creamy Roquefort, '84 12
Dressing, Garden Salad with Tomato-Cream Cheese,
   '79 173
Dressing, Low-Fat Blue Cheese, '00 337
Dressing, Oregano-Feta, '01 57
Dressing, Parmesan, '86 192; '97 326; '01 96, 101
Dressing, Romano, '80 174
Dressing, Roquefort, '79 85; '80 74; '93 128
Dressing, Special Blue Cheese, '80 74
Dressing, Spinach Salad with Zesty Blue Cheese,
   '02 121
Dressing, Tangy Blue Cheese, '87 81
Dressing, Thick Roquefort Cheese, '97 63
Dressing, Zesty Blue Cheese, '79 104
Dumplings, Chicken Ragoût with Cheddar, '94 44
Dumplings, Goat Cheese, '99 70
Egg Medley, Cheddary, '81 M176
Eggs and Cheese, '95 165
Eggs Benedict, Southwest, '03 53
Eggs, Black-and-Blue, '96 90
Eggs, Blue Cheese Stuffed, '93 87
Eggs, Cheddar, '94 M141
Eggs, Cheese-Chive Scrambled, '95 34
Eggs, Chile-Cheese Deviled, '93 87
Eggs, Cottage, '85 44
Eggs, Cottage Cheese Scrambled, '81 142
Eggs, Cottage-Scrambled, '80 49
Eggs, Cream Cheese Scrambled, '81 287; '05 26
Eggs, Marbleized Garlic-Cheese-Stuffed, '96 91
Empanadas, Easy Turkey, '96 63
Enchiladas, Cheese, '81 194; '85 154; '95 311
Enchiladas, Cheesy Sour Cream, '79 25
Enchiladas, Enticing, '99 57
Enchiladas, Healthy Chicken, '02 19
Enchiladas, Meatless, '93 106
Enchiladas, Saucy Cheese, '84 220
Enchiladas, Vegetable-Cheese, '94 42
Fajitas, Chicken, '99 158
Fettuccine, Broccoli-Parmesan, '93 55
Fettuccine, Crab, '98 142
Fettuccine, Creamy, '96 136
Fig Flowers, '96 195
Fillets, Blue Cheese-Walnut Stuffed, '95 327
Fillets, Parmesan, '86 M112
Fillings
   Blintz Filling, '92 84
   Cheese Filling, '89 91
   Chocolate-Cheese Filling, '90 47
   Cinnamon-Cheese Filling, '90 46
   Cream Cheese Filling, '90 170; '97 287; '05 251
   Four Cheese Filling, '97 171
   Lemon-Cheese Filling, '79 68; '88 7
   Orange-Cheese Filling, '90 47
   Orange Filling, Cheese-and-, '93 159
   Ricotta Filling, '80 58
   Spinach and Feta Filling, '97 171
   Spinach-Ricotta Filling, '81 53
Firecrackers, Roquefort, '97 19

Flank Steak, Cheese-Stuffed, '98 182
Flautas, Rancho Ramillete, '96 M125
Flounder au Fromage, Baked, '86 234
Flounder, Cheesy Broiled, '84 69
Fondue, Beer-and-Cheddar, '03 223
Fondue, Nacho, '94 332
Fondue, Pub, '94 332
Fondue, Warm Goat Cheese, '96 234
Fowl, Fancy, '81 76
French Toast, Ham-and-Cheese Oven, '97 172
French Toast, Stuffed, '00 193
Fried Brie, Walnut-, '86 244
Fries, Parmesan Oven, '98 235
Frittata, Bacon-and-Asparagus, '98 136
Frittata, Broccoli-Cheese, '81 243
Frittata, Potato-Bacon, '98 330
Fritters, Cauliflower-Cheddar, '98 25
Fritters, Cheese-Stuffed Potato, '96 153
Fritters, Cheesy Zucchini, '88 44
Frosting. See CHEESE/Desserts.
Gnocchi à la Narciso, '97 246
Gnocchi with Olive Oil, Tomato, and Parmesan, '04 47
Goat Cheese and Greens, '90 54
Gratin with Lima Beans and Egg, New Potato, '01 71
Grits and Cheese, '00 327
Grits, Baked Cheese, '94 240
Grits, Cheddar Cheese, '05 43
Grits, Cheese, '90 102
Grits, Creamy, '96 24
Grits, Garlic, '03 211
Grits, Garlic-and-Herb Cheese, '95 122
Grits, Garlic-Cheese, '88 126; '89 47; '97 58; '99 270
Grits, Good Morning, '87 156
Grits, Grillades and Baked Cheese, '94 240
Grits, Gruyère Cheese, '81 47
Grits, Hot Tomato, '01 131
Grits, Jalapeño Cheese, '85 43
Grits, Margaret's Creamy, '99 18; '00 21
Grits, Parmesan Cheese, '02 233
Grits, Quick Cheese, '83 M203; '96 97
Grits, Quick Double-Cheese, '03 167
Grits, Saga Blue-Chile, '98 202
Grits, Sausage-Cheese, '90 238
Grits, Sliced Cheese, '84 75
Grits, Smoked Gouda, '02 319; '04 173
Grits Squares, Chili-Cheese, '01 86
Grits, Tomato, '03 199
Grits with Black Bean Salsa, Sautéed Smoked Gouda
   Cheese, '03 323
Grits with Green Chiles, Cheese, '95 208
Grouper, Heavenly Broiled, '99 91
Ham-and-Cheese Bundles, '93 63
Ham-and-Cheese Flips, '92 46
Ham and Eggs Mornay, '02 130
Ham and Eggs on Toast with Cheese Sauce, '81 43
Ham-Cheese Chips, '82 34
Ham Dinner, Cheesy, '84 90
Ham, Frosted, '89 71
Ham Towers, Cheesy, '82 M77
Herb Cheese and Asparagus Bundles, Grilled Chile-
   Rubbed Rib Eyes with, '03 326
Hominy, Hot Cheese, '84 77
Hot Dog Deluxe, '97 140
Huevos con Queso, '00 123
Hush Puppies, Cheesy Mexican, '91 201
Kebabs, Swiss-Ham, '81 124
Kielbasa with Beans, Easy Cheesy, '01 28
Lamb Meat Loaf with Feta Cheese, '97 24
Little Bits, '79 196
Loaf, Cheese, '87 92
Loaf, Cheeseburger, '81 236, 276
Loaf, Pepperoni and Cheese, '82 32
Loaves, Sausage-Cheese, '88 235
Mac and Cheese, Creamy, '05 208

Mac and Cheese, Hearty, '05 208
Mac and Cheese, Taco Dinner, '05 208
Macaroni and Cheese, Chicken, '02 63
Macaroni, Cheeseburger, '02 119
Marinated Cheese, '90 244
Mayonnaise, Parmesan, '86 79
Meatballs, Golden Nugget, '82 233
Meatballs, Mock, '81 243
Meat Loaf, Cheeseburger, '03 204
Meat Loaf, Gonzales, '04 206
Meat Loaf, Mozzarella-Layered, '79 71
Meat Loaf Roll, Blue Cheese, '93 247
Monster Eyes, '02 222
Nachos, Southwestern, '96 170
Nachos, Tuna, '96 201
Noodles and Mushrooms, Cheesy, '79 84
Noodles, Blue Cheese, '98 290
Noodles, Cheesy Parmesan, '83 M7
Noodles, Ham and Swiss on, '87 108
Noodles, Parmesan, '83 118
Omelet, Cheddar-Vegetable, '83 205
Omelet, Cheesy Picante, '86 95
Omelet, Cheesy Vegetable, '85 49
Omelet, Dill-Cheese-Ham, '95 33
Omelet, Farmer's Oven-Baked, '03 204
Omelet, Golden Cheese-Shiitake, '95 265
Omelet, Ham and Cheese, '79 262; '80 123
Omelet, Ham-and-Cheese, '02 246
Omelet, Herbed Cheese, '93 47
Omelet, Open-Faced Bacon-and-Potato, '02 246
Omelet, Puffed Cheese, '89 227
Omelets, George's, '80 68
Omelet, Shrimp-and-Cheddar, '84 57
Omelet, Shrimp-and-Cheese, '94 31
Omelet, Spinach, Cheddar, and Bacon, '03 204
Omelet, Spinach-Cheese, '83 119
Omelet, Swiss Oven, '80 189
Omelet, Zippy Cheese, '87 287
Orange Cream Cheese, '91 177
Pancakes, Cottage Cheese, '79 115
Pancakes, Cream Cheese, '97 70
Pancakes, Featherweight, '99 43
Pancakes with Goat Cheese, Sweet Potato, '96 271
Parmesan Crisps, '01 197; '03 142
Parmesan Toasts, '96 66
Pasta and Lentils, Cheesy, '99 287
Pasta, Basil-Cheese, '96 136
Pasta, Easy Taco, '03 124
Pasta, Garlic Shrimp-and-Goat Cheese, '00 174
Pasta, Mamma Mia, '95 25
Pasta, One-Pot, '05 202
Pasta Primavera, Peppery, '02 161
Pasta Stuffed with Five Cheeses, '88 197
Pasta with Parmesan, Creamy, '98 233
Pastries, Greek Spinach-and-Cheese, '96 76
Pastry, Cheese, '88 56
Pastry, Cream Cheese, '82 39; '86 78; '89 136
Pastry Shells, Miniature Cream Cheese, '87 190
Pastry Tart Shells, '85 216
Pâté, Cream Cheese, '80 154
Pâté, Liver-Cheese, '85 276
Patty Shells, Cream Cheese, '81 266; '82 249
Pears, Cheese-Filled, '81 268
Pears Stuffed with Cheese, '82 290
Penne with Spinach and Feta, '03 170; '04 328
Peppers, Macaroni-and-Cheese-Stuffed, '80 65
Peppers with Chicken and Corn, Stuffed, '02 147
Perch, Parmesan-Crusted, '93 91
Pesto, Basil, '03 208
Pesto, Garden, '04 186
Pesto, Homemade, '01 22
Pesto, Ruth's, '96 170
Pie, Breakfast, '86 242
Pie, Broccoli-Cheese, '84 235

Pie, Cheese-Beef, '85 33
Pie, Cheesy Mexican Chicken, '82 142
Pie, Green Chile-Cheese, '84 234
Pie, Ham-and-Cheese, '95 256; '96 75
Pie, Italian Meat, '01 297
Pie, Jack-O'-Lantern Cheeseburger, '00 234
Pie, Mexican Cheese, '82 9; '83 69
Pie, Mincemeat-Cheese, '80 253
Pie, Onion-Cheese, '88 86
Pie, Quick and Cheesy Corn, '82 191
Pie, Savory Summer, '03 182
Pie, Tortilla, '85 M211
Pie, Tumbleweed, '98 205
Pie, Turkey-Cheese, '88 264
Pie, Zucchini-Ham-Cheese, '80 272
Pigs in a Blanket, Mexican, '00 199
Pineapple Gratin, '93 328
Pinwheels, Pepperoni, '96 247
Pizza, Breakfast, '88 288; '97 172
Pizza, Broccoli Supreme, '02 312
Pizza, Cheese-and-Mushroom, '83 226
Pizza, Cheeseburger, '97 318
Pizza, Cheesy Mexican, '00 314
Pizza, Chicken Parmesan, '00 134
Pizza, Double Cheesy Beef-and-Sausage, '86 77
Pizza, Fresh Mozzarella and Basil, '04 58
Pizza, Greek Eggplant, Tomato, and Feta, '01 312
Pizza, Gruyère-Chicken, '87 182
Pizza, Maca-, '99 195
Pizza, Nutty Pesto, '97 267
Pizza, Peppers-and-Cheese, '03 235
Pizza Pie, Meaty, '03 145
Pizza, Portobello, '03 175
Pizza, Portobello-Pine Nut, '99 216
Pizza, Quick 3-Cheese, '00 94
Pizza, Reuben, '03 69
Pizzas, Chicken-and-Three-Cheese French Bread,
    '96 94
Pizza, Seafood Alfredo, '03 236
Pizzas, Eggplant, '98 183
Pizzas, Five-Ring, '96 180
Pizza, Southwestern, '03 146
Pizza Squares, Easy, '02 61
Poblanos with Mango Salsa, Crab-and-Goat Cheese,
    '04 59
Polenta and Green Chiles, Stuffed Red Peppers with
    Cheesy, '04 169
Polenta Squares, Skillet, '94 22
Polenta Triangles, '98 181
Polenta with Cheese and Okra, Baked, '99 232
Popcorn, Bacon-Cheese, '86 74
Popcorn, Basil, Garlic, and Parmesan, '00 223
Popcorn, Cheese, '98 205
Popcorn, Cheesy Barbecue, '95 239
Popcorn, Chili, '00 M223
Popcorn, Sesame-Cheese, '79 220
Pork Chops, Cheese-Stuffed, '84 81
Pork Chops, Garlic-Parmesan, '02 61
Pork Chops Italian, '98 334
Pork Chops, Stuffed, '02 204
Pork Chops with Apples, Parmesan, '93 338
Pork Chops with Ripieno, '97 245
Pork Scaloppine, '04 221
Pork Tenderloin, Southern-Style Stuffed, '99 45
Pork Tenderloin with Blue Cheese, '86 76
Potatoes with Ham, Scalloped, '02 42
Pot Pie, Ham-Broccoli, '03 83
Preserves, Cream Cheese and Peach, '84 264
Pudding, Baked Cheese, '86 78
Pudding, Cheesy Bread, '83 68

Pudding, Corn-Cheese, '80 244
Puff, Egg-and-Cheese, '85 45
Puff, Macaroni and Cheese, '79 5
Puffs, Bavarian Cheese, '80 191
Puffs, Turkey-Cheese, '87 301
Quesadillas, Breakfast Sausage, '04 183
Quesadillas, Easy, '98 M205
Quesadillas, Greek, '03 61
Quesadillas, Quick, '89 87
Quesadillas, Sausage, '90 118
Quesadillas, Western, '97 65
Quesadillas with Chipotle Salsa, Chicken-and-Brie,
    '99 311
Quesadillas with Shrimp and Brie, '94 173
Quiches
    Bacon-Cheese Quiches, Miniature, '83 93
    Benedict Quiche, '80 M107
    Blue Cheese Quiche, '84 52
    Canadian Bacon-and-Brie Quiche, '04 248
    Cheddar-Leek Quiche, '88 198
    Chicken-Olive-Cheddar Quiche, '03 58
    Chiles Rellenos Quiche, '02 321
    Crabmeat-Parmesan Quiche, '03 59
    Cream Cheese Quiche, '96 203
    Eggless Quiche, '87 220
    Green Onion Quiche, Cheesy, '83 194; '84 42
    Ham-and-Cheese Quiches, Individual, '98 24
    Ham-Cheese Quiche, '79 26
    Ham Quiche, Cheesy, '79 127
    Individual Quiches, '98 101
    Jalapeño Quiche, Cheesy, '84 31
    Lorraine, Perfect Quiche, '79 127
    Lorraine, Quiche, '79 40; '80 M108; '99 M218;
        '01 88
    Miniature Cheese Quiches, '80 150
    Mushroom-Spinach-Swiss Quiche, '03 59
    Sausage-Cheddar Quiche, '79 26
    Sausage Quiche, Spicy, '80 M108
    Shrimp-and-Artichoke Quiche, '03 196
    South-of-the-Border Quiche, '93 321
    Spinach Quiche, Cheesy, '81 228
    Spinach Quiches, Triple-Cheese, '00 220
    Squares, Cheesy Hot Quiche, '79 124
    Swiss Alpine Quiche, '90 18
    Swiss-Zucchini Quiche, '82 49
    Tasty Quiche, '82 264
    Tomato Florentine Quiche, '04 332
    Vegetable Quiche, Cheese-, '81 228
    Vegetable Quiche, Light, '97 332
    Veggie Sausage Quiche, Crustless, '03 175
    Zucchini Quiche, Cheesy, '83 312
Ragù with Tortellini, Wild Mushroom, '04 220
Ramekins, Three-Cheese, '79 26
Rarebit, Cheese, '86 78
Rarebit, Tangy Welsh, '88 159
Rarebit, Uptown Welsh, '87 279
Raspberry Brie in Rye, '93 252
Ravioli, Green Bean Alfredo with Cheese, '01 180
Refried Beans, Easy, '99 57
Rice, Chili-Cheesy, '79 43
Risotto, Asparagus, '03 68
Risotto, Crawfish, '99 120
Risotto, Green Bean, '03 68
Risotto, Onion, '03 98
Risotto, Roasted Garlic-and-Cheese, '04 283
Risotto with Parmesan, Broccoli, '99 120
Risotto with Saffron, Pistachio, '98 272
Roll, Cheesy Meat, '82 136
Rolls, Ham-and-Cheese Lettuce, '89 217
Rollups, Pizza, '99 197
Rounds, Parmesan, '79 170
Rounds, Turkey-Mozzarella, '82 3
Salads
    Apple Salad, Cheesy, '86 301

Apple Salad, Swiss-, '84 81
Artichoke-Goat Cheese Salad, '98 118
Asparagus, Roasted-Beet, and Goat Cheese Salad,
    '02 96
Asparagus, Roasted Beet, and Goat Cheese Salad,
    '03 98
Aspic, Blue Cheese, '96 66
Aspic, Cheesy Vegetable, '81 73
Baby Blue Salad, '01 20; '03 178
Baby Lettuces with Vidalia Onion Vinaigrette, Salad
    of, '99 168
Bacon-Lettuce-Mozzarella-and-Tomato Salad,
    '98 209
Baked Goat Cheese Salad, '96 26
Banana Splits, Cottage Cheese-, '87 56
Black Bean-and-Cheese Salad, '92 217
BLT Bread Salad, Italian, '03 90
Blue Cheese Chicken Salad, '94 81
Blue Cheese Salad, '88 48
Blue Cheese Salad with Spicy Pecans, '02 300
Blue Cheese Tossed Salad, '84 195
Bluegrass Salad, '02 255
Bread Salad, Italian, '03 54
Broccoli-Cheese-Pasta Salad, '96 184
Cantaloupe-Cheese Salad, '88 184
Cauliflower with Parmesan and Bacon,
    '96 137
Chicken Salad, Greek, '98 329
Chicken Salad, Parmesan-, '98 234
Chicken Salad with Blue Cheese, '97 97
Citrus-Blue Cheese Salad, '92 220
Coleslaw, Blue Cheese, '89 13; '95 270
Coleslaw, Cottage, '80 64
Cottage Cheese Salad, Different, '85 328; '86 22
Cottage Cheese Salad, Out-of-This-World, '79 44
Couscous Salad with Fennel and Goat Cheese,
    Israeli, '00 312
Cranberry-Cheese Ribbon Salad, '79 241
Cranberry Congealed Salad Parfaits, Frosted, '02 292
Crunchy-Creamy Salad, '88 100
Freeze Salad, Party, '82 145
Fruit-'n'-Nut Salad, Cheesy, '87 56
Fruit Salad, Cottage Cheese-and-, '86 16
Garden Salad, Italian, '99 203
Goat Cheese and Black-Eyed Pea Salad, Fearrington
    House, '95 60
Green Bean Salad with Feta, '04 169
Green Beans-and-Cheese Salad, '91 159
Green Bean, Walnut, and Feta Salad, '96 273;
    '00 321
Greens with Parmesan Walnuts, Mixed, '95 301
Ham-and-Cheese Salad, '88 138
Ham-Pecan-Blue Cheese Pasta Salad, '90 62
Harvest Salad with Cider Vinaigrette, '99 322
Iceberg Wedges, Blue Cheese, '05 160
Italian House Salad, '02 300
Layered Salad, Cheesy, '81 37
Layered Salad, Old-Fashioned, '01 96
Leaf Lettuce Salad with Sweet-and-Sour Dressing,
    Red, '03 28
Lemon-Cheese Salad, '85 240
Lettuce, Cheesy Stuffed, '79 175
Lettuce Salad, Blue Cheese-Stuffed, '94 202
Lime-Cheese Salad, Frosted, '79 286
Macaroni and Cheese Salad, '97 203
Macaroni-Cheese Salad, Dilled, '86 208
Marinated Tomato and Brie Salad, '95 95
Mexican Salad, '81 36
Mold, Ambrosia Cream Cheese, '79 249
Mold, Cheesy Lemon, '79 241
Mold, Creamy Tuna-Cheese, '81 135
Molds, Snowcap Cheese, '79 242
Mozzarella, Avocado, and Tomato Salad, '05 41
Mozzarella-Tomato Basil Salad, Fresh, '02 110

Mushroom Salad, Quick Cheesy-, '89 128
Orange-Cottage Cheese Salad, '79 44
Pasta Salad, Greek, '02 139
Pasta Salad, Smoked Mozzarella, '03 126
Pear-Apple Salad, Blue Cheese-, '81 224
Pear-Swiss Cheese Salad, '91 237
Pea Salad, '98 274
Pea Salad, Cheddar-, '84 82
Pepper Toss, Parmesan, '93 208
"Pig in the Garden" Salad, '92 255
Pine Nut, Rice, and Feta Salad, '96 26; '98 331
Potato Cobb Salad, '03 140
Potato Salad, Blue Cheese-, '91 208
Potato Salad, Cottage Cheese-, '79 147, 285
Potato Salad, Hot Parmesan, '79 78
Potato Salad, Warm Goat Cheese and, '96 234
Ribbon Salad, Christmas, '02 257
Romaine Salad with Raspberry Dressing, '03 28
Roquefort Salad, Creamy, '79 73
Slaw, Blue Cheese-Bacon, '05 91
Spinach-Blue Cheese Salad, '82 166
Spinach Salad with the Blues, '95 66
Suzie or Steven Salad, '98 204
Tomato-Basil-Mozzarella Salad, '95 171
Tomato-Basil Salad, Fresh Mozzarella-, '93 131
Tomatoes, Cottage Cheese Salad in, '86 208
Tomato-Feta Salad, '81 246; '91 168
Tomato-Gruyère-Basil Salad, '99 172
Tomato-Mozzarella Salad, '89 220
Tomato Salad, Cottage-, '85 163
Tortellini Pasta Salad, Cheese, '02 139
Tuna Salad, Cheese-Sauced, '87 M124
Tuna Salad, Swiss, '86 186
Vegetable Congealed Salad, Cheesy-, '86 199
Vinaigrette with Greens, '98 184
Walnut Salad, Gorgonzola-, '96 170
Warm Cheese Salad, '97 246
Warm Goat Cheese Salad, '01 179
Watercress-Orange Salad with Blue Cheese, '04 45
Watercress Salad, '97 249
Ziti-Cheddar Salad, '85 165
Salmon Patties, Cheesy, '89 99
Salsa, Avocado-Feta, '96 15
Salsa, Fiery Steak with Pimiento Cheese, '99 331
Sandwiches
Avocado, Bacon, and Cheese Sandwiches, '87 279
Bacon, Cheese, and Tomato Sandwiches, '84 14
Bacon-Cheese Sandwiches, Grilled, '83 242
Bacon, Pimiento, and Cheese Hoagies, '90 144
Bacon Sandwiches, Open-Faced Cheesy, '80 78
Bagel Sandwiches, Mozzarella-Pepper, '98 145
Bat Sandwiches, '00 234
Beef and Cheese Roll-Ups, Savory, '96 235
Beef, Bacon, and Blue Cheese Sandwiches, '96 23
Black Bean Wraps, '00 211
BLT's, Cheesy, '85 92
Breakfast Sandwiches, '80 52
Breakfast Sandwiches, Cheesy, '90 140
Brown Bread-Cream Cheese Sandwiches, '87 M6
Buns, Snack, '87 279
Burgers, Chicken-Cheese, '04 56
Calzones, Ground Beef, '97 95
Calzones with Italian Tomato Sauce, '03 202
Calzones with Pasta Sauce, '01 54
Checkerboard Cheese Sandwiches, '05 18
Cheesesteaks, Chimichurri, '04 312
Chicken-and-Cheese Sandwiches, Toasted, '85 242
Chicken 'n' Cheese Sandwiches, Grilled, '99 240
Chicken Parmigiana Sandwich, '94 65
Chicken Salad Melts, Open-Faced Cheesy, '00 134
Chicken Sandwiches, Cheesy, '82 190
Chicken Sandwiches, Gouda Lover's, '99 195
Christmas Tree Sandwiches, '92 279
Corned Beef and Cheese Sandwich, '79 214

Crab-and-Cheese Sandwiches, Hot, '87 279
Eggplant Parmesan Sandwiches, '03 213
Eggplant Sandwiches, '99 240
Eggplant, Tomato, and Feta Sandwiches, '98 106
Egg Sandwiches, Open-Faced Cheesy, '86 67
Feta Salad Sandwich, Tuscan, '99 289
Focaccia Sandwiches, '98 53
Fruit-and-Cheese Breakfast Sandwiches, '89 M21
Gingered Tea Sandwiches, '84 116
Good-Start Sandwiches, '99 134
Grilled Bacon, Cheese, and Tomato Sandwiches, '97 170
Grilled Cheese, '97 328
Grilled Cheese-and-Ham Sandwiches, '05 293
Grilled Cheese Meat Loaf Sandwiches, '04 188
Grilled Cheese Sandwiches, '82 M172; '94 167
Grilled Cheese Sandwiches with Tomato, Avocado, and Bacon, '05 213
Grilled Cheese Sandwich, Mexican, '92 63
Grilled Cheeses, Mexican, '97 170
Grilled Chili con Queso Sandwiches, '96 139
Grilled Four-Cheese Sandwich with Tomato, Avocado, and Bacon, '00 199
Grilled Roast Beef-and-Brie Sandwiches, '03 296
Grilled Sandwiches, Tasty, '84 30
Grilled Spinach Fondue Sandwiches, '99 337
Grills, Double Cheese, '97 170
Grills, Triple Cheese, '97 170
Ham-and-Cheese Pita Pockets, '90 271
Ham-and-Cheese Pita Sandwiches, '87 202; '88 44
Ham-and-Cheese Sandwiches, '01 299
Ham-and-Cheese Sandwiches, Hot, '85 299
Ham-and-Cheese Sandwiches, Tiny, '99 87
Ham-and-Cheese Sandwich Round, '94 326
Ham-and-Cheese Sandwich, Tex-Mex, '86 4
Ham and Swiss in the Pocket, '83 31
Ham-and-Swiss Sandwiches, '98 287
Ham-and-Swiss Sandwiches, Tangy, '85 164
Ham-and-Turkey Specials, Cheesy, '84 14
Ham 'n' Cheese Chicken Sandwich, '95 153
Ham Sandwiches, Creamy Blue Cheese-, '87 279
Ham-Swiss-and-Asparagus Sandwiches, '01 52
Herbed Cheese Sandwiches with Artichoke-Tomato Salsa, '96 182
Hot Browns, '98 287
Hot Browns, Baby, '00 107
Hot Browns, Biscuit, '02 94
Hot Browns, Kentucky, '02 94
Hot Browns, Southwestern, '02 94
Hot Browns with Fried Cheese Grits, '02 94
Hot Cheddar Cheese Sandwiches, '97 179
Hot French Cheese Sandwiches, '82 3
Lasagna in a Bun, '90 176
Leafy Cheese Sandwiches, '90 56
Meatball Sandwiches, '04 170
Melts, Bacon-and-Cheese, '04 324
Monte Cristo Sandwiches, '97 319
Monte Cristo Sandwiches, Open-Faced, '01 171
Muffin, Stuffin', '99 193
Muffuletta Loaf, '97 86
Muffulettas, '98 184
"Muffy" Sandwich, Fertitta's, '94 34
Open-Faced Mexican Sandwiches, '98 230
Open-Faced Sandwiches, Super, '97 52
Parmesan-Turkey-Ranch Rollups, '01 177
Party Sandwiches, Duck, '02 48
Party Sandwiches, Easter Bunny, '02 48
Party Sandwiches, Easter Egg, '02 48
Party Sandwiches, Flower, '02 48
Peanut-Cheese-Raisin Sandwiches, '88 140
Philly Firecrackers, '01 142
Pimiento Cheese Finger Sandwiches, '99 86
Pimiento Cheese Sandwiches, '82 278
Pita, Stuffed, '89 87

Pockets, Toasted Cream Cheese-and-Apple, '01 200
Quesadillas, Quick Fiesta, '02 246
Reuben Melts, Southern, '03 69
Reubens, Open-Faced Coleslaw, '03 169
Roast Beef Slices, '02 246
Rollup, Hot Ham-and-Cheese, '01 217
Sausage-Cheese Muffin Sandwiches, '92 M212
Sebastian, The, '94 184
Shrimp-Cheese Sandwiches, '85 242
Smoked Turkey, Mozzarella, and Blackberry Sandwiches, '99 220
Steak Wraps, Cheese-, '00 M335
Stuffed Sandwich, Deli, '98 287
Sub, Chicken, '98 287
Tea Sandwiches, Cheese, '92 276
Tomato-Cheese-Bacon Melts, '99 72
Tomato, Swiss, and Bacon Sandwiches, '04 140
Tortilla Stack-Ups, '92 196
Tuna Cheesies, '82 191
Tuna Melt, Southwestern, '96 201
Turkey-Cheese Dogs, '97 203
Turkey Schoolwich Sandwiches, '00 198
Welsh Rarebit, '00 239
Wrapidos, Tacos, '03 172
Wraps, Western, '99 194
Yummy Sandwiches, '81 229
Sauces
Blue Cheese Sauce, '90 142; '94 320
Blue Cheese Sauce, Fettuccine with, '98 247
Cheddar Cheese Cream Sauce, '05 277
Cheddar Cheese Sauce, '91 286
Cheese Sauce, '79 M156; '81 43, 44, 225; '82 M123; '83 49, 138, 188; '84 57; '85 92; '86 241; '88 78, 272; '89 181, 229; '90 235; '93 48; '02 94; '04 281; '05 333
Cider Sauce, Cheddar-, '98 242
Cilantro Dipping Sauce, Creamy, '03 327
Cottage Cheese Sauce, '87 232
Cream Sauce, Cheesy, '82 79
Devonshire Sauce, Processor, '86 337
Dipping Sauce, Olive Oil-Balsamic, '04 46
Easy Cheese Sauce, '79 22
Garlic-Cheese Sauce, '84 M70
Guilt-Free Cheese Sauce, '93 M95
Lemon-Cheese Sauce, '91 24
Lemony Cheese Sauce, '84 183
Monterey Jack Sauce, '84 293
Mornay Sauce, '80 120; '81 90; '89 195
Mushroom-Cheese Sauce, '83 190; '86 48
Parmesan Cheese Sauce, '79 165; '80 162; '85 143
Parmesan Sauce, '92 17
Parmesan-Sour Cream Sauce, Baked Fish with, '01 209
Pesto Sauce, Walnut-Parmesan, '97 104
Pimiento Cheese Sauce, '02 291; '05 333
Rich Cheese Sauce, '81 89
Roquefort Sauce, '89 321
Seafood Cheese Sauce, '89 240
Swiss Cheese Cream Sauce, '05 277
Swiss Cheese Sauce, '79 35; '87 289; '88 135; '03 52
Swiss Sauce, '83 M195
Swiss Sauce, Creamy, '80 M53
Topper, Vegetable-Cheese Potato, '86 6
Vegetable-Cheese Sauce, '85 M152
Vegetable Sauce, Cheesy, '92 M134
Walnut-Parmesan Pesto Sauce, '96 251
Wine-Cheese Sauce, '00 310
Sausage, Grilled Pork, Cheddar, and Jalapeño, '98 311
Scallops, Baked Gruyère, '92 57
Scallops, Chip and Cheese, '80 301
Scallops Mornay, '80 164
Schnitzel, Swiss, '80 189
Shake, Strawberry-Cheesecake, '92 44

CHEESE
(continued)

Shell, Rice-Cheese, '82 49
Shells, Cheesy Beef-Stuffed, '83 217
Shells, Cream Cheese, '79 2
Shortcakes, Cheesy Chicken, '95 98
Shrimp and Grits, Garlic, '03 246
Shrimp and Pasta with Two Cheeses, '98 49
Shrimp au Gratin, '85 79
Shrimp Palermo, '04 241
Shrimp, Parmesan-Stuffed, '85 103
Shrimp Tartlets, '00 71
Shrimp with Feta Cheese, '00 221
Sirloin with Cherry-Merlot Sauce and Gorgonzola,
   Peppered, '02 320
Smoked Cheddar, Easy, '01 168
Souffleeta, '05 326
Soufflés. *See also* **CHEESE/Desserts.**
   Blue Cheese Soufflé, '91 244
   Cheddar Cheese Soufflé, '98 24
   Cheese Soufflé, '79 72, 261; '94 116
   Chile-Cheese Soufflés, '96 219
   Corn-and-Cheese Soufflé, '88 122
   Cups, Hot Soufflé, '85 284
   Egg Cheese Soufflé, Three-, '87 234
   Grits Soufflé, Garlic-Cheese, '99 18
   Individual Frozen Soufflés, '80 52
   Individual Soufflés, '80 190
   Italian Pizzaola Soufflé, '98 232
   Mexican Pizzaola Soufflé, '98 232
   Parmesan Soufflés, '97 280
   Rice-Cheese Soufflé, '79 270
   Rolled Cheese Soufflé, '89 13
   Spinach Soufflé, Cheese-and-, '98 235
   Spinach Soufflé, Cheesy, '81 53
   Three-Cheese Soufflés, '96 219
   Two, Cheese Soufflé for, '81 226
Soups
   Anytime Soup, Cheesy, '81 307; '82 314; '83 66
   Bacon-Beer Cheese Soup, '87 M7
   Bacon-Topped Cheese Soup, '80 M224
   Beer-Cheese Soup, '84 246
   Bell Pepper-Cheese Chowder, '95 240
   Blue Satin Soup, '98 248
   Broccoli Soup, Cheese-and-, '89 276
   Broccoli Soup, Cheesy-, '86 258
   Broccoli-Swiss Soup, '86 6
   Carrot Soup, Cheesy, '81 262
   Cauliflower Soup, '99 318
   Cheddar Cheese Chowder, '97 30
   Cheddar Chowder, Hearty, '79 16
   Cheddar-Potato Soup, '03 M283
   Chicken Chowder, Cheesy, '92 21
   Chicken-Corn Soup, Cheesy, '97 158
   Chicken Noodle Soup, Creamy, '99 20
   Chicken Soup, Cheesy Mac 'n', '05 292
   Chicken Soup, Fiesta, '04 323
   Chunky Cheese Soup, '98 31
   Cilantro Soup, Cream of, '00 249
   Corn and Cheese Chowder, '80 228
   Cream Cheese Soup, Austrian, '98 M85
   Cream of Cheese Soup, '83 99
   Cream with Greens Soup, '94 277
   Favorite Cheese Soup, Uncle Ed's, '94 228
   Gazebo Cheese Soup, '90 158
   Gazpacho, Shrimp-Cream Cheese, '94 137
   Golden Cheese Chowder, '80 73
   Ham-and-Cheese Chowder, '89 15
   Ham 'n Cheese Chowder, '79 199
   Hearty Cheese Soup, '84 4
   Herbed Cheese Soup, '96 219
   Hot Brown, Soup, '00 318

Hot Cheese Chowder, '89 16
Macaroni and Cheese Soup, '95 264
Mexican Cheese Soup, '97 268
Minestrone, Cheesy, '99 17
Monterey Jack Cheese Soup, '81 112; '85 M211
Onion-Cheese Soup, '87 81
Onion Soup, Double-Cheese, '85 227
Onion Soup, Double Cheese-Topped, '79 49
Oyster-Cheese Soup, '84 213
Pimiento Cheese Soup, Creamy, '05 254
Pimiento "Mac and Cheese" Soup, '97 M325
Potato-and-Wild Rice Soup, Cheesy, '89 16
Potato Soup, Baked, '03 29
Reuben Soup, Cream of, '97 26
Rice Soup, Wildest, '01 66
Roquefort Vichyssoise, Velvety, '83 223
Shrimp-Cheese Soup, '01 145
Swiss-Broccoli Chowder, '80 73
Tomato Soup with Parmesan Cheese, Cream of,
   '86 161
Tortilla Soup, '99 310
Vegetable-Cheese Soup, '89 15
Vegetable-Cheese Soup, Creamy, '81 244
Vegetable Cheese Soup, Creamy, '83 230
Vegetable Chowder, Cheese-, '02 305
Vegetable Chowder, Cheesy, '80 25; '83 20; '00 272;
   '01 18
Vegetable Soup, Cheesy, '80 73; '97 241
Velvet Soup, Cheese, '80 74; '92 193
Yukon Gold-Cheese Chowder, '03 296
Zucchini Soup, Cold, '99 164
Spaghetti, Chicken, '98 329
Spaghetti, Marzetti's, '99 85
Spaghetti, Three-Cheese, '83 105
Spanakopita, '86 58; '96 233
Spiders, Dried Apricot, '96 255
Spreads
   Almond Cheese Spread, '87 292
   Aloha Spread, '83 93
   Apricot Brie Spread, '86 275
   Apricot-Cream Cheese Spread, '82 161; '87 158
   Artichoke-Parmesan Spread, '92 95
   Bacon-Cheese Spread, '83 241
   Bacon-Olive Cream Cheese, '04 196
   Basil-Cheese Roulade, '05 143
   Basil-Cheese Spread, Fresh, '97 108
   Beer Cheese Spread, '81 160; '85 69
   Beer Spread, Cheesy, '87 196
   Blue Cheese Spread, '90 215; '95 79, 92; '97 240
   Boursin Cheese Spread, Buttery, '94 301; '96 318
   Boursin Cheese Spread, Garlic, '94 301
   Butter, Blue Cheese, '97 306
   Caviar-Cream Cheese Spread, '84 256
   Cheddar-Swiss Spread, '99 106
   Cheese Spread, '96 122; '99 24
   Chile-Cheese Spread, '86 297
   Chili Cheese Spread, '93 242
   Chili-Cheese Spread, '99 336
   Chocolate Cheese Spread, '87 292
   Chutney-Onion Cheese Spread, '01 94
   Coconut-Cranberry Cheese Spread, '92 328
   Confetti Cheese Spread, '84 256
   Cottage Cheese Spread, '87 107
   Cottage-Egg Salad Spread, '82 146
   Cream Cheese-and-Olive Pimiento Cheese, '01 169;
      '03 315
   Cream Cheese-Olive Spread, '82 35
   Cream Cheese Spread, Deviled, '81 235
   Cream Cheese Spread, Fruited, '91 306; '93 79
   Cream Cheese Spread, Peachy, '90 M215
   Cream Cheese Spread, Pear-, '93 80
   Cucumber and Cream Cheese Spread, '82 140
   Date-Walnut-Cheese Spread, '96 322
   Edam-Sherry Spread, '84 257

Feta-and-Apple Spread, '99 106
Feta Cheese Spread, '96 265
Feta Spread, Herbed, '00 135
Four-Cheese Spread, '99 106
Fruit and Cheese Spread, '81 245
Fruit-and-Cheese Spread, Nutty, '87 246
Garlic-and-Dill Feta Cheese Spread, '04 238
Garlic Pimiento Cheese Spread, '79 58
German Cheese Spread, '79 82
Gouda Cheese Spread, '90 36
Green Onion-Cheese Spread, '92 24
Gruyère-Apple Spread, '81 160
Ham and Pimiento Spread, '80 285
Hawaiian Cheese Spread, '87 158
Herb-Cream Cheese Spread, '83 24
Herbed Avocado-Cheese Spread, '98 335
Herbed Cheese Spread, '87 247
Herbed Goat Cheese, '01 310
Horseradish Spread, '02 53; '03 139
Horseradish Spread, Cheese-, '84 222
Jalapeño-Cheese Spread, '82 248
Jalapeño Pimiento Cheese, '03 315
Make-Ahead Cheese Spread, '93 324
Mexican Cheese Spread, '90 119
Olive Spread, Cheese-, '79 82
Orange Cheese Spread, '87 292
Parmesan-Spinach Spread, '93 55
Party Spread, Spicy, '97 240
Pecan Pimiento Cheese, '03 315
Pesto-Goat Cheese Spread, '03 208
Pimiento and Three Cheeses, '86 296
Pimiento Cheese, '01 169; '03 139, 315; '05 323
Pimiento Cheese, Bacon-, '05 142
Pimiento Cheese, Chile-, '04 325
Pimiento Cheese, Chunky, '86 295; '88 91
Pimiento Cheese, Creamy, '86 296
Pimiento Cheese, Fabulous, '98 315
Pimiento Cheese, Green Chile-, '01 61
Pimiento Cheese, Incredible, '96 22
Pimiento Cheese, Jalapeño, '98 315; '01 169
Pimiento Cheese, Pecan, '01 169
Pimiento Cheese, Peppered, '01 137
Pimiento Cheese Spread, '82 35; '83 93; '86 127;
   '99 106, 276
Pimiento Cheese Spread, Creamy, '92 159
Pimiento Cheese Spread, Low-Calorie, '85 215
Pimiento Cheese-Stuffed Celery, Light, '05 161
Pimiento Cheese, West Texas, '84 9
Pimiento Cheese, White Cheddar, '99 106
Pineapple-Cheese Spread, '86 126; '91 167
Pineapple-Cream Cheese Spread, '82 35
Rosemary Cheese with Fig Preserves, '02 256
Sandwich Spread, Benedictine, '80 299
Swiss Cheese Spread, '90 60
Tomato-Cheddar Spread, '01 321
Tomato-Cheese Spread, '81 157
Tomato-Cheese Spread, Fiery, '87 196
Tropical Cheese Spread, '95 46
Vegetable Sandwich Spread, '83 174
Waldorf Cheese Spread, '88 173
Zesty Cheese Spread, '82 140
Zippy Cheese Spread, '85 4
Steak Cheese Skillet, Swiss, '80 106
Steak Parmesan, '93 41
Steak, Parmesan Round, '80 106
Steaks, Blue Cheese, '84 171
Steaks, Cheese-Stuffed, '81 17
Steaks, Mexican Pepper-Cheese, '97 190
Strata, Artichoke-Cheese, '90 236
Strata, Tomato-Cheese, '81 209
Stromboli, '88 272; '89 181
Strudel, Chicken-Goat Cheese, '98 28
Strudel, Meatless Mexican, '98 29
Strudel, Reuben, '98 28

Stuffing, Catfish with Cream Cheese, '89 52
Supper Supreme, Sunday, '79 76
Sweet Potato Chips with Blue Cheese, '93 290
Tacos, Easy Skillet, '04 180
Taco Stacks, Soft, '02 54
Tart, Dried Tomato-Cheese, '90 203
Tart, Ham-and-Cheese, '92 332
Tart, Herb-Cheese, '87 98
Tart, Leek-Goat Cheese, '04 109
Tart Milan, '87 70
Tart Shells, Cheese, '88 88
Tart, Southwestern, '04 109
Tarts, Sausage 'n' Cheese, '88 51
Tart, Tomato-Basil, '98 132
Tart, Tomato-Pesto, '00 195
Tenderloin, Stuffed Tuscany, '99 269
Terrine, Italian Cheese, '93 64
Terrine with Goat Cheese, Black Bean, '87 120
Terrine with Tomato-Basil Vinaigrette, Blue Cheese,
    '99 288
Tomato, Basil, and Cheese, '95 165
Topping, Blue Cheese Burger, '93 218
Topping, Breadcrumb, '02 233
Topping, Buttery Parmesan, '05 277
Topping, Cheese, '86 233
Topping, Yogurt-Cheese, '88 55
Tortellini, Creamy, '99 171
Tortellini with Rosemary-Parmesan Sauce, '92 284
Tortillas, Cheesy, '81 62
Tortilla Snack, Two-Cheese, '90 119
Tortilla Stack, Cheesy Chicken-, '86 3
Toss, Ham and Cheese, '79 55
Tostadas, Quick Chicken, '99 159
Trout Florentine, Cheesy, '85 53
Turkey Cutlets, Parmesan, '01 81
Turkey Parmesan, '82 268
Turnovers, Sausage-Cheese, '88 231; '89 22
Twists, Cheese, '92 125
Veal Parmigiana, '81 227
Vegetables
    Artichoke-Cheese Bottoms, Baked, '94 61
    Artichokes, Stuffed, '99 64
    Asparagus-and-Mushroom Tostadas with Goat
        Cheese, '03 242
    Asparagus Mornay, '99 102
    Asparagus on Toast, Creamed, '95 61
    Asparagus Pie, Cheesy, '01 103
    Asparagus Squares, '02 183
    Asparagus with Goat Cheese Sauce, '93 116
    Banana Peppers, Stuffed, '02 55
    Broccoli-and-Eggs au Gratin, '85 289
    Broccoli au Gratin, '82 M20
    Broccoli Bakers, '99 308
    Broccoli Cups, '00 53
    Broccoli Fritters, Cheesy, '79 53
    Broccoli Mac 'n' Cheese, '00 53
    Broccoli Parmesan, '97 302
    Broccoli with Cheese Sauce, '82 107
    Brussels Sprouts with Cheese Sauce, '79 246
    Cabbage, Cheese Scalloped, '81 87; '82 7
    Cabbage Rolls, Southwestern, '97 214
    Cauliflower au Gratin, '82 204; '99 59
    Cauliflower au Gratin, French-Fried, '79 221; '80 82
    Cauliflower, Baked Swiss, '79 100
    Cauliflower, Cheddar, '99 318
    Cauliflower, Cheese-Frosted, '85 68
    Cauliflower, Frosted, '97 105
    Cauliflower Italiano, Cheesy, '82 300
    Cauliflower with Cheese Sauce, '81 101
    Celery, Nutty Stuffed, '03 184
    Cherry Tomatoes, Cheesy, '83 135
    Chiles Rellenos, Cheese, '96 24
    Chiles Rellenos (Stuffed Chiles), '82 220; '83 150
    Corn-and-Swiss Cheese Bake, '92 133

Corn, Creamy Fried Confetti, '02 160
Corn, Grilled Parmesan, '82 127
Eggplant, Cheesy Fried, '90 75
Eggplant, Cheesy Stuffed, '79 188; '82 208
Eggplant, Fried Parmesan, '87 166
Eggplant Parmesan, '82 230; '92 18
Eggplant, Parmesan Fried, '79 189
Eggplant Parmesan, No-Fry, '92 172
Eggplant, Scalloped, '91 223
Fries, Cheesy Oven, '91 187
Green Beans au Gratin, '80 116
Green Beans, Cheese-Topped, '79 100
Green Beans, Cheesy, '80 157
Green Beans, Parmesan, '04 327
Green Beans, Tomato-Feta, '99 59
Green Beans with Blue Cheese, '88 57; '05 177
Green Beans with Roquefort Cheese and Walnuts,
    '02 255
Hash Brown Cheese Bake, '82 50
Hash Browns, Smothered-Covered, '02 248
Jalapeño Cheese Pie, '96 292
Jalapeños, Hot Stuffed, '99 123
Lentils with Cheese, Baked, '84 113
Limas in Onion Shells, Cheese and, '81 86
Loaf, Pureed Vegetable-Cheese, '85 297
Mashed Potatoes, Cheesy, '05 204
Mushrooms, Herbed Cheese-Stuffed, '96 171
Mushrooms, Parmesan Stuffed, '83 115
Mushrooms, Ricotta-Stuffed, '85 20
New Potatoes, Cheesy, '85 156
New Potatoes, Cheesy Jalapeño, '01 89
New Potatoes, Crispy Roasted, '98 166
Okra with Cheese, '80 185
Onion Bake, Cheese, '82 32
Onion Bake, Romano, '90 98
Onions, Cheese-Stuffed, '90 34
Onions, Parmesan, '93 170
Onions, Sherried Cheese, '82 32
Parmesan Vegetables, '97 147
Pie, Savory Summer, '99 159
Pie, Summer Garden, '02 182
Potato-and-Blue Cheese Pastries, '03 258
Potato Boats, Southwestern, '96 33
Potato Bowls, Mashed, '97 199
Potato-Broccoli-Cheese Bake, '80 114
Potato-Cheese Puff, '95 269
Potato Croquettes, Baked, '97 30
Potato Croquettes, Parmesan, '84 210
Potatoes, Accordion, '98 69
Potatoes Alfredo, '89 204
Potatoes-and-Zucchini au Gratin, '84 5
Potatoes au Gratin, '93 90, 217
Potatoes, Bacon-Topped Blue Cheese, '79 46
Potatoes, Basil-Cheese, '90 M316
Potatoes, Blue Cheese, '98 247; '04 214
Potatoes, Blue Cheese Mashed, '92 330
Potatoes, Blue Cheese Stuffed, '81 276; '92 M228
Potatoes, Blue Cheese-Stuffed, '89 69
Potatoes, Breakfast-Stuffed, '00 179
Potatoes, Cheddar, Broccoli, and Ham Stuffed, '04 26
Potatoes, Cheesy, '82 211
Potatoes, Cheesy Bacon-Stuffed, '81 61
Potatoes, Cheesy Caraway, '86 17
Potatoes, Cheesy Chive, '79 46
Potatoes, Cheesy Chive-Stuffed, '91 128
Potatoes, Cheesy Crab-Stuffed, '86 17
Potatoes, Cheesy Frank-Topped, '83 3
Potatoes, Cheesy Mashed, '02 98
Potatoes, Cheesy Scalloped, '96 33
Potatoes, Cheesy Stuffed, '02 175
Potatoes, Chicken-Cheese Stuffed, '86 55
Potatoes, Chili-Cheese, '90 M62
Potatoes, Chive-Cream Cheese Mashed, '92 330
Potatoes, Crab-Stuffed, '99 307

Potatoes, Cream Cheese Mashed, '97 14
Potatoes, Creamy Cheese, '88 M146
Potatoes, Creamy Cheese-and-Chive, '99 308
Potatoes, Creamy Chive-and-Gorgonzola Stuffed,
    '99 308
Potatoes, Feta Cheese, '04 214
Potatoes, Feta Mashed, '92 330
Potatoes, Garlic-Gruyère Mashed, '98 322
Potatoes, Golden, '96 139
Potatoes, Harvest Mashed, '98 248
Potatoes, Horseradish Mashed, '98 69
Potatoes, Italian Mashed, '03 M135
Potatoes, Loaded Garlic Smashed, '01 325
Potatoes, Parmesan, '82 270; '90 M62; '92 M341;
    '93 M46
Potatoes, Parmesan-Cream, '97 54
Potatoes, Parmesan-Paprika, '99 169
Potatoes, Roasted Garlic-Parmesan Mashed, '97 263;
    '00 146
Potatoes Roquefort, '79 211
Potatoes, Stuffed, '01 48; '02 283
Potatoes, Stuffed Mashed, '98 328
Potatoes, Two-Cheese, '80 114
Potatoes with Cheese Sauce, Baked, '83 239
Potatoes with Cheese Sauce, Stuffed, '87 192
Potatoes with Feta Cheese, '84 295; '85 196
Potatoes with Sweet Marjoram and Parmesan
    Cheese, Scalloped, '91 246
Potato Fans, Parmesan-, '88 M190
Potato Gratin, Dual, '93 328
Potato Skins, Cheese, '84 M239
Potato Soufflé, Cheesy, '89 332
Potato Wedges, Parmesan, '95 181
Rice au Gratin, '83 129
Rutabaga au Gratin, '79 254
Spinach-Cheese Puff, '84 96
Spinach, Cheesy Topped, '84 85
Spinach, Creamed, '96 252
Spinach, Easy Italian, '02 235
Spinach-Gorgonzola Custards, Savory, '02 284
Spinach Madeleine, '05 95
Spinach Parmesan, '93 72
Spinach Pie Parma, '96 203
Spinach Pie with Muenster Crust, '95 48
Spinach, Savory Parmesan, '85 68
Spinach with Cheese, Scalloped, '79 8
Spinach with Feta, Lemon, '85 190
Spuds, Mushroom-Swiss, '96 M238
Squash and Tomato Bake, '95 180
Squash Bake, Cheesy, '80 183
Squash Boats, Parmesan-Stuffed, '79 156
Squash, Cheesy Stuffed, '82 134
Squash, Greek-Style, '92 26
Squash Pie, Italian, '02 183
Squash Soufflé, Cheesy, '82 146
Stalks, Splendid, '93 258
Sugar Snap Peas and Goat Cheese, '01 112
Summer Vegetables, Cheesy, '94 119
Sweet Potato Blues, Stacked, '95 290
Sweet Potato Hash Browns, Cheesy, '02 248
Swiss Chard Bundles, '94 48
Tomato Cheese Puffs, '81 48
Tomatoes, Baked Cheddar, '85 43
Tomatoes, Broiled Parmesan, '04 322
Tomatoes, Cheese Herbed-Topped, '86 108
Tomatoes, Cheese-Stuffed, '91 69
Tomatoes, Cheese-Topped, '81 160
Tomatoes, Cheesy Grilled, '79 150
Tomatoes, Cheesy Puff-Top, '86 187
Tomatoes, Cheesy Stuffed, '80 161
Tomatoes, Chile-Cheese Stuffed, '94 141
Tomatoes, Greek, '98 173
Tomatoes, Parmesan, '80 161
Tomatoes, Parmesan-Stuffed, '92 182

Tomatoes, Provençal, '98 267
Tomatoes, Romano Broiled, '80 42
Tomatoes, Spinach-Feta Stuffed, '04 285
Tomatoes with Cheese Sauce over Toast, '88 159
Tomato-Feta Green Beans, '99 59
Tomato Stacks, Fried Green, '02 184
Tomato Tart, '03 158
Tomato Tart, Herbed, '96 94
Tomato with Fresh Mozzarella, Sautéed, '00 163
Turnip au Gratin, '79 289
Turnips au Gratin, '88 229; '89 244
Turnips in Cheese Sauce, '84 229
Vidalia Onions, Baked, '00 102
Yellow Squash with Cheese Sauce, Stuffed, '80 162
Zucchini and Tomato au Gratin, '82 208
Zucchini Fries, Parmesan-, '95 129
Zucchini, Ham and Cheese Stuffed, '79 157
Zucchini, Parmesan, '81 234
Zucchini Parmesan, '81 108; '82 103
Zucchini Pie, Cheesy, '82 103
Zucchini, Southwestern Stuffed, '03 M127
Zucchini with Feta, Greek Grilled, '95 190
Vermicelli, Shrimp and Feta Cheese on, '87 108
Vinaigrette, Blue Cheese, '90 55, 280; '05 233
Vinaigrette, Garlic-Blue Cheese, '92 57
Wafers, Cheese, '95 174; '00 164
Wafers, Hope Farm Cheese, '93 282
Wafers, Italian, '87 36
Wafers, Sage-Pecan Cheese, '93 12
Walnut-Baked Brie, '93 241
Yogurt Cheese, '04 217

CHEESECAKES

Amaretto Cheesecake, '81 150; '99 273
Amaretto Cheesecakes, No-Bake, '00 205
Amaretto-Irish Cream Cheesecake, '90 266
Ambrosia Cheesecake, '02 296
Apple Cheesecake, Dieter's, '86 318
Banana Cheesecake, Chocolate-Wrapped, '99 M48
Bars, Cherry Cheesecake, '97 330
Bavarian Cheesecake, '97 55
Black-and-White Cheesecake, '99 334
Black Forest Cheesecake, '84 74; '89 93; '94 21; '97 330
Blueberries 'n' Cream Cheesecake, '87 140
Blueberry Cheesecake, '00 153; '03 182
Blueberry Cheesecake, Reduced-fat, '00 153
Blueberry Chiffon Cheesecake, '87 76
Brownies, Cheesecake, '85 249
Brown Sugar-and-Spice Cheesecake, '89 93
Butter Pecan Cheesecake, '86 61
Butterscotch Cheesecake, '86 188
Candy Bar Cheesecake, '85 298; '86 120
Cherry Cheesecake, '79 50
Cherry-Topped Cheesecake, '80 23
Chocolate-Almond Cheesecake, '93 53
Chocolate-Amaretto Cheesecake, '85 M294; '93 97
Chocolate-Caramel-Pecan Cheesecake, '91 197
Chocolate Cheesecake, '81 16; '82 305
Chocolate Cheesecake, Rich, '84 74; '85 38
Chocolate Cheesecakes, Tiny, '92 288
Chocolate Cheesecake with Whipped Cream Frosting, '89 42
Chocolate-Cherry Surprise Cheesecake, '05 273
Chocolate Chip Cheesecake, '85 114
Chocolate-Coffee Cheesecake with Mocha Sauce, '05 M316
Chocolate Cookie Cheesecake, '91 298
Chocolate Fudge Cheesecake, '05 M288
Chocolate-Glazed Triple-Layer Cheesecake, '86 315; '90 310

Chocolate Marble Cheesecake, '89 93
Chocolate-Mint Baked Alaska Cheesecake, '94 142
Chocolate-Mint Cheesecake, '91 104
Chocolate-Raspberry Truffle Cheesecake, '91 270
Chocolate Swirl Cheesecake, '84 295; '85 26
Coconut-Chocolate-Almond Cheesecake, '98 322
Coffee Cake, Deep-Dish Cheesecake, '90 50
Cottage Cheese Cheesecake, '80 24
Cream Cheesecake, Rich, '83 270
Crème de Menthe Cheesecake, '82 263; '89 93
Daiquiri Chiffon Cheesecake, '88 66
Deluxe Cheesecake, '80 23
Fruit-Glazed Cheesecake, '80 24; '90 162
Fudge Cheesecake, '98 M213
Fudge-Filled Cheesecake, Warm, '98 34; '03 320
German Chocolate Cheesecake, '87 265; '00 245
Glazed Cheesecake, '83 142
Grasshopper Cheesecake, '80 191
Individual Cheesecakes, So Easy, '85 30
Island Breeze Cheesecake, '03 144
Kahlúa Cheesecake, Heavenly, '83 48
Key Lime Cheesecake with Strawberry-Butter Sauce, '96 87
Key Lime Cheesecake with Strawberry Sauce, '03 55
Key Lime-Coconut Mini-Cheesecakes, '05 159
Lemon Cheesecake, '86 194; '91 308; '92 24
Lemon Cheesecake, Luscious, '90 M196
Lemon Cheesecakes with Raspberry Sauce, Mini, '02 123
Lemon Cheesecake with Orange-Pineapple Glaze, '81 60
Lemon Delight Cheesecake, '95 219
Light-and-Easy Cheesecake, '88 55
Lime Cheesecake with Raspberry Sauce, '00 204
Lime-Goat Cheese Cheesecakes, '05 176
Make-Ahead Cheesecake Pie, '81 233
Marbled Cheesecake, '87 261
Marble Mint Cheesecake, '84 152
Margarita Cheesecake, '92 211; '94 142
Mile-High Cheesecake, '83 334
Mincemeat Cheesecake, Holiday, '00 319
Miniature Cheesecakes, '82 305; '90 170
Mint Cheesecake Bites, '99 282
Mocha Cheesecake, '98 278
Mocha-Chocolate Cheesecake, '88 258
Mocha Swirl Cheesecake, '87 262
New York-Style Cheesecake, '00 205
Orange Cheesecake, '81 84; '85 38
Parfaits, Sugar-Free Peachy Cheesecake, '02 326
Passover Cheesecake, '91 53; '04 86
Passover Cheesecake, Lemony, '02 51
Peach-Caramel Cheesecake, '02 M158
Peaches 'n' Cream Cheesecake, '88 137
Peanut Butter Cheesecake, '94 142
Pear-Berry Cheesecake, '82 M141
Pear-Glazed Cheesecake, '79 67
Pecan Cheesecake, '85 38
Pecan Pie Cheesecake, '02 318; '03 316
Pecan Praline Cheesecake, '03 269
Peppermint Cheesecake, Frozen, '94 143
Petite Cheesecakes, Holiday, '86 321
Phyllo Cheesecakes, Little, '87 275
Piña Colada Cheesecake, '92 70
Piña Colada Cheesecake, Festive, '01 286
Pineapple Cheesecake, '81 32
Pineapple Cheesecake, Ultimate, '85 38
Praline Cheesecake, '83 270; '89 93
Praline-Crusted Cheesecake, '99 295
Pudding with Caramel Syrup, The Ultimate No-Bake Cheesecake Banana, '05 326
Pumpkin Cheesecake, '80 254; '85 280; '96 268
Raspberry-Lemon Sauce, Cheesecake with, '96 30
Raspberry Sauce, Cheesecake with, '87 116
Raspberry Sauce, Frozen Cheesecake with, '84 73

Red Velvet Cheesecake, '04 292
Ricotta Cheesecake, Italian, '95 303
Savory
Cheddar-Chili Cheesecake, '02 251
Chicken Cheesecake, Curried, '90 174
Chicken Cheesecakes, Pesto-, '00 118
Chicken-Chile Cheesecake, '92 42
Feta Cheesecakes, Little, '86 277
Fiesta Cheesecake, '93 273
Ham-and-Asparagus Cheesecake, '90 174; '02 103
Herbed Cheesecakes, '99 182
Reuben Cheesecake, '90 175
Salsa Cheesecake, '98 33
Shrimp-and-Gruyère Cheesecake, '92 57
Smoked Salmon Cheesecake, '99 92
Southwest Cheesecake, '04 293; '05 249
Spinach Appetizer Cheesecake, Savory, '02 M207
Spinach-Herb Cheesecake, '99 139
Spinach-Mushroom Cheesecake, '92 326
Spinach Pesto Cheesecake, '90 175
Sun-Dried Tomato Cheesecake, '03 118
Taco Cheesecake, '00 56
Three-Layer Cheesecake, '99 140
Vegetable Cheesecake, '96 110
Vegetable Cheesecake, Layered, '91 62; '92 51
Vegetable Cheesecake, Roasted, '99 140
Shake, Strawberry-Cheesecake, '92 44
Sour Cream Cheesecake, '86 320
Squares, Cheesecake, '84 151
Strawberry-and-Cream Cheesecake, Irish, '05 273
Strawberry Cheesecake, '02 176, 209
Strawberry Cheesecake, Almost, '86 32
Strawberry-Lemon Cheesecake, '04 237
Sweet Potato Cheesecake, '80 287; '96 312
Tarts, Cream Cheese, '84 74
Three-Layer Cheesecake, '99 140
Tofu Cheesecake, Tropical, '00 204
Ultimate Cheesecake, '98 260
Vanilla Cheesecake, Creamy, '89 93
White Chocolate Cheesecake, '87 44; '88 267; '94 180
Yam Cheesecake, '81 224

CHERRIES

à la Mode, Cherries, '88 202
Bake, Cherry-Apple, '04 29
Bark, Cherry-Pistachio, '00 M41
Bars, Cherry Cheesecake, '97 330
Bars, Delightful Cherry, '86 217
Black Forest Crisp, '02 128
Bread, Cherry Nut, '81 306; '82 36
Bread, Maraschino Cherry Nut, '79 234
Bread, Quick Cherry-Nut, '85 55
Cake, Black Forest Cherry, '83 302
Cake, Black Forest Pudding, '02 210
Cake, Cherry, '79 165
Cake, Cherry Bourbon, '82 287
Cake, Cherry Fudge, '98 214
Cake, Cherry-Pineapple Dump, '02 128
Cake, Cherry Upside-Down, '82 56
Cake, Choco-Cherry, '96 229
Cake, Chocolate-Cherry, '84 200; '86 239
Cake, Cute-as-a-Button Cherry Pound, '95 139
Cake, Dried Cherry, '97 33
Cake, Maraschino Nut, '83 268
Cake, Pineapple-Cherry Dump, '04 91
Cake, Quick Cherry, '81 238
Cake, Upside-Down Sunburst, '87 9
Cake, White Chocolate-Cherry, '88 268
Cheesecake, Black Forest, '89 93; '94 21; '97 330
Cheesecake, Cherry, '79 50
Cheesecake, Cherry-Topped, '80 23
Cheesecake, Chocolate-Cherry Surprise, '05 273
Chocolate-Covered Cherries, '81 286; '84 298; '97 M55
Chocolates, Cherry, '95 321
Chutney, Glazed Ham with Cherry-Peach, '97 315

Cider, Cherry, **'94** 288
Cloud, Cherry-Berry on a, **'79** 94
Cobbler, Berry-Cherry, **'83** 270
Cobbler, Cherry, **'82** 91, 139; **'99** 156
Cobbler, Colossal Cherry, **'89** 137
Cobbler, Double-Cherry Cheesecake, **'03** 21
Cobbler, Fresh Cherry, **'84** 178
Cobbler, Raspberry-Cherry, **'93** 230
Cobbler, Too-Easy Cherry, **'04** 28
Coffee Cake, Cherry, **'94** 49
Coffee Cake, Cherry Blossom, **'80** 21
Coffee Cake, Cinnamon-Cherry, **'98** 330
Compote, Cherry, **'83** 139
Compote, Watermelon-Cherry, **'90** 180
"Concrete," Cardinal Sin, **'94** 113
Cookies, Cherry Bonbon, **'93** 52
Cookies, Cherry Pecan, **'82** 136
Cookies, Chocolate-Cherry, **'85** 324
Cookies, Chocolate-Covered Cherry, **'99** 280
Cookies, Christmas Cherry, **'88** 282
Cookies, Chunky Cherry-Double Chip, **'05** M87
Cookies, Coconut-Cherry, **'79** 292
Cookies, Frosted Chocolate-Cherry, **'89** 294
Cookies, Neapolitan, **'00** 290
Cordial Cherries, **'02** 30
Cordial Hot Chocolate, Cherry, **'02** 220
Cream, Maraschino Russian, **'79** 231
Crêpes, Cherry, **'91** 67
Crêpes Flambé, Cherry, **'79** 18
Crisp, Cherry, **'91** 20
Crisp, Oatmeal Cherry-Apple, **'90** M16
Crowns, Cherry, **'92** 275
Dessert, Cherry Cordial, **'84** 312
Dessert, Holiday Cherry, **'80** 255
Divinity Candy with Sugared Maraschino Cherries, **'01** 271
Divinity, Cherry, **'97** 316
Dried Cherry-Walnut Sweet Rolls, **'03** 235
Drops, Cherry-Almond, **'81** 20
Filling, Cherry, **'83** 302; **'84** 225; **'88** 178
Frosting, Cherry, **'86** 217
Frosting, Cherry-Nut Cream Cheese, **'96** 249
Frosting, Chocolate-Cherry, **'89** 294
Fudge, Cherry Nut, **'83** 315
Glaze, Cherry, **'83** 143; **'93** 52; **'98** 260
Ice Cream, Black Forest, **'88** 203
Ice Cream, Cherry, **'84** 184; **'99** 156
Ice Cream, Cherry-Nut, **'86** 129
Ice Cream, Cherry-Pecan, **'88** 203
Icing, Chunky Cherry, **'03** 94
Jubilee, Cherries, **'79** 18; **'83** 139
Jubilee, Quick Cherries, **'82** M100
Jubilite, Cherries, **'86** 317
Kirsch, Melon Balls and Cherries in, **'91** 91
Muffins, Cherry, **'82** 105
Muffins, Cherry-Nut, **'90** 87
Muffins, Dried Cherry, **'94** 59
Nuggets, Cherry Nut, **'81** 286
Oatmeal, Dried Cherry-and-Pecan, **'05** 126
Pies
 Berry Pie, Cherry-, **'92** 316
 Chocolate-Covered Cherry Pie, **'05** M216
 Coconut Crumb Cherry Pie, **'92** 30
 Cranberry-Cherry Pie, Tart, **'87** 299
 Cream Pie with Almond Pastry, Cherry, **'92** 30
 Dried Cherry-and-Pear Fried Pies, **'00** 213
 Easy Cherry Pie, **'82** M299
 Filling, Dried Cherry Fried Pie, **'96** 109
 Fresh Cherry Pie, **'88** 178
 Lemony Cherry Pie, **'92** 30
 No-Bake Cherry Confetti Pie, **'93** 114
 Pecan Pie, Cherry-, **'92** 30
 Prize-Winning Cherry Pie, **'82** 57
 Red Cherry Pie, **'83** 192

 Scrumptious Cherry Pie, **'83** 250
Pork Roast, Cherry-Glazed, **'91** 84
Pound Cake Loaf, Noel, **'04** 279
Punch, Cranberry-Cherry, **'91** 176
Relish, Cherry-Honey, **'97** 32
Rolls, Cherry-Almond, **'84** M198
Sabayon, Cherries, **'88** 178
Salads
 Apple Salad, Cherry-, **'86** 31
 Best Cherry Salad, **'82** 302
 Bing Cherry-and-Cranberry Salad, **'04** 297
 Bing Cherry-Grapefruit Salad, **'00** 285
 Bing Cherry Salad, **'01** 46
 Chicken Salad, Cherry-Tarragon, **'05** 275
 Cola Salad, Cherry, **'80** 104
 Cola Salad, Cherry-, **'91** 224; **'95** 94
 Congealed Cherry Salad, **'89** 278
 Festive Cherry Salad, **'84** 265
 Fresh Cherry Salad, **'83** 120
 Frozen Black Cherry Salad, **'89** 163
 Frozen Cherry Salad, **'79** 126
 Frozen Cherry Salad, Delicious, **'81** 252
 Fruit Salad, Cherry, **'87** 236
 Honey-Lime Dressing, Cherry Salad with, **'83** 139
 Orange Salad, Cherry-, **'79** 74; **'82** 56
 Port Wine-Cherry Salad, **'86** 11
 Ribbon Salad, Christmas, **'02** 257
 Sherry Dressing, Cherry Salad with, **'79** 165
 Sweet Cherry Salad, **'89** 326
 Wine Salad, Elegant Cherry-, **'82** 56
Salsa, Cherry, **'99** 156
Sauce and Gorgonzola, Peppered Sirloin with Cherry-Merlot, **'02** 320
Sauce, Cherry, **'79** 91; **'83** 276; **'84** 91; **'91** 67
Sauce, Cherry-Wine, **'95** 285; **'97** 132
Sauce, Chocolate-Cherry, **'85** 189
Sauce, Chocolate Cherry, **'87** M165
Sauce, Elegant Cherry, **'79** M156
Sauce, Ham Balls with Spiced Cherry, **'81** 112; **'82** 12
Sauce, Maraschino-Orange, **'96** 164
Sauce, Pork Fillets with Dark Cherry, **'04** 221
Sauce, Roast Ducklings with Cherry, **'86** 312
Sauce, Roast Pork with Spiced Cherry, **'89** 324
Sauce, Royal Cherry, **'85** 224; **'86** 83
Sauce, Smoked Pork Chops with Jalapeño-Cherry, **'01** 208
Sauce, Spicy Cherry, **'83** 244
Scones, Cherry-and-Cream, **'99** 49
Sherried Cherries, **'93** 289
Slump, Cherry, **'83** 139
Snow, Berries on, **'82** 227
Sorbet, Cherry, **'03** 171
Sparkler, Cherry, **'00** 329
Spread, Cherry, **'93** 309
Squares, Cherry, **'97** 273
Squares, Surprise Cherry, **'82** 57
Stuffed Cherries, **'85** 81
Sugared Maraschino Cherries and Mint Sprigs, **'01** 271
Syrup, Cherry-Lemonade, **'86** 214
Tart, Cherry and Blackberry, **'83** 225
Tart, Chocolate-Cherry, **'97** 33
Tart, Fresh Cherry, **'05** 168
Tarts, Cheery Cherry, **'80** 238
Topping, Cherry-Pineapple, **'87** 126
Torte, Black Forest Cherry, **'88** 178
Truffles, Chocolate-Cherry Cordial, **'99** 127
CHICKEN
Acapulco, Chicken, **'84** 32
à la King, Chicken, **'79** 218; **'83** 137; **'87** 197; **'94** 41
à la King, Easy Chicken, **'93** 14
Alfredo, Chicken Fettuccine, **'00** 57
Almond Chicken, **'01** 26
Almond Chicken and Vegetables, **'86** 21
Almond Chicken, Creamy, **'89** 281

Almond Chicken, Spicy, **'88** 150
à l'Orange, Chicken, **'84** 277
Alouette, Chicken, **'91** 295
Andalusia, Chicken, **'87** 103
Appetizers, Chicken-Mushroom, **'88** 210
Appetizers, Sesame Chicken, **'89** 61
Apple Chicken, **'85** 57
Apricot Chicken, **'92** 12
Apricot Chicken Breasts, **'88** 301
Apricot Chicken with Roasted Potato Thins, **'02** 23
Apricot Glaze, Chicken with Tangy, **'98** 275
Ariosto, Shrimp and Chicken, **'79** 31
Arroz con Pollo, **'01** 279
Artichoke Chicken, **'81** 97
Artichoke Hearts, Chicken with, **'88** 54
Artichokes and Mushrooms, Chicken with, **'90** 35
Artichokes, Chicken with, **'02** 314
Artichokes, Italian Chicken and, **'95** 68
Bag, Chicken in a, **'86** M57; **'87** 23
Bake, Chicken, Ham, and Cheese, **'87** 217
Bake, Chicken-Italian Dressing, **'91** 199
Bake, Chicken-Tomato, **'83** 35
Bake, Crispy Chicken, **'83** 115
Baked Breast of Chicken with Marinated Bermuda Onions, **'92** 194
Baked Chicken and Artichoke Hearts, **'82** 260
Baked Chicken and Dressing, **'79** 296
Baked Chicken, Breaded, **'81** 76
Baked Chicken Breasts, **'05** 43
Baked Chicken Breasts, Basic, **'04** 215
Baked Chicken Breasts, Sherried, **'79** 83
Baked Chicken Breasts, Wine-, **'83** 177
Baked Chicken, Buttermilk, **'00** 48; **'01** 212; **'05** 213
Baked Chicken, Citrus Herb, **'85** 303
Baked Chicken, Fancy, **'79** 85
Baked Chicken, Fruity, **'01** 48
Baked Chicken, Herb-, **'82** 229
Baked Chicken in Wine, **'81** 109
Baked Chicken, Italian, **'82** 84
Baked Chicken, Marmalade, **'99** 286
Baked Chicken Parmesan, **'83** 137
Baked Chicken, Tomato-, **'81** 281; **'82** 30
Baked Chicken with Tarragon Sauce, **'94** 126
Baked Chicken with Wine-Soaked Vegetables, **'84** 277
Baked Hen with Cranberry Pan Gravy, **'94** 308
Baked Honey Chicken, **'99** 110
Baked in Wine, Chicken, **'97** 128
Baked Lemon Chicken, **'83** 184
Baked Lemon Chicken, **'85** 190
Baked Mustard Chicken, **'87** 10
Baked Parmesan Chicken, **'83** 320
Baked Pecan Chicken, **'05** 312
Bake, Herb Chicken, **'82** 186
Bake, Individual Chicken, **'90** 279
Bake, Mushroom-Chicken, **'89** 147
Bake, Parslied Chicken, **'90** 65
Bake, Pineapple Chicken, **'82** 120
Bake, Saucy Chicken, **'84** 220
Bake, Savory Chicken, **'98** 31
Bake, Seasoned Chicken, **'94** 278
Ball, Chicken-Cheese, **'93** 216
Ball, Chicken-Curry Cheese, **'85** 118
Balls, Coconut Curried Chicken, **'91** 165
Balls, Curried Chicken, **'91** 98
Banana Chicken with Black Bean Sauce, **'96** 156
Barbecued
 Bake, Barbecued Chicken, **'81** 97
 Braised and Barbecued Chicken, Melt-in-Your-Mouth, **'03** 326
 Chicken, Barbecue, **'86** 122
 Chicken, Barbecued, **'82** 97, 106; **'83** 103; **'85** 144; **'86** 153; **'89** 167
 Chili-Barbecued Chicken, **'98** 170
 Cranberry Chicken, Barbecued, **'83** 178

CHICKEN, Barbecued
(continued)

Glazed Barbecue Chicken, Carambola-, **'92** 246
Golden Barbecued Chicken, **'83** 136
Grilled Barbecued Chicken, **'81** 154
Honey Barbecue Chicken, **'04** 197
Legs and Thighs, Barbecued Chicken, **'94** 94
Lemon Barbecued Chicken, **'93** 215
Marinated Barbecued Chicken, **'79** 90
Old South Barbecued Chicken, **'82** 97; **'83** 103
Orange Barbecued Chicken, **'88** 123
Oven-Baked Barbecue Chicken, **'03** 160
Oven-Barbecued Chicken, Kentucky-Style, **'96** 328
Oven-Barbecued Cranberry Chicken, **'93** 332
Pizza, Barbecue Chicken, **'03** 49
Raspberry-Barbecue Chicken, **'05** 203
Saucy Barbecued Chicken, **'83** 11
South-of-the-Border Barbecued Chicken, **'97** 311
Sweet-and-Spicy Barbecued Chicken, **'01** 316
Tangy Barbecued Chicken, **'86** 186; **'98** 170
White Barbecue Sauce, Chicken with, **'89** M84; **'97** 322
Zesty Barbecued Chicken, **'80** M76
Zippy Barbecued Chicken, **'83** 213
Basil Chicken, **'87** 171
Beer-Can Chicken, **'04** 118
Beer-Can Chicken, Basic, **'03** 130; **'04** 104
Beer-Smothered Chicken, **'01** 107
Bengalese Chicken, **'79** 12
Benne Seed Chicken, **'01** 107
Bird's-Nest Chicken, **'88** 152
Birds of Paradise, **'82** 224
Biscuit, Chicken in a, **'79** 263; **'80** 30
Bites, Curried Chicken, **'85** 40
Bites, Savory Chicken, **'92** 209
Bites with Sweet-Hot Tomato Chutney, Chicken, **'00** 309
Black Bean Puree, Spicy Chicken with, **'97** 48
Black Beans and Oranges, Chicken with, **'00** 94
Boiled Chicken Breasts, **'04** 215
Bourbon Chicken with Gravy, **'94** 252
Bourbon-Laced Tipsy Chicken with Peaches, **'97** 136
Bourbon-Purple Onion Relish, Chicken with, **'95** 253
Bowl, Wild Rice-and-Chicken, **'05** 127
Braised Bourbon Chicken, **'86** 51
Braised Chicken Breast in Lemon Cream Sauce, **'94** 184
Brandado, Chicken, **'84** 195
Breaded Chicken Breasts, **'89** M196
Breast of Chicken, Herbed, **'79** 100
Breasts, Celebrity Chicken, **'95** 60
Breasts Diane, Chicken, **'99** 213
Breasts, Greek Chicken, **'95** 170; **'98** 19
Breasts, Island Chicken, **'84** 68
Breasts Lombardy, Chicken, **'82** 242
Breasts, Salsa-Topped Chicken, **'94** 144
Breasts Saltimbocca, Chicken, **'98** 19
Breasts, Saucy Chicken, **'83** 184; **'87** 167
Breasts with Artichoke-Pepper Sauce, Chicken, **'05** 139
Breasts with Herb Butter, Chicken, **'89** 120
Breasts with Orange-Ginger Sauce, Chicken, **'97** 47
Breasts with Sage Orzo, Chicken, **'98** 169
Brioche Chicken Curry, **'88** 124
Broiled Chicken Breast Tarragon, **'89** 310
Broiled Chicken, Island, **'84** 288
Broth, Easy Microwave Chicken, **'90** M167
B'steeya with Chicken, **'98** 210
Buffalo Chicken Twice-Baked Potatoes, **'04** 184
Bundles, Cheesy Chicken-and-Ham, **'84** 261
Bundles, Chicken-Mushroom, **'80** 157

Bundles, San Antonio-Style Chicken, **'85** 251
Bundles, Southwestern Chicken, **'02** 215
Bundles with Bacon Ribbons, Chicken, **'87** 68
Burgers, Open-Faced Chicken-Onion, **'94** 139
Burgoo, Five-Meat, **'87** 3
Burgoo, Harry Young's, **'87** 3
Burgoo, Kentucky, **'97** 138
Burgoo, Old-Fashioned, **'87** 3
Buttermilk-Pecan Chicken, **'89** 166; **'97** 252
Cacciatore, Chicken, **'99** 213
Cacciatore, Hearty Chicken, **'02** 269
Cajun Chicken over Rice, **'87** 268; **'88** 102; **'89** 67
Cakes, Southwestern Chicken-Corn, **'05** 321
Cakes with Avocado Cream, Southwestern Chicken-and-Corn, **'97** M311
Canapés, Chicken-Cucumber, **'98** 154
Caprese with Tomato-Basil Cream, Chicken, **'99** 240
Caramelized Chicken with Cranberry Conserve, **'98** 320
Cashew Chicken, **'79** 255; **'80** 8; **'83** 21; **'01** 188
Cashew, Chicken, **'88** 38
Cashews, Chicken with, **'79** 207
Casseroles
à la Russell, Chicken, **'95** 175
Almond Casserole, Chicken-, **'94** 199
Artichoke Casserole, Chicken-and-, **'96** 133
Artichokes, Chicken and, **'03** 26
Asparagus Casserole, Chicken-, **'83** 76; **'84** 71
Basil Chicken with Spinach Fettuccine, Creamy, **'97** 328
Breast-of-Chicken Fiesta, **'88** 151
Breasts, Creamy Baked Chicken, **'83** 24
Broccoli, and Cauliflower Casserole, Chicken, **'00** 337
Broccoli Casserole, Chicken-, **'79** 48; **'91** 315
Broccoli-Chicken Casserole, **'82** 33
Brown Rice Bake, Chicken-, **'91** 314
Cacciatore, Chicken, **'80** 39; **'83** 118; **'84** 9; **'86** 42
Cacciatore, Quick Chicken-and-Rice, **'88** 38
Cannelloni with Roasted Red Bell Pepper Sauce, Chicken, **'02** 287
Cassoulet, Easy Chicken, **'00** 43; **'04** 325
Cheesy Chicken Casserole, **'85** 34
Cheesy Chicken Curry Casserole, **'05** 311
Chicken Casserole, **'96** 103, 302
Chilaquiles con Pollo (Tortillas with Chicken), **'81** 66
Chile Chicken with Salsa, Baked, **'88** 147
Chiles Casserole, Chicken-and-, **'93** 107
Chili Bake, Chicken, **'93** 302
Chimichangas, Chicken, **'93** 68; **'94** 30
Chow Mein Chicken Casserole, **'96** 276
Company Chicken Bake, **'80** 301
Countryside Chicken Bake, **'88** 39
D'Iberville, Chicken Casserole, **'04** 182
Dilly Chicken, **'90** 65
Divan Casserole, Chicken, **'82** M203
Divan, Chicken, **'80** M10; **'87** M218
Divan, Curried Chicken, **'80** 83
Divan, Easy Chicken, **'94** 310
Divan, Elegant Crêpes, **'81** 91
Divan, Gourmet Chicken, **'82** 83
Divan, Overnight Chicken, **'83** 198
Divan, Sherried Chicken, **'80** 38
Dressing Casserole, Chicken-and-, **'81** 263
Dressing, Santa Fe Chicken and, **'03** 48
Enchilada Casserole, Easy, **'02** 143
Enchiladas, Baked Chicken-and-Cheese, **'03** 332
Enchiladas, Black Bean-Chicken-Spinach, **'05** 95
Enchiladas, Chicken, **'80** 301; **'86** 296; **'90** 121; **'00** 45; **'03** 214
Enchiladas, Chicken-and-Spinach, **'91** 222
Enchiladas, Chicken-Cheese, **'02** 236
Enchiladas, Chicken-Sour Cream, **'04** 274
Enchiladas, Creamy Chicken, **'97** 250; **'01** M94

Enchiladas, Easy Chicken, **'82** 89; **'86** 231
Enchiladas, Quicker Chicken, **'97** 312
Enchiladas, Three-Cheese Chicken, **'99** 330
Enchiladas Verde, Chicken, **'00** M240
Enchiladas with Tomatillo Sauce, Chicken, **'95** 206
Florentine, Chicken, **'93** 107
Florentine, Chicken-and-Shrimp, **'89** 64
Fontina-Baked Chicken, **'90** 64
Garlic-Spinach Chicken, **'92** 56
Good Chicken Casserole, Simply, **'95** 255
Green Bean Casserole, Chicken-, **'85** 296
Green Bean Casserole, Creamy Chicken-, **'97** 158
Grits, Chicken and, **'95** 263
Grits with Chicken Sausage and Shiitake Mushrooms, Cheese, **'03** 254
Herbed Chicken, French, **'86** 89
Hot-and-Spicy Chicken Dinner, **'94** M94
Jalapeño Chicken Casserole, **'02** 50
King Ranch Casserole, **'02** 210
King Ranch Chicken, **'95** 193; **'99** 330; **'03** 313
King Ranch Chicken Casserole, **'00** 280
King Ranch Chicken Casserole, Light, **'04** 57
Lasagna Bake, Chicken, **'95** 55
Lasagna, Chicken, **'87** M302; **'88** 90; **'92** 197; **'93** 25; **'96** 16
Lasagna, Creamy Ham-and-Chicken, **'95** 88
Lasagna, Easy Mexican, **'03** 22
Lasagna Florentine, Chicken, **'95** 158; **'02** 232
Lasagna, Green Chile-Chicken, **'00** 338
Lasagna, Heavenly Chicken, **'00** 310
Lasagna, Southwestern Chicken, **'03** 173
Linguine, Chicken, **'01** 128
Macaroni-and-Cheese Bake, **'01** 41
Macaroni and Chicken Casserole, **'80** 260
Macaroni Casserole, Chicken-, **'85** 219
Make-Ahead Chicken Casserole, **'84** 241
Manicotti, Creamy Chicken, **'85** 60
Mexicana, Chicken, **'91** M127
Mexican Chicken Casserole, **'82** 143
Mexican Chicken, Cheesy, **'01** 199
Mexican Chicken, Spicy, **'82** 89
Mexi-Chicken Casserole, **'93** 69; **'94** 30
Noodle Casserole, Chicken-, **'94** 286
Noodle Casserole, Chicken, **'01** 308
Noodle Casserole, Chicken and Green, **'80** 32
Orzo, and Spinach Casserole, Chicken, **'02** 124
Oyster-and-Chicken Casserole, **'99** 320
Paella Casserole, **'95** 254
Parmesan, Chicken, **'04** 42
Parmigiana, Chicken, **'80** 190
Parmigiana, Chicken-Eggplant, **'82** 212
Parmigiana, Zesty Chicken, **'00** 19
Pasta Casserole, Chicken-and-, **'97** 192
Pecan Chicken, Lemony, **'96** 82
Pesto-Chicken Casserole, **'94** 231
Poppy Seed Chicken, **'99** 195
Quick Chicken Casserole, **'81** 91
Reuben Casserole, Chicken, **'03** 69
Rice-and-Chicken Casserole, **'87** 154
Rice Casserole, Chicken-, **'86** 52; **'99** 215
Rice Casserole, Chicken and, **'80** 260
Rice Casserole, Creamy Chicken-, **'99** 21
Rice Casserole, Creamy Chicken-and-, **'02** 309
Rice Casserole, Crispy Chicken-and-, **'03** 203
Rice Casseroles, Chicken-and-, **'01** 52
Rice, Chicken and, **'95** 54
Salad, Baked Chicken, **'86** 297; **'87** 176
Scarborough Chicken, **'80** 38
Shrimp-and-Chicken Casserole, **'91** 102
Southwestern Casserole, **'99** 216
Spaghetti Casserole, Chicken-, **'84** 15
Spaghetti, Spicy Chicken, **'02** 327

Spaghetti Squash and Chicken Skillet Casserole, '94 134
Spicy Chicken Bake, '85 251
Squash Casserole, Chicken-, '95 121
Squash-Chicken Casserole, Hearty Tex-Mex, '99 312; '03 107
Sunday Chicken Casserole, '83 290
Superb Casserole, Chicken, '89 83
Supreme Casserole, Chicken, '84 219
Supreme, Hot Chicken, '81 76
Swiss Chicken, '95 54
Swiss Chicken Casserole, '90 67
Swiss Chicken Thighs, '94 282
Tangy Chicken, '85 251
Tetrazzini, Cheesy Chicken, '83 M87
Tetrazzini, Chicken, '79 268; '80 M75; '83 288; '99 61; '00 45; '02 171; '04 221
Tortilla Bake, Chicken, '82 89
Tortilla Casserole, Chicken, '81 166
Unforgettable Chicken Casserole, '04 294
Vegetable-Chicken Bake with Sweet Bacon Dressing, '93 108
Wild Rice Casserole, Chicken-, '84 241; '85 65
Wild Rice Casserole, Chicken-and-, '97 192; '00 257
Wild Rice Casserole, Leslie's Favorite Chicken-and-, '00 209; '03 107
Wild Rice, Chicken and, '79 248
Wild Rice Supreme, Chicken-, '79 77
Cassoulet, '96 328
Cassoulet, Sausage-and-Chicken, '05 237
Celery Skillet, Chicken-and-, '88 6
Chafing Dish Chicken, '82 284
Chalupas, Chicken, '79 185
Chalupas, Chicken-Olive, '81 227
Champagne Chicken, '85 251
Champagne Sauce, Chicken Breasts with, '86 49
Charcoal Broiled Chicken, '79 90
Charlemagne, Chicken, '86 293
Cheesecake, Chicken-Chile, '92 42
Cheesecake, Curried Chicken, '90 174
Cheesecakes, Pesto-Chicken, '00 118
Chili, White, '91 284
Chili, White Bean, '02 20
Chili, White Christmas, '98 266; '02 260
Chili, White Lightning Texas, '92 321
Chimichangas, Chicken, '98 95
Chimichangas, Oven-Fried Chicken, '90 175
Chinese, Chicken, '94 33
Chinese Chicken and Vegetables, '81 212
Chinese Chicken, Lazy Day, '81 3
Chinese-Style Chicken Dinner, '89 247
Chinese-Style Dinner, '84 26
Chop Suey, Chicken, '81 227
Chowder, Cheesy Chicken, '92 21
Chowder, Chicken, '83 20
Chowder, Creamy Chicken-Vegetable, '92 20
Chowder, Curried Chicken-and-Corn, '92 21
Chowder, Mexican Chicken-Corn, '01 18
Chow Mein, Chicken, '90 68; '98 283
Chutney Chicken, '86 249
Cobbler, Spicy Tex-Mex Chicken, '03 324
Cobbler with Caramelized Onions, Chicken, '00 44
Coconut Chicken, '98 20
Coconut Chicken with Fresh Fruit, '93 294
Coconut Milk, Chicken in, '97 202
Cola-Can Chicken, '03 130; '04 104
Company Chicken, '80 39; '83 125
Continental, Chicken, '82 274
Cordon Bleu, Chicken, '81 304; '82 83; '86 37; '93 126
Cordon Bleu, Company Chicken, '82 274
Cordon Bleu, Easy Chicken, '02 175
Cordon Bleu in Mushroom Sauce, Chicken, '86 198
Cordon Bleu, Pasta, '97 327

Corn Flake Chicken, '91 172
Country Captain Chicken, '94 252
Country Poulet, '86 292
Couscous, Chicken with, '97 325
Crabmeat Stuffing, Chicken Breasts with, '85 302
Cracked Wheat, "Fried," '89 31
Cranberry Chicken, '05 272
Cream Cheese Chicken Breasts, '90 234
Creamed Chicken, '82 49, 284; '83 14
Creamed Chicken and Vegetables, '91 90
Creamed Chicken, Company, '82 84
Creamed Chicken in a Shell, '79 138
Creamed Chicken in Biscuit Bowls, '03 222
Creamed Chicken in Patty Shells, '86 123
Creamed Chicken over Confetti Rice Squares, '81 282; '82 31
Creamed Chicken over Cornbread, '86 231
Creamed Chicken Toppers, '99 240
Creamed Ham and Chicken, '81 M74
Creole, Chicken, '86 231; '89 33; '90 146
Creole Chicken, '94 93; '95 261
Creole Chicken and Rice, '92 262
Crêpes, Chicken, '80 39
Crêpes, Chicken-Vegetable, '83 70
Crêpes, Creamy Chicken, '81 200
Crêpes Divan, Elegant, '81 91
Crispy Chicken, '84 152; '01 246
Croissants, Chutney-Chicken, '92 22
Croquettes and Mushroom Sauce, Chicken, '91 220
Croquettes, Chicken, '81 133
Croquettes, Crispy Chicken, '88 206
Crunchy Chicken, Janet's, '96 22
Curried Chicken, '86 43
Curried Chicken, Quick, '89 219; '99 92
Curried Chicken, Regal, '84 110
Curry-and-Spice Chicken, Aromatic, '05 238
Curry, Chicken, '84 110; '85 220; '86 21; '89 219
Curry, Indian-Style Chicken, '97 119
Curry, Turban Chicken, '94 266
Cutlets with Lemon, Chicken, '85 8
Dante's Chicken, '88 25
Delicacy, Chicken, '99 M23
Deviled Chicken, Zesty, '90 232
Dijon Chicken, '81 156; '99 21
Dijon, Chicken, '04 196
Dijon Chicken with Pasta, '90 318
Dijon-Herb Chicken, '89 120
Dilled Chicken Paprika, '86 41
Dinner, Chicken-Mushroom, '81 3
Dinner, Chicken Peach, '79 77
Dinner, Curried Chicken Skillet, '95 47
Dinner, Healthful Chicken, '83 232
Dip, Hot Chicken, '80 86
Dixie Manor, Chicken à la, '85 3
Dressing, Chicken and, '99 42
Dressing, Chicken and Rice, '79 288
Dressing, Chicken Cornbread, '90 159
Dressing, Tipsy Chicken and, '88 151
Drummettes. See also CHICKEN/Wings.
    Down-Home Chicken Drummettes, '93 157
    Fried Chicken Drummettes with Horseradish Sauce, '88 207
    Ginger-Garlic Appetizer Drummettes, '93 157
    Orange-Pecan Chicken Drummettes, '93 158
    Southwestern Chicken Drummettes, '93 158
Drumsticks, Breaded Chicken, '99 110
Drumsticks, Cajun-Style, '87 159
Drumsticks, Tangy, '97 120
Dumplings and Chicken, Biscuit, '99 326
Dumplings, Chicken and, '97 208; '00 111; '01 231; '03 25
Dumplings, Chicken and Potato, '99 326
Dumplings, Chicken and Tortilla, '99 327
Dumplings, Country Chicken and, '85 254

Dumplings, Easy Chicken and, '86 21
Dumplings, Old-Fashioned Chicken and, '79 55; '83 228; '93 302
Dumplings, Quick Chicken and, '95 125; '02 16
Dumplings with Herbed Broth, Chicken and, '95 338
Dumplings with Vegetables, Chicken and, '85 M56
Easy Chicken, '89 M129
Egg Bread, Chicken on, '95 120
Eggs, Chicken-Stuffed, '98 102
Empanadas, '92 156
Enchiladas, Chicken, '04 96
Enchiladas, Chicken-Chile, '97 313
Enchiladas, Creamy, '93 174
Enchiladas, Healthy Chicken, '02 19
Enchiladas Terrificas, '84 32
Enchiladas Verde, Chicken, '93 274
Enchiladas with Spicy Sauce, Chicken, '84 76
Enchiladas with Tomatillo Sauce, Chicken, '94 231
English Muffin Delight, '82 45
en Papillote, Chicken and Vegetables, '86 145
Fajita Fettuccine, '94 84
Fajitas, Beef and Chicken, '02 119
Fajitas, Chicken, '88 231; '89 100; '90 204; '99 158
Fajita Spuds, Chicken, '96 238
Fajita Spuds with Black Bean Salsa, Chicken, '04 25
Fancy Fowl, '81 76; '82 13
Fennel and Mushrooms, Chicken with, '97 93
Fennel, Chicken with, '00 322
Fettuccine, Cajun Chicken, '96 198
Fettuccine, Chicken and Dried Tomatoes over, '98 233
Fettuccine, Chicken-and-Tomatoes over, '90 204
Fettuccine, Chicken-Pecan, '86 52
Fettuccine, Ranch House, '03 123
Fiesta Chicken, Spicy, '84 234
Filling, Chicken, '81 200; '05 117
Filling, Chicken Divan, '81 91
Filling, Chicken-Olive, '81 227
Filling, Crêpe, '96 48
Filling, Curried Chicken, '88 125
Filling Luau, Chicken, '79 81
Fingers, Buttermilk-Pecan Chicken, '93 165
Fingers, Chicken Little, '80 249
Fingers, Herb-Baked Chicken, '86 249
Fingers, No-Fry-Pan Chicken, '91 120
Fingers, Spicy Chicken, '91 162
Fingers with Honey-Horseradish Dip, Chicken, '02 308
Fingers with Honey-Mustard Sauce, Chicken, '05 300
Firecrackers, Texas, '95 96; '99 94
Flautas, '83 199
Flautas with Guacamole, Chicken, '89 226
Florentine with Mushroom Sauce, Chicken, '87 250
Foil, Chicken in, '91 134; '94 93
Foil Supper, Chicken Ole, '04 222
Foil-Wrapped Chicken, '99 108
Fricassee, White Chicken, '98 122
Fried
    Beaumont Fried Chicken, '88 92
    Best Ever Sunday Chicken, '89 234
    Best Fried Chicken, Our, '97 311
    Bites, French-Fried Chicken, '85 160
    Buttermilk Fried Chicken, Company, '86 177
    Cajun Fried Chicken, '01 334
    Cakes with Creole Sauce, Chicken, '02 32, 284
    Cakes with Rémoulade Sauce, Chicken, '00 44
    Cheese-Stuffed Chicken Thighs, Fried, '88 206
    Coconut Chicken Dippers with Wowee Maui Mustard, Crispy, '05 324
    Cream Gravy, Fried Chicken with, '85 241
    Crispy Fried Chicken Breasts, '80 155
    Crunchies, Tex-Mex Chicken, '03 328
    Curried Fried Chicken, '85 160
    Delicious Fried Chicken, '86 156

CHICKEN, Fried
(continued)

Dixie Fried Chicken, '88 14
Drummettes with Horseradish Sauce, Fried Chicken, '88 207
Drumsticks, Buttermilk, '87 175
Edna's Fried Chicken, '99 126
Finger Chicken, '96 89
Fingers, Chicken Almondette, '93 12
Fingers with Come Back Sauce, Fried Chicken, '00 211
Fritters with Lime-Cayenne Mayonnaise, Chicken-and-Mashed Potato, '04 121
Garlic-Flavored Fried Chicken, '79 147
Garlic Fried Chicken, '82 148
Gravy, Fried Chicken, '95 235
Herbed Fried Chicken, '87 91
Herb-Seasoned Fried Chicken, '80 8
Kudzu Fried Chicken, '95 198
Lemon-Fried Chicken, '79 77
Lemon Fried Chicken, '82 275
Mama's Fried Chicken, '02 180
Mandarin Chicken, Crispy, '86 119
Mexican Fried Chicken, '81 166; '87 176
Mom's Fried Chicken, '01 163
Mushroom Sauce, Chicken with, '04 255
Nuggets, Golden Chicken, '80 159
Nuggets, Lemon-Chicken, '87 283
Oven-Fried Chicken, '84 118; '93 90; '95 236; '99 212
Oven-Fried Chicken, Buttermilk, '03 213
Oven-Fried Chicken, Crisp, '94 220
Oven-Fried Chicken, Crunchy, '87 163
Oven-Fried Chicken, Crusty, '79 77
Oven-Fried Chicken Cutlets, '04 81
Oven-Fried Chicken, Golden-Brown, '86 21
Oven-Fried Chicken Legs, Jalapeño, '94 94
Oven-Fried Chicken, Nutty, '85 160
Oven-Fried Chicken, Southern, '86 37
Oven-Fried Chicken, Spicy, '97 307
Oven-Fried Chicken with Honey-Butter Sauce, '85 18
Oven-Fried Parmesan Chicken, '81 97; '82 148
Oven-Fried Pecan Chicken, '84 288
Oven-Fried Sesame Chicken, '79 77
Pan-Fried Chicken, Virginia, '96 142
Peppery Chicken Fried Chicken, '04 57
Picnic Fried Chicken, '01 125
Poppers, Chicken, '01 321
Sesame Chicken, '82 148
Southern Fried Chicken Breasts, '98 20
Southern Fried Chicken, Our Best, '95 235; '00 142; '02 106; '03 178, 310
Special Fried Chicken, '88 220
Spicy Country-Fried Chicken, '82 148
Spicy Fried Chicken, '83 5; '88 129; '94 162
Spinach-Stuffed Chicken Breasts, Fried, '88 206
Stuffed Chicken with Roasted Red Pepper-and-Vidalia Onion Gravy, Southern-Fried, '03 322
Stuffed Fried Chicken, Pimiento Cheese-, '05 322
Sunday Dinner Fried Chicken, '88 110
Super Fried Chicken, '82 148
Sweet 'n' Sour Chicken, '04 311
Timely Fried Chicken, '98 274
Traditional Fried Chicken, '82 148
Walnut Chicken, Deep-Fried, '87 175
Wings, Hot Buffalo, '87 176
Fried Rice, Chicken-Cashew, '99 171
Fruited Chicken en Crème, '83 264
Garden, Chicken-in-a-, '80 18
Garlic Chicken, Forty-Cloves-of-, '95 261
Garlic Chicken, Moroccan, '99 15

Garlic Sauce, Chicken with, '00 270
Ginger-and-Orange Chicken with Broccoli, Spicy, '02 309
Ginger Chicken and Cashews, '85 M11
Ginger-Nut Chicken, '90 M33
Glazed Chicken and Pears, '99 21
Glazed Chicken, Fruit-, '80 211
Glazed Chicken, Wine-, '03 26
Glazed Roasted Chicken, '03 217
Gold Nugget Chicken, '95 120
Gravy, Chicken, '99 34
Gravy, Chicken Smothered in, '99 41
Greek Lemon Chicken, '90 65
Greek-Style Chicken, '05 220
Green Onions, Chicken with Grilled, '01 94
Grilled Bahamian Chicken with Cha-Cha Salsa, '97 160
Grilled Basil Chicken, '93 201
Grilled Chicken, '89 200; '92 170; '94 167
Grilled Chicken and Onions, Grits with, '99 17
Grilled Chicken and Vegetables, '99 200
Grilled Chicken Breasts, '84 172; '04 214
Grilled Chicken Breasts with Fig-and-Melon Compote, '00 163
Grilled Chicken Breasts with Lemon-Yogurt Coleslaw, '98 148
Grilled Chicken, Creole, '04 289
Grilled Chicken, Garlic-, '87 180
Grilled Chicken, Garlic-and-Wine, '00 136
Grilled Chicken, Honey-Glazed, '99 213
Grilled Chicken, Honey-Lime, '96 189; '98 332
Grilled Chicken, Lemon-Herb, '95 87
Grilled Chicken, Lexington-Style, '05 54
Grilled Chicken, Lime-, '02 142; '04 320
Grilled Chicken, Smoky, '85 160
Grilled Chicken, Tea-Thyme, '05 M52
Grilled Chicken Thighs, '05 163
Grilled Chicken Tortas, '01 M187
Grilled Chicken with Basting Sauce, '01 146
Grilled Chicken with Cha-Cha Salsa, '98 333
Grilled Chicken with Creamy Sauce, '01 318
Grilled Chicken with Dill Sauce, '88 162
Grilled Chicken with Spicy Soba Noodles, '00 93
Grilled Chicken with Sweet Soy Slaw and Dipping Sauce, '04 123
Grilled Chicken with Tabbouleh Salad, '91 70
Grilled Chicken with Vegetables Vinaigrette, '91 26
Grilled Chicken with Watermelon-Feta Salad, Herb-, '05 320
Grilled Cumin Chicken, '87 142
Grilled Ginger-Glazed Chicken, '98 166
Grilled Ginger-Orange Chicken, '91 26
Grilled Herbed Chicken Quarters, '96 171
Grilled Jalapeño Chicken, '93 213
Grilled Lime-Jalapeño Chicken, '91 87
Grilled Margarita-Marinated Chicken, '97 167
Grilled Southwestern Chicken with Pineapple Salsa, '04 196
Grilled Sweet Guava Chicken, '05 278
Grilled Tarragon-Dijon Thighs, '97 120
Grilled Teriyaki Chicken, '92 59
Grilled Yogurt-Lemon Chicken, '81 111
Gruyère, Chicken Breasts, '80 189
Gumbo, Chicken, '79 199; '90 26
Gumbo, Chicken-Andouille, '98 14
Gumbo, Chicken and Oyster, '81 198
Gumbo, Chicken-and-Sausage, '89 275; '90 256; '94 20; '00 221; '01 324; '03 313; '04 213
Gumbo, Chicken-Ham-Seafood, '81 6
Gumbo, Chicken-Sausage, '04 288
Gumbo, Combo, '81 198
Gumbo, Easy Chicken, '83 156
Gumbo, Old-Style Shrimp, '98 97
Gumbo, The Gullah House, '92 237
Gumbo, Wild Game, '91 290

Gumbo with Smoked Sausage, Chicken, '81 199
Gumbo Ya Ya, '87 210
Hawaiian Chicken, '82 274
Hawaiian, Chicken, '84 88
Herb Chicken, Smoky, '95 116
Herbed Chicken-and-Rice Bake, '02 215
Herbed Chicken, Sunny, '86 156
Herbed Chicken, Tangy, '87 M302
Herbs and Vegetables, Chicken with Fresh, '02 91
Herb-Seasoned Chicken Breasts, '93 M325
Holiday Chicken Presents, '01 251
Honey Chicken, '82 55; '88 67
Honey-Curry Chicken, '87 36
Honey-Pecan Chicken, '03 147
Honey-Pecan Chicken Strips, '05 188
Honey Sauce, Chicken in, '89 82
Honolulu Chicken, '85 52
Imperial Chicken, '81 238; '98 91
Italian Chicken, '86 122; '91 206
Italian Chicken and Artichokes, '00 219
Italian Chicken Cutlets, '89 82
Italian Chicken-Mozzarella Melt, '95 153
Jalapeño, Easy Chicken, '92 310
Jamaican Jerk Raspberry Chicken, '00 88
Jambalaya, '90 26
Jambalaya, Chicken-and-Sausage, '88 200; '91 216; '01 278; '02 36; '03 201
Jambalaya, 1-2-3, '97 301
Jambalaya, Red Rice, '91 18
Jambalaya, Smoky Cajun, '96 62
Jambalaya with Shrimp, Chicken-and-Ham, '04 99
Jerk Chicken, Jamaican, '96 120; '99 121
Kebabs, Chicken, '87 141; '03 180
Kebabs, Chicken-Avocado, '82 9; '83 68
Kebabs, Chicken-Pineapple, '00 200
Kebabs, Chicken-Vegetable, '03 95
Kebabs, Good-and-Easy Chicken, '85 87
Kebabs, Hawaiian, '85 157
Kebabs, Marinated Chicken, '84 M144
Kebabs, Oriental Chicken, '95 193
Kebabs, Pineapple-Chicken, '86 M328
Kebabs, Sesame Chicken, '82 165
Kebabs, Soy-Chicken, '86 156
Kebabs Supreme, Chicken, '81 124
Kiev, Chicken, '80 39
Kiev, Cranberry Chicken, '87 250
Kiev, Oven-Baked Chicken, '86 37
Kiev, Oven Chicken, '82 83
King Ranch Chicken, '94 26
la France, Chicken, '86 248
Lemonade Chicken, '82 163
Lemon and Wine, Chicken in, '83 281
Lemon-Basil Chicken, '02 91
Lemon Chicken, '81 M138; '86 173; '96 49
Lemon Chicken and Vegetables, '88 118
Lemon Chicken Breasts, '89 18
Lemon Chicken, Sweet, '79 218
Lemon-Chicken, Sweet, '84 69
Lemon-Dill Chicken, '93 19
Lemon-Dill Chicken Sauté, '91 186
Lemon-Frosted Chicken, '88 170
Lemon-Garlic Chicken, '89 M132; '90 35
Lemon-Herb Chicken, '85 127; '00 90
Lemon Marinade, Chicken in, '98 128
Lemon-Pepper Chicken, '89 104
Lemon-Rosemary Chicken, '94 201
Lemon-Spinach Chicken, '97 104
Limeade Chicken, '01 257
Lime Butter, Chicken with, '84 68
Lime Chicken with Grilled Pineapple, '04 88
Lime-Roasted Chicken Breasts, '97 100
Linguine, Chicken-Broccoli, '98 30
Livers
Bits and Livers, Chicken, '84 222

Chopped Chicken Livers, Grandma Rose's, '96 105
en Brochette, Chicken Livers, '84 222
Fried Chicken Livers, '96 105
Garlic Chicken Livers, '96 105
Italian Sauce, Chicken Livers in, '83 117
Kebabs, Rumaki, '82 182
Mushrooms, Chicken Livers with, '81 133
Omelet, Chicken Liver, '82 44
Orange Sauce, Chicken Livers in, '82 218
Party Chicken Livers, '83 242
Pâté, Chicken Liver, '79 153; '81 235; '83 108;
    '84 205; '88 M132
Pâté Maison, '84 222
Potatoes, Chicken Livers and, '82 218
Rice, Chicken Livers with, '80 200; '81 58; '84 292
Rice Dish, Chicken Livers and, '82 218
Risotto, Chicken Livers, '82 218
Roll-Ups, Chicken Liver and Bacon, '80 200; '81 57
Rumaki, '80 M136
Sautéed Chicken Livers, '80 200; '81 57
Scrumptious Chicken Livers, '84 230
Spread, Sherried Liver, '80 86
Stroganoff, Chicken Livers, '80 200; '81 57
Supreme, Chicken Livers, '81 298
Turnovers, Chicken Liver, '79 141
Wine Sauce, Chicken Livers in, '81 104
Wine Sauce, Chicken Livers with Marsala, '81 76
Log, Chicken-Pecan, '81 290
Luzianne, Poulet, '86 197
Macadamia-Mango Chicken, '02 162
Macaroni and Cheese, Chicken, '02 63
Macaroni and Cheese, Spicy Chicken, '02 63
Madrid, Chicken, '97 326
Maple-Balsamic Chicken, '04 195
Marbella, Chicken, '04 34
Marengo, Chicken, '92 70
Marinade, Zesty Chicken, '03 180
Marinara, Chicken, '86 77
Marinated Breast of Chicken, '87 123
Marinated Chicken, '87 61
Marinated Chicken, Balsamic, '98 130
Marinated Chicken, Balsamic-, '05 219
Marinated Chicken Breasts, '90 54
Marinated Chicken, Mojo-, '05 163
Marinated Chicken Quarters, '02 142
Marinated Chicken Strips and Vegetables, '90 110
Marinated Chicken with Mango Salsa, Margarita,
    '05 328
Marsala, Chicken, '83 137; '89 237
Meatballs, White Spaghetti and, '03 34
Medaillons in Pepper Pesto, Chicken-Rice, '90 97
Mediterranean Chicken, '91 27; '94 72
Mediterranean, Chicken, '01 17
Medley, Creamy Ham-and-Chicken, '92 272
Mexican Chicken, '80 124
Mexican Chicken, Cheesy, '02 91
Milano, Chicken, '84 220
Minted Chicken, '81 102
Mojo Chicken with Mandarin-Black Bean Salad, Cuban,
    '05 318
Mole, Chicken, '81 193
Mole Sauce, Chicken with, '93 34
Monterey, Chicken, '82 275
Mornay Sauce, Chicken Breasts in, '81 273
Moroccan Chicken, '00 309
Mousse, Curried Chicken, '95 328
Muffins, Broccoli-Chicken, '96 27
Muffins, Chicken-and-Green Chile, '03 81
Murphy, Chicken, '89 82
Mushroom Sauce, Chicken with, '99 22
Mushrooms, Chicken-Stuffed, '80 162
Mustard Chicken, '80 222; '86 293; '93 239
Mustard Cream Sauce, Chicken in, '92 181
Nachos, Chicken, '84 244

Nuggets, Baked Chicken, '81 149; '89 18
Nuggets, Chicken-Bacon, '03 292; '04 146
Nuggets, Golden Chicken, '80 159; '81 237
Nuggets, Lemon-Chicken, '86 337
Nuggets Supreme, Chicken, '85 160
Nuggets with Pineapple Sauce, Chicken, '84 236
Olé, Chicken-and-Artichoke, '05 59
Olives, Chicken with Green, '03 87
Omelet, Indian, '99 92
Onion-Crusted Chicken, '88 40
Onions, Down-Home Chicken and, '02 271
Orange-Almond Sauce, Chicken in, '79 219; '80 13
Orange-Avocado Chicken, '80 38
Orange Chicken, '83 278; '86 M140
Orange Chicken Breasts with Parslied Rice, '87 242
Orange Chicken, Skillet-Seared, '96 68
Orange, Lime, and Ginger Sauce, Chicken with,
    '92 123
Orange Sauce, Chicken Breasts with, '79 77
Orange Sauce, Chicken in, '83 8
Orange Sauce, Skillet Chicken in, '94 252
Oregano Chicken, '95 84
Oriental Chicken, '80 40, 208; '82 131
Oriental, Chicken, '01 36
Oriental Chicken with Peanuts, '82 236
Oriental Chicken with Pineapple, '86 42
Packets, Chicken, '96 104
Paella, '97 328
Paella, Chicken-Pork-Shrimp, '82 245
Paella, Chicken-Seafood, '88 68
Paella, Shortcut, '01 309
Paella, Shrimp-and-Chicken, '94 168
Paella, Spanish, '85 26
Paella Valenciana, '82 246
Pané Chicken with Sweet-'n'-Spicy Red Pepper Sauce,
    '05 320
Paprika Chicken, '95 125
Parchment, Chicken and Leeks in, '97 290
Parmesan, Chicken, '83 184; '95 210; '00 219
Parmesan Chicken, Crispy, '80 M76
Pasquale, Chicken, '83 67
Pasta and Chicken, Taste-of-Texas, '92 78
Pasta and Garden Vegetables, '87 192
Pasta, Chicken and Bow Tie, '05 49
Pasta, Chicken-and-Broccoli, '87 286
Pasta, Chicken-and-Pepper, '03 199
Pasta, Chicken Caesar, '97 87
Pasta, Chicken Picante, '01 164
Pasta, Mediterranean Chicken and, '03 63
Pasta Platter, Cold, '88 42
Pasta Primavera, Chicken-, '91 72
Pasta, Quick Chicken and, '93 14
Pasta, Spicy Chicken, '02 125
Pasta with Artichokes and Capers, Chicken, '04 129
Pasta with Rosemary, Chicken-Artichoke,
    '98 15
Pastry, Chicken in, '86 122
Pâté, Curried Chicken, '00 106
Pâté, Vegetable-Chicken, '86 66
Peach Sauce, Chicken with, '98 334
Peachy Chicken, '90 212
Peanut Butter-Marmalade Chicken, '81 282; '82 30
Pecan Chicken, '90 54; '99 332
Pecan-Rice Dressing, Chicken with, '85 M57
Pecan-Sausage Stuffing, Chicken Breasts with,
    '94 212
Penne, Cheesy Chicken, '00 289
Penne Pasta, Chicken, Asparagus, and Mushrooms with,
    '98 212
Penne, Spicy Cheesy Chicken, '00 289
Pepper-Sage Chicken, '96 237
Peppers, Chicken Breasts with Curried, '90 227
Peppers, Curried Chicken-Stuffed, '87 19
Peppers, Devilish Chicken, '80 65

Peppers with Chicken and Corn, Stuffed, '02 147
Pesto Chicken and Pasta, '89 M132
Pesto Chicken with Basil Cream, '89 158
Phyllo, Cheese-Stuffed Chicken in, '01 251
Phyllo, Cheesy Chicken in, '02 308
Phyllo, Chicken in, '87 286
Phyllo Pastry, Chicken Breasts in, '91 105
Piccata, Chicken, '83 35; '84 230
Piccata, Herbed Chicken, '88 28
Pie, Biscuit-Topped Chicken, '86 157, 264
Pie, Brunswick Stew-Cornbread, '02 121
Pie, Cheesy Mexican Chicken, '82 142
Pie, Chicken, '81 281; '82 31
Pie, Chicken-and-Egg Pot, '00 98
Pie, Chicken Dumpling, '95 245; '96 55; '00 336
Pie, Chicken Pot, '81 210; '82 114; '84 21; '94 21;
    '95 54, 256; '96 75; '01 282; '03 247
Pie, Chicken-Vegetable Pot, '81 281; '82 30
Pie, Deluxe Chicken, '88 298
Pie, Double-Crust Chicken, '87 111
Pie, Double-Crust Chicken Pot, '90 220
Pie, Easy Chicken Pot, '83 156; '89 218
Pie, Egg-Stra Special Chicken, '86 264
Pie Filling, Pot, '03 247
Pie, Greek Chicken Phyllo, '92 328
Pie in Biscuit Bowls, Chicken Pot, '03 222
Pie, Montezuma Tortilla, '83 199
Pie, Nana's Chicken, '90 25
Pie, Old-Fashioned Chicken Pot, '92 271
Pie, Savory Southern Chicken, '90 24
Pie, Thick 'n' Crusty Chicken Pot, '87 267; '88 102;
    '89 67
Pie with Cheese Crust, Chicken Pot, '86 264
Pilaf, Chicken, '82 246
Pilaf, Chicken-Vegetable, '97 51
Pilau, Chicken, '99 184
Pilau, Chicken-and-Smoked Sausage, '04 204
Piña Colada Chicken, '86 21
Pineapple Chicken, '83 M194; '85 3
Pineapple, Chicken and, '81 281; '82 30
Pineapple Chicken, Oriental, '84 288
Pineapple, Oriental Chicken with, '86 42
Piquant Chicken, '86 76
Piquant, Chicken, '94 19
Pita, Oriental Chicken, '89 216
Pita, Peppery Chicken in, '93 62
Pitas, Acadian Stuffed, '90 177
Pizza, Bistro Grilled Chicken, '05 131
Pizza, Broccoli Supreme, '02 312
Pizza, Chicken, '94 218
Pizza, Chicken-and-Purple Onion, '97 47
Pizza, Chicken Fajita, '03 235
Pizza, Chicken Parmesan, '00 134
Pizza, Gruyère-Chicken, '87 182
Pizza, Mexican Chicken, '97 321
Pizza, Quick 'n' Easy Chicken Barbecue, '04 139
Pizzas, Chicken-and-Three-Cheese French Bread,
    '96 94
Pizza, Southwest Deluxe, '95 268
Pizza, Southwestern, '03 146
Pizza, Tex-Mex Chicken-and-Bacon, '05 325
Pizza with Mango Pico de Gallo, Fajita Chicken, '04 318
Plum Sauce, Chicken with, '82 236
Poached Chicken and Vegetables, Ginger-, '98 229
Poached Chicken Breast in Wine, '91 184
Poached Chicken Breasts, Wine-, '85 58
Poached Chicken Breast with Turned Vegetables and
    Chive Sauce, '94 309
Poached Chicken, Whole, '98 229
Poached Chicken with Black Beans and Salsa, '87 217
Poached Chicken with Creamy Mustard Sauce,
    Champagne-, '94 24
Poblano Chicken, Creamy, '98 42
Polenta, Chicken with, '02 87

Pollo Almendrado (Chicken in Almond Sauce), **'81** 193

Pollo con Calabacita (Mexican Chicken with Zucchini), **'82** 219

Pollo en Mole de Cacahuate (Chicken with Peanut Mole Sauce), **'80** 194

Pollo en Pipián, Mexican, **'88** 31

Poppy Seed Chicken, **'94** 108

Potatoes, Chicken-Cheese Stuffed, **'86** 55

Potatoes, Creamed Beef and Chicken-Topped, **'83** 210

Potatoes, Gumbo, **'95** 22

Potatoes, Sweet-and-Sour-Topped, **'83** 4

Pot, Chicken in a, **'81** 3

Pretzel-Crusted Chicken, **'94** 252

Princess Chicken, **'86** 122

Provolone, Chicken, **'93** 323

Pudding, Chicken, **'05** 22

Puffs, Appetizer Chicken, **'85** 72

Puffs, Chicken Nut, **'81** 260

Quesadillas, Chicken-and-Black Bean, **'96** 288

Quesadillas, Grilled Chicken, **'04** 36

Quesadillas, Sesame-Ginger Chicken, **'00** 147

Quesadillas, Spicy Chicken, **'95** 42

Quesadillas with Chipotle Salsa, Chicken-and-Brie, **'99** 311

Quiche, Chicken Divan, **'88** M125

Quiche, Chicken-Olive-Cheddar, **'03** 58

Quiche, Chicken-Pecan, **'91** 206

Quiche Noël, **'82** 310

Quick, Chicken, **'90** 117

Ragoût with Cheddar Dumplings, Chicken, **'94** 44

Raspberry Chicken, **'97** 66

Rice and Chicken, Salsa, **'99** 109

Rice, Chicken Caruso and, **'89** 177

Rice, Chicken with Curried, **'98** 127

Rice, Island Chicken and, **'04** 165

Rice, Moorish Chicken with, **'98** 127

Rice, One-Dish Chicken and, **'01** 279

Rice Pilaf, Chicken Breasts with Fruited, **'92** 307

Rice, Shortcut Chicken and, **'90** 220

Rice, Spicy Chicken and, **'88** 200

Risotto, Smoked Chicken-and-Roasted Shallot, **'00** 30

Roast Chicken, **'93** 14

Roast Chicken and Brown Rice, **'83** 268

Roast Chicken and Vegetables, **'81** 3

Roast Chicken with Pineapple-Mustard Glaze, **'89** 83

Roast Chicken with Rice, **'95** 261

Roast Chicken with Sautéed Green Beans, Lemon-Garlic, **'05** 43

Roasted Chicken and Potatoes, **'98** 289

Roasted Chicken, Chipotle, **'03** 44

Roasted Chicken, Glazed, **'00** 14; **'01** 327

Roasted Chicken, Herb-, **'87** 155; **'00** 330

Roasted Chicken, Hot Oven-, **'98** 108

Roasted Chicken, Jan's, **'01** 224

Roasted Chicken, Lemon-, **'95** 24

Roasted Chicken, Lemon-Garlic, **'98** 108

Roasted Chicken, Lemon-Thyme, **'03** 44

Roasted Chicken, Peanut-, **'01** 107

Roasted Chicken, Rice-Stuffed, **'88** 38

Roasted Chicken, Savory, **'98** 21

Roasted Chicken, Slow-, **'98** 108

Roasted Chicken with Lemon, Garlic, and Rosemary, **'97** 61

Roasted Chicken with Poblano Vinaigrette and Corn Pudding, **'99** 71

Roasted Chicken with Vegetables, **'98** 108

Roasted Chicken with Wild Rice, Orange-Glazed, **'02** 85

Roasted Citrus Chicken, Clay Oven-, **'98** 108

Roasted Stuffed Chicken, **'98** 109

Rockefeller Chicken, **'79** 219

Rolls à la Swiss, Chicken-and-Ham, **'92** 42

Rolls, Chicken-Asparagus, **'86** M211

Rolls, Crispy Chicken, **'84** 288

Rolls Elégante, Chicken, **'80** 210

Rolls, Hearts of Palm Chicken, **'89** 201

Rolls, Hearty Salad, **'81** 206

Rolls Jubilee, Chicken, **'87** 118

Rolls, Mexican Chicken, **'93** 242

Rolls, Pesto-Stuffed Chicken, **'93** 82

Rolls, Southwestern Cabbage, **'97** 214

Rollups, Cheesy Chicken, **'82** 44

Rollups, Chicken, **'85** 179; **'88** 38

Rollups, Chicken and Spinach, **'80** 90; **'82** M68

Imperial Chicken, **'80** 217

Rollups in Gravy, Chicken, **'83** 184

Rollups, Sunshine Chicken, **'85** 251

Romano, Chicken alla, **'83** M58

Romano, Chicken Breasts, **'79** 218

Romanoff, Chicken, **'84** 292

Roquefort Chicken, **'89** 320

Rosemary Chicken, Pinot Noir Risotto with, **'97** 214

Rotelle, Chicken and Tomato with, **'87** 108

Rub, Paul's Chicken, **'05** 174

Saffron Chicken with Prunes, **'97** 264

Salads

Almond-Chicken Salad Shanghai, **'90** 160

Almond Salad, Chicken-, **'81** 133

Aloha Chicken Salad, **'80** 297

Amandine, Chicken Salad, **'81** 37

Ambrosia, Chicken Salad, **'85** 216

Apple Salad, Chicken-, **'90** 216

Apricot-Chicken Salad, **'99** 163

Apricot Salsa, Chicken with, **'98** 126

Artichoke-Chicken-Rice Salad, **'94** 132

Artichoke-Chicken-Rice Salad, Mediterranean, **'97** 321

Artichokes, Chicken Salad with, **'86** 186

Asian Chicken Salad, **'99** 124

Asparagus-Chicken Salad, **'89** 83

Aspic-Topped Chicken Salad, **'88** 88

Autumn Chicken Salad, **'01** 312

Avocado-Chicken Salad, **'87** 107

Avocado Salad, Chicken-, **'80** 139

Avocado Salad, Fruited Chicken-, **'82** 101

Avocado Salad Platter, Chicken-, **'83** 2

Avocado Salad, Tossed Chicken-, **'80** 4

Avocados, Chicken Salad in, **'85** 216

Baked Chicken Salad, **'86** 297; **'87** 176

Barbecue Chicken Salad, Warm, **'99** 124

Basil-Chicken-Vegetable Salad, **'92** 162

Black-and-Blue Salad, **'00** 337

Black Bean Salad, Chicken-, **'99** 124

Black-Eyed Pea Salad, Chicken-and-, **'97** 305

BLT Chicken Salad, **'87** 144

Blueberry Salad, Chicken-, **'02** 177

Blue Cheese Chicken Salad, **'94** 81

Blue Cheese, Chicken Salad with, **'97** 97

Broccoli-Chicken Salad, **'90** 129; **'00** 53

Buffalo Tenders Salad, **'03** 184

Caesar Salad, Chicken, **'96** 26

Celery Salad, Chicken-, **'81** 187

Chef's Salad, **'98** 209

Cherry-Tarragon Chicken Salad, **'05** 275

Chicken Salad, **'86** 232, 261; **'96** 67; **'05** 65, 94

Chop Suey Salad, **'81** 37

Chunky Chicken Parmesan Salad, **'05** 209

Chutney-Chicken Salad, **'87** 74

Chutney Salad, Chicken, **'82** 108

Cobb Salad, Southern-Style, **'01** 112

Coconut-Chicken Salad, Curried Poached Pears with, **'97** 93

Coleslaw, Chicken, **'84** 2

Cranberry-Pecan Chicken Salad, **'05** 284

Cream Puff Bowl, Chicken Salad in, **'86** 232

Crisp Salad, Crunchy, **'95** 28

Crunchy Chicken Salad, **'86** 157, 207

Curried Chicken-and-Orange Salad, **'87** 144

Curried Chicken-Rice Salad, **'92** 190

Curried Chicken Salad, **'79** 219; **'84** 66; **'85** 96; **'86** 131; **'89** 176

Curried Chicken Salad, Royal, **'96** 200

Curried Chicken Salad with Asparagus, **'81** 36

Dilled Chicken Salad, **'91** 212

Exotic Luncheon Salad, **'83** 210

Fancy Chicken Salad, **'79** 55

Fiesta Chicken Salad, **'05** 223

Filling, Chicken Salad, **'87** 106

Fried Chicken Ginger Salad, **'93** 290

Fried Chicken Salad, Fiesta, **'03** 120

Fruit, Chicken Salad with, **'82** 171

Fruit-Chicken Salad with Blueberry Vinaigrette, Summer, **'00** 154

Fruited Chicken Salad, **'84** 25, 290; **'88** 88; **'90** 318

Fruited Chicken Salad in Avocados, **'87** 41

Fruit Salad, Chicken-, **'82** 79; **'90** 234

Fruit Salad, Chicken-and-, **'01** 178

Fruity Chicken Salad, **'83** 157

Gazpacho-Chicken Salad, **'00** 203

Grapes, Chicken Salad with, **'86** 117

Greek Chicken Salad, **'97** 92; **'98** 329

Green Salad with Chicken, Mixed, **'80** 54

Grilled Asian Chicken Salad, **'96** 158

Grilled Chicken-and-Fruit Salad, **'96** 155

Grilled Chicken on Greens, **'99** 201

Grilled Chicken-Rice Salad, **'98** 148

Grilled Chicken Salad, Moroccan, **'95** 231

Grilled Chicken Salad with Raspberry Dressing, **'95** 202

Hoisin Chicken-and-Pasta Salad, **'99** 125

Honey Chicken Salad, **'04** 51

Horseradish Salad, Chicken-, **'02** 235

Hot Chicken Salad, **'81** 201; **'83** 196; **'98** 290

Hot Chicken Salad, Country Club-Style, **'86** 10

Hot Chicken Salad, Crunchy, **'80** 138

Hot Chicken Salad Pinwheel, **'80** 139

Italian, Chicken Salad, **'89** 18

Lapsang-Poached Chicken Salad, **'05** 135

Layered Chicken Salad, **'89** 162

Lemon-Chicken Salad, Lively, **'00** 16

Macadamia Chicken Salad, **'80** 138

Macaroni-Chicken Salad, **'85** 296; **'86** 302

Macaroni-Chicken Salad, Dilled, **'92** 142

Mama Hudson's Chicken Salad, **'93** 238

Mandarin Chicken, Carousel, **'79** 88

Mango, Chicken Salad with, **'86** 215

Marinated Chicken-Grape Salad, **'85** 74

Marinated Chicken-Raspberry Salad, **'93** 190

Marinated Chicken Strips and Vegetables, **'00** 54

Melts, Open-Faced Cheesy Chicken Salad, **'00** 134

Mexican Chicken Salad, **'85** 84; **'88** 272

Minted Chicken Salad, **'92** 104

Mold, Chicken-Cucumber, **'80** 175

Mold, Chicken Salad, **'83** 80; **'84** 163

Nectarine Chicken Salad, **'79** 175

Noodle Salad, Chicken, **'03** 143

Noodle Salad, Chicken, **'95** 25

Old-Fashioned Chicken Salad, **'83** 79

Oriental Chicken Salad, **'85** 216; **'88** 271; **'91** 43; **'96** 92

Oriental, Chicken Salad, **'90** 146

Overnight Salad, **'97** 305; **'98** 18

Parmesan-Chicken Salad, **'98** 234

Pasta, Chicken-and-Bow Tie, **'01** 164

Pasta-Chicken Salad, Tarragon, **'87** 155

Pasta Salad, Bayou, '00 203
Pasta Salad, Chicken, '88 89
Pasta Salad, Grilled Chicken-, '94 64
Pasta Salad, Zesty Chicken-, '02 186
Peachy Chicken Salad, '97 193
Peanut-Chicken Salad, Sweet, '03 54
Pea Salad, Chicken-, '83 218
Persian Chicken Salad, '81 12
Picnic Salad with Honey-Mustard Dressing,
   Hoover's, '05 184
Pineapple-Chicken Salad Pie, '80 138
Pineapple-Nut Chicken Salad, '83 80
Pocket, Chicken Salad in a, '88 139
Polynesian Chicken Salad, '88 272
Poulet Rémoulade, '87 144
Rice Salad, Chicken-, '81 203; '97 93
Rice Salad, Chicken-and-, '97 92
Rice Salad, Hot Chicken-and-, '83 22
Rice Salad, Nutty Chicken-, '83 157
Ring, Chicken Salad, '90 123
Ring Salad, Chicken Jewel, '83 282
Roasted Chicken Salad, '93 14
Roasted Chicken with Wilted Salad Greens, Tom's,
   '05 185
Roasted Red Pepper Salad, Chicken and, '03 291
Rolls, Hearty Salad, '81 206
Sandwiches, Asian Chicken Salad, '98 223
Sandwiches, Chicken-Salad Finger, '85 119
Sandwiches, Grilled Chicken Salad, '00 164
Sandwiches, Hot Chicken Salad, '96 74
Sherried Chicken-and-Grape Salad, '01 61
South Sea Island Chicken Salad, '97 88
Southwestern Chicken Salad, '88 88
Southwestern Chicken Salad Spirals, '02 58
Spaghetti Salad, Chicken-, '90 146
Spaghetti Salad, Chicken-and-Veggie, '04 129
Special Chicken Salad, '85 82; '87 183; '88 M193
Spicy Chicken Salad with Cabbage Wraps, '04 62
Spicy Chicken Salad with Veggies, '04 177
Spinach-Strawberry Salad, Chicken-, '97 92
Spinach Tossed Salad, Chicken-and-, '83 157
Spread, Chicken Salad Party, '88 M8
Spread, Curried Chicken Salad, '00 68
Spring Salad with Raspberry Vinaigrette, '05 91
Stack-Up Salad, Chicken, '83 80
Strawberry-Chicken Salad, '04 50
Strawberry-Citrus Chicken Salad, '05 84
Strawberry Salad, Chicken-and-, '05 132
Summer Chicken Salad, '83 145
Summery Chicken Salad, '95 138
Super Chicken Salad, '82 174
Supreme, Chicken Salad, '79 107, 152; '89 176
Taco Chicken Salad, Ranch, '97 315
Taco Salad, Chicken, '94 M136
Tahitian Chicken Salad, '84 120
Tarragon Chicken Salad, '90 199
Tarts, Chicken Salad, '84 257
Thai Chicken Salad, '95 177
Tortellini Salad, Chicken, '87 288
Tortilla Salads, Mexican Chicken, '95 129
Tropical Chicken Boats for Two, '82 186
Tropical Chicken Salad, '85 216; '96 127
Tropical Spinach Salad with Grilled Chicken,
   '04 51
Twist, Chicken Salad with a, '84 221
Vegetable-Chicken Salad, '91 287
Vegetable-Chicken Vinaigrette Salad, '86 135
Vegetable Patch Chicken Salad, '04 92
Walnut-Chicken Salad, '89 14; '96 243
Walnut Salad, Sunburst Chicken-and-, '93 91
Wild Rice-and-Chicken Salad, '02 52
Wild Rice-Chicken Salad, '83 146; '99 55; '01 72
Wild Rice Salad, '01 247
Wraps, Lemon-Basil Chicken Salad, '00 216

Saltimbocca alla Romana, Chicken, '80 212
San Antonio-Style Chicken, '81 166
Sandwiches
   Asian Chicken Salad Sandwiches, '98 223
   Bagel Sandwiches, Chicken-Benedict, '96 250
   Baked Chicken Sandwiches, '79 164; '80 130;
      '84 165
   Broiled Chicken Sandwiches with Fresh Salsa, '00 59
   Burgers, Chicken-Cheese, '04 56
   Burritos, Chicken, '01 55
   Cheesy Chicken Sandwiches, '82 190
   Club Sandwiches, Chicken, '86 160
   Crispy Chicken Sandwich, '81 114
   Curried Chicken Tea Sandwiches, '97 23
   Dagwoods, Chicken-Avocado, '96 200; '99 337
   Finger Sandwiches, Chicken-Salad, '85 119
   Focaccia with Roasted Pepper Vinaigrette, Stuffed,
      '00 134; '04 142
   Gouda Lover's Chicken Sandwiches, '99 195
   Grilled Chicken-and-Pesto Clubs, '01 22
   Grilled Chicken 'n' Cheese Sandwiches, '99 240
   Grilled Chicken Salad Sandwiches, '00 164
   Ham 'n' Cheese Chicken Sandwich, '95 153
   Hot Brown Sandwiches, '80 202
   Hot Chicken Salad Sandwiches, '96 74
   Hot Chicken Sandwiches, '83 291
   Jamaican Chicken Sandwich, '95 153
   Jerk Chicken Sandwich, '98 333
   Mandarin Orange Spread Sandwiches, Chicken-,
      '04 259
   Marinated Chicken in a Sandwich, '86 185
   Marinated Chicken Sandwiches, '86 M45
   Open-Faced Sandwiches, Summer, '99 201
   Panini, Chicken Florentine, '02 236
   Parmigiana Sandwich, Chicken, '94 65
   Pita, Fajita in a, '90 177
   Pita Pockets, Chicken-Spinach, '01 66
   Pita Sandwiches, Mango-Chicken, '03 123
   Pitas, Fajita, '99 239
   Pocket, Chicken Salad in a, '88 139
   Pocket Sandwiches, Chicken-Almond, '81 240;
      '83 69
   Pockets, Oriental Stuffed, '79 14
   Puffed Chicken Sandwiches, '82 35
   Rollups, Greek Chicken, '05 128
   Southwestern Chicken Sandwiches, '96 23
   Sub, Chicken, '98 287
   Toasted Chicken-and-Cheese Sandwiches, '85 242
   Wraps, Chicken-and-Bean Slaw, '04 163
   Wraps, Chicken-and-Slaw, '05 222
   Wraps, Chicken-Cranberry, '01 34
   Wraps, Chicken Lettuce, '02 65
   Wraps, Southwestern, '99 238
   Wraps, Thai Chicken-Avocado, '02 206
Sanibel Island Chicken, '97 66
Saté, Chicken, '99 134
Sauce, Chicken Curry, '90 117
Sauce, Creamy Chicken, '81 91
Sauce, Curry, '95 18
Sauce, Fettuccine with Chicken-and-Creamy Herb,
   '01 257
Saucy Chick-Wiches, '81 25; '82 31; '83 34
Sausage with Fennel, Chicken, '98 312
Sauté, Chicken-Apple, '97 48
Sautéed Chicken Breasts, '87 36
Sauté, Savory Chicken, '88 254; '89 120
Sauté, Sherry-Chicken, '87 218
Sauté, Sweet Pepper-Chicken, '89 104
Sauté with Artichokes and Mushrooms, Chicken, '03 57
Scallopini with Lemon Sauce, Chicken, '86 156
Scallopini with Peppers, Chicken, '85 78
Scaloppine in Lemon Sauce, Chicken, '00 166
Scaloppine with Linguine Alfredo, Chicken, '04 96
Scotch Cream, Chicken in, '88 42

Seared Chicken, Zesty, '01 82
Seasoned Browned Chicken, '85 25
Seasoned Chicken, '99 316
Seasoned Chicken, Crunchy, '87 217
Seasoning Blend, Poultry, '88 28
Sesame Chicken, '85 252; '86 122; '97 256; '98 20
Sesame Chicken, Hawaiian, '81 106
Sesame Chicken Strips, '98 250
Sesame Chicken with Noodles, '88 M125
Sesame-Crusted Chicken with Pineapple Salsa, '96 226
Sesame-Dijon Chicken, '98 96
Sesame-Ginger Chicken, '00 219
Shells, Southwestern Stuffed, '99 238
Sherried Chicken, '79 214
Sherried Chicken with Artichokes, '87 143
Sherry Chicken with Rice, '81 97
Shortcakes, Cheesy Chicken, '95 98
Sicilian Chicken, '97 142
Skewers, Taco-Chicken, '99 119
Skewers with Peanut Sauce, Chicken, '02 173; '04 324
Skillet, Cheesy Chicken, '80 115
Skillet Chicken, '81 180
Skillet Chicken Dinner, '86 249; '89 247
Skillet Chicken, Spicy, '94 220
Skillet Company Chicken, '82 60
Skillet, Confetti Chicken, '97 327
Skillet Dinner, Antipasto, '97 327
Skillet Dinner, Chicken-and-Rice, '98 127
Skillet Supper, Chicken-and-Sausage, '03 49
Smoked Chicken, Big "D," '05 175
Smothered Chicken with Lemon Mashed Potatoes,
   '04 180
Snow Peas, Chicken with, '83 187
Soufflé, Chicken-Chestnut, '79 107
Soups
   Artichoke, and Mushroom Soup, Chicken, '92 324
   Asparagus-and-Chicken Soup, Creamy, '95 82
   Bean-Chicken Soup, '99 283
   Bisque, Curried Chicken, '00 144
   Black Bean Soup, Chicken-and-, '05 102
   Broccoli-and-Chicken Soup, '90 202
   Chicken Soup, '81 98
   Chowder, Chicken-and-Roasted Vegetable, '97 21
   Chowder, Chicken Corn, '02 305
   Chowder, Chicken-Vegetable, '04 326
   Chowder, Fiesta, '02 305
   Chowder Sauterne, Chicken, '84 235
   Chunky Chicken-Noodle Soup, '88 12
   Corn Soup, Cheesy Chicken-, '97 158
   Country Chicken-and-Buttermilk Soup, '02 144
   Cream of Chicken Soup, '85 243
   Cream Soup, Chicken-Almond, '92 21
   Curried Chicken Soup, '86 34
   Enchilada Soup, Chicken, '86 22
   Fiesta Chicken Soup, '04 323
   French Soup Maigre, '98 125
   Ham, and Oyster Soup, Chicken, '79 198
   Homemade Chicken Soup, '82 34
   Lime Soup, '88 31
   Mac 'n' Chicken Soup, Cheesy, '05 292
   Mexican Chicken Soup, '84 234; '00 336; '03 63
   Noodle Soup, Chicken, '80 264; '95 45; '98 30
   Noodle Soup, Creamy Chicken, '99 20
   Pepper-and-Chicken Soup, Roasted, '90 58
   Quick Chicken Soup, '86 M72
   Rice Soup, Chicken-and-, '88 236
   Sopa de Lima, '79 211
   Spicy Chicken Soup, '97 268
   Stock, Chicken, '95 18
   Stock, Light Poultry, '90 31
   Tortilla Soup, '98 291; '99 310; '00 98, 110;
      '04 26
   Tortilla Soup, Supereasy, '00 199
   Vegetable Soup, Chicken-, '88 18; '99 60

CHICKEN, Soups
(continued)

Vegetable Soup, Spicy Chicken-, '02 168
Wild Rice Soup, Chicken-and-, '04 26
Wild Rice Soup, Creamy Chicken-and-, '98 M334
Witches' Brew Chicken Soup, '01 205
Southwestern Chicken, '03 180
Soy and Wine, Chicken in, '84 26
Soy-Garlic Chicken, '98 128
Spaghetti, Chicken, '83 105; '87 221; '98 329
Spaghetti, Chicken-Vegetable, '92 281; '98 296
Spanish Chicken, '98 183
Special Occasion Chicken, '91 206
Spiced Chicken, Crunchy, '85 M57
Spiced Fruited Chicken with Almond Rice, '81 195
Spicy Chicken Dish, '87 267; '88 103; '89 66
Spicy Chicken 'n' Dumplings, Quick-and-, '03 325
Spinach Fettuccine, Easy Chicken with, '88 89
Spinach Noodles, Chicken and, '82 19
Spread, Festive Chicken, '87 158
Spread Gift Box, Chicken-Artichoke-Cheese, '00 328
Spread, Low-Fat Chicken, '82 290
Spread, Tasty Chicken, '84 193
Spring Rolls, '99 238
Steamed Dinner, Easy, '83 M314
Stews
Brunswick Chicken Stew, '87 4
Brunswick Stew, '80 264; '97 138, 315; '01 148, 219;
'03 29
Brunswick Stew, Bama, '87 4
Brunswick Stew, Breeden Liles's, '91 14
Brunswick Stew, Chicken, '97 234
Brunswick Stew, Dan Dickerson's, '91 16
Brunswick Stew, Gay Neale's, '91 17
Brunswick Stew, Georgian, '92 35
Brunswick Stew, Jeff Daniel's, '91 16
Brunswick Stew, Sonny Frye's, '87 4
Brunswick Stew, Van Doyle's Family-Size, '91 14
Brunswick Stew, Virginian, '92 34
Brunswick Stew, Virginia Ramsey's Favorite, '91 16
Camp Stew, '02 42
Chicken Stew, '97 26
Chili-Chicken Stew, '90 319
Dumplings, Chicken Stew and, '84 4
Greek-Style Chicken Stew, '03 219
Kale, and Chickpea Stew, Chicken, '98 47
Santa Fe Chicken Stew, '97 193
Speedy Chicken Stew, '03 42
Strader Stew, '89 28
Vegetable Stew, Chicken-and-, '05 235
Zesty Chicken Stew, '02 127
Sticks, Italian Chicken, '98 25
Sticky Chicken, '97 239
Stir-Fry
à l'Orange, Stir-Fry Chicken, '83 82
Apple-Sesame-Chicken Stir-Fry, '92 226
Broccoli Stir-Fry, Chicken-, '82 33
Chinese Chicken Stir-Fry, '90 100
Curry, Stir-Fried Chicken, '87 51
Easy Chicken Stir-Fry, '91 124
Herb-Chicken Stir-Fry, '89 177
Hurry-Up Chicken Stir-Fry, '91 124
Mexican Stir-Fry, '92 126
Orange-Chicken Stir-Fry, '84 68
Orange-Chicken Stir-Fry, Kyoto, '87 96
Pineapple-Chicken Stir-Fry, '89 176
Shiitake-Chicken Stir-Fry, '89 61
Snow Pea Stir-Fry, Chicken and, '95 157
Sweet-and-Sour Chicken Stir-Fry, '98 204
Thai Chicken Stir-Fry, '00 23
Vegetables Stir-Fry Chicken and, '86 249
Vegetables Stir-Fry Chicken-and-, '86 68

Vegetables, Stir-Fry Chicken with, '96 128
Vegetable Stir-Fry, Chicken-, '83 151; '84 13, 141;
'01 175
Vegetable Stir-Fry, Chicken, '00 245
Vegetable Stir-Fry, Chicken and, '82 237
Vegetable Stir-Fry, Chicken-and-, '96 19
Vegetables with Chicken Stir-Fry, '84 195
Zesty Stir-Fried Chicken, '83 82
Zucchini Stir-Fry, Chicken-, '84 50
Stock, Light Poultry, '90 31
Strips, Nutty Chicken, '99 111
Strips with "Come Back" Dipping Sauce, Miss Mary's
Chicken, '96 213
Strips with Honey Sauce, Chicken, '03 27
Strips, Zippy Chicken, '84 205
Stroganoff, Chicken, '99 41
Stroganoff, Chicken-and-Broccoli, '89 M248
Stroganoff, Strolling-Through-the-Holidays, '01 282
Strudel, Chicken-Goat Cheese, '98 28
Strudel with White Wine Gravy, Chicken-Herb, '04 318
Stuffed Alfredo Chicken, '04 56
Stuffed Chicken Breasts, '82 36; '85 291; '88 50;
'89 274
Stuffed Chicken Breasts, Apple-Bacon, '99 313
Stuffed Chicken Breasts, Hawaiian, '99 64
Stuffed Chicken Breasts over Angel Hair, Goat Cheese-,
'97 144
Stuffed Chicken Breasts, Peach-, '79 177
Stuffed Chicken Breasts Sardou, '87 269
Stuffed Chicken Breasts, Walnut-, '85 293
Stuffed Chicken Breasts with Sweet-and-Sour Tomato
Sauce, '01 120
Stuffed Chicken Breasts with White Bean Puree,
'98 270; '02 200
Stuffed Chicken Breasts with White Grape Sauce, '80 38
Stuffed Chicken, Crab-, '84 101
Stuffed Chicken, Creamy Tomato-, '04 16
Stuffed Chicken in Puff Pastry, Spinach-, '92 125
Stuffed Chicken, Rice-, '81 4
Stuffed Chicken Rolls, Spinach-, '86 248
Stuffed Chicken Thighs, '82 84
Stuffed Chicken, Vegetable-, '89 M65
Stuffed Chicken, Wild Rice-, '79 219
Stuffed Chicken with Sautéed Peppers and Mushrooms,
Herb-, '91 26
Stuffed Chicken with Tomato-Basil Pasta, Basil-,
'94 M204
Sunday Chicken, '95 228
Sunshiny Chicken, '81 309
Supremes de Volaille à Blanc (Chicken Breasts in Cream
Sauce), '82 83
Sweet-and-Sour Chicken, '79 106; '83 184; '84 218;
'86 217, 240; '90 161; '91 202; '97 325
Sweet-and-Sour Chicken and Rice, '03 97
Sweet-and-Sour Chicken Nuggets, '90 168
Sweet-and-Sour Chicken Wings, '90 206
Sweet-and-Sour Lemon Chicken, '84 93
Sweet-and-Sour Shrimp and Chicken, '87 267; '88 103;
'89 66
Szechuan Chicken, '83 85; '98 155
Szechuan Chicken with Angel Hair Pasta, '97 91
Szechwan Chicken with Cashews, '81 212
Tacos, Chicken-and-Bean, '93 293
Tacos, Pizza-Flavored Chicken, '95 340
Taco Stacks, Soft, '02 54
Tahitian Chicken, '84 68
Tamales, Chicken, '88 151
Tamales, Helena, '05 112
Tandoori Chicken, '03 165
Tangy Chicken, '85 251; '86 292; '87 35
Tarragon Chicken, '86 231
Tarts, Deviled Chicken, '94 14
Tempura Delight, Chicken, '85 66
Tenders, Buffalo, '03 184

Tenders, Lemon Chicken, '03 184
Teriyaki, Chicken, '80 M76
Teriyaki Chicken, '91 163
Terrine, Chicken-Vegetable, '84 131
Terrine, Cold Chicken-Leek-, '92 145
Terrine Ring, Chicken, '84 132
Terrine, Vegetable-Chicken, '83 224
Texas Rockets, '05 175
Thighs, Balsamic Garlic-and-Herb Chicken,
'05 19
Thighs, Herb-Roasted Chicken, '02 127
Thighs, Honey-Pecan Chicken, '02 127
Thighs, Molasses-Glazed Chicken, '05 85
Thighs, Smoky Chicken, '05 184
Thighs, Sweet Glazed Chicken, '04 202
Tomato Aspic, Chicken in, '84 190
Tomatoes and Sausage, Chicken with, '97 266
Tortilla Stack, Cheesy Chicken-, '86 3
Toss, Quick Chicken, '87 M124
Tostadas, Chicken, '93 204; '95 122
Tostadas, Quick Chicken, '99 159
Undercover Chicken, '97 64
Valencia, Chicken-and-Rice, '85 113
Vegetable Platter, Chicken-and-, '88 M52
Vegetables, Chicken and, '88 165
Vegetables, Jim's Chicken and, '99 237
Vegetables with Ginger-Soy Sauce, Chicken and,
'91 32
Vermicelli, Chicken, '01 237
Vermouth, Chicken and Vegetables, '87 M37
Véronique, Chicken, '84 260; '85 302
Waffles, Southern Chicken-Pecan, '82 231
Walnut Chicken, '85 126
Walnut Chicken and Vegetables, '85 194
Walnut Chicken, Crispy, '90 89
Wellington, Chicken Breasts, '84 22
White Barbecue Sauce, Chicken with, '01 168
White Wine, Chicken in, '81 97
Wild Rice, Chicken and, '01 279
Wild Rice, Chicken-Fried, '89 24; '91 132
Wild Rice, Elegant Chicken with, '80 M76
Wine Sauce, Chicken and Mushrooms in, '81 109
Wine Sauce, Chicken in, '80 8
Wings. *See also* **CHICKEN/Drummettes.**
Broiled Chicken Wings, '80 149
Buffalo Hot Wings, '03 184
Buffalo Wings, '00 203; '05 64
Buffalo Wings, Spicy, '95 239
Chinese Chicken Wings, '96 111
Chipotle Chicken Wings, Sweet-and-Spicy, '04 176
Curried Chicken Wings, '96 110
Honey Chicken Wings, '00 15
Honey Chicken Wings, Grilled, '96 111
Honey-Glazed Chicken Wings, '91 251
Hot 'n' Spicy Chicken Nuggets, '04 132
Maple-Glazed Chicken Wings, '99 110
Oriental-Style Wings, Spicy, '96 215
Satan's Wings, '87 214
Sesame-Maple Chicken Wings, '00 57
Spanish Rice, Chicken Wings with, '00 202
Sweet-and-Hot Citrus Wings, '00 202
Sweet-and-Sour Chicken Wings, '96 110
Tandoori Chicken Wings, '96 110
Teriyaki Chicken Wings, '85 300; '86 18
Wontons, Chicken, '92 284
Wontons with Hoisin Peanut Dipping Sauce, Chicken,
'99 14
Yogurt Chicken, Savory, '91 238; '92 28
Yogurt-Sesame Chicken, '90 216
CHILI
Bake, Chili Hominy, '81 282; '82 58
Basic Chili, '82 M11; '93 326
Basic Chili Embellished, '93 327
Basic Chili Goes Southwest, '93 326

Bean Chili, Spicy 3-, **'03** 291
Bean Chili, Three-, **'00** 34
Beef Chili, Chunky, **'05** 235
Before-and-After Burner, Roy's, **'89** 316
Big-Batch Chili, **'04** 242
Biscuit Bowl, Chili in a, **'98** 224
Black Bean Chili, **'02** 20
Black Bean Chili Marsala, **'95** 16
Bodacious Chili, **'95** 14
Burgers, Open-Face Chili, **'82** 31; **'83** 33
Casserole, Chili, **'90** 176
Casserole, Chili-Rice, **'79** 54
Casserole, Hominy-Chili, **'86** 255
Casserole, Ultimate Chili, **'99** 239
Cheese-Topped Chili, **'82** M11
Cheesy Chili, **'82** 310
Chili, **'87** 17; **'93** 89; **'98** 95
Chilly Night Chili, **'99** 317
Choo-Choo Chili, **'89** 316
Chuck Wagon Chili, **'81** 282; **'82** 57
Chunky Chili, **'82** M282; **'86** 3
Cincinnati Chili, **'96** 18
Cincinnati-Style Chili, **'00** 34
Company Chili, **'82** 311; **'83** 30
con Carne, Beef and Sausage Chili, **'83** 284
con Carne, Chili, **'82** 310; **'83** 30; **'84** 72; **'86** 2; **'03** 19
con Carne, Favorite Chili, **'86** 293
con Carne, Quick-and-Easy Chili, **'86** 2
Cowboy Chili, **'86** 2
Dip, Cheesy Chili, **'80** 150
Dip, Chili, **'82** 161; **'88** 218; **'89** 47; **'91** 143
Dip, Chili-and-Cheese, **'89** 328
Dog, Dinglewood Pharmacy's Scrambled, **'95** 118
Dogs, Chili-Cheese, **'81** M176
Double-Meat Chili, **'79** 269; **'80** 12
Easy Chili, **'82** 310; **'83** 30; **'02** 299
Easy Chili with Beans, **'92** 262
Easy Texas Chili, **'90** 201
Eggplant Chili, **'85** 88
Enchiladas, Chili and, **'00** 55
Firestarter Chili, **'93** 34
Five-Ingredient Chili, **'95** 212
Friday Night Chili, **'86** 228
Game-Day Chili, **'00** 238
Greek Chili, **'95** 16
Hot Dog Chili, **'04** 199
Hot Spiced Chili, **'83** 214
Hotto Lotto Chili, **'89** 316
I-Cious, Chili-, **'89** 315
"In-the-Red" Chili over "Rolling-in-Dough" Biscuits, **'92** 80
Kielbasa Chili, Hearty, **'91** 28
Lolly's Pop Chili, **'89** 316
Lunchtime Chili, **'81** 230
Manicotti, Chili, **'89** 247; **'99** 239
Meat Loaf, Chili, **'81** 275
Meaty Chili, **'81** 282; **'82** 58
Meaty Chili with Beans, **'85** 250
Mexican Chili, **'89** 18
Microwave Chili, **'91** M232
Mom's Chili, **'93** 292
Noodles, Chili with, **'81** 282; **'82** 57
Now, Thatsa Chili, **'95** 16
Out West Chili, **'95** 15
Pastry Cups, Chili in, **'90** 68
Pie, Chili-Tamale, **'82** 9; **'83** 68
Potato Chili, Savory, **'83** 284
Potatoes, Chili-Topped, **'83** 3; **'98** M289
Potatoes, South-of-the-Border Stuffed, **'86** 54
Quick-and-Easy Chili, **'92** 20
Quick and Simple Chili, **'81** 282; **'82** 58
Quick Chili, **'83** 283
Ranch Chili and Beans, **'79** 270; **'80** 11
Red Bean Chili, **'02** 20

Red Bean Chili, Slow-Cooker, **'02** 20
Red Chili, **'93** 108
Red Chili, North Texas, **'87** 303
Rice, Chili with, **'82** M11
Roundup Chili, **'79** 269; **'80** 12
Salad, Chili-Corn Chip Stack-Up, **'04** 242
Salad, Spicy Chili, **'86** 71
Sauce, Chili, **'81** 175; **'94** 287
Sauce, Chili Meat, **'83** 4
Sauce, Chunky Chili, **'85** 188
Sauce, Spicy Chili, **'87** 127
Sausage-Beef Chili, **'86** 232
Sausage Chili, Beefy, **'82** M11
Simple Chili, **'79** 269; **'80** 11
Slow Cooker Cincinnati-Style Chili, **'00** 34
Soup, Chili Bean, **'96** 71
Soup, Chili Vegetable, **'94** 120
South-of-the-Border Chili, **'83** 283; **'91** 283
Southwestern Chili, **'91** 284
Spaghetti, Herbed Chili-, **'84** 222
Speedy Chili, **'92** 66
Spicy Chili, Old-Fashioned, **'79** 269; **'80** 11
Stew, Red Chili, **'95** 226
Strata, Cornbread-Chili, **'03** 100
Supper, Hot Chili, **'99** 279
Surprise, Chili, **'82** 229
Texas Championship Chili, **'81** 54
Texas Chili, Hot, **'80** 222; **'81** 77
Texas-Style Chili, **'82** 311; **'83** 30
Tex-Mex Chili, **'83** 26
Topping, Chili, **'84** 246; **'94** 22
Tree-Hunt Chili, **'87** 292
Turkey-Bean Chili, **'88** M213
Vegetable Chili, **'91** 28; **'97** 179
Vegetarian Chili, **'84** 280, 327; **'91** 284
Veggies Chili, Full-of-, **'00** 294
Venison Chili, **'82** 216; **'86** 3; **'87** 304
Venison Chili, Hot, **'91** 283
Verde, Chili, **'95** 14
White Bean Chili, **'02** 20
White Chili, **'91** 284
White Christmas Chili, **'98** 266; **'02** 260
White Lightning Texas Chili, **'92** 321
Zippy Chili, **'87** 110

CHOCOLATE. *See also* **BROWNIES, COOKIES, FUDGE.**
Apples, Black-and-White Caramel, **'03** M216
Apples, Candy, **'01** M205
Apples on a Stick, Chocolate, **'96** 255
Bags, Chocolate-Raspberry, **'95** 97
Banana Pops, **'84** 44
Bars and Cookies
    Almond Chip Balls, Toasted, **'84** 240
    Almond-Chocolate Bars, **'83** 304
    Almond Cookies, Chocolate-, **'98** 293
    Almond Cream Confections, **'87** 198; **'90** 310
    Almond Surprise Cookies, Chocolate-, **'88** M45
    Almond-Toffee Chocolate Chip Cookies, **'05** 87
    Biscotti, Chocolate Chip-Cinnamon, **'96** 281
    Biscotti, Chocolate-Cinnamon, **'05** 30
    Biscotti, Chocolate-Hazelnut, **'95** 80
    Biscotti Cioccolata, **'93** 268
    Biscotti, Cocoa-Almond, **'96** 280
    Blond Nut Squares, **'82** 156
    Bonbons, Chocolate-Filled, **'89** 162
    Bran Raisin Jumbos, Chocolate-, **'91** 142
    Brazil Squares, **'82** 306
    Brickle Cookies, Chocolate-, **'99** 127
    Butter Cookies, Chocolate-Tipped, **'84** 258; **'90** 312
    Butter Pecan Turtle Bars, **'90** 70
    Butterscotch Bars, Chocolate-, **'81** 197
    By-Cracky Bars, **'84** 212
    Cake Mix Cookies, **'97** 133
    Candy Wrap Cookies, **'04** 139

Cappuccino Cookies, Chocolate, **'01** 315
Caramel-Filled Chocolate Cookies, **'92** 319; **'02** 53
Caramel Layer Squares, Chocolate-, **'79** 83
Cereal Bars, Chewy Chocolate, **'97** 317
Cherry Chocolates, **'95** 321
Cherry Cookies, Chocolate-, **'85** 324
Cherry Cookies, Chocolate-Covered, **'99** 280
Cherry-Double Chip Cookies, Chunky, **'05** M87
Chess Squares, Chocolate, **'92** 45
Chewies, Chocolate, **'93** 216
Chewies, Double Chocolate, **'00** 333
Chewies, Easy Chocolate, **'93** 296; **'94** 234
Chewy Chocolate Chip Squares, **'91** 175
Chewy Chocolate Cookies, **'80** 208; **'97** 166
Chip Bars, Chocolate, **'81** 130
Chip Cookies, **'84** 120
Chip Cookies, Chocolate, **'86** 245; **'90** 193; **'00** 276
Chip Cookies, Chocolate-Chocolate, **'82** 35
Chip Cookies, Mom Ford's Chocolate, **'94** 287
Chippers, Chocolate, **'92** 206
Chips Cookies, Loaded-with-, **'87** 223
Chip Squares, Chocolate, **'83** 170; **'89** 143
Chubbies, Chocolate, **'01** 144
Cinnamon Bars, Chocolate, **'82** 209
Cocoa Drop Cookies, **'80** 217
Cocoa Kiss Cookies, **'85** 171
Coconut Robin's Nests, **'98** M111
Coconut Squares, Chocolate-, **'90** 70
Coconut Swirls, **'97** 274
Coffee Kisses, Chocolate-Dipped, **'96** 313
Congo Squares, **'96** 94
Cranberry-White Chocolate Cookies, **'05** 308
Cream Cheese-Chocolate Chip Cookies, **'02** 229; **'03** 131
Crème de Menthe Bars, Chocolate-, **'86** 245
Crème de Menthe Bites, Chocolate, **'88** 285
Crème de Menthe Squares, **'93** 256
Crispies, Chocolate-Peanut, **'93** 80
Crispy Cookies, Chocolate, **'85** 115
Crumble Bars, Choco-, **'79** 292
Crunch Cookies, Chocolate, **'91** 316
Crunchies, Chocolate, **'92** 50
Cupcake Cookies, **'04** 273
Dainties, Choco-Nut, **'04** M124
Dark Chocolate-Almond Crisps, **'05** M30
Dark Chocolate Chip Cookies, **'05** 87
Date-Nut Chocolate Chip Cookies, Rich, **'92** 207
Deluxe Chocolate Chip Cookies, **'79** 216
Devil Doggies, **'84** 37
Different Chocolate Chip Cookies, **'83** 114
Dipped Cookies, Chocolate-, **'05** M299
Domino Cookies, **'05** 19
Double Chip Cookies, **'81** 301
Double Chocolate Chip Cookies, **'79** 217
Double Chocolate Chunk-Almond Cookies, **'95** 178
Double Chocolate Chunk Cookies, **'05** 181
Double Chocolate Chunk-Peanut Cookies, **'04** 125
Double-Chocolate Cookies, **'95** 272
Doubly-Good Chocolate Cookies, **'82** M185
Dream Bars, Chocolate, **'79** 256; **'82** 298
Drop Cookies, Chocolate, **'84** 36
Easy Cookies, **'00** 133
Favorite Chocolate Chip Cookies, **'05** 142
Fibber McGee Cookies, **'95** 72
Flying Brooms, **'98** 255
Forget 'em Cookies, **'83** 256
Frosted Chocolate-Cherry Cookies, **'89** 294
Fudge Bars, **'86** 93
Fudge Bars, Yummy, **'87** 158
Fudge-Pecan Chewies, Alabama, **'95** 143
Fudge Puddles, **'94** 292
German Chocolate Chess Squares, **'94** 51
Giant Chocolate Chip Cookies, **'84** 119

CHOCOLATE, Bars and Cookies
(continued)

Gingerbread Cookies, Chocolate-, '94 293
Graham Cracker Layered Cookies, Chocolate, '98 94
Jumbo Chocolate Chip Cookies, '82 110
Keyboard Cookies, '94 M330
Kiss Cookies, Chocolate, '03 298
Kissy Cookies, '93 331
Light Chocolate Chip Cookies, '86 46
Log Cookies, Chocolate-Tipped, '87 294
Lollapalooza, '94 194
Macaroon Cookies, Chocolate, '88 217
Macaroons, Chocolate, '83 300; '87 57
Macaroons, White Chocolate Tropical, '00 M166
Magic Cookie Bars, '02 253
Meltaways, Chocolate, '81 302
Melt-Aways, Chocolate Chip, '84 118
Meringue-Chocolate Chip Bars, '84 118
Meringue Cookies, Heavenly Chocolate-Chip,
   '01 218
Meringue Kiss Cookies, '86 121
Mint Chip Cookies, Chocolate-, '86 245
Mint Cookies, Chocolate-, '92 206
Mint Cookies, Chocolate and, '05 308
Mint Snaps, Chocolate-, '83 103; '84 96
Monster Cookies, '84 36
Neapolitan Cookies, '00 290
Nugget Cookies, '79 291
Nut Chews, Chocolate-, '81 92
Nut Freezer Cookies, Chocolate-, '88 217
Nutty Choco Snacks, '83 305
Nutty Oatmeal-Chocolate Chip Cookies, '82 M185
Oatmeal Bars, Chocolate-Topped, '86 110
Oatmeal-Chocolate Chippers, '90 218
Oatmeal-Chocolate Chunk Cookies, Nutty, '01 19
Oatmeal-Chocolate Morsel Cookies, '95 46
Oatmeal Cookies, Chocolate-, '80 105
Oatmeal Cookies, Chocolate Chip-, '84 119
Oatmeal Cookies, Double-Chip, '03 200
Oatmeal-Peanut Butter Chocolate Chip Cookies,
   '92 207
Oatmeal-Raisin Chocolate Chip Cookies, '05 87
Oatmeal-Toffee Lizzies, Crispy, '95 136
Olympic Medal Cookies, '96 180
Orange-Chocolate Cookies, '83 113
Orange Cookies, Chocolate-Dipped, '04 299
Orange Delights, Chocolate-, '93 52
Peanut Bars, Chocolate-, '03 195
Peanut Blossom Cookies, '95 245; '96 55; '97 324
Peanut Butter and Chocolate Chunk Cookies,
   '94 169
Peanut Butter-and-Fudge Bars, '80 M172
Peanut Butter Bars, '84 243
Peanut Butter-Chocolate Chip Cookies, '05 87, 222
Peanut Butter-Chocolate Chip Cookies, Freezer,
   '86 230
Peanut Butter-Chocolate Kiss Cookies, '86 49
Peanut Butter-Chocolate Treats, Crispy, '02 287;
   '03 271
Peanut Butter Cones, Chocolate-, '85 14
Peanut Butter Cookies, Chocolate-, '85 90
Peanut Butter Cookies, Chocolate Chip-, '99 68
Peanut Butter Cups, Chocolate-, '85 14; '97 134
Peanut Butter Fingers, '79 256
Peanut Butter-Kiss Cookies, '03 42
Peanut Butter Squares, Chocolate Chip-, '84 118
Peanut Chip Cookies, Choco-, '92 318
Peanut Cookies, Chocolate-, '83 223
Peanut Cookies, Chocolate Chunk-, '04 125
Pecan-Chocolate Chip Cookies, '05 87
Peppermint Cookies, Chocolate-Chocolate Chip-,
   '97 289

Peppermint Squares, Chocolate-, '81 119
Pinwheel Cookies, '93 316
Pinwheel Cookies, Chocolate, '86 245
Pinwheels, '95 321
Pixies, Chocolate, '00 M155
Pizza Cookies, Candy Shop, '02 299
Polka Dots, '95 272
Praline Bars, '05 M205
Praline-Chocolate Chip Cookies, Crispy, '02 229;
   '03 131
Praline-Chocolate Fudge Bars, Chewy, '04 M330
Pudding Cookies, Chocolate Chip-, '93 21
Pumpkin-Chocolate Chip Cookies, '93 235
Raisin Oatmeal Cookies, Chocolate-, '95 136
Rudolph Cookies, '99 M309
Sachertorte Cookies, '00 155
Sandwich Cookies, Chocolate, '81 192
Sandwich Cookies, Choco-Nut, '84 200
Sandwiches, Chocolate Cookie Ice Cream, '87 147
Scotch Bars, Chewy, '98 M291
Seashells, Chocolate, '91 178
Shortbread Cookies, Chocolate, '99 147
Shortbread, Marble-Topped Hazelnut, '99 M29
Shortbread, Millionaire, '05 M94
Shortbread, Mocha, '05 307
Shortbread, Mocha-Chocolate, '04 173
Shortbread, Peanut-Toffee, '04 329
Shortbread Squares, Mocha-Chocolate, '02 176
Shortbread Wafers, Cocoa, '88 243
Snack Bars, Chocolate, '04 124
Snappers, Jumbo Chocolate, '81 218
Snowball Cookies, Chocolate, '82 295
Snowballs, Chocolate, '03 273
Snowcaps, Smoky Mountain, '00 288
Snowflake Cookies, Chocolate, '89 329
Spice Cookies, Lemon-Iced Chocolate, '97 123
Stick, Chocolate Cookies on a, '05 63
Sugar-Coated Chocolate Cookies, '92 274
Sugar Cookies, Double-Chocolate, '92 206
Super Chocolate Chunk Cookies, '88 217
Supreme Cookies, Chocolate-Chip, '01 218
Surprise Bonbon Cookies, '88 119
Surprise Cookies, Choco, '80 60
Teasers, Chocolate, '87 44
Toffee Cookie Bites, '03 M273
Toffee Treats, '89 330
Turtle Bars, '00 334
Turtle Bars, Gooey, '96 M189
Ultimate Chocolate Chip Cookies, '05 87
Wedding Cookies, Chocolate, '04 275
White Chocolate Chip-Oatmeal Cookies, '99 127;
   '04 43
White Chocolate Cookies, Chunky Macadamia Nut,
   '92 207
White Chocolate-Macadamia Nut Cookies, '94 315
White Chocolate-Orange Dream Cookies, '98 294
Whoopie Pies, '86 246
Witches' Hats, '98 256
Yummy Bars, '92 171
Zucchini Cookies, Spicy, '97 273
Baskets with Berry Cream, Chocolate, '92 118
Beverages
Brandied Chocolate, Flaming, '80 M290
Café au Lait, German Chocolate, '92 264
Café Colombian Royal, '80 M290
Café Mexicano, '92 208
Café Mocha Latte, '01 64
Cappuccino, Chocolate Castle, '84 53
Cocoa Mix, Instant, '86 332
Coffee, Chocolate, '82 43; '97 17
Coffee, Chocolate-Almond, '84 54
Coffee, Chocolate Iced, '01 166
Coffee, Cocoa-, '83 55
Coffee, Fireside, '03 M298

Coffee, Mexican, '83 175, 275; '88 247; '91 78;
   '93 310; '94 97
"Concrete," Abaco Mocha, '94 114
"Concrete," Cardinal Sin, '94 113
"Concrete," Foxtreat, '94 113
Hot Chocolate, '94 290; '04 209
Hot Chocolate, Cherry Cordial, '02 220
Hot Chocolate, Creole, '80 M290
Hot Chocolate Deluxe, '90 272; '00 33
Hot Chocolate, Favorite, '83 55
Hot Chocolate, French, '86 328
Hot Chocolate, Mexican, '98 313; '04 210;
   '04 210,
Hot Chocolate Mix, '04 209
Hot Chocolate Mix, Deluxe, '80 M290
Hot Chocolate Mix, Spicy, '85 278
Hot Chocolate Nog, '02 297
Hot Chocolate, Old-Fashioned, '85 23
Hot Chocolate, Special, '82 5
Hot Chocolate, Spiced, '80 50
Hot Chocolate, Spicy, '85 278
Hot Chocolate, Sugar-and-Spice, '95 34
Hot Chocolate, Tennessee, '96 214
Hot Cocoa, Fudgy, '00 235
Hot Cocoa Mix, '81 287
Hot Cocoa Mix, Minted, '91 316
Hot Cocoa Mix, Mocha-Flavored, '91 316
Hot Cocoa, Quick, '82 5
King Alfonso, '80 259
Malt, Banana-Chocolate, '89 170
Malt, Chocolate, '86 183
Malt, Chocolate-Yogurt, '01 173
Marshmallow Chocolate, Hot Laced, '93 53
Martini, Individual Chocolate, '02 88
Martinis, Chocolate, '02 88
Mexican-Style Chocolate, '81 187
Milk, French Chocolate, '79 38
Mocha Blend, '95 276
Mocha Café au Lait, '05 306
Mocha Cappuccino, '02 M220
Mocha Chocolate Fluff, '89 170
Mocha Cocoa, '83 318
Mocha-Cocoa Mix, Hot, '82 296
Mocha Coffee, '85 M329
Mocha Cream, Café, '84 54
Mocha Deluxe Hot Drink, '82 289
Mocha Espresso, Italian, '82 254
Mocha Frosty, '92 44
Mocha, Hot, '84 60
Mocha Latte, Spiced, '04 333
Mocha Melt, Spiced, '01 240
Mocha, Mexican, '93 M341
Mocha Mix, Spiced, '01 64
Mocha Polka, '89 171
Mocha Punch, '84 58, 166; '95 141
Mocha, Quick Viennese, '79 232
Mocha Spice Mix, Mexican, '00 334
Mocha, Spirited Hot, '91 M260
Mocha Warmer, '97 272
Peppermint Patti, The Peabody, '99 321
Shake, Banana-Mocha, '05 45
Shake, Chocolate-Banana Milk, '94 113
Shake, Chocolate Milk, '05 193
Shake, Chocolate Mint, '89 170
Shake, Mocha-Mint, '02 297
Sipper, Chocolate, '88 83
Smoothie, Chocoholic, '97 173
Smoothie, Chocolate-Mint, '84 166
White Chocolate Latte, '04 210
Bites, Snowy Chocolate, '90 47
Black-Bottom Goodies, '89 251
Bombe, Double-Chocolate, '97 282
Bread, Chocolate Chip-Banana, '90 267
Bread, Chocolate Date-Nut, '81 284

Bread, Chocolate Loaf, '88 M188
Bread, Chocolate-Zucchini, '93 308
Bread, Cocoa-Nut Swirl, '80 257
Bread with Stewed Yard Peaches, Cocoa, '05 23
Brickle Squares, Chocolate, '94 290
Buns, Chocolate-Cinnamon, '85 5
Buns, Chocolate Sticky, '81 300; '82 124
Cakes and Tortes
Almond Cake, Chocolate-, '91 248
Almond Cake with Cherry Filling, Chocolate-,
'84 225
Almond Torte, Chocolate-, '96 M253; '98 273
Amaretto Heart, Chocolate-, '98 56
Angel Cake, Chocolate, '88 128
Angel Cake, Chocolate Truffle, '97 283
Angel Food Cake, Chocolate, '87 21; '90 111; '91 55
Angel Food Cake with Custard Sauce, Chocolate,
'88 259
Angel Squares, Mocha, '98 61
Apricot-Filled Chocolate Torte, '90 107
Banana Cake, Chocolate-, '86 138
Banana Loaf, Chocolate Chip-, '85 115
Banana-Toffee Coffee Cakes, '02 M324
Basket Cake, Chocolate-Strawberry, '98 100
Batter, Chocolate Velvet Cake, '03 M286
Beet Cake, Chocolate, '80 40
Birthday Balloon Cakes, '92 15
Birthday Cake, Fishin'-for-Fun, '93 194
Black Forest Cake, '81 126; '92 174
Black Forest Pudding Cake, '02 210
Black Forest Torte, '88 209
Bourbon-Chocolate Torte, '98 M84
Bourbon-Pecan Cake, Chocolate-, '03 287
Breakfast Cake, Chocolate-Swirl, '04 M41
Brownie Cakes, Birthday Party, '00 199
Brownie Delight, Chocolate, '87 224
Brown Mountain Cake, '84 39
Bûche de Noël, '84 304; '87 241
Bûche de Noël Cake, '82 262
Buttercream Cake, Chocolate, '90 108
Buttermilk Cake, Chocolate-, '00 48
Buttermilk Chocolate Cake, '79 13
Buttermilk Fudge Squares, '99 99
Candy Cake, Chocolate, '81 238
Candy Corn Chocolate Cakes, '00 235
Caramel-Nut Cake, Chocolate-, '83 23
Carrot Cake, Brownie, '92 120
Cheesecake Bites, Mint, '99 282
Cheesecake, Black-and-White, '99 334
Cheesecake, Black Forest, '84 74; '89 93; '94 21;
'97 330
Cheesecake, Candy Bar, '86 120
Cheesecake, Chocolate, '81 16; '82 305
Cheesecake, Chocolate-Almond, '93 53
Cheesecake, Chocolate-Amaretto, '85 M294; '93 97
Cheesecake, Chocolate-Caramel-Pecan, '91 197
Cheesecake, Chocolate-Cherry Surprise, '05 273
Cheesecake, Chocolate Chip, '85 114
Cheesecake, Chocolate Cookie, '91 298
Cheesecake, Chocolate Fudge, '05 M288
Cheesecake, Chocolate-Glazed Triple-Layer, '86 315;
'90 310
Cheesecake, Chocolate Marble, '89 93
Cheesecake, Chocolate-Mint, '91 104
Cheesecake, Chocolate-Mint Baked Alaska,
'94 142
Cheesecake, Chocolate-Raspberry Truffle, '91 270
Cheesecake, Chocolate Swirl, '84 295; '85 26
Cheesecake, Chocolate-Wrapped Banana, '99 M48
Cheesecake, Coconut-Chocolate-Almond,
'98 322
Cheesecake, Fudge, '98 M213
Cheesecake, German Chocolate, '87 265; '00 245
Cheesecake, Marbled, '87 261

Cheesecake, Marble Mint, '84 152
Cheesecake, Mocha, '98 278
Cheesecake, Mocha-Chocolate, '88 258
Cheesecake, Mocha Swirl, '87 262
Cheesecake, Rich Chocolate, '84 74; '85 38
Cheesecakes, Tiny Chocolate, '92 288
Cheesecake, Warm Fudge-Filled, '98 34; '03 320
Cheesecake, White Chocolate, '87 44; '88 267;
'94 180
Cheesecake with Mocha Sauce, Chocolate-Coffee,
'05 M316
Cheesecake with Whipped Cream Frosting,
Chocolate, '89 42
Cherry Cake, Choco-, '96 229
Cherry Cake, Chocolate-, '84 200; '86 239
Cherry Fudge Cake, '98 214
Chewies, Chocolate-Chip, '01 320
Chiffon Cake with Coffee Buttercream, Chocolate,
'95 277
Chocolate Cake, '97 283
Cinnamon Cake, Chocolate-, '93 154
Cocoa Crown Cake, '90 107
Coconut Cake, Chocolate-, '83 23
Coconut Cake, White Chocolate-, '87 263
Coconut-Fudge Cake, '99 206
Coffee Cake, Chocolate-Chip, '79 249
Coffee Cake, Chocolate Chip, '83 231; '97 232;
'04 194
Coffee Cake, Chocolate-Cream Cheese, '03 288
Coffee Cake, Triple-Chocolate, '04 M299
Cola Cake, Quick, '00 120
Cola Cake, Quick Chocolate, '95 56
Crumb Cake, Calico, '87 261
Cupcakes, Banana-Chocolate, '02 187
Cupcakes, Banana-Cocoa, '80 130
Cupcakes, Brownie, '82 280
Cupcakes, Chewy Chocolate, '01 334
Cupcakes, Choco, '03 200
Cupcakes, Chocolate, '92 14
Cupcakes, Chocolate-Brickle Ice-Cream, '01 M172
Cupcakes, Chocolate Chip, '97 108
Cupcakes, Chocolate-Cream Cheese, '03 169
Cupcakes, Chocolate-Peppermint Candy, '03 M287
Cupcakes, Chocolate Surprise, '85 91
Cupcakes, Cinnamon-Chocolate, '81 M139
Cupcakes, Marble Chocolate Chip, '81 239
Cupcakes, Mint-Chocolate Chip Ice-Cream, '01 172
Cupcakes, Mocha, '85 250
Cupcakes, Self-Filled, '80 129
Cupcake Surprises, '01 299
Cups, Black Bottom, '82 279
Custard Cake, Chocolate, '88 175
Decadence, Chocolate, '03 319
Decadent Chocolate Cake, '86 142
Double-Chocolate Torte, '79 67
Easy Chocolate Cake, '80 140
Easy Perfect Chocolate Cake, '99 307
Éclair Cake, Chocolate, '03 206
Extra-Rich Chocolate Cake, '99 271
Father's Day Cake, '92 134
Firewater Cream, Chocolate Torte with, '00 161
Flourless Chocolate Torte, '05 81
IV, Chocolate Cake, '05 322
Frosting, Chocolate Cake with Double, '86 314
Fruitcakes, Chocolate, '95 250
Fudge Cake, '94 M293; '98 110; '99 176
Fudge Cake, Best, '83 301
Fudge Cake, Brown Sugar, '86 316
Fudge Cake, Chocolate, '80 19
Fudge Cake, Coconut-, '99 206
Fudge Cake for Two, '81 205
Fudge Cake, Hot, '99 105
Fudge Cake, One-Foot-in-the-Fire, '90 252
Fudge Cake, Shortbread, '03 M331

Fudge Frosting, Chocolate Cake with, '89 56
Fudge Sundae Cakes, Hot, '00 333
German Chocolate Cake, '81 296; '83 M233; '05 107
German Chocolate Chip Cake, '86 247
German Chocolate Sheet Cake, '03 147
German Chocolate Snack Cake, '02 128
Grandma's Chocolate Cake, '94 133
Graveyard Grumblings, '92 15
Holiday Torte, Chocolate-Vanilla, '01 252
Ice-Cream Torte, Toffee-Coffee, '04 234
Italian Cake, Chocolate, '02 256
Kahlúa Cake, Chocolate, '91 298
Kahlúa Chocolate Cake, '81 303
Layers, Chocolate Cake, '96 229
Loaf Cakes, Chocolate Chip, '98 137
Macadamia-Fudge Cake, '01 278
Marbled Cake, Cocoa, '82 265
Marshmallow Cake, No-Egg Chocolate, '87 M97
Mayonnaise Cake, Chocolate, '83 99
Milk Chocolate Bar Cake, '00 86
Mint Cake, Chocolate-, '03 286
Mint Torte, Chocolate, '94 86
Mississippi Mud Cake, '03 288; '04 136
Mocha Brownie Torte, '85 102
Mocha Cake, Belgian, '84 316
Mocha Cake, Double, '84 311
Mocha Chiffon Cake, Delta, '00 286
Mocha-Chocolate Cake, Dark, '84 311
Mocha Cream Roll, Chocolate-, '84 304
Mocha-Pecan Torte, '86 26
Mocha Torte, '99 66
Mocha Velvet Torte, '92 318
Mousse Cake, Chocolate, '87 264; '98 270; '03 320
Mousse Cake, Chocolate-Peanut Butter, '98 71
Mousse Cake, Strawberry-Studded White Chocolate,
'99 154
Mousse Cake, White Chocolate, '89 160
Mousse Roll, Chocolate, '88 280
Mousse Torte, White Chocolate, '99 154
Nut Cake, Rich Chocolate-, '86 8
Pastry Cake, Chocolate, '91 196
Peanut Butter Cake, Chocolate-, '84 240
Peanut Butter Cake, Fudgy, '85 91
Peanut Butter-Fudge Cake, '96 254; '01 59
Peanut Butter Turtle Torte, '04 316
Peanut Cluster Cake, Chocolate-, '87 184
Pecan Torte, Chocolate-, '89 42
Perfect Chocolate Cake, '82 244; '90 307; '03 318
Petits Fours, Chocolate-Almond, '93 255; '00 72
Piglets, '98 203
Pound Cake, Chocolate, '82 88; '84 10; '89 325;
'94 288; '98 336
Pound Cake, Chocolate Chip, '86 178; '93 105;
'94 100
Pound Cake, Chocolate Marble, '88 16
Pound Cake, Chocolate-Orange, '89 94
Pound Cake, Chocolate-Sour Cream, '83 239;
'92 153
Pound Cake, Chocolate-Swirled, '97 329
"Pound" Cake, Chocolate Velvet, '03 286
Pound Cake, German Chocolate, '97 M254
Pound Cake, Mahogany, '89 207
Pound Cake, Marble, '95 29
Pound Cake, Marbled Pecan, '93 313
Pound Cake, Milk Chocolate, '90 306
Pound Cake, White Chocolate, '91 101
Pound Cake with Frosting, Chocolate, '90 284
Pound Cake with Fudge Frosting, Chocolate, '87 296
Praline Cake, Chocolate-, '01 235
Praline Pecan Cake, Chocolate-, '03 288
Praline Torte, Chocolate, '84 165
Pudding Cake, Hot Fudge, '88 255
Pudding Cake, Warm Chocolate, '92 324
Pudding, Chocolate Cake, '81 99

Chocolate 83

Pumpkin Cake with Little Ghosts, '03 212
Pumpkin, Chocolate, '96 254
Queen's Chocolate Cake, '89 271
Raspberry Cake, Chocolate-, '92 173; '01 M319
Raspberry-Fudge Cake, '97 34
Red Velvet Cake Batter, Chocolate-, '05 286
Red Velvet Cakes, Fluted Chocolate-, '05 287
Red Velvet Layer Cake, Chocolate-, '05 287
Rich Chocolate Cake, '89 43
Rocky Road Cake, '81 178
Roll, Chocolate, '04 85
Roll, Chocolate Cream, '85 317
Roll, Chocolate-Frosted Ice Cream, '84 200
Roll, Chocolate Mousse, '83 290
Roll, Chocolate-Orange, '87 21
Roll, Make-Ahead Chocolate-Mint Cake, '95 220
Rolls, Chocolate Cake, '94 312
Root Beer Float Cake, '04 211
Roulade, Kahlúa-and-Cream, '97 199
Roulage, Chocolate-Cranberry, '94 313
Roulage, Chocolate-Orange, '94 314
Roulage, Mint-Chocolate, '94 314
Royal, Chocolate Cake, '86 239
Royale, Chocolate Torte, '82 263
Rum Cake, Chocolate, '79 67
Sachertorte, '84 253
Sachertorte, Shortcut, '99 M243
Sheet Cake, Chocolate-Caramel, '05 210
Sheet Cake, Texas, '03 19
Shortcake, Chocolate-Raspberry, '95 99
Shortcake, Chocolate-Strawberry, '89 216
Snack Cake, Black Widow, '93 245
Snack Cake, Frosted Chocolate, '90 194
Sour Cream Cake, Chocolate-, '87 222
Sour Cream Cake, Chocolate Chip-, '85 115
Sour Cream Chocolate Cake, '79 282
Spice Potato Cake, Chocolate-, '96 111
Sponge Cake, Chocolaty, '86 60
Strawberry Ice Cream Torte, Chocolate-, '79 7
Sugar Cookie Torte, '79 68
Swiss Chocolate Chip Cake, '87 85
Tannenbaum Temptations, '92 14
Texas Cake, '01 59
Toffee Cake, Chocolate-, '89 335
Tree Cakes, Miniature Chocolate Truffle, '97 M285
Triangle Cake, Chocolate, '85 126
Triple-Chocolate Cake, '05 221
Triple Chocolate Torte, '96 58
Truffle Cake, Chocolate, '89 43
Truffle Cake, Rudolph's Chocolate, '04 M253
Turkey Talk, '92 15
Turtle Cake, '03 287
Turtle Cake Squares, '05 M211
Velvet Cake with Coconut-Pecan Frosting, Chocolate, '03 289
Velvet Cake with Cream Cheese-Butter Pecan Frosting, Chocolate, '03 288
Velvet Cake with Vanilla Buttercream Frosting, Chocolate, '03 287
Velvet Torte, Chocolate, '86 316
Wedding Cake, Double Chocolate, '91 100
Whipped Cream Cake, Chocolate-Mint, '90 265
White Chocolate-Almond Cake, '03 M287
White Chocolate-Cherry Cake, '88 268
White Chocolate Mousse Cake, '89 160
White Chocolate Mousse Cake, Strawberry-Studded, '99 154
White Chocolate Mousse Torte, '99 154
White Chocolate-Raspberry Cake, '98 323

X-Treme Chocolate Double Nut Caramel Ladyfinger Torte, '04 M315
Yule Log, '79 281; '82 289
Zucchini Cake, Chocolate-, '85 156; '02 181
Candies
Almond Hearts, Chocolate-, '03 42
Almond Roca, '86 49
Balls, Buckeye, '00 M280; '01 M322
Bourbon Balls, '83 315; '90 83; '02 30
Bourbon Balls, Chocolate, '84 298
Brittle, Chocolate, '83 315
Brittle, Quick Chocolate, '82 114
Butter Creams, '80 302
Candy Cane Swizzle Sticks, '02 298
Caramels, Chocolate, '91 35
Caramels, Chocolate-Dipped, '02 30
Cherries, Chocolate-Covered, '81 286; '84 298; '97 M55
Cherries, Cordial, '02 30
Chunks of Snow, '02 298
Clusters, Triple Chocolate, '01 242
Coconut Almond Drops, Chocolate-, '87 223
Coconut Joys, '98 282
Coconut Joys, Chocolate-Covered, '98 M282
Coffee Buttons, '99 66
Cracker Candy, '02 30
Cream-Filled Chocolates, Liqueur, '87 258
Creams, Chocolate-Lemon, '98 M235
Crème de Cacao Balls, '86 266
Crème de Menthe Chocolates, '91 36
Crunch, White Chocolate-Peanut Butter, '02 M296
Dark Chocolate Bonbons, '02 297
Drops, Chocolate, '84 111
Fudge, '86 266
Fudge Balls, Strawberry, '93 80
Fudge Bites, Peanut-, '91 M231; '92 M68
Fudge, Cherry Nut, '83 315
Fudge, Chocolate, '82 20
Fudge, Chocolate-Peanut Butter, '87 257; '90 311
Fudge, Coffee-Chip, '86 74
Fudge, Cream Cheese, '84 111
Fudge, Creamy, '81 218
Fudge, Creamy Almond, '95 51
Fudge, Creamy Dark, '82 295
Fudge, Creamy Mocha, '95 51
Fudge, Creamy Pecan, '84 321
Fudge, Diamond, '92 193
Fudge, Dinner Mint, '88 285
Fudge, Double-Good, '79 M263; '95 M50
Fudge, Double Good, '87 M278
Fudge, Double Peanut, '85 91
Fudge, Fast, '79 274
Fudge, Five Pounds of Chocolate, '95 51
Fudge, Four Chips, '92 318
Fudge, Holiday Mocha, '84 298
Fudge, Mama's, '03 279; '05 335
Fudge, Marbled Peanut Butter, '88 65
Fudge, Microwave Chocolate, '92 M50; '02 M31
Fudge, Mint, '95 50
Fudge, Orange-Walnut, '92 288
Fudge, Peanut Butter, '89 307
Fudge-Peanut Butter Chewies, '98 215
Fudge, Pistachio, '83 298
Fudge, Pumpkin, '05 232
Fudge, Quick-and-Easy, '88 M190
Fudge, Quick Nut, '83 316
Fudge Scotch Ring, '79 273
Fudge Squares, Chocolate-Peanut Butter, '97 M54
Fudge, White Chocolate, '92 317; '95 51
Fudge, White Chocolate-Coffee, '94 232
Greeting Card, Chocolate, '83 40
Kentucky Colonels, '79 273
Marshmallow Squares, Chocolate-, '92 M50
Millionaires, '79 M262; '97 M55

Millionaires, Texas, '00 291
Mints, Dinner, '88 66
Molded Candies, '84 40
Nut Clusters, '81 254
Nut Log Candy, Chocolate-, '86 335
Nut Teasers, Chocolate, '91 35
Peanut Brittle, Chocolate-Dipped, '02 M223
Peanut Butter Balls, Chocolate-, '80 87
Peanut Butter Bites, Chocolate-, '92 M317
Peanut Butter-Chocolate Balls, '80 269
Peanut Butter-Chocolate Candy Squares, '82 56
Peanut Butter Creams, '79 273
Peanut Butter Drops, Chocolate-, '92 322
Peanut Clusters, '92 288; '98 M282
Peanut Clusters, Chocolate-, '81 16
Peanutty Clusters, '83 143
Peanutty Swirls, Chocolate, '94 M330
Pecan Clusters, '98 305
Pecan Clusters, Roasted, '90 310
Pecan Clusters, Toasted, '00 M14
Pecan Fritters, Chocolate-Covered, '79 205
Pralines, Chocolate, '92 313; '93 51
Pralines, Chocolate-Mint, '92 313; '93 51
Pralines, Chocolate-Peanut Butter, '92 313; '93 51
Pralines, Mocha, '92 313; '93 51
Pretzels, Chocolate-Covered, '82 295
Raspberry Cream Chocolates, '91 36
Rocky Road, '84 298
Rum Balls, Chocolate, '80 302
Rum Balls, Chocolate-, '88 285
Spiders, Chocolate, '85 236
Spirited Chocolates, '86 278
Tempered Chocolate, '91 35
Tiger Butter, '86 48
Toffee, '01 218
Toffee, English, '79 273
Toffee, Microwave, '92 M317
Toffee, Nutty, '79 M263
Truffles, Almond, '83 298
Truffles, Amaretto Dessert, '86 319
Truffles, Bittersweet, '94 330
Truffles, Chocolate, '85 114; '89 43; '91 108
Truffles, Chocolate-Cherry Cordial, '99 127
Truffles, Chocolate-Kahlúa, '92 285
Truffles, Chocolate Marble, '97 284
Truffles, Chocolate-Praline, '97 284
Truffles, Hazelnut, '97 M54
Truffles, Hazelnut-Chocolate, '03 243
Truffles, Orange-Pecan, '95 92
Truffles, Raspberry-Fudge, '00 M41
Truffles, White Chocolate, '87 45
Truffles, White Chocolate-Praline, '97 284
Truffles, Yule Street, '90 242
Turtle Candies, '93 M41
Velvets, Chocolate, '84 298
White Chocolate Salties, '92 50
White Chocolate Surprises, '91 36
Cannoli, '80 58
Charlotte Russe, Chocolate, '87 74
Charlottes, Mocha, '02 171
Cheese Cups, Chocolate-, '91 142
Cinnamon-Chocolate Cream, '94 199
Cocoa to Chocolate Equivalents, '84 200
Combo, Strawberry-Chocolate, '85 96
Cones, Chocolate-Coffee, '96 M316
Cracker Bites, Miniature Peanut Butter, '02 298
Cream, Chocolate-Almond, '91 108
Cream, Heavenly Chocolate, '88 128
Cream, Strawberries with Chocolate, '85 81
Crème Brûlée, Black-and-White, '98 267; '02 62
Crème Brûlée, Chocolate, '95 323
Crème Brûlée, White Chocolate-Macadamia Nut, '95 323

Crêpes, Chocolate, '86 164
Crêpes, Chocolate Chantilly, '82 183
Crêpes, Chocolate Dessert, '84 84; '85 262
Crêpes, Chocolate Dream, '86 164
Crêpes, Chocolate-Orange, '85 263
Crêpes, Fruit-Filled Chocolate, '89 325
Crescents, Chocolate, '03 283
Croissants, Chocolate-Filled, '96 303
Crust, Chocolate, '87 264; '90 M15; '03 320
Crust, Chocolate-Coconut, '87 261
Crust, Chocolate Crumb, '87 261
Crust, Chocolate-Macadamia Crumb, '96 254
Crust, Chocolate Wafer, '89 42, 93
Cups, Chocolate, '80 207
Cups, Chocolate Crinkle, '93 270
Cups, Chocolate Lace, '87 133
Cups, Chocolate-Mint, '80 71
Cups, Chocolate-Walnut, '85 213
Cups, Miniature Chocolate, '87 132
Custard, Chocolate, '88 258
Custard, Chocolate-Topped Amaretto, '87 M37
Date-Nut Delight, Chocolate, '88 168
Decadence, Chocolate, '89 183
Delights, Choco-Peanut, '99 197
Dessert, Chilled Chocolate, '83 177
Dessert, Chocolate-Almond, '82 306
Dessert, Chocolate-Coffee Frozen, '85 172
Dessert, Chocolate Dream, '83 198
Dessert, Chocolate Ladyfinger, '86 162
Dessert, Chocolate-Mint, '82 100
Dessert, Chocolate-Rum, '81 247
Dessert, Chocolate Truffle, '88 281
Dessert, Choco-Maple Frozen, '86 300; '87 178
Dessert, Cool Chocolate-Mint, '80 109
Dessert, Easy Chocolate, '79 75
Dessert, Frozen Chocolate, '83 76
Dessert, Fudge-Peanut Ice Cream, '88 167
Dessert, Hello Dolly, '95 168
Dessert, Layered Ice Cream, '83 189
Dessert, Nutty Fudgy Frozen, '94 28
Dessert, Peanut-Chocolate, '80 86
Dessert Squares, Chocolate-Blueberry, '87 299
Dessert, Triple Cream, '94 244
Dessert with Kahlúa Cream, Fudge, '91 197
Dip, Chocolate, '92 50
Doughnuts, Chocolate, '83 95
Doughnuts, Chocolate-Covered, '84 55
Doughnuts, Chocolate-Glazed Potato, '85 6
Dream Drops, '99 328
Éclairs, Banana-Chocolate, '01 45
Éclairs, Chocolate, '96 191
Éclairs, Peanut Butter-Chocolate, '01 45
Flan, Layered, '89 45
Fondue, Brandied Chocolate, '93 162
Fondue, Chocolate, '91 142; '05 M281
Fondue, Dessert, '89 281
Fondue, White Chocolate, '92 287
Frostings, Fillings, and Toppings
  Almond Frosting, Chocolate-, '83 241
  Buttercream, Chocolate, '84 156
  Buttercream Frosting, Chocolate, '96 229; '98 M100
  Butter Frosting, Chocolate, '89 271
  Buttermilk Frosting, Chocolate-, '99 99
  Candy Frosting, Chocolate, '81 238
  Cheese Filling, Chocolate-, '90 47
  Cherry Frosting, Chocolate-, '89 294
  Chocolate Filling, '96 316; '03 200; '05 M307
  Chocolate Frosting, '80 M171; '81 265; '82 262;
    '83 79, 99, M233, 253; '84 200; '85 323; '86 8,
    93, 138, 239, 314; '87 M97, 198, 199, 293;
    '89 M25; '90 194, 252, 265, 284, 309; '91 248;
    '92 319; '93 239; '94 133; '96 253, 254; '97 M87,
    254; '99 271; '04 136
  Chocolate Icing, '03 19

Cocoa Frosting, '86 60; '96 253, 254
Coconut Chocolate Frosting, '79 13
Coffee Buttercream Filling, Chocolate-,
  '00 M287
Coffee Frosting, Chocolate-, '84 36; '88 269
Coffee Liqueur Ganache Icing, '05 322
Cola Frosting, '00 120
Cola Frosting, Chocolate-, '95 56
Cranberry Filling, Nutty, '00 M306
Cream Cheese Frosting, Chocolate-, '02 256
Cream, Chocolate, '94 57
Creamy Chocolate Frosting, '85 314; '86 316;
  '87 241; '99 307
Creamy Chocolate Glaze, '82 88
Fluffy Chocolate Frosting, '86 336; '87 58
Fudge Filling, '94 292
Fudge Frosting, '81 303; '87 296; '89 56; '94 51;
  '01 59
Fudge Frosting, Chocolate, '83 105; '00 287
Fudge Frosting, Quick, '81 278
Ganache, Chocolate, '93 255; '97 282; '00 M72;
  '01 M235; '03 M286
Ganache Cream, '92 318
Ganache, Simple Chocolate, '03 M212
Ganache, White Chocolate, '01 253
Glaze, Brownie, '02 M252
Glaze, Chocolate, '81 119; '83 220; '84 10, 55, 253;
  '85 6; '86 315, 316; '89 325; '90 310; '91 M296;
  '93 52; '97 M35, 231; '99 206; '01 M45, M126;
  '05 221, M287
Glaze, Creamy Chocolate, '98 90
Glaze, French Chocolate, '98 M57
Glaze, White Cake with Strawberries and Chocolate,
  '87 76
Glaze, White Chocolate, '01 M45
Gravy, Chocolate, '99 35, 88
Honey Chocolate Frosting, '79 83
Honey Glaze, Chocolate-, '82 306
Hot Fudge Ice Cream Topping, '98 317
Hot Fudge Ice-Cream Topping, '02 109
Kahlúa Frosting, Chocolate, '91 298
Macadamia-Fudge Topping, '01 278
Marshmallow Frosting, Chocolate-, '83 245;
  '04 210
Marzipan Bees, '98 100
Midnight Filling, Chocolate, '96 120
Mint Chocolate Frosting, '99 M176
Mocha Butter Cream Frosting, '79 281
Mocha-Buttercream Frosting, '86 26
Mocha-Chocolate Cream Filling, '05 322
Mocha Cream, '94 47
Mocha Cream Filling, '84 305
Mocha Frosting, '83 301; '84 316; '87 224; '94 292;
  '97 35
Mocha Frosting, Creamy, '82 289; '84 311; '91 248
Mocha Ganache, '04 M260
Nut Frosting, Chocolate, '80 140
Peanut Butter Frosting, Chocolate-, '84 240; '87 222;
  '00 120
Peanut Butter-Fudge Frosting, '87 184
Peanut Topping, Chocolate-, '79 222
Perfect Chocolate Frosting, '90 307; '03 319
Praline Fudge Icing, '04 331
Rich Chocolate Filling, '79 68
Rich Chocolate Frosting, '84 304
Root Beer Frosting, '04 211
Rum Frosting, Chocolate, '79 67
Satiny Chocolate Frosting, '85 126; '89 43
Truffle Filling, Chocolate, '87 69; '04 M253
Velvet Frosting, '02 297
Whipped Cream Frosting, '89 43
White Chocolate Buttercream Frosting, '97 M284
White Chocolate-Cream Cheese Frosting, '94 58;
  '98 323

White Chocolate-Cream Cheese Tiered Cake
  Frosting, '94 125
White Chocolate Filling, '89 160
White Chocolate Frosting, '88 280; '91 101;
  '97 M111; '00 306
Garnishes, Chocolate, '85 16
Garnishes, Lacy Chocolate, '89 43
Gâteau Panache, '83 269
Granola with Chocolate Morsels, '86 69
Grapefruit, Chocolate-Topped, '89 88
Hearts, Crispy Chocolate, '03 M41
Horns, Chocolate-Dipped, '93 197
Ice Cream, Almond-Fudge, '93 205
Ice Cream Balls, Easy, '84 106
Ice Cream Balls, Nutty, '89 72
Ice Cream, Chocolate, '80 176; '86 129
Ice Cream, Chocolate Chunk-Peanut Butter, '85 297;
  '86 120
Ice Cream, Chocolate Cookie, '95 245
Ice Cream, Chocolate-Covered Peanut, '88 203
Ice Cream, Double-Chocolate, '88 203
Ice Cream, Mexican Chocolate, '91 162
Ice Cream, Mint-Chocolate Chip, '88 202
Ice Cream, Mocha, '88 202; '97 M145
Ice Cream, No-Cook Chocolate, '04 179
Ice Cream, No-Cook Chocolate-Almond,
  '04 179
Ice Cream, Orange Pekoe-Chocolate, '99 90
Ice Cream Party Squares, '91 214
Ice Cream Sandwiches, Chocolate, '89 72
Ice-Cream Sandwiches, Chocolate, '04 329
Ice-Cream Sandwiches, Easy Chocolate-Mint, '05 62
Ice-Cream Sandwiches, Mocha-Almond-Fudge,
  '05 62
Ice Cream Squares, Mint-Chocolate Chip, '94 245
Kahlúa Delight, '83 67
Leaves, Chocolate, '88 281; '89 42; '98 270
Loaf, Chocolate Pinwheel, '80 256
Loaves, Chocolate Chip Cheese, '91 299; '92 264
Log, Chocolate Cream, '94 220
Lollipops, Harvest Moon, '02 M223
Mandelbread, Chocolate Chip, '00 282
Meringue Acorns, '93 284
Meringue Fingers, Chocolate-Almond, '84 158
Mexican Fiesta Confection, '82 223
Mint Freeze, Chocolate, '88 167
Mississippi Mud, '96 253
Mocha Alaska Dessert, '84 191
Mocha Chiffon, '86 75
Mocha Delight, Frozen, '96 179
Mocha Dessert, Frozen, '84 311
Mocha Freeze, Royal, '84 53
Mocha Squares, Frozen, '81 187
Molletes, Chocolate, '02 83
Mousse. *See also* **CHOCOLATE/Cakes and Tortes,**
  Pies and Tarts.
  Almond Mousse, Chocolate-, '93 316
  Amaretto-Chocolate Mousse, '86 50
  Amaretto-Chocolate Mousse, Elegant, '86 337
  au Grand Marnier, Chocolate Mousse, '91 296
  Baked Alaska, Chocolate Mousse, '85 195
  Blender Chocolate Mousse, '82 71
  Blender-Quick Chocolate Mousse, '80 269
  Brandy-Chocolate Mousse, '85 102
  Chocolate Mousse, '88 280; '97 282; '02 M277
  Creamy Chocolate Mousse, '87 133
  Dark Chocolate Mousse with Raspberry Sauce,
    '05 31
  Honeyed Chocolate Mousse, '87 223
  Kid-Pleasin' Chocolate Mousse, '90 271
  Loaf with Raspberry Puree, Chocolate Mousse,
    '97 34
  Orange Liqueur, Chocolate Mousse with, '02 315
  Orange Mousse, Chocolate-, '81 16, 205

CHOCOLATE, Mousse
(continued)

Parfait, Chocolate Mousse, '94 90
Parfaits, Chocolate-Peanut Butter Mousse,
'98 71
Present, Chocolate Mousse, '99 281
Quick Chocolate Mousse, '85 87
Rum Mousse, Chocolate, '86 189
Truffle Mousse with Raspberry Sauce, Chocolate,
'95 327
White Chocolate Mousse, '91 247; '93 315; '97 282;
'98 M57, M111
White Chocolate Mousse, Quick, '99 155
Muffins, Banana-Chocolate, '94 197
Muffins, Chocolate Chip, '90 87
Muffins, Fudge Brownie, '95 M50
Muffins, Jumbo Banana-Chocolate Chip, '93 339
Muffins, Peanut Butter-Chocolate Chip, '94 167
Napoleons, Coffee, '95 276
Napoleons, Peanut Butter-and-Chocolate, '94 121
Parfait, Bodacious Peanut, '95 167
Parfaits, Chocolate-Crème de Menthe, '85 161
Parfaits, Chocolate-Mint, '90 M15
Parfaits, Chocolate-Peanut Butter Mousse, '98 71
Parfaits, Chocolate-Peppermint, '88 65
Parfaits, Hooray, '96 259
Parfaits, Mocha-Mallow, '80 219
Parfaits, Speedy, '83 76
Parfait, White Chocolate-Raspberry Swirl,
'93 315
Party Mix, White Chocolate, '03 M289
Pastries, Chocolate-Chestnut, '02 M273
Pecans, Chocolate-Dipped, '05 M269
Pies and Tarts
Almond Pie, Creamy Chocolate-, '85 102
Amandine, Chocolate Pie, '83 300
Amaretto Heavenly Tarts, Chocolate-, '88 4
Amaretto Mousse Pie, Chocolate-, '80 180;
'81 30
Banana-Pecan Cream Pie, Chocolate-, '94 210
Bavarian Pie, Chocolate, '89 326
Berry Pie, Heavenly Chocolate-, '85 102
Best-Ever Chocolate Pie, '88 M45
Black Bottom Mocha-Cream Tart, '92 304
Black Bottom Pie, '82 53
Black-Bottom Pie, '98 161
Bluegrass Chocolate Tarts, '90 84
Bourbon-Chocolate-Pecan Tarts, '96 264
Bourbon Pecan Pie, Chocolate-, '05 134
Bourbon Pie, Chocolate, '88 99
Brownie-Mint Pie, '97 303
Brownie Pie, Crustless, '82 33
Brownie Pie, Frozen Chocolate, '96 57
Caramel Turtle Truffle Tart, '93 M131
Cherry Pie, Chocolate-Covered, '05 M216
Cherry Tart, Chocolate-, '97 33
Chess Pie, Chocolate, '81 161; '86 220; '92 13
Chess Pie, Chocolate-Pecan, '00 60; '02 107
Chess Tarts, Chocolate, '92 214
Chilled Chocolate Pie, '88 99
Chip Pie, Chocolate, '85 114
Coffee Tart, '99 67
Cream Cheese Pie, Chocolate-, '80 69
Cream Cheese Pie, Chocolate, '92 240
Cream Pie, Chocolate, '83 192; '84 49; '87 208;
'94 208
Creamy Chocolate Pie, '85 298; '86 119
Custard Tart, Chocolate, '99 27
Double Chocolate Pie, '82 M282
Easy Chocolate Pie, '83 158
Fox Hunter's Pie, '97 109
French Silk Pie, '80 247

French Silk Tarts, '79 236
Frozen Chocolate-Macadamia Nut Pie, '96 254
Frozen Chocolate Pie, '80 154
Frozen Chocolate Pie with Pecan Crust, '89 291;
'98 180
Fudge Pie, '87 168; '89 252; '01 129
Fudge Pie, Black-and-White, '99 249
Fudge Pie, Chocolate, '98 336
Fudge Pie, Sweetheart, '86 316; '90 313; '03 319
Fudge Truffle-Pecan Tart, '99 315; '02 208
Fudgy Chocolate Malt-Peppermint Pie, '00 313
German Chocolate Pie, '93 129
Heaven, Chocolate, '98 323
Heavenly Chocolate Pie, '87 260
Icebox Pie, Chocolate, '05 157
Ice Cream Pie, Chocolate-, '87 224
Ice Cream Pie, Chocolate, '91 56
Ice Cream Pie, Chocolate-Mint, '81 144
Ice Cream Pie, Chocolate-Peanut Butter, '98 244
Ice Cream Sundae Pie, '94 244
Kahlúa Pie, '83 191
Kentucky Derby Tarts, '79 102
Meringue Pie, Chocolate, '80 238; '82 206; '83 158;
'92 216
Meringue Pie, Chocolate-Filled, '86 121
Microwave Chocolate Pie, '90 M15
Midnight Delights, '95 278
Mint Chocolate Mousse Tarts, '03 283
Mocha Crunch Pie, Chocolate-, '81 136
Mocha Meringue Pie, '80 242
Mocha-Pecan Mud Pie, '05 290
Mocha Pie, '94 168
Mousse Pie, Chocolate, '81 136
Mousse Pie, Chocolate-Amaretto, '80 180; '81 30
Mud Pie, Decadent, '89 252
Mud Pie, Mississippi, '89 26
Mud Pie, Tipsy, '80 255; '97 251
Party Tarts, '95 90
Peanut Butter Cup Pie, Fudgy, '04 211
Peanut Butter Pie, Chocolate-, '85 91
Peanut Butter Swirl Pie, Chocolate-, '87 262
Peanut Butter Tarts, Chocolate-, '92 277
Pecan Chess Pie, Chocolate-, '93 251
Pecan Fudge Pie with Raspberry Sauce, '05 201
Pecan Pie, Bourbon-Chocolate, '98 258
Pecan Pie, Choco-, '82 86
Pecan Pie, Chocolate, '80 237; '83 12; '90 184
Pecan Pie, Chocolate-, '91 272; '02 176
Pecan Tart with Caramel Sauce, Chocolate-, '93 296;
'94 234
Peppermint Brownie Tarts, '05 M288
Pizza Dolce (Italian Sweet Pies), '00 283
Praline Pie, Chocolate-, '86 259
Silk Pie, Chocolate, '88 67
Strawberry-Chocolate Truffle Pie, '89 112
Tin Roof Pie, '85 91
Turtle Pecan Pie, '93 250
Walnut Pie, Chocolate-, '05 134
Whipped Cream Pie, Chocolate, '79 124
White Chocolate-Banana Cream Pie, '94 314
White Chocolate Chess Tart, '95 303
Pineapple with Raspberry Sauce, Chocolate-Drizzled,
'90 57
Pizza, Chocolate, '91 298
Pizza, Chocolate-Peanut Butter, '05 193
Plunge, Chocolate, '94 332; '95 35
Popcorn, Delicious Chocolate, '00 223
Pots de Chocolat, Petits, '82 272
Pots de Crème, '81 15; '84 M145
Pots de Crème au Chocolate, '93 53
Pots de Crème, Chocolate, '93 296; '94 234
Pots de Crème for Two, '89 275
Pots de Crème, Mocha, '88 M45
Pots de Crème, Rum-Flavored, '85 102

Pots de Crème with Orange Meringues, Chocolate,
'95 318
Present, Chocolate Mousse, '99 281
Pudding, Brownie, '79 265; '80 295
Pudding, Chocolate, '02 323
Pudding, Chocolate-Almond, '82 142; '88 24
Pudding, Chocolate-Almond Silk, '96 266
Pudding, Chocolate Biscuit Bread, '94 215
Pudding, Chocolate Bread, '80 8
Pudding, Chocolate Cookie, '03 183
Pudding, Chocolate-Peanut Butter Cookie, '03 183
Pudding, Creamy Chocolate, '83 106
Pudding, Fudge-Banana, '97 331
Pudding, Fudgy Chocolate, '96 285
Pudding, Hot Fudge, '81 208
Pudding, Hot Fudge Sundae Cake, '88 167
Pudding, Mocha-Chocolate Cookie, '03 183
Pudding, Rich Black-and-White, '01 111
Pudding, White Chocolate Bread, '00 M104
Pudding with Custard Sauce, Chocolate Bread, '03 244
Pudding with Lemon Meringue, Chocolate, '88 258
Pudding with Whiskey Sauce, Chocolate Bread, '99 277
Quad, Chocolate, '02 272
Reindeer Food, Magic, '99 M309
Roulage, '90 266
Roulage, Chocolate-Mocha, '80 216
Roulage, Frozen Chocolate, '90 56
Roulage, White Chocolate, '92 230
Sack, Large Chocolate, '93 314
Sack, Small Chocolate, '93 314
Sauces
Amaretto-Chocolate Sauce, '92 154
Bittersweet Chocolate Sauce, '92 319
Champagne-Chocolate Sauce, '05 M282
Cherry Sauce, Chocolate-, '85 189
Cherry Sauce, Chocolate, '87 M165
Chocolate Sauce, '83 189; '84 208, 313; '86 322;
'90 57; '91 56, 57; '93 276; '94 121; '97 178, 331
Cinnamon-Fudge Sauce, '85 141
Classic Chocolate Sauce, '85 207
Creamy Chocolate Sauce, '88 M177
Dark Chocolate Sauce, '93 296; '94 234, 283;
'96 310; '98 336; '05 31
Dark Chocolate Sauce, Poached Pears with,
'90 M141
Double Chocolate Sauce, '83 79
Easy Chocolate Sauce, '92 148
Fudge Sauce, '91 174
Heavenly Chocolate Sauce, '79 79; '82 167
Honey-Chocolate Sauce, '89 251
Hot Fudge Sauce, '82 181, 295; '84 143; '97 255;
'05 193
Hot Fudge Sauce, Easy, '84 69; '94 194
Hot Fudge Sauce, Heavenly, '00 256
Hot Fudge Sauce, Pecan Pie with, '01 306
Hot Fudge Sauce, Quick, '82 212
Kahlúa Chocolate Sauce, '85 155
Mint Sauce, Chocolate-, '93 86; '94 314;
'98 217
Mint Sauce, Quick Chocolate, '86 M58
Mocha Sauce, '98 57; '05 317
Orange Sauce, Chocolate-, '86 165; '94 314
Peanut Butter Sauce, Chocolate-, '79 91, M156
Peppermint Sauce, Chocolate-, '94 205
Praline Sauce, Chocolate-, '85 M295
Semisweet Chocolate Sauce, '00 104
Supreme, Chocolate Sauce, '85 189
Toffee-Fudge Sauce, '89 95
White Chocolate Sauce, '92 164; '96 310; '00 104
Scones, Mocha-Pecan, '97 45
Shavings, Chocolate Hearts and, '86 26
Shell, Chocolate-Coconut Pie, '82 210; '83 100
Shell, Chocolate Pastry, '87 262
Shell, Chocolate Tart, '99 315; '02 208

Shells with Kahlúa Cream, Chocolate, '88 195
S'mores, Grilled Pound Cake, '98 179
S'mores, Indoor, '01 33
Snacks, Chocolate-Peanut Butter, '90 226
Snowballs, Chocolate Mint, '04 M211
Sorbet, Chocolate, '97 111
Soufflé au Chocolat Cointreau, '94 56
Soufflé, Chocolate, '84 317; '94 46
Soufflé, Chocolate Mint, '81 16
Soufflé, Light Chocolate, '83 278
Soufflé with White Chocolate Mousse, Chocolate, '98 57
Soup, Mexican Chocolate, '96 277
Spoons, Dipped Chocolate-Almond, '95 M277
Spread, Chocolate Cheese, '87 292
Stars, White Chocolate, '00 M307
Sticks, Chocolate-Sesame, '91 316
Sticky Buns, Easy Caramel-Chocolate, '95 36
Strawberries, Chocolate-Dipped, '98 M100
Strawberries Dipped in White Chocolate, '90 83
Sundae Dessert, Hot Fudge, '84 313; '86 322
Sundaes, Chocolate Mint, '03 M120
Sundaes, Cocoa-Kahlúa, '83 M58
Sundaes, Cream Cheese Brownie, '03 223
Supreme, Chocolate, '84 94
Tacos, Dessert, '97 141
That's Incredible, '02 322
Torte, Frozen Viennese, '93 171
Trees, Holiday, '02 298
Trifle, Brownie, '03 85
Trifle, Chocolate, '88 258; '93 326
Trifle, Peanut Butter-Brownie, '03 200
Velvet, Chocolate Almond, '81 148
Waffles, Fudge, '94 205
Waffles with Strawberry Cream, Chocolate, '88 153
Whip, Chocolate, '89 326
White Chocolate Ribbons and Bow, '01 253
Yogurt, Mocha Sauce with Chocolate, '92 243
Zuppa Inglese, '99 M267
CHOP SUEY
Cabbage Chop Suey, '81 101
Chicken Chop Suey, '81 227
Salad, Chop Suey, '81 37
CHOWDERS. *See also* **GUMBOS, SOUPS.**
Artichoke-Shrimp Chowder, '03 91
Bell Pepper-Cheese Chowder, '95 240
Bluefish Chowder, '84 282
Broccoli Chowder, '79 16
Cabbage Chowder, Hearty, '80 25
Cheddar Cheese Chowder, '97 30
Cheddar Chowder, Hearty, '79 16
Cheese Chowder, Golden, '80 73
Cheese Chowder, Hot, '89 16
Cheese-Vegetable Chowder, '02 305
Chicken-and-Corn Chowder, Curried, '92 21
Chicken-and-Roasted Vegetable Chowder, '97 21
Chicken Chowder, '83 20
Chicken Chowder, Cheesy, '92 21
Chicken Chowder Sauterne, '84 235
Chicken Corn Chowder, '02 305
Chicken-Corn Chowder, Mexican, '01 18
Chicken-Vegetable Chowder, '04 326
Chicken-Vegetable Chowder, Creamy, '92 20
Clam-and-Sausage Chowder, '94 104
Clam Chowder, '79 182; '81 32; '85 9; '86 36; '89 95; '90 202
Clam Chowder, New England, '86 M72; '98 289
Clam Chowder, Ocracoke, '79 31
Clam Chowder, Shopping Day, '02 305
Clam Chowder, Tomato-, '84 251
Corn and Bacon Chowder, Fresh, '93 203
Corn-and-Bacon Chowder, Southern, '96 166
Corn and Cheese Chowder, '80 228
Corn-and-Poblano Chowder, '03 193

Corn Chowder, '81 128; '83 20; '84 M38; '85 10; '90 202; '91 132; '97 241; '98 31
Corn Chowder, Delicious, '82 279
Fiesta Chowder, '02 305
Fish Chowder, '79 152; '84 M38
Fish Chowder, Basque, '86 36
Fish Chowder, Chunky, '92 331
Fish Chowder, Creamy, '79 16
Fish Chowder, Tasty, '80 188
Green Bean, Mushroom, and Ham Chowder, Creamy, '99 M336
Greens Chowder, Mixed, '97 262
Ham-and-Cheese Chowder, '89 15
Ham and Corn Chowder, '79 16
Ham-and-Corn Chowder, '82 40
Ham Chowder, Creamy, '88 M53
Ham 'n Cheese Chowder, '79 199
Harvest Chowder, '83 317
Mirliton-Corn Chowder, '00 246
Mushroom Chowder, '79 16
Mushroom-Potato Chowder, '92 331
Okra Chowder, Quick, '80 185
Oyster Chowder, '83 229
Oyster-Corn Chowder, '83 211
Potato Chowder with Green Chiles, '00 329
Potato Chowder with Ham, '99 141
Potato-Corn Chowder, '94 66
Potato-Vegetable Chowder, '98 335
Pumpkin-Corn Chowder, '97 219
Red Snapper Chowder, '85 217
Salmon Chowder, '97 125
Sausage-Bean Chowder, '83 20
Seafood Chowder, '85 9; '92 122
Seafood Chowder, Curried, '94 103
Seafood Chowder, So-Quick, '01 18
Seafood Chowder, Southern, '83 20
Shrimp and Corn Chowder, '79 199
Shrimp Chowder, '89 218
Shrimp Chowder, Quick, '04 27
Sweet Potato Chowder, Asian, '97 213
Swiss-Broccoli Chowder, '80 73
Turkey Chowder, '85 10; '91 312
Turkey-Corn Chowder, '81 98; '96 279
Vegetable Chowder, Cheesy, '80 25; '83 20; '00 272; '01 18
Vegetable Chowder, Easy, '97 304
Vegetable Chowder, Hearty, '88 56
Vegetable Chowder, Oven-Roasted, '95 229
White Bean Chowder with Sage Pesto, '97 22
Yukon Gold-Cheese Chowder, '03 296
CHOW MEIN
Beef-and-Vegetable Chow Mein Casserole, '83 313
Chicken Casserole, Chow Mein, '96 276
Chicken Chow Mein, '90 68
Noodles, Chow Mein over Crispy, '85 286
Pork Chow Mein, '80 208; '90 101
Shrimp Chow Mein, '82 30
CHRISTMAS
Beverages
Blossom, Christmas, '99 321
Milk, Santa Claus, '92 281
Punch, Christmas, '84 259; '89 330
Punch, Christmas Eve, '86 314
Punch, Cupid's Creamy Peppermint, '04 253
Punch, Merry Christmas, '79 285
Tea, Christmas Fruit, '83 275; '01 240
Wassail, Christmas, '93 295
Bread, Christmas, '87 296; '88 288
Bread, Norwegian Christmas, '79 234
Bread Stars, '93 286
Buns, Christmas Morning Sticky, '97 245
Cake, Christmas Coconut, '82 262
Cake Loaf, Noel Pound, '04 279
Cake, Rudolph's Chocolate Truffle, '04 M253

Cake, Twinkling Star, '00 306
Candy Canes and Wreaths, Braided, '92 276
Cheese Logs, Candy Cane-, '03 298
Chicken Presents, Holiday, '01 251
Chili, White Christmas, '98 266; '02 260
Chocolate Rudolph Reindeer, '04 M254
Cinnamon Ornaments, '85 284
Coeur à la Crème, Christmas, '86 278
Coffee Cakes, Christmas-Tree, '87 298
Cookies
Calendar, Cookie Advent, '85 325
Candy Canes and Wreaths, Braided, '92 276
Cards, Christmas Cookie, '84 302
Cherry Cookies, Christmas, '88 282
Date Cookies, Christmas, '88 287
Eggnog Christmas Cookies, '79 255
Elf Biscuits, '99 309
Elf Cookie, '80 279, 303
Fruit Squares, Christmas, '88 282
Gingerbread Bowl, Christmas, '93 266
Gingerbread Cookies, '80 278
Gingerbread Men, '99 294
Gingerbread Snowflake Cookies, '98 324
Gingerbread Votives, '98 309
Granny's Christmas Cookies, '02 278
Jammies, Christmas, '95 322
Lizzies, Christmas, '87 257
Moravian Christmas Cookies, '91 282
Mrs. Claus Cookie, '80 279, 303
Nutcracker Cookies, '97 286
Painted Cookies, '86 322
Pfeffernuesse, '01 65
Reindeer Cookies, Jolly, '91 273
Rudolph Cookie, '80 279, 303
Rudolph Cookies, '99 M309
Santa Claus Cookie, '80 278, 303
Santa Cookies, Easy, '95 321
Santa's Whiskers, '85 323
Sleigh Cookie, '80 279, 303
Spiced Christmas Cookies, '87 294
Spritz Cookies, Christmas, '96 314
Strawberries, Christmas, '87 293
Sugarplum Fairy Wands, '97 M286
Sugarplum Sticks, '95 321
Swedish Christmas Cookies, '79 290
Tea Cakes, Victorian Christmas, '02 253
Tree Cookies, Christmas, '93 286
Trees, Christmas, '89 294
Votives, Edible, '98 309
Wreaths, Christmas, '97 288
Corn, Christmas, '93 325
Cottage, Quick-Fix Christmas, '91 280
Cottage, Sugarplum, '88 309
Cranberry Hearts, '93 286
Crostini, Christmas, '94 318
Custard, Boiled Christmas, '95 329
Dessert, White Christmas, '82 261
Dip, Christmas Confetti, '92 279
Divinity, Christmas, '81 286
Doughnuts, Snowy, '93 286
Grittibanz (Swiss Bread Figure), '93 265
Hotcakes, Christmas Tree, '03 305
Icing, Royal, '98 324
Jam, Christmas, '88 288
Jam, Christmas Brunch, '81 286
Jelly, Christmas Freezer, '86 M288
Ketchup, Christmas, '97 254
Loaf, Sweet Christmas, '84 278
Muffins, Dasher's Dill Mini-, '04 252
Munchies, Reindeer, '91 276
Nuggets, Golden North Pole, '99 M309
Orange Baskets, '93 286
Ornaments, Edible, '94 316
Paints, Powdered Sugar, '97 286

CHRISTMAS
(continued)

Pandoro, **'93** 267
Panettone, **'93** 266
Peanut Butter Elf Bites, **'91** 275
Pecans, Christmas, **'03** 300
Pecans, Christmas Eve, **'91** 276
Pie, White Christmas, **'88** 281; **'93** 289
Pinecones, Peanut Butter-Suet, **'93** 286
Pinwheels, Santa's, **'91** 275
Potatoes, Christmas, **'88** 252
Potpourri, Christmas, **'94** 317
Pretzel Garlands, **'93** 286
Pudding with Brandy Sauce, Baked Christmas, **'88** 279
Reindeer Food, Magic, **'99** M309
Reindeer Nibbles, **'92** 280
Relish Tree, Christmas, **'84** 257
Salad, Christmas, **'88** 249
Salad, Christmas Ribbon, **'02** 257
Salad, Christmas Snow, **'82** 266
Salad, Cranberry Christmas, **'79** 243
Salad, Eggnog Christmas, **'86** 281
Salmon with Caribbean Fruit Salsa, Blitzen's Baked, **'04** 252
Sandwiches, Christmas Tree, **'92** 279
Sandwich Wreath, Festive, **'86** 333
Santa's Hat, **'92** 279
Santa's Whiskers, **'85** 323
Scent, Christmas, **'84** 325
Snowman, Marshmallow, **'96** 311
Spices, Barclay House Mulling, **'86** 289
Strata, Christmas Morning, **'95** 282
Strawberries, Christmas, **'87** 293; **'94** 331
Sugarplum Fairy Wands, **'97** M286
Sugar Plums, **'92** 281
Tannenbaum Temptations, **'92** 14
Wine, Christmas Dreams in, **'91** 260
Wreath, Christmas, **'80** 280
Wreath, Della Robbia Fruit, **'87** 294
Wreaths, Braided Candy Canes and, **'92** 276

CHUTNEYS. *See also* PESTOS, RELISHES, SALSAS, SAUCES, TOPPINGS.
Apple Chutney, **'92** 309
Apple Chutney, Sweet-'n'-Hot, **'96** 14
Blueberry Chutney, **'95** 190; **'00** 154
Cantaloupe Chutney, **'00** 108
Cantaloupe Chutney, Fresh, **'97** 148
Cherry-Peach Chutney, Glazed Ham with, **'97** 315
Commander's Chutney, **'87** 245
Cranberry-Amaretto Chutney with Cream Cheese, **'87** 244
Cranberry-and-Apricot Chutney, **'02** 286
Cranberry-Apple Chutney, Quick, **'05** 231
Cranberry Chutney, **'80** 243; **'83** 260; **'84** 265; **'96** 275; **'98** 276, 318
Cranberry Chutney, Texas, **'04** 257
Cranberry-Ginger Chutney, **'00** 253
Cranberry-Orange Chutney, **'79** 292
Cranberry-Pear Chutney, Hot-and-Spicy, **'00** 255
Dressing, Chutney, **'00** 53
Dressing, Warm Chutney, **'02** 242
Fruit Chutney, Autumn, **'88** M230
Fruit Chutney, Fall, **'97** 218
Green Tomato-Cranberry Chutney, **'00** 140
Kiwifruit-Onion Chutney, **'93** 125
Mango Chutney, **'89** 141; **'96** 182; **'03** 123
Mango Chutney, Blue-Ribbon, **'96** 206
Orange-Cranberry Chutney, **'86** 266
Peach Chutney, **'84** 179; **'96** 207
Pear-Apple Chutney, **'89** 141
Pear Chutney, **'95** 251; **'98** 243
Pear Chutney, Sunny, **'01** 281

Pepper Chutney, Jeweled, **'94** 316
Plum Chutney, **'84** 179
Rhubarb Chutney, **'87** 245
Roll, Chutney, **'83** 259
Rosy Chutney, **'80** 120
Sauce, Chutney-Mustard, **'89** 242
Sweet Potato Chutney, **'99** 45
Tomato-Apple Chutney, **'84** 180
Tomato Chutney, **'99** 143

CLAMS
Backyard Clambake, **'81** 92
Bisque, Clam, **'86** 228
Casino, Clams, **'81** 125
Casino, Maryland Clams, **'89** 196
Chase, Clams, **'79** 85
Chowder, Clam, **'79** 182; **'81** 32; **'85** 9; **'86** 36; **'89** 95; **'90** 202
Chowder, Clam-and-Sausage, **'94** 104
Chowder, New England Clam, **'86** M72; **'98** 289
Chowder, Ocracoke Clam, **'79** 31
Chowder, Shopping Day Clam, **'02** 305
Chowder, Tomato-Clam, **'84** 251
Cocktail, Tomato-Clam, **'87** 252
Crisps, Clam, **'80** 151
Dip, Clam, **'79** 151; **'80** 265; **'01** 194
Dip, Hot Clam, **'82** 59; **'89** 48
Dip, Zesty Clam, **'92** 25
Fritters, Clam, **'79** 151; **'86** 71
Linguine, Clam, **'95** 212
Linguine, Quick Clam, **'90** 233
Littleneck Clams with Cilantro-Black Walnut Pesto, **'97** 164
Oreganata, Clams, **'85** 104
Pasta, White Wine-Tomato-and-Clam, **'05** 140
Pizza, Baby Clam, **'87** 182
Puffs, Clam, **'90** 60
Quiche, Clam, **'83** 215
Sauce, Linguine in Clam, **'81** 83
Sauce, Linguine with Clam, **'84** 124; **'88** 90; **'89** 178
Sauce, Linguine with White Clam, **'05** 49
Sauce, Pasta with Clam, **'84** 291
Sauce, Pasta with Pesto-Clam, **'98** 17
Sauce, Tricolor Pasta with Clam, **'93** 272
Sauce, Vermicelli and Sprouts with Red Clam, **'86** 143
Sauce, Vermicelli with Clam, **'85** 295
Sauce with Linguine, Clam, **'84** 9
Shells, Baked Clam, **'87** 94
Soup, Clam Florentine, **'85** 23
Spread, Creamy Clam, **'91** 274
Steamed Clams Chesapeake, **'89** 196

COBBLERS. *See* PIES, PUFFS, AND PASTRIES/Cobblers, Crisps, and Crumbles.

COCONUT
Ambrosia Sorbet, **'04** 317
Apples, Calypso Caramel, **'03** M216
Balls, Coconut-Almond, **'84** 256
Balls, Orange-Nut, **'02** 297
Bars and Cookies
Brownies, Caramel-Coconut-Pecan, **'05** M288
Brownies, Chocolate-Coconut, **'97** 35
Brownies, Coconut-Pecan-Frosted, **'97** 99
Cherry Cookies, Coconut-, **'79** 292
Chocolate Macaroon Cookies, **'88** 217
Clear-the-Cupboard Cookies, **'99** 278; **'02** 176
Crinkle Sunflower Cookies, **'83** 149
Crisp Coconut Cookies, **'89** 162
English Cherubs, **'83** 257
Golden Bars, **'84** 255
Graham Cracker Layered Cookies, **'98** 94
Graham Cracker Layered Cookies, Chocolate, **'98** 94
Granola Bars, Coconut, **'85** 202
Hawaiian Bars, **'84** 153
Kisses, Coconut, **'90** 106

Lace Cookies, Crunchy, **'01** 294
Lemon-Coconut Cookies, **'02** 293
Macadamia Chunk Cookies, Coconut-, **'05** 87
Macadamia Cookies, Coconut-, **'98** 294
Macaroon Cookies, **'03** 282
Macaroons, Chewy Peanut Butter, **'95** 214
Macaroons, Chocolate, **'83** 300
Macaroons, Coconut, **'79** 52
Macaroons, Soft Coconut, **'02** 229; **'03** 131
Macaroons, White Chocolate Tropical, **'00** M166
Magic Cookie Bars, **'02** 253
Mix, Blond Brownie, **'01** 247
Neapolitan Cookies, **'00** 290
No-Bake Bars, Creamy, **'97** 166
Oatmeal-Coconut Cookies, **'80** 218
Oatmeal-Coconut Crispies, **'01** 19
Oatmeal Cookies, Crispy Coconut-, **'93** 80
Peanut Butter-Coconut Cookies, **'83** 113
Robin's Nests, Coconut, **'98** M111
Shortbread, Coconut, **'02** 224
Shortbread Cookies, Coconut, **'93** 316
Squares, Chocolate-Coconut, **'90** 70
Swirls, Coconut, **'97** 274
Toasted Coconut Cookies, **'02** 245
Biscuits, Yummy Coconut, **'95** 99
Bonbons, Coconut-Black Walnut, **'82** 307
Bread, Coconut, **'83** 140
Bread, Pumpkin-Coconut, **'87** 255
Bread, Toasted Coconut-Topped Cream Cheese-Banana-Nut, **'05** 27
Broth with Noodles, Thai Coconut, **'98** 295
Cakes
Angel Cake, Spiked Coconut, **'85** 279
Anniversary Cake, **'00** 117
Apple Coconut Cake, **'80** 226
Banana-Coconut Cake, **'93** 154
Banana Split Cake, **'99** 48
Black Forest Crisp, **'02** 128
Brown Sugar Snack Cake, **'98** 195
Carrot Cake, Fresh Coconut-, **'80** 299
Carrot Cake, Shortcut, **'02** 83
Cheesecake, Ambrosia, **'02** 296
Cheesecake, Coconut-Chocolate-Almond, **'98** 322
Cheesecake, Festive Piña Colada, **'01** 286
Cheesecakes, Key Lime-Coconut Mini-, **'05** 159
Cheesecake, Tropical Tofu, **'00** 204
Chocolate-Coconut Cake, **'83** 23
Christmas Coconut Cake, **'82** 262
Coconut Cake, **'92** 120; **'03** 278; **'05** 335
Coffee Cake, Cranberry-Coconut, **'93** 332
Coffee Cake, Oatmeal-Coconut, **'83** 312
Coffee Cake, Pineapple-Coconut, **'94** 49; **'03** 198
Cream Cake, Coconut, **'81** 179; **'91** 269
Creamy Coconut Cake, **'84** 43
Four-Layer Coconut Cake, **'00** 117
Fresh Coconut Cake, **'80** 289; **'82** 52; **'85** 281
Fudge Cake, Coconut-, **'99** 206
Hibiscus-Nectar Cake, **'96** 248
Holiday Coconut Cake, **'90** 308
Italian Cake, Chocolate, **'02** 256
Italian Cream Cake, **'96** 262
Italian Cream Cake, Fresh Orange, **'02** 294
Italian Cream Cake, Quick, **'99** 307
Layer Cake, Coconut, **'05** M246
Layer Cake, Stately Coconut, **'81** 70
Lemon Cake, Coconut-, **'95** 319
Lemon-Coconut Cream Cake, **'81** 179
Lemon-Coconut Sheet Cake, **'85** 117
MaMa's Coconut Cake, **'97** 71
Orange-Coconut Angel Food Cake, **'94** 294
Party Cake, Gathering of Stars, **'00** 307
Piña Colada Cake, **'99** 117
Pineapple Cake, Coconut-, **'89** 56

Pineapple Cake, Nanny's Famous Coconut-, '97 277
Pineapple-Coconut Cake, '00 86
Pineapple Layer Cake, Coconut-, '80 140
Pound Cake, Coconut, '82 87; '91 224
Pound Cake, Coconut Cream, '84 10
Pound Cake, Coconut-Cream Cheese, '85 297;
　'90 305
Pound Cake, Cream Cheese-Coconut-Pecan,
　'04 280
Quick Coconut-Pineapple Cake, '05 106
Regal Coconut Cake, '83 299
Roll, Coconut-Pineapple Cake, '84 304
Rum-Orange Coconut Cake, '88 224
Sheet Cake, Coconut, '04 136
Spice Cake, Coconut-, '84 255; '87 296
Star Cake, Twinkling, '00 306
Toasted Coconut Cake, '86 60
Unforgettable Coconut Cake, '90 104; '01 330
White Chocolate-Coconut Cake, '87 263
Calypso, Coco-Berry, '89 171
Candy, Coconut, '79 272; '80 250
Caramels, Coconut-Macadamia, '98 305
Chicken Balls, Coconut Curried, '91 165
Chicken, Coconut, '98 20
Chicken Dippers with Wowee Maui Mustard, Crispy
　Coconut, '05 324
Chicken with Fresh Fruit, Coconut, '93 294
Cloud, Coconut, '80 70
Clusters, Pecan-Coconut, '86 M251
Coffee, Coconut, '97 17
Cookies. *See* **COCONUT/Bars and Cookies.**
Cream, Coconut, '00 27
Cream, Orange-Coconut, '84 24
Cream, Red Curry-Coconut, '00 197
Crème Brûlée, Piña Colada, '04 246
Crisp, Tropical Pineapple, '02 232
Crust, Chocolate-Coconut, '87 261
Crust, Coconut, '89 160; '05 157
Custard, Coco Loco, '02 89
Custard, Coconut, '86 109; '97 131
Custard, Coconut Cream, '03 85
Dessert, Chilled Coconut, '83 116
Dessert, Coconut-Caramel, '92 44
Dessert in a Nutshell, '96 318
Dessert, Macaroon-Sherbet Frozen, '79 212
Dip, Coconut-Honey Fruit, '84 171
Dressing, Coconut, '87 251
Dressing, Coconut-Orange, '97 93
Dressing, Orange-Coconut, '80 158
Dressing, Tangy Coconut-Fruit, '84 171
Drink, Coconut-Pineapple, '83 172
Drops, Chocolate-Coconut Almond, '87 223
Filling, Coconut, '81 265; '00 117; '03 329
Filling, Coconut Cream, '84 200
Filling, Coconut-Pecan, '05 107
Filling, Piña Colada, '99 117
Filling, Sour Cream-Coconut, '92 120
Frosting, Coconut, '82 262; '91 269
Frosting, Coconut Chocolate, '79 13
Frosting, Coconut Cream Cheese, '86 60
Frosting, Coconut-Cream Cheese, '04 137; '05 317
Frosting, Coconut Milk, '00 117
Frosting, Coconut-Pecan, '81 296; '83 M233; '84 43,
　322; '97 99; '03 289
Frosting, Creamy Coconut, '80 287
Frosting, Lemon-Coconut, '90 253
Frosting, Nutty Coconut, '86 8
Frosting, Quick Caramel-Coconut-Pecan, '05 211
Frost, Pink Coconut, '79 174; '80 128
Fruit Bowl, Coconut, '83 111
Granola, '99 212
Granola, Pecan-Coconut, '02 70
Ice Cream, Banana-Coconut, '02 164
Ice Cream, Coconut, '98 180

Ice Cream, Coconut Fried, '85 141
Ice Cream, Fresh Coconut, '79 166
Ice Cream, Mint Nectarines with Pineapple-Coconut,
　'05 123
Ice Cream, Mint Peaches with Pineapple-Coconut,
　'05 123
Ice Cream, No-Cook Coconut, '04 179
Ice Cream, Simple Coconut, '02 232
Ice Cream, Toasted Coconut, '00 143
Ice Cream with Sweet Heat Salsa and Cinnamon Crisps,
　South Seas, '04 315
Icing, Chunky Cherry, '03 94
Joys, Chocolate-Covered Coconut, '98 M282
Joys, Coconut, '98 282
Macaroon Charlotte, '81 296
Macaroon-Stuffed Peaches, '79 178
Milk, Chicken in Coconut, '97 202
Mousse, Coconut-Pineapple, '94 198
Muffins, Coconut, '95 214
Muffins, Coconut-Molasses, '82 210
Nests, Strawberry Coconut, '88 136
Nog, Coconut, '83 275
Pears, Spicy Coconut, '83 207
Pecan Coils, Coconut-, '90 196
Pies
　Blender Coconut Pie, '84 236
　Butter Coconut Pie, '01 244
　Buttermilk-Coconut Pie, '94 246
　Buttermilk Pie, Rancher's, '04 208
　Caramel Pies, Coconut-, '87 260
　Cherry Pie, Coconut Crumb, '92 30
　Chess Pie, Coconut, '86 220; '00 60; '02 107
　Coconut Pie, '93 115
　Cream Pie, Coconut, '80 238; '81 136; '82 85;
　　'84 49; '87 207; '89 236; '90 312; '98 161;
　　'02 92; '03 106; '05 110
　Cream Pie, Fresh Coconut, '80 289
　Cream Pie, Surprise Coconut, '92 43
　Creamy Coco-Nana Pie, '00 95
　Crunch Pie, Coconut, '90 105
　Custard Pie, Coconut, '82 33
　French Coconut Pie, '90 162
　Key Lime Pie, Rum-Coconut, '05 157
　Macadamia Nut Pie, Coconut-, '97 110
　Macaroon Pie, Coconut, '88 204
　Magic Coconut Pie, '79 53
　Mock Coconut Pie, '86 200
　Orange Chess Pie, Coconut-, '89 169
　Orange-Coconut Cream Pie, '94 208
　Orange-Coconut Pie, '90 90
　Pecan Chess Pie, Coconut-, '81 248
　Pecan Pie, Coconut, '81 161
　Pineapple-Coconut Chess Pie, '92 214
　Pineapple Pie, Coconut-, '84 256
　Quick Coconut Pie, '83 115
　Shell, Chocolate-Coconut Pie, '82 210; '83 100
　Toasted Coconut Pie, '90 105
Pirate's Painkiller, '99 161
Pudding, Piña Colada Bread, '98 34
Puffs, Coconut, '87 277
Relish, Pineapple-Coconut, '96 323; '97 27
Rice, Coconut, '00 201
Rice, Polynesian Pork Tenderloin with Orange-Curry
　Sauce and Coconut, '04 309
Salad, Cantaloupe Colada, '97 148
Salad, Chunky Fruit-and-Coconut, '84 24
Salad, Curried Poached Pears with Coconut-Chicken,
　'97 93
Salsa, Tropical, '01 60
Sauce, Coconut, '98 34
Sauce, Coconut-Orange, '85 189
Sauce, Creamy Light Coconut, '82 177
Shrimp, Coconut, '00 175
Shrimp, Coconut-Beer, '85 230; '89 23

Shrimp, Coconut Fried, '96 248
Shrimp Martinis with Napa Cabbage Slaw, '02 280
Shrimp with Mustard Sauce, Coconut, '02 245
Shrimp with Orange Dipping Sauce, Coconut-Pecan,
　'03 212
Sipper, Creamy Coconut, '02 298
Soufflé, Coconut, '79 73; '85 212
Spread, Coconut-Cranberry Cheese, '92 328
Spread, Coconut-Pineapple, '93 309
Stir-Fry, Coconut-Beef, '97 18
Sundae, Tropical, '04 179
Sweet Potatoes, Coconut-Broiled, '84 231
Sweet Potatoes, Coconut-Orange, '84 252
Sweet Potatoes, Coconut-Stuffed, '82 204
Tartlets, Zamaani's Nutty Yam, '02 21
Tarts, Coconut-Pecan Cookie, '04 305
Tarts with Macadamia Nut Crusts, Coconut Cream,
　'97 62
Toffee, Hawaiian, '04 235
Topping, Coconut-Pecan, '04 41
Torte, Blitz, '01 65
Trifle, Tropical Rum, '03 85
Tropical Snow, '86 34
COFFEE
Beverages
　After-Dinner Coffee, '81 262
　After-Dinner Coffee, Spiced, '02 270
　Almond-Coffee Delight, '84 115
　Blends, Coffee, '95 276
　Bourbon-Barrel Coffee, '03 233
　Brandied Coffee, '81 244
　Brandy Coffee, '97 17
　Cappuccino, Café, '82 253
　Cappuccino, Chocolate Castle, '84 53
　Cappuccino Coffee Dessert, '92 264
　Cappuccino Cooler, Low-Fat, '01 166
　Cappuccino, Flaming, '79 293
　Cappuccino, Iced, '99 333
　Cappuccino Sipper, '99 29
　Chiller, Royal Cup, '98 218
　Chocolate-Almond Coffee, '84 54
　Chocolate Coffee, '82 43; '97 17
　Cocoa-Coffee, '83 55
　Coconut Coffee, '97 17
　Colombian Royal, Café, '80 M290
　Colonial Coffee, '89 290
　Concentrate, Coffee, '04 68; '05 136
　"Concrete," Abaco Mocha, '94 114
　Cream, Café, '82 312
　Cream, Icy Rum Coffee, '83 172
　Creamy Coffee, '81 244
　Dessert Drink, Simply Super, '83 303
　Dessert, Light Coffee, '88 260
　Diablo, Café, '80 259
　Espresso, Amaretto, '92 263
　Fireside Coffee, '03 M298
　Floats, Maple-Coffee, '86 195
　Freeze, Amaretto-Coffee, '99 161
　Frosted Coffee, '81 244
　Frozen Coffee Cooler, '02 163
　German Chocolate Café au Lait, '92 264
　Hazelnut-Coffee Ice, '94 233
　Holiday Coffee, '90 273
　Hot Buttered Bourbon, '97 17
　Iced Coffee, '04 68
　Iced Coffee, Chocolate, '01 166
　Irish Coffee, Creamy, '79 232
　Irish Coffee, Flaming, '79 293
　Irish Coffee Nog, '84 258; '93 340
　Irish Cream Nog, '82 312
　Kahlúa Beverage Sipper, '99 27
　Kahlúa Delight, Make-Ahead, '84 M89
　Kona Luscious, '84 54
　Liqueur, Coffee-Flavored, '86 266

COFFEE, Beverages
(continued)

Maple Coffee, '97 17; '01 130
Mexican Coffee, '83 175, 275; '88 247; '91 78; '93 310; '94 97
Mexicano, Café, '92 208
Mix, Cappucino, '90 87
Mix, Fireside Coffee, '87 241
Mix, Hot Mocha-Cocoa, '82 296
Mix, Mocha-Flavored Hot Cocoa, '91 316
Mix, Spiced Mocha, '01 64
Mocha Blend, '95 276
Mocha Café au Lait, '05 306
Mocha Cappuccino, '02 M220
Mocha Chocolate Fluff, '89 170
Mocha Cocoa, '83 318
Mocha Coffee, '85 M329
Mocha Cream, Café, '84 54
Mocha Deluxe Hot Drink, '82 289
Mocha Espresso, Italian, '82 254
Mocha Frosty, '92 44
Mocha, Hot, '84 60
Mocha Latte Beverage, '03 46
Mocha Latte, Café, '01 64
Mocha Latte, Spiced, '04 333
Mocha Melt, Spiced, '01 240
Mocha, Mexican, '93 M341
Mocha Milkshake, '89 35
Mocha-Mint Shake, '02 297
Mocha Polka, '89 171
Mocha, Quick Viennese, '79 232
Mocha, Spirited Hot, '91 M260
Mocha, Swiss-Style, '82 253
Mocha Warmer, '97 272
Nog, Brandied Coffee, '86 329
Orange Blend, '95 276
Orange Coffee, '96 313
Orange Coffee, Viennese, '84 54
Pontalba, Café, '92 83
Praline Coffee, '97 17; '01 291
Praline-Flavored Coffee, '87 69
Punch, Chilly Coffee, '01 64
Punch, Coffee, '80 50; '83 275; '88 83
Punch, Coffee-and-Cream, '85 116
Punch, Coffee-Eggnog, '86 281
Punch, Coffee Eggnog, '92 264
Punch, Coffee-Ice Cream, '05 136
Punch, Creamy Coffee, '81 50
Punch, Eggnog-Coffee, '02 297
Punch, "Eye-Opener" Coffee, '92 80
Punch, Irish Coffee-Eggnog, '95 314
Punch, Mocha, '84 58, 166; '86 270; '95 141
Punch, Rich-and-Creamy Coffee, '82 121
Punch, Vanilla-Nut Coffee, '03 282
Refresher, Velvet Coffee, '79 149
Royal, Café, '80 259
Shake, Peach-Coffee Milk, '84 284
Slush, Café Latte, '01 64
Soda, Coffee, '97 272
Spiced Brew, Hot, '91 36
Spiced Coffee, '05 307
Spiced Coffee, Special, '84 284
Spiced-Up Coffee, '89 92
Turkish-Style Coffee, '02 257
Vienna Blend, '95 276
Viennese, Café, '82 254
White Chocolate Latte, '04 210
Buttercream, Coffee, '95 277
Buttons, Coffee, '99 66
Cake, Cappuccino Mousse, '99 154
Cake, Coffee Sponge, '83 229; '91 55
Cake, Extra-Rich Chocolate, '99 271

Cake, Two-Day Coffee Sponge, '86 75
Cheesecake with Mocha Sauce, Chocolate-Coffee, '05 M316
Chill, Coffee-and-Cream, '99 126
Cones, Chocolate-Coffee, '96 M316
Cookies, Chocolate Cappuccino, '01 315
Cookies, Java Shortbread, '94 233
Cream, Coffee, '00 27
Cream Puffs, Java, '81 187
Crème Brûlée, Coffee, '95 323
Crêpes, Coffee Ice Cream, '84 85
Dessert, Chocolate-Coffee Frozen, '85 172
Dip, Kahlúa, '99 139
Fajitas, Java, '96 227
Filling, Chocolate-Coffee Buttercream, '00 M287
Filling, Chocolate Midnight, '96 120
Filling, Coffee, '96 316
Frosting, Chocolate-Coffee, '84 36; '88 269
Frosting, Coffee, '94 86
Frosting, Coffee Buttercream, '99 155
Fudge, Coffee-Chip, '86 74
Fudge, White Chocolate-Coffee, '94 232
Granita, Coffee-Kahlúa, '88 118
Ice Cream, Coffee, '88 202
Ice Cream Crunch, Coffee, '82 182
Icing, Coffee Liqueur Ganache, '05 322
Jam, Coffee-Onion, '05 123
Kisses, Chocolate-Dipped Coffee, '96 313
Mallow, Coffee, '80 109
Meringues with Butterscotch Mousse, Coffee, '93 254
Mocha. *See also* **COFFEE/Beverages.**
Angel Squares, Mocha, '98 61
Blend, Mocha, '95 276
Brownies, Mocha, '87 93
Buttercream, Mocha, '89 42
Cake, Belgian Mocha, '84 316
Cake, Dark Mocha-Chocolate, '84 311
Cake, Delta Mocha Chiffon, '00 286
Cake, Double Mocha, '84 311
Cake, Mocha, '02 87
Cake, Mocha Marble Pound, '99 23
Charlottes, Mocha, '02 171
Cheesecake, Mocha, '98 278
Cheesecake, Mocha-Chocolate, '88 258
Cheesecake, Mocha Swirl, '87 262
Chiffon, Mocha, '86 75
"Concrete," Abaco Mocha, '94 114
Cupcakes, Mocha, '85 250
Dessert, Frozen Mocha, '84 311
Dessert, Mocha Alaska, '84 191
Dessert, Mocha-Almond, '80 289; '81 62
Éclairs, Mocha, '01 45
Filling, Mocha, '80 55; '82 262
Filling, Mocha-Chocolate Cream, '05 322
Filling, Mocha Cream, '81 187; '84 305
Freeze, Royal Mocha, '84 53
Frosting, Creamy Mocha, '82 289; '84 311; '91 248
Frosting, Mocha, '83 301; '84 316; '87 224; '94 292; '97 35; '99 66
Frosting, Mocha Butter Cream, '79 281
Frosting, Mocha-Buttercream, '86 26
Frozen Mocha Delight, '96 179
Frozen Mocha Squares, '81 187
Fudge, Creamy Mocha, '95 51
Ganache, Mocha, '04 M260
Gingerbread, Mocha, '81 207; '82 14
Ice Cream, Mocha, '88 202; '97 M145
Ice-Cream Sandwiches, Mocha-Almond-Fudge, '05 62
Mix, Mexican Mocha Spice, '00 334
Parfaits, Mocha-Mallow, '80 219
Pie, Chocolate-Mocha Crunch, '81 136
Pie, Mocha, '94 168
Pie, Mocha Meringue, '80 242; '88 163

Pie, Mocha Pecan Mud, '00 245
Pots de Crème, Mocha, '88 M45
Pralines, Mocha, '92 313; '93 51
Pudding, Mocha-Chocolate Cookie, '03 183
Pudding, Pecan-Mocha, '89 M130
Roll, Chocolate Mocha Cream, '84 304
Roulage, Chocolate-Mocha, '80 216
Sauce, Mocha, '98 57; '05 317
Sauce with Chocolate Yogurt Mocha, '92 243
Scones, Mocha-Pecan, '97 45
Shake, Banana-Mocha, '05 45
Shortbread, Mocha, '05 307
Shortbread, Mocha-Chocolate, '04 173
Shortbread Squares, Mocha-Chocolate, '02 176
Syrup, Mocha Latte, '03 46
Tart, Black Bottom Mocha-Cream, '92 304
Torte, Mocha, '99 66
Torte, Mocha Brownie, '85 102
Torte, Mocha Mousse, '04 260
Torte, Mocha Velvet, '92 318
Mousse, Coffee, '84 126
Mousse, Coffee-Nut, '86 319
Mousse Present, Chocolate, '99 281
Mousse, Quick-as-a-Wink, '84 311
Napoleons, Coffee, '95 276
Nuggets, Coffee, '95 278
Parfaits, Coffee Crunch, '82 159
Pastry Cream, Coffee, '01 45
Pecans, Coffee 'n' Spice, '88 256
Penuche, Coffee, '98 305
Pie, Coffee, '96 148
Pie, Coffee Cream, '94 209
Pie, Coffee Ice Cream, '79 231
Pie, Coffee Pecan, '82 74
Pie, Decadent Mud, '89 252
Pie, Tipsy Mud, '97 251
Pie, Tiramisù Toffee Trifle, '00 312; '04 195
Pralines, Café au Lait, '92 313; '93 51
Pralines, Plantation Coffee, '86 241
Pudding, French Vanilla Latte, '03 M282
Slush, Caffe Latte, '02 209
Steaks, Coffee-Rubbed Strip, '03 282
Syrup, Coffee, '01 64
Tart, Coffee, '99 67
Tiramisù, '98 280; '00 288; '02 285
Tiramisù, Easy, '00 167
Tiramisù Éclairs, Mini, '03 M41
Torte, Toffee-Coffee Ice-Cream, '04 234
Tortoni, Coffee-Almond, '81 30
Tortoni, Creamy Coffee, '88 268
Turkey Breast, Molasses-Coffee, '05 M289
Wafers, Kahlúa, '99 147
COFFEE CAKES. *See* **CAKES/Coffee Cakes.**
COLESLAW. *See* **SLAWS.**
COLLARD GREENS. *See* **GREENS.**
COOKIES. *See also* **BROWNIES.**
Almond-Anise Biscotti, '93 266
Almond Biscotti, '91 108
Almond Brittle Cookies with Ice Cream Balls, '96 202
Almond Butter Cookies, '79 52
Almond Chip Balls, Toasted, '84 240
Almond Cookies, '83 22, 181; '91 51; '92 176
Almond Cookies, Chewy, '02 258
Almond Cookies, Light, '83 151
Almond Cookies, Skillet, '97 288
Almond Cookies, Swedish, '85 312
Almond Snaps, '92 273
Almond Spritz Cookies, '82 306
Apple-Filled Cookies, '92 311
Apricot Cookies, '95 322
Bars and Squares
Almond Bars, Swedish, '97 322
Almond Brickle Treats, '95 321
Almond Cake Squares, '79 111

Almond-Chocolate Bars, '83 304
Almond Cream Confections, '87 198; '90 310
Apple Butter Bars, '84 153
Apple Kuchen, '79 24
Apple-Oat Snack Squares, '00 332
Apricot-Almond Squares, '95 272
Apricot Bars, '81 247
Apricot Bars, Layered, '01 161
Apricot-Oatmeal Bars, '86 216
Apricot-Raisin Bars, '87 32
Banana Breakfast Bars, '79 124
Blackberry Bars, '87 130
Blackberry-Filled Bars, '79 124
Blackberry Jam Bars, '82 M185
Blondie Swirls, '85 248
Blond Nut Squares, '82 156
Brazil Squares, '82 306
Butter Pecan Pie Squares, '81 262
Butter Pecan Turtle Bars, '90 70
Butterscotch Bars, '82 209; '83 297
By-Cracky Bars, '84 212
Caramel-Pecan Triangles, '99 281
Carrot-Lemon Squares, Golden, '80 40
Carrot Squares, '79 256
Cheesecake Bars, Caramel-Pecan, '05 210
Cherry Bars, Delightful, '86 217
Cherry Squares, '97 273
Cherry Squares, Surprise, '82 57
Choco-Crumble Bars, '79 292
Chocolate-Butterscotch Bars, '81 197
Chocolate-Caramel Layer Squares, '79 83
Chocolate Cereal Bars, Chewy, '97 317
Chocolate Chess Squares, '92 45
Chocolate Chip Bars, '81 130
Chocolate Chip-Peanut Butter Squares, '84 118
Chocolate Chip Squares, '83 170; '89 143
Chocolate Chip Squares, Chewy, '91 175
Chocolate Cinnamon Bars, '82 209
Chocolate-Coconut Squares, '90 70
Chocolate-Crème de Menthe Bars, '86 245
Chocolate Crème de Menthe Bites, '88 285
Chocolate Dream Bars, '79 256; '82 298
Chocolate-Peanut Bars, '03 195
Chocolate-Peanut Crispies, '93 80
Chocolate-Peppermint Squares, '81 119
Cinnamon Chews, '84 110
Cinnamon Sand Bars, '91 178
Citrus Bars, '05 173
Coconut Granola Bars, '85 202
Coffee Bars, Frosted, '79 256
Congo Squares, '96 94
Cranberry-Caramel Bars, '98 277
Cranberry-Cinnamon Granola Bars, '03 26
Crème de Menthe Squares, '93 256
Date Bars, '84 313; '95 322
Date Bars, No-Bake, '79 256
Date Bars, Nutty, '84 153
Date Bars, Walnut-, '03 272
Date-Nut Bars, '80 166
Date-Oat Bars, '80 M172
English Cherubs, '83 257
Fudge Bars, '86 93
Fudge Bars, Yummy, '87 158
German Chocolate Chess Squares, '94 51
Golden Bars, '84 255
Graham Cracker Layered Cookies, '98 94
Graham Cracker Layered Cookies, Chocolate, '98 94
Granola Bars, '83 305; '95 214
Granola Bars, Fruit and Nut, '81 49
Granola Bars, No-Bake, '97 220
Hawaiian Bars, '84 153
Honey Cake Squares, '89 250
Jam-It Bars, '87 159
Jam Squares, '81 M289

Janhagel Cookies, '86 195
Key Lime Bars with Macadamia Crust, '99 282
Layer Squares, Novelty, '90 70
Lemon Bars Deluxe, '79 35
Lemon Bars, Luscious, '01 161
Lemon Bars, Tangy, '86 217
Lemon-Pecan Squares, '89 124
Lemon Squares, '81 197; '97 329
Lemon Yogurt Wheat Bars, '79 93
Lime Squares, '79 2
Magic Cookie Bars, '02 253
Marmalade Biscuit Squares, '79 193
Meringue-Chocolate Chip Bars, '84 118
Mincemeat-Spice Bars, '88 231; '89 22
Mystery Bars, '93 239
Nutmeg Logs, Frosted, '85 324
Nutty Choco Snacks, '83 305
Oatmeal Bars, Chocolate-Topped, '86 110
Oatmeal-Caramel Bars, '85 247
Oatmeal-Date Bars, Layered, '85 10
Peanut Bars, '89 307
Peanut Bars, Chewy, '80 M172
Peanut Butter-and-Fudge Bars, '80 M172
Peanut Butter Bars, '84 243; '93 166
Peanut Butter-Chocolate Treats, Crispy, '02 287; '03 271
Peanut Butter Fingers, '79 256
Peanut Butter Frosts, '84 153
Peanut Butter-Jam Bars, '94 291
Peanut Butter Logs, No-Bake, '84 211
Peanut Butter 'n' Jelly Bars, '83 305
Peanut Butter Squares, '83 116
Peanut Squares, Crispy, '01 M161
Pecan Bars, '82 209
Pecan Bars, Gooey, '94 133
Pecan Squares, '79 205; '90 69; '98 336; '04 271
Pecan Squares, Easy, '81 230
Pecan Squares, Twice-Baked, '79 291
Pecan Sticks, '01 242
Praline Bars, '05 M205
Praline-Chocolate Fudge Bars, Chewy, '04 M330
Pumpkin Bars, '80 40
Pumpkin Nut Bars, '82 217
Raisin Bars, '94 228
Raspberry Bars, '82 209; '84 212
Rhubarb Squares, '91 146
Rhubarb Squares, Rosy, '79 111
Scotch Bars, Chewy, '98 M291
Shortbread, '85 266
Shortbread, Butter-Mint, '99 28
Shortbread, Millionaire, '05 M94
Shortbread, Orange, '91 272
Shortbread Squares, Mocha-Chocolate, '02 176
Snack Bars, Chocolate, '04 124
Strawberry Bars, '81 301
Sushi Bars, '00 50
Sushi Bars, Confetti, '00 50
Toffee Treats, '89 330
Tropical Bars, '80 284
Turtle Bars, '00 334
Turtle Bars, Gooey, '96 189
Walnut-Date Bars, '02 287
Wheat Germ Squares, Spicy, '80 44
Yummy Bars, '92 171
Zucchini Bars, '85 77
Benne Seed Wafers, '96 315; '05 111
Bird's Nest Cookies, '93 284
Biscochos, Betty's, '00 325
Biscotti, Anise, '96 282
Biscotti, Chocolate Chip-Cinnamon, '96 281
Biscotti, Chocolate-Cinnamon, '05 30
Biscotti Cioccolata, '93 268
Biscotti, Cocoa-Almond, '96 280
Biscotti, Fruitcake, '96 281

Biscotti, Orange-Pecan, '01 207
Black-Eyed Susans, '00 291
Bonbon Cookies, Surprise, '88 119
Bourbon Balls, '81 254
Bourbon Balls, Chocolate, '84 298
Bourbon Dunkers, Crunchy, '85 90
Brutti Ma Buoni (Ugly but Good), '93 267
Butter Cookies, '85 322
Butter Cookies, Chocolate-Tipped, '84 258; '90 312
Butter Cookies, Holiday, '92 317
Butter Cookies, Lemon, '01 90
Butter Cookies, Lemon-Basil, '01 117
Butter Cookies, Melt-Away, '81 20
Butter-Nut Strips, '82 167
Butter Pecan Cookies, '82 139
Cake Mix Cookies, '97 133
Candy Wrap Cookies, '04 139
Cats' Tongues, '96 145
Cheesecake Cookies, Chewy, '82 109
Cherry Bonbon Cookies, '93 52
Cherry Crowns, '92 275
Cherry Nut Nuggets, '81 286
Chocolate-Almond Cookies, '98 293
Chocolate-Cherry Cookies, Frosted, '89 294
Chocolate Chewies, Easy, '93 296; '94 234
Chocolate Chip Cookies, '84 120; '86 245; '90 193; '00 276
Chocolate Chip Cookies, Giant, '84 119
Chocolate Chip Melt-Aways, '84 118
Chocolate-Chip Supreme Cookies, '01 218
Chocolate Chunk-Peanut Cookies, '04 125
Chocolate Chunk-Peanut Cookies, Double, '04 125
Chocolate Cookies, Caramel-Filled, '92 319; '02 53
Chocolate Cookies, Chewy, '97 166
Chocolate Cookies, Sugar-Coated, '92 274
Chocolate-Covered Cherry Cookies, '99 280
Chocolate Crunch Cookies, '91 316
Chocolate-Dipped Cookies, '05 M299
Chocolate-Filled Bonbons, '89 162
Chocolate Kiss Cookies, '03 298
Chocolate-Mint Snaps, '83 103; '84 96
Chocolate-Peanut Butter Cones, '85 14
Chocolate-Peanut Butter Cookies, '85 90
Chocolate-Peanut Butter Cups, '85 14
Chocolate Pixies, '00 M155
Chocolate Seashells, '91 178
Chocolate Snappers, Jumbo, '81 218
Chocolate Snowflake Cookies, '89 329
Chocolate Spice Cookies, Lemon-Iced, '97 123
Chocolate-Tipped Log Cookies, '87 294
Chocolate Wedding Cookies, '04 275
Choco-Nut Dainties, '04 M124
Choco-Nut Sandwich Cookies, '84 200
Christmas
    Calendar, Cookie Advent, '85 325
    Candy Canes and Wreaths, Braided, '92 276
    Cards, Christmas Cookie, '84 302
    Cherry Cookies, Christmas, '88 282
    Date Cookies, Christmas, '88 287
    Eggnog Christmas Cookies, '79 255
    Elf Biscuits, '99 309
    Elf Cookie, '80 279, 303
    Fruit Squares, Christmas, '88 282
    Gingerbread Bowl, Christmas, '93 266
    Gingerbread Cookies, '80 278
    Gingerbread Men, '99 294
    Gingerbread Snowflake Cookies, '98 324
    Gingerbread Votives, '98 309
    Granny's Christmas Cookies, '02 278
    Jammies, Christmas, '95 322
    Lizzies, Christmas, '87 257
    Moravian Christmas Cookies, '91 282
    Mrs. Claus Cookie, '80 279, 303

COOKIES, Christmas
(continued)

Nutcracker Cookies, '97 286
Nutcracker Sweets, '02 293
Painted Cookies, '86 322
Pfeffernüesse, '01 65
Reindeer Cookies, Jolly, '91 273
Rudolph Cookie, '80 279, 303
Rudolph Cookies, '99 M309
Santa Claus Cookie, '80 278, 303
Santa Cookies, Easy, '95 321
Santa's Whiskers, '85 323
Sleigh Cookie, '80 279, 303
Spiced Christmas Cookies, '87 294
Spritz Cookies, Christmas, '96 314
Strawberries, Christmas, '87 293
Sugarplum Fairy Wands, '97 M286
Sugarplum Sticks, '95 321
Swedish Christmas Cookies, '79 290
Swedish Holiday Cookies, '01 296
Tree Cookies, Christmas, '93 286
Trees, Christmas, '89 294
Votives, Edible, '98 309
Wreaths, Christmas, '97 288
Cinnamon Balls, '79 23
Cinnamon Sticks, Italian, '93 204
Cinnamon Wafers, '81 192
Cocoa Kiss Cookies, '85 171
Coconut Cookies, Crisp, '89 162
Coconut-Oatmeal Cookies, Crispy, '93 80
Coconut Swirls, '97 274
Coffee Kisses, Chocolate-Dipped, '96 313
Cream, Cookies and, '96 179
Cupcake Cookies, '04 273
Curled Cookies, French, '87 16
Date Balls, '01 90
Drop
Almond Cookies, '97 288; '99 49
Almond Lace Cookies, '98 336
Almond-Toffee Chocolate Chip Cookies, '05 87
Amaretti Cookies, '02 270
Ambrosia Cookies, '81 301; '82 110; '86 313
Apple Butter Spice Cookies, '79 291
Apple Cookies, Fresh, '84 36
Apple-Nut Cookies, '80 228
Apple Oatmeal Cookies, '85 215
Apple-Oatmeal Cookies, '90 218
Apricot Cookies, Frosted, '81 192
Banana Oatmeal Cookies, '79 217
Benne Seed Cookies, '84 318
Breakfast Cookies, '97 52
Breakfast Cookies, Take-Along, '84 59
Brownie Chip Cookies, '90 320
Butterscotch Cookies, '87 58
Butterscotch-Pecan Cookies, '84 36
Candy Bit Cookies, '81 192
Carrot Cookies, '82 137
Carrot Cookies, Frosted, '81 7
Carrot-Orange Cookies, '83 149
Cashew Crunch Cookies, '92 17
Cherry-Almond Drops, '81 20
Cherry-Double Chip Cookies, Chunky, '05 M87
Chip Cookies, Double, '81 301
Chips Cookies, Loaded-with-, '87 223
Chocolate and Mint Cookies, '05 308
Chocolate-Bran Raisin Jumbos, '91 142
Chocolate-Brickle Cookies, '99 127
Chocolate Cappuccino Cookies, '01 315
Chocolate Chewies, '93 216
Chocolate Chewies, Double, '00 333
Chocolate Chip Cookies, '84 120; '86 245; '90 193

Chocolate Chip Cookies, Dark, '05 87
Chocolate Chip Cookies, Deluxe, '79 216
Chocolate Chip Cookies, Different, '83 114
Chocolate Chip Cookies, Double, '79 217
Chocolate Chip Cookies, Favorite, '05 142
Chocolate Chip Cookies, Giant, '84 119
Chocolate Chip Cookies, Jumbo, '82 110
Chocolate Chip Cookies, Light, '86 46
Chocolate Chip Cookies, Mom Ford's, '94 287
Chocolate Chip Cookies, Nutty Oatmeal-, '82 M185
Chocolate Chip Cookies, Ultimate, '05 87
Chocolate Chip-Oatmeal Cookies, '84 119
Chocolate Chip-Peanut Butter Cookies, '99 68
Chocolate Chippers, '92 206
Chocolate Chip-Pudding Cookies, '93 21
Chocolate-Chocolate Chip Cookies, '82 35
Chocolate-Chocolate Chip-Peppermint Cookies, '97 289
Chocolate Chubbies, '01 144
Chocolate Chunk-Almond Cookies, Double, '95 178
Chocolate Chunk Cookies, Double, '05 181
Chocolate Chunk Cookies, Super, '88 217
Chocolate Cookies, Double-, '95 272
Chocolate Cookies, Doubly-Good, '82 M185
Chocolate Crispy Cookies, '85 115
Chocolate Drop Cookies, '84 36
Chocolate Macaroon Cookies, '88 217
Chocolate Macaroons, '83 300; '87 57
Chocolate-Mint Chip Cookies, '86 245
Chocolate-Mint Cookies, '92 206
Chocolate-Nut Chews, '81 92
Chocolate-Oatmeal Cookies, '80 105
Chocolate-Orange Delights, '93 52
Chocolate-Peanut Butter Cups, '97 134
Chocolate-Peanut Cookies, '83 223
Chocolate-Raisin Oatmeal Cookies, '95 136
Chocolate Sandwich Cookies, '81 192
Choco-Peanut Chip Cookies, '92 318
Clear-the-Cupboard Cookies, '99 278; '02 176
Cocoa Drop Cookies, '80 217
Coconut-Cherry Cookies, '79 292
Coconut Cookies, Toasted, '02 245
Coconut Kisses, '90 106
Coconut-Macadamia Chunk Cookies, '05 87
Coconut-Macadamia Cookies, '98 294
Coconut Macaroons, '79 52
Coconut Robin's Nests, '98 M111
Cranberry-Almond Cookies, '98 26
Cranberry-White Chocolate Cookies, '05 308
Cream Cheese-Chocolate Chip Cookies, '02 229; '03 131
Cream Cheese Cookies, '80 282; '02 229; '03 131
Date-Nut Chocolate Chip Cookies, Rich, '92 207
Devil Doggies, '84 37
Easy Cookies, '00 133
English Rocks, '01 295
Fibber McGee Cookies, '95 72
Forget 'em Cookies, '83 256
Fruitcake Cookies, '79 291; '86 320; '88 286; '96 314; '98 294
Fruitcake Cookies, Holiday, '81 301
Fruitcake Drop Cookies, '92 275
Fruit Cookies, Bourbon, '86 334
Fruit Cookies, Spicy Holiday, '83 298
Fruit Drops, Candied, '89 329
Fudge-Pecan Chewies, Alabama, '95 143
Gumdrop Cookies, '79 292
Jack-o'-Lantern Cookies, '87 214
Lace Cookies, '86 8
Lemonade Cookies, '79 51
Lemon Yummies, '81 301
Macadamia Nut White Chocolate Cookies, Chunky, '92 207
Macaroons, Soft Coconut, '02 229; '03 131

Macaroons, White Chocolate Tropical, '00 M166
Melting Moments, '85 191
Meringue Kiss Cookies, '86 121
Meringue Surprise Cookies, '86 320
Mincemeat Drop Cookies, '79 246
Molasses Cookies, Chewy, '87 257
Molasses Cookies, Crispy-Chewy, '90 218
Monster Cookies, '84 36
Nugget Cookies, '79 291
Oatmeal-Chocolate Chippers, '90 218
Oatmeal-Chocolate Chunk Cookies, Nutty, '01 19
Oatmeal-Chocolate Morsel Cookies, '95 46
Oatmeal-Coconut Crispies, '01 19
Oatmeal Cookies, '92 82; '99 280
Oatmeal Cookies, Cake Mix, '96 247
Oatmeal Cookies, Cinnamon, '84 72
Oatmeal Cookies, Crunchy, '85 202
Oatmeal Cookies, Double-Chip, '03 200
Oatmeal Cookies, Easy, '80 105
Oatmeal Cookies, Nutty, '81 130
Oatmeal Cookies, Old-Fashioned, '80 106; '85 250
Oatmeal Cookies, Orange-Glazed, '80 60
Oatmeal Cookies, Peanutty, '80 106; '83 95
Oatmeal Cookies, Pudding-, '98 215
Oatmeal Cookies, Spicy, '81 197; '01 19
Oatmeal Cookies, Toasted, '92 273; '95 136
Oatmeal-Date Cookies, '82 109
Oatmeal Krispies, '85 115
Oatmeal-Peanut Butter Chocolate Chip Cookies, '92 207
Oatmeal-Peanut Butter Cookies, '85 171
Oatmeal-Raisin Chocolate Chip Cookies, '05 87
Oatmeal-Raisin Cookies, '87 221; '93 127
Oatmeal-Raisin Cookies, Frosted, '79 290
Oatmeal-Spice Cookies, Giant, '80 105; '03 59
Oatmeal Sunshine Cookies, '89 59
Oatmeal-Toffee Cookies, '04 234
Oats-and-Peanut Cookies, '89 60
Olympic Medal Cookies, '96 180
Orange-Chocolate Cookies, '83 113
Orange Cookies, Frosted, '83 114
Orange Crinkles, '95 272
Orange Crispies, Grandmom Lucy's, '02 253
Orange Slice Cookies, '98 324
Peanut Butter-Chocolate Chip Cookies, '05 87, 222
Peanut Butter Cookies, No-Bake, '94 197
Peanut Butter Macaroons, Chewy, '95 214
Peanut Butter-Oatmeal Cookies, '81 218
Peanut Butter-Toffee Turtle Cookies, '02 M325
Peanut Cookies, Salted, '87 92
Pecan-Chocolate Chip Cookies, '05 87
Pecan Crispies, '99 337
Pecan Lace Shells, '97 167
Pecan Sandies, Basil-, '97 166
Persimmon Cookies, '96 242
Persimmon-Raisin Cookies, '85 232
Pfeffernüesse, '01 65
Pineapple Cookies, '79 216
Polka Dots, '95 272
Potato Chip Cookies, '86 93
Praline-Chocolate Chip Cookies, Crispy, '02 229; '03 131
Praline Cookies, '91 271
Praline Cookies, Crispy, '02 229; '03 131
Pumpkin-Chocolate Chip Cookies, '93 235
Pumpkin Drop Cookies, '79 206
Pumpkin-Walnut Cookies, Frosted, '82 217
Rainy Day Cookies, '94 168
Raisin Cookies, Alltime Favorite, '80 24
Raisin-Granola Treats, '92 22
Red, White, and Blue Cookies, Chewy, '03 163
Snowcaps, Smoky Mountain, '00 288

Sour Cream Cookies, Southern, '83 113
Sour Cream-Nutmeg Cookies, '85 171
Sugar Biscuits, '04 72
Sugar Cookies, Nutmeg, '79 136
Sugar Cookies, Stir-and-Drop, '92 174
Sunflower Cookies, Crinkle, '83 149
Tea Cakes, Dropped, '90 156
Toffee Crunch Cookies, '93 80
Walnut Spice Kisses, '89 295
White Chocolate Chip-Oatmeal Cookies, '99 127;
  '04 43
White Chocolate-Macadamia Nut Cookies, '94 315
White Chocolate-Orange Dream Cookies, '98 294
Zucchini Cookies, Spicy, '97 273
Easter Basket and Eggs, '95 101
Eggnog Logs, '92 274
Finikia, '96 21
Flying Brooms, '98 255
Ginger Cookies, '85 306; '96 314
Ginger Crinkles, '83 149
Ginger-Oatmeal Sorghum Cookies, '00 230; '02 230
Gingersnaps, '79 146; '91 299; '92 264
Gingersnaps, Best-Ever, '79 208
Hamburger Cookies, '00 171
Hazelnut Bonbons, Crisp, '97 274
Hazelnut Cookies, '84 111
Hazelnut Crinkle Cookies, '98 294
Hazelnut-Lemon Logs, '84 117
Heavenly Delights, '85 324
Jumbles, Mrs. Jemison's, '97 133
Keyboard Cookies, '94 M330
Kissy Cookies, '93 331
Lace Cookies, Crunchy, '01 294
Lace Cookies, Florentine, '88 120
Ladybugs, Cream Cheese, '05 211
Lemon Cookies, '03 298
Lemon Cookies, Sunshine, '86 69
Lemon Crinkle Cookies, '81 287
Lemon Crisps, '95 272
Lemon Thumbprint Cookies, '03 298
Lemon Zephers, '81 172
Lollipop Cookies, '94 196
Macadamia-Oat Snowballs, '92 274
Madeleines, Snow-Capped, '85 120
Mailing Cookies, Tips on, '83 305
Mandel Bread, '97 220; '99 57
Mandelbrot, Rhoda's, '98 243
Meringue Cookies, '98 71
Meringue Cookies, Vanilla, '01 197
Miracle Cookies, '83 149
Mix, Quick, '94 167
Molasses Crinkles, '92 276
Nutcracker Sweets, '02 293
Oat Cookies, Crispy, '88 203; '90 311
Oatmeal Cookies, Special, '81 236
Oat 'n' Cereal Cookies, Crunchy, '05 181
Orange Fingers, '87 57
Peanut Blossom Cookies, '95 245; '96 55; '97 324
Peanut Butter and Chocolate Chunk Cookies,
  '94 169
Peanut Butter-Chocolate Kiss Cookies, '86 49
Peanut Butter-Cinnamon Cookies, '84 30
Peanut Butter Cookies, '82 56
Peanut Butter Cookies, Double-Chip, '89 169
Peanut Butter Cookies, Easy, '92 272
Peanut Butter Cookies, Quick, '86 109; '02 229;
  '03 131
Peanut Butter Cup Cookies, '03 298
Peanut Butter-Kiss Cookies, '03 42
Peanut Butter-Oatmeal Cookies, '84 72
Peanut Butter Temptations, '84 29
Peanut-Date Balls, '81 92
Peanut Truffle Cookies, '93 212
Pecan-Butter Cookies, '83 113

Pecan Crescent Cookies, '85 324
Pecan Crescents, '04 284
Pecan Pie Cookies, '92 289; '00 290
Pecan Sticks, Crispy, '00 258
Peppermint Candy Cookies, '88 286
Peppermint Crescents, '03 273
Peppermint Sandwich Cookies, '92 277
Peppermint Wreaths, Melt-Away, '85 324
Pizza Cookies, Candy Shop, '02 299
Pizzelles, '83 298
Pumpkin Cookies, Peppy, '89 253
Refrigerator
Almond Crescents, '97 273
Almond Crunch Cookies, Texan-Size, '91 236
Almond Sand Dollar Cookies, '05 130
Apple Rugelach, '97 220
Apricot Kolaches, '83 84
Berliner Kranse, '96 311
Biscotti, Chocolate-Hazelnut, '95 80
Biscotti, Light, '91 310
Brown Sugar-Pecan Cookies, '91 236
Brown Sugar Wafers, '96 213
Buckin' Bronco Cookies, '90 95
Butter Cookie Dough, Basic, '95 320
Butter Cookies, '00 288
Butter Cookies, Valentine, '81 20
Cardamom Cookies, '79 12
Cheese Wafers, '00 164
Cheese Wafers, Hope Farm, '93 282
Cherry Chocolates, '95 321
Cherry Pecan Cookies, '82 136
Chocolate-Almond Surprise Cookies, '88 M45
Chocolate-Cherry Cookies, '85 324
Chocolate-Gingerbread Cookies, '94 293
Chocolate Meltaways, '81 302
Chocolate-Nut Freezer Cookies, '88 217
Chocolate Pinwheel Cookies, '86 245
Chocolate Snowball Cookies, '82 295
Chocolate Teasers, '87 44
Choco Surprise Cookies, '80 60
Cinnamon Chip Icebox Cookies, '01 308
Coffee Nuggets, '95 278
Cran-bear-y Bread Cookies, '02 254
Crème de Menthe Cookies, '86 230
Crescents, '85 321
Date-Cream Cheese Rollups, '83 298
Date Moons, '01 295
Date Nut Roll, '79 249
Date Pinwheel Cookies, '02 93
Fruit Rugelach, '97 220
Fudge Puddles, '94 292
Ghosts on a Stick, '00 M235
Gingerbirds, '93 283
Gingerbread Boys, '02 252
Gingerbread Men, '84 299
Gingerbread Men, Miniature, '84 318
Ginger Icebox Cookies, '93 205
Gingersnaps, Raisin, '85 324
Hat Cookies, '01 91
Holiday Garland Cookies, '83 299
Holiday Riches, '83 257
Jack-o'-Lantern Cookies, '95 273
Lemon-Almond Cookies, '02 293
Lemon-Basil Snaps, '05 275
Lemon-Coconut Cookies, '02 293
Lemon Ice Box Cookies, '02 293
Lemon-Pecan Cookies, '02 293
Lemon-Poppy Seed Cookies, '02 293
Lemon Thyme Cookies, '96 124
Linzer Cookies, '02 293
Lollipop Cookies, '95 322
Macaroon Cookies, '03 282
Memory Book Cookies, '92 45
Molasses Cookies, '86 20

Neapolitan Cookies, '00 290
Oatmeal Cookies, Crispy, '89 328
Oatmeal-Date Sandwich Cookies, '83 257
Oatmeal-Toffee Lizzies, Crispy, '95 136
Orange Cookies, Chocolate-Dipped, '04 299
Orange Crispies, '84 205
Orange Refrigerator Cookies, '86 230
Orange-Slice Cookies, '89 294
Peanut Butter-Chocolate Chip Cookies, Freezer,
  '86 230
Peanut Butter-Coconut Cookies, '83 113
Peanut Butter Cookie Ice Cream Sandwiches,
  '93 199
Peanut Butter Cookies, '87 58
Peanut Butter Crisps, '79 50
Peanut Butter Slice-and-Bakes, '82 M185
Peanut Butter Snaps, '81 237
Pecan-Cheese Wafers, '81 119
Pecan Crescent Cookies, '97 274
Pecan Crisps, Sugar, '86 230
Pfeffernusse, German, '98 293
Pinwheel Cookies, '93 316
Raisin-Oatmeal Cookies, '01 19
Raspberry Sandwich Cookies, '82 306
Ravioli, Sweet, '91 107
Ribbon Cookies, '87 293
Sandwich Cookies, Grandmother's, '82 306
Sesame-Cheese Cutouts, '82 296
Shortbread, Brown Sugar, '98 278
Shortbread, Cinnamon, '98 202
Shortbread Cookie Crumbs, '83 298
Shortbread Cookies, '87 58
Shortbread Cookies, Angel, '97 M285
Shortbread Cookies, Crispy, '83 113
Shortbread, Rum-Currant, '98 277
Shortbreads, Pecan-Cornmeal, '04 230
Shortbread Thumbelinas, '05 307
Snowball Surprises, '93 315
Sour Cream Cookies, Dutch, '83 149
Spice Cookies, '03 307
Spice Cookies, Slice-of-, '79 290
Spice-Molasses Cookies, '89 289
Spooky Eyes, '95 273
Spring Bonnet Cookies, '97 111
Springerle, '81 251
Sugar Cookies, Crisp, '84 243
Sugar Cookies, Golden, '88 286
Sugar Cookies, Molasses, '80 270
Sugar Cookies, Pastel, '99 179
Sugar Cookies, Red-, '81 21
Sugar Cookies, Symbol, '91 282
Sugar Cookies, Valentine, '82 20
Sugar 'n Spice Cookies, '81 21
Swedish Cookies, '82 306
Swedish Holiday Cookies, '01 296
Tea Cakes, '02 161
Tea Cakes, Old-Fashioned, '91 72; '99 319
Tea Cakes, Victorian Christmas, '02 253
Tea Cookies, '83 170
Vanilla Crescents, '82 307
Vanilla Slice-and-Bake Cookies, '85 171
Wafers, Italian, '87 36
Walnut Cookies, '81 301; '97 275; '98 35
Watermelon Cookies, '92 179
Rolled
Almond-Filled Wafers, '88 120
Almond Holly Leaves, '86 319
Angel Cookies, '05 308
A-Pees, '97 133
Apricot Cookie Rolls, '80 282
Apricot Kolaches, '94 291
Apricot Wonders, '93 316
Bears, Red-Bellied, '92 277

COOKIES, Rolled
(continued)

Biscochitos, '92 230
Chocolate Cookies, Chewy, '80 208
Cinnamon Cookies, GrandLady's, '00 323
Cinnamon Stars, Swiss, '87 293
Cranberry-Walnut Swirls, '00 290
Cream Cheese Frills, '79 291
Crème de Menthe Cookies, '80 282
Cutout Cookies, Frosted, '85 236
Cutout Cookies, Old-Fashioned, '92 273
Dark Chocolate-Almond Crisps, '05 M30
Date-Filled Cookies, '91 95
Domino Cookies, '05 19
Fruit Cookies, Rolled, '80 15
Fruit-Nut Twists, '82 253
Gingerbread Animal Cookies, '86 70
Gingerbread Cookies, '80 278; '92 343
Gingerbread Man Cookies, '88 227
Gingerbread Men, '85 259; '99 294; '00 297
Gingerbread Men Cookies, '85 319
Gingerbread People, '92 312
Gingerbread Snowflake Cookies, '98 324
Ginger Cookies, Swedish, '85 323
Grandmother's Cookies, '85 319
Ice Box Filled Cookies, '79 112
Lemon Pecan Dainties, '80 208
Lemony Cutout Cookies, '85 323
Maple Sandwich Cookies, '85 322
Mincemeat Cookies, '79 51
Mincemeat Sweetheart Cookies, '87 293
Oat Crispies, '83 96
Oatmeal-Coconut Cookies, '80 218
Oatmeal Cookies, Date-Filled, '86 314
Oatmeal Cookies, Slice-and-Bake,
'80 105
Oatmeal Nut Crispies, '80 208
Orange-Pecan Cookies, '88 119
Ornaments, Edible, '94 316
Peanut Butter Cookies, Double, '80 209
Peanuttiest Cookies, Crisp, '88 65
Pear Mincemeat Cookies, '84 264
Pecan Cookies, Easy, '80 208
Peppermint Cookies, '95 322
Pinwheels, '95 321
Polvorones, '00 123
Pueblo Indian Cookies, '95 228
Pumpkin Cookies, Great, '91 234
Raspberry Swirl Cookies, '90 111
Rugelach, '92 252
Sand Tarts, '00 323
Scones, Currant, '84 117
Sherry Snaps, '87 94
Shortbread, Apricot-Almond, '99 29
Shortbread Cookies, '99 147
Shortbread Cookies, Butter Pecan,
'80 282
Shortbread Cookies, Chocolate, '99 147
Shortbread Cookies, Coconut, '93 316
Shortbread, Easy Roll-Out, '81 21
Shortbread, Raspberry, '99 29
Shortbread Sugarplums, Pecan-, '83 298
Snowflake Cookies, '92 278
Snow Flurries, '92 275
Stick, Chocolate Cookies on a, '05 63
Stick, Cookies on a, '05 63
Strawberry Cookie Tarts, '89 112
Sugar Cookies, '94 271
Sugar Cookies, Crescent, '87 294
Sugar Cookies, Molasses, '80 270
Sugar Cookies, Moravian, '85 321
Sugar Cookies, Old-Fashioned, '86 313

Sugar Cookies, Orange, '89 329
Sugar Cookies, Rolled, '79 291
Sweetheart Cookies, '93 53
Tea Cake Hat Cookies, '04 84
Tea Cakes, '02 161
Tea Cakes, Back-Home, '90 156
Teacakes, Currant, '80 88
Tea Cakes, Decorative, '90 156
Tea Cakes, Grandma's, '90 156
Teacakes, Old-Fashioned, '84 43
Tea Cakes, Sorghum, '85 239
Wafers, Kahlúa, '99 147
Sachertorte Cookies, '00 155
Sandwich Cookies, Viennese, '87 293
Sesame Cookies, Italian, '85 311
Shortbread, '85 266
Shortbread, Brown Sugar, '93 331
Shortbread, Coconut, '02 224
Shortbread Cookie, Old-Fashioned, '88 242
Shortbread Cookies, Java, '94 233
Shortbread Cookies, Praline, '88 242
Shortbread Cookies, Spiced, '88 242
Shortbread Madeleines, Orange, '88 242
Shortbread, Marble-Topped Hazelnut,
'99 M29
Shortbread, Mocha, '05 307
Shortbread, Peanut Butter, '95 321
Shortbread, Peanut-Toffee, '04 329
Shortbread, Raspberry, '02 33
Shortbread, Scottish, '94 242; '95 34
Shortbread Wafers, Cocoa, '88 243
Snickerdoodles, '04 223
Snowballs, Chocolate, '03 273
Snow Cookies, '99 167
Spice Cookies, '87 M278
Spice Thins, '95 322
Spider Cookies, '93 M166
Spooky Ghosts, '98 M256
Spritz Cookies, '04 284
Spritz Cookies, Butter, '91 175
Spritz Hearts, '91 107
Sugar Cookies, '97 288; '03 298
Sugar Cookies, Cinnamon, '84 73
Sugar Cookies, Double-Chocolate, '92 206
Sugar Cookies, Holiday, '04 331
Sugar Cookies, Molasses, '82 140
Sugar Cookies, Sour Cream, '79 51
Sugar Cookies, Winning, '97 108
Swedish Heirloom Cookies, '81 129; '90 311
Tea Cakes, Brandied Apricot, '91 241
Tea Cakes, Mexican, '81 196
Tea Cakes, Royal Raspberry, '02 253
Thumbprint Cookies, Childhood, '85 323
Thumbprint Cookies, Praline, '89 328
Toffee Cookie Bites, '03 M273
Turkey Treats, '93 256
Turtle Cookies, Snappin', '85 323
Waffle Cookies, Brownie, '86 245
Walnut Cookies, Simply, '91 236
Wedding Cookies, '82 M185; '00 332
Whoopie Pies, '86 246
Witches' Hats, '98 256
CORN
Bacon and Caramelized Onion, Corn with,
'99 94
Bake, Corn-and-Swiss Cheese, '92 133
Baked Corn, Creamy, '90 60
Balls, Zesty Corn Dressing, '82 307
Beef "Tenders," Corn, and Tomatoes with Chipotle-Lime
Cream, Tex-Mex Grilled, '05 329
Beignets, Lobster-and-Roasted Corn, '00 51
Boil, Monroe County Corn, '96 167
Cabbage Rolls, Southwestern, '97 214
Cakes, Southwestern Chicken-Corn, '05 321

Cakes with Avocado Cream, Southwestern Chicken-and-
Corn, '97 M311
Cakes with Smoked Salmon Salsa, Corn-and-Black
Bean, '96 272
Casseroles
Baked Corn, Creamy, '02 234
Baked Jack Corn, '97 86
Bean Casserole, Corn-and-, '90 208
Broccoli-Corn Casserole, '83 313
Cheese Casserole, Corn and, '81 128
Cheesy Corn Bake, '98 244
Chili-Corn Casserole, '88 266
Corn Casserole, '79 247; '89 126; '93 141
Creamy Corn, '79 213; '90 207
Escalloped Corn, '79 251
Fresh Corn Casserole, '80 165
Green Bean-and-Corn Casserole, '88 123;
'99 36
Green Chile Casserole, Corn-and-, '89 68
Hamburger-Corn Bake, '99 58
Hominy-and-Corn Casserole, '97 291
Jalapeño-Corn Casserole, '83 256
Moussaka, Corn, '87 190
Oyster-and-Corn Bake, '83 34; '84 44
Rice Casserole, Corn-, '01 46
Salami-Corn Casserole, '80 209
Scalloped Corn, '80 164; '81 128; '86 111;
'88 218
Scalloped Corn, Baked, '85 290
Scalloped Corn, Elegant, '86 268
Scalloped Corn for Two, '82 208
Sour Cream, Baked Corn with, '86 170
Squash-and-Corn Casserole, Easy, '03 69
Tomato Casserole, Corn and, '81 127
Tomato Casserole, Corn-and-, '84 145
Zucchini Bake, Corn-, '79 178
Chiles Rellenos with Walnut Cream Sauce, Havarti-and-
Corn-Stuffed, '93 M275
Chili, White Bean, '02 20
Christmas Corn, '93 325
Cob
Baked Corn on the Cob, Seasoned, '82 134
Barbecued Corn on the Cob, '81 128
Basil Corn on the Cob, Fresh, '00 M170
Chili Corn on the Cob, '03 M185
Corn on the Cob, '79 122
Foil-Baked Corn on the Cob, '81 128
Foiled Corn on the Cob, '80 165
Garlic-Chive Butter, Corn on the Cob with, '01 331
Grill, Corn on the, '94 161; '97 191
Grilled Corn in the Style of Oaxaca, '04 134
Grilled Corn-on-the-Cob, '90 166
Grilled Corn on the Cob with Red Chile Paste,
'05 118
Grilled Corn with Jalapeño-Lime Butter, '01 158;
'04 178
Grilled Corn with Maple Vinaigrette, '98 171
Grilled Parmesan Corn, '82 127
Herb Butter, Corn-on-the-Cob with, '84 160
Herb Butter Sauce, Corn with, '79 150
Hickory-Smoked Corn, '85 145
Lemony Corn on the Cob, '89 200
Mexican Corn on the Cob, '96 167
Microwaved Corn on the Cob, '80 M122
Parmesan Corn on the Cob, '88 M187
Parslied Corn, '90 155
Roasted Camp Corn, '05 174
Roasted Red Pepper Corn, '91 122
Spicy Corn-on-the-Cob, '84 149
Spicy Corn on the Cob, '87 M151
Cold-Pack Corn, '81 216
Combo, Field Peas, Okra, and Corn, '01 214
Combo, Zucchini-Corn, '86 218
Cornbread, Sour Cream, '96 17

Creamed Corn, '97 136; '02 16
Creamed Corn, Freezer-Fresh, '96 46
Creamed Corn, Skillet, '02 204
Creamed Corn, Southern-Style, '81 M165; '92 201
Creamed Fresh Corn, '82 158
Cream-Style Corn, '80 127; '85 106
Creamy Corn, '79 213; '90 207
Creole Corn, '81 128
Creole, Corn-and-Okra, '89 127
Creole, Okra-Corn, '83 157
Crêpes, Blue-Corn, '97 197
Crêpes with Beef Filling, Blue-Corn, '97 197
Curried Corn and Celery, '86 192
Curried Corn and Sweet Red Peppers, '95 47
Custard, Fresh Corn, '89 127
Deviled Corn, '86 192
Dinner, Corn-and-Ham Skillet, '83 190
Dip, Corn-and-Field Pea, '01 177
Dip, Quick Fiesta, '99 M197
Dip, Roasted Corn-and-Avocado, '91 279
Dressing, Corny Cornbread, '99 258
Flan, Corn, '98 246; '99 25
Flan, Corn-Chive, '94 172
Fresh Corn, Seasoned, '83 M147
Fried Confetti Corn, Creamy, '02 160
Fried Corn, '89 127; '94 158
Fried Corn, Buttermilk, '96 167; '00 184
Fried Corn, Skillet, '83 190
Frittata, Corn-and-Squash, '89 144
Frittata, Skillet Corn, '87 90
Fritters, Corn, '86 192; '94 22; '98 207
Fritters, Corn-and-Crab, '97 227
Fritters, Corn-Jalapeño, '96 153
Fritters, Golden Corn, '80 165; '81 128
Fritters, Skillet-Fried Corn, '85 14
Grilled Corn and Squash, '02 122
Hush Puppies, Corn Soufflé, '98 M328
Hush Puppies with Corn, '83 286; '84 17
Indian Corn, '96 287
Jus, Chile Corn, '00 197
Limping Susan, '90 155
Macque Choux (Smothered Corn), '94 236
Maque Choux, Cajun Corn, '01 284
Meat Loaf, Corny, '86 68
Medley, Corn-and-Okra, '99 203
Medley, Okra-Corn-Tomato, '81 159
Medley, Peas-and-Corn, '85 138
Medley, Skillet Corn, '86 192
Medley, Summer Garden, '84 158
Medley, Zucchini-and-Corn, '80 298; '81 25
Mexican Corn, '80 157, 165
Mexican Corn, Spicy, '93 90
Mexi-Corn, '82 M21
Mexicorn, '96 189
Mexicorn, Black Bean, '96 189
Mexicorn Main Dish, '96 189
Muffins, Corn, '98 313
Muffins, Corn-Oat, '89 108
Muffins, Southwestern Corn, '02 212
Muffins, Sunny Corn, '96 166
Muffins, Tex-Mex Corn, '92 253; '93 144
Okra and Corn in Cream, '79 160
Okra, Corn, and Peppers, '87 M151
Okra, Corn, and Tomatoes, '95 203
Pancakes, Corn, '93 43
Peppers, Corn-Stuffed, '84 104
Peppers, Ham-and-Corn Stuffed, '81 87
Peppers with Chicken and Corn, Stuffed, '02 147
Pie, Quick and Cheesy Corn, '82 191
Pies, Maque Choux, '02 182
Pie with Fresh Tomato Salsa, Buttercrust Corn, '95 181
Poblanos, Corn-Stuffed, '97 269
Pork Chops, Mexican, '99 108

Pork Chops, Southwestern, '98 131
Posole, '95 226
Pudding, Baked Corn, '83 314
Pudding, Corn, '79 276; '81 128; '86 192; '90 219; '98 124; '99 71, 270
Pudding, Corn-Cheese, '80 244
Pudding, Cornmeal, '05 43
Pudding, Creamy Corn, '81 267
Pudding, Dashiell Corn, '98 274
Pudding, Easy Corn, '83 280
Pudding, Fresh Corn, '80 157, 165; '89 172
Pudding, Green Tomato-Tomatillo-Corn, '04 103
Pudding, Southwestern Corn, '01 165; '03 178
Pudding, Sweet Corn, '05 66
Pudding, Tee's Corn, '95 318; '01 165; '03 178
Puppies, Corn, '97 140
Quesadillas, Chorizo, Black Bean, and Corn, '00 148
Quesadillas, Poblano-and-Corn, '01 333
Quesadilla Torta, '97 325
Quiche, Jalapeño-Corn, '85 122
Quick Corn Fix-Up, '81 M4
Relish, Corn, '81 129, 175; '83 189; '84 107; '85 136; '87 120, 245; '92 241
Relish Dogs, Corn, '85 192
Relish, Easy Corn, '83 260
Relish, Quick Corn, '90 13
Relish, Summer Corn, '89 127
Relish, Sweet Corn, '93 119
Relish, Sweet White Corn-and-Tomato, '00 130
Relish, Tomato, Basil and Corn, '05 321
Relish, Virginia Corn, '79 283
Rice with Corn, Tex-Mex, '03 129
Salads
    Avocado-Corn-Poblano Salad, '01 320
    Bean Salad, Mexicorn-, '96 184
    Broccoli-Corn Salad, '87 24
    Chilled Corn Salad, '79 20
    Colorful Corn Salad, '00 139
    Confetti Corn Salad, '96 168
    Corn Salad, '80 247; '81 139; '85 236; '91 27; '95 214; '02 234
    Festive Corn Salad, '92 263
    Fresh Corn Salad, '91 126; '94 162
    Garden Medley Salad, '80 122
    Marinated Corn-Bean Salad, '87 9
    Marinated Corn Salad, '89 126
    Pea Salad, Corn-and-, '90 181
    Roasted Corn-and-Black Bean Salad, '05 209
    Roasted Corn Salad, '97 196
    Shoepeg Corn Salad, '81 23
    Shuck Salad, Corn-in-the-, '93 236
    Slaw, Corn and Cabbage, '79 135
    Tabbouleh Salad, Southwestern, '01 216
    Tangy Corn Salad, '88 176
    Tasty Corn Salad, '84 289
    Wheat Berry-and-Roasted Corn Salad, '94 175
    Wild Rice-and-Corn Salad, '98 288
    Zucchini-Corn Marinated Salad, '98 236
Salsa, Avocado-Corn, '94 201; '99 335
Salsa, Black Bean-and-Corn, '94 80; '05 297
Salsa, Black Bean-Corn, '96 126; '04 322
Salsa, Corn, '00 164
Salsa, Corn-Black Bean, '96 15
Salsa, Grilled Corn, '99 162
Salsa, Mexi-Corn, '91 182
Salsa Pork Chops, Black Bean-and-Corn, '01 320
Salsa, Spicy Corn, '93 322
Salsa, Sweet Corn, '95 156
Salsa with Black Beans and Corn, Southwestern, '96 275
Salsa, Yellowfin Tuna with Corn, Pepper, and Tomato, '94 164
Salsa, Zesty Corn, '02 193
Sauce, Fresh Corn, '98 43

Sauté, Corn, '80 165
Sautéed Corn and Okra, '84 158
Sauté, Spicy Okra-Tomato-Corn, '04 327
Skillet, Zucchini-and-Corn, '01 137
Smoked Corn, '01 169
Soufflé, Corn-and-Cheese, '88 122
Soufflés, Zucchini-Corn, '97 203
Soufflé, Zucchini-and-Corn, '83 265
Soups
    Bisque, Crab-and-Corn, '87 137
    Bourbon Soup, Corn-and-, '92 194
    Chicken-Corn Soup, Cheesy, '97 158
    Chowder, Chicken Corn, '02 305
    Chowder, Corn, '81 128; '83 20; '84 M38; '85 10; '90 202; '91 132; '97 241; '98 31
    Chowder, Corn and Cheese, '80 228
    Chowder, Corn-and-Poblano, '03 193
    Chowder, Curried Chicken-and-Corn, '92 21
    Chowder, Delicious Corn, '82 279
    Chowder, Fresh Corn and Bacon, '93 203
    Chowder, Ham and Corn, '79 16
    Chowder, Ham-and-Corn, '82 40
    Chowder, Mexican Chicken-Corn, '01 18
    Chowder, Mirliton-Corn, '00 246
    Chowder, Oyster-Corn, '83 211
    Chowder, Potato-Corn, '94 66
    Chowder, Pumpkin-Corn, '97 219
    Chowder, Shrimp and Corn, '79 199
    Chowder, Southern Corn-and-Bacon, '96 166
    Chowder, Turkey-Corn, '81 98; '96 279
    Corn Soup, '80 56; '85 243; '87 156
    Crab Soup, Fresh Corn-and-, '92 183
    Cream of Corn Soup, '90 210
    Favorite Corn Soup, '85 155
    Gazpacho, Tomato-Avocado-Corn, '97 182
    Grilled Corn Soup, '87 121
    Pimiento-Corn Soup, '89 126
    Pumpkin-Corn Soup with Ginger-Lime Cream, '95 227
    Shrimp-and-Corn Soup, '84 88
    Sweet Corn Soup with Crab, '02 159
    Sweet Corn Soup with Shiitakes and Shrimp, '99 168
    Tortilla Soup, '98 291
Spoonbread, Corn, '97 301
Spoonbread, Corn and Bacon, '81 129
Spoonbread, Corn-Cheese, '88 9
Spread, Corn-and-Walnut, '96 26
Stew, Frogmore, '00 174, 336
Succotash, '02 16
Succotash, Easy, '80 165
Succotash, Garden, '04 160
Succotash, Savory, '96 63
Timbales, Corn-and-Zucchini, '92 100
Tomatoes-and-Corn, Creole-Style, '84 142
Tomatoes, Corn-Stuffed, '82 270
Tomatoes, Stuffed, '96 82
Tomatoes with Corn, Baked, '80 161
Vinaigrette, Okra-Corn-and-Tomato, '90 173
Waffles, Corn, '01 24
Waffles, Corn-Chile, '94 206
Waffles with Cilantro-Lime Butter, Corn, '02 109
Whole Kernel Corn, '85 106
Zucchini and Corn, '86 177
Zucchini and Corn, Dilled, '83 173
Zucchini, Corn and, '83 190
CORNBREADS. See also HUSH PUPPIES.
Bake, Bacon, Zucchini, and Cornbread, '99 123
Bake, Cornbread Tamale, '79 163
Basic Cornbread, '99 257; '02 141
Batter, Cornbread Crust, '03 20
Beef Cornbread, Cheesy, '81 242
Biscuits, Cornmeal-Jalapeño, '94 214

CORNBREADS

(continued)

Bites, Corn Dog, '85 245
Black-Eyed Pea Cornbread, '98 44
Black-Eyed Pea Cornbread, One-Dish, '03 215
Bowls, Cornbread, '95 58
Buttermilk Cornbread, '79 34; '82 70; '99 235
Carrot Cornbread, '80 89; '81 163
Casserole, Bean-and-Cornbread, '92 243
Casserole, Beef, Bean, and Cornbread, '99 215
Casserole, Cornbread, '81 91
Casserole, Cornbread Skillet, '83 243; '84 101
Cheddar Cornbread, '83 285; '84 17
Cheddar-Jalapeño Cornbread, '85 3
Cheese-and-Onion Cornbread, '05 35
Chicken over Cornbread, Creamed, '86 231
Chile-Cheese Cornbread, '87 171
Chile Cornbread, '86 254
Confetti Cornbread, '94 170
Cornbread, '80 272; '86 231; '87 197; '92 324; '93 122;
  '01 234
Cornish Hens, Cranberry-Cornbread Stuffed,
  '95 325
Cottage Cheese Cornbread, '80 90
Cowboy Cornbread, '81 188
Cracklin' Cornbread, '92 216
Cracklin' Cornbread, Grannie's, '98 252
Cracklin' Cornbread, Southern, '80 119
Crackling Cornbread, '85 200
Crackling Cowboy Cornbread, '82 114
Crêpes, Cornbread, '98 42
Crêpes, Goat Cheese-Filled Cornbread, '98 43
Crêpes, Southwestern Cornbread, '98 42
Crispy Cornbread, '92 340
Croutons, Cornbread, '93 192; '05 45
Croutons, Honeyed Cornbread, '94 106
Crust, Turkey and Peppers in Cornbread,
  '95 312
Crusty Cornbread, '85 255
Dieter's Cornbread, '87 164
Dressings
  Biscuit Dressing, Cornbread-, '79 296
  Cakes, Southwestern Cornbread Dressing, '01 233
  Chicken and Dressing, '99 42
  Chicken Cornbread Dressing, '90 159
  Cornbread Dressing, '86 286; '88 254; '92 267;
    '98 269; '00 259; '02 249; '03 231
  Corny Cornbread Dressing, '99 258
  Crawfish-Cornbread Dressing, '99 257
  Fruited Cornbread Dressing, '80 262
  Green Chile-Cornbread Dressing, '93 306; '94 296
  Herb-Seasoned Cornbread Dressing, '83 315
  Kentucky Cornbread Dressing, '86 281
  Light Cornbread Dressing, '92 324
  Louise's Cornbread Dressing, '03 251
  Nannie's Cornbread Dressing, '95 306
  Old-Fashioned Cornbread Dressing, '84 321
  Oyster-Cornbread Dressing, Ma E's Traditional,
    '96 35
  Quail and Dressing, '99 42
  Quail Stuffed with Cornbread Dressing, '93 280
  Roast Turkey and Cornbread Dressing, '89 324
  Sage-Cornbread Dressing, '84 283
  Sage Dressing, Cornbread-, '80 262
  Sausage, and Pecan Cornbread, '99 257
  Sausage-Cornbread Dressing, '95 289
  Sausage-Cornbread Dressing, Turkey with, '83 287
  Sausage Dressing, Cornbread-, '82 307; '85 280
  Sausage Dressing, Cornbread-and-, '83 213
  Savory Cornbread Dressing, '88 303
  Slow-Cooker Cornbread Dressing, '05 270
  Spoonbread Dressing, Southwestern-Style, '94 273

Sweet Cornbread Dressing, '97 303
Texas Cornbread Dressing, '82 243
Dumpling Dough, Cornbread Dressing, '03 239
Easy Cornbread, '94 158
Fresh Cornbread, '80 165
Green Chile Cornbread, '82 134
Herbed Cornbread, '90 214
Hoecake, Hot Water, '81 56
Hoecakes, Green Onion, '88 112
Honey Cornbread, '83 286; '84 17
Honey-Sweet Cornbread, '05 137
Hot Water Cornbread, '88 92
Hot-Water Cornbread, '01 29; '02 107; '03 112;
  '04 25
Hot-Water Cornbread, Bacon-Cheddar, '01 29; '02 107;
  '04 25
Hot-Water Cornbread, Baked, '01 29; '02 107; '04 25
Hot-Water Cornbread, Country Ham, '01 29; '02 107;
  '04 25
Hot-Water Cornbread, Southwestern, '01 29; '02 107;
  '04 25
Jalapeño Cornbread, '85 200; '94 78; '98 178
Jalapeño Cornbread, Beefy, '82 142
Jalapeño Pepper Bread, '83 121
Lacy Corncakes, '81 242
Lightbread, Corn, '81 137
Light Bread, Corn, '00 270
Light Cornbread, Old Southern, '81 242
Loaded Cornbread, '99 214
Loaf, Cornbread, '85 200
Menfolks' Cornbread, '82 156
Mexican Cornbread, '80 198; '81 137; '84 140, 242;
  '93 182; '01 247
Mexican Cornbread, Hot, '83 286; '84 17
Mexican Cornbread, Quick, '81 242
Mexican Flatbread, '80 197
Mex-Tex Cornbread, Lynda's, '01 273
Muffins
  Angel Cornbread Muffins, Heavenly, '98 43
  Blue Corn Muffins, '89 145; '92 52; '94 114
  Broccoli Cornbread Muffins, '03 81
  Cheesy Cornbread Muffins, '88 M275
  Cornmeal Muffins, '80 90; '88 92; '96 248
  Corn Muffins, '82 M282; '84 16
  Corn-Oat Muffins, '89 166
  Four-Grain Muffins, '80 46
  Jalapeño-Corn Muffins, '93 164
  Miniature Cornmeal Muffins, '93 119
  Parmesan Corn Muffins, '01 255
  Quick Corn Muffins, '88 15
  Sage-Corn Muffins, '83 207
  Sour Cream Corn Muffins, '95 176
  Southern Cornbread Muffins, '85 201
  Spicy Cornbread Muffins, '90 59
  Sunny Corn Muffins, '96 166
  Tex-Mex Corn Muffins, '93 144
  Tomato Corn Muffins, '81 137
  Yeast Muffins, Cornmeal, '92 49
Mush, '81 215
Old-Fashioned Cornbread, '81 242
Onion Cornbread, '88 283
Onion Cornbread, Sweet, '98 252
Onion-Topped Cornbread, '84 153
Oysters Casino on Cornbread, '79 34
Paprika Cornbread, '90 213
Pastry, Cornmeal, '81 140
Pecan Cornbread, '94 169; '98 252
Picante Cornbread, '94 169
Pie, Beef-and-Onion Cornbread, '01 298
Pie, Brunswick Stew-Cornbread, '02 121
Pie, Cornbread-Sausage-Apple, '87 171
Pie, Cornbread-Tamale, '92 123
Pie, Sausage-and-Cornbread, '90 25
Puff, Cornmeal, '82 42

Quick-and-Easy Cornbread, '83 9
Quick Cornsticks, '81 192
Salad, Cornbread, '87 172
Salad, Dianne's Southwestern Cornbread, '04 133
Salad, Layered Cornbread-and-Turkey, '02 141;
  '05 147
Salad, Layered Southwest Cornbread-and-Turkey,
  '05 147
Salad, Mexican Cornbread, '95 210
Salad, Sara's Grilled Chicken-Cornbread, '05 184
Sandwiches, Open-Faced Shrimp-Cornbread,
  '02 141
Seasoned Cornbread, '90 320
Serrano Chile Blue Cornbread, '94 114
Skillet Cornbread, '81 31; '84 102; '85 200; '90 13;
  '97 137; '00 22; '01 291; '03 112
Soufflé Cornbread, '96 34
Sour Cream Cornbread, '81 137; '96 17
Southern Cornbread, '79 123; '81 56; '83 12
Southern Corncakes, '88 166
Spinach Cornbread, '95 49
Spoonbread, '81 138
Spoonbread, Cheddar, '82 196
Spoonbread, Golden, '83 286; '84 17
Spoonbread, Old Virginia, '84 102
Spoonbread, Ozark, '85 202
Spoon Cornbread, '98 252
Sticks
  Angel Corn Sticks, '84 20
  Blue Ribbon Corn Sticks, '84 102
  Buttermilk Corn Sticks, '80 120; '01 319; '05 218
  Cornbread Sticks, '87 15
  Corn Sticks, '79 275; '89 54; '90 214; '00 43
  Favorite Corn Sticks, '85 202
  Firecracker Corn Sticks, '85 241
  Garlic-Thyme Corn Sticks, '93 242
  Golden Cornbread Sticks, '94 213
  Old-Fashioned Corn Sticks, '90 232
  Pimiento-Cheese Corn Sticks, '03 20
  Quick Corn Sticks, '88 15
  Savory Corn Sticks, '93 33
  Southern Corn Sticks, '81 242
Strata, Cornbread-Chili, '03 100
Stuffed Cornish Hens, Cranberry-Cornbread-,
  '95 325
Stuffed Peppers, Barbecued Shrimp and Cornbread-,
  '97 261
Stuffing, Cornbread, '94 305
Stuffing, Pork Chops with Cornbread-Apple,
  '99 14
Stuffing, Spicy Pecan-Cornbread, '01 207
Super-Moist Cornbread, '02 260
Supper, Cornbread-Vegetable, '97 319
Supreme, Cornbread, '93 67
Sweet Potato Cornbread, '05 252
Swiss Cheese Cornbread, '79 60
Toasted Cornbread, '82 174
Tomatoes, Cornbread-Stuffed, '97 169; '02 213
Topping, Cornbread, '01 215, 298
Ultimate Cornbread, '80 90
Vicksburg Cornbread, '96 35
Waffles, Cornbread, '79 265; '91 90; '98 42;
  '03 205
Waffles, Cornmeal, '85 201
Wampus Bread, '81 305; '82 36
CORNISH HENS
à l'Orange, Cornish Hens, '95 325
Barley-Mushroom Stuffing, Cornish Hens with,
  '97 242
Brandied Cornish Hens, '81 259
Brown Rice, Cornish Hens with, '82 275
Buttered Cornish Hens, Brandy-, '79 292; '80 32
Cajun-Fried Cornish Hens, '95 326
Casserole, Cornish Hens-and-Rice, '92 267

Chutney-Mustard Glaze, Game Hens with, '93 66
Company Cornish Hens, '83 263
Cranberry Cornish Hens, '86 303
Cranberry-Orange Sauce, Cornish Hens with, '86 119
Cranberry Sauce, Cornish Hens with, '79 180
Elegant Cornish Hens, '80 227; '81 52
Flambé, Cornish Hens, '80 227; '81 52
Fruited Stuffing, Cornish Hens with, '90 191
Glazed Cornish Hens, Apricot-, '80 84; '87 306
Glazed Cornish Hens, Asian, '00 111
Glazed Cornish Hens, Jelly-, '89 193; '93 251
Glazed Cornish Hens, Orange-, '83 267; '99 293;
   '00 292
Glazed Stuffed Cornish Hens, Orange-, '84 M89
Grilled Cornish Hens, '88 243; '92 59
Grilled Cornish Hens, Asian, '99 41
Grilled Cornish Hens, Orange-Glazed, '86 250
Grilled Cornish Hens with Tropical Fruit, '97 310
Herbed Cornish Hens, '82 271
Marinated Cornish Hens, Sherry-, '91 148
Mesquite-Smoked Cornish Hens, '92 144
Orange-Ginger Hens with Cranberry Salsa, '98 321
Orange Glaze, Cornish Hens with, '79 244
Pecan-Cornbread Stuffing, Cornish Hens with Spicy,
   '01 206
Port and Sour Cream, Cornish Hens in, '86 323
Roast Cornish Hens, '86 89
Roasted Cornish Hens, Herb-, '88 29
Roasted Cornish Hens, Lemon, '82 260
Roasted Cornish Hens with Vegetables, Tarragon,
   '94 79
Roasted Rock Cornish Hens, '82 66
Smoked Cornish Hens, '86 142, 154; '88 168
Stuffed Cornish Hens, '85 261
Stuffed Cornish Hens, Apricot-, '84 6
Stuffed Cornish Hens, Cranberry-Cornbread, '95 325
Stuffed Cornish Hens, Rice-, '82 302
Tarragon, Cornish Hens, '95 326
Tarragon, Cornish Hens with, '83 143
Teriyaki Cornish Hens, '86 198
Texas-Style Game Hens, '87 61
Vermouth, Cornish Hens in, '86 33
Wild Rice Stuffing, Cornish Hens with, '79 222; '80 64;
   '82 136

COUSCOUS
Chicken, Moroccan Garlic, '99 15
Chicken with Couscous, '97 325
Cranberry-and-Toasted Pecan Couscous, '05 M259
Currants, Pine Nuts, and Pork, Couscous with,
   '00 295
Fruit, Couscous with Mixed, '95 232
Lemon Couscous, '96 154; '00 99; '02 237
Orange-Ginger Couscous, '00 295
Parmesan Couscous, Quick, '05 203
Peas and Feta, Couscous with, '01 158
Raisins, Almonds, and Lemon, Couscous with,
   '00 295
Red Beans and Couscous, '99 22
Roasted Asparagus-and-Hazelnut Couscous, '04 60
Salad, Basil-and-Tomato Couscous, '94 175
Salad, Couscous-and-Garbanzo, '02 65
Salad, Curried Couscous, '91 44
Salad, Mediterranean Couscous, '03 127
Salad, Shrimp-and-Couscous, '96 157
Salad with Dried Tomato Vinaigrette, Couscous,
   '96 244
Salad with Fennel and Goat Cheese, Israeli Couscous,
   '00 312
Shrimp, Hot Red Curry, '02 125
Spinach-and-Onion Couscous, '98 23
Tabbouleh Couscous, '96 251; '97 103; '02 200
Tabbouleh Salad, '91 70
Vegetables and Couscous, '96 136
Vegetables with Couscous, Curried, '04 328

CRAB
Appetizers
Balls, Crabmeat, '88 150
Ball, Spicy Crab, '01 332
Bites, Crabmeat, '97 98
Bites, Crab-Zucchini, '84 M216
Bites, Spicy Crab, '91 165
Broiled Crab Meltaways, '93 287
Cakes and Dijon Sauce, Mini Crab, '03 92
Cakes, Crab, '01 245
Cakes, Crab-and-Scallop, '02 165
Cakes, Miniature Crab, '96 306
Cakes with Cress Sauce, Baked Crab, '96 176
Cakes with Jalapeño Tartar Sauce, Chesapeake Bay
   Crab, '96 69
Cakes with Maui Sauce, Crab, '99 310
Canapés, Cheesy Crab, '86 262
Canapés, Crab, '93 130
Canapés, Crabmeat, '88 150
Canapés, Hot Crab, '86 70; '87 239
Chafing Dish Crabmeat, '89 284
Cherry Tomatoes, Crab-Stuffed, '82 289; '88 78
Cocktail Puffs, '91 106
Cocktail, Sherried Avocado-Crabmeat, '87 95
Deviled Crab, Devilish, '85 264
Dip, Cheese-Crab, '91 200
Dip, Creamy Crab, '80 M135
Dip, Festive Crab, '92 285
Dip, Hot Cheese and Crab, '81 261
Dip, Hot Crab, '93 269; '97 89; '05 124
Dip, Hot Crab-and-Cheese, '94 282
Dip, Hot Crabmeat, '95 154
Dip, Oven-Baked Crab, '82 59
Dip, Tangy Crab, '83 5
Dip, Trawler Crab, '93 238
Hors d'Oeuvre, Crabmeat, '94 236
Imperial, Crab, '02 103
Mold, Crab, '85 318
Mousse, Crab, '79 117; '95 327
Mousse, Crabmeat, '90 190; '91 244; '94 159
Mushroom Caps, Crab-Stuffed, '84 160
Mushrooms, Crab-Stuffed, '81 190; '97 102
Mushrooms Stuffed with Crab, '82 249
Oysters, Crabmeat Stuffed, '94 328
Pâté, Crab, '79 233
Pot Stickers, Hoisin Crab, '96 92
Puffs, Crab, '80 20; '84 269
Puffs, Crabmeat, '99 335
Salsa with Sesame Wontons, Spicy Crab-and-Ginger,
   '01 283
Sandwiches, Miniature Crab Cake, '96 306
Snacks, Crab, '83 93
Snow Peas, Crab-Stuffed, '85 288
Spread, Baked Crab, '80 86
Spread, Best-Ever Crab, '98 60
Spread, Crab, '93 167
Spread, Crabmeat-Horseradish, '90 292
Spread, Crab Soufflé, '85 4
Spread, Hot Artichoke-Crab, '85 81
Spread, Layered Crabmeat, '83 127; '04 69
Spread, Superb Crab, '81 235
Topping, Crabmeat, '91 64
au Gratin, Crabmeat, '86 154
au Gratin, Crab, Shrimp, and Artichoke, '90 240
Baked Avocado-and-Crabmeat, '84 119
Bake, Easy Crab, '95 209
Bake, Quick Crab, '87 192
Benedict, Crab, '92 63
Benedict, Lion, '93 121
Blue Crabs, Festive, '85 103
Blue Crabs, Spicy Steamed, '84 162
Blue Crabs, Steamed, '89 195; '02 141
Bow Ties with Crab and Vegetables, '98 233
Broiled Crab and Avocado, '79 116

Brunch Scramble, Crabmeat, '95 32
Burgers, Crab, '00 58
Burgers, Potato-Crusted Crab, '94 139
Cakes, Baltimore Crab, '92 117
Cakes, Chesapeake Bay Crab, '89 194; '95 155
Cakes, Country Crab, '95 20
Cakes, Crab, '81 125; '90 71; '91 122; '98 140, 222;
   '99 267
Cakes, Crispy Fried Crab, '80 119
Cakes, Down-East Crab, '79 151
Cakes, Faidley's Crab, '01 97
Cakes, Gulf Coast Crab, '94 71
Cakes, Maryland Crab, '05 105
Cakes, Mock Crab, '95 159
Cakes Our Way, Crab, '01 145
Cakes, Uncle Frank's Crab, '05 124
Cakes, Victoria Crab, '92 195
Cakes, Virginia Jumbo Lump Crab, '97 180
Cakes with Collard Greens and Roasted-Garlic Beurre
   Blanc, Down-South Crab, '03 324
Cakes with Sweet White Corn-and-Tomato Relish,
   Crab, '00 130
Cakes with Tomato Cream, Crab, '94 70
Casserole, Crab, '79 228
Casserole, Crab-and-Mushroom, '89 96
Casserole, Crab-and-Shrimp, '84 71
Casserole, Crab-Egg, '80 260
Casserole, Crabmeat-Broccoli, '84 232
Casserole, Creamy Crab and Spinach, '80 3
Casserole, Deviled Crab, '91 238; '92 27
Casserole, Easy Crab, '93 270
Chicken, Crab-Stuffed, '84 101
Cornbread, Crab with Chile, '86 254
Creamed Crabmeat with Artichoke Hearts, '93 26
Crêpes, Crab, '79 165
Crêpes, Sautéed Crab, '84 84
Crisps, Crab, '79 63
Delight, Crab-and-Egg, '84 261
Deviled Crab, '85 104; '92 117
Dressed Crab, '82 276
Dressing, Crabmeat-and-Oyster, '02 243
Eggs New Orleans, Crabmeat and, '82 45
Eggs, Shrimp and Crab Scrambled, '79 261
Eggs Stuffed with Crabmeat, '04 18
Étouffée, Crab-and-Shrimp, '89 96
Fettuccine, Crab, '98 142
Filling, Crab, '89 13
Flounder, Crab-Stuffed, '80 120
Fresh Crab, Preparing, '82 127
Fried Soft-Shell Crabs, '95 154
Fritters, Corn-and-Crab, '97 227
Fritters, Crab, '98 142
Gravy, Tomato-and-Crabmeat Cream, '04 165
Gumbo, Shrimp-Crab, '03 111
Hash with Three-Pepper Hollandaise, Lump Crab,
   '96 52
Imperial, Crab, '79 82, 116; '89 194; '95 155; '96 148
Imperial, Crabmeat, '82 311; '83 72
Imperial, Easy Crab, '93 128
Imperial, Elegant Crab, '83 245
Imperial, Pineapple-Crab, '84 M286
Imperial, Speedy Crabmeat, '90 M112
Karen, Crabmeat, '93 49
Lasagna, Crabmeat, '96 290
Lasagna, Crabmeat-and-Spinach, '04 292
Lobster Tails, Crab-Stuffed, '95 326
Marinière, Mashed Potatoes with Crab, '99 165
Melts, Open-Faced Crab, '01 171
Meunière, Soft-Shell Crab, '80 57
Mold, Cream Cheese-Crabmeat, '90 71
Mushrooms on Toast Points, Crabmeat and, '82 M91
Oysters and Crabmeat, Creamy, '83 211
Poblanos with Mango Salsa, Crab-and-Goat Cheese,
   '04 59

CRAB

(continued)

Polenta, Crab, '00 277
Potatoes, Cheesy Crab-Stuffed, '86 17
Potatoes, Crabmeat-Topped, '83 3; '95 22
Potatoes, Crab-Stuffed, '91 311; '92 26; '99 307
Puff, Crab, '79 116
Puff, Shrimp-Crab, '79 57
Quesadillas with Mango Salsa, Beefy Crab, '00 124
Quiche, Almond-Topped Crab, '79 127
Quiche, Crab, '82 M122, 243
Quiche, Crabmeat-Parmesan, '03 59
Quiche, Quick Crab, '84 96
Quiche, Sherried Crab, '83 180
Quiche, Simple Crab, '85 207
Ravigote, Crabmeat, '82 250; '92 329
Redfish with Shrimp and Crab, Coastal Bend,
    '01 281
Relish, Crabmeat, '99 198
Salads
    Asparagus Salad, Crab-and-, '92 141
    Avocado Salad, Crab-, '81 114
    Avocados, Crab-Stuffed, '86 73
    Avocado with Crabmeat, '86 119
    Blue Crab Salad with Asian Vinaigrette, '98 142
    Cakes with Greens and Dijon Dressing, Crab,
        '96 176
    Caribbean Crabmeat Salad with Creamy Gingered
        Dressing, '97 263
    Chesapeake Crab Salad, '89 195
    Congealed Salad with Crabmeat-and-Asparagus,
        '84 86
    Crabmeat Salad, '91 169
    Cucumber-and-Crab Salad, '98 208
    Delightful Crab Salad, '87 145
    Louis, Crab, '95 94
    Luncheon Salad, Crab, '00 17
    Luncheon Salad, Crabmeat, '82 207
    Macaroni-Crabmeat Salad, '81 153
    Marinated Crab-and-Endive Salad, '93 22
    Rémoulade, Crabmeat, '93 280
    Shrimp Pasta Salad, Crabmeat-, '86 208
    Tomato Salad, Crab-Stuffed, '80 148
    Wild Rice Salad, Crab-, '86 207
    Wild Rice Salad, Crab and, '79 116
Sandwiches, Avocado-Crabmeat, '83 2
Sandwiches, Crab Cake, '02 60
Sandwiches, Crabmeat, '84 285
Sandwiches, Deluxe Crabmeat, '81 M74
Sandwiches, Hot Crab-and-Cheese, '87 279
Sandwiches, Mango-Crab Salad, '99 72
Sandwiches, Open-Face Crab Tomato, '81 29
Sandwiches, Open-Faced Crab, '87 106
Sandwiches, Puffy Crab, '83 291
Sauce, Cajun Shrimp-and-Crab, '05 206
Sauce Piquante, Crab and Shrimp, '83 92
Sauce, Quick Crab Marinara, '85 M151
Sauce, Stone Crab Mustard, '80 3
Sauce, Tangy Stone Crab, '80 3
Sautéed Crabmeat, Roussos, '84 88
Shrimp Bundles, Crab-Stuffed, '81 176
Shrimp, Crab-Stuffed, '84 259
Soft-Shell Crabs, Chesapeake, '89 194
Soft-Shell Crabs, Fried Stuffed, '98 140
Soups
    Beaufort Crab Soup, '92 238
    Bisque, Crab, '88 251
    Bisque, Crab-and-Corn, '87 137
    Bisque, Crab-and-Leek, '94 104
    Bisque, Crab-and-Spinach, '97 241
    Bisque, Stone Crab, '96 86
    Chowder, Maryland Crab, '97 23

Corn-and-Crab Soup, Fresh, '92 183
Corn Soup with Crab, Sweet, '02 159
Crabmeat Soup, '84 123
Cream of Crab Soup, '88 302
Cream of Crab Soup, Steamboat's, '81 127
Creamy Crab Soup, '80 M224
Elegant Crab Soup, '80 188
Gazpacho, Crab, '97 181
Gumbo, Crab and Shrimp, '81 200
Gumbo, Shrimp-Crab, '98 15
Gumbo with Whole Crabs, Seafood, '85 2
Old-Fashioned Crab Soup, '90 71
Plantation Crab Soup, '92 237
Quick Crab Soup, '84 279
She-Crab Soup, '03 137; '05 98
She-Crab Soup with Marigold, '79 32
Spread, Crabmeat, '79 81
Stroganoff, Crab, '79 116
Strudel, Crab-and-Mushroom, '98 28
Stuffed Soft-Shell Crabs, '83 91
Stuffed Soft-Shell Crabs, Steamboat's, '81 127
Stuffing, Chicken Breasts with Crabmeat, '85 302
Stuffing, Crabmeat, '94 68
Stuffing, Tropical Orange Roughy with Crab,
    '99 122
Supreme, Crab, '79 181
Tomatoes, Crab-and-Avocado Stuffed, '94 141
Tostadas, Crab, '93 203
Veal with Crabmeat, New Orleans, '86 94

CRACKERS
Bacon-Wrapped Crackers, '93 280
Bisque Crackers, Easy, '83 252
Blue Cheese Crisps, '96 106
Bone Crackers, '01 204
Bread, Sesame Cracker, '87 2
Cheddar Crackers, '84 236
Cheese Cracker Nibbles, '84 328
Cheese Crisps, Peppered, '98 107
Cranberry Crackers, '99 258
Critter Crackers, '93 193
Dessert Crackers, '87 3
Fennel-Rye Crackers, '87 2
Florida Crackers, '86 179
Hot Nut Crackers, '90 206
Hush Puppies, Cracker, '80 99
Oatmeal-Wheat Germ Crackers, '84 236
Olive-Rye Snack Crackers, '84 191
Pie, Cracker, '79 113
Snack Crackers, '00 133
Snackers, Cracker, '86 229; '93 197
Soup Nuts, '96 106
Tortilla-Lime Crackers, '99 17
Vegetable Crackers, '96 105

CRANBERRIES
Acorn Squash, Cranberry-Filled, '81 M231
Ambrosia, Glazed Cranberry, '00 269
Beverages
    Apple-Berry Sparkler, '93 104
    Apple Berry Sparkler, '94 100
    Beach Brew, '91 177
    Cabernet Cranberries, '00 327
    Cider, Mulled Cranberry, '99 278
    Cider, Spiced Cranberry, '84 261; '98 278
    Cocktail, Hot Cranberry, '89 310
    Cocktail, Orange-Cranberry, '01 103
    Cocktails, Sea Breeze, '97 161
    Cooler, Cranberry, '86 229; '01 93
    Cooler, Cranberry Tea, '01 322
    Cubes, Cranberry, '95 201
    Daiquiris, Cranberry, '81 245
    Fizz, Cranberry-Ginger, '99 93
    Float, Sparkling Cranberry, '86 195
    Frappé, Cranberry, '82 263
    Juice, Sparkling Cranberry, '88 275

Lemonade, Cranberry, '05 205
Lemonade, Spiced Cranberry, '87 292
Mulled Cranberry Drink, '92 12; '03 36
New Orleans, Mr. Funk of, '95 57
Punch, Cranberry, '83 275; '85 90; '99 290
Punch, Cranberry-Cherry, '91 176
Punch, Cranberry-Cinnamon, '86 270
Punch, Cranberry Percolator, '88 248
Punch, Cranberry-Pineapple, '00 284
Punch, Cranberry-Wine, '01 242
Punch, Cran-Grape-Tea, '92 209
Punch, Holiday Cranberry, '85 265
Punch, Hot Cranberry, '80 288; '84 41, 319;
    '85 265
Punch, Hot Spiced, '80 250
Punch, Pink Lady, '81 100
Punch, Sparkling Cranberry, '85 277; '95 101
Punch, Spiced Cranberry, '89 290
Punch, Tart Cranberry, '83 318
Raspberry Drink, Cranberry-, '97 154
Red Roosters, '87 147
Refresher, Cranberry-Vodka, '91 210
Sangría, Cranberry, '95 238
Shake, Cranberry, '83 171
Shimmer, Cranberry, '98 168
Slush, Cranberry-Rum, '84 259
Smoothie, Cranberry, '86 183; '91 307
Soda, Cranberry-Orange, '79 148
Sparkler, Cranberry-Apple, '05 61
Spritzer, Cranberry, '91 66; '92 265
Spritzers, Cranberry, '89 213
Tea, Cranberry, '94 131; '97 121, 160; '04 63
Tea, Cranberry-Apple, '88 169
Tea, Cranberry-Raspberry Herb, '05 61
Tea, Holiday Cranberry, '03 233
Tea, Mulled Cranberry, '01 240
Tea, Pink Sangría, '95 200
Wassail, Cranberry, '88 289
Wine Cup, Cranberry, '85 23
Biscuits, Cranberry-Orange-Glazed, '04 280;
    '05 335
Brandied Cranberries, '86 269; '95 306
Bread, Cranberry, '79 242
Bread, Cranberry-Banana, '80 281; '90 294
Bread, Cranberry Fruit-Nut, '79 275
Bread, Cranberry-Orange, '87 244
Bread, Cranberry-Orange Nut, '80 288
Bread, Orange-Cranberry, '85 266
Bread, Raisin-Cranberry, '81 305; '82 36
Brie, Warmed Cranberry, '01 245
Butter, Cranberry, '97 307
Casserole, Cranberry-Apple, '83 311
Casserole, Sweet Potatoes-and-Berries, '84 231
Cheese Box, Cranberry-, '03 238
Chicken, Barbecued Cranberry, '83 178
Chicken, Cranberry, '05 272
Chicken Kiev, Cranberry, '87 250
Chunks of Snow, '02 298
Chutney, Cranberry, '80 243; '83 260; '84 265; '96 275;
    '98 276, 318
Chutney, Cranberry-and-Apricot, '02 286
Chutney, Cranberry-Ginger, '00 253
Chutney, Cranberry-Orange, '79 292
Chutney, Green Tomato-Cranberry, '00 140
Chutney, Hot-and-Spicy Cranberry-Pear, '00 255
Chutney Melt, Brie-and-Cranberry, '98 M318
Chutney, Orange-Cranberry, '86 266
Chutney, Quick Cranberry-Apple, '05 231
Chutney, Texas Cranberry, '04 257
Chutney with Cream Cheese, Cranberry-Amaretto,
    '87 244
Coffee Cake, Cranberry, '81 14; '90 159
Coffee Cake, Cranberry-Coconut, '93 332

Coffee Cake, Cranberry Crunch, '97 231
Coffee Cake, Cranberry-Nut, '81 250
Coffee Cake, Cranberry-Orange, '82 283
Compote, Pear-Cranberry, '02 196
Conserve, Apple-Cranberry, '82 308
Conserve, Caramelized Chicken with Cranberry, '98 320
Conserve, Cranberry, '79 243; '83 279; '85 266; '03 278
Conserve, Cranberry-Coriander, '04 287
Cornish Hens, Cranberry, '86 303
Cornish Hens, Cranberry-Cornbread Stuffed, '95 325
Couscous, Cranberry-and-Toasted Pecan, '05 M259
Crackers, Cranberry, '99 258
Cream, Cranberry, '90 66
Croissant, Turkey-Cranberry, '96 320

Desserts
Apple Dessert, Cranberry, '80 253
Apples, Cranberry, '99 246
Bake, Hot Cranberry, '91 250
Bars, Cranberry-Caramel, '98 277
Bars, Cranberry-Cinnamon Granola, '03 26
Bread Pudding, Stuffed Pumpkin with Cranberry-Raisin, '02 231
Cake Batter, Cranberry-Pecan, '05 287
Cake, Cranberry-Ambrosia, '01 271
Cake, Cranberry Upside-Down, '87 8
Cake, Orange-Cranberry, '85 314
Cloud, Cranberry, '90 287
Cobbler, Cranberry, '81 275
Cobbler, Cranberry-and-Apple, '84 306; '90 294
Cobbler, Cranberry-Peach, '92 322
Cobbler, Cran-Blueberry, '04 28
Cobbler, Easy Cranberry, '86 260
Cobbler Roll, Cranberry, '80 288; '81 248
Cobbler with Cinnamon Biscuits, Cranberry-Apple, '99 256
Compote, Apple-Cranberry, '04 237
Compote, Berry, '81 275
Compote, Cranberry, '97 264
Cookies, Cran-bear-y Bread, '02 254
Cookies, Cranberry-Almond, '98 26
Cookies, Cranberry-White Chocolate, '05 308
Crêpes, Cranberry, '85 262
Crisp, Cranberry-Pear, '83 207; '97 16
Crunch, Apple-Cranberry, '86 300; '87 178
Crusts, Cranberry-Pecan, '02 198
Dumplings, Apple-Cranberry, '00 16
Filling, Cranberry-Ambrosia, '01 271
Filling, Cranberry-Pecan, '04 305
Filling, Nutty Cranberry, '00 M306
Glaze, Cranberry, '84 306
Ice, Cranberry-Apple, '82 290
Ice, Tangy Cranberry, '87 305
Ice, Tart Cranberry-Orange, '86 317
Jubilee, Cranberries, '85 312; '90 293
Jubilee, Tasty Cranberry, '84 305; '85 189
Mousse, Cran-Apple, '93 255
Orange Surprise, Cran-, '94 143
Pie, Apple-Cranberry, '97 276; '99 M269
Pie, Autumn Apple, '79 205
Pie, Berry-Apple, '88 251
Pie, Cran-Apple, '92 304
Pie, Cranberry-Apple, '79 264
Pie, Cranberry-Apple Holiday, '81 M269
Pie, Cranberry-Apple-Raisin, '98 270
Pie, Cranberry-Pecan, '92 316
Pie, Cranberry-Raisin, '80 283; '85 316
Pie, Cranberry Streusel, '98 258
Pie, Cran-Raspberry, '87 244
Pie, Festive Cranberry Freezer, '84 306
Pie, Frosty Cranberry, '79 249
Pie, Nutty Cranberry, '82 M298

Pie, Peach-Cranberry, '83 249
Pies, Honeyed Apple-Cranberry Fried, '02 214
Pie, Tart Cranberry-Cherry, '87 299
Pie, Walnut-Cranberry, '87 259
Pizzas, Cranberry Dessert, '96 320
Pockets, Cranberry, '96 320
Pudding, Cranberry, '84 306
Roulage, Chocolate-Cranberry, '94 313
Rugalach, Cranberry-Pecan, '04 305
Sherbet, Cranberry, '88 280
Sorbet, Cranberry, '82 251
Sorbet, Cranberry Juice, '85 259
Soufflé, Cranberry-Topped Holiday, '84 306
Supreme, Cranberry, '85 280
Surprise Dessert, Cranberry, '79 242
Swirls, Cranberry-Walnut, '00 290
Tart, Cranberry-Apple, '97 M316
Tart, Cranberry-Nut, '84 305
Tartlets, Fresh Cranberry, '87 244
Tart, Rustic Apple-Cranberry, '01 M314
Tarts, Cranberry-Cream Cheese, '80 154
Tarts, Cranberry Holiday, '83 279
Tarts, Cran-Raspberry Meringue, '92 286
Dip, Cranberry Fruit, '89 60
Dip, Cranberry-Horseradish, '85 65
Dipper's Delight, '98 93
Dressing, Cranberry-Orange, '91 287
Dressing, Orange Salad with Honey-Berry, '89 250
Frosted Cranberries, '82 280
Fruit Bake, Cranberry-Mustard, '90 287
Glaze, Chili-Cranberry, '98 320
Glaze, Cranberry, '84 306; '86 171; '88 244
Glaze, Cranberry-Honey, '89 273
Gravy, Baked Hen with Cranberry Pan, '94 308
Ham, Cranberry Broiled, '88 301
Ham, Cranberry Glazed, '81 274
Ham, Cranberry-Orange Glazed, '81 295
Hearts, Cranberry, '93 286
Jam, Christmas, '88 288
Jam, Christmas Brunch, '81 286
Jelly, Cranberry-Wine, '81 290
Ketchup, Christmas, '97 254
Lamb, Cranberry Leg of, '90 52
Loaf, Apricot-Cranberry, '79 235
Loaf, Cranberry-Ham, '82 M77
Meatballs, Cranberry, '05 310
Mexican Cranberries, '94 273
Muffins, Cranberry, '81 249; '05 313
Muffins, Cranberry Oat Bran, '89 107
Muffins, Cranberry-Orange, '04 209
Muffins, Cranberry-Pecan, '84 269
Muffins, Cranberry Streusel Cake, '88 M274
Muffins, Miniature Cranberry, '90 294
Mustard, Cranberry, '05 320
Orange Delight, Cranberry-, '90 168
Orange 'n' Jellied Cranberry Sauce Stacks, '05 270
Oranges, Brandied Cranberry, '98 309
Popcorn, Trick or Treat, '03 210
Pork Chops, Cranberry, '88 288; '90 53
Pork Chops, Orange-Cranberry, '86 335; '87 84
Pork, Cranberry, '90 293
Pork Loin, Cranberry-Glazed, '04 251
Pork Roast, Berry Barbecued, '80 288
Relish, Cran-Apple, '84 300
Relish, Cranberry, '81 275; '83 144; '85 258, 264; '86 283; '87 245; '91 257; '92 341; '95 318; '98 310; '02 276
Relish, Cranberry-Black Bean, '03 243
Relish, Cranberry-Nut, '86 275
Relish, Cranberry-Orange, '81 M289; '88 254; '99 15
Relish, Cranberry-Pear, '85 232
Relish, Frozen Cranberry, '95 302
Relish, Holiday Cranberry, '88 304

Relish, Lemony Cranberry, '79 243
Relish, Old-Fashioned Cranberry, '82 297
Relish, Roasted Acorn Squash with Cranberry, '05 234
Relish, Tipsy Cranberry, '92 M310
Ring, Cranberry, '90 291
Rolls, Cranberry, '00 244
Rolls, Cranberry-Pineapple, '86 275

Salads
Apple Salad, Cranberry-, '02 255; '05 65
Bing Cherry-and-Cranberry Salad, '04 297
Cheese Ribbon Salad, Cranberry-, '79 241
Chicken Salad, Cranberry-Pecan, '05 284
Christmas Salad, Cranberry, '79 243
Congealed Cranberry Salad, '90 124
Congealed Salad, Cranberry, '91 296; '02 292; '05 334
Congealed Salad, Lemon-Cranberry, '87 311
Congealed Salad Parfaits, Frosted Cranberry, '02 292
Cranberry Salad, '88 250; '99 290
Cup, Berry Grapefruit, '79 242
Festive Cranberry Salad, '81 264, 296
Frosted Cranberry Salad, '90 288
Frozen Cranberry-Pineapple Salad, '91 237
Green Salad, Cranberry-Topped, '87 311
Holiday Cranberry Salad, '82 266, 288; '95 301
Holiday Jewel Salad, '81 252
Holiday Salad, Cranberry, '89 277
Jellied Cranberry Salad, '83 279; '85 281
Layered Cranberry Salad, '84 322; '86 325
Mold, Cranberry, '79 250
Mold, Cranberry-Apple, '89 277
Mold, Cranberry Gelatin, '92 271
Oriental, Cranberry, '79 126
Pear-and-Cranberry Wild Rice Salad, '03 199
Relish Salad, Cranberry, '05 245
Ring, Cranberry Salad, '80 247
Ring, Spicy Peach-Cranberry, '85 264
Spinach-and-Cranberry Salad with Warm Chutney Dressing, '02 242
Strawberry-Cranberry-Orange Salad, '05 249
Strawberry-Jícama Salad, Cranberry-, '02 300
Tart Cranberry Salad, '79 286
Whipped Cream Salad, Cranberry-, '83 261
Wild Rice-and-Cranberry Salad, '99 272
Sauce, Fresh Cranberry, '04 271

Sauces
Apple Sauce, Cranberry-, '92 203
Apricot Sauce, Fresh Cranberry-, '87 243
Baked Cranberry Sauce, '88 257
Cranberry Sauce, '86 278; '88 280; '92 269
Double Cranberry-Apple Sauce, '03 231
Dried Cranberry Sauce, Pork Medaillons with Port Wine and, '95 330
Fresh Cranberry Sauce, '79 283; '84 275; '04 271
Holiday Cranberry Sauce, '02 M311
Jalapeño-Cranberry Sauce, '92 310
Jezebel Sauce, Cranberry, '03 250
Juice Sauce, Cranberry, '85 224; '86 83
Orange Sauce, Cornish Hens with Cranberry-, '86 119
Orange Sauce, Cranberry-, '05 218
Raisin Sauce, Baked Ham with Cranberry-, '88 244
Salsa, Cranberry, '98 321; '99 316; '00 269; '01 254
Salsa, Cranberry-Citrus, '97 290
Salsa, Cranberry-Jalapeño, '01 234
Salsa, Grilled Turkey Breast with Cranberry, '95 252
Salsa with Sweet Potato Chips, Cranberry, '93 332
Spiced Cranberry Sauce, '96 267
Tart Cranberry Sauce, '83 261
Wine Sauce, Cranberry, '83 276
Scones, Cranberry, '95 283

CRANBERRIES

(continued)

Scones, Cranberry-Orange, '97 45
Scones, Merry Cranberry-Nut Yeast, '99 274
Spiced Cranberries, '82 254, 287
Spread, Coconut-Cranberry Cheese, '92 328
Spread, Cranberry Ambrosia-Cream Cheese, '00 308
Spread, Cranberry-Butter, '99 86
Stuffing, Cranberry, '04 246
Stuffing, Cranberry-Orange-Pecan, '01 249
Stuffing, Cranberry-Pecan, '96 309
Stuffing, Crown Roast of Pork with Cranberry-Sausage, '88 49
Sugared Cranberries, '04 279
Triangles, Cranberry-Nut, '04 273
Turkey Loaf, Cranberry-Glazed, '86 171
Vinaigrette, Cranberry, '98 321; '05 247
Vinegar, Cranberry, '91 288
Wild Rice, Cranberry-Almond, '04 204
Wild Rice, Cranberry-Pear, '83 279
Wraps, Chicken-Cranberry, '01 34

CRAWFISH

Boil, Crawfish, '01 95
Borscht, Crawfish, '92 84
Cakes with Cilantro-Lime Cream, Crawfish, '98 129
Casserole, Crawfish Pasta, '97 106
Delicacy, Crawfish, '99 M23
Dressing, Crawfish-Cornbread, '99 257
Dressing, Louisiana Crawfish, '90 103
Dressing, Pecan, Rice, and Crawfish, '00 252
Étouffée, Crawfish, '83 91; '86 156; '90 103; '94 239; '02 85
Étouffée, Quick Crawfish, '05 57
Étouffée, Traditional Crawfish, '05 56
Fettuccine, Crawfish, '96 98
Fettuccine, Crawfish and Tasso, '96 290
Jambalaya, Crawfish, '05 118
Lasagna, Crawfish, '91 89
Mushrooms, Crawfish-Stuffed, '86 258
Pasta, Creamy Crawfish, '03 277
Risotto, Crawfish, '99 120
Salad, Dilled Crawfish, '83 126
Soft-Shell Crawfish on Eggplant, '88 222
Spaghetti, Crawfish, '85 104
Stroganoff, Crawfish, '91 89
Trout Stuffed with Crawfish, Bacon-Wrapped, '99 54

CRÈME BRÛLÉE. *See* **CUSTARDS.**

CRÈME FRAÎCHE

Crème Fraîche, '85 39; '91 99; '01 275; '02 312
Sauce, Crème Fraîche, '79 281; '93 135

CRÊPES

Apple Breakfast Crêpes, '97 331
Basic Crêpes, '84 83; '86 38; '04 245
Beef Crêpes, Sherried, '85 M29
Beef Roulades, '80 80
Beggar's Purses with Smoked Salmon, '04 244
Blintzes, Cheese, '92 84
Blue-Corn Crêpes, '97 197
Blue-Corn Crêpes with Beef Filling, '97 197
Bran Crêpes, '83 70; '86 44
Breakfast Crêpes, Country-Style, '79 22
Brunch Crêpes, Nutritious, '80 44
Brunch Crêpes, Royal, '81 44
Cannelloni Crêpes, '86 143
Cheese and Mushroom Crêpes, '81 88
Cheese Blintzes, '82 146; '83 71
Cheesy Party Wedges, '84 84
Chicken Crêpes, '80 39
Chicken Crêpes, Creamy, '81 200
Chicken-Vegetable Crêpes, '83 70
con Queso, Crêpes, '96 48

Coquilles St. Jacques Crêpes, '83 13
Cornbread Crêpes, '98 42
Cornbread Crêpes, Goat Cheese-Filled, '98 43
Cornbread Crêpes, Southwestern, '98 42
Cornmeal Sombreros, '93 277
Crab Crêpes, '79 165
Crab Crêpes, Sautéed, '84 84
Crêpes, '82 38, 46, 146, 240; '83 13, 71, 122, 127, 205, 282; '84 186; '86 216; '87 126; '88 295; '89 44; '90 157; '91 24; '92 41, 88; '93 123; '94 116; '96 191; '97 332; '98 266; '99 25, 166; '00 310
Cups, Florentine Crêpe, '89 44

Desserts

Amandine, Crêpes Gelée, '83 126
Amaretto-and-Orange Crêpes, '86 260
Banana Crêpes Flambé, '84 262
Basic Dessert Crêpes, '82 183; '85 262; '86 275
Cheese Blintzes, '82 146
Cherry Crêpes, '91 67
Cherry Crêpes Flambé, '79 18
Chocolate Chantilly Crêpes, '82 183
Chocolate Crêpes, '86 164
Chocolate Crêpes, Fruit-Filled, '89 325
Chocolate Dessert Crêpes, '84 84; '85 262
Chocolate Dream Crêpes, '86 164
Chocolate-Orange Crêpes, '85 263
Coffee Ice Cream Crêpes, '84 85
Cranberry Crêpes, '85 262
Dessert Crêpes, '84 84; '86 260; '87 290; '88 134
Dixie Dessert Crêpes, '79 222
Fruit Crêpes, Tropical, '87 77
Fruit Filling, Crêpes with, '81 96
Lemon Crêpes with Fruit Filling, '82 46
Low-Calorie Crêpes, '87 77
Mango-Pineapple Crêpes, '86 216
Orange Dream Crêpes, '82 183
Peach Crêpes, '82 184
Peach Crêpes, Fresh, '84 186
Plain Crêpes, '83 70
Processor Crêpes, Basic, '87 289; '88 135
Raspberry Crêpes, '87 126
Raspberry Crêpes with Yogurt Filling, Fresh, '93 123
Spicy Dessert Crêpes, '84 262
Strawberry Dessert Crêpes, '83 122
Strawberry Ice Cream Crêpes, '87 290; '88 135
Suzette, Raspberry Crêpes, '84 84
Suzettes, Light Crêpes, '83 71
Tropical Crêpes, '86 275
Whole Wheat Crêpes, '83 70
Divan, Elegant Crêpes, '81 91
Eggplant Crêpes with Marinara Sauce, Mini, '99 266
Entrée Crêpes, '79 264
Fajita Crêpes, '94 116
Filling, Crêpe, '96 48
Florentine Crêpe Pie, '79 34
Florentine, Crêpes, '80 190
Ham-and-Egg Crêpes, '83 204
Ham-and-Egg Crêpes with Mushroom Sauce, '82 46
Italian Crêpes, '90 157
Light Crêpes, '86 143
Mushroom-Cheese Crêpes, '87 289; '88 135
Plain Crêpes, '83 70
Processor Crêpes, Basic, '87 289; '88 135
Sausage Crêpes, '88 295
Sausage Crêpes, Cheesy, '82 240; '83 71
Sausage-Filled Crêpes, '79 39; '98 266; '99 25
Shellfish Crêpes in Wine-Cheese Sauce, '00 310
Spinach-Ricotta Crêpes, '81 52
Steak Crêpes, Special, '91 24
Turkey Crêpes, '92 41
Turkey Crêpes, Elegant, '83 282
Virginia Crêpes, '79 264
Whole Wheat Crêpes, '80 44; '83 70
Zucchini Crêpes, '79 157

CRISPS. *See* **PIES, PUFFS, AND PASTRIES/Cobblers, Crisps, and Crumbles.**

CROUTONS

Bagel Croutons, '93 192
Bourbon Croutons, '93 234
Bread Croutons, Hawaiian, '94 107
Bread, Quick Crouton, '90 138
Celery Croutons, '79 16
Cheese Grits Croutons and Vidalia Onion-Balsamic Vinaigrette, Southern Spinach Salad with, '04 316
Cinnamon Pound Cake Croutons, '93 161
Cornbread Croutons, '93 192; '05 45
Cornbread Croutons, Honeyed, '94 106
Creole Croutons, '02 121
Crispy Croutons, '05 207
Crispy Italian Croutons, '84 126
Crostini, '92 56
Croûtes, Croutons and, '93 30
Croutons, '86 M288
Curried Croutons, '00 322
Dilled Croutons, '93 161
Egg Roll Fan, Sesame, '94 107
Fried Okra Croutons, Salad Greens and Veggies with, '96 178
Garlic Croutons, '92 71; '05 247
Garlic-Flavored Croutons, '86 47
Goat Cheese-and-Chive Croutons, '01 312
Herb Croutons, '81 150
Microwave Croutons, '86 M227
Parslied Croutons, Carrot-and-Butternut Squash Soup with, '97 217
Pita Croutons, '93 192; '96 64; '98 329
Prosciutto Croutons, '99 89
Pumpernickel Croutons, '94 62
Seasoned Croutons, '96 326
Spiced Croutons, '00 317
Sweet Croutons, '00 296
Tortilla Triangles, '94 107
Vegetable-Flavored Croutons, '84 148

CRUMBLES. *See* **PIES, PUFFS, AND PASTRIES/ Cobblers, Crisps, and Crumbles.**

CUCUMBERS

Bisque, Shrimp-Cucumber, '79 172
Canapés, Chicken-Cucumber, '98 154
Canapés, Cucumber, '95 88
Canapés, Shrimp-and-Cucumber, '93 164
Chips, Cucumber, '85 176
Cool Cucumbers, '84 152
Creamy Cucumbers, '92 62
Delights, Cucumber, '84 117
Dills, Lazy Wife, '87 149
Dip, Cucumber-Cheese Vegetable, '83 128
Dip, Cucumber-Yogurt, '99 93
Dip, Refreshing Dill, '99 324
Dressing, Benedictine, '98 83
Dressing, Creamy Cucumber Salad, '82 79
Dressing, Cucumber, '80 74; '90 144
Dressing, Cucumber-Curry, '89 179
Dressing, Cucumber-Mint, '87 153
Dressing, Cucumber-Radish, '00 99
Dressing, Tomato, Onion, and Cucumber in Italian, '81 83
Fried Cucumber Fingers, '86 146
Gazpacho, '00 118; '02 130
Gazpacho Blanco, '01 177
Gazpacho, Pineapple, '01 85
Gazpacho-Stuffed Endive, '95 287
Gazpacho, White, '97 181
Lemony Cucumbers, '89 102
Marinated Cucumbers and Artichokes, '82 111
Marinated Cucumbers and Squash, '86 146
Marinated Shrimp and Cucumber, '91 166
Pasta, Asian Cucumbers and, '96 177

Pepper Combo, Cucumber-and-, **'88** 176
Pickled Cucumber Rounds, Easy, **'90** 143
Pickled Onion and Cucumber, **'02** 126
Pickles, Cucumber Sandwich, **'81** 174
Pickles, Dill, **'81** 174
Pickles, Freezer Cucumber, **'99** 87
Pickles, Hot-and-Sweet Freezer, **'04** 160
Pickles, Lime, **'96** 206
Pickles, Mixed, **'81** 174
Pickles, Peppery Texas, **'04** M161
Pickles, Quick Sweet, **'87** 149
Pickles, Sour Cucumber, **'85** 176
Pickles, Sweet Icicle, **'85** 176
Pico de Gallo, **'98** 174
Red Snapper Rolls, Cucumber-Stuffed, **'83** 176
Relish, Cucumber, **'85** 176; **'96** 23
Rounds, Cucumber, **'88** 78
Rounds, Cucumber-Dill, **'05** 96
Salads
  Almond Salad, Cucumber-, **'86** 147
  Asian Greens, Cucumber, **'98** 66
  Aspic, Shrimp-Cucumber, **'83** 108
  Bean Salad, Cucumber-, **'83** 81
  Congealed Salad, Pineapple-Cucumber, **'83** 118
  Cool Cucumber Salad, **'03** 165
  Cooler, Simple Cucumber, **'86** 147
  Crab Salad, Cucumber-and-, **'98** 208
  Creamy Cucumber Salad, **'86** 147; **'92** 97; **'01** 56;
    '02 258
  Dilled Cucumber and Tomato Salad, **'81** 153
  Dilled Cucumber on Tomatoes, **'84** 142
  Dilled Cucumber Salad, **'82** 229; **'92** 72; **'93** 65
  Grapefruit-Cucumber Salad, **'80** 100
  Layered Lebanese Salad, **'05** 148
  Marinated Cucumber Salad, **'82** 111
  Marinated Cucumber-Tomato Salad, **'02** 167
  Marinated Tomato-and-Cucumber Salad, **'92** 216
  Mold, Asparagus-Cucumber, **'85** 252
  Mold, Chicken-Cucumber, **'80** 175
  Mold, Creamy Cucumber, **'84** 164
  Mold, Cucumber Salad, **'82** 111; **'83** 81, 253
  Mold, Lemon-Cucumber, **'87** 90
  Mousse, Cucumber, **'79** 11; **'88** 121
  Mousse with Dill Sauce, Cucumber, **'95** 216
  Pineapple Salad, Cucumber-, **'84** 124
  Potato Salad with Cucumbers and Tomatoes, **'03** 92
  Roast Beef Salad, Cucumber-, **'89** 162
  Roasted Red Bell Pepper Dressing, Cucumber Salad
    with, **'03** 28
  Scallions, Cukes and, **'91** 168
  Slaw, Creamy Cucumber, **'89** 49
  Sour Cream, Cucumbers in, **'79** 52; **'80** 178
  Tomato-and-Cucumber Salad, **'05** 69
  Tomato-and-Cucumber Summer Salad, **'93** 141
  Tomato-Cucumber-Onion Salad, **'81** 239
  Tomato-Cucumber Salad, **'86** 218; **'92** 199
  Tomato-Cucumber Salad with Yogurt-Herb Dressing,
    '92 96
  Tomato Salad, Cucumber-, **'90** 144
  Tomato Salad, Cucumber-and-, **'01** 127
  Tuna Boats, Cucumber, **'83** 136
  Vinaigrette Oriental, Cucumber-, **'85** 198; **'86** 147
  Winter Fruit-and-Cucumber Salad, **'02** 274
  Yogurt-Cucumber Salad, **'82** 122
  Yogurt Salad, Cucumber-, **'87** 33
Salsa, Cucumber, **'95** 131
Salsa, Cucumber-Dill, **'95** 107
Salsa, Cucumber-Radish, **'01** 187
Salsa, Radish-Cucumber, **'04** 119
Sandwiches, Cucumber, **'88** 159; **'90** 81; **'94** 14; **'97** 99;
  '00 208
Sandwiches, Cucumber Pinwheel, **'85** 120
Sandwiches, Cucumber-Salmon-Watercress, **'03** 111
Sandwiches, Dainty Cucumber, **'81** 119

Sandwiches, Watercress-Cucumber, **'97** 108
Sandwiches with Dill, Cucumber-Salmon, **'02** 131
Sauce, Cucumber, **'82** 111; **'84** M286; **'92** 41
Sauce, Cucumber-and-Yogurt Dipping, **'02** 172
Sauce, Cucumber Cream, **'92** 33
Sauce, Cucumber-Dill, **'86** 5; **'91** 62; **'92** 51
Sauce, Cucumber Dipping, **'94** 47
Sauce, Cucumber-Yogurt, **'03** 44
Sauce, Lamb Burgers with Cucumber, **'98** 102
Sauce, Lemony Cucumber, **'89** 245
Sauce, London Broil Sandwiches with Yogurt-
  Cucumber, **'01** 162
Sauce, Sour Cream-Cucumber, **'05** 207
Sauce, Tomato-Cucumber, **'98** 45
Sauce, Tuna Steaks with Cucumber, **'97** 180
Sauce, Tzatziki, **'04** 108; **'05** 82
Sauce, White Bean Spread with Creamy Cucumber,
  '00 178
Sauce, Yogurt-Cucumber, **'04** 216
Sesame Cucumbers, **'85** 85
Sherbet, Jalapeño-Mint, **'98** 202
Slices, Cheesy Cucumber, **'84** 80
Slices, Fresh Cucumber, **'86** 177
Soup, Chilled Cucumber, **'79** 144
Soup, Chilled Cucumber-Buttermilk, **'95** 134
Soup, Cold Cucumber, **'79** 130; **'81** 130
Soup, Cold Minted Cucumber, **'86** 34
Soup, Cold Potato-Cucumber, **'88** 160
Soup, Cream of Cucumber, **'81** 98
Soup, Creamy Cucumber, **'80** 171
Soup, Cucumber-Dill, **'01** 176
Soup, Cucumber-Yogurt, **'82** 157; **'83** 205
Soup, Dilled Cucumber, **'90** M167
Soup with Dill Cream, Cucumber, **'00** 130
Sour Cream, Cucumber and Onion in, **'81** 69
Sour Cream, Cucumbers and, **'93** 203
Sour Cream, Cucumbers in, **'99** 243
Spread, Cucumber, **'79** 295; **'80** 31; **'93** 158
Spread, Cucumber and Cream Cheese, **'82** 140
Spread, Cucumber-Yogurt, **'00** 135
Spread, Shrimp-Cucumber, **'79** 81
Stuffed Cucumbers, **'81** 237
Tartlets, Smoked Salmon and Cucumber, **'95** 216
Tomatoes, Cucumber-Stuffed Cherry, **'88** 262
Topping, Lamb Pockets with Dilled Cucumber,
  '87 104
Vichyssoise, Cucumber, **'94** 90
Vichyssoise with Mint Cream, Cucumber, **'98** 246
CUPCAKES. See **CAKES/Cupcakes.**
CURRY
Almonds, Cauliflower and Peas with Curried,
  '79 221
Appetizers
  Almonds, Curried, **'82** 297
  Bites, Curried Swiss, **'85** 220
  Cheese Ball, Chicken-Curry, **'85** 118
  Cheese Ball, Curried Shrimp, **'86** 135
  Chicken Balls, Coconut Curried, **'91** 165
  Chicken Balls, Curried, **'91** 98
  Chicken Bites, Curried, **'85** 40
  Chicken Tea Sandwiches, Curried, **'97** 23
  Dip and Vegetable Platter, Curry, **'89** 327
  Dip, Curried, **'81** 262
  Dip, Curry, **'80** 84; **'81** 9; **'85** 132; **'86** 184; **'87** 25;
    '99 138
  Dip, Curry-Onion, **'93** 313
  Dip, Tuna-Curry, **'84** 31
  Hazelnuts, Curried, **'93** 301
  Nuts, Spicy Curried, **'82** 250
  Pecans, Curried, **'91** 208
  Popcorn Mix, Curried, **'86** 326
  Sandwiches, Curried Tea, **'91** 314
  Sauce, Curry, **'94** 54
  Shrimp Balls, Curried, **'94** 180

Spread, Broccamoli Curry, **'88** 55
Spread, Curried Chutney, **'89** 283
Spread, Curried Shrimp, **'87** 158
Spread, Curry-Almond Cheese, **'01** 238
Apples, Curried, **'93** 252
Apricots, Curried, **'91** 315
Bananas, Fillets with Horseradish Sauce and Curried,
  '85 230
Beef and Rice, Curried, **'88** 164
Beef Dinner, Curried, **'83** 4
Beef Pitas, Curried, **'85** 220
Beef Steak, Curried, **'88** 60
Beef Stir-Fry, Curried, **'01** 162
Bisque, Curried Butternut-Shrimp, **'01** 248
Bread, Honey-Curry, **'89** 250
Butter, Tomato-Curry-Orange, **'93** 159
Carrots and Pineapple, Curried, **'90** 228
Casserole, Curry Pea, **'87** 154
Casserole, Vegetable-Curry, **'91** 286; **'92** 27
Cauliflower Bake, Curried, **'01** 49
Cauliflower, Curried, **'91** 315
Chicken. See also **CURRY/Appetizers, Salads.**
  Bisque, Curried Chicken, **'00** 144
  Brioche, Chicken Curry, **'88** 124
  Casserole, Cheesy Chicken Curry, **'05** 311
  Cheesecake, Curried Chicken, **'90** 174
  Chowder, Curried Chicken-and-Corn, **'92** 21
  Country Captain Chicken, **'94** 252
  Curried Chicken, **'86** 43
  Curry, Chicken, **'84** 110; **'85** 220; **'86** 21;
    '89 219
  Divan, Curried Chicken, **'80** 83
  Filling, Curried Chicken, **'88** 125
  Fried Chicken, Curried, **'85** 160
  Honey-Curry Chicken, **'87** 36
  Indian-Style Chicken Curry, **'97** 119
  Mousse, Curried Chicken, **'95** 328
  Pâté, Curried Chicken, **'00** 106
  Peppers, Chicken Breasts with Curried, **'90** 227
  Peppers, Curried Chicken-Stuffed, **'87** 19
  Quick Curried Chicken, **'89** 219; **'99** 92
  Regal Curried Chicken, **'84** 110
  Sauce, Chicken Curry, **'90** 117
  Skillet Dinner, Curried Chicken, **'95** 47
  Soup, Curried Chicken, **'86** 34
  Spice Chicken, Aromatic Curry-and-, **'05** 238
  Stir-Fried Chicken Curry, **'87** 51
  Turban Chicken Curry, **'94** 266
  Wings, Curried Chicken, **'96** 110
Chops, Pineapple-Curry Glazed, **'82** 106
Chowder, Curried Seafood, **'94** 103
Corn and Celery, Curried, **'86** 192
Corn and Sweet Red Peppers, Curried, **'95** 47
Cream, Red Curry-Coconut, **'00** 197
Croutons, Curried, **'00** 322
Dressing, Cucumber-Curry, **'89** 179
Dressing, Curried, **'84** 115; **'00** 217
Dressing, Curry, **'80** 242; **'82** 78; **'97** 63
Eggs, Curried Deviled, **'93** 87
Eggs, Saucy Shrimp-Curried, **'84** 143
Fish, Curried Baked, **'87** 5
Fish, Curry-Baked, **'91** 196
Fruit, Almond-Curried, **'83** 261
Fruit Bake, Curried, **'87** 241
Fruit, Baked Curried, **'03** 247
Fruit, Hot Curried, **'79** 225; **'81** 264; **'84** 287; **'95** 72
Fruit Medley, Curried, **'95** 329
Ham and Peaches, Curried, **'82** 60
Ham Steak, Curried, **'82** 120
Ham with Rice, Curried, **'80** 111
Hurry Curry, **'79** 103
Kheema, Indian, **'81** 226
Lamb Curry, Creamy, **'04** 202
Lamb Curry with Rice, **'80** 83; **'81** 10

CURRY

(continued)

Lamb with Cucumber-Yogurt Sauce, Curried Leg of, '03 44
Lamb with Rice Mold, Curried, '85 36
Mayonnaise, Curry, '95 66
Meat Loaf, Curried, '86 43
Mushrooms, Curried, '84 214
Navy Beans, Curried, '00 201
Nuts, Spicy Curried, '82 250
Onions, Curried, '90 34
Pasta with Apple, Curried, '02 68
Peas with Almonds, Curried, '88 M294
Pecans, Curried, '91 208
Pineapple, Curried, '03 201
Pork Chops, Curried Apricot, '89 191
Pork Tenderloin, Curried, '86 76
Rice and Shrimp, Curried, '83 231
Rice, Chicken with Curried, '98 127
Rice, Curried, '90 183; '97 51; '98 237; '04 21
Rice, Curry-Spiced, '86 M226
Rice Mix, Fruited Curry-, '86 326
Rice Mold, Curried, '85 36
Rice, Quick Curried, '86 81
Rice with Almonds, Curried, '83 M285
Rice with Curry, Raisin, '85 83
Rice with Pineapple, Curried, '79 142
Salad Dressing, Curry, '96 326
Salads
Apple-Raisin Salad, Curried, '80 24
Broccoli Salad, Curried, '86 225
Chicken-and-Orange Salad, Curried, '87 144
Chicken-Rice Salad, Curried, '92 190
Chicken Salad, Curried, '79 219; '84 66; '85 96; '86 131; '89 176
Chicken Salad, Royal Curried, '96 200
Chicken Salad Spread, Curried, '00 68
Chicken Salad with Asparagus, Curried, '81 36
Coleslaw, Curried, '85 139
Coleslaw, Curried Pineapple, '88 172
Couscous Salad, Curried, '91 44
Gift, Curried Salad, '96 326
Indian Curry Salad, Hot, '83 23
Melon and Shrimp Curry Salad, '97 129
Pears with Coconut-Chicken Salad, Curried Poached, '97 93
Potato Salad, Curried, '99 137
Rice Salad, Curried, '80 84; '85 147, 220; '96 240
Rice Salad, Curry, '89 146
Shrimp Salad, Aloha, '95 46
Shrimp Salad, Curried, '00 217
Spinach Salad, Curry, '80 242
Tuna Salad, Curried, '86 208
Tuna Salad with Grapes, Curried, '87 201
Turkey Salad, Chutney Curried, '98 314
Turkey Salad, Curried, '88 140
Sandwiches, Curried BLT, '93 158
Sauce, Asparagus with Curry, '90 17
Sauce, Curried Rum, '91 164
Sauce, Curried Sour Cream, '90 174
Sauce, Curry, '79 156; '83 138; '84 M71; '95 18; '97 170; '99 92
Sauce, Curry-Mustard, '96 249
Sauce, Halibut with Orange-Curry, '87 91
Sauce, Pineapple-Curry, '79 252
Sauce, Turkey Slices with Curried Cream, '91 60
Seasoning Salt, Gourmet, '97 254
Shrimp, Curried, '84 110
Shrimp Curry, '99 91
Shrimp Curry, Creamy, '90 145

Shrimp, Curry-Ginger, '00 316
Shrimp Curry, Polynesian, '89 23
Shrimp Curry, Sour Cream, '80 83
Shrimp Curry, Sour Cream and, '81 10
Shrimp, Hot Red Curry, '02 125
Shrimp Malai Curry, '84 110
Shrimp, Quick Curried, '84 M198
Snapper, Honey-Curried, '85 181
Soup, Cold Curried Pea, '91 120
Soup, Cream of Curried Peanut, '02 242
Soup, Curried, '81 130
Soup, Curried Acorn Squash-and-Apple, '03 221
Soup, Curried Butternut Squash, '05 234
Soup, Curried Carrot, '82 157
Soup, Curried Chicken, '86 34
Soup, Curried Mushroom, '84 M89
Soup, Curried Pumpkin, '96 242
Soup, Curried Turkey, '86 332
Spread, Curried Chicken Salad, '00 68
Spread, Curried Shrimp, '87 158
Spread, Curried Turkey, '92 16
Spread, Curry, '93 159
Stir-Fry, Indian, '92 126
Tomatoes, Curried Green, '93 138
Topping, Curry Salad, '96 326
Tuna-Apple Sandwiches, Curried, '00 247
Tuna Melts, Curried, '95 46
Turkey Pie, Crumb-Crust Curried, '86 265
Vegetable Curry, '99 91; '04 217
Vegetables, Curried, '89 219
Vegetables with Couscous, Curried, '04 328
Vegetables with Curry, Stir-Fried, '87 51
Vinaigrette, Ginger-Curry, '97 146
Vinaigrette, Warm Curry, '93 107
Walnuts, Sugared Curried, '05 281
CUSTARDS. *See also* **MOUSSES, PUDDINGS.**
Acorn Squash, Custard-Filled, '86 334
Almond Crème Custard with Raspberries, '88 174
Amaretto Custard, Chocolate-Topped, '87 M37
Amaretto Custard, Range-Top, '87 77
Amaretto Custard with Raspberries, '86 152
Ambrosia, Custard Sauce, '84 256
Baked Custard, '80 219
Baked Custard, Creamy, '86 7
Baked Custard, Easy, '85 52
Baked Vanilla Custard, '82 129
Blackberry Custard, '99 132
Boiled Christmas Custard, '95 329
Boiled Custard, Favorite, '81 181
Boiled Custard, Perfect, '81 34
Cake, Chocolate Custard, '88 175
Cake, Southern Custard Crêpe, '99 166
Caramel Custard, '01 237
Chocolate Custard, '88 258
Citrus Custard with Fresh Fruit, '93 70
Coco Loco Custard, '02 89
Coconut Cream Custard, '03 85
Coconut Custard, '86 109; '97 131
Corn Custard, Fresh, '89 127
Crema, '80 175
Crème Brûlée, Almond, '95 323
Crème Brûlée, Basic, '95 323
Crème Brûlée, Berry, '95 323
Crème Brûlée, Black-and-White, '98 267; '02 62
Crème Brûlée, Chocolate, '95 323
Crème Brûlée, Coffee, '95 323
Crème Brûlée, Double Raspberry, '95 323
Crème Brûlée, Ginger, '95 323
Crème Brûlée, Onion, '95 324
Crème Brûlée, Orange, '95 323
Crème Brûlée, Peppermint, '95 323
Crème Brûlée, Piña Colada, '04 246
Crème Brûlée, Roasted Garlic, '95 324

Crème Brûlée, Roquefort-and-Black Pepper, '95 324
Crème Brûlées, Savory, '95 324
Crème Brûlée, Sweet Potato, '02 275
Crème Brûlée, White Chocolate-Macadamia Nut, '95 323
Crème Patissière, '84 207
Easy Custard with Nutmeg, '90 316
Filling, Creamy Custard, '81 180
Filling, Custard, '82 52, 298; '85 281
Filling, Egg Custard, '87 14
Flans
Almendra, Flan, '80 199
Almond-Orange Flan, '04 241
Apricot Flan, '99 146
Baked Flan with Caramel, '92 231
Blackberry Flan, '79 182
Caramel-Crowned Flans, '90 227
Columbia's Flan, '05 120
Corn-Chive Flan, '94 172
Corn Flan, '98 246; '99 25
Cream Cheese Flan, '03 328
de Leche (Flan with Milk), Flan, '92 169
de Queso, Flan, '95 303
Flaming Flan, '85 313
Flan, '88 247
Individual Flans, '85 52
Layered Flan, '89 45
Luscious Flan, '90 56
Orange Flan, '84 95
Pineapple Flan, '01 85
Pumpkin Flan, '82 217
Spanish Flan, '85 51, 311
Sweet Potato Flan, '95 291
Goat Cheese Custard, '96 285
Ice Cream, Vanilla Custard, '96 145; '00 143
Lemon-Buttermilk Custards, '89 49
Lemon Custard in Meringue Cups, '80 295; '81 172
Mexican Custard, Light, '88 149
Napoleon Cream, '84 138
Orange Custard Pudding, '88 174
Peach Custard Dessert, Fresh, '86 162
Pears in Custard, Poached, '88 20
Pie, Apple Custard, '88 236
Pie, Carrot Custard, '79 45
Pie, Coconut Custard, '82 33
Pie, Custard Pecan, '87 184
Pie, Old-Fashioned Egg Custard, '82 261
Pie, Perfect Custard, '82 92
Pie, Quick 'n' Easy Custard, '96 28
Pie, Strawberry Custard, '00 81
Pie, Warm Apple-Buttermilk Custard, '99 98
Preserves, Custard, '98 126
Pumpkin Custard, '88 279
Rice Custard, Baked, '92 308
Sauce, Bourbon Custard, '95 271
Sauce, Buttermilk Custard, '96 183
Sauce, Custard, '85 41; '88 154, 251, 259; '89 291; '97 16, 313; '03 244, 318
Sauce, Fresh Berries with Raspberry Custard, '88 163
Sauce, Vanilla Custard, '99 27
Spinach-Gorgonzola Custards, Savory, '99 313; '02 284
Stirred Custard, '92 45; '99 126
Stirred Custard, Old-Fashioned, '85 52
Stirred Custard over Fruit, '84 83
Stirred Custard, Sherried Gel with, '99 126
Tart, Chocolate Custard, '99 27
Tocino del Cielo, '93 29
Trifle Custard, '03 84
Vanilla Cream, '83 M115
Vanilla Custard, '99 27
Vanilla Custard, Pecan Pie with Chilled, '00 331

DATES

Ball, Date-Nut, '92 326

Bars and Cookies
Balls, Date, '01 90
Balls, Date-Nut, '85 10
Balls, Peanut-Date, '81 92
Brownies, Date-and-Almond, '88 217
Chocolate Chip Cookies, Rich Date-Nut, '92 207
Christmas Date Cookies, '88 287
Cranberry-Caramel Bars, '98 277
Date Bars, '84 313; '95 322
Filled Cookies, Date-, '91 95
Fruit Cookies, Rolled, '80 15
Moons, Date, '01 295
No-Bake Date Bars, '79 256
Nut Bars, Date-, '80 166
Nutty Date Bars, '84 153
Oat Bars, Date-, '80 M172
Oatmeal-Date Bars, Layered, '85 10
Oatmeal-Date Cookies, '82 109
Oatmeal-Date Sandwich Cookies, '83 257
Pinwheel Cookies, Date, '02 93
Squares, Date, '90 49
Walnut-Date Bars, '02 287; '03 272

Breads
Apple-Date-Nut Ring, '90 212
Banana Loaves, Tropical Date-, '95 143
Chocolate Date-Nut Bread, '81 284
Muffins, Carrot-Date-Nut, '86 262
Muffins, Date, '79 142
Muffins, Date-Nut, '84 75; '99 234
Muffins, Miniature Date, '02 171
Muffins, Orange-Date, '92 119; '97 243; '05 215
Muffins, Surprise Date, '79 216
Nut Bread, Date-, '85 306
Nut Loaf, Date-, '85 10
Persimmon Date-Nut Bread, '82 218
Walnut Loaf, Blue Ribbon Date-, '80 15
Whole Wheat Date-Nut Bread, '04 208
Wine-Date Nut Bread, '82 253
Cake, Bourbon, '98 277
Cake, Date Nut, '79 176; '80 5
Cake, Fresh Apple-Date, '83 300
Cake, Orange-Date, '94 60
Cake, Orange Date-Nut, '01 285
Cake, Pumpkin Date, '79 251
Cake, Queen Bee, '81 237
Cake Roll, Date-Nut, '89 94
Cake Squares, Apple-Date Dream, '85 10
Candy, Date, '89 308
Candy, Date Loaf, '80 302
Cheese, Nutty Date Dessert, '87 299
Chocolate Date-Nut Delight, '88 168
Conserve, Brandied Date, '85 315
Cupcakes, Date, '84 7
Dessert Squares, Date, '89 255
Dressing, Date, '87 57
Filling, Apple-Date, '83 301
Filling, Date, '80 15; '83 257; '86 314
Filling, Date Cream, '81 303
French Toast, Stuffed, '02 105
June Bugs, '85 11
Logs, Date, '79 274
Muffins, Date, '00 239
Pastries, Date-Filled Cheese, '83 259
Pie, Date-Pecan, '80 15
Pie, Dried Fruit, '83 249
Pudding, Steamed Date, '79 86
Relish, Lemon-Date, '96 271
Rice), Basted Dates and Basted Rice (Date-Nut, '96 158
Roll, Date Nut, '79 249
Rollups, Date-Cream Cheese, '83 298
Salad, Festive Fruit, '80 16

Sandwich, Date-Nut Lettuce, '94 202
Sauce, Date-Nut Sundae, '82 167
Spread, Apple-Date, '91 231; '92 67
Spread, Breakfast Date, '84 7
Spread, Date-Orange-Nut, '02 59
Spread, Date-Walnut, '87 292
Spread, Date-Walnut-Cheese, '96 322
Stuffed Date Drops, '97 247
Stuffed Dates, Apricot-, '80 250

DESSERT OF THE MONTH

Bananas, Caramelized, '99 49
Beverage Sipper, Kahlúa, '99 27
Bombe, Double-Chocolate, '97 282
Brownies à la Mode, Magnolias Cream Cheese, '97 M178
Cake, Banana Split, '99 48
Cake, Best Carrot, '97 230
Cake, Buttermilk Pound, '99 98
Cake, Chocolate-Peanut Butter Mousse, '98 71
Cake, German Carrot-Hazelnut, '97 230
Cake, Mama's Coconut, '97 71
Cake, Nanny's Famous Coconut-Pineapple, '97 277
Cake, Pastel, '97 173
Cake, Pecan-Carrot, '99 223
Cake with Coconut Custard, Supreme Banana, '97 131
Cake with Wine Jelly, Pound, '98 125
Candied Rose Petals, '98 57
Caramels, Coconut-Macadamia, '98 305
Cheesecake, Bavarian, '97 55
Cheesecake, Chocolate-Wrapped Banana, '99 M48
Cheesecake, Praline-Crusted, '99 295
Cheesecake, Warm Fudge-Filled, '98 34
Cobbler à la Mode, Apple, '97 16
Cobbler with Custard Sauce, Apricot, '97 16
Coffee Buttons, '99 66
Cookies, Chocolate-Brickle, '99 127
Cookies, Chocolate Shortbread, '99 147
Cookies, Gingerbread Snowflake, '98 324
Cookies, Orange Slice, '98 324
Cookies, Shortbread, '99 147
Cookies, White Chocolate Chip-Oatmeal, '99 127
Cream, Spanish, '99 27
Crisp, Cranberry-Pear, '97 16
Crust, Gingersnap, '98 161
Crust, Peanut-Graham, '99 49
Crust, Vanilla Wafer, '98 216
Custard, Coconut, '97 131
Custard, Vanilla, '99 27
Filling, Pineapple, '97 277
Frosting, Amaretto Buttercream, '98 57
Frosting, Chocolate-Buttermilk, '99 99
Frosting, Citrus Cream Cheese, '99 223
Frosting, Cream Cheese, '97 230, 277
Frosting, Mocha, '99 66
Frosting, Seven-Minute, '97 71
Ganache, Chocolate, '97 282
Glaze, Buttermilk, '97 230; '99 98
Glaze, Chocolate, '97 231
Glaze, Pineapple, '97 55
Heart, Chocolate-Amaretto, '98 56
Ice Cream, Mocha, '97 M145
Ice Cream, Rum-Raisin, '97 145
Ice Cream Sandwiches, '99 147
Icing, Royal, '98 324
Jelly, Wine, '98 125
Meringue, '97 109
Mousse, Chocolate, '97 282
Mousse Parfaits, Chocolate-Peanut Butter, '98 71
Mousse, White Chocolate, '97 282; '98 M57, M111
Pecan Clusters, '98 305
Penuche, Coffee, '98 305
Pie, Black-and-White Fudge, '99 249

Pie, Black-Bottom, '98 161
Pie, Caramel Meringue, '97 109
Pie, Coconut Cream, '98 161
Pie, Coconut-Macadamia Nut, '97 110
Pie, Fox Hunter's, '97 109
Pie, Georgia Peach-and-Praline, '98 196
Pie, Lemony Ice Cream, '99 207
Pie, Maverick Lunar, '98 111
Pie, Peach Melba, '98 216
Pie, Pear Streusel, '97 109
Pie, Raspberry Baked Alaska, '98 216
Pie, Red, White, and Blueberry, '98 162
Pie, Triple Mint Ice Cream, '98 217
Pie, Warm Apple-Buttermilk Custard, '99 98
Pralines, '99 295
Pralines, Buttermilk, '99 99
Preserves, Custard, '98 126
Pudding, Lemon Cake, '98 35
Pudding, Piña Colada Bread, '98 34
Sauce, Caramel, '97 178
Sauce, Chocolate, '97 178
Sauce, Chocolate-Mint, '98 217
Sauce, Coconut, '98 34
Sauce, Custard, '97 16
Sauce, Mocha, '98 57
Sauce, Raspberry, '98 216
Sauce, Vanilla Custard, '99 27
Sherbet, Buttermilk, '99 99
Shortcake, Warm Blueberry-Nectarine, '97 205
Soufflé with White Chocolate Mousse, Chocolate, '98 57
Soup, Fresh Fruit, '98 196
Spritzers, Raspberry, '99 207
Squares, Buttermilk Fudge, '99 99
Strudel, Autumn-Apple, '98 253
Strudel, Fig, '98 253
Strudel, Pear, '98 253
Tart, Apricot-Nut, '99 249
Tart, Bakewell, '97 110
Tart, Chocolate Custard, '99 27
Tart, Coffee, '99 67
Tart, Golden Peach Meringue, '98 197
Tart, Upside-Down Apple, '98 35
Tea, Almond-Lemonade, '99 207
Torte, Mocha, '99 66
Truffles, Chocolate-Cherry Cordial, '99 127
Wafers, Kahlúa, '99 147
Waffles with Apples and Caramel, Gingerbread, '98 M237

DESSERTS. *See also* AMBROSIA; BROWNIES; CAKES; CHEESECAKES; COOKIES; CUSTARDS; ICE CREAMS; MERINGUES; MOUSSES; PIES, PUFFS, AND PASTRIES; PUDDINGS; SHERBETS; SOUFFLÉS/Dessert.

Alaska, Peachy Melba, '88 266
Alaskas, Brownie, '83 299
Almond Dessert, Sour Cream-, '92 120
Amaretto Cream Tortoni, '85 161

Apple
Bake, Apple-Almond, '02 M209
Baked Alaska, Apple, '80 226
Baked Apples and Pear, Honey-, '97 303
Baked Apples, Imperial, '82 273
Baked Apples, Orange-Pecan, '85 45
Baked Apples, Pecan-and-Dried Fruit, '03 269
Baked Apples with Orange Sauce, '84 314
Baked Mincemeat-Filled Apples, '80 276
Brandied Apples, '81 248
Brandied Apples and Cream, '82 M237
Brown Betty, Apple, '83 213
Caramel Apples, Old English, '85 231
Charlotte, Apple, '99 84
Cheese Crisp, Apple-, '92 235

(continued)

Cinnamon Apples with Brandied Date Conserve, '85 315
Compote, Apple-Cranberry, '04 237
Compote, Apricot-Apple, '98 17
Cooked Apples, '93 338
Cranberry Apple Dessert, '80 253
Cranberry Apples, '99 246
Cranberry Crunch, Apple-, '86 300; '87 178
Crisp, Delicious Apple, '82 303
Crisp, Granola Apple, '85 78
Crumble, Whole Wheat-Apple, '90 M213
Delight, Apple, '80 109
Dumplings, Apple, '82 273; '00 96
Dumplings, Quick Apple, '01 185
Dumplings with Orange Hard Sauce, Apple, '88 224
Dutch Apple Dessert, Creamy, '91 19
Enchiladas, Apple, '99 63
Flambé, Hot Apples and Rum, '92 88
Flan, Apple, '81 309
Fritters, Apple, '82 273
Fritters with Lemon Sauce, Apple, '01 184
Golden Apples, '82 254
Honey-Baked Apple Dessert, '90 M213
Kuchen, Apple, '79 24
Melting Apples, '88 19
Nut Crunch, Apple-, '82 M238
Oatmeal Cherry-Apple Crisp, '90 M16
Orange-Apple Crisp, '80 295
Pecan Apples, Taffy, '99 247
Pizza, Apple-Pineapple Dessert, '00 313
Poached Lemon Apples, Chilled, '86 182
Quesadillas, Apple Pie 'n' Cheddar, '03 61
Rings, Apple, '85 232
Rings, Cinnamon Apple, '82 M237
Roasted Apples, Orange-Ginger, '01 184
Saucy Apples 'n' Pears, '96 72
Sour Cream Apple Squares, '82 262
Sundae, Hot Apple Spice, '92 239
Apricot-Apple Compote, '98 17
Apricot Cream, Peachy-, '86 163
Avocado Whip, '79 107
Baklava, '96 20
Banana
Alaska, Banana Split, '87 10
Baked Bananas, '96 163
Baked Bananas, Coffee-Kissed, '98 279
Baked Bananas with Orange Sauce, '79 115
Berry Supreme, Banana-, '81 205
Boats, Banana, '00 173
Candied Bananas, '83 179
Caramelized Bananas, '99 49
Cream Dessert, Banana, '81 180
Flambé, Banana-Peach, '85 316
Flip, Banana, '83 303
Foster, Bananas, '79 18; '83 M114; '86 139; '88 20; '96 99
Foster, Elegant Bananas, '81 59
Foster for Two, Bananas, '80 115
Foster, Tropical Bananas, '79 231
Glacé, Bananas, '96 46
Pie, Layered Banana Split, '83 189
Pops, Banana, '83 60; '84 44
Pops, Orange-Banana, '82 129
Praline Bananas, '84 313
Regal Bananas, '85 46
Soufflé, Banana Daiquiri, '84 317
Spiced Bananas with Rum Sauce, '99 247
Split, Banana-Berry, '05 193
Splits, French Toast Banana, '96 M164

Supreme, Bananas, '84 256
Tropical Bananas, Easy, '00 141
Bavarian Cream with Fresh Fruit, '88 137
Bavarian Cream with Raspberry Sauce, '91 180
Bavarian Dessert, Light, '86 6
Berried Treasure, '89 124
Berries on Snow, '82 227
Berries with Raspberry Custard Sauce, Fresh, '88 163
Berry Basket, Summer, '84 158
Berry Compote, '81 275
Berry Grapefruit Cup, '79 242
Beverages. *See also* **BEVERAGES.**
Berry Smoothie, Four-, '97 173
Brandy Alexander, '92 283
Brandy Float, Blazing, '85 314
Cappuccino Coffee Dessert, '92 264
Champagne Delight, '83 304
Chocoholic Smoothie, '97 173
Coconut Sipper, Creamy, '02 298
Creamy Dessert Drink, '86 131
Golden Dream, '82 100
Grape Juice-Fruit Refresher, '86 182
Ice Cream Ginger Fizz, '83 303
Nog, Hot Chocolate, '02 297
Orange-Banana Smoothie, '97 173
Pineapple Smoothie, '97 172
Pineapple Smoothie, Peachy-, '97 173
Punch, Eggnog-Coffee, '02 297
Punch, Milk, '02 298
Shake, Mocha-Mint, '02 297
Strawberry Smoothie, '97 173
Super Dessert Drink, Simply, '83 303
Birds' Nests, '04 84
Birds' Nests, Peanut-Butter, '04 84
Biscotti, Light, '91 310
Biscuits, Elf, '99 309
Biscuits, Sugar, '03 85
Biscuits, Sweet Little, '85 305
Biscuits with Balsamic Strawberries, Anise, '02 170
Blackberries and Dumplings, '86 196
Blackberries Chantilly, '99 130
Blackberry Dessert Tamales, '94 190
Blackberry Flan, '79 182
Blueberries and Cointreau, '82 100
Blueberry-Amaretto Squares, '83 220
Blueberry Crumble, '81 84
Blueberry Crunch, '96 146
Blueberry Crunch, Fresh, '82 143
Blueberry Delight, '96 17
Blueberry Dessert, Easy, '89 M130
Blueberry Dream, '88 94
Blueberry Pizza, '96 147
Blueberry Yum Yum, '98 91
Boysenberries and Cream Supreme, '82 133
Bread, Fry, '85 155
Bread with Stewed Yard Peaches, Cocoa, '05 23
Brie, Almond-Raspberry, '94 M89
Brownie Ice Cream Sandwich Shells, '88 195
Brûlé, Petit, '93 219
Buñuelos, '80 199
Buñuelos, King-Size, '86 5
Butter-Nut Strips, '82 167
Butterscotch Drops, '01 33
Butterscotch Fantastic, '83 76
Cakes, Funnel, '83 250
Cakes, Spanish Wind, '84 157
Cannoli, '80 58; '91 20
Cantaloupe Compote, '81 147
Cantaloupe Cream Delight, '82 179
Cantaloupe Delight, '89 204
Caramel Dessert Biscuits, '95 36
Caramel Fondue, '94 331; '95 35
Caramel Surprise, '88 202
Champagne Shooters, '02 280

Charlotte, Macaroon, '81 296
Charlotte, Peach, '79 68
Charlotte, Pineapple, '90 288
Charlotte Russe, '80 71; '82 M142; '90 288
Charlotte Russe, Chocolate, '87 74
Charlotte Russe, Fresh Lemon, '80 13
Charlotte Russe, Lemon, '84 192
Charlotte Russe, Wine Jelly and, '82 305
Charlotte Russe with Strawberry Sauce, '92 85
Charlottes, Mocha, '02 171
Cheese Blintzes, '82 146; '83 71
Cheese Kuchen, '86 84
Cheese Molds, Heavenly Dessert, '85 209
Cheese, Nutty Date Dessert, '87 299
Cheese Squares, Lemony Cream, '82 159
Cherries à la Mode, '88 202
Cherries Jubilee, '79 18; '83 139
Cherries Jubilee, Quick, '82 M100
Cherries Jubilite, '86 317
Cherries Sabayon, '88 178
Cherries, Sherried, '93 289
Cherry-Berry on a Cloud, '79 94
Cherry Compote, '83 139
Cherry Dessert, Holiday, '80 255
Chocolate. *See also* **DESSERTS/Frozen, Sauces.**
Almond Dessert, Chocolate-, '82 306
Almond Meringue Fingers, Chocolate-, '84 158
Bags, Chocolate-Raspberry, '95 97
Baskets with Berry Cream, Chocolate, '92 118
Black-Bottom Goodies, '89 251
Bombe, Double-Chocolate, '97 282
Brickle Squares, Chocolate, '94 290
Brownie-Mint Dessert, '82 227
Buttercream, Chocolate, '84 156
Charlotte Russe, Chocolate, '87 74
Chilled Chocolate Dessert, '83 177
Cinnamon-Chocolate Cream, '94 199
Coffee Mallow, '80 109
Cones, Chocolate-Coffee, '96 M316
Cream, Heavenly Chocolate, '88 128
Crêpes, Chocolate Dream, '86 164
Crêpes, Fruit-Filled Chocolate, '89 325
Cups, Chocolate, '80 207
Cups, Chocolate Crinkle, '93 270
Cups, Chocolate Lace, '87 133
Cups, Chocolate-Mint, '80 71
Cups, Miniature Chocolate, '87 132
Date-Nut Delight, Chocolate, '88 168
Decadence, Chocolate, '89 183
Dip, Chocolate, '92 50
Dream Dessert, Chocolate, '83 198
Easy Chocolate Dessert, '79 75
Fondue, Chocolate, '05 M281
Fondue, Dessert, '89 281
Fondue, White Chocolate, '92 287
Fudge Dessert with Kahlúa Cream, '91 197
Hearts, Crispy Chocolate, '03 M41
Hello Dolly Dessert, '95 168
Ladyfinger Dessert, Chocolate, '86 162
Loaves, Chocolate Chip Cheese, '91 299; '92 264
Log, Chocolate Cream, '94 220
Midnight Delights, '95 278
Mint Dessert, Chocolate-, '82 100
Mint Dessert, Cool Chocolate-, '80 109
Mississippi Mud, '96 253
Peanut-Chocolate Dessert, '80 86
Pizza, Chocolate, '91 298
Plunge, Chocolate, '94 332; '95 35
Pots de Chocolat, Petits, '82 272
Pots de Crème, '81 15; '84 M145
Pots de Crème au Chocolate, '93 53
Pots de Crème, Chocolate, '93 296; '94 234
Pots de Crème for Two, '89 275

Pots de Crème, Mocha, '88 M45
Pots de Crème, Rum-Flavored, '85 102
Pots de Crème with Orange Meringues, Chocolate,
  '95 318
Quad, Chocolate, '02 272
Roll, Chocolate Cream, '85 317
Roll, Chocolate Mousse, '83 290
Roulage, '90 266
Roulage, Chocolate-Cranberry, '94 313
Roulage, Chocolate-Mocha, '80 216
Roulage, Chocolate-Orange, '94 314
Roulage, Mint-Chocolate, '94 314
Roulage, White Chocolate, '92 230
Rum Dessert, Chocolate-, '81 247
Sack, Large Chocolate, '93 314
Sack, Small Chocolate, '93 314
Shells with Kahlúa Cream, Chocolate, '88 195
Squares, Chocolate-Blueberry Dessert,
  '87 299
Strawberry-Chocolate Combo, '85 96
Sundae Dessert, Hot Fudge, '84 313
Supreme, Chocolate, '84 94
Trifle, Chocolate, '88 258; '93 326
Truffle Dessert, Chocolate, '88 281
Turtle Bars, Gooey, '96 M189
Waffles with Strawberry Cream, Chocolate,
  '88 153
Cinnamon Crisps, '93 106
Coconut Cloud, '80 70
Coconut Dessert, Chilled, '83 116
Coeur à la Crème, Christmas, '86 278
Coffee-Almond Tortoni, '81 30
Coffee-and-Cream Chill, '99 126
Cookies and Cream, '96 179
Corn, Indian, '96 287
Cottage Cheese Dessert, Creamy, '87 191
Crackers, Dessert, '87 3
Cranberries, Brandied, '86 269
Cranberries Jubilee, '85 312; '90 293
Cranberry Apple Dessert, '80 253
Cranberry Bake, Hot, '91 250
Cranberry Compote, '97 264
Cranberry Dessert Pizzas, '96 320
Cranberry Jubilee, Tasty, '84 305
Cranberry-Pear Crisp, '97 16
Cranberry Pockets, '96 320
Cranberry Supreme, '85 280
Cranberry Surprise Dessert, '79 242
Cream, Bavarian, '86 M165
Cream Cheese, Chunky, '85 306
Cream Cheese Eggs, '99 118
Cream Cheese, Fruited, '85 306
Cream Cheese Squares, Lemony, '82 159
Cream, Molded French, '85 311; '99 72
Cream Puffs, Captivating, '81 180
Cream Puffs, Java, '81 187
Cream Puffs, Strawberry, '81 95
Cream Puffs, Tutti-Frutti, '79 231
Cream Puff Tree, '96 310
Cream, Spanish, '99 27
Crème Celeste, '88 94
Crème d'Ange, '83 91
Crème Patissière, '84 207
Crêpes, Basic Dessert, '82 157; '86 275
Crêpes, Dessert, '86 260; '87 290; '88 134
Crêpes, Dixie Dessert, '79 222
Crêpes Flambé, Cherry, '79 18
Crêpes, Strawberry Dessert, '83 122
Crêpes Suzettes, Light, '83 71
Date Dessert Squares, '89 255
Date-Nut Balls, '85 10
De-Light-Ful Dessert, '95 220
Dip, Citrus-Cream Cheese, '03 93
Dip, Orange-Flavored Cream Cheese, '03 93

Dip, Orange Marmalade-Cream Cheese, '03 93
Dip, Pink Lemonade-Lime, '04 133
Doughnuts, Orange Spiced, '79 136
Doughnut Stacks, Mini-, '05 58
Dough, Peanut Butter Fun, '00 171
Dumplings, Apple, '00 96
Éclair Cake, '93 42
Éclairs, Miniature Orange, '95 92
Éclairs, Mini Tiramisù, '03 M41
Éclairs, Minted Miniature, '88 66
Éclairs, Pistachio-Cream, '91 296
Éclairs with Pecan Sauce, '83 219
Eggnog Dessert, '95 314
Figs, Sugar-Crusted, '96 195
Flan. *See* CUSTARDS.
Frozen
  After Dinner-Drink Dessert, '82 100
  Almond Crunch, Frozen, '94 283
  Amaretto Chantilly, '89 14
  Amaretto Freeze, '82 182
  Amber Bombe, '80 255
  Applesauce Fluff, '91 173
  Apricot Fluff, Frozen, '86 242
  Apricot Freeze, '82 10
  Baked Alaska, '84 105; '85 295
  Baked Alaska, Apple, '80 226
  Baked Alaska, Brownie, '80 66
  Baked Alaska, Chocolate Mousse, '85 195
  Banana Pops, Yummy, '01 231
  Banana Pudding Parfait Pops, '96 180
  Banana Split Alaskas, '87 10
  Banana Split Pie, Layered, '83 189
  Banana Split Terrine, '96 164
  Bars, Creamy No-Bake, '97 166
  Bombe, Caramel-Toffee, '00 112
  Bombe, Ice Cream, '90 269
  Bombe with Raspberry Sauce, Creamy, '89 322
  Caffe Latte Slush, '02 209
  Cantaloupe Cream, Frozen, '82 159
  Cantaloupe Whip, '89 198
  Caramel-Toffee Bombe, '93 214
  Cassata, '01 125
  Charlotte, Spumoni, '90 193
  Cherry Cordial Dessert, '84 312
  Chocolate Almond Velvet, '81 148
  Chocolate-Coffee Frozen Dessert, '85 172
  Chocolate Dessert, Frozen, '83 76
  Chocolate Mint Freeze, '88 167
  Chocolate Roulage, Frozen, '90 56
  Chocolate-Walnut Cups, '85 213
  Chocolate Whip, '89 326
  Choco-Maple Frozen Dessert, '86 300; '87 178
  Cinnamon Ice Cream Sombreros, '93 276
  Citrus Cup, Snowball, '79 2
  Coconut-Caramel Dessert, '92 44
  Coffee Dessert, Light, '88 260
  Coffee Ice Cream Crunch, '82 182
  Coffee Tortoni, Creamy, '88 268
  Cookies 'n' Cream Dessert, Gold-Dusted,
    '94 271
  Cream, Betty's Holiday, '95 303
  Cream Dessert, Triple, '94 244
  Elegant Ending, '86 145
  Frappé, Hawaiian, '81 178
  Fruit Cream Freeze, '82 144
  Fruit Cups, Frozen, '93 197
  Fruit Freeze, Holiday, '88 283
  Fruit Ice, Mixed, '88 85
  Fudge-Peanut Ice Cream Dessert, '88 167
  Fudgy Frozen Dessert, Nutty, '94 28
  Grand Marnier Cream, '84 312
  Grapefruit Freeze, '93 242; '00 241
  Grasshopper Freeze, Creamy, '81 180
  Ice-Cream Angel Dessert, Triple Mint, '93 86

  Ice Cream Balls, Cinnamon-Chip, '00 198
  Ice Cream Bombe, '82 305
  Ice Cream Delight, '80 69
  Ice Cream Dessert, Caramel, '95 36
  Ice Cream Dessert, Decadent, '91 56
  Ice Cream Dessert, Layered, '83 189; '84 94, 105; '
    86 163
  Ice Cream Dessert, Mint, '88 66
  Ice Cream Dessert, Rocky Road, '00 332
  Ice Cream Dessert, Toffee, '87 110
  Ice Cream Party Squares, '91 214
  Ice Cream Pumpkin, '96 255
  Ice Cream Sandwiches, Chocolate Cookie,
    '87 147
  Ice Cream-Toffee Dessert, '00 176; '03 182
  Ice-Cream Torte, Toffee-Coffee, '04 234
  Ice Cream Treats, Crunchy, '86 300; '87 178
  Ice, Hazelnut-Coffee, '94 233
  Ice, Lemon, '01 330
  Ice, Mimosa, '94 24
  Lemon-Chiffon Frozen Yogurt, '85 54
  Lemon Cream, Frozen, '83 118
  Lime-Mint Refresher, '82 144
  Lime Whip, '89 199
  Little Bits, '79 196
  Macaroon-Sherbet Frozen Dessert, '79 212
  Mint Patty Alaska, '80 219
  Mocha Alaska Dessert, '84 191
  Mocha Delight, Frozen, '96 179
  Mocha Dessert, Frozen, '84 311
  Mocha Freeze, Royal, '84 53
  Mocha Squares, Frozen, '81 187
  Orange Alaska, '83 177
  Orange Dessert, Frozen, '92 44
  Oranges Grand Marnier, '92 82
  Ozark Pudding, Frozen, '88 127
  Peach Freeze, Creamy, '82 144
  Peach Torte, Frozen, '93 135
  Peanut Butter Delight, Frozen, '88 137
  Pineapple Delight, Fresh, '79 111
  Pineapple-Orange Bars, '82 129
  Pops, Banana, '83 60; '84 44
  Pops, Berry, '99 133
  Pops, Cherry-Berry Lemonade, '03 89
  Pops, Deep Blue Sea, '94 143
  Pops, Fruit, '87 168
  Pops, Hawaiian Orange-Pineapple, '94 143
  Pops, Kiwi Margarita, '99 133
  Pops, Orange-Banana, '82 129
  Pops, Orange Float, '99 132
  Pops, Peach, '04 141
  Pops, Pineapple-Yogurt, '91 173
  Pops, Purple People Eater, '99 132
  Pops, Sangría, '99 133
  Pops, Strawberry, '04 141
  Pops, Strawberry-Cinnamon, '99 132
  Pops, Strawberry-Orange, '03 179
  Popsicles, Smoothie Strawberry, '82 112
  Praline Freeze, '89 60
  Pumpkin Dessert, Frozen, '88 167
  Rainbow Delight, Frozen, '84 105
  Raspberry Dessert, Frozen, '84 192
  Raspberry Fluff, '89 198
  Sherbet Ambrosia Cups, '82 159
  Sherbet Dessert, Layered, '87 109
  Strawberry Cups, Frozen, '91 173
  Strawberry Delight, Frozen, '82 112, 174
  Strawberry Freeze, '04 141
  Strawberry Frost, '82 24; '83 154
  Strawberry Puff, '82 5
  Strawberry Whip, '89 198
  Sundaes, Waffle Taco, '05 M62
  Texas Tornadoes for Grown-Ups, '94 143
  Toffee Dessert, Ice Cream-, '04 82

DESSERTS, Frozen
(continued)

Torte, Frozen Viennese, '93 171
Tortoni, Apricot-Yogurt, '95 124
Turtle Dessert, '04 127
Vanilla Almond Crunch, '93 243
Vanilla Frozen Yogurt, '87 125
Vanilla Soufflé, Frozen, '79 230; '82 173
Watermelon Frost, '86 196
Watermelon, Looks-Like, '03 179

Fruit

Amaretto Crème on Fresh Fruit, '93 176
Bake, Nutty Fruit, '83 127
Beauberries Bordeaux, '98 18
Bowl, Fresh Fruit, '89 137
Caribbean Fruit Dessert, '84 314
Cheese, and Nuts, Fruit, '93 324
Cheese, Luscious Fresh Fruit with, '79 153
Chilled Fruit with Dressing, '85 222
Combo, Fresh Fruit, '86 178
Compote, Baked Fruit, '80 276; '84 314
Compote, Baked Mustard Fruit, '85 47
Compote, Champagne Fruit, '81 309; '82 124
Compote, Chilled Fruit, '83 123
Compote, Citrus, '98 17
Compote, Dried Fruit, '98 18
Compote, Fresh Fruit, '79 162; '82 197, 272; '84 82;
  '94 190
Compote, Fruit, '86 330
Compote, Gingered Fruit, '88 184
Compote, Hot Fruit, '81 203; '83 53
Compote, Jícama-Fruit, '92 49
Compote, Mixed Fruit, '93 123
Compote, Warm Praline Fruit, '85 260
Compote, Wine Fruit, '81 272
Compote with Caramel Syrup, Fruit, '98 313
Crisp, Fruit, '94 168
Cup, Fruit, '81 141; '91 202
Cup with Rum, Fruit, '83 55
Curried Fruit, Hot, '95 72
Dumplings, Delicious Fruit, '97 210
Flame, Sherried Fruit, '85 313
Flaming Fruit Dessert, '83 302
Fondue, Fruitcake, '84 258
Fruitini, '05 283
Gazpacho, Tropical, '95 204
Gingered Fruit, '83 151
Glazed Fruit, '85 83
Hot Fruit Delight, '83 281
Island Fruit Chill, '98 180
Kebabs with Mint Marinade, '82 157
Lemon Curd, Fresh Fruit with, '88 21
Marinated with Kirsch, Mixed Fruit, '03 86
Medley, Chinese Fruit, '83 22
Medley, Fancy Fruit, '84 82
Medley, Fresh Fruit, '81 141
Medley, Frosty Fruit, '82 226
Medley of Fruit, Tropical, '86 53
Meringue Shells, Fruited, '87 32
Mint-Balsamic Tea, Fresh Fruit with, '95 232
Orange, Fruit Dessert, '84 314
Planter's Punch Dessert, '95 175
Rainbow Fruit Dessert, '85 108
Soup Dessert, Fruit, '79 172
Soup, Fresh Fruit, '98 196
Spiced Fruit Delight, '82 229
Spiced Fruit Dessert, '82 50
Tequila, Fruit in, '82 223
Trifle, Tropical, '95 204
Turnovers, Fruit, '79 150
Gâteau Panache, '83 269
Gel with Stirred Custard, Sherried, '99 126

Glacé, Sabayon, '89 306
Grahams, Caramel-Apple, '04 M183
Grahams, Peanut Butter-Apple, '04 M183
Grahams, Praline, '92 239
Honeydew-Berry Dessert, '83 120
Honeydew Melon with Grapes, '91 91
Ice-Cream Dessert, Toffee, '97 134
Jelly, Rosy Wine, '85 306
Jelly, Wine, '98 125
Kahlúa Cream, '87 134
Kahlúa Delight, '83 67
Kahlúa Delight, Make-Ahead, '84 M89
Kahlúa Velvet Dessert, '85 M294
Kiwi and Cream in Meringue Cups, '81 279
Kiwi-and-Orange Dessert, '93 295
Kiwi-Berry Pizza, '86 198
Kiwifruit Pizza, '89 306
Kiwi Jubilee, '83 120
Kugel, Apricot Noodle, '92 251
Kugel, Sweet, '90 254
Ladyfingers, Creamy Berry, '05 36
Lemon Angel Rolls with Raspberry Sauce, '94 294
Lemon-Cream Cheese Dessert, '84 95
Lemon Cups, Baked, '87 128
Lemon Curd, '89 334; '04 259, 279
Lemon Curd with Berries, '90 102
Lemon Delight, '82 227
Lemon Dessert, Layered, '88 134
Lemon Solid, '93 279
Little Nothings, '79 135
Lollapalooza, '94 194
Lollipops, Harvest Moon, '02 M223
Madeleines, '88 79
Mango Dessert Tamales, '94 190
Mango Pan Dowdy, '83 150
Maple Nut Dessert, '81 84
Maraschino Russian Cream, '79 231
Margarita Tacos, '97 167
Maverick Lunar Pie, '98 111
Melon Ball Compote, '85 157
Melon Balls and Cherries in Kirsch, '91 91
Melon Balls in Watermelon Sauce, '79 177
Melon-Mint Julep, '86 196
Melons in Mint Sauce, '85 164
Melon Wedges with Berry Sauce, '86 178
Meringue Baskets with Fresh Fruit and Ice Cream,
  '98 179
Meringue Cream Cups, Lemon, '84 23
Meringue Flowers, '84 156
Meringue, Piping, '84 156
Meringues, Baked Pear, '85 232
Meringues, Strawberry, '84 188
Mocha-Almond Dessert, '80 289; '81 62
Mocha Chiffon, '86 75
Nectarines Royale, '85 132
Nectarines with Pineapple-Coconut Ice Cream, Mint,
  '05 123
Noodle Casserole, Sweet, '02 238
Nuggets, Golden North Pole, '99 M309
Oatmeal Cherry-Apple Crisp, '90 M16
Omelet, Puffy Dessert, '00 35
Orange. *See also* **DESSERTS/Frozen, Sauces.**
  Baked Apples, Orange-Pecan, '85 45
  Baked Orange Elegance, '80 13
  Baskets, Orange, '81 308
  Caramelized Oranges, Italian, '05 101
  Champagne Oranges, '93 83
  Chiffon Dessert, Orange, '93 295
  Cream Dessert, Orange, '80 254; '84 165
  Cream, Orange, '81 12
  Cream, Orange Chantilly, '84 156
  Cream, Orange-Coconut, '84 24
  Crisp, Orange-Apple, '80 295
  Curd, Fresh Orange, '02 294

Delight, Pumpkin-Orange, '86 321
Dip, Creamy Orange, '84 117
Doughnuts, Orange Spiced, '79 136
Éclairs, Miniature Orange, '95 92
Flambé, Dessert Orange, '85 313
Frosted Oranges, '83 270
Fruit Dessert Orange, '84 314
Grand Marnier, Oranges, '92 82
Kiwi-and-Orange Dessert, '93 295
Molded Dessert, Orange, '83 302
Parfaits, Chilled Orange, '80 219
Parfaits, Orange Cream, '94 198
Pears Flambé, Orange-Poached, '85 313
Poached Oranges, Wine-, '84 M323
Rice Cream with Mandarin Oranges, '85 317
Sections with Chocolate and Raspberry Sauce,
  Orange, '97 33
Slices, Burgundy-Spiced Orange, '93 294
Soufflé, Chilled Orange, '84 317; '86 189
Soufflé, Frozen Orange, '79 211
Soufflé, Orange Dessert, '83 206
Strawberries with Brandied Orange Juice, '82 160
Tapioca Crème, Orange-, '82 M283
Tapioca Fluff, Orange, '87 31
Pancakes, Dessert Ginger, '88 153
Pancakes, Luau Dessert, '88 154
Parfaits
Blackberries-and-Cream Parfait, '87 129
Cheesecake Parfaits, Sugar-Free Peachy, '02 326
Chocolate-Crème de Menthe Parfaits, '85 161
Chocolate-Mint Parfaits, '90 M15
Chocolate Mousse Parfait, '94 90
Chocolate-Peanut Butter Mousse Parfaits, '98 71
Chocolate-Peppermint Parfaits, '88 65
Coffee Crunch Parfaits, '82 159
Eggnog Bavarian Parfait, '79 255
Family, Parfait, '94 130
Hooray Parfaits, '96 229
Kiwi Parfait, '86 199; '87 55
Lemon-Blueberry Layered Dessert, '05 206
Lime Parfaits, '80 153
Mocha-Mallow Parfaits, '80 219
Orange Cream Parfaits, '94 198
Orange Parfaits, Chilled, '80 219
Peach Parfait, '82 166
Peanut Butter Parfaits, Crunchy, '79 176; '80 6
Peppermint Parfait, '93 315
Pineapple Parfait, '84 83
Speedy Parfaits, '83 76
Strawberry-Lemon Parfaits, '84 198
Strawberry Meringue Parfaits, '02 62
Strawberry Parfait, '79 99
Strawberry Parfaits, Frosty, '85 213
Strawberry Parfait, Surprise, '86 151
Strawberry Shortcake Parfaits, Super Fast, '05 196
Strawberry-Yogurt Parfait, Crunchy, '79 124
Surf-and-Sand Parfaits, '93 169
Tropical Trilogy Parfait, '92 247
White Chocolate-Raspberry Swirl Parfait,
  '93 315
Pavlova, '92 101
Peach. *See also* **DESSERTS/Frozen, Sauces.**
Baked Peaches, '92 179
Blueberry Dessert, Peach-, '92 184
Brandy Peaches, '85 275
Caramel Peaches, '93 134
Cardinale, Peach, '89 155
Champagne, Peaches, '79 146
Charlotte, Peach, '79 68
Compote, Berry-Peach, '82 133
Compote, Peach-Berry, '89 112
Cream, Bavarian Peach, '82 171
Cream, Peach Almond, '82 108
Cream, Peaches and, '95 196

Cream, Peachy-Apricot, '86 163
Crisp, Gingered Peach, '97 303
Crisp, Peach, '92 13
Custard Dessert, Fresh Peach, '86 162
Dumplings, Peach, '85 177
Foster, Peaches, '86 240
Ginger Peaches with Rum, '84 M323
Gingersnap Peaches, '85 M329
Honeyed Peaches 'n' Cream, '93 134
Layered Peach Dessert, '95 196
Marinated Peaches, '91 91
Melba, Peach, '81 83; '83 M114
Melt-Away Dessert, Peachy, '87 298
Mint Peaches with Pineapple-Coconut Ice Cream,
    '05 123
Oven-Baked Peaches with Ginger, '82 170
Parfait, Peach, '82 166
Quick Peach Dessert, '85 178
Sherbet Cooler, Peachy, '91 187
Spiced Peach Dessert, '83 9
Spiced Peaches with Nutty Dumplings, '87 164
Split, Peach, '85 277
Stewed Yard Peaches, '05 23
Strawberry Sauce, Peaches with, '85 8
Stuffed Peaches, Macaroon-, '79 178
Stuffed Peach Halves, '86 196
Sundaes Flambé, Peach, '81 88
Trifle, Peach, '92 179
Wine Sauce, Peaches in, '79 184
Peanut Butter Dessert, '92 164
Peanut-Buttery Dessert, Crunchy, '92 204
Pear. *See also* **DESSERTS/Sauces.**
Amaretto Pears with Meringue, '90 M58
Baked Apples and Pear, Honey-, '97 303
Baked in Molasses-Port Sauce, Pears, '97 195
Baked Pears à la Mode, '95 129
Baked Pears Elegant, '91 48
Belle Helene, Pears, '86 164
Blue, Pears, '99 246
Coconut Pears, Spicy, '83 207
Crème Chantilly, Holiday Pears with, '91 297
Crème de Menthe Pears, '94 50
Crisp, Cranberry-Pear, '97 16
Crisp, Raspberry-Pear, '89 109
Dumplings, Pear, '97 210
Flaming Pears, '84 313
Gratin, Pear-Blue Cheese, '93 328
Maple-Sugared Pears, '81 232
Meringues, Baked Pear, '85 232
Orange-Caramel Sauce, Pears with, '95 281
Poached in Red Wine, Pears, '83 302
Poached Pear Fans with Raspberry-Orange Sauce,
    '88 22
Poached Pears, Champagne-, '01 289
Poached Pears Flambé, Orange-, '85 313
Poached Pears in Custard, '88 20
Poached Pears in Wine, '82 194
Poached Pears, Lemon, '82 74
Poached Pears, Vanilla, '90 57
Poached Pears with Berry Sauce, Wine-, '86 144
Poached Pears with Dark Chocolate Sauce,
    '90 M141
Poached Pears with Honey-Yogurt Sauce, '92 306
Poached Pears with Raspberry Sauce, '84 213;
    '87 69; '88 223
Poached Pears with White Caramel Sauce, '99 28
Red Wine, Pears in, '82 254
Sautéed Pears, '03 195
Stewed Pears, '98 280
Stuffed Pears, Almond-, '83 207
Sundaes, Quick Pear, '86 71
Pecans, Sugared, '82 167
Peppermint Bavarian, '80 153
Peppermint Fondue, '94 332

Peppermint Wafer Dessert, '79 176; '80 7
Pineapple-Almond Delight, '85 96
Pineapple Boats with Rum Sauce, '97 192
Pineapple Dessert Chimichangas, '86 4
Pineapple Filling, '97 277
Pineapple, Meringue-Topped, '84 178
Pineapple 'n' Cream, '88 202
Pineapple, Scalloped, '79 106; '82 254
Pineapple Skewers with Rum Sauce, Grilled, '04 247
Pineapple, Stuffed, '00 160
Pineapple with Natillas Sauce, Baked, '83 179
Pineapple with Raspberry Sauce, Chocolate-Drizzled,
    '90 57
Pizza Dessert, Rocky Road, '99 196
Pizzelles, '83 298
Plum Crunch, Layered, '86 174
Plums in Port Wine, '97 176
Port Wine Jelly with Whipped Cream, '84 254
Pots de Crème, Easy, '93 281
Praline Horns, '96 316
Profiteroles, '84 208
Prune Bavarian, '86 223
Prunes in Merlot, '98 18
Pumpkin Chiffon, '82 216; '86 283; '88 260
Pumpkin Chiffon Dessert, '88 128
Pumpkin Flan, '97 219
Pumpkin Mold, '82 311
Pumpkin-Orange Delight, '86 321
Pumpkin Swirl, Easy, '93 234
Quesadillas, Dessert, '02 54
Raspberry Bites, Creamy, '05 36
Raspberry Dream, '83 108
Raspberry-Jellyroll Dessert, '85 95
Raspberry Jellyrolls, '93 M255
Raspberry-Pear Crisp, '89 109
Raspberry Prunes, '82 124
Raspberry-Strawberry Bavarian, '89 15
Reindeer Food, Magic, '99 M309
Rhubarb Crisp, '91 146; '92 130
Rhubarb-Strawberry Bavarian, '86 140
Rhubarb Whip, '79 112
Rice Cream with Mandarin Oranges, '85 317
Roulage, Toffee-Pecan, '94 312
Rum Balls, '93 314
Sabayon, '93 272
Sabayon, Champagne, '00 288
Santa's Hat, '92 279
Sauces
Almond-Vanilla Custard Sauce, '88 M177
Amaretto-Chocolate Sauce, '92 154
Amaretto-Cinnamon Sauce, '93 171
Amaretto Cream Sauce, '03 330
Amaretto-Strawberry Sauce, '87 M165
Ambrosia Sauce, Hot, '89 335
Apple Ambrosia Sauce, '89 95
Apple-Cinnamon Sauce, '93 42
Apple Dessert Sauce, '87 M165
Apple Dessert Sauce, Spicy, '82 177
Apple Topping, Spicy, '87 125
Apricot Ice Cream Sauce, '91 57
Apricot Sauce, '82 212
Apricot-Walnut Hard Sauce, '88 153
Banana-Pineapple Sauce, '83 48
Bananas Foster Sauce, '03 94
Banana Sundae Sauce, '84 275
Berry Mimosa Sauce, '90 315
Berry Sauce, '87 290; '88 135; '94 130; '95 103
Bittersweet Chocolate Sauce '92 319
Blackberry Sauce, '86 152; '94 232
Blueberry-Lemon Sauce, '01 117
Blueberry Sauce, '88 155; '89 M130; '94 122;
    '95 135
Blueberry Topping, '87 125
Bourbon Cream Sauce, '98 84

Bourbon Praline Sauce, '81 170
Bourbon Sauce, '93 51; '98 336; '01 223; '03 66;
    '05 119
Brandied Hard Sauce, '80 264; '83 250;
    '85 313
Brandy-Butter Sauce, '79 230
Brandy-Macadamia Sauce, '82 311
Brandy Sauce, '88 279; '98 119
Bread Pudding Sauce, '04 235
Brown Sugar Sauce, '90 314
Buttered Rum Sauce, '83 249
Buttered Rum Sauce, Hot, '88 204
Buttermilk Custard Sauce, '96 183
Buttermilk Sauce, '95 183
Butter Pecan Sauce, '91 174
Butter-Rum Sauce, '95 134
Butterscotch-Pecan Sauce, '82 212
Caramel-Raisin Sauce, '88 127
Caramel Sauce, '79 79; '91 56, 180; '93 210, 235,
    296; '94 234; '95 308; '96 284, 310; '97 178;
    '00 52, 256; '01 313; '03 194
Caramel Sauce, Easy, '87 38
Caramel Sauce, The Best Ever, '03 216
Caramel Sauce, White, '92 195
Champagne-Chocolate Sauce, '05 M282
Cherry-Pineapple Topping, '87 126
Cherry Sauce, '79 91
Cherry Sauce, Elegant, '79 M156
Cherry-Wine Sauce, '97 132
Chocolate and Raspberry Sauce, Orange Sections
    with, '97 33
Chocolate-Cherry Sauce, '85 189
Chocolate Cherry Sauce, '87 M165
Chocolate-Mint Sauce, '93 86; '94 314; '98 217
Chocolate Mint Sauce, Quick, '86 M58
Chocolate-Orange Sauce, '86 165; '94 314
Chocolate-Peanut Butter Sauce, '79 91, M156
Chocolate-Peppermint Sauce, '94 205
Chocolate-Praline Sauce, '85 M295
Chocolate Sauce, '83 189; '84 208, 313; '86 322;
    '90 57; '91 56, 57; '93 276; '94 121;
    '97 178, 331
Chocolate Sauce, Classic, '85 207
Chocolate Sauce, Creamy, '88 M177
Chocolate Sauce, Dark, '93 296; '94 234, 283;
    '96 310; '98 336; '05 31
Chocolate Sauce, Double, '83 79
Chocolate Sauce, Easy, '92 148
Chocolate Sauce, Heavenly, '79 79; '82 167
Chocolate Sauce, Semisweet, '00 104
Chocolate Sauce Supreme, '85 189
Cinnamon-Blueberry Sauce, '86 11
Cinnamon-Butter Sauce, '00 254
Cinnamon-Fudge Sauce, '85 141
Cinnamon Sauce, Apple Pie with Hot,
    '88 210
Coconut-Orange Sauce, '85 189
Coconut Sauce, '98 34
Coconut Sauce, Creamy Light, '82 177
Cranberry Jubilee, Tasty, '85 189
Cranberry Sauce, '86 278; '88 280
Crème Anglaise, '92 164
Crème Fraîche Sauce, '79 281; '93 135
Custard Sauce, '85 41; '88 154, 251, 259; '89 291;
    '97 16, 313; '03 244, 318
Date-Nut Sundae Sauce, '82 167
Fig Sauce, '79 140
Fruit Dessert Sauce, Hot, '87 299
Fruit Puree, '94 190
Fruit Sauce, Golden, '89 281
Fruit Sauce, Quick, '82 212
Fudge Sauce, '91 174
Fudge Sauce, Easy Hot, '84 69; '94 194
Fudge Sauce, Heavenly Hot, '00 256

Fudge Sauce, Hot, '82 181, 295; '84 143; '97 255;
  '05 193
Fudge Sauce, Quick Hot, '82 212
Golden Sauce, '88 267
Hard Sauce, '80 265; '82 14
Hard Sauce, Special, '86 318
Honey-Chocolate Sauce, '89 251
Honey-Orange Sauce, '85 108
Honeyscotch Sundae Sauce, '82 167
Honey-Yogurt Sauce, '92 307
Kahlúa Chocolate Sauce, '85 155
Lemon Cream Sauce, '93 200
Lemon Dessert Sauce, '87 M165
Lemon Sauce, '84 258, 306; '85 77, 190; '91 240;
  '96 283; '01 184; '04 98
Lemon Sauce, Tart, '85 191
Lemon Sauce, Zesty, '97 318
Lemon-Vanilla Sauce, '02 231
Mandarin Dressing, '89 137
Mandarin Orange Sauce, '89 204
Mango Sauce, '83 120
Marshmallow Sauce, '91 91
Melba Sauce, '87 77
Mint Sauce, '96 127
Mint Sauce, Party, '82 212
Mocha Sauce, '98 57; '05 317
Orange Dessert Sauce, '86 337; '87 58
Orange Hard Sauce, '88 225
Orange Sauce, Fresh, '85 209
Peach-Berry Sauce, '87 M165
Peach-Blueberry Pancake Sauce, '82 177
Peach Blueberry Sauce, '81 170
Peach-Praline Sauce, '85 161
Peach Sauce, '84 144
Peach Sauce, Creamy, '85 189
Peach Sauce, Fresh, '87 167
Peanut Butter Ice Cream Sauce, '84 30
Peanut Butter Sauce, '03 289
Peanut Dessert Sauce, '86 M251
Pear Sauce, '92 164
Pecan Sauce, '83 219
Piña Colada Topping, Chunky, '87 125
Pineapple Ice Cream Sauce, '81 M289
Pineapple-Rhubarb Sauce, '88 94
Pineapple-Rum Sauce, '84 275
Plum Sauce, Fresh, '94 129
Praline Ice Cream Sauce, '85 189
Praline Ice Cream Sauce, Southern, '86 M227
Praline Sauce, '83 25; '84 143; '89 95; '92 282;
  '93 214; '94 206, 312; '96 285
Raspberry-Amaretto Sauce, '88 130
Raspberry-Lemon Sauce, Cheesecake with, '96 30
Raspberry-Orange Sauce, '88 22; '92 154
Raspberry-Peach Topping, '87 126
Raspberry Sauce, '82 289; '83 108; '84 73, 213;
  '87 69, 117, 183; '88 267; '89 183, 322; '91 96,
  180, 270; '92 130; '93 82, 99, 315; '94 295;
  '95 327; '96 183, 310; '98 157, 216; '99 167, 259;
  '02 123; '03 319; '04 33; '05 31, 201
Raspberry Sauce, Crimson, '79 91; '85 30
Raspberry Sauce Dessert, '80 147
Raspberry Sauce Flambé, '84 142
Raspberry Sauce, Fresh, '93 120
Rhubarb Sauce, Chilled, '88 94
Rum-Butter Sauce, '86 301
Rum-Fruit Sauce, '84 312
Rum-Raisin Sauce, '84 7; '94 295
Rum Sauce, '88 32; '94 241; '03 244
Rum Sauce, Brown Sugar-, '85 231
Rum Sauce, Hot, '79 86

Rum Sundae Sauce, '93 162
Sherry Sauce, '84 109
Spicy Sauce, '93 52
Strawberries Arnaud Sauce, '93 50
Strawberry-Banana Topping, '87 125
Strawberry-Butter Sauce, '96 87
Strawberry-Orange Sauce, '96 95
Strawberry-Peach Sauce, '92 154
Strawberry Sauce, '84 144; '87 93, 198; '92 85;
  '94 121; '03 55
Strawberry Sauce, Brandied, '88 196
Strawberry Sauce, Fresh, '82 177
Strawberry Sauce, Old-Fashioned, '94 130
Strawberry Sauce, Peaches with, '85 8
Strawberry Sauce with Crunchy Topping, '81 170
Strawberry Sauce with Dumplings, '84 314
Taffy Dessert Sauce, '86 20
Tea-Berry Sauce, '94 130; '99 334
Toffee-Fudge Sauce, '89 95
Toffee Sauce, '94 72
Vanilla Cream Sauce, '05 260
Vanilla Crème Sauce, '94 243; '96 155
Vanilla Custard Sauce, '99 27
Vanilla-Nutmeg Sauce, '02 208
Vanilla Sauce, '97 M15
Watermelon Sauce, Melon Balls in, '79 177
Whiskey Sauce, '90 230; '92 87, 93; '99 277
White Caramel Sauce, '99 28
White Chocolate Sauce, '92 164; '96 310; '00 104
Savarin, '79 171
Sherbet-Cantaloupe Surprise, '91 105
S'mores, Indoor, '01 33
Sopaipillas, '80 197; '88 112; '91 78
Sopaipillas, Pineapple, '83 179
Soufflés
Banana Daiquiri Soufflé, '84 317
Brandy Alexander Soufflé, '82 173; '83 M114
Chocolate-Mint Soufflé, '81 16
Chocolate Soufflé, Light, '83 278
Chocolate Soufflé with White Chocolate Mousse,
  '98 57
Coconut Soufflé, '85 212
Daiquiri Soufflé, Elegant, '80 69
Devonshire Soufflé, Chilled, '88 279
Gingerbread Soufflés with Lemon Cream, '04 300
Grand Marnier Soufflé, '79 281
Grand Marnier Soufflés, '03 318
Grasshopper Soufflé, '81 248; '86 188
Kahlúa Soufflé, '82 173
Lemon-Lime Soufflé, Cold, '84 24
Lemon Soufflé, '82 170
Lemon Soufflé, Tart, '85 82
Orange Dessert Soufflé, '83 206
Orange Soufflé, Chilled, '84 317; '86 189
Orange Soufflé, Frozen, '79 211
Pineapple Dessert Soufflé, '80 153
Raspberry Soufflé, '86 188
Raspberry-Topped Soufflé, '85 317
Spiced Soufflés with Lemon Whipped Cream,
  '05 255
Vanilla Soufflé, Frozen, '79 230; '82 173
Vanilla Soufflés with Vanilla Crème Sauce, '96 155
Soup, Sherry-Berry Dessert, '91 180
Spumoni and Berries, '91 204
Sticky Fingers, '03 M168
Strawberry. *See also* **DESSERTS/Frozen, Parfaits,
Sauces.**
Almond Cream with Fresh Strawberries, '87 93
Arnaud, Strawberries, '93 50
Balsamic Strawberries, '02 170
Banana-Berry Supreme, '81 205
Bavarian, Raspberry-Strawberry, '89 15
Bavarian, Rhubarb-Strawberry, '86 140
Best-Dressed Berries, '96 317

Brandied Orange Juice, Strawberries with,
  '82 160
Carousel, Strawberry, '91 247
Cheese Delight, Strawberry, '79 50
Cherry-Berry on a Cloud, '79 94
Chilled Strawberry Dessert, '84 164
Chocolate Combo, Strawberry-, '85 96
Coconut Nests, Strawberry, '88 136
Compote, Peach-Berry, '89 112
Cream Cheese Dessert, Strawberry-, '83 123
Cream in Vanilla Lace Cups, Strawberry, '98 93
Cream Puffs, Strawberry, '81 95
Cream, Strawberries and, '82 100
Cream, Strawberries 'n', '90 30
Cream, Strawberries with Strawberry, '84 108
Crêpes, Strawberry Dessert, '83 122
Deep-Fried Strawberries, '84 109
Delight, Strawberry, '81 85
Dipped Strawberries, '94 17
Dip, Strawberries with Brown Sugar-and-Sour
  Cream, '03 93
Dip, Strawberries with Fluffy Cream Cheese,
  '03 93
Dip, Strawberries with Mint Yogurt, '03 93
Dip, Strawberries with Vanilla Pudding, '03 93
French Cream, Strawberries with, '83 191
Frost, Strawberry, '81 279; '82 24; '83 154
Glazed Strawberry Dessert, '84 33
Honeydew-Berry Dessert, '83 120
Jamaica, Strawberries, '85 161; '93 239
Juliet, Strawberries, '84 82
Lemon Dessert, Strawberry-, '86 162
Marsala, Strawberries, '88 171
Meringues, Strawberry, '84 188
Napoleons, Strawberry, '81 126
Pizza, Kiwi-Berry, '86 198
Pizza, Strawberry, '79 94
Raspberry Custard Sauce, Fresh Berries with,
  '88 163
Rock Cream with Strawberries, Old-Fashioned,
  '90 125
Romanoff, Strawberries, '84 108; '88 95; '91 126
Romanoff, Strawberry-Almond, '98 99
Ruby Strawberries, '82 100
Sabayon, Strawberries, '79 94
Shortcake Squares, Strawberry, '85 122
Soup, Sherry-Berry Dessert, '91 180
Spumoni and Berries, '91 204
Strawberry Dessert, '83 123
Stuffed Strawberries with Walnuts, '85 122;
  '86 124
Summer Strawberry Dessert, '92 143
Sweet-and-Sour Strawberry Dessert, '92 54
Swirl, Strawberry, '84 108
Trifle, Easy Strawberry, '88 201
Yogurt Delight, Strawberry, '85 77
Yogurt Dessert, Strawberry-, '90 295
Zabaglione, Strawberries, '81 95
Sundaes
Apple Spice Sundae, Hot, '92 239
Berry Sundaes, Very, '03 126
Brownie Sundaes, Cream Cheese, '03 223
Cantaloupe Sundae, '89 166
Chocolate Mint Sundaes, '03 M120
Cocoa-Kahlúa Sundaes, '83 M58
Hot Fudge Sundae Dessert, '86 322
Mauna Loa Sundaes, '80 126
Peach Sundaes Flambé, '81 88
Pear Sundaes, Quick, '86 71
S'mores Sundaes, '05 257
Strawberry Sundaes, Hot, '81 M5
Sushi, Crisp Rice Cereal, '00 50
Syrup, Madeira, '98 247
Tacos, Dessert, '97 141

Tea Cakes and Fresh Strawberries, Telia's, '98 110
That's Incredible, '02 322
Tiramisù, '91 21; '94 295; '98 280; '00 288; '02 285
Tiramisù, Easy, '00 167
Toffee Dessert, English, '88 136
Torte, Mocha Mousse, '04 260
Torte, Peanut Butter Turtle, '04 316
Torte, X-Treme Chocolate Double Nut Caramel
    Ladyfinger, '04 M315
Tortilla Baskets, '94 97
Tortilla Triangles with Fruit Salsa, Sweet, '02 54
Trees, Holiday, '02 298
Trifles
    Angel Food Trifle, '91 184
    Banana Pudding Trifle, '98 273
    Brownie Trifle, '03 85
    English Trifle, '93 289
    Individual Trifles, Easy, '92 239
    Island Trifle, '92 238
    Jumbleberry Trifle, '03 84
    Lemon-Blueberry Trifle, '88 210
    Lemon Trifle, All Seasons, '95 219
    Olde English Trifle, '95 331
    Peach Trifle, Georgia, '04 169
    Peanut Butter-Brownie Trifle, '03 200
    Pineapple Angel Food Trifle, '93 86
    Raspberry Trifle, '88 259
    Raspberry Trifles, Individual, '99 112
    Rum Trifle, '86 322
    Savannah Trifle, '80 121
    Strawberry-Sugar Biscuit Trifle, '03 84
    Strawberry Trifle, Easy, '88 201
    Toffee Trifle, '94 168
    Tropical Rum Trifle, '03 85
Tropical Snow, '86 34
Vacherin Moka, '80 55
Vanilla Cream, '83 M115
Vanilla Lace Cups, '98 M93
Vanilla Sherry Dessert, Glorified, '81 85
Waffles, Banana Split, '89 205
Waffles with Apples and Caramel, Gingerbread,
    '98 M237
Waffles with Mandarin Orange Sauce, Dessert Pumpkin,
    '89 204
Waffle, Whole Wheat Dessert, '79 92
White Christmas Dessert, '82 261
Wine Jelly, Rosy, '85 306
Yule Log, '79 281; '82 289
Zabaglione with Fruit, Champagne Vanilla, '00 31
Zuppa Inglese, '99 M267
DOUGHNUTS
Applesauce Doughnuts, '81 203
Applesauce Drop Doughnuts, '90 70
Banana Doughnuts, '86 137
Beignets, '84 56
Cake Doughnuts, Quick, '82 226
Chocolate-Covered Doughnuts, '84 55
Chocolate Doughnuts, '83 95
Cinnamon Puffs, '81 209; '01 126
Dutch Doughnuts, '81 50
Fry Bread, '84 140
Glazed Doughnuts, '83 94
Hanukkah Doughnuts with Strawberry Preserves,
    '01 M275
Jelly-Filled Doughnuts, '84 55
Orange Spiced Doughnuts, '79 136
Pineapple Drop Doughnuts, '83 95
Potato Doughnuts, Chocolate-Glazed, '85 6
Potato Doughnuts, Old-Fashioned, '84 56
Puffs, Doughnut, '86 85
Puffs, Wheat Quick Doughnut, '85 278
Pumpkin Doughnut Drops, '90 323
Quick Doughnuts and Doughnut Holes,
    '01 126

Raised Doughnuts, '01 126
Snowy Doughnuts, '93 286
Spice Doughnuts, '84 56
Stacks, Mini-Doughnut, '05 58
Sufganiyot (Jelly-Filled Doughnuts), '90 255
Whole Wheat Doughnuts, '84 56
DOVE. *See* **GAME.**
DRESSINGS. *See also* **SALAD DRESSINGS,**
    STUFFINGS.
Andouille Sausage, Apple, and Pecan Dressing, '02 249
Cajun Dressing, '82 307
Chicken and Dressing, Baked, '79 296
Cornbread
    Biscuit Dressing, Cornbread-, '79 296
    Cakes, Southwestern Cornbread Dressing, '01 233
    Chicken and Dressing, '99 42
    Chicken Cornbread Dressing, '90 159
    Cornbread Dressing, '86 286; '88 254; '92 267;
        '98 269; '00 259; '02 249; '03 231
    Corny Cornbread Dressing, '99 258
    Crawfish-Cornbread Dressing, '99 257
    Fruited Cornbread Dressing, '80 262
    Green Chile-Cornbread Dressing, '93 306;
        '94 296
    Herb-Seasoned Cornbread Dressing, '83 315
    Kentucky Cornbread Dressing, '86 281
    Light Cornbread Dressing, '92 324
    Louise's Cornbread Dressing, '03 251
    Nannie's Cornbread Dressing, '95 306
    Old-Fashioned Cornbread Dressing, '84 321
    Oyster-Cornbread Dressing, Ma E's Traditional,
        '96 35
    Quail and Dressing, '99 42
    Quail Stuffed with Cornbread Dressing, '93 280
    Sage-Cornbread Dressing, '84 283
    Sage Dressing, Cornbread-, '80 262
    Sausage, and Pecan Dressing, Cornbread, '99 257
    Sausage-Cornbread Dressing, '95 289
    Sausage-Cornbread Dressing, Turkey with,
        '83 287
    Sausage Dressing, Cornbread-, '82 307; '85 280
    Sausage Dressing, Cornbread-and-, '83 213
    Savory Cornbread Dressing, '88 303
    Slow-Cooker Cornbread Dressing, '05 270
    Squash Dressing, '01 160
    Sweet Cornbread Dressing, '97 303
    Texas Cornbread Dressing, '82 243
    Turkey and Cornbread Dressing, Roast, '89 324
Corn Dressing Balls, Zesty, '82 307
Crabmeat-and-Oyster Dressing, '02 243
Crawfish Dressing, Louisiana, '90 103
Creole Dressing, '95 289
Eggplant Dressing, '90 236
Fruit-and-Pecan Dressing, '84 252
Fruit Dressing, Baked, '87 253
Giblet Dressing, '91 255
Grandmother's Dressing, '91 254
Green Onion Dressing, '96 17
Grits Dressing, '93 306; '94 296
Oyster Bread Dressing, '82 251
Oyster Dressing, '79 250
Peanut Dressing, Roast Turkey with, '79 283
Pecan, Rice, and Crawfish Dressing, '00 252
Pecan-Rice Dressing, Chicken with, '85 M57
Pecan-Sage Dressing, '80 262
Pretzel Dressing, '86 280
Rice Dressing, '91 217; '01 222
Rice Dressing, Chicken and, '79 288
Rice Dressing, Mexican, '87 253
Rice Dressing, Roast Turkey with, '82 286
Rice Dressing, Southern, '99 256
Roasted Garlic Dressing, '99 269
Sausage-Apple Dressing, '93 305; '94 296
Sausage Dressing, '86 280

Sausage Dressing, Harvest, '88 254
Seasoned Dressing, Stuffed Turkey Breast with,
    '83 320; '84 128
Spoonbread Dressing, Southwestern-Style, '94 273
Squash Dressing, '83 315; '86 280; '95 290
Squash Dressing, Turkey with, '87 248
Turkey and Dressing, Easy, '79 296
Turkey-and-Dressing Pie, '84 326
Turkey Dressing, '85 298
Turkey Dressing, Fruited, '99 257
Whole Wheat-Mushroom Dressing, '84 283
Zucchini Dressing, '86 282
DUCK. *See* **GAME.**
DUMPLINGS
Apple Dumpling Cobbler, '04 29
Apple Dumplings, '82 273; '00 96
Apple Dumplings, Cinnamon, '97 M330
Apple Dumplings, Old-Fashioned, '84 226
Apple Dumplings, Quick, '01 185
Apple Dumplings with Maple-Cider Sauce,
    '95 288
Apple Dumplings with Orange Hard Sauce,
    '88 224
Beef Stew with Dumplings, '84 3
Biscuit Dumplings and Chicken, '99 326
Blackberries and Dumplings, '86 196
Blackberry Dumplings, '97 253
Cheddar Dumplings, Chicken Ragoût with, '94 44
Chicken and Dumplings, '97 208; '00 111; '01 231;
    '03 25
Chicken and Dumplings, Country, '85 254
Chicken and Dumplings, Easy, '86 21
Chicken and Dumplings, Old-Fashioned, '79 55;
    '83 228; '93 302
Chicken and Dumplings, Quick, '95 125; '02 16
Chicken and Dumplings with Herbed Broth,
    '95 338
Chicken and Dumplings with Vegetables, '85 M56
Chicken Dumpling Pie, '96 55
Chicken 'n' Dumplings, Quick-and-Spicy, '03 325
Chicken Stew and Dumplings, '84 4
Cilantro-Cornmeal Dumplings, Bean Ragout with,
    '97 209
Cornbread Dressing Dumpling Dough, '03 239
Cornbread Dressing Dumplings, Turkey Soup with,
    '03 239
Cornmeal Dumplings, Turnip Greens with, '82 211
Drop Dumplings, Burgundy Stew with, '83 125
Fruit Dumplings, Delicious, '97 210
Gnocchi à la Narciso, '97 246
Gnocchi with Olive Oil, Tomato, and Parmesan, '04 47
Goat Cheese Dumplings, '99 70
Green Peas and Dumplings, '80 102
Old-Fashioned Dumplings, '81 191
Parsley Dumplings, Beef Stew with, '81 76; '82 13;
    '85 M246
Peach Dumplings, '80 143; '85 177; '96 172
Pear Dumplings, '97 210
Pie, Chicken Dumpling, '00 336
Pork Dumplings, Make-Ahead, '03 64
Potato Dumplings, Chicken and, '99 326
Potato Dumplings, Venison Stew with, '87 304
Pot Roast with Dumplings, '98 245
Sesame Dumplings, Steamed, '97 208
Shrimp with Dumplings, Stewed, '79 31
Spinach and Dumplings, '00 85
Strawberry Sauce with Dumplings, '84 314
Tomato Dumplings, '88 144; '97 209
Tortilla Dumplings, Chicken and, '99 327

EGGNOG
    Beverages
        Blender Eggnog, '93 341

EGGNOG, Beverages
(continued)

Breakfast Nog, Speedy, '82 47
Christmas Eggnog, '87 242
Cider Nog, Hot, '98 241
Cider Nog, Hot Apple, '84 42
Coconut Nog, '83 275
Coffee Nog, Brandied, '86 329
Cooked Custard Eggnog, '91 305
Creamy Eggnog, '80 259; '83 303; '85 300
Creamy Eggnog, Aunt Kat's, '01 287
Easy Eggnog, '91 305
Edenton Eggnog, '84 251
Eggnog, '83 318
Egg Nog, '00 274
Holiday Brew, '81 265
Holiday Eggnog Deluxe, '79 232
Hot Chocolate Nog, '02 297
Irish Coffee Nog, '84 258; '93 340
Irish Cream Nog, '82 312
Mock Eggnog with Orange and Nutmeg,
    '92 323
Orange Spiced Nog, '82 48
Punch, Coffee-Eggnog, '86 281
Punch, Coffee Eggnog, '92 264
Punch, Creamy Nog, '01 240
Punch, Eggnog-Coffee, '02 297
Punch, Holiday Eggnog, '86 281
Punch, Irish Coffee-Eggnog, '95 314
Punch, Peppermint-Eggnog, '90 273
Sparkling Eggnog, '79 232
Thick and Creamy Eggnog, '80 261
Bread, Eggnog, '83 294
Cake, Eggnog-Pecan Pound, '95 313
Cake, Eggnog Pound, '90 253
Casserole, Sweet Potato-Eggnog, '95 291
Cookies, Eggnog Christmas, '79 255
Dessert, Eggnog, '95 314
French Toast, Eggnog, '95 313
Parfait, Eggnog Bavarian, '79 255
Pie, Eggnog, '80 254; '83 205; '86 317; '87 295
Pie, Eggnog Chiffon, '86 281
Pie, Fluffy Eggnog, '81 M269
Salad, Eggnog Christmas, '86 281
Tarts, Creamy Eggnog, '79 255

EGGPLANT
Almonds, Eggplant with, '79 179
Appetizer, Eggplant, '83 187
Appetizer, Grilled Eggplant, '95 198
Balsamic-Flavored Eggplant, '95 342
Barbecue Eggplant, '02 180
Biscuit Cakes, Tomato-Eggplant, '95 170
Cakes, Eggplant, '95 196
Caponata, '87 166; '98 50
Caponata alla Siciliana, '02 269
Caponata, Sicilian-Style, '01 124
Casseroles
    Bake, Eggplant, '80 82
    Cakes, Eggplant, '95 196
    Chiles Rellenos, Eggplant, '91 86
    Creole Eggplant, '86 110
    Crêpes with Marinara Sauce, Mini Eggplant,
        '99 266
    Easy Eggplant Casserole, '80 202
    Eggplant Casserole, '81 205; '84 217; '93 44;
        '94 214
    Elegant Eggplant Casserole, '82 168
    Flavorful Eggplant Casserole, '79 92
    Frittata, Fresh Vegetable, '93 140
    Heavenly Eggplant, '93 293
    Italian Eggplant, '84 216
    Italian-Style Eggplant and Zucchini, '79 289; '80 26

Lebanese Eggplant, '81 24
Mexican Eggplant, '83 187
Moussaka, '87 166; '90 68; '97 94
Moussaka Casserole, '79 179
Moussaka, Potatoes, '93 44
Noodle Casserole, Eggplant and, '82 230
Oyster Louisiane, Eggplant-and-, '95 196
Parmesan, Eggplant, '82 230; '83 186; '84 215;
    '86 53; '92 18; '95 84; '01 53
Parmesan, No-Fry Eggplant, '92 172
Parmesan with Feta, Eggplant, '03 174
Parmigiana, Chicken-Eggplant, '82 212
Parmigiana, Eggplant, '81 19; '82 186; '95 197;
    '01 310
Potato-Eggplant Casserole, '87 166
Sausage Bake, Eggplant-, '85 221
Sausage Casserole, Eggplant-, '84 215
Sausage-Pasta Casserole, Freezer Eggplant-,
    '95 197
Scalloped Eggplant, '91 223
Spanish Eggplant, '79 21
Spicy Hot Eggplant Casserole, '93 92
Spinach Casserole, Eggplant-, '99 217
Stuffed Eggplant, Spinach-and-Basil, '02 147
Super Eggplant Casserole, '80 202
Supreme, Eggplant, '79 188; '86 170
Tomato Casserole, Eggplant-and-, '83 187
Caviar, Eggplant, '88 262; '99 217
Caviar, Homemade Cowboy, '94 64
Caviar with Tapenade, Eggplant, '92 194
Crawfish on Eggplant, Soft-Shell, '88 222
Creole, Eggplant, '82 107; '83 86; '86 110
Dip, Eggplant, '96 275
Dressing, Eggplant, '90 236
Easy Eggplant, '87 M151
French-Fried Eggplant, '81 204
Fried Eggplant, '79 178; '83 187; '88 111; '03 158
Fried Eggplant, Cheesy, '90 75
Fried Eggplant, Oven-, '91 187
Fried Eggplant, Parmesan, '79 189
Fried Parmesan Eggplant, '87 166
Fritters, Eggplant, '91 211; '05 128
Georgian Eggplant with Walnuts, '01 87
Gravy, Roast Duck with Sweet Potato-Eggplant,
    '83 90
Grilled Eggplant, '80 202; '89 174
Grilled Eggplant, Sage-, '96 269
Italiano, Eggplant, '91 212
Italian Style, Eggplant, '01 111
Jackstraw Eggplant, '82 230
Julienne, Eggplant, '85 221
Main Dish, Sausage-Eggplant, '80 211
Medley, Eggplant-Shrimp, '79 188
Mexicano, Eggplant à la, '82 229
Parmigiana, Eggplant, '01 310
Patties, Eggplant, '83 186
Pizza, Eggplant, '85 221
Pizza, Garden Eggplant, '05 127
Pizza, Greek Eggplant, Tomato, and Feta, '01 312
Pizzas, Eggplant, '98 183
Provençal, Eggplant, '92 82
Ratatouille, Eggplant-Zucchini, '81 205
Relish, Eggplant, '95 342
Salad, Eggplant, '90 99
Sandwiches, Baked Eggplant, '82 230
Sandwiches, Eggplant, '99 240
Sandwiches, Eggplant Parmesan, '03 213
Sandwiches, Eggplant, Tomato, and Feta, '98 106
Sandwiches, Open-Face Eggplant, '95 124
Sautéed Eggplant and Zucchini, '82 96
Sauté, Eggplant, '96 135
Slices, Quick Eggplant, '90 75
Soup, Eggplant Supper, '85 221
Soup, Herbed Eggplant, '90 173

Spaghetti Squash with Sesame Eggplant, '92 252
Spicy Eggplant, '99 217
Spicy Oriental Eggplant, '96 130
Spread, Eggplant, '86 278
Spread, Eggplant-Mushroom, '92 156
Squash, Eggplant and, '83 187
Stacks, Eggplant, '91 211
Sticks, Ned's Eggplant, '95 309
Stuffed
    à la Creole, Eggplant, '96 177
    Baked Stuffed Eggplant, '81 133
    Beefy Stuffed Eggplant, '81 204
    Cheesy Stuffed Eggplant, '79 188; '82 208
    Creole Stuffed Eggplant, '82 230
    Eggplant, Stuffed, '80 158
    Ham-Stuffed Eggplant, '80 162
    Italian-Stuffed Eggplant, '90 74
    Mushroom-Stuffed Eggplant, '83 136
    Ratatouille-Bran Stuffed Eggplant, '86 44
    Ratatouille-Stuffed Eggplant, '83 187
    Rolled Stuffed Eggplant, '80 63
    Sausage Stuffed Eggplant, '81 204
    Sausage-Stuffed Eggplant, '91 211
    Seafood Stuffed Eggplant, '79 187
    Shrimp-Stuffed Eggplant, '92 99
Supper, Beef-and-Eggplant, '84 291
Tophats, Eggplant, '79 188
Vinaigrette, Italian Eggplant, '03 125
Zaalouk, Eggplant, '98 210
EGGS. *See also* **QUICHES, SOUFFLÉS.**
Armadillo Eggs, '97 270; '05 139
Baked Egg Crisps, '83 57
Baked Eggs Florentine, '86 M12
Baked Eggs in Spinach Nests, '82 70
Baked in Mushroom Sauce, Eggs, '93 47
Bake, Egg and Rice, '83 119
Bedeviled Eggs, '86 67
Benedict, Bacon-and-Tomato Eggs, '87 195
Benedict, Country Ham Eggs, '03 52
Benedict, Easy Eggs, '80 M268
Benedict, Eggs, '79 40, 254; '85 49; '98 55
Benedict, Light Eggs, '93 M68
Benedict, Lion, '93 121
Benedict, Shrimp-and-Grits Eggs, '03 53
Benedict, Southwest Eggs, '03 53
Benedict, Traditional Eggs, '03 52
Benedict with Cheese Sauce, Eggs, '81 225
Brandied Cream Sauce, Eggs in, '82 70
Bread, Butter-Egg, '85 269
Bread, County Fair Egg, '87 68
Bread, Easter Egg, '84 94; '96 88
Breakfast Eye-Openers, '82 231
Breakfast, Farmer's, '81 44
Breakfast, Mexican, '00 194
Brunch Eggs, '85 44
Brunch, Texas, '82 70
Bunwiches, '80 92
Burritos, Brunch, '91 77
Burritos, Potato-and-Egg, '02 72
Burritos, Tex-Mex Egg, '95 34
Casseroles
    Apple-Egg Casserole, '85 44
    Bacon and Egg Casserole, '81 225
    Bacon-and-Egg Casserole, '03 166
    Bacon-and-Ham Casserole, Cheesy, '01 256
    Bacon Casserole, Egg-and-, '85 248
    Bel-Mar, Eggs, '90 92
    Breakfast Bake, '85 45
    Breakfast Casserole, '01 130, 243
    Breakfast Casserole, Hearty Healthy, '05 325
    Broccoli-and-Egg Casserole, '86 324
    Broccoli-and-Eggs au Gratin, '85 289
    Brunch Casserole, Southwestern, '03 197
    Brunch Casserole with Creole Sauce, '98 98

Brunch Egg Casserole, '86 329
Brunch Eggs, '98 93
Bruncheon Eggs, '83 83
Campfire Casserole, '00 173
Cheese-and-Egg Casserole, '99 268
Cheese Casserole, Egg-and-, '84 293
Cheese-Egg-Zucchini Casserole, '84 114
Cheesy Egg Casserole, '81 244; '86 15
Chile Eggs, '88 80
Crab-Egg Casserole, '80 260
Creole Eggs, '82 42
Egg Casserole, '83 311; '98 98
Frittata, Fresh Vegetable, '93 140
Ham and Egg Casserole, Breakfast, '79 253
Layered Eggs, '96 97
Mushroom Casserole, Egg-, '83 49
Potato-Egg Casserole, Cheesy, '84 5
Potatoes and Eggs au Gratin, '79 107
Sausage-and-Egg Casserole, '94 284
Sausage Breakfast Casserole, '81 270
Sausage Egg Bake, '81 225
Sausage-Egg Bake, Smoked, '85 248
Sausage-Egg Casserole, '86 M12
Scrambled Egg Casserole, '80 51; '86 241
Scrambled Egg Casserole, Saucy, '89 213
Soufflé Casserole, Egg, '83 55
Spinach and Egg Casserole, '82 270
Squash and Egg Casserole, '80 146
Strata, Cheese-Rice, '81 176
Strata, English Muffin Breakfast, '03 100
Strata, Sausage, '84 101
Strata, Tomato-Bacon, '03 100
Strata, Tomato-Cheese, '81 209
Strata, Turkey-Cheddar-Broccoli, '03 100
Sunday Egg Casserole, '95 100
Zucchini-Egg Casserole, '84 M113
Cheddar Eggs, '94 M141
Cheese, Eggs and, '95 165
Cottage Eggs, '85 44
Crabmeat and Eggs New Orleans, '82 45
Creamed Eggs à la Asparagus, '81 201
Creamed Eggs, Broccoli and, '83 84
Creamed Eggs in Patty Shells, '80 M267
Creamed Eggs in Toast Cups, '83 83
Creole, Eggs, '92 86
Creole, Skillet Eggs, '85 143
Crêpes, Ham-and-Egg, '83 204
Crêpes with Mushroom Sauce, Ham-and-Egg, '82 46
Croissant Eggwiches, '91 160
Croquettes, Tuna-Egg, '80 275
Delight, Bacon-and-Egg, '85 143
Delight, Crab-and-Egg, '84 261
Delight, Mushroom-Egg, '83 14
Deviled Eggs. See EGGS/Stuffed.
Dip, Festive Egg, '79 285
Dressing, Egg, '86 79
Eagle Nest Egg, '99 194
Featherbed Eggs, '93 122
Florentine, Eggs, '79 39; '83 56
Florentine-Style Eggs, '82 38
Foo Yong, Egg, '80 19; '86 232
Foo Yong Noodles, Egg, '98 233
Foo Yong Patties, '80 223
Foo Yong, Shrimp Egg, '83 22
Frittata, Avocado-and-Black Bean, '02 212
Frittata, Bacon-and-Asparagus, '98 136
Frittata, Bell Pepper, '96 204
Frittata, Broccoli-Cheese, '81 243
Frittata, Corn-and-Squash, '89 144
Frittata, Firecracker Pasta, '94 230
Frittata, Ham-and-Broccoli, '98 101
Frittata, Potato, '89 145
Frittata, Potato-Bacon, '95 269; '98 330

Frittata, Spinach, '81 53
Frittata, Vegetable, '92 48; '93 183
Garden District Eggs, '04 66
Ham and Eggs à la Swiss, '88 158
Ham and Eggs, Creamed, '82 40
Ham and Eggs, Creamy, '87 286
Ham and Eggs on Toast with Cheese Sauce, '81 43
Ham and Eggs, Savory, '82 231
Hard-Cooked Eggs (garnish), '82 280
Hash Brown Skillet Breakfast, '82 5
Herb Sauce, Eggs in, '88 80
Hominy, Bacon, Eggs, and, '85 143
Huevos con Queso, '00 123
Huevos Rancheros, '82 197; '91 77; '02 72
Huevos Rancheros, Spicy, '05 221
Medley, Cheddary Egg, '81 M176
Mexicana, Eggs, '82 146
Mornay, Ham and Eggs, '02 130
Mound, Frosted Egg, '79 33
Muffin, Stuffin', '99 193
Mushroom Eggs, Sherried, '83 49
Mushrooms and Eggs in Patty Shells, '85 143; '88 197
Mushrooms and Eggs, Saucy, '79 138
Nests, Fluffy Egg, '79 128
Omelets
    Apple Omelet Stack, '94 50
    Bacon-and-Potato Omelet, Open-Faced, '02 246
    Baked Omelets, '94 50
    Biscuits, Deluxe Omelet, '98 101
    Broccoli-Mushroom Omelet, '85 45
    Cheese Omelet, Herbed, '93 47
    Cheese Omelet, Puffed, '89 227
    Cheese Omelet, Zippy, '87 287
    Cheese-Shiitake Omelet, Golden, '95 265
    Cheesy Picante Omelet, '86 95
    Chicken Liver Omelet, '82 44
    Country Omelets, '91 128
    Creole Sauce, Omelets with, '89 228
    Dessert Omelet, Puffy, '00 35
    Dill-Cheese-Ham Omelet, '95 33
    Fines Herbes, Omelette aux, '92 82
    Fluffy Omelet, '84 56
    George's Omelets, '80 68
    Ham and Cheese Omelet, '79 262; '80 123
    Ham-and-Cheese Omelet, '02 246
    Indian Omelet, '99 92
    Italian Omelet, '92 47
    Mexican Omelet, '79 128; '81 225
    Mexican Omelet, Easy, '88 114
    Mushroom Omelet, Rolled, '82 70
    Mushroom Sauce, Puffy Omelets with, '85 40
    Olé Omelet, '87 M124
    Olé, Omelet, '94 31
    Oven-Baked Omelet, Farmer's, '03 204
    Oyster Omelets, Smoked, '84 96
    Potato Omelet, Family-Size, '94 31
    Potato-Sprout Omelet, '79 128
    Primavera, Omelet, '87 71
    Rising Sun Omelet, '82 281; '83 42
    Rolled Omelet, '89 228
    Sandwich, Omelet, '86 95
    Sausage Filling, Omelet with, '81 43
    Sausage Omelet, Puffy, '80 M268
    Shrimp-and-Cheddar Omelet, '84 57
    Shrimp-and-Cheese Omelet, '94 31
    Shrimp-and-Vegetable Oven Omelet, '99 286
    Sour Cream-Ham Omelet, '79 261
    Spanish Omelet, '81 201; '83 243; '84 101; '00 35
    Spanish Omelet with Fresh Avocado Salsa, '02 247
    Spanish-Style Omelets, '83 188
    Spinach, Cheddar, and Bacon Omelet, '03 204
    Spinach-Cheese Omelet, '83 119
    Strawberry-Sour Cream Omelet, '89 229

    Sunrise Omelet, '83 289
    Swiss Oven Omelet, '80 189
    Tarragon Omelet, '89 144
    Tex-Mex Omelet con Carne, '81 209
    Vegetable Omelet, Beefy, '83 188
    Vegetable Omelet, Cheddar-, '83 205
    Vegetable Omelet, Cheesy, '85 49
    Vegetable Omelet, Fresh, '84 211
    Vegetable Omelet, Golden, '82 M123
    Vegetable Omelet, Puffy, '83 188
    Vegetable-Pasta Oven Omelet, '99 286
    Vegetarian Omelet, '84 114
    Veggie Omelet, Creamy, '02 248
    White Wine Omelet, '79 103
    Yogurt-Avocado Omelet, '81 33
    Zucchini Omelet, '81 99
Oso Grande, Eggs, '98 279
Paint, Egg Yolk, '86 322
Peanut Butter Easter Eggs, '87 86
Pickled Eggs, Beet, '84 287
Pickled Eggs, Rosy, '86 68
Pickled Eggs, Spiced, '84 288
Pie, Country Breakfast, '93 M328
Pie, Egg Custard, '99 82
Pie, Egg-Stra Special Chicken, '86 264
Pie, Old-Fashioned Egg Custard, '82 261
Pillows, Egg, '92 332
Pizza, Breakfast, '85 44
Pizza, Ham-and-Eggs Crescent, '93 47
Poached Eggs, '92 87, 93; '93 121; '03 53
Poached Eggs, Basic, '82 58
Poached Eggs, Easy, '03 70
Poached Eggs, French-Style, '82 58
Poached Eggs, Microwave, '02 M131
Potatoes with Eggs and Meat, '91 311; '92 25
Potato Nests, Mashed, '94 141
Pot Pie, Chicken-and-Egg, '00 98
Puff, Egg-and-Cheese, '85 45
Quesadillas, Bacon-and-Egg, '05 88
Rancheros, Easy Eggs, '88 81
Rice, Egg Fried, '79 252; '80 19
Roll-Ups, Spicy Egg, '90 140
Roulade with Mushroom Filling, Egg, '88 84
Salads
    Asparagus-and-Egg Salad, '86 305
    Bacon-Horseradish Egg Salad, '94 181
    Club, Shrimp-Egg Salad, '02 203
    Club, Sweet-Pickle Egg Salad, '02 203
    Deviled Egg Salad, '83 124
    Egg Salad, '05 209
    Ham-and-Egg Potato Salad, '86 84
    Ham 'n Egg Salad, '81 36
    Rice Salad, Egg-, '84 18; '86 169
    Sandwiches, Egg Salad, '03 179
    Sandwiches, Egg Salad Club, '02 203
    Shrimp-and-Egg Salad Sandwiches, '94 182
    Shrimp-Egg Salad, Tossed, '80 4
    Smoked Salmon-and-Egg Salad, '02 203
    Spread, Cottage-Egg Salad, '82 146
    Spread, Egg Salad, '86 127
    Tacos, Mexican Egg Salad, '94 181
    Tuna-Egg Salad, '81 135
    Vegetable and Egg Salad, Green, '79 191
    Yolkless Egg Salad, '94 181
Sandwiches, BLT Breakfast, '04 171
Sandwiches, Breakfast, '82 M123; '89 M230
Sandwiches, Confetti, '79 236
Sandwiches, Eggsclusive, '79 164; '80 130
Sandwiches, Eggs-Tra Special, '81 240; '83 69
Sandwiches, Open-Faced Cheesy Egg, '86 67
Sandwiches, Open-Face Egg, '83 292; '84 78; '86 160
Sandwiches, Saucy Egg, '91 160
Sardou, Eggs, '92 93

Saucy Eggs, **'83** 84
Saucy Eggs on Toast, **'81** 209
Sauté, Vegetable-Egg, **'96** 204
Scotch Eggs, **'79** 261; **'83** 289; **'98** 101
Scrambled
  Bacon-and-Eggs Scramble, **'80** M267
  Buttermilk Scrambled Eggs, **'79** 72
  Casserole, Saucy Scrambled Egg, **'89** 213
  Casserole, Scrambled Egg, **'80** 51; **'86** 241
  Cheese-Chive Scrambled Eggs, **'95** 34
  Cottage Cheese Scrambled Eggs, **'81** 142
  Cottage-Scrambled Eggs, **'80** 49
  Country Eggs, **'86** 330
  Country-Style Scrambled Eggs, **'79** 22
  Crabmeat Brunch Scramble, **'95** 32
  Cream Cheese Scrambled Eggs, **'81** 287;
   '05 26
  Creamy Scrambled Eggs, **'90** 82
  Empanadas, Bacon 'n' Egg Breakfast, **'02** 324
  Enchiladas, Scrambled Egg, **'97** 153
  Home-Style Scrambled Eggs, **'84** 66
  Mexican-Style Scrambled Eggs, **'85** 50
  Migas, **'87** 180; **'94** 26; **'98** 312
  Onion Scrambled Eggs, Creamy, **'83** M203
  Pizza, Sausage-and-Scrambled Egg, **'05** 88
  Shrimp and Crab Scrambled Eggs, **'79** 261
  Sonora, Eggs, **'80** 196
  Spanish Scrambled Eggs, **'83** 49; **'84** 60
  Special Scrambled Eggs, **'81** 103
  Supreme, Scrambled Eggs, **'79** 39
  Tacos, Sausage-Egg Soft, **'05** 26
  Tostadas, Scrambled Egg, **'86** 95
  Veggie Scramble, **'01** 288
  Wild Rice, Scrambled Eggs with, **'80** 42
Soufflés, Little Egg, **'83** 57
Soufflé, Three-Egg Cheese, **'87** 234
Soup, Egg Drop, **'83** 21; **'86** 16
Soup, Egg-Drop, **'85** M12
Soup, Egg Flower, **'81** 307; **'82** 313; **'83** 65
Soup, Egg-Lemon, **'96** 88
Soup, Lemon-Egg Drop, **'93** 81
Soup, Spinach Egg Drop, **'03** 65
Spread, Cottage-Egg Salad, **'82** 146
Spread, Egg Salad, **'86** 127
Spread, Egg, Sour Cream, and Caviar, **'85** 279
Spread, Ham-and-Egg, **'79** 59
Spread, Vegetable-Egg, **'87** 106
Stuffed
  Bacon-Stuffed Eggs, **'97** 52; **'00** 70; **'04** 290
  Black-and-Blue Eggs, **'96** 90
  Blue Cheese Stuffed Eggs, **'93** 87
  Chicken-Stuffed Eggs, **'98** 102
  Crabmeat, Eggs Stuffed with, **'04** 18
  Creamed Eggs, **'86** 67
  Creamy Stuffed Eggs, **'84** 143
  Crunchy Stuffed Eggs, **'86** 67
  Deluxe, Eggs, **'82** 79
  Deviled Eggs, **'86** 176; **'94** 161; **'01** 299
  Deviled Eggs, Bacon, **'86** 136
  Deviled Eggs, Barbecue, **'05** 167
  Deviled Eggs, Basic, **'03** 88
  Deviled Eggs, Best, **'80** 159
  Deviled Eggs, Buttery Dijon, **'05** 93
  Deviled Eggs, Chile-Cheese, **'93** 87
  Deviled Eggs, Chive-Tarragon, **'05** 93
  Deviled Eggs, Creamed, **'82** 79
  Deviled Eggs, Curried, **'93** 87
  Deviled Eggs, Easy, **'82** 127
  Deviled Eggs, Mexican, **'04** 93
  Deviled Eggs, Nippy, **'80** 217

Deviled Eggs, Pimiento-, **'84** 143
Deviled Eggs, Saucy, **'82** 80
Deviled Eggs Surprise, **'79** 83
Deviled Eggs, Sweet, **'93** 88
Deviled Eggs, Tex-Mex, **'97** 247
Deviled Eggs with Capers, **'05** 93
Deviled Eggs with Smoked Oysters, **'84** 161
Deviled Eggs, Zesty, **'84** 205
Deviled Green Goblin Eggs, **'02** 222
Devil's Island Eggs, **'82** 79
Double-Stuffed Eggs, **'00** 70
Eggs, Stuffed, **'80** 155; **'88** 95
Garlic-Cheese-Stuffed Eggs, Marbleized, **'96** 91
Green Eggs and Ham, **'96** 90
Ham Devils, **'93** 88
Herb-Sour Cream Stuffed Eggs, **'93** 87
Mustard Eggs, Spicy, **'84** 143
Pecan-Stuffed Deviled Eggs, **'04** 93
Pecan-Stuffed Eggs, **'80** 78
Shrimp-Curried Eggs, Saucy, **'84** 143
Shrimp-Stuffed Eggs, **'00** 70
Spicy-Sweet Deviled Eggs, **'04** 198
Spinach-and-Bacon Eggs, Double Stuffed,
  '00 M333
Stuffed Eggs, Easy, **'93** 87
Tomato Slices, Stuffed Eggs-and-, **'84** 152
Tuna-Stuffed Eggs, **'83** 83
Substitute, Homemade Egg, **'92** 47
Sunny-Side-Up Eggs, **'79** 38
Tacos, Breakfast, **'80** 43
Tamales, Breakfast, **'00** 122
Tomatoes, Bacon-and-Egg-Stuffed, **'80** 162
Tortilla, Potato, **'00** 85
Tortillas, Chorizo and Egg, **'81** 193
Tortillas, Egg-and-Sausage, **'83** 246; **'84** 42
Tulsa Eggs, **'87** 95

ENCHILADAS
American Enchiladas, **'81** 170
Apple Enchiladas, **'99** 63
Bean Enchiladas, Spicy, **'88** 18
Bean Enchiladas, Three-, **'91** 133
Black Bean-Chicken-Spinach Enchiladas, **'05** 95
Black Bean 'n' Spinach Enchiladas, **'05** 95
Breakfast Enchiladas, **'04** 281; **'05** 333
Casserole, Easy Enchilada, **'02** 143
Casserole, Enchilada, **'87** 287
Casserole, Firecracker Enchilada, **'80** 260
Casserole, Green Enchilada, **'79** 76
Casserole, Lightened Texas-Style Enchilada,
  '05 247
Casserole, Sour Cream Enchilada, **'82** 113
Casserole, Texas-Style Enchilada, **'05** 247
Cheese Enchiladas, **'81** 194; **'85** 154; **'95** 311
Cheese Enchiladas, Saucy, **'84** 220
Chicken-and-Cheese Enchiladas, Baked, **'03** 332
Chicken-and-Spinach Enchiladas, **'91** 222
Chicken-Cheese Enchiladas, **'02** 236
Chicken-Chile Enchiladas, **'97** 313
Chicken Enchiladas, **'80** 301; **'86** 296; **'90** 121; **'00** 45;
  '03 214; **'04** 96
Chicken Enchiladas, Creamy, **'97** 250;
  '01 M94
Chicken Enchiladas, Easy, **'82** 89; **'86** 231
Chicken Enchiladas, Healthy, **'02** 19
Chicken Enchiladas, Quicker, **'97** 312
Chicken Enchiladas, Three-Cheese, **'99** 330
Chicken Enchiladas Verde, **'93** 274; **'00** M240
Chicken Enchiladas with Spicy Sauce, **'84** 76
Chicken Enchiladas with Tomatillo Sauce,
  '94 231; **'95** 206
Chicken-Sour Cream Enchiladas, **'04** 274
Chili and Enchiladas, **'00** 55
Creamy Enchiladas, **'93** 174
Dove Enchiladas, **'85** 270

Duck Enchiladas with Red Pepper-Sour Cream,
  Smoked, **'87** 121
Egg Enchiladas, Scrambled, **'97** 153
Enticing Enchiladas, **'99** 57
Green Chile Enchiladas, **'02** 188
Green Chile-Sour Cream Enchiladas,
  '84 234
Hot and Saucy Enchiladas, **'81** 141; **'82** 6
Meatless Enchiladas, **'93** 106
New Mexican Flat Enchiladas, **'85** 244
Pie, Enchilada, **'83** 155
Poblano-Shrimp Enchiladas, **'00** 311
Pork Enchiladas, **'97** M94
Quicker Enchiladas, **'96** 103
Sauce, Enchilada, **'81** 194
Sauce, Red Chile Enchilada, **'85** 245
Shrimp Enchiladas, **'01** 104
Shrimp Enchiladas in Tomatillo Sauce,
  '95 310
Skillet Enchiladas, **'82** 89
Smothered Enchiladas, **'05** 59
Soup, Chicken Enchilada, **'86** 22
Soup, Shrimp Enchilada, **'94** 103
Sour Cream Enchiladas, **'83** 200; **'87** 37
Sour Cream Enchiladas, Cheesy, **'79** 25
Spinach Enchiladas, **'83** 60; **'84** 14
Terrificas, Enchiladas, **'84** 32
Weeknight Enchiladas, **'93** 63
ESCARGOTS
Provençal, Escargots, **'82** 238; **'83** 156
ESCAROLE. *See* **GREENS.**

FAJITAS
Beef and Chicken Fajitas, **'02** 119
Beef Fajitas, **'88** 233
Beef Fajita Salad, **'91** 70
Beef Fajitas with Pico de Gallo, **'04** 61
Casserole, Fajita, **'97** 96
Chicken Fajita Pizza, **'03** 235
Chicken Fajitas, **'88** 231; **'89** 100; **'90** 204;
  '99 158
Chicken Fajita Spuds, **'96** 238
Chicken Fajita Spuds with Black Bean Salsa,
  '04 25
Crêpes, Fajita, **'94** 116
Fajitas, **'84** 233
Favorite Fajitas, **'86** 114
Fettuccine, Fajita, **'94** 84
Java Fajitas, **'96** 227
Pico de Gallo, Fajitas with, **'98** 87
Pita, Fajita in a, **'90** 177
Pitas, Fajita, **'99** 239
Plum Good Fajitas, **'94** 115
Pork Fajitas, Pronto, **'05** 223
Slow Cooker Fajitas, **'02** 43
Tex-Mex Fajitas, **'01** 188
Turkey Fajitas, **'01** 108
Vietnamese Fajitas (Bo Nuong Xa), **'05** 117
FETTUCCINE
Alfredo, Fettuccine, **'80** 236; **'86** 158
Alfredo, Southwestern Fettuccine, **'05** 186
Blue Cheese Noodles, **'98** 290
Blue Cheese Sauce, Fettuccine with, **'98** 247
Broccoli and Sausage, Pasta with, **'97** 266
Broccoli, Fettuccine with, **'90** 97
Broccoli-Parmesan Fettuccine, **'93** 55
Chicken-and-Creamy Herb Sauce, Fettuccine with,
  '01 257
Chicken and Dried Tomatoes over Fettuccine,
  '98 233
Chicken and Pasta, Pesto, **'89** M132
Chicken-and-Tomatoes over Fettuccine, **'90** 204
Chicken-Artichoke Pasta with Rosemary, **'98** 15
Chicken Fettuccine Alfredo, **'00** 57

Chicken Fettuccine, Cajun, '96 198
Chicken Pasta with Artichokes and Capers, '04 129
Chicken-Pecan Fettuccine, '86 52
Chicken with Pasta, Dijon, '90 318
Cordon Bleu, Pasta, '97 327
Crab Fettuccine, '98 142
Crawfish and Tasso Fettuccine, '96 290
Crawfish Fettuccine, '96 98
Creamy Fettuccine, '92 283; '96 136
Eggplant Sauté, '96 135
Fajita Fettuccine, '94 84
Greens, Pasta with, '95 211
Ham-and-Asparagus Fettuccine, '94 84
Parsley, Fettuccine with, '83 115
Peas and Pasta, '93 139
Pepper Pasta, '89 321
Poppy Seeds, Fettuccine with, '91 48
Portobello-Alfredo Sauce, Fettuccine with, '04 135
Primavera, Fettuccine, '89 238; '94 85
Primavera, Fettuccini, '04 64
Prosciutto, Party Pasta with, '94 176
Ranch House Fettuccine, '03 123
Salmon Fettuccine, '90 123
Scallop-Mushroom Fettuccine, '96 198
Seafood Pasta, Herbed, '04 255
Shrimp and Andouille Alfredo Sauce Over Pasta, Cajun, '05 57
Shrimp-and-Creamy Herb Sauce, Fettuccine with, '01 257
Shrimp and Tomatoes, Fettuccine with, '96 198
Shrimp Elégante, '83 48
Shrimp Fettuccine, '94 84; '96 210
Shrimp-Herb Fettuccine, '01 308
Shrimp-Tomato Pasta, '98 172
Shrimp with Dried Tomato Pesto, Fettuccine and, '94 249
Shrimp with Fettuccine, Dilled, '99 141
Spinach Alfredo Fettuccine, '01 164
Spinach Fettuccine, '82 179
Spinach, Fettuccine and, '88 90
Spinach Fettuccine, Creamy Basil Chicken with, '97 328
Spinach Fettuccine, Easy Chicken with, '88 89
Spinach Fettuccine, Fresh, '83 60
Spinach Fettuccine with Mustard Greens, '94 247
Spinach Sauce, Fettuccine with, '84 329
Supreme, Fettuccine, '83 288; '86 333
Tetrazzini, Smoked Turkey, '02 286
Thai-Style Noodles with Peanut Basil Sauce, '98 133
Tomato-Olive Pasta Toss, '86 209
Vegetable Fettuccine, '83 312
Vegetables, Fettuccine and, '97 178
Vegetables, Noodles with Spring, '02 125

FIGS
Baked Fig Bites, '02 160
Cake, Fig, '79 32; '99 314; '02 166
Cake, Fig Preserve, '79 140; '84 316
Cake, Fig Preserves, '89 335
Cobbler, Cajun Fig, '94 196
Cobbler, Fig, '79 140
Cobbler, Fig-and-Raspberry, '02 160
Cobbler, Super Fig, '86 206
Coffee Cake, Easy Fig, '80 116
Compote, Grilled Chicken Breasts with Fig-and-Melon, '00 163
Flowers, Fig, '96 195
Ice Cream, Fig, '87 139
Ice Cream, No-Cook Fig-Mint, '04 179
Jam, Fig, '86 206
Marinated Grilled Figs, '96 194
Muffins, Fig, '86 206
Pickled Figs, '79 140
Pies with Fruit Salsa, Lone Star Fried, '97 124

Pork Loin, Fig-Balsamic Roasted, '03 45
Preserves, Fig, '79 140; '82 150; '89 140; '96 195; '00 175
Preserves, Quick Strawberry-Fig, '96 194
Preserves, Rosemary Cheese with Fig, '02 256
Prosciutto, Walnuts, and Cream, Figs with, '96 194
Pudding, Fig-Walnut, '03 244
Sauce, Fig, '79 140
Snacks, Sliced Fig, '86 206
Strudel, Fig, '98 253
Sugar-Crusted Figs, '96 195

FILLINGS
Savory
Baria, '97 91
Beef Filling, '80 81
Broccoli Filling, '81 44
Chicken Divan Filling, '81 91
Chicken Filling, '81 200; '05 117
Chicken Filling, Curried, '88 125
Chicken Filling Luau, '79 81
Chicken-Olive Filling, '81 227
Chicken Salad Filling, '87 106
Crab Filling, '89 13
Crêpe Filling, '96 48
Four Cheese Filling, '97 171
Green Tomato Pie Filling, '01 141
Mushroom Filling, '81 89; '88 84
Omelet Filling, Greek, '80 68
Omelet Filling, Spanish, '80 68
Peanut Filling, '93 211
Pesto, '89 158
Pot Pie Filling, '03 247
Shrimp and Dill Filling, '97 171
Shrimp Filling, '89 320
Shrimp Salad Filling, '87 106
Spinach and Feta Filling, '97 171
Spinach Filling, '95 316
Spinach-Mushroom Filling, '80 215
Spinach-Ricotta Filling, '81 53

Sweet
Almond Cream Filling, '85 320; '91 248
Almond Filling, '87 301; '96 316
Almond Filling, Ground, '87 14
Amaretto Filling, '87 241
Apple-Date Filling, '83 301
Apple Filling, '85 5; '96 53; '97 239
Apple Filling, Dried, '85 242; '87 229
Apricot Filling, '83 84; '86 107; '93 316; '01 330
Blackberry Curd Filling, '05 182
Blintz Filling, '92 84
Butterscotch Filling, '91 271; '02 323
Caramel Filling, '88 278; '03 287
Caramel Whipped Cream Filling, '96 312
Chantilly Crème, '80 280
Cheese-and-Orange Filling, '93 159
Cheese Filling, '89 91
Cherry Filling, '83 302; '84 225; '88 178
Cherry Fried Pie Filling, Dried, '96 109
Chocolate Buttercream, '84 156
Chocolate-Cheese Filling, '90 47
Chocolate-Coffee Buttercream Filling, '00 M287
Chocolate Filling, '96 316; '03 200; '05 M307
Chocolate Filling, Rich, '79 68
Chocolate Midnight Filling, '96 120
Chocolate Truffle Filling, '87 69; '04 M253
Cinnamon-Cheese Filling, '90 46
Cinnamon Roll Filling, '03 247
Citrus Filling, '02 221
Coconut Cream Filling, '84 200
Coconut Filling, '81 265; '00 117; '03 329
Coconut-Pecan Filling, '05 107
Coffee Filling, '96 316
Coffee Pastry Cream, '01 45

Cran-Apple Mousse, '93 255
Cranberry-Ambrosia Filling, '01 271
Cranberry Filling, Nutty, '00 M306
Cranberry-Pecan Filling, '04 305
Cream Cheese Filling, '90 170; '97 287; '04 273; '05 251
Cream Filling, '83 220; '84 37; '87 198; '90 311
Crème Fraîche, '91 99
Custard Filling, '82 52, 298; '85 281
Custard Filling, Creamy, '81 180
Custard Filling, Egg, '87 14
Date Cream Filling, '81 303
Date Filling, '80 15; '83 257; '86 314
Dried Apple Filling, '05 108
Fluffy Filling, '81 192; '86 246
Fluffy White Filling, '90 252
Fruit Filling, '94 245
Fruit Filling, Nutty, '99 306
Fruit Fried Pie Filling, Mixed, '96 109
Fruit-Nut Filling, '80 289
Fudge Filling, '94 292
Grand Marnier Pastry Cream, '01 45
Honey Filling, '88 287
Honey-Walnut Filling, '80 21
Lane Cake Filling, '89 55; '96 144
Lemon-Apricot Filling, '90 105
Lemon-Cheese Filling, '79 68; '88 7; '03 317
Lemon Cream, '91 119
Lemon Cream Filling, '84 23; '87 14
Lemon Filling, '81 172; '84 137; '85 191; '86 235; '87 293; '89 312; '90 308; '94 122; '95 319; '97 255; '99 118
Lemon Filling, Creamy, '80 70
Lemon Icebox Pie Filling, '03 104
Lemon-Orange Filling, '81 71
Lime Icebox Pie Filling, '03 104
Mascarpone Filling, '02 146
Mint-Cream Filling, '96 229
Mocha-Chocolate Cream Filling, '05 322
Mocha Cream Filling, '81 187; '84 305
Mocha Filling, '80 55; '82 262
Napoleon Cream, '84 138
Nut-and-Fruit Filling, '84 263
Nut Filling, '91 35
Orange-Cheese Filling, '90 47
Orange Cream Filling, '99 118
Orange Curd Filling, '96 120
Orange Curd, Fresh, '02 294
Orange Filling, '79 229; '86 336; '87 84; '88 224; '89 287; '96 316
Orange Icebox Pie Filling, '03 104
Orange-Pineapple Fried Pie Filling, '96 109
Pastry Cream, Luscious, '82 304
Peach Filling, '89 154; '90 107; '96 119
Peach Pie Filling, Fresh, '95 195
Peanut Butter Filling, '96 229
Peanut Butter Pastry Cream, '01 45
Pecan Filling, '04 305
Pecan Pie Filling, '98 254; '03 316
Peppermint Filling, '81 119; '89 254
Piña Colada Filling, '99 117
Pineapple Filling, '80 140; '83 179; '84 153; '89 57; '97 277
Praline Buttercream, '95 243
Praline Cream Filling, '03 332
Praline Filling, '89 328
Raisin Filling, '90 86
Raspberry Filling, '90 111
Ricotta Filling, '80 58
Sour Cream-Coconut Filling, '92 120
Strawberry-Lemon Filling, '04 137
Vanilla Pastry Cream, '01 45
Whipped Cream Filling, '90 265, 307; '99 307; '03 319

FILLINGS, Sweet
(continued)

White Chocolate Cream Filling, '92 230
White Chocolate Filling, '89 160
FISH. *See also* **CLAMS, CRAB, CRAWFISH,**
    LOBSTER, OYSTERS, SALMON,
    SCALLOPS, SEAFOOD, SHRIMP, TUNA.
Amandine, Fillet of Fish, '80 M54
Amberjack Sandwiches, Grilled, '91 195
Asparagus Divan, Fish-, '87 128
Baked
    Almond Baked Fish, '88 270; '89 203
    Barbecue Sauce, Baked Fish with, '84 92
    Creamy Baked Fillets, '84 91
    Crunchy Baked Fish Fillets, '85 217
    Fast Fish Bake, '85 218
    Herbed Fish and Potato Bake, '79 287; '80 34
    Lemon-Celery Sauce, Baked Fillets in, '84 91
    Saucy Fish Bake, '79 75
    Southern Baked Fish, '82 73
Beer-Batter Fish, '85 68
Blackened Fish, '05 119
Bluefish Chowder, '84 282
Broiled Fish Fillets Piquante, '84 91
Broiled Herb Fish Fillets, '79 99
Cakes, Fish, '85 54
Catfish
    Amandine, Mandarin Catfish, '84 183
    Amandine, Spicy Catfish, '89 52
    Appetizer, Layered Catfish, '92 209
    Baked Catfish, '94 67
    Baked Catfish, Barbecue, '02 51
    Baked Catfish, Cajun-, '02 218
    Baked Lemon-Dill Catfish, '05 216
    Barbecued Catfish, '80 157
    Barbecued Catfish, Lemon, '88 271; '89 202
    Battered Catfish and Chips, '02 140
    Blackened Catfish, '97 82
    Breaded Catfish with Creole Sauce, '90 28
    Breaded Herbed Fish Fillets, '91 121
    Broiled Manchac, Catfish, Middendorf's, '84 183
    Cakes, Catfish, '94 70
    Cakes, Creole Catfish, '97 82
    Caribbean Catfish with Spicy Island Sweet Potatoes, '04 310
    Cream Cheese Stuffing, Catfish with, '89 52
    Crispy Catfish, '03 101
    Crunchy Catfish, '02 256
    Dip, Layered Catfish, '03 185; '05 55
    Eldorado de Colorado, Catfish, '84 183
    Fingers, Crackermeal Catfish, '89 53
    Fingers with Curried Rice, Crunchy Catfish, '04 20
    Fried Catfish, '82 135; '83 169; '00 172; '04 100
    Fried Catfish, Classic, '97 82; '01 135
    Fried Catfish, Crisp, '82 242
    Fried Catfish, Crisp-, '88 110
    Fried Catfish, Delta-Style, '04 121
    Fried Catfish, Front Porch, '96 233
    Fried Catfish, Front-Porch, '02 166
    Fried Catfish, Golden, '80 99
    Fried Catfish, Jack's, '04 164
    "Fried" Catfish with Lemon Cream, Spicy, '03 212
    Fried Lemon-Rosemary Catfish, '02 319
    Fry, Burk's Farm-Raised Catfish, '95 158
    Fry, Catfish, '84 184
    Grilled Catfish Cajun-Style, '90 129
    Grilled Catfish Over Mixed Greens, '04 326
    Grilled Catfish with Red Salsa, '90 172
    Grilled Catfish with Relish, '92 54
    Grilled Fish with Heather Sauce, Catfish Inn's, '84 182
    Gumbo, Catfish, '90 278; '91 216

Jack's Catfish, '99 32
Kiev-Style, Catfish, '84 184
Lafitte, Catfish, '97 83
Lime-Orange Catfish, '02 22
Louisiana, Catfish, '93 291
Meunière, Catfish, '80 57
Microwave Catfish, '89 M52
Mousse, Catfish, '92 327
Nuggets, Cornmeal-Crusted Catfish, '05 44
Nuggets with Spicy Tartar Sauce, Hushpuppy-
    Battered Catfish, '04 313
Oven-Baked Catfish with Tartar Sauce, '01 316
Oven-Fried Catfish, '95 106; '99 174
Oven-Fried Catfish, Crispy, '05 256
Oven-Fried Catfish, Southern, '87 163
Pan-fried Catfish, Light and Crispy, '05 198
Pan-fried Catfish, Quick, '05 170
Parmesan, Catfish, '79 184; '86 210; '99 91
Parmesan Catfish, '92 309
Pasta with Catfish and Artichokes, '90 123
Pecan, Catfish, '85 53
Pecan Catfish, '98 329
Pecan Catfish with Lemon Sauce, '03 185; '05 56
Pecan with Lemon-Thyme-Pecan Butter, Catfish, '04 68
Pilaf, Catfish, '94 171
Potato-Crusted Catfish and Chips, '02 140
Potato-Crusted Catfish with Warm Pinto Bean-and-
    Bacon Salsa, '03 331
Ranchero Catfish, '04 322
Sandwiches, Fried Catfish, '02 60
Sesame, Catfish, '81 106
Smoked Catfish, '84 47
South by Southwest Catfish with Guacamole Aioli, '04 314
Southern-Fried Catfish and Chips, '02 140
Spicy Catfish, '01 209
Spicy Catfish with Vegetables and Basil Cream, '03 56
Spicy-Seasoned Catfish, '89 M66
Spread, Best-Ever Catfish, '98 60
Stew, Cajun-Style Catfish, '88 12
Stir, Catfish, '84 184
Stuffed Catfish, Crown Room's Shrimp-, '84 182
Stuffed Catfish, Soufflé-, '84 183
Taco Appetizers, Fish, '04 324
Tacos, Baja-Style Fried Catfish, '04 311
Tacos, Southern-Style Fish, '05 327
Ceviche in Avocado Shells, '81 33
Ceviche (Marinated Raw Fish), '80 194; '82 220
Ceviche, Mexican-Style, '88 115
Chart, Fat and Lean Fish, '85 180
Chowder, Chunky Fish, '92 331
Chowder, Creamy Fish, '79 16
Chowder, Fish, '79 152; '84 M38
Chowder, Tasty Fish, '80 188
Corned Fish, '79 32
Dinner, Jollof Rice, '91 230; '92 325
Dip, Smoked Fish, '84 46
en Papillote, Fish with Snow Peas, '86 144
Fillet of Fish à l'Orange, '89 180
Fillets, Lemon-Coated, '80 M53
Florentine, Fish, '86 35
Florentine in Parchment, Fish, '87 22
Flounder
    Amandine, Flounder, '89 M196
    Ambassador, Flounder, '86 234
    Aspic, Fish 'n, '84 190
    Baked Flounder, '79 31; '90 316
    Baked Flounder au Fromage, '86 234
    Baked Flounder Supreme, '79 75
    Broiled Flounder, '88 28; '89 310
    Broiled Flounder, Cheesy, '84 69
    Broiled Flounder, Pesto, '86 150

Broil, Flounder-Grapefruit, '85 53
Caesar's Fish, '90 76
Casserole, Green Chile-and-Fish, '84 32
Chowder, Basque Fish, '86 36
Creole Flounder with Lemon Couscous, '00 99
Creole-Style Flounder, '85 180
Crunchy Flounder, Quick, '90 76
Crust, Fish in a, '84 294
Delight, Fish, '86 M212
Dijon, Flounder, '85 95
Fried Fish, '79 151
Fried Fish, Crispy, '84 92
Fried Flounder, Crispy, '84 93
Fried Flounder, Seasoned, '79 214
Grilled Flounder Fillets, '83 213
Hollandaise-Shrimp Sauce, Flounder with, '86 234
Italian Fish, '88 270; '89 203
Monterey, Fish, '84 293
Nicole, Flounder, '85 217
Oven-Fried Fish Fillets, '79 75
Papillote, Ocean, '84 M287
Poached Fish with Greek Sauce, '91 M183
Rolls, Vegetable-Filled Fish, '86 M251
Rollups, Shrimp-Stuffed, '82 234
Royal Flounder Fillets, '91 128
Sesame Flounder, '89 33
Shrimp Sauce, Flounder Fillets in, '83 227
Stuffed Flounder, Crab-, '80 120; '81 176
Stuffed Flounder Fillets, '86 234
Stuffed Flounder, Grand Lagoon, '94 68
Stuffed Flounder Rolls, Vegetable-, '87 6
Stuffed Flounder Rolls with Citrus Sauce, '85 180
Stuffed with Shrimp, Flounder, '88 51
Thermidor, Flounder, '85 190
Vegetable Medley, Flounder-, '85 217
Wine Sauce, Fillet of Flounder in, '80 179; '81 30
Wrap, Fish in a, '97 64
Fresh Fish, Preparing, '82 127
Fried Fish, Golden, '82 134
Fried Fish, Sephardic-Style, '00 324
Fried Fish, Southern, '92 168
Grecian Seafood, '97 314
Greek Fish with Vegetable Sauce, '82 72
Grilled Fish and Vegetables, '89 179
Grilled Fish, Easy, '91 194
Grilled Fish with Caribbean Salsa, Montego Bay, '96 70
Grill Fish, How to Charcoal-, '84 48
Grouper
    Baked Fish, '98 122
    Baked Grouper, Creamy, '85 292
    Batter-Fried Grouper Sandwiches, '96 197
    Breaded Grouper Fillets, '89 M36
    Broiled Grouper, Heavenly, '99 91
    Creole Fish, '87 M79
    Fingers, Grouper, '00 167
    Gourmet Fish, '86 71
    Grilled Grouper, '86 185
    Grilled Herbed Grouper, '99 178
    Grilled Marinated Grouper, '90 166
    Guadalajara Grouper, '98 17
    Herb-Coated Fish, '86 M112
    Hot Spicy Grouper, '94 78
    Macadamia, Grouper, '85 127
    Marinated Grouper, Garlic-Basil, '94 160
    Pan-Fried Fish Fillets, '91 196
    Pan-Fried Grouper with Vanilla Wine Sauce, '94 241
    Parmesan Fillets, '86 M112
    Pesto Grouper with Orzo, '97 321
    Sauté, Shrimp-and-Grouper, '87 91
    Spectacular, Grouper, '84 163

Steamed Fish and Vegetables, '91 32
Stuffed Fillets, Apple-Carrot, '88 M192
Tarragon Fillets, Easy, '00 14
Vegetables, Grouper with Confetti, '88 M189
Vegetables, Grouper with Sautéed, '90 M233
Gumbo, Easy Fish, '81 6
Haddock, Baked, '80 179; '81 30
Haddock Fillets in White Wine, '90 76
Haddock Fillets with Zucchini Stuffing, '88 M191
Haddock Italiano, '81 M4
Halibut, Chinese-Style Fried, '80 179; '81 30
Halibut Steaks Italiano, '88 M191
Halibut Steak, Wine-Herb, '94 171
Halibut with Champagne Sauce, Baked, '90 29
Halibut with Cider, '79 182
Halibut with Orange-Curry Sauce, '87 91
Halibut with Swiss Sauce, '83 M195
Hash, Smoked Fish, '92 306
Heroes, Neptune, '84 281
Herring Dip, Yogurt, '80 232
Italian Fish, Easy, '86 M112
Kebabs, Fish's, '98 223
Mackerel Creole, '80 126
Mackerel, Lemon-Baked, '79 182
Mackerel, Rosemary-Garlic, '92 200
Mackerel, Smoked Salmon or, '84 46
Mahimahi in Grape Sauce, '91 218
Mahi Mahi, Macadamia, '88 164
Mahimahi, Middle Eastern, '96 92
Mahi-Mahi with Lemon Mayonnaise, '99 178
Mahi-Mahi with Parsleyed Tomatoes, Broiled, '05 130
Marinated Beer-Battered Fish, '86 180
Mix, Fish Herb, '98 51
Monkfish, Greek-Style, '87 M79
Mullet, Festive, '79 75
Mullet, Smoked, '84 47
Mullet Spread, '94 159

Orange Roughy
Asian-Inspired Orange Roughy, '99 122
Baked Fish with Parmesan-Sour Cream Sauce,
  '01 209
Basil-Orange Roughy with Vegetables, '92 98
Caper Sauce, Fish in, '95 209
Caribbean Fish, '99 109
Curried Baked Fish, '87 5
Curry-Baked Fish, '91 196
Dijon, Orange Roughy, '99 122
Fillets, Crispy Baked, '99 90
Fillets, Quick Fish, '96 196
Fillets Tomatillo, '94 135
Fillets with Herb Sauce, Orange Roughy, '91 29
Kiwi Orange Roughy, '87 193
Mustard Fish, Spicy, '99 90
Oven-Fried Fish, '91 172; '94 172
Oven-Fried Fish, Mexi-Style, '90 76
Pan-Fried Roughy with Tomato-Basil Salsa, '99 123
Pecan Roughy with Brown Butter Sauce, '91 64
Pesto-Crusted Orange Roughy, '96 156
Sour Cream, Fish with, '89 180
Spinach Pesto, Orange Roughy with, '88 M192
Steamed Orange Roughy with Herbs, '95 189
Stew, Fish-and-Vegetable, '87 220
Stir-Fry, Orange Roughy, '98 50
Stir-Fry, Orange Roughy-and-Vegetable, '91 50
Tropical Orange Roughy with Crab Stuffing,
  '99 122
Vegetable-Topped Orange Roughy, '93 67
Perch Fillets, Buttery Baked, '81 134
Perch, Parmesan-Crusted, '93 91
Poached Fish in Creamy Swiss Sauce, '80 M53
Po'boys, Zesty Fish, '03 120
Pollock with Summer Squash Relish, '92 200
Potatoes, Fish-Stuffed, '92 306
Potato Platter, Fish-and-, '89 M248

Redfish Court Bouillon, '83 290; '84 93
Redfish with Shrimp and Crab, Coastal Bend,
  '01 281
Salad, Smoked Fish-Potato, '84 233
Salad, Smoky Seafood, '84 46
Sautéed Seafood Platter, '83 89
Scamp, Tangy Broiled, '87 5
Sea Bass, Hong Kong-Style, '96 196
Seasoning Blend, Fish-and-Seafood, '88 28
Seviche Cocktail, '83 258
Shad Roe with Lemon-Butter Sauce, Baked, '84 252
Shark, Marinated, '79 151
Skillet Fish Dinner, '88 199
Skillet Fish, Spicy, '03 165
Smoked Fish, '92 305
Smoked Fish Log, '85 144

Snapper
Baked Snapper à l'Orange, '85 181
Baked Snapper and Stuffing, '82 72
Baked Snapper with Tarragon Stuffing, '82 136
Blackened Red Snapper, '90 27
Captain's Spicy One, '81 125
Caribbean Banana Fish, '95 202
Caribbean Snapper, '87 5
Chowder, Red Snapper, '85 217
Company Red Snapper, '82 72
Destin, Snapper, '88 222
Dill, Snapper with, '84 190
Fingers with Banana Salsa, Snapper, '96 85
Glazed Snapper with Rosemary, '98 51
Grilled Snapper with Orange-Almond Sauce,
  '01 158
Gumbo, Savannah Snapper, '94 105
Honey-Curried Snapper, '85 181
Horseradish-Crusted Red Snapper, '96 227
Huachinango à la Veracruzana (Veracruz-Style Red
  Snapper), '80 193
Lemon Sauce, Red Snapper with, '01 83
Louisiane, Red Snapper, '85 217
Orangy Snapper, '88 23
Oven-Fried Snapper, '90 75
Pecan-Crusted Snapper with Crabmeat Relish,
  Lemony, '99 198
Peppered Snapper with Creamy Dill Sauce, '94 42
Poached Fish with Vegetables, '89 332; '90 18
Poached Red Snapper, '85 127
Poached Snapper, '83 101
Provençal, Snapper, '91 M170
Rome, Fillet of Snapper, '80 57
Southwestern Snapper, '91 195
Spanish-Style Fillets, '86 M112
Spicy Snapper, '89 179
Stuffed Red Snapper Rolls, Cucumber-, '83 176
Stuffed Red Snapper with Lime, '83 246
Stuffed Snapper, '87 138
Vegetables, Yellowtail Snapper with Julienne,
  '93 31
Veracruz, Red Snapper, '88 149; '92 142
Wine Sauce, Red Snapper in, '85 138
Sole Divan, '87 21
Sole Fillets, Herbed, '82 21
Sole Fillets in Wine Sauce, '81 109
Sole in Papillote, '82 22
Sole Provençal, Fillet of, '85 78
Sole Royale, '89 104
Sole, Saucy, '82 M68
Sole Véronique, '85 181
Sole with Cucumber Sauce, '84 M286
Soup with Garlic Mayonnaise, Rich Fish, '92 56
Spread, Smoked Fish, '92 305
Steaks, Soy Fish, '86 M112
Stock, Fish, '95 19; '00 65
Stock, Homemade Fish, '92 237
Surprise, Fish, '84 231

Sweet-and-Sour Fish, '80 M54
Swordfish, Foil-Baked, '87 5
Swordfish, Mediterranean, '02 237
Swordfish Salad, '00 18
Swordfish-Shiitake Skewers, '97 168
Swordfish, Skewered, '86 256
Swordfish Steaks, Orange-Ginger Marinated, '93 271
Swordfish Steak with Chervil Butter, '91 147
Swordfish Stir-Fry, '96 128
Swordfish with Caper Sauce, Grilled, '95 230
Swordfish with Cashew-and-Cracked Pepper Crust,
  '96 196
Tacos, Barbecued Fish, '95 339
Tilapia Tacos, Shredded Grilled, '05 16

Trout
Amandine, Classic Trout, '96 202; '01 110
Amandine, Fish, '85 179
Amandine, Gaston's Trout, '96 232
Amandine, Orange Lake, '80 99
Amandine, Trout, '99 53
Baked Fish Fillets, Creamy, '85 217
Baked Trout, '95 106
Cakes with Lemon-Butter Sauce, Mountain Trout,
  '92 337
Cornmeal-Crusted Trout, '99 52
Delmonico, Trout, '80 57
Fillets with Capers, Trout, '95 252
Florentine, Cheesy Trout, '85 53
Grilled Rainbow Trout with Mushroom Stuffing,
  '97 162
Grilled Trout, '95 106
Grilled Trout with Ginger and Soy Sauce,
  '85 228
Laurie, Trout, '88 270; '89 202
Pecan-Crusted Trout with Orange Sauce,
  '98 M82
Poached Trout, '95 106
Salad with Black Pepper Vinaigrette, Trout-and-
  Tomato, '98 284
Smoked Trout, '84 47
Spread, Smoked Trout, '84 47
Stuffed Rainbow Trout, '93 121
Stuffed Trout, Sweet Onion-, '99 52
Stuffed with Crawfish, Bacon-Wrapped Trout, '99 54
Sunshine Trout, '84 M286
Tomato Sauce, Fish in, '85 75
Wine Sauce, Trout in, '80 180; '81 31
Two, Fish for, '92 60
Vegetable Dinner, Fish-and-, '91 196
Vegetables, Cheesy Fish and, '94 254
Veracruz Fish with Shrimp, '86 130
Whitefish Spread, Smoked, '92 58

FLAN. *See* **CUSTARDS/Flans.**
FOKTY. *See* **FROM OUR KITCHEN.**
FONDUE
Beer-and-Cheddar Fondue, '03 223
Caramel Fondue, '94 332; '95 35
Cheese Fondue, '81 40
Cheese Fondue, Party, '92 20
Chocolate Fondue, '91 142; '05 M281
Chocolate Fondue, Brandied, '93 162
Chocolate Plunge, '94 332; '95 35
Dessert Fondue, '89 281
Fruitcake Fondue, '84 258
Goat Cheese Fondue, Warm, '96 234
Nacho Fondue, '94 332; '95 35
Peppermint Fondue, '94 332; '95 35
Pub Fondue, '94 332; '95 35
Spinach Fondue Sandwiches, Grilled, '99 337
Swiss Cheese Fondue, '91 48
White Chocolate Fondue, '92 287
FRANKFURTERS
Appetizer Franks, Saucy, '84 M12
Appetizers, Bourbon Frankfurter, '85 207

FRANKFURTERS

(continued)

Bacon-Wrapped Franks, '81 202
Barbecued Frankfurters, '83 144; '84 M12
Barbecued Frankfurters, Oven-, '83 11
Barbecued Franks, '85 192
Barbecue, Tangy Frank, '79 63
Beans and Franks, '85 142
Beans and Franks, Hawaiian Baked, '80 136
Beans and Franks, Jiffy, '91 M172
Beans-and-Franks, Polynesian, '84 M11
Beans, Stove-Top Franks 'n', '88 201
Beany Hot Dogs, '82 190
Cabbage with Apples and Franks, '87 42
Casserole, Hot Doggie, '88 200
Casserole, Layered Frankfurter, '79 64
Chafing Dish Franks, '83 143
Chili-Cheese Dogs, '81 M176
Chili, Hot Dog, '04 199
Corn Dog Bites, '85 245; '93 79
Corn Dogs and Taters, '02 57
Corn Dogs, Favorite, '83 144
Corn Puppies, '97 140
Corn Relish Dogs, '85 192
Crusty Franks, '80 166
Delicious, Hot Dogs, '81 202
Deluxe, Hot Dog, '97 140
Family-Style Franks, '79 54
Fried Hot Dogs, '02 56
Grilled Stuffed Franks, '82 163
Hash Browns, Franks and, '80 166
Hawaiian Franks, '81 202
Jubilee, Hot Dog, '81 113
Kraut and Franks, Beany, '79 64
Marrow's Famous Dogs, '04 198
Mexicali Hot Dogs, '82 131
Mexican Franks, '93 78
Pickled Party Franks, '83 174
Pigs in a Blanket, '95 178
Pigs in a Blanket, Mexican, '00 199
Pigs on a Roll, Three Little, '98 203
Pizza Dogs, Grilled, '97 139
Pizzas, Hot Dog, '93 78
Potatoes, Cheesy Frank-Topped, '83 3
Potatoes, Frank-Filled, '84 M11
Potluck Dish, Frankaroni, '88 201
Rollups, Wienie, '02 186
Sandwiches, Frankfurter, '84 M11
Sauce, Hot Diggity Dog, '93 198
Saucy Franks, '88 201
Scrambled Dog, Dinglewood Pharmacy's,
  '95 118
Skillet Dinner, Frankfurter, '80 166
Skillet, Frankfurter-Cabbage, '80 166
Skillet, Hot Dog and Spaghetti, '83 144
Sloppy Joe Dogs, '85 192
Soup, Split Pea and Frankfurter, '79 64
Spanish Frankfurters, '80 166
Spicy Frankfurters, '81 202
Stuffed Franks and Potatoes, '81 202
Supper, Hot Dog, '93 78
Taco Dogs, '02 M57
Tipsy Franks, '85 52
Wiener Worms, '02 223

FRENCH TOAST

Almond French Toast, '88 62
Amandine, Baked Toast, '82 47
Amaretto French Toast, '98 280
Apple French Toast, '98 55
au Fromage, French Toast, '88 288
Baked Apple French Toast, '03 M283
Banana Splits, French Toast, '96 M164

Caramel-Pecan French Toast, '03 328
Caramel-Soaked French Toast, '03 307
Caribbean French Toast, '92 46
Cinnamon French Toast, '84 211
Cinnamon Toasty Fruity Delight, '00 193
Cottage-Topped French Toast, '85 49
Croissant French Toast with Fresh Strawberry Syrup,
  '05 132
Easy French Toast, '82 M172
Eggnog French Toast, '95 313
English Muffin French Toast, '00 179
Grand Marnier Fruit Sauce, French Toast with,
  '90 93
Ham-and-Cheese Oven French Toast, '97 172
Macadamia French Toast, '86 96
Macadamia Nut French Toast, '95 282
Make-Ahead French Toast with Strawberry Sauce,
  '02 131
Orange Butter, French Toast with, '81 42
Orange French Toast, '83 292; '84 78; '86 329
Orange Sauce, French Toast with, '82 47
Oven-Baked French Toast, '82 47; '90 192
Oven-Baked French Toast, Easy, '93 195
Overnight French Toast, '89 227
Overnight French Toast Deluxe, '79 216
Overnight Oven-Baked French Toast, '05 283
Pain Perdu, '04 67
Pain-Perdu Po-Boy, '93 291
Painted French Toast, '98 206
Peach-Filled French Toast, '98 160
Peachy French Toast, '98 56
Peanut Butter and Jelly French Toast, '00 198
Peanut Butter French Toast, '93 166
Potato-Crusted Texas Toast, '94 142
Pound Cake French Toast, '04 33
Praline French Toast, '98 55
Sandwiches, Strawberry-French Toast, '91 160
Slender French Toast, '86 103
Stuffed French Toast, '96 52; '98 55, 313; '00 193;
  '02 105
Stuffed French Toast, Orange-, '98 54
Stuffed French Toast, Three Cheese, '93 122
Waffled French Toast, '82 47

FRITTERS

Apple Fritter Rings, '88 44
Apple Fritters, '81 105; '82 273; '85 14; '97 153
Apple Fritters with Lemon Sauce, '01 184
Apple Holiday Fritters, '86 314
Banana Fritters, '79 213
Beet Fritters, '96 36
Blueberry Fritters, '85 152
Broccoli-Cauliflower Fritters, '02 45
Broccoli Fritters, Cheesy, '79 53
Buñuelos, '93 29; '05 295
Cauliflower-Cheddar Fritters, '98 25
Chicken-and-Mashed Potato Fritters with Lime-Cayenne
  Mayonnaise, '04 121
Clam Fritters, '79 151; '86 71
Corn-and-Crab Fritters, '97 227
Corn Fritters, '86 192; '94 22; '98 207
Corn Fritters, Golden, '80 165; '81 128
Corn Fritters, Skillet-Fried, '85 14
Corn-Jalapeño Fritters, '96 153
Crab Fritters, '98 142
Eggplant Fritters, '91 211; '05 128
Ham Fritters, '82 39
Ham Fritters with Creamy Sauce, '81 105
Honey Puffs, '96 153
Leek-and-Potato Fritters, '00 324
Matzoh-and-Honey Fritters, '05 81
Okra, Fritter-Fried, '86 218
Okra Fritters, '79 160; '98 159
Orange Fritters, Puffy, '81 169
Oyster Fritters, '79 31; '97 20

Pear Fritters, Ol' Timey, '86 51
Pecan Fritters, Chocolate-Covered, '79 205
Pineapple Fritters, '88 112; '00 238
Potato Fritters, Cheese-Stuffed, '96 153
Potato-Ham Fritters, '98 249
Shrimp Fritters, '00 238
Squash Fritters, '89 68
Squash-Jalapeño Fritters, '98 249
Sweet Potato Fritters, '88 44
Sweet Potato Fritters, Golden, '79 9
Zucchini Fritters, '81 163
Zucchini Fritters, Cheesy, '88 44

FROG LEGS

Crispy Frog Legs, '80 99
Fried Frog Legs, '88 110

FROM OUR KITCHEN (FOK)

Alcohol, substituting in recipes, '92 314; '99 148;
  '00 66; '01 138
Almond brickle chips, '02 28
  substitute for, '02 28
Almonds, salted, '00 330
Aluminum foil, '02 100, 216
Apples, '84 227, 228
  adding to meat loaf, '98 138
  amounts to buy, '84 228
  preventing browning after cutting, '84 228
  selecting for cooking, '84 227, 228
  selecting for eating, '84 227, 228
  storing, '84 228; '01 202
Appliances, kitchen. *See* **FOK/Dishwasher, Food
  processor, Freezer, Kitchen, Microwave oven,
  Ovens, Refrigerator, Slow cooker.**
Arrowroot, as a thickening agent, '83 147
Artichokes, '00 66; '03 30
  discoloration of, '03 30
Asparagus, '01 118
  pickled, '04 174
  selecting, '01 118
  storing, '01 118
Avocados, '03 132
  preserving color of, '03 132
  removing the seed from, '03 132
  softening, '96 76
  storing, '03 132
Bacon
  cooking, '00 330; '01 335
  freezing, '02 28
Baking soda, as ice melter, '98 36
Barbecue, '94 155. *See also* **FOK/Grilling.**
  bottled sauces, '00 180
  chicken, '94 155
  recipe, Barbecue Ribs, '99 68
  tongs, using to reach things, '97 206
Basil
  fresh, '03 208
  recipes for purees, '03 208
Bay leaves, removing from soups, '95 314;
  '96 51
Beans, canned, '01 98
  baked, '01 166
  black bean dip, '05 102
Beans, dried, '88 4; '99 250
  amount of folate in, '99 250
  baked, '01 166
  buying, '88 4
  cooking, '88 4; '99 100
  soaking, '88 4; '03 30
  storing, '88 4
Beans, green, steaming, '03 132
Beef, '83 38; '92 65, 66; '94 140; '04 130
  barbacoa, '02 148
  bresaola, '02 148
  browning, '83 38; '02 132
  buying, '83 38; '90 276; '92 65; '04 130

churrascos, '02 148
cooking methods, '83 38
fat content of, '92 65, 66; '94 140; '04 130
freezing, '02 178
freezing cooked, '02 28
handling properly, '87 208; '94 140; '96 76; '01 335
making gravy from pan drippings, '83 38
marinating, '02 46
removing fat from browned, '02 132
selecting (chart), '02 100
stir-frying, '01 335
storing, '94 140
tenderizing, '83 38
Beers
selecting, '99 250; '00 250
tasting, '99 250; '00 250
types of, '99 250; '00 250
Berries. *See also* **FOK/Blueberries.**
selecting, '99 148
storing, '99 148
Beverages, '83 191; '90 276, 277; '97 174; '98 218. *See also* **FOK/Alcohol, Beers, Buttermilk, Coffee, Eggnog, Ice, Tea, Water, Wines.**
chilling quickly, '96 21
determining amounts to buy for entertaining, '90 276, 277
as food preservative, '02 70
freezing, '92 314
garnishing, '97 56
glasses, '97 184
ice cubes of tea and fruit juice, '01 260
ice molds, '86 331
limeade, '03 224
placement of in basic table setting, '90 182
placement of when entertaining, '90 277
recipe, Chocolate Iced Coffee, '01 166
recipe, Low-Fat Cappuccino Cooler, '01 166
recipe, Mint Juleps, '04 94
recipe, Royal Cup Chiller, '98 218
substituting for alcohol in recipes, '92 314; '99 148; '00 66
sugar syrup, recipe, '03 224
Biscuits, '89 211, 212; '92 52. *See also* **FOK/Breads, Rolls, Yeast.**
baking, '89 211, 212
cutting dough, '89 211; '95 30; '97 36
freezing, '89 212
kneading, '92 52
making dough for, '89 211; '92 52
reheating, '89 212
removing burned bottoms from, '96 51
storing leftovers, '89 212
using food processor to make, '89 211, 212; '96 256
Blackberries, '05 182
recipe, Blackberry Curd Filling, '05 182
recipe, Blackberry Juice, '05 182
Blueberries, '04 148
buying, '04 148
freezing, '01 166; '03 148; '04 148
freezing before adding to batter, '98 138
serving amounts, '00 156
storing, '00 156; '01 166; '03 148
washing, '00 156; '04 148
Bouillon cubes, '00 100
Breads, '82 198; '84 92; '89 268; '92 52, 102, 314; '93 183. *See also* **FOK/Biscuits, Muffins, Rolls, Yeast.**
commercial products, '03 148
cutting, '91 144, 145
doubling recipes, '91 22
freezing, '89 268; '90 315; '91 95; '92 102
as gifts, '91 95
metal dough scraper, '90 126; '92 52

microwave oven, '89 268
in pudding, '00 128
purchasing, '03 148
quick breads, '84 92; '89 268; '04 224
recipe, Bread Dough Basket, '04 64
recipe, Icebox Rolls, '04 130
refrigerated products, '01 202
rising procedures, '87 12; '89 268; '98 72
selecting fresh, '01 202
serving warm, '01 260
substituting oat flour, '00 28
testing for doneness, '84 92; '92 314
yeast breads, '84 92; '87 12; '89 268; '92 314
yeast rolls, '83 323
Broccoli, '84 249
cutting, '93 132
preparing, '84 249
selecting, '84 249
Broths. *See* **FOK/Soups.**
Brussels sprouts, '84 249
preparing, '84 249
selecting, '84 249
Butter, '82 189; '95 314; '99 296; '00 300
availability of, '82 189
balls, how to make, '82 189
clarifying, '82 189; '97 232
curls, how to make, '82 189
fat content of, '82 189; '00 300
softening, '00 300
storing, '82 189; '00 300
substituting for in baked goods, '90 314; '97 134
Buttermilk
adding to bottled salad dressings, '00 66
freezing, '92 314; '97 72
powdered, '00 66
substitutes for, '00 66
Butterscotch, '98 238
Cactus (Nopales), '94 29
cooking, '94 29
selecting, '94 29
storing, '94 29
Cakes, '89 57, 58; '91 144, 200, 201; '92 154, 155, 314; '94 59; '00 128. *See also* **FOK/Fruitcakes.**
assembling Twinkling Star Cake, '00 330
baking techniques, '89 57; '98 218
cheesecakes, cutting, '96 140
cheesecakes, disguising cracks in, '96 112
cheesecakes, eliminating cracks in, '91 300
cooling, '92 155; '99 128, 328
cutting, '91 144; '92 314; '95 30
decorating, '94 59; '99 328
dry ingredients, '87 12; '92 155
freezing, '89 58; '90 314, 315; '99 328; '02 316
frosting, '89 57, 58; '02 316
as gifts, '02 316
greasing pans, '92 314; '05 314
jellyroll cakes, '92 314
mixing procedures, '89 57; '92 154, 155; '99 328
pan sizes, '92 154, 314; '96 332; '00 128
personalized cakepans, '04 148
pound cakes '84 92, 319 (baking tips chart); '92 154, 155; '00 206; '03 102
repairing disasters, '96 21
server, '02 316
as snacks, '91 200, 201
storing, '89 57, 58; '92 155; '99 328; '01 300
substituting flours, '92 155
testing for doneness, '84 92; '92 155; '96 112, 332
Campsite cooking, '86 172
cleaning up, '86 172
making lists, '86 172

packing, '86 172
planning, '86 172
Candy
crushing hard, '96 21, 76; '02 28
as dessert topping, '02 194
recipe, Sugared Rabbits, '04 94
using leftover in baking, '01 220
Canning fruits and vegetables, '84 180; '89 141, 142; '93 136, 137; '99 180. *See also* **FOK/Paraffin.**
and altitude, '03 148
boiling water bath, '84 180; '89 141, 142; '91 300; '93 136, 137; '03 148
equipment, '93 137; '97 278; '99 180; '00 156; '03 148
packing, '84 180; '89 141, 142; '03 148
safety, '84 180; '89 141, 142; '91 300; '93 137; '03 148
steam pressure method of, '84 180; '89 141, 142
sterilizing equipment, '03 148
Caramel, '98 238; '00 66; '05 224
Casseroles
doubling recipes, '91 22, 23, 96; '01 335
freezing, '90 314; '91 96; '96 112; '03 274
preventing spoilage of, '87 208
using oats in, '00 28
Cast-iron cookware, '93 33; '99 50; '04 48
caring for, '93 33; '99 50
cleaning, '99 50
seasoning, '93 33; '99 50
Cauliflower, '84 249
cutting, '93 132
maintaining color of during cooking, '01 118
preparing, '84 249; '99 100
selecting, '84 249
Celery, chopping, '01 202
Centerpieces, '90 205; '97 232; '01 335
Easter, '04 94
entrée as, '04 276
Cereal, hot, adding oat bran to, '00 28
Champagne. *See* **FOK/Wines.**
Cheese, '82 109
browning, '01 50
buying, '85 210; '90 276
cheese straws, '02 216
cooking with, '85 210; '87 12; '01 98
freezing, '89 12; '85 211; '02 28
fresh mozzarella, '04 174
grating, '00 224
handling properly, '87 208
melting, '01 50
preshredded combinations, '01 138
rinds of, '01 138
serving, '85 210, 211; '02 240; '04 276
shredding, '95 31 (illustration)
as snacks, '91 200, 201
storing, '85 210
waxed coverings of, '01 138
Cheesecakes. *See* **FOK/Cakes.**
Chicken, '87 12; '88 39; '94 155, 253
barbecuing, '94 155
boning, '88 39
cooking, '87 12; '88 39; '95 246; '97 112
cutting up, '94 253
handling properly, '87 208; '99 128; '03 50
marinating, '02 46
microwaving, '88 39
packaging of, '88 39; '02 148
pounder, '04 204
preparing for stir-frying, '91 160; '01 335
recipe, Chicken-and-Smoked Sausage Pilau, '04 204
Children in the kitchen, '91 92; '92 102, 207
gadgets for, '00 206
Chili, types of, '03 30
China, '88 301
removing marks from, '88 301

FROM OUR KITCHEN, China
(continued)

storing, '88 301
washing, '88 301
Chinese cooking, '85 76
equipment, '85 76
garnishing, '85 76
preparing food for, '85 76
Chocolate, '86 246, 247; '92 314; '93 317; '00 224
dipping, '86 330, 331; '04 94
garnishing with, '86 247; '93 317; '94 59; '96 230, 256
illustrations for chocolate sacks, '93 317
kinds of, '86 246, 247
measuring, '01 118
melting, '92 314; '93 317; '96 21, 332; '02 46
storing, '01 220; '02 46
substitutions, '86 246, 247; '00 156
using to line pie shells, '97 36
white chocolate, '86 246, 247; '94 59
Cholesterol, '90 72
and food labels, '90 72
Cleaning up. *See* **FOK/Recipe preparation.**
Clothing for "chefs," '97 278
Club soda, using to remove stains, '96 304
Coconut, '98 238
Coffee
accessories, '04 30
beverages, '98 218
freezing excess, '98 306
recipe, Chocolate Iced Coffee, '01 166
recipe, Low-Fat Cappuccino Cooler, '01 166
using spices in to enhance flavor of, '00 224
Commercial food products
baking mix, '03 132
breads, '03 148
frozen cheese wafer dough, '05 144
frozen roll dough, '03 224
jalapeño jelly, '03 186
olive oil, '03 102
pickles and pickle relish, '03 102
seasoning blend, '03 132
vinegars, '03 102
Computer, index online, '01 300
Cookbooks, '02 148, 240
creating keepsake, '03 274
making notations in, '96 160
Cookies, '91 234; '92 207, 208; '95 30
baking, '92 208; '98 326; '02 216
cooling, '92 208; '96 208; '98 326
crushing, '95 30
equipment, '92 208; '00 100, 330
freezing, '90 314; '92 207, 208; '02 216, 316
freezing dough, '97 112
as gifts, '91 95
mixing procedures, '92 207
recipe, Chocolate Chip-Peanut Butter Cookies, '99 68
shaped cookie cutters, '97 56
slicing dough, '96 140, 230; '97 112
storing, '92 208; '01 300
testing for doneness, '84 92
uneven baking, '00 330
using dough as piecrust, '01 335
using oats in dough, '00 28
Cooking directions, basic, '87 12, 208. *See also* **FOK/Handling food properly, Recipe preparation.**
chicken, '87 12
shrimp, '87 12
Cooking oils, '98 112; '01 50, 118
best for frying, '02 216

checking for freshness, '02 216
flavored, '01 50
infusing, '05 182
reusing, '02 216
storing used, '02 216
varieties of, '98 112; '02 216
Cooking spray. *See* **FOK/Vegetable cooking spray.**
Cooking torch, '01 50, 118
Cookware, '85 329; '86 227; '90 50; '93 33, 183, 220; '03 70. *See also* **FOK/Cast-iron cookware, Kitchen.**
broken, '02 46
caring for, '85 329; '93 33, 183
keeping metal handles cool, '97 184
for microwave, '86 227
selecting, '85 329; '86 227; '93 220; '01 220
Corn, '04 64
buttering on the cob, '03 186
cutting from the cob, '96 192
grating, '02 178
removing silks, '98 198
Cornbread, '87 16; '02 28
cornmeal, '87 16
ingredients in, '87 16
making cornbread, '87 16
Cornmeal, '87 16
making cornbread, '87 16
understanding the label, '87 16
Cornstarch, '83 146, 147
adding to hot mixture, '01 335
as a thickening agent, '83 146, 147
Couscous, '01 50
Crab, cracking, '95 156
Crackers, '02 28
Cranberries, '04 30
buying, '92 314
enhancing canned sauce, '99 296
freezing, '92 314; '02 28; '04 30
frosted cranberries (garnish), '82 280
Crystal, '88 300, 301
removing discolorations and stains, '88 300, 301
repairing chips, '88 300
storing, '88 300
washing, '88 300, 301
Custards
preparing and storing properly (chart), '87 208
testing for doneness, '84 92
thickening, '83 147
Cutting boards, '87 208; '98 138, 198
acrylic, '87 208
cleaning, '87 208; '99 224
food safety, '87 208; '02 28
wooden, '87 208
Desserts. *See also* **FOK/Butterscotch, Cakes, Candy, Caramel, Cookies, Custards, Fruits, Garnishes, Meringue, Piecrust, Puddings, Soufflés, Tarts.**
gelatin molds, '99 100
glazing pastries, '01 50
sauces, '01 335
topping, '02 194
using ready-made products, '97 174
using toasted oats as topping, '00 28
Dishwasher, '87 130
freshening interior, '02 194
Dressing/Stuffing
preparing ahead, '01 260
Drying foods, '93 23
cherry tomatoes, '93 23
equipment, '93 23
safety, '93 23
uses for, '93 23
Eggnog, freezing, '92 314

Eggplant
cooking, '01 166
peeling, '01 166
types of, '01 166
Egg rolls, '05 50
recipe, Egg Rolls, '05 50
Eggs, '83 147, 214; '89 26. *See also* **FOK/Meringue.**
cooking methods, '83 214; '98 112
cooking omelets, '00 46
eggshell vases and candy dishes, '04 94
handling properly, '87 208 (chart)
pasteurized egg substitute, '89 26
poached, recipe, '03 70
preventing curdling, '82 198; '83 147
separating, '01 335
using oat bran in, '00 28
using raw egg whites, '91 300
using raw egg yolks, '89 26
yolks, thick and lemon colored, '83 214
Entertaining, '84 122, 123; '88 276; '90 182, 276, 277; '91 300; '94 17, 18; '02 316; '03 274
accumulating supplies for, '02 148
beverage glasses, '97 184
cleaning up, '02 46
decorating, '02 194
determining amounts of food to buy, '90 276 (chart)
determining traffic flow, '84 122, 123; '86 191; '90 276, 277
during the holidays, '03 274
making preparations for, '84 122; '86 191; '94 17, 18; '96 21; '97 154; '02 148
outdoors, '86 191; '96 230; '03 148, 176
presenting food, '84 122; '88 276; '97 56, 174; '98 112; '01 260; '02 194; '04 276; '05 102
"referral coffee," '97 154
sandwich bar for, '05 28
seafood server, '03 224
selecting menus for, '84 122; '86 191; '88 276; '90 276; '97 308; '02 178
serving food safely, '91 300; '96 230
setting up a bar for, '90 277
sharing recipes, '97 72
table setting, '90 182 (illustration), 276; '96 192; '97 184; '01 335
tailgating, '96 230
Web site, '05 314
Equivalents of ingredients, '91 22, 23
Etiquette, '90 225
basic manners at the table, '90 225; '96 208
tipping in restaurants, '96 140
Fat, dietary, '82 189; '90 72; '91 200, 201; '92 65, 66; '93 207
in beef, '92 65, 66
in butter, '82 189; '90 314
eliminating in snacks, '91 200, 201
and food labels, '90 72; '92 65; '93 207
in margarine, '82 189; '90 314
removing excess from foods, '00 300
storing, '82 189
Fish, '84 48; '87 79, 80; '90 130; '94 105, 106. *See also* **FOK/Seafood, Shellfish, Shrimp, Surimi.**
boning, '96 256
buying, '84 48; '87 79, 80; '90 130; '94 106; '97 112; '99 68; '01 220
cooking, '87 80; '01 220; '05 198
deep frying, '98 238
eliminating odors on hands, '82 109
fat fish, '87 79
freezing, '87 80; '02 28; '05 198
grilling, '84 48; '92 52
handling properly, '87 208
lean fish, '87 79
market forms of, '87 79; '01 220; '02 194

recipe, Light and Crispy Pan-fried Catfish, '05 198
selecting, '02 194; '05 198
selecting fish for grilling, '84 48; '90 130
storing, '87 80; '90 130; '94 105, 106; '97 112; '01 220
substituting, '90 130
thawing, '87 80; '90 130; '05 198
transporting fresh, '94 105, 106
Flour, '82 197, 198; '04 224
all purpose, '82 197, 198; '87 12; '99 224; '04 224
bread, '99 224; '04 224
cake flour, '82 197, 198; '87 12; '04 224
cracked wheat, '82 197, 198
measuring, '00 180
oat flour, '00 28
self rising, '99 224; '04 224
sifting, '82 197, 198; '87 12
Southern flours, '04 224
storing, '82 197, 198; '00 180
types of, '82 197, 198; '96 256; '99 224; '04 224
whole wheat, '99 224
Flowers, '94 59; '96 304
crystallizing edible, '94 59; '99 100
edible, '96 304
keeping fresh, '99 100
toxic, '96 304
Food processor, '82 109; '86 13
chopping nuts, '92 314; '95 208
easy cleanup, '01 50
Food safety. See FOK/Handling food properly.
Freezer, '83 14, 15; '86 50, 51; '87 112, 208; '93 83, 84; '02 28
amount of food to store in, '87 112
casseroles in, '87 112
checking temperature of, '01 166
cleaning, '84 11; '87 112
cleaning out, '01 30
constant freezer temperature, '86 50; '99 50
defrosting, '87 112; '99 50
foods that don't freeze well, '01 98
foods that freeze well, '86 50; '87 112; '90 314, 315; '01 98; '02 28; '03 186, 274
fruits in, '87 112
labeling foods in, '84 11; '86 51; '87 112; '00 100; '03 186
leftovers, freezing safely, '87 112; '96 140, 160; '99 50; '02 28
organizing foods in, '87 112; '02 28
and power loss, '83 14, 15; '93 83, 84
preventing sogginess of particular foods to be frozen, '87 112
refreezing foods, '83 15; '93 83, 84; '99 50
reheating frozen foods, '87 112
sausage, '87 238
storage times, '03 186
storing nuts in, '01 50
vegetables in, '87 112
wraps and containers for freezing foods, '86 50, 51; '87 112; '02 28; '03 274
Fruitcakes, '83 285; '86 331; '95 343
purchasing candied fruit for, '92 314
shortcut for, '99 224
storing, '83 285; '86 331
Fruits, '83 94; '85 233; '89 141, 142; '92 248, 249, 250; '01 30. See also FOK/Apples, Avocados, Berries, Blueberries, Coconut, Cranberries, Garnishes, Grapefruit, Kiwifruit, Lemons, Mangoes, Melons, Oranges, Peaches, Pears, Persimmons, Raspberries, Strawberries, Tangerines, Tomatillos.
candied, '02 28
canning, '84 180; '89 141, 142
in centerpieces, '90 205

as "containers" for food, '97 174
cooking with, '97 36
dressing for fruit salad, '97 134
exotic fruits, '92 248, 249, 250; '02 240
fall fruits, '85 233
freezing, '87 112
grating citrus peel, '95 314; '96 140; '98 138; '00 28
health benefits of, '00 46
nutritive values of, '92 248, 249, 250
preparing, '92 248, 249, 250; '97 134; '02 178
preserving cut, '02 70, 178
pureeing, '01 335
selecting, '84 186, 187; '92 248, 249, 250
as snacks, '91 200, 201
storing, '83 94; '92 248, 249, 250; '01 98, 166, 300; '02 132, 148; '03 176
using yogurt instead of puree, '97 206
winter fruits, '04 30
Frying foods, '84 211; '88 112, 113; '01 118. See also FOK/Lard.
cooking fat to use, '88 113
equipment, '88 113
fish, '05 198
safety, '90 22
techniques, '88 113
Gardening, '98 112
Garlic, '93 182; '00 100
baker, '94 332
conversions of bottled for fresh, '99 50
freezing, '01 335
press, '94 332; '97 134
storing, '03 70
tool for peeling easily, '97 154
Garnishes, '82 138, 280; '89 100; '90 108; '93 317; '94 59; '96 230, 256; '04 276. See also FOK/Flowers.
butter curls, '82 189
candy holly leaves, '99 328
chocolate, '86 247; '94 59; '96 230, 256
chocolate leaves, '96 230
chocolate sacks, '93 317
containers as garnishes, '97 174
curling garnishes, '89 100
eggs, hard-cooked, '82 280
fruit garnishes, '82 280; '96 230; '97 36
illustrations, '89 100; '90 108; '93 317
making ahead, '89 100
pastry garnishes, '96 230; '04 276
piped garnishes, '82 280; '86 330; '90 108
soup garnish, '96 160
sugar, lemon, '97 56
sugar, powdered, '96 51
utensils for creating, '89 100; '90 108
vegetable garnishes, '82 280; '89 100, 243; '95 343
whipped cream, '86 330
Gelatin, '83 124, 125; '91 300
chilling, '83 124; '86 13
molds, determining size of, '82 313
molds, substituting, '99 100
softening, '91 300
unmolding, '83 124, 125; '86 330
using fresh fruits and vegetables in, '91 300
Gifts of food, '86 289; '91 95, 96; '95 343; '96 112; '02 132; '05 284, 314
assembling, '02 178
containers for, '86 289; '91 95, 96; '98 36; '00 224; '05 314
freezing, '91 95, 96; '95 343
gift baskets, '02 178
mailing, '86 289; '95 343
mail orders from favorite restaurants, '97 308
recipe, Holiday Herb Butter, '05 284
recipe, Italian Parmesan Herb Mix, '05 284
recipe, Sweet-Hot Honey Mustard, '05 284
safety of, '02 132

storing, '91 95, 96; '02 132
wrapping, '86 289; '95 343
Gifts, nonfood, '97 134; '98 326; '00 330; '01 300
coupons, '02 316
gift certificates, '97 308
Gingerroot, '94 29
cooking with, '92 314; '94 29; '01 335
freezing, '98 138
grating, '98 138
selecting, '94 29
in stir-frying, '92 314
storing, '92 314; '98 138
Glasses, cleaning stemmed, '02 46
Gloves, disposable, '96 76; '03 50
Granita, '00 156
Grapefruit, '01 30
sectioning, '04 48
Grating
citrus rind, '95 314; '96 140; '98 138
corn, fresh, '02 178
Gravies, '83 38; '86 330
serving and storing properly, '87 208 (chart)
thickening, '00 28
Greens
arugula, '03 224
cleaning, '96 304; '97 206; '03 30
radicchio, '97 232
Grilling, '82 109; '83 191; '84 48; '86 172; '88 145, 146; '92 202; '93 103, 104; '00 128. See also FOK/Smoking (cooking method).
avoiding flare-ups, '88 145; '92 202; '99 148, 180
basting, '82 109; '88 146; '93 103
charcoal, '82 109; '93 103, 104; '00 128
cleanup, '93 104
cooking times, '95 194 (chart)
direct/indirect cooking methods, '88 145; '93 103, 104; '95 194; '97 206; '99 148
equipment, '82 109; '88 146; '92 52; '93 103; '95 274; '99 148; '02 132
flavoring with wood chips, '88 145; '93 103; '00 128
kebabs, '88 146; '93 103; '99 180; '00 128
safety, '99 148; '02 132
temperature of fire, '82 109; '88 145, 146; '95 195
thermometer, '93 103, 104; '95 195; '99 148
Grits
eliminating lumps in, '97 154; '00 224
leftover, '05 224
storing, '00 224
Grocery shopping, '84 11; '91 187, 188; '00 206; '05 50
best time for, '84 11
comparative shopping, '91 188
determining best values, '91 188 (chart)
making lists for, '82 312; '83 248; '84 11; '00 206; '01 98
planning menus, '82 312; '83 284; '84 11
saving time and money, '91 187, 188; '00 206; '05 50
stocking up, '91 188
transporting cold and frozen items, '00 206; '01 118
using coupons, '91 188
Ham, '89 333, 334; '90 276
cooking in microwave oven, '89 333, 334
determining amount to buy for entertaining, '90 276
freezing, '89 334
preparing, '89 333, 334
reducing saltiness during cooking, '97 134
selecting, '89 333
storing, '89 334
Handling food properly, '87 208; '89 26; '91 300; '92 202; '93 23, 83, 84; '96 76, 230; '99 224; '01 330. See also FOK/Beef, Canning, Chicken, Eggs, Fish, Turkey.
chart, '87 208

egg whites, raw, '91 300
egg yolks, raw, '89 26
holiday hot lines, '97 278; '98 306
irradiating foods, '02 100
transporting food, '01 220
when entertaining, '91 300; '96 230
when grilling, '99 148
Herbs, '85 58; '89 121; '99 208. *See also*
  FOK/Seasonings, Spices.
amounts to use, '89 121; '95 30
chart '89 121
cooking with, '85 58
as decoration, '01 118
drying, '85 58; '98 198
freezing, '85 58
gathering fresh, '85 58; '89 121
mint, '02 132
rosemary, '00 28
sage, '01 260
storing, '85 58; '89 121; '98 198; '00 206;
  '03 176
substituting, '01 118
substituting fresh for salt, '99 208
types of, '99 208
using fresh, '00 206; '02 132
Holiday
baking, '98 326
entertaining, '03 274
hot lines, '97 278; '98 306; '01 300;
  '03 274
Honey, '02 100
Ice
dry ice, '82 14, 15
freezing beverages as ice cubes, '01 260
molds, '86 331
Ice cream, '82 171; '86 215; '00 156
adding fresh fruit to homemade, '82 171
fat content of, '00 156
homemade, '82 171; '03 176
varieties of, '86 215
Ingredients, uncommon, '97 232; '02 28
Jams and jellies
commercial, '03 186
jars for, '03 148
storing, '02 132
Kitchen, '83 191; '84 10, 11, 148, 149; '90 22, 50;
  '93 220; '94 332
aluminum foil cooking bags, '99 68
appliances, '87 130
baking pans, '98 138; '99 128; '00 128, 250; '02 46;
  '05 314
baking stone, '99 68; '02 46
basic equipment, '90 50; '93 220; '94 332; '97 56,
  308; '98 138; '00 128, 224; '02 46
cleaning, '02 148
cookware, '85 329; '90 50; '93 220; '96 160;
  '98 326; '03 70
countertops, '84 148, 149
fire extinguisher for, '99 50
gadgets, '86 13; '90 126; '94 332; '95 343; '97 154;
  '98 36, 218; '00 28, 206, 224; '01 50, 118, 138,
  300; '02 194, 316
keeping cool in summer, '83 191
knives, '91 144, 145
organizing, '84 10, 11
safety in, '84 37; '90 22; '96 256
shears, '91 160; '92 52
toolbox, '96 21
Kiwifruit, peeling, '95 31 (illustration)
Knives, '84 11; '91 144, 145; '01 260

buying, '91 144, 145; '03 50
sharpening, '91 144, 145
storing, '84 11; '03 50
using properly, '86 13; '91 144, 145
varieties of, '91 144, 145 (illustration);
  '03 50
Labels, food, '90 72; '92 65; '93 207; '94 140
chart, '90 72
margarine or "spread" labels, '97 134
sample label, '93 207
"sell by" date, '99 128
understanding, '90 72; '93 207
Lamb, '88 59; '02 70
buying, '88 59; '01 98
cooking, '88 59; '95 105 (chart); '01 98
seasoning, '95 105
selecting, '88 59; '01 98
storing, '88 59; '95 105 (chart); '01 98
Lard, '96 160
Lasagna noodles, no-cook, '00 180
Lavosh, '00 66
Leftovers, '82 313; '87 112, 208; '92 314; '95 30, 274;
  '96 230; '05 50
bread slices, '82 313
buns, '82 313
freezing, '87 112, 208; '92 314; '01 30; '02 28
of grits, '05 224
of ham, '01 30
of jams and jellies, '97 232
storing, '01 30, 166; '02 178
of turkey, '01 30
using, '02 178
Lemons
using for routine kitchen cleanup, '96 51
using juice as a substitute in recipes,
  '00 66
Lettuce, '86 80; '95 67
coring, '86 80
mâche, '04 30
selecting, '86 80
storing, '86 80
types of, '86 80 (illustration)
yields, '86 80
Limes, '01 98
List making, '82 312; '83 284; '84 11, 122; '86 172
and grocery shopping, '88 165; '91 188
and meal planning, '82 312; '83 284; '84 11;
  '91 188
telephone numbers for emergencies, '84 37
Low-fat, low-calorie foods
substituting fresh herbs for salt, '99 208
using frozen juice concentrate as a sweetener,
  '99 208
using lemon or lime juice, '99 208
Lunch, packing for kids, '00 224
Mailing food, '86 289
Mangoes, '94 192
Manners. *See* **FOK/Etiquette.**
Margarine, '82 189
availability of, '82 189
colored, '02 70
diet margarine, '82 189
fat content of, '82 189; '90 314
storing, '82 189
substituting in baked goods, '90 314; '97 137
Marinating, '88 165; '95 30
containers to use, '87 208; '02 100
vinaigrette, '04 204
Masa harina, '94 192
Mayonnaise
recipe, Béarnaise Mayonnaise, '05 144
recipe, Fresh Herb Mayonnaise, '05 144
recipe, Homemade Mayonnaise, '99 180
recipe, Lemon-Rosemary Mayonnaise, '05 144

Meal planning, '82 312, 313; '83 191, 284; '84 122,
  123; '86 13; '88 165, 276; '99 30. *See also*
  FOK/Campsite cooking, Snacks.
advance planning, '82 312, 313; '86 172
for a crowd, '82 313; '86 191
family dinners, '03 30
for holidays, '83 284
making lists, '82 312; '83 284; '84 11, 122; '86 172
party menus, '82 313; '84 122, 123; '86 191; '88 276
for specific recipes in 2001, '01 67
Measuring, '85 192, 193; '86 13; '98 36; '04 224
butter, '85 192, 193
determining cup measurement of dish, '85 193;
  '96 332
dry measuring utensils, '85 192, 193; '00 224;
  '04 224
how to measure accurately, '85 192, 193
liquid measuring utensils, '85 192, 193
salt, '01 138
seasonings, '03 176
sifting ingredients for, '82 197, 198; '85 192, 193;
  '87 12
solid shortening, '85 192, 193
Meat loaf, '02 46
additives, '98 138
Meats, '89 191, 192; '91 300; '92 202; '99 224;
  '05 102. *See also* **FOK/Beef, Pork.**
alternatives to, '02 148
garnishing, '97 56
handling properly, '87 208; '99 224; '03 50
meat-cure mix, '91 300
pounder, '04 204
serving safely, '87 208; '91 300; '03 102
standing time, '89 192
suggested cooking temperatures, '89 191, 192;
  '92 202
tenderizer, '02 316
using a meat thermometer, '89 191, 192; '92 202
Melons, '88 183
cantaloupe, '88 183
enhancing flavor of, '00 206
honeydew, '88 183
selecting, '88 183
storing, '88 183
watermelon, '88 183; '96 192; '98 198
Meringue, '83 214
baking, '83 214
browning, '01 50
equipment, '83 214
humidity, effects of, '83 214
making, '83 214
powder, '92 314; '04 94
preventing weeping, '83 214; '95 246; '02 194
recipe, Dream Drops, '99 328
Microwave oven, '83 191; '84 211; '86 113, 227;
  '87 130; '92 176; '99 296; '02 288
cleaning, '87 130; '99 128
cookware for, '86 227
drying herbs in, '98 198
features, '86 113
melting chocolate in, '02 46
recipe, Microwave Fudge, '91 92
removing odors from, '99 30
roasting peppers in, '92 176
safety when using, '91 92; '00 28
sizes, '86 113
steaming vegetables in, '99 296; '02 70
using to clean microwave cookware, '98 256
variations of, '86 113
wattage, '86 113
Milk, as cooling agent to burning taste buds,
  '01 138
Mirlitons, '00 250; '01 260
Muffins, preparing ahead, '97 174

Mushrooms
dried, '01 202
as garnish, '82 280
portobello, '03 176
preparing, '00 180; '01 202; '03 176 (recipe)
serving, '02 194
shiitake, '97 232
slicing, '98 198
storing, '92 314; '01 202
varieties of, '01 202
Noodles
cooking, '00 100
rinsing, '00 100
Nopales. *See* FOK/Cactus.
Nutrition, '90 72; '91 200, 201; '92 65
food labels, '90 72; '92 65
snacks, '91 200, 201
Nuts
storing, '02 132
storing in freezer, '01 50
toasting frozen, '01 50
Oats
types of, '00 28; '03 30
uses for, '00 28
Okra
cooking, '01 166
types of, '01 166
Oils. *See* FOK/Cooking oils, Olive oils, Sesame oil,
Vegetable oil, Walnut oil.
Olive oils, '89 175; '98 112; '01 50
commercial, '03 102
flavored, '89 175
selecting, '89 175
storing, '89 175
using to store garlic, '03 70
varieties of, '89 175; '98 112
Onions, '88 87; '95 30; '98 36
caramelizing, '98 72
chopping, '92 314; '95 246; '97 134
cooking with, '88 87
eliminating odor on hands, '82 109; '94 332; '96 51
extracting onion juice, '88 87
grating, '92 314; '95 30; '97 134; '01 335
OSO Onions, '04 30
paste, '98 218
recipe, Caramelized Onions, '04 30
selecting, '88 87
substituting for shallots in recipes, '00 100
using in salads, '96 192
varieties of, '88 87 (illustrations)
Oranges
types of, '99 250; '01 30
using in recipes, '99 250
Outdoor cooking. *See* FOK/Campsite cooking,
Grilling, Smoking (cooking method).
Ovens, '83 191; '84 211; '86 113; '87 130
checking oven temperature, '96 230; '01 98
cleaning, '87 130; '01 335
convection, '86 113
conventional, '86 113
microwave, '83 191; '84 211; '86 113, 227; '87 130;
'92 176
preheating, '86 13
racks, cleaning, '01 260
Pancakes, '04 148
adding fruit to batter, '04 148
batter, '04 148
cooking, '04 148
as dessert, '02 70
recipe, Lemon-Blueberry Pancakes, '04 148
Pan sizes, '96 332; '97 112 (chart); '00 128;
'01 98
Paraffin, '89 244
as a seal in canning, '84 180; '89 142; '91 300

Parchment paper, '99 250
Parsley, keeping fresh, '98 72
Pastas, '87 177; '96 208
basic categories, '87 177
cooking, '87 177; '95 30; '05 242
measuring, '87 177
recipe, Fettuccine Primavera, '04 64
reheating, '87 177; '95 31
salads, '02 240; '05 242
storing, '87 177; '03 186
substituting, '87 177
Pastry. *See* FOK/Piecrust.
Peaches
kinds of, '02 178
overripe fruit, uses for, '97 174
selecting, '02 178
Peanut butter, '96 256
storing, '01 202
Peanuts, '83 228, 229
boiling, '83 228
chopping, '83 229
roasting, '83 228
Pears, '85 233
cooking, '85 233; '00 250
peeling, '85 233
ripening, '85 233; '02 216
selecting, '85 233
storing, '02 216
types of, '02 216
Peas, black-eyed
recipe, Marinated Black-Eyed Peas,
'01 30
recipe, Pickled Black-Eyed Peas, '01 30
Peas, dried, '88 4
buying, '88 4
cooking, '88 4; '00 180
soaking, '88 4
storing, '88 4
Pecans, '83 228, 229; '94 59
chopping, '83 229; '95 208
as garnish, '94 59
toasting, '83 228
Pepper, ground, cayenne, or red, '98 58
pepper mill, '02 316
Peppers, '85 4; '92 176; '94 29; '95 208
cooking stuffed, '01 118
dried chiles, '01 202
freezing, '85 4; '02 132
as garnish, '82 280; '89 100
removing skins of, '85 4; '02 132
roasting, '92 176; '02 132
selecting, '94 29; '01 202
storing, '94 29
substituting, '85 4
types of, '85 4; '98 218; '01 166, 202
working with hot peppers, '85 4; '94 29; '95 208;
'01 202
Persimmons, '85 233; '00 250
freezing, '85 233; '00 250
preparing, '85 233
selecting, '85 233; '00 250
types of, '00 250
Pesto
paste, '98 218
as a spread, '00 206
storing, '00 206
using, '02 316
Pickles, '87 150
pickling vegetables, '87 150
relishes, '03 102
spoilage, '87 150
Picnic
storage containers for, '03 176
supplies, '03 176

Piecrust, '82 234; 235; '92 52, 314; '94 210; '95 246;
'96 76
crumb crust, '99 250
equipment, '82 234; '94 332; '95 208
finishing, '82 234; '98 36
flavor variations of, '97 72; '00 330; '01 335
glazing, '82 235
lining with melted chocolate, '97 36
mixing, '82 234; '92 52; '95 246
phyllo dough, leftover, '02 178
preventing overbrowning, '92 314; '95 30
preventing sogginess, '86 330; '91 300; '92 314
puff pastry, '97 56
recipe, Water-Whipped Baked Pastry Shell, '95 246
refrigerated dough, '05 164
rolling, '82 234; '92 314
using cookie dough as, '01 335
variations of, '82 234, 235
Pineapple
adding to pancakes, '02 70
juice as food preservative, '02 178
Planning meals. *See* FOK/Meal planning.
Plastic containers, storing, '99 250
Poaching, '85 127
eggs, '85 127
equipment, '85 127
fish, '85 127
fruits, '85 127
liquid to use, '85 127
Pomegranate seeds, '00 250
freezing, '00 250
using, '00 250
Popcorn, '00 224
restoring moisture to dry kernels, '00 224
Pork. *See also* FOK/Ham.
carnitas, '02 148
cooking, '95 246
nutritional value, '98 198
recipe, Barbecue Ribs, '99 68
Potatoes, '84 210, 211. *See also* FOK/Sweet Potatoes.
adding to soups and stews, '02 46
Easter Egg Potatoes, '04 94
frozen prepared, '02 46
instant, '02 46
methods of mashing, '97 278
preparing, '84 210, 211; '97 206; '99 100; '00 206;
'01 335
selecting, '84 210, 211; '98 256
storing, '84 211; '98 256; '03 70
using to absorb too much pepper or salt in cooking,
'96 76
Poultry. *See* FOK/Chicken, Turkey.
Pound cakes. *See* FOK/Cakes.
Pressure cooker, using to cook peas, '00 180
Puddings, '86 330; '96 256. *See also* FOK/Custards.
bread, '00 128
preventing "skin" from forming, '86 330
Pumpkins, '85 233
as jack-o'-lanterns, '97 232
preparing for cooking, '85 233
selecting, '85 233
as a side dish, '01 220
storing, '85 233
substituting canned for fresh, '98 256
using pumpkin shell as serving container, '98 256
Raisins
chopping, '02 316
freezing, '02 316
selecting, '02 316
storing, '02 316
using in recipes, '02 316
Raspberries
making sauce, '92 314
morsels, '02 28

Recipe preparation, '86 13; **'91** 22, 23; **'93** 235;
  '96 76; **'99** 30; **'01** 98. *See also* **FOK/Cooking
  directions, Handling food properly,
  Substitutions.**
  baking techniques, **'89** 57; **'98** 218; **'02** 100
  cleaning up, **'86** 13; **'95** 31 (illustration); **'98** 198,
    256; **'99** 100, 128, 224; **'00** 66, 206, 330; **'01** 50,
    166, 300; **'02** 216, 316
  cutting recipes for smaller yields, **'97** 184; **'02** 194
  determining solutions to problems, **'93** 235;
    '96 21, 76
  doubling recipes, **'91** 22, 23; **'92** 66; **'95** 30; **'01** 335;
    '02 194; **'03** 274
  enhancing recipes, **'00** 156; **'02** 148
  equipment, **'86** 13; **'96** 160, 208; **'98** 218; **'01** 260;
    '02 100, 240; **'03** 274
  following instructions in *Southern Living Annual
    Recipes,* **'02** 240
  freezing berries, **'98** 138
  frying, **'02** 216
  greasing bakeware, **'98** 238; **'01** 335
  measuring, **'86** 13; **'95** 274; **'02** 100
  mistakes in, **'01** 50
  parchment paper, **'99** 250
  planning menus, **'86** 13; **'02** 178
  preparing ingredients, **'86** 13; **'95** 30, 31
    (illustration), 208; **'00** 156, 206; **'02** 288
  presentation, **'99** 128, 148; **'02** 194
  securing wooden spoons on cook pots, **'00** 300
  shortcuts in, **'96** 256; **'05** 70
  tasting along the way, **'98** 138
  trying new recipes, **'01** 202
  tubes of paste: onion, pesto, tomato, **'98** 218
  utensils, **'86** 13; **'01** 98
Recipes
  creating handmade cookbooks, **'03** 274
  enlarging copies of, **'01** 260
  organizing, **'98** 198; **'03** 274
  prize-winning tips, **'04** 48
  recording, **'02** 316
Recycling, '92 28; **'02** 148
  items to be recycled, **'92** 28
  packaging of products, **'92** 28
  setting up home recycling center, **'92** 28
  the three Rs, **'92** 28
Refrigerator, '83 94; **'87** 130; **'01** 98
  canned foods (opened), **'83** 94
  checking temperature of, **'01** 166
  cleaning, **'84** 11; **'87** 130; **'01** 166
  cleaning out, **'00** 300
  dairy products, **'83** 94
  food storage chart, **'83** 94
  meats, **'83** 94
Relishes, '03 102
Rhubarb, freezing, '01 118
Rice, '87 46; **'05** 50
  cooking, **'95** 30; **'98** 238; **'01** 335; **'02** 216
  flavoring, **'87** 46; **'01** 335
  fried rice, **'05** 50
  mixes, **'04** 204
  preparing, **'87** 46
  ready-to-eat, **'04** 204
  recipe, Cranberry-Almond Wild Rice,
    '04 204
  recipe, Fried Rice 101, **'05** 50
  recipe, Pecan Rice, **'04** 204
  recipe, Saffron Rice Pilaf, **'04** 204
  reheating, **'87** 46
  storing, **'87** 46
  types of, **'87** 46; **'99** 208; **'01** 220

Rolls, '83 323. *See also* **FOK/Biscuits, Breads,
  Yeast.**
  frozen roll dough, **'03** 224
  glazing, **'83** 323
  recipe, Cheddar Crescents, **'05** 70
  recipe, Lemon-Orange Rolls, **'05** 70
  removing burned bottoms from, **'96** 51
  variations of, **'83** 323
  yeast, **'83** 323
Rosemary, **'00** 28
Roux, '87 211, 212
  color of, **'87** 211, 212
  cooking temperature, **'87** 211
  cooking times, **'87** 211
  ingredient amounts, **'87** 211
  microwave roux, **'87** 211, 212
  oven roux, **'87** 211
  reducing fat in roux, **'87** 212
  utensils to use, **'87** 212
Safety, '84 37, 180; **'90** 22; **'91** 92, 300. *See also*
  FOK/Handling food properly.
  canning fruits and vegetables, **'84** 180; **'91** 300
  extinguishing a range-top fire, **'99** 50
  first aid for burns, **'90** 22; **'99** 50
  in the kitchen, **'84** 37; **'90** 22; **'96** 256; **'99** 50
  preventing burns in the kitchen, **'84** 37; **'90** 22
  when serving food, **'91** 300
  when using the microwave, **'91** 92; **'00** 28
Salad dressings, '97 184
  adding flavor to bottled dressings, **'00** 66
  recipe, Fresh Lemon Vinaigrette, **'04** 30; **'05** 242
  recipe, Grandpa Jim's Salad Dressing, **'01** 182
  recipe, Sugar-and-Vinegar Dressing, **'04** 174
Salads, '82 313; **'91** 300
  congealed, **'82** 313; **'91** 300
  equipment, **'94** 332
  recipe, Confetti Pasta Salad, **'05** 242
  recipe, Cranberry-Pecan Chicken Salad, **'05** 284
  using toasted oats as topping, **'00** 28
  washing salad greens, **'97** 36
Salsa
  using leftover for soup, **'00** 206
  using as a marinade, **'02** 46
Salt
  as cleaning agent on dishes, **'01** 335
  measuring, **'01** 138
  types of, **'01** 138
  using on boil overs in oven, **'01** 335
Sandwiches, '05 28
  bar for entertaining, **'05** 28
  fillings for, **'05** 28
  grilled, **'05** 28
  grill press for, **'05** 28
  on the road, **'02** 194
  storing finger sandwiches, **'01** 335
Sauces, '83 146, 147; **'92** 314; **'94** 274; **'95** 30
  chilling quickly, **'86** 13
  reduction sauces, **'94** 274; **'96** 332
  thickening, **'83** 146, 147; **'00** 28
Sausage, '87 238
  classifications of, **'87** 238
  freezing, **'87** 238; **'02** 28
  meat-cure mix, **'91** 300
  mock, **'00** 330
Scallops, '99 180
  amounts to buy, **'99** 180
  cooking, **'99** 180
  selecting, **'99** 180
  types of, **'99** 180
Seafood, '90 130; **'01** 220. *See also* **FOK/Crab, Fish,
  Scallops, Shellfish, Shrimp, Surimi.**
Seasonings, '92 121, 344; **'93** 182; **'96** 304. *See also*
  FOK/Herbs, Oils, Spices.
  bouquet garni, **'03** 30

  frozen seasoning blend, **'03** 132
  Greek seasoning, **'03** 132
  how to use, **'03** 176
  measuring, **'03** 176
  in recipes, **'91** 22
  recipes for seasoning blends, **'92** 121
  storing, **'82** 198; **'84** 11; **'92** 121; **'98** 36;
    '03 208
  substitutions, **'92** 344; **'01** 118; **'03** 132
Secrets from the *Southern Living* Test Kitchens,
  '02 240
Sesame oil, **'01** 118
Shelf life, '83 65
  of canned foods, **'83** 65
  chart, **'83** 65
  of packaged mixes, **'83** 65
  of staples, **'83** 65
Shellfish, '94 105, 106
  buying, **'94** 106
  cooking, **'01** 220
  storing, **'01** 220
  transporting fresh, **'94** 105, 106
Sherbet, **'00** 156
Shopping. *See* **FOK/Grocery shopping.**
Shrimp, '87 12; **'94** 105, 106; **'00** 180
  amounts to buy, **'00** 180
  cooking, **'87** 12; **'00** 180
  deveining, **'92** 52; **'01** 138
  freezing, **'00** 224
  grilling, **'92** 52
  recipe, Grandpa Jim's Shrimp Sauce,
    '01 182
  recipe, Shrimp Cocktail Sauce, **'01** 182
  recipe, Shrimp Sauce, **'01** 182
  selecting, **'94** 106
  serving, **'03** 224
  storing, **'00** 180
  transporting fresh, **'94** 105
Sifting, '82 197, 198; **'85** 192, 193; **'87** 12
  flour, **'82** 197, 198; **'87** 12
  powdered sugar, **'85** 192; **'87** 12
Silver, '88 300
  avoiding spotting and pitting, **'88** 300
  buying sterling, **'02** 178
  cleaning, **'88** 300
  removing tarnish from, **'88** 300
  serving spoons, **'99** 296
  storing, **'88** 300
Slow cookers, using to serve food, **'03** 224
Smoking (cooking method), '95 116
  adding the food, **'95** 116
  cleaning the smoker, **'95** 117
  filling the water pan, **'95** 116
  maintaining the temperature, **'95** 116
  soaking the wood, **'95** 116
  starting the fire, **'95** 116
Snacks, '91 200, 201; **'01** 118
  health bars, **'02** 100
  nutritious, **'91** 200, 201
  planning, **'91** 200, 201
  recipes for, **'91** 200, 201
  on the road, **'02** 194
Sodium, '90 72
  content of in surimi, **'90** 130
  and food labels, **'90** 72
Sorbet, '00 156
  homemade, **'03** 176
Soufflés, '84 92
  testing for doneness, **'84** 92
Soups, '89 30; **'95** 274; **'96** 160; **'00** 206. *See also*
  FOK/Stews.
  as appetizers, **'98** 112; **'00** 206
  bouillons, **'00** 250
  broths, **'89** 30; **'98** 138; **'00** 100; **'01** 98

dashi, '00 100
freezing, '89 30
as gifts, '91 95
presentation, '98 112
pureeing, '99 250
recipe, Chicken-and-Black Bean Soup, '05 102
recipe for broth, '03 274
reheating, '89 30
removing bay leaf, '95 314
stocks, '89 30; '95 30
storing, '89 30
Sour cream, as cooling condiment to spicy foods, '01 202
Spaghetti sauce, substituting vegetable juice for tomato
     sauce, '98 256
Spices, '87 297; '99 180. See also FOK/Herbs, Seasonings.
     amounts to use, '87 297; '99 208
     buying, '87 297; '98 58
     checking for freshness, '84 11; '87 297; '98 58
     grinding your own, '87 297; '98 58
     soothing burning taste buds, '01 138
     sprinkle opening, '99 180
     storing, '82 198; '84 11; '87 297; '98 58
     substituting, '87 297; '01 118
     toasting, '98 58
     using to enhance coffee, '00 224
     whole spices, '87 297; '98 58
Spinach
     eliminating excess moisture from, '02 240
     freezing, '02 132
     nutritional value of, '02 132, 240
     using frozen, '02 240
Squash, winter, '88 229, 230; '00 250
     cooking, '88 229, 230
     determining amount to buy, '88 229
     selecting, '88 229, 230
     storing, '88 229, 230
     types of, '88 229, 230
Stains, removing, '96 304; '99 100; '02 194
Stews, baking in oven, '98 256
Stir frying, '95 30; '01 335
Stocks. See FOK/Soups.
Storage containers
     for jams, jellies, and preserves, '03 148
     for picnics, '03 176
Strawberries, '82 109
     buying, '82 109
     freezing, '01 118
     as garnish, '82 138
     preparing, '99 100
Substitutions, '92 344; '96 208; '98 256; '00 100
     alcohol, '92 314; '99 148; '00 66; '01 138
     emergency substitutions, '92 344 (chart); '00 66;
          '01 220
     flour, '99 224
     herbs and spices, '01 118
     lemon juice, '99 100
     light ingredients, '00 100
     using tofu as a substitution, '99 128
     vinegar, '99 100; '00 66
Sugar, '85 19
     making colored sugar, '86 331
     making lemon sugar, '97 56
     measuring, '85 19; '87 12
     preventing brown sugar from drying out, '85 19
     sifting powdered sugar, '85 192; '87 12
     softening brown, '98 198
     substitutions, '85 19
     types of, '85 19
Surimi, '90 130
Sweet potatoes, '88 208; '00 250. See also FOK/
     Potatoes.
     cooking, '88 208; '00 250; '01 220
     handling, '88 208
     selecting, '88 208

storing, '88 208; '00 250
substituting canned for fresh, '88 208
yams, '88 208
Syrups, commercial, '04 130
Table setting, '90 182, 225
     centerpieces, '90 205; '98 72; '01 335
     for formal entertaining, '90 182
     illustration, '90 182
Tahini (sesame seed paste), '96 304
     storing, '01 202
Tamales, '94 192. See also FOK/Masa harina.
     making tamale dough, '94 192
Tangerines, types of, '01 30
Tapioca, as a thickening agent, '83 147
Tarts, '95 274
Tea, '85 120, 121
     brewing, '85 120,121
     storing, '85 121
     types of, '85 120, 121
Templates for holiday gift box cake, '03 308
Thawing food, '83 14, 15; '86 330; '87 208; '88 165
     turkey, '83 284; '86 330
Thermometers, '89 191, 192; '92 202; '98 306
     deep-fat frying, '84 37
     instant-read, '89 191, 192; '92 202, 314; '93 104;
          '03 102
     meat, '89 191, 192; '92 202
     storing, '89 192; '92 202
     testing for accuracy, '89 192; '92 202; '96 230
Thickening agents, '83 146, 147. See also FOK/
     Arrowroot, Cornstarch, Eggs, Oats, Tapioca.
Tofu, '99 128
Tomatillos, about, '97 232
Tomatoes, '85 181, 182; '93 23; '95 30
     drying cherry tomatoes, '93 23
     enhancing flavor of, '01 335
     freezing leftover paste, '96 160
     frying, '01 118
     as garnish, '82 280; '89 100
     paste, '98 218
     peeling large amount of, '82 138; '85 181, 182
     recipe, Marinated Dried Cherry Tomatoes, '93 23
     ripening, '85 181
     seeding, '85 182
     selecting, '85 181
     slicing, '85 181, 182
     storing, '85 181; '00 206
     stuffing, '85 182
Tortillas, '95 44; '00 224; '03 132
     equipment, '95 44
     how to cook, '95 44
     how to shape, '95 44
     recipe, Flour Tortillas, '95 44
     reheating, '95 44
     storing, '95 44
     using for quesadillas, '00 156
     using leftover, '01 202; '03 132
     as wraps, '03 132
Transporting food, '01 220
     for road trips, '02 194
Turkey, '83 284, 285; '93 306, 307
     carving, '93 306, 307
     chart, '83 285
     cooking, '83 284, 285; '86 330; '98 306;
          '02 288
     cuts of, '01 260
     deep-frying, '00 300
     determining amounts to buy for entertaining,
          '90 276; '99 296
     handling properly, '87 208
     leftovers, storing, '83 285; '98 306; '02 288
     recipe, Benny Sauce Marinated Turkey, '98 306
     roasting, '02 288
     selecting fresh or frozen, '99 296; '02 288

stuffing, '83 284; '98 306
thawing, '83 284; '86 330; '98 306; '99 296;
     '00 300; '02 288
trussing, '02 288
Turnips, '01 220
U.S. Department of Agriculture (USDA), '89 142;
     '90 72; '92 65, 202; '93 83; '02 100
Vegetable cooking spray, '92 208; '98 138
     cleanup, easy, '82 198, 314; '84 48; '92 314;
          '93 104; '95 31; '01 50
Vegetable oil, '82 189; '84 211; '88 112, 113; '98 112
     deep-fat frying thermometer, '84 37; '88 113
     preventing fire, '84 37; '88 112, 113
Vegetables, '82 138; '83 94; '84 180, 211, 249; '86 140,
     141; '89 243, 244; '92 344; '93 132; '94 29, 92;
     '95 30. See also FOK/Broccoli, Brussels
          sprouts, Canning, Cauliflower, Celery, Corn,
          Garnishes, Greens, Lettuce, Mirlitons,
          Mushrooms, Onions, Peas, Peppers, Potatoes,
          Pumpkins, Rhubarb, Squash, Sweet potatoes,
          Tomatoes, Turnips.
     basic cooking methods, '82 138; '84 249; '94 29, 92
          (chart)
     blackening to remove skins, '01 50
     broths, '00 100
     canning, '84 180; '93 136, 137
     as centerpiece, '01 335
     as "containers" for food, '97 174
     cutting, '86 13; '92 52; '93 132; '94 29; '96 21;
          '98 72; '01 202, 260
     determining amounts to buy for entertaining,
          '90 276
     enhancing flavor of steamed, '01 30
     exotic, '01 166
     freezing, '87 112; '01 260, 335
     grilling, '83 191; '92 52; '95 274; '97 56
     growing your own, '98 112
     health benefits of, '00 46
     julienning, '02 316
     microwaving, '82 138; '83 191; '99 296
     "perking up," '01 335
     pre-packaged, '02 70
     preparing, '86 140, 141; '89 243, 244; '98 238;
          '99 100
     seasoning, '94 92 (chart)
     selecting, '84 249; '86 140, 141; '89 243, 244;
          '94 29
     steaming, '99 296; '01 30; '02 70
     stir-frying, '82 138; '83 191
     storing, '83 94; '84 211; '86 140, 141; '89 243, 244;
          '94 29; '96 208; '01 98; '02 132; '03 176
     substitutions, '92 344
     winter vegetables, '84 249; '88 229; '01 30
Vinegar
     flavored, '03 102
     as a stain remover, '99 100
     as a substitute in recipes, '99 100; '00 66
     using to enhance flavors, '99 100; '01 30
Walnut oil, '01 118
Water, adding flavor to bottled or tap water,
     '96 21
Web sites, watermelon, '98 198
Whipping cream, '97 72
     stabilizer, '02 216
White chocolate. See FOK/Chocolate.
Wines, '85 292, 293; '98 162; '99 30, 328
     adding fresh ginger to, '01 335
     amounts to buy for entertaining, '99 328
     champagne, '85 293; '96 21; '98 306; '99 328
     chilling, '99 328
     cooking with, '00 46; '01 335; '02 132
     freezing, '00 46; '02 132
     mirin, '00 100
     removing the cork, '99 328

selecting, **'85** 292; **'99** 30, 68, 100, 128, 224, 328;
  '00 46; **'01** 300
selecting in restaurants, **'96** 140
serving, **'85** 292, 293; **'99** 328; **'00** 46
storing, **'85** 292
substituting for in recipes, **'00** 46
sugar content of, **'99** 328
Wok cooking, '85 76
  equipment, **'85** 76
  preparing food for, **'85** 76
Yams. *See* **FOK/Sweet potatoes.**
Yeast, '89 268; **'04** 224. *See also* **FOK/Biscuits,**
  Breads, Rolls.
  kinds of, **'89** 268
  proofing, **'01** 50
  using leftover, **'99** 50; **'01** 335
Yogurt
  drinkable, **'02** 194
  frozen, **'00** 156
  instead of fruit puree, **'97** 206
  as a substitute for buttermilk in recipes, **'00** 66
FROSTINGS. *See also* **FILLINGS, GLAZES,**
  TOPPINGS.
Almond Buttercream Frosting, **'97** 61; **'99** 155
Almond-Butter Frosting, **'86** 107
Amaretto Buttercream Frosting, **'98** 57
Amaretto Frosting, **'86** 246
Apricot Frosting, **'81** 192
Banana-Nut Frosting, **'79** 115
Boiled Frosting, **'90** 45; **'92** 14; **'93** 318
Bourbon Buttercream Frosting, **'03** 286
Bourbon Frosting, **'88** 236
Brandy Cream Frosting, **'86** 239
Browned Butter Frosting, **'97** 247
Brown Sugar Frosting, **'79** 13; **'87** 296; **'91** 236;
  '01 201
Brown Sugar Meringue Frosting, **'81** 70
Butter Cream Frosting, **'88** 279
Buttercream Frosting, **'85** 322; **'92** 230; **'93** 53, 285;
  '96 96; **'98** 155; **'00** 235, 244; **'03** 200; **'05** 308
Buttercream Frosting, White, **'93** 337
Buttercream Icing, **'83** 73
Buttercream, Spiced, **'84** 226
Butter Frosting, **'80** 129
Butter Frosting, Browned, **'86** 248
Butter Frosting, Williamsburg, **'81** 120; **'82** 23
Buttermilk Frosting, **'85** 249
Butter Pecan Frosting, **'80** 229
Butter Whip Frosting, **'96** 119
Caramel-Coconut-Pecan Frosting, Quick, **'05** 211
Caramel Frosting, **'81** 278, M289; **'82** 314; **'83** 43;
  '84 39, 263; **'86** 239; **'87** 265; **'89** 55, 236;
  '90 307; **'98** 195; **'00** 52; **'03** 329
Caramel Frosting, Creamy, **'81** 71
Caramel Frosting, Easy, **'87** 39
Caramel Frosting, Favorite, **'83** 106
Caramel Frosting, Quick, **'04** 55; **'05** 211
Caramel-Pecan Frosting, Quick, **'05** 211
Carob Frosting, **'85** 218
Carolina Dream Frosting, **'88** 278
Cheese Spread, Tropical, **'95** 46
Cherry Frosting, **'86** 217
Cherry Icing, Chunky, **'03** 94
Cherry-Nut Cream Cheese Frosting, **'96** 249
Chocolate
  Almond Frosting, Chocolate-, **'83** 241
  Buttercream Frosting, Chocolate, **'96** 229;
    '98 M100
  Butter Frosting, Chocolate, **'89** 271
  Buttermilk Frosting, Chocolate-, **'99** 99

Candy Frosting, Chocolate, **'81** 238
Cherry Frosting, Chocolate-, **'89** 294
Chocolate Frosting, **'80** M171; **'81** 265; **'82** 262;
  '83 79, 99, M233, 253; **'84** 200; **'85** 323; **'86** 8,
  93, 138, 239, 314; **'87** M97, 198, 199, 293;
  '89 M25; **'90** 194, 252, 265, 284, 309; **'91** 248;
  '92 319; **'93** 239; **'94** 133; **'96** 253, 254; **'97** M87,
  254; **'99** 271; **'04** 136
Chocolate Icing, **'03** 19
Coca-Cola Frosting, **'02** 181
Cocoa Frosting, **'86** 60
Coconut Chocolate Frosting, **'79** 13
Coffee Frosting, Chocolate-, **'84** 36; **'88** 269
Cola Frosting, **'81** 238; **'00** 120
Cola Frosting, Chocolate-, **'95** 56
Cream Cheese Frosting, Chocolate-, **'02** 256
Creamy Chocolate Frosting, **'85** 314; **'86** 316;
  '87 241; **'99** 307
Fluffy Chocolate Frosting, **'86** 336; **'87** 58
Fudge Frosting, **'81** 303; **'87** 296; **'89** 56; **'94** 51;
  '01 59
Fudge Frosting, Chocolate, **'83** 105; **'00** 287
Fudge Frosting, Quick, **'81** 278
Ganache, Chocolate, **'93** 255; **'01** M235
Honey Chocolate Frosting, **'79** 83
Kahlúa Frosting, Chocolate, **'91** 298
Marshmallow Frosting, Chocolate-, **'83** 245;
  '04 210
Mint Chocolate Frosting, **'99** M176
Mocha Buttercream, **'89** 42
Mocha Butter Cream Frosting, **'79** 281
Mocha-Buttercream Frosting, **'86** 26
Mocha Frosting, **'83** 301; **'84** 316; **'87** 224; **'94** 292;
  '97 35; **'99** 66
Mocha Frosting, Creamy, **'82** 289; **'84** 311;
  '91 248
Nut Frosting, Chocolate, **'80** 140
Peanut Butter Frosting, Chocolate-, **'84** 240; **'87** 222;
  '00 120
Peanut Butter-Fudge Frosting, **'87** 184
Perfect Chocolate Frosting, **'90** 307; **'03** 319
Rich Chocolate Frosting, **'84** 304
Root Beer Frosting, **'04** 211
Rum Frosting, Chocolate, **'79** 67
Satiny Chocolate Frosting, **'85** 126; **'89** 43
Velvet Frosting, **'02** 297
White Chocolate Buttercream Frosting,
  '97 M284
White Chocolate-Cream Cheese Frosting, **'94** 58;
  '98 323
White Chocolate-Cream Cheese Tiered Cake
  Frosting, **'94** 125
White Chocolate Frosting, **'88** 280; **'91** 101; **'97** 111;
  '00 306
White Chocolate Ganache, **'01** 253
Cinnamon-Cream Cheese Frosting, **'03** 332
Cinnamon-Cream Frosting, **'84** 311
Cinnamon Frosting, Buttery, **'81** M139
Cinnamon Roll Icing, **'03** 247
Coconut Cream Cheese Frosting, **'86** 60
Coconut-Cream Cheese Frosting, **'04** 137; **'05** 317
Coconut Frosting, **'82** 262; **'91** 269
Coconut Frosting, Creamy, **'80** 287
Coconut Frosting, Nutty, **'86** 8
Coconut Milk Frosting, **'00** 117
Coconut-Pecan Frosting, **'81** 296; **'83** M233;
  '84 43, 322; **'97** 99; **'03** 289
Coffee Buttercream, **'95** 277
Coffee Buttercream Frosting, **'99** 155
Coffee Frosting, **'94** 86
Coffee Liqueur Ganache Icing, **'05** 322
Cola Frosting, **'81** 238; **'02** 298
Colored Frostings, **'90** 21; **'00** 61
Cream Cheese-Butter Pecan Frosting, **'03** 288

Cream Cheese Frosting, **'79** 45; **'80** 140, 253, 299;
  '82 135, 244; **'83** 105, 215, M233; **'84** 201, 255,
  315, 316; **'85** 118, 121; **'86** 217, 337; **'87** 58;
  '90 305, 308; **'92** 120; **'93** 20; **'94** 254; **'95** 139;
  '96 282; **'97** 230, 277, 330; **'98** 275; **'99** 307, 315;
  '01 34, 185, 244, 271; **'02** 83, 209, 323; **'03** 55,
  315; **'05** 232, 287, 299
Cream Cheese Frosting, Deluxe, **'80** 120
Cream Cheese Frosting, Fluffy, **'80** 245
Cream Cheese Frosting, Nutty, **'85** 117; **'96** 263
Creamy Frosting, **'04** 83
Crème Chantilly, **'87** 9; **'91** 297
Crème de Menthe Frosting, **'86** 245; **'93** 256; **'97** 35
Decorating Techniques, Cake, **'83** 72, 240
Decorator Frosting, **'82** 20, 307; **'83** 106; **'87** 86;
  '91 282; **'93** 285; **'01** 91
Decorator Frosting, Creamy, **'79** 117
Decorator Frosting, Green, **'93** 286
Decorator Frosting, Yellow, **'93** 283
Divinity Frosting, **'79** 229; **'01** 270
Fluffy Frosting, **'79** 246; **'86** 235; **'88** 268; **'89** 254;
  '90 308
Fluffy White Frosting, **'90** 105; **'95** 319; **'01** 330
Fondant, Faux, **'98** M154
Fondant, Rolled, **'92** 69
Fondant Teapot Spout, Handle, Daisies, and Butterflies,
  '04 83
Ganache Cream, **'92** 318
Grapefruit Frosting, **'89** 308
Heavenly Frosting, **'80** 140
Lemon
  Buttercream Frosting, Lemon, **'83** 301; **'86** 61;
    '91 247; **'03** 105
  Butter Cream Frosting, Lemon-, **'85** 117
  Coconut Frosting, Lemon-, **'90** 253
  Cream Cheese Frosting, Lemon-, **'81** 157
  Creamy Lemon Frosting, **'79** 93
  Lemon Frosting, **'85** 191; **'86** 217; **'93** 81
  Orange-Lemon Frosting, **'88** 92
  White Frosting, Lemony, **'88** 7; **'03** 317
Lime Buttercream Frosting, **'03** 105
Maple Frosting, **'82** 217; **'85** 322; **'96** 17
Meringue Frosting, **'86** 336; **'87** 84; **'99** 118
Meringue Frosting, Italian, **'98** 70
Microwave Frosting, Easy, **'05** M63
Mint Cream Frosting, **'93** 216
Mint Frosting, **'88** 80
Never Fail Frosting, **'86** 314
Orange
  Buttercream Frosting, Orange, **'80** 70; **'99** 117;
    '03 105
  Butter Frosting, Orange, **'83** 300
  Cream Cheese Frosting, Citrus, **'99** 223
  Cream Cheese Frosting, Orange, **'81** 70; **'82** 16;
    '92 19
  Cream Cheese Frosting, Orange-, **'04** 258
  Cream Frosting, Orange, **'81** 207; **'82** 14
  Creamy Orange Frosting, **'83** 24, 241
  Lemon Frosting, Orange-, **'88** 92
  Orange Frosting, **'81** 7; **'86** 61; **'88** 119
Panocha Frosting, **'89** 296
Peanut Butter Frosting, **'83** 223; **'84** 153; **'85** 34
Peanut Butter Swirl Frosting, **'86** 109
Peanut Frosting, Creamy, **'80** 87
Pecan-Cream Cheese Frosting, **'02** 294
Pecan Frosting, **'86** 86
Peppermint Birthday Cake Frosting, Pink, **'92** 269
Peppermint Cream Cheese Frosting, **'98** 308
Peppermint Frosting, Quick, **'98** 308
Pineapple-Cream Cheese Frosting, **'95** 160
Piping Icing, **'92** 69
Piping Icing, Tips for, **'84** 302
Powdered Sugar Frosting, **'96** 319
Praline Frosting, **'01** 235

Praline Fudge Icing, '04 331
Quick Pour Frosting, '85 119
Royal Icing, '80 278; '81 21; '83 73; '84 303; '85 323;
   '87 295; '88 309; '91 281; '98 324; '02 49
Rum Buttercream Frosting, '99 117
Rum Cream, '88 154, 224
Satin Icing, '05 246
Sea Foam Frosting, '81 211; '91 271
Seven-Minute Double Boiler Frosting, '81 278
Seven-Minute Frosting, '80 289; '83 299, 301; '87 296;
   '89 55, 57; '94 98, 99; '97 71
Snow Peak Frosting, '82 53; '85 281
Spiced Cream, '89 215
Strawberry Buttercream Frosting, '04 55
Strawberry Frosting, '89 184
Toffee Frosting, English, '85 125
Vanilla Buttercream Frosting, '92 239; '94 99; '96 229;
   '97 111; '99 117; '03 286
Vanilla Frosting, '84 36; '85 236; '92 14, 274
Vanilla-Rum Frosting, '85 324
Whipped Cream Frosting, '83 229; '85 125; '87 263;
   '89 43; '93 86; '96 229; '03 105; '05 107
White Chocolate-Cream Cheese Frosting, '94 58
White Frosting, '83 268
White Frosting, Fluffy, '81 278
White Frosting, Luscious, '81 71

FRUIT. *See also* specific types.
Acorn Squash, Fruited, '85 235
Acorn Squash, Fruit-Stuffed, '81 295
Appetizers
  Bowl, Sparkling Fresh Fruit, '80 146
  Brie, Tropical Breeze, '94 M18
  Brown Sugar Dip with Fruit, Buttery, '90 243
  Canapés, Fruit-Topped, '85 80
  Cascade, Fruit, '86 104
  Cheese Ball, Fruit-and-Nut, '91 251
  Cup, Appetizer Fruit, '86 131
  Curried Rum Sauce, Tropical Fruit with, '91 164
  Dip, Ginger Fruit, '90 110
  Dip, Orange Fruit, '96 190
  Dips, Fun Fruit, '01 109
  Fresh Fruit, Mint Dip with, '87 146
  Fresh Fruit with Lemon Sauce, '82 290
  Kebabs with Coconut Dressing, Fruit, '87 251
  Mix, Trash, '01 204
  Picks, Fruit on, '80 159
  Soup, Cold Fresh Fruit, '87 157
  Soup, Swedish Fruit, '82 313; '83 65
  Spread, Fruit and Cheese, '81 245
  Spread, Fruited Cream Cheese, '91 306
  Spread, Nutty Fruit-and-Cheese, '87 246;
    '02 164
Bake, Cranberry-Mustard Fruit, '90 287
Baked Curried Fruit, '03 247
Baked Fruit, Gingered, '81 232
Baked Fruit, Ginger-Orange, '93 313
Baked Spiced Fruit, '89 305
Bake, Hot Fruit, '81 270
Bake, Mustard Fruit, '90 291
Bake, Nutty Fruit, '83 127
Bars, Fruit and Nut Granola, '81 49
Beets, Fruited, '97 28
Beverages
  Apricot Fruit Flip, '91 18
  Batida, Citrus, '02 274
  Blender Fruit Beverage, '83 318
  Breakfast Drink, Yummy, '01 133
  Breakfast Fruit Juicy, '86 176
  Brew, Fruity Witches', '95 273
  Brunch Punch, '04 281; '05 335
  Champagne Fruit Slush, '90 322
  Champions' Cooler, '96 M181
  Cider, Warm Citrus, '01 46
  Citrus Blush, '98 197

  Cocktails, Sea Breeze, '97 161
  Cooler, Four-Fruit, '86 101
  Cooler, Fruited Wine, '86 176
  Cooler, Fruit Juice, '92 67
  Coolers, Fruit, '98 197
  Cooler, Speedy Spring, '02 58
  Float, Frosty Fruit, '87 159
  Four-Fruit Refresher, '79 174
  Frappé, Hootenanny, '89 110
  Freeze, Berry, '05 220
  Honey-Yogurt Smoothie, Fruited, '88 231;
    '89 23
  Ice Ring, '03 141
  Ice Ring, Easy, '03 141
  Ice Tropical, '79 174
  Lemonade, Cherry-Berry, '03 89
  Patio Blush, '99 93
  Punch, Autumn Harvest, '96 277
  Punch, Brunch, '05 335
  Punch, Can-Can Fruit, '94 122
  Punch, Caribbean, '95 173
  Punch, Champagne, '03 141
  Punch, Citrus-Wine, '98 197
  Punch, Cottontail, '02 48
  Punch, Emerald Sea, '04 163
  Punch, Florida Fruit, '92 247
  Punch for a Bunch, '95 90
  Punch, Fresh Fruit, '98 155
  Punch, Fruit, '83 52; '01 106; '02 162
  Punch, Fruited Ice-Cube, '98 197
  Punch, Fruit Juice, '96 214
  Punch, Fruit Juice-and-Vodka, '96 214
  Punch, Fruit Juicy Rum, '91 175
  Punch, Fruit Slush, '91 278
  Punch, Golden Fruit, '80 299; '83 56; '96 278
  Punch, Happy New Year, '98 26
  Punch, Holiday Fruit, '79 232
  Punch, Holiday Hot Fruit, '92 286
  Punch, Hot Cider, '03 233
  Punch, Hot Fruit, '83 33
  Punch, Hot Spiced, '96 214
  Punch, Hot Spiced Rum, '96 214
  Punch, Hurricane, '00 61
  Punch, Margarita, '98 88
  Punch, Mixed Fruit, '90 207; '95 239
  Punch, Party Fruit, '82 137
  Punch, Passion Fruit, '90 169
  Punch, Pineapple Fruit, '02 49
  Punch, Poinsettia, '02 251
  Punch, Polka Dot, '95 178
  Punch, Slushy Fruit, '98 92
  Punch, Southern Fresh Fruit, '99 70
  Punch, Southern Fruit, '95 238
  Punch, Spiced Fruit, '88 2
  Punch, Spirited Fruit, '81 100
  Punch, Summertime Fruit, '80 160
  Punch, Sunset, '96 278
  Punch, Tropical Fruit, '81 51; '83 176; '90 169
  Refresher, Fruit, '91 203
  'ritas, Fruit, '94 157
  Sangría, '00 122
  Sangría, Garden, '01 100
  Sangría, Mock Tea, '99 336
  Sangría, Texas White, '02 86
  Sangría, Three-Fruit, '89 212
  Shake, Frosty Fruit, '87 23
  Shake, Tangy Fruit, '95 129
  Shake, Three-Fruit Yogurt, '01 173
  Shake, Tropical, '93 212; '04 21
  Sipper by the Glass, Fresh Mint-Citrus, '03 89
  Sipper, Fresh Mint-Citrus, '03 89
  Slush, Fruit, '96 157
  Slushy, Fruit, '80 146
  Slushy, Fruit Parfait, '02 185

  Smoothie, Citrus, '98 17
  Smoothie, Fruit, '89 87
  Smoothie, Two-Fruit, '89 182
  Smoothie, Yogurt-Fruit, '03 25
  Sparkle, Fruit, '99 289
  Sparkle, Tangerine, '98 54
  Spritzer, Fruit, '01 174
  Tea, Christmas Fruit, '83 275; '01 240
  Tea, Citrus Iced, '00 139
  Tea Cooler, Fruited, '94 131
  Tea, Fruit-and-Mint Iced, '98 84
  Tea, Fruited Mint, '88 79; '91 81
  Tea, Fruity Mint, '04 143
  Tea, Hot Russian, '97 274
  Tea, Hot Spiced Fruit, '87 242
  Tea, Refreshing Fruit, '97 122
  Tea-Ser, Tropical, '95 200
  Tea, Spiced Iced, '97 121
  Three-Fruit Drink, '79 38; '80 50; '87 199
  Tropical Fruit Drink, '85 43
  Tropical Fruit Whisper, '89 212
  Tropical Refresher, '96 157
  Wassail, '97 240; '99 268
  Wassail, Golden, '96 278
  Wassail, Winter, '03 295
  Whiskey Sours, '03 258
  Whiskey Sour Slushies, '04 106
  Whiskey Sours, Slushy, '03 258
Boats, Honeydew Fruit, '81 147
Bowl, White Grape Juice Fruit, '00 160
Braid, Fruit-and-Cheese, '86 214
Brandied Fruit, Hot, '80 48
Bread, Cranberry Fruit-Nut, '79 275
Bread, Fruity Banana, '95 78
Bread, Kahlúa Fruit-Nut, '79 235
Canning and Preserving
  Apple Rings, Cinnamon, '85 107
  Berries (except Strawberries), '80 128
  Conserve, Dried Fruit, '82 308
  Dehydration Chart, Fruit and Vegetable, '84 147
  Freezing Chart, Fruit, '85 187
  Jam, Tri-Berry Lemon, '98 214
  Juices, Fruit, '85 107
  Mixed Fruit, Unsweetened, '83 182
  Peaches, '80 128
  Peaches and Pears, '85 106
  Peaches, Honey-Sweet, '85 107
  Preserves, Fruity, '98 214
  Syrup, Fruit, '86 176
Chafing Dish Fruit, '89 305
Cheesecake, Island Breeze, '03 144
Chilled Fruit with Dressing, '85 222
Chutney, Autumn Fruit, '88 M230
Chutney, Fall Fruit, '97 218
Compotes
  Amaretto-Hot Fruit Compote, '90 250
  Baked Fruit Compote, '80 276; '84 314;
    '87 228
  Baked Mustard Fruit Compote, '85 47
  Beauberries Bordeaux, '98 18
  Brandied Fruit Compote, '96 286
  Champagne Fruit Compote, '81 309; '82 124
  Chilled Fruit Compote, '83 123
  Citrus Compote, '98 17
  Citrus Compote with Caramel Syrup, '98 313
  Dried Fruit Compote, '98 18
  Festive Fruit Compote, '94 279
  Fresh Fruit Compote, '79 162; '82 197, 272; '84 82;
    '94 190
  Fruit Compote, '86 330
  Gingered Fruit Compote, '88 184
  Hot Fruit Compote, '81 203; '83 53; '86 324;
    '90 124; '03 307
  Jícama-Fruit Compote, '92 49

FRUIT, Compotes
(continued)

Mixed Fruit Compote, '93 123
Praline Fruit Compote, Warm, '85 260
Pudding Compote, Fresh Fruit, '86 151
Raspberry Puree, Fruit Compote with, '88 81
Shortcakes with Fruit Compote, Cinnamon-Crunch, '03 194
Wine Fruit Compote, '81 272
Couscous with Mixed Fruit, '95 232
Cup, Mixed Fruit, '94 60
Cup, Tipsy Fruit, '81 268
Curried Fruit, Almond-, '83 261
Curried Fruit Bake, '87 241
Curried Fruit, Hot, '79 225; '81 264; '84 287; '95 72
Delight, Fruit, '86 131
Delight, Hot Fruit, '83 281
Delight, Winter Fruit, '80 243
Desserts. *See also* **FRUIT/Fruitcakes.**
Amaretto Crème on Fresh Fruit, '93 176
Angel Cakes with Almond Sugar, Mixed-Berry, '02 175
Balls, Fruit, '82 296; '84 299
Bars, Citrus, '05 173
Bavarian Cream with Fresh Fruit, '88 137
Biscotti, Fruitcake, '96 281
Brandied Fruit Starter, '82 249
Bread Pudding, Old-Fashioned, '01 223
Bread Pudding with Vanilla Cream Sauce, Berry, '05 260
Brie with Fresh Fruit, Caramel, '90 266
Briwatts with Fruit, '98 211
Cake, Fruit-and-Cereal Brunch, '88 263
Cake, Fruit and Spice, '87 M97
Cake, Fruited Pound, '81 265
Cake, Fruity Ice Cream, '87 110
Cake, Holiday Lane, '99 306
Cake, Southern Custard Crêpe, '99 166
Cake, Spicy Fruited Carrot, '85 117
Cake, Stately Fruit-and-Nut, '84 226
Caribbean Fruit Dessert, '84 314
Cassata, '01 125
Cheese, and Nuts, Fruit, '93 324
Cheesecake, Fruit-Glazed, '80 24; '90 162
Cobbler, Apple-Berry, '04 330
Cobbler, Fruit, '99 33
Cobbler, Mixed-Berry, '02 214
Cobbler, Quick Fruit, '91 20
Cobbler, Three-Berry, '04 29
Cobbler, Too-Easy Berry, '04 28
Cookies, Bourbon Fruit, '86 334
Cookies, Fruitcake, '79 291; '86 320; '88 286; '96 314; '98 294
Cookies, Fruitcake Drop, '92 275
Cookies, Holiday Fruitcake, '81 301
Cookies, Rolled Fruit, '80 15
Cookies, Spicy Holiday Fruit, '83 298
Cream Cheese, Fruited, '85 306
Cream Freeze, Fruit, '82 144
Cream Puffs, Tutti-Frutti, '79 231
Crêpes, Fruit-Filled Chocolate, '89 325
Crêpes, Tropical, '86 275
Crêpes, Tropical Fruit, '87 77
Crisp, Fruit, '94 168
Cup, Fruit, '81 141
Cup, Snowball Citrus, '79 2
Cup, Vanilla Fruit, '80 183
Curried Fruit, Hot, '95 72
Custard over Fruit, Stirred, '84 83
Custard with Fresh Fruit, Citrus, '93 70
Drops, Candied Fruit, '89 329

Dumplings, Delicious Fruit, '97 210
Elegant Fruit, '91 91
English Rocks, '01 295
Filling, Crêpes with Fruit, '81 96
Filling, Fruit, '94 245
Filling, Fruit-Nut, '80 289
Filling, Lemon Crêpes with Fruit, '82 46
Filling, Mixed Fruit Fried Pie, '96 109
Filling, Nutty Fruit, '99 306
Filling, Tutti-Frutti, '79 231
Flaming Fruit Dessert, '83 302
Freeze, Holiday Fruit, '88 283
Fresh Fruit with Cheese, Luscious, '79 153
Frozen Fruit Cream, '94 129
Frozen Fruit Cups, '93 197
Fruitini, '05 283
Glaze, Berry, '00 312
Glazed Fruit, '85 83
Ice Cream, Tutti-Frutti, '86 129
Ice, Fruit, '86 176
Ice, Mixed Fruit, '81 178; '88 85
Ice, Three-Fruit, '02 51
Ice, Tropical, '99 105
Island Fruit Chill, '98 180
Kebabs, Fruit, '86 181
Kebabs with Mint Marinade, Fruit, '82 157
Lemon Curd, Fresh Fruit with, '88 21
Marinated Fruit Bowl, '80 297
Marinated with Kirsch, Mixed Fruit, '03 86
Meringue Baskets with Fresh Fruit and Ice Cream, '98 179
Meringue Shells, Fruit-Filled, '86 151
Meringues, Tropical, '98 71
Parfait, Tropical Trilogy, '92 247
Pie, Bumbleberry, '97 163
Pie, Crispy-Crust Fruit, '88 68
Pie, Frozen Hawaiian, '05 157
Pie, Fruitcake, '80 237
Pie, Fruited Cheese, '92 228
Pie, Fruit-Topped Vanilla Cream, '84 49
Pie, Japanese Fruit, '80 238
Pies, Baked Fruit, '84 7
Pizza, Peanut Butter-Fruit, '94 60
Planter's Punch Dessert, '95 175
Pops, Cherry-Berry Lemonade, '03 89
Pops, Fruit, '87 168
Pudding, Fruited Rice, '86 95
Pudding, Summer, '98 217; '04 159
Puff, Giant Fruit, '85 72
Puff Pastry Baskets, Tropical, '93 177
Puree, Fruit, '94 190
Rainbow Fruit Dessert, '85 108
Refresher, Grape Juice-Fruit, '86 182
Ribbons, Sugared Fruit, '02 295
Rugelach, Fruit, '97 220
Rumtopf, '95 142
Sabayon, Champagne, '00 288
Sauce, Fruit, '81 177
Sauce, Golden Fruit, '89 281
Sauce, Hot Fruit Dessert, '87 299
Sauce, Quick Fruit, '82 212
Sauce, Rum-Fruit, '84 312
Shells, Fruited Meringue, '87 32
Sherbet, Freezer Fruit, '86 334
Sherbet, Frozen Fruit, '79 155
Sherbet, Fruit Punch, '86 129
Sherbet, Instant Fruit, '85 158
Sherried Fruit Flame, '85 313
Slush, Refreshing Fruit, '82 35
Sorbet, Tropical, '97 110
Soup Dessert, Fruit, '79 172
Soup, Fresh Fruit, '98 196
Spiced Fruit Dessert, '82 50
Split, Banana-Berry, '05 193

Squares, Christmas Fruit, '88 282
Strudels, Dried Fruit, '01 48
Sugarplum Sticks, '95 321
Sundaes, Very Berry, '03 126
Tart, Double Citrus, '05 55
Tart, Fancy Fruit, '82 128; '91 119
Tart, Fresh Fruit, '84 178; '90 58
Tart, King Cake Fruit, '96 57
Tartlets, Fresh Fruit, '93 96
Tart, Open-Face Fruit, '84 207
Tart, Rainbow Fruit, '82 304
Tarts, Bowl-Me-Over Fresh Fruit, '93 200
Tequila, Fruit in, '82 223
Topping, Fruity Dessert, '82 167
Trifle, Jumbleberry, '03 84
Trifle, Olde English, '95 331
Trifle, Tropical Rum, '03 85
Turnovers, Fruit, '79 150
Winter Fruit with Custard Sauce, '88 251
Zabaglione with Fruit, Champagne Vanilla, '00 31

Dips
Citrus-Cream Cheese Dip, '03 93
Coconut-Honey Fruit Dip, '84 171
Cranberry Fruit Dip, '89 60
Cream Cheese Dip, Fruited, '88 261
Fresh Fruit Dip, '80 265; '95 94
Ginger Fruit Dip, '96 110
Heavenly Fruit Dip, '81 160
Honey-Sour Cream Dip, Fresh Fruit with, '90 180
Marshmallow Fruit Dip, '84 171
Orange Fruit Dip, '96 190
Quick Fruit Dip, '90 110
Sweet Fruit Dip, '89 328
Tropical Dip for Fruit, '91 252
Yogurt Dip, Fruited, '84 171
Dressings. *See also* **FRUIT/Salads, Stuffing.**
Avocado Fruit Salad Dressing, '82 93
Baked Fruit Dressing, '87 253
Coconut-Fruit Dressing, Tangy, '84 171
Cornbread Dressing, Fruited, '80 262
Fluffy Fruit Dressing, '79 69
Fresh Fruit Dressing, '87 134
Lime-Honey Fruit Salad Dressing, '87 81
Marmalade-Fruit Dressing, '84 171
Nutty Fruit Dressing, '88 68
Pecan Dressing, Fruit-and-, '84 252
Salad Dressing for Fruit, '86 40
Salad, Dressing for Fruit, '87 81
Salad Dressing, Fruit, '79 69; '93 184
Salad Dressing, Snappy Fruit, '05 160
Turkey Dressing, Fruited, '99 257
Whipped Cream Fruit Dressing, '79 270
Dried Fruit Baked Apples, Pecan-and-, '03 269
Fresh Fruit Combo, '86 178
Fresh Fruit with Lemon-Yogurt Dressing, '93 17
Fresh Fruit with Lime Syrup, '05 220
Fruitcakes
Applesauce Fruitcake, '83 258
Aronowitz Fruitcake, '86 285
Black Cake (A Kwanzaa Fruitcake), '01 292
Bourbon Fruitcake, '85 315
Brandy Fruitcake, '82 261
Burgundy Fruitcake, '85 292
Cake Mix Fruit Cake, '95 248
Chocolate Fruitcakes, '95 250
Classic Fruitcake, '91 258
Favorite Fruitcake, Family, '88 284
Fondue, Fruitcake, '84 258
Grandmother's Fruitcake, '95 248
Japanese Fruitcake, '83 268; '90 252
Jeweled Fruitcake, '88 260
Jill's Fruitcake, '95 249

Kentucky Fruitcake, '86 266
Layered Fruitcake, '87 265
Lemon Fruitcake, '83 258
Light Fruitcake, '90 309
Loaf, Fruitcake, '96 286
Mom's Fruitcake, '85 321
No-Bake Fruitcake, '95 249
Old-South Fruitcake, '79 289
Regal Fruitcake, '83 257
Sherry-Nut Fruitcake, '84 266; '00 299
White Fruitcake, '80 280; '85 316; '00 299; '03 248
Zucchini Fruitcake, '88 284
Garnishes, '82 280; '85 339
Gazpacho, Berry, '97 181
Gazpacho, Citrus, '96 70
Gingered Fruit, '83 151
Granola, Fruity, '84 148
Granola, Mixed Fruit, '01 290; '05 240
Grilled Fruit with Honey Yogurt, '95 87
Hawaiian Fruit Dish, '82 112
Hot Fruit Delight, '83 281
Kebabs, Fruit, '86 181; '89 85
Kebabs, Fruity Mermaid, '91 177
Kebabs, Grilled Fruit, '97 147
Kebabs, Winter Fruit, '89 34
Main Dishes
  Brisket, Mixed Fruit Tzimmes with, '93 114
  Chicken Breasts with Fruited Rice Pilaf, '92 307
  Chicken en Crème, Fruited, '83 264
  Chicken, Fruit-Glazed, '80 211
  Chicken, Fruity Baked, '01 48
  Chicken with Almond Rice, Spiced Fruited, '81 195
  Chicken with Fresh Fruit, Coconut, '93 294
  Chuck Roast, Fruited, '91 289
  Cornish Hens with Fruited Stuffing, '90 191
  Cornish Hens with Tropical Fruit, Grilled, '97 310
  Goose, Fruit- and Pecan-Stuffed, '83 268
  Goose, Fruited Stuffed Wild, '88 248
  Goose, Fruit Stuffed, '83 320
  Ham Slice, Fruited, '83 M317
  Poblanos Stuffed with Pork and Fruit, '97 269
  Pork Chops, Fruited, '87 194
  Pork Chops, Fruited Stuffed, '86 197
  Pork Chops, Fruit-Stuffed, '82 136
  Pork Chops, Fruit-Topped, '94 41
  Pork Chops with Rice, Fruit-Glazed, '82 73
  Pork Loin, Fruitcake-Stuffed, '95 250
  Pork Loin, Roast, '01 222
  Pork Medaillons with Fresh Fruit, '97 104
  Pork Pilaf, Fruited, '82 246
  Pork Tenderloins, Fruit-Stuffed, '87 270
  Pork Tenderloin with Fruit Stuffing and Shiitake
    Sauce, '97 218
  Pot Roast, Fruited, '90 211
  Salad, Main Dish Fruit, '83 119
  Shrimp with Louis Sauce, Citrus-Marinated,
    '03 66
  Spareribs, Fruit-Stuffed, '79 14
  Turkey-and-Fruit Kebabs, '88 140
  Turkey Breast, Citrus-Rosemary, '02 270
Marinade, Citrus, '04 51
Marinade, Fruit with Lime, '98 92
Marinated Fruit, '91 67
Marinated Fruit, Minted, '92 138
Marmalade, Citrus, '97 32
Marmalade, Delicious Fruit, '81 285
Marmalade, Fruited Onion, '96 323; '97 27
Marmalade, Spicy Blueberry-Citrus, '03 135
Medleys
  Baked Fruit Medley, '81 297
  Barley, Vegetable, and Fruit Medley, '05 127
  Chilled Fruit Medley, '84 60
  Chinese Fruit Medley, '83 22
  Cup Medley, Fruit, '85 47

Curried Fruit Medley, '95 329
Fancy Fruit Medley, '84 82
Fresh Fruit Medley, '81 141
Frosty Fruit Medley, '82 226
Fruit Medley, '89 235
Midsummer Fruit Medley, '88 182
Minted Fruit Medley, '80 182
Tropical Medley of Fruit, '86 53
Mélange, Fruit, '88 M295
Mélange, Melon, '84 139
Mint-Balsamic Tea, Fresh Fruit with, '95 232
Mix, Dried Fruit, '92 22; '96 286
Mixed Fruit Grand, '02 212
Mix, Trash, '01 204
Muesli, Bran-and-Fruit, '91 134
Muesli, Homestyle, '91 315
Muffins, Fruit-and-Bran, '04 22
Muffins, Fruited Wheat, '79 93
Nuggets, Dried Fruit, '86 326
Oatmeal, Fruited, '88 19
Pick, Fruit-on-a-, '90 179
Pilaf, Mixed Fruit, '05 205
Preserving. See **FRUIT/Canning and Preserving.**
Relish, Fresh Fruit, '95 158
Rémoulade, Citrus, '05 69
Rhapsody, Fruit, '80 158
Rice, Far East Fruited, '81 175
Rice Mix, Fruited, '90 267; '97 317
Rice Mix, Fruited Curry-, '86 326
Rice Pilaf, Fruit-and-Vegetable, '84 196
Rice Pilaf, Fruited, '04 271
Rice, Sweet Jamaican, '96 71
Salads
  Almond-Citrus Salad, '96 274; '01 42
  Apricot Fruit Salad, '82 132
  Avocado Citrus Salad, '01 133
  Avocado Fruit Salad, '87 41
  Avocado-Fruit Salad with Honey-Yogurt Dressing,
    '93 172
  Baby Blue Salad, '01 20; '03 178
  Berry-Citrus Twist, '95 100
  Blackberry-Basil Vinaigrette, Fruit Salad with,
    '04 97
  Bowl, Fresh Fruit, '89 137
  Cabbage and Fruit Salad, '79 286
  Cantaloupe, Fruit-Filled, '83 120
  Carrot-and-Seed Salad, Fruity, '86 223
  Carrot-Fruit Toss, '82 235
  Chef Salad, Fruited, '85 222
  Chef's Fruit Salad, '86 35
  Cherry Fruit Salad, '87 236
  Chicken-and-Fruit Salad, '01 178
  Chicken-and-Fruit Salad, Grilled, '96 155
  Chicken-Avocado Salad, Fruited, '82 101
  Chicken-Fruit Salad, '82 79
  Chicken Fruit Salad, '90 234
  Chicken Salad, Autumn, '01 312
  Chicken Salad, Fruited, '84 25, 290; '88 88; '90 318
  Chicken Salad, Fruity, '83 157
  Chicken Salad in Avocados, Fruited, '87 41
  Chicken Salad, Summery, '95 138
  Chicken Salad, Sweet Peanut-, '03 54
  Chicken Salad, Tropical, '96 127
  Chicken Salad with Fruit, '82 171
  Citrus-and-Avocado Salad, '99 26
  Citrus and Greens with Orange-Ginger Dressing,
    '96 240
  Citrus-Cilantro Dressing, Fruit Salad with, '93 310;
    '94 97; '00 160
  Citrus Dressing, Fruit Salad with, '88 6
  Citrus Salad with Sweet-and-Sour Dressing, '01 104
  Citrus-Strawberry Salad, '04 249
  Coconut Fruit Bowl, '83 111

Coconut Salad, Chunky Fruit-and-, '84 24
Coleslaw, Fruited, '83 209; '85 139
Coleslaw, Three-Fruit, '86 250
Colorful Fruit Bowl, '91 58
Colorful Fruit Salad, '82 113
Congealed Fresh Fruit, Jeweled, '95 89
Congealed Salad, Layered Fruit, '05 M146
Cottage Cheese-and-Fruit Salad, '86 16
Cottage-Fruit Split, '86 169
Cracked Wheat-Fruit Salad, '96 240
Cream Dressing, Fruit Salad with, '89 277
Creamy Fruit Salad, '84 265; '04 333
Creamy Holiday Fruit Salad, '90 251
Cup, Fruit, '81 141; '91 202
Cup, Mixed Fruit, '87 233; '94 60
Cups, Honeydew Fruit, '82 179
Cups, Royal Fruit, '81 146
Cup with Mint Dressing, Fresh Fruit, '80 183
Curried Fruit Salad, '85 107
Date Dressing, Fruit Salad with, '87 57
Dressed-Up Fruit, '82 5
Easy Fruit Salad, '80 221
Easy Patio Fruit Salad, '88 184
Fall Salad with Ginger Dressing, '82 194
Favorite Fruit Salad, '99 220
Festive Fruit Salad, '80 16
Freeze, Fruity Lemon, '82 145
Fresh Fruit Salad, '82 165; '97 122
Fresh Fruit Salad with Celery-Honey Dressing,
  '80 42
Fresh Fruit Salad with Celery Seed Dressing, '00 68
Fresh Fruit Salad with Orange-Ginger Syrup,
  '03 167
Fresh Fruit Salad with Poppy Seed Dressing, '91 168
Fresh Fruit with Lime Sauce, '02 68
Frisky Fruit Salad, '85 46
Frozen Fruit Salad, '83 110; '97 158; '00 160
Frozen Fruit Salad, Dreamy, '79 126
Frozen Fruit Salad, Luscious, '81 204
Frozen Fruit Salad, Summertime, '99 111
Frozen Salad Christmas Wreath, '79 241
Fruit Salad, '83 209; '89 277; '03 42
Ginger-and-Lemon Fruit Salad, '05 17
Gingered Fruit Salad, '95 95
Glazed Fruit Salad, '83 48; '84 290
Green-and-Gold Salad with Fresh Citrus Ranch
  Dressing, '04 91
Green Fruit Salad with Honey-Lime Dressing,
  '93 71
Ham Salad, Fruited, '81 36, 146
Harvest Crunch Salad, '05 291
Harvest Salad with Cider Vinaigrette, '99 322
Heavenly Salad, '81 252
Holiday Fruit Salad, '87 236
Honeydew Fruit Bowl, '84 186
Honey Dressing, Fruit Salad with, '87 129;
  '05 137
Honey Fruit Salad, '80 276
Honey-Lemon Dressing, Fruit Salad with, '93 21
Honey-Pecan Dressing, Fruit Salad with, '03 28
Hurry-Up Fruit Salad, '87 236
Jícama-Fruit Salad, '86 83
Jícama Salad, Fruit-, '00 203
Layered Fruit Salad, '84 290; '89 277; '91 58
Lemonade Fruit Salad, '84 24
Lettuce and Fruit Salad with Poppy Seed Dressing,
  '80 152
Main Dish Fruit Salad, '83 119
Marinated Fruit Deluxe, '81 146
Mélange Delight, Fruit, '81 302
Melon-Citrus Mingle, '79 177
Minted Fruit Toss, '99 160
Mint-Gin Fruit Salad, '92 92
Mint Sauce, Fruit Salad with, '88 M96

FRUIT, Salads
(continued)

Mixed Fruit with Sour Cream Sauce, '02 169
Mold, Sherried Fruit, '90 124
Multi-Fruit Salad, '93 184
Nut Salad, Cheesy Fruit-'n'-, '87 56
Old-Fashioned Fruit Salad, '82 80
Orange Cream, Fresh Fruit Salad with, '90 126
Orange Fruit Cup, '91 277
Oriental Dressing, Fruit Salad with, '91 277
Pasta Salad, Fruited, '92 108
Peachy Fruit Salad, '89 206
Persimmon Fruit Salad, '79 206
Pineapple Cream Dressing, Fruit Cups with, '83 81
Pineapple Dressing, Fruit Salad with, '85 207
Pineapple-Fruit Salad, Icy, '87 9
Pita, Fresh Fruit Salad, '02 99
Platter, Fresh Fruit Salad, '92 213
Platter, Fruit Salad, '83 261
Poppy Seed Dressing, Fruit Salad with, '88 78
Potato Salad, Fruity, '85 214
Quick-and-Easy Fruit Salad, '81 99
Raspberry Fruit Mounds, '79 35
Refreshing Fruit Salad, '85 92
Rum, Fruit Cup with, '83 55
Sangría Fruit Cups, '89 34
Shrimp Salad, Fruited, '86 156
Sour Cream Fruit Salad, '80 138
Sparkling Fruit Salad, '82 266
Spiced Autumn Fruit Salad, '87 228
Spiced Fruit Salad, '98 54
Spring Mix Salad, Fruity, '04 105
Springtime Fruit Salad, '81 96
Summer Fruit-Chicken Salad with Blueberry
    Vinaigrette, '00 154
Summer Fruit Salad, '82 164; '92 171
Summer Fruit Salad with Blueberry Vinaigrette,
    '00 154
Summer Salad, Favorite, '80 158
Sunny Fruit Salad, '91 58
Sweet-and-Sour Fruit Salad, '80 13; '84 125
Sweet Potato Fruit Salad, '00 325
Tossed Fruit Salad, '92 106
Tropical Fruit Salad, '89 306; '02 163
Tropical Fruit Salad with Fresh Mint Dressing,
    '84 126
Turkey-Fruit Salad, '79 56
Turkey Fruit Salad, '83 233; '84 244
Turkey Salad, Fruit-and-, '89 176
Turkey Salad, Fruit-and-Spice, '94 325
Turkey Salad, Fruitful, '84 197
Twenty-Four-Hour Fruit Salad, '96 279
Vanilla-Scented Fruit Salad, '05 209
Watermelon Fruit Basket, '84 161
Wheat Salad with Citrus and Mint, '99 163
Winter Fruit-and-Cucumber Salad, '02 274
Winter Fruit Cup, '02 22
Winter Fruit Salad, '80 248; '82 23
Winter Fruit with Poppy Seed Dressing, '95 317
Wreath, Della Robbia Fruit, '87 294
Yogurt Fruit Salad, '81 114; '96 247
Yogurt-Granola Fruit Medley, '91 58
Salsa and Cinnamon Crisps, South Seas Ice Cream with
    Sweet Heat, '04 315
Salsa, Caribbean Fruit, '04 252
Salsa, Cranberry-Citrus, '97 290
Salsa, Fresh Citrus, '03 291
Salsa, Fruit, '97 124; '02 54; '04 168
Salsa, Fruity Black Bean, '05 16
Salsa, Grilled Shrimp with Citrus, '97 141
Salsa, Key Lime Pie with Minted Tropical, '99 333
Salsa, Spicy Summer, '03 186

Salsa, Tropical, '01 60
Salsa with Cinnamon Crisps, Fruit, '01 108
Sandwiches, Fruit-and-Cheese Breakfast, '89 M21
Sandwiches, Glazed Breakfast Fruit, '93 178
Sauce, Citrus Dipping, '97 208
Sauce for Fruit, Tangy, '90 161
Sauce, Grand Marnier Fruit, '90 93
Sauce, Grilled Shrimp with Tropical Fruit,
    '01 195
Sherried Fruit Casserole, '80 284
Sherried Fruit Mélange, '80 158
Snack Mix, Fruity, '03 47
Soup, Chilled Fresh Fruit, '88 160
Soup, Dried Fruit, '79 23
Soup, Fiesta Citrus, '01 176
Soup, Fruit, '87 98
Soup, Yogurt Fruit, '86 176
Spiced Fruit, '79 23
Spiced Fruit, Cold, '90 269
Spiced Fruit Delight, '82 229
Spiced Fruit, Warm, '86 39
Spiced Mixed Fruit, '01 88
Spiced Winter Fruit, '83 262
Spicy Fruit and Veggies with Lime, '04 141
Spicy Tropical Fruit, '04 166
Spread, Fruit, '85 135
Spread, Fruited Cream Cheese, '91 306; '93 79
Spread, Sugarless Fruit, '84 60
Strudel, Fruit Basket, '87 276
Stuffing Mix, Fruited, '89 331
Summer Fruit Fantasy, '91 178
Sundae, Breakfast, '98 206
Syrup, Apricot Fruit, '82 10
Terrine with Raspberry Sauce, Fruit, '98 157
Topping, Fruit, '81 42; '87 225; '89 50; '03 145
Tropical Fruit Fluff, '88 68
Tropical Fruit Tray, '93 72
Twists, Fruit-Nut, '82 253
White Wine, Fruit in, '81 48
Wontons, Fruit-Filled, '85 287
Wreath, Tex-Mex, '96 241

FUDGE

Almond Fudge, Creamy, '95 51
Buttermilk Fudge, '95 52; '97 317
Butterscotch-Peanut Fudge, '98 M282
Butterscotch Rum Fudge, '88 256
Caramel Fudge, '91 273
Cherry Nut Fudge, '83 315
Chocolate Fudge, '82 20
Chocolate Fudge, Five Pounds of, '95 51
Chocolate-Peanut Butter Fudge, '87 257; '90 311
Chocolate-Peanut Butter Fudge Squares, '97 M54
Chunks of Snow, '02 298
Coffee-Chip Fudge, '86 74
Cream Cheese Fudge, '84 111
Creamy Dark Fudge, '82 295
Creamy Fudge, '81 218
Diamond Fudge, '92 193
Double-Good Fudge, '79 M263; '95 M50
Double Good Fudge, '87 M278
Fast Fudge, '79 274
Four Chips Fudge, '92 318
Fudge, '86 266
Mama's Fudge, '03 279; '05 335
Microwave Chocolate Fudge, '92 M50; '02 M31
Microwave Fudge, '91 M92
Mint Fudge, '95 50
Mint Fudge, Dinner, '88 285
Mocha Fudge, Creamy, '95 51
Mocha Fudge, Holiday, '84 298
Nut Fudge, Quick, '83 316
Nutty White Fudge, '81 253
Orange-Walnut Fudge, '92 288
Peanut Butter Chewies, Fudge-, '98 215

Peanut Butter Fudge, '80 302; '89 307; '95 51;
    '02 296
Peanut Butter Fudge, Creamy, '92 240
Peanut Butter Fudge, Marbled, '88 65
Peanut-Fudge Bites, '91 M231; '92 M68
Peanut Fudge, Double, '85 91
Pecan Fudge, Creamy, '84 321
Penuche, '79 272
Pistachio Fudge, '83 298
Pumpkin Fudge, '05 232
Quick-and-Easy Fudge, '88 M190
Scotch Ring, Fudge, '79 273
Sour Cream Fudge, '95 52
Strawberry Fudge Balls, '93 80
Tiger Butter, '86 48
White Chocolate-Coffee Fudge, '94 232
White Chocolate Fudge, '92 317; '95 51

GAME

Birds in Wine Marinade, Game, '94 306
Chili, Double-Meat, '79 269; '80 12
Dove and Sausage Gumbo, '81 199
Dove au Vin, '95 309
Dove Enchiladas, '85 270
Doves, Pan-Roasted, '87 240
Doves, Sherried, '91 290
Duck and Duckling
    Baked Duck, Sherried, '79 224
    Blackberry Sauce, Ducklings with, '82 251
    Breasts, Blackened Duck, '93 259
    Breasts, Charcoaled Marinated Duck,
        '79 226
    Breasts, Smoked Duck, '87 121
    Breasts with Raspberry Sauce, Duck, '87 240
    Breast, Tender Duck, '97 215
    Casserole, Duck and Wild Rice, '79 224
    Enchiladas with Red Pepper-Sour Cream, Smoked
        Duck, '87 121
    Foxfire Duck, '89 241
    Grilled Duck with Orange Sauce, '94 305
    Gumbo, Duck, Oyster, and Sausage, '79 226
    Holiday Duckling, '80 251
    Kebabs with Almond Rice, Grilled Duck, '91 291
    Mallard, Prairie Wings, '83 252
    Muscovy Duck with Parsnip Mash, Honey-Orange-
        Glazed, '97 262
    Orange Duck, Chafing Dish, '79 226
    Orange Gravy, Duck with, '81 259
    Pâté, Duck, '79 226
    Pâté, Duck Liver, '79 227
    Roast Ducklings with Cherry Sauce, '86 312
    Roast Duckling with Orange Sauce, '81 125
    Roast Duckling with Tangerine Stuffing, '90 16
    Roast Duckling with Wine Jelly, '88 243
    Roast Duck with Sweet Potato-Eggplant Gravy,
        '83 90
    Roast Long Island Duckling, '84 87
    Wild Duck, Buffet, '86 268
    Wild Duck with Orange Gravy, Roast, '89 323
    Wild Duck with Pecan Stuffing, '85 269
Goose, Fruit- and Pecan-Stuffed, '83 268
Goose, Fruited Stuffed Wild, '88 248
Goose, Fruit-Stuffed, '83 320
Goose with Currant Sauce, Wild, '87 240
Gumbo, Wild Game, '91 290
Gumbo Ya Ya, '87 210
Pepper Feet, '93 258
Pheasant, Gin-Marinated, '02 250
Pheasant Muscatel, '85 269
Pheasants with Port Wine Sauce, '84 252
Pot Pie with Parmesan Crust, Game, '94 304
Quail
    Bacon-Wrapped Quail, '02 238

Baked Quail with Cornbread Stuffing, '94 305
Baked Quail with Mushroom Gravy, '89 273
Baked Quail with Mushrooms, '81 259
Breasts, Southern Quail, '85 270
Currant Jelly Sauce, Quail with, '86 94
Dressing, Quail and, '99 42
Étouffée, Roasted Quail, '96 34
Foxfire Quail, '89 240
Fried Quail, '82 45
Fried Quail, Seasoned, '88 220
Fried Quail with Onion Gravy, '82 214
Glazed Quail with White Bean Ragoût, Maple-,
  '96 232
Gravy, Georgia Quail with, '87 240
Gravy, Quail Smothered in, '99 41
Grilled Breakfast Quail, '88 220
Grilled Quail, '92 90
Grilled Quail, Asian, '99 41
Grilled Quail with Red Wine-Blackberry Sauce,
  '98 319
Hatcreek Quail, '89 270
J.W. Quail, '89 240
Magnificent Quail, '82 214
Marinated Quail, '80 221
Marinated Quail, Chipotle-, '04 240
Mushrooms, Quail with, '85 138
Orange Sauce in Potato Baskets, Quail with, '86 193
Pan-Roasted Chipotle-Marinated Quail, '98 201
Red Plum Sauce, Quail with, '80 48
Roasted Quail with Cranberry-Orange-Pecan
  Stuffing, '01 249
Smoked Champagne Quail, Sage-, '97 164
Smoked Quail, '93 236
Stroganoff, Quail, '99 41
Stuffed Quail, Hawkeye-, '89 241
Stuffed with Cornbread Dressing, Quail,
  '93 280
Superb, Quail, '81 303
Rabbit, Hickory Barbecued, '82 216
Rabbit, Santa Fe Spanish, '94 307
Squab, Baked Stuffed, '82 260
Turkey, Country-Fried Wild, '94 306
Venison
  Bake, Venison-Vegetable, '87 304
  Burgers, Venison, '87 304
  Chili, Hot Venison, '91 283
  Chili, Venison, '82 216; '86 3; '87 304
  Chutney-Mustard Sauce, Bostick Venison with,
    '89 242
  Country-Fried Venison, '81 233
  Kebabs, Venison, '82 215; '88 249
  Loin, Mushroom-Crusted Venison, '94 302
  Roast, Grilled Venison, '93 278
  Roast, Lillie Bell's Venison, '89 242
  Roast, Venison, '82 226
  Roast with Red Wine Gravy, Venison, '85 270
  Sauce, Venison Reduction, '94 303
  Sausage Balls, Venison, '80 42
  Soup, Venison, '82 216
  Steak, Country-Fried Venison, '83 262
  Steaks, Country-Style Venison, '82 215
  Steaks, Grilled Venison, '82 215
  Stew, Hunter's, '85 270
  Stew, Venison, '86 294
  Stew, Venison Sausage, '87 238
  Stew with Potato Dumplings, Venison, '87 304
  Stock, Venison, '94 302
  Tenderloin Appetizers, Venison, '88 249
  Tomatoes, Venison and, '85 270
GARLIC
Aioli, Mint, '01 71
Asparagus, Marinated, '02 243; '05 105
Asparagus, Oven-Roasted, '05 55
Asparagus with Garlic, Stir-fried, '05 86

Beans, Buzz's Pot of, '03 19
Beans, Molasses Baked, '99 105
Beans, Spicy Black, '04 119
Beef Brisket with Fall Vegetables, '02 237
Beef Tenderloin, Garlic-and-Rosemary, '02 255
Beef Tenderloin, Hampton Place, '04 272
Black Beans and Rice, '05 214
Black Beans, Cuban, '99 56
Boston Butt Roast with Gravy, '05 90
Bread, Barbecue, '99 105
Bread, Buttery Garlic, '02 25, 110
Broccoli, Garlic, '99 46
Bruschetta, Black Truffle, '99 323
Burgers, Spinach-Feta, '99 135
Butter, Garlic, '83 193; '84 108; '95 89; '00 90
Butter, Garlic-Basil, '98 156
Butter, Green Beans with Garlic-Herb, '02 61
Butter, Herb-Pesto, '04 255
Butter, Roasted Garlic, '97 46
Cabbage with Garlic, '04 62
Canapés, Roasted Garlic, '96 95
Casserole, Cajun Shrimp, '05 237
Casserole, Savory Ham-and-Swiss, '01 308
Cauliflower in Browned Butter, '02 45
Cheesesteaks, Chimichurri, '04 312
Chicken and Potatoes, Roasted, '98 289
Chicken Breasts, Greek, '98 19
Chicken Breasts with Artichoke-Pepper Sauce, '05 139
Chicken, Forty-Cloves-of-Garlic, '95 261
Chicken, Garlic-and-Wine Grilled, '00 136
Chicken, Garlic-Spinach, '92 56
Chicken, Glazed Roasted, '00 14; '03 217
Chicken, Grilled Sweet Guava, '05 278
Chicken, Herb-Roasted, '00 330
Chicken, Jan's Roasted, '01 224
Chicken, Lemon-Garlic, '90 35
Chicken Marbella, '04 34
Chicken Mediterranean, '01 17
Chicken, Soy-Garlic, '98 128
Chicken with Green Olives, '03 87
Chicken with Lemon Mashed Potatoes, Smothered,
  '04 180
Chili, Black Bean, '02 20
Chili Con Carne, '03 19
Chili, Game-Day, '00 238
Chili, Spicy 3-Bean, '03 291
Collard Greens, Esau's, '03 17
Confit, Roasted Shallot-Garlic, '94 303
Crawfish Boil, '01 95
Cream, Red Curry-Coconut, '00 197
Crème Brûlée, Roasted Garlic, '95 324
Crisps, Garlic, '99 60
Crostini, Roasted Red Pepper-Feta, '04 69
Croutons, Garlic, '92 71; '05 247
Dip, Zesty Feta, '04 71
Dressing, Basil-and-Garlic, '94 55
Dressing, Fresh Tomato, '00 182
Dressing, Garlic-Ginger Vinaigrette, '92 195
Dressing, Lime-Peanut, '01 26
Dressing, Purple Parrot Sensation, '04 289
Dressing, Rice, '01 222
Dressing, Southern Rice, '99 256
Eggplant Vinaigrette, Italian, '03 125
Eggplant with Walnuts, Georgian, '01 87
Eggs, Garden District, '04 66
Elephant Ears, Garlic-and-Herb Baby, '00 87
Étouffée, Crawfish, '02 85
Étouffée, Quick Crawfish, '05 57
Étouffée, Traditional Crawfish, '05 56
Flatbread, Quick, '00 119
French Bread, Garlic, '05 57
Frijoles, '02 119
Fritters, Shrimp, '00 238
Garbanzo-Black Bean Medley, '99 236

Gazpacho, Classic Tomato, '99 172
Gnocchi with Olive Oil, Tomato, and Parmesan, '04 47
Green Beans, Garlic, '91 159; '00 260; '01 111
Green Beans with Mushrooms, Roasted, '04 182
Green Beans with Pimiento, Tangy, '01 21
Greens with Raspberry Vinaigrette, Gourmet, '00 163
Gremolata, '05 319
Grits, Baked Cheese-and-Garlic, '83 292; '84 78
Grits Casserole, Garlic, '81 47
Grits, Garlic-and-Herb Cheese, '95 122
Grits, Garlic Cheese, '80 47; '81 197
Grits, Garlic-Cheese, '86 180; '88 126; '89 47; '97 58;
  '99 270
Grits, Garlicky Ham-and-Spinach, '94 177
Grits Soufflé, Garlic-Cheese, '99 18
Guacamole, '02 118
Gumbo, Chicken-and-Sausage, '01 324
Gumbo, Green Tomato, '04 314
Hamburgers Teriyaki, '99 332
Ham, Pineapple-Glazed, '03 82
Ham with Garlic and Orange, '05 294
Hash Browns, Rosemary-Garlic, '02 248
Hoppin' John, Esau's, '03 17
Hummus, '02 99
Jelly, Garlic, '99 283
Jelly, Garlic Pepper, '99 221
Journey Cakes, Rosemary-Garlic, '04 99
Kale with Tomatoes, Spicy, '99 243
Lamb Chops, Glazed, '02 66
Lamb Chops with Chipotle and Cilantro Oils, Grilled,
  '02 96; '03 98
Lamb Chops with Mint Aioli, '01 70
Lamb Chops with Minted Apples, '99 230; '00 20
Lamb Extraordinaire, '99 242
Lamb, Mint-Crusted Rack of, '98 118
Lamb, Roast Leg of, '00 275
Lamb Shanks, Braised, '00 62
Leeks, Creamed, '00 222
Leg of Lamb, Garlic-and-Herb Stuffed, '99 241
Leg of Lamb, Roast, '99 242
Leg of Lamb with Port, Roasted, '02 258
Linguine, Grilled Pepper-Pesto, '04 136
Marinade, Basic, '02 19
Marinade, Garlic-Basil, '94 160
Marinade, Italian, '03 180
Marinade, Southwestern, '00 177
Marinade, Zesty Chicken, '03 180
Mashed Potatoes, Golden Buttermilk, '05 298
Mayonnaise, Garlic, '92 56
Mayonnaise, Garlic-Dill, '00 324
Mayonnaise, Roasted Garlic, '97 47
Meatballs, Red Sauce and, '04 17
Meat Loaf, Gonzales, '04 206
Mirlitons, Stuffed, '00 246
Mojo, Yuca with Garlic-Lime, '05 294
Mushrooms, Garlic and, '95 165
Mussels Marinara, '00 283
Oil, Roasted Garlic, '96 122
Olives, Citrus Party, '03 124
Olives Scaciati, '99 266
Panzanella, '00 62
Pasta, Creamy Crawfish, '03 277
Pasta, Tomato-Garlic, '94 177
Pasta with Marinara Sauce, Garlic, '92 78
Peanuts, Hot, '00 278
Penne with Pancetta, '00 51
Pesto, '00 118
Pesto, Basil, '03 208
Pesto, Cilantro, '00 148
Pesto, Dried Tomato, '01 62
Pesto, Garlic, '84 108
Pesto, Homemade, '01 22
Pesto, Lucinda's Garden, '01 100
Pesto, Roasted Garlic-Basil, '98 145

GARLIC

(continued)

Pesto, Roasted Garlic-Rosemary, '97 46
Pickles, Peppery Texas, '04 M161
Pizza Squares, Easy, '02 61
Pork Chops, Garlic-Parmesan, '02 61
Pork Chops, Grilled Asian, '03 271
Pork, Garlic-Orange Roast, '03 277; '05 332
Pork Loin, Garlic-Honey Marinated, '99 334
Pork Loin with Rosemary-Breadcrumb Crust, Grilled, '05 200
Pork Roast, Citrus-and-Garlic, '05 294
Pork Roast, Festive, '01 276; '05 46
Pork, Slow-Roasted, '02 274
Pork, Smoked, '99 81; '03 121
Pork, Stir-fry, '05 241
Pork Tenderloin, Asian, '02 33
Pork Tenderloin, Bourbon-Marinated, '04 168
Pork Tenderloin, Grilled, '02 187
Pork Tenderloin, Honey-Garlic, '01 16
Pork Tenderloins, Honey-Garlic, '01 318
Pork with Garlic, Sweet, '04 17
Potato Bake, Smoky Mashed, '00 214
Potatoes, Creamy Lemon-Poppy Seed Mashed, '03 294
Potatoes, Garlic Mashed, '92 330; '97 308; '02 281
Potatoes, Garlic-Parsley, '90 290
Potatoes, Garlic-Roasted, '95 87
Potatoes, Leek Mashed, '02 98; '03 293
Potatoes, Loaded Garlic Smashed, '01 325
Potatoes, Roasted Garlic Mashed, '95 288
Potatoes, Roasted Garlic-Parmesan Mashed, '97 263; '00 146
Pot Roast, '00 65
Pot Roast, Italian, '02 88
Prime Rib, Smoked, '02 177
Puree, Roasted Garlic, '92 55
Quail, Chipotle-Marinated, '04 240
Red Beans and Rice, Spicy, '02 56
Rémoulade, Braised Shrimp with Garlic, '98 133
Rib Roast, Rosemary-Thyme, '05 248
Rice with Fresh Herbs, '05 68
Risotto, Crawfish, '99 120
Roasted Garlic, '94 177; '96 304
Roasted Garlic-and-Cheese Risotto, '04 283
Roasted-Garlic Beurre Blanc, '03 324
Roasted Garlic Bulbs, '97 46
Roasted Garlic Dressing, '99 269
Roasted Garlic, Herbed, '94 177
Roasted Garlic-Rosemary Bread, '04 16
Roast, Peppered Rib-Eye, '01 122
Roast, Roasted Lime-Cilantro Eye of Round, '04 88
Roast, Rosemary Rib, '03 294
Rollups, Mediterranean, '00 277
Salad, Caesar, '00 19
Salad Dressing, Creamy Garlic, '03 211
Salad, Lemon-Basil Potato, '01 178
Salad, Peanut-Noodle, '02 163
Salsa, Fiery, '01 174
Salsa, Zesty Santa Fe, '03 198
Sandwiches, Shredded Flank Steak Mini-, '05 158
Saté Mixed Grill with Spicy Peanut Sauce, '04 134
Sauce, Brisket Mopping, '03 188
Sauce, Chilled Asparagus with Garlic Dipping, '98 136
Sauce, Come Back, '00 211
Sauce, Crescent City Grill Creole, '04 289
Sauce, Garlic, '92 56
Sauce, Garlic Beurre Blanc, '88 222
Sauce, Lemon-Butter, '99 198
Sauce, Parsley-Garlic, '83 138; '84 M76
Sauce, Pasta, '01 53
Sauce, Paul's Barbecue, '05 175

Sauce, Red Pepper-Garlic, '98 140
Sauce, Red Wine Garlic, '94 250
Sauce, Rémoulade, '04 66
Sauce, Roasted Garlic, '95 268; '98 176
Sauce, Roasted Garlic-Tomato, '97 46
Sauce, Spaghetti with Mint-and-Garlic Tomato, '05 100
Sauce, The, '00 177; '03 312
Scampi, Speedy, '02 161
Shrimp and Andouille Alfredo Sauce Over Pasta, Cajun, '05 57
Shrimp, Barbecue, '00 30
Shrimp Cocktail, Mexican, '00 249
Shrimp, Daufuskie, '00 174
Shrimp di Santo, '99 265
Shrimp, Garlic-and-Rosemary, '01 101; '04 52
Shrimp, Grilled Garlic, '99 178
Shrimp, New Orleans Barbecue, '02 201
Shrimp Scampi, '00 283
Shrimp Stir-Fry, '01 258
Shrimp with Fettuccine, Dilled, '99 141
Shrimp with Smoky Sweet Sauce, Mexican-Grilled, '03 32
Soup, Black Bean, '05 120
Soup, Butternut Squash-Lime, '03 236
Soup, Golden Garlic-and-Potato, '04 214
Soup, Roasted Garlic-and-Basil Tomato, '01 17
Soup, Roasted Red Pepper, '05 72
Soup, Spanish Fiesta, '01 66
Soup, Tortilla, '99 310
Soup with Goat Cheese-and-Chive Croutons, Caramelized Onion, '01 312
Soup with Gremolata, White Bean, '05 319
Spinach Pie, '00 26
Spread, Creamy Potato-Garlic, '02 35
Spread, Cucumber-Yogurt, '00 135
Spread, Tri-Flavored Cream Cheese, '98 134
Steak, Garlic, '84 8
Steaks, Garlic-Herb, '98 169; '99 175
Steaks, Italian Sirloin, '04 61
Sugar Snap Peas, Pickled, '01 112
Tapenade, '00 135
Taquitos with Pork Picadillo, '04 206
Tart, Tomato, '03 158
Tenderloins, Honey-Grilled, '00 126
Torta, Goat Cheese, '04 186
Turkey, Rosemary Roasted, '99 312
Turkey Scaloppine, '04 321
Vegetable Curry, '04 217
Vegetable Medley, Herbed, '99 46; '00 138
Vegetable Medley, Root, '03 260
Vegetables, Bill's Roasted, '00 276
Vegetables, Rosemary Baked, '05 313
Vegetables with Fresh Sage, Roasted, '00 125
Vermicelli with Chunky Vegetable Sauce, '04 180
Vinaigrette, Dijon, '03 237
Vinaigrette, Garlic, '95 65; '03 142
Vinaigrette, Garlic-Blue Cheese, '92 57
Vinaigrette, Roasted Garlic, '97 47
Vinaigrette, Warm Garlic, '00 324
Vinegar, Shallot-Tarragon-Garlic, '93 191
Wings, Sweet-and-Hot Citrus, '00 202

GARNISHES
Boxwood Garland, '02 295
Butter
    Balls, Butter, '82 189; '89 90
    Curls, Butter, '82 51, 189; '89 90
    Molds, Butter, '89 90
Candy Bow, '99 M306
Candy Box, White, '97 M54
Chocolate
    Cups, Chocolate, '80 207
    Cups, Chocolate Crinkle, '93 270

    Cups, Miniature Chocolate, '87 132
    Curls, Chocolate, '85 338
    Hearts and Shavings, Chocolate, '86 26
    Lacy Chocolate Garnishes, '89 43
    Leaves, Chocolate, '88 281; '89 42; '98 270
    Ribbons and Bow, White Chocolate, '01 253
    Sack, Large Chocolate, '93 314
    Sack, Small Chocolate, '93 314
    Stars, White Chocolate, '00 M307
Eggs, Hard-Cooked, '82 280
Flowers
    Candied Flowers and Raspberries, '98 155
    Pansies, Candied, '96 118
    Rose Petals and Mint Leaves, Candied, '99 155
    Rose Petals, Candied, '98 57
    Roses and Leaves, Crystallized, '97 61
    Fondant Teapot Spout, Handle, Daisies, and Butterflies, '04 83
Fruit
    Cherries and Mint Sprigs, Sugared Maraschino, '01 271
    Citrus Cups, '85 339
    Citrus Cups, Notched, '82 280
    Cranberries, Frosted, '82 280; '85 339
    Cranberries, Sugared, '04 279
    Grapes, Frosted, '82 51; '85 339
    Lemon Peel, Candied, '94 199
    Lemon Roses, '82 280; '85 338
    Lemon Slices, Fluted, '82 51
    Orange Rind, Candied, '96 162; '97 32
    Orange Rose, '85 338
    Orange Zest, Candied, '95 320
    Ribbons, Sugared Fruit, '02 295
    Tangerine Segments, Glazed, '02 295
    Vegetable and Fruit Garnishes, '82 280
Ghosts, Little, '03 M212
Guide, Garnishing, '82 138
Holiday Trees, '98 308
Holly Leaves, '99 M306
Marzipan Bees, '98 100
Pastry Garnish, '98 254; '03 317
Pastry Strips, Decorated, '02 M296
Pecans, Spiced, '03 332
Piped Garnishes, '82 280
Rosemary, Sugared, '04 M279
Vegetable
    Broccoli Bouquet, '87 115
    Carrot Curls, '85 338
    Carrot Flowers, '85 338
    Celery Fans, '85 339
    Fruit Garnishes, Vegetable and, '82 280
    Green Onion Fans, '85 339; '05 271
    Green Pepper Cups, '85 339
    Mushrooms, Aztec, '82 51
    Mushrooms, Fluted, '82 280; '85 338
    Onion Mum, '85 339
    Onion Mums, '96 318
    Onion Rose, '87 114
    Radish Rose, '85 339
    Squash Buttercup, '87 114
    Tomato Cups, '85 339
    Tomato Flower, Marinated Pasta in, '87 115
    Tomato Rose, '82 51; '85 338
    Zucchini Fan, '87 114
GIFTS
Bars, Chewy Chocolate Cereal, '97 317
Biscuits with Olive-Parsley Spread, Cream Cheese-and-Olive, '04 238
Brownie Mix, Blond, '01 247
Cake, Gift Box, '96 319
Candy Cane Swizzle Sticks, '02 298
Candy, Cola, '02 298
Cheese Marinade, '04 238
Cookies, Candy Shop Pizza, '02 299

Cookies, Skillet Almond, '97 288
Cracker Bites, Miniature Peanut Butter, '02 298
Cream Cheese Braids, '97 287
Divinity, Cherry, '97 316
Divinity, Lemon, '97 316
Extract, Vanilla, '97 288
Filling, Cream Cheese, '97 287
Frosting, Cola, '02 298
Fudge, Buttermilk, '97 317
Gadgets, Off-the-Wall, '95 332
Gifts That Measure Up, '95 332
Glaze, '99 284
Glaze, Powdered Sugar, '97 287
Hot Handlers, '95 332
Jambalaya Mix, '98 317
Jelly, Garlic, '99 283
Marinated Cheese, Olives, and Peppers, '04 238
Miniature Liqueur Sampler, '95 332
Muffins, Cheese, '97 287
Mustard, Easy Sweet-Tangy, '01 247
Pralines, Cinnamon, '97 317
Rice Mix, Fruited, '97 317
Rice Mix, Seasoned, '01 248
Rolls, Cinnamon, '99 M284
Salad Gift, Asian, '96 327
Salad Gift, Caesar, '96 326
Salad Gift, Curried, '96 326
Sauce, Peach Rib, '01 248
Sauce, Zesty Lemon, '97 318
Snow, Chunks of, '02 298
Soup Mix, Bean, '99 283
Spice Mix, Tex-Mex, '01 247
Spread, Garlic-and-Dill Feta Cheese, '04 238
Topping, Hot Fudge Ice Cream, '98 317
Topping, Maple-Pecan Ice Cream, '98 317
Trees, Holiday, '02 298
Wine Tasting, '95 332
Wreaths, Christmas, '97 288
GLAZES. See also **FILLINGS, FROSTINGS, TOPPINGS.**
Apricot Glaze, '80 280; '82 8; '86 197; '97 60; '98 260
Apricot Glaze for Ham, '85 256
Apricot Glaze, Sweet, '82 304
Apricot-Kirsch Glaze, '87 14
Berry Glaze, '83 225; '00 312
Blueberry Glaze, '83 143
Brandy Glaze, Powdered Sugar-, '86 291
Brownie Glaze, '02 M252
Brown Sugar Glaze, '83 312; '96 268
Buttered Rum Glaze, '03 94
Buttermilk Glaze, '79 140; '81 70; '84 316; '97 230;
    '99 98; '02 166; '03 55
Caramel Glaze, '85 320; '98 195; '02 196
Cherry Glaze, '83 143; '93 52; '98 260
Chili-Cranberry Glaze, '98 320
Chocolate Glaze, '81 119; '83 220; '84 10, 55, 253;
    '85 6; '86 315, 316; '89 325; '90 310; '91 M296;
    '93 52; '97 M35, 231; '99 206; '01 M45, M126;
    '05 M287
Chocolate Glaze, Creamy, '82 88; '98 90
Chocolate Glaze, French, '98 M57
Chocolate-Honey Glaze, '82 306
Cinnamon Glaze, '88 83
Citrus Glaze, '82 128; '89 205
Cranberry Glaze, '84 306; '86 171; '88 244
Cranberry-Honey Glaze, '89 273
Cream Cheese Glaze, '84 150; '94 242
Currant Jelly Glaze, '00 82
Daiquiri Glaze, '93 83
Dijon Glaze, '87 54
Drizzle Glaze, '87 94
Drizzling Icing, '91 35
Guava Glaze, '05 279
Holiday Glaze, Creamy, '03 281

Honey Glaze, '88 287
Honey-Nut Glaze, '87 15
Irish Cream Glaze, '92 287
Kahlúa Glaze, '86 292
Lemon Glaze, '79 285; '86 194; '87 41; '92 269;
    '93 154, 183; '97 123, 332; '01 117
Orange-Bourbon Glaze, '03 249
Orange Butter Glaze, '90 194
Orange Glaze, '79 2; '80 257; '81 34, 107; '82 75, 206;
    '83 33, 114, 140, 267; '84 161; '86 298; '92 263;
    '95 320; '99 293; '03 35, 281, 307
Orange Glaze, Nutty, '80 45
Orange-Pineapple Glaze, '81 60
Paint, Egg Yolk, '86 322
Pineapple Glaze, '83 143; '85 38; '97 55
Powdered Sugar Glaze, '79 24; '82 92, 283; '83 83, 295;
    '85 55; '90 95; '97 287; '04 279
Praline Glaze, '82 196
Raspberry Glaze, '00 88
Root Beer Glaze, '99 196
Rum Glaze, Buttered, '83 220
Scuppernong-Orange Glaze, '98 220
Snowy Glaze, '82 295
Strawberry Glaze, '80 35; '83 142
Sugar Glaze, '86 161; '90 47; '01 89
Teriyaki Glaze, '94 82
Topping Glaze, '87 69
Vanilla Glaze, '85 M89; '89 211; '04 M84; '05 287
White Chocolate Glaze, '01 M45
GOOSE. See **GAME.**
GRANOLA
Apple Crisp, Granola, '85 78
Bars, Coconut Granola, '85 202
Bars, Cranberry-Cinnamon Granola, '03 26
Bars, Fruit and Nut Granola, '81 49
Bars, Granola, '83 305; '95 214
Bars, No-Bake Granola, '97 220
Bread, Honey-Granola, '86 56
Chocolate Morsels, Granola with, '86 69
Crunchy Granola, '81 218; '84 144
Easy Granola, '81 49
Fabulous Granola, '92 213
Fruit Granola, Mixed, '05 240
Fruit Medley, Yogurt-Granola, '91 58
Fruity Granola, '84 148
Gorp, Granola, '89 59
Granola, '79 190; '93 197; '99 212
Healthful Granola, '97 204
Homemade Granola, '84 58
Mix, Bunny Trail, '95 101
Mixed Fruit Granola, '01 290
Mix, Granola, '94 168
Mix, Granola Snack, '86 229
Muffins, Granola, '95 78
Nutty Granola, '90 95
Orange Granola, Sunny, '84 212
Pancakes, Granola-Squash, '94 267
Peanut Butter Granola, '82 296
Peanut Granola, Crunchy, '90 48
Pecan-Coconut Granola, '02 70
Raisin-Granola Treats, '92 22
Reindeer Nibbles, '92 280
Salad, Rudolph's Apple, '02 277
Sunshine Granola, '79 37
Superhero Granola, '98 M206
Toasty Granola, '79 37
Whole Wheat Granola, '82 167
GRAPEFRUIT
Beverages
Cocktails, Sea Breeze, '97 161
Cooler, Grapefruit, '88 81
Drink, Grapefruit, '90 84; '95 238
Freeze, Grapefruit, '93 242
Refresher, Grapefruit, '88 85

Refresher, Grapefruit-Orange, '82 174
Sangría, Grapefruit, '89 92
Spritzer, Pineapple-Grapefruit, '04 143
Spritzers, Grapefruit-White Wine, '96 56;
    '01 319
Tea, Grapefruit, '92 67
Three-Fruit Drink, '80 50
Biscuits, Grapefruit Juice, '83 10
Broiled Grapefruit, '85 7; '96 55
Broiled Grapefruit, Holiday, '88 251
Broiled Grapefruit, Sherried, '80 50
Broil, Flounder-Grapefruit, '85 53
Cake, Fresh Grapefruit, '89 308
Chocolate-Topped Grapefruit, '89 88
Compote, Spicy Grapefruit-Berry, '91 19
Cup, Berry Grapefruit, '79 242
Delight, Winter Fruit, '80 243
Dressing, Grapefruit French, '80 101
Dressing, Grapefruit Salad, '84 262
Freeze, Grapefruit, '00 241
Frosting, Grapefruit, '89 308
Ice, Grapefruit, '91 122
Ice, Pink Grapefruit, '85 304
Marmalade, Combination Citrus, '80 50
Marmalade, Grapefruit, '82 308
Minted Grapefruit, '88 81
Pear-Berry Puree, Grapefruit with, '89 213
Pie, Grapefruit Chess, '01 23
Pie, Grapefruit Meringue, '96 56
Salads
Apple Salad, Grapefruit-, '89 41
Aspic, Grapefruit, '80 297; '82 112; '83 153
Avocado-Grapefruit Salad, '85 26; '93 282
Avocado Salad, Grapefruit-, '83 316; '84 16; '89 41
Banana Salad with Celery Seed Dressing,
    Grapefruit-, '91 237
Bing Cherry-Grapefruit Salad, '00 285
Combo Salad, Grapefruit, '80 50
Congealed Grapefruit Salad, '84 325; '85 279
Congealed Salad, Grapefruit, '83 190
Cucumber Salad, Grapefruit-, '80 100
Grapefruit Salad, '83 124; '84 325; '88 122
Greens and Grapefruit Salad, '95 301
Orange-Grapefruit Salad, '93 294
Orange Salad, Grapefruit-, '91 276
Shrimp Salad, Grapefruit-and-, '88 5
Winter Salad, Grapefruit, '84 24
Sorbet, Grapefruit, '03 171
Sorbet, Grapefruit-Mint, '93 153
Sorbet, Pink Grapefruit and Tarragon, '95 163
Spiced Pink Grapefruit, '96 55
Supreme, Grapefruit, '80 50
Tart, Grapefruit, '04 43
GRAPES
Beverages
Cooler, Grape-Lime, '94 227
Cooler, White Grape-and-Orange, '05 61
Juice, Scuppernong, '98 221
Mulled Grape Juice, '90 21
Punch, Sparkling Grape, '82 48
Punch, Spiced White Grape, '96 170
Punch, White Grape, '90 15
Tea, White Grape Iced, '98 84
Tea, White Grape Juice, '87 57
Blue Cheese-Pecan Grapes, '95 48
Caribbean Grapes, '95 48
Carrots with Grapes, Glazed, '82 287
Chicken Véronique, '84 260; '85 302
Desserts
Beauberries Bordeaux, '98 18
Cobbler, Muscadine, '98 221
Granita, Grape, '88 118
Ice Cream, Scuppernong, '88 216
Ice, Grape, '83 162

GRAPES, Desserts
(continued)

Ice, Muscadine, '82 202
Pie, Grape, '85 212
Pie, Grape Juice, '79 123
Pie, Muscadine, '82 202
Pie, Scuppernong, '88 216
Pops, Purple People Eater, '99 132
Refresher, Grape Juice-Fruit, '86 182
Tart, Green Grape, '87 77
Tarts, Scuppernong Pudding, '98 221
Frosted Grapes, '82 51; '85 339
Glaze, Scuppernong-Orange, '98 220
Green Grapes Supreme, '88 81
Ham Véronique, '85 90
Honeydew Melon with Grapes, '91 91
Honeyed Grapes, '95 47
Jelly, Grape, '89 140
Jelly, Grape-Burgundy Freezer, '85 130
Jelly, Quick Grape, '89 M156
Jelly, Scuppernong, '98 220
Jelly, Thyme-Grape, '89 193
Jelly, Wild Muscadine, '79 32
Marmalade, Muscadine, '98 220
Mold, Double Grape-Cantaloupe, '79 173
Pork Loin, Scuppernong-Orange Glazed,
   '98 220
Salad, Broccoli-Grape, '01 163
Salad, Chicken, '96 67
Salad, Marinated Chicken-Grape, '85 74
Salad Mold, Grape, '83 120
Salad, Sherried Chicken-and-Grape, '01 61
Salad Véronique, Macaroni, '85 164
Salad with Grapes, Chicken, '86 117
Salad with Grapes, Curried Tuna, '87 201
Sauce, Muscadine, '04 231
Sauce, Pears in Muscadine, '88 216
Sauce, White Grape, '80 38
Scallops Véronique, '83 144
Slaw, Grape-Poppy Seed, '86 225
Sole Véronique, '85 181
Spiced Grapes, '98 220
Wild Rice with Grapes, '95 48
GRAVIES. *See also* **SAUCES.**
Black-Eyed Pea Gravy, '87 12
Boston Butt Roast with Gravy, '05 90
Burgundy Gravy, Beef Roast with, '95 263
Chicken Gravy, '99 34
Chive Gravy, Beef and Broccoli with, '88 214
Chocolate Gravy, '99 35, 88
Cranberry Pan Gravy, Baked Hen with, '94 308
Cream Gravy, '88 15; '97 25; '03 68
Cream Gravy, Country-Fried Steak with, '84 8
Cream Gravy, Fried Chicken with, '85 241
Cream Gravy, Fried Pork Chops with, '03 24
Currant Gravy, '83 276
Dill-Cream Gravy, Pork Chops with, '84 81
Fried Chicken Gravy, '95 235
Fried Ripe Tomatoes with Gravy, '82 180
Giblet Gravy, '79 283; '88 253; '03 256
Giblet Gravy, Roast Turkey and, '94 308
Gravy, '88 303
Green Chile-Tomato Gravy, '05 42
Ham with Gravy, Virginia, '86 15
Horseradish Gravy, Filet Mignon with, '92 262
Meat Gravy, '03 68
Milk Gravy, Buttermilk-Marinade Turkey with Peppery,
   '98 311
Mushroom Gravy, '99 34
Mushroom Gravy, Baked Quail with, '89 273
Mushroom Gravy, Minute Steak with, '05 67
Mushroom Gravy, Pot Roast with, '02 90

Mushroom Gravy, Salisbury Steak with, '03 202
Onion-and-Mushroom Gravy, Roast with,
   '00 293
Onion Gravy, Fried Quail with, '82 214
Onion Gravy, Pork Chops in, '99 222
Orange Gravy, '81 259; '89 323
Pancakes and Gravy, Pasta, '05 43
Pork Chops and Gravy, '96 71
Red-Eye Gravy, Country Ham with, '79 37; '99 34
Redeye Gravy, Country Ham with, '86 254; '98 271;
   '00 216
Red-Eye Gravy, Ham and, '88 221
Red Wine Gravy, Venison Roast with, '85 270
Roasted Red Pepper-and-Vidalia Onion Gravy, '03 323
Sage Gravy, '96 269
Salsa Gravy, Country-Fried Steak with Creamy, '05 67
Sausage Gravy, '92 271; '94 20; '97 243; '03 67
Sawmill Gravy, '03 67; '05 110
Shallot Gravy, '02 239
Sour Cream Gravy, '92 301
Sour Cream Gravy, Pot Roast with, '79 17
Southwestern Gravy, '99 34
Sweet Potato-Eggplant Gravy, Roast Duck with,
   '83 90
Tasso Gravy, '92 236; '96 270
Tomato-and-Crabmeat Cream Gravy, '04 165
Tomato Gravy, '93 18; '99 35; '00 216, 330;
   '02 17, 33
Tomato Gravy, Spicy, '95 172
Turkey Gravy, '91 255; '94 306
Turkey Gravy, Quick Herbed, '05 270
Turkey with Gravy, Old-Fashioned Roasted, '04 270
White Wine Gravy, '89 322
White Wine Gravy, Chicken-Herb Strudel with,
   '04 318
White Wine Gravy, Pot Roast in, '81 299
GREENS
Bacon, Shelly Greens and, '96 290
Bake, Grits 'n Greens Dinner, '84 281
Beets 'n' Greens, '95 179
Chowder, Mixed Greens, '97 262
Collard Green Risotto and Pot Liquor, '01 121
Collard Greens, '95 233; '96 272; '03 324
Collard Greens, Esau's, '03 17
Collard Greens, Nana's, '03 278
Collard Greens, Seasoned, '82 211
Collard Greens Soup, '00 293
Collard 'n' Black-Eyed Pea Stew, '04 24
Collard, Raisin, and Pecan Sauté, '05 292
Collards, '79 32
Collards and Sausage, Pasta with, '94 230
Collards Casserole, Parmesan-, '95 233
Collards, Country-Style, '03 252
Collards, Risotto with, '96 203
Collards, Southern-Style, '82 107
Collard Stew, '02 17
Collard Stew, Hearty Ham-and-, '05 236
Collards, Uptown, '92 23; '05 21
Collards with Apples, '98 250
Edna's Greens, '96 144; '00 184
Escarole-and-Bacon Salad, '84 85
Escarole, Easy Cooked, '84 85
Green and Gold, '00 91
Grits and Greens, '95 233
Gumbo z'Herbes, '94 239
Kale, Homestyle, '00 91
Kale, Pasta with Sausage and, '03 279
Kale, Scalloped, '86 224
Kale Soup, Creamy, '96 203
Kale, Sweet-and-Sour, '80 298
Kale with Salsa, Southwest, '94 246
Kale with Tomato and Onion, '92 244
Kale with Tomatoes, Spicy, '99 243
Mustard Greens and Potatoes, '86 224

Mustard Green Soup, Cream of, '93 280
Mustard Greens, Spinach Fettuccine with, '94 247
Mustard Greens-Stuffed Tenderloin, '96 324
Pasta with Beans and Greens, '02 202
Pasta with Greens, '95 211; '96 47
Pasta with Greens, Creamy, '00 91
Pork Tenderloin, Southern-Style Stuffed, '99 45
Pot Pie with Cornbread Crust, Ham-and-Greens,
   '03 20
Risotto with Greens, '96 132
Salad with Warm Pecan Dressing, Mess o' Greens,
   '98 250
Sauce, Cress, '96 176
Stewed Tomatoes and Greens, '95 234
Stir-Fried Greens, '94 33; '97 270
Super-Charged Greens, '01 211
Turnip-and-Carrot Salad, '91 212
Turnip-and-Collard Greens, '92 215
Turnip Green Dip, '91 13
Turnip Green Dip with Jalapeño-Corn Muffins, Hot,
   '93 164
Turnip Greens, '90 13, 232; '95 306
Turnip Greens and Ham Hock, Southern, '80 119
Turnip Greens and Ham Hocks, Southern, '03 220
Turnip Greens and White Bean Bake, '94 246
Turnip Greens, Fresh, '92 339
Turnip Greens, Old-Fashioned, '85 255
Turnip Greens, Saucy, '83 12
Turnip Greens, Simple, '01 211; '02 106
Turnip Greens Stew, '02 17; '04 24
Turnip Greens, Suppertime, '04 34
Turnip Greens with Cornmeal Dumplings, '82 211
Turnip Greens with Turnips, '84 230; '01 211
Watercress-and-Mushroom Salad, '88 104
Watercress Mousse, '88 104
Watercress Soup, '88 104
Watercress Soup, Cream of, '96 66
Watercress Spread, '88 103
Wilted Greens and Red Beans, '05 21
GRILLED. *See also* **BARBECUE.**
Beef
Brisket, Smoked, '01 169
Burgers, All-American Pizza, '92 148
Burgers, Barbara's Big Juicy, '03 M138; '04 M178
Burgers, Beefy Vegetable, '98 143
Burgers, Burgundy, '80 156
Burgers, Favorite, '89 165
Burgers, Grilled Sour Cream, '87 287
Burgers, Italian, '00 326
Burgers, Italian-Style, '05 180
Burgers, Mushroom, '89 164
Burgers, Nutty, '87 185
Burgers, Party, '83 164; '84 39
Burger Spirals, '94 139
Burgers, Sausage, '83 212
Burgers, Seasoned, '85 158
Burgers, Spicy Cheddar-Stuffed, '05 163
Burgers, Spinach, '00 26
Burgers, Steak-House, '87 186
Burgers, Stuffed, '85 159
Burgers, Stuffed Border, '04 127
Burgers, Sweet-and-Savory, '03 163
Burgers, Sweet-and-Sour, '90 128
Burgers, Tortilla, '94 138
Burgers, Triple-Layer, '89 165
Burgers with Caramelized Onions, Beef, '98 143
Burgers with Caramelized Onions, Pepper,
   '00 218
Burgers with Roasted Bell Pepper Ketchup,
   Jalapeño-Stuffed, '97 318
Burgers with Sprouts, '89 164
Burgers with Tahini Sauce, Gyro, '03 183
Cheeseburgers, Fried Green Tomato, '94 138
Cheesesteaks, Chimichurri, '04 312

Eye of Round, Grilled Beef, '82 91
Fajita Salad, Beef, '91 70
Fajitas, Beef and Chicken, '02 119
Fajitas (Bo Nuong Xa), Vietnamese, '05 117
Fajitas, Favorite, '86 114
Fajitas, Java, '96 227
Fajitas, Plum Good, '94 115
Fajitas with Pico de Gallo, '98 87
Filet Mignon, Marinated, '84 171
Fillet, Acapulco, '98 174
Fillets with Orange Cream, Beef, '97 66
Flank Steak and Mushrooms, '87 61
Flank Steak, Cheese-Stuffed, '98 182
Flank Steak, East-West, '04 90
Flank Steak, Easy Greek, '05 207
Flank Steak, Flavorful, '96 32
Flank Steak, Ginger-Marinated, '89 25; '05 216
Flank Steak, Grilled, '80 152; '89 168; '91 80;
    '92 166; '03 146
Flank Steak, Grilled Marinated, '97 182
Flank Steak in Mexican Marinade, '98 128
Flank Steak, Lemon-Lime, '95 55
Flank Steak, Marinated, '82 162; '83 35; '85 86;
    '95 237; '04 118
Flank Steak, Mediterranean, '00 145
Flank Steak, Oriental, '83 178
Flank Steak, Peppery Grilled, '99 157
Flank Steak Pinwheels, '87 141
Flank Steak, Rosemary Grilled, '03 125
Flank Steak Sandwiches with Apple Barbecue Sauce,
    '99 173
Flank Steaks, Delicious Marinated, '83 110
Flank Steak Skewers, Lemon, '02 134
Flank Steak, Soy-Ginger, '02 90
Flank Steaks with Mushrooms, '00 121
Flank Steak, Tangy, '86 184
Flank Steak, Tenderized, '82 105
Flank Steak Teriyaki, '81 110
Flank Steak, Texas, '86 185
Flank Steak with Apple-Bourbon Sauce and Roasted
    Vegetables, Grilled, '99 142
Flank Steak with Black Bean-and-Corn Salsa,
    Grilled, '94 80
Flank Steak with Chili Butter, '00 177
Flank Steak with Horseradish Sauce, Grilled, '02 19
Flank Steak with Molasses Barbecue Glaze, Grilled,
    '00 59
Flank Steak with Salsa, Southwest, '03 95
Flank Steak with Sweet Peppers, Grilled,
    '90 138
Grilled Steaks, '96 172
Hamburgers, Flavorful Grilled, '81 110
Hamburgers, Grilled, '93 198
Hamburgers, Old-Fashioned, '79 149
Hamburgers, Spicy Grilled, '98 158
Hamburgers, Teriyaki, '94 138
Hamburgers Teriyaki, '99 332
Kebabs, Beef, '85 110
Kebabs, Beef-and-Vegetable, '91 148
Kebabs Deluxe, Beef, '82 182
Kebabs, Marinated Beef, '82 105; '85 159
Kebabs, Marinated Steak, '80 184
Kebabs, Meatball, '95 192
Kebabs, Pineapple-Beef, '83 212
Kebabs, Saucy Beef, '83 109
Kebabs, Spicy Grilled, '98 158
Kebabs, Spirited Beef, '87 142
Kebabs, Steak, '93 95
Kebabs, Steak-and-Shrimp, '80 184; '00 124
Kebabs, Teriyaki Beef, '80 207
Kebabs with Rice, Marinated Beef, '84 32
Kebabs with Vegetables, Beef, '90 148
Kebabs with Vegetables, Marinated Beef, '99 292
London Broil, Marinated, '05 84

London Broil Sandwiches with Yogurt-Cucumber
    Sauce, '01 162
London Broil, Teriyaki, '92 282
Marinated Beef on a Stick, '85 234
Mashed Potatoes and Chipotle Cream, Grilled Beef
    with, '02 M320
Medaillons of Beef with Horseradish Cream, '90 96
New York Steaks, Grilled, '05 123
Pigs on a Roll, Three Little, '98 203
Pizza, Taco, '98 176
Poor Boy Fillets, '82 106
Prime Rib, Smoked, '97 161; '02 177
Red Wine Marinade, Beef with, '91 46
Rib-Eye Grill, '02 306
Rib-Eyes, Italian, '98 215
Rib-Eye Steaks, Molasses-Grilled, '05 218
Rib-Eye Steaks, Peppered, '97 46; '00 146; '02 110
Rib Eyes with Herb Cheese and Asparagus Bundles,
    Grilled Chile-Rubbed, '03 326
Rib Eyes with Red Pepper-Polenta Fries and Chile
    Corn Jus, '00 196
Ribs, Baby Loin Back, '01 106
Ribs, Sweet-and-Sour Grilled, '98 331
Roast, Grilled Marinated Beef, '93 141
Roast, Grilled Pepper, '81 110
Round Steak, Tender Grilled, '85 3
Salad, Beef Vinaigrette, '95 177
Salad, Spicy Beef, '02 174
Sirloin Kebabs, Marinated, '82 162
Sirloin, Peppery Grilled, '02 212
Sirloin Salad, Grilled, '94 129
Sirloin Steak, Secret, '81 110
Sirloin Steaks, Italian, '04 61
Sirloin Steaks with Thyme Pesto, '97 182
Sirloin with Zesty Corn Salsa, Cilantro-Garlic,
    '02 193
Steak-and-Onion Sandwiches, '02 126
Steak-and-Vegetable Kebabs, '04 218
Steak, Bourbon, '90 148
Steak Continental, '83 178
Steak, Curried Beef, '88 60
Steak, Grilled Black Pepper, '86 184
Steakhouse Beef, American, '93 15
Steak, Italian, '03 180
Steak, Marinated Bourbon, '95 91
Steak, Mediterranean, '03 180
Steak, Mesquite-Grilled, '85 154
Steak on a Stick, '83 109
Steak, Patio, '87 141
Steak, Pirate, '79 89
Steak Salad Niçoise, Grilled, '98 148
Steaks Balsamico, Grilled, '05 84
Steaks, Blue Cheese, '84 171
Steaks, Garlic-Herb, '99 175
Steaks, Mexican Pepper-Cheese, '97 190
Steak, Spicy Grilled, '97 211
Steaks, Stately, '00 121
Steaks, Sweet-and-Sour Marinated, '83 110
Steaks with Blue Pecan Confetti, Maple-Mustard-
    Glazed Balsamic, '05 330
Steaks with Green Chiles, Grilled, '85 144
Steaks with Spicy Herb Sauce, Asian Grilled,
    '03 280
Steak, Tabasco, '95 207
Steak with Ham-and-Mushroom Sauce, '83 109
Steak with Mushroom Sauce, '83 212
Steak with Pimiento Cheese Salsa, Fiery, '99 331
Steak with Vegetables, Skewered, '81 124
Superburgers, '79 89
Tacos al Carbón, '86 19
Tacos al Carbón, Tailgate, '79 185
Tacos, Jerk Steak, '01 170
Tenderloin, Grilled, '91 166
Tenderloin, Herb Marinated, '83 109

Tenderloin, Marinated Beef, '93 215
Tenderloin Shish Kebabs, Beef, '00 200
Tenderloin with Horseradish Cream, Beef,
    '05 309
Tenderloin with Mushrooms, Beef, '87 115
"Tenders," Corn and Tomatoes with Chipotle-Lime
    Cream, Tex-Mex Grilled Beef, '05 329
Tomatoes and Artichokes, Beef with, '92 282
Tournedos Diables, '87 60
Bratwurst, Grilled, '94 253; '01 159
Bread, Barbecue, '99 105
Bread, Greek, '89 200
Bread, Grilled, '00 88
Bread, Lemony French, '97 147
Burgers, Pizza, '89 165
Cantaloupe Wedges, Grilled, '87 162
Cheddar, Easy Smoked, '01 168

Chicken
Bahamian Chicken with Cha-Cha Salsa, Grilled,
    '97 160
Barbecued Chicken, Grilled, '81 154
Basil Chicken, Grilled, '93 201
Basil-Stuffed Chicken with Tomato-Basil Pasta,
    '94 204
Basting Sauce, Grilled Chicken with, '01 146
Beer-Can Chicken, '04 118
Beer-Can Chicken, Basic, '03 130; '04 104
Breast of Chicken, Marinated, '87 123
Breasts, Grilled Chicken, '84 172; '04 214
Breasts, Marinated Chicken, '90 54
Breasts with Fig-and-Melon Compote, Grilled,
    Chicken, '00 163
Breasts with Lemon-Yogurt Coleslaw, Grilled
    Chicken, '98 148
Bundles with Bacon Ribbons, Chicken, '87 168
Burgers, Open-Faced Chicken-Onion,
    '94 139
Charcoal Broiled Chicken, '79 90
Clubs, Grilled Chicken-and-Pesto, '01 22
Cola-Can Chicken, '03 130; '04 104
Creamy Sauce, Grilled Chicken with, '01 318
Creole Grilled Chicken, '04 289
Cumin Chicken, Grilled, '87 142
Dill Sauce, Grilled Chicken with, '88 162
Fajitas, Beef and Chicken, '02 119
Fajitas, Chicken, '99 158
Foil-Wrapped Chicken, '99 108
Garlic-and-Wine Grilled Chicken, '00 136
Garlic-Grilled Chicken, '87 180
Ginger-Glazed Chicken, Grilled, '98 166
Ginger-Orange Chicken, Grilled, '91 26
Green Onions, Chicken with Grilled, '01 94
Greens, Grilled Chicken on, '99 201
Grilled Chicken, '89 200; '92 170
Grits with Grilled Chicken and Onions, '99 17
Guava Chicken, Grilled Sweet, '05 278
Herbed Chicken Quarters, Grilled, '96 171
Herb-Grilled Chicken with Watermelon-Feta Salad,
    '05 320
Honey-Glazed Grilled Chicken, '99 213
Honey-Lime Grilled Chicken, '96 189;
    '98 332
Jalapeño Chicken, Grilled, '93 213
Jamaican Jerk Chicken, '96 120; '99 121
Jamaican Jerk Raspberry Chicken, '00 88
Kebabs, Chicken, '87 141; '03 180
Kebabs, Chicken-Pineapple, '00 200
Kebabs, Chicken-Vegetable, '03 95
Kebabs, Hawaiian, '85 157
Kebabs, Oriental Chicken, '95 193
Kebabs, Rumaki, '82 182
Kebabs, Sesame Chicken, '92 165
Kebabs, Soy-Chicken, '86 156
Kebabs Supreme, Chicken, '81 124

GRILLED, Chicken
(continued)

Lemonade Chicken, '82 163
Lemon-Herb Grilled Chicken, '95 87
Lemon-Mustard Chicken, '99 109
Lexington-Style Grilled Chicken, '05 54
Lime Chicken with Grilled Pineapple, '04 88
Lime-Grilled Chicken, '02 142; '04 320
Lime-Jalapeño Chicken, Grilled, '91 87
Macadamia-Mango Chicken, '02 162
Margarita-Marinated Chicken, Grilled, '97 167
Marinated Chicken, '87 61
Marinated Chicken Quarters, '02 142
Marinated Chicken with Mango Salsa, Margarita,
'05 328
Mojo-Marinated Chicken, '05 163
Mushroom Bundles, Chicken-, '80 157
Orange, Lime, and Ginger Sauce, Chicken with,
'92 123
Pesto Chicken with Basil Cream, '89 158
Pizza, Bistro Grilled Chicken, '05 M131
Polenta, Chicken with, '02 87
Provolone, Chicken, '93 323
Quesadillas, Grilled Chicken, '04 36
Salad, Chicken-and-Fruit, '01 178
Salad, Chicken-Blueberry, '02 177
Salad, Grilled Asian Chicken, '96 158
Salad, Grilled Chicken-and-Fruit, '96 155
Salad, Grilled Chicken-Pasta, '94 64
Salad, Grilled Chicken-Rice, '98 148
Salad, Moroccan Grilled Chicken, '95 231
Salad, Sara's Grilled Chicken-Cornbread, '05 184
Salad, Strawberry-Chicken, '04 50
Salad, Strawberry-Citrus Chicken, '05 84
Salad, Thai Chicken, '95 177
Salad with Grilled Chicken, Tropical Spinach, '04 51
Salad with Mango Chutney, Grilled Chicken,
'96 182
Salad with Raspberry Dressing, Grilled Chicken,
'95 202
Salsa, Grilled Chicken with Cha-Cha, '98 333
Sandwiches, Chicken-Benedict Bagel, '96 250
Sandwiches, Grilled Chicken Salad, '00 164
Sandwiches, Open-Faced Mexican, '98 230
Sandwiches, Summer Open-Faced, '99 201
Sandwich, Ham 'n' Cheese Chicken, '95 153
Sandwich Jamaican Chicken, '95 153
Sandwich, Jerk Chicken, '98 333
Sandwich, Marinated Chicken in a, '86 185
Saté, Chicken, '99 134
Sausage with Fennel, Chicken, '98 312
Sesame-Ginger Chicken, '00 219
Skewers with Peanut Sauce, Chicken, '02 173;
'04 324
Slaw and Dipping Sauce, Grilled Chicken with Sweet
Soy, '04 123
Smoky Grilled Chicken, '85 160
Soba Noodles, Grilled Chicken with Spicy, '00 93
South-of-the-Border Barbecued Chicken, '97 311
Southwestern Chicken, '03 180
Southwestern Chicken with Pineapple Salsa, Grilled,
'04 196
Soy-Garlic Chicken, '98 128
Tabbouleh Salad, Grilled Chicken with, '91 70
Tarragon-Dijon Thighs, Grilled, '97 120
Tea-Thyme Grilled Chicken, '05 M52
Teriyaki Chicken, '91 163
Teriyaki Chicken, '92 59
Thighs, Grilled Chicken, '05 163
Thighs, Molasses-Glazed Chicken, '05 85
Thighs, Smoky Chicken, '05 184
Tomatillo Salsa, Grilled Chicken with, '02 123

Tortas, Grilled Chicken, '01 M187
Vegetables, Grilled Chicken and, '99 200
Vegetables Vinaigrette, Grilled Chicken and,
'91 26
White Barbecue Sauce, Chicken with, '97 322;
'01 168
Wings, Grilled Honey Chicken, '96 111
Wings, Hot 'n' Spicy Chicken, '04 132
Wings, Maple-Glazed Chicken, '99 110
Yogurt-Lemon Chicken, Grilled, '81 111
Cornish Hens, Asian Grilled, '99 41
Cornish Hens, Grilled, '88 243; '92 59
Cornish Hens, Jelly-Glazed, '93 251
Cornish Hens, Orange-Glazed Grilled, '86 250
Cornish Hens, Sherry-Marinated, '91 148
Cornish Hens with Tropical Fruit, Grilled, '97 310
Crostini, Tomato-and-Goat Cheese, '04 168
Crostini with Olive Tapenade, Grilled, '05 172
Dogs, Marrow's Famous, '04 198
Duck Breasts, Charcoal Marinated, '79 226
Duck Kebabs with Almond Rice, Grilled, '91 291
Duck with Orange Sauce, Grilled, '94 305
Duck with Parsnip Mash, Honey-Orange-Glazed
Muscovy, '97 262
Fennel and Radicchio with Orange Vinaigrette, Grilled,
'95 253
Figs, Marinated Grilled, '96 194
Fish. *See also* **GRILLED/Seafood.**
Amberjack Sandwiches, Grilled, '91 195
Caribbean Fish, '99 109
Catfish Cajun-Style, Grilled, '90 129
Catfish, Lime-Orange, '02 22
Catfish Over Mixed Greens, Grilled, '04 326
Catfish with Red Salsa, Grilled, '90 172
Catfish with Relish, Grilled, '92 54
Easy Grilled Fish, '91 194
Fillets Tomatillo, '94 135
Flounder Fillets, Grilled, '83 213
Grouper, Garlic-Basil Marinated, '94 160
Grouper, Grilled, '86 185
Grouper, Grilled Herbed, '99 178
Grouper, Grilled Marinated, '90 166
Grouper, Hot Spicy, '94 78
Heather Sauce, Catfish Inn's Grilled Fish with,
'84 182
Kebabs, Fish, '98 223
Mahi-Mahi with Lemon Mayonnaise, '99 178
Montego Bay Grilled Fish with Caribbean Salsa,
'96 70
Rainbow Trout with Mushroom Stuffing, Grilled,
'97 162
Salmon Fillets, Fresh Herb-Rubbed, '03 207
Salmon Fillets with Sweet Corn Relish, '93 119
Salmon, Orange-Basil, '97 165
Salmon Quesadilla with Cucumber Salsa, Grilled,
'95 131
Salmon Steaks, Grilled, '94 278
Salmon Steaks, Grilled Herbed, '93 176
Salmon Steaks, Mint-Marinated, '96 175
Salmon Steaks with Lemon-Mustard Sauce, '97 124
Salmon Steaks with Tarragon Butter, '87 155
Salmon Steaks with Tarragon Sauce, Grilled, '97 42
Salmon with Mustard-Molasses Glaze, Grilled,
'01 209
Salmon with Sweet Soy Slaw and Dipping Sauce,
Grilled, '04 123
Salmon with Tangy Dill Sauce, Grilled, '04 320
Snapper with Orange-Almond Sauce, Grilled,
'01 158
Swordfish Salad, '00 18
Swordfish-Shiitake Skewers, '97 168
Swordfish, Skewered, '86 256
Swordfish Steaks, Orange-Ginger Marinated, '93 271
Swordfish Steak with Chervil Butter, '91 147

Swordfish with Avocado-Lime Sauce, Grilled,
'97 127
Swordfish with Caper Sauce, Grilled, '95 230
Tilapia Tacos, Shredded Grilled, '05 16
Trout, Grilled, '95 106
Tuna, Grilled Florida, '93 128
Tuna, Inland Grilled, '96 197
Tuna Sandwiches, Grilled-, '02 173
Tuna Steaks, Grilled, '90 129
Tuna Steaks on Mixed Greens with Lemon-Basil
Vinaigrette, Seared, '94 205
Tuna Steaks with Cucumber Sauce, '97 180
Tuna with Poblano Salsa, Grilled, '91 135
Tuna with Sautéed Vegetables, '98 222
Yellowfin Tuna with Corn, Pepper, and Tomato Salsa,
'94 164
Franks, Grilled Stuffed, '82 163
Fruit Kebabs, Grilled, '97 147
Fruit with Honey Yogurt, Grilled, '95 87
Game Hens, Texas-Style, '87 61
Grits, Grilled Andouille, '04 165
Grits, Hot Grilled, '97 191
Ham. *See* **GRILLED/Pork.**
Lamb
Burgers, Mesquite-Grilled Lamb, '88 59
Chops, Grilled Lamb, '91 163
Chops, Joan's Rosemary Lamb, '97 42
Chops, Peppercorn-Crusted Lamb, '92 142
Chops, Rosemary Grilled Lamb, '03 125
Chops, Smart and Saucy Rosemary-Cherry Lamb,
'02 193
Chops, Teriyaki Lamb, '87 60
Chops with Chipotle and Cilantro Oils, Grilled
Lamb, '02 96; '03 98
Chops with Pineapple-Mint Salsa, Grilled Lamb,
'05 52
Chops with Rosemary Sauce and Wild Rice-Fennel
Pilaf, Grilled Lamb, '97 127
Chops with Shrimp, Lamb, '88 58
Kebabs, Apricot-Grilled Lamb, '98 102
Kebabs, Lamb, '85 159; '95 192; '00 220;
'03 136
Kebabs, Lamb Shish, '93 70
Kebabs, Overnight Shish, '81 124
Kebabs, Rosemary Marinated Lamb, '93 203
Kebabs, Saucy Lamb, '89 167
Kebabs, Savory Lamb, '80 184
Kebabs, Shish, '82 182
Kebabs Teriyaki, Shish, '85 37
Leg of Lamb, Greek-Style, '93 170
Leg of Lamb, Grilled, '96 88; '98 103
Mango Salsa, Grilled Lamb with, '95 104
Patties, Grilled Lamb, '02 167
Rosemary-Skewered Lamb, '97 190
Sandwiches, Lamb, '97 107
Steaks with Béarnaise Sauce, Lamb, '85 37
Sweet Pepper Relish, Grilled Lamb with, '95 104
Liver Kebabs, '80 185
Melon Salad with Orange-Raspberry Vinaigrette,
Grilled, '95 144
Nachos, Smoked, '01 146
Peaches, Grilled Balsamic-Glazed, '02 159
Pecans, Smoky, '01 168
Pie, Pear-Praline, '97 192
Pineapple Boats with Rum Sauce, '97 192
Pineapple Skewers with Rum Sauce, Grilled,
'04 247
Pineapple with Vanilla-Cinnamon Ice Cream, Grilled,
'00 127; '01 195
Pizza Dogs, Grilled, '97 139
Pizza, Grilled, '97 190
Pizzas, Grilled, '93 178; '98 176
Polenta, Grilled, '00 126
Polenta with Black Bean Salsa, Grilled, '93 155

Pork

Burgers, Hearty Sauced Pork, '84 125
Burgers, Sausage, '83 212
Chops, Apricot-Stuffed Pork, '92 219
Chops, Country Pride Pork, '79 159
Chops, Glazed Pork, '86 185
Chops, Grilled Asian Pork, '02 307; '03 271
Chops, Grilled Pork, '88 113; '98 246
Chops, Hawaiian Grilled Pork, '85 159
Chops, Herbed Pork, '97 147
Chops, Honey-Glazed, '97 200
Chops, Lemon-Herb Pork, '84 81
Chops, Marinated Grilled Pork, '81 110
Chops, Mexican Pork, '99 108
Chops on Smoked Gouda Grits, Grilled Maple
    Chipotle Pork, '04 172
Chops, Pineapple-Curry Glazed, '82 106
Chops, Rosemary Pork, '98 329
Chops with Ancho Cream Sauce, Boneless Pork,
    '95 205
Chops with Black-and-White Salsa, Pork, '97 200
Chops with Caramelized Onions, Thai Pork, '05 85
Chops with Garlic Mashed Potatoes, Grilled Pork,
    '02 281
Chops with Jalapeño-Cherry Sauce, Smoked Pork,
    '01 208
Chops with Orange Slices, Saucy Pork, '05 197
Chops with Tangy Barbecue Sauce, Pork, '99 104
Glazed Pork Chops, Bourbon-, '04 44
Ham and Apples, Grilled, '96 M303
Ham, Easy Grilled, '92 134
Ham, Golden Grilled, '79 90
Ham, Hickory-Grilled, '92 81
Ham Kebabs, Honey, '80 156
Ham Kebabs, Swiss-, '81 124
Ham 'n' Cheese Chicken Sandwich, '95 153
Ham Slice, Apricot-Glazed, '93 252
Honey-and-Herb Grilled Pork, '90 148
Jalapeño Grilled Pork, '99 160
Kebabs, Margarita Pork, '98 M223
Kebabs, Pineapple-Pork, '99 144
Kebabs, Spicy Pork, '82 182
Kebabs with Sesame Seeds, Pork, '00 337
Loin, Grandma Ruth's Grilled Pork, '96 250
Loin, Honey-Grilled Pork, '92 219
Loin, Marinated Pork, '01 331
Loin, Minted Pork, '99 96
Loin with Rosemary-Breadcrumb Crust, Grilled
    Pork, '05 200
Maple-Glazed Pork Chops with Pecans and Apples,
    Commune's, '04 102
Medaillons, Grilled Pork, '93 229
Medaillons with Blackberry Sauce, Pork,
    '02 136
Ribs, Adams', '95 236; '00 177; '03 312
Ribs, Baby Back, '04 86
Ribs, Chipotle Grilled Pork, '01 319
Ribs, Jamaican Jerk Raspberry, '00 88
Ribs, Lemon Grilled, '81 154
Ribs McCoy, '04 132
Ribs, Smoky, '84 172
Ribs, Smoky Chipotle Baby Back, '04 87
Ribs with Plum Sauce, Crispy, '98 182
Roast, Company Pork, '99 276
Roast, Grilled Pork, '97 323
Salad, Grilled Pork Cosmopolitan, '04 123
Salsa, Grilled Pork with, '90 128
Saté, Pork, '05 53
Sausage, Grilled Pork, Cheddar, and Jalapeño,
    '98 311
Sausage Pasta, Three Pepper-, '02 122
Sesame Pork, '01 177
Slow-Grilled Pork with Ranch-Barbecue Sauce,
    '05 163

Smoked Pork, '01 233; '03 121
Smoked Pork Shoulder, '01 147
Spareribs, Baked and Grilled, '97 211
Spareribs, Grilled Maple, '99 136
Spareribs, Honey-Glazed, '82 163
Spareribs in Plum Sauce, '99 136
Spareribs, Peach-Glazed, '86 14
Spareribs, Spicy, '89 168
Steaks, Glazed Pork, '83 178
Superburgers, '79 89
Tacos with Cucumber-Radish Salsa, Adobo Grilled
    Pork, '01 186
Tenderloin, Barbecued Pork, '05 245
Tenderloin, Blueberry-Rum Marinated Pork, '05 178
Tenderloin, Coriander-Pepper Pork, '99 145
Tenderloin, Garlic Grilled Pork, '90 172
Tenderloin, Grilled Balsamic Pork, '05 241
Tenderloin, Grilled Marinated Pork, '91 199
Tenderloin, Grilled Pork, '91 163; '94 88; '02 187
Tenderloin, Honey-Garlic Pork, '01 16
Tenderloin, Margarita Pork, '05 85
Tenderloin, Marinated Pork, '84 175
Tenderloin, Molasses-Grilled Pork, '96 265
Tenderloins, Grilled Pork, '88 98; '94 158
Tenderloins, Honey-Grilled, '92 199; '00 126
Tenderloin, Spicy Grilled Pork, '04 96
Tenderloins with Rosemary Pesto, Grilled Pork,
    '01 174; '04 82
Tenderloin Towers, Pork, '86 75
Tenderloin, Tropical Spinach Salad with Grilled
    Pork, '04 51
Tenderloin with Apples, Celery, and Potatoes, Grilled
    Pork, '95 161
Tenderloin with Brown Sauce, Grilled Pork, '89 32
Tenderloin with Gingered Jezebel Sauce, Grilled
    Pork, '04 138
Tenderloin with Lime and Chipotle, Sweet Pork,
    '04 184
Tenderloin with Molasses Sauce, Grilled Pork,
    '97 193
Tenderloin with Mustard Sauce, Pork, '99 145;
    '03 238
Tenderloin with Onion-Balsamic Sauce, Pork,
    '99 44
Tenderloin with Orange-Curry Sauce and Coconut
    Rice, Polynesian Pork, '04 309
Tenderloin with Orange Marmalade, Grilled Pork,
    '03 181
Tenderloin with Parmesan-Pepper Toasts, Herbed
    Pork, '98 242
Tenderloin with Red Wine Sauce, Molasses Pork,
    '02 290
Tenderloin with Sauce Caribe, Jamaican Pork,
    '02 320
Tenderloin with Yogurt and Lime, Grilled Pork,
    '04 216
Tenders, Skewered Pork, '00 200
Quail, Asian Grilled, '99 41
Quail, Grilled, '92 90
Quail, Grilled Breakfast, '88 220
Quail, Marinated, '80 221
Quail, Sage-Smoked Champagne, '97 164
Quail with Red Wine-Blackberry Sauce, Grilled,
    '98 319
Sandwiches, Grilled Garden, '98 315
Saté Mixed Grill with Spicy Peanut Sauce, '04 134
Seafood. *See also* **GRLLED/Fish.**
Brochette, Seafood, '87 96
Oriental Marinade, Seafood in, '98 128
Oysters Mornay, Grilled, '89 195
Oysters Supreme, Smoky, '87 60
Oysters with Paul's Cocktail Sauce, Grilled,
    '05 244
Po'Boy, Grilled Seafood, '96 244

Scallop-Bacon Kebabs, '81 111
Scallop Kebabs, Grilled, '83 101
Scallop Kebabs, Sea, '82 162
Scallops, Grilled Sweet-and-Sour, '01 92
Scallops, Marinated Grilled, '84 171
Scallops Tostada, Grilled, '87 120
Scallops with Cilantro-Lime Vinaigrette, Grilled
    Orange, '94 77
Shrimp and Cornbread-Stuffed Peppers, Barbecued,
    '97 261
Shrimp-and-Scallop Kebabs, Grilled, '92 210
Shrimp and Vegetables, Grilled Parsleyed, '04 256
Shrimp, Grilled, '85 103
Shrimp, Grilled Garlic, '99 178
Shrimp, Grilled Margarita-Marinated, '97 167
Shrimp, Grilled Marinated, '87 173
Shrimp, Grilled Sweet-and-Sour, '97 100
Shrimp, Grilled Zucchini-Wrapped, '98 200
Shrimp Gyros with Herbed Yogurt Spread, Grilled-,
    '02 M169
Shrimp Kebabs, Marinated, '85 158
Shrimp Kebabs, Steak-and-, '80 184; '00 124
Shrimp, Marinated and Grilled, '87 141
Shrimp, Orange, and Watermelon Salad with
    Peppered Peanuts in a Zesty Citrus Dressing,
    Grilled, '04 308
Shrimp Skewers with Vegetable Salsa, '98 32, 223
Shrimp, Stove-Top Smoked, '01 168
Shrimp, Tropical Spinach Salad with Grilled, '04 51
Shrimp with Bacon and Jalapeños, Grilled, '05 M200
Shrimp with Citrus Salsa, Grilled, '97 141
Shrimp with Creamy Tomatillo Sauce, Grilled Jerk,
    '01 332
Shrimp with Smoky Sweet Sauce, Mexican-Grilled,
    '03 32
Shrimp with Tropical Fruit Sauce, Grilled, '01 195
S'mores, Grilled Pound Cake, '98 179
Steak-and-Vegetable Kebabs, '04 218
Tortilla Bites, '95 42
Turkey-and-Fruit Kebabs, '88 140
Turkey Breast, Citrus-Marinated, '94 272
Turkey Breast, Smoky, '89 323
Turkey Breast, Spicy-Sweet Smoked, '03 250
Turkey Breast with Cranberry Salsa, Grilled,
    '95 252
Turkey Burgers, Grilled, '91 61
Turkey Drumsticks, Grilled, '89 168
Turkey, Seasoned Smoked, '97 85
Turkey Steaks, Grilled Marinated, '93 170
Turkey Tenderloins, Lime-Buttered, '92 127
Vegetables
Acorn Squash with Rosemary, Grilled, '96 266
à la Grill, Vegetables, '88 130
Asparagus, Grilled, '00 165; '05 197
Asparagus Salad with Orange Vinaigrette, Grilled,
    '99 102; '01 110
Barbecue Hobo Supper, '99 108
Bell Peppers, Potato-Stuffed Grilled, '05 123
Burgers, Vegetable, '89 164
Cilantro Butter, Grilled Vegetables with, '98 182
Corn and Squash, Grilled, '02 122
Corn-and-Squash Quesadillas, Grilled, '02 123
Corn, Grilled Parmesan, '82 127
Corn in the Style of Oaxaca, Grilled, '04 134
Corn-on-the-Cob, Grilled, '90 166
Corn on the Cob, Lemony, '89 200
Corn on the Cob, Mexican, '96 167
Corn on the Cob with Garlic-Chive Butter,
    '01 331
Corn on the Cob with Red Chile Paste, Grilled,
    '05 118
Corn on the Grill, '94 161; '97 191
Corn, Roasted Camp, '05 174
Corn Salsa, Grilled, '99 162

GRILLED, Vegetables
(continued)

Corn Salsa, Zesty, '02 193
Corn, Smoked, '01 169
Corn Soup, Grilled, '87 121
Corn with Herb Butter Sauce, '79 150
Corn with Jalapeño-Lime Butter, Grilled, '01 158;
   '04 178
Corn with Maple Vinaigrette, Grilled, '98 171
Easy Grilled Veggies, '05 194
Eggplant Appetizer, Grilled, '95 198
Eggplant, Balsamic-Flavored, '95 342
Eggplant, Grilled, '80 202
Eggplant, Sage-Grilled, '96 269
Eggplant Vinaigrette, Italian, '03 125
Gazpacho, Grilled Vegetable, '97 181
Gazpacho, Southwestern Grilled, '00 84
Grilled Vegetables, '84 172; '92 124;
   '96 123, 173
Herbs, Grilled Vegetables with, '00 220
Italian-Style Grilled Vegetables, '92 143
Kebabs, Beef-and-Vegetable, '91 148
Kebabs, Easy Vegetable, '02 142
Kebabs, Fresh Vegetable, '92 101
Kebabs, Grilled Vegetable, '93 170
Kebabs, Tangy Marinated Vegetable, '88 142
Kebabs, Vegetable, '87 116; '01 132
Marinated Grilled Vegetables, '95 162; '00 126
Marinated Vegetables, Grilled, '00 137; '04 133
Medley, Grilled Vegetable, '98 158
Mushroom-Asparagus Salad, Grilled, '02 122
Mushroom Burgers, '97 101; '99 135
Okra and Tomatoes, Grilled, '98 124
Onion Flowers with Pecans, Grilled, '96 217
Onion Salad, Grilled, '99 96
Onions, Grilled Stuffed, '95 180
Onions, Smoky Sweet, '97 191
Onion Stacks, Balsamic, '05 141
Parmesan Vegetables, '97 147
Pasta, Grilled Vegetable, '97 142
Pepper Grill, Three-, '02 122
Pepper Kebabs, Pretty, '90 166
Pepper-Pesto Linguine, Grilled, '04 136
Peppers, Marinated Roasted, '97 123
Pepper Tacos, Grilled, '95 340
Pizza, Grilled Vegetable, '98 176
Pizzas, Grilled Vegetable, '97 323
Poblano Chile con Queso, Roasted, '01 186
Portabello Mushrooms, Grilled, '95 123
Portobello Burger, Grilled, '98 331
Portobello Burgers with Avocado Mayonnaise,
   '00 335
Portobello Mushroom Burgers, '01 144
Portobello Mushrooms and Asparagus, Grilled,
   '02 122
Portobello Mushrooms, Lime-Grilled, '05 18
Portobello Pizza Burgers, Grilled, '00 89
Portobello Pizzas, Grilled, '00 89
Potatoes, Grilled Herb, '84 172
Potatoes, Grilled Irish, '97 53
Potatoes, Grilled Stuffed, '05 123
Potatoes, Italian Grilled, '98 171
Potatoes, Smoked Baked, '97 25
Red Onions, Grilled, '03 139
Romaine Salad with Buttermilk-Chive Dressing,
   Grilled, '04 105
Salad, Avocado-Corn-Poblano, '01 320
Salad, Grilled Marinated Vegetable, '01 143
Salad, Grilled Vegetable, '94 203; '00 146
Sandwiches, Grilled Vegetable, '01 310
Sandwiches, Open-Faced Summer, '01 171
Shiitakes, Grilled, '95 265

Skewers, Grilled Vegetable, '94 160
Squash and Onion, Grilled, '79 150
Squash-and-Pepper Kebabs, Summery, '95 193
Squash and Tomatoes, Grilled Summer, '99 144
Squash Fans, Grilled, '79 150
Squash, Marinated Grilled, '02 110
Sweet Potatoes, Grilled, '93 213
Tomatillo Salsa, '02 123
Tomato, Bell Pepper, and Portobello Salad, Grilled,
   '98 211
Tomatoes, Cheesy Grilled, '79 150
Tomatoes, Grilled, '85 158; '99 173; '04 178
Tomatoes with Basil Vinaigrette, Grilled,
   '97 168
Yellow Squash and Tomatoes, Grilled, '00 102
Zucchini Fans, Grilled, '89 200
Zucchini with Feta, Greek Grilled, '95 190
Venison Kebabs, '82 215; '88 249
Venison Roast, Grilled, '93 278
Venison Steaks, Grilled, '82 215
Wiener Worms, '02 223

GRITS
Bake, Grits 'n Greens Dinner, '84 281
Biscuits, Shrimp-and-Grits, '02 313
Bread, Bacon-Cheddar Grits, '05 83
Bread, Basil Pesto-Cheese Grits, '05 83
Bread, Cheesy Grits, '05 83
Bread, Tomato-Black Olive Grits, '05 83
Cakes, Southwestern Grits, '93 61
Casserole, Garlic Grits, '81 47
Casserole, Grits-Sausage, '84 75; '86 241
Cheese
   Baked Cheese-and-Garlic Grits, '83 292; '84 78
   Baked Cheese Grits, '80 49, 99; '83 311; '85 41;
      '94 240; '01 289
   Baked Cheese Grits, Grillades and, '94 240
   Baked Grits, Swiss-and-Cheddar, '91 71
   Bake, Santa Fe Grits, '00 123
   Casserole, Cheddar Cheese Grits, '05 283
   Casserole, Cheesy Grits, '81 270
   Casserole, Cheesy Shrimp-and-Grits, '03 28
   Cheddar Cheese Grits, '05 43
   Cheese Grits, '86 242; '90 102
   Chicken Sausage and Shiitake Mushrooms, Cheese
      Grits with, '03 254
   Chile-Blue Cheese Grits, '04 240
   Chili-Cheese Grits, '01 86
   Creamy Grits, '96 24
   Creamy Grits, Margaret's, '99 18; '00 21
   Croutons and Vidalia Onion-Balsamic Vinaigrette,
      Southern Spinach Salad With Cheese Grits,
      '04 316
   Crust Batter, Cheese Grits, '03 21
   Double-Cheese Grits, Quick, '03 167
   Fried Cheese Grits, Hot Browns with, '02 94
   Garlic-and-Herb Cheese Grits, '95 122
   Garlic-and-Herb Grits, Baked, '01 326
   Garlic Cheese Grits, '80 47; '81 197
   Garlic-Cheese Grits, '86 180; '88 126; '89 47;
      '97 58; '99 270; '00 215
   Garlic Grits, '00 194; '03 211
   Green Chiles, Cheese Grits with, '95 208
   Grilled Grits, Hot, '97 191
   Grits and Cheese, '00 327
   Gruyère Cheese Grits, '81 47
   Jalapeño Cheese Grits, '85 43
   Jalapeño-Cheese Grits, '00 239; '01 328
   Mexican Cheese Grits, '02 34
   Parmesan Cheese Grits, '02 233
   Quick Cheese Grits, '83 M203; '96 97
   Saga Blue-Chile Grits, '98 202
   Sausage-Cheese Grits, '90 238
   Sautéed Smoked Gouda Cheese Grits with Black
      Bean Salsa, '03 323

   Sliced Cheese Grits, '84 75
   Smoked Gouda Grits, '02 319; '04 173
   Soufflé, Garlic-Cheese Grits, '99 18
   Squares, Chili-Cheese Grits, '01 86
Chicken and Grits, '95 263
Chicken and Onions, Grits with Grilled, '99 17
Chiles Rellenos, Southern-Style, '96 24
Country Grits and Sausage, '83 54
Creamy Grits, '92 237, 238; '93 60; '00 215
Dressing, Grits, '93 306; '94 296
Eggs Benedict, Shrimp-and-Grits, '03 53
Eggs Creole, '92 86
Fried Grits, '83 292; '84 78
Garlic Shrimp and Grits, '03 246
Good Morning Grits, '87 156
Greens, Grits and, '95 233
Grillades and Grits, '88 126; '89 47; '93 62
Grilled Andouille Grits, '04 165
Ham-and-Spinach Grits, Garlicky, '94 177
Italiano, Grits, '92 43
Nassau Grits, '81 47; '99 214
Orange Grits, '81 47
Pan-Fried Grits, '93 62
Patties, Grits, '83 52
Pie, Crustless Grits-and-Ham, '86 103
Pie, Grits Fiesta, '92 43
Pie, Pineapple-Grits, '96 236
Pudding, Grits, '96 28
Quiche, Ham-and-Grits Crustless, '94 89
Risotto, Redneck, '98 107
Salad, Stacked Grits-Spinach, '98 66
Sausage Grits, '86 92
Sausage, Grits with, '99 233
Scrambled Grits, '80 48
Shrimp and Grits, '01 258
Shrimp and Grits, Crook's Corner, '04 102
Shrimp and Grits, Garlic, '05 111
Shrimp and Grits, Garlic-Chili, '00 23
Shrimp and Grits, Spicy, '04 176
Shrimp-Manchego-Chorizo Grits with Red Bean Salsa,
   '97 227
Shrimp Stew and Grits, '80 118
Shrimp Stew over Grits, '88 126; '89 47
Soufflé, Grits, '80 30
Soufflé, Mexican Grits, '79 55
Spoonbread, Grits, '79 38
Spoonbread Grits with Savory Mushroom Sauce,
   '96 236
Stackable Grits, '02 204
Stuffing, Grits, '96 270
Tarts, Shrimp 'n' Grits, '03 254
Timbales, Chives-Grits, '90 172
Timbales, Grits, '88 223
Tomato Grits, '03 199
Tomato Grits, Hot, '95 171; '01 131
Wedges, Southwestern Grits, '04 332
GUACAMOLE. *See* **APPETIZERS/Dips, Guacamole.**
GUMBOS. *See also* **CHOWDERS, JAMBALAYAS,**
   SOUPS, STEWS.
Carolina Gumbo, '95 70
Chicken
   Andouille Gumbo, Chicken-, '98 14
   Chicken Gumbo, '79 199; '90 26
   Easy Chicken Gumbo, '83 156
   Gullah House Gumbo, The, '92 237
   Ham-Seafood Gumbo, Chicken-, '81 6
   Oyster Gumbo, Chicken and, '81 198
   Sausage Gumbo, Chicken-, '04 288
   Sausage Gumbo, Chicken-and-, '89 275; '90 256;
      '94 20; '00 221; '01 324; '03 313; '04 213
   Smoked Sausage, Chicken Gumbo with, '81 199
   Ya Ya, Gumbo, '87 210
Dove and Sausage Gumbo, '81 199
Duck, Oyster, and Sausage Gumbo, '79 226

Fish

Catfish Gumbo, '90 278; '91 216

Easy Fish Gumbo, '81 6

Snapper Gumbo, Savannah, '94 105

Green Tomato Gumbo, '04 314

Ground Beef Gumbo, '87 283

Gumbo, '01 160

Mogumbo, '93 32

Okra Gumbo, '86 210; '91 206; '01 165

Okra Gumbo, Deep South, '79 48

Okra Gumbo Freezer Mix, '86 210; '01 165

Seafood

Cajun Seafood Gumbo, '94 238

Champion Seafood Gumbo, '86 293

Chicken-Ham-Seafood Gumbo, '81 6

Combo Gumbo, '81 198

Crab and Shrimp Gumbo, '81 200

Crabs, Seafood Gumbo with Whole, '85 2

Creole Gumbo, '86 234

Creole Gumbo, Quick, '82 87

Creole Seafood Gumbo, '82 278

Ham and Seafood Gumbo, '81 199

Okra Gumbo, Light Seafood-, '86 155

Oyster Gumbo, Chicken and, '81 198

Seafood Gumbo, '79 198, 286; '80 34; '81 5; '83 90; '84 87, 92; '87 210; '90 154; '96 98

Shrimp-Crab Gumbo, '98 15; '03 111

Shrimp Gumbo, '81 199

Shrimp Gumbo, Old-Style, '98 97

Shrimp Gumbo, Quick, '86 71

Southern Gumbo, '82 242

Spicy Seafood Gumbo, '91 207

Texas Ranch-Style Gumbo, '82 226

Turkey Gumbo, '82 268; '85 258

Wild Game Gumbo, '91 290

z'Herbes, Gumbo, '94 239

HAM. *See also* **PORK.**

Acorn Squash, Ham-Stuffed, '81 239; '83 66

Appetizers

Appetillas, Ham, '93 63

Balls, Appetizer Ham, '82 39

Balls, Fried Ham-and-Cheese, '84 221

Balls, Ham, '86 256; '03 299

Balls with Spiced Cherry Sauce, Ham, '81 112; '82 12

Biscuits, Country Ham in Heart, '86 105

Biscuits, Cured Ham and, '85 320

Biscuits, Kentucky Ham 'n' Angel, '90 83

Biscuits, Petite Ham and Cheese, '79 193

Biscuits, Southern Ham and, '91 12

Biscuits with Country Ham, '90 93

Biscuits with Ham, Ranch, '97 59

Cheesecake, Cheddar-Chili, '02 251

Cheesecake, Ham-and-Asparagus, '02 103

Chips, Ham-Cheese, '82 34

Deviled Ham Twists, '82 86

Dip, Creamy Ham, '93 125

Eggs and Ham, Green, '96 90

Fig Bites, Baked, '02 160

Meat-and-Cheese Appetizers, '87 7

Mousse Pitas, Ham, '95 328

Mushrooms Stuffed with Ham, '97 237

New Potatoes, Ham-Stuffed, '88 211

Nuggets, Cheesy Ham, '81 290

Pâté, Ham, '85 279

Pineapple Nibbles, Ham-, '95 283

Prosciutto Bruschetta and Cantaloupe Chutney, '00 108

Prosciutto, Walnuts, and Cream, Figs with, '96 194

Prosciutto, Watermelon and, '98 164

Prosciutto-Wrapped Asparagus, '91 98

Puffs, Ham-and-Cheese, '86 277

Puffs, Ham-Filled Party, '84 116

Roll, Ham-and-Cheese, '79 234

Rolls, Ham, '79 153

Rollups, Almond-Ham, '89 284

Rollups, Asparagus, '01 239

Rollups, Ham-and-Swiss, '85 113

Sandwiches, Party Ham, '97 240

Sandwiches, Tiny Ham-and-Cheese, '99 87

Spread, Buttery Ham, '95 93; '97 98

Spread, Cold Ham, '82 248

Spread, Country Ham, '87 8

Spread, Ham, '86 126

Spread, Ham and Pimiento, '80 285; '81 56

Stack-Ups, Ham, '96 109

Tapas, Garlic-Ham, '92 175

Tennessee Ham, '95 263

Tennessee Sin, '95 218; '96 204

Turnovers, Chile-Ham, '88 64

Turnovers, Party Ham, '82 39

Apricots, Ham and, '90 53

Artichokes, Ham-Mushroom-Stuffed, '95 228

Baked

Apricot Baked Ham, '84 160

Bourbon Glaze, Baked Ham with, '98 M271; '01 M42

Burgundy Ham, Baked, '94 326

Cranberry-Raisin Sauce, Baked Ham with, '88 244

Festive Baked Ham, '83 263

Maple-Raisin Sauce, Baked Ham with, '83 215

Marinated Baked Ham, '86 94; '88 133

Michelle's Baked Ham, '03 16

Orange-Honey Glaze, Baked Ham with, '90 53

Orange Sauce, Baked Ham with, '86 294

Pineapple-Baked Ham, '86 48

Plum Ham, '80 110

Royale, Ham, '84 260

Slice, Baked Ham, '83 12

Balls, Ham, '84 91; '86 256

Barbecued Ham Slices, '81 110

Beans and Ham, Baked, '05 45

Birming "Ham," '94 229

Biscuits, Blue Cheese-and-Ham Cornmeal, '98 136

Biscuits, Ham, '99 233

Biscuits, Ham-and-Swiss Cheese, '04 209

Biscuits, Ham-Filled Angel, '80 159

Biscuits, Surprise Pull-Apart, '95 46

Black-Eyed Peas and Ham, Quick, '00 336

Black-Eyed Peas, Cajun, '96 218

Black-Eyed Peas, Hearty, '02 107

Black-Eyed Peas with Ham Hocks, '79 122

Bread, Ham-and-Cheese, '86 213

Broiled Ham, Cranberry, '88 301

Brunch Egg Nests, '03 246

Bundles, Ham-and-Cheese, '93 63

Burritos, Breakfast, '97 172

Butterbeans, Smoky Speckled, '04 167

Cakes, Hawaiian Ham, '79 252

Casseroles

Apple Ham Casserole, '79 213

Apples, Baked Ham and, '82 M237

Asparagus Dinner, Ham-, '80 M10

Asparagus Ham Rolls, '91 117

au Gratin, Broccoli-Ham, '90 239

Bacon-and-Ham Casserole, Cheesy, '01 256

Beans with Ham, Baked, '80 136

Breakfast Casserole, '91 285

Breakfast Casserole, Sausage-Ham, '01 54

Broccoli Casserole, Ham and, '81 133

Broccoli Casserole, Quick Ham-, '82 40

Brunch Casserole, Southwestern, '03 197

Cheese Casserole, Ham-and-, '87 78

Cheese Layered Casserole, Ham-and-, '98 160

Chicken, Ham, and Cheese Bake, '87 217

Creamy Ham Casserole, '03 83

Creamy Ham Casseroles, '01 55

Creamy Ham Medley, '84 90

Egg Casserole, '98 98

Egg Casserole, Breakfast Ham and, '79 253

Golden Ham Casserole, '82 119

Ham Casserole, '96 302; '98 314

Harvest Ham Bake, '79 210

Hash Brown-Ham-Cheese Bake, '97 323

Lasagna, Creamy Ham-and-Chicken, '95 88

Lima Casserole, Ham and, '79 192

Macaroni-Ham Casserole, '81 M177; '83 283

Noodle Casserole, Ham and, '80 300

Pasta Casseroles, Hot Brown, '96 290

Potato Casserole, Cheesy Ham-and-, '84 326

Potato Casserole, Ham-and-, '83 M87; '96 103

Potatoes with Ham Bits, Creamy, '87 191

Potato-Pineapple Bake, Ham-, '93 302

Quiche Casserole, '95 32

Rice Casserole, Ham-and-, '84 75

Rice-Stuffed Ham Rolls, '83 190

Rice-Tomato Bake, Ham-, '87 78

Roll Casserole, Ham, '91 M127

Sausage-Ham Breakfast Casserole, '04 332

Spaghetti, Ham-and-Turkey, '95 19

Spinach-and-Ham Rollups, '86 84

Spinach-Ham Rolls, '88 78

Spinach Roll-Ups, Ham and, '81 143

Strata, Baked Ham, '83 283

Strata, Ham, '95 308

Strata, Ham and Broccoli, '80 261

Swiss Casserole, Savory Ham-and-, '01 308

Tetrazzini, Ham, '82 M77; '84 241; '03 174

Turkey Bake, Layered Ham and, '79 252

Vegetable-and-Ham Casserole, '84 91

Cheesecake, Ham-and-Asparagus, '90 174

Cheesy Ham Dinner, '84 90

Cheesy Ham Towers, '82 M77

Chicken-and-Ham Bundles, Cheesy, '84 261

Chicken Breasts Saltimbocca, '98 19

Chicken Medley, Creamy Ham-and-, '92 272

Chowder, Creamy Green Bean, Mushroom, and Ham, '99 336

Chowder, Creamy Ham, '88 M53

Chowder, Ham-and-Cheese, '89 15

Chowder, Ham and Corn, '79 16

Chowder, Ham-and-Corn, '82 40

Chowder, Ham 'n Cheese, '79 199

Chowder with Ham, Potato, '99 141

Citrus-and-Spice Ham, '88 40

Collard Greens, '03 324

Collard Greens, Esau's, '03 17

Cordon Bleu, Chicken, '81 304; '82 83; '93 126

Cordon Bleu, Company Chicken, '82 274

Cordon Bleu, Easy Chicken, '02 175

Cordon Bleu, Veal, '87 219

Country Ham

Biscuits, Country Ham, '94 215

Biscuits, Country Ham in Heart, '86 105

Biscuits with Country Ham, '90 93

Bread with Herb Butter, Country Ham, '86 255; '99 18

Brown Sugar Coating, Country Ham with, '90 88

Chips, Country Ham, '92 338

Cider-Baked Country Ham, '82 195

Cider, Country Ham in Apple, '80 251

Cornbread, Country Ham Hot-Water, '01 29; '02 107; '04 25

Cornbread, Crab with Chile, '86 254

HAM, Country Ham
(continued)

Country Ham, '99 19; '00 298
Eggs Benedict, Country Ham, '03 52
Grits Stuffing, Country Ham with, '96 270
Kentucky Hot Brown, '86 254
Kentucky Jack, '86 254
Oven-Braised Country Ham, '90 87
Oysters and Ham, Edwards', '86 253
Puff, Cheesy Country Ham, '90 88
Quiche, Country Ham, '87 287
Raisin Sauce, Country Ham with, '99 19
Red-Eye Gravy, Country Ham with, '79 37; '99 34
Redeye Gravy, Country Ham with, '86 254; '98 271;
    '00 216
Roasted Country Ham, Edwards', '86 253
Sauce, Country Ham, '90 117; '96 24; '05 109
Shrimp With Country Ham and Capers, Sautéed,
    '04 241
Sotterley Plantation Country Ham, '93 270
Stuffed Country Ham, '90 317
Stuffed Country Ham, Maryland, '88 49
Swirls, Veal-and-Smithfield Ham, '86 253
Tartlets, Country Ham-and-Asparagus, '98 82
Virginia Ham, Buttermilk Biscuits with, '96 142
Virginia Ham with Gravy, '86 15
Wine, Country Ham in, '81 260
Creamed Ham and Chicken, '81 M74
Creamed Ham and Eggs, '82 40
Creamy Ham Towers, '79 138
Crêpes, Ham-and-Egg, '83 204
Crêpes with Mushroom Sauce, Ham-and-Egg,
    '82 46
Croquettes, Ham, '82 119
Curried Ham and Peaches, '82 60
Curried Ham Steak, '82 120
Curried Ham with Rice, '80 111
Deviled Delight, '83 130
Devils, Ham, '93 88
Eggplant, Ham-Stuffed, '80 162
Egg Rolls, Chinese, '96 101
Eggs, Creamy Ham and, '87 286
Eggs on Toast with Cheese Sauce, Ham and, '81 43
Eggs, Savory Ham and, '82 231
Enchiladas, Scrambled Egg, '97 153
Fettuccine, Ham-and-Asparagus, '94 84
Flips, Ham-and-Cheese, '92 46
French Toast, Ham-and-Cheese Oven, '97 172
French Toast, Stuffed, '00 193
Fried Rice, Ham, '04 125
Frittata, Ham-and-Broccoli, '98 101
Fritters, Ham, '82 39
Fritters, Potato-Ham, '98 249
Fritters with Creamy Sauce, Ham, '81 105
Frosted Ham, '89 71
Garlic and Orange, Ham with, '05 294
Glazed
    Apricot-Glazed Ham Slice, '93 252
    Baked Glazed Ham, '01 52
    Bourbon Glaze, Baked Ham with, '98 M271;
        '01 M42
    Bourbon-Glazed Ham, '04 296
    Brown Sugar Glaze, Smithfield Ham with, '86 253
    Cherry-Peach Chutney, Glazed Ham with, '97 315
    Cranberry Glazed Ham, '81 274
    Cranberry-Honey Glaze, Baked Ham with, '89 273
    Cranberry-Orange Glazed Ham, '81 295
    Currant-Glazed Ham, '91 249; '05 104
    Fruited Ham Slice, '83 M317
    Honey-Glazed Ham Slice, '81 104
    Honey-Orange Glazed Ham, '83 320
    Marmalade-Glazed Ham, '89 M196

Molasses-Coffee Glazed Ham, '03 119
    Molasses-Glazed Ham, '84 24
    Orange-Glazed Ham, '89 324
    Orange-Glazed Ham, Sweet, '02 286
    Orange-Honey Glaze, Baked Ham with,
        '90 53
    Peachy Glazed Ham, '96 189
    Pineapple-Glazed Ham, '01 288; '03 82
    Praline-Mustard Glazed Ham, '01 306
    Steak, Glazed Ham, '91 13
    Strawberry-Glazed Ham, '91 84
    Stuffed Ham, Glazed, '84 321
    Sunshine-Glazed Ham, '84 252
    Sweet-and-Sour Glazed Ham, '88 M15
    Sweet-Sour Glazed Ham, '83 311
Green Beans with Ham and Potatoes, '01 223
Green Peppers, Ham-Stuffed, '80 65
Griddle Cakes, Ham, '89 255
Grilled Ham and Apples, '96 M303
Grilled Ham, Easy, '92 134
Grilled Ham, Golden, '79 90
Grilled Ham, Hickory-, '92 81
Grits, Garlicky Ham-and-Spinach, '94 177
Gumbo, Chicken-Ham-Seafood, '81 6
Gumbo, Combo, '81 198
Gumbo, Ham and Seafood, '81 199
Hash Brown Bake, '95 281
Hopping John with Ham, '81 7
Jambalaya, '04 288
Jambalaya, Creole, '87 210; '03 83
Jambalaya de Covington, '87 211
Jambalaya with Shrimp, Chicken-and-Ham, '04 99
Kabobs, Honey Ham, '80 156
Kabobs, Swiss-Ham, '81 124
Loaves
    Chili-Sauced Ham Ring, '81 M122
    Country Ham Loaves, '86 255
    Cranberry-Ham Loaf, '82 M77
    Glazed Ham Loaf, '79 187; '90 212
    Ham Loaf, '79 180; '80 272
    Ham Loaves, '90 235
    Hawaiian Ham Loaf, '79 71
    Pineapple Upside-Down Ham Loaf, '79 253
    Ring, Ham, '84 91
    Saucy Ham Loaf, '86 M328
    Spicy Ham Loaf, '80 110
    Supreme Ham Loaf, '79 242
    Upside-Down Ham Loaf, '82 40
Mac and Cheese, Hearty, '05 208
Mirlitons, Shrimp-and-Ham Stuffed, '03 251
Mirlitons, Stuffed, '00 246
Mornay, Ham and Eggs, '02 130
Muffins, Ham-and-Cheddar, '03 81
Muffins, Ham-and-Cheese, '92 252; '93 144
Muffins, Ham-and-Swiss, '03 81
Muffins, Reduced-Fat Ham-and-Cheddar, '03 81
Noodles, Ham and Swiss on, '87 108
Omelet, Dill-Cheese-Ham, '95 33
Omelet, Ham and Cheese, '79 262; '80 123
Omelet, Ham-and-Cheese, '02 246
Omelet, Rolled, '89 228
Omelet, Sour Cream-Ham, '79 261
Omelets with Creole Sauce, '89 228
Pancakes, Potato-Ham, '96 138
Pancetta, Penne with, '00 51
Patties, Ham, '81 99
Patties, Ham-Sprout, '85 51
Patties, Pineapple-Ham, '80 110
Patties, Spicy Ham, '90 235
Peach Holiday Ham, '04 251
Peas and Ham, Southern, '85 138
Peas and Pasta, '99 68
Peppers, Ham-and-Corn Stuffed, '81 87
Peppers with Rice and Ham, Stuffed, '82 131

Pie, Crustless Grits-and-Ham, '86 103
Pie, Golden Ham, '87 78
Pie, Ham-and-Cheese, '95 256; '96 75
Pie, Ham Pot, '90 25
Pie, Omelet, '00 M35
Pie, Savory Ham-and-Swiss Breakfast, '05 240
Pie, Spaghetti-Ham, '93 19
Pie with Cheese Crust, Ham, '80 286
Pie with Cornbread Crust, Ham-and-Greens Pot,
    '03 20
Pie, Zucchini-Ham-Cheese, '80 272
Pineapple-Flavored Ham, '87 160
Pinto Beans, Ham Hocks, and Rice, '05 46
Pinto Beans with Ham, '97 210
Pinwheels, Ham, '90 235
Pizza, Greek, '03 145
Pizza, Ham-and-Eggs Crescent, '93 47
Pizza, Ham-and-Pineapple, '96 169
Pizzas, Muffuletta, '00 M335
Pizza, Southern Classic, '95 268
Po-Boy, Pain-Perdu, '93 291
Potatoes, Cheddar, Broccoli, and Ham Stuffed, '04 26
Potatoes, Ham Stuffed, '79 210
Potatoes, Ham-Stuffed Baked, '02 52
Potatoes, Jalapeño-Ham Stuffed, '81 M61
Potatoes, Stuffed Mashed, '98 328
Potatoes with Ham, Herbed, '00 318
Pot Pie, Ham-Broccoli, '03 83
Praline Ham, '85 302; '96 303
Prosciutto and Artichoke Hearts, Tortellini Alfredo
    with, '02 322
Prosciutto Croutons, '99 89
Prosciutto, Party Pasta with, '94 176
Prosciutto, Pizza with Artichoke and, '87 182
Quiches
    Cheese Quiche, Ham-, '79 26
    Cheese Quiches, Individual Ham-and-, '98 24
    Cheesy Ham Quiche, '79 127
    Crustless Ham Quiche, '84 235
    Grits Crustless Quiche, Ham-and-, '94 89
    Ham Quiche, '80 110
    Jalapeño Quiche, Cheesy, '84 31
    Mushroom Quiche, Ham-and-, '81 11
    Vegetable Quiche, Ham-and-, '84 326
Raisin Ham, '80 124
Raisin Sauce, Ham with, '82 M76
Red-Eye Gravy, Ham and, '88 221
Red Rice and Ham, '00 289
Rice, Charleston, '97 310
Rice, Fried, '00 273
Rice, Orphan's, '03 32
Rice, Savannah Red, '80 119
Roast of Ham, Brandied, '98 320
Roast, Peachy Ham, '86 118
Rolls à la Swiss, Chicken-and-Ham, '92 42
Rolls, Ham-and-Broccoli, '86 212; '87 82
Rolls, Ham-and-Cheese, '82 3
Rolls, Ham-and-Cheese Lettuce, '89 217
Rolls, Ham-Asparagus, '79 41
Salads
    Apple Salad, Ham-and-, '88 139
    Asparagus with Prosciutto, Marinated, '95 83
    Baked Ham Salad, Crunchy, '83 23
    Boats, Salad, '80 93
    Bread Salad, Italian, '03 54
    Cheese Salad, Ham-and-, '88 138
    Cheese Toss, Ham and, '79 55
    Coleslaw, Ham, '84 195
    Congealed Ham Salad, '81 36
    Egg Salad, Ham 'n, '81 36
    Fruited Ham Salad, '81 36, 146
    Hearty Ham Salad, '82 40
    Italian Ham Salad, Spicy, '85 74
    Macaroni-Ham Salad, '85 218

Macaroni Salad, Ham and, '79 220
Mandarin Ham-and-Rice Salad, '87 145
Noodle Salad, Ham-, '85 249
Pasta Salad, Ham-and-, '90 128
Pasta Salad, Ham-and-Pea, '00 217
Pasta Salad, Ham-Dijon, '92 191
Pasta Salad, Ham-Pecan-Blue Cheese, '90 62
Pasta Salad with Ham, '92 108
Pilaf Mold, Ham, '86 222
Potato Salad, Ham and, '80 272
Potato Salad, Ham-and-, '95 94
Potato Salad, Ham-and-Egg, '86 84
Prosciutto Salad, Melon-and-, '92 191
Rice Salad, Colorful Ham-and-, '90 319
Rice Toss, Ham-, '82 40
Rolls, Hearty Salad, '81 206
Spread, Ham Salad, '87 92
Sweet Potato Salad, Hawaiian Ham-, '82 232
Tropical Ham Salad, '89 175
Watermelon-Prosciutto Salad, '04 171
Sandwiches. *See also* **HAM/Appetizers.**
Asparagus-and-Ham Melt Sandwiches, '88 M96
Asparagus Delight, Ham-, '86 48
Asparagus Sandwiches, Ham-and-, '01 307
Baked Ham Sandwiches, '81 29
Biscuits and Ham, Green Elf, '02 277
Blue Cheese-Ham Sandwiches, Creamy, '87 279
Cheese-and-Ham Striped Tea Sandwiches, Cheshire Claret, '94 16
Cheese Chicken Sandwich, Ham 'n', '95 153
Cheese Sandwiches, Ham-and-, '01 299
Cheese Sandwiches, Hot Ham-and-, '85 299
Cheese Sandwich Round, Ham-and-, '94 326
Cheese Sandwich, Tex-Mex Ham-and-, '86 4
Club Sandwiches, Double-Decker, '91 231; '92 68
Club Sandwich, Italian, '01 22
Croissant Sandwiches, '89 161
Eggs à la Swiss, Ham and, '88 158
Focaccia Sandwiches, '98 53
Focaccia Sandwich, Pesto, '05 131
French Market Sandwiches, '98 230
Giant Ham-and-Pepper Salad Sandwich, '05 204
Giant Ham-and-Pepper Sandwich, '96 74
Grilled Cheese-and-Ham Sandwiches, '05 293
Hamwiches, '96 246
Hideaways, Ham, '81 29
Holiday Ham Sandwiches, '02 286
Hot Browns, '98 287
Hot Ham Sandwiches, '79 214
Hot Rods, Ham, '86 136
Meal-in-One Sandwiches, '80 218
Monte Cristo Sandwiches, '83 134; '97 319
Monte Cristo Sandwiches, Open-Faced, '01 171; '05 222
Muffin, Stuffin', '99 193
Muffuletta, '04 27
Muffuletta, Doodles, '94 35
Muffulettas, '98 184
Open-Faced Sandwiches, '79 214
Open-Face Ham Sandwiches, '82 40; '85 8
Panhandle Sandwiches, '01 56
Pineapple-Ham Sandwich Loaf, '91 167
Pineapple Slaw Sandwiches, Ham-and-, '96 199
Pita Pockets, Ham-and-Cheese, '90 271
Pita Sandwiches, Denver, '86 M12
Pita Sandwiches, Ham-and-Cheese, '87 202; '88 44
Pita, Stuffed, '89 87
Po'Boys, Guacamole-Topped Ham, '04 170
Pocket, Ham and Swiss in the, '83 31
Quesadillas, Quick Fiesta, '02 246
Reuben Melts, Southern, '03 69
Rollup, Hot Ham-and-Cheese, '01 217
Rollups, Creamy Pineapple-and-Ham, '04 163
Rollups, Pizza, '99 197

Salad Sandwich, Tangy Ham, '80 272
Sebastian, The, '94 184
Stroganoff on Cheesy Onion Biscuits, Ham, '95 98
Stuffed Sandwich, Deli, '98 287
Swiss-and-Asparagus Sandwiches, Ham-, '01 52
Swiss Sandwiches, Ham-and-, '98 287
Swiss Sandwiches, Tangy Ham-and-, '85 164
Torta, Mediterranean, '98 23
Turkey and Ham Pine-Berry Sandwiches, '00 59
Turkey Specials, Cheesy Ham-and-, '84 14
Virginia Ham Sandwiches, '80 155
Wraps, Club, '01 23
Yummy Sandwiches, '81 229
Sauce, Steak with Ham-and-Mushroom, '83 109
Scalloped Potatoes with Ham, '02 42
Skillet Dinner, Corn-and-Ham, '83 190
Skillet Dinner, Ham, '85 179
Skillet Ham-and-Vegetables, '84 90
Skillet, Ham-Noodle, '87 78
Skillet, Ham Spaghetti, '83 283
Slice with Cinnamon Apple Rings, Holiday Ham, '90 250
Smoked Ham, '86 92
Soufflé, Virginia Ham Breakfast, '93 121
Soufflé with Cucumber Sauce, Ham, '92 41
Soup, Bean-and-Ham, '04 325
Soup, Chicken, Ham, and Oyster, '79 198
Soup, Creamy Kale, '96 203
Soup, Ham-and-Bean, '84 4; '05 45
Soup, Hearty Ham, '82 4
Soup, Hot Brown, '00 318
Soup, New Year's Day, '00 25
Soup, Pot Liquor, '98 273
Soup, Spicy Ham-and-Bean, '94 322
Spread, Deviled Ham, '79 81
Spread, Ham-and-Egg, '79 59
Spread, Ham Salad, '87 92
Spread, Hawaiian Ham, '87 106
Spread, Horseradish-Ham, '91 167
Stew, Blakely Brunswick, '87 4
Stew, Collard, '02 17
Stew, Collard 'n' Black-Eyed Pea, '04 24
Stew, Ham-and-Black-Eyed Pea, '93 20
Stew, Hearty Ham-and-Collard, '05 236
Stew, Quick Okra, '97 88
Stew, Turnip Greens, '02 17; '04 24
Stir-Fry, Easy Ham, '86 332
Stir-Fry, Ham and Zucchini, '79 47
Stroganoff, Ham, '82 40
Stromboli, '88 272; '89 181
Stuffed Ham, '86 323
Succotash, Savory, '96 63
Superburgers, '79 89
Supper, Top-of-Stove, '86 332
Tart, Ham-and-Cheese, '92 332
Tart Milan, '87 70
Tart, Supreme Ham, '84 22
Tasso Hollandaise, '04 67
Tennessee Ham, '95 263
Turnip Greens and Ham Hock, Southern, '80 119
Turnip Greens and Ham Hocks, Southern, '03 220
Véronique, Ham, '85 90
Waffles, Ham, '80 44
Zucchini, Ham and Cheese Stuffed, '79 157
HEALTHY & LIGHT
Andouille, '92 242
Appetizers
Ambrosia, Sherried, '84 324
Apple-Phyllo Rolls, '88 213
Artichokes, Marinated, '87 250
Artichokes with Herb-Mayonnaise Dip, '84 67
Beets, Blue Cheese-Stuffed, '88 211
Buzzard's Nests, '93 244
Carrot-Cheese Ball, '86 325

Cheese Tartlets, '88 211
Cherry Tomatoes, Crab-Stuffed, '82 289
Cherry Tomatoes, Stuffed, '88 212
Chicken-Mushroom Appetizers, '88 210
Chicken Wontons, '92 284
Chiles Medley, Fiery Pickled, '01 333
Chips, Bagel, '91 138
Chips, Baked Pita, '99 138
Chips, Baked Wonton, '91 138; '99 138
Chips, Cinnamon-and-Sugar Bagel, '91 139
Chips, Cinnamon-and-Sugar Wonton, '91 138
Chips, Corn Tortilla, '91 17
Chips, Garlic Bagel, '91 139
Chips, Garlic Wonton, '91 138
Chips, Lemon-and-Herb Bagel, '91 139
Chips, Lemon-and-Herb Wonton, '91 138
Chips, Light Tortilla, '90 278; '91 257
Chips, Parmesan Cheese Bagel, '91 138
Chips, Parmesan Cheese Wonton, '91 138
Chips, Pita, '89 19; '91 138
Chips, Plantain, '95 M203
Chips, Sweet Potato, '91 138; '95 M203
Chips, Tortilla, '91 137
Crab Ball, Spicy, '01 332
Crab Cakes with Jalapeño Tartar Sauce, Chesapeake Bay, '96 69
Crackers, Cranberry, '99 258
Crostini, Festive, '99 324
Crostini, Spinach-Red Pepper, '03 34
Crudité Platter with Dip, '84 139
Dip, Apple-Berry, '01 109
Dip, Cheese-Herb, '89 20
Dip, Chickpea-and-Red Pepper, '99 138
Dip, Cilantro, '00 248
Dip, Creamy Beef-and-Pasta Sauce, '01 108
Dip, Creamy Ham, '93 125
Dip, Curry, '87 25; '99 138
Dip, Deviled, '87 25
Dip, Dilled Garden, '84 324
Dip, Festive Crab, '92 285
Dip, Garbanzo, '93 94
Dip, Ginger, '99 139
Dip, Kahlúa, '99 139
Dip, Low-Cal Tuna, '87 25
Dip, Marmalade, '99 324
Dip, Monster Mash, '93 244
Dip, Peanut Butter, '01 109
Dip, Pine Nut-Spinach, '99 138
Dip, Quick Fruit, '90 110
Dip, Ranch-Style, '90 138
Dip, Refreshing Dill, '99 324
Dip, Santa Fe Skinny, '94 137
Dips, Fun Fruit, '01 109
Dip, Skinny Ranch, '93 96
Dip, Spinach, '87 25
Dip, Strawberry, '01 109
Dip, Tofu, '86 109
Dip, Vegetable Garden, '85 215
Dumplings, Make-Ahead Pork, '03 64
Eggplant Appetizer, Grilled, '95 198
Empanadas, '04 135
Fruit Kebabs with Coconut Dressing, '87 251
Fruit with Lemon Sauce, Fresh, '82 290
Goat Cheese Wrapped in Phyllo, '99 43
Hummus, '96 158
Hummus, Low-Fat, '99 137
Meatballs, Sweet-and-Sour, '99 325
Mix, Crunchy Snack, '93 94
Mix, Snack, '89 19
Mousse, Shrimp, '87 251
Mushroom-Almond Pastry Cups, '88 210
Mushroom Appetizers, Stuffed, '88 210
Mushrooms, Shrimp-Stuffed, '99 324
Mushrooms, Spinach-Stuffed, '89 M133

Nectarine Cocktail, '85 107
New Potatoes, Ham-Stuffed, '88 211
Nuts, Mexico, '01 27
Orange Halves, Broiled, '85 288
Oysters Bienville, Baked, '90 27
Oysters Italiano, Baked, '89 97
Pasta Bites, Pesto-Cheese, '87 251
Pâté, Black-Eyed Pea, '93 97
Pâté, Lentil, '92 285
Pâté, Mock, '87 251
Pears Stuffed with Cheese, '82 290
Pita Bread Triangles, '88 211
Pita Wedges, Garlic, '93 98
Pizzas, Pita, '89 19
Poblanos with Mango Salsa, Crab-and-Goat Cheese, '04 59
Popcorn, Chili, '91 17
Popcorn Mix, Curried, '86 326
Popcorn with Pizzazz, '93 245
Potato Skin Snack, '91 18
Pretzels, Whole Wheat, '89 20
Quesadillas, Green Chile, '90 121
Quesadillas, Poblano-and-Corn, '01 333
Salsa, Chunky Black-Eyed Pea, '01 333
Salsa with Cinnamon Crisps, Fruit, '01 108
Saté Mixed Grill with Spicy Peanut Sauce, '04 134
Scallop Appetizer, '86 155
Shrimp Cocktail, Mexican, '00 249
Shrimp Dippers, '84 324
Shrimp with Creamy Tomatillo Sauce, Grilled Jerk, '01 332
Shrimp with Marmalade Dip, Oven-Fried, '99 324
Snow Peas, Crab-Stuffed, '85 288
Spinach-Ricotta Phyllo Triangles, '88 212
Spread, Artichoke-Parmesan, '92 95
Spread, Broccamoli Curry, '88 55
Spread, Creamy Potato-Garlic, '02 35
Spread, Feta Cheese, '96 265
Spread, Low-Fat Chicken, '82 290
Spread, Roasted Red Bell Pepper, '97 217
Spread, Smoked Salmon, '84 324
Steak-and-Chestnut Appetizers, Marinated, '84 323
Tabbouleh, '88 211
Tortilla Snacks, Pesto, '89 19
Vegetable Appetizer, Tarragon, '83 277
Vegetable Nachos, '91 17
Yogurt Cheese Appetizer, '04 217
Zucchini Caviar, '88 212
Zucchini Pizzas, '88 212
Zucchini-Shrimp Appetizers, '89 311
Apple-Cheese Bake, '92 225
Apples, Baked, '86 40
Apple Side Dish, Dried, '92 226
Apples, Stuffed Baked, '89 217
Apples with Orange Sauce, Baked, '84 314
Barley, Vegetable, and Fruit Medley, '05 127
Barley, Baked, '91 133
Beans, Molasses Baked, '99 105
Beans, Ranch-Style, '00 43
Beans, Smashed Pinto, '03 129
Beverages
Apple Cooler, '90 14
Apple Julep, '86 103
Apricot Fruit Flip, '91 18
Apricot Mint Cooler, '90 165
Banana Coolers, '91 308
Banana Nog, '82 290
Banana Smoothie, '93 95
Bellini Spritzers, '90 110
Black Russian, Mock, '92 322

Bourbon Blizzard, '92 287
Breakfast Drink, Yummy, '01 133
Brew, Witch's, '93 244
Cantaloupe-Lime Refresher, '01 332
Caribbean Cooler, '95 203
Carrot Cooler, '89 35
Cider, Hot Spiced, '82 290; '99 248
Cocoa, Mocha, '83 318
Cranberry Cocktail, Hot, '89 310
Cranberry Smoothie, '91 307
Eggnog, '83 318
Eggnog with Orange and Nutmeg, Mock, '92 323
Fruit Beverage, Blender, '83 318
Fruit Refresher, '91 203
Fruit Slush, '96 157
Fruit Smoothie, '89 87
Grapefruit Refresher, '88 85
Hot Chocolate, Mexican, '98 313
Kiwi-Peach Slushy, '00 201
Lemon Velvet, '90 15
Milkshake, Mocha, '89 35
Mocha, Hot, '84 60
Orange Juicy, '90 178
Orange-Pineapple Drink, '89 35
Orange Slush, '82 49
Peach Cooler, '86 6
Peach Frosty, '83 318
Peach Refresher, '86 103
Piña Colada, Mock, '92 322
Piña Coladas, '95 203
Pineapple-Banana Slush, '90 14
Pineapple Sparkle, Spiced, '92 322
Pineapple-Yogurt Whirl, '91 132
Punch, Apple-Tea, '85 82
Punch, Citrus, '93 99
Punch, Holiday, '87 252
Punch, Holiday Hot Fruit, '92 286
Punch, Hot Apple, '84 324
Punch, Sparkling Orange, '05 170
Punch, Tart Cranberry, '83 318
Punch, White Grape, '90 15
Scarlet Sipper, '90 198
Shake, Double Strawberry, '00 179
Shake, Frosty Fruit, '87 23
Shake, Get-Up-and-Go, '00 179
Shake, Strawberry-Banana, '89 35
Shake, Strawberry-Orange Breakfast, '87 186
Shake, Strawberry-Pear, '92 139
Shake, Tropical, '00 179
Strawberry Cooler, '83 56
Strawberry Spritzer, '90 14
Tea, Iced Green, '05 196
Tea Mix, Spiced, '86 32
Tea Mix, Sugar-Free Spiced, '91 258
Tofruitti Breakfast Drink, '88 26
Tomato-Clam Cocktail, '87 252
Tomato Refresher, '83 318
Tropical Refresher, '96 157
Vegetable Cocktail, Fresh, '82 165
Virgin Mary, Spicy, '92 323
Watermelon-Berry Slush, '90 137
Breads
Apricot-Orange Bread, '92 285
Apricot-Pecan Bread, '97 266
Banana Bread, '87 72
Banana Bread, Fruity, '95 78
Barbecue Bread, '99 105
Biscuits and Sausage Gravy, '94 20
Biscuits, Angel, '90 28
Biscuits, Buttermilk, '03 24
Biscuits, Cheese-Chive, '94 324
Biscuits, Easy-Bake, '96 157
Biscuits, Herbed, '93 67
Biscuits, Light, '89 53

Biscuits, Oatmeal, '89 108
Biscuits, Orange, '88 85
Biscuits, Whole Wheat, '84 60; '91 222
Biscuits, Yeast, '87 71
Bowls, Italian Bread, '98 292
Breadsticks, Quick, '00 317
Caraway Breadsticks, '89 239
Cinnamon-Oat Bread, '90 135
Cornbread, '92 324
Cornbread, Dieter's, '87 164
Cornbread, Jalapeño, '94 78
Cornbread, Mexican, '93 182
Cornbread Supreme, '93 67
Cornmeal Yeast Bread, '89 54
Corn Sticks, '89 54; '00 43
Cranberry-Banana Bread, '90 294
Crouton Bread, Quick, '90 138
English Muffin Bread, '95 M79
Flatbread, '98 106
Focaccia, Rosemary, '95 190
French Bread, '89 54
French Pistou Bread, Crusty, '97 68
French Toast, Cottage-Topped, '85 49
French Toast, English Muffin, '00 179
French Toast, Slender, '86 103
Garlic Bread, '82 19; '91 204
Herbed Bread, '89 34
Honey-Oat Bread, '89 107
Hush Puppies, Baked, '89 53; '95 108
Loaf, Cheddar Cheese, '00 317
Muffins, All-Bran Oat Bran, '91 134
Muffins, Apple, '84 193
Muffins, Applesauce, '91 141
Muffins, Banana-Oat, '87 188
Muffins, Banana-Raisin, '89 218
Muffins, Blueberry, '91 140, 203
Muffins, Blueberry-Cinnamon, '02 177
Muffins, Bran-Buttermilk, '85 7
Muffins, Corn, '98 313
Muffins, Cornmeal, '91 19
Muffins, Cornmeal Yeast, '92 49
Muffins, Corn-Oat, '89 108
Muffins, Freezer Bran, '91 141
Muffins, Granola, '95 78
Muffins, Green Onion-and-Cream Cheese, '01 289
Muffins, Honey Bran, '88 171
Muffins Made of Bran, '86 103
Muffins, Miniature Cranberry, '90 294
Muffins, Oat Bran, '89 106
Muffins, Oat Bran-Banana, '91 18
Muffins, Oatmeal-Bran, '91 83
Muffins, Orange-Oatmeal, '00 24
Muffins, Parmesan Corn, '01 255
Muffins, Spicy Apple-Oat, '86 45
Muffins, Spicy Cornbread, '90 59
Muffins, Yogurt, '88 55
Oat Bread, Caraway-Raisin, '86 44
Oatmeal-Molasses Bread, '97 194
Onion-Herb Bread, '90 165
Pitas, Puffy, '97 69
Pizza Dough, '04 58
Popovers, Whole Wheat, '05 195
Pumpkin-Pecan Bread, '87 221
Roasted Garlic-Rosemary Bread, '04 16
Rolls, Dinner, '89 312
Rolls, Honey Wheat, '83 278
Rolls, Old-Fashioned Cinnamon, '92 226
Rolls, Parsley-Garlic, '93 319
Rolls, Vegetable Salad, '82 278
Rolls, Whole Wheat, '90 111
Rolls, Yogurt Crescent, '91 123
Rye Loaves, Swedish, '97 68
Sourdough Wedges, '90 199
Spoonbread, '90 200

Swiss Cheese Loaves, Mini, '95 80
Toast Points, Parmesan, '00 316
Toasts, Parmesan-Pepper, '98 242
Toasts, Tomato-Basil, '01 254
Toast Strips, Seasoned, '93 98
Whole Wheat Cardamom Bread, '86 223
Breakfast-in-a-Bowl, '89 87
Burritos, Hot Phyllo, '98 312
Cheese, Yogurt, '04 217
Chorizo, '92 241
Chutney, Blueberry, '95 190
Chutney, Fall Fruit, '97 218
Chutney, Green Tomato-Cranberry, '00 140
Chutney, Mango, '96 182
Chutney, Peach, '96 207
Chutney, Pear, '98 243
Couscous, Lemon, '02 237
Couscous with Mixed Fruit, '95 232
Crab Cakes, Country, '95 20
Cream, Lemon, '03 213
Crêpes, Basic, '86 38
Crêpes, Bran, '83 70; '86 44
Crêpes, Ham-and-Egg, '83 204
Crêpes, Light, '86 143
Crêpes, Low-Calorie, '87 77
Crêpes, Plain, '83 70
Crêpes, Whole Wheat, '83 70
Crisps, Parmesan, '01 197
Croutons, Bagel, '93 192
Croutons, Cornbread, '93 192
Croutons, Garlic, '92 71
Croutons, Pita, '93 192
Croutons, Spiced, '00 317
Crust, Whole Wheat, '94 78
Desserts
Alaska, Orange, '83 177
Alaska, Peachy Melba, '88 266
Ambrosia, Baked, '83 303
Ambrosia, Layered, '88 304
Apple Crisp, Tart, '92 226
Apples à l'Orange, Baked, '90 280
Applesauce Fluff, '91 173
Apples, Caramel-Peanut, '93 M244
Apples, Melting, '88 19
Bananas, Easy Tropical, '00 141
Bananas Foster, '88 20; '96 99
Bananas with Honey, Broiled, '84 175
Bananas with Rum Sauce, Spiced, '99 247
Bars, Apricot-Raisin, '87 32
Bars, Pineapple-Orange, '82 129
Bavarian Dessert, Light, '86 6
Berries, Best-Dressed, '96 317
Biscotti, Chocolate-Cinnamon, '05 30
Biscotti, Chocolate-Hazelnut, '95 80
Biscotti, Light, '91 310
Blackberries and Dumplings, '86 196
Blintzes, Cheese, '83 71
Blueberry Crisp, '84 177
Brownies, Chocolate-Kahlúa, '93 99
Brownies, Chocolate-Walnut, '89 325
Cake, Apple-Nut, '87 76
Cake, Apple Spice, '92 225
Cake, Banana-Coconut, '93 154
Cake, Black Widow Snack, '93 245
Cake, Blueberry Streusel, '92 144
Cake, Blue Ribbon Angel Food, '01 35
Cake, Chocolate Angel Food, '87 21; '90 111
Cake, Chocolate-Cinnamon, '93 154
Cake, Chocolate Custard, '88 175
Cake, Chocolate Pound, '89 325
Cake, Cinderella Fantasy, '98 70
Cake, Cinnamon Swirl, '01 255
Cake, Deluxe Light Banana, '84 314
Cake, Four-Flavor Pound, '91 136

Cake, Frosted Carrot, '92 19
Cake, German Chocolate Sheet, '03 147
Cake, Heavenly Pineapple, '83 303
Cake, Lemon-Poppy Seed, '93 154
Cake, Lightened Hummingbird, '01 34
Cake, Mocha Marble Pound, '99 23
Cake, Orange Angel Food, '96 246
Cake, Orange-Coconut Angel Food, '94 294
Cake, Orange Pound, '87 221
Cake, Pound, '92 94
Cake, Pumpkin, '93 303
Cake, Red Velvet, '93 318
Cake Roll, Lemon, '89 312
Cake Roll, Make-Ahead Chocolate-Mint, '95 220
Cakes, Creamy Lime, '04 89
Cake, Strawberry Yogurt Layer, '94 85
Cake, Warm Chocolate Pudding, '92 324
Cake, Winter Squash-Spice Bundt, '99 248
Cake with Amaretto-Almond Sauce, Angel Food,
    '90 199
Cake with Coffee Frosting, Spice Layer, '94 86
Cake with Custard Sauce, Chocolate Angel Food,
    '88 259
Cake with Pineapple-Orange Sauce, Angel, '84 14
Cake with Raspberry Sauce, Sour Cream Pound, '99 259
Cake with Strawberries and Chocolate Glaze, White,
    '87 76
Cantaloupe Whip, '89 198
Cheesecake, Almost Strawberry, '86 32
Cheesecake, Black Forest, '94 21
Cheesecake, Blueberry Chiffon, '87 76
Cheesecake, Chocolate-Amaretto, '93 97
Cheesecake, Dieter's Apple, '86 318
Cheesecake, Fudge, '98 M213
Cheesecake, Lemon, '91 308
Cheesecake, Lemon Delight, '95 219
Cheesecake, Light-and-Easy, '88 55
Cheesecake, Strawberry-Lemon, '04 237
Cheesecakes with Raspberry Sauce, Mini Lemon,
    '02 123
Cheesecake with Raspberry-Lemon Sauce, '96 30
Cherries Jubilite, '86 317
Chocolate-Bran Raisin Jumbos, '91 142
Chocolate-Cheese Cups, '91 142
Chocolate-Coffee Cones, '96 M316
Chocolate Cream Log, '94 220
Chocolate Cream Roll, '85 317
Chocolate Fondue, '91 142
Chocolate Glaze, '89 325
Chocolate-Orange Roll, '87 21
Chocolate Whip, '89 326
Chocolat, Petits Pots de, '82 272
Cobbler, Cranberry-and-Apple, '90 294
Cobbler, Fresh Cherry, '84 178
Cobbler, New-Fashioned Apple, '91 221
Cobbler, New-Fashioned Blackberry, '87 164
Cobbler, Peach, '84 178
Cobbler, Raspberry-Cherry, '93 230
Coffee Cake, Sour Cream, '93 154
Coffee Dessert, Light, '88 260
Compote, Apple-Cranberry, '04 237
Compote, Baked Fruit, '84 314
Compote, Fresh Fruit, '82 272; '84 82
Compote, Jícama-Fruit, '92 49
Compote, Melon Ball, '85 157
Compote, Spicy Grapefruit-Berry, '91 19
Compote with Caramel Syrup, Citrus, '98 313
Cookies, Almond, '91 51
Cookies, Apple-Oatmeal, '85 215
Cookies, Light Almond, '83 151
Cookies, Light Chocolate Chip, '86 46
Cookies, Meringue, '98 71
Cookies, Oatmeal-Raisin, '87 221; '93 127
Cookies, Sunshine Lemon, '86 69

Cookies, Vanilla Meringue, '01 197
Cranberries Jubilee, '90 293
Cream Puffs, Strawberry-Lemon, '87 75
Crème Anglaise, '05 239
Crêpes, Fruit-Filled Chocolate, '89 325
Crêpes Suzettes, Light, '83 71
Crêpes, Tropical Fruit, '87 77
Crisps, Dark Chocolate-Almond, '05 M30
Crust, Gingersnap, '90 296
Crust, Graham Cracker, '86 32; '88 55; '91 308
Crust, Lattice, '90 294
Custard, Baked Rice, '92 308
Custard, Baked Vanilla, '82 129
Custard, Coconut, '86 109
Custard, Light Mexican, '88 149
Custard over Fruit, Stirred, '84 83
Custard, Range-Top Amaretto, '87 77
Custard with Raspberries, Almond Crème, '88 174
De-Light-Ful Dessert, '95 220
Filling, Almond, '96 316
Filling, Chocolate, '96 316
Filling, Coffee, '96 316
Filling, Lemon, '89 312
Filling, Orange, '96 316
Flambé, Banana-Peach, '85 316
Flan, Luscious, '90 56
Flan, Pumpkin, '97 219
Frosting, Boiled, '93 318
Frosting, Coffee, '94 86
Frosting, Cream Cheese, '01 34
Frosting, Italian Meringue, '98 70
Frosting, Orange-Cream Cheese, '92 19
Fruitcake, Classic, '91 258
Fruitcake, Jeweled, '88 260
Fruit Cup, '91 202
Fruit Dessert, Caribbean, '84 314
Fruit Dessert, Flaming, '83 302
Fruit Dessert Orange, '84 314
Fruit Dessert, Rainbow, '85 108
Fruit Dessert, Spiced, '82 50
Fruit, Gingered, '83 151
Fruit, Glazed, '85 83
Fruit Medley, Fancy, '84 82
Fruit with Lemon Curd, Fresh, '88 21
Fruit with Mint-Balsamic Tea, Fresh, '95 232
Glaze, Lemon, '93 154
Glaze, Orange, '03 35
Honeydew-Berry Dessert, '83 120
Ice, Cranberry-Apple, '82 290
Ice-Cream Freeze, Two-Layered, '01 197
Ice Cream, Vanilla-Cinnamon, '00 127
Ice, Grapefruit, '91 122
Ice, Kiwi, '84 315
Ice Milk, Banana Yogurt, '89 199
Ice Milk, Fresh Strawberry, '92 94
Ice, Mixed Fruit, '88 85
Ice, Peach-Yogurt, '84 83
Ice, Pink Grapefruit, '85 304
Ice, Strawberry, '84 175; '85 108
Ice, Strawberry-Orange, '86 196
Ice, Tangy Cranberry, '87 305
Ice, Tart Cranberry-Orange, '86 317
Ice, Tropical, '99 105
Ice, Watermelon, '91 173
Kiwi Jubilee, '83 120
Lemon Angel Rolls with Raspberry Sauce, '94 294
Lemon Curd with Berries, '90 102
Lime Strips, Candied, '94 137
Lime Whip, '89 199
Mandelbrot, Rhoda's, '98 243
Melon Mélange, '84 139
Melon-Mint Julep, '86 196
Meringue Mixture, Basic, '98 70
Meringue Mushrooms, '96 317

Meringue Shells, Fruited, '87 32
Meringues, Peach Melba, '87 76
Meringues, Tropical, '98 71
Meringues with Buttermilk Custard Sauce, Peach Melba, '96 183
Mocha Sauce with Chocolate Yogurt, '92 243
Mousse, Coffee-Nut, '86 319
Mousse, Peach, '85 54
Mousse, Strawberry-Lemon, '82 128
Mousse with Raspberry Sauce, Dark Chocolate, '05 31
Orange-Mallow Cream, '94 295
Orange Molded Dessert, '83 302
Oranges and Pineapple, Glazed, '86 318
Oranges, Italian Caramelized, '05 101
Parfait, Peach, '82 166
Parfait, Pineapple, '84 83
Parfaits, Super Fast Strawberry Shortcake, '05 196
Pastry, Light, '92 95
Peach-Blueberry Dessert, '92 184
Peach Dessert, Spiced, '83 9
Peaches with Honey-Lime Whip, '85 108
Peaches with Nutty Dumplings, Spiced, '87 164
Peaches with Strawberry Sauce, '85 8
Peach Halves, Stuffed, '86 196
Pear Fans with Raspberry-Orange Sauce, Poached, '88 22
Pears Baked in Molasses-Port Sauce, '97 195
Pears in Custard, Poached, '88 20
Pears in Orange Sauce, Poached, '82 19
Pears Poached in Red Wine, '83 302
Pears, Vanilla Poached, '90 57
Pears with Berry Sauce, Wine-Poached, '86 144
Pears with Honey-Yogurt Sauce, Poached, '92 306
Pears with Meringue, Amaretto, '90 M58
Pie, Buttermilk, '92 95
Pie, Chocolate Bavarian, '89 326
Pie, Eggnog, '83 205
Pie, Fresh Apple, '84 178
Pie, Frozen Chocolate Brownie, '96 57
Pie, Fruited Cheese, '92 228
Pie, Mocha-Pecan Mud, '05 290
Pie, New-Fashioned Pumpkin, '90 296
Pie, Orange Cream, '03 35
Pineapple, Brown Sugar-Baked, '05 170
Pineapple, Meringue-Topped, '84 178
Pineapple with Raspberry Sauce, Chocolate-Drizzled, '90 57
Pineapple with Vanilla-Cinnamon Ice Cream, Grilled, '00 127
Plum Slush, '84 139
Pops, Orange-Banana, '82 129
Pops, Pineapple-Yogurt, '91 173
Praline Horns, '96 316
Prune Bavarian, '86 223
Pudding, Almost Banana, '88 174
Pudding, Apple-Raisin Bread, '88 175
Pudding, Banana, '03 24
Pudding, Chocolate-Almond, '88 24
Pudding, Chocolate-Almond Silk, '96 266
Pudding, Layered Lemon, '82 128
Pudding, Lemon Cake, '92 96
Pudding, Lemon Fluff, '85 304
Pudding, Light Plum, '86 318
Pudding, Old-Fashioned Banana, '92 94
Pudding, Old-Fashioned Bread, '88 175
Pudding, Orange Custard, '88 174
Pudding, Peachy Bread, '88 175
Pudding, Raisin-Pumpkin, '84 315
Pudding, Russian Blueberry-Raspberry, '97 128

Pudding with Crème Anglaise, Brown Sugar Bread, '05 239
Pudding with Whiskey Sauce, Bread, '90 230
Pumpkin Chiffon, '86 283; '88 260
Quesadillas, Apple, '99 248
Raspberry Fluff, '89 198
Raspberry-Pear Crisp, '89 109
Rice Cream with Mandarin Oranges, '85 317
Rice Custard, Baked, '92 308
Roulage, Frozen Chocolate, '90 56
Salsa with Cinnamon Crisps, Fruit, '01 108
Sauce, Buttermilk Custard, '96 183
Sauce, Chocolate, '90 57
Sauce, Creamy Light Coconut, '82 177
Sauce, Custard, '88 259
Sauce, Dark Chocolate, '05 31
Sauce, Golden, '88 267
Sauce, Honey-Orange, '85 108
Sauce, Honey-Yogurt, '92 307
Sauce, Mango, '83 120
Sauce, Melba, '87 77
Sauce, Pineapple-Orange, '84 14
Sauce, Raspberry, '88 267; '93 99; '94 295; '96 183; '99 259; '02 123; '05 31
Sauce, Raspberry-Orange, '88 22
Sauce, Rum-Raisin, '94 295
Sauce, Special Hard, '86 318
Sauce, Spicy Apple Dessert, '82 177
Sauce, Whiskey, '90 230
Sherbet, Blueberry, '04 283
Sherbet, Easy Pineapple, '92 199
Sherbet, Fresh Mint, '88 23
Sherbet, Instant Fruit, '85 158
Sherbet, Lemon, '91 309
Sherbet, Nectarine, '89 199
Sherbet, Peach, '90 179
Sherbet, Pineapple, '84 83; '89 199
Sherbet, Watermelon, '92 124
Shortcake, Strawberry, '92 184
Sorbet, Blackberry-Lemon, '02 85
Sorbet, Blueberry-Kirsch, '83 120
Sorbet, Fresh Orange, '92 143
Sorbet, Mango, '86 196
Sorbet, Pink Grapefruit and Tarragon, '95 163
Sorbet, Strawberry-Champagne, '95 20
Soufflé, Baked Apricot, '88 267
Soufflé, Light Chocolate, '83 278
Soufflé, Orange Dessert, '83 206
Soufflé, Raspberry-Topped, '85 317
Soufflé, Tart Lemon, '85 82
Spumoni and Berries, '91 204
Strawberries Juliet, '84 82
Strawberries Marsala, '88 171
Strawberries 'n' Cream, '90 30
Strawberry Cups, Frozen, '91 173
Strawberry Dessert, Glazed, '84 33
Strawberry Dessert, Summer, '92 143
Strawberry Puff, '82 5
Strawberry Whip, '89 198
Strawberry-Yogurt Dessert, '90 295
Sundaes, S'mores, '05 257
Tapioca Fluff, Orange, '87 31
Tart, Fancy Fruit, '82 128
Tart, Fresh Fruit, '84 178; '90 58
Tart, Green Grape, '87 77
Tart, Kiwifruit-Peach, '88 20
Tartlets, Fresh Fruit, '93 96
Tart, Pear, '92 72
Tarts, Cran-Raspberry Meringue, '92 286
Tart Shell, '87 77; '88 20
Tarts, Orange, '96 317
Tiramisù, '94 295; '02 285
Topping, Blueberry, '87 125
Topping, Cherry-Pineapple, '87 126

Topping, Chunky Piña Colada, '87 125
Topping, Raspberry, '85 317
Topping, Raspberry-Peach, '87 126
Topping, Reduced-Calorie Whipped, '85 55
Topping, Spicy Apple, '87 125
Topping, Strawberry, '86 32
Topping, Strawberry-Banana, '87 125
Torte, Apricot Sponge, '90 59
Torte, Chocolate Mint, '94 86
Torte, Triple Chocolate, '96 58
Tortoni, Apricot-Yogurt, '95 124
Trifle, All Seasons Lemon, '95 219
Trifle, Angel Food, '91 184
Trifle, Olde English, '95 331
Trifle, Raspberry, '88 259
Trifle, Tropical, '95 204
Truffles, Chocolate-Kahlúa, '92 285
Wafers, Cinnamon, '84 324
Watermelon Frost, '86 196
Yogurt, Frozen Fresh Peach, '90 139
Yogurt, Lemon-Chiffon Frozen, '85 54
Yogurt, Vanilla Frozen, '87 125
Di-Calcium Phosphate Solution, '89 138
Dressing, Creamy Lime, '04 46
Dressing, Light Cornbread, '92 324
Dressing, Savory Cornbread, '88 303

Eggs and Omelets

Benedict, Eggs, '85 49
Benedict, Light Eggs, '93 M68
Florentine, Eggs, '83 56
Garden Omelet, '99 174
Italian Omelet, '92 47
Primavera, Omelet, '87 71
Roulade with Mushroom Filling, Egg, '88 84
Scrambled Eggs, Mexican-Style, '85 50
Scrambled Eggs, Spanish, '84 60
Substitute, Homemade Egg, '92 47
Vegetable Omelet, Cheddar-, '83 205
Vegetable Omelet, Cheesy, '85 49
Enchiladas, Three-Bean, '91 133
Fettuccine and Spinach, '88 90
Fettuccine Primavera, '89 238
Filling, Chicken Salad, '87 106
Filling, Mushroom, '88 84
Filling, Shrimp Salad, '87 106
Fruit Kebabs, Winter, '89 34
Fruit Medley, Chilled, '84 60
Fruit, Minted Marinated, '92 138
Fruit Nuggets, Dried, '86 326
Fruit-on-a-Pick, '90 179
Fruit, Warm Spiced, '86 39
Fruit with Lemon-Yogurt Dressing, Fresh, '93 17
Glaze, Cranberry-Honey, '89 273
Glaze, Teriyaki, '94 82
Gnocchi with Olive Oil, Tomato, and Parmesan, '04 47
Granola, Mixed Fruit, '01 290
Grapefruit, Broiled, '85 7
Grits, Baked Cheese, '01 289
Grits, Cheese, '90 102
Grits, Garlic-and-Herb Cheese, '95 122
Guacamole, Mock, '93 36
Ham-and-Cheese Lettuce Rolls, '89 217
Jam, Berry Refrigerator, '89 139
Jam, Blackberry, '89 138
Jam, Blueberry Refrigerator, '89 139
Jam, Plum Refrigerator, '89 139
Jam, Strawberry, '89 138
Jelly, Crabapple, '89 139
Jelly, Grape, '89 140
Kielbasa, '92 242
Lentils, Bean Pot, '01 35
Lentils, Tangy Marinated, '00 94
Linguine with Garlic and Lemon, '88 91

Linguine with Green Beans and Walnut Sauce, '04 128
Linguine with Red Pepper Sauce, '93 127

Low Sodium

Applesauce, Spicy, '82 296
Asparagus with Basil Sauce, '86 33
Beef and Rice, Spicy, '83 231
Beef Burgundy, '83 281
Beef Goulash, '83 231
Beef Roast, French-Style, '89 32
Biscuits, Flaky, '84 228
Bread, Bran-Applesauce, '84 229
Bread, Salt-Free Raisin Batter, '86 33
Breadsticks, Whole Wheat, '84 228
Brussels Sprouts, Calico Citrus, '85 303
Butter, Herbed Unsalted, '82 67
Carrots Madeira, '83 281
Catsup, Spicy Tomato, '83 182
Cereal Snack, Toasted, '85 215
Chicken à l'Orange, '84 277
Chicken-and-Vegetables, Stir-Fry, '86 68
Chicken, Citrus-Herb Baked, '85 303
Chicken, Creole, '89 33
Chicken Dinner, Healthful, '83 232
Chicken, Herb-Baked, '82 229
Chicken in Lemon and Wine, '83 281
Chicken Piccata, '83 35
Chicken-Tomato Bake, '83 35
Chicken with Wine-Soaked Vegetables, Baked, '84 277
Chili Surprise, '82 229
Cookies, Sunshine Lemon, '86 69
Cornish Hens in Vermouth, '86 33
Cornish Hens, Roasted Rock, '82 66
Dressing, Basil, '88 24
Dressing, Lemon-Herb Salad, '82 67
Dressing, Orange-Yogurt, '85 304
Fish, Curried Baked, '87 5
Flank Steak, Marinated, '83 35
Flounder Rolls, Vegetable-Stuffed, '87 6
Flounder, Sesame, '89 33
Fruit Delight, Hot, '83 281
Fruit Delight, Spiced, '82 229
Fruit, Unsweetened Mixed, '83 182
Green Beans, Minted, '84 104
Ice, Pink Grapefruit, '85 304
Jam, Banana, '82 296
Jam, Freezer Peach, '83 182
Lamb Chops, Dijon, '84 277
Lamb Chops, Orange, '83 35
Linguine with Seafood Sauce, '83 232
Meat Loaf, Corny, '86 68
Meat Loaf, Parsleyed, '83 35
Mocha-Cocoa Mix, Hot, '82 296
Mousse, Orange, '86 67
Muffins, Honey-Oatmeal, '84 229
Muffins, Spiced Bran, '84 229
Mustard, Lower Sodium Horseradish, '86 325
Nectarines in Apple Juice, '83 183
Onions, Glazed, '84 104
Pastry Shell, Sesame, '82 67
Peppers, Corn Stuffed, '84 104
Pie, Nutty Pumpkin, '82 67
Pork, Roast Loin of, '84 276
Pork Tenderloin with Brown Sauce, Grilled, '89 32
Potato Bake, Chive-, '82 229
Potatoes, Yogurt-Stuffed, '88 24
Pretzels with Lower Sodium Horseradish Mustard, Herb, '86 325
Pudding, Chocolate-Almond, '88 24
Pudding, Lemon Fluff, '85 304
Ratatouille, '84 105
Rice and Shrimp, Curried, '83 231
Rice, Calico Brown, '86 33
Rolls, Low-Sodium Refrigerator, '82 67
Rolls, Low-Sodium Yeast, '84 228

Salad, Asparagus-and-New Potato, '86 69
Salad, Citrus Green, '85 304
Salad, Dilled Cucumber, '82 229
Salad Mold, Golden Citrus, '85 303
Salad, Mushroom-and-Pepper, '86 68
Salad, Sesame-Citrus Green, '86 33
Salmon, Poached, '83 35
Salmon Steaks, Marinated, '87 6
Sauce, Apple-Horseradish, '82 229
Sauce, Brown, '89 32
Sauce, Green Herb, '83 36
Sauce, Seafood, '83 36
Scallops, Sherried, '83 281
Scampi, Orange, '85 303
Scamp, Tangy Broiled, '87 5
Seasoning Blend, '82 296
Shake, Pineapple-Banana, '85 215
Shrimp Kebabs, Marinated, '84 276
Shrimp, Special Boiled, '83 36
Snapper, Caribbean, '87 5
Snapper, Orangy, '88 23
Soup, Chunky Chicken-Noodle, '88 12
Soup, Chunky Mushroom, '88 12
Soup, Cream of Cauliflower, '88 12
Soup, Spicy Vegetable-Beef, '88 11
Squash Sauté, '82 67
Squash, Vegetable-Stuffed, '84 104
Stew, Cajun-Style Catfish, '88 12
Stew, White Wine, '82 228
Stuffing, Low-Sodium, '82 66
Swordfish, Foil-Baked, '87 5
Tomatoes, Stewed, '83 182
Tomato Puree, Seasoned, '83 182
Tropical Snow, '86 34
Veal, Savory, '83 281
Veal Spaghetti, '84 276
Vegetable Stir-Fry, '84 104
Waffles, Whole Wheat, '84 228
Zucchini, Herbed, '84 104
Zucchini with Baby Carrots, '88 24
Macaroni and Cheese, Baked, '82 199
Macaroni with Pesto, Whole Wheat, '89 238

Main Dishes

Asparagus Roulade, '86 102
Beans and Rice, Red, '90 27
Beans and Rice, Smoky Kidney, '03 290
Beans with Coconut Milk, Spicy, '03 175
Beef, American Steakhouse, '93 15
Beef-and-Barley Rolls, Wine-Sauced, '87 269
Beef and Cauliflower over Rice, '93 94
Beef-and-Rice Dinner, Mexican, '88 199
Beef and Vegetables, Company, '88 234
Beef-and-Vegetable Stir-Fry, '87 22; '99 204
Beef, Bean, and Cornbread Casserole, '99 215
Beef Burgundy, '88 25
Beef Chimichangas, Oven-Fried, '92 124
Beef, Chinese-Style, '87 50
Beef Fajitas, '88 233
Beef Fillets with Black Bean Sauce, Spicy, '97 184
Beef Fillets with Green Peppercorn Sauce, '02 285
Beef Hash, '95 24
Beef Kebabs, Chile-, '94 251
Beef Kebabs, Spirited, '87 142
Beef Kebabs with Rice, Marinated, '84 32
Beef, Marinated Sauerbraten, '93 16
Beef Medallions, Italian, '87 305
Beef Patties, Deviled-, '87 22
Beef Stir-Fry, Chinese, '83 151
Beef Stroganoff, '91 134
Beef Stroganoff, Light, '86 36
Beef Tenderloin Bundles, Peppered, '89 272
Beef Tenderloin for Two, '90 295
Beef Tenderloin Steaks with Peperonata, '97 291
Beef with Asparagus, '90 100

Beef with Ginger, '03 64
Black Beans and Rice, '91 82
Black Beans and Yellow Rice, Easy, '92 308
Burgers, Balsamic-Blue Cheese Portobello, '05 53
Burgers, Barbecued, '89 164
Burgers, Beefy Vegetable, '98 143
Burgers, Black Bean, '98 144
Burgers, Favorite, '89 165
Burgers, Lentil, '95 123
Burgers, Mushroom, '89 164; '97 101
Burgers, Pizza, '89 165
Burgers, Salmon, '98 144
Burgers, Seasoned, '85 158
Burgers, Triple-Layer, '89 165
Burgers, Vegetable, '89 164
Burgers, Walnut, '89 163
Burgers with Caramelized Onions, Beef, '98 143
Burgers with Sprouts, '89 164
Burgers with Tahini Sauce, Gyro, '03 183
Burritos, Cheesy Beef, '85 193
Burritos, Tony's Veggie, '96 289
Burritos, Vegetable, '90 134; '92 138
Cabbage Rolls, Stuffed, '88 18
Cannelloni, '92 17
Carne Guisada, '94 219
Casserole, Bean-and-Cornbread, '92 243
Casserole, Breakfast, '91 285
Casserole, Chicken, Orzo, and Spinach, '02 124
Casserole, Chiles Rellenos, '92 18
Casserole, Confetti Omelet, '05 169
Casserole, Crab-and-Mushroom, '89 96
Casserole, Creamy Chicken-and-Rice, '02 309
Casserole, Freezer Eggplant-Sausage-Pasta, '95 197
Casserole, Low-Fat Spaghetti, '99 215
Casserole, Southwestern, '99 216
Casserole, Turkey-and-Shrimp Florentine, '92 122
Catfish, Baked, '94 67
Catfish, Crispy Oven-Fried, '05 256
Catfish, Lime-Orange, '02 22
Catfish, Oven-Fried, '95 106; '99 174
Catfish, Parmesan, '92 309
Catfish, Southern Oven-Fried, '87 163
Catfish with Creole Sauce, Breaded, '90 28
Catfish with Lemon Cream, Spicy "Fried," '03 212
Chicken à la King, '94 41
Chicken, Almond, '01 26
Chicken and Dumplings, '03 25
Chicken and Dumplings, Old-Fashioned, '93 302
Chicken and Leeks in Parchment, '97 290
Chicken and Rice, Spicy, '88 200
Chicken and Rice, Sweet-and-Sour, '03 97
Chicken and Spinach Noodles, '82 19
Chicken and Vegetables, Ginger-Poached, '98 229
Chicken and Vegetables, Stir-Fry, '86 249
Chicken and Vegetables, Walnut, '85 194
Chicken and Vegetables with Ginger-Soy Sauce, '91 32
Chicken-Apple Sauté, '97 48
Chicken, Aromatic Curry-and-Spice, '05 238
Chicken, Asparagus, and Mushrooms with Penne Pasta, '98 212
Chicken, Baked Honey, '99 110
Chicken Bake, Individual, '90 279
Chicken Bowl, Wild Rice-and-, '05 127
Chicken Breast in Wine, Poached, '91 184
Chicken Breasts, Hawaiian Stuffed, '99 64
Chicken Breasts, Lime-Roasted, '97 100
Chicken Breasts Sardou, Stuffed, '87 269
Chicken Breasts, Wine-Baked, '83 177
Chicken Breasts with Fruited Rice Pilaf, '92 307
Chicken Breasts with Orange-Ginger Sauce, '97 47
Chicken, Buttermilk Oven-Fried, '03 213
Chicken Cacciatore, '86 42

Chicken Cakes with Creole Sauce, '02 284
Chicken Chili Bake, '93 302
Chicken, Chutney, '86 249
Chicken Cordon Bleu, '86 37; '93 126
Chicken, Creamed, '82 49
Chicken, Creamy Tomato-Stuffed, '04 16
Chicken Croquettes and Mushroom Sauce, '91 220
Chicken, Crunchy Oven-Fried, '87 163
Chicken, Curried, '86 43
Chicken Curry, Stir-Fried, '87 51
Chicken Cutlets with Lemon, '85 8
Chicken, Dante's, '88 25
Chicken Dinner, Skillet, '86 249
Chicken Drumsticks, Breaded, '99 110
Chicken Enchiladas, '90 121
Chicken Fingers, Herb-Baked, '86 249
Chicken Fingers, No-Fry-Pan, '91 120
Chicken Fingers with Honey-Horseradish Dip,
    '02 308
Chicken-Fried Wild Rice, '91 132
Chicken Gumbo, '90 26
Chicken, Honey-Pecan, '03 147
Chicken in a Bag, '87 23
Chicken in Foil, '91 134
Chicken in Orange Sauce, '83 8
Chicken in Phyllo, Cheesy, '02 308
Chicken Kebabs, Sesame, '82 165
Chicken Kiev, Oven-Baked, '86 37
Chicken la France, '86 248
Chicken Lasagna, '88 90
Chicken-Leek Terrine, Cold, '92 145
Chicken, Lemon-Frosted, '88 170
Chicken, Lemon-Mustard, '99 109
Chicken, Lemon-Roasted, '95 24
Chicken Marengo, '92 70
Chicken Marsala, '89 237
Chicken, Orange, '83 278
Chicken, Oven-Fried, '93 90
Chicken Paprika, Dilled, '86 41
Chicken Pasta with Artichokes and Capers,
    '04 129
Chicken, Pineapple, '83 M194
Chicken Pot Pie, '94 21
Chicken-Rice Casserole, '99 215
Chicken Rolls, Spinach-Stuffed, '86 248
Chicken, Salsa Rice and, '99 109
Chicken, Savory Roasted, '98 21
Chicken, Sicilian, '97 142
Chicken, Southern Oven-Fried, '86 37
Chicken Spaghetti, '87 221
Chicken Stir-Fry, Apple-Sesame-, '92 226
Chicken Stir-Fry, Chinese, '90 100
Chicken Strips and Vegetables, Marinated, '90 110
Chicken, Sweet-and-Sour, '91 202
Chicken, Tea-Thyme Grilled, '05 M52
Chicken Thighs, Sweet Glazed, '04 202
Chicken Twice-Baked Potatoes, Buffalo, '04 184
Chicken Tostadas, '95 122
Chicken-Vegetable Stir-Fry, '83 151; '84 13
Chicken, Whole Poached, '98 229
Chicken Wings, Maple-Glazed, '99 110
Chicken with Artichoke Hearts, '88 54
Chicken with Artichokes, Sherried, '87 143
Chicken with Black Bean Puree, Spicy, '97 48
Chicken with Black Beans and Oranges, '00 94
Chicken with Broccoli, Spicy Ginger-and-Orange,
    '02 309
Chicken with Grilled Pineapple, Lime, '04 88
Chicken with Mole Sauce, '93 34
Chicken with Mushroom Sauce, '99 22

Chicken with Orange, Lime, and Ginger Sauce,
    '92 123
Chicken with Pineapple, Oriental, '86 42
Chicken with Pineapple Salsa, Sesame-Crusted,
    '96 226
Chicken with Prunes, Saffron, '97 264
Chicken with Roasted Potato Thins, Apricot, '02 23
Chicken with Salsa, Baked Chile, '88 147
Chicken with Spinach Fettuccine, Easy, '88 89
Chicken with Tabbouleh Salad, Grilled, '91 70
Chicken with Tomato-Basil Pasta, Basil-Stuffed,
    '94 M204
Chicken with Vegetables, Stir-Fry, '96 128
Chicken with Wild Rice, Orange-Glazed Roasted,
    '02 85
Chiles Rellenos, Light, '93 156
Chiles Rellenos with Tomatillo Sauce, Roasted,
    '94 203
Chile Verde, Light, '88 148
Chili, '93 89
Chili, Firestarter, '93 34
Chili, Hot Venison, '91 283
Chili, South-of-the-Border, '91 283
Chili, Southwestern, '91 284
Chili, Vegetarian, '91 284
Chili, White, '91 284
Cornbread-Tamale Pie, '92 123
Cornish Hens, Herbed, '82 271
Cornish Hens, Mesquite-Smoked, '92 144
Cornish Hens, Orange-Glazed Grilled, '86 250
Cornish Hens with Vegetables, Tarragon Roasted,
    '94 79
Crab-and-Shrimp Étouffée, '89 96
Crab Burgers, '00 58
Crab Cakes, '91 122
Crabmeat au Gratin, '86 154
Cracked Wheat, "Fried," '89 31
Crawfish Étouffée, '86 156
Crawfish Fettuccine, '96 98
Crêpes, Cannelloni, '86 143
Crêpes, Chicken-Vegetable, '83 70
Eggplant Parmesan, '92 18
Eggplant Parmesan with Feta, '03 174
Enchiladas, Spicy Bean, '88 18
Fajita Fettuccine, '94 84
Fajita in a Pita, '90 177
Fajitas, Java, '96 227
Fajitas, Turkey, '01 108
Fettuccine and Shrimp with Dried Tomato Pesto,
    '94 249
Fettuccine, Ham-and-Asparagus, '94 84
Fettuccine Primavera, '94 85
Fettuccine, Shrimp, '94 84
Filet Mignon with Mushroom Sauce, '94 250
Fillets, Apple-Carrot Stuffed, '88 M192
Fillets Tomatillo, '94 135
Fish and Vegetables, Steamed, '91 32
Fish, Caribbean Banana, '95 202
Fish Dinner, Skillet, '88 199
Fish Fillets, Breaded Herbed, '91 121
Fish Florentine, '86 35
Fish Florentine in Parchment, '87 22
Fish with Greek Sauce, Poached, '91 M183
Flank Steak, Grilled, '03 146
Flank Steak, Grilled Marinated, '97 182
Flank Steak Sukiyaki, '88 233
Flank Steak with Black Bean-and-Corn Salsa,
    Grilled, '94 80
Flank Steak with Molasses Barbecue Glaze, Grilled,
    '00 59
Flank Steak with Noodles, Stuffed, '90 101
Flank Steak with Sweet Peppers, Grilled, '90 138
Flounder, Creole-Style, '85 180
Flounder Rolls with Citrus Sauce, Stuffed, '85 180

Frijoles Rancheros, '88 148
Frittata, Vegetable, '92 48
Game Hens with Chutney-Mustard Glaze, '93 66
Goulash, Hungarian, '92 227
Grits-and-Ham Pie, Crustless, '86 103
Grouper, Grilled Marinated, '90 166
Grouper, Hot Spicy, '94 78
Haddock Fillets with Zucchini Stuffing, '88 M191
Halibut Steaks Italiano, '88 M191
Halibut with Champagne Sauce, Baked, '90 29
Halibut with Swiss Sauce, '83 M195
Hamburger Pie, '84 13
Ham, Pineapple-Glazed, '01 288
Ham-Potato-Pineapple Bake, '93 302
Ham with Cranberry-Honey Glaze, Baked, '89 273
Hopping John with Grilled Pork Medaillons, '93 229
Jambalaya, '90 26
Jambalaya, Black-Eyed Pea, '92 70
Jambalaya, Chicken-and-Sausage, '88 200
Jambalaya, Red Rice, '91 18
Kebabs, Hawaiian, '85 157
Lamb Chops, Broiled, '85 22
Lamb Chops, Joan's Rosemary, '97 42
Lamb Chops, Peppercorn-Crusted, '92 142
Lamb Chops, Smart and Saucy Rosemary-Cherry,
    '02 193
Lamb Chops with Herbs, '90 164
Lamb Chops with Pineapple-Mint Salsa, Grilled,
    '05 52
Lamb Chops with Rosemary Sauce and Wild Rice-
    Fennel Pilaf, Grilled, '97 127
Lamb Curry, Creamy, '04 202
Lamb with Five Spices, Stewed, '92 72
Lasagna, Cheesy Spinach, '83 204; '01 196
Lasagna, Creamy Ham-and-Chicken, '95 88
Lasagna in a Bun, '90 176
Lasagna, Lean, '86 37
Lasagna, Light, '95 212
Lasagna, Spinach-Bean, '92 96
Lasagna, Vegetable, '84 201; '99 97
Lasagna with Cream Sauce, Polenta, '03 237
Lasagna, Won Ton Spinach, '04 129
Lasagna, Zucchini, '85 194
Lentil-and-Rice Supper, '84 202
Lentils-and-Rice Casserole, '93 301
Linguine with Clam Sauce, '88 90
Liver, Creole, '86 108
Liver in Creole Sauce, '87 33
Lobster Tails with Spiced Orange Sauce, '86 155
London Broil, Marinated, '87 32
Mackerel, Rosemary-Garlic, '92 200
Manicotti, Creamy Chipotle, '03 96
Manicotti, Spinach, '82 199
Meat and Potatoes, Italian-Style, '03 97
Meatballs and Vegetables with Horseradish Dressing,
    '91 32
Meatballs, Red Sauce and, '04 17
Meat Loaf, '89 109
Meat Loaf, Curried, '86 43
Meat Loaf, Oriental, '83 M194
Meat Loaf, Parsley, '87 22
Meat Loaf, Summer, '01 162
Meat Loaves, Individual, '00 214
Migas, '98 312
Oatmeal, Dried Cherry-and-Pecan, '05 126
Orange Roughy-and-Vegetable Stir-Fry, '91 50
Orange Roughy, Pesto-Crusted, '96 156
Orange Roughy, Vegetable-Topped, '93 67
Orange Roughy with Herbs, Steamed, '95 189
Orange Roughy with Spinach Pesto, '88 M192
Pasta, Creamy Turkey-Basil, '89 216
Pasta, Mamma Mia, '95 25
Pasta Primavera, Almost, '86 38
Pasta Salad, Main-Dish, '82 199

Pasta, Vegetable Stir-Fry, '96 29
Pasta Verde, '84 201
Pasta with Beans and Greens, '02 202
Pasta with Fennel, '98 46
Pasta with Peanut Sauce, '95 252
Pastichio, '85 194
Penne, Fresh Vegetable, '05 101
Peppers Stuffed with Shrimp-and-Orzo Salad, '91 203
Perch, Parmesan-Crusted, '93 91
Picadillo, Lettuce-Wrapped, '03 193
Pie, Italian Meat, '89 109
Pizza, Breakfast, '90 178
Pizza, Chicken-and-Purple Onion, '97 47
Pizza, Fresh Mozzarella and Basil, '04 58
Pizza, Garden, '89 108
Pizza, Portobello, '03 175
Pizza, Quick 3-Cheese, '00 94
Pizzas, Veggie, '99 97
Pizzas, Veggie Sausage, '00 294
Pizza, Turkey-Vegetable, '90 139
Pizza, Vegetable, '94 218
Pizza, Veggie, '94 78
Pizza, Whole Wheat, '84 33
Polenta with Black Bean Salsa, Grilled, '93 155
Pollock with Summer Squash Relish, '92 200
Pork-and-Noodles Skillet Dinner, '88 199
Pork, Cajun Pecan, '01 27
Pork, Chinese Roast, '91 308
Pork Chop Dinner, '88 25
Pork Chops, An Apple-a-Day, '01 35
Pork Chops, Apricot-Sauced, '85 22
Pork Chops, Creole-Style, '91 49
Pork Chops, Fruit-Topped, '94 41
Pork Chops, Honey-Lime, '91 33
Pork Chops in Gravy, '91 137
Pork Chops with Cream Gravy, Fried, '03 24
Pork Chops with Tangy Barbecue Sauce, '99 104
Pork Chops with Warm Pineapple Salsa, '02 144
Pork Chops with White Bean Puree, '96 226
Pork Chow Mein, '90 101
Pork, Cranberry, '90 293
Pork Loin, Braised Tuscan, '04 202
Pork Loin Roast, Barbecued, '93 34
Pork Medaillons, Grilled, '93 229
Pork Medaillons with Port Wine and Dried Cranberry Sauce, '95 330
Pork, Oven-Roasted Vegetables and, '99 259
Pork Roast, Barbecued, '03 147
Pork Roast, Orange-Glazed, '04 M236
Pork Roast, Oven-Barbecued, '91 50
Pork Roast, Stuffed Crown, '89 272
Pork Saté, '05 53
Pork, Stir-Fried, '87 51
Pork, Sweet-and-Sour, '85 34, 194
Pork Tacos with Pineapple Salsa, '03 128
Pork Tenderloin, Apple-Mushroom, '95 53
Pork Tenderloin, Honey-Mustard, '95 52
Pork Tenderloin, Marinated, '84 175
Pork Tenderloin, Molasses-Grilled, '96 265
Pork Tenderloin, Sesame, '95 53
Pork Tenderloins, Fruit-Stuffed, '87 270
Pork Tenderloin, Spinach-and-Bacon Stuffed, '94 81
Pork Tenderloin with Apples, Celery, and Potatoes, Grilled, '95 161
Pork Tenderloin with Fruit Stuffing and Shiitake Sauce, '97 218
Pork Tenderloin with Lime and Chipotle, Sweet, '04 184
Pork Tenderloin with Molasses Sauce, Grilled, '97 193
Pork Tenderloin with Orange Marmalade, '91 49
Pork Tenderloin with Parmesan-Pepper Toasts, Herbed, '98 242

Pork Tenderloin with Yogurt and Lime, Grilled, '04 216
Pork with Garlic, Sweet, '04 17
Quesadillas, Breakfast Sausage, '04 183
Potatoes, Breakfast-Stuffed, '00 179
Pot Roast, Marinated, '85 21
Quail with Mushroom Gravy, Baked, '89 273
Quesadillas, Chicken-and-Black Bean, '96 288
Quesadillas, Quick, '89 87
Quesadillas, Shrimp-and-Roasted Pepper, '00 215
Quiche, Crustless Veggie Sausage, '03 175
Quiche, Eggless, '87 220
Quiche, Fiesta, '92 47
Quiches, Individual Spinach, '86 38
Quiche, Spinach, '85 49; '91 204
Quiche, Swiss-Zucchini, '82 49
Ravioli, Mediterranean, '93 301
Red Beans and Couscous, '99 22
Red Snapper, Blackened, '90 27
Red Snapper Rolls, Cucumber-Stuffed, '83 176
Red Snapper Veracruz, '88 149; '92 142
Rice-and-Lentil Pilaf, '88 17
Rice, Dirty, '03 147
Risotto with Vegetables, '98 193
Roast Beef, Deli-Style, '93 15
Roast, Roasted Lime-Cilantro Eye of Round, '04 88
Salmon Burgers, '95 24
Salmon Fillets, Cracked Pepper, '00 140
Salmon Fillets with Red Wine Garlic Sauce, '94 250
Salmon in Parchment, '95 311
Salmon Loaf with Cucumber-Dill Sauce, '86 5
Salmon-Pesto Vermicelli, '92 200
Salmon Steaks with Tarragon Sauce, Grilled, '97 42
Salmon with Ginger Vinaigrette, Sesame-Crusted, '95 162
Salmon with Horseradish Sauce, Poached, '91 183
Salmon with Lemon and Olive Oil, Broiled, '04 46
Salmon with Stir-Fried Vegetables, Glazed, '02 69
Salmon with Yellow Pepper Sauce, Poached, '98 230
Sausage, Dieters' Spicy, '85 49
Sausage Patties, Breakfast Turkey, '05 169
Scallop Kebabs, Grilled, '83 101
Scallops, Grilled Sweet-and-Sour, '01 92
Scallops in Vegetable Nests, '91 70
Scallops with Cilantro-Lime Vinaigrette, Grilled Orange, '94 77
Scallops with Orange-Ginger Sauce, Sesame-Crusted, '97 125
Scallops with Tomato-Mango Salsa, Seared, '95 122
Scramble, Veggie, '01 288
Shells, Spinach-Stuffed, '99 64
Shrimp and Pasta, Sautéed, '96 288
Shrimp-and-Spinach Pasta, Creamy, '05 239
Shrimp-and-Vegetable Medley Stir-Fry, '99 205
Shrimp, Barbecued, '90 28
Shrimp, Beer-Broiled, '87 142
Shrimp Cancun en Papillote, '91 136
Shrimp Enchiladas in Tomatillo Sauce, '95 310
Shrimp Étouffée, '90 229
Shrimp Fettuccine, '94 84
Shrimp, Grilled Sweet-and-Sour, '97 100
Shrimp Rémoulade, '03 146
Shrimp Risotto, '00 95; '02 124
Shrimp Skillet, Quick, '87 50
Shrimp, Stir-Fry, '96 129
Shrimp, Sweet-and-Sour, '83 278
Shrimp with Citrus Salsa, Grilled, '97 141
Shrimp with Cranberry-Citrus Salsa, Sautéed, '97 290
Shrimp with Onion and Red Pepper, Sweet-and-Sour, '02 84
Shrimp with Orange Dipping Sauce, Coconut-Pecan, '03 212
Shrimp with Orzo, Fire-Roasted, '99 42

Shrimp with Pasta, Asian, '04 128
Shrimp with Peanut Sauce, '93 303
Shrimp with Roasted Red Pepper Cream, '03 97
Shrimp with Yogurt-Cucumber Sauce, '04 216
Sirloin in Vodka Sauce, '03 96
Sirloin, Mustard Marinated, '94 41
Sirloin Steaks with Thyme Pesto, '97 182
Sirloin with Zesty Corn Salsa, Cilantro-Garlic, '02 193
Snapper à l'Orange, Baked, '85 181
Snapper, Honey-Curried, '85 181
Snapper, Poached, '83 101
Snapper with Creamy Dill Sauce, Peppered, '94 42
Snow Peas and Red Pepper, Sesame, '84 175
Sole Divan, '87 21
Sole Véronique, '85 181
Spaghetti and Meatballs, White, '03 34
Spaghetti, Meaty, '82 19
Spaghetti with Mint-and-Garlic Tomato Sauce, '05 100
Spinach-and-Cheese Calzones, '95 310
Steak au Poivre, '88 232
Steak Diane, '92 306
Steak, Fast-and-Easy Stir-Fried, '87 50
Steak in Red Wine Sauce, Skillet, '85 21
Steak, Italian-Stuffed, '88 232
Steak Kebabs, '82 4; '93 95
Steak lo Mein, '90 100
Steak, Marinated, '88 233
Steak, Mexican Marinated, '88 148
Steak, Mock Country-Fried, '87 163
Steak, Pepper-Beef, '85 21
Stir-Fry, Curried Beef, '01 162
Stroganoff, Creamy Beef, '02 124
Swordfish, Mediterranean, '02 237
Swordfish-Shiitake Skewers, '97 168
Swordfish Stir-Fry, '96 128
Swordfish with Avocado-Lime Sauce, Grilled, '97 127
Swordfish with Caper Sauce, Grilled, '95 230
Tacoritos, '90 133
Tacos, Jerk Steak, '01 170
Tacos, Loaded Veggie, '00 294
Tacos, Skillet Veggie, '01 170
Tacos with Spicy Cream Sauce, Shrimp, '01 170
Tagine, Vegetable, '96 289
Tenderloins, Honey-Grilled, '92 199; '00 126
Tenderloin, Spinach-Stuffed, '89 311
Tofu, Stroganoff, '84 202
Tomato with Tuna Pasta, Stuffed, '88 54
Trout, Baked, '95 106
Trout Fillets with Capers, '95 252
Trout, Grilled, '95 106
Trout, Poached, '95 106
Tuna Croquettes with Parsley Sauce, '86 108
Tuna Steaks on Mixed Greens with Lemon-Basil Vinaigrette, Seared, '94 205
Tuna with Poblano Salsa, Grilled, '91 135
Tuna with Rosemary, Broiled, '93 127
Tuna with Tangy Mustard Sauce, '92 201
Turkey-Asparagus Pilaf, '88 200
Turkey Breast and Gravy, Roast, '88 303
Turkey Breast, Molasses-Coffee, '05 M289
Turkey Breast, Stuffed, '87 270
Turkey Breast with Cranberry Salsa, Grilled, '95 252
Turkey Breast with Special Gravy, Roast, '86 282
Turkey Burgers, '98 22
Turkey, Citrus-and-Herb, '01 254
Turkey Cutlets, Oven-Fried, '91 121
Turkey Cutlets with Pepper Salsa, Spicy, '88 26
Turkey Lasagna, '91 130
Turkey, Lazy Day, '93 93
Turkey Piccata, '91 137

(continued)

Turkey Strips with Roasted Peppers and Beans,
    Herbed, '04 282
Turkey Tenderloins with Lingonberry Sauce, '97 289
Turkey Tenderloin with Raspberry-Chipotle Sauce,
    Jerk, '05 M194
Veal and Carrots, Company, '85 22
Veal, Lemon, '93 35
Veal Marsala, '91 310
Veal Picante, '87 31
Veal Piccata with Capers, '87 142
Veal Scallopini, '83 8
Vegetables and Chicken, Glazed Stir-Fry, '99 205
Vegetarian Supper, '86 222
Veggie-and-Pork Stir-Fry, Mixed, '99 206
Vermicelli and Sprouts with Red Clam Sauce,
    '86 143
Vermicelli, Scallop-Vegetable, '87 143
Zucchini Frittata, '86 103
Zucchini with Pasta, Stuffed, '97 101
Marinade, Soy-and-Ginger, '96 129
Mayonnaise, Adobo, '02 203
Mayonnaise, Basil, '98 144
Mayonnaise, Dried Tomato, '98 144
Mayonnaise, Lemon, '98 144
Mayonnaise, Mediterranean, '98 144
Mayonnaise, Onion, '98 144
Mayonnaise, Roasted Red Pepper, '98 144
Meatballs, '89 237
Meatballs, Turkey, '89 237
Meat Mixture, Basic, '92 241
Muesli, Bran-and-Fruit, '91 134
Navy Beans, Curried, '00 201
Oatmeal, Applesauce, '89 108
Oatmeal, Fruited, '88 19
Olive Oil, Basil-Infused, '95 231
Olive Oil, Lemon-Infused, '95 231
Pancakes, Honey, '91 139
Pancakes, Oatmeal, '89 107
Pancakes, Shredded Wheat, '84 59
Pancakes, Whole Wheat-Oat, '93 16
Pasta, Asian Pesto, '95 189
Pasta-Basil Toss, '87 33
Pasta, Caesar Salad, '95 230
Pasta, Garden, '82 199
Pasta, Grilled Vegetable, '97 142
Pasta Provençale, '88 90
Pasta, Tomato-Basil, '94 204
Peaches, Spicy Baked, '86 39
Pear Breakfast Treat, '87 72
Pears, Champagne-Poached, '01 289
Pears, Wine-Poached, '98 230
Pickles, Lime, '96 206
Pico de Gallo, '96 227; '04 89
Pizza Crust, Special, '90 139
Pizza Crusts, Skillet, '94 218
Pizza on a Bagel, '93 M94
Pizza, Plum-and-Sweet Onion, '98 193
Polenta, Grilled, '00 126
Potatoes, Breakfast-Stuffed, '00 179
Preserves, Fig, '89 140
Preserves, Peach, '89 140
Relish, Cranberry, '86 283; '91 257
Relish, Green Tomato, '98 124
Relish, Holiday Cranberry, '88 304
Relish, Papaya-Basil, '94 82
Relish, Sweet Onion, '96 206
Relish, White Bean, '93 229

Rice

Apple-Cinnamon Rice, '86 249
Black-Eyed Peas, Rice with, '93 66
Blended Rice, '96 68
Brown Rice, Calico, '86 33
Casserole, Colorful Rice, '82 199
Coconut Rice, '00 201
Herb Rice, '91 257
Lime-Flavored Rice, '84 175
Mexican Rice, Spicy, '88 149
Mix, Fruited Curry-Rice, '86 326
Onion Rice, Seasoned, '82 166
Orange Rice, '82 200
Peppered Rice, '82 4
Pilaf, Browned Rice, '87 305
Pilaf, Brown Rice, '90 136; '91 82
Pilaf, Onion Rice, '04 236
Pilaf, Rice-and-Lentil, '88 17
Risotto, Roasted Garlic-and-Cheese, '04 283
Shell, Rice-Cheese, '82 49
Southwestern Rice, '90 121
Spanish Rice with Tofu, '88 26
Tex-Mex Rice with Corn, '03 129
Tomatoes and Basil, Rice with, '95 232
White Rice, Fluffy, '03 65
Wild Rice and Mushrooms, '83 278
Wild Rice Bulgur, '91 83
Wild Rice, Veggie, '00 141
Yellow Rice, '91 136

Salad Dressings

Avocado Sauce, Chunky, '03 128
Balsamic Dressing, '99 259
Blue Cheese Dressing, '82 166
Blue Cheese Dressing, Creamy, '91 307
Blue Cheese Vinaigrette, '90 280
Caper Vinaigrette, '91 310
Cilantro-Lime Vinaigrette, '94 77
Cilantro Vinaigrette, '97 126
Coconut Dressing, '87 251
Creamy Dressing, '93 318
Creole Dressing, '02 69
Cucumber-Mint Dressing, '87 153
Cucumber Salad Dressing, Creamy, '82 79
Curry Dressing, '82 78
Dijon Vinaigrette, '03 237
Dressing, '01 58
French Dressing, Miracle, '82 79
Fruit, Salad Dressing for, '86 40
Gorgonzola Dressing, Creamy, '03 34
Greek Salad Dressing, '03 290
Herb-Mustard Vinaigrette, '02 84
Herb Salad Dressing, '86 40
Honey-Mustard Dressing, '90 111
Horseradish Dressing, '87 152; '91 32
Lemon-Basil Vinaigrette, '94 205
Lemon-Caper Dressing, '96 69
Lemon-Molasses Dressing, '97 195
Lemon-Yogurt Dressing, '93 17
Lemon-Yogurt Slaw or Salad Dressing, '88 54
Lime Dressing, '83 120
Lime-Peanut Dressing, '01 26
Miso-Ginger Dressing, Creamy, '02 144
Orange-Poppy Seed Dressing, '87 187
Oregano-Feta Dressing, '01 57
Papaya Seed Dressing, '95 204
Pineapple-Poppy Seed Dressing, '85 55
Poppy Seed Dressing, '01 56
Raspberry Dressing, '87 153; '95 202
Roasted Red Pepper-Dill Dressing, '02 144
Soy-Sesame Dressing, '87 153
Spicy Southwestern Dressing, '94 136
Spring Garden Dressing, '85 157
Stay Trim Dressing, '86 40
Sweet-and-Sour Dressing, '87 305
Tangy Dressing, '83 9
Thousand Island Dressing, Special, '82 79
Vinaigrette Dressing, '95 231

Vinaigrette, Spicy Lime, '01 217
Wine Vinegar Dressing, '93 126
Yogurt Dressing, '85 59, 215; '88 27
Yogurt Dressing, Sweet-Hot, '86 40
Yogurt-Herb Dressing, '92 96
Yogurt-Honey Poppy Seed Dressing, '83 177

Salads

Ambrosia, Brunch, '83 57
Apple-Apricot Salad, '88 121
Apple-Bran Salad, Lemony, '86 223
Apple Cider Salad Mold, '85 54
Apple Salad, Spicy, '85 215
Apple Salad, Triple, '88 122
Apple Toss, Sesame-, '88 21
Asparagus, Marinated, '84 67
Asparagus Salad, '88 121; '94 67
Asparagus Vinaigrette, Light, '82 50
Aspic, Light Tomato, '85 83
Aspic, Three-Layer, '88 120
Aspic, Tomato-Crab, '85 287
Aspic with Horseradish Dressing, Crisp Vegetable,
    '87 152
Avocado Citrus Salad, '01 133
Barley-Broccoli Salad, '90 135
Barley-Pine Nut Salad, '05 126
Bean-and-Rice Salad, Marinated, '87 152
Bean-and-Veggie Salad, Sweet-and-Hot, '04 184
Bean Salad, Garlic-Herb Two-, '05 209
Bean Salad, Marinated, '85 137, 296
Bean Salad, Supreme, '91 202
Bean Salad with Lime-Mustard Dressing, One-,
    '00 202
Beans with Sprouts, Sweet-and-Sour, '86 32
Beef-and-Broccoli Salad, '87 187
Beef Fajita Salad, '91 70
Beef Salad, Stir-Fry, '96 129
Beet Salad, Fresh, '02 236
Black Bean-and-Barley Salad, '94 174
Black Bean Salad, '89 217
Black-Eyed Pea Salad, '95 203; '99 174
Black-Eyed Pea Salad, Marinated, '93 190
Broccoli-Corn Salad, '87 24
Broccoli Salad, '01 58
Brown Rice-and-Vegetable Salad, '84 202
Brown Rice Confetti Salad, '94 174
Brown Rice-Pine Nut Salad, '05 126
Caesar Salad, '92 71
Caesar Salad, Baby Romaine, '97 128
Cantaloupe, Fruit-Filled, '83 120
Carrot-and-Seed Salad, Fruity, '86 223
Carrot-Pineapple Salad, '91 83
Carrot-Raisin Salad, '84 174
Cauliflower-Vegetable Salad, '85 158
Cherry-Apple Salad, '86 31
Cherry Salad, Fresh, '83 120
Cherry Tomato-Caper Salad, '00 140
Chicken and Roasted Red Pepper Salad, '03 291
Chicken-and-Veggie Spaghetti Salad, '04 129
Chicken-and-Walnut Salad, Sunburst, '93 91
Chicken-Blueberry Salad, '02 177
Chicken-Fruit Salad, '82 79
Chicken Noodle Salad, '95 25
Chicken Parmesan Salad, Chunky, '05 209
Chicken Pasta Salad, '88 89
Chicken-Raspberry Salad, Marinated, '93 190
Chicken Salad, Blue Cheese, '94 81
Chicken Salad, Crunchy, '86 207
Chicken Salad, Grilled Asian, '96 158
Chicken Salad, Moroccan Grilled, '95 231
Chicken Salad, Special, '85 82
Chicken Salad, Tarragon, '90 199
Chicken Salad with Mango Chutney, Grilled, '96 182
Chicken Salad with Raspberry Dressing, Grilled,
    '95 202

Chicken Taco Salad, '94 M136
Chile-Tomato Salad, Spicy, '88 121
Citrus Salad, Tangy, '89 34
Coleslaw, Crunchy, '86 295
Coleslaw, Light and Creamy, '93 318
Coleslaw with Garden Vegetables, '01 57
Composé, Salad, '93 126
Corn Salad, '85 236
Corn Salad, Wheat Berry-and-Roasted, '94 175
Cottage Cheese Salad in Tomatoes, '86 208
Couscous Salad, Basil-and-Tomato, '94 175
Couscous Salad with Dried Tomato Vinaigrette,
    '96 244
Crab-and-Asparagus Salad, '92 141
Crab-Wild Rice Salad, '86 207
Cucumber Mousse, '88 121
Cucumber Salad, Creamy, '01 56
Cucumber Salad, Dilled, '92 72
Cucumber-Yogurt Salad, '87 33
Dijon Vinaigrette, Salad with, '03 237
Egg Salad, '05 209
English Pea-and-Apple Salad, '87 24
Fennel and Radicchio with Orange Vinaigrette,
    Grilled, '95 253
Freezer Salad, '94 118
Fruit Cups, Sangría, '89 34
Fruit Cup, Winter, '02 22
Fruit, Dressed-Up, '82 5
Fruit Salad, Chef's, '86 35
Fruit Salad, Curried, '85 107
Fruit Salad, Vanilla-Scented, '05 209
Fruit with Lime Sauce, Fresh, '02 68
Fruit with Mint-Balsamic Tea, Fresh, '95 232
Garden-Patch Salad Molds, '86 283
Garden Salad, Summer, '87 153
Gazpacho Molded Salad, '92 323
Grapefruit Salad, '88 122
Grape Salad Mold, '83 120
Greek Salad, '03 290
Green Beans with Creamy Tarragon Dressing,
    '93 191
Green Beans with Smoked Almonds, Thyme-Scented,
    '01 57
Green Salad, Mixed, '90 230
Greens, Crimson, '87 153
Greens with Blue Cheese Vinaigrette, Mixed, '90 280
Greens with Raspberry Dressing, Peppery, '95 254
Hominy-Bean Salad, '88 266
Italian Bread Salad, '99 259
Italian Salad, Cheesy, '84 33
Jícama-Orange Salad, '90 122
Layered Salad, '86 35
Legumes, Marinated, '90 197
Lentils-and-Rice Salad, '90 197
Lettuce, Confetti-Stuffed, '87 24
Lettuces with Mustard Vinaigrette, Baby, '93 67
Lima Bean-Tomato Salad, '85 137
Lime-Potato Salad, '02 22
Macaroni-Cheese Salad, Dilled, '86 208
Macaroni-Chicken Salad, Dilled, '92 142
Macaroni-Tuna Salad, Whole Wheat, '84 193
Mandarin Salad Molds, '85 54
Meal-in-One Salad, '86 43
Melon Ball Bowl with Cucumber-Mint Dressing,
    '87 153
Mixed Greens with Raspberries and Walnuts, '98 194
Mushroom-Zucchini Salad, '85 8
New Potato Salad, '84 139
Niçoise, Salad, '86 35
Oriental Salad Bowl, '87 153
Paella Salad, '86 207
Pasta-and-Tomato Salad, Herbed, '92 144
Pasta Salad, '84 139; '89 217
Pasta Salad, Garden, '86 188

Pasta with Apple, Curried, '02 68
Peaches in a Garden Nest, '87 154
Pear Salad with Jícama and Snow Peas, '01 56
Pork Salad, Oriental, '92 140
Pork Salad, Thai, '00 249
Potato-and-Bacon Salad, Roasted, '05 289
Potato Salad, '90 122
Potato Salad, Dill, '99 104
Potato Salad, Hot-and-Light, '93 90
Potato Salad, Layered, '03 183
Potato Salad, Pesto, '90 164
Potato Slices, Marinated, '93 98
Rice-and-Bean Salad, Zesty, '02 84
Rice-and-Vegetable Salad, '86 42
Rice-Shrimp Salad, '92 142
Roasted Corn-and-Black Bean Salad, '05 209
Roasted Tomato-and-Pepper Salad, '01 196
Roasted Vegetable Salad with Dried Peach
    Vinaigrette, '97 265
Romaine Salad with Cashews, '05 195
Romaine with Caper Vinaigrette, Hearts of, '91 310
Salmon-and-Wild Rice Salad, Oriental, '94 173
Salmon Salad, Chilled Poached, '96 68
Seafood Salad Sussex Shores, '93 98
Shrimp-and-Couscous Salad, '96 157
Shrimp-and-Rice Salad, '92 307
Shrimp Salad, Fruited, '86 156
Shrimp Salad, Marinated, '85 82
Slaw, Apple-Carrot, '92 243
Slaw, Cabbage-Pineapple, '92 182
Slaw, Chinese Cabbage, '89 312
Slaw, Green Bean, '95 108
Slaw, Healthy, '92 183
Slaw, Overnight, '05 208
Slaw, Red Cabbage-and-Apple, '87 31
Slaw, Tangy Ginger, '01 92
Slaw, Vegetable, '00 32
Spinach-Blue Cheese Salad, '82 166
Spinach-Kiwifruit Salad, '87 305
Spinach Salad, Citrus, '90 59
Spinach Salad, Tangy, '00 24
Spinach Salad, Wilted, '93 125
Spinach Salad with Orange Dressing, '87 187
Sprout Salad, '90 137
Steak Salad Cups, Pepper, '86 206
Steak Salad with Peach Salsa, '97 183
Strawberry-Pretzel Salad, '03 290
Strawberry Salad, Frozen, '94 119
Sweet Potato Salad with Rosemary-Honey
    Vinaigrette, '98 243
Tabbouleh Salad, '91 70; '94 174; '01 57
Tabbouleh Salad, Southwestern, '01 216
Taco Salad, Beefy, '03 128
Tofu Salad, '88 27
Tomato-Cucumber Salad, '92 199
Tomato-Cucumber Salad with Yogurt-Herb Dressing,
    '92 96
Tomatoes Stuffed with Sea Slaw, '89 96
Tortellini Salad, '89 237
Tossed Salad, Grecian, '04 283
Tuna-and-Cannellini Bean Salad, '86 143
Tuna Chef Salad, '82 78
Tuna-Mac in Tomatoes, '87 188
Tuna-Pasta Salad, '92 141
Tuna Salad, Curried, '86 208
Turkey Waldorf Salad with Yogurt Dressing, '88 53
Turnip Salad, '85 235
Vegetable Salad, Crispy Marinated, '84 193
Vegetable Salad, Grilled, '94 203
Vegetable Salad, Italian, '82 19
Vegetable Salad, Marinated, '84 13
Vegetable Salad, Minted, '88 23
Vegetable Salad, Tarragon-, '85 288
Vegetable Salad, Winter, '86 42

Vegetables, Zesty Marinated, '82 272
White Bean-and-Asparagus Salad, '05 100
White Bean-and-Tuna Salad, '01 35
Wild Rice Salad, '93 191
Wild Rice Salad with Spicy Lime Vinaigrette, '01 217
Salt, Dragon, '03 236
Sandwiches
Bagel, Breakfast on a, '94 66
Bean Burgers with Adobo Mayonnaise, '02 202
Breakfast Sandwiches, Open-Faced, '92 140
Cheese Sandwiches with Artichoke-Tomato Salsa,
    Herbed, '96 182
Chicken Pita, Oriental, '89 216
Chicken Sandwiches, Marinated, '86 M45
Chicken Sandwich with Fresh Salsa, Broiled, '00 59
Crab Sandwiches, Open-Faced, '87 106
Eggplant Parmesan Sandwiches, '03 213
Eggplant Sandwiches, Open-Face, '95 124
Eggplant, Tomato, and Feta Sandwiches, '98 106
Flank Steak Sandwiches with Apple Barbecue Sauce,
    '99 173
Garden Sandwiches, Open-Faced, '87 105
Ham Sandwiches, Open-Face, '85 8
Heroes, Healthy, '90 177
Lamb Pockets with Dilled Cucumber Topping,
    '87 104
London Broil Sandwiches with Yogurt-Cucumber
    Sauce, '01 162
Open-Face Sandwiches, '84 13
Picnic Loaf, Mediterranean, '96 156
Pimiento Cheese Sandwiches, '82 278
Pitas, Acadian Stuffed, '90 177
Pita Sandwiches, '84 139
Pita, Stuffed, '89 87
Pita, Tuna-Veggie Stuffed, '01 216
Pizza Sandwiches, Open-Face, '85 22
Rollup, Hot Ham-and-Cheese, '01 217
Seafood Po'Boy, Grilled, '96 244
Seafood Sandwiches, Caribbean, '98 105
Shrimp Salad Sandwiches, '90 178
Sloppy Toms, '91 51
Tabbouleh Pitas, '98 105
Tofu-Veggie Sandwiches, Open-Face, '86 5
Turkey and Ham Pine-Berry Sandwiches, '00 59
Turkey-in-the-Slaw Sandwich, '90 177
Turkey-Roasted Pepper Sandwiches, Smoked, '94 66
Vegetable Pitas, Garbanzo-, '00 58
Vegetable Pockets, '85 215
Vegetarian Melt, Open-Faced, '87 106
Vegetarian Pita Sandwiches, '84 193
Wraps, Chicken-Cranberry, '01 34
Sauces and Gravies
Alfredo Sauce, '94 84
Avocado Sauce, Chunky, '03 128
Barbecue Sauce, Apple, '99 173
Barbecue Sauce, Easy, '82 178
Barbecue Sauce, LBJ's Texas, '97 42
Barbecue Sauce, Special, '82 177
Barbecue Sauce, Tangy, '99 104
Basil-Brown Butter Sauce, '93 92
Champagne Sauce, '90 29
Cheese Sauce, Guilt-Free, '93 M95
Cream Sauce, '03 237
Creole Sauce, '90 28; '02 284
Cucumber-Dill Sauce, '86 5
Dill Sauce, Creamy, '94 42
Dipping Sauce, Olive Oil-Balsamic, '04 46
Ginger Dipping Sauce, '03 64
Ginger-Soy Sauce, '91 33
Ginger Vinaigrette, '95 162
Gravy, '88 303
Gravy, Sausage, '94 20
Greek Sauce, '91 183
Hollandaise Sauce, Mock, '85 49; '93 68

HEALTHY & LIGHT, Sauces and Gravies
(continued)

Honey-Horseradish Dip, '02 309
Horseradish Sauce, '91 183
Jalapeño Sauce, '93 230
Jalapeño Tartar Sauce, '96 69
Lemon-Chive Sauce, '86 249
Lemon-Molasses Dressing, '97 195
Lemon Sauce, '82 290
Mandarin Sauce, '84 60
Mandarin-Teriyaki Sauce, '96 68
Mango-Pineapple Hot Sauce, '04 183
Marinade, Tangy Light, '82 178
Marinara Sauce, '82 178; '89 239; '92 18
Mediterranean Sauce, '94 83
Mushroom Sauce, '83 205; '91 221
Mushroom Sauce, Spicy Sherried, '89 239
Mustard-Hollandaise Sauce, Mock, '87 269
Mustard Sauce, '87 22
Mustard Sauce, Easy, '94 83
Mustard Sauce, Light, '82 178
Mustard Sauce, Tangy, '92 201
Orange Dipping Sauce, '03 M212
Parmesan Sauce, '92 17
Parsley Sauce, '86 108
Peanut Sauce, Spicy, '04 134
Pesto, Dried Tomato, '94 249
Pesto, Sage, '97 22
Picante Sauce, Processed, '91 257
Pizza Sauce, '84 33
Rancheros Sauce, '88 148
Red Chile Sauce, '94 251
Reduction Sauce, Cider-Port Wine, '96 245
Red Wine Garlic Sauce, '94 250
Roasted Red Pepper Sauce, '00 58
Rosemary-Cherry Sauce, '02 193
Rosemary Sauce, '97 127
Salsa, '88 147
Salsa, Artichoke-Tomato, '96 182
Salsa, Black Bean, '93 155
Salsa, Black Bean-and-Corn, '94 80
Salsa, Cranberry-Citrus, '97 290
Salsa Cruda, '88 148
Salsa, Cucumber-Dill, '95 107
Salsa, Dried Chile, '97 265
Salsa, Fiesta Onion, '94 82
Salsa, Fresh, '00 59
Salsa, Fresh Citrus, '03 291
Salsa, Fresh Vegetable, '98 194
Salsa, Hot Kiwifruit, '94 82
Salsa, Mango, '04 59
Salsa, Peach, '97 183
Salsa, Pepper, '88 26
Salsa, Pineapple, '96 226; '03 128
Salsa, Poblano, '91 135
Salsa, Smoky Three-Bean, '02 202
Salsa, Tomato-Avocado, '94 83
Salsa, Vegetable, '96 208
Salsa Verde, Roasted, '96 182
Salsa, Warm Pineapple, '02 144
Salsa, Zesty Corn, '02 193
Sauerbraten Sauce, '93 16
Seafood Sauce, '89 239
Seafood Sauce, Red, '95 107
Spaghetti Sauce, Lentil, '90 198
Swiss Sauce, '83 M195
Tahini Sauce, '03 183
Tarragon Sauce, '83 56; '97 42
Tartar Sauce, '95 107; '99 174
Tomato Sauce, '85 193, 244
Tomato Sauce, Spicy, '88 19
Vegetable-Cheese Potato Topper, '86 6

White Sauce, Low-Calorie Medium, '87 26
Yogurt-Cucumber Sauce, '04 216
Zesty Sauce, '94 82
Zippy Sauce, '86 44
Sausage, Country, '92 242
Sausage, Italian, '92 242
Seasoning, Herb, '99 63
Shells and Cheese, Creamy, '01 216
Soups and Stews
Asparagus Soup, '84 67
Bean-and-Hominy Soup, '95 23
Bean and Pasta Soup, '94 220
Bean-and-Turkey Soup, '93 319
Bean Soup, Leafy, '86 223
Bean Soup, Quick, '99 97
Beef-and-Barley Vegetable Soup, '89 31
Beef-and-Pepperoni Soup, Italian-Style, '00 316
Beef Stew, '90 230
Beef Stew, Burgundy, '88 234
Beef Stew, Quick, '92 71
Black Bean Soup, '88 266; '98 291
Black Bean Soup, Carolina, '92 139
Black Bean Soup, Marge Clyde's, '96 29
Borscht, Ruby Red, '83 176
Bouillon, Court-, '98 229
Bouillon, Tomato, '83 8
Broccoli Soup, Creamy, '91 307
Broccoli Soup, Light Cream of, '93 17
Broccoli Soup, Mock Cream of, '85 288
Broccoli-Swiss Soup, '86 6
Butternut Soup, '02 68
Butternut Squash-Lime Soup, '03 236
Cantaloupe Soup, '83 120
Carrot-and-Butternut Squash Soup with Parslied
    Croutons, '97 217
Carrot-Leek Soup, '86 34
Carrot Soup, '98 123
Chicken-and-Buttermilk Soup, Country, '02 144
Chicken, Artichoke, and Mushroom Soup, '92 324
Chicken, Kale, and Chickpea Stew, '98 47
Chicken Soup, Curried, '86 34
Chicken-Vegetable Soup, '88 18
Chili, Full-of-Veggies, '00 294
Chili, Spicy 3-Bean, '03 291
Chili Vegetable Soup, '94 120
Chili, Vegetarian, '84 280
Chowder, Basque Fish, '86 36
Chowder, Chicken-and-Roasted Vegetable, '97 21
Chowder, Clam, '86 36; '89 95
Chowder, Corn, '91 132
Chowder, Corn-and-Poblano, '03 193
Chowder, Maryland Crab, '97 23
Chowder, Potato-Corn, '94 66
Chowder, Seafood, '92 122
Chowder with Sage Pesto, White Bean, '97 22
Cilantro Soup, Cream of, '00 249
Corn-and-Crab Soup, Fresh, '92 183
Crab Soup, Cream of, '88 302
Cucumber Soup, Cold Minted, '86 34
Cucumber-Yogurt Soup, '83 205
Fish-and-Vegetable Stew, '87 220
French Market Soup, '92 49
Gazpacho, Chilled, '84 138
Gazpacho, Citrus, '96 70
Gazpacho, Tropical, '95 204
Gumbo, Catfish, '90 278
Gumbo, Chicken-and-Sausage, '94 20
Gumbo, Light Seafood-Okra, '86 155
Gumbo, Seafood, '96 98
Ham-and-Bean Soup, Spicy, '94 322
Hot-and-Sour Soup, '91 50
Mex-Tex Soup, '90 278
Minestrone Soup, '86 144; '91 258
Minestrone Soup Mix, '91 258

Navy Bean Soup, '84 280
New Year's Day Soup, '00 25
Okra-and-Shrimp Soup, '94 323
Peach Soup, '83 120
Pepper-and-Chicken Soup, Roasted, '90 58
Pepper Soup, Spicy, '93 98
Plum Soup, '85 107
Potato Soup, Hearty, '98 292
Roasted Red Pepper Soup, '96 245
Seafood Stew, '84 280
Spinach Egg Drop Soup, '03 65
Spinach Soup, Oriental, '83 151
Split Pea-and-Lentil Soup, Oven-Baked, '00 316
Split Pea Soup, '90 198; '94 322
Squash Bisque, '84 280
Sweet Potato-and-Pear Bisque, '00 317
Sweet Potato-and-Sausage Soup, '95 23
Tomato Soup, '89 217
Tomato Soup, Easy, '84 14
Tomato Soup Plus, '88 170
Tortilla Soup, '94 136; '98 291
Turkey-Tomato Stew, '90 279
Vegetable-Beef Stew, '94 323
Vegetable Soup, '86 187; '88 266; '98 291
Vegetable Soup, Light, '84 280
Vegetable Stew, '00 248
Vegetable Stew, Mixed, '84 13
Wild Mushroom Soup, '04 203
Zucchini Soup with Fresh Vegetable Salsa, Chilled,
    '98 194
Sour Cream, Mock, '83 71, 205
Spice Mix, Tex-Mex, '94 135
Spice Rub, Caribbean, '02 144
Spice Rub, Moroccan, '95 231
Spread, Blue Cheese, '95 79
Spread, Cottage Cheese, '87 107
Spread, Hawaiian Ham, '87 106
Spread, Light Strawberry, '85 55
Spread, Low-Calorie Pimiento Cheese, '85 215
Spread, Peachy-Raisin, '86 326
Spread, Raisin-Nut, '95 79
Spread, Strawberry, '95 79
Spread, Sugarless Fruit, '84 60
Spread, Tasty Chicken, '84 193
Spread, Vegetable-Egg, '87 106
Syrup, Maple, '93 16
Topping, Apple, '89 107
Topping, Oat Crunch, '89 108
Topping, Yogurt-Cheese, '88 55
Tortellini with Rosemary-Parmesan Sauce, '92 284
Tortilla Rollups, '89 87
Vegetables
Acorn Squash, Fruited, '85 235; '90 228
Acorn Squash, Sugar-and-Spice, '05 289
Acorn Squash with Nutmeg, '85 267
Acorn Squash with Rosemary, Grilled, '96 266
Artichokes, Shrimp-Stuffed, '84 67
Artichokes, Stuffed, '99 64
Artichokes Stuffed with Shrimp and Scallops,
    '84 174
Asparagus, Company, '85 82
Asparagus, Stir-Fried, '87 52
Asparagus Vinaigrette, '90 138
Asparagus with Ginger, '04 237
Barley and Vegetables, '91 81
Beans, Lemon-Mint, '88 22
Beans, Texas Ranch, '90 198
Beets, Ginger-Marmalade Glazed, '93 35
Beets, Harvard, '83 M195
Beets, Orange, '91 219
Beets, Orange-Glazed, '86 187
Beets, Pickled, '87 163
Black Bean Terrine with Fresh Tomato Coulis and
    Jalapeño Sauce, '93 230

Black-Eyed Peas, '93 180
Black-Eyed Peas, Creole, '98 22
Black-Eyed Peas, Seasoned, '85 138
Black-Eyed Peas, Spicy Hot, '90 135
Bread Bowl, Veggie, '01 132
Broccoli and Cauliflower, Roasted, '01 132
Broccoli and Walnut Sauté, '95 52
Broccoli Casserole, '88 265
Broccoli, Easy Orange, '85 267
Broccoli, Garlic, '93 35; '95 54
Broccoli, Lemon, '95 53
Broccoli, Pecan, '05 257
Broccoli, Sesame, '85 8
Broccoli Toss, '86 294
Broccoli with Horseradish Sauce, '84 33
Broccoli with Tangy Chive Sauce, Steamed, '83 101
Brussels Sprouts, Casserole of, '86 294
Brussels Sprouts, Glorified, '86 282
Brussels Sprouts in Mustard Sauce, '90 228
Brussels Sprouts, Marinated, '88 265
Brussels Sprouts Medley, '85 267
Bundles, Vegetable, '93 181
Butterbeans, '90 166
Butternut-Orange Bake, '86 295
Cabbage, Skillet, '90 229
Cabbage, Sweet-and-Sour, '86 295
Cabbage with Caraway, '93 181
Carrots and Onions, Herbed, '87 31
Carrots and Pineapple, Curried, '90 228
Carrots, Dilled Baby, '92 145
Carrots, Ginger, '83 9
Carrots, Glazed, '88 304
Carrots, Golden, '85 267
Carrots, Lemon-Dill Steamed, '93 180
Carrots, Light Glazed, '92 227
Carrots, Marinated, '86 108
Carrots Marsala, '83 56
Carrots, Orange-Spiced, '88 18
Carrots Polynesian, Spiced, '88 85
Carrots, Rosemary, '91 219
Carrot Strips, Orangy, '89 312
Carrots, Tropical, '84 34
Carrot-Sweet Potato Puree, '02 M285
Cauliflower Sauté, '94 67
Cauliflower-Snow Pea Medley, '87 305
Celeriac and Carrots, '91 219
Celery-Parmesan Toss, '84 34
Chard with Onion and Apple, Sautéed, '98 48
Cherry Tomatoes, Rosemary-Roasted, '05 257
Corn Casserole, Chili-, '88 266
Corn, Creamy Baked, '90 60
Corn in the Style of Oaxaca, Grilled, '04 134
Corn-on-the-Cob, Grilled, '90 166
Corn Pudding, Fresh, '89 172
Corn, Roasted Red Pepper, '91 122
Corn, Southern-Style Creamed, '92 201
Corn, Spicy Mexican, '93 90
Crêpes, Vegetable-Filled Bran, '86 44
Crunchy Vegetables, '99 43
Curry, Vegetable, '04 217
Eggplant Casserole, Spicy Hot, '93 92
Eggplant, Ratatouille-Bran Stuffed, '86 44
Eggplant, Spicy Oriental, '96 130
English Pea Medley, '85 236
English Peas, Deluxe, '84 68
French Fries, Oven, '91 122
French Fries, Seasoned, '96 245
Fries, Salty Rosemary, '03 213
Fries, Spicy Oven, '02 34
Green Bean Medley, Peppery, '93 181
Green Beans and Potatoes, '91 221
Green Beans, Gingered, '05 290
Green Beans, Herbed, '83 177
Green Beans, Indian-Style, '88 265

Green Beans, Italian, '90 164; '92 183
Green Beans Italiano, '86 144
Green Beans, Lemony, '99 259
Green Beans, Seasoned, '88 304
Green Beans with Mushrooms, '93 89
Green Beans with New Potatoes, '87 164
Green Beans with Oregano, '97 218
Green Beans with Tomatoes, '85 137
Green Tomatoes, '89 174
Green Tomatoes, Oven-Fried, '91 122
Grilled Vegetables, '92 124
Grilled Veggies, Easy, '05 194
Grilled Vegetables, Italian-Style, '92 143
Grilled Vegetables, Marinated, '95 162; '00 126
Hash Brown Casserole, Creamy, '03 193
Hominy, Mexican, '91 133
Kebabs, Marinated Vegetable, '83 M195
Kebabs, Vegetable, '01 132
Kale with Tomato and Onion, '92 244
Kidney Bean Casserole, '90 136
Leeks Vinaigrette, Warm, '98 47
Lima Beans Creole, '85 137
Marinated Vegetables, '88 170; '99 105
Marinated Vegetables, Creole-, '02 69
Medley, Chinese Vegetable, '84 33
Mixed Vegetables, '83 M195
Mushrooms, Flavor-Stuffed, '85 288
Mushrooms, Grilled Portobello, '95 123
Mushrooms, Microwave Portobello, '95 M123
Mushrooms, Sautéed Portobello, '95 123
Mushrooms, Savory Fresh, '85 268
New Potatoes, Herbed, '83 9
New Potatoes, Roasted, '90 138
New Potato Medley, '90 279
Okra-and-Tomato Bake, '89 173
Okra and Tomatoes, Grilled, '98 124
Okra, Corn, and Tomatoes, '95 203
Okra, Oven-Fried, '91 121
Onion-Potato Bake, '83 M195
Onion Rings, Crispy Baked, '93 247
Onions and Wine, Stuffed, '85 268
Onions, Citrus, '04 89
Onions, Roasted Sweet, '04 282
Onions, Stuffed Vidalia, '89 172
Onions Stuffed with Peas, '84 68
Parsnips, Glazed, '91 220
Peas-and-Corn Medley, '85 138
Peas and Ham, Southern, '85 138
Peas and Peppers, Stir-Fried, '87 51
Peperonata, '97 291
Pepper Kebabs, Pretty, '90 166
Peppers, Carrot-and-Cabbage Stuffed, '99 63
Peppers, Stuffed, '84 202
Pilaf, Barley-Vegetable, '91 33
Potato Bake, Smoky Mashed, '00 214
Potato-Cheese Dream, '91 307
Potatoes and Turnips, Scalloped, '85 235
Potatoes au Gratin, '93 90
Potatoes, Buttermilk-Basil Mashed, '95 330
Potatoes, Confetti Twice-Baked, '02 35
Potatoes, Cottage, '93 M92
Potatoes, Cream Cheese Mashed, '02 35
Potatoes, Double-Cheese, '86 6
Potatoes, Herbed, '91 220
Potatoes, Light Scalloped, '89 311
Potatoes, Mexican-Stuffed, '91 131
Potatoes, Mushroom-Dill-Topped, '86 41
Potatoes, Ranch, '05 256
Potatoes, Rosemary-Roasted, '95 20
Potatoes, Scalloped, '92 48
Potatoes, Stuffed, '89 173
Potatoes, Twice Baked Cottage-Style, '91 135
Potatoes, Vegetable-Topped Stuffed, '85 235
Potato Thins, Roasted, '02 23

Potato, Twice-Baked, '90 M295
Potato Wedges, '94 M119
Potato Wedges, Lemon, '88 21
Ragoût, Vegetable, '89 172
Ratatouille, Microwave, '95 M232
Red Cabbage-and-Apple Slaw, '91 309
Rice Toss, Vegetable-, '91 309
Rice, Vegetables and, '93 91
Risotto Primavera, '95 163
Roasted Root Vegetables, Rosemary, '01 255
Roasted Summer Vegetables, '98 213
Rollup, Veggie, '01 109
Rutabaga, Honey, '91 220
Rutabagas, Mashed, '86 295
Sautéed Vegetable Medley, '83 101
Sauté, Tossed Vegetable, '92 138
Snap Beans, Sweet-and-Sour, '89 173
Snow Peas with Red Pepper, '90 102
Spaghetti Squash Sauté, '98 212
Spinach-Gorgonzola Custards, Savory, '02 284
Spinach Quiche, '85 49; '91 204
Spinach Soufflé, '86 108
Spinach with Pine Nuts, Baby, '03 64
Squash Casserole, '87 163
Squash Stuffed with Spinach Pesto, '89 M133
Steamed Garden Vegetables, '93 155
Steamed Herbed Vegetables, '93 M303
Steamed Vegetable Medley, '90 29
Stir-Fried Vegetables, '90 136
Stir-Fried Vegetables with Curry, '87 51
Stir-Fry, Almond-Vegetable, '86 222
Stir-Fry, Mixed Veggie, '99 206
Stir-Fry, Vegetable, '99 204
Stir-Fry, Vegetable Medley, '99 205
Stir-Fry Vegetables, Glazed, '99 205
Sugar Snap Peas with Basil and Lemon, '93 66
Summer Vegetables, '91 136
Summer Vegetables, Cheesy, '94 119
Sweet Potato-Apple Bake, '86 282
Sweet Potato Casserole, '03 M24
Sweet Potatoes-and-Apple Casserole, '90 228
Sweet Potatoes and Onions, Oven-Roasted, '00 24
Sweet Potatoes, Orange-Spice Mashed, '02 34
Sweet Potatoes, Roasted Gingered, '01 92
Sweet Potato Puff, '85 235
Sweet Potato Puree, '92 306
Tomato Coulis, Fresh, '93 230
Tomatoes and Okra, '87 164
Tomatoes, Bean-Stuffed, '84 34
Tomatoes, Cheese Herbed-Topped, '86 108
Tomatoes, Cheesy Puff-Top, '86 187
Tomatoes, Fire-and-Ice, '03 183
Tomatoes, Grilled, '85 158
Tomatoes, Parmesan-Stuffed, '92 182
Tomatoes, Spinach-Topped, '88 265
Tomatoes, Stuffed Scalloped, '90 29
Tomatoes with Basil Vinaigrette, Grilled, '97 168
Tomato Slices, Herbed, '89 173
Torta, Mexican, '88 149
Turnips and Carrots Julienne, '86 295
Turnips, Braised, '91 219
Yellow Squash, Tomato-Stuffed, '00 43
Zucchini-and-Tomato Casserole, '88 265
Zucchini and Tomato with Herbs, '92 182
Zucchini-Basil Delight, '85 267
Zucchini-Basil Scramble, '87 34
Zucchini Dressing, '86 282
Zucchini Fans, '91 33
Zucchini Spears, Oven-Fried, '91 121
Zucchini, Stuffed, '86 187; '89 M133
Zucchini with Feta, Greek Grilled, '95 190
Zucchini with Pecans, '87 31
Vinegar, Raspberry Wine, '93 191
Vinegar, Shallot-Tarragon-Garlic, '93 191

HEALTHY & LIGHT
(continued)

Waffles, Light, '91 139
Waffles, Oat Bran, '92 139
Waffles, Oatmeal, '89 107
Wild Rice-Fennel Pilaf, '97 127
Yogurt Snack, '88 55

HEARTS OF PALM
Chicken Rolls, Hearts of Palm, '89 201
Marinated Asparagus and Hearts of Palm, '90 91
Salad, Different Vegetable, '82 143
Salad, Hearts of Palm, '81 252; '89 276; '96 86
Salad, Hearts-of-Palm, '87 138
Salad, Italian Tossed, '00 167
Salad with Basil-and-Garlic Dressing, Hearts of Palm, '94 55
Salad with Lemon-Dill Vinaigrette, Green, '99 27
Sandwich, Hearts of Palm, '92 191
Spread, Hearts of Palm, '90 293

HOMINY
Bacon, Eggs, and Hominy, '85 143
Bake, Chili Hominy, '81 282; '82 58
Bake, Hominy-Sausage, '88 51
Casserole, Cheesy Hominy, '83 170
Casserole, Chile-Hominy, '81 29
Casserole), Four-Part Hominy (Cheesy Hominy, '96 158
Casserole, Hominy-and-Corn, '97 291
Casserole, Hominy-Chili, '86 255
Caviar, Texas, '86 218
Cheese Hominy, Hot, '84 77
Chiles and Cheese, Hominy with, '86 78
Gold Coast Hominy, '83 52
Jalapeño Hominy, '82 51
Mexican Hominy, '86 255; '91 133, 162
Mexihominy, '96 189
Olé, Hominy, '01 17
Salad, Hominy-Bean, '88 266
Skillet, Hominy-Sausage, '81 29
Soup, Bean-and-Hominy, '95 23
Soup, Black, White, and Red All Over, '95 126
Soup, Southwest, '86 255

HONEY
Ambrosia, Honey Bee, '83 267
Apple Quarters, Honey-Baked, '86 93
Apple Rings, Honey, '80 243
Apples and Pear, Honey-Baked, '97 303
Apples, Honey-Baked, '83 234; '84 244
Apples, Honey-Yogurt, '92 46
Apples, Stuffed, '99 247
Bananas, Honey-Baked, '81 268
Breads
Applesauce-Honey Nut Bread, '87 300
Banana Bread, Honey-, '91 68
Biscuits, Honey Angel, '95 138; '03 111
Buns, Honey-Oat, '98 27
Buns, Honey Oatmeal, '83 154
Cinnamon Swirl Bread, Honey-, '88 287
Cornbread, Honey-Sweet, '05 137
Curry Bread, Honey-, '89 250
Graham Bread, Honey, '99 211
Granola Bread, Honey-, '86 56
Muffins, Banana-Honey-Nut, '88 62
Muffins, Honey Bran, '88 171
Muffins, Honey-Bran, '89 250
Muffins, Honey-Oatmeal, '84 229
Muffins, Honey-Wheat, '83 96; '88 263
Muffins, Oatmeal-Honey, '83 95
Muffins, Orange-Honey, '88 284
Muffins, Peanut Butter-Honey, '82 56
Oat Bread, Honey-, '89 107; '93 232; '98 27
Oatmeal Bread, Honey, '80 60
Pancakes, Buttermilk 'n' Honey, '05 137

Rolls, Dilled Honey-Wheat, '83 254
Rolls, Honey Wheat, '83 278
Rolls, Super Honey, '80 115
Swirl, Honey-Walnut, '80 21
Twist, Honey, '79 80
Wheat Bread, Honey, '85 18, 268
Wheat Bread, Honey-, '91 223
Whole Wheat Honey Bread, '82 65; '83 106
Zucchini-Honey Bread, '89 143
Brie, Honey-Mustard, '91 252
Brownies, Heavenly Honey, '79 83
Butter, Cinnamon-Honey, '89 281
Butter, Honey, '93 309; '94 206; '95 139; '97 307; '03 111
Butter, Honey-Lemon, '04 231
Butter, Honey-Orange, '79 36; '85 19
Butter, Honey-Spice, '05 274
Butter, Pecan-Honey, '05 137
Cake, Honey, '92 250
Cake, Honey-Apple, '99 210
Cake, Honey-Oatmeal, '87 222
Cake, Southern Honey, '89 251
Cake Squares, Honey, '89 250
Carrots, Honey-Glazed, '80 115; '84 121; '85 18; '99 63
Carrots, Honey-Kissed, '84 122
Carrots with Honey, '02 59
Chicken, Baked Honey, '99 110
Chicken, Honey, '82 55; '88 67
Chicken, Honey Barbecue, '04 197
Chicken, Honey-Curry, '87 36
Chicken, Honey-Glazed Grilled, '99 213
Chicken, Honey-Lime Grilled, '96 189; '98 332
Chicken, Honey-Pecan, '03 147
Chicken Strips, Honey-Pecan, '05 188
Chicken Thighs, Honey-Pecan, '02 127
Chicken Wings, Grilled Honey, '96 111
Chicken Wings, Honey-Glazed, '91 251
Chops, Honey-Glazed, '97 200
Citrus-Pear Honey, '05 230
Cornbread, Honey, '83 286; '84 17
Crunch, Honey-and-Spice, '94 290
Dip, Coconut-Honey Fruit, '84 171
Dip, Creamy Honey-Herb, '98 135
Dip, Honey-Horseradish, '02 309
Dip, Peanut Butter-Honey, '85 19
Dressings
Applesauce Salad Dressing, Honey-, '99 210
Basil-Honey Dressing, '97 30
Berry Dressing, Orange Salad with Honey-, '89 250
Buttermilk-Honey Dressing, '96 243
Celery-Honey Dressing, '80 42
Cider Vinegar-Honey Dressing, '05 41
Dijon-Honey Dressing, '89 45; '99 333
Dijon Salad Dressing, Creamy Honey-, '99 245
Dijon Vinaigrette, Honey-, '04 321
French Dressing, Honey, '87 81
Honey Dressing, '79 242; '83 146; '87 129
Lemon Dressing, Fruit Salad with Honey-, '93 21
Lemon Dressing, Honey-, '95 133
Lime Dressing, Honey-, '83 139; '93 71
Lime-Honey Dressing, '92 213
Lime-Honey Fruit Salad Dressing, '87 81
Mustard Dressing, Honey-, '90 55, 111, 146; '00 54; '01 230; '05 185
Orange Salad with Honey Dressing, '89 14
Pecan Dressing, Honey-, '03 28
Salad with Honey Dressing, Fruit, '05 137
Spinach Salad with Honey Dressing, '90 16
Tomato-Honey French Dressing, '81 105
Vinaigrette, Honey-Mustard, '94 249
Vinaigrette, Honey-Orange, '91 255
Vinaigrette, Lemon-Honey, '96 65
Walnut Dressing, Honey-, '93 107
Yogurt Dressing, Honey-, '93 172

Duck with Parsnip Mash, Honey-Orange-Glazed Muscovy, '97 262
Filling, Honey, '88 287
Filling, Honey-Walnut, '80 21
Flavored Honey, '97 30
Fritters, Matzoh-and-Honey, '05 81
Frosting, Honey Chocolate, '79 83
Glaze, Chocolate-Honey, '82 306
Glaze, Cranberry-Honey, '89 273
Glaze, Honey, '88 287
Glaze, Honey-Nut, '87 15
Grapes, Honeyed, '95 47
Ham, Honey-Orange Glazed, '83 320
Ham Slice, Honey-Glazed, '81 104
Ice Cream, Honey, '99 212
Ice Cream, Honey-Vanilla, '95 178
Jelly, Honey-Lemon, '97 29
Kebabs, Honey Ham, '80 156
Leeks, Honey-Glazed, '86 62
Lemon Honey, '94 16; '96 124
Loaves, Hint o' Honey, '81 104
Marinade, Garlic-Honey, '93 102
Marinade, Honey-Mustard, '93 103
Mousse, Honeyed Chocolate, '87 223
Mustard, Honey, '05 203
Mustard, Hot Honey, '93 240
Mustard, Peppered Honey, '95 312
Mustard, Sweet-Hot Honey, '05 284
Onions, Honey, '81 86
Onions, Honey-Paprika Sweet, '92 52
Pancakes, Honey, '91 139
Peaches, Honey-Sweet, '85 107
Peaches 'n' Cream, Honeyed, '93 134
Pear Honey, '90 159
Pear Honey, Gingered, '97 62
Pears, Honey-Baked, '93 47
Pears, Pineapple-Honey, '86 94
Pecans, Honeycomb, '84 300
Pecans, Sugar-and-Honey, '86 319
Pie, Honey Apple, '00 331
Pie, Honeyed Orzo-Pecan, '04 219
Pork Chops, Honey-Lime, '91 33
Pork Chops, Honey-Pecan, '01 82
Pork, Honey-Roasted, '02 282
Pork Loin, Garlic-Honey Marinated, '99 334
Pork Tenderloin, Honey-Garlic, '01 16
Pork Tenderloin, Honey-Mustard, '95 52
Pork Tenderloins, Honey-Garlic, '01 318
Pork Tenderloins, Pepper-Honey, '98 33
Pork Tenderloin with Avocado-Peach Salsa, Honeyed, '02 159
Preserves, Honeyed Peach, '85 130
Puffs, Honey, '96 153
Punch, Honey-Apple, '05 23
Relish, Cherry-Honey, '97 32
Rice, Honey, '85 83
Rutabaga, Honey, '91 220
Salad, Honey Chicken, '04 51
Salad, Honey Fruit, '80 276
Sauces
Barbecue Sauce, Honey, '04 197
Barbecue Sauce, Honey-Mustard, '05 167
Butter Sauce, Honey-, '85 18; '98 45
Chicken in Honey Sauce, '89 82
Chicken Strips with Honey Sauce, '03 27
Chocolate Sauce, Honey-, '89 251
Cinnamon-Pecan-Honey Pancake Sauce, '88 46
Honey Sauce, '99 210
Lemon Mustard Sauce, Honey-, '84 275
Lime Sauce, Honey-, '82 85
Mustard Sauce, Honey-, '85 13
Mustard Sauce, Smoked Ribs with Honey-, '92 168
Orange-Honey Sauce, '97 236
Orange Sauce, Honey-, '85 108

Poppy Seed Sauce, Honey-, '93 13
Sundae Sauce, Honeyscotch, '82 167
Yogurt Sauce, Honey-, '92 307
Shrimp, Tangy Honeyed, '94 32
Smoothie, Fruited Honey-Yogurt, '88 231; '89 23
Smoothie, Honey-Banana, '89 144
Smoothie, Honey-Yogurt, '97 326
Snack Mix, Honey-Nut, '02 187
Snapper, Honey-Curried, '85 181
Spareribs, Honey-Glazed, '82 163
Spread, Honey, '81 229
Spread, Honey Mustard-Butter, '99 86
Spread, Honey-Nut, '87 157; '03 46
Stir-Fry, Honey-Butternut, '93 184
Syrup, Honey, '96 21
Syrup, Maple-Honey-Cinnamon, '85 19
Tart, Honey-Pecan, '99 212
Tea, Honey, '81 105
Tenderloins, Honey-Grilled, '00 126
Tomatoes, Honey-Baked, '02 166
Topping, Honey, '83 154
Turkey Salad, Honey-Mustard, '92 309; '01 230
Vegetables, Honey-Dijon, '98 311
Vegetables, Honey-Glazed Roasted Fall, '99 244
Vegetables, Honey-Mustard Marinated, '93 236
Vegetables, Honey-Roasted, '97 29
Vinaigrette, Sweet Potato Salad with Rosemary-Honey, '98 243
Whip, Peaches with Honey-Lime, '85 108
Yogurt, Orange Slices with Honey, '91 68
HONEYDEW. *See* **MELONS.**
HORS D'OEUVRES. *See* **APPETIZERS.**
HOT DOGS. *See* **FRANKFURTERS.**
HUSH PUPPIES
Acorn Squash Puppies, '94 268
Aunt Jenny's Hush Puppies, '84 88
Bacon Hush Puppies, '91 201
Baked Hush Puppies, '89 53; '95 108
Beer Hush Puppies, Fiery, '86 233
Buttermilk Hush Puppies, '00 172
Corn, Hush Puppies with, '83 286; '84 17
Corn Soufflé Hush Puppies, '98 M328
Cracker Hush Puppies, '80 99
Creole Hush Puppies, '98 43
Easy Hush Puppies, '81 191; '85 14
Golden Hush Puppies, '82 135
Green Onion-Tomato Hush Puppies, '97 84
Hush Puppies, '84 102; '87 15; '92 168; '99 32; '01 148, 325; '05 99
Jalapeño Hush Puppies, '05 99
Lela's Hush Puppies, '04 164
Mexican Hush Puppies, '90 214
Mexican Hush Puppies, Cheesy, '91 201
Mississippi Hush Puppies, '97 84
Onion Hush Puppies, '85 14
Peppery Hush Puppies, '80 221; '88 111
Shrimp Puppies, Hot-to-Trot, '97 84
Squash Puppies, '01 179
Tomato-Onion Hush Puppies, '91 201
Topsail Island Hush Puppies, '79 152

ICE CREAMS. *See also* **SHERBETS.**
Alaska, Apple Baked, '80 226
Alaska, Baked, '84 105; '85 295
Alaska, Brownie Baked, '80 66
Alaska, Mint Patty, '80 219
Alaskas, Banana Split, '87 10
Almond-Fudge Ice Cream, '93 205
Almond Ice Cream, '98 221
Amaretto Freeze, '82 182
Apricot Ice Cream, '99 146
Balls, Almond Ice Cream, '86 315
Balls, Cinnamon-Chip Ice Cream, '00 198

Balls, Cinnamon-Chocolate Chip Ice-Cream, '02 143
Balls, Easy Ice Cream, '84 106
Balls, Nutty Ice Cream, '89 72
Banana-Coconut Ice Cream, '02 164
Banana-Graham Ice Cream, '91 56
Banana-Nut Ice Cream, '00 143
Bananas Foster, Elegant, '81 59
Banana Split Ice Cream, '80 176
Banana Split Pie, Layered, '83 189
Beverages
Almond Float, Nutmeg-, '84 106
Amaretto Breeze, '83 172
Apple Juice Shrub, Shenandoah, '79 282
Banana Flip, '83 303
Banana-Pineapple Milk Shake, '84 59
Banana Smoothie, '87 160
Berry Milk Shake, Double-, '00 81
Berry Smoothie, Four-, '97 173
Brandy Cream, '84 312; '00 271
Cappuccino Cooler, Low-Fat, '01 166
Champagne Delight, '83 304
Chocoholic Smoothie, '97 173
Chocolate-Mint Smoothie, '84 166
Coffee Floats, Maple-, '86 195
Coffee Punch, Creamy, '81 50
Coffee Refresher, Velvet, '79 149
Coffee Soda, '97 272
Cranberry Float, Sparkling, '86 195
Cranberry-Orange Soda, '79 148
Cranberry Shake, '83 171
Fruit Float, Frosty, '87 159
Ginger Fizz, Ice Cream, '83 303
Golden Dream, '82 100
Kahlúa Velvet Frosty, '82 244
Lime Cooler, '87 160
Lime Fizz, '81 172
Lime-Pineapple Punch, '83 142
Mocha Melt, Spiced, '01 240
Mocha Punch, '84 166
Orange Milk Shake, '84 166
Orange Shake, Peachy, '81 156
Peach Frosty, '81 156
Peanut Butter Milkshakes, '85 198
Peanut Butter Shake, '82 48
Pineapple-Buttermilk Shake, '01 173
Pineapple-Buttermilk Shake, Light, '01 173
Pineapple Smoothie, Peachy-, '97 173
Pineapple Soda, '90 179
Pink Soda, Blushing, '90 104
Punch, Coffee-Ice-Cream, '05 136
Punch, Creamy Nog, '01 240
Punch, Parsonage, '79 148
Raisin Shake, Amazin', '86 195
Raspberry Fizz, Rosy, '90 179
Rum Coffee Cream, Icy, '83 172
Shake, Pep, '79 38
Strawberry-Banana Float, '87 160
Strawberry-Banana Shake, Double, '01 173
Strawberry Milkshake, Fresh, '82 113
Strawberry-Pineapple Shake, '84 166
Strawberry Punch, Creamy, '86 195
Strawberry Smoothie, '86 183
Strawberry Soda, Old-Fashioned, '79 149
Tahitian Flower, '87 159
Vanilla Cream, '97 272
Vanilla Frosty, French, '79 148
Whispers, '86 317
Black Forest Ice Cream, '88 203
Blueberry Ice Cream, '88 203
Blueberry-Peach Ice Cream, '00 153
Bombe, Amber, '80 255
Bombe, Ice Cream, '82 305; '90 269
Bombe with Raspberry Sauce, Creamy, '89 322
Bourbon Ice Cream, '87 139

Bourbon-Pecan Ice Cream, '00 260
Bread, Ice-Cream, '05 252
Brownie Dessert, Special-Occasion, '87 139
Brownies, Chocolate Ice Cream, '89 124
Butter Crisp Ice Cream, '92 132
Buttermilk-Lime Ice Cream, '04 103
Butter Pecan Ice Cream, '80 176; '86 129; '88 202
Butter-Pecan Ice Cream, '96 134
Cake for Grown-Ups, Ice Cream, '88 M192
Cake, Fruity Ice Cream, '87 110
Cake, Ice Cream, '86 321; '89 71
Cake, Ice Cream Angel, '83 23
Cake, No-Bake Ice-Cream Angel Food, '05 107
Cake, Praline Ice Cream, '80 84
Candy Crunch Ice Cream, '79 166
Cantaloupe Ice Cream, '79 177
Caramel Ice Cream Dessert, '95 36
Caramel-Vanilla Helado (Caramel-Vanilla Ice Cream), '81 67
Cherry Ice Cream, '84 184; '99 156
Cherry-Nut Ice Cream, '86 129
Cherry-Pecan Ice Cream, '88 203
Chocolate-Almond Ice Cream, No-Cook, '04 179
Chocolate Chunk-Peanut Butter Ice Cream, '85 297; '86 120
Chocolate Cookie Ice Cream, '95 245
Chocolate-Covered Peanut Ice Cream, '88 203
Chocolate Ice Cream, '80 176; '86 129
Chocolate Ice Cream, Double-, '88 203
Chocolate Ice Cream, Mexican, '91 162
Chocolate Ice Cream, No-Cook, '04 179
Cinnamon Ice Cream, '95 126
Cinnamon Ice Cream Sombreros, '93 276
Coconut Ice Cream, '98 180
Coconut Ice Cream, Fresh, '79 166
Coconut Ice Cream, No-Cook, '04 179
Coconut Ice Cream, Simple, '02 232
Coconut Ice Cream, Toasted, '00 143
Coffee Ice Cream, '88 202
Coffee Ice Cream Crunch, '82 182
Cookies and Cream Ice Cream, '88 203
Crêpes, Coffee Ice Cream, '84 85
Crêpes, Strawberry Ice Cream, '87 290
Delight, Ice Cream, '80 69
Dessert, Decadent Ice Cream, '91 56
Dessert, Ice Cream-Toffee, '00 176; '03 182; '04 82
Dessert, Layered Ice Cream, '83 189; '84 94, 105; '86 163
Dessert, Rocky Road Ice Cream, '00 332
Fennel Ice Cream, '95 281
Fig Ice Cream, '87 139
Fig-Mint Ice Cream, No-Cook, '04 179
Frangelica Cream, '89 291
French-Fried Ice Cream, '85 141
Fried Ice Cream, Coconut, '85 141
Fried Ice Cream Puffs, '85 141
Fruit Cream, Frozen, '94 129
Fudge-Peanut Ice Cream Dessert, '88 167
Galore and More, Ice Cream, '91 144
Granitas
Coffee-Kahlúa Granita, '88 118
Ginger Tea Granita, '98 334
Grape Granita, '88 118
Honeydew Granita, '87 162
Mint Tea Granita, '88 117
Orange Granita, '88 118
Raspberry Liqueur Granita, '88 117
Watermelon Granita, '96 179; '98 165; '04 171
Wild Raspberry Tea Granita, '99 89
Hawaiian Frappé, '81 178
Honey Ice Cream, '99 212
Honey-Vanilla Ice Cream, '95 178
Ice Milks
Banana Yogurt Ice Milk, '89 199
Strawberry Ice Milk, Fresh, '92 94

ICE CREAMS
(continued)

Ices

Apricot Yogurt Ice, '81 177
Avocado Ice, '83 179
Champagne Ice, '90 315
Cider Ice, '83 162
Cranberry-Apple Ice, '82 290
Cranberry Ice, Tangy, '87 305
Cranberry-Orange Ice, Tart, '86 317
Fruit Ice, '86 176
Fruit Ice, Mixed, '81 178
Fruit Ice, Three-, '02 51
Grapefruit Ice, '91 122
Grape Ice, '83 162
Kiwi Ice, '84 315
Lemon Ice, '00 176; '01 330; '02 201
Merlot Ice, '93 323
Muscadine Ice, '82 202
Peach Ice, '81 178
Peach-Yogurt Ice, '84 83
Pink Grapefruit Ice, '85 304
Raspberry Ice, '92 268
Strawberry Ice, '84 175; '85 108
Strawberry-Orange Ice, '86 196
Tropical Ice, '99 105
Watermelon Ice, '91 173
Wine Ice, '83 163
Irish Cream Ice Cream, '98 221
Italian-Style Ice Cream, '79 245
Kick-the-Can Ice Cream, '00 171
Layered Ice-Cream Freeze, Two-, '01 197
Lemonade Ice Cream, '88 202
Lemon Ice Cream, '79 142; '83 170; '91 65; '97 160; '00 55
Lemon Ice Cream Tarts, '80 152
Lime Ice Cream, Fresh, '97 160
Loaf, Pink Lemonade Ice Cream, '88 202
Log, Ice Cream Yule, '83 253
Making Ice Cream, About, '82 171
Mango Ice Cream, '86 216
Mint-Chocolate Chip Ice Cream, '88 202
Mint-Chocolate Chip Ice Cream Squares, '94 245
Mint Ice-Cream Angel Dessert, Triple, '93 86
Mint Ice Cream Dessert, '88 66
Mocha Ice Cream, '88 202; '97 M145
Oatmeal in a Slow Cooker with Ice Cream, '99 193
Orange Ice Cream, '97 160
Orange Pekoe-Chocolate Ice Cream, '99 90
Orange-Pineapple Ice Cream, '86 117
Parfaits, Chocolate-Crème de Menthe, '85 161
Parfaits, Coffee Crunch, '82 159
Parfait, Strawberry, '79 99
Parfait, Surprise Strawberry, '86 151
Peach-Almond Ice Cream, '89 156
Peach-Cinnamon Ice Cream, '05 168
Peach Ice Cream, '81 184; '82 171; '83 159; '86 15; '93 135; '98 221
Peach Ice Cream, Creamy, '85 177
Peach Ice Cream, Deluxe, '80 176; '90 314
Peach Ice Cream, Fresh, '95 195
Peach Ice Cream, No-Cook, '04 179
Peach Ice Cream, Summertime, '02 158
Peanut Butter Ice Cream, '81 103; '88 64, 203; '00 143
Peanut Ice Cream, '92 132
Pecan-Caramel Crunch Ice Cream, '02 322
Peppermint Ice Cream, '80 176; '86 129

Pies

Banana Split Pie, Layered, '83 189
Caramel Ice Cream Pie, '82 181
Carrot Ice Cream Pie, '86 200
Chocolate-Ice Cream Pie, '87 224
Chocolate Ice Cream Pie, '91 56
Chocolate-Mint Ice Cream Pie, '81 144
Chocolate-Peanut Butter Ice Cream Pie, '98 244
Coffee Ice Cream Pie, '79 231
Divine Ice Cream Pie, Absolutely, '82 181
Double-Delight Ice Cream Pie, '89 72
Heavenly Ice Cream Pie, '82 181
Kona Ice Cream Pie, '83 189
Lemon Ice Cream Pie, '80 70
Lemony Ice Cream Pie, '99 207
Meringue-Pecan Crust, Ice Cream Pie with, '88 127
Mincemeat Ice Cream Pie, '99 285
Mint Ice Cream Pie, Triple, '98 217
Mocha-Pecan Mud Pie, '05 290
Nutty Ice Cream Pie, '91 180
Orange Cream Pie, '03 35
Peanutty Ice Cream Pie, '82 56
Peppermint Candy-Ice Cream Pie, '87 260
Pumpkin Ice Cream Pie, '81 272
Pumpkin-Ice Cream Pie, '87 243
Rum-Fruit Sauce, Ice Cream Pie with, '84 312
Spectacular, Ice-Cream Pie, '90 314
Strawberry-Lime Ice-Cream Pie, '05 89
Strawberry-Lime Ice-Cream Pie, Spiked, '05 89
Strawberry Smoothie Ice-Cream Pie, '05 89
Sundae Pie, Ice Cream, '94 244
Piña Colada Ice Cream, '91 181
Pineapple-Coconut Ice Cream, Mint Nectarines with, '05 123
Pineapple-Coconut Ice Cream, Mint Peaches with, '05 123
Pineapple-Mint Ice Cream, '84 186
Praline Freeze, '90 48
Praline Ice Cream, '89 318
Pralines and Cream Ice Cream, '82 184; '83 159
Pumpkin, Ice Cream, '96 255
Rainbow Candy Ice Cream, '88 202
Raspberry Ice Cream, '80 176
Raspberry Ice Cream, Fresh, '86 152
Rocky Road Ice Cream Dessert, '00 332
Roll, Chocolate-Frosted Ice Cream, '84 200
Roll, Strawberry Ice Cream, '84 105
Rum-Raisin Ice Cream, '97 145
Salad, Ice Cream, '79 126
Sandwiches, Butter Pecan Ice-Cream, '05 62
Sandwiches, Chocolate Cookie Ice Cream, '87 147
Sandwiches, Chocolate Ice Cream, '89 72
Sandwiches, Chocolate Ice-Cream, '04 329
Sandwiches, Easy Chocolate-Mint Ice-Cream, '05 62
Sandwiches, Ice Cream, '99 147
Sandwiches, Mocha-Almond-Fudge Ice-Cream, '05 62
Sandwiches, Oatmeal Crispy Ice-Cream, '93 199
Sandwiches, Oatmeal-Rum-Raisin Ice-Cream, '05 62
Sandwiches, Peanut Butter Cookie Ice Cream, '93 199
Sandwiches, Peanutty Ice-Cream, '05 62
Sandwich Shells, Brownie Ice Cream, '88 195
Scuppernong Ice Cream, '88 216
Snow Ice Cream, '88 10

Sorbets

Ambrosia Sorbet, '04 317
Apricot-Almond Sorbet, '98 126
Avocado Sorbet, '88 117
Banana-Orange Sorbet, '88 117
Berry Sorbet, Very, '90 85
Blackberry-Lemon Sorbet, '02 85
Blueberry-Kirsch Sorbet, '83 120
Cantaloupe Sorbet, '03 171
Cherry Sorbet, '03 171
Chocolate Sorbet, '97 111
Cran-Apple Spice Sorbet, '93 153
Cranberry Juice Sorbet, '85 259
Cranberry Sorbet, '82 251
Grapefruit-Mint Sorbet, '93 153
Grapefruit Sorbet, '03 171
Lemon Sorbet, '93 153; '03 171
Mango Sorbet, '86 196
Merlot Sorbet, '97 111
Orange Sorbet, '03 171
Orange Sorbet, Fresh, '92 143
Peach Sorbet, '93 153; '97 110
Pear-Lemon Sorbet, '88 116
Pineapple Sorbet, '03 171
Pink Grapefruit and Tarragon Sorbet, '95 163
Raspberry Sorbet, '03 171
Strawberry-Champagne Sorbet, '83 162; '95 20
Strawberry Margarita Sorbet, '89 111
Strawberry-Passion Fruit Sorbet, '98 180
Strawberry Sorbet, '88 117; '93 153; '03 171
Tropical Sorbet, '97 110
Watermelon Sorbet, '92 190; '99 166; '03 171
South Seas Ice Cream with Sweet Heat Salsa and Cinnamon Crisps, '04 315
Spiced Ice Cream, '98 259; '99 26
Squares, Ice Cream Party, '91 214
Straw-Ba-Nut Ice Cream, '80 177
Strawberries and Cream, '92 132
Strawberry-Banana-Nut Ice Cream, '88 203
Strawberry Ice Cream, '80 177; '98 221
Strawberry Ice Cream Crêpes, '88 135
Strawberry Ice Cream, Fresh, '89 111
Strawberry Ice Cream, Homemade, '84 184
Strawberry Ice Cream, No-Cook, '04 179
Strawberry Ice Cream, Old-Fashioned, '79 94
Strawberry Ice Cream, Very, '81 155

Sundaes

Apple Ice Cream Sundaes, Spicy, '86 M195
Cocoa-Kahlúa Sundaes, '83 M58
Hot Fudge Sundae Dessert, '84 313
Ice Cream Sundae, '01 64
Mauna Loa Sundaes, '80 126
Peach Sundaes Flambé, '81 88
Pear Sundaes, Quick, '86 71
Strawberry Sundaes, Hot, '81 M5
Tropical Sundae, '04 179
Toffee Ice Cream, '88 202
Toffee Ice Cream Dessert, '87 110
Toffee Ice-Cream Dessert, '97 134
Treats, Crunchy Ice Cream, '86 300; '87 178
Tropical Paradise, Frozen, '89 206
Turtle Ice Cream, No-Cook, '04 M179
Tutti-Frutti Ice Cream, '86 129
Vanilla-Cinnamon Ice Cream, '00 127; '01 195
Vanilla Custard Ice Cream, '92 148; '96 145; '98 221; '00 143
Vanilla Ice Cream, '80 176; '86 129; '91 174; '04 275
Vanilla Ice Cream, Basic, '88 202
Vanilla Ice Cream, Country, '82 143
Vanilla Ice Cream, No-Cook, '04 179
Vanilla Ice Cream, Old-Fashioned, '97 166
Vanilla Ice Cream Spectacular, '82 166
ICE CUBES. *See* BEVERAGES.
ICINGS. *See* FROSTINGS.

JAMBALAYAS

Black-Eyed Pea Jambalaya, '92 70
Cajun Jambalaya, Smoky, '96 62
Chicken-and-Ham Jambalaya with Shrimp, '04 99
Chicken-and-Sausage Jambalaya, '88 200; '91 216; '01 278; '02 36; '03 201
Crawfish Jambalaya, '05 118
Creole Jambalaya, '81 51; '87 210; '03 83
de Covington, Jambalaya, '87 211
Good Luck Jambalaya, '87 11
Jambalaya, '84 282; '98 317; '03 144; '04 288
Mix, Jambalaya, '98 317
1-2-3 Jambalaya, '97 301

Oven Jambalaya, '84 44
Red Rice Jambalaya, '91 18
Sausage Jambalaya, '80 210; '84 249
Seafood Jambalaya, Three-, '82 126
Shrimp Jambalaya, Creole, '92 99
Smoked Sausage Jambalaya, '79 42
Trail Jambalaya, '93 179
Tuna Jambalaya, '83 44

JAMS AND JELLIES
Apple Jelly, '82 149
Apple Jelly, Spiced, '95 251
Apple-Mint Jelly, '87 134
Apricot Jam, Golden, '80 31
Apricot Jam, Quick-Cooked, '99 146
Banana Jam, '82 296
Basil Jelly, '82 301
Basil Jelly, Tart, '03 135
Blackberry Jam, '82 149; '89 138; '99 M131
Blackberry Jelly, '82 149
Blueberry Jam, '79 120; '85 130
Cantaloupe-Peach Jam, '95 143
Champagne Jelly, '90 248
Chile Piquin Jelly, '94 28
Christmas Brunch Jam, '81 286
Christmas Jam, '88 288
Coffee-Onion Jam, '05 123
Conserves
   Apple-Cranberry Conserve, '82 308
   Blueberry Conserve, '82 149
   Cranberry Conserve, '79 243; '85 266; '03 278
   Cranberry Conserve, Caramelized Chicken with, '98 320
   Cranberry-Coriander Conserve, '04 287
   Fruit Conserve, Dried, '82 308
   Peach Conserve, '79 120
Crabapple Jelly, '79 120; '81 217; '89 139
Cranberry-Wine Jelly, '81 290
Di-Calcium Phosphate Solution, '89 138
Fig Jam, '86 206
Freezer
   Blackberry Jam, Freezer, '84 M181
   Christmas Freezer Jelly, '86 M288
   Garlic Pepper Jelly, '99 221
   Grape-Burgundy Freezer Jelly, '85 130
   Peach Jam, Freezer, '83 182; '84 M182
   Peach-Plum Freezer Jam, '85 130
   Plum Jam, Freezer, '89 M156
   Raspberry Freezer Jam, '84 M181
   Strawberry Freezer Jam, '84 M182
   Strawberry Preserves, Freezer, '82 112
Garlic Jelly, '99 283
Grape Jelly, '89 140
Grape Jelly, Quick, '89 M156
Grape Jelly, Thyme-, '89 193
Green Pepper Jelly, Unusual, '82 132
Green Tomato-Blueberry Jam, '01 140
Green Tomato Jam, '79 121
Honey-Lemon Jelly, '97 29
Jalapeño Jelly, '92 230; '96 292
Jalapeño Pepper Jelly, Quick, '96 275
Kudzu Blossom Jelly, '95 198
Lemon Jam, Tri-Berry, '98 214
Lime Jelly, '94 23
Marmalades
   Apple Marmalade, '79 120
   Blueberry-Citrus Marmalade, Spicy, '03 135
   Blueberry Marmalade, '96 145
   Carrot-Citrus Marmalade, '81 148
   Carrot-Orange Marmalade, '03 134
   Citrus Marmalade, '80 101; '97 32
   Citrus Marmalade, Combination, '80 50
   Citrus Marmalade, Mixed, '81 43
   Fruit Marmalade, Delicious, '81 285
   Grapefruit Marmalade, '82 308

Green Tomato Marmalade, '01 140
Kumquat Marmalade, '90 48
Muscadine Marmalade, '98 220
Onion Marmalade, Fruited, '97 27
Orange Marmalade, '81 42
Orange Marmalade, Sunny, '02 27
Orange-Pineapple Marmalade, '82 150; '89 M156
Peach-Orange Marmalade, '82 150
Pear Marmalade, '79 196
Strawberry-Pineapple Marmalade, '85 130
Tomato Marmalade, '00 170
Watermelon-and-Ginger Marmalade, '98 164
Mint Jelly, '79 121; '82 301; '03 135
Muscadine Jelly, Wild, '79 32
Onion Jelly, '93 135
Peach-Banana Jam, Rosy, '80 142
Peach Jam, '93 135
Peach Jam, Spiced, '00 51
Peach-Rosemary Jam, '03 134
Pear Jam, Paradise, '84 300
Pear Jam, Spiced, '98 214
Pepper Jelly, '79 121
Pineapple Jam, '81 147
Pineapple-Orange Mint Jelly, '92 105
Plum Jelly, '82 150
Port Wine Jelly with Whipped Cream, '84 254
Preserves
   Custard Preserves, '98 126
   Fig Preserves, '79 140; '82 150; '89 140; '96 195; '00 175
   Fruity Preserves, '98 214
   Mango-Pineapple Preserves, '79 137
   Peach Preserves, '81 147; '89 140
   Peach Preserves, Honeyed, '85 130
   Peach Preserves, Old-Fashioned, '82 150
   Pear Preserves, '82 195
   Plum Preserves, '03 161
   Strawberry-Fig Preserves, Quick, '96 194
   Strawberry Preserves, '79 120; '81 96
   Strawberry Preserves Deluxe, '82 150
   Tomato Preserves, '98 214
   Watermelon Preserves, '79 120
Raspberry Jam, Mock, '96 168
Red Bell Pepper Jam, '95 242
Red Pepper Jelly, '89 M156
Red Zinger Jelly, '99 89
Refrigerator
   Berry Refrigerator Jam, '89 139
   Blueberry Refrigerator Jam, '89 139
   Pepper Jelly, Easiest, '03 135
   Plum Refrigerator Jam, '89 139
Rose Geranium Jelly, '82 301
Rosemary Jelly, '82 301
Sage Jelly, '82 301
Sangría Jelly, '93 341
Scuppernong Jelly, '98 220
Southwest Jelly, '03 135
Strawberry Jam, '89 138
Strawberry Jelly, '81 147
Strawberry-Port Jam, '03 134
Thyme Jelly, '82 301
Wine Jelly, '88 243; '98 125
Wine Jelly, Rosy, '85 306
Zucchini Jam, '00 168
JÍCAMA
Compote, Jícama-Fruit, '92 49
French-Fried Jícama, '81 88
Parsleyed Jícama, '81 88
Pico de Gallo, '98 174
Salad, Cranberry-Strawberry-Jícama, '02 300
Salad, Fruit-Jícama, '00 203
Salad, Jícama, '87 123
Salad, Jícama-and-Orange, '88 246
Salad, Jícama-Fruit, '86 83

Salad, Jícama-Orange, '86 83; '90 122
Salad, Pear, Jícama, and Snow Pea, '01 329
Salad with Jícama and Snow Peas, Pear, '01 56
Soup with Crunchy Jícama, Tomatillo, '97 143
Tomatillo Soup with Crunchy Jícama, '92 245
Wreath, Tex-Mex, '96 241

KEBABS
Antipasto Kebabs, '94 144
Beef
   Beef Kebabs, '85 110
   Chile-Beef Kebabs, '94 251
   Deluxe Beef Kebabs, '82 182
   Flank Steak Skewers, Lemon, '02 134
   Grilled Kebabs, Spicy, '98 158
   Hot-and-Spicy Kebabs, '87 193
   Marinated Beef Kebabs, '82 105; '85 159
   Marinated Beef Kebabs with Rice, '84 32
   Marinated Beef Kebabs with Vegetables, '99 292
   Meatball Kebabs, '95 192
   Pineapple-Beef Kebabs, '83 212
   Saucy Beef Kebabs, '83 109
   Shish Kebabs, Beef Tenderloin, '00 200
   Shrimp Kebabs, Steak-and-, '00 124
   Sirloin Kebabs, Marinated, '82 162
   Spirited Beef Kebabs, '87 142
   Steak-and-Shrimp Kebabs, '80 184
   Steak-and-Vegetable Kebabs, '04 218
   Steak Kebabs, '82 4; '93 95
   Steak Kebabs, Barbecued, '79 89
   Steak Kebabs, Marinated, '80 184
   Steak on a Stick, '83 109
   Steak with Vegetables, Skewered, '81 124
   Stick, Beef on a, '99 336
   Teriyaki Beef Kebabs, '80 207
   Vegetable Kebabs, Beef-and-, '91 148
   Vegetables, Beef Kebabs with, '90 148
Cantaloupe Wedges, Grilled, '87 162
Cheese Kebabs, Peppered, '91 279
Fish Kebabs, '98 223
Fruit Kebabs, '86 181; '89 85
Fruit Kebabs, Grilled, '97 147
Fruit Kebabs, Winter, '89 34
Fruit Kebabs with Coconut Dressing, '87 251
Fruit Kebabs with Mint Marinade, '82 157
Fruity Mermaid Kebabs, '91 177
Ham Kebabs, Honey, '80 156
Ham Kebabs, Swiss-, '81 124
Lamb Kebabs, '85 159; '86 90; '92 129; '95 192; '00 220; '03 136
Lamb Kebabs, Apricot-Grilled, '98 102
Lamb Kebabs, Rosemary Marinated, '93 203
Lamb Kebabs, Saucy, '89 167
Lamb Kebabs, Savory, '80 184
Lamb, Rosemary-Skewered, '97 190
Lamb Shish Kebabs, '79 142; '93 70
Liver Kebabs, '80 185
Mixed Grill with Spicy Peanut Sauce, Saté, '04 134
Oysters Brochette, '80 56
Pepper Kebabs, Pretty, '90 166
Pineapple-Pork Kebabs, '99 144
Pineapple Skewers with Rum Sauce, Grilled, '04 247
Pork Kebabs, Margarita, '98 M223
Pork Kebabs, Spicy, '82 182
Pork Kebabs with Sesame Seeds, '00 337
Pork Saté, '05 53
Pork Tenders, Skewered, '00 200
Poultry
   Chicken-Avocado Kebabs, '82 9; '83 68
   Chicken, Garlic-Grilled, '87 180
   Chicken Kebabs, '87 141; '03 180
   Chicken Kebabs, Good-and-Easy, '85 87
   Chicken Kebabs, Marinated, '84 M144

KEBABS, Poultry
(continued)

Chicken Kebabs, Oriental, '95 193
Chicken Kebabs, Pineapple-, '86 M328
Chicken Kebabs, Sesame, '82 165
Chicken Kebabs, Soy-, '86 156
Chicken Kebabs Supreme, '81 124
Chicken Livers en Brochette, '84 222
Chicken-Pineapple Kebabs, '00 200
Chicken Saté, '99 134
Chicken, Sesame, '97 256
Chicken Skewers, Taco-, '99 119
Chicken Skewers with Peanut Sauce, '02 173;
  '04 324
Chicken-Vegetable Kebabs, '03 95
Chicken with Cha-Cha Salsa, Grilled Bahamian,
  '97 160
Duck Kebabs with Almond Rice, Grilled, '91 291
Hawaiian Kebabs, '85 157
Rumaki Kebabs, '82 182
Turkey-and-Fruit Kebabs, '88 140
Salmon Kebabs, '81 182
Scallop-Bacon Kebabs, '81 111
Scallop Kebabs, Grilled, '83 101
Scallop Kebabs, Sea, '82 162
Scallops en Brochette with Vegetables, '80 163
Seafood Brochette, '87 96
Shish Kebabs, '82 182; '85 M112
Shish Kebabs, Overnight, '81 124
Shish Kebabs Teriyaki, '85 37
Shrimp
Appetizer Shrimp Kebabs, '91 251
Bacon and Jalapeños, Grilled Shrimp with, '05 M200
Barbecued Shrimp, '90 28
Grilled Shrimp with Smoky Sweet Sauce, Mexican-,
  '03 32
Jerk Shrimp with Creamy Tomatillo Sauce, Grilled,
  '01 332
Marinated and Grilled Shrimp, '87 141
Marinated Shrimp, Grilled, '87 173
Marinated Shrimp Kebabs, '84 276; '85 158
Scallop Kebabs, Grilled Shrimp-and-, '92 210
Shrimp Kebabs, '80 150, 184
Steak-and-Shrimp Kebabs, '80 184; '00 124
Vegetable Salsa, Shrimp Skewers with, '98 32, 223
Squash-and-Pepper Kebabs, Summery, '95 193
Swordfish-Shiitake Skewers, '97 168
Tomatoes with Basil Vinaigrette, Grilled, '97 168
Vegetable Kebabs, '01 132
Vegetable Kebabs, Easy, '02 142
Vegetable Kebabs, Fresh, '81 158; '92 101
Vegetable Kebabs, Grilled, '93 170
Vegetable Kebabs, Marinated, '83 M195
Vegetable Kebabs, Tangy Marinated, '88 142
Vegetable Skewers, Grilled, '94 160
Venison Kebabs, '82 215; '88 249
Watermelon, Sherried, '92 117
KIWIFRUIT
Chutney, Kiwifruit-Onion, '93 125
Dessert, Kiwi-and-Orange, '93 295
Glacé, Sabayon, '89 306
Ice, Kiwi, '84 315
Jubilee, Kiwi, '83 120
Meringue Cups, Kiwi and Cream in, '81 279
Muffins, Kiwifruit, '87 255
Orange Roughy, Kiwi, '87 193
Parfait, Kiwi, '86 199; '87 55
Pizza, Kiwi-Berry, '86 198; '87 55
Pizza, Kiwifruit, '89 306
Pops, Kiwi Margarita, '99 133
Salad, Peach-and-Kiwi, '90 180
Salad, Spinach-Kiwifruit, '87 305

Salsa, Hot Kiwifruit, '94 82
Slushy, Kiwi-Peach, '00 201
Spritzer, Kiwi-Lemonade, '03 89
Spritzer, Strawberry-Kiwi-Lemonade,
  '03 89
Tart, Kiwifruit, '89 232
Tart, Kiwifruit-Peach, '88 20
KUGEL
Apricot Noodle Kugel, '92 251
Mushroom Matzo Kugel, '00 83
Noodle Casserole, Sweet, '02 238
Nu Awlins Kugel, '94 229
Sweet Kugel, '90 254
Vegetable-Noodle Kugel, '96 228

L
LAMB
Barbecued Lamb, '79 58
Burgers, Mesquite-Grilled Lamb, '88 59
Burgers with Cucumber Sauce, Lamb, '98 102
Burgoo, Five-Meat, '87 3
Casserole, Moussaka, '79 179
Chops
Apples, Lamb Chops with Minted, '00 20
Baked Lamb Chops, Easy, '02 66
Barbecued Lamb Chops, '79 89
Broiled Lamb Chops, '85 22
Broiled Lamb Chops with Southwestern Butter,
  '01 194
Dijonaise, Gourmet Lamb Chops, '82 93
Dijon Lamb Chops, '84 277
Dijon Lamb Chops, Creamy, '04 108; '05 82
Dijon-Rosemary Lamb Chops, '95 285; '99 333
Fried Lamb Chops, '02 66
Glazed Lamb Chops, '02 66
Grilled Lamb Chops, '91 163
Grilled Lamb Chops, Rosemary, '03 125
Grilled Lamb Chops with Chipotle and Cilantro Oils,
  '02 96; '03 98
Grilled Lamb Chops with Pineapple-Mint Salsa,
  '05 52
Grilled Lamb Chops with Rosemary Sauce and Wild
  Rice-Fennel Pilaf, '97 127
Herbs, Lamb Chops with, '90 164
Maple-Glazed Lamb Chops with Zesty Horseradish
  Sauce, '04 284
Mint Aioli, Lamb Chops with, '01 70
Minted Apples, Lamb Chops with, '99 230
Orange Lamb Chops, '83 35
Peppercorn-Crusted Lamb Chops, '92 142
Rosemary-Cherry Lamb Chops, Smart and Saucy,
  '02 193
Rosemary Lamb Chops, Joan's, '97 42
Sage Lamb Chops, '96 M328
Shrimp, Lamb Chops with, '88 58
Teriyaki, Lamb Chops, '85 109
Teriyaki Lamb Chops, '87 60
Curried Lamb with Rice, '82 93
Curried Lamb with Rice Mold, '85 36
Curry, Creamy Lamb, '04 202
Curry with Rice, Lamb, '80 83; '81 10
Fillets of Lamb with Vegetables, '85 36
Grape Leaves, Stuffed, '94 48
Grilled Lamb with Sweet Pepper Relish, '95 104
Kebabs
Grilled Lamb Kebabs, Apricot-, '98 102
Lamb Kebabs, '85 159; '86 90; '92 129; '95 192;
  '00 220; '03 136
Marinated Lamb Kebabs, Rosemary, '93 203
Rosemary-Skewered Lamb, '97 190
Saucy Lamb Kebabs, '89 167
Savory Lamb Kebabs, '80 184
Shish Kebabs, '82 182; '85 M112
Shish Kebabs, Lamb, '79 142; '93 70

Shish Kebabs, Overnight, '81 124
Shish Kebabs Teriyaki, '85 37
Leg of Lamb
Cranberry Leg of Lamb, '90 52
Curried Leg of Lamb with Cucumber-Yogurt Sauce,
  '03 44
Extraordinaire, Lamb, '99 242
Glazed Lamb, Honey-Mustard, '90 52
Glazed Leg of Lamb, '86 90
Greek-Style Leg of Lamb, '93 170
Grilled Lamb with Mango Salsa, '95 104
Grilled Leg of Lamb, '96 88; '98 103
Half of Leg of Lamb, '86 90
Hawaii, Lamb, '81 58
Hunter Sauce, Leg of Lamb with, '95 317
Leg of Lamb, '86 90; '95 285
Mustard Sauce, Leg of Lamb with, '89 71
Roasted Lamb Rosemary, '88 244
Roasted Leg of Lamb with Port, '02 258
Roasted Rosemary Lamb, '86 89
Roast, Garlic-Rolled Lamb, '92 128; '93 113
Roast Leg of Lamb, '87 96; '99 242; '00 275;
  '01 159
Rosemary-Crusted Lamb with Tzatziki Sauce,
  '04 108; '05 82
Sandwiches, Lamb, '97 107
Smoked Leg of Lamb, '98 102
Stuffed Leg of Lamb, '82 93; '87 248
Stuffed Leg of Lamb, Garlic-and-Herb, '99 241
Meatballs with Yogurt Sauce, Lamb, '85 132
Meat Loaf, Greek, '96 251; '97 103
Meat Loaf, Minted Lamb, '93 248
Meat Loaf with Feta Cheese, Lamb, '97 24
Mint-Crusted Lamb, '99 163
Moussaka, '87 166
Patties, Grilled Lamb, '02 167
Pie, Lamb, '90 26
Pilaf, Hearty Lamb, '83 101
Pockets with Dilled Cucumber Topping, Lamb,
  '87 104
Quenelles, Veal-Vermicelli Soup with, '94 14
Rack, Greek Lemon Lamb, '97 247
Rack of Lamb, '89 270
Rack of Lamb, Dijon, '02 276
Rack of Lamb, Marinated, '94 55
Rack of Lamb, Mint-Crusted, '98 118
Rack of Lamb with Cherry-Wine Sauce, Hazelnut-
  Crusted, '95 284
Rack of Lamb with Herb Mustard Glaze, '81 260
Rack, Pistachio-Crusted Lamb, '03 242
Roasted Lamb with Vegetables, '98 266
Roast of Lamb, Crown, '81 58
Roast, Rolled Lamb, '95 285
Salad, Spinach-Lamb, '85 58
Shanks, Barbecued Lamb, '92 128; '93 113
Shanks, Braised Lamb, '00 62
Shanks Braised with Tomatoes, Lamb, '03 87
Shanks Milanaise, Lamb, '82 93
Soup with Spring Vegetables, Lamb, '04 108
Steak, Destin Lamb, '92 129; '93 113
Steaks with Béarnaise Sauce, Lamb, '85 37
Stewed Lamb with Five Spices, '92 72
Stew, Emerald Isle, '95 71
Stew-in-a-Loaf, Lamb, '85 37
Stew, Lamb, '79 293; '88 58
Stew, Lamb-and-Okra, '97 156
Stew with Popovers, Lamb, '94 43
Stir-Fry, Indian, '92 126
LASAGNA
Beefy Lasagna, '80 81
Bun, Lasagna in a, '90 176
Cheesy Lasagna, '82 224; '88 299
Chicken Lasagna, '87 M302; '88 90; '92 197; '93 25;
  '96 16

Chicken Lasagna Bake, '95 55
Chicken Lasagna Florentine, '95 158; '02 232
Chicken Lasagna, Heavenly, '00 310
Chicken Lasagna, Southwestern, '03 173
Crabmeat-and-Spinach Lasagna, '04 292
Crabmeat Lasagna, '96 290
Crawfish Lasagna, '91 89
Cups, Lasagna, '04 293
Easy Lasagna, '92 M197; '93 M24
Egg-Noodle Lasagna, '04 219
Ellie's Lasagna, '02 186
Extra-Easy Lasagna, '00 326
Gourmet White Lasagna, '96 225
Green Chile-Chicken Lasagna, '00 338
Ground Sirloin Lasagna, '03 143
Ham-and-Chicken Lasagna, Creamy, '95 88
Italian Sausage Lasagna, '96 225
Lasagna, '82 119; '83 M6; '98 95
Lean Lasagna, '86 37
Light Lasagna, '95 212
Maria, Lasagna, '90 191
Meatball Lasagna, '00 243; '03 142
Mexican Lasagna, '89 63; '98 283; '01 282
Mexican Lasagna, Easy, '03 22
Microwave Lasagna, '96 M225
Noodles Lasagna, Lots of, '91 M127
One-Step Lasagna, '89 M129
Pizza, Lasagna, '85 285
Polenta Lasagna with Cream Sauce, '03 237
Quick Lasagna, '84 220
Quick 'n Easy Lasagna, '80 M10
Roasted Vegetable-Meat Lasagna, '99 M332
Rolls, Pepper-Topped Lasagna, '89 M36
Rollups, Artichoke-Red Pepper, '02 231
Sausage Lasagna, '83 288
Sausage-Lasagna Rollups, '80 236
Sausage Pinwheels, Lasagna, '79 6
Simple Lasagna, '81 188
South-of-the-Border Lasagna, '84 31
Speedy Lasagna, '05 M252
Spinach-Black Bean Lasagna, '02 44
Supreme, Lasagna, '92 198; '93 24
Taco Lasagna, Fiesta, '05 140
Texas Lasagna, '98 52
Tex-Mex Lasagna, '05 58
Tofu Lasagna, '83 312
Tuna Lasagna, '83 44; '84 123
Turkey Lasagna, '83 239; '91 130
Turkey-Picante Lasagna, '97 93
Two, Lasagna for, '81 91
Vegetable
    Avocado-Vegetable Lasagna, '01 310
    Casserole, Vegetable Lasagna, '92 198; '93 25
    Cheese-Vegetable Lasagna, Saucy, '01 306
    Cheesy Vegetable Lasagna, '79 84
    Colorful Vegetable Lasagna, '87 19
    Florentine, Creamy Lasagna, '91 94
    Florentine, Lasagna, '88 196
    Garden Lasagna, '83 119
    Spaghetti Squash Lasagna, '84 127
    Spinach-Bean Lasagna, '92 96
    Spinach Lasagna, '79 25; '81 243
    Spinach Lasagna, Cheesy, '80 32; '83 204; '01 196
    Spinach Lasagna, Won Ton, '04 129
    Vegetable Lasagna, '84 201; '93 320; '95 211;
        '96 47; '99 97
    Zucchini Lasagna, '85 194
Vintage Lasagna, '79 194
Zesty Lasagna, '87 M188
LEEKS
Bisque, Crab-and-Leek, '94 104
Brussels Sprouts and Almonds, Leeks with, '00 222
Chicken and Leeks in Parchment, '97 290
Creamed Leeks, '00 222

Dilled Lemon-Butter, Leeks in, '90 M98
Dilly Leek Combo, '82 26
Dip, Creamy Leek, '86 77
Fritters, Leek-and-Potato, '00 324
Glazed Leeks, '82 26
Glazed Leeks, Honey-, '86 62
Gratin, Potato-Leek, '05 281
Linguine, Leeks and Peppers with, '98 68
Mashed Potatoes, Creamy Leek, '05 334
Medley, Carrot-and-Leek, '88 102
Orange Sauce, Leeks in, '88 86
Potatoes, Creamy Leek Mashed, '02 291
Potatoes, Leek Mashed, '02 98; '03 293
Quiche, Cheddar-Leek, '88 198
Roasted Leeks, '00 222
Roasted Potatoes, Carrots, and Leeks, '94 276
Soup, Carrot-and-Leek, '02 260
Soup, Carrot-Leek, '86 34
Soup, Cream of Leek, '99 276
Soup, Cream of Mushroom-and-Leek, '01 312
Soup, Cream of Squash and Leek, '04 42
Soup, Leek-and-Potato, '84 112
Soup, Leek-Vegetable, '86 304
Soup, Watercress-and-Leek, '86 161
Tarragon Leeks, '84 66
Tart, Leek-Goat Cheese, '04 109
Tart, Tomato-Leek-Bacon, '03 325
Terrine, Cold Chicken-Leek, '92 145
Veal Cutlets with Leeks and Zinfandel Cream, '96 237
Vinaigrette, Warm Leeks, '98 47
LEMON
Antipasto, Lemon-Vinaigrette Marinated, '04 256
Apples, Chilled Poached Lemon, '86 182
Artichoke Hearts with Lemon, '90 98
Asparagus, Lemon-Marinated, '03 119
Asparagus, Lemon-Sesame, '91 31
Asparagus with Lemon, '98 103
Bagel Chips, Lemon-and-Herb, '91 139
Basil, Cream of Tomato Soup with Lemon, '96 124
Beans, Lemon-Mint, '88 22
Beverages
    Appleade, Hot Spiced Lemon-, '05 23
    Apple Lemonade, '89 212; '03 169
    Berry Delicious Lemonade, '93 205
    Blackberry Lemonade, '99 130; '03 89
    Blueberry Lemonade, '98 179
    Caribbean Cooler, '95 203
    Cayenne Lemonade, '03 169
    Cherry-Berry Lemonade, '03 89
    Claret Lemonade, '93 72
    Concentrate, Lemonade, '89 110
    Cooler, Lemon, '82 48
    Cooler, Watermelon-Lemonade, '04 172
    Cranberry Lemonade, '05 205
    Cranberry Lemonade, Spiced, '87 292
    Cubes, Lemonade, '95 201
    Cubes, Lemonade Ice, '02 48
    Cubes, Lemon-Mint, '95 201
    Dazzling Lemonade, '97 99
    Frappé, Lemon, '92 44
    Fresh Lemonade, '00 139
    Fresh Squeezed Lemonade, '81 172
    Fresh-Squeezed Lemonade, '99 220
    Front Porch Lemonade, '90 156
    Glass, Lemonade by the, '96 161
    Homemade Lemonade, '01 143
    Hot Buttered Lemonade, '88 208; '94 18
    Loaded Lemonade, '01 93
    Margaritas, Lemon-Lime, '94 227
    Margaritas, Mock, '99 120
    Mist, Orange-Lemon, '79 288; '80 35
    Orange-Mint Lemonade, '88 82
    Piña Coladas, '95 203
    Pineapple Lemonade, '93 194

    Pink Lemonade, '01 163
    Punch, Lemonade-Bourbon, '95 287
    Punch, Lemon Balm, '80 42
    Punch, Lemon Champagne, '94 176
    Punch, Pink, '96 190
    Punch, Sparkling Lemonade, '88 276
    Punch, Strawberry-Lemonade, '85 116; '91 175
    Raspberry Lemonade, '03 89
    Raspberry Lemonade, Fizzy, '05 61
    Sipper, Sunshine, '86 179
    Slush, Lemon, '00 271
    Slush, Lemon-Rum, '00 271; '04 240
    Slush, Pink Lemonade, '80 151
    Slush, Strawberry-Lemonade, '03 169
    Southern Breeze, '02 185
    Spritzer, Kiwi-Lemonade, '03 89
    Spritzer, Lemon-Mint, '99 175
    Spritzer, Strawberry-Kiwi-Lemonade, '03 89
    Strawberry Lemonade, '80 160
    Strawberry Lemonade, Fizzy, '05 61
    Sunny Spring Lemonade, '00 70
    Sweetened Preserved Lemons, '95 141
    Sweet-Tart Lemonade, '96 161; '02 160
    Syrup, Cherry-Lemonade, '86 214
    Tea, Almond-Lemonade, '86 229; '99 207
    Tea Cubes, Lemonade with Frozen, '85 161
    Tea, Lemon, '82 156
    Tea, Lemon-Mint, '85 162
    Tea, Minted Lemon Iced, '00 131
    Tea, Sparkling Summer, '96 172
    Tea Tingler, Lemon, '95 200
    Velvet, Lemon, '90 15
    Watermelon Lemonade, '98 165
Breads
    Biscuits, Lemon Drop, '97 332
    Blueberry-Lemon Bread, '85 190
    French Bread, Lemony, '97 147
    Knots, Glazed Lemon, '86 290
    Lemon Bread, '79 275; '87 256
    Muffins, Blueberry-Lemon, '79 7
    Muffins, Fresh Lemon, '79 161
    Muffins, Lemon, '88 119, M275
    Muffins, Lemon-Blueberry, '03 26
    Muffins, Lemon-Poppy Seed, '05 33
    Muffins, Lemon-Raspberry, '92 119; '03 306
    Muffins, Poppy Seed-Lemon, '96 280
    Nut Bread, Lemon-, '79 24
    Pancakes, Lemon-Blueberry, '04 148
    Pecan Bread, Lemon-, '83 54
    Rolls, Lemon-Orange, '05 70
    Scones, Lemon-Poppy Seed, '97 44
    Scones, Lemon-Raisin, '87 69
    Spirals, French Lemon, '81 94
    Tea Bread, Lemon, '92 268; '93 183; '04 209
    Tea Bread, Lemon-Almond, '04 209
    Tea Bread, Lemon-Walnut, '05 59
    Tea Loaf, Lemon-Cream, '84 50
    Toast, Lemon-Garlic, '05 171
Broccoli Goldenrod, Lemon-, '84 M89
Broccoli, Lemon, '88 119; '95 53
Broccoli, Lemon Pepper Steamed, '02 215
Broccoli, Lemony Herbed, '02 45
Brussels Sprouts with Celery, Lemony, '85 25
Butter, Asparagus in Lemon, '80 M123
Butter, Asparagus with Lemon, '87 M151; '98 168
Butter, Catfish Pecan with Lemon-Thyme-Pecan, '04 68
Butter, Citrus, '03 307
Butter, Garlic-Lemon, '04 54
Butter, Green Beans with Lemon-Dill, '99 141
Butter, Honey-Lemon, '04 231
Butter, Lemon, '95 32; '96 124; '02 141
Butter, Lemon-Anchovy, '97 307
Butter, Lemon Pepper, '97 307
Butter, Thyme-Lemon, '96 121

LEMON
(continued)

Cabbage, Lemon-Butter, '88 156
Canapés, Lemon-Cheese, '87 93
Carrot Bundles, Lemon-, '91 80
Carrot Marmalemon, '96 107
Carrots and Rutabaga, Lemon-Glazed, '97 46
Carrots, Lemon, '82 300; '83 111
Carrots, Lemon-Dill Steamed, '93 180
Carrots, Lemon-Glazed, '84 16
Cauliflower, Easy Lemon, '83 322
Cheese Party Bites, Lemon-, '95 160
Cheese Patty, Lemon-Pepper, '84 117
Corn on the Cob, Lemony, '89 200
Couscous, Lemon, '96 154; '00 99; '02 237
Couscous with Raisins, Almonds, and Lemon, '00 295
Cream, Broccoli with Lemon, '89 245
Cream, Lemon, '03 213
Crêpes with Fruit Filling, Lemon, '82 46
Cucumbers, Lemony, '89 102
Curd, Lemon, '94 315
Desserts
 Apples, Chilled Poached Lemon, '86 182
 Bars Deluxe, Lemon, '79 35
 Bars, Lemon Yogurt Wheat, '79 93
 Bars, Luscious Lemon, '01 161
 Bars, Tangy Lemon, '86 217
 Cake Batter, Lemon-Poppy Seed, '05 287
 Cake, Coconut-Lemon, '95 319
 Cake, Easy Lemon, '83 24
 Cake, General Robert E. Lee Orange-Lemon, '88 92
 Cake, Glazed Lemon, '86 70
 Cake, Lemon Angel, '80 147; '97 163
 Cake, Lemon-Coconut Cream, '81 179
 Cake, Lemon-Coconut Sheet, '85 117
 Cake, Lemon Curd Pound, '04 278
 Cake, Lemon Geranium Pound, '01 131
 Cake, Lemon Gold, '83 301
 Cake, Lemon Meringue, '89 296; '99 118
 Cake, Lemon-Pineapple, '86 60, 239
 Cake, Lemon-Poppy Seed, '93 154
 Cake, Lemon Pound, '82 88; '03 94
 Cake, Lemon Pudding, '83 106
 Cake, Lemon-Raspberry, '91 247
 Cake, Lemon-Sour Cream Pound, '87 38
 Cake, Lemon Sour Cream Pound, '01 117
 Cake, Lemon Tea, '82 169
 Cake, Lemony Pound, '96 60
 Cake, Lightly Lemon Coffee, '81 14
 Cake, Luscious Lemon, '93 81
 Cake, Luscious Lemon Layer, '86 61
 Cake, Old-Fashioned Lemon Layer, '85 191
 Cake Roll, Elegant Lemon, '80 70
 Cake Roll, Lemon, '89 312
 Cake, Strawberry-Lemon Sheet, '04 137
 Cake, Sullivan's Lemon-Almond Pound, '04 278
 Cake, Tart Lemon-Cheese, '88 7; '03 317
 Cake with Blueberry Sauce, Buttermilk-Lemon
  Pudding, '95 135
 Cake with Mint Berries and Cream, Lemon Pound,
  '99 183
 Cake, Yogurt-Lemon-Nut, '89 169
 Candied Lemon Peel, '94 199
 Charlotte Russe, Fresh Lemon, '80 13
 Charlotte Russe, Lemon, '84 192
 Cheesecake, Lemon, '86 194; '91 308; '92 24
 Cheesecake, Lemon Delight, '95 219
 Cheesecake, Lemony Passover, '02 51
 Cheesecake, Luscious Lemon, '90 M196
 Cheesecake, Strawberry-Lemon, '04 237
 Cheesecakes with Raspberry Sauce, Mini Lemon,
  '02 123

 Cheesecake with Orange-Pineapple Glaze, Lemon,
  '81 60
 Chocolate-Lemon Creams, '98 M235
 Cookies, Lemon, '03 298
 Cookies, Lemonade, '79 51
 Cookies, Lemon-Almond, '02 293
 Cookies, Lemon-Basil Butter, '01 117
 Cookies, Lemon Butter, '01 90
 Cookies, Lemon-Coconut, '02 293
 Cookies, Lemon Crinkle, '81 287
 Cookies, Lemon Ice Box, '02 293
 Cookies, Lemon-Iced Chocolate Spice, '97 123
 Cookies, Lemon-Pecan, '02 293
 Cookies, Lemon-Poppy Seed, '02 293
 Cookies, Lemon Thumbprint, '03 298
 Cookies, Lemon Thyme, '96 124
 Cookies, Lemony Cutout, '85 323
 Cookies, Sunshine Lemon, '86 69
 Cream Cheese Dessert, Lemon-, '84 95
 Cream, Frozen Lemon, '83 118
 Cream, Lemon, '82 237; '91 119; '04 300
 Cream, Lemon-Blueberry, '92 153
 Cream Puffs, Lemon, '93 254
 Cream Puffs, Strawberry-Lemon, '87 75
 Cream, Strawberries 'n Lemon, '85 120
 Cream, Strawberries with Lemon, '90 170
 Crisp, Lemon-Blackberry, '98 171
 Crisps, Lemon, '95 272
 Cupcakes, Lemonade, '04 163
 Cupcakes, Lemon-Blueberry Ice-Cream, '01 172
 Cupcakes, Lemon Moist, '82 112; '83 153
 Cups, Baked Lemon, '87 128
 Curd, Fresh Fruit with Lemon, '88 21
 Curd, Lemon, '87 139; '89 334; '94 315;
  '04 259, 279
 Curd with Berries, Lemon, '90 102
 Custard in Meringue Cups, Lemon, '80 295; '81 172
 Custards, Lemon-Buttermilk, '89 49
 Dainties, Lemon Pecan, '80 208
 Delight, Lemon, '82 227
 Divinity, Lemon, '97 316
 Filling, Creamy Lemon, '80 70
 Filling, Lemon, '81 172; '84 137; '85 191; '86 235;
  '87 293; '89 312; '90 308; '94 122; '95 319;
  '97 255; '99 118
 Filling, Lemon-Apricot, '90 105
 Filling, Lemon-Cheese, '79 68; '88 7; '03 317
 Filling, Lemon Cream, '84 23; '87 14
 Filling, Lemon Icebox Pie, '03 104
 Filling, Lemon-Orange, '81 71
 Filling, Strawberry-Lemon, '04 137
 Frosting, Creamy Lemon, '79 93
 Frosting, Lemon, '85 191; '86 217; '93 81
 Frosting, Lemon Buttercream, '83 301; '86 61;
  '91 247; '03 105
 Frosting, Lemon-Butter Cream, '85 117
 Frosting, Lemon-Coconut, '90 253
 Frosting, Lemon-Cream Cheese, '81 157
 Frosting, Lemony White, '88 7; '03 317
 Frosting, Orange-Lemon, '88 92
 Fruitcake, Lemon, '83 258
 Glaze, Lemon, '79 285; '86 194; '87 41; '92 269;
  '93 154, 183; '97 123; '01 117
 Ice Cream, Lemon, '79 142; '83 170; '91 65;
  '97 160; '00 55
 Ice Cream, Lemonade, '88 202
 Ice, Lemon, '00 176; '01 330; '02 201
 Layered Dessert, Lemon-Blueberry, '05 206
 Layered Lemon Dessert, '88 134
 Logs, Hazelnut-Lemon, '84 117
 Mandel Bread, '99 57
 Melting Moments, '85 191
 Meringue, Chocolate Pudding with Lemon, '88 258
 Meringue Cream Cups, Lemon, '84 23

 Mousse, Lemon Cloud, '90 90
 Mousse, Strawberry-Lemon, '82 128
 Mousse with Raspberry Sauce, Lemon, '91 96;
  '92 130
 Napoleons, Blueberry-Lemon, '94 122
 Parfaits, Strawberry-Lemon, '84 198
 Pastry Shell, Lemon in, '84 137
 Pears, Lemon Poached, '82 74
 Pie, Angel, '79 123
 Pie, Apple-Lemon Chess, '86 220
 Pie, Aunt Kitty's Lemon, '98 275
 Pie, Best-Ever Lemon Meringue, '94 208
 Pie, Buttermilk Lemon, '81 120; '82 23
 Pie, Buttermilk-Lemon, '88 297
 Pie, Buttermilk-Lemon Cream, '88 99
 Pie, Deluxe Lemon Meringue, '81 172; '90 313
 Pie Filling, Lemon Meringue, '04 110
 Pie, Frozen Lemonade, '92 101
 Pie, Frozen Lemon Cream, '82 86
 Pie, Lemonade, '91 42
 Pie, Lemon-Blueberry Cream, '02 92
 Pie, Lemon-Buttermilk, '91 272
 Pie, Lemon Cheese, '81 136; '82 146
 Pie, Lemon Chess, '79 32; '82 196; '00 60; '02 107;
  '03 217, 259
 Pie, Lemon-Cottage Cheese, '79 44
 Pie, Lemon Cottage Cheese, '81 143
 Pie, Lemon Fluff, '92 342; '93 46
 Pie, Lemon Ice Cream, '80 70
 Pie, Lemon-Lime Chess, '01 23
 Pie, Lemon Meringue, '85 M112; '86 130; '04 110
 Pie, Lemon-Orange, '85 172
 Pie, Lemon Parfait, '94 310
 Pie, Lemon-Pecan, '93 251
 Pie, Lemon-Sour Cream, '82 169
 Pie, Lemon Sponge, '83 192
 Pie, Lemon-Strawberry, '88 127
 Pie, Lemon Twirl, '84 94
 Pie, Lemony Cherry, '92 30
 Pie, Lemony Ice Cream, '99 207
 Pie, Slice of Lemon, '84 23
 Pie, Tart Lemon, '91 275
 Pie, Tart Lemon-Apple, '80 100
 Pie, Whipped Lemon, '79 124
 Pie, Zesty Lemon, '05 157
 Pops, Cherry-Berry Lemonade, '03 89
 Pops, Deep Blue Sea, '94 143
 Pops, Sangría, '99 133
 Pudding, Baked Lemon, '04 295
 Pudding, Layered Lemon, '82 128
 Pudding, Lemon, '79 86; '81 99
 Pudding, Lemon Cake, '92 96; '98 35
 Pudding, Lemon Fluff, '85 304
 Pudding, Lemon-Pear, '96 283
 Pudding, Old-Fashioned Lemon Bread, '88 95
 Roll, Snow-Capped Lemon, '79 68
 Rolls with Raspberry Sauce, Lemon Angel, '94 294
 Sauce, Blueberry-Lemon, '01 117
 Sauce, Cheesecake with Raspberry-Lemon, '96 30
 Sauce, Lemon, '84 258, 306; '85 77, 190; '91 240;
  '96 283; '01 184; '04 98
 Sauce, Lemon Cream, '93 200
 Sauce, Lemon Dessert, '87 M165
 Sauce, Tart Lemon, '85 191
 Sherbet, Lemon, '91 309
 Sherbet, Lemon Cream, '79 114
 Sherbet, Lemon-Pineapple, '96 330
 Sherbet, Refreshing Lemon, '05 133
 Snaps, Lemon-Basil, '05 275
 Solid, Lemon, '93 279
 Sorbet, Blackberry-Lemon, '02 85
 Sorbet, Lemon, '93 153; '03 171
 Sorbet, Pear-Lemon, '88 116
 Soufflé, Cold Lemon-Lime, '84 24

Soufflé, Lemon, **'82** 170, 252; **'94** 199
Soufflés, Quick Lemon Sauce, **'88** 43
Soufflé, Tart Lemon, **'85** 82
Soufflé with Raspberry-Amaretto Sauce, Frozen
Lemon, **'88** 130
Sponge Cups, Lemon, **'83** 10
Squares, Golden Carrot-Lemon, **'80** 40
Squares, Lemon, **'81** 197; **'97** 329
Squares, Lemon-Pecan, **'89** 124
Squares, Lemony Cream Cheese, **'82** 159
Strawberry-Lemon Dessert, **'86** 162
Tart), Caky Flaky Tart (Tart Lemon, **'96** 159
Tart, Double Citrus, **'05** 55
Tart, Double-Decker Lemon, **'04** 111
Tart Filling, Tangy Lemon, **'04** 111
Tarts, Berry Good Lemon, **'91** 119
Tarts, Dainty Lemon, **'82** 304
Tarts, Golden Lemon, **'85** 191
Tart Shells, Lemon, **'88** 195
Tarts, Lemon, **'82** 156; **'83** 79
Tarts, Lemon-Cheese, **'79** 2
Tarts, Lemon Ice Cream, **'80** 152
Tarts, Lemon-Sour Cream, **'81** 304
Tart, Strawberry-Lemon, **'89** 111
Tart, Tangy Lemon, **'01** 245; **'04** 111
Topping, Lemon-Pineapple, **'86** 60
Torte with Raspberry Sauce, Lemon Meringue,
'93 82
Trifle, All Seasons Lemon, **'95** 219
Trifle, Lemon-Blueberry, **'88** 210
Yogurt, Lemon-Chiffon Frozen, **'85** 54
Yummies, Lemon, **'81** 301
Zephers, Lemon, **'81** 172
Dip, Pink Lemonade-Lime, **'04** 133
Dressing
Broccoli with Lemon Dressing, Chilled, **'88** 270
Caper Dressing, Lemon-, **'96** 69
Cream Dressing, Lemon, **'82** 170
Creamy Lemon Dressing, **'88** M193
French Dressing, Green Salad with Lemony, **'85** 67
Herb Dressing, Lemon-, **'97** 92
Herb Dressing, Lemon-and-, **'92** 108
Herb Salad Dressing, Lemon-, **'82** 67
Honey-Lemon Dressing, **'95** 133
Honey-Lemon Dressing, Fruit Salad with, **'93** 21
Lemon Dressing, **'04** 167
Molasses Dressing, Lemon-, **'97** 195
Mustard Dressing, Lemon-, **'02** 52
Pepper Dressing, Lemon-, **'87** 55
Salad Dressing, Lemon, **'79** 8
Tomato Slices with Lemon Dressing, **'87** 167
Vinaigrette, Fresh Lemon, **'04** 30; **'05** 242
Vinaigrette, Lemon, **'04** 169
Yogurt Dressing, Lemon-, **'93** 17
Yogurt Slaw or Salad Dressing, Lemon-, **'88** 54
Glaze, Lemon, **'97** 332
Green Beans, Lemon, **'89** 275
Green Beans, Lemon-Almond, **'05** 218
Green Beans, Lemon-and-Dill, **'05** 17
Green Beans, Lemon-Dill, **'01** 181
Green Beans, Lemon-Pecan, **'04** 285
Green Beans, Lemon-Walnut, **'93** 304
Green Beans, Lemony, **'85** 190; **'99** 259
Green Beans with Lemon, **'03** 66
Honey, Lemon, **'94** 16; **'96** 124
Jam, Tri-Berry Lemon, **'98** 214
Jelly, Honey-Lemon, **'97** 29
Linguine, Lemon, **'97** 228
Main Dishes
Beef, Spicy Lemon Thai, **'97** 320
Beef, Thai Lemon, **'97** 292
Catfish, Baked Lemon-Dill, **'05** 216
Catfish, Fried Lemon-Rosemary, **'02** 319
Catfish, Lemon Barbecued, **'88** 271; **'89** 202

Chicken and Vegetables, Lemon, **'88** 118
Chicken, Baked Lemon, **'85** 190
Chicken Breasts, Lemon, **'89** 18
Chicken, Clay Oven-Roasted Citrus, **'98** 108
Chicken Cutlets with Lemon, **'85** 8
Chicken, Greek Lemon, **'90** 65
Chicken, Grilled Yogurt-Lemon, **'81** 111
Chicken in Lemon and Wine, **'83** 281
Chicken in Lemon Marinade, **'98** 128
Chicken, Lemon, **'81** M138; **'86** 173; **'96** 49
Chicken, Lemonade, **'82** 163
Chicken, Lemon Barbecued, **'93** 215
Chicken, Lemon-Basil, **'02** 91
Chicken, Lemon-Dill, **'93** 19
Chicken, Lemon-Fried, **'79** 77
Chicken, Lemon Fried, **'82** 275
Chicken, Lemon-Frosted, **'88** 170
Chicken, Lemon-Garlic, **'89** M132; **'90** 35
Chicken, Lemon-Garlic Roasted, **'98** 108
Chicken, Lemon-Herb, **'85** 127; **'00** 90
Chicken, Lemon-Herb Grilled, **'95** 87
Chicken, Lemon-Mustard, **'99** 109
Chicken, Lemon-Pepper, **'89** 104
Chicken, Lemon-Roasted, **'95** 24
Chicken, Lemon-Rosemary, **'94** 201
Chicken, Lemon-Spinach, **'97** 104
Chicken, Lemony Pecan, **'96** 82
Chicken Nuggets, Lemon-, **'86** 337; **'87** 283
Chicken Piccata, Herbed, **'88** 28
Chicken Sauté, Lemon-Dill, **'91** 186
Chicken, Sweet-and-Sour Lemon, **'84** 93
Chicken, Sweet Lemon, **'79** 218
Chicken, Sweet Lemon-, **'84** 69
Chicken Tenders, Lemon, **'03** 184
Chicken with Lemon, Garlic, and Rosemary,
Roasted, **'97** 61
Chicken with Sautéed Green Beans, Lemon-Garlic
Roast, **'05** 43
Cornish Hens, Lemon Roasted, **'82** 260
Cutlets, Lemon-Flavored, **'79** 105
Fillets, Lemon-Coated, **'80** M53
Flank Steak, Lemon-Lime, **'95** 55
Flounder Thermidor, **'85** 190
Lamb Rack, Greek Lemon, **'97** 247
Linguine with Garlic and Lemon, **'88** 91
Mackerel, Lemon-Baked, **'79** 182
Pork Chops, Lemon-Herb, **'84** 81; **'89** M132
Pork Chops, Lemony, **'88** 118
Pork Chops, Lemony Pan-Fried, **'03** 205
Pork Piccata, **'94** 57; **'99** 332
Ribs, Lemon Baked, **'81** 166
Ribs, Lemon Grilled, **'81** 154
Salmon with Lemon and Olive Oil, Broiled, **'04** 46
Shrimp and Pasta, Lemon, **'96** 124
Shrimp in Lemon Butter, **'84** 163
Shrimp, Lemon-Garlic Broiled, **'82** 29; **'86** 182
Shrimp, Luscious Lemon, **'88** 150
Snapper with Crabmeat Relish, Lemony Pecan-
Crusted, **'99** 298
Spareribs, Lemony Sweet, **'80** 73
Steak Skewers, Lemon Flank, **'02** 134
Steak with Brandy Sauce, Lemon-Butter, **'85** 78
Tuna with Lemon and Capers, **'97** 180
Turkey-Basil Piccata, **'96** 49
Turkey Piccata, **'91** 137
Turkey Piccata with Caper Sauce, **'98** 49
Veal, Lemon, **'93** 35
Veal Piccata, **'92** 181
Veal Piccata, Lemon, **'86** 118
Veal with Artichoke Hearts, Lemon, **'87** 219
Marinade, Lemon-Soy, **'91** 194
Marmalade, Citrus, **'80** 101
Mashed Potatoes, Lemon, **'04** 181
Mayonnaise, Gremolata, **'00** 136

Mayonnaise, Lemon, **'95** 32; **'98** 144; **'99** 178; **'04** 56
Mayonnaise, Lemon-Basil, **'03** 208
Mayonnaise, Lemon-Cream, **'85** 264
Mayonnaise, Lemon-Dill, **'99** 267
Mold, Cheesy Lemon, **'79** 241
Mold, Lemon-Cucumber, **'87** 90
New Potatoes, Lemon-Buttered, **'84** 149; **'90** 268;
'98 159
New Potatoes, Lemony, **'82** 158
Olive Oil, Lemon-Infused, **'95** 231
Olives, Lemon-Garlic, **'94** 118
Pancakes with Strawberry Butter, Lemon, **'99** 44
Pasta, Lemon-Garlic, **'95** 181
Pilaf, Lemon, **'97** 322
Pilaf, Lemon-and-Pine Nut, **'97** 51
Potatoes, Creamy Lemon-Poppy Seed Mashed, **'03** 294
Potatoes, Herbed Lemon Mashed, **'93** 208
Potatoes, Lemon and Nutmeg, **'80** 36
Potatoes, Lemon-Herb Stuffed, **'83** 173
Potatoes, Lemon-Steamed, **'86** 177
Potatoes, Oregano-and-Lemon Skillet, **'93** 54
Potato Wedges, Lemon, **'88** 21
Potato Wedges, Lemony, **'90** M61
Preserved Lemons, Fresh, **'00** 17
Relish, Lemon-Date, **'96** 271
Relish, Lemony Cranberry, **'79** 243
Rice, Lemon, **'89** 166
Rice, Lemony, **'99** 46
Rice Pilaf, Lemon, **'01** 36; **'04** 82
Risotto, Lemon-Lime, **'97** 213
Roses, Lemon, **'82** 280
Salads
Apple-Bran Salad, Lemony, **'86** 223
Asparagus Salad, Creamy Lemon-, **'93** 116
Cauliflower-Lemon Salad, **'81** 23
Cheese Salad, Lemon-, **'85** 240
Chicken Salad Wraps, Lemon-Basil, **'00** 216
Coleslaw, Lemon-Apple, **'05** 44
Congealed Lemon-Tomato Salad, **'89** 178
Congealed Salad, Lemon-Cranberry, **'87** 311
Congealed Salad, Lemon-Vegetable, **'85** 22
Cream Salad, Lemon-, **'88** 250
Freeze, Fruity Lemon, **'82** 145
Fruit Salad, Ginger-and-Lemon, **'05** 17
Fruit Salad, Lemonade, **'84** 24
Onion Salad, Lemon-, **'85** 252
Pineapple Salad, Lemon-, **'05** 65
Potato Salad, Lemon-Basil, **'97** 63; **'01** 178
Tossed Salad, Lively Lemon, **'00** 16
Sauces
Asparagus with Lemon Sauce, **'86** 62
Barbecue Sauce, Herbed Lemon, **'94** 154; **'98** 334
Barbecue Sauce, Lemony, **'88** M177; **'95** 31
Basting Sauce, Lemon, **'95** 32
Broccoli with Lemon Sauce, **'91** 292; **'92** 256
Broccoli with Lemon Sauce and Pecans, **'86** 71
Brussels Sprouts in Lemon Sauce, **'82** 269
Butter Sauce, Lemon-, **'84** 252; **'92** 337; **'99** 198
Butter Sauce, New Potatoes with Lemon-, **'00** 103
Catfish with Lemon Sauce, Pecan, **'03** 185; **'05** 56
Celery Sauce, Baked Fillets in Lemon-, **'84** 91
Cheese Sauce, Lemon-, **'91** 24
Cheese Sauce, Lemony, **'84** 183
Chicken Scaloppine in Lemon Sauce, **'00** 166
Cream Sauce, Braised Chicken Breast in Lemon,
'94 184
Cream Sauce, Lemon, **'99** 53
Cucumber Sauce, Lemony, **'89** 245
Dill Sauce, Potatoes and Green Beans with Lemon-,
'01 89
Dipping Sauce, Lemon, **'02** 134
Garlic Sauce, Shrimp in Lemon, **'83** 67
Honey-Lemon Mustard Sauce, **'84** 275
Hot Lemon-Herb Sauce, **'91** 286

LEMON, Sauces
(continued)

Lemon Sauce, '82 290
Meunière Sauce, Lemon, '88 222
Mustard Sauce, Salmon Steaks with Lemon-, '97 124
New Potatoes with Lemon Sauce, '86 130
Parsley Sauce, Lemon, '81 106
Parsley Sauce, Lemon-, '93 48
Red Snapper with Lemon Sauce, '01 83
Tartar Sauce, Lemony, '95 32
Tomato-Lemon Sauce, Salmon with Almonds and, '04 23
Vanilla Sauce, Lemon-, '02 231
Veal Scaloppine in Lemon Sauce, '00 166
Zesty Lemon Sauce, '97 318
Slices, Fluted Lemon, '82 51
Soup, Egg-Lemon, '96 88
Soup, Lemon-Egg Drop, '93 81
Spinach, Creamy Lemon, '82 302
Spinach with Feta, Lemon, '85 190
Spinach with Lemon and Pepper, '97 105
Spread, Lemon-Raisin, '01 48
Sprouts, Lemon, '85 288
Squeezers, Lemon, '95 32
Sugar, Lemon-Mint, '95 32
Sugar Snap Peas, Lemon-Scented, '02 282
Sugar Snap Peas with Basil and Lemon, '93 66
Sweetened Preserved Lemons, '95 141
Vegetables, Honey-Glazed Roasted Fall, '99 244
Vegetables, Lemon, '93 83
Vermicelli, Lemon, '84 329
Vinaigrette, Fresh Lemon, '05 242
Vinaigrette, Lemon, '95 31
Vinaigrette, Lemon-Basil, '94 205
Vinaigrette, Lemon-Dill, '99 27
Vinaigrette, Lemon-Honey, '96 65
Vinaigrette, Peppery Lemon, '01 122
Vinegar, Lemon, '95 31; '96 124
Vinegar, Lemon-Mint, '85 124
Vinegar, Raspberry-Lemon, '87 134
Vinegar, Spicy Oregano-Lemon, '85 124
Wild Rice, Pecan-Lemon, '92 211
Wonton Chips, Lemon-and-Herb, '91 138
Yogurt Coleslaw, Grilled Chicken Breasts with Lemon-, '98 148
Zucchini, Lemon-Garlic, '89 226

LENTILS
Baked Lentils with Cheese, '84 113
Bean Pot Lentils, '01 35
Burgers, Lentil, '95 123
Burritos, Lentil, '99 287
Casserole, Lentils-and-Rice, '93 301
Liver, Mock Chopped, '00 281
Marinated Lentils, Tangy, '00 94
Pasta and Lentils, Cheesy, '99 287
Pilaf, Rice-and-Lentil, '88 17
Rice, Lentils and, '99 236
Salad, Lentil-and-Orzo, '03 127
Salad, Lentils-and-Rice, '90 197
Salad, Mediterranean Lentil, '96 239
Salad, Winter, '97 304; '98 19
Samosas, '96 239
Sauce, Lentil Spaghetti, '90 198
Soup, Beefy Lentil, '87 282
Soup, Lentil, '83 292; '86 304; '91 28; '97 304; '98 19
Soup, Oven-Baked Split Pea-and-Lentil, '00 316
Soup, Spanish-Style Lentil, '96 239
Spanish-Style Lentils and Rice, '03 201
Spread, Lentil, '99 288
Stew, Lentil-Rice, '82 232
Supper, Lentil-and-Rice, '84 202
Tacos, Lentil, '88 197

Tex-Mex Lentils, '99 288
Vegetables, Savory Lentils and, '98 29
LIGHT & EASY. *See* **HEALTHY & LIGHT.**
LIME
Beverages
Apple Limeade, Pink, '89 46
Cooler, Grape-Lime, '94 227
Cooler, Lime, '87 160
Daiquiris, Freezer Lime, '79 141
Fizz, Frosty Lime, '90 104
Fizz, Lime, '81 172
Fresh Limeade, '00 139
Fuzz Buzz, '82 160
Limeade, '01 143
Margarita Granita, '02 49
Margaritas, Frosted, '84 115
Margaritas, Frosty, '83 172
Margaritas, Lemon-Lime, '94 227
Margaritas, Mock, '99 120
Margaritas, Orange-Lime, '97 140
Margaritas, Pitcher, '83 175
Pineapple Limeade, '01 235
Punch, Brew-Ha-Ha, '98 255
Punch, Calypso Presbyterian Church Women's Lime, '95 141
Punch, Foamy Lime, '82 264
Punch, Lime, '84 58
Punch, Lime-Pineapple, '83 142
Punch, Lime Slush, '90 273
Punch, Orange-Lime, '82 160
Refresher, Cantaloupe-Lime, '01 332
Rio Grande Limeade, '01 186
Swamp Breeze, '01 146
Tea, Lime, '98 198
Tea, Lime-Mint, '97 122
Butter, Cilantro-Lime, '98 156; '01 24; '02 109
Butter, Grilled Corn with Jalapeño-Lime, '01 158; '04 178
Candied Lime Strips, '94 137
Crackers, Tortilla-Lime, '99 17
Cream, Chipotle-Lime, '05 329
Cream, Cilantro-Lime, '98 129
Cream, Ginger-Lime, '95 227
Desserts
Cake, Key Lime, '91 214
Cake, Lime Icebox Pie, '03 104
Cakes, Creamy Lime, '04 89
Cheesecakes, Key Lime-Coconut Mini-, '05 159
Cheesecakes, Lime-Goat Cheese, '05 176
Cheesecake with Raspberry Sauce, Lime, '00 204
Cheesecake with Strawberry-Butter Sauce, Key Lime, '96 87
Cheesecake with Strawberry Sauce, Key Lime, '03 55
Cream, Lime-Rum, '93 169
Curd, Key Lime, '96 126
Filling, Lime Icebox Pie, '03 104
Frosting, Lime Buttercream, '03 105
Ice Cream, Buttermilk-Lime, '04 103
Ice Cream, Fresh Lime, '97 160
Key Lime Bars with Macadamia Crust, '99 282
Loaf, Lime Layer, '85 96
Mousse Freeze, Luscious Lime, '81 173
Parfaits, Lime, '80 153
Parfaits, Surf-and-Sand, '93 169
Pie, Key Lime, '91 42; '96 171; '00 120; '03 179; '04 254
Pie, Lemon-Lime Chess, '01 23
Pie, Lime Chiffon, '86 130
Pie, Lime Fluff, '84 43
Pie, Manny and Isa's Key Lime, '95 118
Pie, Rum-Coconut Key Lime, '05 157
Pies, Key Lime, '95 86; '97 162
Pies, Lime Party, '92 65
Pie, Spiked Strawberry-Lime Ice-Cream, '05 89

Pie, Strawberry-Lime Ice-Cream, '05 89
Pie with Gingersnap Crust, Margarita-Key Lime, '01 187
Pie with Minted Tropical Salsa, Key Lime, '99 333
Refresher, Lime-Mint, '82 144
Sherbet, Creamy Lime, '84 165
Sherbet, Lime, '82 159; '89 202
Sherbet, Refreshing Lime, '05 133
Soufflé, Cold Lemon-Lime, '84 24
Squares, Lime, '79 2
Tart in Coconut Crust, Key Lime, '89 160
Tartlets, Key Lime Curd, '01 250
Tart, Lime, '98 272
Tart, Lime-and-Macadamia Nut, '03 295
Tart, Lime-Pineapple, '88 6
Tornadoes for Grown-Ups, Texas, '94 143
Whip, Lime, '89 199
Dip, Cilantro-Lime Sour Cream, '05 247
Dip, Lime-Dill, '92 65
Dip, Orange-Lime, '96 248
Dressing, Asparagus with Warm Citrus, '96 M86
Dressing, Creamy Lime, '04 46
Dressing, Honey-Lime, '83 139; '93 71
Dressing, Lime, '79 2; '83 120
Dressing, Lime-Honey, '92 213
Dressing, Lime-Honey Fruit Salad, '87 81
Dressing, Lime-Parsley, '85 131
Dressing, Lime-Peanut, '01 26
Dressing, Lime Sherbet, '80 221
Dressing, One-Bean Salad with Lime-Mustard, '00 202
Dressing, Spinach Salad with Chili-Lime, '94 63
Fruit and Veggies with Lime, Spicy, '04 141
Jelly, Lime, '94 23
Main Dishes
Beef Stir-Fry, Lime-Ginger, '92 65
Bow Ties, Black Beans, and Key Limes, '96 291
Catfish, Lime-Orange, '02 22
Chicken Breasts, Lime-Roasted, '97 100
Chicken, Grilled Lime-Jalapeño, '91 87
Chicken, Honey-Lime Grilled, '96 189; '98 332
Chicken, Limeade, '01 257
Chicken, Lime-Grilled, '02 142; '04 320
Chicken with Grilled Pineapple, Lime, '04 88
Chicken with Lime Butter, '84 68
Chicken with Orange, Lime, and Ginger Sauce, '92 123
Flank Steak, Lemon-Lime, '95 55
Pork Chops, Honey-Lime, '91 33
Pork Tenderloin with Lime and Chipotle, Sweet, '04 184
Pork Tenderloin with Yogurt and Lime, Grilled, '04 216
Red Snapper with Lime, Stuffed, '83 246
Roast, Roasted Lime-Cilantro Eye of Round, '04 88
Swordfish with Avocado-Lime Sauce, Grilled, '97 127
Turkey Tenderloins, Lime-Buttered, '92 127
Veal, Amaretto-Lime, '93 54
Marinade, Fruit with Lime, '98 92
Marinade, Southwestern, '99 141
Marmalade, Citrus, '80 101
Mayonnaise, Flavored, '97 328
Mayonnaise, Lime-Cayenne, '04 121
Mojo, Yuca with Garlic-Lime, '05 294
Muffins, Key Lime, '95 50
Mustard, Key Lime, '94 278
Oil, Cilantro, '03 98
Onions, Citrus, '04 89
Pesto, Cilantro, '98 145
Pickles, Lime, '96 206
Popcorn, Spicy Nut, '02 287
Portobello Mushrooms, Lime-Grilled, '05 18
Rice, Lime-Flavored, '84 175
Risotto, Lemon-Lime, '97 213

Salad, Beef-and-Lime Rice, '03 172
Salad, Emerald, '81 143
Salad, Frosted Lime-Cheese, '79 286
Salad, Lime-Carrot, '92 65
Salad, Lime Congealed, '02 257
Salad, Lime-Potato, '02 22
Salad, Pear-Lime, '84 152
Salad, Pineapple-Lime, '84 320
Salad, Snowy Emerald, '87 311
Salad, Zesty Shredded, '04 324
Sauce, Avocado-Lime, '03 90
Sauce, Creamy Lime, '04 119
Sauce, Fresh Fruit with Lime, '02 68
Sauce, Honey-Lime, '82 85
Sauce, Lime Hollandaise, '93 121
Sauce, Lime-Saffron, '94 71
Sauce, Sour Cream-Lime, '91 286
Slaw, Tangy, '02 215
Sopa de Lima, '79 211
Soup, Butternut Squash-Lime, '03 236
Soup, Lime, '88 31; '02 168
Sour Cream, Lime, '04 324
Sweet Potatoes, Lime, '02 307
Syrup, Fresh Fruit with Lime, '05 220
Vinaigrette, Cilantro-Lime, '94 77
Vinaigrette, Pistachio-Lime, '97 148
Vinaigrette, Spicy Lime, '01 217
Whip, Peaches with Honey-Lime, '85 108

LINGUINE
Alfredo, Bourbon-Pecan, '96 291
Alfredo, Linguine, '04 96
Artichoke and Shrimp Linguine, '95 210
Artichoke Hearts, Pasta with, '86 209
Baked Linguine with Meat Sauce, '01 41
Basil Pasta, Fresh Tomato Sauce over, '93 176
Bay Scallops, Linguine with, '97 201
Beef Stir-Fry, Italian, '99 35
Broccoli Linguine, '98 30
Cacciatore, Hearty Chicken, '02 269
Carbonara, Linguine, '87 108
Casserole, Linguine with Meat Sauce, '03 22
Chicken-and-Pepper Pasta, '03 199
Chicken-Broccoli Linguine, '98 30
Chicken Linguine, '01 128
Chicken, Sicilian, '97 142
Chicken, Taste-of-Texas Pasta and, '92 78
Clam Linguine, '95 212
Clam Linguine, Quick, '90 233
Clam Sauce, Linguine in, '81 83
Clam Sauce, Linguine with, '84 124; '88 90; '89 178
Clam Sauce with Linguine, '84 9
Cracked Pepper Linguine, '97 228
Crawfish Pasta, Creamy, '03 277
Creole Sauce, Pasta with Crescent City Grill, '04 289
Dried Tomato-Basil Pesto Linguine, Flank Steak and, '04 101
Favorite Pasta, My, '95 213
Garlic and Lemon, Linguine with, '88 91
Green Beans and Walnut Sauce, Linguine with, '04 128
Greens, Creamy Pasta with, '00 91
Leeks and Peppers with Linguine, '98 68
Lemon Linguine, '97 228
Mussels Linguine, '90 M112
Parmesan, Creamy Pasta with, '98 233
Pasta Verde, '84 201
Peas and Pasta, '99 68
Pepper-Pesto Linguine, Grilled, '04 136
Pepper-Sausage Pasta, Three, '02 122
Pesto and Pasta, '92 98
Pesto Pasta, Asian, '95 189
Pesto Primavera, '96 170
Primavera, Peppery Pasta, '02 161
Red Pepper Sauce, Linguine with, '93 127
Salad, Pasta, '84 139

Salad Pasta, Caesar, '95 230
Salad, Peanutty Spicy Noodle, '04 72
Salad, Sesame Noodle, '02 186
Sausage and Peppers, Linguine with, '03 170
Seafood Delight, '86 208
Seafood Linguine, '79 227
Seafood Sauce, Linguine with, '83 232
Shrimp and Linguine, Spicy, '92 34
Shrimp and Pasta, Mediterranean, '95 286
Shrimp and Pasta, Sautéed, '96 288
Shrimp Marinara, '84 233
Shrimp Scampi, '00 283
Shrimp, Spicy Pasta and, '97 67
Spinach, Linguine with, '91 30
Tomato-Cream Sauce, Linguine with, '86 158
Tomato Linguine, Two, '05 187
Tomato Sauce with Linguine, Fresh, '02 213
Turkey Scaloppine, '04 321
Vegetables, Noodles with Spring, '02 125
Vegetables, Traveling Linguine with Roasted, '93 178
Verde, Pasta, '84 201
White Clam Sauce, Linguine with, '05 49
Whole Wheat Linguine, '84 177
Zucchini with Pasta, Stuffed, '97 101

LIVER
Appetizers
Chicken Liver and Bacon Roll-Ups, '80 200; '81 57
Chicken Livers, Party, '83 242
Chicken Liver Turnovers, '79 141
Pâté, Chicken Liver, '79 153; '81 235; '83 108; '84 205
Pâté, Country, '86 66
Pâté, Duck Liver, '79 227
Pâté, Liver-Cheese, '85 276
Pâté with Cognac, '86 159
Pâté with Madeira Sauce, Liver, '93 323
Rumaki, '80 M136
Spread, Liver, '89 161
Spread, Sherried Liver, '80 86
Barbecued Liver, '85 219
Beef Liver Patties, '81 277
Beef Liver with Balsamic Vinegar, '98 130
Calf's Liver with Vegetables, '85 219
Chicken
Chopped Chicken Livers, Grandma Rose's, '96 105
en Brochette, Chicken Livers, '84 222
Fried Chicken Livers, '96 105
Garlic Chicken Livers, '96 105
Italian Sauce, Chicken Livers in, '83 117
Marsala Wine Sauce, Chicken Livers with, '81 76
Mushrooms, Chicken Livers with, '81 133
Omelet, Chicken Liver, '82 44
Orange Sauce, Chicken Livers in, '82 218
Party Chicken Livers, '83 242
Pâté, Chicken Liver, '79 153; '81 235; '83 108; '84 205
Potatoes, Chicken Livers and, '82 218
Rice, Chicken Livers with, '80 200; '81 58; '84 292
Rice Dish, Chicken Livers and, '82 218
Risotto, Chicken Livers, '82 218
Roll-Ups, Chicken Liver and Bacon, '80 200; '81 57
Rumaki Kebabs, '82 182
Sautéed Chicken Livers, '80 200; '81 57
Scrumptious Chicken Livers, '84 230
Stroganoff, Chicken Livers, '80 200; '81 57
Supreme, Chicken Livers, '81 298
Turnovers, Chicken Liver, '79 141
Wine Sauce, Chicken Livers in, '81 104
Creole Liver, '85 219; '86 108; '96 236
Creole Sauce, Liver in, '87 33
French-Style Liver, '80 10
Gravy, Liver and, '80 10
Herbs, Liver with, '81 277
Italiano, Liver, '85 219

Kebabs, Liver, '80 185
Loaf, Skillet Liver, '80 11
Mock Chopped Liver, '00 281
Noodle Dinner, Creamy Liver and, '80 11
Saucy Liver, '81 277
Sauté, Liver, '81 277
Spanish-Style Liver, '80 11
Stroganoff, Liver, '79 54
Sweet-and-Sour Liver, '81 277
LIVING LIGHT. *See* **HEALTHY & LIGHT.**
LOBSTER
Beef Tenderloin, Lobster-Stuffed, '87 248
Beef Tenderloin, Stuffed, '00 124
Beignets, Lobster-and-Roasted Corn, '00 51
Clambake, Backyard, '81 92
Crab-Stuffed Lobster Tails, '95 326
Creamy Lobster, '79 181
How to Cook Lobster, '81 169
Medaillons in Garlic-Chive Butter Sauce, Lobster, '90 96
Orange Sauce, Lobster Tails with Spiced, '86 155
Salad, Lobster, '89 249; '90 69
Salad, Lobster and Orange, '82 207
Salad with Tarragon Vinaigrette, Lobster, '97 163
Shooters, Lobster Scallion, '00 197
Soup, Spicy Thai Lobster, '94 102
Taco with Yellow Tomato Salsa and Jicama Salad, Warm Lobster, '87 122
Thermidor, Lobster, '85 103

MACADAMIA
Apples, Calypso Caramel, '03 M216
Beans, Hawaiian-Style Baked, '86 210
Brownies, Macadamia-Fudge Designer, '94 51
Cake, Macadamia-Fudge, '01 278
Caramels, Coconut-Macadamia, '98 305
Chicken, Macadamia-Mango, '02 162
Chunks of Snow, '02 298
Coffee Cake, Macadamia Ring, '85 326
Cookies, Chunky Macadamia Nut White Chocolate, '92 207
Cookies, Coconut-Macadamia, '98 294
Cookies, Coconut-Macadamia Chunk, '05 87
Cookies, White Chocolate-Macadamia Nut, '94 315
Crème Brûlée, White Chocolate-Macadamia Nut, '95 323
Crust, Chocolate-Macadamia Crumb, '96 254
Crust, Key Lime Bars with Macadamia, '99 282
Crusts, Coconut Cream Tarts with Macadamia Nut, '97 62
French Toast, Macadamia, '86 96
French Toast, Macadamia Nut, '95 282
Grouper Macadamia, '85 127
Mahi Mahi, Macadamia, '88 164
Oat Snowball, Macadamia, '92 274
Pie, Coconut-Macadamia Nut, '97 110
Pie, Frozen Chocolate-Macadamia Nut, '96 254
Pie, Hawaiian Banana Cream, '90 105
Pie, Macadamia, '80 238
Pie, Pear-Macadamia, '93 260
Salad, Macadamia Chicken, '80 138
Sauce, Brandy-Macadamia, '82 311
Tart, Lime-and-Macadamia Nut, '03 295
Toffee, Hawaiian, '04 235
Topping, Macadamia-Fudge, '01 278
MACARONI. *See also* **PASTAS.**
Beans, Pasta with, '99 236
Beef and Macaroni, Easy, '02 188
Beef and Macaroni, Skillet, '82 130
Beef-Macaroni Bake, '94 255
Beef-Macaroni Combo, '79 194
Beef 'n' Pasta, Easy Skillet, '02 63
Casserole, Chicken-Macaroni, '85 219

MACARONI

(continued)

Casserole, Macaroni, '84 220; '87 154
Casserole, Macaroni and Chicken, '80 260
Casserole, Macaroni-Ham, '81 M177; '83 283
Casserole, Mushroom-Macaroni, '95 180
Casserole, Spinach-Beef-Macaroni, '83 313
Cheese
Baked Macaroni and Cheese, '82 199; '00 271;
  '02 26; '03 184
Baked Macaroni with Spinach, '99 244
Bake, Macaroni-and-Cheese, '01 41
Blue Cheese and Walnuts, Macaroni with, '02 M208
Blue Cheese, Macaroni and, '93 248; '94 44
Broccoli Macaroni and Cheese, '02 36
Broccoli Mac 'n' Cheese, '00 53
Caramelized Onion Macaroni and Cheese, '04 231
Casserole, Macaroni-Cheese-Beef, '95 125
Cheeseburger Macaroni, '02 119
Chicken Macaroni and Cheese, '02 63
Chicken Macaroni and Cheese, Spicy, '02 63
Creamy Mac and Cheese, '05 208
Creamy Macaroni and Cheese, '93 249; '94 45;
  '02 26
Deluxe, Macaroni-and-Cheese, '79 84
Deluxe, Macaroni and Cheese, '80 236
Divine Macaroni and Cheese, '99 314
Double Cheese Macaroni, '82 224
Eleanor's Macaroni and Cheese, '97 253
Extra Cheesy Macaroni, '00 92
Golden Macaroni and Cheese, '04 24
Gorgonzola Macaroni, '97 28
Hearty Mac and Cheese, '05 208
Italian Macaroni and Cheese, '04 327
Jack-in-the-Macaroni Bake, '93 249; '94 45
Macaroni and Cheese, '83 M7; '88 M147, M90;
  '90 30; '00 273
Mexican Macaroni, '96 73
Mousse, Macaroni, '96 73
Mushroom Bake, Cheesy Macaroni-, '81 243
Mushroom Bake, Macaroni-, '97 96
Old-Fashioned Macaroni and Cheese, '92 215
Peppers, Macaroni-and-Cheese-Stuffed, '80 65
Pizza, Maca-, '99 195
Primavera, Macaroni, '96 73
Puff, Macaroni and Cheese, '79 5
Quick-and-Easy Macaroni and Cheese, '00 15
Salad, Macaroni and Cheese, '97 203
Soup, Cheesy Mac 'n' Chicken, '05 292
Souper Macaroni and Cheese, '00 92
Soup, Macaroni and Cheese, '95 264
Soup, Pimiento "Mac and Cheese," '97 M325
Taco Dinner Mac and Cheese, '05 208
Tasty Macaroni and Cheese, '83 288
Texas Cheeses with Roasted Chiles, Mac and,
  '04 207
Tex-Mex Macaroni and Cheese, '00 92
Thick-and-Rich Macaroni and Cheese, '84 329
Three-Cheese Macaroni, '00 M92
Tomatoes, Macaroni, Cheese, and, '95 213
Tomato Macaroni and Cheese, Spicy, '03 68
Veggie Mac-and-Cheese, '01 111
Wine, Macaroni-and-Cheese with, '86 78
Dinner, Sausage Skillet, '83 29
Glorious Macaroni, '84 76
Ground Beef and Macaroni, '85 218
Mexican Luncheon, '87 192
Oysters with Macaroni, Scalloped, '80 297
Salads
Acini di Pepe Salad, '83 163
Barbecue Macaroni Salad, '82 276
Cheese Salad, Macaroni and, '97 203

Chicken-Pasta Salad, Zesty, '02 186
Chicken Salad, Dilled Macaroni-, '92 142
Chicken Salad, Macaroni-, '85 296; '86 302
Confetti Macaroni Salad, '82 132; '85 297
Crabmeat Salad, Macaroni-, '81 153
Crunchy Macaroni Salad, '82 24
Dilled Macaroni-Cheese Salad, '86 208
Dilled Macaroni Salad, '89 161
Garden Macaroni Salad, '84 290; '92 64
Gourmet Macaroni Salad, '81 253
Ham and Macaroni Salad, '79 220
Ham Salad, Macaroni-, '85 218
Hearty Macaroni Salad, '84 90
Kidney Bean-Salami Pasta Toss, '85 165
Macaroni Salad, '87 92
Olive Clubhouse Salad, '81 114
Overnight Pasta Salad, '82 276
Pineapple Macaroni Salad, '79 220
Refreshing Macaroni Salad, '80 177
Salmon-and-Macaroni Salad, '81 114
Salmon Salad, Macaroni-, '82 232
Shell Macaroni Salad, '92 163
Shell Salad, Macaroni, '87 38
Shrimp Macaroni Salad, '79 220
Shrimp-Macaroni Salad, '85 219
Shrimp Salad, Festive Macaroni-, '85 165
Shrimp Salad, Macaroni-, '85 121
Spiral Macaroni Salad, '82 276
Sweet-and-Sour Macaroni Salad, '85 166
Taco Macaroni Salad, '85 165
Tuna Macaroni Salad, '83 44, 145
Tuna-Macaroni Salad, '84 66
Tuna Salad, Whole Wheat Macaroni-, '84 193
Turkey Macaroni Salad, '83 282
Two, Macaroni Salad for, '81 31
Vegetable Salad, Macaroni-, '86 209
Véronique, Macaroni Salad, '85 164
Supper Supreme, Sunday, '79 76
Tomatoes, Tuna-Mac in, '87 188
Toss, Corkscrew Macaroni, '83 163
Treat, Tuna-Macaroni, '82 131
Whole Wheat Macaroni with Pesto, '89 238

MANGOES

Beef and Rice, Mango-, '88 138
Bread, Mango, '96 205
Cake, Mango, '83 150
Cake, Mango Upside-Down, '05 120
Chicken, Macadamia-Mango, '02 162
Chutney, Blue-Ribbon Mango, '96 206
Chutney, Mango, '89 141; '96 182; '03 123
Cooler, Caribbean, '98 333
Crêpes, Mango-Pineapple, '86 216
Dessert Tamales, Mango, '94 190
Frappé, Mango, '86 216
Ice Cream, Mango, '86 216
Margaritas, Mango, '96 126
Orange Smoothie, Mango-, '86 216
Pan Dowdy, Mango, '83 150
Pico de Gallo, Mango, '04 318
Pie, Green Mango, '79 137
Pie, Mango Cream, '03 122
Pie, Mango-Ginger, '88 138
Pork Loin, Tropical, '96 86
Preserves, Mango-Pineapple, '79 137
Relish, Mango, '89 198
Salad, Fresh Mango, '84 126
Salad, Mango, '79 137; '03 122
Salad Sandwiches, Mango-Crab, '99 72
Salad with Mango, Chicken, '86 215
Salsa, Avocado-Mango, '00 328
Salsa, Black Bean-and-Mango, '05 297
Salsa, Fresh Mango, '00 122
Salsa, Mango, '91 182; '95 104; '98 232; '00 124, 337;
  '02 163; '04 59; '05 328

Salsa, Mango-and-Bell Pepper, '00 247
Salsa, Minted Mango, '96 206
Salsa, Seared Scallops with Tomato-Mango, '95 122
Salsa, Snappy Mango, '05 329
Salsa, Sweet Pepper-Mango, '05 148
Salsa, Tropical, '96 14
Sandwiches, Mango-Chicken Pita, '03 123
Sauce, Mango, '83 120
Sauce, Mango-Pineapple Hot, '04 183
Sauce, Mango-Spiced Rum, '86 215
Slaw, Mango, '93 31; '94 71
Smoothie, Mango, '03 122
Sorbet, Mango, '86 196
Soup, Chilled Mango-Cantaloupe, '96 205
Torta, Mango Chutney, '96 322
Vinegar, Mango-Cilantro, '95 190

MANICOTTI

Cannelloni, '85 60; '92 17
Cheesy Manicotti, '83 216
Chicken Manicotti, Creamy, '85 60
Chili Manicotti, '89 247; '99 239
Chipotle Manicotti, Creamy, '03 96
Ground Beef-and-Tomato Manicotti, '03 257
Make-Ahead Manicotti, '98 68
Meaty Cheese Manicotti, '05 34
Quick Manicotti, '79 6
Sausage-and-Tomato Manicotti, Cheesy, '03 257
Seafood Manicotti, '94 195
Shrimp Manicotti, '97 96
Special Manicotti, '88 50
Spinach Manicotti, '82 199
Stuffed Manicotti, '83 M6
Stuffed Manicotti, Meaty, '00 19
Stuffed Manicotti, Saucy, '83 288
Stuffed Manicotti, Spinach-, '88 255
Zucchini Manicotti, '84 194

MARINADES

Asian Marinade, '99 141
Basic Marinade, '99 141; '02 19
Beef Marinade, Tangy, '86 113
Cheese Marinade, '04 238
Chicken Marinade, Zesty, '03 180
Cinnamon-Soy Marinade, '93 103
Citrus Marinade, '93 103; '04 51
Garlic-Basil Marinade, '94 160
Garlic-Honey Marinade, '93 102
Honey-Mustard Marinade, '93 103
Italian Marinade, '03 180
Lemon Marinade, Chicken in, '98 128
Lemon-Molasses Dressing, '97 195
Lemon-Soy Marinade, '91 194
Light Marinade, Tangy, '82 178
Lime Marinade, Fruit with, '98 92
Marinade, '86 153; '92 283
Mexican Marinade, Flank Steak in, '98 128
Minty Marinade, '92 105
Oriental Marinade, '93 102
Oriental Marinade, Seafood in, '98 128
Raspberry Vinaigrette, '96 275
Southwestern Marinade, '93 102; '99 141; '00 177
Soy-and-Ginger Marinade, '96 129
Sweet-and-Sour Marinade, '86 113
Teriyaki Marinade, '86 114; '93 102
Vegetable Marinade, '92 231

MARMALADES. *See* **JAMS AND JELLIES/**
  Marmalades.

MARSHMALLOWS

Ambrosia, Carrot-Marshmallow, '80 5
Bars, Broadway Brownie, '97 M35
Bars, Chewy Chocolate Cereal, '97 317
Bird's Nests, '95 102
Birds' Nests, '04 84
Brownies, Chewy Marshmallow, '83 306
Brownies, Chocolate-Marshmallow, '01 246

Brownies, Choco-Mallow, '87 198; '90 309
Brownies, No-Bake, '94 330
Cake, Cola, '00 120
Cake, Mississippi Mud, '04 136
Cake, No-Egg Chocolate Marshmallow, '87 97
Chocolate, Hot Laced Marshmallow, '93 53
Coffee Mallow, '80 109
Cream, Orange-Mallow, '94 295
Dip, Marshmallow Fruit, '84 171
Frosting, Chocolate-Marshmallow, '83 245; '04 210
Fudge, Butterscotch-Peanut, '98 M282
Fudge, Peanut Butter, '02 296
Ice Cream Dessert, Rocky Road, '00 332
Monster Mouths, '95 274
Munchies, Pop Graham, '96 28
Parfaits, Mocha-Mallow, '80 219
Pie, Coffee, '96 148
Piglets, '98 203
Pizza Dessert, Rocky Road, '99 196
Popcorn Balls, Marshmallow, '90 226
Pudding, Banana-Mallow, '86 139
Salad, Waldorf, '97 204
Sauce, Marshmallow, '91 91
S'mores, Grilled Pound Cake, '98 179
S'mores, Indoor, '01 33
Squares, Chocolate-Marshmallow, '92 M50
Sugarplum Fairy Wands, '97 M286
Sushi Bars, '00 50
Sushi Bars, Confetti, '00 50
Sushi, Crisp Rice Cereal, '00 50
Treat, Toasty Marshmallow, '00 200

MAYONNAISE
Adobo Mayonnaise, '02 203
Aioli (Garlic Mayonnaise), '88 221
Aioli, Picante, '99 53
Anchovy Mayonnaise, '86 179
Apricot Mayonnaise, '97 320
Avocado Mayonnaise, '00 335
Avocado Mayonnaise, Spicy Salmon Fillets with,
    '02 327
Basil Mayonnaise, '98 144
Béarnaise Mayonnaise, '00 136; '05 144
Caramelized Onion Mayonnaise, '00 218
Cilantro Mayonnaise, '98 51
Citrus Mayonnaise, Creamy, '92 107
Curry Mayonnaise, '95 66
Dill-Garlic Mayonnaise, '92 320
Dill Mayonnaise, '96 197
Dip, Artichokes with Herb-Mayonnaise, '84 67
Dip, Seasoned Mayonnaise Artichoke, '80 87
Dressing, Mayonnaise, '86 11; '00 217
Dressing, Southwestern Mayonnaise, '99 245
Dried Tomato Mayonnaise, '98 144
Flavored Mayonnaise, '94 167; '96 123; '97 328
Garlic-Dill Mayonnaise, '00 324
Garlic Mayonnaise, '92 56
Gremolata Mayonnaise, '00 136
Herbed Mayonnaise, '82 85, 192
Herb Mayonnaise, Fresh, '05 144
Homemade Mayonnaise, '80 155; '90 81; '99 180
Homemade Mayonnaise, Easy, '84 12
Italian Herbed Mayonnaise, '92 320
Lemon-Basil Mayonnaise, '03 208
Lemon-Cream Mayonnaise, '85 264
Lemon-Dill Mayonnaise, '99 267
Lemon Mayonnaise, '95 32; '98 144; '99 178; '04 56
Lime-Cayenne Mayonnaise, '04 121
Mediterranean Mayonnaise, '98 144
Onion Mayonnaise, '98 144
Parmesan Mayonnaise, '86 79
Raspberry Mayonnaise, '97 107
Roasted Garlic Mayonnaise, '97 47
Roasted Red Pepper Mayonnaise, '98 144
Rosemary-Garlic Mayonnaise, '01 322

Russian Mayonnaise, '80 137
Sauce, Herb-Mayonnaise, '85 73
Sauce, Zesty, '97 312
Spread, Dijon-Mayo, '96 199
Tasty Mayonnaise, '82 192
Tex-Mex Mayonnaise, '01 134
Thai Mayonnaise, Spicy, '02 52
Thyme Mayonnaise, '96 121; '00 333
Tomato-Basil Mayonnaise, '00 136; '05 180
Watercress Mayonnaise, '93 119
Wine Mayonnaise, Hot, '81 83

MEATBALLS
Appetizers
Baked Meatballs, '02 25
Bourbon Meatballs, '00 252
Bourbon-Mustard Glazed Meatballs, '05 305
Brandied Meatballs, '83 78
Chafing Dish Meatballs, '81 260
Chestnut Meatballs, '79 110
Chipotle-Barbecue Meatballs, Spicy, '05 305
Cocktail Meatballs, '79 63, 207
Cranberry Meatballs, '05 310
Flavorful Meatballs, '84 206
German Meatballs, Crisp, '92 326
Ham Balls, '86 256
Ham Balls, Appetizer, '82 39
Hawaiian Meatballs, Tangy, '79 129
Polynesian Meatballs, '80 207
Quesadillas, Meatball, '00 242
Red Delicious Meatballs, '85 85
Saucy Party Meatballs, '80 149
Sauerkraut Meatballs, '86 257
Spiced Meatballs, '79 284
Spicy Holiday Meatballs, '01 238
Spicy Party Meatballs, '00 242
Sweet-and-Sour Meatballs, '82 247; '99 325; '05 305
Sweet-and-Sour Meatballs, Spicy, '03 186
Sweet-and-Sour Party Meatballs, '79 233
Tamale Balls, Tangy, '89 60
Tamale Meatballs, '80 194
Zesty Meatballs, '80 250
Bacon Meatballs, Burgundy-, '80 283
Bacon-Wrapped Meatballs, '79 81
Baked Meatballs, '02 25
Beef Balls Heidelberg, '83 164; '84 39
Charleston Press Club Meatballs, '93 129
Chinese Meatballs, '83 116; '87 194
Creole, Meatball-Okra, '83 156
Creole, Meatballs, '82 233
Espanol, Meatballs, '82 110
Golden Nugget Meatballs, '82 233
Gravy, Meatballs in, '79 136
Ham Balls, '84 91; '86 256
Hawaiian Meatballs, '85 86
Italian Meatball Packets, '04 222
Kebabs, Meatball, '95 192
Lamb Meatballs with Yogurt Sauce, '85 132
Lasagna, Meatball, '00 243; '03 142
Meatballs, '89 237
Minestrone, Meatball, '00 242
Mock Meatballs, '81 243
Oven Barbecued Meatballs, '82 233
Pineapple and Peppers, Meatballs with, '90 145
Pizza Meatballs, '85 86
Processor Meatballs, Quick, '87 111
Royal Meatballs, '87 268; '88 102; '89 67
Sandwiches, Meatball, '04 170
Sandwiches, Open-Faced Meatball, '99 239
Sandwich, Giant Meatball, '92 196
Sauce with Meatballs, Pasta, '01 55
Saucy Meatballs, '85 68; '90 122
Sauerbraten Meatballs, '85 85
Sloppy Joe Meatball Hoagies, '00 242
Soup, Mexican Meatball, '98 315

Spaghetti-and-Herb Meatballs, '84 75
Spaghetti and Meatballs, White, '03 34
Spaghetti, Country-Style, '02 25
Spaghetti with Meatballs, '81 38
Spicy Meatballs and Sausage, '79 163
Stew, Meatball, '79 198; '98 30
Stroganoff, Meatball, '81 297; '02 50
Stroganoff, Mushroom-Meatball, '85 85
Swedish Meatballs, '80 80; '86 256
Sweet-and-Sour Meatballs, '82 233, 247; '86 240
Turkey Meatballs, '89 237
Veal Meatballs, European, '85 30
Venison Sausage Balls, '80 42

MEAT LOAF
Alabama Meat Loaf, '04 188
All-American Meat Loaf, '92 341; '93 46
Barbecued Meat Loaf, '80 60; '81 275; '84 50; '87 216
Barbecue Meat Loaf Sandwiches, '04 188
Basic Meat Loaf, '88 M14
Beef Loaf, Glazed, '86 19
Beef Loaves, Individual Barbecued, '95 242
Beef-Vegetable Loaf, '79 164
Blue Cheese Meat Loaf Roll, '93 247
Cheeseburger Loaf, '81 236, 276
Cheeseburger Meat Loaf, '03 204
Cheesy Meat Roll, '82 136
Chili Meat Loaf, '81 275
Corny Meat Loaf, '86 68
Crunchy Meat Loaf Oriental, '79 212
Curried Meat Loaf, '86 43
Easy Meat Loaf, '88 M214; '95 125; '97 24
Elegant Meat Loaf, '89 243
Family-Style Meat Loaf, '93 18
Fennel Meat Loaf, '88 46
German Meat Loaf, '87 216
Gonzales Meat Loaf, '04 206
Greek Meat Loaf, '96 251; '97 103
Green Chile-Tomato Gravy, Meat Loaf with, '05 42
Ham Loaf, '79 180; '80 272
Ham Loaf, Cranberry-, '82 M77
Ham Loaf, Glazed, '79 187; '90 212
Ham Loaf, Hawaiian, '79 71
Ham Loaf, Pineapple Upside-Down, '79 253
Ham Loaf, Saucy, '86 M328
Ham Loaf, Spicy, '80 110
Ham Loaf, Supreme, '79 242
Ham Loaf, Upside-Down, '82 40
Ham Loaves, '90 235
Ham Loaves, Country, '86 255
Ham Ring, '84 91
Ham Ring, Chili-Sauced, '81 M122
Herb-and-Veggie Meat Loaf, '05 161
Hurry-Up Meat Loaf, '82 21
Hurry-Up Meat Loaves, '88 15
Individual Meat Loaves, '81 279; '82 24; '83 154;
    '92 229; '00 214
Italian Meat Loaf, '79 187
Ketchup-and-Bacon-Topped Meat Loaf, Sweet, '03 203
Lamb Meat Loaf with Feta Cheese, '97 24
Liver Loaf, Skillet, '80 111
Meat Loaf, '81 170; '89 109
Mexicali Meat Loaf, '81 275
Mexican Meat Loaf, '87 217
Mini Alabama Meat Loaves, '04 188
Miniature Meat Loaves, '85 24
Mini Mexican Meat Loaves, '02 90
Mini-Teriyaki Meat Loaf, '90 69
Mozzarella-Layered Meat Loaf, '79 71
My-Ami's Meat Loaf, '94 229
Old-Fashioned Meat Loaf, '05 95
Oriental Meat Loaf, '81 M122; '83 M194
Parsleyed Meat Loaf, '83 35
Parsley Meat Loaf, '87 22
Pineapple Loaves, Individual, '81 M121

MEAT LOAF
(continued)

Pizza Meat Loaf, Cheesy, '81 M121
Reuben Loaf, '95 338
Roll, Meat Loaf, '79 129
Sandwiches, Grilled Cheese Meat Loaf, '04 188
Sandwich, Meat Loaf, '01 210
Saucy Meat Loaves, '79 186
Savory Meat Loaf, '87 216
Southwestern Meat Loaf, '93 248
Special Meat Loaf, '89 70
Spicy Meat Loaf, '79 71
Sprout Meat Loaf, '85 51
Stuffed Beef Log, '79 71
Stuffed Meat Loaf, '79 187
Stuffed Meat Loaf, Rolled, '80 80
Sun-Dried Tomatoes and Herbs, Meat Loaf with, '92 192
Supreme, Meat Loaf, '92 33
Swedish Meat Loaf, '81 M121
Sweet 'n' Saucy Meat Loaf, '01 210
Tasty Meat Loaf, '83 213
Teriyaki Meat Loaf, '03 172
Tex-Mex Meat Loaf for Two, '90 234
Tomato Gravy, Meat Loaf with, '00 330
Triple Meat Loaf, '79 186
Turkey Loaf, '92 33
Turkey Loaf, Cranberry-Glazed, '86 171
Turkey Loaf, Ground, '86 171
Turkey Loaf, Herb-and-Veggie, '05 161
Turkey Meat Loaf, Spinach-Stuffed, '97 24
Veal Meat Loaf, '93 292
Vegetable Meat Loaf, '85 M29
Wellington, Meat Loaf, '79 186; '87 284
Wrap, Meat Loaf in a, '89 122

MELONS
Balls and Cherries in Kirsch, Melon, '91 91
Balls, Fiery Sweet Melon, '92 311
Balls, Mellowed-Out Melon, '88 182
Bowl with Cucumber-Mint Dressing, Melon Ball, '87 153

Cantaloupe
Berry-Filled Melon, '86 93
Chutney, Cantaloupe, '00 108
Chutney, Fresh Cantaloupe, '97 148
Compote, Cantaloupe, '81 147
Compote, Melon Ball, '85 157
Cream Delight, Cantaloupe, '82 179
Delight, Cantaloupe, '89 204
Frozen Cantaloupe Cream, '82 159
Fruit-Filled Cantaloupe, '83 120
Fruit Medley, Minted, '80 182
Grilled Cantaloupe Wedges, '87 162
Ice Cream, Cantaloupe, '79 177
Jam, Cantaloupe-Peach, '95 143
Mold, Double-Grape Cantaloupe, '79 173
Pickled Cantaloupe, '99 171
Pickled Cantaloupe, Sweet, '89 197
Pie, Cantaloupe, '86 163
Pie, Cantaloupe Cream, '79 177
Pie, Cantaloupe Meringue, '88 182
Punch, Cantaloupe, '81 147; '00 140
Refresher, Cantaloupe-Lime, '01 332
Salad, Avocado-Melon, '82 164
Salad, Cantaloupe, '86 182
Salad, Cantaloupe-Cheese, '88 184
Salad, Cantaloupe Colada, '97 148
Salad, Cantaloupe Cooler, '79 176
Salad, Cantaloupe Green, '91 126
Salad, Cantaloupe-Pecan, '86 178
Salad, Melon-Berry, '90 180
Salad with Dill Dressing, Melon, '88 182

Salad with Pistachio-Lime Vinaigrette, Cantaloupe-Spinach, '97 148
Sherbet, Cantaloupe, '88 183
Sherbet-Cantaloupe Surprise, '91 105
Sherbet, Frosty Cantaloupe, '82 144
Sorbet, Cantaloupe, '03 171
Soup, Cantaloupe, '83 120; '88 160
Soup, Chilled Cantaloupe, '81 156; '97 148
Soup, Chilled Mango-Cantaloupe, '96 205
Soup, Fresh Cantaloupe, '84 190
Soup, Melon, '80 182
Southern Plantation Cantaloupe, '82 179
Sundae, Cantaloupe, '89 166
Sweet-and-Hot Melon, '92 163
Wedges with Berry Sauce, Melon, '86 178
Whip, Cantaloupe, '89 198
Citrus Mingle, Melon-, '79 177
Compote, Grilled Chicken Breasts with Fig-and-Melon, '00 163
Cooler, Melon, '81 146
Fruit Bowl, Sparkling Fresh, '80 146
Fruit Cup with Mint Dressing, Fresh, '80 183
Fruit Deluxe, Marinated, '81 146

Honeydew
Boats, Honeydew Fruit, '81 147
Bowl, Honeydew Fruit, '84 186
Cooler, Melon Ball, '86 131
Cups, Honeydew Fruit, '82 179
Dessert, Honeydew-Berry, '83 120
Granita, Honeydew, '87 162
Grapes, Honeydew Melon with, '91 91
Salad, Fruited Ham, '81 146
Salad, Melon and Shrimp Curry, '97 129
Salad, Melon-Berry, '90 180
Salad with Apricot Cream Dressing, Honeydew, '84 191
Salad with Dill Dressing, Melon, '88 182
Soup, Melon, '80 182
Wedges with Berry Sauce, Melon, '86 178
Julep, Melon-Mint, '86 196
Julep, Rainbow Melon, '80 183
Mélange, Melon, '84 139
Minted Melon, '96 123
Minted Melon Cocktail, '81 146
Mint Sauce, Melons in, '85 164
Salad, Congealed Melon Ball, '84 125
Salad, Georgia Summer, '92 179
Salad, Melon-and-Prosciutto, '92 191
Salad, Summertime Melon, '82 101
Salad with Orange-Raspberry Vinaigrette, Grilled Melon, '95 144
Salsa, Hot Melon, '95 144
Soup, Swirled Melon, '87 162

Watermelon
Balls, Minted Melon, '87 162
Basket, Watermelon Fruit, '84 161
Compote, Watermelon-Cherry, '90 180
Cookies, Watermelon, '92 179
Cooler, Melon Ball, '86 131
Cooler, Watermelon-Lemonade, '04 172
Cooler, Watermelon-Strawberry, '98 178
Daiquiri, Watermelon, '95 143; '98 165; '04 172
Frost, Watermelon, '86 196
Granita, Watermelon, '96 179; '98 165; '04 171
Ice, Watermelon, '91 173
Lemonade, Watermelon, '98 165
Looks-Like Watermelon, '03 179
Margaritas, Watermelon, '02 185
Marmalade, Watermelon-and-Ginger, '98 164
Mousse, Frozen Watermelon, '91 96; '92 130
Pickles, Watermelon Rind, '81 174; '98 164
Pie, Watermelon, '95 144
Preserves, Watermelon, '79 120
Prosciutto, Watermelon and, '98 164

Punch, Watermelon, '89 204; '92 190; '00 140
Salad, Watermelon-Feta, '05 320
Salad, Watermelon-Prosciutto, '04 171
Salad with Celery-Nut Dressing, Watermelon, '80 182
Salad with Peppered Peanuts in a Zesty Citrus Dressing, Grilled Shrimp, Orange, and Watermelon, '04 308
Salsa, Watermelon, '98 164
Sauce, Melon Balls in Watermelon, '79 177
Sherbet, Light Watermelon, '81 147
Sherbet, Watermelon, '79 155; '92 124
Sherried Watermelon, '92 117
Slush, Watermelon-Berry, '90 137
Sorbet, Watermelon, '92 190; '99 166; '03 171
Soup, Chilled Watermelon, '03 168
Sparkle, Watermelon, '84 191

MERINGUES
Acorns, Meringue, '93 284
Asparagus Meringue, '88 131
Baked Pear Meringues, '85 232
Bars, Meringue-Chocolate Chip, '84 118
Basket, Summer Berry, '84 158
Baskets with Fresh Fruit and Ice Cream, Meringue, '98 179
Cake, Brown Sugar Meringue, '81 70
Cake, Cinderella Fantasy, '98 70
Cake, Orange Meringue, '86 336; '87 84
Cakes, Spanish Wind, '84 157
Coconut Kisses, '90 106
Coffee Kisses, Chocolate-Dipped, '96 313
Coffee Meringues with Butterscotch Mousse, '93 254
Cooked Meringue, '86 130
Cooked Meringue, Easy, '82 207; '83 158
Cookies, Forget 'em, '83 256
Cookies, Heavenly Chocolate-Chip Meringue, '01 218
Cookies, Meringue, '98 71
Cookies, Meringue Kiss, '86 121
Cookies, Meringue Surprise, '86 320
Cookies, Vanilla Meringue, '01 197
Cran-Apple Mousse Filling, Meringues with, '93 254
Cups, Kiwi and Cream in Meringue, '81 279
Cups, Lemon Custard in Meringue, '80 295; '81 172
Cups, Lemon Meringue Cream, '84 23
Dream Drops, '99 328
Fingers, Chocolate-Almond Meringue, '84 158
Flowers, Meringue, '84 156
Frosting, Brown Sugar Meringue, '81 70
Frosting, Italian Meringue, '98 70
Frosting, Meringue, '86 336; '87 84; '99 118
Ghosts, White Meringue, '99 246
Holiday Meringues, '88 280
Meringue, '87 207; '94 208; '97 109
Meringues, '02 62
Mixture, Basic Meringue, '98 70
Mushrooms, Meringue, '96 317
Orange Meringues, '95 318
Parfaits, Strawberry Meringue, '02 62
Pavlova, '92 101
Peach Melba Meringues, '87 76
Peach Melba Meringues with Buttermilk Custard Sauce, '96 183
Pears with Meringue, Amaretto, '90 58
Pineapple, Meringue-Topped, '84 178
Piping Meringue, '84 156
Shell, Cinnamon Meringue, '82 263
Shells, Fruited Meringue, '87 32
Shells, Fruit-Filled Meringue, '86 151
Strawberry Meringues, '84 188
Strawberry Meringue Torte, '88 136
Toffee Meringue Torte, '87 118
Tropical Meringues, '98 71
Vacherin Moka, '80 55

MICROWAVE. Includes microwave conversions. *See also*
CASSEROLES/Microwave.

Appetizers
Bacon-Chestnut Wraps, '84 M216
Brie-and-Cranberry Chutney Melt, '98 M318
Brie Appetizer, Bit-of-, '88 M8
Brie, Baked Honey-Raisin, '05 M258
Brie, Chutney-Bacon, '90 M292
Brie, Tropical Breeze, '94 M18
Canapés, Green Onion, '84 M216
Cheese Log, Toasted Pecan, '86 M288
Cheese Sticks, Peppery, '81 M289
Crab-Zucchini Bites, '84 M216
Dip, Apple, '96 M190
Dip, Bill D's Black-Eyed Pea, '97 M89
Dip, Black-Eyed Pea, '04 M18
Dip, Cheddar-Bacon, '89 M119
Dip, Chili-and-Cheese, '89 M328
Dip, Chipped Beef, '88 M8
Dip, Creamy Crab, '80 M135
Dip, Hot Artichoke Seafood, '85 M212
Dip, Mexican Artichoke, '90 M292
Dip, Monterey Shrimp, '99 M65
Dip, Nacho, '93 M330
Dip, Quick Fiesta, '95 M237; '99 M197
Dip, Quick Pizza, '00 M168
Dip, Shrimp, '88 M261
Dip, Sweet-and-Spicy Mustard, '96 M274
Eggs, Double Stuffed Spinach-and-Bacon, '00 M333
Franks, Saucy Appetizer, '84 M12
Mix, Spicy Party, '81 M138
Mushrooms, Shrimp-Stuffed, '80 M135
Mushrooms, Spinach-Stuffed, '88 M261; '89 M133
Mushrooms, Tipsy, '84 M216
Nachos, Make-Ahead, '80 M135
Nuts, Sherry-Orange, '86 M289
Nuts, Spiced, '91 M316
Pâté, Chicken Liver, '88 M132
Pecans, Spicy, '81 M289
Pizzas, Appetizer, '89 M118
Plantain Chips, '95 M203
Popcorn, Caramel, '86 M212
Popcorn, Garlic, '83 M315
Potato Shell Appetizers, '89 M119
Potato Skins, Cheese, '84 M239
Rumaki, '80 M136
Rumaki, Scallop, '98 M173
Spread, Artichoke-Parmesan, '92 M95
Spread, Chicken Salad Party, '88 M8
Spread, Hearts of Palm, '90 M293
Spread, Hot Beef, '84 M216
Spread, Seafood, '86 M58
Spread, Spinach-Bacon, '92 M310
Sweet Potato Chips, '95 M203
Tostadas, Party, '98 M33
Wings and Ribs, Thai, '97 M225
Apples, Honey-Glazed, '90 M125
Apples, Rosy Cinnamon, '87 M37
Apples, Spicy Poached, '90 M141

Beverages
Café Colombian Royal, '80 M290
Cappuccino, Mocha, '02 M220
Champions' Cooler, '96 M181
Chocolate, Flaming Brandied, '80 M290
Coffee, Fireside, '03 M298
Coffee, Mocha, '85 M329
Fizz, Berry Blue, '03 M164
Hot Chocolate, Creole, '80 M290
Hot Chocolate Mix, Deluxe, '80 M290
Mocha, Mexican, '93 M341
Mocha, Spirited Hot, '91 M260
Spoons, Dipped Chocolate-Almond, '95 M277
Tomato Cocktail, '83 M203
Blanching Chart, Microwave, '80 M181

Breads
Biscuit Bread, Brown Sugar, '02 M224
Breakfast Ring, Almond-Vanilla, '04 M249
Buns, Cinnamon-Apple Breakfast, '00 M198
Caramel Ring, Easy, '85 M89
Cheese-Herb Bread, '84 M144
Chocolate Loaf Bread, '88 M188
Coffee Cake, Cinnamon, '83 M203
Coffee Cake, Orange, '85 M88
Coffee Cake Ring, '85 M89
Coffee Ring, Sugarplum, '83 M37
Egg Bread, Braided, '03 M234
English Muffin Bread, '95 M79
French Toast, Baked Apple, '03 M283
French Toast, Easy, '82 M172
Muffins, Apple-Bran, '85 M89
Muffins, Cheesy Cornbread, '88 M275
Muffins, Cinnamon-Nut, '85 M88
Muffins, Corn, '82 M282
Muffins, Cranberry Streusel Cake, '88 M274
Muffins, Fudge Brownie, '95 M50
Muffins, Lemon, '88 M275
Muffins, Whole Wheat Bran, '88 M274
Pizza Bread Rollups, '04 M35
Pumpkin Bread, Harvest, '90 M215
Rolls, Cherry-Almond, '84 M198
Rolls, Cinnamon, '99 M284
Rolls, Dinner, '93 M326
Rolls, Easy Orange, '89 M131
Tomato-Cheese Bread, '99 M157
Waffles, Honey-Buttered Peanut Butter, '94 M206
Whole Wheat-Rye Bread, '83 M37
Butter, Cinnamon, '01 M309
Butter, Sweet Potato, '95 M290
Chart, Shortcuts, '89 M134
Chutney, Autumn Fruit, '88 M230
Couscous, Cranberry-and-Toasted Pecan, '05 M259
Croutons, '86 M288
Croutons, Microwave, '86 M227

Desserts. *See also* **MICROWAVE/Sauces and Gravies.**
Apple-Almond Bake, '02 M209
Apple Crumble, Whole Wheat-, '90 M213
Apple Dessert, Honey-Baked, '90 M213
Apple-Nut Crunch, '82 M238
Apple Rings, Cinnamon, '82 M237
Apples and Cream, Brandied, '82 M237
Apples, Candy, '01 M205
Apples, Caramel, '89 M231
Apples, Caramel-Peanut, '93 M244
Apples, Easy Baked, '82 M238
Balls, Buckeye, '00 M280; '01 M322
Bananas Foster, '83 M114
Banana Splits, French Toast, '96 M164
Bark, Cherry-Pistachio, '00 M41
Bars, Blackberry Jam, '82 M185
Bars, Chewy Peanut, '80 M172
Bars, Chewy Praline-Chocolate Fudge, '04 M330
Bars, Chewy Scotch, '98 M291
Bars, Date-Oat, '80 M172
Bars, Gooey Turtle, '96 M189
Bars, Peanut Butter-and-Fudge, '80 M172
Bars, Praline, '05 M205
Blueberry Dessert, Easy, '89 M130
Brie, Almond-Raspberry, '94 M89
Brownie Bars, Broadway, '97 M35
Brownies à la Mode, Magnolias Cream Cheese, '97 M178
Brownies, Banana-Split, '03 M43
Brownies, Basic, '97 M34
Brownies, Biscuit Mix, '94 M51
Brownies, Caramel-Coconut-Pecan, '05 M288
Brownies, Caramel-Pecan Filled, '03 M43
Brownies, Chocolate Fudge, '05 M288

Brownies, Chocolate-Mint, '85 M294
Brownies, Cream Cheese, '04 M330
Brownies, Dark Chocolate, '00 M211
Brownies, Double Chocolate, '04 M220
Brownies, Frosted, '97 M87
Brownies, Frosted Peanut Butter, '00 M155
Brownies, Layered, '02 M252
Brownies, Magnolia Cream Cheese, '01 M63
Brownies, Mississippi Mud, '89 M25
Brownies, Mississippi Mud Dessert, '01 M314
Brownies, Nutty Fudge, '80 M171
Brownies, Passover, '98 M104
Brownies, Praline-Pecan, '05 M288
Brownie Squares, Mint Truffle, '05 M254
Brownies, Quick, '87 M302
Brownies with Caramel Frosting, Double Chocolate, '04 M220
Cake Batter, Chocolate Velvet, '03 M286
Cake, Chocolate-Raspberry, '01 319
Cake, Coconut Layer, '05 M246
Cake for Grown-Ups, Ice Cream, '88 M192
Cake, Fruit and Spice, '87 M97
Cake, Fudge, '94 M293
Cake, German Chocolate, '83 M233
Cake, German Chocolate Pound, '97 M254
Cake, No-Egg Chocolate Marshmallow, '87 M97
Cake, Old-Fashioned Carrot, '83 M232
Cake, Peanut Butter, '83 M233
Cake, Shortbread Fudge, '03 M331
Cakes, Miniature Chocolate Truffle Tree, '97 M285
Cakes, Spring's Little, '01 M91
Candies, Turtle, '93 M41
Candy Bow, '99 M306
Candy Box, White, '97 M54
Candy Cups, Rocky Road-Peanut Butter, '04 M330
Caramel Apples, '03 M216
Caramel Apples, Calypso, '03 M216
Charlotte Russe, '82 M142
Cheesecake, Chocolate-Amaretto, '85 M294
Cheesecake, Chocolate Fudge, '05 M288
Cheesecake, Chocolate-Wrapped Banana, '99 M48
Cheesecake, Fudge, '98 M213
Cheesecake, Luscious Lemon, '90 M196
Cheesecake, Peach-Caramel, '02 M158
Cheesecake, Pear-Berry, '82 M141
Cheesecake with Mocha Sauce, Chocolate-Coffee, '05 M316
Cherries, Chocolate-Covered, '97 M55
Cherries Jubilee, Quick, '82 M100
Chocolate-Coffee Cones, '96 M316
Chocolate Hearts, Crispy, '03 M41
Chocolate-Lemon Creams, '98 M235
Chocolate-Marshmallow Squares, '92 M50
Chocolate-Mint Parfaits, '90 M15
Chocolate Mint Snowballs, '04 M211
Chocolate-Peanut Butter Bites, '92 M317
Chocolate Peanutty Swirls, '94 M330
Chocolate Rudolph Reindeer, '04 M254
Clusters, No-Bake Peanut Butter, '05 M211
Clusters, Toasted Pecan, '00 M14
Cobbler, Apple-Pecan, '84 M198
Cobbler, Sweet Potato, '99 M255
Cobbler, Sweet Potato-Apple, '04 M232
Coconut Joys, Chocolate-Covered, '98 M282
Coconut Robin's Nests, '98 M111
Coffee Cakes, Banana-Toffee, '02 M324
Coffee Cake, Triple-Chocolate, '04 M299
Cookie Bites, Toffee, '03 M273
Cookies, Angel Shortbread, '97 M285
Cookies, Chocolate-Almond Surprise, '88 M45
Cookies, Chocolate-Dipped, '05 M299
Cookies, Chunky Cherry-Double Chip, '05 M87
Cookies, Doubly-Good Chocolate, '82 M185
Cookies, Keyboard, '94 M330

Cookies, Nutty Oatmeal-Chocolate Chip, '82 M185
Cookies, Peanut Butter-Toffee Turtle, '02 M325
Cookies, Rudolph, '99 M309
Cookies, Spice, '87 M278
Cookies, Spider, '93 M166
Cookies, Wedding, '82 M185
Cream, Bavarian, '86 M165
Cream, Vanilla, '83 M115
Crème, Orange-Tapioca, '82 M283
Crisp, Pear, '02 M233
Crisps, Dark Chocolate-Almond, '05 M30
Crunch, White Chocolate-Peanut Butter, '02 M296
Crust, Chocolate, '90 M15
Crust, Graham Cracker, '88 M45; '91 M234
Crust, Microwaved Graham Cracker, '82 M141
Cupcakes, Cinnamon-Chocolate, '81 M139
Cups, Vanilla Lace, '98 M93
Custard, Chocolate-Topped Amaretto, '87 M37
Divinity, Peanut, '87 M278
Dumplings, Cinnamon Apple, '97 M330
Éclairs, Mini Tiramisù, '03 M41
Filling, Chocolate, '05 M307
Filling, Chocolate-Coffee Buttercream, '00 M287
Filling, Chocolate Truffle, '04 M253
Filling, Nutty Cranberry, '00 M306
Fondant, Faux, '98 M154
Fondue, Chocolate, '05 M281
Frosting, Buttery Cinnamon, '81 M139
Frosting, Caramel, '81 M289
Frosting, Chocolate, '80 M171; '83 M233; '87 M97;
    '89 M25; '97 M87
Frosting, Chocolate Buttercream, '98 M100
Frosting, Coconut-Pecan, '83 M233
Frosting, Cream Cheese, '83 M233
Frosting, Easy Microwave, '05 M63
Frosting, Mint Chocolate, '99 M176
Frosting, White Chocolate Buttercream, '97 M284
Fudge, Butterscotch-Peanut, '98 M282
Fudge, Double-Good, '79 M263; '95 M50
Fudge, Double Good, '87 M278
Fudge, Microwave, '91 M92
Fudge, Microwave Chocolate, '92 M50; '02 M31
Fudge, Quick-and-Easy, '88 M190
Fudge Squares, Chocolate-Peanut Butter, '97 M54
Ganache, Chocolate, '00 M72; '01 M235; '03 M286
Ganache, Mocha, '04 M260
Ganache, Simple Chocolate, '03 M212
Ghosts, Little, '03 M212
Ghosts on a Stick, '00 M235
Glaze, Brownie, '02 M252
Glaze, Chocolate, '91 M296; '97 M35; '01 M45,
    M126; '05 221, M287
Glaze, French Chocolate, '98 M57
Glaze, Vanilla, '04 M84
Glaze, White Chocolate, '01 M45
Grahams, Caramel-Apple, '04 M183
Grahams, Peanut Butter-Apple, '04 M183
Holly Leaves, '99 M306
Ice Cream, Mocha, '97 M145
Ice Cream, No-Cook Turtle, '04 M179
Jam Squares, '81 M289
Jamwiches, Sweetheart, '03 M41
Jellyrolls, Raspberry, '93 M255
Kahlúa Delight, Make-Ahead, '84 M89
Kahlúa Velvet Dessert, '85 M294
Macaroons, White Chocolate Tropical, '00 M166
Millionaires, '79 M262; '97 M55
Mousse, Chocolate, '02 M277
Mousse, White Chocolate, '98 M57, M111
Napoleons, Caramel-Apple, '01 M313

Nuggets, Golden North Pole, '99 M309
Oatmeal Cherry-Apple Crisp, '90 M16
Oranges, Wine-Poached, '84 M323
Pastries, Chocolate-Chestnut, '02 M273
Pastry, Basic, '81 M268
Pastry, Basic Microwave, '82 M142; '85 M113
Pastry, Double-Crust, '82 M298
Pastry Strips, Decorated, '02 M296
Peaches, Gingersnap, '85 M329
Peach Melba, '83 M114
Peanut Brittle, '79 M263
Peanut Brittle, Chocolate-Dipped, '02 M223
Peanut Brittle, Classic, '02 M223
Peanut Brittle, Popcorn, '02 M223
Peanut Butter Slice-and-Bakes, '82 M185
Peanut Clusters, '98 M282
Peanut-Fudge Bites, '91 M231; '92 M68
Pears with Dark Chocolate Sauce, Poached,
    '90 M141
Pecan Brittle, '91 M272; '02 M223
Pecan Brittle, Microwave, '97 M245
Pecan-Coconut Clusters, '86 M251
Pecans, Chocolate-Dipped, '05 M269
Pie, Apple-Cranberry, '99 M269
Pie, Best-Ever Chocolate, '88 M45
Pie, Caramel-Banana, '86 M165
Pie, Chocolate-Covered Cherry, '05 M216
Pie, Cranberry-Apple Holiday, '81 M269
Pie, Double Chocolate, '82 M282
Pie, Easy Cherry, '82 M299
Pie, Festive Pumpkin, '81 M269
Pie, Fluffy Eggnog, '81 M269
Pie, Frosty Pumpkin-Praline, '91 M234
Pie, Glazed Strawberry, '82 M142
Pie, Lemon Meringue, '85 M112
Pie, Microwave Chocolate, '90 M15
Pie, Nutty Cranberry, '82 M298
Pie, Old-Fashioned Apple, '82 M299
Pie, Old-Fashioned Pecan, '81 M269
Pie, Quick Pumpkin, '88 M230
Pixies, Chocolate, '00 M155
Pizza, Banana Split-Brownie, '96 M164
Plums, Poached, '90 M141
Popcorn Delight, '00 M133
Pots de Crème, '84 M145
Pots de Crème, Mocha, '88 M45
Pralines, '86 M288
Pralines, Old-Fashioned, '89 M318
Pralines, Southern, '79 M263
Pudding, Bread, '89 M130
Pudding, Brown Sugar-Pecan, '86 M165
Pudding, Butternut Squash, '89 M313; '90 M19
Pudding, Chocolate-Almond, '82 M142
Pudding, Creamy Banana, '89 M130
Pudding, Mandarin-Almond, '85 M12
Pudding, Pecan-Mocha, '89 M130
Pudding, Pumpkin, '89 M313; '90 M20
Pudding, White Chocolate Bread, '00 M104
Reindeer Food, Magic, '99 M309
Sachertorte, Shortcut, '99 M243
Shortbread, Marble-Topped Hazelnut, '99 M29
Shortbread, Millionaire, '05 M94
Soufflé, Brandy Alexander, '83 M114
Spooky Ghosts, '98 M256
Squares, Crispy Peanut, '01 M161
Squares, Turtle Cake, '05 M211
Stars, White Chocolate, '00 M307
Sticky Fingers, '03 M168
Strawberries, Chocolate-Dipped, '98 M100
Sugarplum Fairy Wands, '97 M286
Sundaes, Chocolate Mint, '03 M120
Sundaes, Cocoa-Kahlúa, '83 M58
Sundaes, Hot Strawberry, '81 M5
Sundaes, Spicy Apple Ice Cream, '86 M195

Sundaes, Waffle Taco, '05 M62
Tart, Caramel Turtle Truffle, '93 M131
Tart, Cranberry-Apple, '97 M316
Tart, Rustic Apple-Cranberry, '01 M314
Tarts, Peppermint Brownie, '05 M288
Toffee, Microwave, '92 M317
Toffee, Microwave Peanut, '04 M234
Toffee, Nutty, '79 M263
Torte, Bourbon-Chocolate, '98 M84
Torte, Chocolate-Almond, '96 M253
Torte, X-Treme Chocolate Double Nut Caramel
    Ladyfinger, '04 M315
Truffles, Hazelnut, '97 M54
Truffles, Raspberry-Fudge, '00 M41
Truffles, Yule Street, '90 M242
Waffles with Apples and Caramel, Gingerbread,
    '98 M237
Zuppa Inglese, '99 M267
Doughnuts with Strawberry Preserves, Hanukkah,
    '01 M275
Eggs and Omelets
Baked Eggs Florentine, '86 M12
Benedict, Easy Eggs, '80 M268
Benedict, Light Eggs, '93 M68
Casserole, Saucy Scrambled Egg, '89 M213
Casserole, Sausage-Egg, '86 M12
Cheddar Eggs, '94 M141
Creamed Eggs in Patty Shells, '80 M267
Medley, Cheddary Egg, '81 M176
Olé Omelet, '87 M124
Pie, Omelet, '00 M35
Poached Eggs, Microwave, '02 M131
Sausage Omelet, Puffy, '80 M268
Scramble, Bacon-and-Eggs, '80 M267
Scrambled Eggs, Creamy Onion, '83 M203
Vegetable Omelet, Golden, '82 M123
Frostings. See MICROWAVE/Desserts.
Fruit Bake, Cranberry-Mustard, '90 M287
Fruit Compote, Hot, '90 M124
Fruit Mélange, '88 M295
Granola, Superhero, '98 M206
Grits, Quick Cheese, '83 M203
Jam, Blackberry, '99 M131
Jam, Freezer Blackberry, '84 M181
Jam, Freezer Peach, '84 M182
Jam, Freezer Plum, '89 M156
Jam, Raspberry Freezer, '84 M181
Jam, Strawberry Freezer, '84 M182
Jelly, Christmas Freezer, '86 M288
Jelly, Quick Grape, '89 M156
Jelly, Red Pepper, '89 M156
Macaroni and Cheese, '83 M7; '88 M147, M190
Macaroni with Blue Cheese and Walnuts, '02 M208
Main Dishes
Beans and Franks, Jiffy, '91 M172
Beans-and-Franks, Polynesian, '84 M11
Beef Casserole, Easy, '86 M58
Beef Casserole, Layered, '82 M203
Beef Pie, Sensational, '03 M284
Beef Roast, Easy, '89 M65
Beef with Mashed Potatoes and Chipotle Cream,
    Grilled, '02 M320
Beef with Pea Pods, Oriental, '86 M328
Broccoli-Ham au Gratin, '90 M239
Burgers, Barbara's Big Juicy, '93 M138; '04 M178
Burgers, Blue Cheese, '89 M66
Casserole, Mexi, '83 M87
Casserole, Mexican, '92 M22
Casserole, Microwave Mexican, '90 M231
Catfish, Microwave, '89 M52
Catfish, Spicy-Seasoned, '89 M66
Chicken alla Romano, '83 M58
Chicken-and-Broccoli Stroganoff, '89 M248
Chicken and Cashews, Ginger, '85 M11

Chicken-and-Corn Cakes with Avocado Cream, Southwestern, '97 M311
Chicken and Dumplings with Vegetables, '85 M56
Chicken and Pasta, Pesto, '89 M132
Chicken and Spinach Rollups, '82 M68
Chicken-and-Vegetable Platter, '88 M52
Chicken and Vegetables Vermouth, '87 M37
Chicken-Asparagus Rolls, '86 M211
Chicken, Barbecued, '89 M167
Chicken Breasts, Breaded, '89 M196
Chicken Breasts, Herb-Seasoned, '93 M325
Chicken, Crispy Parmesan, '80 M76
Chicken, Crunchy Spiced, '85 M57
Chicken Delicacy, '99 M23
Chicken Dinner, Hot-and-Spicy, '94 M94
Chicken Divan, '80 M10; '87 M218
Chicken Divan Casserole, '82 M203
Chicken Divan Quiche, '88 M125
Chicken, Easy, '89 M129
Chicken Enchiladas, Creamy, '01 M94
Chicken Enchiladas Verde, '00 M240
Chicken, Ginger-Nut, '90 M33
Chicken in a Bag, '86 M57
Chicken Kebabs, Marinated, '84 M144
Chicken Kebabs, Pineapple-, '86 M328
Chicken Lasagna, '87 M302
Chicken, Lemon, '81 M138
Chicken, Lemon-Garlic, '89 M132
Chicken Mexicana, '91 M127
Chicken, Orange, '86 M140
Chicken, Pineapple, '83 M194
Chicken, Tangy Herbed, '87 M302
Chicken, Tea-Thyme Grilled, '05 M52
Chicken Teriyaki, '80 M76
Chicken Tetrazzini, '80 M75
Chicken Tetrazzini, Cheesy, '83 M87
Chicken Toss, Quick, '87 M124
Chicken, Vegetable-Stuffed, '89 M65
Chicken with Noodles, Sesame, '88 M125
Chicken with Pecan-Rice Dressing, '85 M57
Chicken with Tomato-Basil Pasta, Basil-Stuffed, '94 M204
Chicken with White Barbecue Sauce, '89 M84
Chicken with Wild Rice, Elegant, '80 M76
Chicken, Zesty Barbecued, '80 M76
Chiles Rellenos with Walnut Cream Sauce, Havarti-and-Corn-Stuffed, '93 M275
Chili-Cheese Dogs, '81 M176
Chili, Microwave, '91 M232
Chili, Turkey-Bean, '88 M213
Cornish Hens, Orange-Glazed Stuffed, '84 M89
Crab Imperial, Pineapple-, '84 M286
Crabmeat and Mushrooms on Toast Points, '82 M91
Crabmeat Imperial, Speedy, '90 M112
Crab, Shrimp, and Artichoke au Gratin, '90 M240
Crawfish Delicacy, '99 M23
Crêpes, Sherried Beef, '85 M29
Dinner, Easy Steamed, '83 M314
Dogs, Taco, '02 M57
Filet Mignon Patties, Mock, '82 M68
Fillets, Apple-Carrot Stuffed, '88 M192
Fillets, Lemon-Coated, '80 M53
Fillets, Parmesan, '86 M112
Fillets, Spanish-Style, '86 M112
Fish Amandine, Fillet of, '80 M54
Fish-and-Potato Platter, '89 M248
Fish-and-Vegetable Dinner, '91 M196
Fish, Creole, '87 M79
Fish Delight, '86 M212
Fish, Easy Italian, '86 M112
Fish, Herb-Coated, '86 M112
Fish in Creamy Swiss Sauce, Poached, '80 M53
Fish Rolls, Vegetable-Filled, '86 M251
Fish Steaks, Soy, '86 M112

Fish, Sweet-and-Sour, '80 M54
Fish with Greek Sauce, Poached, '91 M183
Flautas, Rancho Ramillete, '96 M125
Flounder Amandine, '89 M196
Flounder, Baked, '90 M316
Frankfurters, Barbecued, '84 M12
Grits, Sausage-Cheese, '90 M238
Grouper Fillets, Breaded, '89 M36
Grouper with Confetti Vegetables, '88 M189
Grouper with Sautéed Vegetables, '90 M233
Haddock Fillets with Zucchini Stuffing, '88 M191
Haddock Italiano, '81 M4
Halibut Steaks Italiano, '88 M191
Halibut with Swiss Sauce, '83 M195
Ham and Apples, Baked, '82 M237
Ham and Apples, Grilled, '96 M303
Ham and Chicken, Creamed, '81 M74
Ham-Asparagus Dinner, '80 M10
Hamburger Patties, '82 M172
Ham Casserole, Macaroni-, '81 M177
Ham Loaf, Cranberry-, '82 M77
Ham Loaf, Saucy, '86 M328
Ham, Marmalade-Glazed, '89 M196
Ham Ring, Chili-Sauced, '81 M122
Ham Roll Casserole, '91 M127
Ham Slice, Fruited, '83 M317
Ham Steak, Glazed, '91 M13
Ham, Sweet-and-Sour Glazed, '88 M15
Ham Tetrazzini, '82 M77
Ham Towers, Cheesy, '82 M77
Ham with Bourbon Glaze, Baked, '98 M271; '01 M42
Ham with Raisin Sauce, '82 M76
Kebabs, Shish, '85 M112
Kielbasa and Cabbage, '89 M196
Lamb Chops, Sage, '96 M328
Lasagna, '83 M6
Lasagna, Easy, '92 M197; '93 M24
Lasagna, Lots of Noodles, '91 M127
Lasagna, Microwave, '96 M225
Lasagna, One-Step, '89 M129
Lasagna, Quick 'n Easy, '80 M10
Lasagna, Roasted Vegetable-Meat, '99 M332
Lasagna Rolls, Pepper-Topped, '89 M36
Lasagna, Speedy, '05 M252
Lasagna, Zesty, '87 M188
Manicotti, Stuffed, '83 M6
Meat Loaf, Basic, '88 M14
Meat Loaf, Cheesy Pizza, '81 M121
Meat Loaf, Easy, '88 M214
Meat Loaf, Oriental, '81 M122; '83 M194
Meat Loaf, Swedish, '81 M121
Meat Loaf, Vegetable, '85 M209
Monkfish, Greek-Style, '87 M79
Mussels Linguine, '90 M112
Orange Roughy with Spinach Pesto, '88 M192
Oysters on the Half Shell, Dressed, '87 M79
Paella, Party, '88 M189
Papillote, Ocean, '84 M287
Patties, Cracked Pepper, '89 M131
Peppers, Beef-Stuffed, '91 M127
Peppers, Hearty Stuffed, '88 M214
Pie, Country Breakfast, '93 M328
Pineapple Loaves, Individual, '81 M121
Pizza, Bistro Grilled Chicken, '05 M131
Pizza Casserole, Microwave, '89 M248
Pizza, Jiffy Jazzed-Up, '83 M314
Pizzas, Muffuletta, '00 M335
Pizza, Taco, '89 M177
Pork Casserole, Cheesy, '81 M74
Pork Chop, Saucy, '86 M140
Pork Chops, Lemon-Herb, '89 M132
Pork Chops, Pineapple, '87 M124
Pork Chops with Apricot Glaze, Stuffed, '89 M36

Pork Enchiladas, '97 M94
Pork Kebabs, Margarita, '98 M223
Pork Loin Roast with Red Currant Sauce, '89 M84
Pork Roast, Orange-Glazed, '04 M236
Potatoes, Chili-Topped, '98 M289
Potatoes, Frank-Filled, '84 M11
Pot Roast, Basic, '81 M208
Pot Roast, Company, '88 M14
Pot Roast with Vegetables, '81 M208
Pot Roast with Vegetables, Marinated, '88 M52
Quesadillas, Easy, '98 M205
Quiche, Benedict, '80 M107
Quiche, Crab, '82 M122
Quiche Lorraine, '80 M108; '99 M218
Quiche, Spicy Sausage, '80 M108
Quiche, Spinach-Mushroom, '81 M74
Quiche, Vegetable, '87 M219
Red Beans and Rice, Easy, '99 M219
Ribs, Sweet-and-Sour, '89 M84
Round Steak over Rice, Burgundy, '90 M33
Salmon Patties, Open-Faced, '87 M218
Sausage and Rice Casserole, Oriental, '82 M123
Sausage Casserole, Easy, '87 M189
Sausage Dinner, Beefy, '80 M9
Sausage-Egg Casserole, '86 M12
Sausage Jambalaya Casserole, '82 M203
Shrimp Creole, '90 M220
Shrimp, Garlic-Buttered, '86 M226
Shrimp in Cream Sauce, '84 M286
Shrimp, Quick Curried, '84 M198
Shrimp, Sweet-and-Sour, '90 M112
Shrimp with Bacon and Jalapeños, Grilled, '05 M200
Sloppy Joes, Pocket, '85 M328
Snapper Provençal, '91 M170
Sole, Saucy, '82 M68
Sole with Cucumber Sauce, '84 M286
Spaghetti, Easy, '83 M317
Spaghetti Pie, '81 M32
Spinach-Tenderloin Pinwheels, '89 M118
Squash with Meat Sauce, Spaghetti, '88 M180
Steak, Onion-Smothered, '87 M189
Taco Pies, Individual, '82 M282
Tacos, Jiffy, '83 M318
Tacos, Microwave, '88 M213
Tortilla Pie, '85 M211
Trout, Sunshine, '84 M286
Trout with Orange Sauce, Pecan-Crusted, '98 M82
Tuna Casserole, Easy, '82 M203
Turkey Breast and Gravy, Savory Seasoned, '89 M309
Turkey Casserole, Crunchy, '89 M282
Turkey Divan, Creamy, '90 M34
Turkey-Noodle-Poppyseed Casserole, '90 M239
Turkey Scaloppine, Easy, '95 M192
Turkey Tenderloin with Raspberry-Chipotle Sauce, Jerk, '05 M194
Veal and Carrots in Wine Sauce, '86 M139
Veal, Italian Style, '82 M68
Welsh Rarebit with Tomatoes and Bacon, '92 M159
Zucchini, Beef-Stuffed, '86 M139
Marmalade, Orange-Pineapple, '89 M156
Mustard, Coarse-and-Sweet, '86 M288
Noodles, Cheesy Parmesan, '83 M7
Pancakes with Apple-Pear Sauce, Oatmeal Mini-, '97 M272
Party Mix, White Chocolate, '03 M289
Pastry, Microwaved Quiche, '81 M74; '82 M122
Pastry, Quiche, '80 M107
Peaches, Bay Laurel, '90 M124
Peaches with Rum, Ginger, '84 M323
Pears, Gingered, '89 M231
Pears, Marmalade Breakfast, '83 M203
Pears, Spiced Fall, '89 M231
Pickles, Peppery Texas, '04 M161

Pineapple, Scalloped, '84 M323
Pizza on a Bagel, '93 M94
Popcorn, Chili, '00 M223
Popcorn Clusters, Caramel-Nut, '00 M223
Pumpkin, Cooked Fresh, '88 M230
Pumpkin Seeds, Seasoned, '91 M234
Pumpkin Seeds, Toasted, '88 M230
Relish, Cranberry-Orange, '81 M289
Relish, Quick Corn, '90 M13
Relish, Spicy Apple, '84 M323
Relish, Tipsy Cranberry, '92 M310
Rice, Almond, '85 M112
Rice, Basic Long-Grain, '83 M285
Rice, Basic Quick-Cooking, '83 M285
Rice, Chicken-Flavored, '84 M144
Rice, Curry-Spiced, '86 M226
Rice, Herb, '91 M257
Rice, Herbed, '83 M285
Rice, Jiffy Spanish, '90 M176
Rice, Oriental, '85 M12, 146
Rice, Parsleyed, '83 M58
Rice Pilaf, Basil, '05 M197
Rice with Almonds, Curried, '83 M285
Risotto, Microwave, '97 M213
Rosemary, Sugared, '04 M279

Salads
   Artichokes with Orzo Salad, '88 M193
   Beef Salad, Tangy, '87 M218
   Chef Salad, Microwave, '90 M146
   Chicken Salad, Special, '88 M193
   Chicken Taco Salad, '94 M136
   Dressing, Raspberry Salad, '03 M28
   Fast-and-Easy Salad, '85 M328
   Fried Okra Salad, '97 M157
   Fruit Congealed Salad, Layered, '05 M146
   Fruit Salad with Mint Sauce, '88 M96
   Green Beans-and-Cheese Salad, '91 M159
   Pork-and-Spinach Salad, Mandarin, '88 M126
   Potato Salad, Chunky, '81 M138
   Potato Salad, German-Style, '88 M194
   Spaghetti Squash Salad, '99 M322
   Spinach Salad, Sweet-Sour, '85 M112
   Spinach Salad, Wilted, '81 M4
   Squash Salad, '03 M184
   Taco Salad Cups, '85 M29
   Tomato-Pasta Salad, '97 M160
   Tuna Salad, Cheese-Sauced, '87 M124

Sandwiches
   Asparagus-and-Ham Melt Sandwiches, '88 M96
   Breakfast Pita Pockets, '89 M21
   Breakfast Sandwiches, '82 M123; '89 M230
   Brown Bread-Cream Cheese Sandwiches, '87 M6
   Burgers, Pizza, '80 M201
   Cheese-Steak Wraps, '00 M335
   Chicken Tortas, Grilled, '01 M187
   Crabmeat Sandwiches, Deluxe, '81 M74
   Frankfurter Sandwiches, '84 M11
   Fruit-and-Cheese Breakfast Sandwiches, '89 M21
   Grilled Cheese Sandwiches, '82 M172
   Hot Brown Sandwiches, '80 M202
   Pita Sandwiches, Denver, '86 M12
   Pita Sandwiches, Hot, '87 M6
   Pizza Sandwiches, Open-Face, '84 M198
   Pork Sandwiches, Party, '88 M273
   Reuben Sandwiches, '80 M201
   Sausage-Cheese Muffin Sandwiches, '92 M212
   Sausage in a Bun, '89 M22
   Tuna Sandwiches, Hot, '86 M194

Sauces and Gravies
   Almond-Vanilla Custard Sauce, '88 M177

Amaretto-Strawberry Sauce, '87 M165
Apple Dessert Sauce, '87 M165
Apple-Pear Sauce, '97 M272
Barbecue Sauce, Lemony, '88 M177
Béchamel Sauce, '84 M239
Blueberry Sauce, '89 M130
Champagne-Chocolate Sauce, '05 M282
Cheese Sauce, '79 M156; '82 M123
Cheese Sauce, Guilt-Free, '93 M95
Cheesy Vegetable Sauce, '92 M134
Cherry Sauce, Elegant, '79 M156
Chocolate Cherry Sauce, '87 M165
Chocolate Mint Sauce, Quick, '86 M58
Chocolate-Peanut Butter Sauce, '79 M156
Chocolate-Praline Sauce, '85 M295
Chocolate Sauce, Creamy, '88 M177
Crab Marinara Sauce, Quick, '85 M151
Cranberry Sauce, Holiday, '02 M311
Cream Sauce, Sherried, '85 M152
Curry Sauce, '79 M156; '84 M71
Dill Sauce, '84 M70
Dill Sauce, Creamy, '79 M156
Garlic Butter Sauce, '05 M253
Garlic-Cheese Sauce, '84 M70
Hollandaise Sauce, '80 M107, M268; '88 M177
Horseradish-Mustard Sauce, Creamy, '88 M177
Horseradish Sauce, '88 M273
Jezebel Sauce, Gingered, '04 M138
Lemon Dessert Sauce, '87 M165
Mint Sauce, '88 M96
Mushroom Sauce, '84 M70
Mustard Sauce, '84 M70
Orange Dipping Sauce, '03 M212
Orange Sauce, '84 M286
Orange Sauce, Sweet, '93 M325
Parsley-Garlic Sauce, '84 M70
Peach-Berry Sauce, '87 M165
Peanut Dessert Sauce, '86 M251
Pineapple Ice Cream Sauce, '81 M289
Praline Ice Cream Sauce, Southern, '86 M227
Sour Cream Sauce, '82 M68
Swiss Sauce, '83 M195
Taco Sauce, '82 M283
Tomato Sauce, Herbed Fresh, '85 M151
Tomato Sauce, Italian, '82 M68
Vanilla Sauce, '97 M15
Vegetable-Cheese Sauce, '85 M152
White Sauce, Basic, '79 M156
Shortcuts, '89 M134
Snack Mix, Make-Ahead, '04 M92

Soups and Stews
   Bacon-Beer Cheese Soup, '87 M7
   Beef Stew with Parsley Dumplings, '85 M246
   Broccoli Soup, '86 M194
   Broccoli Soup, Cream of, '80 M225
   Carrot-Mint Soup, Chilled, '90 M168
   Carrot Soup, Creamy, '92 M218
   Cauliflower Soup, Cream of, '87 M7
   Cheddar-Potato Soup, '03 M283
   Cheese Soup, Bacon-Topped, '80 M224
   Cheese Soup, Monterey Jack, '85 M211
   Chicken-and-Wild Rice Soup, Creamy, '98 M334
   Chicken Broth, Easy Microwave, '90 M167
   Chicken Soup, Quick, '86 M72
   Chili, Basic, '82 M11
   Chili, Beefy Sausage, '82 M11
   Chili, Cheese-Topped, '82 M11
   Chili, Chunky, '82 M11
   Chili with Rice, '82 M11
   Chowder, Corn, '84 M38
   Chowder, Creamy Green Bean, Mushroom, and
     Ham, '99 M336
   Chowder, Creamy Ham, '88 M53
   Chowder, Fish, '84 M38

Chowder, New England Clam, '86 M72
Crab Soup, Creamy, '80 M224
Cream Cheese Soup, Austrian, '98 M85
Cucumber Soup, Dilled, '90 M167
Egg-Drop Soup, '85 M12
Garden Harvest Soup, Italian, '90 M167
Mushroom Soup, '86 M73
Mushroom Soup, Curried, '84 M89
Onion Soup, French, '86 M212
Onion Soup, Shortcut French, '85 M328
Oyster-and-Artichoke Soup, Louisiana, '92 M81
Pea Soup, Spring, '88 M96
Potato-Bacon Soup, '84 M38
Potato Soup, Cream of, '80 M224
Potato-Yogurt Soup, '92 M217
Strawberry Soup Supreme, '81 M144
Tomato-Celery Soup, '83 M58
Tomato-Vegetable Soup, '81 M177
Vegetable Soup, Beefy, '84 M38
Vegetable Soup, Chunky, '89 M283
Spoons, Dipped Chocolate-Almond, '95 M277
Spread, Peachy Cream Cheese, '90 M215
Topper, Sticky Bun Toast, '99 M72
Topping, Streusel, '88 M275
Tortelloni, Roasted Red Pepper-Caesar, '05 M186

Vegetables
   Acorn Rings, Easy Glazed, '81 M231
   Acorn Squash, Cranberry-Filled, '81 M231
   Acorn Squash, Sausage-Stuffed, '81 M231
   Artichokes, '92 M107
   Artichokes, Quick 'n' Easy Whole Cooked,
     '96 M132
   Artichokes, Stuffed, '91 M117
   Artichokes, Whole Cooked, '04 53
   Asparagus-Carrot-Squash Toss, '91 M45
   Asparagus in Lemon Butter, '80 M123
   Asparagus, Lemon-Sesame, '91 M31
   Asparagus-Pea Casserole, '88 M294
   Asparagus with Almond Sauce, '91 M117
   Asparagus with Lemon Butter, '87 M151
   Asparagus with Warm Citrus Dressing, '96 M86
   Beans, Marinated Italian, '86 M226
   Beets, Harvard, '83 M195
   Beets with Sour Cream Dressing, '88 M295
   Black-Eyed Peas, '03 M49
   Black-Eyed Peas, Fresh, '81 M165
   Broccoli au Gratin, '82 M20
   Broccoli Casserole, '05 M276
   Broccoli Casserole, Cheesy, '95 M191
   Broccoli Casserole, Easy, '03 M49
   Broccoli, Chinese, '85 M12
   Broccoli Goldenrod, Lemon-, '84 M89
   Broccoli, Marinated Fresh, '81 M139
   Broccoli-Swiss Cheese Casserole, '85 M211
   Butternut Squash, Apple-Stuffed, '81 M232
   Butternut Squash Ring, '81 M232
   Carrots-and-Celery, Scalloped, '84 M112
   Carrots, Orange-Fennel, '92 M133
   Carrots, Orange-Glazed, '81 M165; '90 M98
   Carrots, Peach-Glazed, '90 M13
   Carrots, Spice-Glazed, '83 M58
   Carrot-Sweet Potato Puree, '00 M32; '02 M285
   Corn-and-Bean Casserole, '90 M208
   Corn Fix-Up, Quick, '81 M4
   Corn, Mexi-, '82 M21
   Corn on the Cob, Chili, '03 M185
   Corn on the Cob, Fresh Basil, '00 M170
   Corn on the Cob, Microwaved, '80 M122
   Corn on the Cob, Parmesan, '88 M187
   Corn on the Cob, Spicy, '87 M151
   Corn, Parslied, '90 M155
   Corn, Seasoned Fresh, '83 M147
   Corn, Southern-Style Creamed, '81 M165
   Eggplant, Easy, '87 M151

Fresh Vegetables, Microwaving, '82 M138
Garden Harvest, '85 M142
Green Bean Gratin, Gourmet, '99 M334
Green Beans, '87 M151
Green Beans Amandine, '82 M20
Green Beans, Bacon-Topped, '80 M123
Green Beans, Baked, '91 M159
Green Beans, French, '90 M208
Green Beans, Garlic, '91 M159
Green Beans, Herbed, '83 M147; '88 M190
Green Beans, Nutty, '88 M187
Green Beans Oriental, '91 M158
Green Beans, Speedy Rosemary, '05 M241
Green Beans, Tangy, '85 M142
Green Beans with Bacon, Sautéed, '05 M160
Green Beans with Marjoram, Fresh, '91 M159
Green Peas, Company, '91 M31
Julienne Vegetables with Walnuts, '86 M251
Kebabs, Marinated Vegetable, '83 M195
Leeks in Dilled Lemon-Butter, '90 M98
Mashed Potatoes, Speedy Garlic, '04 M81
Medley, Garden Vegetable, '91 M45
Medley, Vegetable, '89 M129
Medley, Vegetable-Cheese, '99 M287
Mixed Vegetables, '83 M195
Mushrooms, Microwave Portabello, '95 M123
New Potatoes, Herbed, '83 M148
New Potatoes, Seasoned, '87 M151
New Potato Gratin, Creamy, '01 M320
Okra and Tomatoes, Fresh, '81 M165
Okra, Corn, and Peppers, '87 M151
Okra Medley, '88 M185
Onion-Potato Bake, '83 M195
Onions and Peppers, Sautéed, '83 M148
Onions, Micro-Baked, '82 M32
"Pasta," Garden-Fresh, '94 M134
Peas and Peppers, Minted, '90 M99
Peas in a Potato Nest, '84 M239
Peas with Almonds, Curried, '88 M294
Pepper Cups, Hot Vegetable, '88 M188
Platter, Vegetable, '88 M187
Potato Casserole, Creamy, '84 M113
Potatoes, Basil-Cheese, '90 M316
Potatoes, Blue Cheese Stuffed, '92 M228
Potatoes, Broccoli-Shrimp Stuffed, '92 M228
Potatoes, Cheesy Bacon-Stuffed, '81 M61
Potatoes, Chili-Cheese, '90 M62
Potatoes, Chili-Topped, '98 M289
Potatoes, Cottage, '93 M92
Potatoes, Creamy Cheese, '88 M146
Potatoes, Hearty Stuffed, '89 M282
Potatoes, Italian Mashed, '03 M135
Potatoes, Jalapeño-Ham Stuffed, '81 M61
Potatoes, Micro-Baked, '81 M61
Potatoes, Parmesan, '90 M62; '92 M341; '93 M46
Potatoes, Quick Baked, '92 M134
Potatoes, Quick Browned, '82 M172
Potatoes, Seafood-Stuffed, '95 M192
Potatoes, Shrimp-Sauced, '81 M61
Potatoes, Soufflé, '90 M14
Potatoes, Summertime, '86 M195
Potatoes, Taco-Topped, '93 M18
Potatoes, Twice-Baked, '91 M185
Potatoes with Béchamel Sauce, Stuffed, '84 M239
Potatoes with Chives, '81 M61
Potatoes with Hot Bacon Dressing, '88 M294
Potatoes with Tomato Gravy, Mashed, '02 M17
Potatoes, Zesty Stuffed, '94 M46
Potato Fans, Parmesan, '84 M240
Potato Fans, Parmesan-, '88 M190
Potato, Twice-Baked, '90 M295
Potato Wedges, '94 M119
Potato Wedges, Lemony, '90 M61
Ratatouille, Microwave, '95 M232

Snow Peas and Tomatoes, Basil, '88 M185
Spaghetti Squash with Meat Sauce, '88 M180
Spinach Casserole, '91 M31
Spinach Delight, '84 M144
Spuds, Mushroom-Swiss, '96 M238
Squash, Amarillo, '99 M218
Squash-and-Pepper Toss, Crisp, '87 M152
Squash Bake, Cheddar-, '84 M113
Squash Casserole, Jiffy, '81 M144
Squash Casserole, Southwestern, '05 M217
Squash, Country Club, '88 M16
Squash Medley, Fresh, '81 M165
Squash Mexican, Stuffed, '90 M200
Squash, Stuffed Summer, '02 M181
Squash, Stuffed White, '90 M201
Squash Stuffed with Spinach Pesto, '89 M133
Squash Toss, Simple, '85 M142
Steamed Herbed Vegetables, '93 M303
Stir-Fry, Vegetable, '82 M172
Sweet Potato Casserole, '03 M24
Sweet Potatoes, Applesauce, '91 M292; '92 M256
Sweet Potatoes, Cinnamon-Apple, '95 M23
Sweet Potatoes, Orange-Baked, '88 M294
Tomatoes with Walnut-Rice Stuffing, '91 M102
Tomatoes, Zippy Mustard, '86 M226
Zucchini and Carrots, Julienne, '90 M14
Zucchini Boats, '85 M143
Zucchini-Egg Casserole, '84 M113
Zucchini, Italian, '83 M147
Zucchini, Southwestern Stuffed, '03 M127
Zucchini, Stuffed, '89 M133
Vinaigrette, Apricot, '05 M312
Vinaigrette Dressing and Croutons, '86 M288

MINCEMEAT
Apples, Baked Mincemeat-Filled, '80 276
Apples, Stuffed, '99 247
Bars, Mincemeat-Spice, '88 231; '89 22
Cake, Mincemeat Spice, '79 246
Cakes, Mini-Mincemeat Nut, '88 257
Cheesecake, Holiday Mincemeat, '00 319
Cookies, Mincemeat, '79 51
Cookies, Mincemeat Drop, '79 246
Cookies, Mincemeat Sweetheart, '87 293
Cookies, Pear Mincemeat, '84 264
Homemade Mincemeat, '79 245
Peaches, Mincemeat, '85 178
Peaches with Mincemeat, Brandied, '81 47
Pear Mincemeat, '79 196; '84 264; '88 226
Pies
    Apple-Mincemeat Pie, '85 316
    Cheese Pie, Mincemeat-, '80 253
    Chiffon Pie, Mincemeat, '79 245
    Holiday Mincemeat Pie, '80 282; '87 213
    Ice Cream Pie, Mincemeat, '99 285
    Kentucky Mincemeat Pie, '95 302
    Peach Pie, Mincemeat-, '80 295; '81 188
    Pear Mincemeat Pie, '84 264; '88 226
    Pear-Mincemeat Pie, '98 258
    Pear-Mince Pie, '81 271
    Spirited Mince Pie, '92 316
Pudding, Steamed Mincemeat, '80 264
Salad, Holiday Mincemeat, '85 263
Salad, Mincemeat, '94 282
Stuffing, Mincemeat, '00 319
MINTS. *See* **APPETIZERS/Mints.**
MOUSSES
Amaretto Mousse, '86 188
Apricot Mousse, '82 72; '91 297
Asparagus Mousse Salad, '86 252
Avocado Mousse with Shrimp Salad, '98 333
Butter Pecan Mousse, '95 286
Butterscotch Mousse, '93 254
Catfish Mousse, '92 327

Caviar Mousse, '82 71; '85 86; '92 83
Chicken Mousse, Curried, '95 328
Chocolate
    Almond Mousse, Chocolate-, '93 316
    Amaretto-Chocolate Mousse, '86 50
    Amaretto-Chocolate Mousse, Elegant, '86 337
    au Grand Marnier, Chocolate Mousse, '91 296
    Baked Alaska Chocolate Mousse, '85 195
    Blender Chocolate Mousse, '82 71
    Blender-Quick Chocolate Mousse, '80 269
    Brandy-Chocolate Mousse, '85 102
    Cake, Cappuccino Mousse, '99 154
    Cake, Chocolate Mousse, '87 264; '98 270; '03 320
    Cake, Chocolate-Peanut Butter Mousse, '98 71
    Cake, Strawberry-Studded White Chocolate Mousse, '99 154
    Chocolate Mousse, '88 280; '97 282; '02 M277
    Creamy Chocolate Mousse, '87 133
    Dark Chocolate Mousse with Raspberry Sauce, '05 31
    Honeyed Chocolate Mousse, '87 223
    Kid-Pleasin' Chocolate Mousse, '90 271
    Loaf with Raspberry Puree, Chocolate Mousse, '97 34
    Mint Chocolate Mousse Tarts, '03 283
    Mocha Mousse Torte, '04 260
    Orange Liqueur, Chocolate Mousse with, '02 315
    Orange Mousse, Chocolate-, '81 16, 205
    Parfait, Chocolate Mousse, '94 90
    Peanut Butter Mousse Parfaits, Chocolate-, '98 71
    Pie, Chocolate-Amaretto Mousse, '80 180; '81 30
    Pie, Chocolate Mousse, '81 136
    Present, Chocolate Mousse, '99 281
    Quick-as-a-Wink Mousse, '84 311
    Quick Chocolate Mousse, '85 87
    Roll, Chocolate Mousse, '88 280
    Rum Mousse, Chocolate, '86 189
    Truffle Mousse with Raspberry Sauce, Chocolate, '95 327
    White Chocolate Mousse, '91 247; '93 315; '97 282; '98 57, M111; '99 155
    White Chocolate Mousse, Quick, '99 155
    White Chocolate Mousse Torte, '99 154
Coconut-Pineapple Mousse, '94 198
Coffee Mousse, '84 126
Coffee-Nut Mousse, '86 319
Crabmeat Mousse, '90 190; '91 244; '94 159
Crab Mousse, '79 117; '95 327
Cran-Apple Mousse, '93 255
Crème de Menthe Mousse, '80 109
Cucumber Mousse, '79 11; '88 121
Cucumber Mousse with Dill Sauce, '95 216
Ham Mousse Pitas, '95 328
Horseradish Mousse, '84 126
Lemon Cloud Mousse, '90 90
Lemon Mousse with Raspberry Sauce, '91 96; '92 130
Lime Mousse Freeze, Luscious, '81 173
Macaroni Mousse, '96 73
Margarita Tacos, '97 167
Mustard Mousse, '84 127; '86 184; '95 328
Orange Mousse, '86 69; '94 198
Oyster Mousse, '81 245
Oyster Mousse, Smoked, '84 320; '99 162
Peach Macaroon Mousse, '80 153
Peach Mousse, '85 54
Peppermint Candy Mousse, '82 71; '94 198
Peppermint Mousse, '93 315
Pineapple Mousse, Elegant, '79 230
Pumpkin Mousse, '91 96; '92 130
Raspberry Mousse, '81 34; '04 260
Raspberry Mousse in Chocolate Crinkle Cups, '93 270
Rhubarb Mousse, '88 93
Roquefort Mousse, '82 71
Salmon Dill Mousse, '81 21

MOUSSES
(continued)

Salmon Mousse, Irresistible, '79 284
Sherried Mousse, '81 247
Shrimp Mousse, '79 57; '87 196, 251
Strawberry-Lemon Mousse, '82 128
Strawberry Mousse, '81 95
Strawberry Mousse, Fresh, '82 72
Tuna Mousse, '80 275
Watercress Mousse, '88 104
Watermelon Mousse, Frozen, '91 96; '92 130

MUFFINS
Almond Muffins, '90 87
Almond Muffins, Peachy-, '86 301

Apple
Apple Muffins, '83 96; '84 193; '87 23; '99 234
Applesauce Muffins, '84 284; '91 141
Bite-Size Applesauce Muffins, '82 104
Bran Muffins, Apple-, '85 M89
Caramel-Apple Muffins, '05 210
Carrot Muffins, Apple-, '91 213
Cinnamon Oat Bran Muffins, Apple-, '89 106
Fresh Apple Muffins, '84 264
Oat Muffins, Spicy Apple-, '86 45
Pumpkin-Apple Muffins, '96 242
Spiced Apple Muffins, '79 60
Spice Muffins, Applesauce, '88 236

Banana
Banana Muffins, '80 88; '84 75
Bran Muffins, Banana, '83 48
Chocolate Chip Muffins, Jumbo Banana-, '93 339
Chocolate Muffins, Banana-, '94 197
Cream Cheese-Banana-Nut Muffins, '05 27
Honey-Nut Muffins, Banana-, '88 62
Nut Muffins, Banana-, '93 140
Oat Bran-Banana Muffins, '91 18
Oat Bran Muffins, Banana, '89 106
Oatmeal Muffins, Banana-, '84 20
Oat Muffins, Banana-, '87 188
Orange Muffins, Banana-, '84 148
Poppyseed Muffins, Banana-, '89 205
Praline Muffins, Banana-, '04 21
Raisin Muffins, Banana-, '89 218
Surprise Muffins, Banana, '82 105
Barbecue Muffins, '96 246
Basic Cupcake Muffins, '90 87
Basic Sweet Muffins, '99 234
Berry-and-Spice Whole Wheat Muffins, '05 25
Biscuit Muffins, '98 136

Blueberry
Batter, Blueberry Muffin, '04 200
Blueberry Muffins, '80 143; '91 140, 203; '99 234;
  '04 200,
Bran Muffins, Blueberry-, '89 23
Buttermilk Muffins, Blueberry, '80 16
Cinnamon Muffins, Blueberry-, '02 177
Cream Cheese Muffins, Blueberry-, '86 14
Easy Blueberry Muffins, '81 197
Golden Blueberry Muffins, '79 235
Ice Cream Muffins, Blueberry, '82 143
Lemon-Blueberry Muffins, '03 26
Lemon Muffins, Blueberry-, '79 7
Oat Bran Muffins, Blueberry, '89 106
Oatmeal Muffins, Blueberry-, '87 24
Oat Muffins, Blueberry-, '92 119
Old-Fashioned Blueberry Muffins, '86 161
Speedy Blueberry Muffins, '95 135
Streusel Muffins, Blueberry, '80 46
Streusel Muffins, Blueberry-, '96 146; '01 131
Streusel Topping, Blueberry Muffins with, '88 129
Sweet Muffins, Blueberry, '00 210
Whole-Wheat Muffins, Berry-and-Spice, '05 25

Bran
All-Bran Oat Bran Muffins, '91 134
Apple-Bran Muffins, '85 M89
Apple-Cinnamon Oat Bran Muffins, '89 106
Banana Bran Muffins, '83 48
Banana Muffins, Oat Bran-, '91 18
Banana Oat Bran Muffins, '89 106
Big Batch Moist Bran Muffins, '95 214
Blueberry-Bran Muffins, '89 23
Blueberry Oat Bran Muffins, '89 106
Bran Muffins, '84 53
Buttermilk Muffins, Bran-, '85 7
Cranberry Oat Bran Muffins, '89 107
Easy Bran Muffins, '83 55
Ever-Ready Bran Muffins, '81 106
Fiber Muffins, High-, '85 250
Freezer Bran Muffins, '91 141
Honey Bran Muffins, '88 171
Honey-Bran Muffins, '89 250
Made of Bran, Muffins, '86 103
Maple-Bran Muffins, '90 66
Quick Bran Muffins, '86 85
Raisin Oat Bran Muffins, '89 106
Refrigerator Bran Muffins, '79 6
Sour Cream-Bran Muffins, '87 98
Spiced Bran Muffins, '84 229
Two, Bran Muffins for, '84 211
Whole Wheat Bran Muffins, '88 M274
Breakfast Bites, '86 15
Breakfast Muffins, '04 209
Broccoli-Chicken Muffins, '96 27
Broccoli Cornbread Muffins, '03 81
Butter Muffins, '00 260
Carrot-and-Raisin Muffins, '87 24
Carrot-Date-Nut Muffins, '86 262
Carrot-Pineapple Muffins, '81 6
Carrot-Wheat Muffins, '88 9
Carrot-Zucchini Muffins, '01 200

Cheese
Bacon-and-Cheese Muffins, '89 205
Bacon-Cheese Muffins, '96 280
Caraway-Cheese Muffins, '91 213
Cheddar Muffins, '89 15
Cheddar Muffins, Peppered, '99 234
Cheddar-Raisin Muffins, '91 51
Cheese Muffins, '96 54; '97 287
Chive-and-Cheese Muffins, '04 332
Cornbread Muffins, Cheesy, '88 M275
Cream Cheese-Banana-Nut Muffins, '05 27
Dilly Cheese Muffins, '95 245; '96 55
English Cheese Muffins, '02 41
Green Onion-and-Cream Cheese Muffins, '01 289
Ham-and-Cheddar Muffins, '03 81
Ham-and-Cheddar Muffins, Reduced-Fat, '03 81
Ham-and-Cheese Muffins, '92 252; '93 144
Ham-and-Swiss Muffins, '03 81
Herb-Cheese Muffins, Buttery, '03 232
Marvelous Cheese Muffins, '83 96
Parmesan Cheese Muffins, '04 209
Pepper-Cheese Muffins, '96 280
Pepper Muffin Mix, Cheese-and-, '89 330
Pepper Muffins, Cheese-and-, '84 139
Sandwiches, Sausage-Cheese Muffin, '92 M212
Sausage-and-Cheese Muffins, '03 81
Sausage-Cheese Muffins, '86 213
Sausage Muffins, Cheesy, '92 252; '93 144
Sesame-Cheese Muffins, '86 16; '03 81
Cherry Muffins, '82 105
Cherry Muffins, Dried, '94 59
Cherry-Nut Muffins, '90 87
Chicken-and-Green Chile Muffins, '03 81
Chive Muffins, '91 34
Chocolate Chip Muffins, '90 87
Cinnamon-Nut Muffins, '85 M88

Cinnamon-Pecan Muffins, '84 219
Coconut-Molasses Muffins, '82 210
Coconut Muffins, '95 214
Coffee Cake Muffins, '79 7; '98 160

Corn
Angel Cornbread Muffins, Heavenly, '98 43
Blue Corn Muffins, '89 145; '92 52
Cheesy Cornbread Muffins, '88 M275
Cornmeal Muffins, '80 90; '88 92; '91 19; '96 248
Corn Muffins, '82 M282; '84 16; '98 313
Jalapeño-Corn Muffins, '93 164
Miniature Cornmeal Muffins, '93 119
Oat Muffins, Corn-, '89 108
Parmesan Corn Muffins, '01 255
Quick Corn Muffins, '88 15
Sage-Corn Muffins, '83 207
Sour Cream Corn Muffins, '95 176
Southern Cornbread Muffins, '85 201
Southwestern Corn Muffins, '02 212
Southwestern Muffins, '91 34
Spicy Cornbread Muffins, '90 59
Sunny Corn Muffins, '96 166
Tex-Mex Corn Muffins, '92 253; '93 144
Tomato Corn Muffins, '81 137
Yeast Muffins, Cornmeal, '92 49
Cranberry Muffins, '81 249; '05 313
Cranberry Muffins, Miniature, '90 294
Cranberry Oat Bran Muffins, '89 107
Cranberry-Orange Muffins, '04 209
Cranberry-Pecan Muffins, '84 269
Cranberry Streusel Cake Muffins, '88 M274
Date Muffins, '79 142; '00 239
Date Muffins, Miniature, '02 171
Date Muffins, Orange-, '92 119; '97 243
Date Muffins, Surprise, '79 216
Date-Nut Muffins, '84 75; '99 234
Dill Mini-Muffins, Dasher's, '04 252
Dino-Mite Muffins, '94 197
Egg Muffins, One-, '83 9
English Muffins, '87 49; '88 76
English Muffins, Raisin, '80 75
Fig Muffins, '86 206
French Breakfast Puffs, '96 67
Fruit-and-Bran Muffins, '04 22
Fudge Brownie Muffins, '95 M50
Gingerbread Bites with Orange-Cream Cheese Frosting,
  '04 258
Gingerbread Muffins, '81 285; '00 15
Gingerbread Muffins, Last-Minute, '82 105
Grain Muffins, Four-, '80 46
Granola Muffins, '95 78
Ham-and-Cheddar Muffins, '03 81
Ham-and-Cheddar Muffins, Reduced-Fat, '03 81
Ham-and-Cheese Muffins, '92 252; '93 144
Ham-and-Swiss Muffins, '03 81
Herb Muffins, '96 280
Honey Bran Muffins, '88 171
Honey-Bran Muffins, '89 250
Honey-Oatmeal Muffins, '84 229
Honey-Wheat Muffins, '83 96; '88 263
Jam Muffins, '79 7
Jelly-Filled Muffins, '80 16
Key Lime Muffins, '95 50
Kiwifruit Muffins, '87 255
Lemon Muffins, '88 119, M275
Lemon Muffins, Fresh, '79 161
Lemon-Poppy Seed Muffins, '05 33
Lemon-Raspberry Muffins, '92 119; '03 306
Magic Muffins, '79 244
Mayonnaise Muffins, '83 57; '86 16
Merry Muffins, '82 253
Mix, Quick, '94 167
Mix, Quick Bread, '81 90
Monster Muffins, '94 256

Morning Glory Muffins, '93 327
Muffins, '81 90
Nut Crunch Muffins, Best Ever, '82 65; '83 106
Nut Muffins, Tasty, '79 208
Nutty Muffins, '86 141
Oat
    All-Bran Oat Bran Muffins, '91 134
    Apple-Cinnamon Oat Bran Muffins, '89 106
    Apple-Oat Muffins, Spicy, '86 45
    Banana Muffins, Oat Bran-, '91 18
    Banana Oat Bran Muffins, '89 106
    Banana-Oatmeal Muffins, '84 20
    Banana-Oat Muffins, '87 188
    Batter, Oatmeal Muffin, '04 201
    Best-Ever Oatmeal Muffins, '84 242
    Blueberry Oat Bran Muffins, '89 106
    Blueberry-Oatmeal Muffins, '87 24
    Blueberry-Oat Muffins, '92 119
    Bran Muffins, Oatmeal, '81 236
    Bran Muffins, Oatmeal-, '91 83
    Corn-Oat Muffins, '89 108
    Cranberry Oat Bran Muffins, '89 107
    Honey Muffins, Oatmeal-, '83 95
    Honey-Oatmeal Muffins, '84 229
    Oat Bran Muffins, '89 106
    Oatmeal Muffins, '82 129, 210; '84 72, 140; '92 163;
       '04 201
    Orange-Oatmeal Muffins, '85 202; '00 24
    Raisin Oat Bran Muffins, '89 106
Okra Muffins, Fresh, '93 161
Onion-Dill Muffins, '92 253; '93 144
Orange
    Banana-Orange Muffins, '84 148
    Blossom Muffins, Orange, '96 54
    Cranberry-Orange Muffins, '04 209
    Date Muffins, Orange-, '92 119; '97 243; '05 215
    Ginger Muffins, Orange-, '89 41
    Honey Muffins, Orange-, '88 284
    Honey Spread, Orange Juice Muffins with, '81 229
    Oatmeal Muffins, Orange-, '85 202; '00 24
    Orange Muffins, '79 236; '81 107; '83 54; '89 205;
       '97 271
    Pecan Muffins, Orange-, '83 96; '99 56
    Pecan-Orange Muffins, '97 163
    Raisin Muffins, Orange-, '97 153
    Streusel-Topped Orange Muffins, '84 74
Peach Muffins, Special, '84 74
Peach Streusel Muffins, '03 167
Peanut Butter-Banana Muffins, '03 195
Peanut Butter-Chocolate Chip Muffins, '94 167
Peanut Butter-Honey Muffins, '82 56
Peanut Butter Muffins, '80 86; '87 158; '99 111
Peanut Butter Muffins, Jelly-Topped, '96 279
Peanut Muffins, '91 223
Pear-Ginger Muffins, '91 240
Pecan Muffins, '80 16
Pecan Muffins, Chunky, '88 9
Pecan Muffins, Country, '83 222
Pecan Muffins, Orange-, '83 96; '99 56
Pecan-Orange Muffins, '97 163
Pecan Pie Muffin Batter, '04 200
Pecan-Pie Muffins, '01 206
Pecan Pie Muffins, '04 201
Pineapple Muffins, '81 14, 250
Plum Good Muffins, '83 96
Plum Muffin Batter, Spiced, '04 201
Plum Muffins, Spiced, '04 201
Poppy Seed-Lemon Muffins, '96 280
Poppy Seed Muffins, '81 63; '91 34
Prune Muffins, Miniature, '85 223
Prune Muffins, Spicy, '97 271
Pumpkin-Apple Muffins, '96 242
Pumpkin Muffins, '79 206, 275; '81 272; '04 112
Pumpkin Muffins, Holiday, '03 281

Pumpkin Muffins, Nutty, '86 291
Raisin Muffins, Banana-, '89 218
Raisin Muffins, Breakfast, '84 59
Raisin-Nut Muffins, '92 46
Raisin Oat Bran Muffins, '89 106
Raisin-Pecan Ginger Muffins, '88 9
Raspberry-Streusel Muffins, '96 54
Rum Muffins, Hot Buttered, '96 280
Rum-Nut Muffins, '90 87
Sausage Muffins, '88 52; '95 49
Sour Cream Muffins, '90 283
Sour Cream Muffins, Mini, '88 283
Squash Muffins, '91 69
Strawberry Muffins, '99 234
Sunshine Muffins, '86 9
Sweet Potato Muffins, '81 224; '85 6; '87 280; '92 31
Taylor House Muffins, '96 48
Tea Muffins, '82 105
Tropical Muffins, '84 299
Twin Mountain Muffins, '96 280
Wheat Germ-Prune Muffins, '81 106
Wheat Muffins, Fruited, '79 93
Whole Wheat Bran Muffins, '88 M274
Whole Wheat Raisin Muffins, '85 207
Yam Muffins, '79 7
Yeast Muffins, Quick, '84 69
Yellow Squash Muffins, '81 163
Yogurt-Muesli Muffins, '90 215
Yogurt Muffins, '88 55
Zucchini Muffins, '83 121; '86 146
MUSHROOMS
    Appetizers, Chicken-Mushroom, '88 210
    Artichokes, Ham-Mushroom-Stuffed, '95 228
    Aztec Mushrooms, '82 51
    Balls, Cheese and Mushroom, '79 63
    Canapés, Mushroom, '97 23
    Champignons au Vin, '79 47
    Cheesecake, Spinach-Mushroom, '92 326
    Coquilles St. Jacques, '97 201
    Creamed Mushrooms on Toast, '81 190
    Curried Mushrooms, '84 214
    Dip, Hot Mushroom, '89 48
    Drunk Mushrooms, '83 174
    Egg Rolls, Chinese, '96 101
    Egg Rolls, Scrumptious, '96 101
    Elephant Ears, Mushroom-and-Brie Petite, '00 87
    English Peas with Mushrooms, '98 286
    Filling in a Peel, Mushroom, '84 214
    Filling, Mushroom, '81 89; '82 259; '83 51; '88 84
    Filling, Spinach-Mushroom, '80 215
    Fluted Mushrooms, '82 280
    French-Fried Mushrooms, '82 78
    French-Fried Mushrooms with Tartar Sauce, '86 233
    Garlic and Mushrooms, '95 165
    Gravy, Minute Steak with Mushroom, '05 67
    Gravy, Mushroom, '99 34
    Gravy, Roast with Onion-and-Mushroom, '00 293
    Gravy, Salisbury Steak with Mushroom, '03 202
    Gravy, Shallot, '02 239
    Logs, Mushroom, '84 206
    Main Dishes
        Beef in a Blanket, Bourbon Peppered, '00 109
        Beef, Marinated Stuffed Fillet of, '99 165
        Beef Stroganoff, '03 23
        Beef Tenderloin in Wine Sauce, '02 136
        Beef Tenderloin with Mushrooms, '87 115
        Beef Tenderloin with Mushroom Sauce, '88 3
        Beef Tenderloin with Mushroom-Sherry Sauce,
           '87 306
        Beef Wellingtons, Mini, '01 252
        Bouchées aux Fruits de Mer, '98 267
        Brisket, Saucy, '00 83
        Brunch Egg Nests, '03 246
        Burger, Grilled Portobello, '98 331

Burgers, Balsamic-Blue Cheese Portobello, '05 53
Burgers, Brie-Mushroom, '95 128
Burgers, Grilled Portobello Pizza, '00 89
Burgers, Mushroom, '89 164; '97 101; '99 135
Burgers, Portobello Mushroom, '01 144
Burgers with Avocado Mayonnaise, Portobello,
    '00 335
Cacciatore, Hearty Chicken, '02 269
Casserole, Crab-and-Mushroom, '89 96
Casserole, Egg-Mushroom, '83 49
Casserole, Sausage-Mushroom Breakfast, '86 95
Cassoulet, Easy Chicken, '00 43
Chicken and Mushrooms in Wine Sauce, '81 109
Chicken and Pasta, Mediterranean, '03 63
Chicken-and-Rice Bake, Herbed, '02 215
Chicken, Asparagus, and Mushrooms with Penne
    Pasta, '98 212
Chicken Bake, Mushroom-, '89 147
Chicken Florentine with Mushroom Sauce, '87 250
Chicken Livers with Mushrooms, '81 133
Chicken Madrid, '97 326
Chicken-Mushroom Bundles, '80 157
Chicken-Mushroom Dinner, '81 3
Chicken Sauté with Artichokes and Mushrooms,
    '03 57
Chicken with Artichokes and Mushrooms, '90 35
Chicken with Fennel and Mushrooms, '97 93
Chicken with Lemon Mashed Potatoes, Smothered,
    '04 180
Chicken with Mushroom Sauce, '99 22
Chicken with Sautéed Peppers and Mushrooms,
    Herb-Stuffed, '91 26
Crabmeat and Mushrooms on Toast Points, '82 M91
Creamed Mushrooms in Wild Rice Ring, '80 270
Crêpes, Cheese and Mushroom, '81 88
Crêpes, Coquilles St. Jacques, '83 13
Crêpes, Mushroom-Cheese, '87 289; '88 135
Egg Delight, Mushroom-, '83 14
Eggs, Garden District, '04 66
Eggs, Saucy Mushrooms and, '79 138
Eggs, Sherried Mushroom, '83 49
Filet Mignons with Shiitake Madeira Sauce, '95 265
Filet Mignon with Mushroom Sauce, '94 250
Filets Mignons, Skillet, '03 258
Flank Steak and Mushrooms, '87 61
Flank Steaks with Mushrooms, '00 121
Fricassee, White Chicken, '98 122
Grits with Chicken Sausage and Shiitake
    Mushrooms, Cheese, '03 254
Hamburger Steaks, Mushroom-Stuffed, '99 202
Hot Browns, '98 287
Macaroni-Mushroom Bake, Cheesy, '81 243
Muffin Stacks, Mushroom-Topped, '80 271
Omelet, Broccoli-Mushroom, '85 45
Omelet, Golden Cheese-Shiitake, '95 265
Omelet, Rolled Mushroom, '82 70
Patty Shells, Mushrooms and Eggs in, '85 143;
    '88 197
Pizza, Cheese-and-Mushroom, '83 226
Pizza, Portobello, '03 175
Pizzas, Grilled Portobello, '00 89
Pork Chops, Apricot-Mushroom Stuffed, '95 287
Pork Chops, Italian, '02 307
Pork Chops, Weeknight, '97 200
Pork Chops with Mushrooms, Creamy, '01 137
Pork Loin with Apples and Mushrooms, Roast,
    '92 218
Pork Loin with Mushrooms and Garlic, Roasted,
    '92 301
Pork, Moo Shu, '99 237
Pork Tenderloin, Apple-Mushroom, '95 53
Pork Tenderloin with Fruit Stuffing and Shiitake
    Sauce, '97 218
Portabello Mushrooms, Grilled, '95 123

MUSHROOMS, Main Dishes
(continued)

Portobello-Pine Nut Pizza, '99 216
Pot Roast, Mushroom, '79 17; '96 250
Pot Roast with Mushroom Gravy, '02 90
Quail Stroganoff, '99 41
Quail with Mushroom Gravy, Baked, '89 273
Quail with Mushrooms, '85 138
Quail with Mushrooms, Baked, '81 259
Quesadillas, Spinach, Mushroom, and Cilantro,
   '00 148
Quiche, Ham-and-Mushroom, '81 11
Quiche Lorraine, Mushroom-, '86 242
Quiche, Mushroom, '81 244
Quiche, Spinach-Mushroom, '81 M74
Quiche, Zucchini-Mushroom, '79 127
Ragoût of Wild Mushrooms with Creamy Grits,
   '92 238
Ragù with Tortellini, Wild Mushroom, '04 220
Rib-Eyes, Italian, '98 215
Risotto, Redneck, '98 107
Roast, Savory Chuck, '00 18
Roast with Onion-and-Mushroom Gravy, '00 293
Salisbury Steak with Mushroom Gravy, '03 202
Salmon with Mushrooms and Green Onions, Fresh,
   '93 180
Scallop-Mushroom Fettuccine, '96 198
Scallops and Mushrooms, Creamy, '83 144
Shrimp and Mushrooms with Angel Hair Pasta,
   '92 34
Shrimp-Mushroom Italienne, Green Pasta with,
   '79 170
Sirloin in Vodka Sauce, '03 96
Spaghetti with Mushrooms, Spicy, '85 2
Spinach and Mushrooms with Bow Tie Pasta,
   '95 341
Steak with Ham-and-Mushroom Sauce, '83 109
Steak with Mushroom Sauce, '83 212
Stir-Fry, Shiitake-Chicken, '89 61
Stroganoff, Chicken, '99 41
Stroganoff, Creamy Beef, '02 124
Stroganoff, Mushroom, '81 298
Stroganoff, Mushroom-Meatball, '85 85
Stroganoff, Quail, '99 41
Swordfish-Shiitake Skewers, '97 168
Tart, Smoked Portabello Mushroom, '94 163
Turkey Scaloppine with Angel Hair Pasta, '02 44
Veal-and-Mushrooms Marsala, '89 44
Veal-Cepe Sauté, '89 62
Veal Scallopini with Shiitakes, '99 232
Venison Loin, Mushroom-Crusted, '94 302
Vermicelli with Mushrooms, '79 195
Marinated
Caps, Marinated Mushroom, '83 128
Easy Marinated Mushrooms, '86 217
Herb Mushrooms, Marinated, '86 327
Marinated Mushrooms, '80 82, 270; '81 69; '86 135;
   '91 306; '92 328
Mexican Marinated Mushrooms, '81 66
Rosemary-Red Wine Vinaigrette, Marinated
   Mushrooms in, '97 63
Salad, Marinated Mushroom, '88 215; '90 181
Special Marinated Mushrooms, '83 13
Meringue Mushrooms, '96 317
Pastry Cups, Mushroom-Almond, '88 210
Pâté de Champignon, '93 171
Pâté in Pastry, Turkey-Mushroom, '92 327
Pâté, Mushroom, '89 157
Patty Shells, Mushrooms and Eggs in, '85 143; '88 197
Patty Shells, Mushrooms in, '80 283
Phyllo Bites, Sausage-Mushroom-, '89 284
Piroshki, '92 84

Portabello Mushrooms, Microwave, '95 M123
Portabello Mushrooms, Sautéed, '95 123
Portabello Mushrooms, '03 176
Portobello Mushrooms and Asparagus, Grilled, '02 122
Portobello Mushrooms, Lime-Grilled, '05 18
Potatoes, Shrimp-and-Mushroom Stuffed, '99 308
Quiche, Mushroom-Spinach-Swiss, '03 59
Quiche, Southwestern, '04 41
Rice, Holiday, '98 289
Rollups, Mushroom, '85 318
Salads
Cheesy-Mushroom Salad, Quick, '89 128
Chicken Salad, Asian, '99 124
Fabulous Mushroom Salad, '81 190
Fresh Mushroom Salad, '93 65
Greens, Cucumber Asian, '98 66
Greens with Walnuts, Mixed, '99 107
Grilled Mushroom-Asparagus Salad, '02 122
Marinated Mushroom Salad, '88 215; '90 181
Marinated Mushrooms in Rosemary-Red Wine
   Vinaigrette, '97 63
Pepper Salad, Mushroom-and-, '86 68
Portobello Salad, Grilled, '99 216
Portobello Salad, Grilled Tomato, Bell Pepper, and,
   '98 211
Rice Salad with Fresh Mushrooms, '80 231
Spinach and Mushroom Salad, '80 112
Spinach-Enoki Salad, '89 62
Watercress-and-Mushroom Salad, '88 104
Zucchini Salad, Mushroom-, '85 8
Sandwiches, Toasted Mushroom, '87 281
Sandwiches with Curry-Mustard Sauce, Mushroom
   Bagel, '96 249
Sauces. *See also* **MUSHROOMS/Gravy.**
Artichoke Sauce, Creamy Mushroom-, '05 312
Beef Tenderloin with Mushroom Sauce, '88 3
Chanterelle Brown Sauce, '89 62
Cheese Sauce, Mushroom-, '83 190; '86 48
Chicken Florentine with Mushroom Sauce, '87 250
Chicken with Mushroom Sauce, '99 22; '04 255
Cream Sauce, '03 237
Creole Sauce, '98 98
Dill Sauce, Mushroom-, '80 271
Eggs Baked in Mushroom Sauce, '93 47
Filet Mignon with Mushroom Sauce, '94 250
Ham-and-Mushroom Sauce, Steak with, '83 109
Mole Sauce, Burgundy, '98 174
Mushroom Sauce, '81 90, 200; '82 46; '83 71, 205,
   212; '84 M70; '85 40; '86 198; '87 36, 186, 284;
   '91 221; '03 255
Omelets with Mushroom Sauce, Puffy, '85 40
Onion-Mushroom Sauce, '85 224; '86 84
Portobello-Alfredo Sauce, Fettuccine with, '04 135
Portobello-Marsala Sauce, '05 280
Savory Mushroom Sauce, '96 236
Sherried Mushroom Sauce, Green Beans in, '93 206
Sherried Mushroom Sauce, Spicy, '89 239
Sherry Sauce, Beef Tenderloin with Mushroom-,
   '87 306
Shiitake Madeira Sauce, Filet Mignons with, '95 265
Shiitake Sauce, Pork Tenderloin with Fruit Stuffing
   and, '97 218
Spinach Loaf with Mushroom Sauce, '01 277
Steak with Mushroom Sauce, '83 212
Tomatoes with Mushroom Sauce, Broiled, '81 103
Tuna with Mushroom Sauce, Peppered, '05 72
Vermicelli, Mushroom Sauce Supreme on, '86 158
Wine Sauce, Mushroom-, '84 84; '86 24; '00 125
Zucchini-Mushroom Sauce, '93 71
Shiitakes, Grilled, '95 265
Side Dishes
Acorn Squash-Mushroom Puree, '93 305
à la King, Mushrooms, '89 285
Asparagus and Mushrooms, '85 108

Asparagus-and-Mushroom Sauté, '93 115
Asparagus-and-Mushroom Tostadas with Goat
   Cheese, '03 242
au Gratin, Mushrooms, '81 108
Baked Mushrooms, Creamy, '87 127
Bake, Windsor Mushroom, '88 132
Bread Pudding, Mushroom, '99 58
Casserole, Mushroom, '95 211; '96 47
Casserole, Mushroom-Artichoke, '87 241
Casserole, Mushroom-Cheese, '85 216
Casserole, Mushroom Deluxe, '96 20
Casserole, Mushroom-Macaroni, '95 180
Casserole, Mushroom-Potato, '84 5
Creamed Oyster Mushrooms, '89 61
Dressing, Whole Wheat-Mushroom, '84 283
Eggplant, Mushroom-Stuffed, '83 136
Fresh Mushrooms, Savory, '85 268
Green Bean Casserole, '02 197
Green Beans, Mushroom-Bacon, '91 291; '92 255
Green Beans with Bacon and Mushrooms, '92 13
Green Beans with Mushrooms, '82 21; '93 89
Green Beans with Mushrooms and Sage, '02 314
Green Peas with Mushrooms, '80 101
Heavenly Mushrooms, '87 281
Herbed Mushrooms, '84 214; '88 176
Kugel, Mushroom Matzo, '00 83
Macaroni-Mushroom Bake, '97 96
Mixed-Up Mushrooms, '01 213
Newburg, Mushroom, '88 252
Noodles and Mushrooms, Cheesy, '79 84
Panuchos, Mushroom, '83 51
Pasta 1-2-3, Mushroom, '97 102
Peas and Mushrooms, '83 141
Peas and Mushrooms, Buttered, '82 204
Peas with Mushrooms, Creamy, '84 196
Pepper-Mushroom Medley, '90 98
Pie with Mushrooms, Vidalia Onion, '02 183
Portobello Mushrooms, Lime-Grilled, '05 18
Portobello Mushrooms, Sautéed, '96 273
Potatoes, Buffet, '98 92
Potatoes, Mushroom-Dill-Topped, '86 41
Potatoes, Mushroom Scalloped, '87 191
Quiche, Mushroom, '80 222; '89 285
Quiches, Wild Rice-and-Mushroom, '93 237
Rice, Baked Mushroom, '92 170; '95 84
Rice, Easy Mushroom, '89 286
Rice, Holiday, '98 289
Roasted Green Beans with Mushrooms, '04 182
Sautéed Mushrooms, '84 35
Sautéed Mushrooms, Easy, '81 131
Sautéed Mushroom Spectacular, '83 206
Sauté, Mixed Mushroom, '89 62
Seasoned Mushrooms, '83 291
Sherried Mushrooms, '83 13
Soufflés, Mushroom, '87 282
Sour Cream-Dill Sauce, Mushrooms in, '84 215
Sparkling Mushrooms, '94 24
Spinach and Mushrooms with Bow Tie Pasta, '95 341
Spinach with Mushrooms, '80 19
Stir-Fried Mushrooms with Bacon, '80 123
Supreme, Mushrooms, '84 214
Tarts, Mushroom, '88 161
Tomatoes, Mushroom-Stuffed, '86 218; '96 106
Turnovers, Tiny Mushroom, '86 24
Vermouth, Mushrooms in, '89 203
Wild Mushroom-and-Onion Pot Pies, '98 296
Wild Rice and Mushrooms, '83 278
Wild Rice with Morels, '89 62
Wine Sauce, Mushrooms with, '85 292
Yellow Squash, Mushroom-Stuffed, '84 154
Zesty Mushrooms, '93 218
Zucchini with Mushrooms, Sautéed, '94 135
Soups
Avocado-Mushroom Soup, Creamy, '85 25

Bisque, Brisk Mushroom, '81 190
Chicken, Artichoke, and Mushroom Soup, '92 324
Chowder, Creamy Green Bean, Mushroom, and Ham, '99 M336
Chowder, Mushroom, '79 16
Chowder, Mushroom-Potato, '92 331
Chunky Mushroom Soup, '88 12
Consommé aux Champignons, '79 48
Consommé, Brown Rice, '98 288
Corn Soup with Shiitakes and Shrimp, Sweet, '99 168
Cream of Mushroom-and-Leek Soup, '01 312
Cream of Mushroom Soup, '84 5; '85 93, 261
Creamy Mushroom Soup, '79 243; '81 307
Curried Mushroom Soup, '84 M89
Elegant Mushroom Soup, '83 99
Fresh Mushroom Soup, '81 109; '90 190
Mushroom Soup, '82 286; '86 M73; '94 54
Onion Soup, Mushroom-, '80 25
Oyster-and-Mushroom Soup, '87 39
Rice Soup, Mushroom-, '90 32
Rice Soup, Wildest, '01 66
Sherried Mushroom Soup, '96 104
Shiitake Soup, Cream of, '95 265
Wild Mushroom Soup, '98 281; '04 203
Sour Cream, Mushrooms in, '00 106
Spread, Eggplant-Mushroom, '92 156
Spread, Hot Mushroom, '81 190
Spuds, Mushroom-Swiss, '96 M238
Stewed Anasazi Beans with Mushrooms, '95 226
Strudel, Crab-and-Mushroom, '98 28
Stuffed
Appetizers, Stuffed Mushroom, '88 210
Artichoke-Stuffed Mushrooms, '01 239
Beef-Stuffed Mushrooms, '00 278
Black Olive-Stuffed Mushrooms, '86 258
Canapés, Mushroom, '80 285
Cheese 'n' Bacon-Stuffed Mushrooms, '86 258
Cheese-Stuffed Mushrooms, Elegant, '81 57
Chicken-Stuffed Mushrooms, '80 162
Crab, Mushrooms Stuffed with, '82 249
Crab-Stuffed Mushroom Caps, '84 160
Crab-Stuffed Mushrooms, '81 190; '97 102
Crawfish-Stuffed Mushrooms, '86 258
Delight, Stuffed Mushroom, '87 281
Flavor-Stuffed Mushrooms, '85 288
Florentine, Stuffed Mushrooms, '82 270
Ham, Mushrooms Stuffed with, '97 237
Italian Sausage-Stuffed Mushrooms, '83 127
Parmesan Stuffed Mushrooms, '83 115
Pâté-Stuffed Mushrooms, '85 118
Pecan-Stuffed Mushrooms, '84 261
Pesto-Stuffed Mushrooms, '86 150
Pistachio-Stuffed Mushrooms, '86 141
Ricotta-Stuffed Mushrooms, '85 20
Samurai 'shrooms, '93 258
Sausage-Stuffed Mushrooms, '80 248; '91 164; '05 300
Seasoned Stuffed Mushrooms, '84 206
Shiitakes Parmigiana, Stuffed, '98 25
Shrimp-Stuffed Mushrooms, '80 M135; '99 324
Spinach-Stuffed Mushrooms, '86 81; '88 131, M261; '89 M133
Stems, Mushrooms with, '86 258
Stuffed Mushrooms, '79 212; '81 239; '83 13, 66, 126, 136; '93 172
Vegetable Mushroom Caps, '81 246
Stuffing, Cornish Hens with Barley-Mushroom, '97 242
Stuffing, Grilled Rainbow Trout with Mushroom, '97 162
Stuffing, Sausage-and-Wild Mushroom, '96 267
Tapas, Majorcan Mushroom, '95 159
Tarts, Hot Sherried Mushroom, '83 78
Tipsy Mushrooms, '84 M216

Tomatoes, Veracruz, '97 169
Tomatoes with Curry Sauce, Stuffed, '97 170
Turnovers, Hot Mushroom, '89 285; '97 102
Turnovers, Mushroom, '05 310
MUSSELS. *See* **SEAFOOD.**
MUSTARD
Bourbon Mustard, '93 240
Bread, Mustard, '01 146
Brie, Honey-Mustard, '91 252
Brussels Sprouts Dijon, '96 91
Brussels Sprouts with Shallots and Mustard, '85 258
Butter, Chive-Mustard, '98 156
Butter, Jalapeño-Pecan-Mustard, '03 205
Chicken, Dijon, '99 21
Chicken Dijon, '04 196
Chicken, Lemon-Mustard, '99 109
Chicken, Mustard, '93 239
Coarse-and-Sweet Mustard, '86 M288
Compote, Baked Mustard Fruit, '85 47
Cranberry Mustard, '05 320
Cream, Mustard-Horseradish, '02 53
Dip, Sweet-and-Spicy Mustard, '96 M274
Dressing, Dijon-Honey, '89 45; '99 333
Dressing, Herbed Mustard, '00 145
Dressing, Honey-Mustard, '90 55, 111, 146; '00 54; '01 230; '05 185
Dressing, Lemon-Mustard, '02 52
Dressing, Mustard, '80 112
Dressing, One-Bean Salad with Lime-Mustard, '00 202
Dressing, Tangy Mustard, '93 323
Easy Sweet-Tangy Mustard, '01 247
Fish, Spicy Mustard, '99 90
Flounder Dijon, '85 95
Fruit Bake, Mustard, '90 291
Glaze, Apple-Stuffed Tenderloin with Praline-Mustard, '97 216
Glaze, Game Hens with Chutney-Mustard, '93 66
Glaze, Roast Chicken with Pineapple-Mustard, '89 83
Herbed Mustard, '87 134
Homemade Mustard, '81 77
Homemade Mustard, Zesty, '82 55
Honey Mustard, '05 203
Honey Mustard, Hot, '93 240
Honey Mustard, Peppered, '95 312
Honey Mustard, Sweet-Hot, '05 284
Horseradish Mustard, '93 240
Horseradish Mustard, Lower Sodium, '86 325
Hot German Mustard, '82 298
Hot Mustard, Chinese, '85 12
Hot Mustard, Really, '95 312
Hot Sweet Mustard, '85 12
Jalapeño Mustard, '93 240; '95 312
Key Lime Mustard, '94 278
Lamb Chops, Dijon-Rosemary, '99 333
Marinade, Honey-Mustard, '93 103
Maui Mustard, Wowee, '05 324
Mousse, Mustard, '84 127; '86 184; '95 328
Orange Roughy Dijon, '99 122
Pork Chops, Spicy Brown Mustard, '03 205
Pork Loin, Orange-Dijon, '00 259
Pork Tenderloin, Honey-Mustard, '95 52
Raspberry Mustard, '95 313
Sauces
Asparagus in Mustard Sauce, Chilled, '88 130
Barbecue Sauce, Mustard, '84 173
Chutney-Mustard Sauce, '89 242
Cream Sauce, Chicken in Mustard, '92 181
Cream Sauce, Mustard, '88 61
Creamy Mustard Sauce, '80 272; '86 257; '87 232; '93 240
Creamy Mustard Sauce, Champagne-Poached Chicken with, '94 24
Creole Mustard Sauce, '99 142

Curry-Mustard Sauce, '96 249
Dijon-Caper Cream Sauce, Broiled Salmon with, '98 329
Dijon Horseradish Sauce, '03 297
Dijon Mustard Sauce, Creamy, '04 198
Dijon Sauce, Orange-, '00 259
Easy Mustard Sauce, '94 83
Extra-Special Mustard Sauce, '79 82
Hamburger Steaks with Mustard Sauce, '84 230
Hollandaise Sauce, Mock Mustard-, '87 269
Honey-Lemon Mustard Sauce, '84 275
Honey-Mustard Sauce, '85 13
Honey-Mustard Sauce, Smoked Ribs with, '92 168
Horseradish-Mustard Sauce, Creamy, '88 M177
Hot Mustard Sauce, '93 240
Leg of Lamb with Mustard Sauce, '89 71
Lemon-Mustard Sauce, Salmon Steaks with, '97 124
Light Mustard Sauce, '82 178
Mild Mustard Sauce, '85 224; '86 84
Mustard Sauce, '80 222, 283; '83 21, 321; '84 M70, 289; '85 148; '86 185; '87 22; '89 122, 333; '90 19, 97; '92 302; '93 118; '99 270; '00 32; '01 102; '02 162, 245·
Pork Tenderloin with Mustard Sauce, '99 145; '03 238
Sausage Sandwiches with Mustard Sauce, '84 250
Scallops with Mustard Sauce, '84 163
Smoked Sausages with Mustard Sauce, '81 56
Sour Cream Sauce, Mustard-, '81 68
Special Mustard Sauce, '01 159
Stone Crab Mustard Sauce, '80 3
Sweet Mustard Sauce, '85 12
Tangy Mustard Sauce, '92 201
Tarragon-Mustard Sauce, Turkey Cutlets with, '93 239
Vinaigrette Sauce, Mustard-, '84 174
Vinegar Sauce, Shrimp with Mustard-, '93 240
Spread, Chive-Mustard, '91 12
Spread, Honey Mustard-Butter, '99 86
Spread, Mustard, '86 105
Sweet Cider Mustard, '95 312
Vegetables, Honey-Dijon, '98 311
Vegetables, Honey-Mustard Marinated, '93 236
Vinaigrette, Baby Lettuces with Mustard, '93 67
Vinaigrette, Dijon, '00 222; '02 18
Vinaigrette, Greens with Dijon, '98 332
Vinaigrette, Herb-Mustard, '02 84
Vinaigrette, Honey-Dijon, '04 321
Vinaigrette, Honey-Mustard, '94 249
Vinaigrette, Mustard, '96 184; '01 102

NECTARINES
Apple Juice, Nectarines in, '83 183
Butter, Nectarine, '79 175
Cobbler with Blueberry Muffin Crust, Nectarine, '04 200
Cocktail, Nectarine, '85 107
Mint Nectarines with Pineapple-Coconut Ice Cream, '05 123
Royale, Nectarines, '85 132
Salad, Nectarine Chicken, '79 175
Sherbet, Nectarine, '89 199
Shortcake, Warm Blueberry-Nectarine, '97 205
NOODLES
Caraway Buttered Noodles, '87 230
Casserole, Eggplant and Noodle, '82 230
Casserole, Sweet Noodle, '02 238
Casserole, Vegetable Noodle, '91 30
Egg Foo Yong Noodles, '98 233
Green Noodles, '80 211
Kugel, Apricot Noodle, '92 251
Kugel, Nu Awlins, '94 229
Kugel, Sweet, '90 254

NOODLES
(continued)

Kugel, Vegetable-Noodle, '96 228
Lo Mein Noodles and Broccoli, '97 18
Main Dishes
  Beef and Noodles, Easy, '83 288
  Beef Bake, Asian Noodle, '98 31
  Beef over Rice Noodles, Shredded, '85 74
  Beefy Noodle Dinner, '81 179
  Cakes with Coconut-Beef Stir-Fry, Noodle, '97 18
  Casserole, Beef-and-Noodles, '84 72
  Casserole, Beef, Cheese, and Noodle, '99 58
  Casserole, Chicken and Green Noodle, '80 32
  Casserole, Chicken-Noodle, '94 286
  Casserole, Chicken Noodle, '01 308
  Casserole, Fabulous Tuna-Noodle, '02 63
  Casserole, Ham, '96 302
  Casserole, Ham and Noodle, '80 300
  Casserole, Sausage and Noodle, '82 123
  Casserole, Sausage-and-Noodle, '95 255
  Casserole, Shrimp-and-Noodle, '90 240
  Casserole, Stroganoff, '98 48
  Casserole, Turkey-Noodle-Poppyseed, '90 239
  Cheesy Noodles and Mushrooms, '79 84
  Chicken and Spinach Noodles, '82 19
  Chicken with Noodles, Sesame, '88 M125
  Chicken with Spicy Soba Noodles, Grilled, '00 93
  Chili with Noodles, '81 282; '82 57
  Chow Mein over Crispy Noodles, '85 286
  Fried Noodles with Shrimp, '02 174
  Ham and Swiss on Noodles, '87 108
  Hamburger-Noodle Bake, '81 140
  Ham-Noodle Skillet, '87 78
  Hoisin Noodles with Shrimp, '98 233
  Italian Sauce with Noodles, '84 250
  Lasagna, Egg-Noodle, '04 219
  Lasagna, Lots of Noodles, '91 M127
  Liver and Noodle Dinner, Creamy, '80 11
  Pad Thai, '97 202
  Pork-and-Noodle Bake, '88 98
  Pork-and-Noodles Skillet Dinner, '88 199
  Ring, Noodle, '85 285
  Sausage and Mixed Vegetables, Pasta with, '87 249
  Sausage-Noodle Bake, '81 92
  Sausage, Pasta with Broccoli and, '87 109
  Scallops and Pasta, Fresh, '83 164
  Sesame Noodles, '01 188
  Shrimp and Noodles, Creamy, '92 100
  Sour Cream-Noodle Bake, '79 55
  Stew with Noodles, Hungarian, '80 263
  Szechuan Noodles with Spicy Beef Sauce, '97 95
  Taco Beef-Noodle Bake, '81 141
  Tempura Udon, '00 93
  Turkey Noodle Bake, '93 243
  Veal Sauce, Noodles with, '80 236
Orange Noodles, '84 177
Pancake, Szechuan Ginger Stir-Fry with Noodle, '97 292
Parmesan Noodles, '83 118
Parmesan Noodles, Cheesy, '83 M7
Parslied Noodles, '85 31
Ramen Noodle Satay, '98 233
Salad, Chicken Noodle, '95 25
Salad, Ham-Noodle, '85 249
Salad, Noodle Chicken, '03 143
Salad, Peanut-Noodle, '02 163
Salad, Ramen Noodle, '88 41; '97 18; '02 24
Salad, Sesame Noodle, '02 186
Soup, Chicken Noodle, '80 264; '95 45; '98 30
Soup Mix, Turkey-Noodle, '89 330
Soup, Turkey-Noodle, '91 312
Spinach with Noodles, Creamed, '84 29

Thai Coconut Broth with Noodles, '98 295
Vegetables, Noodles with Spring, '02 125
White Noodles, '80 211
NUTS. *See also* **ALMONDS; APPETIZERS/Nuts;
  MACADAMIA; PEANUTS; PECANS;
  WALNUTS.**

OATMEAL
Applesauce Oatmeal, '89 108
Bake, Pear-Oatmeal, '89 208
Bars and Cookies
  Apple-Nut Cookies, '80 228
  Apple-Oatmeal Cookies, '85 215; '90 218
  Apple-Oat Snack Squares, '00 332
  Apricot-Oatmeal Bars, '86 216; '04 331
  Banana Oatmeal Cookies, '79 217
  Breakfast Cookies, '97 52
  Breakfast Cookies, Take-Along, '84 59
  Brownies, Elephant Stomp, '03 43
  Brownies, Oat, '89 59
  Brownies, Oatmeal, '87 199
  Brownies, Oat 'n' Crunch, '91 233
  Cake Mix Oatmeal Cookies, '96 247
  Caramel Bars, Oatmeal-, '85 247
  Carrot Cookies, Oatmeal-, '94 292
  Cereal Cookies, Crunchy Oat 'n,' '05 181
  Chocolate Chip Cookies, '00 276
  Chocolate Chip Cookies, Nutty Oatmeal-, '82 M185
  Chocolate Chip-Oatmeal Cookies, '84 119
  Chocolate Chippers, Oatmeal-, '90 218
  Chocolate Chunk Cookies, Double, '05 181
  Chocolate Chunk Cookies, Nutty Oatmeal-, '01 19
  Chocolate Morsel Cookies, Oatmeal-, '95 46
  Chocolate-Oatmeal Cookies, '80 105
  Chocolate-Raisin Oatmeal Cookies, '95 136
  Chocolate-Topped Oatmeal Bars, '86 110
  Cinnamon Oatmeal Cookies, '84 72
  Clear-the-Cupboard Cookies, '99 278; '02 176
  Coconut Cookies, Oatmeal-, '80 218
  Coconut Crispies, Oatmeal-, '01 19
  Coconut-Macadamia Cookies, '98 294
  Coconut-Oatmeal Cookies, Crispy, '93 80
  Crackers, Oatmeal-Wheat Germ, '84 236
  Cranberry-Caramel Bars, '98 277
  Crispies, Oat, '83 96
  Crispy Oat Cookies, '88 203; '90 311
  Crispy Oatmeal Cookies, '89 328
  Crunchy Oatmeal Cookies, '85 202
  Date Bars, Layered Oatmeal-, '85 10
  Date Cookies, Oatmeal-, '82 109
  Date-Filled Oatmeal Cookies, '86 314
  Date-Oat Bars, '80 M172
  Date Sandwich Cookies, Oatmeal-, '83 257
  Double-Chip Oatmeal Cookies, '03 200
  Easy Oatmeal Cookies, '80 105
  Fibber McGee Cookies, '95 72
  Fudge Bars, Yummy, '87 158
  Ginger-Oatmeal Sorghum Cookies, '00 230;
    '02 230
  Granola Bars, '83 305
  Granola Bars, No-Bake, '97 220
  Krispies, Oatmeal, '85 115
  Lace Cookies, '86 8
  Lace Cookies, Crunchy, '01 294
  Layered Oatmeal-Date Bars, '85 10
  Macadamia-Oat Snowballs, '92 274
  Nut Crispies, Oatmeal, '80 208
  Nutty Oatmeal Cookies, '81 130
  Oatmeal Cookies, '92 82; '99 280
  Old-Fashioned Oatmeal Cookies, '80 106; '85 250
  Olympic Medal Cookies, '96 180
  Orange-Glazed Oatmeal Cookies, '80 60
  Orange Slice Cookies, '98 324

Peanut Butter Chocolate Chip Cookies, Oatmeal-,
    '92 207
  Peanut Butter Cookies, Oatmeal-, '85 171
  Peanut Butter-Oatmeal Cookies, '81 218; '84 72
  Peanut Cookies, Oats-and-, '89 60
  Peanutty Oatmeal Cookies, '80 106; '83 95
  Pudding-Oatmeal Cookies, '98 215
  Raisin Chocolate Chip Cookies, Oatmeal-, '05 87
  Raisin Cookies, Frosted Oatmeal-, '79 290
  Raisin Cookies, Oatmeal-, '87 221; '93 127
  Raisin-Oatmeal Cookies, '01 19
  Red, White, and Blue Cookies, Chewy, '03 163
  Slice-and-Bake Oatmeal Cookies, '80 105
  Special Oatmeal Cookies, '81 236
  Spice Cookies, Giant Oatmeal-, '80 105; '03 59
  Spicy Oatmeal Cookies, '81 197; '01 19
  Sunshine Cookies, Oatmeal, '89 59
  Toasted Oatmeal Cookies, '92 273; '95 136
  Toffee Cookies, Oatmeal-, '04 234
  Toffee Lizzies, Crispy Oatmeal-, '95 136
  White Chocolate Chip-Oatmeal Cookies, '99 127;
    '04 43
Breads
  Biscuits, Oatmeal, '89 108
  Blueberry-Oatmeal Bread, '83 139
  Buns, Honey-Oat, '98 27
  Buns, Honey Oatmeal, '83 154
  Buttermilk-Oatmeal Bread, '97 212
  Caraway-Raisin Oat Bread, '86 44
  Dill-Oat Bread, '91 95
  Herbed Oatmeal Pan Bread, '97 243
  Honey-Oat Bread, '89 107; '98 27
  Honey Oatmeal Bread, '80 60
  Loaf, Banana-Oat Tea, '87 256
  Loaf, Pumpkin-Oatmeal, '81 49
  Molasses Bread, Oatmeal-, '97 194
  Muffin Batter, Oatmeal, '04 201
  Muffins, Banana-Oat, '87 188
  Muffins, Banana-Oatmeal, '84 20
  Muffins, Best-Ever Oatmeal, '84 242
  Muffins, Blueberry-Oat, '92 119
  Muffins, Blueberry-Oatmeal, '87 24
  Muffins, Corn-Oat, '89 108
  Muffins, Honey-Oatmeal, '84 229
  Muffins, Oat Bran, '89 106
  Muffins, Oat Bran-Banana, '91 18
  Muffins, Oatmeal, '82 129, 210; '84 72, 140;
    '92 163; '04 201
  Muffins, Oatmeal Bran, '81 236
  Muffins, Oatmeal-Bran, '91 83
  Muffins, Oatmeal-Honey, '83 95
  Muffins, Orange-Oatmeal, '85 202; '00 24
  Muffins, Spicy Apple-Oat, '86 45
  Oatmeal Bread, '81 236, 300; '92 212; '97 130
  Oatmeal Raisin Bread, '81 14
  Oatmeal-Raisin Bread, '83 59
  Oat-Molasses Bread, '82 139
  Rolls, Oatmeal-Cinnamon-Pecan, '96 50
  Rolls, Oatmeal Dinner, '01 44
  Round Oatmeal Bread, '84 20
  Whole Wheat-Oatmeal Bread, '87 85
Breakfast Oatmeal Surprise, '93 178
Breakfast Oatmeal, Swiss Style, '81 49
Burgers, Black Bean, '98 144
Burgers, Pinto, '98 51
Burgers, Spicy Bean, '00 84
Cake, Applesauce-Oatmeal, '92 119
Cake, Dutch Oatmeal, '83 95
Cake, Golden Apple-Oatmeal, '86 301
Cake, Honey-Oatmeal, '87 222
Cake, Oatmeal, '01 58
Cake, Saucy Pudding, '98 196
Cereal, Full-of-Fiber Hot, '89 208
Coffee Cake, Oatmeal-Coconut, '83 312

Crisp, Oatmeal Cherry-Apple, '90 M16
Crust, Nutty Oat, '89 251
Dried Cherry-and-Pecan Oatmeal, '05 126
Fruited Oatmeal, '88 19
Granola, '99 212
Granola, Crunchy, '81 218; '84 144
Granola, Easy, '81 49
Granola, Fruity, '84 148
Granola, Healthful, '97 204
Granola, Homemade, '84 58
Granola, Mixed Fruit, '01 290
Granola, Sunny Orange, '84 212
Granola, Superhero, '98 M206
Hamburgers, Meatless Walnut, '96 243
Ice Cream Sandwiches, Oatmeal Crispy, '93 199
Ice-Cream Sandwiches, Oatmeal-Rum-Raisin,
    '05 62
Ice-Cream Sandwiches, Peanutty, '05 62
Mix, Rolled Oats, '84 72
Muesli, '89 208
Muesli, Homestyle, '91 315
Pancakes, Oat, '89 227
Pancakes, Oatmeal, '80 44; '89 107
Pancakes, Oatmeal-Brown Sugar, '88 203
Pancakes, Whole Wheat-Oat, '93 16
Pancakes with Apple-Pear Sauce, Oatmeal Mini-,
    '97 M272
Piecrust, Crisp Cereal, '83 100
Piecrust, Oatmeal, '79 79
Slow Cooker with Ice Cream, Oatmeal in a, '99 193
Topping, Oat Crunch, '89 108
Topping, Oatmeal Cookie, '95 291
Waffles, Banana-Oatmeal, '94 206
Waffles, Oatmeal, '89 107
Waffles, Oatmeal-Nut, '83 96

OILS. *See also* **SEASONINGS.**
Basic Recipe, '96 122
Basil-Infused Olive Oil, '95 231
Basil Oil, '96 122
Black Pepper Oil, '96 122
Chile Pepper Oil, '96 122
Chili Oil, '96 234
Chipotle Oil, '02 97; '03 98
Chive Oil, '96 122
Cilantro Oil, '02 97; '03 98
Dill Oil, '96 122
Ginger Oil, '96 122
Lemon-Infused Olive Oil, '95 231
Mint Oil, '96 122
Oregano Oil, '96 122
Parsley Oil, '96 234
Roasted Garlic Oil, '96 122
Rosemary Oil, '96 122; '02 122
Sage Oil, '96 122
Thyme Oil, '96 122
Vanilla Oil, '94 243

OKRA
Bake, Okra-and-Tomato, '89 173
Bake, Okra-Tomato, '80 298; '81 26
Bake, Tomato-and-Okra, '03 158
Bisque, Okra-and-Shrimp, '97 156
Caponata, Okra, '97 157
Casserole, Okra, '79 160
Chowder, Quick Okra, '80 185
Combo, Field Peas, Okra, and Corn, '01 214
Corn, and Peppers, Okra, '87 M151
Corn, and Tomatoes, Okra, '95 203
Cream, Okra and Corn in, '79 160
Creole, Corn-and-Okra, '89 127
Creole, Meatball-Okra, '83 156
Creole Okra, '81 182
Creole, Okra, '02 234
Creole, Okra-Corn, '83 157
Dills, Okra, '97 157

Étouffée, Okra, '98 207
Fresh Okra and Tomatoes, '87 89
Fried
    Cheese, Okra with, '80 185
    Crispy Fried Okra, '86 169
    Croutons, Salad Greens and Veggies with Fried Okra,
        '96 178
    Crunchy Fried Okra, '01 165
    Deep-Fried Okra, '90 154
    Fingers, Okra, '85 196
    French-Fried Okra, '82 126
    Fried Okra, '79 122; '86 211; '87 89; '88 111;
        '00 205; '03 311
    Fritter-Fried Okra, '86 218
    Fritters, Okra, '79 160; '92 133; '98 159
    Green Tomatoes, Fried Okra and, '93 160; '01 325
    Green Tomatoes, Okra and, '79 160
    Nutty Okra, '03 136
    Old-Time Fried Okra, '80 185
    Oven-Fried Okra, '91 121
    Pods, Fried Okra, '00 205
    Potatoes, Fried Okra and, '97 136
    Potato Fry, Okra-, '81 159
    Puffs, Okra, '83 157
    Rellenos, Okra, '97 156
    Salad, Fried Okra, '97 M157; '04 167
Goulash, Okra, '93 160
Grilled Okra and Tomatoes, '98 124
Gumbo, Deep South Okra, '79 48
Gumbo Freezer Mix, Okra, '86 210; '01 165
Gumbo, Light Seafood-Okra, '86 155
Gumbo, Okra, '86 210; '91 206; '01 165
Gumbo, Old-Style Shrimp, '98 97
How to Can Okra, '80 127
Medley, Corn-and-Okra, '99 203
Medley, Okra, '88 M185
Medley, Okra-Corn-Tomato, '81 159
Muffins, Fresh Okra, '93 161
Pickled Okra, '98 177
Pickles, Okra, '81 173
Pilaf, Okra, '80 185; '82 126; '93 160
Pilau, Okra, '99 184
Plantation Okra, '82 126
Polenta with Cheese and Okra, Baked, '99 232
Salad, Okra, '90 155
Salad, Okra-Walnut, '04 291
Salad with Feta, Marinated Green Bean-and-Okra,
    '00 131
Sautéed Corn and Okra, '84 158
Sauté, Spicy Okra-Tomato-Corn, '04 327
Skillet Okra, '95 179
Soup, Charleston Okra, '87 156
Soup, Okra, '05 98
Soup, Okra-and-Shrimp, '94 323
Soup, Sausage and Okra, '80 209
Soup with Fou-Fou, Okra, '96 325
Stewed Okra, Southern, '82 134
Stew, Lamb-and-Okra, '97 156
Stew, Old-Fashioned Okra, '84 158
Stew, Quick Okra, '97 88
Stir-Fried Okra, '96 177
Stir-Fried Okra, Simple, '03 166
Surprise, Okra, '79 160; '84 158
Tomato Combo, Okra-, '83 157
Tomatoes and Okra, '86 170; '87 164; '00 182
Tomatoes, Fresh Okra and, '81 M165
Tomatoes, Okra and, '80 185; '81 139; '92 215; '98 286
Tomatoes with Okra, '85 106
Vinaigrette, Okra-Corn-and-Tomato, '90 173

OLIVES
Antipasto, Easy, '85 114
Antipasto, Grandpa's, '98 183
Appetizers, Cheesy Olive, '85 113
Appetizers, Cheesy-Olive, '87 246

Ball, Blue Cheese-Olive, '82 248
Ball, Olive Cheese, '80 258
Balls, Pumpkin Patch Cheese, '99 245
Biscuits with Olive-Parsley Spread, Cream Cheese-and-
    Olive, '04 238
Biscuits with Sun-Dried Tomato Spread and Bacon,
    Cream Cheese-and-Olive, '02 313
Biscuits with Tapenade, Cream Cheese-and-Olive, '02 313
Black Olives, Shrimp Spaghetti with, '85 13
Black Olive-Stuffed Mushrooms, '86 258
Bread, Olive, '93 78
Bread, Olive-Dill Casserole, '92 16
Bread, Tomato-Black Olive Grits, '05 83
Bruschetta, Caper-and-Olive, '00 276
Butter, Mediterranean, '97 307
Butter, Olive, '91 295
Casserole, Turkey-Olive, '87 268
Caviar, Mexican, '98 135
Chalupas, Chicken-Olive, '81 227
Cheesecake, Three-Layer, '99 140
Cheese, Cream Cheese-and-Olive Pimiento, '01 169;
    '03 315
Chicken-and-Rice Valencia, '85 113
Chicken Breasts, Greek, '98 19
Chicken, Spanish, '98 183
Cream Cheese, Bacon-Olive, '04 196
Crostini, Festive, '98 183
Crostini, Olive, '02 205
Dip, Monterey Shrimp, '99 65
Elephant Ears Provençale, Baby, '00 87
Filling, Chicken-Olive, '81 227
Greek Olive Cups, '99 221
Green Olives, Chicken with, '03 87
Lemon-Garlic Olives, '94 118
Marinated Cheese, Olives, and Peppers, '04 238
Marinated Green Beans with Tomatoes, Olives, and
    Feta, '03 163
Marinated Olives, '01 187
Marinated Olives and Peppers, '04 71
Marinated Olives, Balsamic, '02 135
Marinated Olives, Caliente, '95 177
Marinated Olives, Herb-, '92 176
Monster Eyes, '02 222
Muffuletta Loaf, '97 86
Muffulettas, '98 184
Olivata, '04 159
Orzo, Mozzarella-and-Olive, '97 249
Party Olives, Citrus, '03 124
Pesto, Olive-Rosemary, '01 317
Pizzas, Eggplant, '98 183
Pork Chops, Greek-Style Baked, '04 44
Potatoes, Olive, '80 114
Potatoes, Tangy Olive, '04 214
Quiche, Chicken-Olive-Cheddar, '03 58
Relish, Flank Steak with Tomato-Olive, '03 210
Relish with Coriander, Green Olive, '96 323;
    '97 27
Salad, Doodles Olive, '94 35
Salad, Greek Chicken, '97 92; '98 329
Salad, Greek Pasta, '02 139
Salad, Italian Olive, '94 35
Salad, Mexican Olive, '85 84
Salad Mix, Muffy, '94 34
Salad, Olive, '98 184; '00 335; '04 27
Salad, Olive Clubhouse, '81 114
Salad, Olive-Potato, '85 114
Salad with Sherry Vinaigrette, Shrimp, Orange, and
    Olive, '93 177
Salsa, Olive, '00 277
Sandwich, Deli Stuffed, '98 287
Sandwiches, Bacon-Olive Party, '04 196
Sandwiches, Goat Cheese-Olive, '04 272
Sandwiches, Mini Muffuletta Bacon-Olive Party,
    '04 196

OLIVES

(continued)

Sandwiches, Olive-Nut Spread, '04 259
Sandwiches, Olive Tea, '02 252
Sandwiches, Rolled Olive, '01 241
Sauce, Roasted Red Pepper, '98 16
Scaciati, Olives, '99 266
Snack, Open-Faced Cheese-and-Olive, '89 97
Spread, Antipasto, '81 25
Spread, Cheese-Olive, '79 82
Spread, Cream Cheese-Olive, '82 35
Spread, Creamy Olive, '81 290; '05 311
Spread, Feta-and-Apple, '99 106
Spread, Tomatoes with Olive, '85 114
Stuffed Olives, Almond-, '88 95
Tapenade, '92 194; '00 135; '01 70; '04 194
Tapenade, Grilled Crostini with Olive, '05 172
Toss, Cauliflower-Olive, '85 198; '86 147
Toss, Tomato-Olive Pasta, '86 209

OMELETS

Apple Omelet Stack, '94 50
Bacon-and-Potato Omelet, Open-Faced, '02 246
Baked Omelets, '94 50
Broccoli-Mushroom Omelet, '85 45
Casserole, Confetti Omelet, '05 169
Cheese Omelet, Herbed, '93 47
Cheese Omelet, Puffed, '89 227
Cheese Omelet, Zippy, '87 287
Cheese-Shiitake Omelet, Golden, '95 265
Cheesy Picante Omelet, '86 95
Chicken Liver Omelet, '82 44
Country Omelets, '91 128
Creole Sauce, Omelets with, '89 228
Dessert Omelet, Puffy, '00 35
Dill-Cheese-Ham Omelet, '95 33
Filling, Greek Omelet, '80 68
Filling, Spanish Omelet, '80 68
Fluffy Omelet, '84 56
Garden Omelet, '99 174
George's Omelets, '80 68
Ham and Cheese Omelet, '79 262; '80 123
Ham-and-Cheese Omelet, '02 246
Indian Omelet, '99 92
Mexican Omelet, '79 128; '81 225
Mushroom Omelet, Rolled, '82 70
Mushroom Sauce, Puffy Omelets with, '85 40
Olé Omelet, '87 M124
Olé, Omelet, '94 31
Oven-Baked Omelet, Farmer's, '03 204
Oyster Omelets, Smoked, '84 96
Pie, Omelet, '00 M35
Potato Omelet, Family-Size, '94 31
Potato-Sprout Omelet, '79 128
Primavera, Omelet, '87 71
Rising Sun Omelet, '82 281; '83 42
Rolled Omelet, '89 228
Sandwich, Omelet, '86 95
Sausage Filling, Omelet with, '81 43
Sausage Omelet, Puffy, '80 M268
Shrimp-and-Cheddar Omelet, '84 57
Shrimp-and-Cheese Omelet, '94 31
Shrimp-and-Vegetable Oven Omelet, '99 286
Sour Cream-Ham Omelet, '79 261
Spanish Omelet, '81 201; '83 243; '84 101; '00 35
Spanish Omelet with Fresh Avocado Salsa, '02 247
Spanish-Style Omelets, '83 188
Spinach, Cheddar, and Bacon Omelet, '03 204
Spinach-Cheese Omelet, '83 119
Strawberry-Sour Cream Omelet, '89 229
Sunrise Omelet, '83 289
Swiss Oven Omelet, '80 189
Tarragon Omelet, '89 144

Tex-Mex Omelet con Carne, '81 209
Vegetable Omelet, Beefy, '83 188
Vegetable Omelet, Cheddar-, '83 205
Vegetable Omelet, Cheesy, '85 49
Vegetable Omelet, Fresh, '84 211
Vegetable Omelet, Golden, '82 M123
Vegetable Omelet, Puffy, '83 188
Vegetable-Pasta Oven Omelet, '99 286
Vegetarian Omelet, '84 114
Veggie Omelet, Creamy, '02 248
White Wine Omelet, '79 103
Yogurt-Avocado Omelet, '81 33
Zucchini Omelet, '81 99

ONIONS

Appetizers, Bacon-Onion, '94 290
Bake, Cheese Onion, '82 32
Baked Onions, Micro-, '82 M32
Baked Onions, Spicy, '84 65
Baked Onions, Sweet-and-Sour, '90 34
Bake, Four Onion, '93 304
Bake, Onion-Potato, '83 M195
Bake, Romano Onion, '90 98
Barbecued Onions, '88 86
Beans, Buzz's Pot of, '03 19
Beans, Hearty Baked, '01 259
Beans, K.C. Baked, '98 244; '03 107
Beef à la Beer, '98 64
Beef à la Mode, '98 122
Beef and Onions, Smothered, '85 293
Beef Stroganoff, '03 23
Black Beans, Cuban, '99 56
Black-Eyed Peas, '03 M49
Black-Eyed Peas, Hearty, '02 107
Black-Eyed Peas, Michelle's, '03 16
Black-Eyed Peas, Pickled, '01 30

Breads

Biscuits, Cheesy Onion, '95 98
Buns, Cheesy Onion, '85 5
Buns, Onion-Cheese, '88 218
Buns, Potato-Caramelized Onion, '03 234
Cheese Bread, Onion-, '79 180; '81 8
Cheese Supper Bread, Onion-, '83 112
Cornbread, Cheese-and-Onion, '05 35
Cornbread, Onion, '88 283
Cornbread, Onion-Topped, '84 153
Cornbread, Sweet Onion, '98 252
Dill Bread, Easy Onion-, '85 5
Easy Onion Bread, '81 162
Flatbread, Parmesan-Onion, '98 65
Flatbread, Quick, '00 119
Focaccia, Mustard-and-Onion, '90 321; '92 97
Focaccia, Onion, '93 77
Focaccia, Roquefort-and-Onion, '98 54
French Bread, Onion-Cheese, '89 29
French Onion Bread, '91 90
Herb Bread, Onion-, '90 165
Herb Bread, Toasted Onion-, '83 266
Hush Puppies, Onion, '85 14
Hush Puppies, Tomato-Onion, '91 201
Loaves, Onion Twist, '84 300
Muffins, Onion-Dill, '92 253; '93 144
Parmesan Bread, Onion-, '84 284
Poppy Seed Twist, Onion-, '97 242
Rolls, Onion-and-Sesame, '95 292
Rolls, Onion-Bacon, '99 47
Rolls, Onion Twist, '89 288
Rolls, Poppy Seed Onion, '81 63
Rye Bread, Onion-, '99 55
Burgers, Open-Faced Chicken-Onion, '94 139
Burritos, Potato-and-Egg, '02 72
Butter, Onion, '86 253
Cakes, Black-Eyed Pea, '01 32
Caponata alla Siciliana, '02 269

Caramelized Onion-and-Gorgonzola Mashed Potatoes, '01 256
Caramelized Onion-and-Pecan Brussels Sprouts, '99 254
Caramelized Onion BLT, '03 90
Caramelized Onion Macaroni and Cheese, '04 231
Caramelized Onion Mayonnaise, '00 218
Caramelized Onions, '03 90, 235; '05 259
Caramelized Onions, Beef Burgers with, '98 143
Caramelized Onions, Chicken Cobbler with, '00 44
Caramelized Onions, Green Beans with, '95 288; '00 33
Caramelized Onions, Mediterranean, '96 273
Caramelized Onions, Pepper Burgers with, '00 218
Caramelized Onions, Potato Casserole with, '03 231
Caramelized Onions, Potato-Horseradish Gratin with, '99 314
Caramelized Onions, Thai Pork Chops with, '05 85
Carrots, Scalloped, '02 129
Carrots with Bacon and Onion, Glazed, '87 200; '02 283
Casserole, Cheesy Onion, '79 101
Chard with Onion and Apple, Sautéed, '98 48
Cheese Onions, Sherried, '82 32
Chicken and Onions, Down-Home, '02 271
Chicken in Coconut Milk, '97 202
Chicken, Onion-Crusted, '88 40
Chicken Sandwich, Jerk, '98 333
Chicken, Slow-Roasted, '98 108
Chicken with Rice, Moorish, '98 127
Chili, White Christmas, '98 266
Chutney, Cranberry, '98 276
Collard Greens, Esau's, '03 17
Confit, Roasted Shallot-Garlic, '94 303
Corn, Skillet Creamed, '02 204
Couscous, Spinach-and-Onion, '98 23
Crème Brûlée, Onion, '95 324
Crunch Sticks, Onion Crescent, '90 206
Curried Onions, '90 34
Custards, Savory Spinach-Gorgonzola, '02 284
Deluxe, Broccoli-Onion, '81 75
Dip, Cheesy Onion, '83 145
Dip, Chunky Onion, '84 257
Dip, Cream Cheese-Onion, '79 236
Dip, Curry-Onion, '93 313
Dip, Swiss-Onion, '95 93
Dressing, Cornbread, '98 269
Dressing, Green Pepper-Onion Salad, '84 12
Dressing, Onion-French, '84 283

Fried

Beer-Battered Onion Rings, '92 52
Buttermilk Batter-Fried Onion Rings, '02 131
Crisp Fried Onion Rings, '84 65
Crispy Fried Onion Rings, '80 108
Crispy Onion Rings, '86 110
Deluxe Fried Onion Rings, '80 108
Easy Onion Rings, '80 108
Favorite Fried Onion Rings, '81 86
French-Fried Onion Rings, '88 111
French-Fried Onion Rings Supreme, '80 109
Green Onions, Fried, '81 106
Leonard's-Style Onion Rings, '90 120
Rings, Fried Onion, '83 85; '85 69
Rings, South-of-the-Border Onion, '96 217
Glazed Apple and Onion, Pork Chops with Mustard-, '01 47
Glazed Carrots and Onions, '83 25; '87 128
Glazed Onions, '84 104; '97 306; '99 24
Gourmet Onions, '81 86
Gravy, Fried Quail with Onion, '82 214
Gravy, Pork Chops in Onion, '99 222
Gravy, Roast with Onion-and-Mushroom, '00 293
Gravy, Southwestern, '99 34
Green Beans, Lorraine's, '99 319
Green Beans with Onion and Basil, Italian, '03 241
Green Beans with Purple Onion, Spicy, '98 286

Green Onions
  Biscuits, Cheesy Onion, '01 330
  Butterbeans with Bacon and Green Onions, '96 267
  Canapés, Green Onion, '84 M216
  Cheese Ball, Pinecone, '98 265
  Crostini, Green Onion, '96 93
  Cukes and Scallions, '91 168
  Dip, Onion, '94 21
  Dressing, Green Onion, '96 17
  Eggs, Creamy Onion Scrambled, '83 M203
  Fans, Green Onion, '05 271
  Grilled Green Onions, Chicken with, '01 94
  Hoecakes, Green Onion, '88 112
  Hush Puppies, Green Onion-Tomato, '97 84
  Lima Beans and Scallions, Fresh, '82 133
  Lobster Scallion Shooters, '00 197
  Mayonnaise, Mediterranean, '98 144
  Muffins, Green Onion-and-Cream Cheese, '01 289
  Pie, Green Onion, '98 159
  Pie, Tumbleweed, '98 205
  Pork-and-Onions with Bean Sauce, '85 76
  Potatoes, Green Onion-and-Bacon Mashed, '02 110
  Quiche, Cheesy Green Onion, '83 194; '84 42
  Relish, Green Onion, '84 65
  Salad, Bacon 'n' Onion Potato, '05 188
  Salmon with Mushrooms and Green Onions, Fresh, '93 180
  Sauce, Onion-Mushroom, '85 224; '86 84
  Sautéed Onions and Peppers, '83 M148
  Scallion Hoe Cake Medaillons, Skillet Hoppin' John with, '02 326
  Soup, Creamed Green Onion, '83 82
  Soup, Green Onion, '84 112
  Spread, Chutney-Onion Cheese, '01 94
  Spread, Green Onion-Cheese, '92 24
  Teasers, Green Onion, '82 42
  Tempura-Battered Green Onions, '96 93
  Grilled Onion Flowers with Pecans, '96 217
  Grilled Squash and Onion, '79 150
  Grits with Grilled Chicken and Onions, '99 17
  Hamburger Steaks, Smothered, '00 289
  Hash Browns, Smothered-Covered, '02 248
  Herbed Carrots and Onions, '87 31
  Herbed Onions, '84 149
  Honey Onions, '81 86
  Hush Puppies, Corn Soufflé, '98 M328
  Italian Dressing, Tomato, Onion, and Cucumber in, '81 83
  Jam, Coffee-Onion, '05 123
  Kale with Tomato and Onion, '92 244
  Kuchen, Onion, '90 34
  Loaf, Poppy-Onion, '04 35
  Marinade, Basic, '99 141; '02 19
  Marmalade, Fruited Onion, '96 323; '97 27
  Mayonnaise, Onion, '98 144
  Meat Loaf, French Market, '02 33
  Meat Loaf, Moist-and-Saucy, '99 270
  Medley, Cabbage-Onion-Sweet Pepper, '96 252; '97 28
  Mums, Onion, '96 318
  Oven-Browned Onions, '02 221
  Patties, Potato-Onion, '95 269
  Pearl Onions, Beef Burgundy with, '81 108
  Pearl Onions, Glazed, '85 258
  Pearl Onions, Green Beans with Roasted Red Peppers and, '93 260
  Pearl Onions, Snap Peas and, '89 280
  Pearl Onions, Sweet-and-Sour, '96 216
  Peas with Onions, Buttered, '80 242
  Pickled Cocktail Onions, '89 197
  Pickled Refrigerator Onion Rings, '84 265
  Pie, Beef-and-Onion Cornbread, '01 298
  Pie, Onion, '82 191
  Pie, Summer Garden, '02 182

  Pilau, Sausage, '99 184
  Polenta Triangles, '98 181
  Pork Chops with Onions, Pan-fried, '05 43
  Potatoes and Onions, Cheesy, '00 275
  Pot Pie with Cranberry-Pecan Crusts, Turkey, '02 198
  Pot Roast, Root Beer, '04 212
  Pot Roast, Sweet-and-Sour, '99 291
  Pudding, Kathy's Onion, '95 318
  Quiche, Onion, '83 121
  Red Onions, Grilled, '03 139
  Relish, Hot, '01 123
  Relish, Pepper-Onion, '84 180
  Rice, Braised, '98 45
  Rice Pilaf, Greek, '01 146
  Rice, Red, '97 138
  Rice, Seasoned Onion, '82 166
  Risotto, Easy Baked, '99 120
  Risotto with Saffron, Pistachio, '98 272
  Roasted Celery Root, Carrots, and Onions, '98 293
  Roasted Onion Guacamole, '00 334
  Roasted Onions, Rosemary, '98 16
  Roasted Sweet Potatoes and Onions, '01 234
  Roast, Pumpernickel, '97 234
  Ropa Vieja, '98 20
  Salad, Bacon 'n' Onion Potato, '05 188
  Salad, Classic Broccoli-Raisin, '02 24
  Salad Dressing, Vinaigrette, '02 25
  Salad, Lemon-Onion, '85 252
  Salad, Lettuce-Wedge, '02 65
  Salad, Roasted Onion, '95 65; '03 142
  Salad, Tomato-Cucumber-Onion, '81 239
  Salad, Tomato-Red Onion, '04 181
  Salad with Onion and Celery, Potato, '02 138
  Salad with Peppered Cheese Crisps, Roasted Onion Pasta, '98 107
  Salsa Salpicon, '03 33
  Salsa Verde, '96 160
  Sandwiches, Steak-and-Onion, '02 126
  Sauce, Beef Tenderloin with Five-Onion, '98 272
  Sauce, Brussels Sprouts in Onion, '81 308
  Sauce, Come Back, '00 211
  Sauce, Creole, '02 32
  Sauce, Green Barbecue, '02 183
  Sauce, Onion, '82 72; '87 248
  Sauce, Onion-Balsamic, '99 44
  Sauce, Onion Cream, '87 232
  Sauce, Onion-Parsley, '85 148
  Sauce, Pepper-Onion, '84 125
  Sauce, Sweet 'n' Saucy, '01 210
  Sauerbraten, '98 278
  Sautéed Apples, Onions, and Pears over Spinach, '94 212
  Selecting and Storing Onions, '84 65
  Shallot Salad, Caramelized, '96 308
  Shells, Cheese and Limas in Onion, '81 86
  Shrimp Bourbon, '00 125
  Shrimp, Marinated, '98 317
  Shrimp with Onion and Red Pepper, Sweet-and-Sour, '02 84
  Soufflé, Onion, '79 247
Soups
  Caramelized French Onion Soup, '00 218
  Caramelized Onion Soup with Goat Cheese-and-Chive Croutons, '01 312
  Cheese Onion Soup, Double-, '85 227
  Cheese Soup, Onion-, '87 81
  Classic Onion Soup, '84 65
  Creamy Onion Soup, '90 211
  Double Cheese-Topped Onion Soup, '79 49
  Easy Onion Soup, '85 226
  French Onion-Beef Soup, '87 54
  French Onion Soup, '79 49; '80 188; '83 126; '85 226; '86 M212; '90 31; '93 246; '04 243
  French Onion Soup, Shortcut, '85 M328

  French Onion Soup, Toasty, '81 306
  Green Onion Soup, '84 112
  Green Onion Soup, Creamed, '83 82
  Mexican Onion Soup, '04 243
  Mushroom-Onion Soup, '80 25
  Onion Soup, '99 96
  Oven-Browned Onion Soup, '79 49
  Potato Soup, Creamy Onion-and-, '92 51; '97 304
  Rich Onion Soup, '85 226
  Superb Onion Soup, '81 86
  Three-Onion Soup, '96 217
  Tomato-Onion Soup, '04 243
  Vichyssoise, '86 181
  Vidalia Onion Soup, Beefy, '97 212
  Sour Cream, Cucumber and Onion in, '81 69
  Spaghetti with Smothered Onions, '97 229
  Spinach with Crowder Peas, '00 159
  Spread, Braunschweiger-Onion, '79 82
  Squares, Creamy Onion, '79 48
  Squares, Sausage-Onion, '83 112
  Squash, Basil Summer, '01 180
  Squash, Creole, '01 180
  Steak, Onion-Smothered, '87 M189
  Stew, Beef-and-Onion, '87 18
Stuffed
  Baked Onions, Stuffed, '82 32
  Baked Stuffed Onions, '83 135
  Baked Sweet Onions, '98 130
  Broccoli-Stuffed Onions, '84 154
  Cheese-Stuffed Onions, '90 34
  Peas, Onions Stuffed with, '84 68
  Ratatouille-Stuffed Onions, '96 91
  Sweet Onions, Stuffed, '91 79
  Vidalia Onions, Stuffed, '89 172
  Wine, Stuffed Onions and, '85 268
  Stuffing, Rice-and-Onion, '88 246
Sweet
  Applesauce, Sweet Onion, '02 319
  Baked Sweet Onions, '91 79
  Balsamic Onion Stacks, '05 141
  Blossom, Onion, '94 226
  Butter, Sweet Onion, '93 124
  Cabbage, Scalloped, '01 43
  Cakes, Southwestern Cornbread Dressing, '01 233
  Caramelized Florida Sweet Onions, Balsamic, '94 163
  Caramelized Onion, Corn with Bacon and, '99 94
  Caramelized Onion, Green Beans with, '00 33
  Caramelized Onions, '00 218; '01 61; '03 90; '04 30
  Casserole, French Onion, '95 26
  Casserole, Sweet Onion, '00 103
  Chutney, Kiwifruit-Onion, '93 125
  Citrus Onions, '04 89
  Creole Onions, '82 32
  Eye of Round, Slow Cooker Spicy Marinated, '99 291
  Eye of Round, Spicy Marinated, '99 291
  Flatbread, Quick, '00 119
  Grilled Stuffed Onions, '95 180
  Honey-Paprika Sweet Onions, '92 52
  Hot Onions, Sweet-, '85 139
  Jelly, Onion, '93 135
  Marinated Bermuda Onions, '92 194
  Oven-Roasted Sweet Potatoes and Onions, '00 24
  Parmesan Onions, '93 170
  Pickled Onion and Cucumber, '02 126
  Pie, Onion, '00 283
  Pie, Onion-Cheese, '88 86
  Pizza, Chicken-and-Purple Onion, '97 47
  Pizza, Plum-and-Sweet Onion, '98 193
  Pot Pies, Wild Mushroom-and-Onion, '98 296
  Puddings, Onion, '02 126
  Pudding, Sweet Onion, '00 260; '02 310
  Relish, Onion, '91 79

ONIONS, Sweet
(continued)

Relish, Purple Onion, '95 253
Relish, Sweet Onion, '93 124; '96 206; '99 204
Ribs and Onions, Tangy, '99 136
Rice Pilaf, Onion, '04 236
Rings, Crispy Baked Onion, '93 247
Risotto, Onion, '99 94; '02 97; '03 98
Risotto, Sweet Onion, '03 217
Roasted Sweet Onions, '04 282
Salad Bowl, Spinach-and-Onion, '81 157
Salad, Grilled Onion, '99 96
Salad, Marinated Orange-Onion, '91 231; '92 68
Salad, Orange-Onion, '89 41
Salad, Tomato-and-Onion, '05 167
Salad, Tomato-and-Sweet Onion, '05 141
Salsa, Fiesta Onion, '94 82
Sauce, Spicy, '99 291
Sauce, Vidalia Onion, '99 52
Shortcake, Onion, '92 51
Slaw, Sweet Onion, '98 171
Smoky Sweet Onions, '97 191
Stir-Fry, Sweet Onion-Asparagus, '98 135
Stuffed Onions, Florentine, '05 141
Stuffed Sweet Onions, '91 79
Tart, Caramelized Onion, '99 96
Tarts, Sweet Onion, '95 229
Tomatoes and Okra, '00 182
Trout, Sweet Onion-Stuffed, '99 52
Vidalia Deep Dish, '89 120
Vidalia Onion-Balsamic Vinaigrette, '04 317
Vidalia Onion Dip, Baked, '02 88
Vidalia Onion Gravy, Roasted Red Pepper-and-,
    '03 323
Vidalia Onion Pie with Mushrooms, '02 183
Vidalia Onion Sauté, '89 119
Vidalia Onions, Baked, '00 102
Vidalia Onions, Cheesy Baked, '01 145
Vidalia Onion Soufflé, '04 167
Vidalia Onions, Stuffed, '89 172
Vidalia Onions with Pecans and Roasted Carrots,
    Roasted, '92 340
Vidalia Sandwiches on Salt-Rising Bread, '79 145
Vidalias, Marinated, '89 119
Vidalia-Tomato Salad, '84 65
Vinaigrette, Spinach Salad with Apple-Onion,
    '94 276
Vinaigrette, Vidalia Onion, '99 168
Sweet Potatoes with Cumin, Mashed, '99 244
Swordfish, Mediterranean, '02 237
Taters, Buck's, '95 72
Toasties, Onion, '97 225
Turkey, New Year's, '97 255
Turnips and Onions, '83 242
Veal and Onions, Herbed, '79 108
Vinaigrette, Asian, '97 146
Vinegar Sauce, Whole Onions with Warm, '94 172
ON THE LIGHT SIDE. *See* HEALTHY & LIGHT.
ORANGES. *See also* AMBROSIA.
Appetizer, Orange-Berry, '85 81
Apples, Orange-Ginger Roasted, '01 184
Apples, Orange-Glazed, '82 51
Baked Fruit, Ginger-Orange, '93 313
Baked Oranges, '79 247; '89 41
Baked Orange Slices, '89 88
Baskets, Orange, '93 286
Beverages
    Blend, Orange, '95 276
    Blush, Orange, '80 51
    Brandy Smash, Orange, '99 30
    Breakfast Eye-Opener, '87 199
    Champagne with Orange Juice, '91 71
    Cider, Apple-Orange, '92 20
    Cider, Hot Mulled Apple-Orange, '97 301
    Cocktail, Citrus Wine, '99 93
    Cocktail, Orange-Champagne, '79 39
    Cocktail, Orange-Cranberry, '01 103
    Cocktail, Tomato-Orange Juice, '83 169
    Coffee, Orange, '96 313
    Coffee, Viennese Orange, '84 54
    Cooler, Apricot-Orange-Carrot, '96 108
    Cooler, Citrus, '82 160
    Cooler, Orange Tea, '05 216
    Cooler, White Grape-and-Orange, '05 61
    Cruising Drink, '00 167
    Cubes, Florida, '95 201
    Flip, Orange-Banana, '82 48
    Flips, Orange Blossom, '80 51
    Frosty, Orange, '86 101
    Frosty Sours, '81 156
    Jogger's Sunrise, '93 213
    Jubilee, Orange, '03 305
    Juicy, Orange, '90 178
    Lemonade, Orange-Mint, '88 82
    Liqueur, Orange, '81 287
    Magnolia Blossoms, '87 72
    Magnolias, '82 196
    Margaritas, Orange-Lime, '97 140
    Mimosa, '04 106
    Mist, Orange-Lemon, '79 288; '80 35
    Nog, Orange Spiced, '82 48
    Pick-Me-Up, Orange, '80 232
    Pineapple Drink, Orange-, '89 35
    Pirate's Painkiller, '99 161
    Punch, Champagne, '96 277; '98 310
    Punch, Champagne Blossom, '99 290
    Punch, Citrus Party, '83 141
    Punch, Orange Blossom, '83 142
    Punch, Orange-Lime, '82 160
    Punch, Orange-Mint, '82 121
    Punch, Orange Sherbet Party, '83 142
    Punch, Orange Soda, '87 214
    Punch, Pineapple-Orange, '85 236
    Punch, Refreshing Orange, '81 39
    Punch, Sparkling Orange, '05 170
    Refresher, Grapefruit-Orange, '82 174
    Sangría, '81 67
    Sangría, Easy Citrus, '80 218
    Sangría, Orange, '81 237
    Shake, Orange Milk, '84 166
    Shake, Peachy Orange, '81 156
    Shake, Pineapple-Orange-Banana, '97 172
    Shake, Strawberry-Orange Breakfast, '87 186
    Shake, Tropical, '87 200
    Sipper, Sunset Vodka-Orange, '05 122
    Slush, Banana-Orange, '80 48; '81 155
    Slush, Orange, '82 49
    Slush, Strawberry-Orange, '83 172
    Slush, Vodka-Orange, '89 92
    Smoothie, Mango-Orange, '86 216
    Smoothie, Orange-Banana, '97 173
    Smoothie, Tropical, '81 50
    Soda, Cranberry-Orange, '79 148
    Soda, Homemade Orange, '03 141
    Sunrise, Bourbon, '01 326
    Sunshine Fizz, '92 44
    Syrup, Orange, '96 161
    Tea, Marmalade, '98 330
    Tea, Pineapple-Orange Herb, '05 61
    Thing, Orange, '04 290
    Whip, Orange-Banana, '95 244
    Whiskey Sours, Frozen Orange-, '92 67
Breads
    Anise-Orange Bread, '83 295
    Apricot-Orange Bread, '92 285
    Baba au Orange, '86 138
    Biscuits, Cranberry-Orange-Glazed, '04 280; '05 335
    Biscuits, Orange, '88 85
    Blueberry-Orange Bread, '87 140; '02 21
    Breakfast Ring, Orange, '81 229
    Coffee Cake, Cranberry-Orange, '82 283
    Coffee Cake, Nutty Orange, '95 160
    Coffee Cake, Orange, '85 M88
    Coffee Cake, Orange Butter, '89 229
    Coffee Cake, Orange Marmalade Swirl, '81 107
    Coffee Cake, Orange-Pecan, '86 86
    Coffee Ring, Caramel-Orange, '80 45
    Cranberry Bread, Orange-, '85 266
    Cranberry-Orange Bread, '87 244
    Cream Cheese-Banana-Nut Bread, Orange-Pecan-
        Topped, '05 27
    Cream Cheese Bread, Orange-, '82 210
    Doughnuts, Orange Spiced, '79 136
    French Toast, Orange, '83 292; '84 78; '86 329
    French Toast with Orange Sauce, '82 47
    Kulich, '01 87
    Muffins, Banana-Orange, '84 148
    Muffins, Cranberry-Orange, '04 209
    Muffins, Orange, '79 236; '81 107; '83 54; '89 205;
        '97 271
    Muffins, Orange Blossom, '96 54
    Muffins, Orange-Date, '92 119; '97 243; '05 215
    Muffins, Orange-Ginger, '89 41
    Muffins, Orange-Honey, '88 284
    Muffins, Orange-Oatmeal, '85 202; '00 24
    Muffins, Orange-Pecan, '83 96; '99 56
    Muffins, Orange-Raisin, '97 153
    Muffins, Pecan-Orange, '97 163
    Muffins, Streusel-Topped Orange, '84 74
    Muffins with Honey Spread, Orange Juice, '81 229
    Nut Bread, Blueberry-Orange, '84 141
    Nut Bread, Cranberry-Orange, '80 288
    Nut Bread, Orange-, '82 75
    Nut Loaf, Orange, '80 226
    Pecan Bread, Glazed Orange-, '81 250
    Pecan Bread, Orange-, '79 148
    Pecan Loaves, Orange-, '79 215
    Poppy Seed Bread, Orange-Scented, '04 300
    Puffs, Upside-Down Orange, '83 57
    Pumpkin Bread, Orange-, '87 300
    Rolls, Apricot-Orange Sweet, '03 235
    Rolls, Citrus-Pecan, '03 256
    Rolls, Easy Orange, '89 M131
    Rolls, Frosted Hot Orange, '80 257
    Rolls, Glazed Orange, '90 194
    Rolls, Kitchen Express Orange, '98 252
    Rolls, Lemon-Orange, '05 70
    Rolls, Luscious Orange, '86 298
    Rolls, Orange, '80 22; '82 17; '88 79; '96 321;
        '01 257
    Rolls, Orange Butter, '82 206; '83 33
    Rolls, Speedy Orange, '89 287
    Rye Bread, Swedish Orange-, '85 111
    Scones, Cranberry-Orange, '97 45
    Scones, Orange-Pecan, '94 215; '01 72
    Scones with Orange Butter, Double-Orange, '97 44
    Tea Bread, Orange, '79 234
    Toast, Orange Praline, '79 36
    Toast Topper, Orange, '79 36
    Whole Wheat Orange Bread, '85 5
Broiled Orange Halves, '85 288
Broth, Tortellini in Citrus, '99 292
Butter, Citrus, '97 307
Butter, Honey-Orange, '79 36; '85 19
Butter, Orange, '81 8, 42; '90 323; '92 319; '94 115;
    '97 44
Butter, Orange-Pecan, '84 75; '97 15
Butter, Prune-Orange, '92 49
Butter, Tomato-Curry-Orange, '93 159
Chutney, Cranberry-Orange, '79 292

Chutney, Orange-Cranberry, '86 266
Couscous, Orange-Ginger, '00 295
Cranberry Oranges, Brandied, '98 309
Cranberry Sauce Stacks, Orange 'n' Jellied, '05 270
Cream, Beef Fillets with Orange, '97 66
Cream Cheese, Orange, '91 177
Cream, Orange, '90 126

Desserts

Alaska, Orange, '83 177
Ambrosia, Pineapple-Orange, '88 252
Apples, Orange-Pecan Baked, '85 45
Apples with Cookie Crumbs, Orange Baked, '95 271
Apples with Orange Sauce, Baked, '84 314
Baked Orange Elegance, '80 13
Balls, Orange, '94 331
Balls, Orange-Nut, '02 297
Bananas Foster, Orange-Glazed, '91 91
Bananas with Orange Sauce, Baked, '79 115
Bars, Pineapple-Orange, '82 129
Baskets, Orange, '81 308
Biscochos, Betty's, '00 325
Biscotti, Orange-Pecan, '01 207
Cake, Aztec Pound, '96 61
Cake, Chocolate-Orange Pound, '89 94
Cake, Fresh Orange, '83 300
Cake, Fresh Orange Chiffon, '88 179
Cake, Fresh Orange Italian Cream, '02 294
Cake, General Robert E. Lee Orange-Lemon, '88 92
Cake, Mandarin Orange, '83 24
Cake, Mandarin-Rum, '84 150
Cake, Orange, '86 61; '95 320
Cake, Orange Angel Food, '96 246
Cake, Orange Blossom, '96 162
Cake, Orange Butter, '95 46
Cake, Orange Chiffon, '91 56
Cake, Orange-Coconut Angel Food, '94 294
Cake, Orange-Cranberry, '85 314
Cake, Orange Cream, '99 118
Cake, Orange-Date, '94 60
Cake, Orange Date-Nut, '01 285
Cake, Orange Liqueur, '87 84
Cake, Orange Marmalade, '85 53
Cake, Orange Meringue, '86 336; '87 84
Cake, Orange Nut, '80 70
Cake, Orange-Nut Butter, '80 254
Cake, Orange-Pecan Crunch, '83 10
Cake, Orange-Pecan Pound, '93 13
Cake, Orange-Pecan-Spice Pound, '02 295
Cake, Orange Pound, '87 84, 221; '92 69
Cake, Orange Rum, '79 2
Cake, Orange-Slice, '81 264
Cake, Orange Streusel, '88 10
Cake, Pig Pickin', '04 112
Cake, Praline-Filled Carrot, '03 332
Cake, Rum-Orange Coconut, '88 224
Cake, Sour Cream-Orange Pecan Pound, '89 207
Cake Squares, Apple-Orange, '84 150
Cake Squares, Orange, '81 34
Cake Squares, Orange-Pumpkin, '83 242
Cake, Williamsburg Orange, '81 120; '82 23
Cake with Orange Icebox Pie Filling, Orange
  Chiffon, '03 105
Candied Orange Peel, '81 286
Candied Orange Rind, '96 162; '97 32
Candied Orange Zest, '95 320
Caramelized Oranges, Italian, '05 101
Champagne Oranges, '93 83
Cheesecake, Orange, '81 84; '85 38
Chiffon Dessert, Orange, '93 295
Chocolate-Orange Delights, '93 52
Chocolate-Orange Roll, '87 21
Cookies, Carrot-Orange, '83 149
Cookies, Chocolate-Dipped Orange, '04 299
Cookies, Frosted Orange, '83 114

Cookies, Orange-Chocolate, '83 113
Cookies, Orange-Glazed Oatmeal, '80 60
Cookies, Orange-Pecan, '88 119
Cookies, Orange Refrigerator, '86 230
Cookies, Orange-Slice, '89 294
Cookies, Orange Slice, '98 324
Cookies, Orange Sugar, '89 329
Cookies, White Chocolate-Orange Dream, '98 294
Cran-Orange Surprise, '94 143
Cream Dessert, Orange, '80 254; '84 165
Cream, Orange, '81 12; '00 27
Cream, Orange Chantilly, '84 156
Cream, Orange-Coconut, '84 24
Cream, Orange-Mallow, '94 295
Cream, Orange Whipped, '88 83
Crème Brûlée, Orange, '95 323
Crème, Orange-Tapioca, '82 M283
Crêpes, Amaretto-and-Orange, '86 260
Crêpes, Chocolate-Orange, '85 263
Crêpes, Orange Dream, '82 183
Crinkles, Orange, '95 272
Crispies, Grandmom Lucy's Orange, '02 253
Crispies, Orange, '84 205
Crisp, Orange-Apple, '80 295
Cupcakes, Orange, '97 32
Curd, Fresh Orange, '02 294
Dip, Creamy Orange, '84 117
Dip, Orange-Flavored Cream Cheese, '03 93
Dip, Orange Marmalade-Cream Cheese, '03 93
Éclairs, Miniature Orange, '95 92
Filling, Citrus, '02 221
Filling, Lemon-Orange, '81 71
Filling, Orange, '79 229; '86 336; '87 84; '88 224;
  '96 316
Filling, Orange Cream, '99 118
Filling, Orange Curd, '96 120
Filling, Orange Icebox Pie, '03 104
Filling, Orange-Pineapple Fried Pie, '96 109
Fingers, Orange, '87 57
Flambé, Dessert Orange, '85 313
Flan, Almond-Orange, '04 241
Flan, Orange, '84 95
Frosted Oranges, '83 270
Frosting, Citrus Cream Cheese, '99 223
Frosting, Creamy Orange, '83 24, 241
Frosting, Orange, '81 7; '86 61; '88 119
Frosting, Orange Butter, '83 300
Frosting, Orange Buttercream, '80 70; '99 117;
  '03 105
Frosting, Orange Cream, '81 207; '82 14
Frosting, Orange-Cream Cheese, '81 70; '82 16;
  '92 19; '04 258
Frosting, Orange-Lemon, '88 92
Frozen Orange Dessert, '92 44
Fruit Dessert Orange, '84 314
Fudge, Orange-Walnut, '92 288
Glazed Oranges and Pineapple, '86 318
Grand Marnier, Oranges, '92 82
Grand Marnier, Oranges in, '95 142
Grand Oranges and Strawberries, '03 119
Granita, Orange, '88 118
Ice Cream, Orange, '97 160
Ice Cream, Orange-Pineapple, '86 117
Ice, Strawberry-Orange, '86 196
Ice, Tart Cranberry-Orange, '86 317
Juice, Strawberries with Brandied Orange, '82 160
Kiwi-and-Orange Dessert, '93 295
Meringues, Orange, '95 318
Molded Dessert, Orange, '83 302
Mousse, Chocolate-Orange, '81 16, 205
Mousse, Orange, '86 69; '94 198
Mousse with Orange Liqueur, Chocolate, '02 315
Parfaits, Chilled Orange, '80 219
Parfaits, Orange Cream, '94 198

Pastry Cream, Grand Marnier, '01 45
Peanut Brittle, Orange, '80 302
Pears Flambé, Orange-Poached, '85 313
Pears in Orange Sauce, Poached, '82 19
Pears, Orange Poached, '80 218
Pie, Coconut-Orange Chess, '89 169
Pie, Florida Orange, '91 43
Pie, Frosty Orange, '90 296
Pie, Lemon-Orange, '85 172
Pie, Orange Ambrosia, '80 237
Pie, Orange Chess, '88 204; '01 23
Pie, Orange Chiffon, '87 260
Pie, Orange-Coconut, '90 90
Pie, Orange-Coconut Cream, '94 208
Pie, Orange Cream, '03 35
Pie, Orange Dream, '02 93
Pie, Orange Meringue, '81 12, 309
Pie, Orange-Pecan, '79 282; '83 222
Pie, Sweet Potato-Orange, '88 207
Pie, Tangerine Chess, '01 23
Poached Oranges, Wine-, '84 M323
Pops, Hawaiian Orange-Pineapple, '94 143
Pops, Orange-Banana, '82 129
Pops, Orange Float, '99 132
Pops, Strawberry-Orange, '03 179
Pralines, Orange, '92 313; '93 51
Pudding, Mandarin-Almond, '85 M12
Pudding, Orange, '81 85; '82 111; '83 153
Pudding, Orange Custard, '88 174
Pumpkin-Orange Delight, '86 321
Rice Cream with Mandarin Oranges, '85 317
Roulage, Chocolate-Orange, '94 314
Sections with Chocolate and Raspberry Sauce,
  Orange, '97 33
Sherbet Ambrosia Cups, '82 159
Sherbet, Banana-Orange, '83 162
Sherbet, Orange, '79 155
Sherbet, Three-Ingredient Orange, '01 105
Sherbet with Blackberry Sauce, Orange, '94 232
Shortbread Madeleines, Orange, '88 242
Shortbread, Orange, '91 272
Shortcake, Fresh Orange, '80 100
Shortcake, Orange-Strawberry, '95 100
Slices, Burgundy-Spiced Orange, '93 294
Sorbet, Banana-Orange, '88 117
Sorbet, Fresh Orange, '92 143
Sorbet, Orange, '03 171
Soufflé, Chilled Orange, '84 317; '86 189
Soufflé, Frozen Orange, '79 211
Soufflé, Grand Marnier, '79 281
Soufflé, Orange Dessert, '83 206
Special, Orange Blossom, '79 48
Squares, Orange-Crunch, '86 136
Squash Brûlée, Orange-, '94 267
Tapioca Fluff, Orange, '87 31
Tart, Double Citrus, '05 55
Tartlets, Creamy Citrus, '02 136
Tarts, Frozen Orange, '80 154
Tarts, Orange, '96 317
Tarts, Orange Curd, '92 193
Topping, Whipped Orange, '80 254
Truffles, Orange-Pecan, '95 92
Turnovers, Orange-Apple, '99 294
Whipped Cream, Orange, '02 315
Dip, Creamy Orange, '87 247
Dip, Marmalade, '99 324
Dip, Orange Fruit, '96 190
Dip, Orange-Lime, '96 248
Dip, Orange Sour Cream, '79 208
Dip, Spicy Orange, '85 230

Dressings

Blossom Dressing, Orange, '82 266
Citrus-Cilantro Dressing, '00 160
Citrus-Herb Dressing, '04 182

ORANGES, Dressings
(continued)

Citrus Ranch Dressing, Fresh, '04 91
Coconut Dressing, Orange-, '80 158
Coconut-Orange Dressing, '97 93
Cranberry-Orange Dressing, '91 287
Curd Dressing, Orange-, '93 22
Hot Citrus Dressing, '00 108
Mandarin Dressing, '89 137
Marmalade-Fruit Dressing, '84 171
Nutmeg Dressing, Carrot-Raisin Salad with Orange-,
'98 19
Orange Dressing, '81 141; '97 129
Poppy Seed Dressing, Orange-, '87 187
Vinaigrette Dressing, Tangy Orange, '93 46
Vinaigrette, Grilled Asparagus Salad with Orange,
'99 102
Vinaigrette, Grilled Fennel and Radicchio with
Orange, '95 253
Vinaigrette, Honey-Orange, '91 255
Vinaigrette, Orange, '96 65; '97 229; '98 288
Vinaigrette, Orange-Raspberry, '95 144; '96 155;
'01 178
Yogurt Dressing, Orange-, '85 304
Filling, Cheese-and-Orange, '93 159
Filling, Orange, '89 287
Filling, Orange-Cheese, '90 47
French Toast, Orange-Stuffed, '98 54
Fritters, Puffy Orange, '81 169
Glaze. *See* ORANGES/Sauces and Glazes.
Grand Oranges, '01 131
Granola, Sunny Orange, '84 212
Gravy, Orange, '81 259; '89 323
Grits, Orange, '81 47
Honey Yogurt, Orange Slices with, '91 68
Jelly, Pineapple-Orange Mint, '92 105
Main Dishes
Catfish Amandine, Mandarin, '84 183
Catfish, Lime-Orange, '02 22
Chicken à l'Orange, '84 277
Chicken à l'Orange, Stir-Fry, '83 82
Chicken Breasts with Orange-Ginger Sauce, '97 47
Chicken Breasts with Orange Sauce, '79 77
Chicken Breasts with Parslied Rice, Orange, '87 242
Chicken, Crispy Mandarin, '86 119
Chicken Drummettes, Orange-Pecan, '93 158
Chicken, Grilled Ginger-Orange, '91 26
Chicken in Orange-Almond Sauce, '79 219; '80 13
Chicken in Orange Sauce, '83 8
Chicken in Orange Sauce, Skillet, '94 252
Chicken Livers in Orange Sauce, '82 218
Chicken, Orange, '83 278; '86 M140
Chicken, Orange-Avocado, '80 38
Chicken, Orange Barbecued, '88 123
Chicken, Skillet-Seared Orange, '96 68
Chicken Stir-Fry, Kyoto Orange-, '87 96
Chicken Stir-Fry, Orange-, '84 68
Chicken with Black Beans and Oranges, '00 94
Chicken with Broccoli, Spicy Ginger-and-Orange,
'02 309
Chicken with Orange, Lime, and Ginger Sauce,
'92 123
Chicken with Wild Rice, Orange-Glazed Roasted,
'02 85
Chuck Roast, Orange Marinated, '85 179
Cornish Hens, à l'Orange, '95 325
Cornish Hens, Orange-Glazed, '83 267; '99 293;
'00 292
Cornish Hens, Orange-Glazed Grilled, '86 250
Cornish Hens, Orange-Glazed Stuffed, '84 M89
Cornish Hens with Cranberry-Orange Sauce, '86 119
Cornish Hens with Orange Glaze, '79 244

Duck, Chafing Dish Orange, '79 226
Duck with Orange Sauce, Grilled, '94 305
Duck with Parsnip Mash, Honey-Orange-Glazed
Muscovy, '97 262
Fish à l'Orange, Fillet of, '89 180
Halibut with Orange-Curry Sauce, '87 91
Ham, Cranberry-Orange Glazed, '81 295
Ham, Orange-Glazed, '89 324
Ham, Sweet Orange-Glazed, '02 286
Ham with Garlic and Orange, '05 294
Hens with Cranberry Salsa, Orange-Ginger, '98 321
Lamb Chops, Orange, '83 35
Lobster Tails with Spiced Orange Sauce, '86 155
Porc à l'Orange, '80 242
Pork Chops, Orange, '84 81
Pork Chops, Orange-Cranberry, '86 335; '87 84
Pork Chops, Orange-Glazed, '81 234; '82 25; '83 39;
'91 84
Pork Chops with Orange Slices, Saucy, '05 197
Pork, Garlic-Orange Roast, '03 277
Pork Loin, Orange-Dijon, '00 259
Pork Loin, Scuppernong-Orange Glazed, '98 220
Pork Roast, Orange-Glazed, '04 M236
Pork Tenderloins, Orange-Cranberry Glazed, '00 314
Pork Tenderloin with Orange Marmalade, '91 49
Pork Tenderloin with Orange Marmalade, Grilled,
'03 181
Roast Pork, Garlic-Orange, '05 332
Salmon, Orange-Basil, '97 165
Scallops with Orange-Ginger Sauce, Sesame-
Crusted, '97 125
Scampi, Orange, '85 303
Shrimp in Orange Sauce, '99 292; '00 292
Snapper à l'Orange, Baked, '85 181
Snapper, Orangy, '88 23
Spareribs, Orange-Glazed, '84 296
Spareribs with Orange Barbecue Sauce, '83 11
Swordfish Steaks, Orange-Ginger Marinated, '93 271
Turkey Breast with Orange-Raspberry Glaze, '91 253
Turkey-Orange Skillet, Oriental, '86 284
Turkey Slices, Orange-, '90 53
Mandarin Orange Spread Sandwiches, Chicken-,
'04 259
Marmalade, Carrot-Orange, '03 134
Marmalade, Orange, '81 42
Marmalade, Orange-Pineapple, '82 150; '89 M156
Marmalade, Peach-Orange, '82 150
Marmalade, Sunny Orange, '02 27
Noodles, Orange, '84 177
Nuts, Sherry-Orange, '86 M289
Pancakes, Orange-Yogurt, '87 225
Pancakes with Sunshine Orange Sauce, Orange, '97 70
Pears and Oranges, Spicy, '89 305
Pears, Marmalade Breakfast, '83 M203
Pears, Orange-Glazed, '79 247
Pecans, Orange, '84 299; '87 292
Pecans, Orange-Glazed, '97 225
Popcorn, Orange, '86 230
Prunes, Orange-Spiced, '85 224
Relish, Cranberry-Orange, '81 M289; '88 254; '99 15
Rice à l'Orange, '90 236
Rice, Miami, '96 86
Rice, Orange, '79 43; '81 175; '82 200
Rice, Orange-Herb, '89 286
Rice Pilaf, Orange, '05 219
Salads
Almond Salad, Orange-, '99 107
Ambrosia Supreme, Orange, '79 37
Aspic, Orange-and-Carrot, '86 199
Avocado-Orange Salad, '91 44
Avocado Salad, Orange-, '99 331
Beet Salad, Orange-and-, '88 43
Broccoli-Orange Salad, '94 281
Buttermilk Salad, Orange-, '95 134

Carrot Salad, Orange-, '80 89; '84 325
Carrot-Tangerine Salad, '83 316; '84 16
Cauliflower Salad, Orange-, '82 266
Cherry-Orange Salad, '79 74; '82 56
Chicken-and-Orange Salad, Curried, '87 144
Chicken Salad, '96 67
Chicken Salad, Persian, '81 12
Company's Coming Salad, '96 64
Congealed Salad, Pineapple-Orange, '83 218
Cottage Cheese Salad, Orange-, '79 44
Cranberry-Orange Delight, '90 168
Creamy Orange Salad, '84 124
Cup, Orange Fruit, '91 277
Cups, Citrus Salad in Orange, '85 47
Cups, Orange, '86 92
Cups, Orange Salad, '85 40
Fennel Salad, Tuscan, '02 170
Frosted Orange Salad, '81 154; '83 123
Grapefruit-Orange Salad, '91 276
Grapefruit Salad, Orange-, '93 294
Grilled Shrimp, Orange, and Watermelon Salad with
Peppered Peanuts in a Zesty Citrus Dressing,
'04 308
Honey-Berry Dressing, Orange Salad with, '89 250
Honey Dressing, Orange Salad with, '89 14
Jeweled Orange Salad, '83 210
Jícama-and-Orange Salad, '88 246
Jícama-Orange Salad, '86 83; '90 122
Lobster and Orange Salad, '82 207
Mandarin-Black Bean Salad, '05 319
Mandarin Chicken, Carousel, '79 88
Mandarin Ham-and-Rice Salad, '87 145
Mandarin Orange-and-Almond Salad, '05 291
Mandarin Orange and Pineapple Salad, '82 266
Mandarin Orange-Lettuce Salad, '92 79
Mandarin Orange Salad, '81 252; '84 161
Mandarin Orange Salad, Congealed, '89 327
Mandarin Orange Tossed Salad, '92 303
Mandarin Pork-and-Spinach Salad, '88 M126
Mandarin Rice Salad, '88 271
Mandarin Salad, Bacon-, '02 87
Mandarin Salad, Broccoli-, '93 325
Mandarin Salad Molds, '85 54
Mandarin Salad Oriental, '02 175
Mandarin Spinach Salad, '85 163
Mandarin Tossed Salad, '89 12
Marinated Orange-Onion Salad, '91 231; '92 68
Mimosa Salad, '98 310
Minted Orange Salad, '92 105
Onion Salad, Orange-, '89 41
Pear Salad, Orange-, '84 164
Poppy Seed Salad, Orange-, '98 87; '03 121
Quick Orange Salad, '87 80
Red Cabbage Citrus Salad, '94 72
Romaine Salad, Orange-, '84 325; '87 239
Scallop Salad, Thai-Rific Orange, '04 317
Sesame-Citrus Green Salad, '86 33
Sherbet Salad, Orange, '81 154
Shrimp-and-Orange Rice Salad, Zesty, '87 155
Shrimp, Orange, and Olive Salad with Sherry
Vinaigrette, '93 177
Shrimp Salad, Orange-, '84 197
Slaw, Cabbage-Orange, '79 135
Spinach-and-Orange Salad, '86 15
Spinach, Hot Spiked, '97 195
Spinach-Orange Salad, Warm, '00 112
Spinach Salad, Orange-, '83 316; '84 16
Strawberry-Cranberry-Orange Salad, '05 249
Strawberry Salad with Orange-Curd Dressing,
Orange-, '93 22
Sunshine Delight, '86 117
Surprise Salad, Orange, '79 12
Tropical Orange Salad, '92 97
Turkey-in-the-Orange Salad, '93 21

Turkish Salad, '96 137

Walnut Salad, Orange, '80 246

Watercress-Orange Salad with Blue Cheese, '04 45

Sauces and Glazes

Almond Sauce, Grilled Snapper with Orange-, '01 158

Bourbon Glaze, Orange-, '03 249

Butter Glaze, Orange, '90 194

Caramel Sauce, Pears with Orange-, '95 281

Chocolate-Orange Sauce, '86 165; '94 314

Coconut-Orange Sauce, '85 189

Cranberry-Orange Sauce, '05 218

Curry Sauce and Coconut Rice, Polynesian Pork Tenderloin with Orange-, '04 309

Dessert Sauce, Orange, '86 337; '87 58

Dijon Sauce, Orange-, '00 259

Dipping Sauce, Orange, '03 M212

Fresh Orange Glaze, '88 179

Fresh Orange Sauce, '85 209

Ginger Sauce, Chicken Breasts with Orange-, '97 47

Ginger Sauce, Sesame-Crusted Scallops with Orange-, '97 125

Hard Sauce, Orange, '88 225

Honey-Orange Sauce, '85 108

Honey Sauce, Orange-, '97 236

Liqueur Sauce, Orange, '86 142

Mandarin Orange Sauce, '89 204

Mandarin Sauce, '84 60

Mandarin-Teriyaki Sauce, '96 68

Maraschino-Orange Sauce, '96 164

Nutty Orange Glaze, '80 45

Orange Glaze, '79 2; '80 257; '81 34, 107; '82 75, 206; '83 33, 114, 140, 267; '84 161; '86 298; '92 263; '95 320; '99 293; '02 221; '03 35, 281, 307

Orange Sauce, '82 47; '83 10, 277; '84 M286; '86 294; '98 83

Pineapple Glaze, Orange-, '81 60

Pineapple-Orange Sauce, '84 14

Raspberry-Orange Sauce, '88 22; '92 154

Salsa, Orange-Black Bean, '98 231

Scuppernong-Orange Glaze, '98 220

Shrimp in Orange Sauce, '99 292; '00 292

Strawberry-Orange Sauce, '96 95

Sunshine Orange Sauce, '97 70

Sweet Orange Sauce, '93 M325

Syrup, Orange, '80 228; '89 254; '96 164; '97 32; '02 295; '05 240

Syrup, Orange-Ginger, '03 167

Syrup, Orange Marmalade, '96 27

Sauté, Orange-Watercress, '98 83

Slices, Spicy Orange, '81 12

Snack Balls, Orange-Almond, '95 214

Soup, Carrot-Orange, '79 172

Special, Orange Blossom, '88 158

Spread, Date-Orange-Nut, '02 59

Spread, Orange Cheese, '87 292

Spread, Tropical Cheese, '95 46

Stuffing, Cranberry-Orange-Pecan, '01 249

Vegetables

Asparagus with Orange Butter Sauce, '85 43

Asparagus with Orange Sauce, '83 46

Beets, Glazed Orange, '02 138

Beets, Orange, '91 219

Beets, Orange-Ginger, '80 137

Beets, Orange-Glazed, '81 167; '85 289; '86 187; '99 24

Beets, Spicy Orange, '94 280

Broccoli, Easy Orange, '85 267

Broccoli with Orange Sauce, '80 243; '04 285

Brussels Sprouts, Orange, '84 34

Butternut-Orange Bake, '86 295

Cabbage Cooked in Orange Juice, '97 129

Carrots and Turnips, Sunset Orange, '94 213

Carrots in Orange Sauce, '82 107

Carrots, Julienned Orange, '04 297

Carrots, Orange-Fennel, '92 133

Carrots, Orange-Glazed, '79 12; '81 M165; '90 M98

Carrots, Orange-Raisin, '80 24

Carrots, Orange-Spiced, '88 18

Carrot Strips, Orangy, '89 312

Celery in Orange Sauce, '79 70

Green Peas in Orange Sauce, '88 97

Leeks in Orange Sauce, '88 86

Peas, Orange-Ginger, '04 294

Potatoes, Orange Mashed, '96 33

Rutabaga, Glazed, '99 284

Squash à l'Orange, '85 230

Sweet Potatoes, Candied, '01 49

Sweet Potatoes, Coconut-Orange, '84 252

Sweet Potatoes in Orange Cups, '82 272

Sweet Potatoes, Orange, '86 279

Sweet Potatoes, Orange-Baked, '88 M294

Sweet Potatoes, Orange-Glazed, '81 223; '83 280

Sweet Potatoes, Orange-Spice Mashed, '02 34

Sweet Potatoes, Pineapple-Orange, '96 46

Sweet Potato-Orange Bake, '83 226

Sweet Potato-Stuffed Orange Cups, '81 223

Vinegar, Orange, '95 31

ORZO

Chicken, Orzo, and Spinach Casserole, '02 124

Grouper with Orzo, Pesto, '97 321

Marinara on Beds of Spinach and Orzo, '93 320

Mozzarella-and-Olive Orzo, '97 249

Pie, Honeyed Orzo-Pecan, '04 219

Primavera, Orzo, '92 192

Sage Orzo, Chicken Breasts with, '98 169

Salad, Artichokes with Orzo, '88 M193

Salad, Confetti Orzo, '92 173

Salad, Lentil-and-Orzo, '03 127

Salad, Peppers Stuffed with Shrimp-and-Orzo, '91 203

Salad, Shrimp-and-Orzo, '99 182

Salad, Summer Vegetable-and-Orzo, '00 165

Salad with Sesame Dressing, Orzo, '96 137

Shrimp with Orzo, Fire-Roasted, '99 42

Three-Grain Rice, '95 166

OYSTERS

Appetizers

Annapolis, Oysters, '89 195

Artichoke Oysters, '96 154

Bacon, Oysters in, '83 211

Barbecued Oysters, '82 247

Bienville, Baked Oysters, '90 27

Bienville, Oysters, '93 257

Casino, Oysters à la, '80 296

Creamed Oysters, '92 254

Dip, Smoked Oyster, '79 233

Dressed Oysters on the Half Shell, '87 M79

Fried Bacon-Wrapped Oysters, '02 103

Fritters, Oyster, '97 20

Grilled Oysters with Paul's Cocktail Sauce, '05 244

Mousse, Oyster, '81 245

Mousse, Smoked Oyster, '84 320

Spread, Smoked Oyster, '91 64

Stuffed Oysters, Crabmeat, '94 328

Baked Oysters, Bacon-, '86 132

Baked Oysters Italiano, '89 97

Baked Oysters on the Half Shell, '93 269

Bake, Oyster-and-Corn, '83 34; '84 44

Bisque, Oyster, '83 252; '96 276; '99 320

Brochette, Oysters, '80 56

Casserole, Oyster-and-Spinach, '83 34; '84 44

Casserole, Oyster-and-Wild Rice, '83 34; '84 44

Chesapeake, Oysters, '92 254

Chowder, Oyster, '83 229

Chowder, Oyster-Corn, '83 211

Dressing, Crabmeat-and-Oyster, '02 243

Dressing, Ma E's Traditional Oyster-Cornbread, '96 35

Dressing, Oyster, '79 250

Dressing, Oyster Bread, '82 251

Eggplant-and-Oyster Louisiane, '95 196

Fresh Oysters, Preparing, '82 127

Fried Bacon-Wrapped Oysters, '02 103

Fried Oysters, '85 104; '99 320

Fried Oysters, Delicious, '83 212

Fried Oysters, Southern, '88 111

Fried Raw Oysters, '81 135; '82 14

Fritters, Oyster, '79 31

Grilled Oysters Mornay, '89 195

Gumbo, Chicken and Oyster, '81 198

Gumbo, Duck, Oyster, and Sausage, '79 226

Gumbo, Seafood, '83 90; '87 210

Johnny Reb, Oysters, '82 42

Loaves, Spinach-Oyster, '84 213

Main Dishes

Baked Oysters over Toast Points, '84 214

Bienville, Oysters, '79 182

Buccaneer, Oysters, '87 40

Casserole, Oyster, '79 228

Casserole, Oyster-and-Chicken, '99 320

Casserole, Wild Rice-Oyster, '86 256

Cornbread, Oysters Casino on, '79 34

Crabmeat, Creamy Oysters and, '83 211

Creamed Oysters in Acorn Squash, '97 20

Creamed Oysters, Pan-Fried Grits with, '93 62

Crêpes, Virginia, '79 264

Fried Buffalo Oysters, '05 48

Fried Oyster Bubbles, '80 296

Fried Oysters, Southwest, '03 45; '05 48

Fry, Hangtown, '80 297

Gino, Oysters à la, '81 126

Ham, Edwards' Oysters and, '86 253

Landmark, Oyster, '84 88

Loaf, Crusty Oyster, '92 254

Mornay, Seafood, '83 67

Omelets, Smoked Oyster, '84 96

Pie, Turkey-and-Oyster, '82 267

Pilaf, Oyster, '97 20

Poor Boys, Oyster-and-Bacon, '87 40

Rockefeller, Oysters, '98 222; '03 272

Rockefeller, Southern Oysters, '80 212

Sandwich, Oyster Submarine, '80 92

Sautéed Oysters, '86 132

Sautéed Seafood Platter, '83 89

Scalloped Oysters, '79 225; '84 213; '86 132; '90 249; '95 318; '99 321; '05 47

Scalloped Oysters with Macaroni, '80 297

Shrimp Sauce, Oysters in, '87 40

Smoky Oysters Supreme, '87 60

Stewed in Cream, Oysters, '93 50

St. Jacques, Oysters, '80 103

Stuffing, Roast Turkey with Oyster, '80 251

Mousse, Smoked Oyster, '99 162

Nachos, Texas Oyster, '87 39

Patty Shells, Oysters in, '83 212; '85 257

Pie, Creole Oyster, '84 214

Pierre, Oysters, '02 102

Po'boys, Dressed Mini Oyster, '01 33

Po'boys, Dressed Oyster, '02 184

Po' Boys, Fried Buffalo Oyster, '05 48

Scalloped Oysters, '79 225; '84 213; '95 318

Smoked Oysters, Deviled Eggs with, '84 161

Soup, Chicken, Ham, and Oyster, '79 198

Soup, Louisiana Oyster-and-Artichoke, '92 81

Soup, Oyster, '79 228; '83 211; '02 102

Soup, Oyster-and-Artichoke, '97 21

Soup, Oyster-and-Mushroom, '87 39

Soup, Oyster-Cheese, '84 213

Soup, Oyster-Turnip, '94 328

Spinach Salad with Oysters and Red Wine Vinaigrette, '94 327

Stew, Company Oyster, '80 297

Stew, Golden Oyster, '86 132

OYSTERS

(continued)

Stew, Holiday Oyster, '85 264
Stew, Oyster, '80 221; '05 48
Stew, Oyster-Broccoli, '89 242
Stew, Oyster-Sausage, '89 242
Stew, Potato-Oyster, '89 243
Topless Oysters, '01 249
Wild Rice and Oysters, '92 339

Pancakes

Ambrosia Pancakes with Orange Syrup, '89 254
Apple-Filled Pancake, '86 96
Apple Pancakes with Caramel Sauce, Baked, '04 249
Apple Pancakes with Cider Sauce, Spicy, '87 224
Applesauce Pancakes, '79 114
Apple-Topped Pancakes, '93 339
Apricot Delight, '81 42
Baked Pancake, Arkansas German-, '96 53
Banana-Nut Pancakes, '98 160
Banana Pancakes, '03 305
Banana Pancakes with Peanut Butter and Jelly Syrups,
   '01 24
Best Pancakes, '99 194
Black Bean Pancakes with Gazpacho Butter, '92 86
Blueberry Buttermilk Pancakes, '79 114
Blueberry Pancakes, '85 152; '89 138
Blueberry Pancakes, Sour Cream, '81 164
Blue Cornmeal-Blueberry Pancakes, '94 115
Bran Pancakes with Cinnamon Syrup, '91 315
Buttermilk Griddle Cakes, '81 120; '82 22
Buttermilk 'n' Honey Pancakes, '05 137
Buttermilk Pancakes, '83 243; '84 101; '97 256
Buttermilk Pancakes with Fruit Topping, '89 50
Christmas Tree Hotcakes, '03 305
Cornmeal Batter Cakes, '87 16
Cornmeal Pancakes, Hearty, '88 129
Corn Pancakes, '93 43
Cottage Cheese Pancakes, '79 115
Cracklin' Cakes, Grannie's, '98 252
Cream Cheese Pancakes, '97 70
Dessert Pancakes, Luau, '88 154
Easy Pancakes, '92 203
Featherweight Pancakes, '99 43
Fluffy Pancakes, '86 137
Fruit Topping, Pancakes with, '81 42
Gingerbread Pancakes, '84 242; '95 282; '96 27
Ginger Pancakes, Dessert, '88 153
Gorditas with Turkey Mole, '03 18
Griddle Cakes, Levee Camp, '03 29
Ham Griddle Cakes, '89 255
Honey Pancakes, '91 139
Island Pancakes, '87 225
Latkes, '90 254
Latkes, Potato, '97 252
Latkes, Sweet Potato, '01 275
Lemon-Blueberry Pancakes, '04 148
Lemon Pancakes with Strawberry Butter, '99 44
Maple-Bacon Oven Pancake, '89 255
Mix, Quick Bread, '81 90
Noodle Pancake, Szechuan Ginger Stir-Fry with,
   '97 292
Oatmeal-Brown Sugar Pancakes, '88 203
Oatmeal Mini-Pancakes with Apple-Pear Sauce,
   '97 M272
Oatmeal Pancakes, '80 44; '89 107
Oat Pancakes, '89 227
Orange Pancakes with Sunshine Orange Sauce, '97 70
Orange-Yogurt Pancakes, '87 225
Oven-Baked Pancake for Two, '89 227
Pancakes, '81 90

Pasta Pancakes and Gravy, '05 43
Peach Pancake, Baked, '97 71
Peanut Butter Pancakes, '97 271
Pecan Pancakes, '03 305
Pecan Pancakes, Toasted, '99 43
Popover Pancake, Brunch, '96 28
Potato-Chive Pancakes, Quick, '04 248
Potato-Ham Pancakes, '96 138
Potato Pancake, '85 20
Potato Pancakes, '79 115; '89 144
Potato Pancakes, German, '98 279
Potato Pancakes, Leftover, '96 138
Potato Pancakes, Moist, '80 36
Potato Pancakes, Old-Fashioned, '96 138
Potato Pancakes, Parsley-, '96 251; '97 103
Potato-Two Potato Pancakes, One, '96 138
Pumpkin Pancakes, '80 228
Refrigerator Pancakes, Overnight, '93 196
Rice Pancakes, '85 147
Sauce, Cinnamon-Pecan-Honey Pancake, '88 46
Sauce, Peach-Blueberry Pancake, '82 177
Sausage Rollups, Pancake-, '83 246; '84 42
Sausage Wedges, Pancake-, '93 196
Sour Cream-Blueberry Morning Pancakes with Wild
   Blueberry-and-Peach Topping, '05 326
Sour Cream Pancakes, '79 213
Sour Cream Pancakes, Fluffy, '79 209
Sour Cream Pancakes with Fruit Topping, '90 142
Squash Pancakes, Granola-, '94 267
Strawberry Pancakes, '84 219
Supper Pancake, '86 242
Suppertime Pancakes, '03 278
Sweet Potato-Chive Pancakes, Quick, '04 248
Sweet Potato Pancakes, '87 280
Sweet Potato Pancakes with Goat Cheese, '96 271
Vegetable Pancakes, '88 297; '98 236
Vegetable-Rice Pancakes, '93 43
Veggie Pancakes, '00 85
Wheat Germ-Banana Pancakes, '79 114
Wheat Germ Pancakes, '86 242
Wheat Pancakes, Shredded, '84 59
Wheat Quick Pancakes, '85 278
Whole Grain Pancakes, '93 123
Whole Wheat-Oat Pancakes, '93 16
Whole Wheat Pancakes, '83 18
Wild Rice Pancakes, '02 238
Zucchini Pancakes, '93 43

PARSNIPS

Broccoli and Parsnips with Horseradish, '02 235
Candied Parsnips, '86 224
Fried Parsnips, '96 36
Glazed Carrots and Parsnips, '02 129
Glazed Parsnips, '91 220
Mash, Parsnip, '97 263
Medley, Parsnip-Carrot, '96 36
Scalloped Root Vegetables, '98 310
Soufflé, Golden Parsnip, '83 266
Soup, Butternut Squash-Parsnip, '05 36
Soup, Gingered Carrot-and-Parsnip, '03 221
Sugar-Crusted Parsnips, '88 229

PASTAS. *See also* **COUSCOUS; FETTUCCINE;
   LASAGNA; LINGUINE; MACARONI;
   MANICOTTI; NOODLES; ORZO;
   SALADS/Pasta; SPAGHETTI.**

Angel Hair, Goat Cheese-Stuffed Chicken Breasts over,
   '97 144
Angel Hair Pasta, Scallops and, '99 176
Angel Hair Pasta, Shrimp and Mushrooms with, '92 34
Angel Hair Pasta, Szechuan Chicken with, '97 91
Angel Hair Pasta, Turkey Scaloppine with, '02 44
Angel Hair Pasta with Shrimp and Asparagus, '92 100
Angel Hair Pasta with Tomato Cream Sauce, '93 292
Angel Hair Pasta with Veal and Shrimp, '04 223
Antipasto, Pasta, '85 286

Asparagus Pasta with Toasted Pecans, '04 90
Asparagus, Tomatoes, and Shrimp, Garlicky Pasta with,
   '95 82
Bacon Pasta, '97 52; '05 224
Bake, Cheesy Pasta, '02 161
Bake, Layered Pasta, '04 326
Bake, Three-Cheese Pasta, '05 54
Basil-Cheese Pasta, '96 136
Beans and Greens, Pasta with, '02 202
Beans and Pasta, '99 35
Beans, Pasta with, '99 236
Bow Tie Pasta, Chicken and, '05 49
Bow Tie Pasta, Spinach and Mushrooms with, '95 341
Bow-Tie Pesto, '94 231
Bow Ties, Black Beans, and Key Limes, '96 291
Bow Ties with Crab and Vegetables, '98 233
Bow-Tie with Marinara, '94 64
Broccoli Pasta, '84 176
Cabbage and Cheese Sauce, Pasta with, '00 105
Cannelloni, '85 60; '92 17
Cannelloni with Roasted Red Bell Pepper Sauce,
   Chicken, '02 287
Casserole, Crawfish Pasta, '97 106
Casserole, Freezer Eggplant-Sausage-Pasta, '95 197
Casseroles, Hot Brown Pasta, '96 290
Catfish and Artichokes, Pasta with, '90 123
Cherry Tomatoes over Pasta, Herbed, '95 229
Chicken-and-Broccoli Pasta, '87 286
Chicken and Pasta, Mediterranean, '03 63
Chicken, Bird's-Nest, '88 152
Chicken Caesar Pasta, '97 87
Chicken Pasta, Spicy, '02 125
Chicken Picante Pasta, '01 164
Clam Sauce, Pasta with, '84 291
Collards and Sausage, Pasta with, '94 230
Cucumbers and Pasta, Asian, '96 177
Curried Pasta with Apple, '02 68
Dinner, One-Pot Pasta, '00 173
Dressing, Pasta Salad, '86 121
Fennel, Pasta with, '98 46
Frittata, Firecracker Pasta, '94 230
Garden-Fresh "Pasta," '94 M134
Garlic Pasta with Marinara Sauce, '92 78
Green Pasta with Shrimp-Mushroom Italienne, '79 170
Greens, Pasta with, '96 47
Herb-and-Tomato Pasta, '96 122
Italian Pasta, Weeknight, '03 48
Late-Night Pasta Chez Frank, '95 228
Lemon Shrimp and Pasta, '96 124
Lentils, Cheesy Pasta and, '99 287
Mamma Mia Pasta, '95 25
Mediterranean Pasta, '95 341; '96 122
Minestrone, Dixie, '94 230
Minestrone, Mama's Mexican, '05 254
Mostaccioli Alfredo, '91 47
Mostaccioli Casserole, '04 316
One-Pot Pasta, '05 202
Oregano Pasta, '84 176
Pancakes and Gravy, Pasta, '05 43
Pastitsio, '99 167
Penne, Cheesy Chicken, '00 289
Penne, Fresh Vegetable, '05 101
Penne, Garden Sauté with, '98 207
Penne Pasta, Chicken, Asparagus, and Mushrooms with,
   '98 212
Penne Pasta, Spicy Vegetables with, '04 195
Penne, Spicy Cheesy Chicken, '00 289
Penne with Greek-Style Tomato Sauce, '05 187
Penne with Pancetta, '00 51
Penne with Spinach and Feta, '03 170; '04 328
Peppery Pasta, '94 164
Pesto and Pasta, '92 98
Pesto-Clam Sauce, Pasta with, '98 17
Pie, Broccoli-and-Turkey Pasta, '88 269

Pimiento Pasta, '84 176
Potpourri, Pasta, '94 33
Primavera
  Almost Pasta Primavera, '86 38
  Chicken-Pasta Primavera, '91 72
  Creamy Pasta Primavera, '95 167
  Garden Spiral Primavera, '91 30
  Pasta Primavera, '85 86; '89 105; '93 168; '97 228
  Smoked Turkey Pasta Primavera, '90 84
  Tomato-Pasta Primavera, '86 209
Prosciutto, Party Pasta with, '94 176
Provençale, Pasta, '88 90
Pumpkin Pasta, '98 241
Ravioli, Green Bean Alfredo with Cheese, '01 180
Ravioli, Homemade, '87 230
Ravioli in Basil-Cream Sauce, Beef, '05 293
Ravioli, Mediterranean, '93 301
Ravioli Pasta, Homemade, '87 231
Ravioli, St. Louis Toasted, '95 117
Ravioli with Creamy Pesto Sauce, '92 79
Red Wine-Tomato-and-Steak Pasta, '05 140
Rigatoni with Sausage and Bell Peppers, '05 215
Rotelle, Chicken and Tomato with, '87 108
Rotelle, Shrimp, '85 165
Rotini, Baked, '01 185
Rotini Romano, '87 193
Salad Dressing, Herbed Pasta, '96 106
Salads
  Acini di Pepe Salad, '83 163
  Artichoke-Pasta Salad, '94 180
  Asian Peanut-and-Pasta Salad, '03 127
  Bayou Pasta Salad, '00 203
  Bean-Pasta Salad, Marinated, '94 167; '97 328
  Bean Salad, Pasta-, '86 169
  Beef-Pasta Salad, Spicy, '01 311
  Bow Tie Pasta, '01 164
  Broccoli-Cauliflower Pasta Salad, '88 269
  Broccoli-Cheese-Pasta Salad, '96 184
  Chicken-and-Bow Tie Pasta, '01 164
  Chicken-and-Pasta Salad, Hoisin, '99 125
  Chicken Pasta Salad, '88 89
  Chicken-Pasta Salad, Grilled, '94 64
  Chicken-Pasta Salad, Zesty, '02 186
  Chicken Salad, Tarragon Pasta-, '87 155
  Confetti Pasta Salad, '05 242
  Confetti-Pasta Salad, Easy, '92 220
  Crabmeat-Shrimp Pasta Salad, '86 208
  Crunchy Pasta Salad, '85 166
  Fruited Pasta Salad, '92 108
  Garden Pasta Salad, '86 188
  Greek Pasta Salad, '02 139; '05 130
  Ham-and-Pasta Salad, '90 128
  Ham-and-Pea Pasta Salad, '00 217
  Ham-Dijon Pasta Salad, '92 191
  Ham, Pasta Salad with, '92 108
  Ham-Pecan-Blue Cheese Pasta Salad, '90 62
  Herbed Pasta-and-Tomato Salad, '92 144
  Italian Salad, '87 145
  Luncheon Pasta Salad, '90 191
  Main-Dish Pasta Salad, '82 199
  Mediterranean Pasta Salad, '05 220
  Oriental Pasta Salad, '90 63
  Overnight Pasta Salad, '82 276
  Pasta Salad, '84 139; '86 120; '87 36; '89 217;
    '90 62, 91; '00 213; '01 127
  Pesto Pasta Salad, Fresh, '01 61
  Pistachio-Pasta Salad, '86 141
  Presto Pasta Salad, '90 63
  Ratatouille Pasta Salad, '90 74
  Ravioli Salad, Caesar, '95 183
  Roasted Onion Pasta Salad with Peppered Cheese
    Crisps, '98 107
  Rotelle Salad, Crunchy, '86 209
  Rotini Salad, '88 42

Salmon-Pasta Salad, '87 9
Salmon Salad Shells, '85 286
Seafood Pasta Salad, '90 62
Seashell Salad, '86 209
Shell Salad, Tossed, '91 256
Shrimp Pasta Salad with Green Goddess Dressing,
  '02 139
Shrimp Salad, Pasta-and-, '83 163
Smoked Mozzarella Pasta Salad, '03 126
Southwestern Pasta Salad, '94 278
Tomato-Pasta Salad, '97 M160
Tortellini Pasta Salad, Cheese, '02 139
Tortellini-Pesto Salad, '92 22
Tortellini Salad, '89 237; '02 186
Tortellini Salad, Chicken, '87 288
Tortellini Salad, Garden, '91 44
Tortellini Salad, Terrific, '96 134
Tuna-Pasta Salad, '91 43; '92 141; '00 247
Tuna Pasta Salad, '92 108
Turkey 'n' Pasta Salad, Ranch-Style, '94 184
Vegetable Pasta Salad, '89 256; '91 143
Vegetable-Pasta Salad, '92 167
Vegetable Salad, Pasta-, '95 238
Veggie Salad, Pasta-, '96 106
Vermicelli Salad, Shrimp, '88 139
Vermicelli Vinaigrette Salad, '82 189
Ziti-Cheddar Salad, '85 165
Sauce, Pasta, '01 53
Sauce, Pecan Pasta, '96 262
Sausage and Bell Peppers, Pasta with, '02 63
Sausage and Kale, Pasta with, '03 279
Sausage and Pasta, Skillet, '97 267
Scallops and Pasta, Fresh, '83 164
Scampi, Speedy, '02 161
Shells
  Bake, Quick Crab, '87 192
  Bites, Pesto-Cheese Pasta, '87 251
  Casserole, Seashell-Provolone, '80 189
  Casserole, Turkey, '96 302
  Cavatini, '94 214
  Cheese, Creamy Shells and, '01 216
  Florentine, Layered Pasta, '00 56
  Florentine Pasta Shells, '00 326
  Garden Pasta Medley, '89 256
  Greens and Bacon, Shelly, '96 290
  Italiano, Pasta, '01 41
  Jumbo Seashells Florentine, '79 6
  Peppers and Broccoli, Pasta with, '91 69
  Seafood and Pasta, '90 234
  Spinach Shells, '97 50
  Stuffed Shells, Cheesy Beef-, '83 217
  Stuffed Shells, Mexican, '91 87
  Stuffed Shells, Sausage-, '96 102
  Stuffed Shells, Southwestern, '93 234; '99 238
  Stuffed Shells, Spinach-, '85 60; '87 20; '99 64
  Stuffed with Five Cheeses, Pasta, '88 197
  Taco Pasta, Easy, '03 124
  Tuna Pasta, Stuffed Tomato with, '88 54
Shrimp-and-Goat Cheese Pasta, Garlic, '00 174
Shrimp and Pasta, '91 207
Shrimp and Pasta, Herbed, '92 329; '97 228
Shrimp and Pasta with Cream Sauce, '98 295
Shrimp and Pasta with Creole Cream Sauce, '05 49
Shrimp and Pasta with Two Cheeses, '98 49
Shrimp-and-Spinach Pasta, '01 258
Shrimp-and-Spinach Pasta, Creamy, '05 239
Shrimp Elégante, '83 48
Shrimp-Pasta Medley, '88 302
Shrimp Scampi, '95 209
Shrimp Scampi, Pasta with, '01 83
Shrimp with Pasta, Asian, '04 128
Smoked Salmon-Caper-and-Dill Pasta, '98 169
Snappy Pasta, '83 164
Soup, Bean and Pasta, '94 220

Spaghettini with Green Beans and Walnut Brown Butter,
  '03 170
Spinach-Mustard Twist, '86 209
Spinach Pesto-Pasta, '91 314
Steak with Pasta and Sesame-Ginger Butter, '99 142
Straw and Hay Pasta, '80 211
Summer Pasta, '04 223
Toasted Rice and Pasta, '95 57
Tomato-Basil Pasta, '94 204
Tomatoes and Basil, Pasta with Fresh, '98 233
Tomato-Garlic Pasta, '94 177
Tomato Pasta, Italian, '93 201
Tomato Pasta, Southwestern, '93 201
Tortellini. *See also* **PASTAS/Salads.**
  Alfredo with Prosciutto and Artichoke Hearts,
    Tortellini, '02 322
  Carbonara, Creamy Tortellini, '99 171
  Carbonara, Tortellini, '91 47
  Citrus Broth, Tortellini in, '99 292
  Creamy Tortellini, '99 171
  Kebabs, Antipasto, '94 144
  Parsley-Caper Sauce, Tortellini with, '93 175
  Ragù with Tortellini, Wild Mushroom, '04 220
  Rosemary-Parmesan Sauce, Tortellini with, '92 284
  Shrimp and Tortellini, '92 34
  Soup, Japanese Tortellini, '96 330
  Soup, Sausage-Tortellini, '99 20
  Soup, Seafood-Tortellini, '97 324
  Soup, Spinach-Tortellini, '99 317
  Soup, Tortellini, '98 68; '00 14
  Soup with Tortellini, Italian Sausage, '88 46
  Spinach Tortellini with Tomato Sauce, '88 302
  Tapas with Spicy Ranch Dip, Tortellini, '98 318
  Tomatoes, Quick Pasta and, '92 180
  Tomato Pesto Dip with Tortellini, Creamy, '00 196
Tortelloni, Roasted Red Pepper-Caesar, '05 M186
Toss, Garden Pasta, '00 57
Toss, Pasta-Basil, '87 33
Tricolor Pasta with Clam Sauce, '93 272
Turkey-Basil Pasta, Creamy, '89 216
Vegetable Pasta, Grilled, '97 142
Vegetables and Pasta, Roasted, '93 184
Vegetable Sauce, Pasta with, '83 163
Vegetables, Pasta and, '89 255
Vegetables, Pasta and Garden, '87 192
Vegetable Stir-Fry Pasta, '96 29
Verde, Pasta, '84 201
Vermicelli
  Anchovy-Garlic Sauce over Vermicelli, '86 158
  Casserole, Chicken-and-Pasta, '97 192
  Chicken and Pasta, Quick, '93 14
  Chicken Vermicelli, '01 237
  Clam Sauce, Pasta with, '84 291
  Clam Sauce, Vermicelli with, '85 295
  Frittata, Pasta, '85 286
  Garden Pasta, '82 199
  Lemon Vermicelli, '84 329
  Mushroom Sauce Supreme on Vermicelli, '86 158
  Mushrooms, Vermicelli with, '79 195
  Pie, Spinach-Pasta, '85 286
  Platter, Cold Pasta, '88 42
  Red Clam Sauce, Vermicelli and Sprouts with,
    '86 143
  Rice with Vermicelli, Buttery, '02 258
  Salmon-Pesto Vermicelli, '92 200
  Scallop-Vegetable Vermicelli, '87 143
  Shrimp and Feta Cheese on Vermicelli, '87 108
  Soup with Quenelles, Veal-Vermicelli, '94 114
  Spinach Sauce, Vermicelli with Fresh, '89 256
  Tetrazzini, Chicken, '02 171; '04 221
  Tomato Pasta, Caribbean, '93 201
  Tomato Sauce, Vermicelli with, '83 164
  Toss, Asparagus-Vermicelli, '00 102
  Vegetable Sauce, Vermicelli with Chunky, '04 180

PASTAS
(continued)

Vinaigrette, Italian Pasta, '92 78
Ziti, Baked, '94 65; '05 214
Ziti with Sausage and Broccoli, '95 340

PÂTÉS

Black-Eyed Pea Pâté, '91 12; '93 97
Braunschweiger Pâté, '83 251
Champignon, Pâté de, '93 171
Cheese Pâté, Chutney-, '84 152
Cheese Pâté, Chutney-Glazed, '02 279
Cheese Pâté, Four-, '89 284
Cheese Pâté, Layered, '86 105
Cheese Pâté, Sherry, '95 215
Chicken Liver Pâté, '79 153; '81 235; '83 108; '84 205;
　'88 M132
Chicken Pâté, Curried, '00 106
Chutney-and-Blue Cheese Pâté, '02 279
Cognac, Pâté with, '86 159
Country Pâté, '86 66
Crab Pâté, '79 233
Cream Cheese Pâté, '80 154
Duck Liver Pâté, '79 227
Duck Pâté, '79 226
en Croûte, Pâté, '86 65
Ham Pâté, '85 279
Lentil Pâté, '92 285
Lima Bean-and-Fresh Herb Pâté, '04 70
Liver-Cheese Pâté, '85 276
Liver Pâté with Madeira Sauce, '93 323
Maison, Pâté, '84 222
Mock Pâté, '87 251
Mushroom Pâté, '89 157
Pastry, Pâté, '86 65
Pork Pâté with Spinach and Cream, '83 224
Shrimp Pâté on Crostini, '98 316
Shrimp Pâté with Dill Sauce, '85 39
Spread, Quick Pâté, '84 117
Turkey-Mushroom Pâté in Pastry, '92 327
Vegetable-Chicken Pâté, '86 66
Wine Pâté, '90 36

PEACHES

Alaska, Peachy Melba, '88 266
Ambrosia, Peach, '83 53
Baked Peaches, '92 179
Baked Peaches and Sausage, '82 50
Baked Peaches, Spicy, '86 39
Baked Peaches with Ginger, Oven-, '82 170
Bay Laurel Peaches, '90 124
Beverages
　Bellini, '01 89
　Bellinis, '88 77
　Bellinis, Frosted, '97 122
　Bellinis, Mint, '02 136
　Bellini Spritzers, '90 110
　Christmas Blossom, '99 321
　Cooler, Peach, '85 198; '86 6
　Cream, Peaches 'n' Almond, '86 229
　Daiquiris, Peach, '90 322
　Frost, Peach, '89 155
　Frosty, Peach, '81 156; '83 318
　Fuzz Buzz, '82 160
　Petals, Peach, '90 104
　Pick-Me-Up, Peach, '89 183
　Refresher, Peach, '86 103
　Refresher, Peach Yogurt, '03 166
　Shake, Get-Up-and-Go, '00 179
　Shake, Peach Melba, '02 158
　Shake, Peach Melba Sundae, '93 134
　Shake, Peachy Orange, '81 156
　Shake, Pep, '79 38
　Slush, Peach, '04 141

Slushy, Kiwi-Peach, '00 201
Smash, Peach, '88 161
Smoothie, Banana-Peach Buttermilk, '04 22
Smoothie, Peachy-Pineapple, '97 173
Smoothie, Strawberry-Peach, '89 182
Tea, Peach Iced, '02 181
Bombe with Raspberry Sauce, Creamy, '89 322
Brandied Peaches with Mincemeat, '81 47
Brandy Peaches, '85 275
Bread, Georgia Peach, '79 161
Bread, Peach, '82 170
Bread, Tipsy Peach, '02 21
Butter, Golden Peach, '91 178
Cake, Fresh Peach, '85 178
Cake, Peach-Almond Pound, '89 86
Cake, Peaches and Cream, '80 142
Cake, Peaches-and-Cream, '96 118
Cake, Peach Upside-Down, '87 8
Cake, Peachy Almond-Butter, '90 107
Cake, Peachy Picnic, '79 178
Caramel Peaches, '93 134
Cardinale, Peach, '89 155
Champagne, Peaches, '79 146
Charlotte, Peach, '79 68
Cheesecake, Peach-Caramel, '02 M158
Cheesecake, Peaches 'n' Cream, '88 137
Cobblers
　Apricot Cobbler, Peach-, '99 255
　Blueberry Cobbler, Peachy, '80 143
　Blueberry-Peach Cobbler, No-Dough, '86 177
　Caramel Cobbler, Peach-, '86 300; '87 178
　Cranberry-Peach Cobbler, '92 322
　Crinkle, Peach, '91 20
　Crisp, Peach, '83 113; '92 13; '93 134
　Double Crust Peach Cobbler, '03 310
　Easy Peach Cobbler, '97 137; '99 206
　Easy Peach Cobbler, Too-, '04 28
　Fresh Peach Cobbler, '82 139; '89 154
　Grenadine-Peach Cobbler, '85 178
　Lattice-Topped Peach Cobbler, '79 154
　Old-Fashioned Peach Cobbler, '82 170
　Peach Cobbler, '83 175; '84 178; '90 219; '95 264
　(Peach Cobbler), I Fall to Peaches, '96 159
　Pecan-Peach Cobbler, '04 120
　Praline Biscuits, Peach Cobbler with, '92 180
　Quick Peach Cobbler, '79 215; '81 142
　Spicy Peach Cobbler, '85 178
　Supreme, Peach Cobbler, '81 184; '90 313
Compote, Berry-Peach, '82 133
Compote, Peach-Berry, '89 112
Crabapple Peaches, Broiled Pork Chops with,
　'81 83
Cream, Bavarian Peach, '82 171
Cream Cheese, Peachy, '92 289
Cream, Honeyed Peaches 'n', '93 134
Cream, Peach Almond, '82 108
Cream, Peaches and, '95 196
Cream, Peachy-Apricot, '86 163
Crêpes, Fresh Peach, '84 186
Crêpes, Peach, '82 184
Crisp, Gingered Peach, '97 303
Crisp, Peach-and-Raspberry, '02 232
Crumble, Easy Peach, '83 116
Curried Ham and Peaches, '82 60
Custard Dessert, Fresh Peach, '86 162
Dessert, Layered Peach, '95 196
Dessert, Peach-Blueberry, '92 184
Dessert, Peachy Melt-Away, '87 298
Dessert, Quick Peach, '85 178
Dip, Creole Peach, '80 142
Dip, Peachy, '92 179
Dressing, Peach, '90 180
Dumplings, Peach, '80 143; '85 177; '96 172
Filling, Peach, '89 154; '90 107; '96 119

Flambé, Banana-Peach, '85 316
Flambé, Peach Sundaes, '81 88
Flip, Peach, '79 217
Fluff, Peach, '95 176
Foster, Peaches, '86 240
Freeze, Creamy Peach, '82 144
French Toast, Peach-Filled, '98 160
French Toast, Peachy, '98 56
Frost, Peach, '84 164
Ginger Peaches with Rum, '84 M323
Gingersnap Peaches, '85 M329
Grilled Balsamic-Glazed Peaches, '02 159
Honey-Lime Whip, Peaches with, '85 108
Ice Cream, Blueberry-Peach, '00 153
Ice Cream, Creamy Peach, '85 177
Ice Cream, Deluxe Peach, '80 176; '90 314
Ice Cream, Fresh Peach, '95 195
Ice Cream, No-Cook Peach, '04 179
Ice Cream, Peach, '81 184; '82 171; '83 159; '86 15;
　'93 135; '98 221
Ice Cream, Peach-Almond, '89 156
Ice Cream, Peach-Cinnamon, '05 168
Ice Cream, Summertime Peach, '02 158
Ice, Peach, '81 178
Ice, Peach-Yogurt, '84 83
Jam, Spiced Peach, '00 51
Ketchup, Peach, '95 306
Ketchup, Spicy Peach, '03 139
Main Dishes
　Chicken Breasts, Peach-Stuffed, '79 177
　Chicken Peach Dinner, '79 77
　Chicken, Peachy, '90 212
　Chicken with Peaches, Bourbon-Laced Tipsy,
　　'97 136
　Chicken with Peach Sauce, '98 334
　Ham, Peach Holiday, '04 251
　Ham, Peachy Glazed, '96 189
　Ham Roast, Peachy, '86 118
　Ham with Cherry-Peach, Chutney, Glazed, '97 315
　Pork Chops, Peachy, '89 310
　Pork Loin Dijonnaise with Peach Sauce, '97 87
　Pork Steaks, Peachy, '79 166
　Spareribs, Peach-Glazed, '86 14
Marinated Peaches, '91 91
Melba, Peach, '81 83; '83 M114
Meringues, Peach Melba, '87 76
Meringues with Buttermilk Custard Sauce, Peach
　Melba, '96 183
Mint Peaches with Pineapple-Coconut Ice Cream,
　'05 123
Mold, Peachy Berry Cream, '83 130
Mousse, Peach, '85 54
Mousse, Peach Macaroon, '80 153
Muffins, Peach Streusel, '03 167
Muffins, Peachy-Almond, '86 301
Muffins, Special Peach, '84 74
Nest, Peaches in a Garden, '87 154
Pancake, Baked Peach, '97 71
Pancake, Brunch Popover, '96 28
Parfait, Peach, '82 166
Parfaits, Sugar-Free Peachy Cheesecake, '02 326
Pies
　Blackberry Pie, Peach-and-, '89 136
　Blueberry-Peach Pie, '94 158
　Chiffon Pie, Peach, '89 155
　Cranberry Pie, Peach-, '83 249
　Cream Pie, Peaches-and-, '81 184
　Filling, Fresh Peach Pie, '95 195
　Fresh Peach Pie, '82 170; '95 195
　Fresh Peach Pie, Elizabeth and Phoebe's, '96 119
　Fried Peach Pies, '81 272
　Fried Pies, Delicious, '83 84
　Fried Pies, Easy Peach, '85 178
　Fried Pies, Ginger-Peach, '00 212

Georgia Peach-and-Praline Pie, '98 196
Little Peach Pies, '86 303
Luscious Peach Pie, '81 136
Melba Pie, Peach, '98 216
Mincemeat-Peach Pie, '80 295; '81 188
Praline Pie, Peach, '89 136
Quick Peach Pie, '89 252
Rhubarb-Peach Pie, '86 140
Pops, Peach, '04 141

Preservation
Butter, Peach, '82 308
Chutney, Peach, '84 179; '96 207
Conserve, Peach, '79 120
Honey-Sweet Peaches, '85 107
Jam, Cantaloupe-Peach, '95 143
Jam, Freezer Peach, '83 182; '84 M182
Jam, Peach, '93 135
Jam, Peach-Plum Freezer, '85 130
Jam, Peach-Rosemary, '03 134
Jam, Rosy Peach-Banana, '80 142
Marmalade, Peach-Orange, '82 150
Mincemeat Peaches, '85 178
Pears, Peaches and, '85 106
Pickled Peaches, Perfect, '85 178
Pickles, Peach, '85 177; '99 170
Preserves, Custard, '98 126
Preserves, Honeyed Peach, '85 130
Preserves, Old-Fashioned Peach, '82 150
Preserves, Peach, '81 147; '89 140
Relish, Peach, '85 136
Spiced Peaches, Brandy, '80 142
Preserves, Cream Cheese and Peach, '84 264
Pudding, Peachy Bread, '88 175
Puffs, Peach Sweet Potato, '87 280

Salads
Chicken Salad, Peachy, '97 193
Cream Salad, Peaches-and-, '83 108
Easy Peach Salad Supreme, '79 177
Fluff, Peach, '95 176
Frosted Peach Salad, '82 145
Frozen Peach Salad, '82 54
Fruit Salad, Peachy, '89 206
Georgia Peach Salad, '80 142
Indian Chief Salad, '96 287
Kiwi Salad, Peach-and-, '90 180
Party Salad, Peach, '84 290
Pickled Peach Salad, '80 104; '85 264; '04 269
Pinwheel Salad, Peach, '79 11
Ring, Spicy Peach-Cranberry, '85 264
Slaw, Party Peach, '86 250
Spiced Peach Salad, '94 68
Summer Salad, Georgia, '92 179
Sunny Day Salad, '96 90

Sauces
Berry Sauce, Peach-, '87 M165
Blueberry Pancake Sauce, Peach-, '82 177
Blueberry Sauce, Peach-, '81 170
Chicken with Peach Sauce, '98 334
Creamy Peach Sauce, '85 189
Fresh Peach Sauce, '87 167
Fresh Peach Sauce, Creamy, '79 177
Peach Sauce, '84 144; '92 203
Praline Sauce, Peach-, '85 161
Rib Sauce, Peach, '01 248
Salsa, Avocado-Peach, '02 159
Salsa, Fresh Peach, '95 195
Salsa, Peach, '91 183; '96 14; '97 183
Salsa, Peachy Green Tomato, '99 143
Strawberry-Peach Sauce, '92 154
Tangy Peach Sauce, '96 89
Sherbet Cooler, Peachy, '91 187
Sherbet, Peach, '90 179
Sherbet, Three-Ingredient Peach, '01 105
Shortcakes, Southern Peach-and-Blueberry, '05 318

Shortcakes, Spicy Peach, '89 154
Sorbet, Peach, '93 153; '97 110
Soup, Chilled Peach, '97 159
Soup, Cream of Peach, '99 207
Soup, Peach, '83 120, 180
Soup, Peach-Plum, '87 157
Spiced Peach Dessert, '83 9
Spiced Peaches, '91 72, 148
Spiced Peaches, Ginger, '86 15
Spiced Peaches with Nutty Dumplings, '87 164
Split, Peach, '85 277
Spread, Peachy Cream Cheese, '90 M215
Spread, Peachy-Raisin, '86 326
Stewed Yard Peaches, '05 23
Strawberry Sauce, Peaches with, '85 8
Stuffed Peaches, Macaroon-, '79 178
Stuffed Peach Halves, '86 196
Sweet Potatoes and Peaches, '86 11
Tart, Cream Cheese-Peach, '99 169
Tart, Golden Peach Meringue, '98 197
Tart, Kiwifruit-Peach, '88 20
Tart, Peach Cream, '90 173
Tarts, Peachy Keen, '91 118
Tart with Brandy Sauce, Peach, '98 119
Topping, Peach, '94 22
Topping, Raspberry-Peach, '87 126
Topping, Wild Blueberry-and-Peach, '05 326
Torte, Frozen Peach, '93 135
Trifle, Georgia Peach, '04 169
Trifle, Peach, '92 179
Vinaigrette, Roasted Vegetable Salad with Dried Peach, '97 265
Vinegar, Peach-Mint, '95 190
Wine Sauce, Peaches in, '79 184
Yogurt, Frozen Fresh Peach, '90 139

PEANUT BUTTER
Apple, Piggy, '94 194
Bird's Nests, '95 102
Birds' Nests, Peanut-Butter, '04 84
Bread, Peanut Butter, '86 171; '88 64; '99 111
Bread, Peanut Butter Streusel-Topped Cream Cheese-Banana-Nut, '05 27
Cake, Chocolate-Peanut Butter, '84 240
Cake, Chocolate-Peanut Butter Mousse, '98 71
Cake, Fudgy Peanut Butter, '85 91
Cake, Peanut Butter, '79 51; '83 M233
Cake, Peanut Butter-and-Jelly, '85 34
Cake, Peanut Butter-Banana, '80 87
Cake, Peanut Butter-Fudge, '96 254; '01 59
Cake, Peanut Butter Swirl, '86 109

Candies
Balls, Buckeye, '00 M280; '01 M322
Balls, Chocolate-Peanut Butter, '80 87
Balls, No-Cook Candy, '85 14
Balls, Peanut Butter-Chocolate, '80 269
Bites, Chocolate-Peanut Butter, '92 M317
Bites, Peanut Butter Elf, '91 275
Chocolate Peanutty Swirls, '94 M330
Clusters, No-Bake Peanut Butter, '05 M211
Creams, Peanut Butter, '79 273
Crunch, White Chocolate-Peanut Butter, '02 M296
Cups, Rocky Road-Peanut Butter Candy, '04 M330
Drops, Chocolate-Peanut Butter, '92 322
Eggs, Peanut Butter Easter, '87 86
Fudge Bites, Peanut-, '91 M231; '92 M68
Fudge, Chocolate-Peanut Butter, '87 257; '90 311
Fudge, Creamy Peanut Butter, '92 240
Fudge, Diamond, '92 193
Fudge, Double-Good, '79 M263; '95 M50
Fudge, Double Peanut, '85 91
Fudge, Four Chips, '92 318
Fudge, Marbled Peanut Butter, '88 65
Fudge, Peanut Butter, '80 302; '89 307; '95 51; '02 296

Fudge-Peanut Butter Chewies, '98 215
Fudge Squares, Chocolate-Peanut Butter, '97 M54
Peanut Butter Candy, '93 166
Pralines, Chocolate-Peanut Butter, '92 313; '93 51
Pralines, Peanut Butter, '92 313; '93 51
Squares, Peanut Butter-Chocolate Candy, '82 56
Tiger Butter, '86 48
Yummies, Peanut Butter, '83 223
Cheese Ball, Peanut Butter-, '86 136
Cheesecake, Peanut Butter, '94 142
Chicken, Maple-Balsamic, '04 195
Chicken, Peanut Butter-Marmalade, '81 282; '82 30
Chicken Strips, Nutty, '99 111
"Concrete," All Shook Up, '94 114
Cones, Chocolate-Peanut Butter, '85 14

Cookies
Bars, Chewy Chocolate Cereal, '97 317
Bars, Peanut Butter, '84 243; '93 166
Bars, Peanut Butter-and-Fudge, '80 M172
Bars, Peanut Butter-Jam, '94 291
Bars, Peanut Butter 'n' Jelly, '83 305
Black-Eyed Susans, '00 291
Brownies, Chocolate Chip-Peanut Butter, '84 73
Brownies, Chocolate-Peanut Butter Chip, '91 306
Brownies, Elephant Stomp, '03 43
Brownies, Frosted Peanut Butter, '92 272; '00 M155
Brownies, Peanut Butter, '87 199
Chocolate Chip Cookies, Freezer Peanut Butter-, '86 230
Chocolate Chip Cookies, Peanut Butter-, '05 87, 222
Chocolate Chip-Peanut Butter Cookies, '99 68
Chocolate Chunk Cookies, Peanut Butter and, '94 169
Chocolate Chunk-Peanut Cookies, '04 125
Chocolate Chunk-Peanut Cookies, Double, '04 125
Chocolate Kiss Cookies, Peanut Butter-, '86 49
Chocolate-Peanut Bars, '03 195
Chocolate-Peanut Butter Cookies, '85 90
Chocolate-Peanut Butter Cups, '97 134
Chocolate Treats, Crispy Peanut-, '02 287
Choco-Peanut Chip Cookies, '92 318
Choco Surprise Cookies, '80 60
Cinnamon Cookies, Peanut Butter-, '84 30
Coconut Cookies, Peanut Butter-, '83 113
Crisp Peanuttiest Cookies, '88 65
Crisps, Peanut Butter, '79 50
Cup Cookies, Peanut Butter, '03 298
Cups, Chocolate-Peanut Butter, '85 14
Double Chip Cookies, '81 301
Double-Chip Peanut Butter Cookies, '89 169
Double Peanut Butter Cookies, '80 209
Easter Basket and Eggs, '95 101
Easy Peanut Butter Cookies, '92 272
Kiss Cookies, Peanut Butter-, '03 42
Logs, No-Bake Peanut Butter, '84 211
Macaroons, Chewy Peanut Butter, '95 214
Miracle Cookies, '83 149
Monster Cookies, '84 36
No-Bake Peanut Butter Cookies, '94 197
Oatmeal Cookies, Double-Chip, '03 200
Oatmeal Cookies, Peanut Butter-, '81 218; '84 72
Oatmeal-Peanut Butter Chocolate Chip Cookies, '92 207
Oatmeal-Peanut Butter Cookies, '85 171
Olympic Medal Cookies, '96 180
Peanut Blossom Cookies, '95 245; '96 55; '97 324
Peanut Butter Cookies, '82 56; '87 58
Quick Peanut Butter Cookies, '86 109; '02 229; '03 131
Shortbread, Peanut Butter, '95 321
Slice-and-Bakes, Peanut Butter, '82 M185
Snaps, Peanut Butter, '81 237
Spooky Eyes, '95 273
Spooky Ghosts, '98 M256

PEANUT BUTTER, Cookies
(continued)

    Squares, Chocolate Chip-Peanut Butter, '84 118
    Squares, Crispy Peanut, '01 M161
    Squares, Peanut Butter, '83 116
    Temptations, Peanut Butter, '84 29
    Treats, Crispy Peanut Butter-Chocolate, '03 271
    Truffle Cookies, Peanut, '93 212
    Turtle Cookies, Peanut Butter-Toffee, '02 M325
Cooler, Peanut Butter, '84 115
Cracker Bites, Miniature Peanut Butter, '02 298
Cupcakes, Chocolate Surprise, '85 91
Delights, Choco-Peanut, '99 197
Dessert, Crunchy Peanut-Buttery, '92 204
Dessert, Peanut Butter, '92 164
Dessert, Rocky Road Pizza, '99 196
Dip, Indonesian, '96 190
Dip, Peanut Butter, '86 135; '01 109
Dip, Peanut Butter-Honey, '85 19
Dip, Peanut Butter Lovers', '93 162
Dough, Peanut Butter Fun, '00 171
Eclairs, Peanut Butter-Chocolate, '01 45
Filling, Peanut Butter, '96 229
Fingers, Peanut Butter, '79 256
French Toast, Peanut Butter, '93 166
French Toast, Peanut Butter and Jelly, '00 198
Frosting, Chocolate-Peanut Butter, '84 240; '87 222;
    '00 120
Frosting, Creamy Peanut, '80 87
Frosting, Peanut Butter, '83 223; '84 153; '85 34
Frosting, Peanut Butter-Fudge, '87 184
Frosting, Peanut Butter Swirl, '86 109
Frosts, Peanut Butter, '84 153
Frozen Peanut Butter Delight, '88 137
Grahams, Peanut Butter-Apple, '04 M183
Granola, Peanut Butter, '82 296
Hearts, Crispy Chocolate, '03 M41
Ice Cream, Chocolate Chunk-Peanut Butter, '85 297;
    '86 120
Ice Cream, Peanut Butter, '81 103; '88 64, 203; '00 143
Ice Cream Sandwiches, Peanut Butter Cookie, '93 199
Milkshakes, Peanut Butter, '85 198
Monster Mouths, '95 274
Mousse Parfaits, Chocolate-Peanut Butter, '98 71
Muffins, Jelly-Topped Peanut Butter, '96 279
Muffins, Peanut Butter, '80 86; '87 158; '99 111
Muffins, Peanut Butter-Banana, '03 195
Muffins, Peanut Butter-Chocolate Chip, '94 167
Muffins, Peanut Butter-Honey, '82 56
Napoleons, Peanut Butter-and-Chocolate, '94 121
Nuggets, Golden North Pole, '99 M309
Pancakes, Peanut Butter, '97 271
Parfait, Bodacious Peanut, '95 167
Parfaits, Crunchy Peanut Butter, '79 176; '80 6
Pastry Cream, Peanut Butter, '01 45
Pie, Chocolate-Peanut Butter, '85 91
Pie, Chocolate-Peanut Butter Ice Cream, '98 244
Pie, Chocolate-Peanut Butter Swirl, '87 262
Pie, Fluffy Peanut Butter, '94 246
Pie, Fudgy Peanut Butter Cup, '04 211
Pie, Peanut Butter, '85 275; '86 109; '89 252
Pie, Peanut Butter-Banana, '01 315
Pie, Peanut Butter Cream, '79 50; '88 65
Pie, Peanut Butter Meringue, '84 30
Pie, Tin Roof, '85 91
Pie, "Working for Peanuts," '93 115
Pinecones, Peanut Butter-Suet, '93 286
Pizza, Chocolate-Peanut Butter, '05 193
Pizza, Peanut Butter-Fruit, '94 60
Pudding, Chocolate-Peanut Butter Cookie, '03 183
Pudding, Peanut Butter, '85 95; '88 32; '00 27
Pudding, Peanut Butter-Banana, '93 340; '05 44

Rollups, Peanut Butter, '99 103
Salad Dressing, Peanut Butter, '03 195
Salad, Thai Green Apple, '99 111
Sandwiches, Peanut Butter-and-Jelly "Fish," '91 177
Sandwiches, Peanut-Cheese-Raisin, '88 140
Sandwiches, Spider, '93 193
Sandwich, Peanut Butter Breakfast, '82 55
Sauce, Chocolate-Peanut Butter, '79 91, M156
Sauce, Hoisin Peanut Dipping, '99 14
Sauce, Pasta with Peanut, '95 252
Sauce, Peanut, '99 134; '02 173; '04 324
Sauce, Peanut Butter, '03 289
Sauce, Peanut Butter Barbecue, '81 233
Sauce, Peanut Butter Ice Cream, '84 30
Sauce, Spicy Peanut, '96 93; '04 134
Shake, PBJ, '93 292
Shake, Peanut Butter, '82 48
Shake, Peanut Butter-Banana, '97 172
Snacks, Chocolate-Peanut Butter, '90 226
Soup, Cream of Curried Peanut, '02 242
Soup, Cream of Peanut, '92 193; '93 288
Soup, Cream of Peanut Butter, '84 29
Soup, Creamy Peanut, '79 50
Soup, Peanut Butter, '89 28
Spread, Peanut Butter, '92 21; '96 90
Syrups, Banana Pancakes with Peanut Butter and Jelly,
    '01 24
Tarts, Chocolate-Peanut Butter, '92 277
Tarts, Peanut Butter, '97 329
Topping, Streusel, '03 195
Torte, Peanut Butter Turtle, '04 316
Trifle, Peanut Butter-Brownie, '03 200
Vinaigrette, Sesame-Soy, '97 180
Waffles, Honey-Buttered Peanut Butter, '94 M206
Wings and Ribs, Thai, '97 M225

PEANUTS
Appetizer, Fiery Cheese-and-Chutney, '04 177
Apples, Caramel-Peanut, '93 M244
Apples, Peanutty Stuffed, '85 25
Balls, Peanut-Date, '81 92
Bananas, Nutty, '79 251
Bars, Chewy Chocolate Cereal, '97 317
Bars, Chewy Peanut, '80 M172
Bars, Fruit and Nut Granola, '81 49
Bars, Peanut, '89 307
Beef Stir-Fry, Peanutty, '95 157
Bread, Peanut, '87 184
Bread, Peanut Lover's, '93 211
Cake, Chocolate-Caramel-Nut, '83 23
Cake, Chocolate-Peanut Cluster, '87 184
Cakes, Nutty, '89 50
Cake, Super Peanutty Layer, '83 222
Candies
    Brittle, Chocolate-Dipped Peanut, '02 M223
    Brittle, Classic Peanut, '02 M223
    Brittle, Cooktop, '02 223
    Brittle, Golden Peanut, '83 223
    Brittle, Never-Fail Peanut, '79 273
    Brittle, Orange Peanut, '80 302
    Brittle, Peanut, '79 M263; '80 87; '84 298; '92 240
    Brittle, Popcorn Peanut, '02 M223
    Brittle with Crushed Peanuts, '87 184
    Chocolate Nut Teasers, '91 35
    Chocolate-Peanut Crispies, '93 80
    Clusters, Chocolate-Peanut, '81 16
    Clusters, Nut, '81 254
    Clusters, Peanut, '87 184; '92 288; '98 M282
    Clusters, Peanutty, '83 143
    Divinity, Peanut, '85 233; '87 M278
    Filling, Nut, '91 35
    Fudge, Butterscotch-Peanut, '98 M282
    Fudge, Double Peanut, '85 91
    Squares, Caramel-Peanut, '85 247
    Toffee, Microwave Peanut, '04 M234

Celery, Nutty Stuffed, '03 184
Chesapeake Nuts, '93 269
Chicken, Ginger-Nut, '90 M33
Chicken, Peanut-Roasted, '01 107
Chicken Strips, Nutty, '99 111
Chicken with Peanuts, Oriental, '82 236
Cookies, Chocolate Chunk-Peanut, '04 125
Cookies, Chocolate-Peanut, '83 223
Cookies, Crisp Peanuttiest, '88 65
Cookies, Double Chocolate Chunk-Peanut, '04 125
Cookies, Fibber McGee, '95 72
Cookies, Oats-and-Peanut, '89 60
Cookies, Peanutty Oatmeal, '80 106; '83 95
Cookies, Salted Peanut, '87 92
Crunchy Munchies, '94 196
Crust, Peanut-Graham, '99 49
Crust, Peanut-Graham Cracker, '79 50
Crust, Sweet Potatoes with Peanut, '93 212
Dessert, Fudge-Peanut Ice Cream, '88 167
Dessert, Peanut-Chocolate, '80 86
Dressing, Lime-Peanut, '01 26
Dressing, Peanut-Ginger, '95 177
Dressing, Roast Turkey with Peanut, '79 283
Filling, Peanut, '93 211
Frosting, Creamy Peanut, '80 87
Fruit Dressing, Nutty, '88 68
Granola, Crunchy Peanut, '90 48
Granola, Superhero, '98 M206
Hearts, Crispy Chocolate, '03 M41
Hot Chili Nuts, '81 254
Hot Peanuts, '00 278
Ice Cream, Chocolate-Covered Peanut, '88 203
Ice Cream, Peanut, '92 132
Mix, Jalapeño Nut, '96 27
Mix, Nutty Snack, '92 22
Mix, Starry Snack, '00 329
Muffins, Peanut, '91 223
Okra, Nutty, '03 136
Pad Thai, '97 202
Pesto and Pasta, Spinach-Peanut, '93 212
Pesto, Thai Peanut, '98 145
Pie, Caramel-Nut Crunch, '94 244
Pie, Caramel-Peanut, '86 259
Pie, Peanut Raisin, '79 85
Pie, Peanutty Ice Cream, '82 56
Pie, "Working for Peanuts," '93 115
Polvorones, '00 123
Popcorn and Peanuts, Candied, '82 295
Popcorn Clusters, Caramel-Nut, '00 M223
Popcorn, Crazy Mixed-Up, '97 245
Popcorn, Oriental, '98 205
Power Munch, '96 180
Puff Nibbles, '84 191
Reindeer Food, Magic, '99 M309
Salad, Asian Peanut-and-Pasta, '03 127
Salad, Broccoli-Peanut, '92 35
Salad, Eight-Layer, '99 107
Salad, Green Bean-Peanut, '86 117
Salad, Nutty Cabbage, '87 42
Salad, Nutty Green, '87 168
Salad, Peanut-Apple, '80 5
Salad, Peanut-Noodle, '02 163
Salad, Peanutty Spicy Noodle, '04 72
Salad, Sweet Peanut-Chicken, '03 54
Sauce, Hot Indonesian Peanut, '93 211
Sauce, Peanut Dessert, '86 M251
Sauce, Peanut Hot, '86 305
Sauce, Pork Chops with Peanut, '83 29
Sauce, Shrimp with Peanut, '93 303
Sauce, Thai Dipping, '97 236
Sauce, Thai-Style Noodles with Peanut Basil, '98 133
Shortbread, Peanut-Toffee, '04 329
Slaw, Banana-Nut, '86 250
Slaw, Chinese Peanut, '93 212

Slaw, Nutty Cabbage, '88 218
Slaw, Peanut, '85 139
Slaw, Peanutty-Pear, '86 250
Snack Mix, Sweet 'n' Savory, '03 199
Snack, Toasted Cereal, '85 215
Soup, Chilled Peanut, '79 130
Soup, Creamy Peanut, '79 50
Soup, Peanut, '87 184; '00 325
Spiced Nuts, '91 M316
Spicy Nuts, '82 161
Spread, Cheddar-Swiss, '99 106
Sugar-and-Spice Peanuts, '04 197
Sugared Peanuts, '82 249

PEARS
Amaretto Pears with Meringue, '90 M58
Appetizers, Pear-Pecan, '96 262
Apples 'n' Pears, Saucy, '96 72
Baked Apples and Pear, Honey-, '97 303
Baked in Molasses-Port Sauce, Pears, '97 195
Baked Pears à la Mode, '95 129
Baked Pears Elegant, '91 48
Baked Pears, Honey-, '93 47
Belle Helene, Pears, '86 164
Braised Red Cabbage and Pears, '01 298
Bread, Pear, '80 218
Cake, Caramel-Glazed Pear, '02 196
Cake, Ginger-Pear Upside-Down, '97 205
Cake, Pear Preserve, '85 52
Cake, Pear Preserves, '00 139
Cakes with Praline Sauce, Pear, '96 284
Cake, Upside-Down Sunburst, '87 9
Cake with Caramel Drizzle, Pear, '86 247
Cheesecake, Pear-Berry, '82 141
Cheesecake, Pear-Glazed, '79 67
Chicken and Pears, Glazed, '99 21
Chutney, Sunny Pear, '01 281
Cobbler, Best Ever Pear, '82 194
Cobbler, Citrus-Pear Honey, '05 230
Cobbler, Ginger-Pear, '03 232
Cobbler, Pear-Ginger, '01 214
Cobbler with Oatmeal Muffin Crust, Caramel Apple-
     Pear, '04 201
Coconut Pears, Spicy, '83 207
Compote, Pear-Cranberry, '02 196
Cookies, Pear Mincemeat, '84 264
Cream, Pears in Orange, '84 245
Crème Chantilly, Holiday Pears with, '91 297
Crème de Menthe Pears, '94 50
Crisp, Cranberry-Pear, '83 207; '97 16
Crisp, Pear, '02 M233; '05 214
Crisp, Raspberry-Pear, '89 109
Crostini, Pear-and-Gorgonzola, '02 314
Crumble, Pear, '85 221
Dressing, Pear, '83 146
Dumplings, Pear, '97 210
en Croûte, Pears, '93 210
Flaming Pears, '84 313
Fritters, Ol' Timey Pear, '86 51
Gingered Pears, '89 M231
Gratin, Pear-Blue Cheese, '93 328
Honey, Citrus-Pear, '05 230
Honey, Gingered Pear, '97 62
Meringues, Baked Pear, '85 232
Muffins, Pear-Ginger, '91 240
Muscadine Sauce, Pears in, '88 216
Orange-Caramel Sauce, Pears with, '95 281
Pan-Roasted Pears, Beef Tenderloin with, '02 197
Pies
Apple-Pear Pie, '83 249
Apple-Pear Pull-Up Pie, '98 259
Apple Pie, Natural Pear-, '88 226
Backyard Pear Pie, '93 237
Cheddar-Pear Pie, '02 197
Crumble Pie, Pear, '83 207

Deep-Dish Pear Pie, '80 219
Delicious Pear Pie, '88 226
Double-Crust Pear Pie, '82 194
French Pear Pie, '87 213
Fried Pies, Dried Cherry-and-Pear, '00 213
Ginger-Pear Pie, '93 48
Macadamia Pie, Pear-, '93 260
Mincemeat Pie, Pear, '84 264; '88 226
Mincemeat Pie, Pear-, '98 258
Mince Pie, Pear-, '81 271
Praline Pie, Pear-, '97 192
Rhubarb-Raspberry Pear Pie, '95 119
Streusel Pie, Pear, '83 234; '84 244; '97 109
Tennessee Pear Pie, '85 230
Poached
Belle Helene, Pears, '86 164
Blue, Pears, '99 246
Caramel Sauce, Poached Pears with White, '99 28
Champagne-Poached Pears, '01 289
Curried Poached Pears with Coconut-Chicken Salad,
     '97 93
Custard, Poached Pears in, '88 20
Dark Chocolate Sauce, Poached Pears with,
     '90 M141
Honey-Yogurt Sauce, Poached Pears with, '92 306
Lemon Poached Pears, '82 74
Orange Poached Pears, '80 218
Orange-Poached Pears Flambé, '85 313
Orange Sauce, Poached Pears in, '82 19
Raspberry-Orange Sauce, Poached Pear Fans with,
     '88 22
Raspberry Sauce, Poached Pears with, '84 213;
     '87 69; '88 223
Red Wine, Pears in, '82 254
Red Wine, Pears Poached in, '83 302
Stewed Pears, '98 280
Vanilla Poached Pears, '90 57
Wine-Poached Pears, '98 230
Wine, Poached Pears in, '82 194
Wine-Poached Pears with Berry Sauce, '86 144
Pork Chops with Pears, Rosemary-Crusted, '01 316
Preservation
Butter, Pear, '85 130
Butter, Spiced Pear, '80 218
Chutney, Hot-and-Spicy Cranberry-Pear, '00 255
Chutney, Pear, '95 251; '98 243
Chutney, Pear-Apple, '89 141
Honey, Pear, '90 159
Jam, Paradise Pear, '84 300
Jam, Spiced Pear, '98 214
Marmalade, Pear, '79 196
Mincemeat, Pear, '79 196; '84 264; '88 226
Peaches and Pears, '85 106
Pickles, Mustard Pear, '79 196
Preserves, Pear, '82 195
Relish, Aunt Glennie's Pear, '95 305
Relish, Pear, '79 196
Relish, Peppery Pear, '89 141
Pudding, Lemon-Pear, '96 283
Puree, Grapefruit with Pear-Berry, '89 213
Relish, Cranberry-Pear, '85 232
Roasted Bacon-Wrapped Pears, Field Greens with,
     '05 230
Salads
Blue Cheese-Pear-Apple Salad, '81 224
Bluegrass Salad, '02 255
Celery Salad, Pear-and-, '87 56
Crunchy Pear Salad, '83 234; '84 244
Festive Fruit Salad, '80 16
Fresh Pear Salad with Asian Sesame Dressing,
     '02 196
Golden Pear Salad, '91 58
Harvest Salad with Cider Vinaigrette, '99 322
Jícama, and Snow Pea Salad, Pear, '01 329

Jícama and Snow Peas, Pear Salad with, '01 56
Lime Salad, Pear-, '84 152
Orange-Pear Salad, '84 164
Pineapple-Pear Delight, '82 54
Raspberry Cream, Pear Salad with, '00 311
Royal Pear Salad, '84 265
Sautéed Apples, Onions, and Pears over Spinach,
     '94 212
Slaw, Peanutty-Pear, '86 250
Slaw, "Think Pink," '94 247
Spinach Salad, Festive Pear-and-, '85 131
Spinach Salad with Sautéed Pears, '94 237
Swiss Cheese Salad, Pear-, '91 237
Wild Rice Salad, Pear-and-Cranberry, '03 199
Sauce, Apple-Pear, '97 M272
Sauce, Pear, '92 164
Sautéed Pears, '03 195
Shake, Strawberry-Pear, '92 139
Shortcakes, Ginger-Pear, '03 194
Side Dishes
Baked Pears, Honey-, '93 47
Bake, Pear-Oatmeal, '89 208
Blue Cheese Sauce, Brunch Pears with, '90 142
Breakfast Pears, Marmalade, '83 M203
Breakfast Treat, Pear, '87 72
Casserole, Pear-Sweet Potato, '86 280
Crème de Menthe Pears, '94 50
Filled Pears, Cheese-, '81 268
Glazed Pears, Orange-, '79 247
Oranges, Spicy Pears and, '89 305
Plate, Pretty Pear, '89 225
Ruby Pears, '81 288
Soda Pop Pears, '95 55
Spiced Fall Pears, '89 M231
Spiced Pears, '89 305
Stuffing, Acorn Squash with Pear, '01 293
Sugared Pears, Maple-, '81 232
Wild Rice, Cranberry-Pear, '83 279
Wine, Pears in Red, '82 254
Sorbet, Pear-Lemon, '88 116
Soup, Pumpkin-Pear, '92 234
Spread, Pear-Cream Cheese, '93 80
Strudel, Pear, '98 253
Stuffed Pears, Almond-, '83 207
Stuffed with Cheese, Pears, '82 290
Sundaes, Quick Pear, '86 71
Tart, Almond-Pear, '01 253
Tart, Pear, '82 304; '92 72
Tart, Raspberry-Almond Pear, '05 230
Tart with White Caramel Sauce, Pear, '92 195
Whip, Pear, '89 94

PEAS
Baked Peas, Chinese-Style, '86 305
Black-Eyed. See also **PEAS/Salads.**
Best Ever Plain Ole Peas, '88 2
Black-Eyed Peas, '93 180; '03 M49
Bread, Black-Eyed Pea, '02 224
Cajun Black-Eyed Peas, '96 218
Cajun Peas, '88 3
Cakes, Black-Eyed Pea, '01 32
Casserole, Reunion Pea, '87 11
Caviar, Texas, '86 218; '99 84; '01 160, 257
Chinese Peas, '88 3
con Queso, Black-Eyed Pea, '96 274
Cornbread, Black-Eyed Pea, '98 44
Cornbread, One-Dish Black-Eyed Pea, '03 215
Creole Black-Eyed Peas, '86 252; '98 22
Creole Black-Eyes and Rice, '85 6
Delight, Tomato-Pea, '84 196
Dinner, Black-Eyed Pea Skillet, '86 6
Dip, Bill D's Black-Eyed Pea, '97 M89
Dip, Black-Eyed Pea, '81 8; '04 M18
Dip, Chili-and-Black-Eyed Pea, '92 155

PEAS, Black-Eyed
(continued)

Easy Black-Eyed Peas, '99 204
Farmer's Beans and Rice with Rosemary Biscuits, '99 16
Flips, Pea, '80 7
Fresh Black-Eyed Peas, '81 M165
Gravy, Black-Eyed Pea, '87 12
Ham Hocks, Black-Eyed Peas with, '79 122; '89 16
Hearty Black-Eyed Peas, '85 7; '00 22; '02 107
Hopping Good Peas, '80 7
Hopping John, '80 7; '90 12; '96 272
Hopping John, Skillet, '79 10
Hopping John Stuffing, Pork Roast with, '01 25
Hopping John with Grilled Pork Medaillons, '93 229
Hopping John with Ham, '81 7
Hoppin' John, '02 271; '05 21
Hoppin' John Waffle Stack, '04 19
Hoppin' John with Scallion Hoe Cake Medaillons, Skillet, '02 326
Hummus, Black-Eyed Pea, '94 123; '03 60
Jalapeño Black-Eyed Peas, '88 166
Jambalaya, Black-Eyed Pea, '92 70
Jambalaya, Good Luck, '87 11
Marinated Black-Eyed Peas, '82 156; '88 101; '01 30
Mexican Black-Eyed Peas, '84 327
Mexicano, Black-Eyed Peas, '79 10
Mexi-Peas, '88 3
Michelle's Black-Eyed Peas, '03 16
Passion Peas, '89 17
Pâté, Black-Eyed Pea, '91 12; '93 97
Pickled Black-Eyed Peas, '79 10; '01 30
Pinwheels, Black-Eyed Pea, '85 300; '86 18
Potatoes, Black-Eyed Pea-Spinach-Stuffed, '95 22
Quick Black-Eyed Peas and Ham, '00 336
Relish, Zesty Black-Eyed Pea, '95 56
Rice, Black-Eyed Peas with, '83 12; '90 208; '91 13
Rice with Black-Eyed Peas, '93 66
Salsa, Black-Eyed Pea, '93 164
Salsa, Chunky Black-Eyed Pea, '01 333
Sausage, Black-Eyed Peas with, '86 7
Seasoned Black-Eyed Peas, '85 138
Soup, Beefy Black-Eyed, '85 6
Soup, Black-Eyed Pea, '97 213
Soup, New Year's Day, '00 25
Southern-Style Black-Eyed Peas, '82 107
South-of-the-Border Black-Eyed Peas, '86 7
Spaghetti, Black-Eyed Pea, '81 7
Special, Black-Eyed Pea, '86 7
Spicy Black-Eyed Peas, '92 23
Spicy Black-Eyed Peas, Hot-and-, '84 9; '99 235
Spicy Hot Black-Eyed Peas, '81 8
Spicy-Hot Black-Eyed Peas, '90 135
Spread, Black-Eyed Pea, '86 77
Stew, Collard, '02 17
Stew, Collard 'n' Black-Eyed Pea, '04 24
Stew, Ham-and-Black-Eyed Pea, '93 20
Stew with Rice, Black-Eyed Pea, '04 19
Sweet-and-Sour Black-Eyed Peas, '85 290
Sweet-and-Sour Peas, '88 3
Tasty Black-Eyed Peas, '89 68
Vinaigrette, Black-Eyed Pea, '86 7
Casserole, Curry Pea, '87 154
Couscous with Peas and Feta, '01 158
Crowder Peas, Peppered Tuna with, '00 159
Crowder Peas, Spinach with, '00 159
Dip, Corn-and-Field Pea, '01 177
English. *See also* **PEAS/Salads.**
Baked Tuna and Peas in Wine Sauce, '83 196
Braised Belgian Endive and Peas, '93 22
Braised Rice and Peas, '79 101
Broil, Tomato-English Pea, '83 192

Buttered Peas and Mushrooms, '82 204
Buttered Peas with Onions, '80 242
Carrots and Peas, Mint-Glazed, '90 291
Casserole, Asparagus-and-English Pea, '86 324
Casserole, Asparagus and Peas, '80 152
Casserole, Asparagus-Pea, '88 M294
Casserole, Cauliflower-Pea, '85 260
Casserole, Cheesy English Pea, '83 216
Casserole, English Pea-Pimiento, '83 207
Casserole, Quick Fresh English Pea, '84 145
Casserole Supreme, Pea, '82 281; '83 32
Cauliflower and Peas with Curried Almonds, '79 221; '80 82
Cauliflower, Peas and, '82 288
Celery, Deluxe Peas and, '81 267
Celery, Peas and, '93 289
Company Green Peas, '91 31
Continental, Peas, '84 254
Country-Style Peas, '80 101
Country Style, Peas, '81 101
Creamed Peas and New Potatoes, '79 102
Creole Peas, Quick, '84 123
Curried Peas with Almonds, '88 M294
Deluxe English Peas, '84 68
Deviled Peas in Toast Cups, '86 280
Dumplings, Green Peas and, '80 102
Glazed English Peas, '83 111
Italian Peas, '81 83
Lettuce Peas, French, '86 62
Medley, English Pea, '85 236
Medley, Spring Pea, '83 141
Minted Peas, '83 141; '87 56
Mushrooms, Creamy Peas with, '84 196
Mushrooms, English Peas with, '98 286
Mushrooms, Green Peas with, '80 101
Mushrooms, Peas and, '83 141
Onions Stuffed with Peas, '84 68
Orange-Ginger Peas, '04 294
Orange Sauce, Green Peas in, '88 97
Party Peas, '79 102
Pasta, Peas and, '99 68
Perfection, Peas to, '94 321
Pignoli, Peas, '83 190
Potatoes with Dill, Peas and, '99 67
Potato Nest, Peas in a, '84 M239
Rice, Cashew Fried, '99 171
Rice, Holiday Peas and, '86 328
Rice, Peas and, '88 97
Rice with Green Peas, '87 45
Risotto with Shellfish and Peas, '96 131
Sauce, Green Pea, '83 22
Sautéed Peas and Bacon, '89 331
Scallions, Peas and, '80 101
Sherry, Peas with, '80 102
Soup, Chilled Pea, '84 181
Soup, Cold Curried Pea, '91 120
Soup Elégante, Pea, '79 53
Soup, English Pea, '96 56
Soup, Fresh Pea, '86 181
Soup, Mardi Gras, '96 56
Soup, Pea, '99 67
Soup, Peppery Pea, '82 271
Soup, Potato-Pea, '94 90
Soup, Spring Pea, '88 M96
Special Peas, '88 97; '95 133
Field Pea Patties, '00 158
Field Peas and Spinach, '99 169
Field Peas, Okra, and Corn Combo, '01 214
Green Peas with Crispy Bacon, '04 60
Ham, Southern Peas and, '85 138
Hoppin' John, Esau's, '03 17
Medley, Peas-and-Corn, '85 138
Mess of Peas, A, '00 158
Pasta, Peas and, '93 139

Pecan Peas, Hot, '05 85
Peppery Peas O' Plenty, '04 34
Pigeon Peas, Rice with, '92 157
Pink-Eyed Pea Salsa, '00 158
Rice and Peas, Caribbean, '02 275
Salads
Asparagus Salad, Peas-and-, '83 141
Black-Eyed Pea-and-Sweet Potato Salad, '01 198
Black-Eyed Pea Salad, '80 112; '86 225; '88 92, 221; '90 173; '95 203; '97 305; '98 52; '99 174
Black-Eyed Pea Salad, Black Bean and, '03 54
Black-Eyed Pea Salad, Fearrington House Goat Cheese and, '95 60
Black-Eyed Pea Salad, Marinated, '93 190
Black-Eyed Pea Salad, Overnight, '81 280
Black-Eyed Pea Salad with Benedictine Dressing, '98 83
Black-Eyed Peas, Zesty, '89 147
Black-Eyed Salad, Hot Bacon and, '85 7
Cauliflower and Pea Salad, Savory, '81 280
Cauliflower-Pea Salad, '87 231
Cheddar-Pea Salad, '84 82
Chicken-and-Black-Eyed Pea Salad, '97 305
Chicken-Pea Salad, '83 218
Chilled Dilly Peas, '90 143
Corn-and-Pea Salad, '90 181
Creamy Pea Salad, '80 111
Crunchy Pea Salad, '90 143; '00 103
Dilled Pea Salad, '97 305; '98 18
Dilled Peas-and-Potatoes Vinaigrette, '01 327
English Pea-and-Apple Salad, '87 24
English Pea Salad, '81 280; '90 143
English Pea Salad, Cauliflower-, '95 66
English Pea Salad, Lettuce-, '91 208
English Pea Salad, Marinated, '82 54
Field Pea Salad, Mixed, '00 325
Green Pea Salad, '96 88
Hoppin' John Salad, '96 64; '01 250
Marinated Pea Salad, '81 204
Mexi-Pea Salad, '81 7
Minted Pea Salad, '91 119
Pasta Salad, Ham-and-Pea, '00 217
Pea Salad, '98 274
Plentiful P's Salad, '87 12
Rice-Pea Salad, '85 163
Snow Pea Salad, Pear, Jícama, and, '01 329
Snow Peas, Pear Salad with Jícama and, '01 56
Special Peas, '95 133
Special Pea Salad, '83 239
Sugar Snap Pea Salad, '86 115
Three Pea Salad, '84 290
Snow. *See also* **PEAS/Salads.**
Basil Snow Peas and Tomatoes, '88 M185
Beef and Snow Peas, Oriental, '79 105
Beef with Pea Pods, Oriental, '86 M328
Cashew Pea Pods, '92 343
Chicken with Snow Peas, '83 137
Chinese Peas, Easy, '83 206
Crunchy Snow Peas and Dip, '86 62
en Papillote, Fish with Snow Peas, '86 144
Medley, Cauliflower-Snow Pea, '87 305
Peas and Snow Peas, '88 67
Peppers, Minted Peas and, '90 M99
Pineapple, Snow Peas and, '91 120
Piquant, Snow Peas, '79 21
Red Pepper, Snow Peas with, '90 102
Sesame Snow Peas and Red Pepper, '84 175
Shrimp Combo, Snow Pea-, '79 57
Shrimp with Snow Peas, '85 75
Skillet Snow Peas with Celery, '84 123
Slaw, Zesty, '97 324
Stir-Fried Peas and Peppers, '87 51
Stir-Fry, Beef and Pea, '82 98
Stir-Fry Beef and Pea Pods, '80 19

Stir-Fry, Beef and Snow Pea, '82 98
Stir-Fry Beef and Snow Peas, '83 22
Stir-Fry, Chicken and Snow Pea, '95 157
Stir-Fry, Potato-Snow Pea, '86 173
Stuffed Snow Peas, '84 80
Stuffed Snow Peas, Crab-, '85 288
Tomatoes, Snow Peas and, '83 111
Soup, Country-Style Pea, '86 267
Soup, Cream Pea, '90 211
Soup, French Market, '94 317
Soup Mix, French Market, '94 317
Soup, Oven-Baked Split Pea-and-Lentil, '00 316
Soup, Pea-and-Watercress, '93 162
Soup, Split Pea, '88 235; '89 17; '90 198; '94 322
Soup, Split Pea and Frankfurter, '79 64
Sugar Snap
Appetizers, Sugar Snap Pea, '86 115
Basil and Lemon, Sugar Snap Peas with, '93 66
Bell Peppers, Sugar Snap Peas with, '03 255
Champagne Dressing, Sugar Snap Peas with, '99 166
Creamed Sugar Snaps and Carrots, '93 139
Dilled Peas and Potatoes Vinaigrette, '00 102
Dip, Sugar Peas with, '86 170
Dip, Sugar Snap, '88 91
Goat Cheese, Sugar Snap Peas and, '01 112
Lemon-Scented Sugar Snap Peas, '02 282
Pearl Onions, Snap Peas and, '89 280
Peppers, Sugar Snaps and, '93 139
Pickled Sugar Snap Peas, '01 112
Potato Salad with Sugar Snap Peas, '91 120
Roasted Garlic Dressing, Snap Peas with, '99 269
Steamed Sugar Snap Peas, '99 71; '04 174
Vegetable Medley, Spring, '86 115
PECANS. *See also* **PRALINE.**
Acorn Squash with Molasses and Pecans, '85 205
Appetizers
Ball, Date-Nut, '92 326
Ball, Deviled Pecan, '80 258
Ball, Party Pecan Cheese, '81 235
Ball, Pecan Cheese, '83 127
Ball, Pinecone Cheese, '98 265
Balls, Date-Nut, '85 10
Ball, Tuna-Pecan, '87 94
Barbecued Pecans, '83 222
Bites, Cheesy Pecan, '82 248
Blue Cheese Logs, '04 53
Brie, Kahlúa-Pecan, '92 289
Brie with Brown Sugar and Nuts, '03 282
Brown Sugar Pecans, '81 266
Candied Nuts, '81 261
Cheese Brick, '99 170
Cheese Ring, '05 33
Chesapeake Nuts, '93 269
Chicken Fingers, Buttermilk-Pecan, '93 165
Christmas Eve Pecans, '91 276
Christmas Pecans, '03 300
Citrusy Pecans, '03 292; '04 146
Coffee 'n' Spice Pecans, '88 256
Cranberry-Nut Triangles, '04 273
Crisps, Blue Cheese, '98 285
Curried Nuts, Spicy, '82 250
Curried Pecans, '91 208
Deviled Nuts, '93 118
Glazed Pecans, '81 254; '82 136
Grapes, Blue Cheese-Pecan, '95 48
Greek Olive Cups, '99 221
Honeycomb Pecans, '84 300
Hot-and-Spicy Pecans, '89 161
Hot Pepper Pecans, '85 4
Hot Smoky Pecans, '98 173
Log, Chicken-Pecan, '81 290
Log, Roquefort Pecan, '89 247
Log, Toasted Pecan Cheese, '86 M288
Mexico Nuts, '01 27

Mix, Jalapeño Nut, '96 27
Mushrooms, Pecan-Stuffed, '84 261
Nippy Nuts, '93 301
Orange-Glazed Pecans, '97 225
Orange Nuts, Sherry-, '86 M289
Orange Pecans, '84 299; '87 292
Pear-Pecan Appetizers, '96 262
Pepper Pecans, '87 137; '93 79
Pesto-Spiced Nuts, '95 173
Popcorn Balls, Nutty, '88 227
Quick Party Nuts, '04 197
Roasted Bacon Pecans, '96 262
Roasted Pecans, Creole, '01 241
Rolls, Blue Cheese, '00 210
Salted Pecans, Southern, '80 285
Sandwiches, Olive Tea, '02 252
Savory Southern Pecans, '95 240
Shortbread, Jalapeño-Pecan, '03 108
Smoky Pecans, '01 168
Spiced Nuts, '91 M316
Spiced Pecans, '79 296; '80 31; '81 286
Spicy Pecans, '81 M289; '93 279; '01 206
Spread, Carrot-Pecan, '96 108
Spread, Nutty Carrot, '94 123
Spread Sandwiches, Olive-Nut, '04 259
Sticks, Pecan, '01 242
Sugar-and-Spice Nuts, '05 274
Sugar and Spice Pecans, '82 297
Sugar-and-Spice Pecans, '86 121; '94 272
Sweet-and-Spicy Pecans, '92 321; '00 334; '01 20
Tarts, Apricot-Pecan-Brie, '97 236
Tarts, Toasty Southern Pecan, '95 329
Toasted Chili Pecans, '85 154
Toasted Pecans, '84 321; '86 229; '03 300
Toasted Pecans, Buttery, '88 77
Torte, Showstopping Appetizer, '98 319
Wafers, Pecan-Cheese, '81 119
Wafers, Sage-Pecan Cheese, '93 12
Apples, Caramel, '03 M216
Apples, Orange-Pecan Baked, '85 45
Apples, Pecan-and-Dried Fruit Baked, '03 269
Apples, Taffy Pecan, '99 247
Balls, Orange-Nut, '02 297
Bars, Creamy No-Bake, '97 166
Biscuits, Elf, '99 309
Blueberry Yum Yum, '98 91
Bourbon Balls, '02 30
Bourbon-Pecan Alfredo, '96 291
Breads
Apple-Nut Bread, '85 281
Applesauce Nut Bread, '81 305
Applesauce-Pecan Bread, '90 66
Apricot-Nut Loaf, Tasty, '82 10
Apricot-Pecan Bread, '82 10
Banana-Nut Bread, '86 8, 70; '04 259
Banana-Nut-Raisin Bread, '81 59
Biscuit Braid, Apple-Pecan, '02 326
Biscuit Bread, Brown Sugar, '02 M224
Biscuits, Nutty Tea, '89 210
Biscuits, Peppered Pork with Pecan, '01 33
Biscuits with Cinnamon Butter, Cinnamon-Pecan, '01 309
Bourbon-Pecan Bread, '93 308; '96 27
Buns, Nutty, '86 290
Cheddar-Nut Bread, '85 41; '03 42
Cherry Nut Bread, '81 306; '82 36
Cherry-Nut Bread, Quick, '85 55
Chocolate Date-Nut Bread, '81 284
Coconut-Pecan Coils, '90 196
Cornbread, Pecan, '94 169; '98 252
Crescent Twists, Pecan, '99 47; '03 36
Date-Nut Loaf, '85 10
French Toast, Caramel-Pecan, '03 328
Fritters, Broccoli-Cauliflower, '02 45

Kahlúa Fruit-Nut Bread, '79 235
Lemon-Pecan Bread, '83 54
Maple-Nut Coffee Twist, '86 290
Maraschino Cherry Nut Bread, '79 234
Mini-Cinnis, Mama's, '02 41
Monkey Bread Bites, '04 333
Muffin Batter, Pecan Pie, '04 200
Muffins, Banana-Nut, '93 140
Muffins, Cherry-Nut, '90 87
Muffins, Chunky Pecan, '88 9
Muffins, Cinnamon-Nut, '85 M88
Muffins, Cinnamon-Pecan, '84 219
Muffins, Coffee Cake, '98 160
Muffins, Country Pecan, '83 222
Muffins, Cranberry-Pecan, '84 269
Muffins, Date, '00 239
Muffins, Date-Nut, '99 234
Muffins, Nutty Pumpkin, '86 291
Muffins, Orange-Pecan, '83 96; '99 56
Muffins, Pecan, '80 16
Muffins, Pecan-Orange, '97 163
Muffins, Pecan-Pie, '01 206
Muffins, Pecan Pie, '04 201
Muffins, Raisin-Nut, '92 46
Muffins, Raisin-Pecan Ginger, '88 9
Muffins, Rum-Nut, '90 87
Orange-Nut Bread, '82 75
Orange Nut Loaf, '80 226
Orange-Pecan Bread, '79 148
Orange-Pecan Bread, Glazed, '81 250
Orange-Pecan Loaves, '79 215
Persimmon Date-Nut Bread, '82 218
Pineapple-Nut Bread, '79 215
Pineapple-Pecan Loaf Bread, '87 256
Popovers, Giant Pecan, '83 208
Prune-Nut Bread, '87 255; '91 55
Pull-Away Bread, Cinnamon, '98 137
Pumpkin Muffins, '04 112
Pumpkin-Nut Bread, '83 294
Pumpkin-Pecan Bread, '87 221; '02 224
Roll, Banana-Nut, '85 112
Rolls, Buttered Rum-Nut, '86 291
Rolls, Caramel-Nut, '86 312
Rolls, Cinnamon-Pecan, '98 251
Rolls, Citrus-Pecan, '03 256
Rolls, Easy Cinnamon-Pecan, '89 307
Rolls, Oatmeal-Cinnamon-Pecan, '96 50
Rolls, Pecan, '81 62
Rolls, Pecan-Golden Raisin Sweet, '03 235
Scones, Merry Cranberry-Nut Yeast, '99 274
Scones, Mocha-Pecan, '97 45
Scones, Orange-Pecan, '94 215; '01 72
Strawberry-Nut Bread, '79 24
Whole Wheat Date-Nut Bread, '04 208
Whole Wheat Nut Bread, '04 208
Whole Wheat Raisin-Nut Bread, '04 208
Wine-Date Nut Bread, '82 253
Brittle, Chocolate, '83 315
Brittle, Microwave Pecan, '97 M245
Brittle, Pecan, '91 272; '02 M223
Broccoli, Pecan, '05 257
Broccoli with Lemon Sauce and Pecans, '86 71
Butter, Beehive, '00 68
Buttered Pecans, Green Beans with, '92 61
Butter, Jalapeño-Pecan-Mustard, '03 205
Butter, Orange-Pecan, '84 75; '97 15
Butter, Pecan, '97 307
Butter, Pecan-Honey, '05 137
Cakes
Apple-Pecan Cake, '92 167
Banana-Nut Cake, '92 120
Banana Split Cake, '99 48
Bourbon-Pecan Cake, '84 25
Butter Brickle Loaf Cakes, '98 137

PECANS, Cakes
(continued)

Butter Pecan Cake, '80 229
Butter Pecan Cake, Caramel-Filled, '88 278
Candy Bar Cake, '98 90
Carrot Cake, Pecan-, '99 223
Carrot Cake, Praline-Filled, '03 332
Cheesecake, Butter Pecan, '86 61
Cheesecake, Chocolate-Caramel-Pecan, '91 197
Cheesecake, Lemony Passover, '02 51
Cheesecake, Pecan, '85 38
Cheesecake, Pecan Pie, '02 318; '03 316
Cheesecake, Pecan Praline, '03 269
Cheesecake, Praline, '83 270; '89 93
Chocolate-Bourbon-Pecan Cake, '03 287
Chocolate-Nut Cake, Rich, '86 8
Chocolate-Praline Pecan Cake, '03 288
Cinnamon-Pecan Crumb Cakes, '05 288
Cinnamon Swirl Cake, '01 255
Coffee Cake, Apple-Pecan, '84 242
Coffee Cake, Cinnamon-Pecan, '87 69
Coffee Cake, Nutty Orange, '95 160
Coffee Cake, Orange-Pecan, '86 86
Coffee Cake, Pecan-Topped, '81 41
Coffee Cake, Triple-Chocolate, '04 M299
Cupcakes, Apple-Nut, '82 279
Date Nut Cake, '79 176; '80 5
Dump Cake, Tropical, '02 128
Fruitcake, Sherry-Nut, '00 299
Fruitcake, White, '00 299
Funnel Cakes, Nutty, '91 233
Kentucky Pecan Cake, '84 263
Maple Nut Cake, '96 17
Mississippi Mud Cake, '04 136
Orange Date-Nut Cake, '01 285
Orange-Nut Butter Cake, '80 254
Orange Nut Cake, '80 70
Orange-Pecan Crunch Cake, '83 10
Pear Cake, Caramel-Glazed, '02 196
Pecan Cake, '97 256
Pie Cake, Pecan, '98 254; '03 316
Pineapple-Pecan Upside-Down Cake, '84 25
Pineapple Upside-Down Cake, Spiced, '02 214
Pound Cake, Bourbon-Pecan, '91 270
Pound Cake, Brown Sugar-Rum, '96 60
Pound Cake, Butterscotch-Pecan, '92 153
Pound Cake, Cream Cheese-Bourbon-Pecan, '04 280
Pound Cake, Cream Cheese-Coconut-Pecan, '04 280
Pound Cake, Eggnog-Pecan, '95 313
Pound Cake, Gentleman's, '00 287
Pound Cake, Marbled Pecan, '93 313
Pound Cake, Orange-Pecan, '93 13
Pound Cake, Orange-Pecan-Spice, '02 295
Pound Cake, Pecan, '01 253
Pound Cake, Praline, '82 88
Pound Cake, Sour Cream-Orange Pecan, '89 207
Praline Glaze, Pecan Cake with, '82 196
Praline Ice Cream Cake, '80 84
Praline-Pecan Cakes, '05 286
Roulade, Pecan, '87 183
Roulage, Toffee-Pecan, '94 312
Shortcake, Banana-Pecan, '93 43
Sour Cream-Pecan Cake Batter, '05 286
Sweet Potato Cake with Citrus Filling, '02 221
Candy, Chocolate-Nut Log, '86 335
Candy, Cola, '02 298
Candy, Divinity, '01 271
Caramel Corn, Nutty, '92 317
Caramelized Onion-and-Pecan Brussels Sprouts, '99 254
Caramel O's, '99 196
Caramel-Pecan Triangles, '99 281

Carrots and Celery with Pecans, '84 254
Cassata, '01 125
Casserole, Carrot-Pecan, '93 44; '98 231; '02 282
Catfish, Crispy, '03 101
Catfish Pecan, '85 53
Catfish, Pecan, '98 329
Catfish Pecan with Lemon-Thyme-Pecan Butter, '04 68
Catfish with Lemon Sauce, Pecan, '03 185; '05 56
Cheese, Pecan Pimiento, '01 169; '03 315
Chicken, Baked Pecan, '05 312
Chicken, Buttermilk-Pecan, '89 166; '97 252
Chicken Drummettes, Orange-Pecan, '93 158
Chicken, Honey-Pecan, '03 147
Chicken, Lemony Pecan, '96 82
Chicken, Nutty Oven-Fried, '85 160
Chicken, Oven-Fried Pecan, '84 288
Chicken, Pecan, '90 54; '99 332
Chicken Strips, Honey-Pecan, '05 188
Chicken Thighs, Honey-Pecan, '02 127
Chocolate Date-Nut Delight, '88 168
Chocolate-Dipped Pecans, '05 M269
Clusters, Pecan, '81 266; '98 305
Clusters, Pecan-Coconut, '86 M251
Clusters, Roasted Pecan, '85 233; '90 310; '03 315
Clusters, Toasted Pecan, '00 M14
Coating, Salmon Bake with Pecan-Crunch, '95 209
Cobbler, Apple-Pecan, '84 M198
Cobbler, Apple-Pecan Pie, '04 200
Cobbler, Blueberry-Pecan, '00 154; '03 106
Cobbler, Pecan-Peach, '04 120
Coffee, Praline-Flavored, '87 69
Collard, Raisin, and Pecan Sauté, '05 292
Cookies
Bars, Butter Pecan Turtle, '90 70
Bars, Gooey Pecan, '94 133
Bars, Pecan, '82 209
Biscotti, Orange-Pecan, '01 207
Brownie Mix, Blond, '01 247
Brownies, Caramel-Pecan Filled, '03 M43
Brownies, Chocolate-Glazed, '01 143
Brownies, Chocolate-Pecan, '81 64
Brownies, Coconut-Pecan-Frosted, '97 99
Brownies, Double-Chocolate, '04 100
Brownies, Layered, '02 M252
Brownies, Nutty Blonde, '81 64
Brownies, Nutty Cocoa, '81 64
Brownies, Nutty Fudge, '80 M171
Brownies, Praline, '93 243
Brownies, Praline-Pecan, '05 M288
Brown Sugar-Pecan Cookies, '91 236
Butter Cookies, Pecan-, '83 113
Butter Pecan Cookies, '82 139
Butter Pecan Shortbread Cookies, '80 282
Butterscotch-Pecan Cookies, '84 36
Cheese Crispies, Pecan-, '87 168
Cherry Nut Nuggets, '81 286
Cherry Pecan Cookies, '82 136
Chocolate Chip Cookies, Pecan-, '05 87
Chocolate Chubbies, '01 144
Chocolate Cookies, Chewy, '97 166
Chocolate-Nut Chews, '81 92
Chocolate-Nut Freezer Cookies, '88 217
Cinnamon Cookies, GrandLady's, '00 323
Crescent Cookies, Pecan, '85 324; '97 274
Crescents, Pecan, '04 284
Crispies, Pecan, '99 337
Cupcake Cookies, '04 273
Date Balls, '01 90
Easy Pecan Cookies, '80 208
English Rocks, '01 295
Fruitcake Cookies, '98 294
Fudge-Pecan Chewies, Alabama, '95 143
Graham Cracker Layered Cookies, '98 94
Icebox Cookies, Cinnamon Chip, '01 308

Lemon-Pecan Cookies, '02 293
Lemon Pecan Dainties, '80 208
Oatmeal-Chocolate Chip Cookies, Nutty, '82 185
Oatmeal-Chocolate Chunk Cookies, Nutty, '01 19
Oatmeal Cookies, Nutty, '81 130
Oatmeal Nut Crispies, '80 208
Orange-Pecan Cookies, '88 119
Pfeffernüesse, '01 65
Pie Cookies, Pecan, '92 289; '00 290
Praline-Chocolate Chip Cookies, Crispy, '02 229; '03 131
Praline Cookies, '91 271
Praline Cookies, Crispy, '02 229; '03 131
Praline Shortbread Cookies, '88 242
Praline Thumbprint Cookies, '89 328
Sandies, Basil-Pecan, '97 166
Sand Tarts, '00 323
Scotch Bars, Chewy, '98 M291
Shells, Pecan Lace, '97 167
Shortbreads, Pecan-Cornmeal, '04 230
Squares, Butter Pecan Pie, '81 262
Squares, Congo, '96 94
Squares, Easy Pecan, '81 230
Squares, Lemon-Pecan, '89 124
Squares, Pecan, '79 205; '90 69; '98 336; '04 271
Squares, Twice-Baked Pecan, '79 291
Sticks, Crispy Pecan, '00 258
Sugar Pecan Crisps, '86 230
Sugarplum Sticks, '95 321
Wedding Cookies, '00 332
White Chocolate Chip-Oatmeal Cookies, '04 43
Cornmeal Rounds, Pecan-, '95 99
Couscous, Cranberry-and-Toasted Pecan, '05 M259
Crunch, Apple-Nut, '82 M238
Crunchy Munchies, '94 196
Cupcakes, Apple-Nut, '82 279
Dessert, Maple Nut, '81 84
Dessert, Nutty Fudgy Frozen, '94 28
Dessert, Turtle, '04 127
Divinity, Mrs. Floyd's, '00 315
Dressing, Andouille Sausage, Apple, and Pecan, '02 249
Dressing, Chicken with Pecan-Rice, '85 M57
Dressing, Cornbread, Sausage, and Pecan, '99 257
Dressing, Crabmeat-and-Oyster, '02 243
Dressing, Fruit-and-Pecan, '84 252
Dressing, Honey-Pecan, '03 28
Dressing, Louise's Cornbread, '03 251
Dressing, Mess o' Greens Salad with Warm Pecan, '98 250
Dressing, Pecan, Rice, and Crawfish, '00 252
Dressing, Pecan-Sage, '80 262
Dressing, Watermelon Salad with Celery-Nut, '80 182
Dumplings, Spiced Peaches with Nutty, '87 164
Eggs, Pecan-Stuffed, '80 78
Eggs, Pecan-Stuffed Deviled, '04 93
Fettuccine, Chicken-Pecan, '86 52
Filling, Cranberry-Pecan, '04 305
Filling, Fruit-Nut, '80 289
Filling, Nut, '91 35
Filling, Nutty Fruit, '99 306
Filling, Pecan, '04 305
Filling, Pecan Pie, '98 254; '03 316
Fritters, Chocolate-Covered Pecan, '79 205
Frosting, Banana-Nut, '79 115
Frosting, Butter Pecan, '80 229
Frosting, Cherry-Nut Cream Cheese, '96 249
Frosting, Chocolate Nut, '80 140
Frosting, Coconut-Pecan, '81 296; '83 M233; '84 43, 322; '97 99; '03 289
Frosting, Cream Cheese-Butter Pecan, '03 288
Frosting, Divinity, '01 270
Frosting, Nutty Coconut, '86 8
Frosting, Nutty Cream Cheese, '85 117; '96 263
Frosting, Pecan, '86 86

Frosting, Pecan-Cream Cheese, '02 294
Fruit Compote, Warm Praline, '85 260
Fudge, Buttermilk, '97 317
Fudge, Cherry Nut, '83 315
Fudge, Creamy Pecan, '84 321
Fudge, Nutty White, '81 253
Fudge-Peanut Butter Chewies, '98 215
Fudge, Quick Nut, '83 316
Garnish, Pastry, '98 254; '03 317
Glaze, Buttered Rum, '03 94
Glazed Nuts, '88 222
Glazed Pecan Halves, '02 295
Glaze, Honey-Nut, '87 15
Glaze, Praline, '82 196
Goose, Fruit- and Pecan-Stuffed, '83 268
Grahams, Praline, '92 239
Granola, Nutty, '90 95
Granola, Pecan-Coconut, '02 70
Green Beans, '97 263
Green Beans, Lemon-Pecan, '04 285
Green Beans, Nutty, '88 M187
Ham, Praline, '85 302; '96 303
Ice Cream, Banana-Nut, '00 143
Ice Cream, Bourbon-Pecan, '00 260
Ice Cream, Butter Pecan, '80 176; '86 129; '88 202
Ice Cream, Butter-Pecan, '96 134
Ice Cream, Cherry-Nut, '86 129
Ice Cream, Cherry-Pecan, '88 203
Ice Cream, Pecan-Caramel Crunch, '02 322
Ice Cream, Praline, '89 318
Ice Cream, Pralines and Cream, '82 184; '83 159
Ice-Cream Sandwiches, Butter Pecan, '05 62
Ice Cream, Straw-Ba-Nut, '80 177
Ice Cream, Strawberry-Banana-Nut, '88 203
Millionaires, '97 M55
Mousse, Butter Pecan, '95 286
Oatmeal, Dried Cherry-and-Pecan, '05 126
Onion Flowers with Pecans, Grilled, '96 217
Onions with Pecans and Roasted Carrots, Roasted
    Vidalia, '92 340
Orange Pecans, '84 299; '87 292
Pancakes, Pecan, '03 305
Pancakes, Toasted Pecan, '99 43
Peas, Hot Pecan, '05 85
Penuche, Coffee, '98 305
Pesto, '00 118
Pesto, Cilantro-Pecan, '04 36
Pesto, Garden, '04 186
Pies and Pastries
  Baklava, '96 20
  Bourbon-Chocolate Pecan Pie, '98 258
  Bourbon-Pecan Pie, '85 90
  Bourbon-Pecan Pie, Frozen, '89 251
  Bourbon-Pecan Pumpkin Pie, '87 264
  Caramel-Pecan Apple Pie, '85 247
  Caramel-Pecan Pie, '88 282; '05 269
  Cherry-Pecan Pie, '92 30
  Chess Pie, Chocolate-Pecan, '00 60; '02 107
  Chocolate-Banana-Pecan Cream Pie, '94 210
  Chocolate-Bourbon Pecan Pie, '05 134
  Chocolate Fudge Pie, '98 336
  Chocolate-Pecan Chess Pie, '93 251
  Chocolate Pecan Pie, '80 237; '83 12; '90 184
  Chocolate-Pecan Pie, '91 272; '02 176
  Chocolate-Praline Pie, '86 259
  Choco-Pecan Pie, '82 86
  Cinnamon-Almond-Pecan Pie, '98 89
  Coconut-Pecan Chess Pie, '81 248
  Coconut Pecan Pie, '81 161
  Coffee Pecan Pie, '82 74
  Cranberry-Pecan Crusts, '02 198
  Cranberry-Pecan Pie, '92 316
  Cranberry Pie, Nutty, '82 298
  Crust, Nutty Oat, '89 251

Crust, Pecan, '86 317; '89 291; '98 180
Crust, Spiced Nut, '87 295
Custard Pecan Pie, '87 184
Date-Pecan Pie, '80 15
Fudge Pie with Raspberry Sauce, Pecan, '05 201
Golden Pecan Pie, '81 266
Grandmother's Pecan Pie, '86 269
Holiday Pecan Pie, '81 296
Honey-Pecan Finger Pies, '90 184
Hot Fudge Sauce, Pecan Pie with, '01 306
Ice Cream Pie, Nutty, '91 180
Individual Pecan Pies, '85 295
Layered Pecan Pie, '83 305
Lemon-Pecan Pie, '93 251
Louisiana Pecan Pie, '92 83
Maple-Pecan Pie, '81 266
Mascarpone Pecan Pie, '05 299
Maverick Lunar Pie, '98 111
Mincemeat Ice Cream Pie, '99 285
Miniature Pecan Pies, '79 205; '86 13
Mississippi Pecan Pie, '98 146
Mocha Pecan Mud Pie, '00 245
Mocha-Pecan Mud Pie, '05 290
Molasses-Pecan Pie, '86 259
Mom's Pecan Pie, '02 249
Mystery Pecan Pie, '02 249
Old-Fashioned Pecan Pie, '81 M269
Orange-Pecan Pie, '79 282; '83 222
Orzo-Pecan Pie, Honeyed, '04 219
Peach Praline Pie, '89 136
Pecan Pie, '79 251; '80 57; '85 255; '90 312;
    '92 234; '98 275; '01 244
Praline Pastries, '89 318
Praline-Topped Pumpkin Pie, '00 332
Pumpkin-Pecan Pie, '85 233, 282
Pumpkin Pie, Nutty, '82 67
Raisin-Pecan Pie, '87 213
Shell, Pecan Pastry, '97 275; '98 36
Simmie's Pecan Pie, '00 254
Special, Old Pecan Street, '93 251
Spicy Pecan Pie, '84 240
Strudel, Autumn-Apple, '98 253
Sweet Potato-Pecan Pie, '83 90
Tart, Apricot-Nut, '99 249
Tart, Fudge Truffle-Pecan, '99 315; '02 208
Tart, Honey-Pecan, '99 212
Tartlets, Kentucky Derby, '00 107
Tartlets, Zamaani's Nutty Yam, '02 21
Tarts, Apple-Pecan, '80 282
Tarts, Bourbon-Chocolate-Pecan, '96 264
Tarts, Easy Pecan, '84 313
Tarts, Pecan, '81 266
Tarts, Special Pecan, '87 224
Tart with Caramel Sauce, Chocolate-Pecan, '93 296;
    '94 234
Tart with Praline Cream, Pecan, '90 256
Tassies, Teatime, '84 321
Texas Pecan Pie, '83 159
Texas Star Pecan Pie, '90 184
Tiny Pecan Pies, '79 225
Turtle Pecan Pie, '93 250
Vanilla Custard, Pecan Pie with Chilled, '00 331
Popcorn Balls, Nutty, '88 227
Popcorn, Crazy Mixed-Up, '97 245
Popcorn, Spicy Nut, '02 287
Popcorn, Trick or Treat, '03 210
Popovers, Pecan, '01 206
Pork, Cajun Pecan, '01 27
Pork Chops, Honey-Pecan, '01 82
Pork Chops with Beer Sauce, Pecan-Breaded, '95 266
Pork Chops with Pecans and Apples, Commune's
    Maple-Glazed, '04 102
Pork Loin, Apricot-Pecan Stuffed, '94 274
Pork Loin Roast, Festive, '03 255

Praline Freeze, '89 60; '90 48
Praline Pecans, '97 285; '05 286
Pudding, Brown Sugar-Pecan, '86 M165
Pudding, Pecan-Mocha, '89 M130
Pudding with Hot Rum Sauce, Apple-Nut, '79 86
Quad, Chocolate, '02 272
Quiche, Chicken-Pecan, '91 206
Rice, Island, '98 276
Rice, Nutted, '85 269
Rice, Orphan's, '03 32; '04 218
Rice, Pecan, '85 53; '04 204
Rice, Shrimp-and-Scallop Sauté with Pecan, '90 317
Rice, Speedy Skillet Pecan, '04 328
Roll, Date Nut, '79 249
Rolls, Pecan, '79 285
Roughy with Brown Butter Sauce, Pecan, '91 64
Roulade, Pecan, '87 183
Rugalach, Cranberry-Pecan, '04 305
Salad, Apple-Nut, '80 226
Salad, Beet-Nut, '79 74
Salad, Cantaloupe-Pecan, '86 178
Salad, Creamy Carrot-Nut, '86 331
Salad, Endive, Bacon, and Pecan, '89 12
Salad, Ham-Pecan-Blue Cheese Pasta, '90 62
Salad, Spinach-Pecan, '89 128; '01 284
Salad, Strawberry-Nut, '94 132
Salad, Watercress, '97 249
Sandwiches, Rolled Olive, '01 241
Sauces
  Bourbon Praline Sauce, '81 170
  Butter Pecan Sauce, '91 174
  Butter Sauce, Pecan-, '91 65
  Butterscotch-Pecan Sauce, '82 212
  Chocolate-Praline Sauce, '85 M295
  Cinnamon-Pecan-Honey Pancake Sauce, '88 46
  Date-Nut Sundae Sauce, '82 167
  Éclairs with Pecan Sauce, '83 219
  Pasta Sauce, Pecan, '96 262
  Peach-Praline Sauce, '85 161
  Pecan Sauce, '83 219
  Praline Ice Cream Sauce, '85 189
  Praline Ice Cream Sauce, Southern, '86 M227
  Praline Sauce, '83 25; '84 143; '89 95; '92 282;
      '94 206, 312
  Tartar Sauce, Pecan, '03 101
Shrimp with Orange Dipping Sauce, Coconut-Pecan,
    '03 212
Snack Mix, Honey-Nut, '02 187
Spiced Pecans, '03 332
Spicy Pecans, '01 206; '02 304
Spread, Beet-and-Pecan Sandwich, '99 274
Spread, Honey-Nut, '87 157
Spread, Nutty Cream Cheese, '89 327
Spread, Pimiento Cheese, '99 106, 276
Spread, Raisin-Nut, '95 79
Squash, Apple-and-Pecan-Filled, '88 228
Sticky Bun Toast Topper, '99 M72
Stuffing, Chicken Breasts with Pecan-Sausage, '94 212
Stuffing, Cranberry, '04 246
Stuffing, Cranberry-Orange-Pecan, '01 249
Stuffing, Cranberry-Pecan, '96 309
Stuffing, Pecan, '79 292; '80 32
Stuffing, Piglet's, '04 270
Stuffing, Spicy Pecan-Cornbread, '01 207
Stuffing, Wild Duck with Pecan, '85 269
Sugar-and-Honey Pecans, '86 319
Sugared Pecans, '82 167; '01 271
Sugared Pecans, Cabbage-Apple Salad with, '05 91
Sugarplums, Pecan Shortbread, '83 298
Sweet-and-Spicy Pecans, '00 81, 334; '03 178
Sweet-and-Spicy Texas Pecans, '02 306
Sweet Potato Cakes, '01 105
Sweet Potato Stacks, Bourbon-, '04 246
Syrup, Chunky Pecan, '85 278

PECANS
(continued)

Syrup, Maple-Nut, '80 228
Tarts, Coconut-Pecan Cookie, '04 305
Tarts, Pecan-Raisin, '03 246
Tarts, Pecan-Raisin Mini-, '03 246
Toasted Pecans, Asparagus Pasta with, '04 90
Toast, Orange Praline, '79 36
Toffee, Bourbon-Pecan, '04 235
Toffee, Microwave, '92 M317
Toffee, Mildred's, '04 235
Toffee, Nutty, '79 M263
Toffee, Pecan, '00 42
Topping, Apple-Nut, '93 162
Topping, Butter-Pecan, '95 158
Topping, Cinnamon-Pecan, '85 277
Topping, Coconut-Pecan, '04 41
Topping, Crunchy Cereal, '96 216
Topping, Maple-Pecan Ice Cream, '98 317
Topping, Nutty, '85 256
Topping, Pecan, '94 36
Topping, Streusel, '96 216; '01 214; '04 194
Torte, Apricot, '02 220
Torte, Carob-Pecan, '85 218
Torte, Chocolate-Pecan, '89 42
Torte, Graham Cracker-Nut, '97 275; '98 35
Torte, Ground Pecan, '04 273
Torte, Heavenly Pecan, '81 266
Torte, Mocha-Pecan, '86 26
Torte, X-Treme Chocolate Double Nut Caramel
    Ladyfinger, '04 M315
Trout with Orange Sauce, Pecan-Crusted, '98 M82
Turkey Burgers, Toasted Pecan, Cranberry, and
    Gorgonzola, '05 320
Turkey Cutlets, Pecan-Crusted, '94 282
Vinaigrette, Pecan, '00 162
Waffles, Pecan, '87 225
Waffles, Pumpkin-Nut, '86 96
Waffles, Southern Chicken-Pecan, '82 231
Wild Rice, Nutty, '05 278
Wild Rice, Pecan-Lemon, '92 211
with Lemon Sauce, Pecan Catfish, '05 56
Zucchini with Pecans, '87 31

PEPPERMINT
Bavarian, Peppermint, '80 153
Brownies, Chocolate-Peppermint, '88 262
Brownies, Pistachio-Mint, '94 50
Brownie Squares, Mint Truffle, '05 M254
Brownies, Southern Chocolate-Mint, '93 216
Butter Mints, '03 300
Cake, Chocolate-Mint, '03 286
Cake, Peppermint Candy, '89 254
Cake, Red Velvet Peppermint, '98 308
Cheesecake Bites, Mint, '99 282
Cheesecake, Frozen Peppermint, '94 143
Chocolate Mint Freeze, '88 167
Cookies, Chocolate-Chocolate Chip-Peppermint,
    '97 289
Cookies, Peppermint, '95 322
Cookies, Peppermint Candy, '88 286
Cookies, Peppermint Sandwich, '92 277
Crème Brûlée, Peppermint, '95 323
Crescents, Peppermint, '03 273
Cupcakes, Chocolate-Peppermint Candy, '03 M287
Dessert, Peppermint Wafer, '79 176; '80 7
Dessert, Triple Mint Ice-Cream Angel, '93 86
Filling, Mint-Cream, '96 229
Filling, Peppermint, '81 119; '89 254
Flip, Hot Peppermint, '86 329
Fondue, Peppermint, '94 332; '95 35
Frosting, Mint Cream, '93 216
Frosting, Peppermint Cream Cheese, '98 308

Frosting, Pink Peppermint Birthday Cake, '92 269
Frosting, Quick Peppermint, '98 308
Hot Cocoa Mix, Minted, '91 316
Ice Cream, Peppermint, '80 176; '86 129
Mints, Party, '79 273; '81 119
Mousse, Peppermint, '93 315
Mousse, Peppermint Candy, '82 71; '94 198
Parfait, Peppermint, '93 315
Parfaits, Chocolate-Peppermint, '88 65
Patties, Peppermint, '86 278
Peabody Peppermint Patti, The, '99 321
Pie, Brownie-Mint, '97 303
Pie, Fudgy Chocolate Malt-Peppermint, '00 313
Pie, Peppermint Candy-Ice Cream, '87 260
Pie, Triple Mint Ice Cream, '98 217
Pralines, Chocolate-Mint, '92 313; '93 51
Punch, Cupid's Creamy Peppermint, '04 253
Rounds, Peppermint, '94 19
Sauce, Chocolate-Peppermint, '94 205
Shortbread, Butter-Mint, '99 28
Snowball Surprises, '93 315
Soufflé, Chocolate Mint, '81 16
Special Mints, '99 323
Squares, Chocolate-Peppermint, '81 119
Tarts, Peppermint Brownie, '05 M288
Twists, Mint, '86 106
Wreaths, Melt-Away Peppermint, '85 324

PEPPERS
Antipasto, Grandpa's, '98 183
Appetizers, Basil-Pepper, '98 133
Banana Peppers, Stuffed, '02 55
Banana Peppers, Stuffed Hungarian Yellow, '00 132
Bell Peppers, Pasta with Sausage and, '02 63
Burritos, Breakfast, '99 103
Casserole, Southwestern, '99 216
Cherry Pepper Appetizers, Fiery Stuffed, '97 269
Chicken with Angel Hair Pasta, Szechuan, '97 91
Chile
    Adobo Mayonnaise, '02 203
    Adobo, Puerco en, '88 116
    Ancho Base, '95 205
    Ancho-Beer Mashers, '98 248
    Ancho Chile Butter, '99 93
    Ancho Chile Cream, '87 121
    Ancho Chile Sauce, '87 122
    Ancho Chile Succotash with Serrano Chile Polenta,
        '98 104
    Ancho Cream Sauce, Boneless Pork Chops with,
        '95 205
    Ancho Mashers, '03 243
    Casserole, Chile-Cheese, '82 90
    Casserole, Chile 'n' Cheese Breakfast, '88 57
    Casserole, Chiles Rellenos, '79 84; '84 31, 234;
        '92 18
    Casserole, Chili-Corn, '88 266
    Casserole, Chili-Rice, '79 54
    Casserole, Mexican Rice, '83 31
    Casserole, Sausage-Chile Rellenos, '88 52
    Caviar, Mexican, '98 135
    Cheesecake, Chicken-Chile, '92 42
    Cheese, Chile-Pimiento, '04 325
    Cheeses, Mexican Grilled, '97 170
    Chicken, Jamaican Jerk, '99 121
    Chicken Madrid, '97 326
    Chicken with Salsa, Baked Chile, '88 147
    Chimichangas (Fried Burritos), '81 196; '85 244
    Chipotle Baby Back Ribs, Smoky, '04 87
    Chipotle-Barbecue Meatballs, Spicy, '05 305
    Chipotle-Barbecue Sausage Bites, Spicy, '05 305
    Chipotle-Black Bean Dip, Creamy, '05 247
    Chipotle Butter, '01 234
    Chipotle Caesar Dressing, '04 119
    Chipotle Caesar Salad, '04 119
    Chipotle Chicken Wings, Sweet-and-Spicy, '04 176

Chipotle Cream, Grilled Beef with Mashed Potatoes
    and, '02 M320
Chipotle 'Cue Sauce, Smoky, '04 87
Chipotle Grilled Pork Ribs, '01 319
Chipotle Hollandaise Sauce, '03 53
Chipotle-Lime Cream, '05 329
Chipotle Manicotti, Creamy, '03 96
Chipotle-Marinated Quail, '04 240
Chipotle-Marinated Quail, Pan-Roasted, '98 201
Chipotle Oil, '02 97; '03 98
Chipotle Pepper Butter, '97 307
Chipotle Pork Chops on Smoked Gouda Grits,
    Grilled Maple, '04 172
Chipotle Pork on Smoked Gouda Grits with Sweet
    Onion Applesauce, Maple-, '02 319
Chipotle Roasted Chicken, '03 44
Chipotle Rub, '04 87
Chipotle Salsa, Chicken-and-Brie Quesadillas with,
    '99 311
Chipotle Tostadas, Chickpea-, '01 54; '03 181
con Queso, Chile, '80 194
con Queso Supreme, Chile, '80 265
Dip, Artichoke-Chile, '98 234
Dip, Cheese-and-Chile, '83 31
Dip, Hot Chile, '82 248
Dip, Hot Chile-Beef, '83 218
Dipsy Devil, '00 132
Dressing, Southwestern Mayonnaise, '99 245
Egg Rolls, Chiles Rellenos, '86 296
Eggs, Chile, '88 80
Enchiladas, Chicken-Chile, '97 313
Enchiladas, New Mexican Flat, '85 245
Green Chile-and-Fish Casserole, '84 32
Green Chile Biscuits, '04 233
Green Chile Casserole, Corn-and-, '89 68
Green Chile-Cheddar Cheese with Avocado-Mango
    Salsa, Smoky, '00 328
Green Chile-Cheese Pie, '84 234
Green Chile-Chicken Lasagna, '00 338
Green Chile-Cornbread Dressing, '93 306
Green Chile Enchiladas, '02 188
Green Chile, Muffins, Chicken-and-, '03 81
Green Chile-Pimiento Cheese, '01 61
Green Chile Quiche, '83 31
Green Chile Quiche, Squash-and-, '88 143
Green Chile Sauce, '82 220
Green Chiles, Cheese Grits with, '95 208
Green Chile-Sour Cream Enchiladas, '84 234
Green Chiles, Potato Chowder with, '00 329
Green Chiles, Rice and, '83 152
Green Chiles, Stuffed, '93 208
Green Chiles, Stuffed Red Peppers with Cheesy
    Polenta and, '04 169
Green Chiles, Stuffed Squash with, '83 148
Green Chile-Tomato Gravy, '95 42
Grits, Chile-Blue Cheese, '04 240
Grits, Saga Blue-Chile, '98 202
Jelly, Chile Piquin, '94 28
Jus, Chile Corn, '00 197
Kebabs, Chile-Beef, '94 251
Logs, Chile-Cheese, '05 64
Oil, Chile Pepper, '96 122
Okra Dills, '97 157
Pickled Chiles Medley, Fiery, '01 333
Pickles, Peppery Texas, '04 M161
Pico de Gallo, '97 141; '98 87
Poblano-and-Cheese Casserole, Zesty, '05 311
Poblano-and-Corn Quesadillas, '01 333
Poblano Chicken, Creamy, '98 42
Poblano Chile con Queso, Roasted, '01 186
Poblano Chowder, Corn-and-, '03 193
Poblano-Cilantro Pesto, Central Market's, '04 101
Poblano Salad, Avocado-Corn-, '01 320
Poblanos, Corn-Stuffed, '97 269

Poblano-Shrimp Enchiladas, '00 311
Poblanos Stuffed with Pork and Fruit, '97 269
Poblanos with Mango Salsa, Crab-and-Goat Cheese, '04 59
Poblanos with Walnut Cream Sauce, Pork-Stuffed, '01 229
Poblano Vinaigrette, '99 71
Pork Chops, Chile Pepper, '02 210
Potatoes, Chile Mashed, '00 161
Pudding, Southwestern Corn, '03 178
Quiche, Chile Pepper, '82 224
Quiche, Chiles Rellenos, '02 321
Quiche, Shrimp, '83 50
Red Chile Enchilada Sauce, '85 245
Red Chile Paste, '05 118
Red Chile Powder, '85 245
Red Chile Sauce, '85 245; '94 251; '95 17
Rellenos, Cheese Chiles, '96 24
Rellenos, Chiles (Stuffed Chiles), '82 220; '83 150; '88 116; '89 226
Rellenos Potatoes, Papa's, '96 238
Rellenos, Roasted Chiles, '95 64
Rellenos, Southern-Style Chiles, '96 24
Rellenos with Tomatillo Sauce, Roasted Chiles, '94 203
Rellenos with Walnut Cream Sauce, Havarti-and-Corn-Stuffed Chiles, '93 M275
Rice, Chili-Cheesy, '79 43
Rice, Hot Pepper, '92 310
Roasted Chiles, Mac and Texas Cheeses with, '04 211
Rollups, Cream Cheese, '98 134
Salad, Spicy Chile-Tomato, '88 121
Salsa, Double Chile, '91 182
Salsa, Dried Chile, '97 265
Salsa, Pepper, '88 26
Salsa with Homemade Tostados, Hot Chile, '88 115
Salsa, Zesty Santa Fe, '03 198
Sauce, Drunken, '03 33
Sauce, Pepper, '01 211; '02 106
Sauce, Racy Pesto, '97 67
Sauce, Tex-Mex Secret, '04 127
Serrano Chile Blue Cornbread, '94 114
Serrano Chile Polenta, '98 104
Serrano Salsa, Roasted, '95 207
Soufflés, Chile-Cheese, '96 219
Spread, Chile-Cheese, '02 205
Squash, Chile, '84 77
Squash, Mexican, '83 31
Steaks, Mexican Pepper-Cheese, '97 190
Tacos, Shrimp-and-Pepper Soft, '95 339
Tamales, Hot, '83 51
Tamales, Sweet, '83 52
Turnovers, Chile-Ham, '88 64
Verde, Chili, '95 14
Verde, Light Chile, '88 148
Verde Sauce, '93 275; '00 241
Vinaigrette, Hot Chile, '98 200
Waffles, Corn-Chile, '94 206
Cornbread, Lynda's Mex-Tex, '01 273
Cornbread, Mexican, '01 247
Dip, Pepperoncini-Cream Cheese, '91 252
Dressing, Jeweled Hot Bacon, '97 196
Eggs, Tex-Mex Deviled, '97 247
Fajitas with Pico de Gallo, '98 87
Fillet, Acapulco, '98 174
Filling, Crêpe, '96 48
Firecrackers, Texas, '95 96
Frittata, Bell Pepper, '96 204

Green
Beans, Frolickers Baked, '03 92
Beef and Green Peppers, '79 104
Beefed-Up Peppers, '82 186
Black Beans, Traditional Cuban, '98 21

Bread, Pepper, '85 156
Casserole, Peppered Pork Chop, '82 25
Casserole, Peppery Potato, '95 182
Chicken Peppers, Devilish, '80 65
Coleslaw, Memphis-Style, '98 104
Coleslaw, Old-Fashioned, '99 235
Coleslaw, Sour Cream, '99 220
Cups, Potato Salad in Pepper, '79 78
Deluxe, Peppers, '81 159
Dressing, Green Pepper-Onion Salad, '84 12
Fried Pepper Strips, '82 208
Gazpacho, White, '97 181
Hamburger Steak, '99 45
Jelly, Pepper, '79 121
Jelly, Unusual Green Pepper, '82 132
Linguine, Leeks and Peppers with, '98 68
Meatballs with Pineapple and Peppers, '90 145
Meat Loaf, French Market, '02 33
Medley, Pepper-Mushroom, '90 98
Mexican Green Peppers, '80 65
Muffins, Cheese-and-Pepper, '84 139
Onions, Baked Sweet, '98 130
Oriental Radishes, '01 101
Pizza Peppers, '83 135
Pork, Sweet-and-Sour, '00 110
Potato Salad 'n' Peppers, '83 135
Ratatouille, '85 92
Relish, Pepper, '83 183
Relish, Pepper-Onion, '84 180
Rice, Charleston, '97 310
Rice, Red, '97 138
Salad, Ruby-and-Emerald, '85 79
Sauce, Green Bell Pepper, '97 261
Sauce, Pepper-Onion, '84 125
Sauce, Red or Green Pepper, '91 85
Sausage and Peppers, Italian, '84 9
Sautéed Onions and Peppers, '83 M148
Sauté, Tomato-Pepper, '84 142
Soup, Green Pepper, '88 250
Soup, Mexican Cheese, '97 268
Spaghetti with Pork and Peppers, '98 131
Spread, Roasted Pepper, '94 123
Squash Oregano, Summer, '97 165
Stacks, Pepper-Cheese, '87 80
Steak and Rice, Pepper, '81 17
Steak, Pepper, '81 273; '85 57; '88 113
Steak, Pepper-Beef, '85 21
Steak, Simple Pepper, '01 82
Stir-Fried Sweet Peppers with Tomatoes, '93 207
Stir-Fry Steak, Pepper, '81 240
Stuffed Green Peppers, '03 62
Stuffed Green Peppers, Beefy, '81 86
Stuffed Green Peppers, Ham-, '80 65
Stuffed Pepper Medley, '82 131
Stuffed Peppers, '81 239; '83 66; '84 202
Stuffed Peppers, Beef-, '84 154; '85 146; '91 M127
Stuffed Peppers, Corn-, '84 104
Stuffed Peppers, Curried Chicken-, '87 19
Stuffed Peppers for Two, '80 84
Stuffed Peppers, Ham-and-Corn, '81 87
Stuffed Peppers, Hearty, '88 M214
Stuffed Peppers, Macaroni-and-Cheese-, '80 65
Stuffed Peppers, Rice-, '80 65; '99 241
Stuffed Peppers, Shrimp-, '80 162; '86 131, 197; '97 268
Stuffed Peppers, Spinach-, '82 180
Stuffed Peppers with Rice and Ham, '82 131
Stuffed with Beef, Peppers, '84 72
Taco Peppers, '81 86
Turkey with Peppers, '92 182
Veal and Peppers, Spaghetti with, '81 201; '82 14
Grilled Pepper-Pesto Linguine, '04 136
Grill, Three-Pepper, '02 122
Grits, Mexican Cheese, '02 34

Guacamole Crisps, '98 173
Hush Puppies, Mississippi, '97 84

Jalapeño
Afterburners, '03 159
Beans, Texas Pinto, '01 65
Biscuits, Cornmeal-Jalapeño, '94 214
Black-Eyed Peas, Jalapeño, '88 166
Bread, Jalapeño Pepper, '83 121
Brussels Sprouts, Spicy, '02 307
Burgers with Roasted Bell Pepper Ketchup, Jalapeño-Stuffed, '97 318
Butter, Grilled Corn with Jalapeño-Lime, '01 158; '04 178
Butter, Jalapeño, '97 306
Butter, Jalapeño-Chili, '98 156
Butter, Jalapeño-Pecan-Mustard, '03 205
Casserole, Jalapeño Corn, '83 256
Casserole, Jalapeño Rice, '81 66
Celery, Jalapeño Stuffed, '79 70
Cheese, Jalapeño Pimiento, '98 315; '01 169
Cheese, Shrimp with Herbed Jalapeño, '87 112
Cheesy Jalapeño Peppers, '80 195
Chicken Casserole, Jalapeño, '02 50
Chicken, Grilled Jalapeño, '93 213
Chicken, Grilled Lime-Jalapeño, '91 87
Chicken, Easy Jalapeño, '92 310
Chicken Legs, Jalapeño Oven-Fried, '94 94
Chutney, Jeweled Pepper, '94 316
Chutney, Mango, '03 123
Coleslaw, Jalapeño, '97 26
con Queso, Chili, '80 194; '97 25
Cornbread, Beefy Jalapeño, '82 142
Cornbread, Cheddar-Jalapeño, '85 3
Cornbread, Jalapeño, '85 200; '94 78; '98 178
Cornbread, Southwestern Hot-Water, '01 29
Cups, Hot Vegetable Pepper, '88 M188
Dip, Mexican Fiesta, '98 234
Dressing, Creamy Jalapeño-Cilantro, '04 311
Eggs, Armadillo, '97 270
Eggs, Mexican Deviled, '04 93
Fried Jalapeños, '96 292
Fritters, Corn-Jalapeño, '96 153
Fritters, Squash-Jalapeño, '98 249
Grits, Jalapeño Cheese, '85 43
Grits, Jalapeño-Cheese, '00 239; '01 328
Guacamole, Margarita, '97 167
Heroes, Open-Faced Jalapeño, '90 144
Hominy, Jalapeño, '82 51
Hush Puppies, Jalapeño, '05 99
Jelly, Easiest Pepper, '03 135
Jelly, Jalapeño, '92 230; '96 292
Jelly, Mint, '03 135
Jelly, Quick Jalapeño Pepper, '96 275
Jelly, Southwest, '03 135
Loaf, Jalapeño-Cheese, '84 76
Muffins, Jalapeño-Corn, '93 164
Mustard, Jalapeño, '93 240; '95 312
Nachos, Smoked, '01 146
Nachos, Tuna, '96 201
New Potatoes, Cheesy Jalapeño, '01 89
Nut Mix, Jalapeño, '96 217
Onion Rings, South-of-the-Border, '96 217
Pickled Jalapeño Peppers, '93 136
Pico de Gallo, '04 32
Pie, Jalapeño Cheese, '96 292
Pimiento Cheese, Jalapeño, '03 315
Pork, Jalapeño Grilled, '99 160
Pork Tenderloin, Jalapeño-Glazed, '03 186
Pork Tenderloins, Pepper-Honey, '98 33
Potatoes, Jalapeño, '84 39
Potatoes, Jalapeño-Ham Stuffed, '81 M61
Puffs, Cajun Hot, '94 277
Quesadillas, Bacon-Jalapeño-Tomato, '95 240
Quesadillas, Western, '97 65

PEPPERS, Jalapeño
(continued)

Quiche, Cheesy Jalapeño, '84 31
Quiche, Jalapeño-Corn, '85 122
Quiche Squares, Cheesy Hot, '79 124
Rice, Hot Pepper, '92 310
Rice, Jalapeño, '79 43
Rice, Jalapeño Hot, '80 126
Rollups, Mexican, '98 134
Salad, Jalapeño Potato, '97 64
Salsa, Cranberry-Jalapeño, '01 234
Salsa, Double Chile, '91 182
Salsa, Hot, '98 135
Salsa Picante, '84 108
Salsa Picante, Homemade, '81 67
Salsa Verde, Roasted, '96 182
Salsa, Watermelon, '98 164
Sauce, Fried Green Tomatillos with Jalapeño
　Dipping, '97 143
Sauce, Hot Chile, '92 156
Sauce, Jalapeño, '80 193; '93 230
Sauce, Jalapeño-Cranberry, '92 310
Sauce, Jalapeño Tartar, '96 69; '98 129
Sauce, San Antonio Hot, '84 291
Sausage, Grilled Pork, Cheddar, and Jalapeño,
　'98 311
Sherbet, Jalapeño-Mint, '98 202
Shortbread, Jalapeño-Pecan, '03 108
Spread, Jalapeño-Cheese, '82 248
Squares, Jalapeño Cheese, '80 195
Stuffed Jalapeño Peppers, '96 215
Stuffed Jalapeño Peppers, Fried, '95 22
Stuffed Jalapeños, '98 234
Stuffed Jalapeños, Fiery Fried, '90 118
Stuffed Jalapeños, Hot, '99 123
Stuffed Jalapeños, Shrimp-, '88 115
Tacos, Shrimp-and-Pepper Soft, '95 339
Texas Rockets, '05 175
Vinegar, Southwest, '94 200
Ketchup, Jalapeño-Stuffed Burgers with Roasted Bell
　Pepper, '97 318
Lamb, Rosemary-Skewered, '97 190
Linguine with Sausage and Peppers, '03 170
Marinated Roasted Peppers, '97 123
Meatball Packets, Italian, '04 222
Olives, Marinated, '01 187
Pasta, Chicken-and-Pepper, '03 199
Pasta, Three Pepper-Sausage, '02 122
Pasta with Peppers and Broccoli, '91 69
Peas, A Mess of, '00 158
Pico de Gallo, '04 61
Pizza, Mexican Chicken, '97 321
Pizza, Peppers-and-Cheese, '03 235
Pork Chops with White Rice, '02 312
Red
Bread, Roasted Red Bell Pepper, '95 241
Brie en Croûte, Stuffed, '97 162
Bruschetta, Red-and-Green, '01 62
Bruschetta, Roasted Red Pepper, '00 278
Butter, Fillet of Beef with Red Pepper, '96 32
Butter, Roasted Red Bell Pepper, '95 242
Carrots, Balsamic Baby, '02 43
Cheese, Grilled, '97 328
Crêpes, Goat Cheese-Filled Cornbread, '98 43
Crostini, Roasted Peppers-Feta Cheese, '96 87
Crostini, Spinach-Red Pepper, '03 34
Cucumber-and-Pepper Combo, '88 176
Cups, Hot Vegetable Pepper, '88 M188
Curried Corn and Sweet Red Peppers, '95 47
Dip, Chickpea-and-Red Pepper, '99 138
Dressing, Roasted Red Pepper-Dill, '02 144
Focaccia, Rosemary-Red Pepper, '01 307

Fries, Red Pepper-Polenta, '00 196
Green Beans with Shallots and Red Bell Pepper,
　'97 251
Hummus, Red Pepper, '00 132; '02 31; '05 97
Jam, Red Bell Pepper, '95 242
Jelly, Red Pepper, '89 M156
Marinated Cheese, Olives, and Peppers, '04 238
Marinated Mirlitons, Artichokes, and Peppers,
　'00 246
Marinated Olives and Peppers, '04 71
Mayonnaise, Roasted Red Pepper, '98 144
Okra, Corn, and Peppers, '87 M151
Pasta with Greens, Creamy, '00 91
Peas and Peppers, Minted, '90 M99
Peas and Peppers, Stir-Fried, '87 51
Pizza, Red Pepper Hummus, '01 56
Pizza, Roasted Pepper, '94 218
Potatoes with Sweet Red Peppers, '87 192
Puree, Red Pepper, '93 275; '00 241
Rémoulade Sauce, Red Pepper, '01 145
Roasted Pepper-Tomato Bruschetta, '02 213
Roasted Pepper Vinaigrette, '04 142
Roasted Red Bell Pepper Dressing, '03 28
Roasted Red Pepper-and-Vidalia Onion Gravy,
　'03 323
Roasted Red Pepper-Caesar Tortelloni, '05 M186
Roasted Red Pepper Cream, Shrimp with, '03 97
Roasted Red Pepper-Feta Crostini, '04 69
Roasted Red Pepper Rémoulade, '04 144
Roasted Red Pepper Salad, Chicken and, '03 291
Roasted Red Peppers and Pearl Onions, Green Beans
　with, '93 260
Roasted Red Peppers, Potato Salad with, '04 100
Rollups, Artichoke-Red Pepper, '02 231
Rollups, Roasted Red Pepper, '98 285
Roll with Cilantro Hollandaise Sauce, Southwestern,
　'99 16
Round Steak, Red Pepper, '88 214
Salad, Broccoli and Red Pepper, '83 224
Salad, Roasted Red Pepper-and-Green Bean,
　'99 322
Salad, Roasted Red Pepper and Watercress, '90 55
Salad, Tuna-and-Red Pepper, '93 143
Salad with Avocado, Potato, '98 332
Salsa, Roasted Red Pepper, '01 100
Sandwiches, Mozzarella-Pepper Bagel, '98 145
Sandwiches, Smoked Turkey-Roasted Pepper, '94 66
Sauce, Linguine with Red Pepper, '93 127
Sauce, Red Bell Pepper, '99 267
Sauce, Red or Green Pepper, '91 85
Sauce, Red Pepper, '98 322; '02 165
Sauce, Red Pepper-Garlic, '98 140
Sauce, Roasted Red Bell Pepper, '02 287
Sauce, Roasted Red Pepper, '98 16; '00 58
Sauce, Sweet-'n'-Spicy Red Pepper, '05 321
Sautéed Peppers and Mushrooms, Herb-Stuffed
　Chicken with, '91 26
Shrimp with Onion and Red Pepper, Sweet-and-Sour,
　'02 84
Slaw, Napa Cabbage, '02 280
Snow Peas and Red Pepper, Sesame, '84 175
Snow Peas with Red Pepper, '90 102
Soup, Chilled Roasted Pepper and Tomato, '01 128
Soup, Chilled Sweet Red Pepper, '93 69
Soup, Cream of Roasted Sweet Red Pepper, '95 65
Soup, Creamy Bell Pepper 'n' Tomato, '05 293
Soup, Red Bell Pepper, '98 104
Soup, Roasted Red Pepper, '96 245; '05 72
Soup, Spicy Pepper, '93 98
Spinach with Red Pepper Ribbons, Holiday, '03 260
Spread, Roasted Red Bell Pepper, '97 217
Squash-and-Pepper Toss, Crisp, '87 M152
Stuffed Grilled Bell Peppers, Potato-, '05 123
Stuffed Peppers with Chicken and Corn, '02 147

Stuffed Red Peppers with Cheesy Polenta and Green
　Chiles, '04 169
Sugar Snap Peas with Bell Peppers, '03 255
Tomatoes, Scalloped, '00 183
Vinaigrette, Roasted Bell Pepper, '99 70
Vinaigrette, Roasted Pepper, '00 134
Zucchini, Roasted, '02 89
Relish, Grandma's Pepper, '04 158
Relish, Hot, '01 123
Roasted Pepper Quesadillas, Shrimp-and-, '00 215
Roasted Peppers and Beans, Herbed Turkey Strips with,
　'04 282
Roasted Tomato-and-Pepper Salad, '01 196
Salad, Gazpacho-Chicken, '00 203
Salad, Grilled Tomato, Bell Pepper, and Portobello,
　'98 211
Salad, Hot Tomato, '05 129
Salad, Pasta, '00 213
Salad, Winter Cabbage, '98 284
Salsa, '01 273
Salsa, Banana, '96 85
Salsa, Caribbean, '96 70
Salsa, Cha-Cha, '97 160
Salsa, Cherry, '99 156
Salsa, Corn, '00 164
Salsa, Fiery, '01 174
Salsa, Fresh Tomatillo, '97 143
Salsa, Mango, '02 163
Salsa, Mango-and-Bell Pepper, '00 247
Salsa, Roasted, '95 130
Salsa, Sweet Pepper-Mango, '05 148
Sandwich, Giant Ham-and-Pepper, '96 74
Sauce, Creamy Roasted Pepper, '96 183
Sauce, Miss Kitty's Chili, '04 231
Sausage and Peppers with Parmesan Cheese Grits,
　'02 233
Scallops and Angel Hair Pasta, '99 176
Shrimp, Charleston Harbor Pickled, '99 275
Shrimp, Marinated, '98 317
Shrimp Rellenos, '00 174
Skillet, Pork-Pepper, '01 309
Soup, Mardi Gras, '96 56
Soup, Roasted Yellow Bell Pepper, '96 56
Steak and Rice, Skillet Pepper, '04 326
Stuffed Peppers, Barbecued Shrimp and Cornbread-,
　'97 261
Stuffed Peppers, Carrot-and-Cabbage, '99 63
Stuffed Peppers, Spicy, '98 243
Sweet
Chicken Breasts with Curried Peppers, '90 227
Chicken Sauté, Sweet Pepper-, '89 104
Chicken Scaloppine with Peppers, '85 78
Chicken, Sicilian, '97 142
Chowder, Bell Pepper-Cheese, '95 240
Flank Steak with Sweet Peppers, Grilled, '90 138
Green Beans and Pepper Strips, '86 170
Kebabs, Pretty Pepper, '90 166
Kebabs, Summery Squash-and-Pepper, '95 193
Marinated Roasted Peppers, '92 176
Medley, Cabbage-Onion-Sweet Pepper, '96 252;
　'97 28
Medley, Rainbow Pepper, '91 126
Parmesan Pepper Toss, '93 208
Pasta, Peppery, '94 164
Pesto, Pepper, '89 103; '90 97
Relish, Confetti Pepper, '91 195
Relish, Sweet Pepper, '95 104
Roasted Bell Peppers in Olive Oil, '95 242
Roasted Peppers, Marinated, '87 90
Roasted Peppers with Balsamic Vinaigrette, '94 128
Salad, Chilled Turkey-and-Pepper Stir-Fry, '88 140
Salad, Mixed Pepper, '89 103
Salad, Mushroom-and-Pepper, '86 68
Salad, Three-Pepper, '91 162

Salsa, Mixed Pepper, '91 181
Salsa, Yellowfin Tuna with Corn, Pepper, and
Tomato, '94 164
Sausage and Peppers, '95 165
Sausage, Sweet Peppery, '95 69
Sautéed Sweet Peppers, '89 102
Sauté, Julienne Pepper, '89 104
Soup, Bell Pepper, '89 103
Soup, Roasted Pepper-and-Chicken, '90 58
Soup, Sweet Pepper, '93 277
Spread, Roasted Pepper, '94 123
Stuffed with Shrimp-and-Orzo Salad, Peppers,
'91 203
Sugar Snaps and Peppers, '93 139
Tacos, Grilled Pepper, '95 340
Topping, Rainbow Pepper, '90 117
Terrine with Tomato-Basil Vinaigrette, Blue Cheese,
'99 288
Turkey and Peppers in Cornbread Crust, '95 312
Yellow Pepper Sauce, '02 165
Yellow Pepper Sauce, Poached Salmon with, '98 230

PERSIMMONS
Bread, Persimmon, '80 228
Bread, Persimmon Date-Nut, '82 218
Cake, Persimmon, '79 205
Cookies, Persimmon, '96 242
Cookies, Persimmon-Raisin, '85 232
Pie, Persimmon, '79 206
Pudding, Persimmon, '79 206; '00 254
Salad, Persimmon Fruit, '79 206

PESTOS. *See also* **RELISHES, SALSAS, SAUCES,**
TOPPINGS.
Basil Pesto, '03 208; '04 101
Basil Pesto Focaccia, '00 195
Bow-Tie Pesto, '94 231
Butter, Pesto, '97 307
Cilantro-Black Walnut Pesto, Littleneck Clams with,
'97 164
Cilantro-Pecan Pesto, '04 36
Cilantro Pesto, '98 145; '00 148
Dip, Pesto, '95 93; '97 226
Dip with Tortellini, Creamy Tomato Pesto, '00 196
Dried Tomato-Basil Pesto, '04 101
Fresh Pesto, '86 150
Garden Pesto, '04 186
Garden Pesto, Lucinda's, '01 100
Garlic Pesto, '84 108
Goat Cheese, Pesto, '03 110
Homemade Pesto, '01 22
Nuts, Pesto-Spiced, '95 173
Olive-Rosemary Pesto, '01 317
Pasta, Asian Pesto, '95 189
Pasta, Pesto and, '92 98
Peanut Pesto, Thai, '98 145
Pepper Pesto, '89 103; '90 97
Pesto, '80 242; '96 207; '00 118
Pizza, Nutty Pesto, '97 267
Poblano-Cilantro Pesto, Central Market's, '04 101
Primavera, Pesto, '96 170
Roasted Garlic-Basil Pesto, '98 145
Roasted Garlic-Rosemary Pesto, '97 46
Rosemary Pesto, Grilled Pork Tenderloins with, '04 82
Ruth's Pesto, '96 170
Sage Pesto, '97 22
Sauce, Pasta with Pesto-Clam, '98 17
Sauce, Pesto, '89 280; '91 94; '95 267
Sauce, Racy Pesto, '97 67
Sauce, Walnut-Parmesan Pesto, '96 251; '97 104
Shortbread, Pesto, '03 108
Spinach-Peanut Pesto and Pasta, '93 212
Spinach Pesto-Pasta, '91 314
Spinach Pesto Sauce, '93 59
Tart, Tomato-Pesto, '00 195
Thyme Pesto, Sirloin Steaks with, '97 182

Tomatoes Pesto, '86 150
Tomato Pesto, Dried, '90 204; '94 249; '01 62
Torte, Pesto, '02 278
PETITS FOURS. *See* CAKES/Petits Fours.
PHEASANT. *See* GAME.
PICANTE SAUCE. *See* SALSAS, SAUCES.
PICKLES
Asparagus, Pickled, '83 46; '04 161
Beet Pickles, '81 210
Beets, Easy Pickled, '80 137
Beets, Pickled, '81 216; '97 229; '02 138
Broccoli, Pickled, '81 308
Cantaloupe, Sweet Pickled, '89 197
Carrots, Pickled, '93 12
Chayote Squash Pickles, '89 197
Cucumber Chips, '85 176
Cucumber Pickles, Freezer, '99 87
Cucumber Pickles, Sour, '85 176
Cucumber Rounds, Easy Pickled, '90 143
Cucumber Sandwich Pickles, '81 174
Dill Pickle Rémoulade, '04 311
Dill Pickles, '81 174
Dill Pickles, Fried, '84 206
Dills, Lazy Wife, '87 149
Eggs, Beet Pickled, '84 287
Eggs, Spiced Pickled, '84 288
Figs, Pickled, '79 140
Fire-and-Ice Pickles, '94 316
Green Tomato Pickles, '87 134; '01 141
Hot-and-Sweet Freezer Pickles, '04 160
Icicle Pickles, Sweet, '85 176
Jalapeño Peppers, Pickled, '93 136
Lime Pickles, '96 206
Mixed Pickles, '81 174
No-Cook Sweet-and-Spicy Pickles, '04 176
Okra Dills, '97 157
Okra Pickles, '81 173
Onion Rings, Pickled Refrigerator, '84 265
Onions, Pickled Cocktail, '89 197
Peaches, Perfect Pickled, '85 178
Peach Pickles, '85 177; '99 170
Pear Pickles, Mustard, '79 196
Peppery Texas Pickles, '04 M161
Pineapple, Pickled, '79 24
Problem Chart, Pickle, '85 176
Squash Pickles, '81 174; '87 150; '97 119; '99 170
Sweet Pickles, Quick, '87 149
Tempura Dill Pickles, '04 123
Watermelon Rind Pickles, '81 174; '84 106; '98 164
Yellow Squash, Pickled, '93 136
Zucchini, Dilled Fresh, '81 174
PIES, PUFFS, AND PASTRIES
Almond Pie, Toasted, '86 163
Ambrosia Pie, '79 284
Angel Pie, '79 123; '80 238
Apple. *See also* PIES, PUFFS, AND PASTRIES/
Cobblers, Crisps, and Crumbles; Pastries;
Tarts; Turnovers.
Amandine Pie, Apple-, '89 215
American Apple Pie, '91 197
Applesauce Pie, '98 259; '99 26; '01 213
Autumn Apple Pie, '79 205
Berry-Apple Pie, '88 251
Blackberry-Apple Pie, '87 130
Bourbon Pie, Apple-, '95 302
Brandy-Apple Pie, '86 301
Brandy Raisin-Apple Pie, '83 192
Buttermilk Custard Pie, Warm Apple-, '99 98
Cake, Apple Pie, '82 226
Chess Pie, Apple-Lemon, '86 220
Cider Pie, Apple, '84 227
Cinnamon Crème, Apple Pie with Warm, '99 337
Cinnamon Sauce, Apple Pie with Hot, '88 210
Covered Apple Cake, '89 317

Cran-Apple Pie, '92 304
Cranberry-Apple Holiday Pie, '81 M269
Cranberry-Apple Pie, '79 264
Cranberry-Apple-Raisin Pie, '98 270
Cranberry Pie, Apple-, '97 276; '99 M269
Cream Cheese Pie, Apple-, '81 247
Custard Pie, Apple, '88 236
Dutch Apple Pie, '81 105; '82 273
Easy-Crust Apple Pie, '87 11
Fresh Apple Pie, '84 178
Fried Apple Pies, '81 217; '86 302; '88 112, 225;
'94 61
Fried Pies, Honeyed Apple-Cranberry, '02 214
Georgie's Apple Pie, '02 325
Grandmother's Apple Pie, '87 212
Granny Smith Apple Pie, '01 143
Grated Apple Pie, '83 304
Holiday Apple Pie, '87 260
Honey Apple Pie, '00 331
Lemon-Apple Pie, Tart, '80 100
Maple Pie, Apple-, '97 276
Mexican Apple Pie, '94 97
Mincemeat Pie, Apple-, '85 316
No-Crust Apple Pie, '88 204
Old-Fashioned Apple Pie, '82 M299; '88 94
Pear-Apple Pie, Natural, '88 226
Pear Pie, Apple-, '83 249
Pear Pull-Up Pie, Apple-, '98 259
Pineapple Pie, Apple-, '97 276
Praline-Apple Pie, '99 331; '05 251
Raisin Brandy Pie, Apple-, '89 58
Red Apple Pie, '79 282
Upside-Down Southern Apple Pie, '88 226
Apricot Cream Fried Pies, '00 212
Apricot Fried Pies, '86 269
Apricot Hand Pies, Dried, '98 259
Apricot Pies, Fried, '95 215
Apricot Pies, Special, '94 60
Apricot Pie, Yogurt-, '85 132
Apricot Surprise Pie, '88 99
Banana Cream Pie, '84 48; '87 207
Banana Cream Pie, Hawaiian, '90 105
Banana Pie with Hot Buttered Rum Sauce, '88 204
Bavarian Cream Pie, '79 281
Blackberry Cream Pie, '81 132
Blackberry Pie, '84 141; '86 152
Blackberry Pie, Creamy, '88 179
Blackberry Pie, Fresh, '03 164
Black Walnut Pie, '97 275; '98 35
Blueberry. *See also* **PIES, PUFFS, AND**
PASTRIES/Cobblers, Crisps, and Crumbles.
Banana Pie, Blueberry-, '93 115
Chilled Blueberry Pie, '89 136
Cream Cheese Pie, Blueberry-, '88 154
Cream Pie, Blueberry, '84 142
Cream Pie, Fresh Blueberry, '80 144
Fresh Blueberry Pie, '83 183; '85 152
Kuchen, Blueberry, '80 143
Lemon-Blueberry Cream Pie, '02 92
Old-Fashioned Blueberry Pie, '89 136
Peach Pie, Blueberry-, '94 158
Red, White, and Blueberry Pie, '98 162
Sour Cream Pie, Blueberry-, '83 183
Spicy Blueberry Pie, '96 147
Streusel Pie, Fresh Blueberry, '89 137
Boston Cream Pie, '83 220
Bourbon Pie, Kentucky, '84 87
Boysenberry Pie, '82 133
Brownie Pie, Crustless, '82 33
Bumbleberry Pie, '97 163
Buttermilk Chess Pie, '92 214
Buttermilk-Lemon Cream Pie, '88 99
Buttermilk Lemon Pie, '81 120; '82 23
Buttermilk-Lemon Pie, '88 297

PIES, PUFFS, AND PASTRIES
(continued)

Buttermilk Pie, '82 53; '83 158; '88 93; '92 95; '98 290
Buttermilk Pie, Lemon-, '91 272
Buttermilk Pie, Old-Fashioned, '79 72
Buttermilk Pie, Rancher's, '04 208
Butterscotch Cream Pie, '84 48; '87 207
Butterscotch Meringue Pie, '83 158
Butterscotch Pie, '97 212
Cantaloupe Cream Pie, '79 177
Cantaloupe Meringue Pie, '88 182
Cantaloupe Pie, '86 163
Caramel-Banana Pie, '86 M165
Caramel Banana Pie, Luscious, '79 115
Caramel Meringue Pie, '97 109
Caramel-Nut Crunch Pie, '94 244
Caramel-Peanut Pie, '86 259
Caramel Pie, '96 72
Caramel Pie, Burnt, '82 53
Caviar Pie, '79 154
Cheese. *See also* **PIES, PUFFS, AND**
 PASTRIES/Crusts, Pastries, Tarts, Turnovers,
 Vegetable.
 Apple-Cream Cheese Pie, '81 247
 Blueberry-Cream Cheese Pie, '88 154
 Chocolate-Cream Cheese Pie, '80 69
 Chocolate Cream Cheese Pie, '92 240
 Cottage Cheese Pie, '82 85
 Cream Puffs with Chicken Salad, Cheesy, '86 260
 Fruited Cheese Pie, '92 228
 Hors d'Oeuvre Pie, Cheesy, '88 91
 Lemon Cheese Pie, '81 136; '82 146
 Lemon-Cottage Cheese Pie, '79 44
 Lemon Cottage Cheese Pie, '81 143
 Make-Ahead Cheesecake Pie, '81 233
 Mascarpone Cream Pie with Berry Glaze, '00 312
 Mincement-Cheese Pie, '80 253
 Phyllo Cheesecakes, Little, '87 275
 Tiramisù Toffee Trifle Pie, '00 312
 Yogurt-Cheese Pie, '82 121
Cherry-Berry Pie, '92 316
Cherry Confetti Pie, No-Bake, '93 114
Cherry Cream Pie with Almond Pastry, '92 30
Cherry Pie, Chocolate-Covered, '05 M216
Cherry Pie, Coconut Crumb, '92 30
Cherry Pie, Easy, '82 299
Cherry Pie, Fresh, '88 178
Cherry Pie, Lemony, '92 30
Cherry Pie, Prize-Winning, '82 57
Cherry Pie, Red, '83 192
Cherry Pie, Scrumptious, '83 250
Chess Pie, Brown Sugar, '86 220
Chess Pie, Buttermilk, '92 214
Chess Pie, Classic, '00 60; '02 107
Chess Pie, Old-Fashioned, '86 220
Chocolate. *See also* **PIES, PUFFS, AND**
 PASTRIES/Crusts, Ice Cream, Pastries, Tarts.
 Almond Pie, Creamy Chocolate-, '85 102
 Amandine, Chocolate Pie, '83 300
 Amaretto Mousse Pie, Chocolate-, '80 180; '81 30
 Banana-Pecan Cream Pie, Chocolate-, '94 210
 Bavarian Pie, Chocolate, '89 326
 Berry Pie, Heavenly Chocolate-, '85 102
 Best-Ever Chocolate Pie, '88 M45
 Black Bottom Pie, '82 53
 Black-Bottom Pie, '98 161
 Black Bottom Pie, Weidmann's, '95 118
 Bourbon Pecan Pie, Chocolate-, '05 134
 Bourbon Pie, Chocolate, '88 99
 Cake, Chocolate Pastry, '91 196
 Chess Pie, Chocolate, '81 161; '86 220; '92 13
 Chess Pie, Chocolate-Pecan, '00 60; '02 107

Chilled Chocolate Pie, '88 99
Chip Pie, Chocolate, '85 114
Coffee Cream Pie, '94 209
Cream Cheese Pie, Chocolate-, '80 69
Cream Cheese Pie, Chocolate, '92 240
Cream Pie, Chocolate, '83 192; '84 49; '87 208;
 '94 208
Creamy Chocolate Pie, '85 298; '86 119
Double Chocolate Pie, '82 M282
Easy Chocolate Pie, '83 158
Fox Hunter's Pie, '97 109
French Silk Pie, '80 247
Frozen Chocolate Brownie Pie, '96 57
Frozen Chocolate-Macadamia Nut Pie, '96 254
Frozen Chocolate Pie, '80 154
Frozen Chocolate Pie with Pecan Crust, '89 291;
 '98 180
Fudge Pie, '87 168; '89 252; '01 129
Fudge Pie, Chocolate, '98 336
Fudge Pie, Sweetheart, '86 316; '90 313
German Chocolate Pie, '93 129
Heaven, Chocolate, '98 323
Heavenly Chocolate Pie, '87 260
Icebox Pie, Chocolate, '05 157
Meringue Pie, Chocolate, '80 238; '82 206; '83 158;
 '92 216
Meringue Pie, Chocolate-Filled, '86 121
Microwave Chocolate Pie, '90 M15
Mint Pie, Brownie-, '97 303
Mocha Crunch Pie, Chocolate-, '81 136
Mocha Pie, '94 168
Mousse Pie, Chocolate, '81 136
Mud Pie, Decadent, '89 252
Mud Pie, Mississippi, '89 26
Mud Pie, Tipsy, '80 255; '97 251
Peanut Butter Pie, Chocolate-, '85 91
Peanut Butter Swirl Pie, Chocolate-, '87 262
Pecan Chess Pie, Chocolate-, '93 251
Pecan Fudge Pie with Raspberry Sauce, '05 201
Pecan Pie, Bourbon-Chocolate, '98 258
Pecan Pie, Choco, '82 86
Pecan Pie, Chocolate, '80 237; '83 12; '90 184
Pecan Pie, Chocolate-, '91 272; '02 176
Pecan Pie, Turtle, '93 250
Peppermint Pie, Fudgy Chocolate Malt-, '00 313
Pizza Dolce (Italian Sweet Pies), '00 283
Praline Pie, Chocolate-, '86 259
Silk Pie, Chocolate, '88 67
Strawberry-Chocolate Truffle Pie, '89 112
Walnut Pie, Chocolate-, '05 134
Whipped Cream Pie, Chocolate, '79 124
White Chocolate-Banana Cream Pie, '94 314
Christmas Pie, White, '88 281; '93 289
Cobblers, Crisps, and Crumbles
 à la Mode, Apple Cobbler, '97 16
 Apple Bake, Cinnamon-, '04 29
 Apple-Berry Cobbler, '04 330
 Apple Brown Betty, '05 232
 Apple Cobbler, Country, '99 255
 Apple Cobbler, Easy, '83 174
 Apple Cobbler for Two, '85 261
 Apple Cobbler, New-Fashioned, '91 221
 Apple Crisp, '84 122; '98 215
 Apple Crisp, Tart, '92 226
 Apple Dumpling Cobbler, '04 29
 Apple-Gingerbread Cobbler, '03 21; '04 219
 Apple-Pear Cobbler with Oatmeal Muffin Crust,
 Caramel, '04 201
 Apple-Pecan Cobbler, '84 M198
 Apple-Pecan Pie Cobbler, '04 200
 Apple-Vinegar Biscuit Cobbler, '01 215
 Apple Walnut Cobbler, '79 154
 Apple-Walnut Cobbler, '81 248
 Apricot Cobbler with Custard Sauce, '97 16

Apricot Cobble Up, '82 138
Berry-Cherry Cobbler, '83 270
Berry Cobbler, Mixed-, '02 214
Berry Cobbler, Three-, '04 29
Berry Cobbler, Too-Easy, '04 28
Berry Crisp, '83 130
Blackberry-Almond Cobbler, '81 132
Blackberry Cobbler, '82 139; '83 175; '99 131;
 '02 17
Blackberry Cobbler, Deep-Dish, '80 186
Blackberry Cobbler, Deluxe, '81 132
Blackberry Cobbler, Juicy, '89 137
Blackberry Cobbler, New-Fashioned, '87 164
Blackberry Cobbler, Southern, '81 132
Blueberry Buckle, '85 30
Blueberry Cobbler, '83 175
Blueberry Cobbler, Easy, '83 183
Blueberry Cobbler, Fresh, '80 144
Blueberry Cobbler, Peachy, '80 143
Blueberry Cobbler, Warm, '98 153
Blueberry Crisp, '84 177
Blueberry Crunch, Fresh, '82 143
Blueberry, Huckle-Buckle, '86 151
Blueberry-Peach Cobbler, No-Dough, '86 177
Blueberry-Pecan Cobbler, '00 154; '03 106
Blueberry Pinwheel Cobbler, '87 140
Blueberry Slump, Quick, '91 20
Blueberry Upside-Down Cobbler, '96 146
Boysenberry Cobbler, '82 133
Caramel-Applesauce Cobbler with Bourbon-Pecan
 Ice Cream, '00 260
Cherry-Apple Bake, '04 29
Cherry Cheesecake Cobbler, Double-, '03 21
Cherry Cobbler, '82 91, 139; '99 156
Cherry Cobbler, Colossal, '89 137
Cherry Cobbler, Fresh, '84 178
Cherry Cobbler, Too-Easy, '04 28
Cherry Crisp, '91 20
Cherry Slump, '83 139
Citrus-Pear Honey Cobbler, '05 230
Cranberry-and-Apple Cobbler, '84 306; '90 294
Cranberry-Apple Cobbler with Cinnamon Biscuits,
 '99 256
Cranberry Cobbler, '81 275
Cranberry Cobbler, Easy, '86 260
Cranberry Cobbler Roll, '80 288; '81 248
Cranberry-Peach Cobbler, '92 322
Cranberry-Pear Crisp, '83 207; '97 16
Cran-Blueberry Cobbler, '04 28
Fig-and-Raspberry Cobbler, '02 160
Fig Cobbler, '79 140
Fig Cobbler, Cajun, '94 196
Fig Cobbler, Super, '86 206
Fruit Cobbler, '99 33
Fruit Cobbler, Quick, '91 20
Ginger-Pear Cobbler, '03 232
Grenadine-Peach Cobbler, '85 178
Lemon-Blackberry Crisp, '98 171
Muscadine Cobbler, '98 221
Nectarine Cobbler with Blueberry Muffin Crust,
 '04 200
Peach-and-Raspberry Crisp, '02 232
Peach-Apricot Cobbler, '99 255
Peach-Caramel Cobbler, '86 300; '87 178
Peach Cobbler, '83 175; '84 178; '90 219; '95 264
Peach Cobbler, Double Crust, '03 310
Peach Cobbler, Easy, '97 137; '99 206
Peach Cobbler, Fresh, '82 139; '89 154
(Peach Cobbler), I Fall to Peaches, '96 159
Peach Cobbler, Lattice-Topped, '79 154
Peach Cobbler, Old-Fashioned, '82 170
Peach Cobbler, Quick, '79 215; '81 142
Peach Cobbler, Spicy, '85 178
Peach Cobbler Supreme, '81 184; '90 313

Peach Cobbler, Too-Easy, '04 28
Peach Cobbler with Praline Biscuits, '92 180
Peach Crinkle, '91 20
Peach Crisp, '83 113; '92 13; '93 134
Peach Crumble, Easy, '83 116
Pear Cobbler, Best Ever, '82 194
Pear Crisp, '02 M233; '05 214
Pear Crumble, '85 221
Pear-Ginger Cobbler, '01 214
Pecan-Peach Cobbler, '04 120
Pineapple-Apple Betty, '85 46
Pineapple Crisp, Tropical, '02 232
Plum Brown Betty, Bourbon-, '97 177
Plum Cobbler, '99 254; '03 161
Plum Cobbler, Crunchy, '88 152
Plum Cobbler with Spiced Plum Muffin Crust,
   '04 201
Pumpkin Crisp, '05 269
Raspberry-Cherry Cobbler, '93 230
Strawberry Cobbler, Fresh, '96 84
Strawberry-Rhubarb Cobbler, '88 93
Strawberry-Rhubarb Cobbler, Rosy, '79 154
Strawberry-Rhubarb Crisp, '95 119
Sweet Potato-Apple Cobbler, '04 M232
Sweet Potato Cobbler, '99 255; '01 214
Vegetable Cobbler, Autumn, '01 215

Coconut
Blender Coconut Pie, '84 236
Butter Coconut Pie, '01 244
Buttermilk-Coconut Pie, '94 246
Caramel Pies, Coconut-, '87 260
Cherry Pie, Coconut Crumb, '92 30
Chess Pie, Coconut, '86 220; '00 60; '02 107
Chess Pie, Coconut-Orange, '89 169
Chess Pie, Coconut-Pecan, '81 248
Cloud, Coconut, '80 70
Coconut Pie, '93 115
Cream Pie, Coconut, '80 238; '81 136; '82 85;
   '84 49; '87 207; '89 236; '90 312; '98 161;
   '02 92; '03 106; '05 110
Cream Pie, Fresh Coconut, '80 289
Cream Pie, Surprise Coconut, '92 43
Creamy Coco-Nana Pie, '00 95
Crunch Pie, Coconut, '90 105
Custard Pie, Coconut, '82 33
French Coconut Pie, '90 162
Macadamia Nut Pie, Coconut-, '97 110
Macaroon Pie, Coconut, '88 204
Magic Coconut Pie, '79 53
Mock Coconut Pie, '86 200
Orange-Coconut Cream Pie, '94 208
Orange-Coconut Pie, '90 90
Pecan Pie, Coconut, '81 161
Pineapple Pie, Coconut-, '84 256
Puffs, Coconut, '87 277
Quick Coconut Pie, '83 115
Toasted Coconut Pie, '90 105
Coffee Cream Pie, '94 209
Coffee Pie, '96 148
Cracker Pie, '79 113
Cranberry-Cherry Pie, Tart, '87 299
Cranberry Freezer Pie, Festive, '84 306
Cranberry Pie, Frosty, '79 249
Cranberry Pie, Nutty, '82 M298
Cranberry Pie, Walnut-, '87 259
Cranberry-Raisin Pie, '80 283; '85 316
Cranberry Streusel Pie, '98 258
Cran-Raspberry Pie, '87 244
Cream Pie, Texas, '81 181
Crème de Menthe Pie, Quick, '88 127
Crusts. *See also* **PIES, PUFFS, AND PASTRIES/**
   Pastries.
Black Iron Skillet Piecrust, Universal, '99 33
Brown Sugar Crust, '92 118

Butter Crust, '90 173
Cereal Piecrust, Crisp, '82 209; '83 100
Cheese Crust, '80 286; '86 264
Cheese Grits Crust Batter, '03 21
Chocolate-Coconut Crust, '87 261
Chocolate-Coconut Pie Shell, '82 210; '83 100
Chocolate Crumb Crust, '87 261
Chocolate Crust, '87 264; '90 M15
Chocolate Cups, '80 207
Chocolate-Macadamia Crumb Crust, '96 254
Chocolate Wafer Crust, '89 42, 93
Cinnamon Meringue Shell, '82 263
Coconut Crust, '89 160; '05 157
Cookie Crust, Spicy, '88 7
Cornbread Crust Batter, '03 20
Cracker Crust, '88 97
Cranberry-Pecan Crusts, '02 198
Crumb Crust, Cheesy, '88 86
Crust, '89 272
Decorating Pie Crusts, '83 248
Deluxe Piecrust, '79 79
Gingersnap Crumb Crust, '96 279
Ginger Snap Crust, '88 138
Gingersnap Crust, '89 93; '90 296; '98 161; '01 187
Graham Cracker Crust, '79 45; '86 32; '87 139, 243;
   '88 M45, 55, 67; '89 93, 326; '90 296; '91 197,
   M234, 308; '94 310
Graham Cracker Crust, Microwaved, '82 M141
Graham Cracker Crust, Peanut-, '79 50
Graham Cracker Crusts, '97 162
Graham Crust, Peanut-, '99 49
Italian Sweet Crust, Plum Pie with, '79 162
Lattice Crust, '90 294
Macadamia Nut Crusts, Coconut Cream Tarts with,
   '97 62
Nut Crust, Spiced, '87 295
Nutty Oat Crust, '89 251
Oatmeal Piecrust, '79 79
Parmesan Crust, '94 304
Pecan Crust, '86 317; '89 291; '98 180
Perfect Piecrust, Making, '82 234
Pizza Crust, '80 233; '83 226; '86 77
Pizza Crust, Crispy, '87 181
Rice-Cheese Shell, '82 49
Rice Crust, Crispy, '84 43
Spice Crust, '82 298
Sugar Cookie Crust, '93 131
Tart Crust, '84 178; '90 58; '97 86
Vanilla Wafer Crust, '98 216
Wafer Crust, '02 209
Whole Wheat Crust, '82 298
Custard Pie, Egg, '99 82
Custard Pie, Old-Fashioned Egg, '82 261
Custard Pie, Perfect, '82 92
Custard Pie, Quick 'n' Easy, '96 28
Daiquiri Pie, '79 68
Daiquiri Pie, Daring, '92 191
Dream Pie, '80 90
Eggnog Chiffon Pie, '86 281
Eggnog Pie, '80 254; '83 205; '86 317; '87 295
Eggnog Pie, Fluffy, '81 M269
Empanadas de Calabaza (Pumpkin Empanadas), '94 28
Fried Pies, '96 109
Fried Pies, Delicious, '83 84
Fried Pies, Dried Cherry-and-Pear, '00 213
Fried Pies with Fruit Salsa, Lone Star, '97 124
Fried Strawberry Pies, '02 147
Frozen Hawaiian Pie, '05 157
Fruitcake Pie, '80 237
Fruit Pie, Crispy-Crust, '88 68
Fruit Pie, Dried, '83 249
Fruit Pie, Japanese, '80 238
Fruit Pies, Baked, '84 7
Grapefruit Chess Pie, '01 23

Grapefruit Meringue Pie, '96 56
Grape Juice Pie, '79 123
Grape Pie, '85 212
Grasshopper Freeze, Creamy, '81 180
Grasshopper Pie, '83 145
Ice Cream
Absolutely Divine Ice Cream Pie, '82 181
Caramel Ice Cream Pie, '82 181
Carrot Ice Cream Pie, '86 200
Chocolate-Ice Cream Pie, '87 224
Chocolate Ice Cream Pie, '91 56
Chocolate-Mint Ice Cream Pie, '81 144
Chocolate-Peanut Butter Ice Cream Pie, '98 244
Coffee Ice Cream Pie, '79 231
Delight, Ice Cream, '80 69
Double-Delight Ice Cream Pie, '89 72
Heavenly Ice Cream Pie, '82 181
Kona Ice Cream Pie, '83 189
Lemon Ice Cream Pie, '80 70
Lemony Ice Cream Pie, '99 207
Meringue-Pecan Crust, Ice Cream Pie with, '88 127
Mincemeat Ice Cream Pie, '99 285
Mint Ice Cream Pie, Triple, '98 217
Mocha-Pecan Mud Pie, '05 290
Nutty Ice Cream Pie, '91 180
Orange Cream Pie, '93 35
Peanut Butter Cup Pie, Fudgy, '04 211
Peanutty Ice Cream Pie, '82 56
Peppermint Candy-Ice Cream Pie, '87 260
Pumpkin Ice Cream Pie, '81 272
Pumpkin-Ice Cream Pie, '87 243
Rum-Fruit Sauce, Ice Cream Pie with, '84 312
Spectacular, Ice-Cream Pie, '90 314
Strawberry-Lime Ice-Cream Pie, '05 89
Strawberry-Lime Ice-Cream Pie, Spiked, '05 89
Strawberry Smoothie Ice-Cream Pie, '05 89
Sundae Pie, Ice Cream, '94 244
Jamwiches, Sweetheart, '03 M41
Kahlúa Pie, '83 191
Key Lime Pie, '91 42; '96 171; '00 120; '03 179;
   '04 254
Key Lime Pie, Manny and Isa's, '95 118
Key Lime Pie, Rum-Coconut, '05 157
Key Lime Pies, '95 86; '97 162
Key Lime Pie with Gingersnap Crust, Margarita-,
   '01 187
Key Lime Pie with Minted Tropical Salsa, '99 333
Lemon
Aunt Kitty's Lemon Pie, '98 275
Blueberry Cream Pie, Lemon-, '02 92
Buttermilk-Lemon Cream Pie, '88 99
Buttermilk Lemon Pie, '81 120; '82 23
Buttermilk-Lemon Pie, '88 297
Buttermilk Pie, Lemon-, '91 272
Cheese Pie, Lemon, '81 136; '82 146
Cherry Pie, Lemony, '92 30
Chess Pie, Apple-Lemon, '86 220
Chess Pie, Lemon, '79 32; '82 196; '00 60; '02 107;
   '03 217, 259
Chess Pie, Lemon-Lime, '01 23
Cottage Cheese Pie, Lemon-, '79 44
Cottage Cheese Pie, Lemon, '81 143
Cream Pie, Frozen Lemon, '82 86
Filling, Lemon Icebox Pie, '03 104
Filling, Lemon Meringue Pie, '04 110
Fluff Pie, Lemon, '92 342; '93 46
Frozen Lemonade Pie, '92 101
Heavenly Pie, '83 158
Ice Cream Pie, Lemon, '80 70
Lemonade Pie, '91 42
Magnolia Pie, '94 210
Meringue Pie, Best-Ever Lemon, '94 208
Meringue Pie, Deluxe Lemon, '81 172; '90 313
Meringue Pie, Lemon, '85 M112; '86 130; '04 110

Orange Pie, Lemon-, '85 172
Parfait Pie, Lemon, '94 310
Pastry Shell, Lemon in, '84 137
Pecan Pie, Lemon-, '93 251
Slice of Lemon Pie, '84 23
Sour Cream Pie, Lemon-, '82 169
Sponge Pie, Lemon, '83 192
Strawberry Pie, Lemon-, '88 127
Tart Lemon-Apple Pie, '80 100
Tart Lemon Pie, '91 275
Twirl Pie, Lemon, '84 94
Whipped Lemon Pie, '79 124
Zesty Lemon Pie, '05 157
Lime Chiffon Pie, '86 130
Lime Fluff Pie, '84 43
Lime Party Pies, '92 65
Macadamia Pie, '80 238
Main Dish. *See also* **PIES, PUFFS, AND**
      PASTRIES/Tarts, Turnovers.
Artichoke Pie, '79 25
Barbecue Pot Pie with Cheese Grits Crust, '03 21
Barbecue Pot Pie with Mashed Potato Crust, '03 21
Beef-and-Onion Cornbread Pie, '01 298
Beef in a Blanket, Bourbon Peppered, '00 109
Beef Pies, Carry-Along, '80 224; '81 56
Beef Pie, Sensational, '03 M284
Beef Pies, Fried, '96 108
Beef Pies, Savory, '01 230
Beef Pot Pie, Oriental, '92 253
Beef Pot Pies with Yorkshire Pudding Topping,
      '93 45
Beef Roast Pot Pie, '88 296
Beef Wellingtons, Mini, '01 252
Bouchées aux Fruits de Mer, '98 267
Breakfast Pie, '86 242
Breakfast Pie, Country, '93 M328
Broccoli-and-Turkey Pasta Pie, '88 269
Broccoli-Beef Pie, '83 196
Brunch Egg Nests, '03 246
Brunswick Stew-Cornbread Pie, '02 121
Burrito Pie, Mexican, '87 287
Calzones, All-Star Pizza, '95 308
Calzones, Easy, '99 133
Cheese-Beef Pie, '85 33
Cheeseburger Pie, '89 121
Cheeseburger Pie, Jack-O'-Lantern, '00 234
Cheese Pie, Mexican, '82 9; '83 69
Chicken-and-Egg Pot Pie, '00 98
Chicken Breasts in Phyllo Pastry, '91 105
Chicken Breasts Wellington, '84 22
Chicken Cobbler, Spicy Tex-Mex, '03 324
Chicken Cobbler with Caramelized Onions, '00 44
Chicken, Company Creamed, '82 84
Chicken Dumpling Pie, '95 245; '96 55; '00 336
Chicken in Pastry, '86 122
Chicken in Phyllo, '87 286
Chicken in Phyllo, Cheese-Stuffed, '01 251
Chicken in Phyllo, Cheesy, '02 308
Chicken in Puff Pastry, Spinach-Stuffed, '92 125
Chicken Phyllo Pie, Greek, '92 328
Chicken Pie, '81 281; '82 31
Chicken Pie, Biscuit-Topped, '86 157, 264
Chicken Pie, Cheesy Mexican, '82 142
Chicken Pie, Deluxe, '88 298
Chicken Pie, Double-Crust, '87 111
Chicken Pie, Egg-Stra Special, '86 264
Chicken Pie, Nana's, '90 25
Chicken Pie, Savory Southern, '90 24
Chicken Pot Pie, '81 210; '82 114; '84 21; '94 21;
      '95 54, 256; '96 75; '01 282; '03 247

Chicken Pot Pie, Double-Crust, '90 220
Chicken Pot Pie, Easy, '83 156; '89 218
Chicken Pot Pie in Biscuit Bowls, '03 222
Chicken Pot Pie, Old-Fashioned, '92 271
Chicken Pot Pie, Thick 'n' Crusty, '87 267; '88 102;
      '89 67
Chicken Pot Pie with Cheese Crust, '86 264
Chicken Presents, Holiday, '01 251
Chicken Salad in Cream Puff Bowl, '86 232
Chicken-Vegetable Pot Pie, '81 281; '82 30
Chili-Tamale Pie, '82 9; '83 68
Cornbread-Sausage-Apple Pie, '87 171
Cornbread-Tamale Pie, '92 123
Corn Burger Pie, '83 156
Country Pie, '83 155
Enchilada Pie, '83 155
Fish in a Crust, '84 294
Game Pot Pie with Parmesan Crust, '94 304
Green Chile-Cheese Pie, '84 234
Grits-and-Ham Pie, Crustless, '86 103
Grits Fiesta Pie, '92 43
Ham-and-Cheese Pie, '95 256; '96 75
Ham and Eggs Mornay, '02 130
Ham-and-Greens Pot Pie with Cornbread Crust,
      '03 20
Ham-and-Swiss Breakfast Pie, Savory, '05 240
Ham-Broccoli Pot Pie, '03 83
Hamburger Pie, '81 92; '84 13
Hamburger Pie, Deep-Dish, '00 334
Ham Pie, Golden, '87 78
Ham Pie with Cheese Crust, '80 286
Ham Pot Pie, '90 25
Ham Towers, Cheesy, '82 77
Hot Dog Deluxe, '97 140
Lamb Pie, '90 26
Meat-and-Potato Pie, '84 23
Meat Loaf in a Wrap, '89 122
Meat Pie, Continental, '95 256; '96 75
Meat Pie, Italian, '89 109; '01 297
Meat Pie, Mexicali, '81 194
Meat Pie, Old-Fashioned, '82 110
Meat Pie, Reuben, '80 189
Meat Pies, Cornish, '84 23
Meat Pies, Natchitoches, '84 21; '91 241
Omelet Pie, '00 M35
Oyster Pie, Creole, '84 214
Pancake, Supper, '86 242
Pea Flips, '80 7
Pineapple-Chicken Salad Pie, '80 138
Pizza Pie, Meaty, '03 145
Pot Pie Filling, '03 247
Pulled Pork Tortilla Pie with Snappy Mango Salsa,
      Cuban, '05 329
Sausage-and-Cornbread Pie, '90 25
Sausage Log, Phyllo, '84 294
Sausage Pizza Pie, Link-, '85 33
Seafood Pie, Hot, '80 32
Shepherd Pie, '83 116
Shepherd's Pie, '92 168; '00 55
Shepherd's Pie, Shortcut Greek, '05 238
Shrimp Puffs, Luncheon, '85 72
Sombrero Pie, '81 140
Spaghetti-Ham Pie, '93 19
Spaghetti Pie, '81 32
Spaghetti Pie, Weeknight, '95 312
Spanakopita, '86 58
Spinach-Pasta Pie, '85 286
Taco Pie, '88 256
Taco Pie, Crescent, '80 80
Taco Pie, Double-Crust, '88 272; '89 180
Taco Pies, Individual, '82 M282
Torta Mexican Style, '89 122
Tortilla Pie, '85 M211; '96 135
Tortilla Pie, Montezuma, '83 199

Tumbleweed Pie, '98 205
Tuna Pie with Cheese Roll Crust, '80 286
Tuna-Rice Pie, '84 123
Turkey-and-Dressing Pie, '84 326
Turkey-Cheese Pie, '88 264
Turkey Pie, '80 285
Turkey Pie, Crumb-Crust Curried, '86 265
Turkey Pie, Golden, '79 253
Turkey Pie, Lattice-Topped, '81 277; '82 7
Turkey Pie, Potato-Topped, '86 265
Turkey Pot Pie, '86 265; '90 24; '93 45
Turkey Pot Pie with Biscuit Crust, '98 296
Turkey Pot Pie with Cranberry-Pecan Crusts, '02 198
Turkey-Sausage Pie, '01 297
Turkey-Vegetable-Sausage Cobbler, '04 325
Vegetable-Beef Pies, '80 286
Zucchini-Ham-Cheese Pie, '80 272
Mango Cream Pie, '03 122
Mango-Ginger Pie, '88 138
Mango Pie, Green, '79 137
Mincemeat Chiffon Pie, '79 245
Mincemeat-Peach Pie, '80 295; '81 188
Mincemeat Pie, Holiday, '80 282; '83 250; '87 213
Mincemeat Pie, Kentucky, '95 302
Mincemeat Pie, Pear, '84 264; '88 226
Mince Pie, Spirited, '92 316
Mint Pie, Candy-Crust, '92 191
Mocha Meringue Pie, '80 242; '88 163
Molasses Pie, '86 20
Muscadine Pie, '82 202
Nesselrode Pie, Fluffy, '87 261
Orange Ambrosia Pie, '80 237
Orange Blossom Special, '79 48
Orange Chess Pie, '88 204; '01 23
Orange Chiffon Pie, '87 260
Orange-Coconut Pie, '90 90
Orange Dream Pie, '02 93
Orange Meringue Pie, '81 12, 309
Orange Pie, Florida, '91 43
Orange Pie, Frosty, '90 296
Papaya Pie, '86 53
Pastries. *See also* **PIES, PUFFS, AND**
      PASTRIES/Crusts.
Almond Combs, '84 136
Almond Pastry, '85 177; '89 317; '92 30
Apple Bundles, Quick, '04 242
Apple Dumplings, Old-Fashioned, '84 226
Apple Flan, '81 309
Apple Foldovers, '84 136
Apple Roll, '82 178
Apple Rolls, Luscious, '88 225
Apples, Crescent Roll, '05 231
Apple Squares, '92 311
Apple Strudel, '85 259; '89 267; '92 269; '97 238
Apricot-Cream Cheese Pastries, '03 245
Apricot Pastries, '83 297
Apricot Pinwheels, '87 276
Baklava, '96 20
Blackberry Roll, '82 178
Blueberry Kuchen, '80 143
Brie en Croûte, Stuffed, '97 162
Briwatts with Fruit, '98 211
Buñuelos, '05 295
Burritos, Hot Phyllo, '98 312
Butter Pastry, Golden, '84 22
Calzones, Spinach-and-Cheese, '95 310
Calzones, Surprise, '00 282
Camembert Bars, '86 58
Cannoli, '80 58
Cheddar Cheese Pastry, '80 219; '82 194
Cheddar Pastry, '86 206
Cheese Danish, '97 31
Cheese Pastries, Date-Filled, '83 259

Cheese Pastry, '88 56
Cheese Puffs, '97 240
Cheese Puffs, Mexican, '87 8
Cheese Rolls, '80 286
Chicken, B'steeya with, '98 210
Chicken Puffs, Appetizer, '85 72
Chipped Beef Spread in Puff Pastry, '98 M335
Chocolate-Chestnut Pastries, '02 M273
Chocolate Pastry Shell, '87 262
Chocolate-Raspberry Bags, '95 97
Cinnamon-Apple Rolls, '02 215
Citrus Pastry, Hint-of-, '93 260
Coconut Puffs, '87 277
Cornmeal Dough, '05 112
Cornmeal Pastry, '81 140
Cornmeal Pastry Cups, '90 69
Cornucopia, Pastry, '95 307
Cream Cheese Danish, '98 325
Cream Cheese Pastries, '80 250
Cream Cheese Pastry, '82 39; '86 24, 78; '89 136;
   '96 228, 264
Cream Cheese Pastry Mini Shells, '99 180
Cream Cheese Pastry Shells, '86 13
Cream Cheese Pastry Shells, Miniature, '87 190
Cream Cheese Patty Shells, '81 266; '82 249
Cream Cheese Shells, '79 2
Cream Horns, '84 137
Cream Puff Pastry, '85 72; '96 191
Cream Puffs, '98 316
Cream Puffs, Captivating, '81 180
Cream Puff Tree, '96 310
Danish Pastry Puffs, '85 311
Double-Crust Pastry, '81 105; '82 85, M298;
   '83 248; '85 191; '87 299; '88 94, 178
Double-Crust Pastry, Flaky, '82 57
Dumplings, Apple-Cranberry, '00 16
Éclairs, Banana-Chocolate, '01 45
Éclairs, Chocolate, '96 191
Éclairs, Mocha, '01 45
Éclairs, Peanut Butter-Chocolate, '01 45
Éclairs, Pistachio-Cream, '91 296
Éclairs, Strawberry Cream, '01 45
Éclairs, Vanilla Cream-Filled, '01 45
Éclairs with Pecan Sauce, '83 219
Elephant Ears, Garlic-and-Herb Baby, '00 87
Elephant Ears, Mushroom-and-Brie Petite, '00 87
Elephant Ears, Parmesan-Pepper Baby, '00 87
Elephant Ears Provençale, Baby, '00 87
Elephant Ears, Southwestern Baby, '00 87
Empanadas, '92 156
Empanadas, Pork Picadillo, '03 60
Empanadas, Pumpkin, '82 223
Feta Squares, '02 59
Fig Snacks, Sliced, '86 206
Firecrackers, Texas, '99 94
Flaky Pastry, '80 224; '81 56, 210; '83 156
Fruit Basket Strudel, '87 276
Fruit Puff, Giant, '85 72
Garnish, Pastry, '98 254; '03 317
German Pastries, '86 78
Gingersnap Crust, '01 187
Greek Olive Cups, '99 221
Guava Puffs, '92 247
Java Cream Puffs, '81 187
Lemon Cream Puffs, '93 254
Light Pastry, '92 95
Make-Ahead Pastry, '82 209; '83 100
Maple Cream Coffee Treat, '90 50
Mexican Fiesta Confection, '82 223
Microwave Pastry, Basic, '82 M142; '85 M113
Mix, Perfect Pastry, '81 142
Mocha Pastry Shell, '81 136
Mushroom-Almond Pastry Cups, '88 210
Napoleon, Giant Apple, '99 282

Napoleons, '84 138
Napoleons, Banana, '00 50
Napoleons, Berry, '94 120
Napoleons, Blueberry, '96 147
Napoleons, Blueberry-Lemon, '94 122
Napoleons, Caramel-Apple, '01 M313
Napoleons, Coffee, '95 276
Napoleons, Peanut Butter-and-Chocolate, '94 121
Napoleons, Strawberry, '81 126
Never Fail Pastry, '79 79
Orange Shortcake, Fresh, '80 100
Palmiers, '87 277
Papaya-Pineapple Roll, '94 18
Paste Pastry, Common, '94 17
Pastry, '82 85, 139, 259; '83 84, 91, 175; '84 21, 23;
   '87 212, 267; '88 103, 198, 225; '89 67, 137, 154,
   214, 267; '91 23, 241; '92 84, 157; '98 272;
   '99 131; '00 95, 170
Pastry, Basic, '79 282; '81 M268; '82 114; '84 48;
   '89 215; '91 119; '94 210
Pâté Pastry, '86 65
Pear Dumplings, '97 210
Pears en Croûte, '93 210
Pecan Pastry Shell, '97 275; '98 36
Phyllo Baskets, Walnut-, '93 210
Phyllo Bowls, '95 58
Phyllo Cheesecakes, Little, '87 275
Phyllo-Cheese Triangles, '87 246
Phyllo, Goat Cheese Wrapped in, '99 43
Phyllo Nests, Nutty, '87 277
Phyllo Tartlet Shells, '95 216
Pineapple Phyllo Bundles, '87 277
Piroshki, '92 84
Pistachio Twists, '02 164
Plum Kuchen, '79 161
Potato-and-Blue Cheese Pastries, '03 258
Potatoes, Phyllo, '02 219
Praline Pastries, '89 318
Preserve-Filled Foldovers, '80 7
Processor Pastry, '87 67
Processor Pie Dough, Quick Food, '84 219
Profiteroles, '84 208
Profiteroles with Warm Cranberry Compote,
   Pumpkin-Spiced, '97 264
Puff Pastry, Basic, '84 135
Puff Pastry Baskets, '93 177
Puff Pastry Baskets, Tropical, '93 177
Puff Pastry Bowls, '95 58
Puff Pastry, Quick, '84 207
Puffs, Blue Cheese, '04 18
Puffs, Blue Cheese-and-Bacon, '01 236
Puffs, Cocktail, '91 106
Puffs, Sweet, '89 91
Quiche Pastry, '80 M107
Quiche Pastry, Microwaved, '81 M74; '82 M122
Raisin Pastry Bites, '90 86
Raspberry-Nut Strudel, '83 304
Raspberry Party Puffs, '90 170
Roquefort Firecrackers, '97 19
Rugalach, Cranberry-Pecan, '04 305
Rugelach, '85 276
Samosas, '89 266
Savory Pastry, '90 24
Seasoned Pastry, '79 253
Sesame Pastry Shell, '82 67
Shell, Pastry, '84 31, 127; '87 262; '89 236; '93 289;
   '94 158
Shell, Perfect Pastry, '81 142
Shells, Pastry, '83 93
Shell, Water-Whipped Baked Pastry, '95 246
Shortcake Pastry, '80 100
Shrimp Bundles with Chive Butter Sauce, Crispy,
   '03 91
Sopaipillas, '89 268

Spanakopita, '96 233
Spinach and Artichokes in Puff Pastry, '00 277
Spinach-and-Cheese Pastries, Greek, '96 76
Spinach-Artichoke-Tomato Puffs, '95 284
Spinach Strudels, '93 249
Sticks, Sugared Piecrust, '02 17
Strawberry Cream Puffs, '81 95
Strawberry-Lemon Cream Puffs, '87 75
Strips, Decorated Pastry, '02 M296
Strudel, Autumn-Apple, '98 253
Strudel, Chicken-Goat Cheese, '98 28
Strudel, Crab-and-Mushroom, '98 28
Strudel, Fig, '98 253
Strudel, Meatless Mexican, '98 29
Strudel, Pear, '98 253
Strudel, Reuben, '98 28
Strudels, Dried Fruit, '01 48
Strudel with White Wine Gravy, Chicken-Herb,
   '04 318
Sugar Cookie Pastry, '91 119
Tart Pastry, '89 232; '90 92; '91 118
Tart Pastry, Heart, '87 14
Tart Shell, '87 77; '88 20
Tart Shell, Chocolate, '99 315; '02 208
Tart Shells, '82 304; '83 279; '85 300; '86 18, 105;
   '88 4; '90 84; '91 13
Tart Shells, Cheese, '88 88
Tart Shells, Cheese Pastry, '85 216
Tart Shells, Tea, '85 120
Timbale Shells, '82 108
Triple-Crust Pastry, '80 186
Turkey-Mushroom Pâté in Pastry, '92 327
Tutti-Frutti Cream Puffs, '79 231
Vegetable Oil Pastry, '91 204
Whole Wheat Pastry, '81 229
Peach. *See also* **PIES, PUFFS, AND PASTRIES/**
   Cobblers, Crisps, and Crumbles; Tarts.
Blackberry Pie, Peach-and-, '89 136
Blueberry-Peach Pie, '94 158
Chiffon Pie, Peach, '89 155
Cranberry Pie, Peach-, '83 249
Cream Pie, Dried Peach, '84 146
Cream Pie, Peaches-and-, '81 184
Filling, Fresh Peach Pie, '95 195
Fresh Peach Pie, '82 170; '95 195
Fresh Peach Pie, Elizabeth and Phoebe's, '96 119
Fried Peach Pies, '81 272
Fried Pies, Easy Peach, '85 178
Fried Pies, Ginger-Peach, '00 212
Georgia Peach-and-Praline Pie, '98 196
Little Peach Pies, '86 303
Luscious Peach Pie, '81 136
Melba Pie, Peach, '98 216
Mincemeat-Peach Pie, '80 295; '81 188
Praline Pie, Peach, '89 136
Quick Peach Pie, '89 252
Rhubarb-Peach Pie, '86 140
Peanut Butter-Banana Pie, '01 315
Peanut Butter Cream Pie, '79 50; '88 65
Peanut Butter Cup Pie, Fudgy, '04 211
Peanut Butter Meringue Pie, '84 30
Peanut Butter Pie, '85 275; '86 109; '89 252
Peanut Butter Pie, Fluffy, '94 246
Peanut-Raisin Pie, '79 85
Peanuts" Pie, "Working for, '93 115
Pear
Backyard Pear Pie, '93 237
Cheddar-Pear Pie, '02 197
Crumble Pie, Pear, '83 207
Deep-Dish Pear Pie, '80 219
Delicious Pear Pie, '88 226
Double-Crust Pear Pie, '82 194
French Pear Pie, '87 213
Fried Pies, Dried Cherry-and-Pear, '00 213

PIES, PUFFS, AND PASTRIES, Pear
(continued)

Ginger-Pear Pie, '93 48
Macadamia Pie, Pear-, '93 260
Mincemeat Pie, Pear, '84 264; '88 226
Mincemeat Pie, Pear-, '98 258
Mince Pie, Pear-, '81 271
Praline Pie, Pear-, '97 192
Streusel Pie, Pear, '83 234; '84 244; '97 109
Tennessee Pear Pie, '85 230
Pecan. *See also* PIES, PUFFS, AND
      PASTRIES/Crusts, Pastries, Tarts.
Bourbon-Chocolate Pecan Pie, '98 258
Bourbon Pecan Pie, '85 90
Bourbon-Pecan Pie, Frozen, '89 251
Bourbon-Pecan Pumpkin Pie, '87 264
Butter Pecan Pie Squares, '81 262
Caramel-Pecan Apple Pie, '85 247
Caramel-Pecan Pie, '88 282; '05 269
Cherry-Pecan Pie, '92 30
Chess Pie, Chocolate-Pecan, '02 107
Chocolate-Banana-Pecan Cream Pie, '94 210
Chocolate-Bourbon Pecan Pie, '05 134
Chocolate-Pecan Chess Pie, '93 251; '00 60
Chocolate Pecan Pie, '80 237; '83 12; '90 184
Chocolate-Pecan Pie, '91 272; '02 176
Choco-Pecan Pie, '82 86
Cinnamon-Almond-Pecan Pie, '98 89
Coconut-Pecan Chess Pie, '81 248
Coconut Pecan Pies, '81 161
Coffee Pecan Pie, '82 74
Cranberry-Pecan Pie, '92 316
Custard Pecan Pie, '87 184
Date-Pecan Pie, '80 15
Fudge Pie with Raspberry Sauce, Pecan, '05 201
Golden Pecan Pie, '81 266
Grandmother's Pecan Pie, '86 269
Holiday Pecan Pie, '81 296
Honey-Pecan Finger Pies, '90 184
Hot Fudge Sauce, Pecan Pie with, '01 306
Individual Pecan Pies, '85 295
Layered Pecan Pie, '83 305
Lemon-Pecan Pie, '93 251
Louisiana Pecan Pie, '92 83
Maple-Pecan Pie, '81 266
Mascarpone Pecan Pie, '05 299
Miniature Pecan Pies, '79 205; '86 13
Mississippi Pecan Pie, '98 146
Mocha Pecan Mud Pie, '00 245
Molasses-Pecan Pie, '86 259
Mom's Pecan Pie, '02 249
Mystery Pecan Pie, '02 249
Old-Fashioned Pecan Pie, '81 M269
Orange-Pecan Pie, '79 282; '83 222
Orzo-Pecan Pie, Honeyed, '04 219
Pecan Pie, '79 251; '80 57; '85 255; '90 312;
      '92 234; '98 275; '01 244
Pumpkin-Pecan Pie, '85 233, 282
Pumpkin Pie, Nutty, '82 67
Raisin-Pecan Pie, '87 213
Simmie's Pecan Pie, '00 254
Special, Old Pecan Street, '93 251
Spicy Pecan Pie, '84 240
Sweet Potato-Pecan Pie, '83 90
Texas Pecan Pie, '83 159
Texas Star Pecan Pie, '90 184
Tiny Pecan Pies, '79 225
Turtle Pecan Pie, '93 250
Vanilla Custard, Pecan Pie with Chilled, '00 331
Persimmon Pie, '79 206
Pineapple-Coconut Chess Pie, '92 214
Pineapple-Grits Pie, '96 236

Pineapple Pie, '80 237; '89 252
Pineapple Pie, Double-Crust, '82 85
Pineapple Pie, Fresh, '91 178
Pistachio Pie, '80 56
Plum Cream Pie, Easy, '86 174
Plum Pie, Streusel-Topped, '88 153
Plum Pie with Italian Sweet Crust, '79 162
Pumpkin
Autumn Pumpkin Pie, '87 213
Bourbon-Pecan Pumpkin Pie, '87 264
Chiffon Pie, Pumpkin, '84 312
Cracked Caramel-Pumpkin Pie, '99 254
Festive Pumpkin Pie, '81 M269
Fluffy Pumpkin Pie, '80 283
Frosty Pumpkin Pie, '96 279
Gingersnap Streusel Pumpkin Pie, '01 315
Ice Cream Pie, Pumpkin, '81 272
Ice Cream Pie, Pumpkin-, '87 243
Layered Pie, Elegant Pumpkin-Walnut, '02 244
Mama's Pumpkin Pie, '96 242
Meringue, Pumpkin Pie with, '92 268
New-Fashioned Pumpkin Pie, '90 296
Nutty Pumpkin Pie, '82 67
Pecan Pie, Pumpkin-, '85 233, 282
Praline Pie, Frosty Pumpkin-, '91 M234
Praline Pie, Pumpkin, '80 244
Praline-Topped Pumpkin Pie, '00 332
Quick Pumpkin Pie, '88 M230
Rich Pumpkin Pie, '86 292
Sour Cream-Pumpkin Pie, '84 263
Spiced Nut Crust, Pumpkin Pie in, '87 295
Spicy Pumpkin Pies, '83 322
Supreme, Pumpkin Pie, '82 217
Traditional Pumpkin Pie, '85 256
Raisin Pie, '83 220
Raisin Pie, Spiced, '84 148
Raspberry Baked Alaska Pie, '98 216
Raspberry Cream Pie, '94 209
Rhubarb-Peach Pie, '86 140
Rhubarb-Raisin Pie, '79 112
Rhubarb-Raspberry Pear Pie, '95 119
Rum Bisque Pie, '79 123
Rum Cream Pie, '85 212
Scuppernong Pie, '88 216
Sour Cream Pie, '86 260
Sour Cream Pie, Tropical, '79 176; '80 6
Strawberry Angel Pie, '88 136
Strawberry-Banana Glazed Pie, '81 181
Strawberry Custard Pie, '00 81
Strawberry-Glaze Pie, '81 141
Strawberry Pie, Chilled, '82 112
Strawberry Pie, Easy, '02 146
Strawberry Pie, Glazed, '82 M142
Strawberry-Rhubarb Pie, '98 99; '05 132
Strawberry Yogurt Pie, '80 232
Strawberry-Yogurt Pie, '85 122; '86 124
Tangerine Chess Pie, '01 23
Tarts
Almond-Apple Tart, '01 253
Almond-Pear Tart, '01 253
Almond Tart, '89 232
Almond Tassies, Lucky, '91 13
Almond Tea Tarts, '85 120
Apple-Cranberry Tart, Rustic, '01 M314
Apple-Cream Cheese Tart, '96 228
Apple Cream Tart, '84 207
Apple-Pecan Tarts, '80 282
Apple Tart, Creamed, '94 17
Apple Tart, Deluxe, '84 227
Apple Tarts, Brandied, '96 284; '99 28
Apple Tart, Upside-Down, '98 35
Apple Tart with Cheese Pastry, '88 225
Apricot-Almond Tart, '97 99
Apricot-Apple Crumb Tart, '94 60

Apricot-Nut Tart, '99 249
Apricot-Pecan-Brie Tarts, '97 236
Apricot Tarts, '79 282; '88 281
Bakewell Tart, '97 110
Berry Tartlets, Fresh, '91 98
Berry Tart, Pick-a-, '91 118
Blackberry Pudding Tarts, '93 200; '00 147
Blackberry Supremes, '99 179
Black Bottom Mocha-Cream Tart, '92 304
Blue Cheese Appetizer Tarts, '85 300; '86 18
Bouilli, Tarte à la, '83 92
Bourbon-Chocolate-Pecan Tarts, '96 264
Caramel Tarts, '82 43
Caramel Tarts, Tiny, '99 179
Caramel Turtle Truffle Tart, '93 M131
Cheese Tart, Herb-, '87 98
Cheese Tartlets, '88 211
Cherry and Blackberry Tart, '83 225
Cherry Tart, Fresh, '05 168
Cherry Tarts, Cheery, '80 238
Chess Tarts, '90 83
Chicken Salad Tarts, '84 257
Chicken Tarts, Deviled, '94 14
Chocolate-Amaretto Heavenly Tarts, '88 4
Chocolate-Cherry Tart, '97 33
Chocolate Chess Tarts, '92 214
Chocolate Custard Tart, '99 27
Chocolate-Peanut Butter Tarts, '92 277
Chocolate-Pecan Tart with Caramel Sauce, '93 296;
      '94 234
Chocolate Tarts, Bluegrass, '90 84
Citrus Tart, Double, '05 55
Citrus Tartlets, Creamy, '02 136
Coconut Cream Tarts with Macadamia Nut Crusts,
      '97 62
Coconut-Pecan Cookie Tarts, '04 305
Coffee Tart, '99 67
Country Ham-and-Asparagus Tartlets, '98 82
Cranberry-Apple Tart, '97 M316
Cranberry-Cream Cheese Tarts, '80 154
Cranberry Holiday Tarts, '83 279
Cranberry-Nut Tart, '84 305
Cranberry Tartlets, Fresh, '87 244
Cran-Raspberry Meringue Tarts, '92 286
Cream Cheese-Peach Tart, '99 169
Cream Cheese Tarts, '84 74; '90 312
Derby Tarts, Miniature, '90 92
Eggnog Tarts, Creamy, '79 255
French Silk Tarts, '79 236
Fruit Tart, Fancy, '82 128; '91 119
Fruit Tart, Fresh, '84 178; '90 58
Fruit Tart, King Cake, '96 57
Fruit Tartlets, Fresh, '93 96
Fruit Tart, Open-Face, '84 207
Fruit Tart, Rainbow, '82 304
Fruit Tarts, Bowl-Me-Over Fresh, '93 200
Fudge Pie, Sweetheart, '03 319
Fudge Truffle-Pecan Tart, '99 315; '02 208
Grapefruit Tart, '04 43
Grape Tart, Green, '87 77
Grasshopper Tarts, '80 220; '89 275
Ham-and-Cheese Tart, '92 332
Ham Tart, Supreme, '84 22
Heart Tarts, '87 14
Honey-Pecan Tart, '99 212
Kentucky Derby Tartlets, '00 107
Kentucky Derby Tarts, '79 102
Key Lime Curd Tartlets, '01 250
Key Lime Tart in Coconut Crust, '89 160
Kiwifruit-Peach Tart, '88 20
Kiwifruit Tart, '89 232
Lady Baltimore Tarts, '88 282
Leek-Goat Cheese Tart, '04 109
Lemon-Cheese Tarts, '79 2

Lemon Ice Cream Tarts, '80 152
Lemon-Sour Cream Tarts, '81 304
Lemon Tart), Caky Flaky Tart (Tart, '96 159
Lemon Tart, Double-Decker, '04 111
Lemon Tart Filling, Tangy, '04 111
Lemon Tarts, '82 156; '83 79
Lemon Tarts, Berry Good, '91 119
Lemon Tarts, Dainty, '82 304
Lemon Tarts, Golden, '85 191
Lemon Tart Shells, '88 195
Lemon Tart, Tangy, '01 245; '04 111
Lime-and-Macadamia Nut Tart, '03 295
Lime-Pineapple Tart, '88 6
Lime Tart, '98 272
Little Bits, '79 196
Midnight Delights, '95 278
Milan, Tart, '87 70
Miniature Tarts, '96 120
Mint Chocolate Mousse Tarts, '03 283
Mushroom Tarts, '88 161
Mushroom Tarts, Hot Sherried, '83 78
Onion Tart, Caramelized, '99 96
Orange Curd Tarts, '92 193
Orange Tarts, '96 317
Orange Tarts, Frozen, '80 154
Party Tarts, '95 90
Peach Cream Tart, '90 173
Peach Meringue Tart, Golden, '98 197
Peach Tart with Brandy Sauce, '98 119
Peachy Keen Tarts, '91 118
Peanut Butter Tarts, '97 329
Pear Tart, '82 304; '92 72
Pear Tart, Raspberry-Almond, '05 230
Pear Tart with White Caramel Sauce, '92 195
Pecan-Raisin Mini-Tarts, '03 246
Pecan-Raisin Tarts, '03 246
Pecan Tarts, '81 266
Pecan Tarts, Easy, '84 313
Pecan Tarts, Special, '87 224
Pecan Tarts, Toasty Southern, '95 329
Pecan Tart with Praline Cream, '90 256
Peppermint Brownie Tarts, '05 M288
Picadillo Tarts, '91 279
Pine Nut Tart, '97 86
Pommes, La Tarte aux, '80 125
Portabello Mushroom Tart, Smoked, '94 163
Potato Tarts, Phyllo, '98 69
Prune Tarts, Brandied, '85 223
Puddin' Pies, President Tyler's, '80 43
Pumpkin Tarts, No-Bake, '86 291
Raspberry-Almond Tarts, '99 280
Raspberry-Brie Tartlets, '04 287
Raspberry Jelly Tarts, '00 208
Rutabaga-Spinach Tart, '98 274
Sausage 'n' Cheese Tarts, '88 51
Scuppernong Pudding Tarts, '98 221
Seafood Tartlets, '87 247
Shrimp 'n' Grits Tarts, '03 254
Shrimp Tart, '87 70
Shrimp Tartlets, '00 71
Southwestern Tart, '04 109
Spinach Tarts, '82 249
Squash Tart, '96 83
Strawberry Dream Tart, '92 118
Strawberry-Lemon Tart, '89 111
Strawberry-Mascarpone Tart, '02 146
Strawberry Tart, '84 138; '89 272; '00 82; '01 71
Strawberry Tarts, '80 70
Sweet Onion Tarts, '95 229
Teatime Tassies, '84 321
Tomato-Basil Tart, '98 132
Tomato-Cheese Tart, Dried, '90 203
Tomato-Leek-Bacon Tart, '03 325
Tomato-Pesto Tart, '00 195; '02 108

Tomato-Pesto Tarts, Mini, '02 108
Tomato Tart, '03 158
Tomato Tart, Fresh, '95 170
Tomato Tart, Herbed, '96 94
White Chocolate Chess Tart, '95 303
Yam Tartlets, Zamaani's Nutty, '02 21
Tin Roof Pie, '85 91
Tiramisù Toffee Trifle Pie, '04 195
Transparent Pie, '80 238
Turnovers
Applesauce Turnovers, '05 231
Apple Turnovers, Baked, '93 338
Apple Turnovers, Delicious, '86 25
Apple Turnovers, Fried, '81 161
Apple Turnovers, Puffy, '87 276
Apricot Turnovers, Fried, '86 24
Cheesy Sesame Seed Turnovers, '91 252
Chicken Liver Turnovers, '79 141
Cranberry Pockets, '96 320
Fruit Turnovers, '79 150
Ham Turnovers, Party, '82 39
Meat Turnovers, '86 326
Mushroom Turnovers, '05 310
Mushroom Turnovers, Hot, '89 285; '97 102
Mushroom Turnovers, Tiny, '86 24
Orange-Apple Turnovers, '99 294
Reuben Turnovers, '94 253
Roast Beef Turnovers, '88 273; '89 180
Salmon-Spinach Turnovers, '83 44
Sausage-Cheese Turnovers, '88 231
Turkey Turnovers, Home-Style, '94 325
Turkey Turnovers, Mexican, '02 245
Turnip-Bacon Turnovers, '04 213
Turnip Turnovers, '04 212
Vegetable Turnovers, '86 24
Vanilla Cream Pie, Fruit-Topped, '84 49
Vegetable. *See also* **PIES, PUFFS, AND**
PASTRIES/Tarts, Turnovers.
Artichoke Flan, '96 22
Asparagus Pie, Cheesy, '01 103
Asparagus Squares, '02 183
Broccoli-Cheese Pie, '84 235
Butternut Squash Chiffon Pie, '83 296; '84 285
Butternut Squash Pie, '80 40; '87 212
Butternut Squash Pie, Spicy, '80 296
Carrot Custard Pie, '79 45
Carrot Pie, '83 117
Cauliflower-Carrot Pie, '82 191
Corn Pie, Quick and Cheesy, '82 191
Corn Pie with Fresh Tomato Salsa, Buttercrust,
'95 181
Florentine Crêpe Pie, '79 34
Green Onion Pie, '98 159
Green Tomato Pie, '79 195; '01 141
Green Tomato Pie Filling, '01 141
Jalapeño Cheese Pie, '96 292
Maque Choux Pies, '02 182
Mushrooms in Patty Shells, '80 283
Onion-Cheese Pie, '88 86
Onion Pie, '82 191; '00 283
Pinto Bean Pie, '80 40
Ratatouille Pie, '88 198
Scallopini Pie, '94 133
Spaghetti Squash Pie, '80 186
Spinach Pie, '82 191; '88 56; '00 26
Spinach Pie, Greek, '85 59
Spinach, Pie Pan, '94 195
Spinach Pie Parma, '96 203
Spinach Pie, Super Special, '04 60
Spinach Pie with Muenster Crust, '95 48
Squash Pie, Italian, '02 183
Squash Pie, Savory, '00 170
Squash Pie, Spicy, '85 9
Summer Garden Pie, '02 182

Summer Pie, Savory, '99 159; '03 182
Sweet Potato Cream Pie, Southern, '87 260
Sweet Potato Meringue Pie, '81 126; '83 225
Sweet Potato-Orange Pie, '88 207
Sweet Potato-Pecan Pie, '83 90
Sweet Potato Pie, '79 207; '85 255, 275; '86 269;
'89 289; '96 131, 326; '00 232; '01 243; '04 331
Sweet Potato Pie, Carolina, '89 295
Sweet Potato Pie, No-Crust, '84 236
Sweet Potato Pie, Old-Fashioned, '79 9
Sweet Potato Pie, Speedy, '90 219
Sweet Potato Pone Pie, '80 288
Tomato Pie, '88 198; '97 249; '02 172
Vidalia Onion Pie with Mushrooms, '02 183
Wild Mushroom-and-Onion Pot Pies, '98 296
Yam Pie, Louisiana, '81 223
Zucchini Pie, '98 236
Zucchini Pie, Cheesy, '82 191
Zucchini Pie, Italian-Style, '83 43
Watermelon Pie, '95 144
PIMIENTO
Asparagus with Pimientos, '98 286
Ball, Pimiento Cheese, '80 258
Bread, Pimiento-Cheese, '85 223
Casserole, English Pea-Pimiento, '83 207
Corn Sticks, Pimiento-Cheese, '03 20
Eggs, Pimiento-Deviled, '84 143
Green Beans with Pimiento, Tangy, '00 170; '01 21
Hoagies, Bacon, Pimiento, and Cheese, '90 144
Pasta, Pimiento, '84 176
Popovers, Pimiento, '79 138
Salsa, Fiery Steak with Pimiento Cheese, '99 331
Sandwiches, Pimiento Cheese, '82 278
Sandwiches, Pimiento Cheese Finger, '99 86
Sauce, Cauliflower with Pimiento, '87 232
Sauce, Pimiento Cheese, '02 291
Soup, Cream of Pimiento, '96 45; '01 72
Soup, Pimiento "Mac and Cheese," '97 M325
Spreads
Cheddar-Swiss Spread, '99 106
Cheese, Cream Cheese-and-Olive Pimiento, '01 169;
'03 315
Cheese, Fabulous Pimiento, '98 315
Cheese, Jalapeño Pimiento, '01 169; '03 315
Cheese, Pecan Pimiento, '01 169; '03 315
Cheese, Pimiento, '01 169; '03 139
Chunky Pimiento Cheese, '86 295
Creamy Pimiento Cheese, '86 296
Creamy Pimiento Cheese Spread, '92 159
Feta-and-Apple Spread, '99 106
Four-Cheese Spread, '99 106
Garlic Pimiento Cheese Spread, '79 58
Green Chile-Pimiento Cheese, '01 61
Ham and Pimiento Spread, '80 285; '81 56
Jalapeño Pimiento Cheese, '98 315
Low-Calorie Pimiento Cheese Spread, '85 215
Peppered Pimiento Cheese, '01 137
Pimiento Cheese Spread, '82 35; '83 93; '86 127;
'99 106, 276
Three Cheeses, Pimiento and, '86 296
West Texas Pimiento Cheese, '84 9
White Cheddar Pimiento Cheese, '99 106
Topping, Pimiento, '83 93
Vinaigrette, Pimiento, '00 167
PINEAPPLE
Acorn Squash, Pineapple-Stuffed, '84 255
Appetizer, Shrimp-Pineapple, '85 80
Applesauce, Hot Spiced, '01 60
Bacon-Wrapped Pineapple Chunks, '84 25
Baked Pineapple, '83 261; '84 287; '05 160
Bake, Pineapple, '79 251; '96 84
Bake, Pineapple-Cheese, '79 106
Ball, Pineapple Cheese, '81 160
Ball, Pineapple-Cheese, '84 26

PINEAPPLE
(continued)

Beans, Hawaiian-Style Baked, '86 210
Beets with Pineapple, '79 249; '82 204
Betty, Pineapple-Apple, '85 46
Beverages
  Blue Woo-Woo, '94 226
  Bole, '97 245
  Coconut-Pineapple Drink, '83 172
  Cooler, Pineapple, '90 207
  Float, Pineapple Sherbet, '79 148
  Hot Buttered Pineapple Drink, '91 260
  Lemonade, Pineapple, '93 194
  Limeade, Pineapple, '01 235
  Milk Shake, Banana-Pineapple, '84 59
  Milkshake, Pineapple, '87 199
  Milk Shake, Pineapple, '94 113
  Nectar, Hot Pineapple, '90 21
  Nog, Speedy Breakfast, '82 47
  Orange-Pineapple Drink, '89 35
  Piña Coladas, '95 203; '96 127
  Piña Colada Slush, '95 90
  Punch, Brew-Ha-Ha, '98 255
  Punch, Champagne, '99 30
  Punch, Cranberry-Pineapple, '00 284
  Punch, False-Kick, '82 121
  Punch, Frosty Pineapple, '91 66
  Punch, Hot Pineapple, '82 264
  Punch, Lime-Pineapple, '83 142
  Punch, Pineapple, '79 174; '80 128
  Punch, Pineapple-Citrus, '96 134
  Punch, Pineapple Fruit, '02 49
  Punch, Pineapple-Gin, '95 140
  Punch, Pineapple-Mint, '88 209
  Punch, Pineapple-Orange, '85 236
  Punch, Pineapple Sherbet, '95 141
  Punch, Spiced Pineapple, '83 33; '92 66
  Sangría, Pineapple, '91 176
  Shake, Light Pineapple-Buttermilk, '01 173
  Shake, Pineapple-Banana, '85 215
  Shake, Pineapple-Buttermilk, '01 173
  Shake, Pineapple-Orange-Banana, '97 172
  Shake, Strawberry-Pineapple, '84 166
  Shake, Tropical, '00 179
  Slush, Pineapple, '88 82
  Slush, Pineapple-Banana, '90 14
  Smoothie, Easy Pineapple, '00 199
  Smoothie, Peachy-Pineapple, '97 173
  Smoothie, Pineapple, '97 172
  Smoothie, Quick Banana-Pineapple, '93 195
  Soda, Pineapple, '90 179
  Spiced Pineapple Sparkle, '92 322
  Spritzer, Pineapple-Grapefruit, '04 143
  Strawberry Slush, Pineapple-, '94 227
  Tea, Pineapple, '93 165
  Tea, Pineapple-Orange Herb, '05 61
  Wassail, Pineapple, '01 240
  Wassail, Pineapple-Apricot, '83 275
  Yogurt Whirl, Pineapple-, '91 132
Breads
  Apricot Bread, Pineapple-, '84 7
  Buns, Easy Pineapple, '85 14
  Carrot Bread, Pineapple-, '79 106
  Carrot-Pineapple Bread, '82 210
  Coffee Cake, Pineapple-Coconut, '94 49; '03 198
  Doughnuts, Pineapple Drop, '83 95
  Hawaiian Loaf, '80 225
  Muffins, Carrot-Pineapple, '81 6
  Muffins, Morning Glory, '93 327
  Muffins, Pineapple, '81 14, 250
  Muffins, Sunshine, '86 9
  Nut Bread, Pineapple-, '79 215

Pecan Loaf Bread, Pineapple-, '87 256
Pineapple Bread, '83 139
Puffs, Pineapple Breakfast, '98 326
Rolls, Cranberry-Pineapple, '86 275
Rolls, Pineapple Angel, '89 72
Cabbage with Pineapple, Red, '97 215
Carrots and Pineapple, Curried, '90 228
Carrots, Pineapple, '83 198
Citrus, Pineapple and Fresh, '89 206
Curried Pineapple, '03 201
Desserts
  Ambrosia, Pineapple-Orange, '88 252
  Baked Pineapple, Brown Sugar-, '05 170
  Baked Pineapple with Natillas Sauce, '83 179
  Bars, Pineapple-Orange, '82 129
  Basket, Summer Berry, '84 158
  Boats with Rum Sauce, Pineapple, '97 192
  Cake, Banana Split, '99 48
  Cake, Cajun, '87 138
  Cake, Carrot, '98 275
  Cake, Cherry-Pineapple Dump, '02 128
  Cake, Coconut-Pineapple, '89 56
  Cake, Coconut-Pineapple Layer, '80 140
  Cake, Express Pineapple Upside-Down, '03 65
  Cake, Fresh Pineapple Upside-Down, '97 204
  Cake, Heavenly Pineapple, '83 303
  Cake, Hummingbird, '03 315
  Cake, Lemon-Pineapple, '86 60, 239
  Cake, Lightened Hummingbird, '01 34
  Cake, Nanny's Famous Coconut-Pineapple, '97 277
  Cake, Pig Pickin', '04 112
  Cake, Pineapple-Cherry Dump, '04 91
  Cake, Pineapple-Coconut, '00 86
  Cake, Pineapple-Pecan Upside-Down, '84 25
  Cake, Pineapple Pound, '79 148
  Cake, Pineapple Right-Side-Up Snack, '99 28
  Cake, Pineapple Upside-Down, '80 102; '88 10
  Cake, Quick Coconut-Pineapple, '05 106
  Cake Roll, Coconut-Pineapple, '84 304
  Cake Roll, Pineapple Upside-Down, '96 162
  Cake, Skillet Pineapple Upside-Down, '85 242;
    '03 65
  Cake, Spiced Pineapple Upside-Down, '02 214
  Cake, Stacked Pineapple Upside-Down,
    '86 239
  Cake, Tropical Dump, '02 128
  Cake, Zucchini-Pineapple, '95 160
  Charlotte, Pineapple, '90 288
  Cheesecake, Festive Piña Colada, '01 286
  Cheesecake, Pineapple, '81 32
  Cheesecake, Tropical Tofu, '00 204
  Cheesecake, Ultimate Pineapple, '85 38
  Chimichangas, Pineapple Dessert, '86 4
  Chocolate-Drizzled Pineapple with Raspberry Sauce,
    '90 57
  Cookies, Pineapple, '79 216
  Cream, Pineapple 'n', '88 202
  Crème Brûlée, Piña Colada, '04 246
  Crêpes, Mango-Pineapple, '86 216
  Crisp, Tropical Pineapple, '02 232
  Delight, Fresh Pineapple, '79 111
  Delight, Pineapple-Almond, '85 96
  Filling, Orange-Pineapple Fried Pie, '96 109
  Filling, Pineapple, '80 140; '83 179; '84 153; '89 57;
    '97 277
  Flan, Pineapple, '01 85
  Frappé, Hawaiian, '81 178
  Fritters, Pineapple, '88 112
  Frosting, Pineapple-Cream Cheese, '95 160
  Frozen Tropical Paradise, '89 206
  Glaze, '01 286
  Glazed Oranges and Pineapple, '86 318
  Glaze, Orange-Pineapple, '81 60
  Glaze, Pineapple, '83 143; '85 38; '97 55

Grilled Pineapple with Vanilla-Cinnamon Ice Cream,
    '00 127; '01 195
  Ice Cream, Mint Nectarines with Pineapple-Coconut,
    '05 123
  Ice Cream, Mint Peaches with Pineapple-Coconut,
    '05 123
  Ice Cream, Orange-Pineapple, '86 117
  Ice Cream, Pineapple-Mint, '84 186
  Meringue-Topped Pineapple, '84 178
  Mint Dessert, Pineapple-, '96 127
  Mousse, Coconut-Pineapple, '94 198
  Mousse, Elegant Pineapple, '79 230
  Noodle Casserole, Sweet, '02 238
  Papaya-Pineapple Roll, '94 18
  Parfait, Pineapple, '84 83
  Pears, Pineapple-Honey, '86 94
  Phyllo Bundles, Pineapple, '87 277
  Pie, Apple-Pineapple, '97 276
  Pie, Coconut-Pineapple, '84 256
  Pie, Double-Crust Pineapple, '82 85
  Pie, Fresh Pineapple, '91 178
  Pie, Pineapple, '80 237; '89 252
  Pie, Pineapple-Chicken Salad, '80 138
  Pie, Pineapple-Coconut Chess, '92 214
  Pie, Pineapple-Grits, '96 236
  Pie, Rancher's Buttermilk, '04 208
  Pizza, Apple-Pineapple Dessert, '00 313
  Pops, Hawaiian Orange-Pineapple, '94 143
  Pops, Pineapple-Yogurt, '91 173
  Pudding, Piña Colada Bread, '98 34
  Pudding, Pineapple, '80 102
  Pudding with Bourbon Sauce, Pineapple-Apple
    Bread, '05 119
  Pudding with Vanilla-Nutmeg Sauce, Pineapple-
    Apple Bread, '02 208
  Sauce, Banana-Pineapple, '83 48
  Sauce, Pineapple Ice Cream, '81 M289
  Sauce, Pineapple-Orange, '84 14
  Sauce, Pineapple-Rum, '84 275
  Sherbet, Buttermilk, '99 99
  Sherbet, Creamy Pineapple, '79 155
  Sherbet, Easy Pineapple, '92 199
  Sherbet, Lemon-Pineapple, '96 330
  Sherbet, Pineapple, '81 177; '84 83; '89 199
  Skewers with Rum Sauce, Grilled Pineapple, '04 247
  Sopaipillas, Pineapple, '83 179
  Sorbet, Pineapple, '03 171
  Soufflé, Pineapple Dessert, '80 153
  Spritz, Pineapple, '86 94
  Stuffed Pineapple, '00 160
  Sundaes, Mauna Loa, '80 126
  Tart, Lime-Pineapple, '88 6
  Topping, Cherry-Pineapple, '87 126
  Topping, Lemon-Pineapple, '86 60
  Topping, Pineapple, '86 239
  Trifle, Pineapple Angel Food, '93 86
  Tropical Snow, '86 34
Dip, Cheesy Pineapple, '80 249
Dip, Pineapple-Ginger, '86 104
Dressing, Fruit Salad with Pineapple, '85 207
Dressing, Pineapple Cream, '83 81
Dressing, Pineapple-Poppy Seed, '85 55
Fried Pineapple, '81 232
Fritters, Pineapple, '00 238
Gazpacho, Pineapple, '01 85
Glaze, Pineapple, '83 143; '84 26; '85 38
Gratin, Pineapple, '93 328
Ham-Pineapple Nibbles, '95 283
Hawaiian Dream Boats, '86 151
Jam, Pineapple, '81 147
Jelly, Pineapple-Orange Mint, '92 105
Main Dishes
  Beans and Franks, Hawaiian Baked, '80 136
  Beefburgers Hawaiian, '86 137

Burgers, Pineapple, '82 169
Chicken and Pineapple, '81 281; '82 30
Chicken and Rice, Island, '04 165
Chicken Bake, Pineapple, '82 120
Chicken Breasts, Hawaiian Stuffed, '99 64
Chicken, Hawaiian Sesame, '81 106
Chicken Oriental, '01 36
Chicken, Oriental Pineapple, '84 288
Chicken, Piña Colada, '86 21
Chicken, Pineapple, '83 M194; '85 3
Chicken Stir-Fry, Pineapple-, '89 176
Chicken, Sweet-and-Sour, '97 325
Chicken with Grilled Pineapple, Lime, '04 88
Chicken with Pineapple-Mustard Glaze, Roast,
   '89 83
Chicken with Pineapple, Oriental, '86 42
Chops, Pineapple-Curry Glazed, '82 106
Crab Imperial, Pineapple-, '84 M286
Flank Steak in Mexican Marinade, '98 128
Franks, Hawaiian, '81 202
Fried Rice, Spicy Shrimp-and-Pineapple, '03 285
Ham, Citrus-and-Spice, '88 40
Ham Loaf, Pineapple Upside-Down, '79 253
Ham Patties, Pineapple-, '80 110
Ham, Pineapple-Baked, '86 48
Ham, Pineapple-Flavored, '87 160
Ham, Pineapple-Glazed, '01 288; '03 82
Ham-Potato-Pineapple Bake, '93 302
Ham Sandwich Loaf, Pineapple-, '91 167
Kebabs, Chicken-Pineapple, '00 200
Kebabs, Pineapple-Beef, '83 212
Kebabs, Pineapple-Chicken, '86 M328
Kebabs, Pineapple-Pork, '99 144
Loaves, Individual Pineapple, '81 M121
Loaves, Mini Teriyaki, '98 224
Meatballs, Chinese, '87 194
Meatballs, Polynesian, '80 207
Meatballs with Pineapple and Peppers, '90 145
Meat Loaf, Teriyaki, '98 224
Pizza, Ham-and-Pineapple, '96 169
Pork and Pineapple, Polynesian, '83 102
Pork Chops, Hawaiian, '86 212
Pork Chops, Pineapple, '87 M124
Pork, Pineapple, '82 60
Pork, Pineapple Sweet-and-Sour, '82 120
Pork Roast, Pineapple, '79 41
Pot Roast, Hawaiian, '81 298
Pot Roast, Polynesian, '80 59
Shrimp Oriental, '01 36
Marmalade, Orange-Pineapple, '82 150; '89 M156
Marmalade, Strawberry-Pineapple, '85 130
Melts, Pineapple-Turkey, '03 196
Pears, Pineapple-Honey, '86 94
Pickled Pineapple, '79 24
Preserves, Mango-Pineapple, '79 137
Puro de Piña, '02 82
Relish, Cranberry, '98 310
Relish, Pineapple-Coconut, '96 323; '97 27
Rice with Pineapple, Curried, '79 142
Rollups, Creamy Pineapple-and-Ham, '04 163
Salad Dressing, Pineapple, '81 36
Salads
   Boat Aloha, Pineapple, '80 102
   Boats Ahoy, Pineapple, '80 148
   Buttermilk Salad, Pineapple-, '82 80
   Carrot-Pineapple Salad, '91 83
   Celery Salad, Pineapple-, '85 95
   Chicken Salad, Pineapple-Nut, '83 80
   Chicken Salad, South Sea Island, '97 88
   Citrus, Pineapple and Fresh, '89 206
   Coleslaw, Curried Pineapple, '88 172
   Congealed Salad, Lime, '02 257
   Congealed Salad, Pineapple-Cucumber, '83 118
   Congealed Salad, Pineapple-Orange, '83 218

Cranberry-Pineapple Salad, Frozen, '91 237
Cucumber-Pineapple Salad, '84 124
Daiquiri Salad, Pineapple, '84 232
Delight, Pineapple-Pear, '82 54
Fresh Pineapple Boats, '83 153
Frosted Salad, Heavenly, '79 286
Frosty Pineapple Salad, '89 278
Frozen Salads, Paper Cup, '00 176
Fruit Salad, Icy Pineapple-, '87 9
Lemon-Pineapple Salad, '05 65
Lime Salad, Pineapple-, '84 320
Macaroni Salad, Pineapple, '79 220
Mandarin Orange and Pineapple Salad, '82 266
Mold, Minted Pineapple, '85 240
Shrimp Salad, Aloha, '95 46
Slaw, Apple-Pineapple, '79 241
Slaw, Cabbage-Pineapple, '92 182
Slaw, Colorful Pineapple, '86 250
Slaw, Pineapple, '94 49; '99 26
Slaw, Pineapple-Almond, '92 171
Slaw Sandwiches, Ham-and-Pineapple, '96 199
Slaw, Zesty, '97 324
Waldorf, Pineapple, '97 86
Waldorf Salad, Pineapple, '92 97
Salsa, Cranberry, '99 316
Salsa, Grilled Lamb Chops with Pineapple-Mint, '05 52
Salsa, Pineapple, '96 226; '03 128; '04 196; '05 86
Salsa, Spicy Pineapple, '97 165
Salsa, Warm Pineapple, '02 144
Sandwich, Pineapple-Turkey, '01 85
Sauce, Banana-Pineapple, '83 48
Sauce, Jezebel, '81 29; '82 55
Sauce, Mango-Pineapple Hot, '04 183
Sauce, Maui, '99 310
Sauce, Pineapple, '84 236; '92 203
Sauce, Pineapple-Curry, '79 252
Sauce, Pineapple-Rhubarb, '88 94
Sauce, Raisin-Pineapple, '82 177
Sauce, Sweet-and-Sour Pineapple, '85 66
Scalloped Pineapple, '79 106; '82 254; '84 M323
Shells, Pineapple, '96 127
Skewered Pineapple and Strawberries, '84 251
Slicing Pineapples, Instructions for, '82 94
Snow Peas and Pineapple, '91 120
Spiced Pineapple, '80 102; '02 239
Spread, Coconut-Pineapple, '93 309
Spread, Hawaiian Cheese, '87 158
Spread, Pineapple-Cheese, '86 126; '91 167
Spread, Pineapple-Cream Cheese, '82 35
Spread, Pineapple Sandwich, '84 166
Spritz, Pineapple, '86 94
Sweet Potatoes, Pineapple-Orange, '96 46
Vinaigrette, Black Pepper-Pineapple, '97 181
PITA. See APPETIZERS/Pita; BREADS;
   SANDWICHES/Pita.
PIZZA
   Appetizers
      Appetizer Pizzas, '89 M118
      Bites, Pizza, '95 244
      Cocktail Pizzas, '79 110
      Dip, Pizza, '99 65
      Dip, Quick Pizza, '00 M168
      Horns, Pizza, '89 214
      Party Pizzettes, '80 192
      Pita Pizzas, '89 19
      Shellfish Pizza, '91 224
      Shrimp Pizza Wedges, '89 158
      Slices, Pizza, '84 269
      Snacks, Pizza Party, '86 262
      Snacks, Tasty Little Pizza, '79 248
      Squares, Pizza, '87 168
      Turnovers, Little Pizza, '85 327
      Zucchini Pizzas, '88 212
   Artichoke and Prosciutto, Pizza with, '87 182

Bagel, Pizza on a, '93 M94
Bake, Upside-Down Pizza, '98 224
Barbecue Chicken Pizza, '03 49
Bayou Pizza, The Best of the, '95 268
Beef-and-Sausage Pizza, Double Cheesy, '86 77
Blazing Sunset Pizza, '95 267
Bobolis, Easy Cheesy, '92 278
Bread, Pizza Batter, '85 56
Breakfast Pizza, '85 44; '88 288; '90 140, 178; '97 172;
   '00 193
Broccoli Supreme Pizza, '02 312
Burger, Pizza, '87 185
Burgers, All-American Pizza, '92 148
Burgers, Easy Pizza, '82 190
Burger Snacks, Pizza-, '84 30
Burgers, Pizza, '80 M201; '81 73; '89 165
Calzone, '85 94
Calzones, All-Star Pizza, '95 308
Casserole, Beefy Pizza, '05 217
Casserole, Microwave Pizza, '89 M248
Casserole, Pizza, '88 273; '89 181
Casserole, Quick Pizza, '83 266
Casserole, Upside-Down Pizza, '03 284
Cheese-and-Mushroom Pizza, '83 226
Cheeseburger Pizza, '97 318
Cheese Pizza, Quick 3-, '00 94
Chicken-and-Bacon Pizza, Tex-Mex, '05 325
Chicken-and-Purple Onion Pizza, '97 47
Chicken-and-Three-Cheese French Bread Pizzas, '96 94
Chicken Barbecue Pizza, Quick 'n' Easy, '04 139
Chicken Fajita Pizza, '03 235
Chicken Parmesan Pizza, '00 134
Chicken Pizza, '94 218
Chicken Pizza, Bistro Grilled, '05 M131
Chicken Pizza, Mexican, '97 321
Chicken Pizza, Southwestern, BBQ, '05 33
Chicken Pizza with Mango Pico de Gallo, Fajita,
   '04 318
Clam Pizza, Baby, '87 182
Crusts
   Crispy Pizza Crust, '87 181; '89 64
   Parmesan Pizza Crust, '93 58
   Pizza Crust, '80 233; '83 226; '85 243; '86 77;
      '04 208
   Skillet Pizza Crusts, '94 218
   Special Pizza Crust, '90 139
   Thick Crust, '81 214
   Thin Crust, '81 214
   Whole Wheat Crust, '94 78
   Whole Wheat Pizza Crust, '93 58
Cups, Pizza, '81 215
Deep-Dish Mediterranean Pizza, '80 163
Deep-Dish Pizza, '01 29
Deep-Dish Pizza Luncheon Pie, '80 286
Deep-Dish Vegetarian Pizza, '85 243
Dessert
   Apple-Pineapple Dessert Pizza, '00 313
   Banana Split-Brownie Pizza, '96 M164
   Blueberry Pizza, '96 147
   Chocolate-Peanut Butter Pizza, '05 193
   Chocolate Pizza, '91 298
   Cookie, Pizza, '90 49
   Cookies, Candy Shop Pizza, '02 299
   Cranberry Dessert Pizzas, '96 320
   Dolce (Italian Sweet Pies), Pizza, '00 283
   Kiwi-Berry Pizza, '86 198; '87 55
   Kiwifruit Pizza, '89 306
   Peanut Butter-Fruit Pizza, '94 60
   Rocky Road Pizza Dessert, '99 196
   Strawberry Pizza, '79 94
Dogs, Grilled Pizza, '97 139
Dough, Pizza, '04 58
Easy Pizza, '92 181
Eggplant Pizza, '85 221

PIZZA

(continued)

Eggplant Pizza, Garden, '05 127
Eggplant Pizzas, '98 183
Eggplant, Tomato, and Feta Pizza, Greek, '01 312
Fiesta Pizza, '00 85
Five-Ring Pizzas, '96 180
French Bread, Pizza on, '82 131
Garden Pizza, '89 108
Greek Pizza, '03 145
Grilled Pizza, '97 190
Grilled Pizzas, '93 178; '98 176
Ground Beef Pizza, Cheesy, '03 62
Gruyère-Chicken Pizza, '87 182
Ham-and-Eggs Crescent Pizza, '93 47
Ham-and-Pineapple Pizza, '96 169
Hamburger Pizza, Quick, '85 243
Herb Pizza, Easy, '92 99
Homemade Pizza, Best Ever, '80 233
Hot Dog Pizzas, '93 78
Hummus Pizza, Red Pepper, '01 56
Individual Pizzas, '03 219
Italian-Style Pizza, Original, '87 182
Jazzed-Up Pizza, Jiffy, '83 M314
King Henry Pizza, The, '95 267
Lasagna Pizza, '85 285
Maca-Pizza, '99 195
Meatballs, Pizza, '85 86
Meat Loaf, Cheesy Pizza, '81 121
Meaty Pizza Pie, '03 145
Mexican Pizza, '94 218, 327; '99 119; '02 72
Mexican Pizza, Cheesy, '00 314
Mozzarella and Basil Pizza, Fresh, '04 58
Muffuletta Pizzas, '00 M335
Pan Pizza, Quick, '86 160
Pepperoni Pizza, Thick 'n' Crusty, '85 244
Pepper Pizza, Roasted, '94 218
Peppers-and-Cheese Pizza, '03 235
Peppers, Pizza, '83 135
Pesto Pizza, '87 182; '94 218
Pesto Pizza, Nutty, '97 267
Phyllo Pizza, '94 91
Pie, Pizza, '91 23
Pita Pizza Snack, '94 193
Plum-and-Sweet Onion Pizza, '98 193
Pocket Pizzas, Easy, '90 168
Popcorn, Pizza-Flavored, '85 236
Portobello-Pine Nut Pizza, '99 216
Portobello Pizza, '03 175
Portobello Pizza Burgers, Grilled, '00 89
Portobello Pizzas, Grilled, '00 89
Potato Pizzas, Roasted, '99 16
Pumpkins, Pizza, '98 255
Quiche, Pizza, '86 53
Quick Little Pizzas, '88 227
Reuben Pizza, '03 69
Roasted Vegetable-and-Goat Cheese Pizza, '05 176
Rollups, Pizza, '99 197
Rollups, Pizza Bread, '04 M35
Salad Pizza, '87 182
Sandwiches, Open-Face Pizza, '82 3; '83 85; '84 M198;
        '85 22
Sandwich, Giant Pizza, '80 93
Sauce, Pizza, '84 33; '85 285; '00 314
Sauce, Traditional Pizza, '95 267
Sausage-and-Scrambled Egg Pizza, '05 88
Sausage-Pepperoni Pizza, Spicy, '83 226
Sausage Pizza Pie, Link-, '85 33
Sausage-Potato Pizza, '01 199
Scones, Pizza, '03 207
Seafood Alfredo Pizza, '03 236
Shellfish Pizza, '91 224

Shrimp-and-Dried Tomato Pizza, '97 49
Sicilian Pizza, '01 125
Snacks, Pizza, '01 231
Southern Classic Pizza, '95 268
Southwest Deluxe Pizza, '95 268
Southwestern Pizza, '03 146
Speedy Pizza, '81 214
Squares, Easy Pizza, '02 61
Sticks, Pizza, '98 255
Sunburst, Pizza, '94 245
Supreme, Pizza, '81 214
Swiss Steak, Pizza, '02 36
Taco Pizza, '89 M177; '98 176; '00 293
Tacos, Pizza-Flavored Chicken, '95 340
Tostada Pizza, '81 16; '82 13
Turkey-Vegetable Pizza, '90 139
Two-Way Pizza, '79 93
Upside-Down Pizza, '91 185
Vegetable Pizza, '89 64; '94 218
Vegetable Pizza, Grilled, '98 176
Vegetable Pizzas, Grilled, '97 323
Vegetarian Pizza, Deep-Dish, '85 243
Vegetarian Processor Pizza, '89 225
Veggie Pizza, '94 78
Veggie Pizzas, '99 97
Veggie Pizza, Southwestern, '95 126
Veggie Sausage Pizzas, '00 294
Wedges, Toasted Pizza Crust, '03 280
Whole Wheat Pizza, '84 33
Wide-Eyed Pizzas, '90 94

PLANTAINS

Chips, Plantain, '95 M203
Chips), Tostones de Plátano (Plantain, '92 158
Fried Plantains, '99 121

PLUMS

Betty, Bourbon-Plum Brown, '97 177
Brandied Plums, '97 176
Bread Pudding, Refrigerator Plum, '97 177
Bread, Sugar Plum, '80 256
Butter, Plum, '88 152
Cake, Plum, '97 177
Chutney, Plum, '84 179
Cobbler, Crunchy Plum, '88 152
Cobbler, Plum, '99 254; '03 161
Cobbler with Spiced Plum Muffin Crust, Plum, '04 201
Coffee Cake, Plum Preserves, '02 211
Crunch, Layered Plum, '86 174
Fajitas, Plum Good, '94 115
Ham, Plum, '80 110
Jam, Freezer Plum, '89 M156
Jam, Peach-Plum Freezer, '85 130
Jam, Plum Refrigerator, '89 139
Jelly, Plum, '82 150
Kuchen, Plum, '79 161
Muffin Batter, Spiced Plum, '04 201
Muffins, Plum Good, '83 96
Muffins, Spiced Plum, '04 201
Pheasant, Gin-Marinated, '02 250
Pie, Easy Plum Cream, '86 174
Pie, Streusel-Topped Plum, '88 153
Pie with Italian Sweet Crust, Plum, '79 162
Pizza, Plum-and-Sweet Onion, '98 193
Poached Plums, '90 M141
Port Wine, Plums in, '97 176
Preserves, Plum, '03 161
Pudding, Flamed Plum, '84 276
Pudding-Gelatin Mold, Plum, '86 300; '87 178
Pudding, Light Plum, '86 318
Pudding, Old-Fashioned Plum, '80 264
Pudding, Plum, '79 281
Salad, Crisp Plum, '03 161
Salsa, Plum, '97 176
Sauce, Chinese Plum, '82 237
Sauce, Crispy Ribs with Plum, '98 182

Sauce, Fresh Plum, '94 129; '97 176
Sauce, Gingered Plum, '87 175
Sauce, Plum, '80 249; '82 40; '88 152
Sauce, Quail with Red Plum, '80 48
Sauce, Spareribs in Plum, '99 136
Sauce, Spicy Plum, '86 11
Slush, Plum, '84 139
Soup, Chilled Plum, '03 161
Soup, Chilled Purple Plum, '79 162
Soup, Peach-Plum, '87 157
Soup, Plum, '85 107
Soup, Plum-and-Wine, '00 144

POLENTA

Baked Polenta with Cheese and Okra, '99 232
Basic Polenta, '95 164
Cheesy Polenta and Green Chiles, Stuffed Red Peppers
        with, '04 169
Chicken with Polenta, '02 87
Crab Polenta, '00 277
Fries, Red Pepper-Polenta, '00 196
Grilled Polenta, '00 126
Grilled Polenta with Black Bean Salsa, '93 155
Lasagna with Cream Sauce, Polenta, '03 237
Sausage, Polenta with, '93 32
Serrano Chile Polenta, '98 104
Triangles, Polenta, '98 181

POMEGRANATE

Cider, Mulled Pomegranate, '05 309
Cocktail, Pomegranate-Champagne, '05 282
Salad Dressing, Pomegranate, '96 241
Syrup, Pomegranate, '96 241
Wreath, Tex-Mex, '96 241

POPCORN

Asian Popcorn, Quick-and-Easy, '00 223
Bacon-Cheese Popcorn, '86 74
Balls, Marshmallow Popcorn, '90 226
Balls, Nutty Popcorn, '88 227
Basil, Garlic, and Parmesan Popcorn, '00 223
Cake, Popcorn-Gumdrop, '87 262
Candied Popcorn and Peanuts, '82 295
Caramel
        Baked Caramel Corn, '81 218
        Candy, Caramel Corn, '84 243
        Caramel Corn, '88 64
        Caramel Popcorn, '79 219; '86 M212
        Clusters, Caramel-Nut Popcorn, '00 M223
        Crispy Caramel Corn, '04 112
        Crispy Caramel Popcorn, '85 247
        Crunch, Caramel, '95 165
        Crunch Popcorn, Caramel, '96 255
        Ghoul's Hands, '94 256
        Nutty Caramel Corn, '92 317
        Oven-Made Caramel Corn, '91 233
Cheese Popcorn, '98 205
Cheesy Barbecue Popcorn, '95 239
Chili Popcorn, '91 17; '95 166; '00 M223
Chocolate Popcorn, Delicious, '00 223
Cinnamon-Popcorn Crunch, '86 136
Crazy Mixed-Up Popcorn, '97 245
Delight, Popcorn, '00 M133
Flavored Popcorn, '98 205
Garlic Popcorn, '83 M315
Harvest Popcorn, '84 300
Herb-Seasoned Popcorn, '94 122
Honey-and-Spice Crunch, '94 290
Kettle Corn, '04 187
Mexican Popcorn, '98 205
Mix, Curried Popcorn, '86 326
Mix, Party, '96 306; '97 322; '98 234
Munchies, Pop Graham, '96 28
Nut Popcorn, Spicy, '02 287; '03 272
Nutty Popcorn, '85 208
Orange Popcorn, '86 230
Oriental Popcorn, '86 74; '98 205

Peanut Brittle, Popcorn, '02 M223
Pizza-Flavored Popcorn, '85 236
Pizzazz, Popcorn with, '93 245
Pretzel Popcorn, '84 30
Ranch Popcorn, '98 205
Rosemary Popcorn with Pine Nuts, '00 223
Scramble, Popcorn, '87 185
Sesame-Cheese Popcorn, '79 220
Spiced Popcorn Snack, '87 8
Tex-Mex Popcorn, '05 204
Trick or Treat Popcorn, '03 210

PORK. *See also* **BACON, CASSEROLES, HAM, SAUSAGE.**
Apple Cider Pork and Vegetables, '97 210
Backbone and Rice, Pork, '03 252
Backbones, Smoked Country-Style, '82 162
Bake, Pork-and-Noodle, '88 98
Bake, Pork Spaghetti, '81 11
Barbecue
  Bannister's Barbecue, '92 166
  Barbecued Pork, '80 72
  Chops, Barbecued Pork, '81 10
  Chops, Barbecued Stuffed, '87 229
  Chops, Marinated Barbecued Pork, '79 90
  Chops, Oven-Barbecued Pork, '81 234; '82 26; '83 40
  Chops with Tangy Barbecue Sauce, Pork, '99 104
  Home-Style Barbecue, '88 145
  Quesadillas, Barbecue, '02 121
  Ribs, Apple Barbecued, '80 111
  Ribs, Barbecue, '99 68
  Ribs, Barbecued, '80 111; '85 159; '91 205
  Ribs, Barbecued Country-Style, '95 237
  Ribs, Country-Style Barbecued, '79 42
  Ribs, Herbed Barbecued, '86 185
  Ribs, Oven-Barbecued Pork, '88 132
  Ribs, Slow-Cooker Barbecue, '03 160
  Ribs, Smoky Barbecued, '80 111
  Ribs, Tangy Barbecued, '83 160
  Ribs with Blender Barbecue Sauce, '90 12
  Roast, Barbecued Pork, '82 11; '03 147
  Roast, Barbecued Pork Loin, '93 34
  Roast, Barbecue Pork, '82 97; '83 104
  Roast, Berry Barbecued Pork, '80 288
  Roast, Oven-Barbecued Pork, '91 50
  Sandwiches, Barbecue Pork, '00 23
  Shoulder, Barbecued Pork, '81 111; '82 11
  Shoulder, Barbecue Pork, '00 274
  Spaghetti, Barbecue, '02 121
  Spareribs, Apple-Barbecue, '90 160
  Spareribs, Barbecued, '81 112; '82 12; '86 232; '95 236
  Spareribs, Barbecued Country-Style, '80 73
  Spareribs, Easy Barbecued, '82 97; '83 104
  Spareribs, Saucy Barbecued, '79 14
  Spareribs, Southern Barbecued, '79 90
  Spareribs, Spicy Barbecued, '84 93
  Spareribs, Tangy Barbecued, '82 106
  Spareribs with Orange Barbecue Sauce, '83 11
  Spicy Barbecued Pork, '84 296
  Sundae, Barbecue, '02 121
Bean Sauce, Pork-and-Onions with, '85 76
Brunch Eggs, '85 44
Burgers, Hearty Sauced Pork, '84 125
Burgoo, Five-Meat, '87 3
Burgoo, Harry Young's, '87 3
Burgoo, Kentucky, '97 138
Burritos, '80 196
Burritos, Meat-and-Bean, '81 194
Cabbage Leaves, Stuffed, '00 270
Calabaza Guisada con Puerco (Pumpkin Cooked with Pork), '80 193
Casserole, Cheesy Pork, '81 M74
Casserole, Pork, '83 116
Cassoulet, '96 328

Chalupa, Bean, '80 223
Chalupas, Pork, '83 160
Chile Verde, Light, '88 148
Chili, Double-Meat, '79 269; '80 12
Chili Verde, '95 14
Chops. *See also* **PORK/Barbecue.**
  Apple-a-Day Pork Chops, An, '01 35
  Apple and Onion, Pork Chops with Mustard-Glazed, '01 47
  Apple-Kraut Pork Chops, '84 50
  Apple Pork Chops, '91 198
  Apple Pork Chops, Spicy, '87 230
  Apples, Pork Chops with Minted, '00 21
  Apricot-Sauced Pork Chops, '85 22
  Arlo, Pork, '87 229
  Baked Pork Chops and Apples, '81 10
  Baked Pork Chops, Greek-Style, '04 44
  Bake, Fiesta Pork, '79 265
  Balsamic Pork Chops, '01 128, 208
  Balsamic Pork Chops with Apples, '03 204
  Barbecue-Battered Pork Chops, '04 139
  Beans, Pork Chops with Baked, '93 18
  Black Bean-and-Corn Salsa Pork Chops, '01 320
  Boneless Pork Chops with Ancho Cream Sauce, '95 205
  Bourbon-Braised Pork Chops, '85 89
  Broiled Pork Chops, '89 191
  Broiled Pork Chops with Crabapple Peaches, '81 83
  Burritos with Pico de Gallo, Pork, '97 140
  Cajun Pecan Pork, '01 27
  Calypso Loin Chops with Mango Salsa, '98 232
  Carne Adovada, '91 162
  Casserole, Peppered Pork Chop, '81 235; '82 25; '83 39
  Casserole, Pork Chop, '94 255
  Casserole, Pork Chop-Vegetable, '90 208
  Cheesy Pork Chops, '83 102
  Chile Pepper Pork Chops, '02 210
  Chili Chops, '87 10
  Chili, Spicy 3-Bean, '03 291
  Chinese Pork Chops, '97 320
  Cider Pork Chops, '02 307; '03 271
  Cider-Sauced Pork Chops, '86 213; '87 81
  Company Pork Chops, '85 109
  Cornbread-Apple Stuffing, Pork Chops with, '99 14
  Costillas Rellenos (Stuffed Pork Chops), '82 219
  Country Pride Pork Chops, '79 159
  Couscous with Currants, Pine Nuts, and Pork, '00 295
  Cranberry Pork, '90 293
  Cranberry Pork Chops, '80 288; '90 53
  Creamy Gravy, Pork Chops and, '81 207
  Creamy Pork Chops, '01 208
  Creole Pork Chops, '83 102
  Creole-Style Pork Chops, '91 49
  Crusted Pork Chops, Flavorful, '04 44
  Curried Apricot Pork Chops, '89 191
  Dill-Cream Gravy, Pork Chops with, '84 81
  Dinner, Pork Chop, '80 84; '81 180; '88 25
  Dumplings, Make-Ahead Pork, '03 64
  Enchiladas, Pork, '97 M94
  Fajitas, Pronto Pork, '05 223
  Farm-Style Pork Chops, '02 42
  Fiesta, Pork Chops, '86 118
  Fried Pork Chops with Cream Gravy, '03 24
  Fried Pork Chops with Roasted Vegetables, '98 153
  Fruited Pork Chops, '87 194
  Fruit-Topped Pork Chops, '94 41
  Garlic-Parmesan Pork Chops, '02 61
  Garlic Sauce, Pork in, '04 181
  Glazed Apple Pork Chops, '86 300
  Glazed Chops, Honey-, '97 200
  Glazed Chops, Pineapple-Curry, '82 106
  Glazed Chops with Vegetables, '98 132
  Glazed Pork Chops, '86 185
  Glazed Pork Chops, Apple-, '84 212; '87 35

  Glazed Pork Chops, Bourbon-, '04 44
  Glazed Pork Chops, Ginger-, '05 203
  Glazed Pork Chops, Orange-, '81 234; '82 25; '83 39; '84 234; '91 84
  Glazed Pork Chops with Green Mole Sauce, Tamarind-, '95 266
  Glazed Pork Chops with Pecans and Apples, Commune's Maple-, '04 102
  Glazed Pork Chops with Rice, Fruit-, '82 73
  Glazed Pork Steaks, '83 178
  Gourmet Pork Chops, '79 180
  Gravy, Pork Chops and, '96 71
  Gravy, Pork Chops in, '91 137
  Grilled Asian Pork Chops, '02 307; '03 271
  Grilled Maple Chipotle Pork Chops on Smoked Gouda Grits, '04 172
  Grilled Pork Chops, '88 113; '98 246
  Grilled Pork Chops, Hawaiian, '85 159
  Grilled Pork Chops, Marinated, '81 110
  Grilled Pork Chops with Garlic Mashed Potatoes, '02 281
  Hawaiian Pork Chops, '86 212; '87 82
  Herbed Pork Chops, '97 147
  Herb-Peppered Pork Chops, '98 60
  Holiday Pork Chops, '05 313
  Honey-Lime Pork Chops, '91 33
  Honey-Pecan Pork Chops, '01 82
  Italiano, Pork Chops, '80 72
  Italian, Pork Chops, '79 47; '98 334
  Italian Pork Chops, '02 307; '03 271
  Jardinière, Pork Chops, '81 112; '82 12
  Lemon-Herb Pork Chops, '84 81; '89 M132
  Lemony Pork Chops, '88 118
  Marinated Pork Chops, '89 249
  Meal for Two, Pork Chop, '81 273
  Mexican Pork Chops, '99 108
  Moo Shu Pork, '99 237
  Moroccan Spiced Pork Chops, '01 230
  Mushrooms, Creamy Pork Chops with, '01 137
  Mustard-Apricot Pork Chops, '89 225
  Onion Gravy, Pork Chops in, '99 222
  Orange-Cranberry Pork Chops, '86 335; '87 84
  Orange Pork Chops, '84 81
  Oriental Pork Chops, '84 81; '90 212
  Pan-Fried Pork Chops, '02 16
  Pan-Fried Pork Chops, Lemony, '03 205
  Pan-fried Pork Chops with Onions, '05 43
  Parmesan Pork Chops with Apples, '93 338
  Peachy Pork Chops, '89 310
  Peanut Sauce, Pork Chops with, '83 29
  Pecan-Breaded Pork Chops with Beer Sauce, '95 266
  Pineapple Pork Chops, '87 M124
  Pineapple Salsa, Pork Chops with Warm, '02 144
  Pleasing Pork Chops, '79 125
  Polynesian Pork and Pineapple, '83 102
  Potatoes and Chops, Easy Scalloped, '00 289
  Potatoes, Pork Chops and Scalloped, '98 16
  Potato Scallop, Pork Chops and, '82 114
  Pretzel Pork Chops, '01 208
  Rice, Pork Chops and Spanish, '83 103; '85 293
  Rice, Pork Chops with White, '02 312
  Rice, Savannah Pork Chops and, '00 236
  Ripieno, Pork Chops with, '97 245
  Risotti, Pork Chops, '81 234; '82 26
  Rosemary-Crusted Pork Chops with Pears, '01 316
  Rosemary Pork Chops, '98 329
  Salad, Thai Pork, '00 249
  Salsa, Pork Chops with Black-and-White, '97 200
  Saté, Pork, '05 53
  Saucy Company Pork Chops, '83 102
  Saucy Pork Chop, '86 M140
  Saucy Pork Chops with Orange Slices, '05 197
  Saucy Pork Dinner, '97 26
  Sauerkraut, Pork Chops and, '88 98

PORK, Chops
(continued)

Savory Pork Chops, '87 194
Sherry-Apple Pork Chops, '88 40
Sherry, Chops in, '79 125
Skillet Dinner, Pork, '98 131; '00 335
Skillet Dinner, Pork Chop, '79 125
Skillet Pork Chops, Easy, '79 255
Skillet, Pork-Pepper, '01 309
Smoked Pork Chops with Jalapeño-Cherry Sauce, '01 208
Sour Cream Sauce, Pork Chops with, '83 102
Southwestern Pork Chops, '98 131
Southwest Pork in Black Bean Sauce, '05 139
Spaghetti with Pork and Peppers, '98 131
Special, Pork Chop, '79 81
Spicy Brown Mustard Pork Chops, '03 205
Stew with Rice, Black-Eyed Pea, '04 19
Stir-Fry, Mixed Veggie-and-Pork, '99 206
Stir-fry Pork, '05 241
Stuffed Baked Pork Chops, '79 222; '80 64
Stuffed Pork Chops, '84 195; '86 89; '02 204
Stuffed Pork Chops, Apple-, '79 125
Stuffed Pork Chops, Apple-Crumb, '81 234; '82 26; '83 39
Stuffed Pork Chops, Apple-Sage, '04 250
Stuffed Pork Chops, Apricot-, '86 76; '92 219; '03 49
Stuffed Pork Chops, Apricot-Mushroom, '95 287
Stuffed Pork Chops, Braised, '87 249
Stuffed Pork Chops, Cheese-, '84 81
Stuffed Pork Chops, Easy, '81 10
Stuffed Pork Chops, Fruit-, '82 136
Stuffed Pork Chops, Fruited, '86 197
Stuffed Pork Chops, Rice-, '83 102
Stuffed Pork Chops with Apricot Glaze, '89 M36
Stuffed with Prunes, Pork Chops, '84 7
Sweet-and-Sour Apple Sauce, Pork Chops with, '98 132
Sweet-and-Sour Pork Chops, '83 160
Sweet Potatoes, Pork Chops with, '96 269
Tacos with Pineapple Salsa, Pork, '03 128
Thai Pork Chops with Caramelized Onions, '05 85
Tuscan Pork Chops, '03 205
Vegetable Pork Chops, Skillet, '85 179
Vegetables, Golden Chops with, '89 218
Vegetables, Pork Chops and Garden, '88 297
Weeknight Pork Chops, '97 200
White Bean Puree, Pork Chops with, '96 226
Chorizo, Simple, '04 207
Chow Mein, Pork, '80 208; '90 101
Combo, Vegetable-Pork, '85 113
Curry, Hurry, '79 103
Cutlets, Apple-Glazed Pork, '92 181
Dinner, Pork-and-Noodles Skillet, '88 199
Dumplings, Steamed Sesame, '97 208
Egg Rolls, '86 81
Egg Rolls, Chinese, '96 101
Eggrolls, Shrimp and Pork, '82 240; '83 18
Egg Rolls, Vietnamese, '96 101
Eggs, Tulsa, '87 95
Empanadas, Pork Picadillo, '03 60
Fillets with Dark Cherry Sauce, Pork, '04 221
Hominy, Mexican, '86 255
Hot-and-Spicy Pork, '81 228
Kebabs, Spicy Pork, '82 182
Kebabs with Sesame Seeds, Pork, '00 337
Kung Pao Pork, '96 49
Leg of Pork with Cranberry Glaze, '88 244
Loin with Rosemary-Breadcrumb Crust, Grilled Pork, '05 200
Maple-Chipotle Pork on Smoked Gouda Grits with Sweet Onion Applesauce, '02 319
Marinated Pork Strips, '92 219

Meatballs in Gravy, '79 136
Meatballs, Sauerkraut, '86 257
Meatballs, Tangy Hawaiian, '79 129
Meat Loaf
Alabama Meat Loaf, '04 188
Family-Style Meat Loaf, '93 18
Italian Meat Loaf, '79 187
Mini Alabama Meat Loaves, '04 188
Mozzarella-Layered Meat Loaf, '79 71
Savory Meat Loaf, '87 216
Skillet Liver Loaf, '80 11
Stuffed Meat Loaf, '79 187
Swedish Meat Loaf, '81 M121
Triple Meat Loaf, '79 186
Meat Mixture, Basic, '92 241
Oriental, Pork, '81 212
Paella, Chicken-Pork-Shrimp, '82 245
Pâté, Country, '86 66
Pâté en Croûte, '86 65
Pâté with Spinach and Cream, Pork, '83 224
Picadillo II, '93 72
Picadillo, Taquitos with Pork, '04 206
Pie, Continental Meat, '95 256; '96 75
Pies, Natchitoches Meat, '84 21; '91 241
Pie, Sombrero, '81 140
Pilaf, Fruited Pork, '82 246
Pineapple Pork, '82 60
Poblanos Stuffed with Pork and Fruit, '97 269
Poblanos with Walnut Cream Sauce, Pork-Stuffed, '01 229
Polynesian Pork, '85 78
Posole, '95 226
Pot Pie with Cheese Grits Crust, Barbecue, '03 21
Quesadillas, Barbecued Pork, '04 187
Rack of Pork, Herb-Crusted, '97 262
Ribs. *See also* **PORK/Barbecue.**
Adams' Ribs, '95 236; '00 177; '03 312
Baby Back Ribs, '04 86
Baby Back Ribs, Barbecued, '97 234
Baby Back Ribs, Smoky Chipotle, '04 87
Baby Back Ribs, Sweet-and-Sour, '04 87
Baby Loin Back Ribs, John Wills's, '90 120
Baked and Grilled Spareribs, '97 211
Baked Ribs, Easy, '86 20
Baked Ribs, Lemon, '81 166
Chinese Spareribs, '81 10
Chinese-Style Spareribs, '02 93
Crispy Ribs with Plum Sauce, '98 182
Ginger Pork Ribs, '96 100
Glazed Spareribs, '88 98
Glazed Spareribs, Honey-, '82 163
Glazed Spareribs, Orange-, '84 296
Glazed Spareribs, Peach-, '86 14
Grilled Maple Spareribs, '99 136
Grilled Pork Ribs, Chipotle, '01 319
Grilled Ribs, Lemon, '81 154
Jamaican Jerk Raspberry Ribs, '00 88
Lemony Sweet Spareribs, '80 73
Maple Spareribs, '99 136
McCoy, Ribs, '04 132
Plantation Ribs, '84 217
Plum Sauce, Spareribs in, '99 136
Puerco en Adobo, '88 116
Rub, Paul's Pork Ribs, '05 174
Saucy Oven Spareribs, '80 207
Saucy-Sweet Ribs, '81 166
Smoked Baby Back Ribs, Big "D," '05 174
Smoked Ribs, '88 169
Smoked Ribs with Honey-Mustard Sauce, '92 168
Smoky Oven Ribs, '81 166
Smoky Ribs, '84 172
Spareribs, Southern, '95 116
Spicy Spareribs, '89 168
Spicy-Sweet Ribs and Beans, '02 299; '03 314
Stuffed Spareribs, Fruit-, '79 14

Sweet-and-Sour Ribs, '89 M84
Sweet-and-Sour Spareribs, '83 21
Tangy Ribs and Onions, '99 136
Thai Wings and Ribs, '97 M225
Rice, Pork Fried, '89 99
Risotto, Pork, '82 60
Roasts. *See also* **PORK/Barbecue.**
à l'Orange, Porc, '80 242
Apples and Mushrooms, Roast Pork Loin with, '92 218
Arista of Pork, '81 260
Barbecue Pork, Tabb's, '05 166
Boston Butt Roast with Gravy, '05 90
Braised Pork, Brown Sugar, '84 36
Braised Tuscan Pork Loin, '04 202
Brunswick Stew, Easy, '00 138
Chalupa Dinner Bowl, '05 238
Chinese Roast Pork, '91 308
Citrus-and-Garlic Pork Roast, '05 294
Company Pork Roast, '99 276
Crickhollow Roast Pork, '99 200
Crown Pork Flambé, Stuffed, '83 263
Crown Pork Roast, Stuffed, '89 272
Crown Pork Roast with Cranberry-Pecan Stuffing, '96 309
Crown Pork Roast with Cranberry Stuffing, Johnston County, '04 245
Crown Roast of Pork, Royal, '80 252
Crown Roast of Pork, Stuffed, '86 323
Crown Roast of Pork with Cranberry-Sausage Stuffing, '88 49
Dijonnaise with Peach Sauce, Pork Loin, '97 87
Festive Pork Loin Roast, '03 255
Festive Pork Roast, '01 276; '05 46
Fig-Balsamic Roasted Pork Loin, '03 45
Fried Pork Bites, Zesty, '05 90
Garlic-Orange Roast Pork, '03 277; '05 332
Glazed-and-Spiced Pork Loin, Apricot-, '05 259
Glazed Pork Loin, '87 229
Glazed Pork Loin, Cranberry-, '04 251
Glazed Pork Loin, Scuppernong-Orange, '98 220
Glazed Pork Roast, Cherry-, '91 84
Glazed Pork Roast, Orange-, '04 M236
Grilled Pork, Honey-and-Herb, '90 148
Grilled Pork, Jalapeño, '99 160
Grilled Pork Loin, Grandma Ruth's, '96 250
Grilled Pork Loin, Honey-, '92 219
Grilled Pork Roast, '97 323
Grilled Pork with Ranch-Barbecue Sauce, Slow-, '05 163
Honey-Roasted Pork, '96 251; '02 282
Indonesian Pork Roast, '81 227
Italian Pork Roast, '91 238; '92 27
Jezebel Sauce, Pork Roast with, '02 218
Loin of Pork, Roast, '84 276
Loin, Roast Pork, '88 221; '01 222
Loin Roast with Red Currant Sauce, Pork, '89 M84
Mandarin Pork Roast, '83 47
Marinated Pork Loin, '01 331
Marinated Pork Loin, Garlic-Honey, '99 334
Marinated Pork Roast, '80 71; '84 260
Minted Pork Loin, '99 96
Mix, Mexican Meat, '00 292
Orange-Dijon Pork Loin, '00 259
Peppercorn Pork Roast, '97 248
Pernil (Pork Roast), '92 157
Pineapple Pork Roast, '79 41
Pineapple Sweet-and-Sour Pork, '82 120
Polynesian Pork, '05 90
Pulled Pork Tortilla Pie with Snappy Mango Salsa, Cuban, '05 329
Raisin Sauce, Pork Loin with, '02 278
Rio Grande Pork Roast, '84 35, 296
Roasted Pork, '01 233, 237

Roasted Pork Loin, '96 32
Roasted Pork Loin with Mushrooms and Garlic, '92 301
Rolled Pork with Rhubarb Sauce, '96 134
Sandwiches, Easy Spanish Pork Dip, '04 312
Slow-Roasted Pork, '02 274
Smoked Boston Butt, '01 129
Smoked Pork, '99 81; '01 233; '03 121
Smoked Pork Loin Mahogany, '91 148
Smoked Pork Shoulder, '82 225; '01 147
Spiced Cherry Sauce, Roast Pork with, '89 324
Stew, Baja Pork, '98 283
Stew, Brunswick, '01 219
Stuffed Pork Loin, Apricot-Pecan, '94 274
Stuffed Pork Loin, Fruitcake-, '95 250
Stuffed Pork Loin Roast, Prune-, '80 29
Stuffed Pork Loin with Cider Sauce, Spiced-and-, '05 258
Stuffed Pork Rib Roast, Sausage-, '94 240
Stuffed Pork Roast, '81 111; '82 12; '85 229
Stuffed Pork Shoulder, '81 11
Stuffed Pork, Spinach-and-Herb, '89 193
Stuffed with Wild Rice, Pork Loin, '84 35
Stuffing, Pork Roast with Hopping John, '01 25
Tomato Sauce, Pork Roast with, '87 249
Tropical Pork Loin, '96 86
Tuscan Pork Loin, '05 296
Zesty Pork Roast, '85 179
Salad, Fiesta, '05 58
Salad, Mandarin Pork-and-Spinach, '88 M126
Salad, Oriental Pork, '92 140
Salad, "Pig in the Garden," '92 255
Salad, Pork-'n'-Bean, '87 83
Salad, Thai Green Apple, '99 111
Sandwiches, Party Pork, '88 M273
Sandwiches with Rosemary-Garlic Mayonnaise, Adobo
    Pork, '01 322
Sauce, Italian Meat, '01 160
Sausage, Pork, '81 55; '97 243
Sauté, Plum Delicious Pork, '89 105
Scaloppine, Pork, '04 221
Sesame Pork on Mixed Greens, Hot, '97 19
Sesame Pork Rounds, '89 122
Sloppy Joes, Pork, '86 294
Soup, Guadalajara, '88 30
Soup, Homemade, '79 198
Soup, Pork-and-Black Bean, '05 32
Soup, Pork Rind, '03 33
Spring Rolls with Sweet Chili Sauce, Shanghai, '01 236
Steaks, Herbed Pork, '80 72
Steaks, Peachy Pork, '79 166
Stew, Bama Brunswick, '87 4
Stew, Breeden Liles's Brunswick, '91 14
Stew, Brunswick, '80 264; '97 315; '03 29
Stew, Camp, '02 42
Stew, Dan Dickerson's Brunswick, '91 16
Stew, Easy Brunswick, '92 280; '99 235; '05 292
Stew, Georgian Brunswick, '92 35
Stew, Pancho Villa, '94 44
Stew, Sonny Frye's Brunswick, '87 4
Stew, Virginia Ramsey's Favorite Brunswick, '91 16
Stir-Fried Pork, '87 51
Stir-Fried Pork in Garlic Sauce, '84 141
Stir-Fry Pork and Cashews, '01 16
Strata, English Muffin Breakfast, '03 100
St. Tammany, Pork, '82 260
Swedish Porkburgers, '79 42
Sweet-and-Pungent Pork, '86 118
Sweet-and-Sour Pork, '79 42; '80 72, 227; '81 26, 104,
    111; '82 12; '84 218; '85 34, 194; '86 241;
    '90 317; '92 219
Tamales, '80 195
Tamales, Hot, '83 51
Tasso Fettuccine, Crawfish and, '96 290
Tasso Gravy, '96 270
Tempting Twosome, '81 240

Tenderloin
    Apple Butter Pork Tenderloin, '99 145
    Apple-Ginger Pork Tenderloin, '86 75
    Apple-Mushroom Pork Tenderloin, '95 53
    Apricot Sauce, Pork Tenderloin with, '99 44
    Asian Pork Tenderloin, '02 33
    Asian Pork Tenderloin with Spicy Sweet Potatoes,
        '02 207
    Barbecued Pork Tenderloin, '05 245
    Blackberry Sauce, Pork Medaillons with, '02 136
    Blue Cheese, Pork Tenderloin with, '86 76
    Cacciatore, Pork, '95 69
    Coriander-Pepper Pork Tenderloins, '99 145
    Cornmeal Biscuits, Pork Tenderloin on, '04 257
    Curried Pork Tenderloin, '86 76
    Danish Pork Tenderloin, '82 186
    Deep-Fried Whole Pork Tenderloin with Mint Sauce,
        '04 313
    Fruit Stuffing and Shiitake Sauce, Pork Tenderloin
        with, '97 218
    Garlic, Sweet Pork with, '04 17
    Glazed Pork Tenderloin, '90 315
    Glazed Pork Tenderloin, Ginger-, '05 203
    Glazed Pork Tenderloin, Jalapeño-, '03 186
    Glazed Pork Tenderloins, Orange-Cranberry, '00 314
    Grilled Balsamic Pork Tenderloin, '05 241
    Grilled Marinated Pork Tenderloin, '91 199
    Grilled Pork Medaillons, '93 229
    Grilled Pork Tacos with Cucumber-Radish Salsa,
        Adobo, '01 186
    Grilled Pork Tenderloin, '88 98; '91 163; '94 88; '02 187
    Grilled Pork Tenderloin, Garlic, '90 172
    Grilled Pork Tenderloin, Molasses-, '96 265
    Grilled Pork Tenderloins, '94 158
    Grilled Pork Tenderloin, Spicy, '04 96
    Grilled Pork Tenderloins with Rosemary Pesto,
        '01 174; '04 82
    Grilled Pork Tenderloin, Tropical Spinach Salad
        with, '04 51
    Grilled Pork Tenderloin with Apples, Celery, and
        Potatoes, '95 161
    Grilled Pork Tenderloin with Brown Sauce, '89 32
    Grilled Pork Tenderloin with Gingered Jezebel
        Sauce, '04 138
    Grilled Pork Tenderloin with Molasses Sauce, '97 193
    Grilled Pork Tenderloin with Orange Marmalade, '03 181
    Grilled Pork Tenderloin with Yogurt and Lime, '04 216
    Grilled Pork with Salsa, '90 128
    Grilled Tenderloins, Honey-, '92 199; '00 126
    Herb-Crusted Pork Tenderloin with Horseradish-
        Roasted New Potatoes, '98 168
    Herbed Pork Tenderloin with Parmesan-Pepper
        Toasts, '98 242
    Honeyed Pork Tenderloin with Avocado-Peach Salsa,
        '02 159
    Honey-Garlic Pork Tenderloin, '01 16
    Honey-Garlic Pork Tenderloins, '01 318
    Honey-Mustard Pork Tenderloin, '95 52
    Honey-Mustard Pork Tenderloin with Miniature
        Buttermilk Biscuits, '02 103
    Jamaican Jerk Pork Sandwiches with Apricot
        Mayonnaise, '97 320
    Jamaican Pork Tenderloin with Sauce Caribe,
        '02 320
    Kebabs, Margarita Pork, '98 M223
    Kebabs, Pineapple-Pork, '99 144
    Lamb Extraordinaire, '99 242
    Margarita Pork Tenderloin, '05 85
    Marinated Pork Tenderloin, '84 175
    Marinated Pork Tenderloin, Blueberry-Rum, '05 178
    Marinated Pork Tenderloin, Bourbon-, '04 168
    Marinated Pork Tenderloin with Jezebel Sauce,
        '96 212
    Marsala, Pork, '90 35

    Medaillons in Mustard Sauce, Pork, '90 96; '00 32
    Medaillons of Pork with Vegetables, '88 223
    Medaillons with Chutney Sauce, Pork, '87 35
    Medaillons with Fresh Fruit, Pork, '97 104
    Medaillons with Port Wine and Dried Cranberry
        Sauce, Pork, '95 330
    Molasses Pork Tenderloin with Red Wine Sauce,
        '02 290; '05 332
    Mustard Sauce, Pork Tenderloin with, '92 302;
        '99 145; '03 238
    Onion-Balsamic Sauce, Pork Tenderloin with, '99 44
    Orange Marmalade, Pork Tenderloin with, '91 49
    Oven-Roasted Vegetables and Pork, '99 259
    Parmigiana, Easy Pork, '94 57
    Peking Pork Tenderloin, '93 173
    Peppered Bacon-Wrapped Pork Tenderloin, '02 55
    Peppered Pork with Pecan Biscuits, '01 33
    Pepper-Honey Pork Tenderloins, '98 33
    Piccata, Pork, '94 57; '99 332
    Piccata, Pork Tenderloin, '86 76
    Pinwheels, Herbed Pork, '92 23
    Pinwheels, Spinach-Tenderloin, '89 M118
    Platter, Tenderloin, '79 42
    Polynesian Pork Tenderloin with Orange-Curry
        Sauce and Coconut Rice, '04 309
    Roasted Pork Tenderloins, Herb-, '00 96
    Roast Pork Tenderloin, '84 35
    Rosemary Pesto, Pork Tenderloin with, '98 16
    Salad, Grilled Pork Cosmopolitan, '04 123
    Salad with Spicy Tomato Dressing, Pork-and-Rice,
        '03 143
    Sandwiches, Beef and Pork Tenderloin, '80 175
    Sandwiches, Pork Tenderloin, '00 333
    Sandwiches with Bourbon Sauce, Pork Tenderloin,
        '02 53
    Sandwiches with Cranberry-Coriander Conserve,
        Pork Tenderloin, '04 286
    Scaloppine Marsala, Pork, '94 57
    Scaloppine, Olive-Pork, '89 191
    Sesame Pork, '01 177
    Sesame Pork Tenderloin, '95 53
    Skewered Pork Tenders, '00 200
    Spiced Pork Tenderloin with Chili-Cranberry Glaze,
        '98 320
    Spiked Pork Tenderloin with Sunny Pear Chutney,
        '01 280
    Stir-Fry, Sweet-and-Sour Pork, '03 92
    Stuffed Pork Tenderloin, '00 213
    Stuffed Pork Tenderloins, Fruit-, '87 270
    Stuffed Pork Tenderloin, Southern-Style, '99 45
    Stuffed Pork Tenderloin, Spinach-and-Bacon, '94 81
    Stuffed Tenderloin with Praline-Mustard Glaze,
        Apple-, '97 216
    Sunrise Pork Tenderloin, '79 103
    Sweet-and-Sour Pork, '00 110
    Sweet Pork Tenderloin with Lime and Chipotle, '04 184
    Towers, Pork Tenderloin, '86 75
    Vegetables, Pork Tenderloin with, '01 122
Terrine, Jeweled Pork, '84 130
Terrine of Pork and Veal, '93 287
Turnip Greens, Simple, '01 211
Wontons, Crispy Fried, '83 21
POTATOES. See also SWEET POTATOES.
Accordion Potatoes, '98 69
Anna, Potatoes, '97 53
Anna with Rosemary, Potatoes, '84 290
Appetizers, Fiery Stuffed Cherry Pepper, '97 269
Appetizers, Potato Shell, '89 M119
Bacon Dressing, Potatoes with Hot, '88 M294
Bake, Chive-Potato, '82 229
Baked. See also POTATOES/Stuffed.
    Avocado-Topped Potatoes, '83 3
    Beef and Chicken-Topped Potatoes, Creamed, '83 210
    Broccoli-and-Almond-Topped Potatoes, '83 3

Broccoli-Topped Baked Potatoes, '86 17
Buck's Taters, '95 72
Buffalo Chicken Twice-Baked Potatoes, '04 184
Cheese Sauce, Baked Potatoes with, '83 239
Cheesy Frank-Topped Potatoes, '83 3
Chili Potatoes, Roasted, '97 53
Chili-Topped Potatoes, '83 3; '98 M289
Crabmeat-Topped Potatoes, '83 3; '95 22
Croquettes, Baked Potato, '97 30
Easy Oven-Baked Potatoes, '82 202
Frank-Filled Potatoes, '84 M11
Fries, Baked Potato, '96 90
Garden Potato Cups, '83 76
Garden-Topped Potatoes, '83 4
Gumbo Potatoes, '95 22
Mexican-Topped Potatoes, '83 3
Micro-Baked Potatoes, '81 M61
Million Dollar Potatoes, '83 210
Mushroom-Dill-Topped Potatoes, '86 41
Mushroom Filling in a Peel, '84 214
New Potatoes, Baked, '90 90
Parmesan-Cream Potatoes, '97 54
Pleated Potatoes, Baked, '93 54
Quick Baked Potatoes, '92 M134
Quick Potatoes, '94 283
Rosemary-Baked Potatoes, '95 23
Rosemary-Roasted Potatoes, '95 20
Salad, Baked Potato, '97 319
Salmon-Topped Potatoes, '84 124
Sausage-Vegetable-Topped Potatoes, '98 29
Shrimp-Sauced Potatoes, '81 M61
Skins, Baked Potato, '86 81
Skins, Cheese Potato, '84 M239
Skins, Cheesy Potato, '82 78
Smoked Baked Potatoes, '97 25
Southwestern Potato Boats, '96 33
Sweet-and-Sour-Topped Potatoes, '83 4
Taco-Baked Potatoes, '84 119
Taco-Topped Potatoes, '93 M18
Twice-Baked Potatoes, Confetti, '02 35
Wedges, Potato, '94 M119
Bake, Ham-Potato-Pineapple, '93 302
Bake, Herbed Fish and Potato, '79 287
Bake, Onion-Potato, '83 M195
Bake, Potato, '83 209
Barbecued Potatoes, '91 311; '92 26
Basil-Cheese Potatoes, '90 M316
Basque-Style Potatoes, '79 46
Beans and Potatoes, Down-Home, '85 254
Beans and Potatoes, Snap, '98 177
Beef Hash, '99 62
Beets, Potato-Stuffed, '83 234
Blini with Sour Cream and Caviar, Potato, '01 274
Breads
Biscuits, Potato-Bacon, '94 214
Bowls, Irish Tater Bread, '96 111
Buns, Potato-Caramelized Onion, '03 234
Dough, Potato Sourdough Bread, '94 324; '95 77
Lightbread, Potato, '80 225
Loaves, Potato, '86 162
Old-Fashioned Potato Bread, '86 57
Potato Bread, '85 56
Rolls, Easy Potato, '89 287
Rolls, Feathery Light Potato, '81 305; '82 36
Rolls, Homemade Potato, '82 252
Rolls, Potato, '81 300; '99 290
Rolls, Potato Sourdough, '94 325; '95 77
Rolls, Potato Sourdough Cinnamon, '94 325; '95 77
Rolls, Potato Yeast, '87 53; '98 92
Rolls, Refrigerated Potato, '83 254

Rolls, Refrigerator Potato, '87 15
Rolls, Southern Potato, '86 299
Rolls, Super Potato, '85 145
Rolls, Supreme Potato, '82 130
Rolls, Whole Wheat Potato, '89 50
Sourdough Bread, Potato, '94 325; '95 77
Starter Food, '94 324; '95 77
Starter, Potato Sourdough, '94 324; '95 77
Toast, Potato-Crusted Texas, '94 142
Yeast, Potato, '87 53
Breakfast, Farmer's, '81 44
Breakfast Potatoes, '91 68
Breakfast Potatoes, Mexican, '81 209
Brisket, Aunt Suzi's, '02 321
Broiled Marinated Potatoes, '93 54
Browned Potatoes, Quick, '82 M172
Burgers, Potato-Crusted Crab, '94 139
Burritos, Breakfast, '99 103
Burritos, Potato-and-Egg, '02 72
Candy, Potato, '79 273
Caraway Potatoes, '85 85
Caraway Potatoes, Cheesy, '86 17
Casseroles
Au Gratin Potato Casserole, '05 250
au Gratin, Potatoes, '93 90, 217; '02 197
au Gratin, Potatoes and Eggs, '79 107
au Gratin, Potatoes-and-Zucchini, '84 5
au Gratin, Shredded Potatoes, '89 69
Beef Casserole, Easy, '00 208
Beefy Potato Casserole, '03 218
Breakfast Casserole, Potato, '80 52
Broccoli-Cheese Bake, Potato-, '80 114
Brunch for a Bunch, '88 57
Buffet Potatoes, '98 92
Campfire Casserole, '00 173
Caramelized Onions, Potato Casserole with, '03 231
Cheddar Cheese Potatoes, Double, '00 331
Cheese Casserole, Potato-, '79 101
Cheese Dream, Potato-, '91 307
Cheese Potatoes, Creamy, '88 M146
Cheese Potatoes, Double-, '86 6
Cheese Potatoes, Two-, '80 114
Cheesy Potato Casserole, '80 244; '83 53; '92 229
Cheesy Potatoes, '82 211
Cheesy Potatoes and Onions, '00 275
Chicken Livers and Potatoes, '82 218
Chive Potatoes, Cheesy, '79 46
Christmas Potatoes, '88 252
Cottage Potatoes, '89 69
Creamy Potato Bake, '82 201
Creamy Potato Casserole, '84 M113
Creamy Potatoes with Ham Bits, '87 191
Deviled Potatoes, Hot, '84 296; '85 196
Easy Potato Casserole, '80 114
Egg Casserole, Cheesy Potato-, '84 5
Eggplant Casserole, Potato-, '87 166
Escalloped Potatoes, '01 239
Fish and Potato Bake, Herbed, '80 34
Fluffy Potato Casserole, '80 268
Gourmet, Potatoes, '80 114
Gratin, Potato-and-Rutabaga, '96 237
Gratin, Potato-Butternut Squash-and-Gruyère, '01 43
Gratin, Potato-Leek, '05 281
Gratin, Smoky Potato, '00 233
Gratin with Caramelized Onions, Potato-Horseradish, '99 314
Gruyère Casserole, Potato-and-, '05 248
Gruyère Potatoes, '83 193
Ham-and-Potato Casserole, '83 M87; '96 103
Ham-and-Potato Casserole, Cheesy, '84 326
Hash Brown Breakfast Casserole, '03 306
Hash Brown Breakfast Casserole, Sausage-, '03 218
Hash Brown Casserole, Cheesy, '03 218
Hash Brown Casserole, Creamy, '03 193

Hash Brown Cheese Bake, '82 50
Hash Brown-Cheese Bake, '97 323
Hash Brown-Ham-Cheese Bake, '97 323
Hash Brown Potato Casserole, '81 40
Holiday Potato Casserole, '92 302
Irish Potato Casserole, '81 263
Italian Casserole, '80 81
Italian-Style Potatoes, '89 69
Jalapeño Potatoes, '84 39
Lemon and Nutmeg Potatoes, '80 36
Lorraine, Potatoes, '87 190
Mashed Potato Bake, Smoky, '00 214; '01 21
Mashed-Potato Bake, Swirled, '03 293
Mashed Potato Casserole, '85 296; '99 223
Mashed Potato Casserole, Three-Cheese, '03 72
Meat and Potatoes, Italian-Style, '03 97
Missy Potatoes, '85 259
Moussaka, Potatoes, '93 44
Mushroom-Potato Casserole, '84 5
Olive Potatoes, '80 114
Pepper Jack-Potato Casserole, '03 218
Peppery Potato Casserole, '95 182
Potato Casserole, '87 190; '99 274
Processor Potato Casserole, '86 159
Rosemary's Potatoes, '98 53
Russian Potatoes, '03 255
Saucy Potato Casserole, '81 276
Saucy Potatoes for Company, '82 202
Sausage-Potato Casserole, '86 217
Sausage-Spud Bake, Sunday Night Spicy Cheesy, '03 331
Scalloped Potatoes, '82 300; '83 211; '92 48
Scalloped Potatoes and Turnips, '85 235
Scalloped Potatoes, Cheesy, '83 82; '96 33
Scalloped Potatoes, Light, '89 311
Scalloped Potatoes, Mushroom, '87 191
Scalloped Potatoes, Out-of-This-World, '04 296
Scalloped Potatoes, Party, '87 191
Scalloped Potatoes, Pork Chops and, '98 16
Scalloped Potatoes, Skillet, '79 46
Scalloped Potatoes, Special, '88 162
Scalloped Potatoes, Wayside, '79 283
Scalloped Potatoes, Winter Herb Garden, '99 289
Scalloped Potatoes with Pimiento, '81 75
Scalloped Potatoes with Sweet Marjoram and
    Parmesan Cheese, '91 246
Scallop, Pork Chops and Potato, '82 114
Shoestring Potato Tuna Bake, '82 211
Sour Cream Potatoes, '84 39
Swirled Mashed-Potato Bake, '02 98
Thyme-Potato Bake, '96 121
Tomato Bake, Potato-, '86 17
Tomato Casserole, Saucy Potato-, '79 46
Caviar Potatoes, '84 80
Charcoal Potatoes, '88 129
Chicken and Potatoes, Roasted, '98 289
Chicken Fajita Spuds with Black Bean Salsa, '04 25
Chicken, Spanish, '98 183
Chili-Cheese Potatoes, '90 M62
Chili, Savory Potato, '83 284
Chowder. *See* **POTATOES/Soups.**
Colcannon, '90 64
Corn Dogs and Taters, '02 57
Cottage Potatoes, '89 69; '93 M92
Creamed Potatoes, '83 25
Cream-Wine Sauce, Potatoes in, '86 18
Creole Potatoes, '87 138
Crisps, Potato, '96 175
Croquettes, Parmesan Potato, '84 210
Croquettes, Potato, '87 116
Doughnuts, Chocolate-Glazed Potato, '85 6
Doughnuts, Old-Fashioned Potato, '84 56
Dumplings, Chicken and Potato, '99 326
Dumplings, Venison Stew with Potato, '87 304
Egg, Eagle Nest, '99 194

Eggs and Meat, Potatoes with, '91 311; '92 25
Fans, Parmesan Potato, '84 M240
Feta Cheese, Potatoes with, '84 295; '85 196
Fish-and-Potato Platter, '89 M248
Fried
  Almond-Fried Potatoes, '82 25
  Bacon-Fried Taters, '02 55
  Baskets, Potato, '86 193; '99 166
  Battered Catfish and Chips, '02 140
  Boxty, '02 67
  Catfish and Chips, Potato-Crusted, '02 140
  Catfish with Warm Pinto Bean-and-Bacon Salsa,
    Potato-Crusted, '03 331
  Chips, Homemade Potato, '82 25
  Crinkle-Cut Fries, '99 59; '04 122
  French Fries, '99 59; '04 122
  French Fries, Ranch-Seasoned, '05 93
  French Fries, Seasoned, '96 245
  Herb French Fries, '82 211
  Herb-Fried Potatoes, '82 25
  Latkes, '84 318; '90 254
  Latkes, Potato, '97 252; '00 281
  Latkes, Simple Potato, '05 272
  Latkes with Lemon-Date Relish, Potato, '96 271
  Nests with Savory Shavings, Potato, '84 209
  Okra and Potatoes, Fried, '97 136
  Okra-Potato Fry, '81 159
  Oven French Fries, '91 122
  Oven-Fried Potatoes, '82 25
  Oven Fries, Cheesy, '91 187
  Oven Fries, Parmesan, '98 235
  Oven Fries, Spicy, '02 34
  Patties, Fried Potato, '82 25; '93 54
  Patties, Potato-Onion, '95 269
  (Plantain Chips), Tostones de Plátano, '92 158
  Puffs, Potato, '80 36
  Rosemary Fries, Salty, '03 213
  Shavings, Savory, '84 209
  Southern-Fried Catfish and Chips, '02 140
  Southern-Fried Potatoes, '82 25; '97 53
  Special Potatoes, '83 169
  Steak Fries, Seasoned, '04 127
  Waffle Chips, '99 59; '04 122
  Wedges, Beer-Batter Potato, '83 211
Frittata, Potato, '89 145
Frittata, Potato-Bacon, '95 269; '98 330
Fritters, Cheese-Stuffed Potato, '96 153
Fritters, Leek-and-Potato, '00 324
Fritters, Potato-Ham, '98 249
Fritters with Lime-Cayenne Mayonnaise, Chicken-and-
  Mashed Potato, '04 121
Garlic-Parsley Potatoes, '90 290
Garlic Potatoes, '84 296; '85 196
Gnocchi à la Narciso, '97 246
Golden Potatoes, '96 139
Gratin, Dual Potato, '93 328
Gratin Potatoes, '02 276
Green and Gold, '00 91
Green Beans and Potatoes, '91 221
Green Beans with Ham and Potatoes, '01 223
Grilled Herb Potatoes, '84 172
Grilled Irish Potatoes, '97 53
Grilled Potatoes, Italian, '98 171
Hash, Beef, '95 24
Hash Brown Bake, '95 281
Hash Brown Potatoes, '81 48
Hash Browns, Carrot, '96 107
Hash Browns, Cheesy Sweet Potato, '02 248
Hash Browns, Company, '79 268; '80 14
Hash Browns, Convenient, '95 135
Hash Browns, Franks and, '80 166
Hash Brown Skillet Breakfast, '82 5
Hash Browns, Rosemary-Garlic, '02 248
Hash Browns, Smothered-Covered, '02 248

Hash Browns, Sweet Potato, '02 248
Hash with Rosemary, Potato, '98 16
Herb Butter, Potatoes with, '81 276
Herbed Potatoes, '91 220
Herbed Potatoes with Ham, '00 318
Herb Potatoes, '88 134
Italiano, Potatoes, '89 174
Mashed
  Ancho-Beer Mashers, '98 248
  Ancho Mashers, '03 243
  Bake, Creamy Potato, '88 41
  Bake, Smoky Mashed Potato, '00 214; '01 21
  Bake, Swirled Mashed-Potato, '02 98
  Basic Mashed Potatoes, '92 330
  Beef with Mashed Potatoes and Chipotle Cream,
    Grilled, '02 M320
  Bites, Mashed Potato, '98 249
  Blue Cheese Mashed Potatoes, '92 330
  Bowls, Mashed Potato, '97 199
  Buttermilk-Basil Mashed Potatoes, '95 330
  Buttermilk Mashed Potatoes, Golden, '05 298
  Caramelized Onion-and-Gorgonzola Mashed
    Potatoes, '01 256
  Casserole, Mashed Potato, '85 296; '99 223
  Casserole, Three-Cheese Mashed Potato, '03 72
  Celery Potatoes, Whipped, '94 305; '99 45; '01 212
  Celery Root Mashed Potatoes, '98 293
  Cheese Mashed Potatoes, Three-, '00 112
  Cheesy Mashed Potatoes, '02 98; '05 204
  Chile Mashed Potatoes, '00 161
  Chive-Cream Cheese Mashed Potatoes, '92 330
  Chive Mashed Potatoes, '97 308
  Chive Potatoes, Creamy, '00 109
  Crab Marinière, Mashed Potatoes with, '99 165
  Cream Cheese Mashed Potatoes, '97 14; '02 35
  Creamy Mashed Potatoes, '00 315
  Crust, Barbecue Pot Pie with Mashed Potato, '03 21
  Dill-Sour Cream Mashed Potatoes, '92 330
  Duchesse, Potatoes, '84 210
  Duchess Potatoes, '93 288
  Feta Mashed Potatoes, '92 330
  Fix-Ahead Mashed Potatoes, '89 70
  Flank Steak, Mashed Potato-Stuffed, '01 25
  Fluffy Potatoes, '84 296; '85 196
  Garlic-Gruyère Mashed Potatoes, '98 322
  Garlic-Herb Mashed Potatoes, '05 218
  Garlic Mashed Potatoes, '92 330; '93 328; '97 308;
    '02 281; '05 42
  Garlic Mashed Potatoes, Speedy, '04 M81
  Garlic Smashed Potatoes, Loaded, '01 325
  Good Old Mashed Potatoes, '92 215
  Green Onion-and-Bacon Mashed Potatoes, '02 110
  Harvest Mashed Potatoes, '98 248
  Herbed Lemon Mashed Potatoes, '93 208
  Horseradish Mashed Potatoes, '98 69, 118
  Italian Mashed Potatoes, '03 M135
  Jazzy Mashed Potatoes, '87 192
  Leek Mashed Potatoes, '02 98; '03 293
  Leek Mashed Potatoes, Creamy, '02 291; '05 334
  Lemon Mashed Potatoes, '04 181
  Lemon-Poppy Seed Mashed Potatoes, Creamy, '03 294
  Mexican Mashed Potatoes, '92 330
  Nest, Peas in a Potato, '84 M239
  Nests, Mashed Potato, '94 141
  Old-Fashioned Mashed Potatoes, '89 234
  Orange Mashed Potatoes, '96 33
  Parsnip Mash, '97 263
  Pesto Mashed Potatoes, '92 330
  Quick-and-Easy Mashed Potatoes, '93 41
  Ranch Potatoes, '05 256
  Roasted Garlic Mashed Potatoes, '95 288
  Roasted Garlic-Parmesan Mashed Potatoes, '97 263;
    '00 146
  Seasoned Potatoes, '87 253

Simple Mashed Potatoes, '05 271
Snow-Capped Potatoes, '84 255
Stuffed Mashed Potatoes, '98 328
Sweet-and-Savory Mashed Potatoes, Baked, '02 244
Three-Potato Mash, '05 271
Thunderbolt Potatoes, '94 213
Tomato Gravy, Mashed Potatoes with, '02 M17
Topping, Mashed Potato, '89 243
Turnips and Potatoes, '79 254
Twice-Baked Mashed Potatoes, '04 97
Mexican-Style Potatoes, '91 78
Mustard Greens and Potatoes, '86 224
Mustard Potatoes, '79 32
New Potatoes
  Baked New Potatoes, '90 90
  Basil Cream Sauce, New Potatoes with, '91 46
  Blue Cheese Potatoes, '98 247; '04 214
  Browned New Potatoes, '86 244
  Caviar Potatoes, Appetizer, '86 223
  Chard and Potatoes, Creamy, '98 250
  Cheese Potatoes, Double-, '86 6
  Cheesy New Potatoes, '85 156
  Creamed Peas and New Potatoes, '79 102
  Creamy Potatoes and Broccoli, '92 61
  Feta Cheese Potatoes, '04 214
  Garden New Potatoes, '91 80
  Garlic New Potatoes, '92 54
  Gratin, Creamy New Potato, '01 M320
  Gratin with Lima Beans and Egg, New Potato, '01 71
  Green Beans with New Potatoes, '87 164
  Ham-Stuffed New Potatoes, '88 211
  Herbed New Potatoes, '81 102; '83 9, M148
  Herb-Roasted Potatoes, '01 89
  Jalapeño New Potatoes, Cheesy, '01 89
  Lemon-Buttered New Potatoes, '84 149; '90 268; '98 159
  Lemon-Butter Sauce, New Potatoes with, '00 103
  Lemon-Dill Sauce, Potatoes and Green Beans with, '01 89
  Lemon Sauce, New Potatoes with, '86 130
  Lemony New Potatoes, '82 158
  Medley, New Potato, '90 279
  Medley, Potato, '92 61
  Parsley-Chive Sauce, New Potatoes with, '84 212
  Parsley New Potatoes, '79 122
  Roasted Caraway Potatoes, '96 82
  Roasted New Potatoes, '90 138
  Roasted New Potatoes, Crispy, '98 166
  Roasted New Potatoes, Herb-Crusted Pork
    Tenderloin with Horseradish-, '98 168
  Roasted Potatoes, Jan's, '01 224
  Salad, Asparagus-and-New Potato, '86 69
  Salad, New Potato, '84 120, 139; '94 162; '01 142
  Seasoned New Potatoes, '87 M151
  Skillet, Potato-Vegetable, '92 61
  Steamed Potatoes, Lemon-, '86 177
  Summertime Potatoes, '86 M195
Olive Potatoes, Tangy, '04 214
Omelet, Family-Size Potato, '94 31
Omelet, Open-Faced Bacon-and-Potato, '02 246
Omelet, Potato-Sprout, '79 128
Omelets, Country, '91 128
Oven Potatoes, Crispy, '82 96
Pancake, Potato, '85 20
Pancakes, German Potato, '98 279
Pancakes, Leftover Potato, '96 138
Pancakes, Moist Potato, '80 36
Pancakes, Old-Fashioned Potato, '96 138
Pancakes, One Potato-Two Potato, '96 138
Pancakes, Parsley-Potato, '96 251; '97 103
Pancakes, Potato, '79 115; '89 144
Pancakes, Potato-Ham, '96 138
Pancakes, Quick Potato-Chive, '04 248
Parmesan-Paprika Potatoes, '99 169
Parmesan Potatoes, '82 270; '90 M62; '92 M341; '93 M46
Parmesan-Potato Fans, '88 M190

POTATOES
(continued)

Parmesan Potato Wedges, '95 181
Parslied Potatoes, '86 18
Pastries, Potato-and-Blue Cheese, '03 258
Patties, Thunderbolt Potato, '94 213
Peas and Potatoes Vinaigrette, Dilled, '00 102
Peas and Potatoes with Dill, '99 67
Peppers, Potatoes with Sweet Red, '87 192
Phyllo Potatoes, '02 219
Pie, Country Breakfast, '93 M328
Pie, Meat-and-Potato, '84 23
Pie, Potato-Topped Turkey, '86 265
Pie, Shepherd's, '00 55
Pizza, Sausage-Potato, '01 199
Pizzas, Roasted Potato, '99 16
Point Clear Potatoes, '02 250
Pork Tenderloin with Apples, Celery, and Potatoes, Grilled, '95 161
Pudding, Carrot-Potato, '94 279
Puff, Potato-Cheese, '95 269
Puffs, Celeried Potato, '89 279
Quiche, Crustless Potato, '83 49
Red Potatoes, Green Beans and, '03 158
Roasted Green Beans, Potatoes, and Fennel, '00 322
Roasted Potatoes, '99 60
Roasted Potatoes, Carrots, and Leeks, '94 276
Roasted Potatoes, Garlic-, '95 87, 342
Roasted Potatoes, Oven-, '98 103; '05 44
Roasted Potatoes, Two-Color Rosemary, '05 18
Roasted Potato Thins, '02 23
Roasted Potato Trio, '00 311; '02 310
Rolls. *See* **POTATOES/Breads.**
Rosemary, Potatoes Anna with, '84 209
Roses, Potato, '81 246
Sage Potatoes, '94 320
Salads
    Any Day Potato Salad, '81 154
    Avocado, Potato Salad with, '98 332
    Avocado-Potato Salad with Horseradish Dressing, '96 200
    Bacon 'n' Onion Potato Salad, '05 188
    Bacon Potato Salad, '05 171
    Bacon-Topped Potato Salad, '85 59
    Baked Potato Salad, '97 319
    Basil Potato Salad, '94 178
    Bean Salad, Potato-, '82 301
    BLT Potato Salad, '05 213
    Blue Cheese-Potato Salad, '91 208
    Broccoli-Potato Salad, Hot, '85 23
    Charletta's Potato Salad, '98 153
    Chunky Potato Salad, '81 M138
    Cobb Salad, Potato, '03 140
    Colorful Potato Salad, '01 94
    Confetti Potato Salad, '80 5; '88 16
    Corned Beef-Potato Salad, '85 213
    Corned Beef Salad, Potato-, '81 36
    Cottage Cheese-Potato Salad, '79 147, 285
    Creamy Potato Salad, '80 178; '88 171; '92 241; '98 175; '01 334
    Creole Potato Salad, '99 136
    Cucumbers and Tomatoes, Potato Salad with, '03 92
    Curried Potato Salad, '99 137
    Deluxe Potato Salad, '80 155
    Dill-and-Sour Cream Potato Salad, '93 105; '94 100
    Dilled Potato Salad with Feta, '05 128
    Dill Potato Salad, '85 213; '94 179; '99 104
    Dill Potato Salad, Hot, '79 78
    Dutch Potato Salad, Hot, '86 297; '87 176
    Festive Potato Salad, '89 315
    Fipps Family Potato Salad, '02 138
    Fish-Potato Salad, Smoked, '84 233
    French-Style Potato Salad, '88 171

    Fruity Potato Salad, '85 214
    Garden Patch Potato Salad, '84 82
    German Potato Salad, '82 134, 239; '84 18; '92 169; '97 195; '98 175
    German Potato Salad, Hot, '79 78; '94 254
    German-Style Potato Salad, '83 23; '88 M194
    Goat Cheese and Potato Salad, Warm, '96 234
    Grecian Potato Salad, '82 55
    Greek Potato Salad, '98 276
    Green Bean-Potato Salad, '83 80; '01 181; '04 142
    Green Bean-Red Potato Salad, '96 175
    Green Bean-Red Potato Salad, Layered, '05 146
    Green Bean Salad, Potato-and-, '00 162
    Ham-and-Egg Potato Salad, '86 84
    Ham and Potato Salad, '80 272
    Ham-and-Potato Salad, '95 94
    Herbed Potato Salad, '87 171; '94 164
    Horseradish Potato Salad, '98 175
    Hot-and-Light Potato Salad, '93 90
    Hot Potato Greens, '97 20
    Hot Potato Salad, '79 78; '81 276; '86 10
    Hot Potato Salad Supreme, '79 78
    Jalapeño Potato Salad, '97 64
    Joy's Potato Salad, '99 83
    Layered Creamy Potato Salad, '81 23
    Layered Potato Salad, '03 183
    Lemon-Basil Potato Salad, '97 63; '01 178
    Light Potato Salad, '02 138
    Lime-Potato Salad, '02 22
    Marinated Potato-Apple Salad, '05 41
    Marinated Potato Slices, '93 98
    Mediterranean Spring Salad, '80 148
    Mustard Potato Salad, '86 302
    New Potato Salad, '84 120, 139; '94 162; '01 142
    New Potato Salad, Asparagus-and-, '86 69
    Niçoise, Salad, '03 35
    Olive-Potato Salad, '85 114
    Onion and Celery, Potato Salad with, '02 138
    Parmesan Potato Salad, Hot, '79 78
    Parslied Potato Salad, '85 240
    Patio Potato Salad, '90 160
    Peas-and-Potatoes Vinaigrette, Dilled, '01 327
    Pepper Cups, Potato Salad in, '79 78
    Peppers, Potato Salad 'n', '83 135
    Pesto Potato Salad, '90 164
    Pickle-Potato Salad, Sweet, '85 213
    Pickle, Potato Salad with Sweet, '02 138
    Pole Bean-Potato Salad, Hot, '79 74
    Potato Salad, '90 122; '94 160; '00 195; '01 163; '03 163
    Red Potato Salad, '93 119; '96 172; '02 138
    Roasted New Potato Salad, '04 91
    Roasted Potato-and-Bacon Salad, '05 289
    Roasted-Potato Salad, Creamy, '97 161
    Roasted Red Peppers, Potato Salad with, '04 100
    Salmon-Potato Salad, '87 285
    Saucy Potato Salad, '87 123
    Savory Potato Salad, '80 30
    Shrimp-and-Potato Salad, '96 211
    Smoked Salmon Potato Salad, '97 64
    Sour Cream Potato Salad, '79 104; '80 79; '99 137
    Sour Cream-Potato Salad, '84 149
    Southern-Style Potato Salad, '04 199
    South-of-the-Border Potato Salad, '94 178
    Spicy Potato Salad, '97 305
    Steak Salad Niçoise, Grilled, '98 148
    Sugar Snap Peas, Potato Salad with, '91 120
    Sweet and Sour Potato Salad, '80 152
    Sweet-and-Sour Potato Salad, '92 106
    Tri Club Potato Salad, '92 166
    Tuna-Potato Salad, '84 289
    Vegetable Potato Salad, '03 136
    Warm Potato-and-Sausage Salad, '96 25
    Warm Potato Salad with Smoked Sausage, '97 267
Scalloped Potatoes and Chops, Easy, '00 289

Scalloped Potatoes, Barbecue, '04 139
Scalloped Potatoes with Ham, '02 42
Scalloped Root Vegetables, '98 310
Seasoned Potatoes, Simple, '01 259
Skillet Potatoes, Oregano-and-Lemon, '93 54
Skillet Potatoes, Peppy, '86 110
Skins, Baked Potato, '86 81
Skins, Cheesy Potato, '82 78
Skin Snack, Potato, '91 18
Slims, Potato, '81 276
Soufflé, Cheesy Potato, '89 332
Soufflé Potatoes, '84 295; '85 196; '90 14
Soups
    Asparagus-Potato Soup, '85 23
    Asparagus Soup, '98 290
    Bacon Soup, Potato-, '84 M38
    Baked Potato Soup, '91 311; '92 26; '03 29
    Beet Soup, Potato-, '88 156
    Bisque, Spinach-Potato, '86 66
    Bisque, Squash, '98 290
    Carrot Soup, Potato-, '88 297
    Celery-and-Potato Soup, '84 279
    Cheddar-Potato Soup, '03 M283
    Cheesy Potato-and-Wild Rice Soup, '89 16
    Chowder, Mushroom-Potato, '92 331
    Chowder, Potato-Corn, '94 66
    Chowder, Potato-Vegetable, '98 335
    Chowder with Green Chiles, Potato, '00 329
    Chowder with Ham, Potato, '99 141
    Chowder, Yukon Gold-Cheese, '03 296
    Cream of Potato Soup, '80 M224; '82 21
    Cream of Potato Soup, Golden, '86 302
    Creamy Potato Soup, '81 19, 98; '84 112
    Cucumber-Potato Soup, Chilled, '85 93
    Cucumber Soup, Cold Potato-, '88 160
    Easy Potato Soup, '92 17
    Garlic-and-Potato Soup, Golden, '04 214
    Hearty Potato Soup, '98 292
    Holiday Potato Soup, '79 236
    Irish Potato Soup, '99 54
    Kale Soup, Creamy, '96 203
    Leek-and-Potato Soup, '84 112
    Leek Soup, Cream of, '99 276
    Onion-and-Potato Soup, Creamy, '92 51; '97 304
    Pea Soup, Potato-, '94 90
    Potato Soup, '82 278; '83 292; '92 263
    Sausage-Potato Soup, '80 25
    Sausage Soup, Easy Potato-, '98 315
    Special Potato Soup, '82 3
    Subtle Potato Potage, '80 78
    Three-Potato Soup, '86 16
    Vichyssoise, '86 181
    Vichyssoise with Mint Cream, Cucumber, '98 246
    Yogurt Soup, Potato-, '92 217
Spread, Creamy Potato-Garlic, '02 35
Steak 'n Potatoes, Skillet, '81 18
Stew, Frogmore, '00 174, 336
Stew, Meatball, '98 30
Stew, Potato-Oyster, '89 243
Stir-Fry, Potato, '93 240
Stir-Fry, Potato-Snow Pea, '86 173
Stuffed
    Alfredo, Potatoes, '89 204
    Bacon-Stuffed Potatoes, '86 193
    Bacon-Stuffed Potatoes, Cheesy, '81 M61
    Baked Potatoes, Stuffed, '83 322; '00 293
    Baked Stuffed Potatoes, '84 38
    Barbecue Potatoes, Double-Stuffed, '05 162
    Béchamel Sauce, Stuffed Potatoes with, '84 M239
    Black-Eyed Pea-Spinach-Stuffed Potatoes, '95 22
    Blue Cheese Potatoes, Bacon-Topped, '79 46
    Blue Cheese Stuffed Potatoes, '81 276
    Blue Cheese-Stuffed Potatoes, '89 69
    Breakfast-Stuffed Potatoes, '00 179

Broccoli Bakers, **'99** 308
Broccoli-Shrimp Stuffed Potatoes, **'92** M228
Caviar Potatoes, Appetizer, **'86** 223
Cheddar, Broccoli, and Ham Stuffed Potatoes, **'04** 26
Cheese-and-Chive Potatoes, Creamy, **'99** 308
Cheese Sauce, Stuffed Potatoes with, **'87** 192
Cheesy Stuffed Potatoes, **'02** 175
Chicken-Cheese Stuffed Potatoes, **'86** 55
Chicken Fajita Spuds, **'96** 238
Chive-and-Gorganzola Stuffed Potatoes, Creamy, **'99** 308
Chives, Potatoes with, **'81** M61
Chive-Stuffed Baked Potatoes, **'79** 52
Chive-Stuffed Potatoes, Cheesy, **'91** 128
Chive-Stuffed Potatoes, Creamy, **'80** 268
Crab-Stuffed Potatoes, **'91** 311; **'92** 26; **'99** 307
Crab-Stuffed Potatoes, Cheesy, **'86** 17
Creamy Stuffed Baked Potatoes, **'86** 55
Creamy Stuffed Potatoes, **'79** 211
Fish-Stuffed Potatoes, **'92** 306
Fluffy Stuffed Potatoes, **'86** 223
Franks and Potatoes, Stuffed, **'81** 202
Grilled Stuffed Potatoes, **'05** 123
Ham-Stuffed Baked Potatoes, **'02** 52
Ham Stuffed Potatoes, **'79** 210
Hearty Stuffed Potatoes, **'89** M282
Herb Stuffed Potatoes, **'79** 211
Jalapeño-Ham Stuffed Potatoes, **'81** M61
Lemon-Herb Stuffed Potatoes, **'83** 173
Mexican-Stuffed Potatoes, **'91** 131
Mushroom-Swiss Spuds, **'96** M238
Patchwork Potatoes, **'86** 54
Rellenos Potatoes, Papa's, **'96** 238
Roquefort, Potatoes, **'79** 211
Savory Stuffed Potatoes, **'81** 101
Seafood-Stuffed Potatoes, **'95** M192
Shrimp-and-Mushroom Stuffed Potatoes, **'99** 308
Shrimp Boats, **'79** 57
Shrimp-Stuffed Potatoes, Creamy, **'80** 36
South-of-the-Border Stuffed Potatoes, **'86** 54
Stuffed Potatoes, **'89** 173; **'01** 48; **'02** 283
Summertime Potatoes, **'86** M195
Tuna Stuffed Potatoes, **'79** 210
Twice Baked Cottage-Style Potatoes, **'91** 135
Twice-Baked Potato, **'90** M295
Twice-Baked Potatoes, **'83** 227; **'91** 185
Vegetable-Topped Stuffed Potatoes, **'85** 235
Yogurt-Stuffed Potatoes, **'88** 24
Zesty Stuffed Potatoes, **'94** M46
Tacos, Breakfast, **'91** 316
Tarts, Phyllo Potato, **'98** 69
Tortilla Campesina, **'89** 85
Tortilla Espanola, **'92** 175
Tortilla, Potato, **'00** 85
Vinaigrette, Potato-Broccoli, **'85** 84
Wedges, Lemon Potato, **'88** 21
Wedges, Lemony Potato, **'90** M61
POULTRY. *See* **CHICKEN, CORNISH HENS, GAME, TURKEY.**
PRALINE. *See also* **CANDIES/Praline.**
Almonds, Praline, **'97** 285
Bananas, Praline, **'84** 313
Bars, Chewy Praline-Chocolate Fudge, **'04** M330
Bars, Praline, **'05** M205
Brownies, Praline, **'93** 243
Brownies, Praline-Pecan, **'05** M288
Buns, Praline, **'90** 195
Buttercream, Praline, **'95** 243
Cake, Chocolate-Praline, **'01** 235
Cake, Chocolate-Praline Pecan, **'03** 288
Cake, Praline, **'81** 162
Cake, Praline Cream, **'01** 272
Cake, Praline-Filled Carrot, **'03** 332
Cake, Praline Ice Cream, **'80** 84

Cake, Praline Pound, **'82** 88
Cakes, Praline-Pecan, **'05** 286
Cheesecake, Pecan Praline, **'03** 269
Cheesecake, Praline, **'83** 270; **'89** 93
Cheesecake, Praline-Crusted, **'99** 295
Coffee, Praline, **'97** 17; **'01** 291
Coffee, Praline-Flavored, **'87** 69
Compote, Warm Praline Fruit, **'85** 260
Cookies, Crispy Praline, **'03** 131
Cookies, Crispy Praline-Chocolate Chip, **'03** 131
Cookies, Praline, **'91** 271
Cookies, Praline Shortbread, **'88** 242
Cookies, Praline Thumbprint, **'89** 328
Cream, Praline, **'01** 272
Filling, Praline, **'89** 328
Filling, Praline Cream, **'03** 332
Freeze, Praline, **'89** 60; **'90** 48
French Toast, Praline, **'98** 55
Frosting, Praline, **'01** 235
Glaze, Apple-Stuffed Tenderloin with Praline-Mustard, **'97** 216
Glaze, Praline, **'82** 196
Ham, Praline, **'85** 302; **'96** 303
Horns, Praline, **'96** 316
Ice Cream, Praline, **'89** 318
Ice Cream, Pralines and Cream, **'82** 184; **'83** 159
Icing, Praline Fudge, **'04** 331
Muffins, Banana-Praline, **'04** 21
Pastries, Praline, **'89** 318
Pecans, Praline, **'97** 285; **'05** 286
Pie, Chocolate-Praline, **'86** 259
Pie, Frosty Pumpkin-Praline, **'91** M234
Pie, Georgia Peach-and-Praline, **'98** 196
Pie, Peach Praline, **'89** 136
Pie, Pear-Praline, **'97** 192
Pie, Praline-Apple, **'99** 331; **'05** 251
Pie, Praline-Topped Pumpkin, **'00** 332
Pie, Pumpkin Praline, **'80** 244
Powder, Praline, **'95** 243
Sauce, Bourbon Praline, **'81** 170
Sauce, Chocolate-Praline, **'85** M295
Sauce, Peach-Praline, **'85** 161
Sauce, Praline, **'83** 25; **'84** 143; **'89** 95; **'92** 282; **'93** 214; **'94** 206, 312; **'96** 285
Sauce, Praline Ice Cream, **'85** 189
Sauce, Southern Praline Ice Cream, **'86** M227
Sweet Potatoes and Apples, Praline, **'03** 260
Sweet Potatoes, Praline-Topped, **'98** 96
Toast, Orange Praline, **'79** 36
Torte, Chocolate Praline, **'84** 165
Torte, Lucy's Apricot Praline, **'95** 243
Torte, Praline-Pumpkin, **'01** 285
PRESERVES. *See* **JAMS AND JELLIES.**
PRESSURE COOKER
Carrots Polynesian, **'79** 45
Chicken Marengo, **'92** 70
Jambalaya, Black-Eyed Pea, **'92** 70
Meat Mix, Mexican, **'00** 292
Pot Roast with Vegetables, **'00** 18
Roast Beef, Pressure Cooker, **'01** 86
Roast, Pressure-Cooker, **'91** 289
Roast with Onion-and-Mushroom Gravy, **'00** 293
Stew, Quick Beef, **'92** 71
PRETZELS
Brownies, Saucepan Pretzel, **'85** 171
Chocolate-Covered Pretzels, **'82** 295
Dressing, Pretzel, **'86** 280
Flying Brooms, **'98** 255
Frosted Pretzels, **'92** 280
Garlands, Pretzel, **'93** 286
Herb Pretzels with Lower Sodium Horseradish Mustard, **'86** 325
Homemade Pretzels, **'84** 159; **'91** 185
Nuggets, Golden North Pole, **'99** M309

Popcorn, Pretzel, **'84** 30
Reindeer Food, Magic, **'99** M309
Salad, Strawberry-Pretzel, **'03** 290
Soft Pretzels, **'83** 18
Soft Pretzels, Chewy, **'87** 159
Whole Wheat Pretzels, **'89** 20
PRUNES
Bavarian, Prune, **'86** 223
Bread, Prune-Nut, **'87** 255; **'91** 55
Butter, Prune-Orange, **'92** 49
Cake and Sauce, Prune, **'85** 118
Cake, Prune, **'85** 223
Cake, Spicy Prune, **'79** 136
Chicken with Prunes, Saffron, **'97** 264
Compote, Baked Prune, **'94** 50
Merlot, Prunes in, **'98** 18
Muffins, Miniature Prune, **'85** 223
Muffins, Spicy Prune, **'97** 271
Muffins, Wheat Germ-Prune, **'81** 106
Orange-Spiced Prunes, **'85** 224
Pork Chops Stuffed with Prunes, **'84** 7
Pork Loin Roast, Prune-Stuffed, **'80** 29
Raspberry Prunes, **'82** 124
Relish, Peppy Prune, **'90** 227
Stuffed Prunes, **'85** 47
Tarts, Brandied Prune, **'85** 223
Tzimmes, **'95** 102
PUDDINGS. *See also* **CUSTARDS, MOUSSES.**
Almond Cream, **'00** 27
Apple-Nut Pudding with Hot Rum Sauce, **'79** 86
Applesauce-Graham Cracker Pudding, **'81** 34
Banana
Almost Banana Pudding, **'88** 174
Banana Pudding, **'82** 53; **'84** 94; **'85** 255; **'88** 16, 32; **'03** 24
Basic Banana Pudding, **'81** 59
Best-Ever Banana Pudding, **'00** 332
Cheesecake Banana Pudding with Caramel Syrup, The Ultimate No-Bake, **'05** 326
Creamy Banana Pudding, **'89** M130
Cupcakes, Banana Pudding Ice-Cream, **'01** 173
Delicious Banana Pudding, **'80** 9
Fudge-Banana Pudding, **'97** 331
Graham Banana Pudding, **'02** 62
Mallow Pudding, Banana-, **'86** 139
No-Bake Banana Pudding, **'91** 172; **'99** 197
Old-Fashioned Banana Pudding, **'92** 94
Over-the-Moon Banana Pudding, **'03** 140
Peanut Butter-Banana Pudding, **'93** 340; **'05** 44
Pops, Banana Pudding Parfait, **'96** 180
Sour Cream Banana Pudding, **'98** 90
Sugar Biscuits, Banana Pudding with, **'04** 72
Surprise Banana Pudding, **'86** 7
Trifle, Banana Pudding, **'98** 273
Beach, The, **'95** 168
Black-and-White Pudding, Rich, **'01** 111
Blackberry Pudding Tarts, **'93** 200; **'00** 147
Blueberry-Raspberry Pudding, Russian, **'97** 128
Bread
Almond-Cream Cheese Bread Pudding with Amaretto Cream Sauce, Layered, **'03** 330
Amish Bread Pudding, **'80** 8
Apple-Raisin Bread Pudding, **'88** 175
Apricot Bread Pudding, **'85** 24
Bananas Foster Bread Pudding, **'04** 235
Berry Bread Pudding with Vanilla Cream Sauce, **'05** 260
Biscuit Pudding, **'79** 86; **'93** 51
Blueberry Bread Pudding, **'88** 154; **'03** 119
Blueberry-Lemon Sauce, Bread Pudding with, **'01** 117
Bread Pudding, **'89** M130; **'90** 219
Brown Sugar Bread Pudding with Crème Anglaise, **'05** 239
Buttermilk Bread Pudding with Butter-Rum Sauce, **'95** 134

PUDDINGS
(continued)

Cheesy Bread Pudding, '83 68
Chocolate Biscuit Bread Pudding, '94 215
Chocolate Bread Pudding, '80 8
Chocolate Bread Pudding with Custard Sauce, '03 244
Chocolate Bread Pudding with Whiskey Sauce, '99 277
Cinnamon-Raisin Bread Pudding, '01 315
Cinnamon Toast Pudding with Caramel Sauce, '96 284
Cranberry-Raisin Bread Pudding, Stuffed Pumpkin
    with, '02 231
Croissant Bread Pudding, '03 66
Custard Sauce, Bread Pudding with, '97 313
Durfee's Bread Pudding, '96 48
Fig-Walnut Pudding, '03 244
French Bread Pudding, '85 231
Lemon Bread Pudding, Old-Fashioned, '88 95
Mushroom Bread Pudding, '99 58
Old-Fashioned Bread Pudding, '83 213; '88 175;
    '00 105; '01 223
Old-Fashioned Bread Pudding with Bourbon Custard
    Sauce, '95 271
Old-Fashioned Bread Pudding with Rum Sauce, '88 32
Peachy Bread Pudding, '88 175
Piña Colada Bread Pudding, '98 34
Pineapple-Apple Bread Pudding with Bourbon
    Sauce, '05 119
Pineapple-Apple Bread Pudding with Vanilla-
    Nutmeg Sauce, '02 208
Plum Bread Pudding, Refrigerator, '97 177
Pumpkin Bread Pudding, '98 240
Raisin Bread Pudding, '94 215
Raisin Bread Pudding with Bourbon Sauce, '98 336
Rosemary-Tasso Bread Pudding, '00 104
Sauce, Bread Pudding, '04 235
Spiced Bread Pudding, '93 52
Sweet Potato Bread Pudding, '94 241
Sweet Roll Pudding, '96 283
Tennessee Bread Pudding with Bourbon Sauce,
    '93 51
Vanilla Sauce, Bread Pudding with, '97 M15
Whiskey Sauce, Bread Pudding with, '80 58;
    '90 230; '92 93
White Chocolate Bread Pudding, '00 M104
Brownie Pudding, '79 265; '80 295
Brown Sugar-Pecan Pudding, '86 M165
Butternut Squash Pudding, '89 M313; '90 M19
Cake, Apple Pudding, '01 47
Cake, Black Forest Pudding, '02 210
Cake, Carrot Pudding, '83 24
Cake, Danish Pudding, '91 269
Cake, Lemon Pudding, '83 106
Cake Pudding, Chocolate, '81 99
Cake Pudding, Hot Fudge Sundae, '88 167
Cake Pudding, Lemon, '92 96; '98 35
Cake Pudding, Wine, '79 230
Cake, Saucy Pudding, '98 196
Cake with Blueberry Sauce, Buttermilk-Lemon
    Pudding, '95 135
Chocolate-Almond Pudding, '82 M142; '88 24
Chocolate-Almond Silk Pudding, '96 266
Chocolate Cookie Pudding, '03 183
Chocolate-Peanut Butter Cookie Pudding, '03 183
Chocolate Pudding, '02 323
Chocolate Pudding, Creamy, '83 106
Chocolate Pudding, Fudgy, '96 285
Chocolate-Rum Dessert, '81 247
Christmas Pudding, '79 230
Christmas Pudding, Flaming, '85 312
Christmas Pudding with Brandy Sauce, Baked, '88 279
Coconut Cream, '00 27
Coffee Cream, '00 27

Cookies, Pudding-Oatmeal, '98 215
Cranberry Pudding, '84 306
Finger Painting Never Tasted So Good, '95 167
French Vanilla Latte Pudding, '03 M282
Frozen Ozark Pudding, '88 127
Fruit Pudding Compote, Fresh, '86 151
Hansel Pudding, '80 9
Holland Rusk Pudding, Yia Yia's, '93 124
Hot Fudge Pudding, '81 208
Kugel, Nu Awlins, '94 229
Lemon Fluff Pudding, '85 304
Lemon-Pear Pudding, '96 283
Lemon Pudding, '79 86; '81 99
Lemon Pudding, Baked, '04 295
Lemon Pudding, Layered, '82 128
Mandarin-Almond Pudding, '85 M12
Mocha-Chocolate Cookie Pudding, '03 183
Orange Cream, '00 27
Orange Custard Pudding, '88 174
Orange Pudding, '81 85; '82 111; '83 153
Orange-Tapioca Creme, '82 M283
Peanut Butter-Banana Pudding, '93 340
Peanut Butter Pudding, '85 95; '88 32; '00 27
Peanut Parfait, Bodacious, '95 167
Pecan-Mocha Pudding, '89 M130
Persimmon Pudding, '00 254
Pineapple Pudding, '80 102
Plum Pudding, '79 281
Plum Pudding, Flamed, '84 276
Plum Pudding-Gelatin Mold, '86 300; '87 178
Plum Pudding, Light, '86 318
Plum Pudding, Old-Fashioned, '80 264
Pumpkin Pudding, '89 M313; '90 M20
Pumpkin Pudding, Baked, '80 244
Raisin-Pumpkin Pudding, '84 315
Raspberry Pudding, '92 92
Rice
    Amaretto Rice Pudding, '86 334
    Apple Rice Pudding, '91 217
    Brown Rice Pudding, '85 77
    Creamy Rice Pudding, '81 51, 205
    English Rice Pudding, '04 98
    Fruited Rice Pudding, '81 205; '86 95
    Fudgy Rice Pudding, '81 205
    Old-Fashioned Rice Pudding, '85 147; '03 285
    Raisin-Rice Pudding, '87 46
    Velvety Rice Pudding, '81 205
Rum Pudding with Raspberry Sauce, '82 288
Savory
    Carrot-Potato Pudding, '94 279
    Cheese Pudding, Baked, '86 78
    Chicken Pudding, '05 22
    Corn-Cheese Pudding, '80 244
    Cornmeal Pudding, '05 43
    Corn Pudding, '79 276; '81 128; '86 192; '90 219;
        '98 124; '99 71, 270
    Corn Pudding, Baked, '83 314
    Corn Pudding, Creamy, '81 267
    Corn Pudding, Dashiell, '98 274
    Corn Pudding, Easy, '83 280
    Corn Pudding, Fresh, '80 157, 165; '89 172
    Corn Pudding, Southwestern, '01 165; '03 178
    Corn Pudding, Sweet, '05 66
    Corn Pudding, Tee's, '95 318; '01 165; '03 178
    Green Tomato-Tomatillo-Corn Pudding, '04 103
    Grits Pudding, '96 28
    Onion Pudding, Kathy's, '95 318
    Onion Puddings, '02 126
    Onion Pudding, Sweet, '02 310
    Persimmon Pudding, '79 206
    Rosemary-Tasso Bread Pudding, '00 104
    Squash Pudding, '82 277; '83 15
    Sweet Onion Pudding, '00 260
    Sweet Potato Pudding, '79 244; '86 52

Turnip Pudding, '94 213
Yorkshire Pudding, '80 252; '98 86
Yorkshire Puddings, Mini Prime Ribs and, '01 283
Scuppernong Pudding Tarts, '98 221
Snowflake Pudding, '85 30
Snow White Pudding, '85 77
Steamed Date Pudding, '79 86
Steamed Ginger Pudding, '96 283
Steamed Holiday Pudding, '84 275
Steamed Mincemeat Pudding, '80 264
Summer Pudding, '98 217; '04 159
Tipsy Pudding, Parson's, '80 156
Vanilla Cream, '00 27
Vanilla Pudding, '88 32
Vanilla Pudding, Creamy, '83 227
Woodford Pudding, '79 86
PUMPKIN
Baked Pumpkin, '82 217
Bars and Cookies
    Cake Bars, Pumpkin, '80 245
    Chocolate Chip Cookies, Pumpkin-, '93 235
    Drop Cookies, Pumpkin, '79 206
    Great Pumpkin Cookies, '91 234
    Jack-o'-Lantern Cookies, '87 214
    Nut Bars, Pumpkin, '82 217
    Peppy Pumpkin Cookies, '89 253
    Pumpkin Bars, '80 40
    Walnut Cookies, Frosted Pumpkin-, '82 217
Bisque, Spicy Pumpkin, '86 67
Breads
    Brother Boniface's Pumpkin Bread, '98 26
    Coconut Bread, Pumpkin-, '87 255
    Cream Cheese and Preserves, Pumpkin Bread with,
        '84 264
    Cream Cheese-Pumpkin Bread, '05 251
    Empanadas, '02 82
    Gingerbread with Caramel Sauce, Pumpkin, '93 235
    Harvest Pumpkin Bread, '90 M215
    Harvest Pumpkin Loaf, '85 232
    Holiday Pumpkin Bread, '03 281
    Moist Pumpkin Bread, '80 245
    Muffins, Holiday Pumpkin, '03 281
    Muffins, Monster, '94 256
    Muffins, Nutty Pumpkin, '86 291
    Muffins, Pumpkin, '79 206, 275; '81 272; '04 112
    Muffins, Pumpkin-Apple, '96 242
    Nut Bread, Pumpkin-, '83 294
    Oatmeal Loaf, Pumpkin-, '81 49
    Orange-Pumpkin Bread, '87 300
    Pancakes, Pumpkin, '80 228
    Pecan Bread, Pumpkin-, '87 221; '02 224
    Pumpkin Bread, '81 8; '05 232
    Rolls, Pumpkin, '87 254
    Spiced Pumpkin Bread, '91 233
Cake Bars, Pumpkin, '80 245
Cake, Pumpkin, '81 272; '93 303; '98 241
Cake, Pumpkin Date, '79 251
Cake, Pumpkin Kahlúa, '86 292
Cake, Pumpkin Layer, '80 245
Cake, Pumpkin Pound, '92 235
Cake, Pumpkin Spice, '05 232
Cake Squares, Orange-Pumpkin, '83 242
Cake with Little Ghosts, Pumpkin, '03 212
Calabaza Guisada con Puerco (Pumpkin Cooked with
    Pork), '80 193
Cheese Ball, Pumpkin, '02 222
Cheesecake, Pumpkin, '80 254; '85 280; '96 268
Chiffon, Pumpkin, '82 216; '86 283; '88 260
Chips, Pumpkin, '98 241
Chocolate Pumpkin, '96 254
Chowder, Pumpkin-Corn, '97 219
Cooked Fresh Pumpkin, '88 M230
Cookies. *See* **PUMPKIN/Bars and Cookies.**
Crisp, Pumpkin, '05 269

Cupcakes, Pumpkin, '85 121
Custard, Pumpkin, '88 279
Delight, Pumpkin-Orange, '86 321
Dessert, Frozen Pumpkin, '88 167
Dessert, Pumpkin Chiffon, '88 128
Dip, Pumpkin Pie, '01 242
Doughnut Drops, Pumpkin, '90 323
Empanadas de Calabaza (Pumpkin Empanadas), '94 28
Empanadas, Pumpkin, '82 223
Flan, Pumpkin, '82 217; '97 219
Fudge, Pumpkin, '05 232
Ice Cream Pumpkin, '96 255
Mold, Pumpkin, '82 311
Mousse, Pumpkin, '91 96; '92 130
Pasta, Pumpkin, '98 241
Pies
    Autumn Pumpkin Pie, '87 213
    Bourbon-Pecan Pumpkin Pie, '87 264
    Chiffon Pie, Pumpkin, '84 312
    Cracked Caramel-Pumpkin Pie, '99 254
    Festive Pumpkin Pie, '81 M269
    Fluffy Pumpkin Pie, '80 283
    Frosty Pumpkin Pie, '96 279
    Gingersnap Streusel Pumpkin Pie, '01 315
    Ice Cream Pie, Pumpkin, '81 272
    Ice Cream Pie, Pumpkin-, '87 243
    Layered Pie, Elegant Pumpkin-Walnut, '02 244
    Mama's Pumpkin Pie, '96 242
    Meringue, Pumpkin Pie with, '92 268
    New-Fashioned Pumpkin Pie, '90 296
    Nutty Pumpkin Pie, '82 67
    Pecan Pie, Pumpkin-, '85 233, 282
    Praline Pie, Frosty Pumpkin-, '91 M234
    Praline Pie, Pumpkin, '80 244
    Praline-Topped Pumpkin Pie, '00 332
    Quick Pumpkin Pie, '88 M230
    Rich Pumpkin Pie, '86 292
    Sour Cream-Pumpkin Pie, '84 263
    Spiced Nut Crust, Pumpkin Pie in, '87 295
    Spicy Pumpkin Pies, '84 322
    Supreme, Pumpkin Pie, '82 217
    Traditional Pumpkin Pie, '85 256
Pizza Pumpkins, '98 255
Profiteroles with Warm Cranberry Compote, Pumpkin-
    Spiced, '97 264
Pudding, Baked Pumpkin, '80 244
Pudding, Pumpkin, '89 M313; '90 M20
Pudding, Pumpkin Bread, '98 240
Pudding, Raisin-Pumpkin, '84 315
Puree, Pumpkin, '00 296
Risotto with Shrimp, Pumpkin, '98 240
Roll, Pumpkin, '79 206; '91 297; '04 297
Sauce, Beurre Blanc, '98 240
Sauce, Pumpkin Seed, '88 246
Seeds, Roasted Pumpkin, '03 211
Seeds, Santa Fe, '02 145
Seeds, Seasoned Pumpkin, '91 234
Seeds, Toasted Pumpkin, '88 M230; '98 241
Soup, Cream of Pumpkin, '93 234
Soup, Creamy Southwestern Pumpkin, '03 221
Soup, Curried Pumpkin, '96 242
Soup, Pumpkin, '79 48
Soup, Pumpkin-Pear, '92 234
Soup, Pumpkin-Tomato, '86 291
Soup Stock, Pumpkin, '00 296
Soup with Ginger-Lime Cream, Pumpkin-Corn, '95 227
Soup with Sweet Croutons, Pumpkin, '00 296
Stuffed Pumpkin with Cranberry-Raisin Bread Pudding,
    '02 231
Swirl, Easy Pumpkin, '93 234
Tarts, No-Bake Pumpkin, '86 291
Torte, Praline-Pumpkin, '01 285
Waffles, Pumpkin, '95 282
Waffles, Pumpkin-Nut, '86 96

Waffles with Mandarin Orange Sauce, Dessert Pumpkin,
    '89 204
PUNCH. See BEVERAGES/Alcoholic, Punch.

QUAIL. See GAME/Quail.
QUESADILLAS
Apple Pie 'n' Cheddar Quesadillas, '03 61
Apple Quesadillas, '99 248
Bacon-and-Egg Quesadillas, '05 88
Bacon-Jalapeño-Tomato Quesadillas, '95 240
Barbecue Quesadillas, '02 121
Caramel-Apple Quesadillas, '05 223
Chicken-and-Black Bean Quesadillas, '96 288
Chicken-and-Brie Quesadillas with Chipotle Salsa,
    '99 311
Chicken Quesadillas, Grilled, '04 36
Chicken Quesadillas, Sesame-Ginger, '00 147
Chicken Quesadillas, Spicy, '95 42
Chorizo, Black Bean, and Corn Quesadillas, '00 148
Corn-and-Squash Quesadillas, Grilled, '02 123
Crab Quesadillas with Mango Salsa, Beefy, '00 124
Dessert Quesadillas, '02 54
Easy Quesadillas, '98 M205
Greek Quesadillas, '03 61
Green Chile Quesadillas, '90 121
Meatball Quesadillas, '00 242
Poblano-and-Corn Quesadillas, '01 333
Pork Quesadillas, Barbecued, '04 187
Quick Fiesta Quesadillas, '02 246
Quick Quesadillas, '89 87; '02 143
Reuben Quesadillas, '05 131
Roasted Vegetable Quesadillas, '04 322
Salmon Quesadilla with Cucumber Salsa, Grilled, '95 131
Sausage Quesadillas, '90 118
Sausage Quesadillas, Breakfast, '04 183
Shrimp-and-Roasted Pepper Quesadillas, '00 215
Spinach, Mushroom, and Cilantro Quesadillas, '00 148
Torta, Quesadilla, '97 325
Vegetable Quesadillas, '97 65
Vegetable Quesadilla with Roasted Salsa, Northern New
    Mexican, '95 130
Western Quesadillas, '97 65
QUICHES
Artichoke Quiche, '91 71
Asparagus-Tomato Quiche, '88 198
Broccoli Quiche, Easy, '82 34
Broccoli Quiche, Italian, '85 45
Broccoli-Rice Quiche, '81 228
Casserole, Quiche, '95 33
Cauliflower Quiche, '83 86
Cheese
    Bacon-Cheese Quiches, Miniature, '83 93
    Blue Cheese Quiche, '84 52
    Canadian Bacon-and-Brie Quiche, '04 248
    Cheddar-Leek Quiche, '88 198
    Chiles Rellenos Quiche, '02 321
    Cream Cheese Quiche, '96 203
    Green Onion Quiche, Cheesy, '83 194; '84 42
    Ham-and-Cheese Quiches, Individual, '98 24
    Ham-Cheese Quiche, '79 26
    Ham Quiche, Cheesy, '79 127
    Jalapeño Quiche, Cheesy, '84 31
    Mexican Cheese Pie, '83 69
    Miniature Cheese Quiches, '80 150
    Sausage-Cheddar Quiche, '79 26
    Sealed with a Quiche, '95 135
    Spinach Quiche, Cheesy, '81 228
    Spinach Quiches, Triple-Cheese, '00 220
    Squares, Cheesy Hot Quiche, '79 124
    Squares, Quiche, '84 222
    Swiss Alpine Quiche, '90 18
    Swiss-Zucchini Quiche, '82 49
    Tarragon Cocktail Quiches, '84 127

Vegetable Quiche, Cheese-, '81 228
Zucchini Quiche, Cheesy, '83 312
Chicken Divan Quiche, '88 M125
Chicken-Olive-Cheddar Quiche, '03 58
Chicken-Pecan Quiche, '91 206
Chile Pepper Quiche, '82 224
Clam Quiche, '83 215
Crabmeat-Parmesan Quiche, '03 59
Crab Quiche, '82 M122, 243
Crab Quiche, Almond-Topped, '79 127
Crab Quiche, Quick, '84 96
Crab Quiche, Sherried, '83 180
Crab Quiche, Simple, '85 207
Eggless Quiche, '87 220
Fiesta Quiche, '92 47
Green Chile Quiche, '83 31
Individual Quiches, '98 101
Jalapeño-Corn Quiche, '85 122
Lorraine, Classic Quiche, '81 131
Lorraine, Mushroom-Quiche, '86 242
Lorraine, Peppery Quiche, '81 228
Lorraine, Perfect Quiche, '79 127
Lorraine, Quiche, '79 40; '80 M108; '99 M218; '01 88
Meat
    Bacon-Cheese Quiches, Miniature, '83 93
    Bacon Quiche, '85 60
    Bacon Quiche, Spinach-and-, '00 240
    Benedict Quiche, '80 M107
    Canadian Bacon-and-Brie Quiche, '04 248
    Ham-and-Cheese Quiches, Individual, '98 24
    Ham-and-Grits Crustless Quiche, '94 89
    Ham-and-Mushroom Quiche, '81 11
    Ham-and-Vegetable Quiche, '84 326
    Ham-Cheese Quiche, '79 26
    Ham Quiche, '80 110
    Ham Quiche, Cheesy, '79 127
    Ham Quiche, Country, '87 287
    Ham Quiche, Crustless, '84 235
    Mexican Quiche Cups, '02 72
    Sausage-Apple Quiche, Crustless, '87 70
    Sausage-Cheddar Quiche, '79 26
    Sausage Quiche, Easy, '79 261
    Sausage Quiche, Italian, '81 200
    Sausage Quiche, Spicy, '80 M108
    Sausage Quiche, Zucchini-, '83 122
Mexicali Quiche with Avocado Topping, '93 309; '94 96
Miniature
    Bacon-Cheese Quiches, Miniature, '83 93
    Cheese Quiches, Miniature, '80 150
    Individual Ham-and-Cheese Quiches, '98 24
    Individual Spinach Quiches, '86 38
    Olive Quiche Appetizers, '86 159
    Shrimp Miniquiches, '87 146
    Spinach Quichelets, '87 67
    Spinach Quiches, '01 241
    Spinach Quiches, Miniature, '82 38
    Squares, Quiche, '84 222
    Tarragon Cocktail Quiches, '84 127
    Wild Rice-and-Mushroom Quiches, '93 237
Mushroom Quiche, '80 222; '81 244; '89 285
Noël, Quiche, '82 310
Onion Quiche, '83 121
Pastry, Microwaved Quiche, '81 M74; '82 M123
Pastry, Quiche, '80 M107
Pizza Quiche, '86 53
Potato Quiche, Crustless, '83 49
Salmon-and-Dill Quiche, '03 58
Salmon Quiche, '82 87; '87 38
Shrimp-and-Artichoke Quiche, '03 196
Shrimp Quiche, '83 50
South-of-the-Border Quiche, '93 321
Southwestern Quiche, '04 41
Spinach
    Bacon Quiche, Spinach-and-, '00 240

QUICHES, Spinach
(continued)

Cheese Spinach Quiches, Triple-, '00 220
Cheesy Spinach Quiche, '81 228
Crustless Spinach Quiche, '84 235
Greek Spinach Quiche, '86 10
Individual Spinach Quiches, '86 38
Miniature Spinach Quiches, '82 38
Mushroom Quiche, Spinach-, '81 M74
Mushroom-Spinach-Swiss Quiche, '03 59
No-Crust Spinach Quiche, '90 142
Spinach Quiche, '81 44; '85 49; '91 204
Spinach Quichelets, '87 67
Spinach Quiches, '01 241
Tomato Florentine Quiche, '04 332
Springtime Quiche, '83 122
Squash-and-Green Chile Quiche, '88 143
Tasty Quiche, '82 264
Vegetable Quiche, '87 M219
Vegetable Quiche, Light, '97 332
Veggie Sausage Quiche, Crustless, '03 175
Zucchini Frittata, '86 103
Zucchini-Mushroom Quiche, '79 127
Zucchini Pie, Italian-Style, '83 43
Zucchini-Sausage Quiche, '83 122

QUICK & EASY
Appetizers
Bacon-Cheese Fingers, '00 133
Brie, Chutney-Bacon, '90 M292
Brie in Rye, Raspberry, '93 252
Bruschetta, Roasted Pepper-Tomato, '02 213
Cashews, Caribbean, '04 196
Caviar, Homemade Cowboy, '94 64
Caviar, Texas, '01 257
Cereal Bites, Buttery, '89 97
Cheese-and-Olive Snack, Open-Faced, '89 97
Cheese Ball, '91 200
Cheese Ball, Apple, '98 250
Cheese Ball, Peppered, '94 118
Cheese Fondue, Party, '92 20
Cheese Loaf, Four-Layer, '99 222
Cheese Snack, '89 98
Chicken-Cheese Ball, '93 216
Chicken Strips, Sesame, '98 250
Cinnamon Sticks, '95 244
Cocktail Smoky Links, '90 168
Crackers, Snack, '00 133
Crackers, Tomato-Blue Cheese, '02 213
Cream Cheese, Bacon-Olive, '04 196
Dip and Vegetable Platter, Curry, '89 327
Dip, Bean, '89 97
Dip, Cheese-Crab, '91 200
Dip, Chili-and-Cheese, '89 M328
Dip, Corn-and-Field Pea, '01 177
Dip, Fiesta, '92 263
Dip, Meaty Cheese, '92 160
Dip, Mexican Artichoke, '90 M292
Dip, Quick Nacho, '90 168
Dip, Super Seafood, '90 292
Dip, Sweet Fruit, '89 328
Dip with Tortellini, Creamy Tomato Pesto, '00 196
Guacamole, '96 160
Ham Appetillas, '93 63
Jelly, Garlic Pepper, '99 221
Kielbasa, Sweet-and-Sour, '89 327
Meatballs, Spicy Party, '00 242
Mushrooms, Marinated, '91 306
Nachos, Tex-Mex, '89 97
Nuts, Quick Party, '04 197
Olive Cups, Greek, '99 221
Olives, Lemon-Garlic, '94 118
Parmesan Cheese Bites, '99 221; '02 108

Peanuts, Sugar-and-Spice, '04 197
Pepperoni Pie Hors d'Oeuvres, '98 251
Pistachios, Spicy, '04 197
Pizza Bites, '95 244
Quesadillas, Quick, '02 143
Rollups, Spinach, '98 251
Sandwiches, Bacon-Olive Party, '04 196
Sandwiches, Mini Muffuletta Bacon-Olive Party, '04 196
Spread, Buttery Boursin Cheese, '94 301
Spread, Cheese, '99 24
Spread, Chunky Artichoke, '89 98
Spread, Crabmeat-Horseradish, '90 292
Spread, Creamy Clam, '91 274
Spread, Fruited Cream Cheese, '91 306
Spread, Garlic Boursin Cheese, '94 301
Spread, Hearts of Palm, '90 M293
Spread, Nutty Cream Cheese, '89 327
Spread, Shrimp, '96 104
Spread, Tuna, '91 305
Apples, Curried, '93 252
Beans, Baked, '01 127, 334
Beans, Refried, '96 160
Beans, Skillet Barbecued, '93 217
Beverages
Cider, Apple-Orange, '92 20
Cocktail, Orange-Cranberry, '01 103
Margaritas, Blue, '02 143
Orange-Banana Whip, '95 244
Punch, Percolator, '91 306
Punch, Pink, '96 190
Shake, Chocolate Milk, '05 193
Tea, Easy Mint, '91 187
Black Beans and Rice, '89 178
Black Beans and Yellow Rice, '95 126
Breads
Biscuit Bowls, '03 222
Biscuits, Cheese Garlic, '03 185
Biscuits, Deluxe Omelet, '98 101
Biscuits, Easy Cheddar, '01 103
Biscuits, Easy Herb, '90 283
Biscuits, Green Chile, '04 233
Biscuits, Lightnin' Cheese, '90 283
Biscuits, Quick, '89 30
Breadsticks, Italian Cheese, '95 126
Breadsticks, Sesame-Cheese, '97 31
Cinnamon Loaves, '99 260
Cinnamon Loaves, Miniature, '99 260
Croissants, Cream Cheese, '92 159
Crostini, Feta-Tomato, '92 159
Danish, Cheese, '97 31
Focaccia, Basil Pesto, '00 195
Focaccia, Herb, '97 31
French Bread, Chive-Garlic, '89 29
French Bread, Lemony, '97 147
French Bread, Onion-Cheese, '89 29
Garlic Bread, '04 288
Garlic Bread, Buttery, '02 25
Garlic Bread, Quick, '90 283
Greek Bread, '89 200
Mayonnaise Bread, '89 29
Mini-Cinnis, Mama's, '02 41
Muffins, Barbecue, '96 246
Muffins, English Cheese, '02 41
Muffins, Orange-Pecan, '99 56
Muffins, Sour Cream, '90 283
Parmesan-Wine Bread, '97 31
Pizza Crust Wedges, Toasted, '03 280
Rolls, Almond Crescent, '90 283
Rolls, Cinnamon Tea, '92 263
Rolls, Mayonnaise, '90 283
Rolls, Orange, '01 257
Rolls, Spoon, '91 275
Scones, Classic Cream, '02 41
Sesame Knots, '89 29

Waffles with Cilantro-Lime Butter, Corn, '02 109
Butter, Cilantro, '98 182
Butter, Cilantro-Lime, '01 24; '02 109
Butter, Cinnamon, '92 319
Butter, Garlic, '00 90
Butter, Green Peppercorn, '90 117
Butter, Orange, '92 319
Butter, Southwestern, '92 320
Coffee Cake, Cowboy, '95 84
Desserts
Apple Dessert, Creamy Dutch, '91 19
Apples and Pear, Honey-Baked, '97 303
Apples 'n' Pears, Saucy, '96 72
Apricot-Almond Squares, '95 272
Banana-Berry Split, '05 193
Bars, Gooey Turtle, '96 M189
Bars, Peanut Butter, '93 166
Blueberry Slump, Quick, '91 20
Brownies, Chocolate-Peanut Butter Chip, '91 306
Brownies, Gooey, '97 133
Brownies, No-Bake, '94 330
Brownies, Rich, '95 84
Cake, Carrot-Raisin, '01 58
Cake Dessert Sandwich, Grilled Pound, '94 171
Cake, Éclair, '93 42
Cake, Ice Cream, '89 71
Cake, Oatmeal, '01 58
Cake, Peanut Butter-Fudge, '01 59
Cake, Texas, '01 59
Cake with Strawberry-Banana Topping, Pound, '89 200
Candies, Turtle, '93 M41
Candy, Peanut Butter, '93 166
Cherry Crisp, '91 20
Chocolate Crunchies, '92 50
Chocolate Dip, '92 50
Chocolate-Marshmallow Squares, '92 M50
Chocolate-Peanut Butter Cups, '97 134
Chocolate Peanutty Swirls, '94 M330
Cobbler, Quick Fruit, '91 20
Cookies, Cake Mix, '97 133
Cookies, Cake Mix Oatmeal, '96 247
Cookies, Double-Chocolate, '95 272
Cookies, Easy, '00 133
Cookies, Keyboard, '94 M330
Cookies, Spider, '93 166
Cranberry-Orange Delight, '90 168
Cream Dessert, Triple, '94 244
Cupcakes, Chewy Chocolate, '01 334
Cupcake Surprises, '01 299
Frosting, Fudge, '01 59
Fruit Kebabs, Grilled, '97 147
Fudge, Creamy Peanut Butter, '92 240
Fudge, Microwave Chocolate, '92 M50
Ice-Cream Balls, Cinnamon-Chocolate Chip, '02 143
Ice Cream Balls, Nutty, '89 72
Ice Cream, Chocolate Cookie, '95 245
Ice Cream, Cinnamon, '95 126
Ice-Cream Dessert, Toffee, '97 134
Ice Cream Sandwiches, Chocolate, '89 72
Ice Cream-Toffee Dessert, '00 176
Ice, Lemon, '00 176
Ice, Mimosa, '94 24
Lemon Crisps, '95 272
Omelet, Puffy Dessert, '00 35
Orange Balls, '94 331
Orange Crinkles, '95 272
Peach Crinkle, '91 20
Peach Crisp, Gingered, '97 303
Pie, Blueberry-Banana, '93 115
Pie, Brownie-Mint, '97 303
Pie, Caramel, '96 72
Pie, Caramel-Nut Crunch, '94 244
Pie, Chocolate Cream Cheese, '92 240

Pie, Coconut, '93 115
Pie, Decadent Mud, '89 252
Pie, Double-Delight Ice Cream, '89 72
Pie, Fudge, '89 252
Pie, Ice Cream Sundae, '94 244
Pie, No-Bake Cherry Confetti, '93 114
Pie, Peanut Butter, '89 252
Pie, Pineapple, '89 252
Pie, Quick Peach, '89 252
Pie, Tart Lemon, '91 275
Pie, "Working for Peanuts," '93 115
Pizza, Chocolate-Peanut Butter, '05 193
Polka Dots, '95 272
Praline Grahams, '92 239
Pudding, No-Bake Banana, '91 172
Sauce, Hot Fudge, '05 193
Sauce, Toffee, '94 72
Sherbet Cooler, Peachy, '91 187
Sherbet, Lemon-Pineapple, '96 330
Strawberries, Christmas, '94 331
Sundae, Hot Apple Spice, '92 239
Topping, Hot Fudge Ice Cream, '98 317
Topping, Hot Fudge Ice-Cream, '02 109
Topping, Maple-Pecan Ice Cream, '98 317
Trifles, Easy Individual, '92 239
Truffles, Bittersweet, '94 330
White Chocolate Salties, '92 50
Dressing, Sweet Cornbread, '97 303
Egg Roll-Ups, Spicy, '90 140
Eggs, Chicken-Stuffed, '98 102
Eggs, Deviled, '01 299
Eggs, Scotch, '98 101
Fettuccine and Vegetables, '97 178
Fettuccine, Spinach Alfredo, '01 164
Fettuccine with Poppy Seeds, '91 48
French Toast, Peanut Butter, '93 166
Glaze, Orange, '92 263
Linguine, Fresh Tomato Sauce with, '02 213
Macaroni and Cheese, Baked, '03 184

Main Dishes
Antipasto Kebabs, '94 144
Barbecue, Chuck Roast, '96 71
Beans and Franks, Jiffy, '91 M172
Beef and Broccoli, Quick, '91 123
Beef Burgundy, '95 69
Beef Roll-Ups, Mexican, '90 176
Bow-Tie with Marinara, '94 64
Burgers, Garlic Turkey, '99 135
Burgers, Mushroom, '99 135
Burgers, Spinach-Feta, '99 135
Burritos, Tex-Mex, '95 34
Burritos, Vegetarian, '93 319
Casserole, Beef, '01 199
Casserole, Chicken, '96 103; '96 302
Casserole, Chicken-and-Pasta, '97 192
Casserole, Chicken-and-Wild Rice, '97 192
Casserole, Chili, '90 176
Casserole, Creamy Chicken-Green Bean, '97 158
Casserole, Easy Enchilada, '02 143
Casserole, Ham, '96 302
Casserole, Ham-and-Potato, '96 103
Casserole, Ham Roll, '91 M127
Casserole, Holiday Leftovers, '04 232
Casserole, Macaroni-Cheese-Beef, '95 125
Casserole, Quiche, '95 33
Casserole, Tuna, '96 103
Casserole, Turkey, '96 302
Casserole, Vegetarian, '96 302
Chicken à la King, '93 14
Chicken and Artichokes, Italian, '95 68; '00 219
Chicken and Bow Tie Pasta, '05 49
Chicken and Dumplings, Quick, '95 125
Chicken and Pasta, Quick, '93 14
Chicken and Potato Dumplings, '99 326

Chicken and Potatoes, Roasted, '98 289
Chicken and Rice, Creole, '92 262
Chicken and Tortilla Dumplings, '99 327
Chicken, Biscuit Dumplings and, '99 326
Chicken Breasts, Lemon, '89 18
Chicken Breasts, Salsa-Topped, '94 144
Chicken Breast Tarragon, Broiled, '89 310
Chicken, Cajun Fried, '01 334
Chicken Caruso and Rice, '89 177
Chicken, Cheesy Mexican, '01 199; '02 91
Chicken, Corn Flake, '91 172
Chicken Delicacy, '99 M23
Chicken, Grilled, '89 200
Chicken, Honey-Lime Grilled, '96 189
Chicken in Biscuit Bowls, Creamed, '03 222
Chicken in Mustard Cream Sauce, '92 181
Chicken in Pita, Peppery, '93 62
Chicken-Italian Dressing Bake, '91 199
Chicken, Lemon, '96 49
Chicken, Lemon-Basil, '02 91
Chicken, Lemon-Garlic, '90 35
Chicken, Lemon-Herb, '00 90
Chicken, Lemon-Pepper, '89 104
Chicken, Limeade, '01 257
Chicken, Mediterranean, '94 72
Chicken Mexicana, '91 M127
Chicken Nuggets, Baked, '89 18
Chicken Nuggets, Sweet-and-Sour, '90 168
Chicken, Oregano, '95 84
Chicken Packets, '96 104
Chicken, Paprika, '95 125
Chicken Parmesan, '00 219
Chicken Picante Pasta, '01 164
Chicken Pot Pie, Easy, '89 218
Chicken Pot Pie in Biscuit Bowls, '03 222
Chicken, Quick, '90 117
Chicken, Quick Curried, '89 219
Chicken, Roast, '93 14
Chicken Sauté, Lemon-Dill, '91 186
Chicken Sauté, Sweet Pepper-, '89 104
Chicken, Sesame-Ginger, '00 219
Chicken Skillet Dinner, Curried, '95 47
Chicken Stir-Fry, Thai, '00 23
Chicken, Szechuan, '98 155
Chicken Thighs, Balsamic Garlic-and-Herb, '05 19
Chicken Tostadas, '93 204
Chicken with Artichokes and Mushrooms, '90 35
Chicken with Creamy Mustard Sauce, Champagne-
  Poached, '94 24
Chicken with Fennel and Mushrooms, '97 93
Chicken with Fresh Herbs and Vegetables, '02 91
Chicken with Sweet Soy Slaw and Dipping Sauce,
  Grilled, '04 123
Chili and Enchiladas, '00 55
Chili, Easy Texas, '90 201
Chili, Quick-and-Easy, '92 20
Chili, Vegetable, '97 179
Chili with Beans, Easy, '92 262
Chimichangas, Oven-Fried Chicken, '90 M175
Chops with Vegetables, Golden, '89 218
Cornish Hens, Jelly-Glazed, '93 251
Crab Bake, Easy, '95 209
Crab Imperial, Easy, '93 128
Crabmeat Brunch Scramble, '95 32
Crab Tostadas, '93 203
Crawfish Delicacy, '99 M23
Eggplant Sauté, '96 135
Eggs, Cheese-Chive Scrambled, '95 34
Enchiladas, Cheese, '95 311
Enchiladas, Pork, '97 M94
Enchiladas, Quicker, '96 103
Enchiladas, Weeknight, '93 63
Fettuccine, Ranch House, '03 123
Fettuccine with Chicken-and-Creamy Herb Sauce, '01 257

Fettuccine with Shrimp-and-Creamy Herb Sauce,
  '01 257
Filet Mignon with Horseradish Gravy, '92 262
Fish, Caesar's, '90 76
Fish in Caper Sauce, '95 209
Fish, Mexi-Style Oven-Fried, '90 76
Fish, Oven-Fried, '91 172
Flank Steak, Cheese-Stuffed, '98 182
Flautas, '00 293
Flounder, Broiled, '89 310
Flounder, Quick Crunchy, '90 76
Frittata, Ham-and-Broccoli, '98 101
Grouper, Guadalajara, '98 17
Grouper with Sautéed Vegetables, '90 M233
Haddock Fillets in White Wine, '90 76
Ham-and-Cheese Bundles, '93 63
Hamburgers Mexicali, '93 217
Hamburgers Teriyaki, '89 309
Ham, Peachy Glazed, '96 189
Ham Slice, Apricot-Glazed, '93 252
Jambalaya, '98 317
Kielbasa-Vegetable Dinner, '91 274
Lasagna, Ellie's, '02 186
Lasagna, Lots of Noodles, '91 M127
Lasagna, Meatball, '00 243
Lasagna, Speedy, '05 M252
Lasagna, Turkey-Picante, '97 93
Lasagna, Vegetable, '93 320
Linguine, Leeks and Peppers with, '98 68
Linguine, Quick Clam, '90 233
Linguine with Clam Sauce, '89 178
Linguine with White Clam Sauce, '05 49
Mac and Cheese, Creamy, '05 208
Mac and Cheese, Hearty, '05 208
Mahimahi Grape Sauce, '91 218
Manicotti, Make-Ahead, '98 68
Marinara on Beds of Spinach and Orzo, '93 320
Meatballs, Baked, '02 25
Meat Loaf, Easy, '95 125
Meat Loaf, Teriyaki, '03 172
Mexican Stack-Up, '95 69
Mexicorn Main Dish, '96 189
Omelet, Dill-Cheese-Ham, '95 33
Omelet, Family-Size Potato, '94 31
Omelet Olé, '94 31
Omelet, Shrimp-and-Cheese, '94 31
Omelet, Spanish, '00 35
Pancakes, Apple, '01 24
Pancakes with Peanut Butter and Jelly Syrups,
  Banana, '01 24
Pasta, Basil-Cheese, '96 136
Pasta, Easy Taco, '03 124
Pasta Florentine, Layered, '00 56
Pasta Primavera, Peppery, '02 161
Pasta with Cabbage and Cheese Sauce, '00 105
Pasta with Pesto-Clam Sauce, '98 17
Pasta with Sausage and Kale, '03 279
Pasta with Shrimp, '01 164
Pasta with Tomato Cream Sauce, Angel Hair, '93 292
Peppers, Beef-Stuffed, '91 M127
Pie, Omelet, '00 M35
Pie, Shepherd's, '00 55
Pizza, Bistro Grilled Chicken, '05 M131
Pizza, Chicken Fajita, '03 235
Pizza, Peppers-and-Cheese, '03 235
Pizza, Sausage-and-Scrambled Egg, '05 88
Pizza, Sausage-Potato, '01 199
Pizza, Seafood Alfredo, '03 236
Pizza Squares, Easy, '02 61
Pizza, Taco, '89 177; '00 293
Pork Cacciatore, '95 69
Pork Chops and Gravy, '96 71
Pork Chops and Scalloped Potatoes, '98 16
Pork Chops, Balsamic, '01 208

Pork Chops, Creamy, '01 208
Pork Chops, Garlic-Parmesan, '02 61
Pork Chops, Herbed, '97 147
Pork Chops, Lemony Pan-Fried, '03 205
Pork Chops, Peachy, '89 310
Pork Chops, Pretzel, '01 208
Pork Chops, Spicy Brown Mustard, '03 205
Pork Chops, Tuscan, '03 205
Pork Chops with Jalapeño-Cherry Sauce, Smoked,
   '01 208
Pork Cutlets, Apple-Glazed, '92 181
Pork, Kung Pao, '96 49
Pork Marsala, '90 35
Pork Sauté, Plum Delicious, '89 105
Pork, Sesame, '01 177
Pork, Stir-fry, '05 241
Pork Tenderloin, Grilled Marinated, '91 199
Potatoes, Chili-Topped, '98 M289
Potatoes, Stuffed Baked, '00 293
Potatoes with Ham, Herbed, '00 318
Quesadillas, Bacon-and-Egg, '05 88
Quesadillas, Meatball, '00 242
Quesadillas, Reuben, '05 131
Quesadillas, Western, '97 65
Ravioli in Basil-Cream Sauce, Beef, '05 293
Rib-Eye Steaks with Roquefort Glaze, '89 310
Rice-and-Black Bean Tostadas, '97 65
Roast, Easy Rump, '93 217
Roast with Onion-and-Mushroom Gravy, '00 293
Salmon Bake with Pecan-Crunch Coating, '95 209
Salmon with Sweet Soy Slaw and Dipping Sauce,
   Grilled, '04 123
Sausage Dinner, Italian, '91 218
Sausage, Sweet Peppery, '95 69
Scallops in Vermouth-Cream Sauce, '96 49
Scampi, Speedy, '02 161
Seafood and Pasta, '90 234
Shrimp-and-Black Bean Tostadas, '93 204
Shrimp and Cabbage, Asian, '00 105
Shrimp and Grits, Garlic-Chili, '00 23
Shrimp and Pasta with Creole Cream Sauce, '05 49
Shrimp and Wine Sauce, '98 50
Shrimp, Boiled, '04 147
Shrimp Creole, Easy, '95 68
Shrimp, Fiery Cajun, '91 218
Shrimp Scampi, '95 209
Shrimp Stir-Fry, Cajun, '92 127
Shrimp Versailles, '90 233
Shrimp with Green Peppercorn Tartar Sauce, Boiled,
   '94 144
Sloppy Joes, '91 172
Snapper, Oven-Fried, '90 75
Snapper with Rosemary, Glazed, '98 51
Sole Royale, '89 104
Spaghetti and Meat Sauce, Quick, '94 64
Spaghetti Carbonara, '03 123
Spaghetti, Country-Style, '02 25
Spaghetti Pie, Weeknight, '95 312
Spaghetti with Fresh Tomato Sauce, '96 135
Steak and Gravy, Zippy, '90 35
Steak, Chicken-Fried, '05 67
Steak in Pepper Cream, '94 117
Steak Parmesan, '93 41
Steak with Creamy Salsa Gravy, Country-Fried, '05 67
Steak with Mushroom Gravy, Minute, '05 67
Stir-Fry Beef and Asparagus, '91 124
Stir-Fry, Chicken and Snow Pea, '95 157
Stir-Fry, Easy Chicken, '91 124
Stir-Fry, Hurry-Up Chicken, '91 124
Stir-Fry, Indian, '92 126

Stir-Fry, Italian, '92 126
Stir-Fry, Mexican, '92 126
Stir-Fry, Orange Roughy, '98 50
Stir-Fry, Peanutty Beef, '95 157
Stir-Fry, Sausage, '98 156
Stroganoff, Beef, '92 20
Swiss Steak, Easy, '00 90
Swiss Steak Monterey, '99 23
Taco Dinner Mac and Cheese, '05 208
Tacos, Chicken-and-Bean, '93 293
Tacos, Easy, '96 159
Tacos Wrapidos, '03 172
Tortilla Pie, '96 135
Tuna, Grilled Florida, '93 128
Turkey à la King, '04 232
Turkey and Peppers in Cornbread Crust, '95 312
Turkey-Basil Piccata, '96 49
Turkey Cutlets, Parmesan, '01 81
Turkey Divan, Quick, '89 178
Turkey Mignons, Sesame-Crusted, '01 81
Turkey Mignons with Creamy Wine Sauce, Sesame-
   Crusted, '02 109
Turkey Sauté, '89 105
Turkey Scaloppine, Easy, '95 M192
Turkey Tenders, Baked, '01 81
Turkey Tenders, Sautéed, '01 81
Turkey Tetrazzini, '00 318
Turkey with Peppers, '92 182
Veal Marsala, '91 218
Veal Piccata, '92 181
Vegetarian Sauté, '95 69
Ziti, Baked, '94 65
Mayonnaise, Dill-Garlic, '92 320
Mayonnaise, Italian Herbed, '92 320
Meat Mix, Mexican, '00 292
Mix, Fish Herb, '98 51
Mix, Jambalaya, '98 317
Mostaccioli Alfredo, '91 47
Pancakes, Easy, '92 203
Pasta Bake, Cheesy, '02 161
Pineapple, Baked, '05 160
Pizza, Breakfast, '90 140
Pizza, Southwestern Veggie, '95 126
Popcorn Delight, '00 M133
Quiches, Individual, '98 101
Relish, Quick Corn, '90 M13
Rice, Baked Mushroom, '95 84
Rice, Cajun Dirty, '04 288
Rice, Curried, '98 237
Rice, Jiffy Spanish, '90 M176
Rice, Picadillo, '98 237
Rice Primavera, '98 237

Salads and Salad Dressings
   Apple Salad, '00 176
   Asparagus and Tomatoes with Herb Vinaigrette, '99 56
   Bacon-Lettuce-Mozzarella-and-Tomato Salad, '98 209
   Banana Split Salad, '91 58
   Bean Salad, Quick, '89 128
   Bean Salad, Sweet, '01 46
   Beef-and-Lime Rice Salad, '03 172
   Bing Cherry Salad, '01 46
   Broccoli-Cauliflower Salad, '00 90
   Carrot Salad, Harvest, '89 128
   Chef's Salad, '98 209
   Chicken-and-Bow Tie Pasta, '01 164
   Chicken-Pasta Salad, Grilled, '94 64
   Chicken-Pasta Salad, Zesty, '02 186
   Chicken-Rice Salad, '97 93
   Chicken Salad Italian, '89 18
   Chicken Salad, Peachy, '97 193
   Chicken Salad, Roasted, '93 14
   Chicken Salad, Vegetable Patch, '04 92
   Citrus and Greens, Holiday, '03 280
   Coleslaw, Old-Fashioned Sweet, '93 128

Corn Salad, Festive, '92 263
Cucumber-and-Tomato Salad, '01 127
Cucumber Salad with Roasted Red Bell Pepper
   Dressing, '03 28
Dressing, '01 127
Frozen Salads, Paper Cup, '00 176
Fruit Bowl, Colorful, '91 58
Fruit Medley, Yogurt-Granola, '91 58
Fruit Salad Dressing, Snappy, '05 160
Fruit Salad, Frozen, '97 158
Fruit Salad, Layered, '91 58
Fruit Salad, Sunny, '91 58
Fruit Salad with Honey-Pecan Dressing, '03 28
Fruit Salad, Yogurt, '96 247
Greek Salad, '94 202
Green-and-Gold Salad with Fresh Citrus Ranch
   Dressing, '04 91
Green Salad, Garlic-Tarragon, '92 79
Honey-Pecan Dressing, '03 28
Iceberg Wedges, Blue Cheese, '05 160
Iceberg Wedges, Caesar, '05 160
Iceberg Wedges, Greek, '05 160
Leaf Lettuce Salad with Sweet-and-Sour Dressing,
   Red, '03 28
Lettuce Salad, Blue Cheese-Stuffed, '94 202
Mandarin Orange-Lettuce Salad, '92 79
Marinara Vinaigrette, '94 64
Marinated Salad, '91 186
Mexican Salad, '94 202
Mushroom Salad, Quick Cheesy-, '89 128
Pasta, Bow Tie, '01 164
Pasta Salad, '90 62; '01 127
Pasta Salad Dressing, '01 164
Pasta Salad, Ham-Pecan-Blue Cheese, '90 62
Pasta Salad, Oriental, '90 63
Pasta Salad, Presto, '90 63
Pasta Salad, Seafood, '90 62
Pear Salad, Golden, '91 58
Pork Cosmopolitan Salad, Grilled, '04 123
Potato Salad, Creamy, '01 334
Raspberry Salad Dressing, '03 M28
Red Cabbage Citrus Salad, '94 72
Roasted New Potato Salad, '04 91
Roasted Red Bell Pepper Dressing, '03 28
Romaine Salad with Raspberry Dressing, '03 28
Roquefort Dressing, '93 128
Sesame Noodle Salad, '02 186
Shrimp Salad, '04 147
Shrimp Salad, Aloha, '95 46
Slaw, Freezer, '99 260
Slaw, German Cabbage, '00 105
Spinach-Pecan Salad, '89 128
Squash Salad, '03 M184
Steak-and-Spinach Salad with Hot Pan Dressing, '05 19
Summer Italian Salad, Quick, '92 79
Sweet-and-Sour Dressing, '03 28
Tomato-Asparagus Salad, '92 79
Tomato Flower Salad, '89 128
Tomato-Gruyère-Basil Salad, '99 172
Tortellini Salad, '02 186
Tuna-and-White Bean Salad, '98 209
Vegetable Potato Salad, '03 136
Vinaigrette Dressing, '93 41
Vinaigrette Salad Dressing, '02 25
Wild Rice-and-Shrimp Salad, '02 109
Wild Rice-Chicken Salad, '99 55
Wild Rice-Shrimp Salad, '99 55
Zucchini Salad, '89 128

Sandwiches
   Avocado Deluxe Sandwiches, '99 72
   BLT Breakfast Sandwiches, '04 171
   BLT Croissants, '93 158
   BLT in Pita Pockets, '93 158
   BLT Sandwiches, Curried, '93 158

Breakfast Sandwiches, Cheesy, '90 140
Cheddar Cheese Sandwiches, Hot, '97 179
Chicken 'n' Cheese Sandwiches, Grilled, '99 240
Chicken Parmigiana Sandwich, '94 65
Chicken Toppers, Creamed, '99 240
Cream Cheese Croissants, '92 159
Focaccia Sandwich, Pesto, '05 131
Ham-and-Cheese Sandwiches, '01 299
Ham-and-Pineapple Slaw Sandwiches, '96 199
Hamwiches, '96 246
Hoagies, Sloppy Joe Meatball, '00 242
Lettuce Sandwich, Date-Nut, '94 202
Mango-Crab Salad Sandwiches, '99 72
Meatball Sandwiches, Open-Faced, '99 239
Pepperoni Pinwheels, '96 247
Pesto-Sandwich, Grilled Italian, '94 170
Pitas, Fajita, '99 239
Pizzas, Easy Pocket, '90 168
Pork Sandwiches, Barbecue, '00 23
Reuben Sandwiches, Open-Face, '91 199
Reubens, Spicy Coleslaw, '04 63
Rollups, Parmesan-Turkey-Ranch, '01 177
Spinach Fondue Sandwich, Grilled, '94 171
Tomato-Cheese-Bacon Melts, '99 72
Tuna Melts, Curried, '95 46
Tuna Roll Sandwiches, '96 199
Turkey Sandwich, Waffle-Grilled, '94 170
Vegetable Pita Sandwiches, '96 199
Welsh Rarebit with Tomatoes and Bacon, '92 M159
Wraps, Spicy Chicken Salad with Cabbage, '04 62
Wraps, Turkey, '00 318

Sauces
Basil and Cream Sauce, '90 117
Chervil-and-Savory Sauce, '90 117
Chicken Curry Sauce, '90 117
Country Ham Sauce, '90 117
Cranberry-Apple Sauce, '92 203
Garlic Butter Sauce, '05 M253
Marinara Sauce, '94 64
Peach Sauce, '92 203
Picante-Bean Sauce, '96 220
Pineapple Sauce, '92 203
Salsa, Texas, '96 160
Salsa, Vegetable, '96 220
Salsa Verde, '96 160
Shrimp Sauce, '94 147
Spaghetti Sauce, Slow-Simmered, '96 72
Tomato-Basil Sauce, '96 220
Tomato Sauce, Dried, '96 220; '99 135
Tomato Sauce, Spicy Gingered, '96 220
Wine Sauce, Creamy, '01 81; '02 109
Seasoning Blend, Taco, '96 159
Snack Mix, Make-Ahead, '04 M92

Soups and Stews
Asparagus Soup, Creamy, '94 225
Black-Eyed Pea Soup, '97 213
Black, White, and Red All Over Soup, '95 126
Broccoli-and-Chicken Soup, '90 202
Brunswick Stew, Easy, '05 292
Cheese-Vegetable Chowder, '02 305
Chicken-and-Wild Rice Soup, '04 26
Chicken Corn Chowder, '02 305
Chicken-Corn Soup, Cheesy, '97 158
Chicken Soup, Cheesy Mac 'n', '05 292
Chicken Stew, Santa Fe, '97 193
Chili Bean Soup, '96 71
Clam Chowder, '90 202
Clam Chowder, New England, '98 289
Clam Chowder, Shopping Day, '02 305
Corn Chowder, '90 202
Fiesta Chowder, '02 305
French Soup Maigre, '98 125
Garlic-and-Potato Soup, Golden, '04 214
Gazpacho, Classic Tomato, '99 172

Gumbo, Chicken-Sausage, '04 288
Hot Brown Soup, '00 318
Jambalaya, '04 288
Minestrone, Meatball, '00 242
Mushroom Soup, Sherried, '96 104
Potato Soup, '92 263
Shrimp Chowder, '89 218
Shrimp Chowder, Quick, '04 27
Steak Soup, '99 260
Sweet Potato Chowder, Asian, '97 213
Taco Soup, '94 225; '99 36
Tortellini Soup, '98 68
Tortellini Soup, Japanese, '96 330
Tortilla Soup, '90 201; '04 26
Turkey Soup with Green Chile Biscuits, Fiesta, '04 233
Vegetable-Beef Stew, Shortcut, '89 218
Vegetable Soup, Spicy, '93 293
Veggie Soup, Quick, '91 31
Vidalia Onion Soup, Beefy, '97 212
White Bean Soup, '90 201
White Bean Soup, Spicy, '94 225
Spaghetti with Tomatoes and Garlic, '91 47
Spread, Creamy Pimiento Cheese, '92 159
Spread, Cucumber, '93 158
Spread, Curry, '93 159
Spread, Dijon-Mayo, '96 199
Spread, Garlic-Butter, '96 199
Tart, Tomato-Pesto, '00 195
Toast Topper, Sticky Bun, '99 M72
Topping, Rainbow Pepper, '90 117
Tortellini Carbonara, '91 47

Vegetables
Asparagus, Chilled Sesame, '03 67
Asparagus, Lemon-Sesame, '91 M31
Asparagus Pie, Cheesy, '01 103
Beets, Winter, '02 283
Black-Eyed Peas, Easy, '99 204
Broccoli Casserole, Cheesy, '95 M191
Broccoli Parmesan, '97 302
Broccoli, Sesame, '03 67
Brussels Sprouts and Baby Carrots, Glazed, '97 302
Cabbage, Creole, '00 105
Cabbage Stir-Fry, '04 62
Cabbage Stir-Fry, Spicy, '04 62
Cabbage with Garlic, '04 62
Cajun Vegetable Sauté, '92 62
Carrot Relish, '03 67
Carrots, Peach-Glazed, '90 M13
Carrots with Bacon and Onion, Glazed, '02 283
Corn-and-Okra Medley, '99 203
Corn and Sweet Red Peppers, Curried, '95 47
Corn, Creamy Baked, '02 234
Corn on the Cob, Chili, '03 M185
Corn on the Cob, Lemony, '89 200
Corn Pudding, '98 124
Corn-Rice Casserole, '01 46
Cucumbers, Creamy, '92 62
Eggplant, Heavenly, '93 293
Eggplant Parmesan, '95 84
Eggplant Sauté, '96 135
Green Bean-and-Corn Casserole, '99 36
Green Beans, Chinese, '96 330
Green Beans, Gingered, '02 283
Green Beans, Pesto, '03 185
Green Beans with Bacon, Sautéed, '05 M160
Green Beans with Buttered Pecans, '92 61
Green Beans with Garlic-Herb Butter, '02 61
Green Beans with Lemon, '03 66
Green Peas, Company, '91 M31
Grilled Vegetables with Cilantro Butter, '98 182
Marinated Vegetables, '99 36
Marinated Veggies, '01 127
'Maters, Zippy, '99 172
Mexicorn, '96 189

Mexicorn, Black Bean, '96 189
Mexihominy, '96 189
Mushrooms, Sparkling, '94 24
Okra Creole, '02 234
Okra, Nutty, '03 136
Parmesan Vegetables, '97 147
Potatoes au Gratin, '93 217
Potatoes, Blue Cheese, '04 214
Potatoes, Blue Cheese Stuffed, '92 M228
Potatoes, Broccoli-Shrimp Stuffed, '92 M228
Potatoes, Feta Cheese, '04 214
Potatoes, Italian Mashed, '03 M135
Potatoes, Quick-and-Easy Mashed, '93 41
Potatoes, Seafood-Stuffed, '95 M192
Potatoes, Soufflé, '90 M14
Potatoes, Tangy Olive, '04 214
Quesadillas, Vegetable, '97 65
Spinach Casserole, '91 M31
Spinach, Easy Italian, '02 235
Squash Fritters, '99 203
Squash, Skillet, '92 62
Stir-Fry, Convenient Vegetable, '95 157
Stir-Fry, Fresh, '97 179
Stir-Fry, Vegetable, '98 156
Succotash, Quick, '97 302
Sweet Onion Relish, '99 204
Tomatoes, Baked Ranch, '94 72
Tomatoes, Cold Italian, '99 173
Tomatoes, Cornbread-Stuffed, '02 213
Tomatoes, Grilled, '99 173
Tomato-Pesto Tart, '02 108
Tomato-Pesto Tarts, Mini, '02 108
Zucchini and Carrots, Julienne, '90 M14
Zucchini and Carrots, Sautéed, '92 62
Zucchini Fans, Grilled, '89 200
Vinaigrette, Asian, '00 105
Waffles, '01 24
Waffles, Corn, '01 24
Waffles, Rice, '98 124

QUINCE
Compote, Baked Quince, '96 241

RAGOÛTS
Bean Ragoût with Cilantro-Cornmeal Dumplings, '97 209
Chicken Ragoût with Cheddar Dumplings, '94 44
Salmon-and-Vegetable Ragoût, '96 45
Veal-and-Artichoke Ragoût, '94 43
Vegetable Ragoût, '89 172; '98 181
Vegetables, Ragoût of Summer, '98 119
White Bean Ragoût, '96 232

RAISINS
Bars, Raisin, '94 228
Breads
Banana-Nut-Raisin Bread, '81 59
Biscuits, Buttermilk-Raisin, '92 338
Biscuits, Cinnamon-Raisin Breakfast, '93 159
Biscuits, Glazed Raisin, '89 210
Boule, Walnut-Raisin Pumpernickel, '02 259
Buns, Hot Cross, '01 88
Buns, Rum-Raisin, '80 22
Butternut-Raisin Bread, '79 25
Caraway-Raisin Oat Bread, '86 44
Chicken Salad on Raisin Bread, Curried, '85 96
Cinnamon Pull-Aparts, Raisin, '82 205; '83 32
Cinnamon Raisin Bread, '80 22
Cranberry Bread, Raisin-, '81 305; '82 36
Homemade Raisin Bread, '87 300
Irish Bread, '02 67
Muffins, Banana-Raisin, '89 218
Muffins, Breakfast Raisin, '84 59
Muffins, Carrot-and-Raisin, '87 24
Muffins, Cheddar-Raisin, '91 51
Muffins, Orange-Raisin, '97 153

RAISINS, Breads
(continued)

Muffins, Raisin English, '80 75
Muffins, Raisin-Nut, '92 46
Muffins, Raisin-Pecan Ginger, '88 9
Muffins, Whole Wheat Raisin, '85 207
Oatmeal Raisin Bread, '81 14
Oatmeal-Raisin Bread, '83 59
Pastry Bites, Raisin, '90 86
Pumpkin Bread, Holiday, '03 281
Rolls, Pecan-Golden Raisin Sweet, '03 235
Rolls, Raisin Cinnamon, '81 107
Rolls, Raisin-Cinnamon, '91 240
Rollups, Sweet Raisin, '86 290
Round Raisin Bread, '89 230
Saffron Bread, '96 50
Salt-Free Raisin Batter Bread, '86 33
Scones, Currant, '84 117; '92 332
Scones, Lemon-Raisin, '87 69
Teacakes, Currant, '80 88
Whole Wheat Bread, Raisin-, '93 77
Whole Wheat Raisin-Nut Bread, '04 208
Bugs in a Rug, '95 178
Butter, Almond-Raisin, '02 258
Butter, Raisin, '81 272
Cake, Carrot-Raisin, '01 58
Cake, Saucy Pudding, '98 196
Cake, Spicy Raisin Layer, '79 230
Cake, Winter Squash-Spice Bundt, '99 248
Candy, Mixed Raisin, '84 111
Carrots, Orange-Raisin, '80 24
Chocolate-Bran Raisin Jumbos, '91 142
Chutney, Cranberry, '98 318
Chutney, Pear, '98 243
Coffee Cake, Cinnamon-Raisin, '93 180
Coffee Cake, Spicy Raisin, '88 63
Conserve, Cranberry, '03 278
Cookies, Alltime Favorite Raisin, '80 24
Cookies, Chocolate-Raisin Oatmeal, '95 136
Cookies, Frosted Oatmeal-Raisin, '79 290
Cookies, Fruitcake, '98 294
Cookies, Nugget, '79 291
Cookies, Oatmeal, '99 280
Cookies, Oatmeal-Raisin, '87 221; '93 127
Cookies, Oatmeal-Raisin Chocolate Chip, '05 87
Cookies, Persimmon-Raisin, '85 232
Cookies, Pudding Oatmeal, '98 215
Cookies, Raisin-Oatmeal, '01 19
Cookies, Spice, '03 307
Cookies, Spicy Oatmeal, '01 19
Couscous with Raisins, Almonds, and Lemon, '00 295
Currants, Pine Nuts, and Pork, Couscous with, '00 295
Filling, Raisin, '90 86
Gingersnaps, Raisin, '85 324
Granola Gorp, '89 59
Granola, Healthful, '97 204
Granola, Superhero, '98 206
Granola Treats, Raisin-, '92 22
Gravy, Currant, '83 276
Ham, Raisin, '80 124
Ice Cream, Rum-Raisin, '97 145
Ice-Cream Sandwiches, Oatmeal-Rum-Raisin, '05 62
Mix, Raisin-Nut Party, '83 60
Mix, Starry Snack, '00 329
Onions, Glazed, '97 306
Pie, Apple-Raisin Brandy, '89 58
Pie, Brandy Raisin-Apple, '83 192
Pie, Cranberry-Apple-Raisin, '98 270
Pie, Cranberry-Raisin, '80 283; '85 316
Pie, Peanut-Raisin, '79 85
Pie, Raisin, '83 220
Pie, Raisin-Pecan, '87 213

Pie, Rhubarb-Raisin, '79 112
Pie, Spiced Raisin, '84 148
Pork Chops, An Apple-a-Day, '01 35
Preserves, Plum, '03 161
Pudding, Apple-Raisin Bread, '88 175
Pudding, Cinnamon-Raisin Bread, '01 315
Pudding, Raisin Bread, '94 215
Pudding, Raisin-Pumpkin, '84 315
Pudding, Raisin-Rice, '87 46
Pudding, Stuffed Pumpkin with Cranberry-Raisin
    Bread, '02 231
Pudding with Bourbon Sauce, Raisin Bread, '98 336
Relish, Apple-Raisin, '03 83
Relish, Raisin, '92 310
Rice, Curried, '98 237
Rice, Island, '98 276
Rice Pilaf, Persian, '02 167
Rice with Curry, Raisin, '85 83
Salad, Carrot-Raisin, '83 117; '84 174; '87 10
Salad, Classic Broccoli-Raisin, '02 24
Salad, Creamy Broccoli-Raisin, '92 106
Salad, Curried Apple-Raisin, '80 24
Salad with Orange-Nutmeg Dressing, Carrot-Raisin,
    '97 305; '98 19
Sandwiches, Peanut-Cheese-Raisin, '88 140
Sandwich, Raisin Country, '91 168
Sauce, Baked Ham with Cranberry-Raisin, '88 244
Sauce, Caramel-Raisin, '88 127
Sauce, Ham with Raisin, '82 M76
Sauce, Raisin, '83 59, 215; '84 91, 275; '87 127; '89 58;
    '99 19; '02 278
Sauce, Raisin-Pineapple, '82 177
Sauce, Rum-Raisin, '84 7; '94 295
Shake, Amazin' Raisin, '86 195
Shortbread, Rum-Currant, '98 277
Slaw, Sweet Potato-Currant, '93 246
Snack Mix, Apple Spice-Raisin, '05 222
Spread, Creamy Raisin, '90 36
Spread, Lemon-Raisin, '01 48
Spread, Peachy-Raisin, '86 326
Spread, Raisin-Nut, '95 79
Tarts, Pecan-Raisin, '03 246
Tarts, Pecan-Raisin Mini-, '03 246
RASPBERRIES
Appetizer, Orange-Berry, '85 81
Bars, Raspberry, '82 209; '84 212
Bavarian, Raspberry-Strawberry, '89 15
Beverages
    "Concrete," Foxtreat, '94 113
    Cooler, Raspberry, '89 171
    Cranberry-Raspberry Drink, '97 154
    Cubes, Berry-Good, '95 201
    Fizz, Rosy Raspberry, '90 179
    Kir, Raspberry, '86 183
    Lemonade, Dazzling, '97 99
    Lemonade, Fizzy Raspberry, '05 61
    Lemonade, Raspberry, '03 89
    Punch, Raspberry-Rosé, '87 242
    Punch, Raspberry Sherbet, '95 141
    Punch, Raspberry Sparkle, '84 57
    Punch, Sunset, '96 278
    Shake, Peach Melba Sundae, '93 134
    Shake, Raspberry-and-Banana, '89 183
    Shakes, Raspberry Milk, '95 238
    Shrub, Berry, '95 29
    Shrub, Red Raspberry, '97 132
    Slush, Watermelon-Berry, '90 137
    Smoothie, Four-Berry, '97 173
    Southern Breeze, '02 185
    Spritzers, Raspberry, '99 207
    Syrup, Berry, '96 161
    Tea, Cranberry-Raspberry Herb, '05 61
    Tea, Rasp-Berry Good, '95 200
    Tea, Sangría, '94 131

Biscuits, Raspberry-Almond, '93 160
Bisque, Banana-Raspberry, '93 161
Bites, Creamy Raspberry, '05 36
Bordeaux, Beauberries, '98 18
Brie, Almond-Raspberry, '94 M89
Brie in Rye, Raspberry, '93 252
Brownies, Raspberry, '92 274; '97 M35
Cake, Blackberry-Raspberry Truffle, '03 245
Cake, Chocolate-Raspberry, '92 173; '01 M319
Cake, Lemon-Raspberry, '91 247
Cake Loaf, Pretty and Pink Pound, '96 60
Cake, Raspberry-Fudge, '97 34
Cake, White Chocolate-Raspberry, '98 323
Candied Flowers and Raspberries, '98 155
Cheesecake, Chocolate-Raspberry Truffle, '91 270
Chicken, Jamaican Jerk Raspberry, '00 88
Chicken, Raspberry, '97 66
Chicken, Raspberry-Barbecue, '05 203
Chocolate Cups, Miniature, '87 132
Chocolate-Raspberry Bags, '95 97
Chocolates, Raspberry Cream, '91 36
Cobbler, Berry-Cherry, '83 270
Cobbler, Fig-and-Raspberry, '02 160
Cobbler, Raspberry-Cherry, '93 230
Coffee Cake, Raspberry, '83 112
Coffee Cake, Raspberry-Cheese, '97 231
Compote, Berry, '81 275
Compote, Berry-Peach, '82 133
Compote, Spicy Grapefruit-Berry, '91 19
Cookies, Raspberry Swirl, '90 111
Cream, Pear Salad with Raspberry, '00 311
Crème Brûlée, Berry, '95 323
Crème Brûlée, Double Raspberry, '95 323
Crêpes, Raspberry, '87 126
Crêpes Suzette, Raspberry, '84 84
Crêpes with Yogurt Filling, Fresh Raspberry, '93 123
Crisp, Peach-and-Raspberry, '02 232
Crisp, Raspberry-Pear, '89 109
Custard with Raspberries, Almond Crème, '88 174
Custard with Raspberries, Amaretto, '86 152
Dessert, Frozen Raspberry, '84 192
Dessert, Raspberry-Jellyroll, '85 95
Dessert, Raspberry Sauce, '80 147
Dream, Raspberry, '83 108
Filling, Raspberry, '90 111
Fluff, Raspberry, '89 198
Gazpacho, Berry, '97 181
Glaze, Raspberry, '00 88
Glaze, Turkey Breast with Orange-Raspberry,
    '91 253
Granita, Raspberry Liqueur, '88 117
Granita, Wild Raspberry Tea, '99 89
Ice Cream, Fresh Raspberry, '86 152
Ice Cream, Raspberry, '80 176
Ice, Raspberry, '92 268
Jam, Berry Refrigerator, '89 139
Jam, Mock Raspberry, '96 168
Jam, Raspberry Freezer, '84 M181
Jellyrolls, Raspberry, '93 M255
Lemon Curd with Berries, '90 102
Mayonnaise, Raspberry, '97 107
Mousse in Chocolate Crinkle Cups, Raspberry, '93 270
Mousse, Raspberry, '81 34; '04 260
Muffins, Lemon-Raspberry, '92 119; '03 306
Muffins, Raspberry-Streusel, '96 54
Mustard, Raspberry, '95 313
Napoleons, Berry, '94 120
Parfait, White Chocolate-Raspberry Swirl, '93 315
Pie, Bumbleberry, '97 163
Pie, Cherry-Berry, '92 316
Pie, Cran-Raspberry, '87 244
Pie, Raspberry Baked Alaska, '98 216
Pie, Raspberry Cream, '94 209
Pie, Rhubarb-Raspberry Pear, '95 119

Prunes, Raspberry, '82 124
Pudding, Raspberry, '92 92
Pudding, Russian Blueberry-Raspberry, '97 128
Puffs, Raspberry Party, '90 170
Puree, Chocolate Mousse Loaf with Raspberry, '97 34
Puree, Fruit Compote with Raspberry, '88 81
Ribs, Jamaican Jerk Raspberry, '00 88
Salads and Salad Dressings
  Aspic, Raspberry-Tomato, '05 65
  Chicken-Raspberry Salad, Marinated, '93 190
  Frozen Raspberry Salad, '79 287; '80 35
  Fruit Mounds, Raspberry, '79 35
  Greens with Raspberries and Walnuts, Mixed, '98 194
  Maple Dressing, Bibb Salad with Raspberry-, '91 246
  Mixed Greens with Raspberry Dressing, '97 50
  Mold, Raspberry Holiday, '84 253
  Peppery Greens with Raspberry Dressing, '95 254
  Raspberry Dressing, '87 153; '95 202
  Raspberry Salad, '86 286
  Raspberry Salad Dressing, '94 158; '03 M28
  Ribbon Salad, Raspberry, '87 236
  Vinaigrette, Gourmet Greens with Raspberry, '00 163
  Vinaigrette, Orange-Raspberry, '95 144; '96 155
  Vinaigrette, Raspberry, '94 249; '96 275; '97 146;
    '98 184; '05 91
  Walnut Salad, Raspberry-, '94 158
  Wine Salad, Raspberry-, '91 256
Sauces
  Amaretto Sauce, Raspberry-, '88 130
  Barbecue Sauce, Raspberry-, '05 203
  Berry Sauce, '94 130
  Chipotle Sauce, Jerk Turkey Tenderloin with
    Raspberry-, '05 M194
  Chocolate and Raspberry Sauce, Orange Sections
    with, '97 33
  Crimson Raspberry Sauce, '79 91; '85 30
  Custard Sauce, Fresh Berries with Raspberry, '88 163
  Duck Breasts with Raspberry Sauce, '87 240
  Flambé, Raspberry Sauce, '84 142
  Fresh Raspberry Sauce, '93 120
  Lemon Sauce, Cheesecake with Raspberry-, '96 30
  Lime Cheesecake with Raspberry Sauce, '00 204
  Melba Sauce, '87 77
  Mimosa Sauce, Berry, '90 315
  Orange Sauce, Raspberry-, '88 22; '92 154
  Peach-Berry Sauce, '87 M165
  Poached Pears with Raspberry Sauce, '87 69; '88 223
  Raspberry Sauce, '82 289; '83 108; '84 73, 213;
    '87 69, 117, 183; '88 267; '89 183, 322; '91 96,
    180, 270; '92 130; '93 82, 99, 315; '94 295;
    '95 327; '96 183, 310; '98 157, 216; '99 167, 259;
    '02 123; '03 319; '04 33; '05 31, 201
  Tea-Berry Sauce, '94 130; '99 334
Sherbet, Raspberry, '83 162
Sherbet, Raspberry-Buttermilk, '05 133
Shortbread, Raspberry, '99 29; '02 33
Shortcake, Chocolate-Raspberry, '95 99
Sorbet, Raspberry, '03 171
Soufflé, Raspberry, '86 188
Soufflé, Raspberry-Topped, '85 317
Soup, Chilled Raspberry, '81 130
Soup, Raspberry, '00 144
Soup, Sherry-Berry Dessert, '91 180
Spirited Raspberries, '95 142
Strudel, Raspberry-Nut, '83 304
Sweet Potatoes, Raspberry, '87 280
Tart, Bakewell, '97 110
Tartlets, Fresh Berry, '91 98
Tartlets, Raspberry-Brie, '04 287
Tart, Pick-a-Berry, '91 118
Tart, Raspberry-Almond Pear, '05 230
Tarts, Berry Good Lemon, '91 119
Tarts, Cran-Raspberry Meringue, '92 286
Tarts, Raspberry-Almond, '99 280

Tarts, Raspberry Jelly, '00 208
Tea Cake, Raspberry, '91 271
Tea Cakes, Royal Raspberry, '02 253
Topping, Raspberry, '85 317
Topping, Raspberry-Peach, '87 126
Trifle, Raspberry, '88 259
Trifles, Individual Raspberry, '99 112
Truffles, Raspberry-Fudge, '00 M41
Vinaigrette, Raspberry, '04 50; '05 91
Vinegar, Raspberry, '97 146
Vinegar, Raspberry-Lemon, '87 134
Vinegar, Raspberry-Thyme, '95 190
Vinegar, Raspberry Wine, '93 191

RELISHES. *See also* **CHUTNEYS, PESTOS, SALSAS,
    SAUCES, TOPPINGS.**
  Antipasto Relish, '86 327
  Apple-Celery Relish, '89 141
  Apple-Raisin Relish, '03 83
  Apple Relish, '96 323; '97 27
  Apple Relish, Spicy, '84 M323
  Avocado Relish, '87 120
  Beet Relish, '84 179
  Beet Relish, Colorful, '85 136
  Black Bean-Tomatillo Relish, '87 121
  Black-Eyed Pea Relish, Zesty, '95 56
  Cabbage Relish, '83 260
  Cabbage Relish, Spanish, '95 270
  Carrot Relish, '03 67
  Cherry-Honey Relish, '97 32
  Chow Chow, '82 196
  Chowchow, '87 150; '00 158
  Chowchow, Nannie's, '95 250
  Confit, Roasted Shallot-Garlic, '94 303
  Corn-and-Tomato Relish, Sweet White, '00 130
  Corn Relish, '81 129, 175; '83 189; '84 107; '85 136;
    '87 120, 245; '92 241
  Corn Relish, Easy, '83 260
  Corn Relish, Quick, '90 13
  Corn Relish, Summer, '89 127
  Corn Relish, Sweet, '93 119
  Corn Relish, Virginia, '79 283
  Crabmeat Relish, '99 198
  Cran-Apple Relish, '84 300
  Cranberry-Black Bean Relish, '03 243
  Cranberry-Nut Relish, '86 275
  Cranberry-Orange Relish, '81 M289; '88 254; '99 15
  Cranberry-Pear Relish, '85 232
  Cranberry Relish, '81 275; '83 144; '85 258, 264;
    '86 283; '87 245; '91 257; '92 341; '95 318;
    '98 310; '02 276
  Cranberry Relish, Frozen, '95 302
  Cranberry Relish, Holiday, '88 304
  Cranberry Relish, Lemony, '79 243
  Cranberry Relish, Old-Fashioned, '82 297
  Cranberry Relish, Roasted Acorn Squash with, '05 234
  Cranberry Relish, Tipsy, '92 M310
  Cucumber Relish, '85 176; '96 23
  Eggplant Relish, '95 342
  Fruit Relish, Fresh, '95 158
  Garden Relish, '83 259
  Garden Relish, End-of-the-, '80 179
  Green Olive Relish with Coriander, '96 323; '97 27
  Green Onion Relish, '84 65
  Green Tomato Relish, '96 168; '98 124
  Green Tomato Sweet Relish, '93 136
  Horseradish Relish, '01 60
  Hot Relish, '01 123
  India Relish, '84 179
  Jerusalem Artichoke Relish, '89 197
  Kraut Relish, '91 232
  Lemon-Date Relish, '96 271
  Mango Relish, '89 198
  Onion Relish, '91 79
  Onion Relish, Sweet, '93 124; '96 206; '99 204

  Orange Slices, Spicy, '81 12
  Papaya-Basil Relish, '94 82
  Peach Relish, '85 136
  Pear Relish, '79 196
  Pear Relish, Aunt Glennie's, '95 305
  Pear Relish, Peppery, '89 141
  Pepper-Onion Relish, '84 180
  Pepper Relish, '83 183
  Pepper Relish, Confetti, '91 195
  Pepper Relish, Grandma's, '04 158
  Pepper Relish, Sweet, '95 104
  Pineapple-Coconut Relish, '96 323; '97 27
  Plums, Brandied, '97 176
  Prune Relish, Peppy, '90 227
  Purple Onion Relish, '95 253
  Raisin Relish, '92 310
  Salad, Relish, '84 121
  Sauerkraut Relish, '85 136
  Summer Squash Relish, Pollock with, '92 200
  Tomato, Basil and Corn Relish, '05 321
  Tomato-Olive Relish, Flank Steak with, '03 210
  Tomato Relish, '85 188
  Tomato Relish, Easy, '80 126
  Vegetable Relish, '90 147
  Vegetable Relish, Eight-, '84 179
  White Bean Relish, '93 229
  Zucchini Relish, '87 200
  Zucchini Relish, Sweet, '95 159
RHUBARB
  Ambrosia, Rhubarb, '88 93
  Bavarian, Rhubarb-Strawberry, '86 140
  Cake, Rhubarb Upside-Down, '00 87
  Chutney, Rhubarb, '87 245
  Cobbler, Rosy Strawberry-Rhubarb, '79 154
  Cobbler, Strawberry-Rhubarb, '88 93
  Crisp, Rhubarb, '91 146; '92 130
  Crisp, Strawberry-Rhubarb, '95 119
  Mousse, Rhubarb, '88 93
  Pie, Bumbleberry, '97 163
  Pie, Rhubarb-Peach, '86 140
  Pie, Rhubarb-Raisin, '79 112
  Pie, Rhubarb-Raspberry Pear, '95 119
  Pie, Strawberry-Rhubarb, '98 99; '05 132
  Salad, Rhubarb, '91 146; '92 129
  Salad, Rhubarb Congealed, '86 140
  Salad, Tart Rhubarb, '91 146; '92 129
  Sauce, Chilled Rhubarb, '88 94
  Sauce, Pineapple-Rhubarb, '88 94
  Sauce, Rolled Pork with Rhubarb, '96 134
  Squares, Rhubarb, '91 146; '92 129
  Squares, Rosy Rhubarb, '79 111
  Whip, Rhubarb, '79 112
RICE
  Almond Rice, '81 195; '85 M112; '89 100; '91 291
  à l'Orange, Rice, '90 236
  Apple-Cinnamon Rice, '86 249
  Arabic Rice, '94 200
  Asparagus, Rice and, '93 324
  Bacon-Chive Rice, '83 129
  Balls, Rice, '81 51
  Basic Long-Grain Rice, '83 M285
  Basic Molding Rice, '86 221
  Basic Quick-Cooking Rice, '83 M285
  Basic Rice, '79 64
  Beans and Rice. *See also* **RICE/Salads.**
    Black Beans and Rice, '80 222; '89 178; '91 82;
      '95 309; '05 214
    Black Beans and Yellow Rice, '95 126
    Black Beans and Yellow Rice, Easy, '92 308
    Black Beans with Yellow Rice, '82 2
    Cajun Peas, '88 3
    Cajun Red Beans and Rice, '83 26
    Caribbean Beans and Rice, '99 121
    Creole Beans and Rice, '80 223

RICE, Beans and Rice
(continued)

Farmer's Beans and Rice with Rosemary Biscuits, '99 16
Kidney Beans and Rice, Smoky, '03 290
New Orleans Red Beans and Rice, '97 235
Pinto Beans, Ham Hocks, and Rice, '05 46
Red Beans and Rice, '80 58; '83 89; '84 37; '87 45; '90 27; '96 218; '02 35
Red Beans and Rice, Delta, '98 146
Red Beans and Rice, Easy, '90 220; '99 M219
Red Beans and Rice, Spicy, '02 56
Red Beans and Rice with Sausage, '05 125
Sausage, Beans, and Rice, Texas, '84 296
South Texas Beans and Rice, '85 252
Beans with Coconut Milk, Spicy, '03 175
Black-Eyed Peas, Rice with, '93 66
Black-Eyed Peas with Rice, '83 12; '90 208; '91 13
Black-Eyes and Rice, Creole, '85 6
Blended Rice, '96 68
Braised Rice, '98 45
Braised Rice and Peas, '79 101
Brown Rice
Brown Rice, '82 275
Calico Brown Rice, '86 33
Casserole, Brown Rice, '87 118
Chicken and Brown Rice, Roast, '83 268
Chicken-Brown Rice Bake, '91 314
Confetti Rice, '89 146
Consommé, Brown Rice, '98 288
Cornish Hens with Brown Rice, '82 275
Garden Rice, '92 12
Mix, Fruited Curry-Rice, '86 326
Mix, Fruited Rice, '97 317
Pancakes, Vegetable-Rice, '93 43
Parmesan, Brown Rice, '84 196
Pecan Rice, '85 53
Pilaf, Brown Rice, '90 136; '91 82
Pudding, Brown Rice, '85 77
Rolls, Crunchy Cabbage-Rice, '85 32
Salad, Brown Rice-and-Vegetable, '84 202
Salad, Brown Rice Confetti, '94 174
Salad, Brown Rice-Pine Nut, '05 126
Salad, Orange Vinaigrette Rice, '98 288
Salad, Zesty Rice-and-Bean, '02 84
Spanish Brown Rice, '84 196
Stew, Lentil-Rice, '82 232
Stuffing, Tomatoes with Walnut-Rice, '91 102
Vegetables and Rice, '93 91
Brussels Sprouts and Rice, '79 288; '80 26
Buttery Rice with Vermicelli, '02 258
Cabbage Leaves, Stuffed, '00 270
Calas, Easy, '92 89
Calas, Quick, '96 64
Calico Rice, '85 83
Carrots and Rice, Sweet, '05 203
Casseroles. *See also* **RICE/Brown Rice, Wild Rice.**
Almond Rice, '91 291
au Gratin, Rice, '83 129
au Gratin Supreme, Rice, '86 78
Baked Rice, '94 270
Baked Spicy Rice, '96 125
Beef and Rice, Spiced, '84 285
Black-Eyed Peas with Rice, '83 12
Broccoli-Rice Casserole, '81 101
Broccoli with Rice, Holiday, '87 252
Chantilly, Rice, '86 82
Cheese-Parslied Rice, '89 99
Chicken and Rice, '95 54
Chicken and Rice Casserole, '80 260
Chicken-and-Rice Casserole, Creamy, '02 309
Chicken-and-Rice Casserole, Crispy, '03 203
Chicken-and-Rice Casseroles, '01 52

Chicken Casserole, '96 302
Chicken Casserole, Rice-and-, '87 154
Chicken-Rice Casserole, '86 52; '99 215
Chicken-Rice Casserole, Creamy, '99 21
Chiles, Rice-and-Cheese con, '89 99
Chiles, Rice and Green, '83 152
Chili-Cheesy Rice, '79 43
Chili-Rice Casserole, '79 54
Colorful Rice Casserole, '82 199
Cornish Hens-and-Rice Casserole, '92 267
Corn-Rice Casserole, '01 46
Fiesta Rice, '84 76
French Rice, '83 24
Golden Rice, '79 270
Green Rice Bake, '79 43
Green Rice Casserole, '95 181
Ham-and-Rice Casserole, '84 75
Ham Casserole, '98 314
Ham-Rice-Tomato Bake, '87 78
Jalapeño Rice Casserole, '81 66
Lentils-and-Rice Casserole, '93 301
Lentils and Rice, Spanish-Style, '03 201
Mexican Rice Casserole, '83 31
Mushroom Rice, Baked, '92 170; '95 84
Mushroom Rice, Easy, '89 286
Pepper Rice, Hot, '92 310
Red Rice, Savannah, '95 27
Rice Casserole, '87 45
Sausage-and-Rice Bake, Creole, '88 58
Sausage and Rice Casserole, Oriental, '82 M123
Sausage Casserole, Skillet, '99 123
Sausage-Rice Casserole, '82 50; '83 75
Shrimp and Rice Casserole, '79 228
Shrimp-and-Rice Casserole, '94 328
Shrimp Casserole, Spicy, '96 62
Spanish Rice Casserole, '79 192
Spinach Rice, '85 146
Squash Casserole, Creamy Rice and, '95 26
Strata, Cheese-Rice, '81 176
Vegetarian Casserole, '96 302
Zucchini-Rice Casserole Italiano, '89 146
Charleston Rice, '97 310
Chicken-Flavored Rice, '84 M144
Coconut Rice, '00 201
Coconut Rice, Polynesian Pork Tenderloin with Orange-Curry Sauce and, '04 309
Consommé Rice, '80 246
Cooler, Rice-and-Cinnamon, '00 139
Cream with Mandarin Oranges, Rice, '85 317
Creole Rice, '90 183
Cumin Rice, '85 83
Curried Rice, '90 183; '97 51; '98 237; '04 21
Curried Rice, Quick, '86 81
Curried Rice with Almonds, '83 M285
Curried Rice with Pineapple, '79 142
Curry-Spiced Rice, '86 M226
Custard, Baked Rice, '92 308
(Date-Nut Rice), Basted Dates and Basted Rice, '96 158
Dirty Rice, '86 142
Dirty Rice, Cajun, '04 288
Dressing, Crabmeat-and-Oyster, '02 243
Dressing, Pecan, Rice, and Crawfish, '00 252
Dressing, Rice, '91 217; '01 222
Dressing, Roast Turkey with Rice, '82 286
Dressing, Southern Rice, '99 256
Empanadas, Easy Turkey, '96 63
Fried Rice
Bacon Fried Rice, '80 115
Calas, Easy, '92 89
Calas, Quick, '96 64
Cashew Fried Rice, '99 171
Chicken-Cashew Fried Rice, '99 171
Easy Fried Rice, '84 76
Egg Fried Rice, '79 252; '80 19

Fried Rice, '83 129; '84 197; '88 67; '00 273
Fried Rice 101, '05 50
Ham Fried Rice, '04 125
Pork Fried Rice, '89 99
Refried Rice, Shrimp and, '89 176
Sausage, Fried Rice with, '83 12
Shrimp-and-Pineapple Fried Rice, Spicy, '03 285
Special, Fried Rice, '80 56
Turkey Fried Rice, '83 282
Turkey "Fried" Rice, '00 97
Two, Fried Rice for, '81 31
Ginger Rice, Fluffy, '83 102
Glorified Rice, '83 129
Grape Leaves, Stuffed, '94 48
Green Peas, Rice with, '87 45
Green Rice, Celebrity, '81 207
Herbed Rice, '83 M285; '93 278
Herb Rice, '91 257
Herbs, Rice with Fresh, '05 68
Holiday Rice, '98 289
Honey Rice, '85 83
Hopping John, Skillet, '79 10
Hoppin' John, '05 21
Hoppin' John, Esau's, '03 17
Indian Rice, '96 202
Island Rice, '98 276
Jardin, Rice, '01 106
Journey Cakes, '04 99
Journey Cakes, Rosemary-Garlic, '04 99
Journey Cakes, Tomato, Parmesan, and Kalamata Olive, '04 99
Lemon Rice, '89 166
Lemony Rice, '99 46
Lentils and Rice, '99 236
Lime-Flavored Rice, '84 175
Lyonnaise, Rice, '83 151
Main Dishes. *See also* **RICE/Beans and Rice, Brown Rice, Casseroles, Pilaf, Risotto, Wild Rice.**
Arroz con Pollo, '01 279
Beef and Cauliflower over Rice, '93 94
Beef and Rice, Curried, '88 164
Beef-and-Rice Dinner, Mexican, '88 199
Beef and Rice, Mango-, '88 138
Beef and Rice, Spicy, '83 231
Beef over Rice Noodles, Shredded, '85 74
Beef Rollups with Rice, Royal, '79 105
Beef Tips on Rice, '85 87
Black-Eyed Peas with Rice, '90 208
Boudin, Old-Fashioned, '85 250
Cabbage Rolls, Stuffed, '88 18
Chicken-and-Rice Bake, Herbed, '02 215
Chicken-and-Rice Cacciatore, Quick, '88 38
Chicken and Rice, Creole, '92 262
Chicken and Rice Dressing, '79 288
Chicken and Rice, Island, '04 165
Chicken and Rice, One-Dish, '01 279
Chicken and Rice, Shortcut, '90 220
Chicken-and-Rice Skillet Dinner, '98 127
Chicken and Rice, Spicy, '88 200
Chicken and Rice, Sweet-and-Sour, '03 97
Chicken-and-Rice Valencia, '85 113
Chicken Breasts, Celebrity, '95 60
Chicken Caruso and Rice, '89 177
Chicken Livers and Rice Dish, '82 218
Chicken Livers with Rice, '80 200; '81 58; '84 292
Chicken over Confetti Rice Squares, Creamed, '81 282; '82 31
Chicken over Rice, Cajun, '88 102; '89 67
Chicken-Rice Medaillons in Pepper Pesto, '90 97
Chicken, Rice-Stuffed, '81 4
Chicken, Rice-Stuffed Roasted, '88 38
Chicken, Roasted Stuffed, '98 109
Chicken, Salsa Rice and, '99 109
Chicken, Sanibel Island, '97 66
Chicken with Curried Rice, '98 127

Chicken with Pecan-Rice Dressing, '85 M57
Chicken with Rice, Moorish, '98 127
Chicken with Rice, Roast, '95 261
Chicken with Rice, Sherry, '81 97
Chili with Rice, '82 11
Cornish Hens, Rice-Stuffed, '82 302
Curried Rice, '97 51
Dirty Rice, '03 147
Dirty Rice, Hot, '93 219
Egg and Rice Bake, '83 119
Fruited Rice, Far East, '81 175
Ham Rolls, Rice-Stuffed, '83 190
Ham with Rice, Curried, '80 111
Hoppin' John with Scallion Hoe Cake Medaillons, Skillet, '02 326
Indian Rice, '79 64
Jollof Rice Dinner, '91 230; '92 325
Lamb Curry with Rice, '80 83; '81 10
Lentil-and-Rice Supper, '84 202
Meatballs Paprikash with Rice, '85 31
Mexican Dinner, Quick, '98 224
Oriental Rice, '85 146
Paella, Chicken-Pork-Shrimp, '82 245
Paella, Seafood, '82 245
Paella, Spanish, '85 26
Paella Valenciana, '82 246
Pancakes, Rice, '85 147
Peppers, Beef-Stuffed, '85 146
Peppers, Rice-Stuffed, '80 65; '99 241
Pepper Steak and Rice, '81 17
Peppers with Rice and Ham, Stuffed, '82 131
Pork Chops and Rice, Savannah, '00 236
Pork Chops and Spanish Rice, '83 103; '85 293
Pork Chops, Rice-Stuffed, '83 102
Pork Chops with White Rice, '02 312
Pork Roast with Hopping John Stuffing, '01 25
Red Rice, '92 235
Red Rice Jambalaya, '91 18
Sausage and Rice, Italian, '86 53
Shrimp and Refried Rice, '89 176
Shrimp and Rice, Oriental, '90 183
Shrimp and Sausage Rice, '79 64
Shrimp-and-Scallop Sauté with Pecan Rice, '90 317
Shrimp Creole in a Rice Ring, '86 222
Shrimp, Curried Rice and, '83 231
Shrimp Sauté, Confetti, '97 104
Skillet Dinner, Antipasto, '97 327
Skillet, Hamburger-Rice, '00 236
Strudel, Meatless Mexican, '98 29
Tostadas, Rice-and-Black Bean, '97 65
Tuna-Rice Pie, '84 123
Turkey and Rice, Herbed, '97 327
Turkey with Rice Dressing, Roast, '82 286
Medley, Rice, '79 270
Mélange, Rice, '87 240
Mexican Rice
Dinner, Quick Mexican, '98 224
Dressing, Mexican Rice, '87 253
Jalapeño Hot Rice, '80 126
Jalapeño Rice, '79 43
Mexican Rice, '83 85; '85 147; '91 217; '01 273
Mold, Chile-Rice, '86 221
Orphan's Rice, '03 32
Spanish Rice, '81 51; '83 209; '90 183; '94 27
Spanish Rice, Chicken Wings with, '00 202
Spanish Rice, Jiffy, '90 176
Spanish Rice, Pork Chops and, '83 103; '85 293
Spanish Rice with Tofu, '88 26
Spanish-Style Rice, '83 152
Spicy Mexican Rice, '88 149
Tex-Mex Rice with Corn, '03 129
Miami Rice, '96 86
Mix, Fruited Rice, '90 267
Mix, Herb-Rice, '91 257

Mix, Seasoned Rice, '01 248
Mold, Curried Rice, '85 36
Mold, Saffron Rice, '86 221
Mushroom Rice, Baked, '92 170; '95 84
Nutted Rice, '85 269
Orange-Herb Rice, '89 286
Orange Rice, '79 43; '81 175; '82 200
Oriental Rice, '85 M12, 146
Orphan's Rice, '04 218
Oven Rice, '83 89
Paella, Garden, '82 245
Paella Rice Mix, '94 168
Paella, Roasted-Vegetable, '04 89
Pancakes, Rice, '85 147
Parsleyed Rice, '83 M58
Parsley Rice, '84 197; '85 95
Parslied Rice, '87 167, 243
Parslied Rice, Creamy, '88 255
Peas and Rice, '88 97
Peas and Rice, Holiday, '86 328
Peas, Caribbean Rice and, '02 275
Pecan Rice, '04 204
Pecan Rice, Speedy Skillet, '04 328
Peppered Rice, '82 4
Picadillo Rice, '98 237
Pigeon Peas, Rice with, '92 157
Pilaf
Apricot Rice Pilaf, '99 146
Basil Rice Pilaf, '05 M197
Browned Rice Pilaf, '87 305
Brown Rice Pilaf, '90 136; '91 82
Chicken-and-Smoked Sausage Pilau, '04 204
Chicken Pilaf, '82 246
Chicken Pilau, '99 184
Chicken-Vegetable Pilaf, '97 51
Cinnamon Rice Pilaf, '01 229
Fruit-and-Vegetable Rice Pilaf, '84 196
Fruited Pork Pilaf, '82 246
Fruited Rice Pilaf, '04 271
Fruited Rice Pilaf, Chicken Breasts with, '92 307
Greek Rice Pilaf, '01 146
Ham Pilaf Mold, '86 222
Lemon-and-Pine Nut Pilaf, '97 51
Lemon Pilaf, '97 322
Lemon Rice Pilaf, '01 36; '04 82
Lentil Pilaf, Rice-and-, '88 17
Near-Eastern Pilaf, '82 246
Okra Pilaf, '80 185; '82 126; '93 160
Okra Pilau, '99 184
Onion Rice Pilaf, '04 236
Orange Rice Pilaf, '05 219
Oyster Pilaf, '97 20
Persian Rice Pilaf, '02 167
Rice Pilaf, '86 82; '87 229; '88 42; '89 286
Saffron Rice Pilaf, '04 204
Sausage Pilau, '99 184
Savory Pilaf, '83 93
Shrimp Pilaf, '82 246
Shrimp Pilau, '99 184
Turkey-Asparagus Pilaf, '88 200
Turkey-Rice Pilaf, '86 284
Turkish Pilaf, '79 184
White Rice Pilaf, '97 238
Wild Rice-Fennel Pilaf, '97 127
Pork Backbone and Rice, '03 252
Primavera, Rice, '98 237
Pudding, Amaretto Rice, '86 334
Pudding, Apple Rice, '91 217
Pudding, Creamy Rice, '81 51, 205
Pudding, English Rice, '04 98
Pudding, Fruited Rice, '81 205; '86 95
Pudding, Fudgy Rice, '81 205
Pudding, Old-Fashioned Rice, '85 147; '03 285
Pudding, Raisin-Rice, '87 46

Pudding, Velvety Rice, '81 205
Quiche, Broccoli-Rice, '81 228
Quick-Cook Rice with Fresh Herbs, '05 69
Raisin Rice with Curry, '85 83
Red Rice, '97 138; '00 289; '02 119
Red Rice and Ham, '00 289
Red Rice, Savannah, '80 119; '89 286
Ring, Oregano Rice, '86 222
Ring, Rice-Carrot, '79 246
Ring with Beets, Rice, '79 225
Risotto
alla Milanese, Risotto, '85 228
Asparagus Risotto, '03 68
Baked Risotto, Easy, '99 120
Broccoli Risotto with Parmesan, '99 120
Chicken-and-Roasted Shallot Risotto, Smoked, '00 30
Collard Green Risotto and Pot Liquor, '01 121
Collards, Risotto with, '96 203
Crawfish Risotto, '99 120
Creamy Risotto, '03 285
Green Bean Risotto, '03 68
Greens, Risotto with, '96 132
Lemon-Lime Risotto, '97 213
Microwave Risotto, '97 M213
Onion Risotto, '99 94; '02 97; '03 98
Pinot Noir Risotto with Rosemary Chicken, '97 214
Pistachio Risotto with Saffron, '98 272
Primavera, Risotto, '95 163; '00 138
Pumpkin Risotto with Shrimp, '98 240
Risotto, '95 280
Roasted Garlic-and-Cheese Risotto, '04 283
Seafood Risotto, '95 280
Shellfish and Peas, Risotto with, '96 131
Shrimp and Asparagus, Risotto with, '03 86
Shrimp Risotto, '00 95; '02 124
Southwestern Risotto, '92 211
Sweet Onion Risotto, '03 217
Tomato-Basil Risotto, '95 269
Vegetables, Risotto with, '98 193
Rolls, Shrimp-and-Romaine, '97 197
Saffron Rice, '79 43; '93 282; '97 51
Saffron Rice Mold, '86 221
Salads
Artichoke-Chicken-Rice Salad, '94 132
Artichoke-Chicken-Rice Salad, Mediterranean, '97 321
Artichoke Hearts, Rice Salad with, '80 232
Artichoke-Rice Salad, '80 178; '81 41; '85 81; '01 144
Avocado Salad, Rice-and-, '89 146
Bacon, Rice Salad with, '79 52
Bean-and-Rice Salad, Marinated, '87 152
Bean Salad, Rice-and-, '85 22
Beans-and-Rice Salad, '91 44
Beef-and-Lime Rice Salad, '03 172
Black Bean-and-Rice Salad, '00 327
Cabbage Salad with Honey-Dijon Vinaigrette, Rice-, '04 321
Chicken-and-Rice Salad, '97 92
Chicken-and-Rice Salad, Hot, '83 22
Chicken-Rice Salad, '81 203; '97 93
Chicken-Rice Salad, Grilled, '98 148
Chicken-Rice Salad, Nutty, '83 157
Chutneyed Rice Salad, '88 100
Colorful Rice Salad, '81 253
Confetti Rice Salad, '80 232
Crunchy Rice Salad, '82 302
Curried Chicken-Rice Salad, '92 190
Curried Rice Salad, '80 84; '85 147, 220; '96 240
Curry Rice Salad, '89 146
Egg-Rice Salad, '84 18; '86 169
Ham-and-Rice Salad, Colorful, '90 319
Ham-and-Rice Salad, Mandarin, '87 145
Ham-Rice Toss, '82 40
Hearty Rice Salad, '82 233

RICE, Salads
(continued)

Herbed Rice Salad, '96 123
Hoppin' John Salad, '96 64
Lentils-and-Rice Salad, '90 197
Mandarin Rice Salad, '88 271
Mardi Gras Rice, '91 217
Molded Gazpacho-Rice Salad, '86 221
Mushrooms, Rice Salad with Fresh, '80 231
Paella Salad, '86 207
Pea Salad, Rice-, '85 163
Pebble Salad, '91 27
Pine Nut, Rice, and Feta Salad, '96 26; '98 331
Pork-and-Rice Salad with Spicy Tomato Dressing, '03 143
Primavera Salad, Rice, '00 131
Red Rice Salad, Charleston, '79 146
Rice Salad, '79 74; '81 51
Salmon-Rice Salad, '84 289
Shrimp-and-Orange Rice Salad, Zesty, '87 155
Shrimp and Rice Salad, '80 231; '82 207
Shrimp-and-Rice Salad, '92 307
Shrimp-Rice Salad, Baked, '83 22
Shrimp-Rice Salad, Tangy, '84 66
Shrimp Salad, Rice-, '79 270; '92 142
Shrimp Salad, Rice-and-, '83 82
Spinach-Rice Salad, '94 63
Tomatoes and Basil, Rice with, '95 232
Tuna-Rice Salad, '87 202
Vegetable-Rice Salad, '80 148; '83 198; '85 87
Vegetable Salad, Rice-and-, '86 42
Zesty Rice Salad, '81 23
Savory Rice, '89 201
Seasoned Onion Rice, '82 166
Seasoned Rice, '79 244; '83 212
Seasoned Rice, Pork Sausage-, '00 236
Shell, Rice-Cheese, '82 49
Shrimp Over Rice, Texas Pesto, '03 327
Shrimp with Rice, '03 219
Soufflé, Rice-Cheese, '79 270
Soup, Chicken-and-Rice, '88 236
Soup, Mushroom-Rice, '90 32
Soup, Tomato-and-Rice, '85 24
Soup, Turkey-Rice, '90 89
Southern Rice, '90 250
Southwestern Rice, '90 121
Spanish Rice. *See* **RICE/Mexican Rice.**
Spicy Rice, '83 215; '85 256; '99 214
Steak and Rice, Skillet Pepper, '04 326
Steamed Rice, Oven-, '89 226
Stew with Rice, Black-Eyed Pea, '04 19
Strata, Cheese-Rice, '81 176
Stuffing, Pork Roast, with Hopping John, '01 25
Stuffing, Rice, '95 290
Stuffing, Rice-and-Onion, '88 246
Succotash, Savory, '96 63
Sweet Jamaican Rice, '96 71
Three-Grain Rice, '95 166
Timbales, Green Rice, '97 62
Timbales, Rice, '94 32
Timbales, Spinach-Rice, '88 271
Toasted Herb Rice, '04 295
Toasted Rice and Pasta, '95 57
Tomatoes and Basil, Rice with, '95 232
Tomatoes, Italian-Style, '97 169
Tomato Rice, '02 169
Tortilla Bites with Sesame-Soy Dipping Sauce, '02 145
Toss, Succotash Rice, '05 218
Vegetable-Rice Toss, '91 309
Vegetables, Rice with, '79 64; '85 83
Vegetables, Rice with Spring, '96 132
Waffles, Rice, '98 124
Waldorf Rice, '84 281

White Rice, Fluffy, '03 65
White Rice, The Ultimate, '05 279
Wild Rice. *See also* **RICE/Pilaf.**
Almond Wild Rice, '86 50
Belvedere, Wild Rice, '86 82
Bulgur, Wild Rice, '91 83
Casserole, Chicken-and-Wild Rice, '97 192; '00 257
Casserole, Chicken-Wild Rice, '84 241; '85 65
Casserole, Duck and Wild Rice, '79 224
Casserole, Leslie's Favorite Chicken-and-Wild Rice, '00 209; '03 107
Casserole, Oyster-and-Wild Rice, '83 34; '84 44
Casserole, Sausage and Wild Rice, '83 196
Casserole, Sausage-Wild Rice, '84 250
Casserole, Turkey-and-Sausage Wild Rice, '03 239
Casserole, Veal and Wild Rice, '79 180
Casserole, Wild Rice, '82 199; '95 176
Casserole, Wild Rice-Oyster, '86 256
Chicken and Wild Rice, '79 248; '01 279
Chicken Bowl, Wild Rice-and-, '05 127
Chicken-Fried Wild Rice, '89 24; '91 132
Chicken Rollups, '88 38
Chicken, Wild Rice-Stuffed, '79 219
Chicken-Wild Rice Supreme, '79 77
Chicken with Wild Rice, Elegant, '80 M76
Chicken with Wild Rice, Orange-Glazed Roasted, '02 85
Cranberry-Almond Wild Rice, '04 204
Cranberry-Pear Wild Rice, '83 279
Creole, Wild Rice-and-Shrimp, '84 292
Dressed-Up Wild Rice, '92 60
Eggs with Wild Rice, Scrambled, '80 42
Gourmet Wild Rice, '89 271
Grapes, Wild Rice with, '95 48
Morels, Wild Rice with, '89 62
Mushrooms, Wild Rice and, '83 278
Nutty Wild Rice, '05 278
Oysters, Wild Rice and, '92 339
Pancakes, Wild Rice, '02 238
Pear-and-Cranberry Wild Rice Salad, '03 199
Pecan-Lemon Wild Rice, '92 211
Popped Wild Rice, '85 65
Pork Loin Stuffed with Wild Rice, '84 35
Quiches, Wild Rice-and-Mushroom, '93 237
Ring, Creamed Mushrooms in Wild Rice, '80 270
Ring, Wild Rice, '83 253
Salad, Crab and Wild Rice, '79 116
Salad, Crab-Wild Rice, '86 207
Salad, Orange Vinaigrette Rice, '98 288
Salad, Oriental Salmon-and-Wild Rice, '94 173
Salad, Springtime Wild Rice, '88 100
Salad, Wild Rice, '85 65; '89 147; '93 191; '01 247
Salad, Wild Rice-and-Chicken, '02 52
Salad, Wild Rice-and-Corn, '98 288
Salad, Wild Rice-and-Cranberry, '99 272
Salad, Wild Rice-and-Kidney Bean, '01 175
Salad, Wild Rice-and-Roasted Vegetable, '99 316
Salad, Wild Rice-and-Shrimp, '02 109
Salad, Wild Rice-Chicken, '83 146; '99 55; '01 72
Salad, Wild Rice-Green Apple, '92 90
Salad, Wild Rice-Shrimp, '99 55
Salad, Wild Tuna, '95 243
Salad with Spicy Lime Vinaigrette, Wild Rice, '01 217
Sausage and Wild Rice, '85 65
Sausage, Wild Rice and, '86 268
Scallops and Wild Rice, '90 129
Soup, Cheesy Potato-and-Wild Rice, '89 16
Soup, Chicken-and-Wild Rice, '04 26
Soup, Creamy Chicken-and-Wild Rice, '98 M334
Soup, Tomato-Beef-Wild Rice, '04 42
Soup, Wildest Rice, '01 66
Stuffing, Cornish Hens with Wild Rice, '79 222; '80 64; '82 136
Turkey Breast, Wild Rice-Stuffed, '97 281
Veggie Wild Rice, '00 141

Yellow Rice, '91 136
Yellow Rice, Black Beans with, '82 2
Yellow Rice, Easy Black Beans and, '92 308
Yellow Rice with Water Chestnuts, '85 24
RISOTTO. *See* **RICE/Risotto.**
ROLLS AND BUNS. *See also* **BREADS.**
Angel's Wing Rolls, '95 329
Apple Pinwheel, Quick, '85 42
Beer-Parmesan Rolls, '03 259
Blueberry Pinwheels, '82 205
Broccoli-Cheddar Rolls, '91 21
Buttered Rum-Nut Rolls, '86 291
Butterscotch Pinwheels, '90 49
Cajun Bread Knots, '03 63
Caramel-Chocolate Sticky Buns, Easy, '95 36
Caramel Rolls, Easy, '90 195
Caramel Sticky Buns, '00 52
Centerpiece Rolls, '94 276
Cheese-Apricot Sweet Rolls, '90 195
Cherry-Almond Rolls, '84 M198
Cinnamon
Breakfast Buns, Cinnamon-Apple, '00 M198
Breakfast Rolls, Cinnamon, '00 243
Chocolate-Cinnamon Buns, '85 5
Cinnamon Buns, '91 68
Cinnamon Rolls, '79 80; '88 290; '92 270; '96 321; '98 325; '99 M284; '01 44, 242; '03 247
Cream Cheese-Filled Cinnamon Rolls, '02 327
Crisps, Cinnamon, '81 113
Dough, Cinnamon Roll, '03 247
Easy Cinnamon Rolls, '85 290
Filling, Cinnamon Roll, '03 247
Glazed Cinnamon Rolls, '86 312
Icing, Cinnamon Roll, '03 247
Mini-Cinnis, Mama's, '02 41
Old-Fashioned Cinnamon Rolls, '86 298; '90 196; '92 226
Pecan Rolls, Cinnamon-, '98 251
Pecan Rolls, Easy Cinnamon-, '89 307
Potato Sourdough Cinnamon Rolls, '94 325; '95 77
Raisin Cinnamon Pull-Aparts, '82 205; '83 32
Raisin Cinnamon Rolls, '81 107
Raisin-Cinnamon Rolls, '91 240
Rollups, Cinnamon Toast, '99 194
Spiral Cinnamon Rolls, '82 205; '83 32
Sticky Buns, Cinnamon, '83 244
Tea Rolls, Cinnamon, '92 263
Tiny Cinnamon Rolls, '97 271; '98 330
Twists, Cinnamon, '83 53
Cornmeal Rolls, '79 60; '89 184
Crescent
Almond Crescent Rolls, '90 283
Apricot-Cheese Crescents, '99 284
Apricot Crescents, '90 181
Butter Crescent Rolls, '95 292
Butter-Rich Crescent Rolls, '81 211
Buttery Crescent Rolls, '83 180
Cheddar Crescents, '05 70
Chocolate Crescents, '03 283
Crescent Rolls, '84 267; '89 235
Deep South Crescent Rolls, '82 309; '83 16
Easy Crescent Rolls, '79 60
Festive Crescents, '80 281
French-Style Crescent Rolls, '82 288
Hurry-Up Crescent Rolls, '97 50
Pecan Crescent Twists, '03 36
Yogurt Crescent Rolls, '91 123
Croissants, Cream Cheese, '92 159
Crunchy Rolls, '97 160
Dinner
Dinner Rolls, '79 251; '89 312; '93 M326
Fancy Dinner Rolls, '86 299
Freezer Dinner Rolls, '90 251
How to Shape Dinner Rolls, '83 323
Italian Dinner Rolls, '83 254

Italiano Dinner Rolls, '85 32
Oatmeal Dinner Rolls, '01 44
Refrigerator Dinner Rolls, '81 78
Sour Cream Dinner Rolls, '97 253
Whole Wheat Dinner Rolls, '91 53
Dried Cherry-Walnut Sweet Rolls, '03 235
Garlic Rolls, Easy, '86 234
Italian Bread Knots, '03 63
Jam Teasers, '81 8
Lemon Knots, Glazed, '86 290
Lemon-Orange Rolls, '05 70
Mayonnaise Rolls, '90 283
Nutty Buns, '86 290
Onion-and-Sesame Rolls, '95 292
Onion-Bacon Rolls, '99 47
Onion Buns, Cheesy, '85 5
Onion-Cheese Buns, '88 218
Onion Rolls, Poppy Seed, '81 63
Onion Twist Rolls, '89 288
Orange
Apricot-Orange Sweet Rolls, '03 235
Butter Rolls, Orange, '82 206; '83 33
Easy Orange Rolls, '89 M131
Frosted Hot Orange Rolls, '80 257
Glazed Orange Rolls, '90 194
Kitchen Express Orange Rolls, '98 252
Luscious Orange Rolls, '86 298
Orange Rolls, '80 22; '82 17; '88 79; '96 321; '01 257
Speedy Orange Rolls, '89 287
Parker House Rolls, Italian, '99 47
Parmesan Rolls, '79 181
Parsley-Garlic Rolls, '93 319
Pecan-Golden Raisin Sweet Rolls, '03 235
Pineapple Buns, Easy, '85 14
Potato
Caramelized Onion Buns, Potato-, '03 234
Easy Potato Rolls, '89 287
Feathery Light Potato Rolls, '81 305; '82 36
Homemade Potato Rolls, '82 252
Potato Rolls, '81 300; '99 290
Refrigerated Potato Rolls, '83 254
Refrigerator Potato Rolls, '87 15
Sourdough Cinnamon Rolls, Potato, '94 325; '95 77
Sourdough Rolls, Potato, '94 325; '95 77
Southern Potato Rolls, '86 299
Super Potato Rolls, '85 145
Supreme Potato Rolls, '82 130
Whole Wheat Potato Rolls, '89 50
Yeast Rolls, Potato, '87 53
Pull-Apart Buns, Easy, '83 100
Pumpkin Rolls, '87 254
Quick Rolls, '95 245; '96 54
Raisin Rollups, Sweet, '86 290
Refrigerator
Big-Batch Rolls, '88 289
Bran Rolls, '85 145
Brioche, Morrison House, '96 53
Buttermilk Refrigerator Rolls, '81 120; '82 22
Butter Rolls, Homemade, '00 137
Caramel Breakfast Rolls, '79 193
Caramel-Nut Rolls, '86 312
Caramel Sticky Buns, Overnight, '00 52
Cloverleaf Refrigerator Rolls, '80 256
Croissants, '83 54
Herb Rolls, '98 325
Icebox Rolls, '80 242
Lemon Spirals, French, '81 94
Low-Sodium Refrigerator Rolls, '82 67
Overnight Rolls, '86 233
Parker House Refrigerator Rolls, '82 310; '83 17
Party Refrigerator Rolls, '79 248
Party Rolls, '98 251
Potato Rolls, Refrigerated, '83 254
Potato Rolls, Refrigerator, '87 15

Refrigerator Rolls, '82 287; '91 53
Reuben Buns, '88 298
Sour Cream Rolls, '80 71
Sour Cream Yeast Rolls, '85 259; '90 17; '93 232; '00 33
Spoon Rolls, '87 15; '91 275
Sweet Rolls, Yummy, '80 281
Three-Day Refrigerator Rolls, '86 306
Twists, Austrian, '80 45
Wixie's Refrigerator Rolls, '99 82
Yeast Rolls, Refrigerator, '81 296, 307; '82 309;
'83 17, 118; '91 80; '98 109, 325
Reuben Rolls, Snappy, '02 58
Romano Sesame Rolls, '87 144
Rum Rolls, Easy, '79 287; '80 35
Sesame Knots, '89 29
Snack Buns, '87 279
Southwestern Knots, '03 63
Sticky Buns, Christmas Morning, '97 245
Sweet Rolls, Quick Breakfast, '90 195
Toasted Rolls with Herb Butter, '89 70
Wheat
Dinner Rolls, Whole Wheat, '91 53
Easy Whole Wheat Rolls, '86 286; '87 74
Feather Rolls, Shredded Wheat, '82 309; '83 16
Hearty Whole Wheat Bread and Rolls, '79 92
Honey Wheat Rolls, '83 278
Honey-Wheat Rolls, Dilled, '83 254
Light Wheat Rolls, '87 254
Pan Rolls, Whole Grain, '89 256
Petite Whole Wheat Rolls, '85 146
Potato Rolls, Whole Wheat, '89 50
Wholesome Whole Wheat Rolls, '92 31
Whole Wheat Buns, '86 236
Whole Wheat Rolls, '79 275; '90 111; '96 50
Yeast. *See also* **ROLLS AND BUNS/Cinnamon,**
    Crescent, Dinner, Potato, Refrigerator, Wheat.
Anise Rolls, '89 91
Baguettes and Rolls, '98 168
Basic Angel Rolls, '89 72
Best-Ever Yeast Rolls, '90 46
Blueberry Buns, Deluxe, '81 164
Bolillos, '88 247; '02 81
Bow Ties, '96 321
Bran Yeast Rolls, '87 116
Butter-and-Herb Rolls, '86 306
Butterhorn Rolls, '89 288
Butterhorns, '84 267
Buttermilk Rolls, Quick, '83 155
Buttermilk Yeast Rolls, '79 59
Butter Rolls, '00 257
Butter Rolls, Homemade, '01 21
Caraway Puffs, '82 174
Cheese Buns, Hurry-Up, '81 300
Cheese Crescents, '82 18
Chocolate Sticky Buns, '81 300; '82 124
Citrus-Pecan Rolls, '03 256
Cloverleaf Rolls, '82 18; '96 321
Cloverleaf Rolls, Light, '83 290
Coconut-Pecan Coils, '90 196
Cornmeal Yeast Rolls, '86 177
Cottage Cheese Rolls, '81 78
Cranberry-Pineapple Rolls, '86 275
Cranberry Rolls, '00 244
Cream Cheese Pinches, '87 85
Crescent Rolls, '97 199
Double Whammie Yeast Rolls, '05 323
Dough, Basic Roll, '82 17
Dough, Sweet Roll, '79 80
Easy Yeast Rolls, '81 78; '86 16; '03 256
Fantan Rolls, French, '80 276
Finger Rolls, '83 254
Hard Rolls, '86 85, 306
Herb Rolls, '01 44
Holiday Sparkle Rolls, '83 296

Honey-Oat Buns, '98 27
Honey Oatmeal Buns, '83 154
Honey Rolls, Super, '80 115
Hot Cross Buns, '81 77; '95 100; '01 88
Hot Rolls, Best, '00 97
Hurry-Up Yeast Rolls, '90 90
Icebox Rolls, '04 70
Jam Kolaches, '85 290
Low-Sodium Yeast Rolls, '84 228
Make-Ahead Yeast Rolls, '95 307
Mollets, '02 83
Mollets, Chocolate, '02 83
Mollets, Pink, '02 83
Mollets, Red, '02 83
Mollets, Yellow, '02 83
Moravian Feast Buns, '83 295
Oatmeal-Cinnamon-Pecan Rolls, '96 50
Onion Buns, Cheesy, '85 5
Onion Twist Rolls, '89 288
Overnight Yeast Rolls, '96 321
Pan Rolls, '88 76
Pan Rolls, Brown-and-Serve, '91 52
Parkerhouse Rolls, Super, '81 78
Pecan Rolls, '81 62
Pepperoni Rolls, Ground-, '83 244
Pineapple Angel Rolls, '89 72
Pinwheel Rolls, Sweet, '90 46
Potato Yeast Rolls, '98 92
Praline Buns, '90 195
Pumpernickel Rolls, German-Style, '02 259
Pumpernickel Rolls with Caraway, German-Style,
'02 259
Puro de Piña, '02 82
Quick Yeast Rolls, '84 267; '95 45
Refrigerator Yeast Rolls, '81 296, 307; '82 309;
'83 17, 118; '91 80; '98 109, 325
Rounds, Individual Bread, '83 159
Rum Buns, '81 299
Rum-Raisin Buns, '80 22
Saffron Rolls, '83 296
Semitas, '02 81
Sesame Buns, '82 17
60-Minute Rolls, '96 321
Slow-Rise Yeast Rolls, '97 131
Sourdough Hot Rolls, '82 201
Special Rolls, Extra-, '88 257
Speedy Yeast Rolls, '82 309; '83 17
Spoon Rolls, '04 47
Spoon Rolls, Make-Ahead, '05 221
S Rolls, '96 321
Sticky Buns, '80 23
Sweet Potato Rolls, '93 172; '97 107
Sweet Rolls, Mexican, '81 285
Tasty Rolls, '90 85
Two-Seed Bread Knots, '05 334
Wixie's Yeast Rolls, '03 121
Yam Rolls, Golden, '86 299
RUTABAGAS
au Gratin, Rutabaga, '79 254
Bacon, Rutabaga with, '83 243
Boiled Rutabagas, '86 224
Buttered Rutabagas, '81 274
Creamy Rutabaga, '79 254
Fried Rutabaga, '99 285
Glazed Carrots and Rutabaga, Lemon-, '97 46
Glazed Rutabaga, '88 229; '99 284
Gratin, Potato-and-Rutabaga, '96 237
Honey Rutabaga, '91 220
Mashed Rutabagas, '86 295
Mash, Rutabaga-Carrot, '02 275
Roasted Rutabaga, Greek-, '99 285
Simple Rutabaga, '83 243
Skillet, Rutabaga-Cabbage, '99 285
Soufflé, Rutabaga, '01 213

RUTABAGAS
(continued)

Steamed Rutabagas, **'81** 274
Tart, Rutabaga-Spinach, **'98** 274
Whip, Rutabaga, **'95** 179

SALAD DRESSINGS. *See also* MAYONNAISE.

Almond Salad Dressing, **'81** 37
Apple Dressing, **'83** 181; **'92** 216
Apricot Dressing, **'99** 245
Artichoke Dressing, **'84** 126
Asian Dressing, **'00** 93
Asian Salad Dressing, **'96** 327
Avocado Cream, **'92** 158
Avocado Dressing, **'80** 15; **'92** 321; **'96** 138
Avocado Sauce, Chunky, **'03** 128
Bacon Dressing, Hot, **'84** 12
Bacon Dressing, Jeweled Hot, **'97** 196
Balsamic Dressing, **'95** 281; **'96** 137; **'99** 259
Banana-Poppy Seed Dressing, **'98** 184
Barbecue Dressing, **'99** 124
Barbecue Salad Dressing, **'80** 74
Basil-and-Garlic Dressing, **'94** 55
Basil Dressing, **'88** 24
Basil-Honey Dressing, **'97** 30
B. B.'s Salad Dressing, **'91** 65
Benedictine Dressing, **'98** 83
Blender Dressing, **'80** 78
Buttermilk-Chive Dressing, **'04** 105
Buttermilk Dressing, Down-Home, **'84** 114
Buttermilk-Honey Dressing, **'96** 243
Buttermilk Salad Dressing, **'79** 69
Caesar Dressing, Chipotle, **'04** 119
Caesar Salad Dressing, **'82** 94
Caesar Salad Dressing, Creamy, **'96** 326
Celery-Honey Dressing, **'80** 42
Celery Seed Dressing, **'82** 265; **'05** 291
Celery Seed Salad Dressing, **'82** 94
Cheese
   Barbecue Salad Dressing, Cheesy-, **'92** 255
   Blue Cheese-Buttermilk Dressing, **'01** 112
   Blue Cheese Dressing, **'79** 69; **'82** 166; **'86** 233;
      '90 286; **'97** 98; **'98** 248; **'99** 244; **'00** 217; **'03** 72
   Blue Cheese Dressing, Creamy, **'81** 150; **'91** 307
   Blue Cheese Dressing, Low-Fat, **'00** 337
   Blue Cheese Dressing, Special, **'80** 30
   Blue Cheese Dressing, Tangy, **'87** 81
   Blue Cheese Dressing, Zesty, **'79** 104
   Blue Cheese Salad Dressing, **'82** 94
   Blue Cheese Salad Dressing, Creamy, **'86** 123
   Dairy Land Salad Dressing, **'86** 85
   Fluff Dressing, Cheese, **'91** 256
   Gorgonzola Dressing, Creamy, **'03** 34
   Oregano-Feta Dressing, **'01** 57
   Parmesan Dressing, **'86** 192; **'97** 326; **'01** 96, 101
   Romano Dressing, **'80** 174
   Roquefort Cheese Dressing, Thick, **'97** 63
   Roquefort Dressing, **'79** 85; **'80** 74; **'93** 128
   Roquefort Dressing, Creamy, **'84** 12
Chutney Dressing, **'00** 53
Chutney Dressing, Warm, **'02** 242
Cider Vinegar-Honey Dressing, **'05** 41
Citrus-Cilantro Dressing, **'93** 310; **'94** 97; **'00** 160
Citrus Dressing, **'85** 92
Citrus Dressing, Black Bean Salsa with, **'01** 60
Citrus Ranch Dressing, Fresh, **'04** 91
Coconut Dressing, **'87** 251
Coconut-Orange Dressing, **'97** 93
Cooked Dressing, **'99** 82
Cooked Salad Dressing, **'90** 231
Cranberry-Orange Dressing, **'91** 287

Creamy Dressing, **'79** 159; **'83** 81; **'85** 26; **'92** 45, 241;
   '93 318; **'95** 66
Creamy Salad Dressing, **'83** 181
Creole Dressing, **'02** 69
Cucumber-Curry Dressing, **'89** 179
Cucumber Dressing, **'80** 74; **'90** 144
Cucumber-Mint Dressing, **'87** 153
Cucumber-Radish Dressing, **'00** 99
Cucumber Salad Dressing, Creamy, **'82** 79
Curried Dressing, **'84** 115; **'00** 217
Curry Dressing, **'80** 242; **'82** 78; **'97** 63
Curry Salad Dressing, **'96** 326
Date Dressing, **'87** 57
Delightful Salad Dressing, **'83** 181
Dijon Dressing, **'94** 282; **'96** 176
Dijon-Honey Dressing, **'89** 45; **'99** 333
Dill Dressing, **'88** 182
Dill Dressing, Creamy, **'91** 213
Dilly Dressing, **'80** 74
Egg Dressing, **'86** 79
French
   Creamy French Dressing, **'81** 60; **'90** 286
   French Dressing, **'89** 46
   Grapefruit French Dressing, **'80** 101
   Honey French Dressing, **'87** 81
   Miracle French Dressing, **'82** 79
   Onion-French Dressing, **'84** 283
   Piquant French Dressing, **'87** 202; **'88** 43
   Sassy French Dressing, **'99** 245
   Spicy French Dressing, **'81** 150; **'86** 123
   Sweet French Dressing, **'82** 94
   Tangy French Dressing, **'84** 12
   Tomato-Honey French Dressing, **'81** 105
Fruit
   Avocado Fruit Salad Dressing, **'82** 93
   Coconut-Fruit Dressing, Tangy, **'84** 171
   Creamy Fruit Salad Dressing, **'82** 94
   Dressing for Fruit Salad, **'87** 81
   Fluffy Fruit Dressing, **'79** 69
   Fresh Fruit Dressing, **'87** 134
   Fruit Salad Dressing, **'79** 69; **'93** 184
   Lime-Honey Fruit Salad Dressing, **'87** 81
   Marmalade-Fruit Dressing, **'84** 171
   Red Fruit Salad Dressing, **'83** 231
   Salad Dressing for Fruit, **'86** 40
   Snappy Fruit Salad Dressing, **'05** 160
   Sweet-and-Sour Fruit Dressing, **'84** 125
   Whipped Cream Fruit Dressing, **'79** 270
Garden Dew Dressing, **'86** 50
Garlic-Herb Salad Dressing, Creamy, **'84** 66
Garlic Salad Dressing, **'86** 123
Garlic Salad Dressing, Creamy, **'03** 211
Ginger Dressing, **'82** 194; **'88** 61; **'90** 160; **'93** 290; **'96** 127
Grandpa Jim's Salad Dressing, **'01** 182
Grapefruit Salad Dressing, **'84** 262
Greek Dressing, **'02** 139
Greek Goddess Dressing, **'81** 150
Greek Salad Dressing, **'90** 286; **'03** 290
Green Goddess Dressing, **'02** 139
Green Pepper-Onion Salad Dressing, **'84** 12
Guacamole Dressing, **'92** 64
Herb Dressing, **'80** 122; **'03** 35
Herb Dressing, Lite, **'02** 18
Herbed Salad Dressing, **'88** 29; **'99** 245
Herb-Mayonnaise Sauce, **'85** 73
Herb Salad Dressing, **'86** 40
Honey-Applesauce Salad Dressing, **'99** 210
Honey-Dijon Salad Dressing, Creamy, **'99** 245
Honey Dressing, **'79** 242; **'83** 146; **'87** 129
Honey-Lemon Dressing, **'95** 133
Honey-Lime Dressing, **'83** 139; **'93** 71
Honey-Mustard Dressing, **'90** 55, 111, 146; **'00** 54;
   '01 230; **'05** 185
Honey-Pecan Dressing, **'03** 28

Honey-Walnut Dressing, **'93** 107
Horseradish Dressing, **'96** 200
Italian
   Cream Dressing, Italian, **'89** 83
   Creamy Italian-American Salad Dressing, **'79** 69
   Grapefruit Salad Dressing, **'84** 262
   Italian Dressing, **'79** 52; **'85** 261; **'89** 166
   Italian Salad Dressing, **'80** 82; **'84** 12
   Sour Cream Italian Dressing, **'89** 45
   Special Italian Dressing, **'79** 190
Lemon-and-Herb Dressing, **'92** 108
Lemon-Caper Dressing, **'96** 69
Lemon Cream Dressing, **'82** 170
Lemon Dressing, **'04** 167
Lemon Dressing, Creamy, **'88** M193
Lemon-Herb Dressing, **'97** 92
Lemon-Herb Salad Dressing, **'82** 67
Lemon-Molasses Dressing, **'97** 195
Lemon-Mustard Dressing, **'02** 52
Lemon-Pepper Dressing, **'87** 55
Lemon Salad Dressing, **'79** 8
Lime Dressing, **'79** 2; **'83** 120
Lime Dressing, Creamy, **'04** 46
Lime-Honey Dressing, **'92** 213
Lime-Parsley Dressing, **'85** 131
Lime-Peanut Dressing, **'01** 26
Lime Sherbet Dressing, **'80** 221
Magnificent Seven Salad Dressing, **'89** 45
Margarita Dressing, **'94** 107
Mayonnaise Dressing, **'86** 11; **'00** 217
Mayonnaise Dressing, Herbed-, **'86** 119
Mayonnaise Dressing, Southwestern, **'99** 245
Mint Dressing, **'80** 183
Mint Dressing, Fresh, **'84** 126
Miso-Ginger Dressing, Creamy, **'02** 144
Mix, Salad Dressing, **'99** 245
Mustard Dressing, **'80** 112
Mustard Dressing, Herbed, **'00** 145
Mustard Dressing, Tangy, **'93** 323
Olive Oil Dressing, **'84** 266
Olive Oil, Flavored, **'89** 193
Orange Blossom Dressing, **'82** 266
Orange-Coconut Dressing, **'80** 158
Orange Cream, **'90** 126
Orange-Curd Dressing, **'93** 22
Orange Dressing, **'81** 141
Orange-Poppy Seed Dressing, **'87** 187
Oregano Dressing, **'86** 141
Oriental Dressing, **'91** 277
Oriental Salad Dressing, **'96** 93
Papaya Seed Dressing, **'95** 204
Paprika Dressing, **'86** 191
Pasta Salad Dressing, **'86** 121; **'01** 164
Pasta Salad Dressing, Herbed, **'96** 106
Peach Dressing, **'90** 180
Peanut Butter Salad Dressing, **'03** 195
Peanut-Ginger Dressing, **'95** 177
Pear Dressing, **'83** 146
Pepper Dressing, **'80** 174
Peppery Salad Dressing, **'79** 69
Pesto Salad Dressing, **'86** 150
Pineapple Cream Dressing, **'83** 81
Pineapple-Poppy Seed Dressing, **'85** 55
Pineapple Salad Dressing, **'81** 36
Pomegranate Salad Dressing, **'96** 241
Poppy Seed Dressing, **'80** 152; **'81** 63, 252; **'83** 153, 316;
   '84 16; **'86** 123, 305; **'88** 78; **'91** 169; **'92** 191;
   '93 65, 168; **'96** 240; **'01** 56
Poppy Seed Dressing, Blender, **'79** 176
Poppy Seed Dressing, Tart, **'03** 241
Purple Parrot Sensation Dressing, **'04** 289
Raspberry Dressing, **'87** 153; **'95** 202
Raspberry Salad Dressing, **'94** 158; **'03** M28
Red Wine Dressing, **'98** 246

Rémoulade Dressing, '86 123
Rémoulade Sauce, '99 164
Roasted Red Bell Pepper Dressing, '03 28
Roasted Red Pepper-Dill Dressing, '02 144
Rosemary Dressing, '81 131
Rum Dressing, '80 139
Russian Dressing, '80 4
Russian Sour Cream Dressing, '79 55
Russian-Style Dressing, '83 181
Russian-Style Salad Dressing, '86 305
Salad Dressing, '90 161; '04 317
Sesame Dressing, '96 137
Sesame-Poppy Seed Dressing, '05 55
Sesame Seed Dressing, '87 81
Sesame-Soy Dressing, '93 106
Slaw Dressing, Sweet, '98 184
Sour Cream Dressing, '82 165; '86 331
Sour Cream-Horseradish Dressing, '00 17
Sour Cream Sauce, '87 233; '02 169
Southwestern Dressing, Spicy, '94 136
Southwestern Salad Dressing, Creamy, '94 278
Soy Dressing, '86 191
Soy-Ginger Salad Dressing, '96 123
Soy-Sesame Dressing, '87 153
Spicy Dressing, '80 55
Spinach Salad Dressing, '83 181; '93 250
Stay Trim Dressing, '86 40
Strawberry Dressing, Creamy, '84 161
Sugar-and-Vinegar Dressing, '04 174
Sweet-and-Sour Dressing, '80 247; '84 70, 161; '85 163;
    '87 305; '89 62; '91 126; '94 281; '03 28
Sweet-and-Sour Dressing, Citrus Salad with, '01 104
Sweet-Sour Dressing, '80 246
Tangy Dressing, '83 9
Tangy Red Dressing, '86 191
Tangy Salad Dressing, '80 146; '84 115
Tarragon Dressing, '90 55
Thousand Island Dressing, '80 74; '81 104; '83 135; '86 123
Thousand Island Dressing, Special, '82 79
Tomato Dressing, Fresh, '00 182
Tomato Dressing, Spicy, '03 143
Tomato Salad Dressing, Fresh, '83 193
Tossed Salad Dressing, '84 115
Touchdown Salad Dressing, '81 197
Vanilla Oil, '94 243

Vinaigrette
Apple Cider Vinaigrette, '98 284; '01 306; '05 201
Apple-Ginger Vinaigrette, '05 230
Apricot Vinaigrette, '02 120
Asian Vinaigrette, '97 146; '98 142; '00 105
Balsamic Vinaigrette, '99 230; '00 81; '01 20; '03 178
Balsamic Vinaigrette, Tangy, '03 101
Basic Vinaigrette, '94 249
Basil-Red Wine Vinaigrette, '96 65
Basil Vinaigrette, '93 106; '97 146; '02 275
Basil Vinaigrette, Fresh, '04 51
Beet Vinaigrette, '97 229
Blackberry-Basil Vinaigrette, '04 97
Black Pepper-Pineapple Vinaigrette, '97 181
Black Pepper Vinaigrette, '98 284
Blueberry Vinaigrette, '00 154
Blue Cheese Vinaigrette, '89 45; '90 55, 280; '05 233
Caper Vinaigrette, '91 310
Cider Vinaigrette, '99 322
Cilantro-Lime Vinaigrette, '94 77
Cilantro Vinaigrette, '97 126
Cinnamon Vinaigrette, '05 133
Citrus Dressing, Hot, '00 108
Cranberry Vinaigrette, '98 321; '05 247
Creamy Vinaigrette, '98 130
Croutons, Vinaigrette Dressing and, '86 M288
Curry Vinaigrette, Warm, '93 107
Dijon Vinaigrette, '95 301; '00 222; '02 18; '03 237
Dill Vinaigrette, '05 173

Garlic-Blue Cheese Vinaigrette, '92 57
Garlic-Chive Vinaigrette, '91 44
Garlic Dressing, '79 269; '80 14
Garlic-Ginger Vinaigrette Dressing, '92 195
Garlic Vinaigrette, '95 65; '03 142
Ginger-Curry Vinaigrette, '97 146
Greens and Vinaigrette, '98 168
Greens, Vinaigrette with, '98 184
Herbed Vinaigrette, '93 120
Herb-Mustard Vinaigrette, '02 84
Herb Vinaigrette, Fresh, '99 183
Honey-Dijon Vinaigrette, '04 321
Honey-Mustard Vinaigrette, '94 249
Honey-Orange Vinaigrette, '91 255
Hot Chile Vinaigrette, '98 200
Italian Vinaigrette, Red, '97 46
Lemon-Basil Vinaigrette, '94 205
Lemon-Dill Vinaigrette, '99 27
Lemon-Honey Vinaigrette, '96 65
Lemon Vinaigrette, '95 31; '04 169
Lemon Vinaigrette, Fresh, '04 30; '05 242
Lemon Vinaigrette, Peppery, '01 122
Lime Vinaigrette, Spicy, '01 217
Maple-Cider Vinaigrette, '05 281
Maple-Walnut Vinaigrette, '04 45
Marinara Vinaigrette, '94 64
Mint Vinaigrette, '02 65
Mustard Vinaigrette, '96 184; '01 102
Orange-Raspberry Vinaigrette, '95 144; '96 155; '01 178
Orange Vinaigrette, '96 65; '97 229; '98 288
Orange Vinaigrette Dressing, Tangy, '92 341; '93 46
Oregano Vinaigrette, '00 331
Oregano-Vinaigrette Dressing, '79 113
Papaya Vinaigrette Dressing, '95 206
Parsley Dressing, Sweet, '02 120
Peach Vinaigrette, Roasted Vegetable Salad with
    Dried, '97 265
Pecan Vinaigrette, '00 162
Pimiento Vinaigrette, '00 167
Pistachio-Lime Vinaigrette, '97 148
Poppy Seed Vinaigrette, '94 249
Raspberry Vinaigrette, '94 249; '96 275; '97 146;
    '98 184; '04 50; '05 91
Red Grapefruit-Lemon Vinaigrette, Salad with, '05 161
Red Wine Vinaigrette, '94 327
Roasted Bell Pepper Vinaigrette, '99 70
Roasted Garlic Vinaigrette, '97 47
Roasted Pepper Vinaigrette, '00 134
Rose Vinaigrette, '01 121
Sesame Dressing, Asian, '02 196
Sesame-Soy Vinaigrette, '97 180; '01 195
Soy Vinaigrette, '97 18
Strawberry-Balsamic Vinaigrette, '05 84
Sweet-and-Sour Balsamic Vinaigrette, '97 146
Sweet-and-Sour Dressing, '02 24
Sweet-Hot Vinaigrette, '04 105
Tarragon Vinaigrette, '94 201
Tomato-Basil Vinaigrette, '99 288
Tomato Vinaigrette, Dried, '93 272
Vanilla Vinaigrette, '94 242
Versatile Vinaigrette, '93 140
Vidalia Onion-Balsamic Vinaigrette, '04 317
Vidalia Onion Vinaigrette, '99 168
Vinaigrette, '94 179; '95 61; '99 107; '01 329
Vinaigrette Dressing, '79 171; '87 138; '89 12, 220,
    256; '90 173; '92 303; '93 41; '95 231; '97 250
Vinaigrette Salad Dressing, '02 25
White Wine Vinaigrette, '89 46
Wine Vinegar Dressing, '92 91; '93 126
Walnut Dressing, '99 125
Whipped Cream Salad Dressing, '82 145
Wine Dressing, Creamy, '85 20

Yogurt
Coconut Dressing, '87 251

Creamy Dressing, '93 318
Cucumber-Mint Dressing, '87 153
Dill Dressing, '88 182
Dilled Yogurt Dressing, Low-Cal, '05 128
Garden Dressing, Spring, '85 157
Ginger-Yogurt Dressing, '81 302
Herb Dressing, Yogurt-, '92 96
Honey-Lime Dressing, '93 71
Honey-Mustard Dressing, '90 111
Honey Poppy Seed Dressing, Yogurt-, '83 177
Honey-Yogurt Dressing, '93 172
Horseradish Dressing, '87 152; '91 32
Lemon-Yogurt Dressing, '93 17
Lemon-Yogurt Slaw or Salad Dressing, '88 54
Orange-Yogurt Dressing, '85 304
Strawberry Dressing, Creamy, '84 161
Sweet-Hot Yogurt Dressing, '86 40
Tangy Yogurt, '02 258
Yogurt Dressing, '85 59, 215; '88 27
Yogurt Salad Dressing, '79 69
Zesty Salad Dressing, '92 60

SALADS. *See also* **AMBROSIA, ASPIC, SLAWS.**
Acini di Pepe Salad, '83 163
Alfalfa-Celery Salad, Overnight, '82 97
Almond-Citrus Salad, '01 42
Antipasto, Easy, '85 114
Antipasto, Pasta, '85 286
Antipasto Salad, '84 66; '89 145
Antipasto, Salad, '96 161
Antipasto Salad, Layered, '92 220

Apple. *See also* **SALADS/Congealed, Waldorf.**
Apple Salad, '87 233; '00 176
Avocado-Apple Salad with Maple-Walnut
    Vinaigrette, '04 45
Beet Salad, Apple-, '91 237
Blue Cheese Dressing, Apple Salad with, '87 103
Blue Cheese-Pear-Apple Salad, '81 224
Bran Salad, Lemony Apple-, '86 223
Cabbage-Apple Salad with Sugared Pecans, '05 91
Carrot Salad, Apple-, '85 22
Cheesy Apple Salad, '86 301
Chicken-Apple Salad, '90 216
Cranberry-Apple Salad, '02 255
Crunchy Apple Salad, '80 138
Double Apple Salad, '84 227
English Pea-and-Apple Salad, '87 24
Fennel-and-Apple Salad, '00 321
Fresh Apple Salad, '81 207
Frozen Apple-Cream Salad, '82 80
Grapefruit-Apple Salad, '89 41
Lemony Apple Salad, '05 241
Nut Salad, Apple-, '80 226
Peanut-Apple Salad, '80 5
Raisin Salad, Curried Apple-, '80 24
Rudolph's Apple Salad, '02 277
Sesame-Apple Toss, '88 21
Snow Salad, Apple, '81 224
Spicy Apple Salad, '85 215
Spinach Salad, Apple-, '99 222; '02 230
Stuffed Apple Ring Salad, '91 198
Stuffed Apple Salad, '92 266
Summer Apple Salad, '80 149
Swiss-Apple Salad, '84 81
Thai Green Apple Salad, '99 111
Turkey-Apple Salad, '88 123; '90 181
Wedges with Poppyseed Dressing, Apple, '86 131
Zucchini Salad, Apple-and-, '97 216
Apricot Salad, Frosted, '80 248
Artichoke-Goat Cheese Salad, '98 118
Artichoke-Pasta Salad, '94 180
Artichoke-Rice Salad, '80 178; '81 41; '85 81; '01 144
Artichoke Salad, '86 333
Artichoke Salad, Marinated, '83 241; '95 66
Artichokes Vinaigrette, '88 101

SALADS
(continued)

Artichokes with Orzo Salad, '88 M193
Artichoke-Tomato Salad, '82 239
Asian Salad Gift, '96 327
Asparagus. *See* **ASPARAGUS/Salads.**
Australian Outback Salad, '92 45
Autumn Salad with Maple-Cider Vinaigrette, '05 281
Avocado Acapulco, '83 2
Avocado and Zucchini Salad, Creamy, '79 208
Avocado-Apple Salad with Maple-Walnut Vinaigrette, '04 45
Avocado-Bread Salad, '02 210
Avocado Citrus Salad, '01 133
Avocado-Corn-Poblano Salad, '01 320
Avocado Garbanzo Salad, '81 33
Avocado-Grapefruit Salad, '85 26; '93 282
Avocado-Melon Salad, '82 164
Avocado-Orange Salad, '91 44
Avocado Salad, '81 195; '82 9; '83 69; '92 246; '97 250;
      '02 99
Avocado Salad, Citrus-, '82 265
Avocado Salad, Spanish, '87 41
Avocados, Salmon-Stuffed, '86 74
Avocados, Shrimp-Filled, '83 2
Avocado with Crabmeat, '86 119
Baby Blue Salad, '00 81; '01 20; '03 178
Bacon-Lettuce-Mozzarella-and-Tomato Salad, '98 209
Bacon-Mandarin Salad, '02 87
Banana Salad, '87 80
Banana Salad, Frozen, '82 80, 132
Bananas, Nutty, '79 251
Barley-Broccoli Salad, '90 135
Barley-Pine Nut Salad, '05 126
Barley Salad, '92 212
Bean
      Black Bean-and-Barley Salad, '94 174
      Black Bean and Black-Eyed Pea Salad, '03 54
      Black Bean-and-Cheese Salad, '92 217
      Black Bean-and-Rice Salad, '00 327
      Black Bean Salad, '89 217; '97 196; '98 208; '01 198
      Black Bean Salad, Mandarin-, '05 319
      Black Bean Salad, Roasted Corn-and-, '05 209
      Chicken-Black Bean Salad, '99 124
      Chickpea Salad, '01 55
      Chilled Bean Salad, '80 178
      Confetti Bean Salad, '01 198
      Cucumber-Bean Salad, '83 81
      Fennel-Salad, Bean-and-, '01 198
      Five-Bean Salad, Hot, '81 149
      Four-Bean Salad, '79 20; '84 82
      Full o' Beans Salad, '81 38
      Garbanzo Salad, '82 2
      Garbanzo Salad, Avocado-, '81 33
      Garbanzo Salad, Couscous-and-, '02 65
      Green Bean-and-Okra Salad with Feta, Marinated,
            '00 131
      Green Bean-and-Tomato Salad, '86 180
      Green Bean-Peanut Salad, '86 117
      Green Bean-Potato Salad, '83 80; '01 181
      Green Bean-Red Potato Salad, '96 175
      Green Bean-Red Potato Salad, Layered, '05 146
      Green Bean Salad, '87 90
      Green Bean Salad, Cold, '84 106
      Green Bean Salad, Crispy, '82 239
      Green Bean Salad, German, '92 169
      Green Bean Salad, Hot, '86 298; '87 176
      Green Bean Salad in Tomatoes, '01 181
      Green Bean Salad, Lettuce and, '80 79
      Green Bean Salad, Molded, '85 252
      Green Bean Salad, Paprika-, '86 191
      Green Bean Salad, Pickled, '82 239
      Green Bean Salad, Roasted Red Pepper-and-, '99 322

Green Bean Salad, Speedy, '84 283
Green Bean Salad, Tomato-and-, '97 162
Green Bean Salad with Feta, '04 169
Green Beans-and-Cheese Salad, '91 159
Green Beans, Dill-Icious, '98 53
Green Beans, Marinated, '83 145
Green Beans, Marinated Dill, '05 129
Green Beans Vinaigrette, '83 25
Green Beans Vinaigrette, Kentucky Wonder, '94 158
Green Bean, Walnut, and Feta Salad, '96 273; '00 321
Hacienda Salad, '81 67
Hominy-Bean Salad, '88 266
Hot German-Style Bean Salad, '91 314
Kidney Bean Salad, Wild Rice-and-, '01 175
Kidney Bean-Salami Pasta Toss, '85 165
Layered Southwestern Salad, '01 97
Lima Beans, Chilly, '81 206
Lima Bean-Tomato Salad, '85 137
Lima Salad), You Lima My Life (Paprika, '96 159
Marinated Bean-and-Rice Salad, '87 152
Marinated Bean-Pasta Salad, '94 167; '97 328
Marinated Bean Salad, '85 137, 296; '89 314;
      '93 312; '94 167; '98 331
Marinated Bean Salad, Crunchy, '84 197
Marinated Corn-Bean Salad, '87 9
Mexican Salad, '81 113; '94 202
Mexican-Style Salad, '83 240
Mexican Tossed Salad, '81 280
Mixed Bean Salad, '83 217
Niçoise, Salad, '86 35
Overnight Fiesta Salad, '83 80
Pasta-Bean Salad, '86 169
Pinto Salad, '86 169
Pole Bean-Potato Salad, Hot, '79 74
Pork-'n'-Bean Salad, '87 83
Potato-Bean Salad, '82 301
Quick Bean Salad, '89 128
Rice-and-Bean Salad, '85 22
Rice-and-Bean Salad, Zesty, '02 84
Rice Salad, Beans-and-, '91 44
Sandwiches, Bean Salad, '81 243
Saucy Bean Salad, '84 18
Sausage Salad, Bean-and-, '91 313
Six-Bean Salad, Colorful, '87 82
Southwest Salad, '81 113; '03 280
Spicy Bean Salad, '96 46
Sprout Salad, Bean, '82 113
Supreme Bean Salad, '91 202
Sweet-and-Hot Bean-and-Veggie Salad, '04 184
Sweet-and-Sour Bean Salad, '85 198; '86 147
Sweet Bean Salad, '01 46
Tabbouleh Salad, Southwestern, '01 216
Tangy Bean Salad, '05 158
Two-Bean Salad, Garlic-Herb, '05 209
White Bean-and-Asparagus Salad, '05 100
White Bean-and-Tuna Salad, '01 35
White Bean-and-Tuna Salad Sandwiches,
      '02 31
White Bean Salad, Tuna-and-, '98 209
White Beans, Caesar Salad with, '93 30
White Bean-Tuna Salad, '98 208
Beet-and-Sugared Walnut Salad with Orange
      Vinaigrette, Roasted, '97 229
Beet, Apple, and Walnut Salad, '98 269
Beet Salad, Fresh, '02 236
Beet Salad, Marinated, '83 216
Beets and Cauliflower, Chilled, '80 137
Berry Grapefruit Cup, '79 242
Black Cherry Salad, Frozen, '89 163
Blue Cheese-Pear-Apple Salad, '81 224
Blue Cheese Salad, '88 48
Blue Cheese Salad with Spicy Pecans, '02 300
Bluegrass Salad, '02 255
Boats, Salad, '80 93

Bok Choy Salad, '01 129
Bread Salad, Italian, '03 54
Bread Salad, Italian BLT, '03 90
Broccoli. *See also* **SALADS/Cauliflower.**
      Broccoli Salad, '82 24; '85 249; '90 292; '95 95;
            '99 84; '00 213; '01 58
      Carrot-Broccoli Salad, '99 26
      Cauliflower, and Carrot Salad, Broccoli, '04 140
      Cauliflower Pasta Salad, Broccoli-, '88 269
      Cauliflower Salad, Broccoli-, '92 97; '00 90
      Cauliflower Salad, Broccoli and, '81 280
      Cauliflower Salad, Broccoli 'n', '90 32
      Cauliflower Salad, Creamy Broccoli and, '81 23
      Cauliflower Toss, Crunchy Broccoli and, '83 25
      Cheese-Pasta Salad, Broccoli-, '96 184
      Chilled Broccoli with Lemon Dressing, '88 270
      Corn Salad, Broccoli-, '87 24
      Creamy Broccoli Salad, '79 143
      Crunchy Broccoli Salad, '83 39
      Curried Broccoli Salad, '86 225
      Fresh Broccoli Salad, '82 34; '87 103
      Grape Salad, Broccoli-, '01 163
      Mandarin Salad, Broccoli-, '93 325
      Marinated Broccoli, '81 40
      Marinated Broccoli Salad, '83 240
      Medley, Broccoli, '81 206
      Orange Salad, Broccoli-, '94 281
      Peanut Salad, Broccoli-, '92 35
      Raisin Salad, Classic Broccoli-, '02 24
      Raisin Salad, Creamy Broccoli-, '92 106
      Ramen Noodle Salad, '02 24
      Red Pepper Salad, Broccoli and, '83 224
      Supreme, Broccoli Salad, '83 260
      Sweet Broccoli Slaw Salad, '05 91
      Warm Broccoli Salad, '92 35
Brussels Sprouts Salad, '87 233
Cabbage and Fruit Salad, '79 286
Cabbage Salad, '87 120, 233
Cabbage Salad, Austrian Hash with, '95 262
Cabbage Salad, Chinese, '81 271; '05 142
Cabbage Salad, Garden, '81 210
Cabbage Salad, Nutty, '87 42
Cabbage Salad, Overnight, '79 83
Cabbage Salad, Tangy, '82 55; '05 162
Cabbage Salad, Wilted, '94 281
Cabbage Salad, Winter, '98 284
Cabbage, Sweet-Sour Red, '79 5
Caesar
      Caesar Salad, '80 112; '86 80; '92 71; '99 265;
            '00 19; '02 269
      Chicken Caesar Salad, '96 26
      Chipotle Caesar Salad, '04 119
      Easy Caesar Salad, '87 116
      Easy Spicy Caesar Salad, '05 122
      Flippo Caesar Salad, '87 61
      Gift, Caesar Salad, '96 326
      Greek Caesar Salad, '96 64
      Iceberg Wedges, Caesar, '05 160
      Margarita Salad, Caesar, '94 107
      Maui Caesar Salad, '94 107
      Mock Caesar Salad, '92 283
      Oriental Caesar Salad, '94 107
      Romaine Caesar Salad, Baby, '97 128
      Southern Caesar Salad, '94 106
      Turkey Caesar Salad, '93 320
      White Beans, Caesar Salad with, '93 30
Cantaloupe-Cheese Salad, '88 184
Cantaloupe Colada Salad, '97 148
Cantaloupe Cooler Salad, '79 176
Cantaloupe-Pecan Salad, '86 178
Cantaloupe Salad, '86 182
Cantaloupe-Spinach Salad with Pistachio-Lime
      Vinaigrette, '97 148
Caponata, Sicilian-Style, '01 124

Carrot
Apple-Carrot Salad, '85 22
Broccoli Salad, Carrot-, '99 26
Caraway Salad, Carrot-, '89 105
Dill Salad, Carrot-and-, '02 129; '03 99
Favorite Carrot Salad, '80 33
Fruit Toss, Carrot-, '82 235
Harvest Carrot Salad, '89 128
Honey-Sweet Carrot Salad, '89 161
Marinated Carrots, Creamy, '87 200
Orange-Carrot Salad, '80 89; '84 325
Raisin Salad, Carrot-, '83 117; '84 174; '87 10
Raisin Salad with Orange-Nutmeg Dressing, Carrot-,
    '97 305; '98 19
Ring, Festive Carrot, '82 16
Seed Salad, Fruity Carrot-and-, '86 223
Shredded Carrot Salad, '80 178
Simple Carrot Salad, '82 101; '84 152
Sunshine Carrot Salad, '82 132
Sweet-and-Sour Carrot Salad, '98 211
Tangerine Salad, Carrot-, '83 316; '84 16
Turkey-Carrot Salad, '86 283
Turnip-and-Carrot Salad, '91 212
Zucchini Salad, Carrot-and-, '83 240
Cauliflower. *See also* **SALADS/Broccoli.**
Beets and Cauliflower, Chilled, '80 137
Broccoli, Cauliflower, and Carrot Salad, '04 140
Broccoli-Cauliflower Salad, '00 90
Broccoli Crunch, Cauliflower, '88 216
Broccoli Salad, Cauliflower-, '79 20
Broccoli Toss, Cauliflower-, '82 54
Broccoli Toss, Italian Cauliflower-, '88 269
Brussels Sprouts Salad, Cauliflower-, '83 240
Cauliflower Salad, '79 221; '80 83; '81 225; '84 291;
    '85 240, 279; '92 36
Celery-and-Cauliflower Salad, '83 39
Corned Beef-Cauliflower Salad, '83 16
Creamy Cauliflower Salad, '82 102; '04 36
Crunchy Cauliflower Salad, '80 4; '82 75
English Pea Salad, Cauliflower-, '95 66
Layered Cauliflower Salad, '83 240
Marinated Cauliflower Salad, '82 303; '84 232
Olive Toss, Cauliflower-, '85 198; '86 147
Orange-Cauliflower Salad, '82 266
Parmesan and Bacon, Cauliflower with, '96 137
Pea Salad, Cauliflower-, '87 231
Pea Salad, Savory Cauliflower and, '81 280
Sweet-and-Sour Cauliflower Salad, '81 2
Vegetable Salad, Cauliflower-, '85 158
Celery Salad, '79 70
Cheese Salad, Warm, '97 246
Cheesy Italian Salad, '84 33
Chef's
Bowl, Chef's Salad, '84 66
Chef's Salad, '86 186; '98 209
Combination Chef's Salad, '86 47
Fruited Chef Salad, '85 222
Fruit Salad, Chef's, '86 35
Garden Salad, Chef's, '83 146
Mexican Chef Salad, '85 84; '92 64
Microwave Chef Salad, '90 M146
Vinaigrette Chef's Salad, '81 9
Zucchini Chef's Salad, '83 143
Cherry-Orange Salad, '79 74; '82 56
Cherry Salad, Delicious Frozen, '81 252
Cherry Salad, Fresh, '83 120
Cherry Salad, Frozen, '79 126
Cherry Salad with Honey-Lime Dressing, '83 139
Cherry Salad with Sherry Dressing, '79 165
Chicken. *See also* **SALADS/Congealed.**
Almond-Chicken Salad Shanghai, '90 160
Almond Salad, Chicken-, '81 133
Aloha Chicken Salad, '80 297
Amandine, Chicken Salad, '81 37

Ambrosia, Chicken Salad, '85 216
Apple Salad, Chicken-, '90 216
Apricot-Chicken Salad, '99 163
Apricot Salsa, Chicken with, '98 126
Artichoke-Chicken-Rice Salad, '94 132
Artichoke-Chicken-Rice Salad, Mediterranean, '97 321
Artichokes, Chicken Salad with, '86 186
Asian Chicken Salad, '99 124
Asparagus-Chicken Salad, '89 83
Aspic-Topped Chicken Salad, '88 88
Autumn Chicken Salad, '01 312
Avocado-Chicken Salad, '87 107
Avocado Salad, Chicken-, '80 139
Avocado Salad, Fruited Chicken, '82 101
Avocado Salad Platter, Chicken-, '83 2
Avocado Salad, Tossed Chicken-, '80 4
Avocados, Chicken Salad in, '85 216
Baked Chicken Salad, '86 297; '87 176
Barbecue Chicken Salad, Warm, '99 124
Basil-Chicken-Vegetable Salad, '92 162
Black-and-Blue Salad, '00 337
Black Bean Salad, Chicken-, '99 124
Black-Eyed Pea Salad, Chicken-and-, '97 305
BLT Chicken Salad, '87 144
Blueberry Salad, Chicken-, '02 177
Blue Cheese Chicken Salad, '94 81
Blue Cheese, Chicken Salad with, '97 97
Bow Tie Pasta, Chicken-and-, '01 164
Broccoli-Chicken Salad, '90 129; '00 53
Buffalo Tenders Salad, '03 184
Caesar Salad, Chicken, '96 26
Celery Salad, Chicken-, '81 187
Cherry-Tarragon Chicken Salad, '05 275
Chicken Salad, '86 232, 261; '96 67; '05 65, 94
Chop Suey Salad, '81 37
Chunky Chicken Parmesan Salad, '05 209
Chutney-Chicken Salad, '87 74
Chutney Salad, Chicken, '82 108
Cobb Salad, Southern-Style, '01 112
Coconut-Chicken Salad, Curried Poached Pears with,
    '97 93
Coleslaw, Chicken, '84 2
Cranberry-Pecan Chicken Salad, '05 284
Cream Puff Bowl, Chicken Salad in, '86 232
Crisp Salad, Crunchy, '95 28
Crunchy Chicken Salad, '86 157, 207
Curried Chicken-and-Orange Salad, '87 144
Curried Chicken-Rice Salad, '92 190
Curried Chicken Salad, '79 219; '84 66; '85 96;
    '86 131; '89 176
Curried Chicken Salad on Raisin Bread, '85 96
Curried Chicken Salad, Royal, '96 200
Curried Chicken Salad with Asparagus, '81 36
Dilled Chicken Salad, '91 212
Fancy Chicken Salad, '79 55
Fiesta Chicken Salad, '05 223
Filling, Chicken Salad, '87 106
Fried Chicken Ginger Salad, '93 290
Fried Chicken Salad, Fiesta, '03 120
Fruit, Chicken Salad with, '82 171
Fruit-Chicken Salad with Blueberry Vinaigrette,
    Summer, '00 154
Fruited Chicken Salad, '84 25, 290; '88 88; '90 318
Fruited Chicken Salad in Avocados, '87 41
Fruit Salad, Chicken-, '82 79; '90 234
Fruit Salad, Chicken-and-, '01 178
Fruity Chicken Salad, '83 157
Gazpacho-Chicken Salad, '00 203
Grapes, Chicken Salad with, '86 117
Greek Chicken Salad, '97 92; '98 329
Green Salad with Chicken, Mixed, '80 54
Grilled Asian Chicken Salad, '96 158
Grilled Chicken-and-Fruit Salad, '96 155
Grilled Chicken-Cornbread Salad, Sara's, '05 184

Grilled Chicken on Greens, '99 201
Grilled Chicken-Rice Salad, '98 148
Grilled Chicken Salad, Moroccan, '95 231
Grilled Chicken Salad with Mango Chutney, '96 182
Hoisin Chicken-and-Pasta Salad, '99 125
Honey Chicken Salad, '04 51
Horseradish Salad, Chicken-, '02 235
Hot Chicken Salad, '81 201; '83 196; '98 290
Hot Chicken Salad, Country Club-Style, '86 10
Hot Chicken Salad, Crunchy, '80 138
Hot Chicken Salad Pinwheel, '80 139
Italian, Chicken Salad, '89 18
Lapsang-Poached Chicken Salad, '05 135
Layered Chicken Salad, '89 162
Lemon-Chicken Salad, Lively, '00 16
Macadamia Chicken Salad, '80 138
Macaroni-Chicken Salad, '85 296; '86 302
Macaroni-Chicken Salad, Dilled, '92 142
Mama Hudson's Chicken Salad, '93 238
Mandarin Chicken, Carousel, '79 88
Mango, Chicken Salad with, '86 215
Marinated Chicken-Grape Salad, '85 74
Marinated Chicken-Raspberry Salad, '93 190
Marinated Chicken Strips and Vegetables, '00 54
Melts, Open-Faced Cheesy Chicken Salad, '00 134
Mexican Chicken Salad, '85 84; '88 272
Mexican Chicken Tortilla Salads, '95 129
Minted Chicken Salad, '92 104
Nectarine Chicken Salad, '79 175
Noodle Chicken Salad, '03 143
Noodle Salad, Chicken, '95 25
Old-Fashioned Chicken Salad, '83 79
Oriental Chicken Salad, '85 216; '88 271; '91 43; '96 92
Oriental, Chicken Salad, '90 146
Overnight Salad, '97 305; '98 18
Parmesan-Chicken Salad, '98 234
Pasta-Chicken Salad, Tarragon, '87 155
Pasta Salad, Chicken, '88 89
Pasta Salad, Grilled Chicken-, '94 64
Pasta Salad, Zesty Chicken-, '02 186
Peachy Chicken Salad, '97 193
Peanut-Chicken Salad, Sweet, '03 54
Pea Salad, Chicken-, '83 218
Persian Chicken Salad, '81 12
Picnic Salad with Honey-Mustard Dressing,
    Hoover's, '05 184
Pineapple-Chicken Salad Pie, '80 138
Pineapple-Nut Chicken Salad, '83 80
Pocket, Chicken Salad in a, '88 139
Polynesian Chicken Salad, '88 272
Poulet Rémoulade, '87 144
Rice Salad, Chicken-, '81 203; '97 93
Rice Salad, Chicken-and-, '97 92
Rice Salad, Curried Chicken-, '92 190
Rice Salad, Grilled Chicken-, '98 148
Rice Salad, Hot Chicken-and-, '83 22
Rice Salad, Nutty Chicken-, '83 157
Roasted Chicken Salad, '93 14
Roasted Chicken with Wilted Salad Greens, Tom's,
    '05 185
Roasted Red Pepper Salad, Chicken and, '03 291
Sandwiches, Asian Chicken Salad, '98 223
Sandwiches, Chicken-Salad Finger, '85 119
Sandwiches, Grilled Chicken Salad, '00 164
Sandwiches, Hot Chicken Salad, '96 74
Sherried Chicken-and-Grape Salad, '01 61
South Sea Island Chicken Salad, '97 88
Southwestern Chicken Salad, '88 88
Southwestern Chicken Salad Spirals, '02 58
Spaghetti Salad, Chicken-, '90 146
Spaghetti Salad, Chicken-and-Veggie, '04 129
Special Chicken Salad, '85 82; '87 183; '88 M193
Spicy Chicken Salad with Cabbage Wraps, '04 62
Spicy Chicken Salad with Veggies, '04 177

Spinach-Strawberry Salad, Chicken-, **'97** 92
Spinach Tossed Salad, Chicken-and-, **'83** 157
Spread, Chicken Salad Party, **'88** M8
Spread, Curried Chicken Salad, **'00** 68
Spring Salad with Raspberry Vinaigrette, **'05** 91
Stack-Up Salad, Chicken, **'83** 80
Strawberry-Chicken Salad, **'04** 50
Strawberry-Citrus Chicken Salad, **'05** 84
Strawberry Salad, Chicken-and-, **'05** 132
Summer Chicken Salad, **'83** 145
Summery Chicken Salad, **'95** 138
Super Chicken Salad, **'82** 174
Supreme, Chicken Salad, **'79** 107, 152; **'89** 176
Taco Chicken Salad, Ranch, **'97** 315
Taco Salad, Chicken, **'94** M136
Tahitian Chicken Salad, **'84** 120
Tarragon Chicken Salad, **'90** 199
Tarts, Chicken Salad, **'84** 257
Thai Chicken Salad, **'95** 177
Thai Lettuce Folds, **'94** 47
Tortellini Salad, Chicken, **'87** 288
Tortilla Salads, Mexican Chicken, **'95** 129
Tropical Chicken Boats for Two, **'82** 186
Tropical Chicken Salad, **'85** 216; **'96** 127
Twist, Chicken Salad with a, **'84** 221
Vegetable-Chicken Salad, **'91** 287
Vegetable Patch Chicken Salad, **'04** 92
Walnut-Chicken Salad, **'89** 14; **'96** 243
Walnut Salad, Sunburst Chicken-and-, **'93** 91
Wild Rice-and-Chicken Salad, **'02** 52
Wild Rice-Chicken Salad, **'83** 146; **'99** 55; **'01** 72
Wraps, Lemon-Basil Chicken Salad, **'00** 216
Citrus and Greens, Holiday, **'03** 280
Citrus-Blue Cheese Salad, **'92** 220
Citrus Salad, **'87** 103
Citrus Salad Bowl, **'86** 335; **'87** 83
Citrus Salad in Orange Cups, **'85** 47
Citrus Salad, Southern-Style, **'84** 262
Citrus Salad, Tangy, **'89** 34
Citrus Vinaigrette Salad, **'86** 192
Congealed
Apple-Apricot Salad, **'88** 121
Apple Cider Salad, **'83** 123
Apple Cider Salad Mold, **'85** 54
Apple Crunch Salad, **'84** 232; **'86** 331
Apple Salad, Congealed, **'85** 252
Apple Salad, Triple, **'88** 122
Apricot Congealed Salad, **'02** 256
Apricot Fruit Salad, **'82** 132
Apricot Nectar Salad, **'83** 218; **'87** 236
Apricot Salad, **'81** 251; **'83** 123
Apricot Salad, Creamy, **'85** 263
Asheville Salad, **'86** 199
Asparagus-Cucumber Mold, **'85** 252
Asparagus Mold, **'80** 104
Asparagus Mousse Salad, **'86** 252
Asparagus Salad, **'88** 121
Asparagus Salad, Congealed, **'83** 260
Asparagus Salad, Creamy Lemon-, **'93** 116
Asparagus Salad, Tart, **'81** 203
Avocado Crunch Salad, Congealed, **'85** 26
Avocado Salad, Congealed, **'84** 266
Avocado Salads, Congealed, **'87** 42
Beet-Nut Salad, **'79** 74
Beet Salad Mold, **'82** 267
Beet Salad, Pickled, **'83** 234
Beet Salad, Tangy, **'86** 199
Berry Salad, Layered, **'79** 173
Bing Cherry-and-Cranberry Salad, **'04** 297
Bing Cherry-Grapefruit Salad, **'00** 285

Bing Cherry Salad, **'01** 46
Broccoli Salad, Congealed, **'84** 124
Cantaloupe, Southern Plantation, **'82** 179
Carrot-Nut Salad, Creamy, **'86** 331
Carrot-Pineapple Salad, **'91** 83
Carrot Salad, **'82** 137
Cauliflower-Lemon Salad, **'81** 23
Cheese Molds, Snowcap, **'79** 242
Cherry-Apple Salad, **'86** 31
Cherry Cola Salad, **'80** 104
Cherry-Cola Salad, **'91** 224; **'95** 94
Cherry Fruit Salad, **'87** 236
Cherry-Salad, Best, **'82** 302
Cherry Salad, Congealed, **'89** 278
Cherry Salad, Festive, **'84** 265
Cherry Salad, Port Wine-, **'86** 11
Cherry Salad, Sweet, **'89** 326
Cherry-Wine Salad, Elegant, **'82** 56
Chicken-Cucumber Mold, **'80** 175
Chicken Jewel Ring Salad, **'83** 282
Chicken-Pea Salad, **'83** 218
Chicken Salad Mold, **'83** 80; **'84** 163
Chicken Salad Ring, **'90** 123
Chile-Tomato Salad, Spicy, **'88** 121
Christmas Salad, **'88** 249
Christmas Snow Salad, **'82** 266
Citrus Mold, Sparkling, **'86** 331
Citrus Salad Mold, Golden, **'85** 303
Corned Beef Salad, **'80** 104
Corned Beef Salad, Molded, **'82** 86
Crabmeat-and-Asparagus, Congealed Salad with, **'84** 86
Cranberry-Apple Mold, **'89** 277
Cranberry-Apple Salad, **'05** 65
Cranberry Congealed Salad, **'91** 296; **'02** 292; **'05** 334
Cranberry Congealed Salad Parfaits, Frosted, **'02** 292
Cranberry Gelatin Mold, **'92** 271
Cranberry Mold, **'79** 250
Cranberry-Orange Delight, **'90** 168
Cranberry Relish Salad, **'05** 245
Cranberry Ring, **'90** 291
Cranberry Salad, **'99** 290
Cranberry Salad, Congealed, **'90** 124
Cranberry Salad, Festive, **'81** 264, 296
Cranberry Salad, Frosted, **'90** 288
Cranberry Salad, Holiday, **'82** 266, 288; **'95** 301
Cranberry Salad, Jellied, **'83** 279; **'85** 281
Cranberry Salad, Layered, **'84** 322; **'86** 325
Cranberry Salad Ring, **'80** 247
Crème de Menthe Salad, **'82** 122
Creole Salad, **'79** 147
Cucumber Mold, Creamy, **'84** 164
Cucumber Mousse, **'88** 121
Cucumber-Pineapple Salad, **'84** 124
Cucumber Salad, Creamy, **'86** 147; **'92** 97
Cucumber Salad Mold, **'82** 111; **'83** 81, 253
Eggnog Christmas Salad, **'86** 281
Egg Salad, Deviled, **'83** 124
Emerald Salad, **'81** 143
Emerald Salad, Snowy, **'87** 311
Fall Salad with Ginger Dressing, **'82** 194
Frosted Salad, Heavenly, **'79** 286
Fruit Congealed Salad, Layered, **'05** M146
Fruit, Jeweled Congealed Fresh, **'95** 89
Fruit Mold, Sherried, **'90** 124
Fruit Salad, Cherry, **'87** 236
Fruit Salad, Sparkling, **'82** 266
Fruit Salad, Spiced Autumn, **'87** 228
Garden-Patch Salad Molds, **'86** 283
Garden Salad, Molded, **'86** 199
Gazpacho Molded Salad, **'92** 323
Gazpacho Salad Mold, **'87** 311
Gazpacho Salad, Molded, **'79** 159

Gazpacho Salad with Avocado Cream, Congealed, **'92** 158
Grape-Cantaloupe Mold, Double, **'79** 173
Grapefruit Congealed Salad, **'83** 190
Grapefruit-Orange Salad, **'91** 276
Grapefruit Salad, **'83** 124; **'84** 325; **'88** 122
Grapefruit Salad, Congealed, **'84** 325; **'85** 279
Grape Salad Mold, **'83** 120
Green Bean Salad, Molded, **'85** 252
Green Spring Salad, **'83** 124
Ham Salad, Congealed, **'81** 36
Holiday Jewel Salad, **'81** 252
Horseradish Salad, **'85** 66
Layered Congealed Salad, **'81** 143
Layered Holiday Salad, **'81** 252
Layered Salad, Make Ahead, **'81** 296
Layer Mold, Three-, **'82** 54
Lemon-Cheese Salad, **'85** 240
Lemon-Cranberry Congealed Salad, **'87** 311
Lemon-Cream Salad, **'88** 250
Lemon-Cucumber Mold, **'87** 90
Lemon Mold, Cheesy, **'79** 241
Lemon-Onion Salad, **'85** 252
Lemon-Pineapple Salad, **'05** 65
Lemon-Tomato Salad, Congealed, **'89** 178
Lemon-Vegetable Congealed Salad, **'85** 22
Lime-Carrot Salad, **'92** 65
Lime-Cheese Salad, Frosted, **'79** 286
Lime Congealed Salad, **'02** 257
Lime Sherbet Salad, **'80** 104
Mandarin Orange Salad, Congealed, **'89** 327
Mandarin Salad Molds, **'85** 54
Melon Ball Salad, Congealed, **'84** 125
Mimosa Salad, **'98** 310
Mincemeat Salad, **'94** 282
Mincemeat Salad, Holiday, **'85** 263
Molds, Perfection, **'81** 153
Mosaic Salad, **'89** 313
Orange-Buttermilk Salad, **'95** 134
Orange-Pear Salad, **'84** 164
Orange Salad, Creamy, **'84** 124
Orange Salad, Frosted, **'81** 154; **'83** 123
Orange Salad, Jeweled, **'83** 210
Orange Sherbet Salad, **'81** 154
Orange Surprise Salad, **'79** 12
Peach-Cranberry Ring, Spicy, **'85** 264
Peaches-and-Cream Salad, **'83** 108
Peach Fluff, **'95** 176
Peach Frost, **'84** 164
Peach Party Salad, **'84** 290
Peach Pinwheel Salad, **'79** 11
Peach Salad, Pickled, **'80** 104; **'85** 264
Peach Salad, Spiced, **'94** 68
Peachy Berry Cream Mold, **'83** 130
Pear-Lime Salad, **'84** 152
Pear Salad, Royal, **'84** 265
Pickled Peach Salad, **'04** 269
Pimiento Salad, Sunshine, **'84** 124
Pineapple-Buttermilk Salad, **'82** 80
Pineapple-Cucumber Congealed Salad, **'83** 118
Pineapple Daiquiri Salad, **'84** 232
Pineapple-Lime Salad, **'84** 320
Pineapple Mold, Minted, **'85** 240
Pineapple-Orange Congealed Salad, **'83** 218
Pineapple-Pear Delight, **'82** 54
Raspberry Fruit Mounds, **'79** 35
Raspberry Holiday Mold, **'84** 253
Raspberry Ribbon Salad, **'87** 236
Raspberry Salad, **'86** 286
Raspberry-Wine Salad, **'91** 256
Rhubarb Congealed Salad, **'86** 140
Rhubarb Salad, **'91** 146; **'92** 129
Rhubarb Salad, Tart, **'91** 146; **'92** 129
Ribbon Salad, Christmas, **'02** 257

Roquefort Salad, Creamy, '79 73
Ruby-and-Emerald Salad, '85 79
Salmon Salad, Chilly, '80 104
Sangría Salad, '86 331
Shrimp Salad, '84 221
Strawberry-Nut Salad, '94 132
Strawberry-Pretzel Salad, '03 290
Strawberry Salad, Hidden Treasure, '79 11
Strawberry-Wine Salad Mold, '83 261
Sunshine Delight, '86 117
Tomato Mold, Tangy, '79 74
Tomato Ring, Tangy, '84 164
Tomato Salad, Frozen, '84 52
Tomato-Vegetable Ring, '81 302
Tuna-Cheese Mold, Creamy, '81 135
Tuna Ring, Creamy, '80 275
Tuna Salad, Congealed, '84 163
Tuna Salad, Creamy, '82 87, 208
Tuna Salad, Luncheon, '81 135
Vegetable Congealed Salad, Cheesy-, '86 199
Vegetable Congealed Salad, Fresh, '91 229
Vegetable Relish Salad, '82 267
Vegetable Salad, Congealed, '79 276
Vegetable Salad, Congealed Fresh, '82 240
Waldorf Salad, Congealed, '82 80
Waldorf Salad, Molded, '84 326
Corn-and-Pea Salad, '90 181
Cornbread-and-Turkey Salad, Layered, '05 147
Cornbread-and-Turkey Salad, Layered Southwest, '05 147
Cornbread Salad, '87 172
Cornbread Salad, Dianne's Southwestern, '04 133
Cornbread Salad, Mexican, '95 210
Corn-in-the-Shuck Salad, '93 236
Corn Salad, '80 247; '81 139; '85 236; '91 27; '95 214; '02 234
Corn Salad, Chilled, '79 20
Corn Salad, Colorful, '00 139
Corn Salad, Confetti, '96 168
Corn Salad, Festive, '92 263
Corn Salad, Fresh, '91 126; '94 162
Corn Salad, Marinated, '89 126
Corn Salad, Roasted, '97 196
Corn Salad, Shoepeg, '81 23
Corn Salad, Tangy, '88 176
Corn Salad, Tasty, '84 289
Cottage Cheese-Banana Splits, '87 56
Cottage Cheese Salad, Different, '85 328; '86 22
Cottage Cheese Salad in Tomatoes, '86 208
Cottage Cheese Salad, Out-of-This-World, '79 44
Cottage-Tomato Salad, '85 163
Couscous Salad, Curried, '91 44
Couscous Salad, Mediterranean, '03 127
Couscous Salad with Dried Tomato Vinaigrette, '96 244
Couscous Salad with Fennel and Goat Cheese, Israeli, '00 312
Cranberry. See also SALADS/Congealed.
Apple Salad, Cranberry-, '02 255
Cheese Ribbon Salad, Cranberry-, '79 241
Christmas Salad, Cranberry, '79 243
Cloud, Cranberry, '90 287
Cranberry Salad, '88 250
Frozen Cranberry-Pineapple Salad, '91 237
Holiday Salad, Cranberry, '89 277
Oriental, Cranberry, '79 126
Spinach-and-Cranberry Salad with Warm Chutney Dressing, '02 242
Strawberry-Jícama Salad, Cranberry-, '02 300
Tart Cranberry Salad, '79 286
Whipped Cream Salad, Cranberry-, '83 261
Wild Rice-and-Cranberry Salad, '99 272
Crunchy-Creamy Salad, '88 100
Cucumber-Almond Salad, '86 147
Cucumber and Tomato Salad, Dilled, '81 153
Cucumber Cooler, Simple, '86 147
Cucumber Mousse, '79 11

Cucumber Mousse with Dill Sauce, '95 216
Cucumber Salad, Cool, '03 165
Cucumber Salad, Creamy, '01 56; '02 258
Cucumber Salad, Dilled, '82 229; '92 72; '93 65
Cucumber Salad, Marinated, '82 111
Cucumber Salad with Roasted Red Bell Pepper Dressing, '03 28
Cucumbers and Artichokes, Marinated, '82 111
Cucumbers, Cool, '84 152
Cucumbers in Sour Cream, '79 52; '80 178
Cucumber-Tomato Salad, '90 144
Cucumber-Tomato Salad, Marinated, '02 167
Cucumber-Vinaigrette Oriental, '85 198; '86 147
Cucumber-Yogurt Salad, '87 33
Cukes and Scallions, '91 168
Curried Salad Gift, '96 326
Curry Salad, Hot Indian, '83 23
Eggplant Salad, '90 99
Egg-Rice Salad, '84 18; '86 169
Egg Salad, '05 209
Egg Salad, Bacon-Horseradish, '94 181
Egg Salad Club Sandwiches, '02 203
Egg Salad Club, Sweet-Pickle, '02 203
Egg Salad, Green Vegetable and, '79 191
Egg Salad Sandwiches, '03 179
Egg Salad Spread, Cottage-, '82 146
Egg Salad Tacos, Mexican, '94 181
Egg Salad, Yolkless, '94 181
Endive, Bacon, and Pecan Salad, '89 12
Endive-Tomato Starburst Salad, '93 323
Endive with Arugula Tabbouleh, '98 67
Escarole-and-Bacon Salad, '84 85
Fennel and Radicchio with Orange Vinaigrette, Grilled, '95 253
Fennel Salad, Marinated, '93 56
Fennel Salad, Tuscan, '02 170
Field Greens with Roasted Bacon-Wrapped Pears, '05 230
Fish. See also SALADS/Seafood.
Confetti Salad, '80 4
Crawfish Salad, Dilled, '83 126
Meal-in-One Salad, '82 232
Salmon-and-Egg Salad, Smoked, '02 203
Salmon-and-Macaroni Salad, '81 114
Salmon-and-Wild Rice Salad, Oriental, '94 173
Salmon on Mixed Greens with Creamy Dill Dressing, '93 143
Salmon-Pasta Salad, '87 9
Salmon-Rice Salad, '84 289
Salmon Salad, '89 99
Salmon Salad, Broiled, '92 108
Salmon Salad, Chilled Poached, '96 68
Salmon Salad, Crunchy, '81 148
Salmon Salad, Scandinavian, '98 208
Salmon Salad Shells, '85 286
Salmon Salad, Simple, '91 23
Salmon Salad, Summertime, '82 207
Salmon-Spinach Salad, '87 145
Salmon-Stuffed Avocados, '86 74
Swordfish Salad, '00 18
Trout-and-Tomato Salad with Black Pepper Vinaigrette, '98 284
Tuna-and-Almond Salad, Crunchy, '04 72
Tuna-and-Cannellini Bean Salad, '86 143
Tuna-and-Red Pepper Salad, '93 143
Tuna-and-White Bean Salad, '98 209
Tuna Chef Salad, '82 78
Tuna-Egg Salad, '81 135
Tuna Macaroni Salad, '83 44
Tuna-Macaroni Salad, '83 145; '84 66
Tuna-Mac in Tomatoes, '87 188
Tuna-Pasta Salad, '91 43; '92 141; '00 247
Tuna Pasta Salad, '92 108
Tuna-Potato Salad, '84 289
Tuna-Rice Salad, '87 202

Tuna Salad, Cheese-Sauced, '87 M124
Tuna Salad, Company, '87 201
Tuna Salad, Crunchy, '87 201
Tuna Salad, Curried, '86 208
Tuna Salad, Favorite, '82 208
Tuna Salad, Flavorful, '81 37
Tuna Salad, Fresh Greens and, '80 55
Tuna Salad, Layered, '84 221
Tuna Salad, My Best, '05 328
Tuna Salad Rolls, Hot, '84 281
Tuna Salad Sandwiches, White Bean-and-, '02 31
Tuna Salad, Swiss, '86 186
Tuna Salad, White Bean-, '98 208
Tuna Salad, White Bean-and-, '01 35
Tuna Salad, Whole Wheat Macaroni-, '84 193
Tuna Salad, Wild, '95 243
Tuna Salad with Grapes, Curried, '87 201
Tuna-Taco Salad, '87 145
Freezer Salad, '94 118
Fruit. See also SALADS/Congealed.
Almond-Citrus Salad, '96 274
Ambrosia, Mixed Fruit, '83 10
Avocado Citrus Salad, '01 133
Avocado Fruit Salad, '87 41
Avocado-Fruit Salad with Honey-Yogurt Dressing, '93 172
Banana Split Salad, '91 58
Berry-Citrus Twist, '95 100
Blackberry-Basil Vinaigrette, Fruit Salad with, '04 97
Cabbage and Fruit Salad, '79 286
Chef Salad, Fruited, '85 222
Chef's Fruit Salad, '86 35
Chicken-and-Fruit Salad, '01 178
Chicken-and-Fruit Salad, Grilled, '96 155
Chicken-Fruit Salad, '82 79; '90 234
Chicken Salad, Fruited, '84 25, 290; '88 88; '90 318
Chicken Salad, Fruity, '83 157
Chicken Salad in Avocados, Fruited, '87 41
Chicken Salad with Fruit, '82 171
Chilled Fruit with Dressing, '85 222
Citrus-and-Avocado Salad, '99 26
Citrus and Greens with Orange-Ginger Dressing, '96 240
Citrus-Cilantro Dressing, Fruit Salad with, '93 310; '94 97; '00 160
Citrus Dressing, Fruit Salad with, '88 6
Citrus Salad with Sweet-and-Sour Dressing, '01 104
Citrus-Strawberry Salad, '04 249
Coconut Fruit Bowl, '83 111
Coconut Salad, Chunky Fruit-and-, '84 24
Colorful Fruit Salad, '82 113
Cottage Cheese-and-Fruit Salad, '86 16
Cottage-Fruit Split, '86 169
Cracked Wheat-Fruit Salad, '96 240
Cream Dressing, Fruit Salad with, '89 277
Creamy Fruit Salad, '84 265
Creamy Holiday Fruit Salad, '90 251
Cups, Royal Fruit, '81 146
Cups, Sangría Fruit, '89 34
Cups with Pineapple Cream Dressing, Fruit, '83 81
Curried Fruit Salad, '85 107
Date Dressing, Fruit Salad with, '87 57
Delight, Fruit, '86 131
Dressed-Up Fruit, '82 5
Easy Fruit Salad, '80 221
Easy Patio Fruit Salad, '88 184
Favorite Fruit Salad, '99 220
Festive Fruit Salad, '80 16
Fresh Fruit Bowl, Sparkling, '80 146
Fresh Fruit Cup with Mint Dressing, '80 183
Fresh Fruit Salad, '82 165; '97 122
Fresh Fruit Salad Pita, '02 99
Fresh Fruit Salad with Celery-Honey Dressing, '80 42
Fresh Fruit Salad with Celery Seed Dressing, '00 68
Fresh Fruit Salad with Orange-Ginger Syrup, '03 167
Fresh Fruit Salad with Poppy-Seed Dressing, '80 137

SALADS, Fruit
(continued)

Fresh Fruit Salad with Poppy Seed Dressing, '91 168
Fresh Fruit with Lemon Sauce, '82 290
Fresh Fruit with Lime Sauce, '02 68
Frisky Fruit Salad, '85 46
Frozen Fruit Salad, '83 110; '97 158; '00 160
Frozen Fruit Salad, Dreamy, '79 126
Frozen Fruit Salad, Luscious, '81 204
Frozen Fruit Salad, Summertime, '89 111
Frozen Salad, Christmas Wreath, '79 241
Frozen Salads, Paper Cup, '00 176
Fruit Salad, '83 209; '89 277; '03 42
Ginger-and-Lemon Fruit Salad, '05 17
Gingered Fruit Salad, '95 95
Glazed Fruit Salad, '83 48; '84 290
Green-and-Gold Salad with Fresh Citrus Ranch
     Dressing, '04 91
Green Fruit Salad with Honey-Lime Dressing, '93 71
Harvest Crunch Salad, '05 291
Hawaiian Fruit Dish, '82 112
Heavenly Salad, '81 252
Holiday Fruit Salad, '87 236
Honeydew Fruit Boats, '81 147
Honeydew Fruit Bowl, '84 186
Honey Dressing, Fruit Salad with, '87 129; '05 137
Honey Fruit Salad, '80 276
Honey-Lemon Dressing, Fruit Salad with, '93 21
Honey-Pecan Dressing, Fruit Salad with, '03 28
Hurry-Up Fruit Salad, '87 236
Jícama-Fruit Salad, '86 83
Jícama Salad, Fruit-, '00 203
Layered Fruit Salad, '84 290; '89 277; '91 58
Lemonade Fruit Salad, '84 24
Lemon Freeze, Fruity, '82 145
Lettuce and Fruit Salad with Poppy Seed Dressing, '80 152
Main Dish Fruit Salad, '83 119
Marinated Fruit Bowl, '80 297
Marinated Fruit Deluxe, '81 146
Medley, Chilled Fruit, '84 60
Medley, Fruit Cup, '85 47
Mélange Delight, Fruit, '81 302
Melon Balls in Watermelon Sauce, '79 177
Melon-Citrus Mingle, '79 177
Melon Cocktail, Minted, '81 146
Melon Cooler, '81 146
Melon Mélange, '84 139
Melon Salad, Summertime, '82 101
Melon Salad with Orange-Raspberry Vinaigrette,
     Grilled, '95 144
Minted Fruit Medley, '80 182
Minted Fruit Toss, '99 160
Mint-Gin Fruit Salad, '92 92
Mint Sauce, Fruit Salad with, '88 M96
Mixed Fruit Cup, '87 233
Mixed Fruit Salad, Banana-, '79 270
Mixed Fruit with Sour Cream Sauce, '02 169
Multi-Fruit Salad, '93 184
Nut Salad, Cheesy Fruit-'n'-, '87 56
Old-Fashioned Fruit Salad, '82 80
Orange Cream, Fresh Fruit Salad with, '90 126
Orange Fruit Cup, '91 277
Oriental Dressing, Fruit Salad with, '91 277
Party Freeze Salad, '82 145
Pasta Salad, Fruited, '92 108
Peachy Fruit Salad, '89 206
Persimmon Fruit Salad, '79 206
Picks, Fruit on, '80 159
Pineapple Dressing, Fruit Salad with, '85 207
Pineapple-Fruit Salad, Icy, '87 9
Platter, Fresh Fruit Salad, '92 213
Platter, Fruit Salad, '83 261

Poppy Seed Dressing, Fruit Salad with, '88 78
Quick-and-Easy Fruit Salad, '81 99
Refreshing Fruit Salad, '85 92
Rhapsody, Fruit, '80 158
Rum, Fruit Cup with, '83 55
Salad, Creamy Fruit, '04 333
Sherried Fruit Melange, '80 158
Shrimp Salad, Fruited, '86 156
Sour Cream Fruit Salad, '80 138
Spiced Fruit Salad, '98 54
Spring Mix Salad, Fruity, '04 105
Springtime Fruit Salad, '81 96
Summer Fruit-Chicken Salad with Blueberry
     Vinaigrette, '00 154
Summer Fruit Salad, '82 164; '92 171
Summer Fruit Salad with Blueberry Vinaigrette, '00 154
Summer Salad, '93 179
Summer Salad, Favorite, '80 158
Summer Salad, Georgia, '92 179
Sunny Day Salad, '96 90
Sunny Fruit Salad, '91 58
Sunny Salad, '80 138
Sweet-and-Sour Fruit Salad, '80 13; '84 125
Sweet Potato Fruit Salad, '00 325
Tossed Fruit Salad, '92 106
Tropical Fruit Salad, '89 306; '02 163
Tropical Fruit Salad with Fresh Mint Dressing, '84 126
Turkey Salad, Fruit-and-, '89 176
Turkey Salad, Fruit-and-Spice, '94 325
Twenty-Four-Hour Fruit Salad, '96 279
Vanilla Fruit Cup, '80 183
Vanilla-Scented Fruit Salad, '05 209
Watermelon Fruit Basket, '84 161
White Wine, Fruit in, '81 48
Winter Fruit-and-Cucumber Salad, '02 274
Winter Fruit Cup, '02 22
Winter Fruit Delight, '80 243
Winter Fruit Salad, '80 248; '82 23
Winter Fruit with Poppy Seed Dressing, '95 317
Wreath, Della Robbia Fruit, '87 294
Wreath, Tex-Mex, '96 241
Yogurt Fruit Salad, '81 114; '96 247
Yogurt-Granola Fruit Medley, '91 58
Gazpacho Salad, '91 313
Goat Cheese Salad, Warm, '01 179
Gorgonzola-Walnut Salad, '96 170
Grapefruit-Apple Salad, '89 41
Grapefruit-Avocado Salad, '83 316; '84 16; '89 41
Grapefruit-Banana Salad with Celery Seed Dressing, '91 237
Grapefruit Combo Salad, '80 50
Grapefruit-Cucumber Salad, '80 100
Grapefruit Winter Salad, '84 24
Greek Salad, '87 103; '93 208; '94 160, 202; '03 290
Greek Salad, Dawn's World-Famous, '98 276
Greek-Style Salad, '91 27
Green. *See also* **SALADS/Caesar, Spinach.**
Apple and Brie, Salad Greens with, '93 241
Baby Lettuces with Vidalia Onion Vinaigrette, Salad
     of, '99 168
Balsamico, Insalata, '94 46
Balsamic-Pesto Salad, '96 274
B.B.'s Salad Dressing, Green Salad with, '91 65
Bibb Salad, Tossed, '87 128
Bibb Salad with Fried Green Tomatoes, Kentucky, '01 121
Bibb Salad with Raspberry-Maple Dressing, '91 246
BLT Salad, Layered, '01 96
Boston Lettuce and Watercress Salad, '93 65
Bouquet, A Salad, '91 44
California Green Salad, '81 84
Cantaloupe Green Salad, '91 126
Chinese Green Salad, '88 48
Citrus Green Salad, '85 304
Citrus Salad, Southern-Style, '84 262
Collard Greens Salad, '96 325

Combination Salad Bowl, '85 132
Combo Salad Bowl, '81 9
Company's Coming Salad, '79 113; '96 64
Cranberry-Topped Green Salad, '87 311
Crimson Greens, '87 153
Crunchy Green Salad, '89 321
Cucumber Asian Greens, '98 66
Dijon Vinaigrette, Greens with, '98 332
Dijon Vinaigrette, Salad with, '03 237
Endive Salad, Avocado-, '94 88
Endive-Watercress Salad, '93 22
Fast-and-Easy Salad, '85 M328
Fenron Salad, '79 85
Garden Salad, '85 92; '89 166; '92 60
Garden Salad Centerpiece, '83 171
Garden Salad, Herbed, '85 328; '86 22
Garden Salad, Summer, '87 153
Garden Salad Toss, '81 9
Garden Salad with Buttermilk Dressing, '96 94
Garden Salad with Rosemary Dressing, Fresh, '81 131
Garlic-Tarragon Green Salad, '92 79
Goat Cheese and Greens, '90 54
Goat Cheese Salad, Baked, '96 26
Gourmet Greens with Raspberry Vinaigrette, '00 163
Grapefruit Salad, Greens and, '95 301
Grecian Green Salad, '84 266
Grecian Tossed Salad, '79 174
Herbed Earl Grey Vinaigrette, Salad Greens with, '99 89
Hill Country Salad, '81 9
Hot Chile Vinaigrette, Greens with, '98 200
Iceberg Wedges, Blue Cheese, '05 160
Iceberg Wedges, Greek, '05 160
Lemon-Dill Vinaigrette, Green Salad with, '99 27
Lemony French Dressing, Green Salad with, '85 67
Lettuce, Cheesy Stuffed, '79 175
Lettuce, Confetti-Stuffed, '87 24
Lettuce, Delicate Garden, '87 62
Lettuce-English Pea Salad, '91 208
Lettuce, Garden-Stuffed, '83 135
Lettuce Salad, Blue Cheese Stuffed, '94 202
Lettuce Salad, French, '84 187
Lettuce Salad, Tennessee-Killed, '88 86
Lettuce Salad, Wilted, '82 302
Lettuce Salad, Wilted Bacon-and-, '85 69
Lettuces with Mustard Vinaigrette, Baby, '93 67
Lettuce-Wedge Salad, '02 65
Lettuce Wedges with Blue Cheese Dressing, Iceberg,
     '00 217; '03 72
Lettuce Wedges with Pimiento Dressing, '84 212
Lettuce, Wilted, '86 269
Lettuce with Sour Cream Dressing Deluxe, '88 48
Marinated Cheese Dressing, Green Salad with, '93 206
Mediterranean Salad, '90 99
Mesclun with Tarragon Dressing, '90 55
Mess o' Greens Salad with Warm Pecan Dressing,
     '98 250
Mint-Fresh Green Salad, '92 105
Mixed Green Salad, '90 230
Mixed Green Salad, Wilted, '85 69
Mixed Green Salad with Chicken, '80 54
Mixed Greens, Hot Sesame Pork on, '97 19
Mixed Greens Salad, '87 62
Mixed Greens with Blue Cheese Vinaigrette, '89 274;
     '90 280
Mixed Greens with Creamy Garlic Dressing, '04 322
Mixed Greens with Parmesan Walnuts, '95 301
Mixed Greens with Raspberries and Walnuts, '98 194
Mixed Greens with Raspberry Dressing, '97 50
Mixed Greens with Roquefort Firecrackers, '97 19
Mixed Greens with Seasoned Almonds and Tangy
     Balsamic Vinaigrette, '03 101
Mixed Greens with Tarragon Vinaigrette, '95 326
Mixed Greens with Toasted Almonds and Apple
     Cider Vinaigrette, '05 201

Mixed Greens with Walnuts, '99 107
Nutty Green Salad, '87 168
Orange-Poppy Seed Salad, '98 87
Oriental, Green Salad, '85 92
Peppery Greens with Raspberry Dressing, '95 254
Purple Parrot Sensation Salad, '04 289
Ranch House Salad with Pecan Vinaigrette, '00 162
Red-and-Green Salad, '90 55
Red Leaf Lettuce Salad with Sweet-and-Sour Dressing, '03 28
Rich Green Salad, '99 203
Robust Salad, '90 181
Romaine Salad, Tangy, '80 155
Romaine Salad with Buttermilk-Chive Dressing, Grilled, '04 105
Romaine Salad with Cashews, '05 195
Romaine Salad with Raspberry Dressing, '03 28
Romaine-Spinach Salad, '89 123
Romaine Toss, Crunchy, '00 30
Romaine Toss, Easy, '00 97
Romaine with Caper Vinaigrette, Hearts of, '91 310
Salmagundi Salad, '83 146
Savory Green Salad, '82 74
Sensational Salad, '84 320
Sesame-Citrus Green Salad, '86 33
Shredded Salad, Zesty, '04 324
Shrimp, Green Salad with, '88 49
Simply Good Salad, '85 131
Southwest Salad, Easy, '03 47
Soy Dressing, Green Salad with, '86 191
Spring Salad, '87 62
Spring Salad, Mediterranean, '80 148
Spring Salad Wedges, '87 62
Summer Salad, Berry Delicious, '05 179
Summer Salad, Crisp, '85 92
Summertime Salad, '79 143; '84 195
Sweet-and-Sour Green Salad, '94 281
Tangy Wilted Salad, '85 69
Tarragon Salad, '97 165
Tossed Mixed Green Salad, '84 126
Tossed Salad, Blue Cheese, '84 195
Tossed Salad, Boston, '84 85
Tossed Salad, Colorful, '90 55
Tossed Salad, Radish-Dressed, '79 104
Veggies with Fried Okra Croutons, Salad Greens and, '96 178
Vinaigrette, Greens and, '98 168
Vinaigrette with Greens, '98 184
Watercress-and-Mushroom Salad, '88 104
Watercress Salad, '97 249
Watercress Salad, Roasted Red Pepper and, '90 55
Wilted Salad Greens, '05 185
Winter Green Holiday Salad with Cranberry Vinaigrette, '98 321
Winter Salad, '95 280
Greens, Grilled Catfish Over Mixed, '04 326
Guacamole Salad, '80 14; '87 181
Guacamole-Tomato Salad, '81 302
Harvest Salad with Cider Vinaigrette, '99 322
Hearts of Palm Salad, '81 252; '89 276; '96 86
Hearts-of-Palm Salad, '87 138
Herb Salad, '87 90
Honeydew Salad with Apricot Cream Dressing, '84 191
Hoppin' John Salad, '96 64
Ice Cream Salad, '79 126
Indian Chief Salad, '96 287
Italian Bread Salad, '99 259
Italian House Salad, '02 300
Italian Salad, '87 145
Jícama-and-Orange Salad, '88 246
Jícama-Orange Salad, '86 83; '90 122
Jícama Salad, '87 123
Layered Lebanese Salad, '05 148
Layered Overnight Salad, '90 319

Layered Salad, '86 35, 79
Layered Salad, Cheesy, '81 37
Layered Salad Deluxe, '81 153
Layered Salad, Hearty, '86 79
Layered Salad, Majestic, '86 79
Layered Salad, Make-Ahead, '81 296
Layered Salad, Mexican, '02 65
Layered Salad, Old-Fashioned, '01 96
Layered Salad, Overnight, '81 188
Layered Salad, Tex-Mex, '03 201
Layer Salad, Eight-, '99 107
Legumes, Marinated, '90 197
Lentil-and-Orzo Salad, '03 127
Lentil Salad, Mediterranean, '96 239
Lentils-and-Rice Salad, '90 197
Macaroni. *See* **SALADS/Pasta.**
Magnolia Blossom Salad, '89 123
Main-Dish Salad, '86 191
Mandarin, Salad, '84 231
Mandarin Spinach Salad, '85 163
Mandarin Tossed Salad, '89 12
Mango Salad, '79 137; '03 122
Mango Salad, Fresh, '84 126
Meal in a Bowl, '96 138
Meal-in-One Salad, '86 43
Meat
  Beef-and-Broccoli Salad, '87 187
  Beef-and-Lime Rice Salad, '03 172
  Beef Fajita Salad, '91 70
  Beef-Pasta Salad, Spicy, '01 311
  Beef Salad, Gingered, '88 61
  Beef Salad Niçoise, '99 159
  Beef Salad, Peking, '88 60
  Beef Salad, Spicy, '02 174
  Beef Salad, Stir-Fry, '96 129
  Beef Salad, Tangy, '87 M218
  Beef Salad, Western-Style, '93 321
  Beef Salad with Cilantro, '97 202
  Beef Salad, Zesty, '79 56
  Beef Vinaigrette Salad, '95 177
  Chili-Corn Chip Stack-Up Salad, '04 242
  Chili Salad, Spicy, '86 71
  Committee, Salad by, '87 288
  Corned Beef-Cauliflower Salad, '83 16
  Corned Beef-Potato Salad, '85 213
  Corned Beef Salad, '80 104
  Corned Beef Salad, Molded, '82 86
  Corned Beef Salad, Potato-, '81 36
  Corned Beef Salad, Vegetable-, '80 148
  Dude Ranch Salad, '80 15
  Fiesta Salad, '05 58
  Ham-and-Apple Salad, '88 139
  Ham-and-Cheese Salad, '88 138
  Ham and Cheese Toss, '79 55
  Ham and Macaroni Salad, '79 220
  Ham-and-Pasta Salad, '90 128
  Ham-and-Pepper Salad Sandwich, Giant, '05 204
  Ham-and-Rice Salad, Colorful, '90 319
  Ham-and-Rice Salad, Mandarin, '87 145
  Ham-Dijon Pasta Salad, '92 191
  Ham 'n Egg Salad, '81 36
  Ham-Noodle Salad, '85 249
  Ham-Rice Toss, '82 40
  Ham Salad, Congealed, '81 36
  Ham Salad, Crunchy Baked, '83 23
  Ham Salad, Fruited, '81 36, 146
  Ham Salad, Hearty, '82 40
  Ham Salad Sandwich, Tangy, '80 272
  Ham Salad, Spicy Italian, '85 74
  Ham Salad Spread, '87 92
  Ham Salad, Tropical, '89 175
  Ham-Sweet Potato Salad, Hawaiian, '82 232
  Mexican Dinner Salad, '98 330
  Mexican Salad in a Shell, '86 4

Mexican Salad Supper, '82 9; '83 68
Paella Salad, '86 207
"Pig in the Garden" Salad, '92 255
Pork-and-Rice Salad with Spicy Tomato Dressing, '03 143
Pork-and-Spinach Salad, Mandarin, '88 M126
Pork Cosmopolitan Salad, Grilled, '04 123
Pork Salad, Oriental, '92 140
Pork Salad, Thai, '00 249
Roast Beef Salad, '80 223; '81 56; '90 318
Roast Beef Salad, Cucumber-, '89 162
Rolls, Hearty Salad, '81 206
Sirloin Salad, Grilled, '94 129
Steak-and-Spinach Salad with Hot Pan Dressing, '05 19
Steak Salad Cups, Pepper, '86 206
Steak Salad, Greek, '92 107
Steak Salad Niçoise, Grilled, '98 148
Steak Salad with Peach Salsa, '97 183
Taco Salad, '79 56; '83 145; '84 221; '85 84; '89 332; '90 20; '02 188
Taco Salad, Beefy, '03 128
Taco Salad Cups, '85 M29
Taco Salad, Party, '97 19
Taco Salad, Spicy, '87 287
Melon-and-Prosciutto Salad, '92 191
Melon Balls, Minted, '87 162
Melon-Berry Salad, '90 180
Melon Salad with Dill Dressing, '88 182
Mexican Salad with Avocado Dressing, '92 321
Mexicorn-Bean Salad, '96 184
Middle Eastern Salad, '87 107
Minestrone Salad, '79 220
Mix, Muffy Salad, '94 34
Mozzarella, Avocado, and Tomato Salad, '05 41
Mozzarella-Tomato-Basil Salad, Fresh, '93 131
Mozzarella-Tomato Basil Salad, Fresh, '02 110
Mushroom-and-Pepper Salad, '86 68
Mushroom-Asparagus Salad, Grilled, '02 122
Mushroom Salad, Fabulous, '81 190
Mushroom Salad, Fresh, '93 65
Mushroom Salad, Marinated, '88 215; '90 181
Mushroom Salad, Quick Cheesy-, '89 128
Mushrooms in Rosemary-Red Wine Vinaigrette, Marinated, '97 63
Mushroom-Zucchini Salad, '85 8
Niçoise, Salad, '03 35
Okra-Corn-and-Tomato Vinaigrette, '90 173
Okra Salad, '90 155
Okra Salad, Fried, '97 M157; '04 167
Okra-Walnut Salad, '04 291
Olive Clubhouse Salad, '81 114
Olive Salad, '98 184; '00 335; '04 27
Olive Salad, Doodles, '94 35
Olive Salad, Italian, '94 35
Olive Salad, Mexican, '85 84
Onion Salad, Grilled, '99 96
Onion Salad, Roasted, '95 65; '03 142
Orange
  Almond Salad, Orange-, '99 107
  Avocado Salad, Orange-, '99 331
  Beet Salad, Orange-and-, '88 43
  Carrot Salad, Orange-, '80 89; '84 325
  Cauliflower Salad, Orange-., '82 266
  Cottage Cheese Salad, Orange-, '79 44
  Cups, Orange, '86 92
  Cups, Orange Salad, '85 40
  Grapefruit Salad, Orange-, '93 294
  Honey-Berry Dressing, Orange Salad with, '89 250
  Honey Dressing, Orange Salad with, '89 14
  Mandarin Orange-and-Almond Salad, '05 291
  Mandarin Orange and Pineapple Salad, '82 266
  Mandarin Orange-Lettuce Salad, '92 79
  Mandarin Orange Salad, '81 252; '84 161
  Mandarin Orange Tossed Salad, '92 303
  Mandarin, Salad, '84 231

SALADS, Orange
(continued)

Mandarin Salad Oriental, '02 175
Mandarin Spinach Salad, '85 163
Mandarin Tossed Salad, '89 12
Marinated Orange-Onion Salad, '91 231; '92 68
Onion Salad, Orange-, '89 41
Poppy Seed Salad, Orange-, '03 121
Quick Orange Salad, '87 80
Romaine Salad, Orange-, '84 325; '87 239
Shrimp Salad, Orange-, '84 197
Spinach Salad, Orange-, '83 316; '84 16
Strawberry Salad with Orange-Curd Dressing,
    Orange-, '93 22
Tropical Orange Salad, '92 97
Walnut Salad, Orange, '80 246
Watercress-Orange Salad with Blue Cheese, '04 45
Oriental Salad Bowl, '87 153
Orzo Salad, Confetti, '92 173
Orzo Salad with Sesame Dressing, '96 137
Paella Salad, '86 207
Pasta
Artichoke-Pasta Salad, '94 180
Asian Peanut-and-Pasta Salad, '03 127
Bayou Pasta Salad, '00 203
Bean-Pasta Salad, Marinated, '94 167
Bean Salad, Pasta-, '86 169
Beef-Pasta Salad, Spicy, '01 311
Bow Tie Pasta, '01 164
Bow Tie Pasta, Chicken-and-, '01 164
Broccoli-Cauliflower Pasta Salad, '88 269
Caesar Salad Pasta, '95 230
Chicken Pasta Salad, '88 89
Chicken-Pasta Salad, Grilled, '94 64
Chicken-Pasta Salad, Zesty, '02 186
Chicken Salad, Tarragon Pasta-, '87 155
Cold Pasta Platter, '88 42
Confetti Pasta Salad, '05 242
Confetti-Pasta Salad, Easy, '92 220
Crabmeat-Shrimp Pasta Salad, '86 208
Crunchy Pasta Salad, '85 166
Fruited Pasta Salad, '92 108
Garden Pasta Salad, '86 188
Greek Pasta Salad, '02 139; '05 130
Ham-and-Pasta Salad, '90 128
Ham-and-Pea Pasta Salad, '00 217
Ham, Pasta Salad with, '92 108
Ham-Pecan-Blue Cheese Pasta Salad, '90 62
Herbed Pasta-and-Tomato Salad, '92 144
Hoisin Chicken-and-Pasta Salad, '99 125
Luncheon Pasta Salad, '90 191
Macaroni and Cheese Salad, '97 203
Macaroni-Cheese Salad, Dilled, '86 208
Macaroni-Chicken Salad, '85 296; '86 302
Macaroni-Chicken Salad, Dilled, '92 142
Macaroni-Crabmeat Salad, '81 153
Macaroni-Ham Salad, '85 218
Macaroni Salad, '87 92
Macaroni Salad, Barbecue, '82 276
Macaroni Salad, Confetti, '82 132; '85 297
Macaroni Salad, Crunchy, '82 24
Macaroni Salad, Dilled, '89 161
Macaroni Salad for Two, '81 31
Macaroni Salad, Garden, '84 290; '92 64
Macaroni Salad, Gourmet, '81 253
Macaroni Salad, Ham and, '79 220
Macaroni Salad, Hearty, '84 90
Macaroni Salad, Pineapple, '79 220
Macaroni Salad, Refreshing, '80 177
Macaroni Salad, Shell, '92 163
Macaroni Salad, Spiral, '82 276
Macaroni Salad, Sweet-and-Sour, '85 166

Macaroni Salad, Taco, '85 165
Macaroni Salad, Turkey, '83 282
Macaroni Salad Véronique, '85 164
Macaroni-Salmon Salad, '82 232
Macaroni Shell Salad, '87 38
Macaroni-Shrimp Salad, '85 121
Macaroni-Shrimp Salad, Festive, '85 165
Macaroni Toss, Corkscrew, '83 163
Macaroni-Tuna Salad, Whole Wheat, '84 193
Macaroni-Vegetable Salad, '86 209
Main-Dish Pasta Salad, '82 199
Marinated Bean-Pasta Salad, '97 328
Mediterranean Pasta Salad, '05 220
Mediterranean Salad, '95 132
Medley, Garden Pasta, '89 256
Noodle Salad, Peanutty Spicy, '04 72
Noodle Salad, Sesame, '02 186
Oriental Pasta Salad, '90 63
Overnight Pasta Salad, '82 276
Pasta Salad, '84 139; '86 120; '87 36; '90 62, 91;
    '00 213; '01 127
Pesto Pasta Salad, Fresh, '01 61
Pistachio-Pasta Salad, '86 141
Plentiful P's Salad, '87 12
Presto Pasta Salad, '90 63
Ramen Noodle Salad, '88 41
Ratatouille Pasta Salad, '90 74
Ravioli Salad, Caesar, '95 183
Roasted Onion Pasta Salad with Peppered Cheese
    Crisps, '98 107
Rotelle Salad, Crunchy, '86 209
Rotini Salad, '88 42
Seafood Pasta Salad, '90 62
Seashell Salad, '86 209
Shell Salad, Tossed, '91 256
Shrimp Pasta Salad with Green Goddess Dressing,
    '02 139
Shrimp Salad, Pasta-and-, '83 163
Smoked Mozzarella Pasta Salad, '03 126
Snappy Pasta, '83 164
Southwestern Pasta Salad, '94 278
Spaghetti Salad, '82 277; '84 205
Spaghetti Salad, Chicken-, '90 146
Spinach-Mustard Twist, '86 209
Tomato-Pasta Salad, '97 M160
Tortellini Pasta Salad, Cheese, '02 139
Tortellini-Pesto Salad, '92 22
Tortellini Salad, '89 237; '02 186
Tortellini Salad, Chicken, '87 288
Tortellini Salad, Garden, '91 44
Tortellini Salad, Terrific, '96 134
Turkey 'n' Pasta Salad, Ranch-Style, '94 184
Vegetable Salad, Pasta-, '95 238
Veggie Salad, Pasta-, '96 106
Vermicelli Vinaigrette Salad, '82 189
Vinaigrette, Italian Pasta, '92 78
Ziti-Cheddar Salad, '85 165
Pea
Asparagus Salad, Peas-and-, '83 141
Black-Eyed Pea Salad, '80 112; '86 225; '88 92, 221;
    '90 173; '95 203; '97 305; '98 52; '99 174
Black-Eyed Pea Salad, Chicken-and-, '97 305
Black-Eyed Pea Salad, Fearrington House Goat
    Cheese and, '95 60
Black-Eyed Pea Salad, Marinated, '93 190
Black-Eyed Pea Salad, Overnight, '81 280
Black-Eyed Pea Salad with Benedictine Dressing, '98 83
Black-Eyed Peas, Marinated, '82 156
Black-Eyed Peas, Zesty, '89 147
Black-Eyed Pea Vinaigrette, '86 7
Black-Eyed Salad, Hot Bacon and, '85 7
Cauliflower and Pea Salad, Savory, '81 280
Cauliflower-Pea Salad, '87 231
Cheddar-Pea Salad, '84 82

Chicken-Pea Salad, '83 218
Corn-and-Pea Salad, '90 181
Creamy Pea Salad, '80 111
Crunchy Pea Salad, '90 143; '00 103
Dilled Pea Salad, '97 305; '98 18
English Pea-and-Apple Salad, '87 24
English Pea Salad, '81 280; '90 143
English Pea Salad, Cauliflower-, '95 66
English Pea Salad, Marinated, '82 54
Field Pea Salad, Mixed, '00 325
Green Pea Salad, '96 88
Hoppin' John Salad, '01 250
Marinated Pea Salad, '81 204
Mexi-Pea Salad, '81 7
Minted Pea Salad, '91 119
Pea Salad, '98 274
Plentiful P's Salad, '87 12
Special Peas, '95 133
Special Pea Salad, '83 239
Sugar Snap Pea Salad, '86 115
Three Pea Salad, '84 290
Peach-and-Kiwi Salad, '90 180
Peaches in a Garden Nest, '87 154
Peach Salad, Frosted, '82 145
Peach Salad, Frozen, '82 54
Peach Salad, Georgia, '80 142
Peach Salad Supreme, Easy, '79 177
Peanut-Apple Salad, '80 5
Peanut-Noodle Salad, '02 163
Pear-and-Celery Salad, '87 56
Pear-and-Cranberry Wild Rice Salad, '03 199
Pear-and-Spinach Salad, Festive, '85 131
Pear, Jicama, and Snow Pea Salad, '01 329
Pear Plate, Pretty, '89 225
Pear Salad, Crunchy, '83 234; '84 244
Pear Salad, Golden, '91 58
Pear Salad with Asian Sesame Dressing, Fresh, '02 196
Pear Salad with Jícama and Snow Peas, '01 56
Pear Salad with Raspberry Cream, '00 311
Pear-Swiss Cheese Salad, '91 237
Pepper-Cheese Stacks, '87 80
Pepperoni-and-Broccoli Salad, '83 216
Pepper Salad, Mixed, '89 103
Pepper Salad, Roasted Tomato-and-, '01 196
Pepper Salad, Three-, '91 162
Pineapple Boat Aloha, '80 102
Pineapple Boats Ahoy, '80 148
Pineapple Boats, Fresh, '83 153
Pineapple-Celery Salad, '85 95
Pineapple Salad, Frosty, '89 278
Pineapple Waldorf, '97 86
Pineapple Waldorf Salad, '92 97
Pita Salad Sandwiches, '83 134
Pizza, Salad, '87 182
Plum Salad, Crisp, '03 161
Portobello Salad, Grilled, '99 216
Potato Salads, Cold
Any Day Potato Salad, '81 154
Asparagus-and-New Potato Salad, '86 69
Avocado, Potato Salad with, '98 332
Avocado-Potato Salad with Horseradish Dressing, '96 200
Bacon 'n' Onion Potato Salad, '05 188
Bacon Potato Salad, '05 171
Bacon-Topped Potato Salad, '85 59
Baked Potato Salad, '97 319
Basil Potato Salad, '94 178
Bean Salad, Potato-, '82 301
BLT Potato Salad, '05 213
Blue Cheese-Potato Salad, '91 208
Charletta's Potato Salad, '98 153
Chunky Potato Salad, '81 M138
Cobb Salad, Potato, '03 140
Confetti Potato Salad, '80 5; '88 16
Corned Beef-Potato Salad, '85 213

Corned Beef Salad, Potato-, '81 36
Cottage Cheese-Potato Salad, '79 147, 285
Creamy Potato Salad, '80 178; '88 171; '92 241; '98 175; '01 334
Creole Potato Salad, '99 136
Cucumbers and Tomatoes, Potato Salad with, '03 92
Curried Potato Salad, '99 137
Deluxe Potato Salad, '80 155
Dill-and-Sour Cream Potato Salad, '93 105; '94 100
Dilled Potato Salad with Feta, '05 128
Dill Potato Salad, '85 213; '94 179; '99 104
Festive Potato Salad, '89 315
Fipps Family Potato Salad, '02 138
Fish-Potato Salad, Smoked, '84 233
French-Style Potato Salad, '88 171
Fruity Potato Salad, '85 214
Garden Patch Potato Salad, '84 82
Grecian Potato Salad, '82 55
Greek Potato Salad, '98 276
Green Bean-Potato Salad, '83 80; '01 181; '04 142
Green Bean-Red Potato Salad, '96 175
Green Bean-Red Potato Salad, Layered, '05 146
Green Bean Salad, Potato-and-, '00 162
Ham-and-Egg Potato Salad, '86 84
Ham and Potato Salad, '80 272
Ham-and-Potato Salad, '95 94
Herbed Potato Salad, '87 171; '94 164
Horseradish Potato Salad, '98 175
Jalapeño Potato Salad, '97 64
Joy's Potato Salad, '99 83
Layered Creamy Potato Salad, '81 23
Layered Potato Salad, '03 183
Light Potato Salad, '02 138
Lime-Potato Salad, '02 22
Marinated Potato-Apple Salad, '05 41
Marinated Potato Slices, '93 98
Mustard Potato Salad, '86 302
New Potato Salad, '84 120, 139; '94 162; '01 142
Olive-Potato Salad, '85 114
Onion and Celery, Potato Salad with, '02 138
Parslied Potato Salad, '85 240
Patio Potato Salad, '90 160
Peas-and-Potatoes Vinaigrette, Dilled, '01 327
Peppers, Potato Salad 'n', '83 135
Pickle-Potato Salad, Sweet, '85 213
Pickle, Potato Salad with Sweet, '02 138
Potato Salad, '90 122; '94 160; '00 195; '01 163; '03 163
Red Potato Salad, '93 119; '96 172; '02 138
Roasted New Potato Salad, '04 91
Roasted-Potato Salad, Creamy, '97 161
Roasted Red Peppers, Potato Salad with, '04 100
Salmon-Potato Salad, '87 285
Salmon Potato Salad, Smoked, '97 64
Saucy Potato Salad, '87 123
Savory Potato Salad, '80 30
Shrimp-and-Potato Salad, '96 211
Sour Cream Potato Salad, '79 104; '80 79; '99 137
Sour Cream-Potato Salad, '84 149
Southern-Style Potato Salad, '04 199
South-of-the-Border Potato Salad, '94 178
Spicy Potato Salad, '97 305
Spring Salad, Mediterranean, '80 148
Sweet and Sour Potato Salad, '80 152
Sweet Potato-Apple Salad, '96 240
Sweet Potato Fruit Salad, '00 325
Sweet Potato Salad, '05 171
Sweet Potato Salad, Black-Eyed Pea-and-, '01 198
Sweet Potato Salad, Fresh, '86 226
Tri Club Potato Salad, '92 166
Tuna-Potato Salad, '84 289

Potato Salads, Hot or Warm
Baked Potato Salad, '97 319
Broccoli-Potato Salad, Hot, '85 23
Colorful Potato Salad, '01 94

Dill Potato Salad, Hot, '79 78
Dutch Potato Salad, Hot, '86 297; '87 176
Fipps Family Potato Salad, '02 138
German Potato Salad, '82 134, 239; '84 18; '92 169; '97 195; '98 175
German Potato Salad, Hot, '79 78; '94 254
German-Style Potato Salad, '83 23; '88 M194
Goat Cheese and Potato Salad, Warm, '96 234
Greens, Hot Potato, '97 20
Lemon-Basil Potato Salad, '97 63; '01 178
Light Potato Salad, '02 138
Light Potato Salad, Hot-and-, '93 90
Onion and Celery, Potato Salad with, '02 138
Parmesan Potato Salad, Hot, '79 78
Pepper Cups, Potato Salad in, '79 78
Pesto Potato Salad, '90 164
Pickle, Potato Salad with Sweet, '02 138
Pole Bean-Potato Salad, Hot, '79 74
Potato Salad, Hot, '79 78; '81 276; '86 10
Red Potato Salad, '02 138
Roasted Potato-and-Bacon Salad, '05 289
Sausage Salad, Warm Potato-and-, '96 25
Savory Potato Salad, '80 30
Smoked Sausage, Warm Potato Salad with, '97 267
Sugar Snap Peas, Potato Salad with, '91 120
Supreme, Hot Potato Salad, '79 78
Sweet-and-Sour Potato Salad, '92 106
Sweet Potato Salad, '05 171
Sweet Potato Salad with Rosemary-Honey Vinaigrette, '98 243
Vegetable Potato Salad, '03 136
Radish Toss, Chilled, '01 101
Ramen Noodle Salad, '97 18
Raspberry Salad, Frozen, '79 287; '80 35
Raspberry-Walnut Salad, '94 158
Red Cabbage Citrus Salad, '94 72
Red Grapefruit-Lemon Vinaigrette, Salad with, '05 161
Relish Salad, '84 121
Rémoulade, Dill Pickle, '04 311
Rice. *See also* SALADS/Vegetable.
Artichoke-Chicken-Rice Salad, Mediterranean, '97 321
Artichoke Hearts, Rice Salad with, '80 232
Artichoke-Rice Salad, '80 178; '81 41; '85 81; '01 144
Avocado Salad, Rice-and-, '89 146
Bacon, Rice Salad with, '79 52
Bean-and-Rice Salad, Marinated, '87 152
Bean Salad, Rice-and-, '85 22
Bean Salad, Zesty Rice-and-, '02 84
Beans-and-Rice Salad, '91 44
Beef-and-Lime Rice Salad, '03 172
Brown Rice-and-Vegetable Salad, '84 202
Brown Rice Confetti Salad, '94 174
Brown Rice-Pine Nut Salad, '05 126
Cabbage Salad with Honey-Dijon Vinaigrette, Rice-, '04 321
Chicken-and-Rice Salad, '97 92
Chicken-and-Rice Salad, Hot, '83 22
Chicken-Rice Salad, '81 203; '97 93
Chicken-Rice Salad, Curried, '92 190
Chicken-Rice Salad, Grilled, '98 148
Chicken-Rice Salad, Nutty, '83 157
Chutneyed Rice Salad, '88 100
Colorful Rice Salad, '81 253
Confetti Rice Salad, '80 232
Crunchy Rice Salad, '82 302
Curried Rice Salad, '80 84; '85 147, 220; '96 240
Curry Rice Salad, '89 146
Egg-Rice Salad, '84 18; '86 169
Ham-and-Rice Salad, Colorful, '90 319
Ham-and-Rice Salad, Mandarin, '87 145
Ham-Rice Toss, '82 40
Hearty Rice Salad, '82 233
Herbed Rice Salad, '96 123
Madras Salad, '86 82

Mandarin Rice Salad, '88 271
Mardi Gras Rice, '91 217
Meal-in-One Salad, '86 43
Molded Gazpacho-Rice Salad, '86 221
Mushrooms, Rice Salad with Fresh, '80 231
Orange Vinaigrette Rice Salad, '98 288
Paella Salad, '86 207
Pea Salad, Rice-, '85 163
Pebble Salad, '91 27
Pine Nut, Rice, and Feta Salad, '96 26; '98 331
Pork-and-Rice Salad with Spicy Tomato Dressing, '03 143
Primavera Salad, Rice, '00 131
Red Rice Salad, Charleston, '79 146
Rice Salad, '79 74; '81 51
Ring, Rice-Carrot, '79 246
Shrimp and Rice Salad, '80 231; '82 207
Shrimp-and-Rice Salad, '92 307
Shrimp-Rice Salad, Tangy, '84 66
Shrimp Salad, Rice-, '79 270; '92 142
Shrimp Salad, Rice-and-, '83 82
Spinach-Rice Salad, '94 63
Tomatoes and Basil, Rice with, '95 232
Tuna Salad, Wild, '95 243
Vegetable-Rice Salad, '80 148; '83 198; '85 87
Wild Rice-and-Chicken Salad, '02 52
Wild Rice-and-Corn Salad, '98 288
Wild Rice-and-Cranberry Salad, '99 272
Wild Rice-and-Kidney Bean Salad, '01 175
Wild Rice-and-Roasted Vegetable Salad, '99 316
Wild Rice-and-Shrimp Salad, '02 109
Wild Rice-Chicken Salad, '83 146; '99 55
Wild Rice-Green Apple Salad, '92 90
Wild Rice Salad, '85 65; '89 147; '93 191; '01 247
Wild Rice Salad, Crab-, '86 207
Wild Rice Salad, Crab and, '79 116
Wild Rice Salad, Oriental Salmon-and-, '94 173
Wild Rice Salad, Springtime, '88 100
Wild Rice Salad with Spicy Lime Vinaigrette, '01 217
Wild Rice-Shrimp Salad, '99 55
Zesty Rice Salad, '81 23
Roasted Butternut Squash Salad with Blue Cheese Vinaigrette, '05 233
Roasted Red Pepper-and-Green Bean Salad, '99 322
Sandwich, Tuscan Feta Salad, '99 289
Sauerkraut Salad, '80 178; '97 195
Sauerkraut Salad, Crunchy, '87 9
Seafood. *See also* SALADS/Fish, Shrimp.
Baked Seafood Salad, '86 10
Blue Crab Salad with Asian Vinaigrette, '98 142
Crab-and-Asparagus Salad, '92 141
Crab-and-Endive Salad, Marinated, '93 22
Crab and Wild Rice Salad, '79 116
Crab-Avocado Salad, '81 114
Crab Cakes with Greens and Dijon Dressing, '96 176
Crab Louis, '95 94
Crab Luncheon Salad, '00 17
Crabmeat, Avocado with, '86 119
Crabmeat Luncheon Salad, '82 207
Crabmeat Salad, '91 169
Crabmeat Salad with Creamy Gingered Dressing, Caribbean, '97 263
Crabmeat-Shrimp Pasta Salad, '86 208
Crab Mousse, '79 117
Crab Salad, Chesapeake, '89 195
Crab Salad, Cucumber-and-, '98 208
Crab Salad, Delightful, '87 145
Crab Salad Sandwiches, Mango-, '99 72
Crab-Wild Rice Salad, '86 207
Fleur-de-lis Salad, '99 164
Hot Seafood Salad, '79 117; '80 164
Lobster and Orange Salad, '82 207
Lobster Salad, '89 249; '90 69
Lobster Salad with Tarragon Vinaigrette, '97 163

SALADS, Seafood
(continued)

Paella Salad, '86 207
Polynesian Seafood Salad, '79 57
Scallop Salad, Thai-Rific Orange, '04 317
Seafood Salad, '90 88
Sewee Preserve's Seafood Salad, '05 173
Smoky Seafood Salad, '84 46
Sussex Shores, Seafood Salad, '93 98
Tropical Salad, '85 91
Sesame-Almond Salad, '89 123
Shallot Salad, Caramelized, '96 308
Shrimp
Aloha Shrimp Salad, '95 46
Artichoke Salad, Shrimp-and-, '04 50
Avocado Salad, Shrimp and, '80 266
Avocados, Shrimp-Filled, '83 2
Avocado Stuffed with Shrimp Salad, '82 207
Baked Shrimp-Rice Salad, '83 22
Bowl, Mediterranean Shrimp, '80 174
Caribbean Shrimp-and-Black Bean Salad, '93 143
Coastal Shrimp Salad, '00 17
Couscous Salad, Shrimp-and-, '96 157
Creamy Shrimp Salad, '79 56
Croissants, Shrimp Salad on, '96 175
Curried Shrimp Salad, '00 217
Curry Salad, Melon and Shrimp, '97 129
Egg Salad Club, Shrimp-, '02 203
Egg Salad, Tossed Shrimp-, '80 4
Endive Salad, Shrimp-, '85 73
Filling, Shrimp Salad, '87 106
Fruited Shrimp Salad, '86 156
Grapefruit-and-Shrimp Salad, '88 5
Green Salad with Shrimp, '88 49
Grilled Shrimp, Orange, and Watermelon Salad with
    Peppered Peanuts in a Zesty Citrus Dressing, '04 308
Half Shell, Shrimp Salad on the, '86 73
Individual Shrimp Salads, '83 146
Layered Shrimp Salad, '88 100
Macaroni Salad, Shrimp, '90 220
Macaroni Salad, Shrimp-, '85 219
Marinated Shrimp Salad, '85 82; '93 321; '99 169
Mousse, Shrimp, '79 57
Old Bay Shrimp Salad, '05 188
Orange, and Olive Salad with Sherry Vinaigrette,
    Shrimp, '93 177
Orange-Shrimp Salad, '84 197
Oriental Shrimp Salad, '91 313
Orzo Salad, Peppers Stuffed with Shrimp-and-, '91 203
Orzo Salad, Shrimp-and-, '99 182
Pasta Salad with Green Goddess Dressing, Shrimp,
    '02 139
Pastry, Shrimp Salad in, '86 105
Picnic Shrimp Salad, '95 182
Potato Salad, Shrimp-and-, '96 211
Rémoulade, Shrimp, '90 255
Rice-and-Shrimp Salad, '83 82
Rice Salad, Shrimp and, '80 231; '82 207
Rice Salad, Shrimp-and-, '92 307
Rotelle, Shrimp, '85 165
Salad, Shrimp, '04 147
Sandwiches, Shrimp-and-Egg Salad, '94 182
Sandwiches, Shrimp Salad, '90 178
Shrimp Salad, '81 94; '86 186; '93 238; '98 333;
    '05 65, 95
Super Shrimp Salad, '81 37
Tangy Shrimp-Rice Salad, '84 66
Vegetable-Shrimp Salad, '79 190
Vermicelli Salad, Shrimp, '88 139
Wild Rice-and-Shrimp Salad, '02 109
Wild Rice-Shrimp Salad, '99 55
Zesty Shrimp-and-Orange Rice Salad, '87 155

Southwestern Spiral Salad, '98 66
Spaghetti Squash Salad, '99 M322
Spaghetti Squash Salad, Marinated, '94 134
Spinach
Apple-Onion Vinaigrette, Spinach Salad with,
    '94 276
Apple Salad, Spinach-, '90 89; '92 13; '97 308
Apple Salad with Cinnamon Vinaigrette, Fresh
    Spinach-and-, '05 44
Apple-Spinach Salad, '97 14; '99 222; '02 230
Apricot Salad, Spinach-, '94 63
Apricot Vinaigrette, Spinach Salad with, '02 120
Arranged Spinach Salad, '91 210; '92 160
Bacon Salad, Spinach and, '81 143
Beet Salad, Spinach-, '83 227
Blue Cheese Dressing, Spinach Salad with Zesty, '02 121
Blue Cheese Salad, Spinach-, '82 166
Blues, Spinach Salad with the, '95 66
Chili-Lime Dressing, Spinach Salad with, '94 63
Citrus Dressing, Spinach Salad with, '88 133
Citrus Spinach Salad, '90 59
Combination Spinach Salad, '85 327; '86 22
Cranberry Salad with Warm Chutney Dressing,
    Spinach-and-, '02 242
Creamy Dressing, Crisp Spinach Salad with, '83 81
Creamy Spinach Salad, '83 60
Crunchy Spinach Salad, '80 147; '81 225
Curry Spinach Salad, '80 242
Dijon Spinach Salad, '89 282
Dried Tomato Vinaigrette, Spinach Salad with, '93 272
Easy Spinach, Pear, and Blue Cheese Salad, '05 41
Easy Spinach Salad, '91 249
Endive Salad with Warm Vinaigrette, Spinach-, '05 291
Enoki Salad, Spinach-, '89 62
Festive Spinach Salad, '80 247
French Spinach Salad, '79 8
Fresh Spinach Salad, '82 73; '83 240; '84 15, 77; '86 130
Fresh Spinach Salad Delight, '80 146
Garlic-Ginger Vinaigrette Dressing, Spinach Salad
    with, '92 195
Green Spinach Salad, '79 142
Grits-Spinach Salad, Stacked, '98 66
Honey Dressing, Spinach Salad with, '90 16
Hot Bacon Dressing, Spinach Salad with, '82 211
Hot Citrus Dressing, Spinach Salad with, '00 108
Hot Spiked Spinach, '97 195
Kiwifruit Salad, Spinach-, '87 305
Lamb Salad, Spinach-, '85 58
Layered Spinach Salad, '80 5; '89 163
Lettuce Salad, Layered Spinach-, '84 266
Mandarin Spinach Salad, '85 163
Minted Spinach Salad, '94 63
Mushroom Salad, Spinach and, '80 112
Mustard Twist, Spinach-, '86 209
Onion Salad Bowl, Spinach-and-, '81 157
Orange Dressing, Spinach Salad with, '87 187
Orange Salad, Spinach-and-, '86 15
Orange Salad, Warm Spinach-, '00 112
Orange-Spinach Salad, '83 316; '84 16
Oriental Spinach Salad, '82 23
Oysters and Red Wine Vinaigrette, Spinach Salad
    with, '94 327
Parsley Dressing, Spinach Salad with Sweet, '02 120
Pear-and-Spinach Salad, Festive, '85 131
Pecan Salad, Spinach-, '89 128; '01 284
Pickled Spinach, '81 69
Poppy Seed Dressing, Spinach Salad with, '91 210;
    '92 160
Pork-and-Spinach Salad, Mandarin, '88 M126
Raspberry Cream Dressing, Spinach Salad with, '94 321
Rice Salad, Spinach-, '94 63
Russian Dressing, Spinach Salad with, '79 144
Salmon-Spinach Salad, '87 145
Sesame Salad, Spinach-, '91 211; '92 160

Sesame Spinach Salad, '90 292
Southern Spinach Salad, '80 55
Southern Spinach Salad with Cheese Grits Croutons
    and Vidalia Onion-Balsamic Vinaigrette, '04 316
Special Spinach Salad, '80 78
Spicy Dressing, Fresh Spinach with, '80 55
Spinach Salad, '82 102; '86 302; '87 62; '88 299;
    '92 281, 341; '93 46, 65; '03 246
Springtime Spinach Salad, '81 114
Sprout Salad, Fresh Spinach-, '82 281; '83 42
Steak-and-Spinach Salad with Hot Pan Dressing, '05 19
Strawberry Salad, Spinach-and-, '05 55
Strawberry Salad with Tart Poppy Seed Dressing,
    Spinach-and-, '03 241
Strawberry-Spinach Salad, '91 169; '93 168
Sun-Dried Tomato Salad, Spinach and, '93 250
Supreme, Spinach Salad, '79 243
Sweet-Sour Spinach Salad, '85 M112
Tangy Spinach Salad, '00 24
Tossed Spinach Salad, '01 159
Tropical Spinach Salad, '90 231
Tropical Spinach Salad with Grilled Chicken, '04 51
Tropical Spinach Salad with Grilled Pork Tenderloin,
    '04 51
Tropical Spinach Salad with Grilled Shrimp, '04 51
Wilted, Spinach Salad, '81 M4; '89 123; '91 210;
    '92 160; '93 125
Zesty Spinach Salad, '79 88
Sprout Salad, '90 137
Sprout Salad, Crunchy, '98 52
Sprout Salad, Spanish, '85 327; '86 22
Squash Salad, '03 M184
Strawberry-Cranberry-Orange Salad, '05 249
Strawberry-Jícama Salad, Cranberry-, '02 300
Strawberry Salad, Frozen, '94 119
Strawberry Salad with Cinnamon Vinaigrette, '05 133
Strawberry Yogurt Salad, '80 232
Suzie or Steven Salad, '98 204
Tabbouleh, '85 148; '93 70; '99 175
Tabbouleh Salad, '91 70; '92 212; '94 174; '01 57
(Tabbouleh Salad), Boot Scoot Tabbouli, '96 159
Taco Salad, '79 56; '83 145; '84 221; '85 84; '89 332; '90 20
Taco Salad Cups, '85 M29
Taco Salad, Meatless, '81 204
Taco Salad, Party, '97 19
Taco Salad, Spicy, '87 287
Tart Cranberry Salad, '79 286
Tofu Salad, '88 27
Tomato. *See also* **SALADS/Congealed.**
Artichoke-Tomato Salad, '82 239
Asparagus and Tomatoes with Herb Vinaigrette, '99 56
Asparagus Salad, Tomato-, '92 79
Avocado Salad, Tomato-, '86 74
Basil-and-Tomato Couscous Salad, '94 175
Basil-Mozzarella Salad, Tomato-, '95 171
Bibb Salad with Fried Green Tomatoes, Kentucky, '01 121
Charred Tomato Salad, '01 158
Cherry Tomato-Caper Salad, '00 140; '02 32
Cherry Tomato Salad, '87 156
Cottage Cheese Salad in Tomatoes, '86 208
Cottage-Tomato Salad, '85 163
Cucumber-and-Tomato Salad, '01 127
Cucumber and Tomato Salad, Dilled, '81 153
Cucumber-Onion Salad, Tomato-, '81 239
Cucumber Salad, Tomato-, '86 218; '92 199
Cucumber Salad with Yogurt-Herb Dressing,
    Tomato-, '92 96
Cucumber Summer Salad, Tomato-and-, '93 141
Cucumber-Tomato Salad, '90 144
Endive-Tomato Starburst Salad, '93 323
Feta Lettuce Salad, Tomato-, '05 207
Feta Salad, Tomato-, '81 246; '91 168; '05 207
Flower Salad, Tomato, '89 128

Grape Tomatoes with Capers, '01 329
Green Bean Salad, Tomato-and-, '97 162
Gruyère-Basil Salad, Tomato-, '99 172
Guacamole-Tomato Salad, '81 302
Herbed Tomatoes, '83 173
Herb Salad, Tomato-, '89 220
Hot Tomato Salad, '05 129
Italian BLT Bread Salad, '03 90
Italian Tomato Salad, '01 124
Lima Bean-Tomato Salad, '85 137
Marinated Cucumber-Tomato Salad, '02 167
Marinated Salsa Tomatoes, '82 164
Marinated Tomato and Brie Salad, '95 95
Marinated Tomato-and-Cucumber Salad, '92 216
Marinated Tomatoes, '85 156, 163; '89 174, 202
Marinated Tomato Slices, '83 193
Mozzarella Salad, Tomato-, '89 220
Mozzarella-Tomato-Basil Salad, Fresh, '93 131
Napoleon, Tomato, '00 182
Okra-Corn-and-Tomato Vinaigrette, '90 173
Onion, and Cucumber in Italian Dressing, Tomato, '81 83
Onion Salad, Tomato-and-, '05 167
Onion Salad, Tomato-and-Sweet, '05 141
Oregano, Tomatoes, '83 145
Pasta Salad, Tomato-, '97 M160
Petal Salad, Tomato, '79 88
Red Onion Salad, Tomato-, '04 181
Refresher, Tomato, '81 94
Relish Salad, Tomato, '83 111
Roasted Tomato-and-Pepper Salad, '01 196
Slices with Lemon Dressing, Tomato, '87 167
Stuffed Tomatoes, Avocado-, '82 101
Stuffed Tomatoes, Cold, '80 100
Stuffed Tomato Salad, Artichoke-, '82 101
Stuffed Tomato Salad, Crab-, '80 148
Stuffed Tomato Salad, Oriental-, '82 101
Stuffed with Sea Slaw, Tomatoes, '89 96
Summer Tomato Salad, '94 201
Summer Tomato Treat, '79 143
Trout-and-Tomato Salad with Black Pepper
    Vinaigrette, '98 284
Tuna with Warm Tomato Salad, '97 179
Vidalia-Tomato Salad, '84 65
Vinaigrette, Tomato-Basil, '87 89
Vinaigrette, Tomatoes, '84 106
Watercress-Tomato Salad, '85 132
Tossed Salad, Grecian, '04 283
Tossed Salad, Italian, '00 167; '05 202
Tossed Salad with Parmesan Dressing, '86 192
Turkey
Bacon Dressing, Turkey Salad with Hot, '87 285
Bake, Turkey Salad, '79 253
Carrot Salad, Turkey-, '86 283
Cobb Salad, Southern-Style Turkey, '05 214
Curried Turkey Salad, '88 140
Curried Turkey Salad, Chutney, '98 314
Fruit-and-Spice Turkey Salad, '94 325
Fruitful Turkey Salad, '84 197
Fruit Salad, Turkey-, '79 56
Fruit Salad, Turkey, '83 233; '84 244
Holiday Turkey Salad, '84 320
Honey-Mustard Turkey Salad, '92 309; '01 230
Hot Turkey Salad, '86 10, 297; '87 176
Layered Cornbread-and-Turkey Salad, '02 141
Layered Turkey Salad, '86 332; '92 220
Macaroni Salad, Turkey, '83 282
Main Dish Turkey Salad with Cranberry Vinaigrette
    and Garlic Croutons, '05 246
Orange Salad, Turkey-in-the-, '93 21
Polynesian Turkey Salad, '87 285
Ranch-Style Turkey 'n' Pasta Salad, '94 184
Sandwiches, Turkey Salad Pita, '87 202; '88 43
Smoked, Turkey Salad, '96 184
Southwestern, Turkey Salad, '91 313

Stir-Fry Salad, Chilled Turkey-and-Pepper, '88 140
Straw Salad, Turkey-in-the-, '96 286
Taco Salad, Turkey, '95 25
Turkey Salad, '90 318
Waldorf Salad with Yogurt Dressing, Turkey, '88 53
Walnut Salad, Turkey-, '03 239
Walnuts, Turkey Salad with Sautéed, '86 117
Zucchini Salad, Turkey-, '85 74
Turkish Salad, '96 137
Turnip-and-Carrot Salad, '91 212
Turnip Salad, '85 235
Turnip Salad, Irish, '94 178
Vegetable. *See also* **SALADS/Congealed, Pasta.**
Antipasto Salad Platter, Mediterranean, '05 220
Antipasto, Vegetable, '85 263
Basil-Chicken-Vegetable Salad, '92 162
Bean Salad, Veggie-, '04 328
Boats, Salad, '80 93
Calico Salad, '82 35
Cauliflower-Vegetable Salad, '85 158
Chicken Salad, Vegetable-, '91 287
Chilled Vegetable Salad, '00 285
Chinese Salad, '80 4
Colorful Vegetable Salad, '04 34
Composée, Salad, '79 171
Composé, Salad, '93 126
Corned Beef Salad, Vegetable-, '80 148
Creamy Vegetable Salad, '79 47
Creole Salad, '79 147
Crunchy Vegetable Salad, '79 11; '80 217; '83 216
Different Vegetable Salad, '82 143
Easy Vegetable Salad, '83 316; '84 16
Extravaganza, Salad, '87 233
Garden Marinade, '81 23
Garden Medley Salad, '80 122
Garden Salad, '85 92; '87 62; '89 166; '92 60
Garden Salad Bowl, '82 239
Garden Salad with Tomato-Cream Cheese Dressing,
    '79 173
Greek Salad, Garden, '86 173
Greek Salad, Quick, '02 24
Greek Vegetable Salad, '99 202
Green-and-White Vegetable Salad, '79 286
Green Vegetable and Egg Salad, '79 191
Green Vegetable Salad, Overnight, '80 5
Grilled Marinated Vegetable Salad, '01 143
Grilled Vegetable Salad, '94 203; '00 146
Healthy Salad, '95 133
Horseradish Dressing, Vegetable Salad with, '92 85
Italian Garden Salad, '99 203
Italian Vegetable Salad, '81 253; '82 19
Layered Vegetable Salad with Parmesan Dressing, '01 96
Loaded Veggie Salad, '03 58
Luncheon Salad, '84 232
Marinade, Fresh Vegetable, '83 209
Marinade, Garden, '81 23
Marinade, Medley, '79 20
Marinade, Tossed Vegetable, '84 266
Marinated Combo Salad, '82 267
Marinated Garden Salad, '00 178
Marinated Garden Vegetables, '87 252
Marinated Mixed Vegetables, '89 276; '92 106
Marinated Salad, '83 170; '91 186
Marinated Salad, Eight-Vegetable, '80 218
Marinated Salad, Zesty, '90 90
Marinated Summer Salad, '81 153
Marinated Tex-Mex Salad, '93 106
Marinated Vegetable-Bacon Bowl, '79 191
Marinated Vegetable Patch Salad, '84 232
Marinated Vegetables, '79 146; '81 239; '85 67; '88 4, 170
Marinated Vegetable Salad, '79 106, 143; '81 280;
    '82 163; '83 260; '84 13; '87 243; '92 64, 91;
    '97 219; '02 211; '05 129
Marinated Vegetable Salad, Crispy, '84 193

Marinated Vegetable Salad, Fresh, '86 173
Marinated Vegetables, Creole-, '02 69
Marinated Vegetables, Sweet-and-Sour, '83 266
Marinated Vegetables, Zesty, '82 272
Marinated Veggies, '01 127
Marinate, Fresh Vegetable, '80 33; '81 230
Meal-in-One Salad, '82 232
Medley Salad, Vegetable, '88 86
Mexican Salad, '81 36, 113
Minted Vegetable Salad, '88 23; '98 158
Mixed Vegetable Salad, '80 115; '81 302; '82 239;
    '83 317; '84 16; '86 136
Next-Day Vegetable Salad, '83 81
Oriental Salad, Make-Ahead, '82 163
Oriental Vegetable Salad, '84 290
Overnight Vegetable Salad, '90 33
Panzanella, '00 62
Party Vegetable Salad, '86 79
Pasta and Vegetables, '89 255
Pasta Salad, Vegetable, '89 256; '91 143
Pasta Salad, Vegetable-, '92 167
Pebble Salad, '91 27
Pita Bread Salad, '95 86
Primavera Salad, '93 140
Primavera Salad, Rice, '00 131
Quick Summer Italian Salad, '92 79
Radish-Vegetable Salad with Parmesan Dressing, '01 101
Rainbow Salad, '02 18
Rainbow Vegetable Salad, '83 111
Red, White, and Green Salad, '90 18
Refrigerated Vegetable Salad, '84 120
Rice-and-Vegetable Salad, '86 42
Riviera, Salade, '89 12
Roasted Vegetable Salad, Wild Rice-and-, '99 316
Rolls, Picnic Salad, '79 127
Rolls, Vegetable Salad, '82 278
Senator's Salad, '79 191
Seven-Layer Vegetable Salad, '79 88
Spaghetti-Vegetable Salad, '97 196
Spring Vegetable Salad, '88 48
Sprout Salad, Crunchy, '96 45
Summer Salad with Citrus Marinade, '92 133
Summer Vegetable-and-Orzo Salad, '00 165
Swedish Vegetable Salad, '82 23
Sweet-and-Sour Vegetable Salad, '81 25
Tangy Vegetable Toss, '79 144
Tarragon-Vegetable Salad, '85 288
Tomato, Bell Pepper, and Portobello Salad, Grilled, '98 211
Tossed Salad, Lively Lemon, '00 16
Variety Salad, '79 113
Vegetable Salad, '98 92; '00 136
Vinaigrette Salad, Vegetable-Chicken, '86 135
Vinaigrette, Vegetables, '82 225, 290
Walnuts, Vegetable Salad with, '86 118
Warm Vegetable Salad, '95 174
Winter Salad, '97 304
Winter Vegetable Salad, '86 42
Winter Vegetable Salad, Baked, '04 45
Waldorf. *See also* **SALADS/Congealed.**
Creamy Waldorf Salad, '87 311
Deluxe Waldorf Salad, '83 81
Frozen Waldorf Salad, '79 126; '82 145
Jiffy Waldorf Salad, '88 100
New Wave Waldorf Salad, '92 36
Old-Fashioned Waldorf Salad, '81 295
Overnight Waldorf Salad, '81 309
Pineapple Waldorf, '97 86
Pineapple Waldorf Salad, '92 97
Southern Classic Waldorf Salad, '92 36
Tropical Waldorf Salad, '89 12
Turkey Waldorf Salad with Yogurt Dressing, '88 53
Waldorf Salad, '89 278; '97 204
Winter Waldorf Salad, '04 245
Watercress Orange Salad, '04 45

SALADS
(continued)

Watercress Salad, '79 144
Watercress-Tomato Salad, '85 132
Watermelon-Feta Salad, '05 320
Watermelon-Prosciutto Salad, '04 171
Watermelon Salad with Celery-Nut Dressing, '80 182
Watermelon Sparkle, '84 191
Wheat Berry-and-Roasted Corn Salad, '94 175
Wheat Salad with Citrus and Mint, '99 163
Winter Salad, '98 19
Yogurt-Cucumber Salad, '82 122
Yogurt Salad, Frozen, '92 303
Zucchini-Artichoke Salad, '91 229
Zucchini Chef's Salad, '83 143
Zucchini-Corn Marinated Salad, '98 236
Zucchini, Marinated, '80 33
Zucchini Salad, '82 104; '87 103; '89 128
Zucchini Salad, Marinated, '82 164; '90 32
Zucchini Salad, Summer, '95 229

SALMON
Almonds and Parsley, Salmon with, '05 68
Almonds and Tomato-Lemon Sauce, Salmon with, '04 23
Baked Salmon with Caribbean Fruit Salsa, Blitzen's, '04 252
Bake with Pecan-Crunch Coating, Salmon, '95 209
Ball, Salmon, '80 149; '86 262
Ball, Smoky Salmon Cheese, '82 247
Barbecued Salmon, '81 181
Bisque, Smoked Salmon-Whiskey, '00 65
Blackened Salmon with Mango Salsa, '00 337
Broiled Salmon with Dijon-Caper Cream Sauce, '98 329
Broiled Salmon with Lemon and Olive Oil, '04 46
Burgers, Salmon, '89 98; '95 24; '98 144
Canapés, Smoked Salmon, '99 140
Carbonara, Salmon, '83 43
Casserole, Salmon, '81 22
Cheesecake, Smoked Salmon, '99 92
Chili-Rubbed Salmon, '97 124
Chilled Salmon with Dill Sauce, '84 285
Chowder, Salmon, '97 125
Cracked Pepper Salmon Fillets, '00 140
Croquettes, Baked Salmon, '81 22
Dip, Extra-Creamy Smoked Salmon, '03 240
Fettuccine, Salmon, '00 123
Fillets with Avocado Mayonnaise, Spicy Salmon, '02 327
Fillets with Red Wine Garlic Sauce, Salmon, '94 250
Fillets with Sweet Corn Relish, Salmon, '93 119
Florentine, Salmon, '83 43
Glazed Salmon, Caramelized Maple-and-Garlic-, '01 275
Glazed Salmon with Stir-Fried Vegetables, '02 69
Grilled Salmon with Mustard-Molasses Glaze, '01 209
Grilled Salmon with Sweet Soy Slaw and Dipping Sauce, '04 123
Grilled Salmon with Tangy Dill Sauce, '04 320
Herb-Rubbed Salmon Fillets, Fresh, '03 207
Kebabs, Salmon, '81 182
Loaf, Easy Salmon, '80 4
Loaf, Savory Salmon, '92 33
Loaf with Cucumber-Dill Sauce, Salmon, '86 5
Log, Salmon, '81 22
Log, Salmon Party, '98 154
Mousse, Irresistible Salmon, '79 284
Mousse, Salmon, '83 79
Mousse, Salmon Dill, '81 21
Mushrooms and Green Onions, Fresh Salmon with, '93 180
Orange-Basil Salmon, '97 165
Pan-Grilled Salmon, '00 295
Parchment, Salmon in, '95 311
Pasta, Smoked Salmon-Caper-and-Dill, '98 169
Patties, Cheesy Salmon, '89 99
Patties, Open-Faced Salmon, '87 M218
Patties, Salmon, '92 215

Patties with Lemon-Cheese Sauce, Salmon, '91 24
Patties with Sauce, Salmon, '88 164
Poached Salmon, '83 35
Poached Salmon with Emerald Sauce, '90 63
Poached Salmon with Horseradish Sauce, '91 183
Poached Salmon with Yellow Pepper Sauce, '98 230
Potatoes, Salmon-Topped, '84 124
Quesadilla with Cucumber Salsa, Grilled Salmon, '95 131
Quiche, Salmon, '82 87; '87 38
Quiche, Salmon-and-Dill, '03 58
Ragoût, Salmon-and-Vegetable, '96 45
Roll, Salmon Party, '83 127
Salads
Avocados, Salmon-Stuffed, '86 74
Broiled Salmon Salad, '92 108
Chilly Salmon Salad, '80 104
Crunchy Salmon Salad, '81 148
Greens with Creamy Dill Dressing, Salmon on Mixed, '93 143
Macaroni Salad, Salmon-and-, '81 114
Macaroni-Salmon Salad, '82 232
Pasta Salad, Salmon-, '87 9
Poached Salmon Salad, Chilled, '96 68
Potato Salad, Salmon-, '87 285
Potato Salad, Smoked Salmon, '97 64
Rice Salad, Salmon-, '84 289
Salmon Salad, '89 99
Scandinavian Salmon Salad, '98 208
Shells, Salmon Salad, '85 286
Simple Salmon Salad, '91 23
Smoked Salmon-and-Egg Salad, '02 203
Spinach Salad, Salmon-, '87 145
Summertime Salmon Salad, '82 207
Wild Rice Salad, Oriental Salmon-and-, '94 173
Salsa, Smoked Salmon, '96 272
Sandwiches, Cucumber-Salmon-Watercress, '03 111
Sandwiches with Dill, Cucumber-Salmon, '02 131
Scalloped Salmon, '81 273
Scalloped Salmon for Two, '89 98
Scaloppine with Vegetable Confetti and Pernod Sauce, Salmon, '94 172
Sesame-Crusted Salmon with Ginger Vinaigrette, '95 162
Smoked Salmon, '95 114
Smoked Salmon and Cucumber Tartlets, '95 216
Smoked Salmon, Beggar's Purses with, '04 244
Smoked Salmon, Drizzled, '88 91
Smoked Salmon or Mackerel, '84 46
Soufflé, Fresh Salmon, '81 182
Spread, Salmon, '81 149
Spread, Salmon-and-Horseradish, '87 146
Spread, Smoked Salmon, '84 324; '98 285
Spread with Capers, Smoked Salmon, '98 49
Steaks, Baked Salmon, '85 54
Steaks, Glazed Salmon, '86 256
Steaks, Grilled Herbed Salmon, '93 176
Steaks, Grilled Salmon, '94 278
Steaks, Marinated Salmon, '87 6
Steaks, Mint-Marinated Salmon, '96 175
Steaks, Oven-Fried Salmon, '81 181
Steaks with Dill Sauce, Salmon, '85 164
Steaks with Lemon-Mustard Sauce, Salmon, '97 124
Steaks with Tarragon Butter, Salmon, '87 155
Steaks with Tarragon Sauce, Grilled Salmon, '97 42
Teriyaki Salmon, Glazed, '97 124
Terrine, Layered Salmon-and-Spinach, '84 132
Turnovers, Salmon-Spinach, '83 44
Vermicelli, Salmon-Pesto, '92 200
SALSAS. *See also* **CHUTNEYS, PESTOS, RELISHES, SAUCES, TOPPINGS.**
Apricot Salsa, '98 126
Artichoke-Tomato Salsa, '96 182
Avocado-Corn Salsa, '94 201; '99 335
Avocado-Feta Salsa, '96 15; '05 298
Avocado-Mango Salsa, '00 328

Avocado-Peach Salsa, '02 159
Avocado Salsa, '91 182
Avocado Salsa, Fresh, '02 247
Banana Salsa, '96 85
Bean Salsa, Smoky Three-, '02 202
Black-and-White Salsa, Pork Chops with, '97 200
Black Bean-and-Corn Salsa, '94 80; '05 297
Black Bean-and-Corn Salsa Pork Chops, '01 320
Black Bean-and-Mango Salsa, '05 297
Black Bean-Corn Salsa, '96 126; '04 322
Black Bean Salsa, '93 155; '94 161; '97 226; '00 122; '03 146, 323; '04 25
Black Bean Salsa, Chunky, '03 25
Black Bean Salsa, Fruity, '05 16
Black Bean Salsa with Citrus Dressing, '01 60
Black-Eyed Pea Salsa, '93 164
Black-Eyed Pea Salsa, Chunky, '01 333
Blueberry Salsa, '05 179
Broiled Salsa Parmesan, '98 33
Caribbean Salsa, '96 70
Cha-Cha Salsa, '97 160; '98 333
Cheesecake, Salsa, '98 33
Cherry Salsa, '99 156
Chile Salsa, Double, '91 182
Chile Salsa with Homemade Tostados, Hot, '88 115
Chipotle Salsa, Chicken-and-Brie Quesadillas with, '99 311
Chunky Salsa, '86 130; '90 206
Citrus Salsa, Fresh, '03 291
Citrus Salsa, Grilled Shrimp with, '97 141
Colorful Salsa, '99 119
Corn-Black Bean Salsa, '96 15
Corn, Pepper, and Tomato Salsa, Yellowfin Tuna with, '94 164
Corn Salsa, '00 164
Corn Salsa, Grilled, '99 162
Corn Salsa, Spicy, '93 322
Corn Salsa, Sweet, '95 156
Corn Salsa, Zesty, '02 193
Crab-and-Ginger Salsa with Sesame Wontons, Spicy, '01 283
Cranberry-Citrus Salsa, '97 290
Cranberry-Jalapeño Salsa, '01 234
Cranberry Salsa, '98 321; '99 316; '00 269; '01 254
Cruda, Salsa, '87 180; '88 148
Cucumber-Dill Salsa, '95 107
Cucumber-Radish Salsa, '01 187
Cucumber Salsa, '95 131
Dried Chile Salsa, '97 265
Fiery Salsa, '01 174
Fresh Salsa, '95 42; '00 59; '04 274
Fresh Summer Salsa, '87 89
Fruit Salsa, '97 124; '02 54; '04 168
Fruit Salsa, Caribbean, '04 252
Fruit Salsa with Cinnamon Crisps, '01 108
Garden Salsa, '91 182
Green Salsa, Creamy, '91 162
Green Tomato Salsa, Peachy, '99 143
Hill Country Salsa, '97 123
Homemade Salsa, '05 59
Hot Mexican Salsa, '85 136
Hot Salsa, '98 135
Kale with Salsa, Southwest, '94 246
Kiwifruit Salsa, Hot, '94 82
Mango-and-Bell Pepper Salsa, '00 247
Mango Salsa, '91 182; '95 104; '98 232; '00 124, 337; '02 163; '04 59; '05 328
Mango Salsa, Fresh, '00 122
Mango Salsa, Minted, '96 206
Mango Salsa, Snappy, '05 329
Melon Salsa, Hot, '95 144
Mexi-Corn Salsa, '91 182
Olive Salsa, '00 277
One-Minute Salsa, '95 93
Onion Salsa, Fiesta, '94 82
Orange-Black Bean Salsa, '98 231

Papaya Salsa, '94 173
Papaya Salsa, Asparagus Salad with, '97 144
Party Salsa, Quick, '03 292
Peach Salsa, '91 183; '96 14; '97 183
Peach Salsa, Fresh, '95 195
Pepper Salsa, '88 26
Pepper Salsa, Mixed, '91 181
Picante, Homemade Salsa, '81 67
Picante, Salsa, '04 41
Picante with Shrimp, Salsa, '92 210
Pimiento Cheese Salsa, Fiery Steak with, '99 331
Pineapple-Mint Salsa, Grilled Lamb Chops with, '05 52
Pineapple Salsa, '96 226; '03 128; '04 196; '05 86
Pineapple Salsa, Spicy, '97 165
Pineapple Salsa, Warm, '02 144
Pink-Eyed Pea Salsa, '00 158
Pinto Bean-and-Bacon Salsa, Warm, '03 331
Plum Salsa, '97 176
Poblano Salsa, '91 135
Quick Party Salsa, '04 146
Radish-Cucumber Salsa, '04 119
Red Bean Salsa, '97 227
Red Salsa, '90 172
Roasted Red Pepper Salsa, '01 100
Roasted Salsa, '95 130
Roasted Salsa Verde, '96 182
Salpicon, Salsa, '03 33
Salsa, '80 196; '87 217; '88 147; '97 171; '01 273; '03 95
Santa Fe Salsa, Zesty, '03 198
Serrano Salsa, Roasted, '95 207
Simple Salsa, '01 60
Smoked Salmon Salsa, '96 272
Southwestern Salsa with Black Beans and Corn, '96 275
Spaghetti, Salsa, '00 58
Strawberry Salsa, Balsamic, '02 86
Summer Salsa, '98 172
Summer Salsa, Spicy, '03 186
Sweet Heat Salsa and Cinnamon Crisps, South Seas Ice
    Cream with, '04 315
Sweet Pepper-Mango Salsa, '05 148
Sweet Salsa, '98 174
Texas Salsa, '96 160
Tomatillo Salsa, '92 245; '02 123
Tomatillo Salsa, Fresh, '97 143
Tomatillo Salsa, Grilled Chicken with, '02 123
Tomatillo Salsa, Roasted, '95 64
Tomato-Avocado Salsa, '94 83
Tomato-Basil Salsa, Pan-Fried Roughy with, '99 123
Tomato-Mango Salsa, Seared Scallops with, '95 122
Tomato Salsa, '87 120; '96 15; '02 118
Tomato Salsa, Fresh, '91 182; '95 181; '01 249
Tomato Salsa, Roasted, '95 64
Tomato Salsa, Three, '93 138
Tropical Rainbow Salsa, '94 161
Tropical Salsa, '96 14; '01 60
Tropical Salsa, Key Lime Pie with Minted, '99 333
Vegetable Salsa, '96 208, 220
Vegetable Salsa, Fresh, '98 194
Vegetable Salsa, Greek, '98 32
Vegetable Salsa, Shrimp Skewers with, '98 32, 223
Verde, Salsa, '91 182; '96 160
Warm-and-Spicy Salsa, '99 279
Watermelon Salsa, '98 164
Yellow Tomato Salsa, '87 122
Zucchini-Carrot Salsa, '05 298

SANDWICHES
Apple Breakfast Sandwiches, '92 332
Apple-Cinnamon Breakfast Sandwiches, '85 298
Apple Party Sandwiches, '92 234
Apple Pockets, Toasted Cream Cheese-and-, '01 200
Apple Sandwiches, '79 164; '80 130
Asparagus Grill Sandwiches, '79 164; '80 130
Asparagus Sandwich, Warm, '99 102
Asparagus Spear Sandwiches, '84 165

Avocado, Bacon, and Cheese Sandwiches, '87 279
Avocado Deluxe Sandwiches, '99 72
Bacon, Cheese, and Tomato Sandwiches, '84 14
Bacon, Cheese, and Tomato Sandwiches, Grilled, '97 170
Bacon-Cheese Sandwiches, Grilled, '83 242
Bacon 'n' Egg Breakfast Empanadas, '02 324
Bacon, Pimiento, and Cheese Hoagies, '90 144
Bacon Sandwiches, Open-Faced Cheesy, '80 78
Bagel, Breakfast on a, '94 66
Bagels, Meal-in-One, '88 159
Bar, Super Summer Sandwich, '91 143
Basket of Sandwiches, Bread, '86 126
Bat Sandwiches, '00 234
Bean Burgers with Adobo Mayonnaise, '02 202
Beef. *See also* **SANDWICHES/Pita.**
    Bacon, and Blue Cheese Sandwiches, Beef, '96 23
    Barbecue Beef Sandwiches, '99 327; '01 136
    Barbecue Beef Sandwiches, Slow-Cooker, '05 64
    Barbecued Beef Sandwiches, '81 25; '82 31; '83 34
    Barbecue Sandwiches, Debate, '97 234
    Barbecue, Slow-Cooker Beef, '02 299
    Beef-Eater Sandwiches, '86 72
    Calzones, Beef-and-Pepperoni, '03 202
    Calzones, Ground Beef, '97 95
    Cheeseburger Biscuits, '79 194
    Cheesesteaks, Chimichurri, '04 312
    Corned Beef and Cheese Sandwich, '79 214
    Corned Beef Sandwiches, '83 291; '85 242; '92 23
    Corned Beef Sandwiches, Barbecued, '83 130
    Corned Beef Sandwiches, Grilled, '87 54
    Dilly Beef Sandwiches, '98 288
    Flank Steak Mini-Sandwiches, Shredded, '05 158
    Flank Steak Sandwiches with Apple Barbecue Sauce,
        '99 173
    French Beef Slice, '79 125
    French Dip Sandwiches, '97 211
    Grilled Cheese Meat Loaf Sandwiches, '04 188
    Grilled Roast Beef-and-Brie Sandwiches, '03 296
    Gumbo Joes, '88 158
    Hot Beef Sandwiches, '00 98
    Jalapeño Heroes, Open-Faced, '90 144
    Kraut Sandwich, Beef-and-, '91 167
    Loaf, Big Wheel, '84 281
    London Broil Sandwiches with Yogurt-Cucumber
        Sauce, '01 162
    Meatball Sandwiches, '04 170
    Meatball Sandwich, Giant, '92 196
    Meat Loaf Sandwich, '01 210
    Meat Loaf Sandwiches, Barbecue, '04 188
    Open-Faced Italian Sandwich, Beef-and-Artichoke,
        '98 22
    Panini Sandwiches, Roast Beef-Cheddar, '05 223
    Philly Sandwiches, Open-Faced, '05 32
    Pizza Sandwiches, Open-Face, '82 3; '83 85;
        '84 M198; '85 22
    Pork Tenderloin Sandwiches, Beef and, '80 175
    Reuben Puffs, '98 231
    Reuben Sandwiches, '80 M201
    Reuben Sandwiches, Broiled, '81 240; '83 69
    Reuben Sandwiches, Crispy, '85 299
    Reuben Sandwiches, Grilled, '81 206
    Reuben Sandwiches, Open-Face, '91 199
    Reuben Sandwich, Rolled, '99 219
    Reubens, Golden-Baked Mini, '01 62
    Reubens, Open-Faced Coleslaw, '03 169
    Reubens, Oven-Grilled, '97 304
    Reubens, Party, '90 61
    Reubens, Spicy Coleslaw, '04 63
    Reubens, Summer, '00 134
    Reuben Turnovers, '94 253
    Roast Beef Hero Sandwich, '91 167
    Roast Beef Slices, '02 246
    Rolls with Mustard-Horseradish Cream, Beef, '02 53
    Roll-Ups, Savory Beef and Cheese, '96 235

Sloppy Joes, '91 172
Steak-and-Onion Sandwiches, '02 126
Steak Bagel Sandwiches, '96 249
Steak Sandwiches, '96 136
Steak Stroganoff Sandwiches, '85 110
Taco Joes, '91 167
Tenderloin Picnic Sandwiches, Beef, '90 91
Wake-Up Sandwiches, '84 58
Wraps, Cheese-Steak, '00 M335
BLT Breakfast Sandwiches, '04 171
BLT, Caramelized Onion, '03 90
BLT Croissants, '93 158
BLT Sandwiches, Curried, '93 158
BLT Sandwiches, Italian, '02 230
BLT's, Cheesy, '85 92
Breakfast Sandwiches, '80 52; '82 M123; '89 M230
Breakfast Sandwiches, Cheesy, '90 140
Breakfast Sandwiches, Open-Faced, '92 140
Brown Bread-Cream Cheese Sandwiches, '87 M6
Bunwiches, '80 92
Burgers, Balsamic-Blue Cheese Portobello, '05 53
Burgers, Chicken-Cheese, '04 56
Burgers, Toasted Pecan, Cranberry, and Gorgonzola
    Turkey, '05 320
Calla Lily Sandwiches, '91 106
Calzone, '85 94
Calzones, Surprise, '00 282
Calzones with Italian Tomato Sauce, '03 202
Calzones with Pasta Sauce, '01 54
Cheddar Cheese Sandwiches, Hot, '97 179
Cheese Sandwiches, Checkerboard, '05 18
Cheese Sandwiches, Hot French, '82 3
Cheese Sandwiches, Leafy, '90 56
Cheese Sandwiches with Artichoke-Tomato Salsa,
    Herbed, '96 182
Cheese Tea Sandwiches, '92 276
Chicken. *See also* **SANDWICHES/Pita.**
    Bagel Sandwiches, Chicken-Benedict, '96 250
    Baked Chicken Sandwiches, '79 164; '80 130; '84 165
    Broiled Chicken Sandwiches with Fresh Salsa, '00 59
    Cheese Chicken Sandwich, Ham 'n', '95 153
    Cheese Sandwiches, Toasted Chicken-and-, '85 242
    Cheesy Chicken Sandwiches, '82 190
    Chutney-Chicken Croissants, '92 22
    Club Sandwiches, Chicken, '86 160
    Creamed Chicken Toppers, '99 240
    Crispy Chicken Sandwich, '81 114
    Curried Chicken Salad on Raisin Bread, '85 96
    Curried Chicken Tea Sandwiches, '97 23
    Dagwoods, Chicken-Avocado, '96 200; '99 337
    English Muffin Delight, '82 45
    Finger Sandwiches, Chicken-Salad, '85 119
    Focaccia with Roasted Pepper Vinaigrette, Stuffed,
        '00 134
    Gouda Lover's Chicken Sandwiches, '99 195
    Grilled Chicken-and-Pesto Clubs, '01 22
    Grilled Chicken 'n' Cheese Sandwiches, '99 240
    Hot Chicken Sandwiches, '83 291
    Jamaican Chicken Sandwich, '95 153
    Jerk Chicken Sandwich, '98 333
    Mandarin Orange Spread Sandwiches, Chicken-, '04 259
    Marinated Chicken in a Sandwich, '86 185
    Marinated Chicken Sandwiches, '86 M45
    Mozzarella Melt, Italian Chicken-, '95 153
    Open-Faced Mexican Sandwiches, '98 230
    Open-Faced Sandwiches, Summer, '99 201
    Panini, Chicken Florentine, '02 236
    Parmigiana Sandwich, Chicken, '94 65
    Puffed Chicken Sandwiches, '82 35
    Rollups, Greek Chicken, '05 128
    Salad Melts, Open-Faced Cheesy Chicken, '00 134
    Salad Sandwiches, Asian Chicken, '98 223
    Salad Sandwiches, Grilled Chicken, '00 164
    Salad Sandwiches, Hot Chicken, '96 74

SANDWICHES, Chicken
(continued)

Salad with Artichokes, Chicken, **'86** 186
Salad Wraps, Lemon-Basil Chicken, **'00** 216
Saucy Chick-Wiches, **'81** 25; **'82** 31; **'83** 34
Southwestern Chicken Sandwiches, **'96** 23
Spread, Tasty Chicken, **'84** 193
Sprout Sandwiches, Polynesian, **'85** 51
Sub, Chicken, **'98** 287
Tortas, Grilled Chicken, **'01** M187
Wraps, Chicken-Cranberry, **'01** 34
Wraps, Thai Chicken-Avocado, **'02** 206
Chili con Queso Sandwiches, Grilled, **'96** 139
Christmas Tree Sandwiches, **'92** 279
Club Sandwich Bar, Easy, **'91** 279
Club Sandwiches, Double-Decker, **'91** 231; **'92** 68
Club Sandwiches, Egg Salad, **'02** 203
Club Sandwiches, Tangy, **'80** 93
Club Sandwich, Italian, **'01** 22
Clubs, Cobb, **'01** 22
Club, Shrimp-Egg Salad, **'02** 203
Club, Sweet-Pickle Egg Salad, **'02** 203
Confetti Sandwiches, **'79** 236
Crab Burgers, Potato-Crusted, **'94** 139
Cream Cheese Party Sandwiches, Nutty, **'00** 119
Crostini, Feta-Tomato, **'92** 159
Cucumber Pinwheel Sandwiches, **'85** 120
Cucumber-Salmon-Watercress Sandwiches, **'03** 111
Cucumber Sandwiches, **'88** 159; **'90** 81; **'94** 14; **'97** 99; **'00** 208
Cucumber Sandwiches, Dainty, **'81** 119
Curried Tea Sandwiches, **'91** 314
Date-Nut Lettuce Sandwich, **'94** 202
Deli Stuffed Sandwich, **'98** 287
Dried Tomato-and-Basil Sandwiches, **'99** 274
Eggplant Sandwiches, **'99** 240
Eggplant Sandwiches, Baked, **'82** 230
Eggplant Sandwiches, Open-Face, **'95** 124
Eggplant, Tomato, and Feta Sandwiches, **'98** 106
Egg Salad Sandwiches, **'03** 179
Egg Sandwiches, Open-Face, **'83** 292; **'84** 78; **'86** 160
Egg Sandwiches, Open-Faced Cheesy, **'86** 67
Egg Sandwiches, Saucy, **'91** 160
Eggsclusive Sandwiches, **'79** 164; **'80** 130
Eggs-Tra Special Sandwiches, **'81** 240; **'83** 69
Eggwiches, Croissant, **'91** 160
Feta Salad Sandwich, Tuscan, **'99** 289
Fish. *See also* **SANDWICHES/Pita.**
Amberjack Sandwiches, Grilled, **'91** 195
Catfish Sandwiches, Fried, **'02** 60
Grouper Sandwiches, Batter-Fried, **'96** 197
Heroes, Neptune, **'84** 281
Po'boys, Zesty Fish, **'03** 120
Salmon Sandwiches with Dill, Cucumber-, **'02** 131
Tuna-Apple Sandwiches, Curried, **'00** 247
Tuna Burgers, Zippy, **'81** 135
Tuna Cheesies, **'82** 191
Tuna Club Sandwiches, **'83** 134
Tuna Melts, **'02** 60
Tuna Melts, Curried, **'95** 46
Tuna Melts, Hot, **'95** 126; **'96** 201
Tuna Melt, Southwestern, **'96** 201
Tuna Melts, Southwestern, **'95** 127
Tuna Melts, Tempting, **'88** 158
Tuna Salad Rolls, Hot, **'84** 281
Tuna Salad Sandwiches, White Bean-and-, **'02** 31
Tuna Salad, Swiss, **'86** 186
Tuna Sandwich Boats, **'91** 166
Tuna Sandwiches, French Toasted, **'80** 275
Tuna Sandwiches, Grilled-, **'02** 173
Tuna Sandwiches, Hot, **'85** 299; **'86** M194
Tuna Waffle-Wich, Hot, **'88** 272; **'89** 181

Focaccia Sandwiches, **'98** 53
Focaccia Sandwich, Pesto, **'05** 131
Focaccia with Roasted Pepper Vinaigrette, Stuffed, **'04** 142
Frankfurter Sandwiches, **'84** M11
French Toast Sandwiches, Strawberry-, **'91** 160
Fruit-and-Cheese Breakfast Sandwiches, **'89** M21
Fruit Sandwiches, Glazed Breakfast, **'93** 178
Garden Sandwiches, Grilled, **'98** 315
Garden Sandwiches, Open-Faced, **'87** 105
Garden, The, **'83** 134
Goat Cheese-Olive Sandwiches, **'04** 272
Good-Start Sandwiches, **'99** 134
Grilled Bacon, Cheese, and Tomato Sandwiches, **'97** 170
Grilled Cheese, **'97** 328
Grilled Cheese Sandwiches, **'82** M172; **'94** 167
Grilled Cheese Sandwiches with Tomato, Avocado, and Bacon, **'05** 213
Grilled Cheese Sandwich, Mexican, **'92** 63
Grilled Cheeses, Mexican, **'97** 170
Grilled Four-Cheese Sandwich with Tomato, Avocado, and Bacon, **'00** 199
Grilled Sandwiches, Tasty, **'84** 30
Grilled Vegetable Sandwiches, **'01** 310
Grills, Double Cheese, **'97** 170
Grills, Triple Cheese, **'97** 170
Guacamole Sandwiches, **'82** 9; **'83** 68
Guacamole Subs, **'84** 293
Ham. *See also* **SANDWICHES/Pita.**
Asparagus-and-Ham Melt Sandwiches, **'88** M96
Asparagus Sandwiches, Ham-and-, **'01** 307
Baked Ham Sandwiches, **'81** 29
Basket of Sandwiches, Bread, **'86** 126
Blue Cheese-Ham Sandwiches, Creamy, **'87** 279
Cheese-and-Ham Striped Tea Sandwiches, Cheshire Claret, **'94** 16
Cheese Chicken Sandwich, Ham 'n', **'95** 153
Cheese Rolls, Ham-and-, **'82** 3
Cheese Sandwiches, Ham-and-, **'01** 299
Cheese Sandwiches, Hot Ham-and-, **'85** 299
Cheese Sandwiches, Tiny Ham-and-, **'99** 87
Cheese Sandwich Round, Ham-and-, **'94** 326
Cheese Sandwich, Tex-Mex Ham-and-, **'86** 4
Country Ham Loaves, **'86** 255
Croissant Sandwiches, **'89** 161
Deviled Delight, **'83** 130
French Market Sandwiches, **'98** 230
Giant Ham-and-Pepper Salad Sandwich, **'05** 204
Giant Ham-and-Pepper Sandwich, **'96** 74
Grilled Cheese-and-Ham Sandwiches, **'05** 293
Grinder Sandwich, **'85** 299
Hamwiches, **'96** 246
Hideaways, Ham, **'81** 29
Holiday Ham Sandwiches, **'02** 286
Hot Ham Sandwiches, **'79** 214
Hot Rods, Ham, **'86** 136
Loaf, Big Wheel, **'84** 281
Muffuletta, **'04** 27
Omelet Sandwich, **'86** 95
Open-Face Ham Sandwiches, **'82** 40; **'85** 8
Open-Face Sandwiches, **'84** 13
Panhandle Sandwiches, **'01** 56
Party Ham Sandwiches, **'97** 240
Pineapple-Ham Sandwich Loaf, **'91** 167
Pineapple Slaw Sandwiches, Ham-and-, **'96** 199
Po-Boy, Pain-Perdu, **'93** 291
Po'Boys, Guacamole-Topped Ham, **'04** 170
Quesadillas, Quick Fiesta, **'02** 246
Reuben Melts, Southern, **'03** 69
Rollups, Creamy Pineapple-and-Ham, **'04** 163
Salad Boats, **'80** 93
Salad Sandwich, Tangy Ham, **'80** 272
Sebastian, The, **'94** 184
Swiss-and-Asparagus Sandwiches, Ham-, **'01** 52

Swiss, Ham and Eggs à la, **'88** 158
Swiss Sandwiches, Ham-and-, **'98** 287
Swiss Sandwiches, Tangy Ham-and-, **'85** 164
Turkey and Ham Pine-Berry Sandwiches, **'00** 59
Turkey Specials, Cheesy Ham-and-, **'84** 14
Virginia Ham Sandwiches, **'80** 155
Yummy Sandwiches, **'81** 229
Hamburgers, Meatless Walnut, **'96** 243
Hearts of Palm Sandwich, **'92** 191
Heroes, Healthy, **'90** 177
Hero, E-Z, **'92** 63
Hot Browns, **'98** 287
Hot Brown Sandwiches, **'80** M202
Hot Browns, Baby, **'00** 107; **'03** 238
Hot Browns, Biscuit, **'02** 94
Hot Browns, Kentucky, **'02** 94
Hot Browns, Southwestern, **'02** 94
Hot Browns with Fried Cheese Grits, **'02** 94
Italian Pesto Sandwich, Grilled, **'94** 170
Lamb Sandwiches, **'97** 107
Loaf, Mediterranean Picnic, **'96** 156
Mayflower Sandwiches, **'96** 287
Meal-in-One Sandwiches, **'80** 218
Meatball Sandwiches, Open-Faced, **'99** 239
Melts, Bacon-and-Cheese, **'04** 324
Monte Cristo Sandwiches, **'83** 134; **'97** 319
Monte Cristo Sandwiches, Open-Faced, **'01** 171; **'05** 222
Mozzarella-Pepper Bagel Sandwiches, **'98** 145
Muffaletta-Style Po-Boys, **'83** 230
Muffin Stacks, Mushroom-Topped, **'80** 271
Muffuletta Bacon-Olive Party Sandwiches, Mini, **'04** 196
Muffuletta, Doodles, **'94** 35
Muffuletta Loaf, **'97** 86
Muffuletta, Napoleon House, **'94** 35
Muffulettas, **'98** 184
"Muffy" Sandwich, Fertitta's, **'94** 34
Mushroom Bagel Sandwiches with Curry-Mustard Sauce, **'96** 249
Mushroom Sandwiches, Toasted, **'87** 281
Olive-Nut Spread Sandwiches, **'04** 259
Olive Sandwiches, Rolled, **'01** 241
Olive Tea Sandwiches, **'02** 252
Open-Faced Sandwiches, **'79** 214
Open-Faced Sandwiches, Super, **'97** 52
Open-Faced Summer Sandwiches, **'01** 171
Orange Blossom Special, **'88** 158
Party Sandwiches, Bacon-Olive, **'04** 196
Party Sandwiches, Double-Filled, **'93** 159
Party Sandwiches, Duck, **'02** 48
Party Sandwiches, Easter Bunny, **'02** 48
Party Sandwiches, Easter Egg, **'02** 48
Party Sandwiches, Flower, **'02** 48
Peanut Butter-and-Jelly "Fish" Sandwiches, **'91** 177
Peanut Butter-and-Jelly Sandwiches, Christmas Tree, **'85** 319
Peanut Butter Breakfast Sandwich, **'82** 55
Peanut-Cheese-Raisin Sandwiches, **'88** 140
Philly Firecrackers, **'01** 142
Pigs in a Blanket, **'03** 167
Pimiento Cheese Finger Sandwiches, **'99** 86
Pimiento Cheese Sandwiches, **'82** 278
Pineapple-Turkey Melts, **'03** 196
Pita
Alfalfa Pocket Bread Sandwiches, **'82** 282; **'83** 41
Avocado Salad-Hummus Pita, **'02** 99
Bavarian Pita Sandwiches, **'83** 31
Bean Salad Sandwiches, **'81** 243
Beef Pitas, Curried, **'85** 220
Beef Pocket Sandwich, Saucy, **'80** 92
Beef Salad Pocket Sandwiches, **'83** 267
BLT in Pita Pockets, **'93** 158
Breakfast Pita Pockets, **'89** M21

Chef's Salad, '86 186
Chicken-Almond Pocket Sandwiches, '81 240; '83 69
Chicken Pita, Oriental, '89 216
Chicken Salad in a Pocket, '88 139
Chicken-Spinach Pita Pockets, '01 66
Denver Pita Sandwiches, '86 M12
Dried Beef Pita Sandwiches, '86 160
Fajita Pitas, '99 239
Falafel Sandwiches, '96 23
Fruit Salad Pita, Fresh, '02 99
Garbanzo-Vegetable Pitas, '00 58
Ham-and-Cheese Pita Pockets, '90 271
Ham-and-Cheese Pita Sandwiches, '87 202; '88 44
Ham and Swiss in the Pocket, '83 31
Hearty Pocket Sandwiches, '80 93
Hot Pita Sandwiches, '83 217; '87 M6
Lamb Pockets with Dilled Cucumber Topping, '87 104
Mango-Chicken Pita Sandwiches, '03 123
Oriental Stuffed Pockets, '79 14
Pita Sandwiches, '84 139
Salad Sandwiches, Pita, '83 134
Shrimp Pitas, '05 188
Sloppy Joe Pocket Sandwiches, '81 200
Spinach-Walnut Pitas, '87 202; '88 43
Steaks, Greek Pocket, '81 262
Stuffed Pita, '89 87
Stuffed Pitas, Acadian, '90 177
Tabbouleh Pitas, '98 105
Taco Pitas, '83 31
Tuna-in-a-Pita Pocket, '87 202
Tuna Pockets, '88 139
Tuna Roll Sandwiches, '96 199
Turkey-Mozzarella Rounds, '82 3
Turkey Salad Pita Sandwiches, '87 202; '88 43
Vegetable Pita Sandwiches, '96 199
Vegetable Pockets, '85 215
Vegetarian Pita Sandwiches, '84 193
Pizza Sandwiches, Open-Face, '82 3; '83 85; '84 M198; '85 22
Pizza Sandwich, Giant, '80 93
Po' Boys, Fried Buffalo Oyster, '05 48
Po' Boys, Fried Green Tomato, '05 330
Pork Dip Sandwiches, Easy Spanish, '04 312
Pork Sandwiches, Barbecue, '00 23
Pork Sandwiches, Party, '88 M273
Pork Sandwiches with Apricot Mayonnaise, Jamaican Jerk, '97 320
Pork Sandwiches with Rosemary-Garlic Mayonnaise, Adobo, '01 322
Pork Tenderloin Sandwiches, '00 333
Pork Tenderloin Sandwiches with Bourbon Sauce, '02 53
Pork Tenderloin Sandwiches with Cranberry-Coriander Conserve, '04 286
Pork with Pecan Biscuits, Peppered, '01 33
Portobello Mushroom Burgers, '01 144
Portobello Pizza Burgers, Grilled, '00 89
Pound Cake Dessert Sandwich, Grilled, '94 171
Raisin Country Sandwich, '91 168
Rarebit, Tangy Welsh, '88 159
Rarebit, Uptown Welsh, '87 279
Rarebit, Welsh, '00 239
Rarebit with Tomatoes and Bacon, Welsh, '92 M159
Rollups, Parmesan-Turkey-Ranch, '01 177
Salad Rolls, Hearty, '81 206
Salami Sandwiches, Open-Faced, '87 279
Sausage and Pepper Loaves, Italian, '83 11
Sausage Burgers, '96 102
Sausage-Cheese Loaves, '88 235
Sausage-Cheese Muffin Sandwiches, '92 M212
Sausage in a Sleeping Bag, '98 206
Sausage Sandwiches with Mustard Sauce, '84 250
Sausage Sandwich, Italian, '80 92
Sausage Sloppy Joes, Italian, '86 160
Sausage-Stuffed French Loaf, '90 19

Seafood. *See also* **SANDWICHES/Pita.**
Caribbean Seafood Sandwiches, '98 105
Club Sandwich, South Seas, '84 282
Crab-and-Cheese Sandwiches, Hot, '87 279
Crab Burgers, '00 58
Crab Cake Sandwiches, '02 60
Crab Cake Sandwiches, Miniature, '96 306
Crabmeat Sandwiches, '84 285
Crabmeat Sandwiches, Avocado-, '83 2
Crabmeat Sandwiches, Deluxe, '81 M74
Crab Melts, Open-Faced, '01 171
Crab Salad Sandwiches, Mango-, '99 72
Crab Sandwiches, Open-Faced, '87 106
Crab Sandwiches, Puffy, '83 291
Crab Tomato Sandwiches, Open-Face, '81 29
English Muffin Delight, '82 45
Hot Brown, Seafood, '88 158
Oyster-and-Bacon Poor Boys, '87 40
Oyster Loaves, Spinach-, '84 213
Oyster Po'boys, Dressed, '02 184
Oyster Po'boys, Dressed Mini, '01 33
Oyster Submarine Sandwich, '80 92
Po'Boy, Grilled Seafood, '96 244
Shrimp-and-Egg Salad Sandwiches, '94 182
Shrimp Burgers, '03 110
Shrimp-Cheese Sandwiches, '85 242
Shrimp-Cornbread Sandwiches, Open-Faced, '02 141
Shrimp Destin, '82 29
Shrimp Gyros with Herbed Yogurt Spread, Grilled-, '02 169
Shrimp Po' Boys, '97 312
Shrimp Po'boys, '02 184
Shrimp Rolls, '03 162; '05 188
Shrimp Salad, '86 186
Shrimp Salad on Croissants, '96 175
Shrimp Salad Sandwiches, '90 178
Sloppy Joe Meatball Hoagies, '00 242
Sloppy José Sandwiches with Cilantro Slaw, '05 324
Sloppy Toms, '91 51
Snack Buns, '87 279
Snackwiches, '88 172
Spider Sandwiches, '93 193
Spinach Fondue Sandwiches, Grilled, '99 337
Spinach Fondue Sandwich, Grilled, '94 171
Spinach Sandwiches, Fresh, '85 59
Squash Sandwiches, Skillet, '98 144
Stacking Sandwiches, '86 127
Sticky Fingers, '03 M168
Stromboli, '88 272
Stuffed Sandwich, Italian, '99 15
Stuffin' Muffin, '99 193
Submarine Sandwiches, Superb, '84 250
Sweet Smoky Sandwiches, '97 219
Tea Sandwiches, Gingered, '84 116
Tempting Twosome, '81 240; '83 69
Tofu-Veggie Sandwiches, Open-Face, '86 5
Tomatillo Sandwiches, Open-Faced, '92 246
Tomato-Cheese-Bacon Melts, '99 72
Tomatoes with Cheese Sauce over Toast, '88 159
Tomato Sandwiches, Fried Green, '04 145
Tomato Sandwiches, Miniature, '00 130
Tomato Sandwich, Floyd's Favorite, '95 172; '00 182
Tomato, Swiss, and Bacon Sandwiches, '04 140
Torta, Mediterranean, '98 23
Tortilla Stack-Ups, '92 196
Tuna. *See* **SANDWICHES/Fish, Pita.**
Turkey and Ham Pine-Berry Sandwiches, '00 59
Turkey-Asparagus Sandwiches, '96 74
Turkey, Bacon, and Havarti Sandwich, '05 92
Turkey-Cheese Dogs, '97 203
Turkey-Cheese Puffs, '87 301
Turkey-Cranberry Croissant, '96 320
Turkey Hero Sandwiches, '92 196
Turkey Hero with Garlic Sauce, '90 145

Turkey-in-the-Slaw Sandwich, '90 177
Turkey Melt, Loaded, '05 159
Turkey Melts, Oven-Grilled Loaded, '05 159
Turkey, Mozzarella, and Blackberry Sandwiches, Smoked, '99 220
Turkey Open-Facers, '82 190
Turkey-Roasted Pepper Sandwiches, Smoked, '94 66
Turkey Sandwiches with Cranberry Salsa, '00 269
Turkey Sandwich, Hot, '93 306
Turkey Sandwich, Pineapple-, '01 85
Turkey Sandwich, Waffle-Grilled, '94 170
Turkey Schoolwich Sandwiches, '00 198
Turkey Tea Sandwiches, '99 86
Turkey Turnovers, Mexican, '02 245
Turkey Wraps, Smoked, '01 61
Vegetable Garden Heroes, '84 14
Vegetable Puff Sandwich, '85 51
Vegetable Salad Rolls, '82 278
Vegetable Sandwiches, Creamy, '97 122
Vegetarian Melt, Open-Faced, '87 106
Vegewiches, '99 86
Veggie Sandwich, Big, '92 196
Victoria Sandwiches, '94 16
Vidalia Sandwiches on Salt-Rising Bread, '79 145
Watercress-Cucumber Sandwiches, '97 108
Watercress Sandwiches, '90 82
Wraps
Black Bean Wraps, '00 211
BLT Wrap, '04 298
BLT Wraps, '05 224
BLT Wrap, Southwest, '03 90
Chicken-and-Bean Slaw Wraps, '04 163
Chicken-and-Slaw Wraps, '05 222
Chicken-Avocado Wraps, Thai, '02 206
Chicken-Cranberry Wraps, '01 34
Chicken Salad with Cabbage Wraps, Spicy, '04 62
Chicken Salad Wraps, Lemon-Basil, '00 216
Club Wraps, '01 23
Garden Wrap, '03 168
Mediterranean Wrap, '03 168
Roast Beef Wraps, Tangy-and-Sweet, '05 92
Smoked Turkey Wraps, '01 61
Tacos Wrapidos, '03 172
Turkey Lettuce Wraps, Crispy Ginger-and-Garlic Asian, '05 325
Turkey Wrap, '03 168
Turkey Wraps, '00 318
Wreath, Festive Sandwich, '86 333
Zucchini Sandwiches, Open-Faced, '88 159
SAUCES. *See also* **CHOCOLATE/Sauces;**
       CHUTNEYS; DESSERTS/Sauces; GRAVIES;
       MARINADES; MUSTARD/Sauces; PESTOS;
       RELISHES; SALSAS; SYRUPS; TOPPINGS.
Aioli, Mint, '01 71
Aioli, Picante, '99 53
Alfredo Sauce, '94 84
Almond Sauce, Asparagus with, '91 117
Ancho Chile Cream, '87 121
Ancho Chile Sauce, '87 122
Anchovy-Garlic Sauce over Vermicelli, '86 158
Artichoke-Pepper Sauce, Chicken Breasts with, '05 139
Avgolemono Sauce, '94 48
Avocado Sauce, Chunky, '03 128
Balsamic Sauce, '98 319
Barbecue
Apple Barbecue Sauce, '99 173
Bannister's Barbecue Sauce, '92 166
Barbecue Sauce, '84 172; '86 153; '88 218; '91 16, 205; '93 129; '94 27
Basting Sauce, '90 120
Basting Sauce, Grill, '00 177
Beer Barbecue Sauce, '84 173
Bourbon Barbecue Sauce, '85 90
Chipotle 'Cue Sauce, Smoky, '04 87

SAUCES, Barbecue
(continued)

Cider Vinegar Barbecue Sauce, '01 148
Cola Barbecue Sauce, '03 130; '04 104
Crickhollow Barbecue Sauce, '99 200
Dressed-Up Barbecue Sauce, '84 173
Eastern-Style Barbecue Sauce, '88 145
Easy Barbecue Sauce, '79 90; '82 178
Green Barbecue Sauce, '02 183
Handcrafted Barbecue Sauce, '98 45
Honey Barbecue Sauce, '04 197
Honey-Mustard Barbecue Sauce, '05 167
John Wills's Barbecue Sauce, '92 255
Lemon Barbecue Sauce, Herbed, '94 154; '98 334
Lemony Barbecue Sauce, '95 31
Maple Syrup Barbecue Sauce, '94 154
Mustard Barbecue Sauce, '84 173
Oven Barbecue Sauce, '82 233
Paprika Barbecue Sauce, '79 90
Paul's Barbecue Sauce, '05 175
Peanut Butter Barbecue Sauce, '81 233
Peppery Barbecue Sauce, '00 255
Piquant Barbecue Sauce, '79 159
Ranch-Barbecue Sauce, '05 163
Raspberry-Barbecue Sauce, '05 203
Savory Barbecue Sauce, '86 153
Southwest Barbecue Sauce, Spicy, '94 154
Special Barbecue Sauce, '82 177
Sweet-and-Sour 'Cue Sauce, '04 87
Sweet-and-Tangy Barbecue Sauce, '00 119
Sweet Sauce, '90 120
Tangy Barbecue Sauce, '97 323; '99 104; '00 230
Texas Barbecue Sauce, '99 210
The Sauce, '00 177
Thick and Robust Barbecue Sauce, '94 95
Thick and Sweet Barbecue Sauce, '94 95
Thin and Tasty Barbecue Sauce, '94 95
Tomato Barbecue Sauce, Fresh, '84 172
Vinegar Sauce, Peppery, '01 148
Western-Style Barbecue Sauce, '88 145
White Barbecue Sauce, '94 95; '05 196
White Barbecue Sauce, Chicken with, '89 M84;
    '97 322; '01 168
Zippy Barbecue Sauce, '92 166
Basil and Cream Sauce, '90 118
Basil-Brown Butter Sauce, '93 92
Basil Cream, '89 159
Basil-Cream Sauce, Beef Ravioli in, '05 293
Basil Cream Sauce, New Potatoes with, '91 46
Basil Sauce, '90 85
Basil Sauce, Asparagus with, '86 33
Basting Sauce, '01 106
Basting Sauce, Grilled Chicken with, '01 146
Bean Sauce, Pork-and-Onions with, '85 76
Béarnaise Sauce, '83 138; '85 37; '86 193; '89 201;
    '96 133, 174
Béarnaise Sauce, Blender, '81 90
Béarnaise Sauce, Classic, '86 244
Béarnaise Sauce, Quick, '82 84
Béchamel Sauce, '80 190; '83 277; '84 M239; '87 286;
    '91 94; '96 239
Beef-and-Pasta Sauce Dip, Creamy, '01 108
Beef Sauce, Szechuan Noodles with Spicy, '97 95
Beer Sauce, '95 266
Beurre Blanc Sauce, '98 240
Black Bean Sauce, '93 59; '98 46
Black Bean Sauce, Southwest Pork in, '05 139
Black Bean Sauce, Spicy Beef Fillets with, '97 184
Bordelaise Sauce, '83 138, 262
Bouillon Sauce, '80 8
Bourbon Sauce, '02 53
Brandy-Butter Sauce, '79 230

Brandy Sauce, Carrots in, '83 86
Brandy Sauce, Lemony-Butter Steak with, '85 78
Brisket Mopping Sauce, '03 188
Brisket Red Sauce, '03 188
Broccoli Sauce, '91 85
Brown Butter Sauce, '91 65
Brown Sauce, '89 32; '94 15, 240
Buttermilk Sauce, '84 6
Butter Sauce, '86 268; '05 124
Butter Sauce, Vegetable, '86 174
Caper Sauce, '05 105
Caramel-Brandy Sauce, Steaks with, '03 56
Caramel Sauce, '04 249
Caribe, Jamaican Pork Tenderloin with Sauce, '02 320
Catsup Sauce, '81 228
Catsup Topping, '81 170
Champagne-Saffron Sauce, Scallops with, '93 177
Champagne Sauce, '90 29
Champagne Sauce, Chicken Breasts with, '86 49
Chanterelle Brown Sauce, '89 62
Cheese
    Blue Cheese Sauce, '90 142; '94 320
    Blue Cheese Sauce, Fettuccine with, '98 247
    Brussels Sprouts with Cheese Sauce, '79 246
    Cheddar Cheese Cream Sauce, '05 277
    Cheddar Cheese Sauce, '91 286
    Cheddar-Cider Sauce, '98 242
    Cheese Sauce, '79 M156; '81 43, 44, 225; '82 M123;
        '83 49, 138, 188; '84 57; '85 92; '86 241; '88 78,
        272; '89 181, 229; '90 235; '93 48; '02 94;
        '04 281; '05 333
    Cottage Cheese Sauce, '87 232
    Cream Sauce, Cheesy, '82 79
    Easy Cheese Sauce, '79 22
    Garlic-Cheese Sauce, '84 M70
    Goat Cheese Sauce, Asparagus with, '93 116
    Guilt-Free Cheese Sauce, '93 M95
    Heather Sauce, '84 182
    Lemon-Cheese Sauce, '91 24
    Lemony Cheese Sauce, '84 183
    Monterey Jack Sauce, '84 293
    Mornay Sauce, '80 120; '81 90; '83 138; '84 295;
        '89 195
    Mushroom-Cheese Sauce, '83 190; '86 48
    Parmesan Cheese Sauce, '79 165; '80 162; '85 143
    Parmesan Sauce, '92 17
    Parmesan-Sour Cream Sauce, Baked Fish with, '01 209
    Pimiento Cheese Sauce, '02 291; '05 333
    Rich Cheese Sauce, '81 89
    Roquefort Sauce, '89 321
    Rosemary-Parmesan Sauce, Tortellini with, '92 284
    Seafood Cheese Sauce, '89 240
    Stilton-Portobello Sauce, Beef Filets with, '00 309
    Swiss Cheese Cream Sauce, '05 277
    Swiss Cheese Sauce, '79 35; '87 289; '88 135; '03 52
    Swiss Sauce, '83 M195
    Swiss Sauce, Creamy, '80 M53
    Topper, Vegetable-Cheese Potato, '86 6
    Turnips in Cheese Sauce, '84 229
    Vegetable-Cheese Sauce, '85 M152
    Vegetable Sauce, Cheesy, '92 M134
    Walnut-Parmesan Pesto Sauce, '97 104
    Wine-Cheese Sauce, '00 310
Chervil-and-Savory Sauce, '90 117
Chervil Sauce, '83 128
Chicken-and-Creamy Herb Sauce, Fettuccine with, '01 257
Chicken Curry Sauce, '90 117
Chicken Sauce, Creamy, '81 91
Chile Corn Jus, '00 197
Chile Sauce, Hot, '92 156
Chili Meat Sauce, '83 4
Chili Sauce, '81 175; '94 287
Chili Sauce, Chunky, '85 188
Chili Sauce, Miss Kitty's, '04 231

Chili Sauce, Spicy, '87 127
Chili Sauce, Sweet, '01 237
Chive Butter Sauce, '03 91
Chive Sauce, Steamed Broccoli with Tangy, '83 101
Cider-Port Wine Reduction Sauce, '96 245
Cider Sauce, '87 224; '05 259
Cilantro Cream, '87 121
Cilantro Vinaigrette, '97 126
Clam Sauce, Tricolor Pasta with, '93 272
Cocktail Sauce, '87 128; '90 242
Cocktail Sauce, Boiled Shrimp with, '79 151
Cocktail Sauce, Coastal, '92 254
Cocktail Sauce, Delta, '91 147
Cocktail Sauce, French Fried Zucchini with, '86 146
Cocktail Sauce, Paul's, '05 244
Cocktail Sauce, Southwestern, '98 46
Cocktail Sauce, Spicy, '83 258
Come Back Sauce, '00 211
Corn Sauce, Fresh, '98 43
Country Ham Sauce, '05 109
Cream Sauce, '85 291; '93 157; '01 43; '03 237;
    '05 248
Cream Sauce, Brandied, '82 70
Cream Sauce, Peppery, '88 206
Cream Sauce, Sherried, '84 210; '85 M152
Cream Sauce, Shrimp in, '84 M286
Cream Sauce, Spicy, '82 45
Cream-Wine Sauce, Potatoes in, '86 18
Creamy Sauce, '79 41
Creamy Sauce, Grilled Chicken, with, '01 318
Creolaise Sauce, '83 91, 262
Creole Cream Sauce, Shrimp and Pasta with, '05 49
Creole Sauce, '89 228; '90 28; '92 87; '98 98, 142;
    '02 32, 284
Creole Sauce, Crescent City Grill, '04 289
Creole Sauce, Simple, '05 203
Cress Sauce, '96 176
Cucumber-and-Yogurt Dipping Sauce, '02 172
Cucumber Cream Sauce, '92 33
Cucumber-Dill Sauce, '86 5; '91 62; '92 51
Cucumber Dipping Sauce, '94 47
Cucumber Sauce, '82 111; '84 M286; '92 41
Cucumber Sauce, Lamb Burgers with, '98 102
Cucumber Sauce, Lemony, '89 245
Cucumber Sauce, Tuna Steaks with, '97 180
Cucumber Sauce, White Bean Spread with Creamy,
    '00 178
Cucumber-Yogurt Sauce, '03 44
Cumberland Sauce, '92 309; '00 256
Currant Jelly Sauce, Quail with, '86 94
Currant Sauce, '87 240
Curried Cream Sauce, Turkey Slices with, '91 60
Curried Rum Sauce, '91 164
Curried Sour Cream Sauce, '90 174
Curry-Mustard Sauce, '96 249
Curry Sauce, '79 M156; '83 138; '84 M71; '94 54;
    '95 18; '97 170; '99 92
Curry Sauce, Asparagus with, '90 17
Curry Sauce, Chicken, '90 117
Custard Sauce, '89 291
Custard Sauce, Bourbon, '95 271
Dijon-Caper Cream Sauce, Broiled Salmon with, '98 329
Dijon Horseradish Sauce, '03 297
Dijon Mustard Sauce, Creamy, '04 198
Dijon Sauce, '03 93
Dijon Vinaigrette, '00 222
Dill Sauce, '84 M70, 107; '85 39; '88 162; '95 216;
    '98 157
Dill Sauce, Chilled Salmon with, '84 285
Dill Sauce, Creamy, '79 M156; '94 42
Dill Sauce, Salmon Steaks with, '85 164
Dill Sauce, Tangy, '04 320
Dipper's Delight, '98 93
Dipping Sauce, Citrus, '97 208

Dipping Sauce, "Come Back," '96 213
Dipping Sauce, Creamy Cilantro, '03 327
Dipping Sauce, Fried Green Tomatillos with Jalapeño, '97 143
Dipping Sauce, Ginger, '03 64
Dipping Sauce, Grilled Chicken with Sweet Soy Slaw and, '04 123
Dipping Sauce, Grilled Salmon with Sweet Soy Slaw and, '04 123
Dipping Sauce, Hoisin Peanut, '99 14
Dipping Sauce, Olive Oil-Balsamic, '04 46
Dipping Sauce, Orange, '03 M212
Dipping Sauce, Sesame-Soy, '02 145
Dipping Sauce, Thai, '97 236
Drunken Sauce, '03 33
Dunk Sauce, John's, '97 129
Egg Foo Yong Sauce, '86 232
Emerald Sauce, '90 63
Enchilada Sauce, '81 194
Enchilada Sauce, Red Chile, '85 245
Florentine Sauce, '93 48
Foo Yong Sauce, '80 223
French Sauce, Broccoli with, '81 295
Fruit
Apple-Bourbon Sauce, '99 142
Apple-Horseradish Sauce, '82 229
Apple-Pear Sauce, '97 M272
Apple Sauce, Pork Chops with Sweet-and-Sour, '98 132
Apricot Sauce, '87 172
Apricot-Sauced Pork Chops, '85 22
Apricot Sauce, Pork Tenderloin with, '99 44
Avocado Béarnaise Sauce, '01 317
Avocado-Lime Sauce, '03 90
Avocado-Lime Sauce, Grilled Swordfish with, '97 127
Avocado Sauce, '80 198; '83 200
Avocado-Tomatillo Sauce, '95 206
Blackberry Sauce, Pork Medaillons with, '02 136
Blueberry Sauce, '80 144; '86 248
Cherry-Merlot Sauce and Gorgonzola, Peppered Sirloin with, '02 320
Cherry Sauce, '83 276; '84 91; '91 67
Cherry Sauce, Elegant, '79 M156
Cherry Sauce, Pork Fillets with Dark, '04 221
Cherry Sauce, Roast Ducklings with, '86 312
Cherry Sauce, Roast Pork with Spiced, '89 324
Cherry Sauce, Royal, '85 224; '86 83
Cherry Sauce, Spicy, '83 244
Cherry-Wine Sauce, '95 285
Citrus Sauce, Stuffed Flounder Rolls with, '85 180
Cranberry-Apple Sauce, '92 203
Cranberry-Apple Sauce, Double, '03 231
Cranberry-Apricot Sauce, Fresh, '87 243
Cranberry Jezebel Sauce, '03 250
Cranberry Juice Sauce, '85 224; '86 83
Cranberry-Orange Sauce, '05 218
Cranberry-Raisin Sauce, Baked Ham with, '88 244
Cranberry Sauce, '92 269
Cranberry Sauce, Baked, '88 257
Cranberry Sauce, Cornish Hens with, '79 180
Cranberry Sauce, Fresh, '79 283; '84 275; '04 271
Cranberry Sauce, Holiday, '02 M311
Cranberry Sauce, Spiced, '96 267
Cranberry Sauce, Tart, '83 261
Cranberry Wine Sauce, '83 276
Devonshire Cream, Mock, '81 288
Devonshire Sauce, Processor, '86 337; '87 58
Dipping Sauce, Citrus, '97 208
Fruit Sauce, '81 177
Grand Marnier Fruit Sauce, '90 93
Grape Sauce, Mahimahi in, '91 218
Honey-Lime Sauce, '82 85
Jezebel Sauce, '81 29; '82 55; '93 331; '96 212; '02 219

Jezebel Sauce, Gingered, '04 M138
Lemon Basting Sauce, '95 32
Lemon-Butter Sauce, '84 252; '92 337
Lemon-Butter Sauce, New Potatoes with, '00 103
Lemon-Celery Sauce, Baked Fillets in, '84 91
Lemon-Cheese Sauce, '91 24
Lemon Cream Sauce, '99 53
Lemon Cream Sauce, Braised Chicken Breast in, '94 184
Lemon-Dill Sauce, Potatoes and Green Beans with, '01 89
Lemon Dipping Sauce, '02 134
Lemon Garlic Sauce, Shrimp in, '83 67
Lemon-Herb Sauce, Hot, '91 286
Lemon Meunière Sauce, '88 222
Lemon-Mustard Sauce, Salmon Steaks with, '97 124
Lemon Parsley Sauce, '81 106
Lemon-Parsley Sauce, '93 48
Lemon Sauce, '82 290
Lemon Sauce, Asparagus with, '86 62
Lemon Sauce, Chicken Scallopini with, '86 156
Lemon Sauce, Pecan Catfish with, '03 185; '05 56
Lemon Sauce, Red Snapper with, '01 83
Lemon Sauce, Zesty, '97 318
Lime-Saffron Sauce, '94 71
Lime Sauce, Creamy, '04 119
Lime Sauce, Fresh Fruit with, '02 68
Lime Sauce, Sour Cream-, '91 286
Mandarin-Almond Cream Sauce, '84 183
Mandarin Sauce, '84 60
Mandarin-Teriyaki Sauce, '96 68
Mango-Pineapple Hot Sauce, '04 183
Maraschino-Orange Sauce, '96 164
Mimosa, Sauce, '88 288
Muscadine Sauce, '04 231
Orange-Almond Sauce, Chicken in, '79 219; '80 13
Orange-Almond Sauce, Grilled Snapper with, '01 158
Orange Butter Sauce, Asparagus with, '85 43
Orange-Curry Sauce and Coconut Rice, Polynesian Pork Tenderloin with, '04 309
Orange-Dijon Sauce, '00 259
Orange-Ginger Sauce, Chicken Breasts with, '97 47
Orange-Ginger Sauce, Sesame-Crusted Scallops with, '97 125
Orange-Honey Sauce, '97 236
Orange, Lime, and Ginger Sauce, Chicken with, '92 123
Orange Liqueur Sauce, '86 142
Orange Sauce, '82 47; '83 10, 277; '84 M286; '98 83
Orange Sauce, Asparagus with, '83 46
Orange Sauce, Broccoli with, '04 285
Orange Sauce, Brussels Sprouts in, '86 55
Orange Sauce, Celery in, '79 70
Orange Sauce, Chicken Breasts with, '79 77
Orange Sauce, Grilled Duck with, '94 305
Orange Sauce, Lobster Tails with Spiced, '86 155
Orange Sauce, Shrimp in, '99 292
Orange Sauce, Sunshine, '79 70
Orange Sauce, Sweet, '93 M325
Peach-Blueberry Pancake Sauce, '82 177
Peach-Blueberry Sauce, '81 170
Peach Sauce, '92 203
Peach Sauce, Creamy Fresh, '79 177
Peach Sauce, Pork Loin Dijonnaise with, '97 87
Peach Sauce, Tangy, '96 89
Pineapple-Curry Sauce, '79 252
Pineapple-Rhubarb Sauce, '88 94
Pineapple Sauce, '84 236; '92 203
Pineapple Sauce, Raisin-, '82 177
Plum Sauce, '80 249; '82 40; '88 152
Plum Sauce, Chinese, '82 237
Plum Sauce, Crispy Ribs with, '98 182
Plum Sauce, Fresh, '97 176
Plum Sauce, Gingered, '87 175

Plum Sauce, Red, '80 49
Plum Sauce, Spareribs in, '99 136
Plum Sauce, Spicy, '86 11
Raspberry-Chipotle Sauce, Jerk Turkey Tenderloin with, '05 M194
Rosemary-Cherry Sauce, '02 193
Strawberry-Banana Sauce, '81 41
Strawberry Sauce, Make-Ahead French Toast with, '02 131
Tangy Sauce for Fruit, '90 161
Tomatillo Sauce, '94 231; '95 206; '97 25
Tomatillo Sauce, Grilled Jerk Shrimp with Creamy, '01 332
Tomatillo Sauce, Roasted Chiles Rellenos with, '94 203
Tropical Fruit Sauce, Grilled Shrimp with, '01 195
White Grape Sauce, '80 38
Garlic Buerre Blanc Sauce, '88 222
Garlic-Butter Sauce, '95 327
Garlic Butter Sauce, '05 M253
Garlic-Chive Butter Sauce, '90 96
Garlic-Ginger Butter Sauce, '94 89
Garlic Sauce, '92 56
Garlic Sauce, Chicken with, '00 270
Garlic Sauce, Pork in, '04 181
Garlic Sauce, Roasted, '95 268; '98 176
Garlic Sauce, Stir-Fried Pork in, '84 141
Garlic Sauce, Turkey Hero with, '90 145
Ginger-Soy Sauce, '91 33
Ginger Vinaigrette, '95 162
Greek Sauce, '91 183
Green Bell Pepper Sauce, '97 261
Green Chile Sauce, '82 220
Green Mole Sauce, '95 267
Green Pea Sauce, '83 22
Green Peppercorn Sauce, Beef Fillets with, '02 285
Green Peppercorn Sauce, Beef Tenderloin Filets with, '00 309
Green Sauce, Herbed, '86 244
Grill Basting Sauce, '95 236; '03 312
Guacamole, '89 226
Ham-and-Mushroom Sauce, Steak with, '83 109
Ham Sauce, Country, '90 117; '96 24
Henry Bain Sauce, Beef Tenderloin with, '00 107; '01 20; '04 52
Herb Butter Sauce, Corn with, '79 150
Herb-Mayonnaise Sauce, '85 73
Herb Sauce, '91 29
Herb Sauce, Green, '83 36
Herb Sauce, Spicy, '03 281
Hollandaise Sauce, '80 M107, M268; '81 90; '83 137; '85 295; '86 94; '87 195; '88 58, M177, 222; '89 24; '92 93; '95 86; '98 55; '03 52
Hollandaise Sauce, Blender, '79 39; '82 84, 234
Hollandaise Sauce, Broccoli with, '79 244, 276
Hollandaise Sauce, Broccoli with Mock, '82 272
Hollandaise Sauce, Chipotle, '03 53
Hollandaise Sauce, Classic, '88 53
Hollandaise Sauce, Easy Dilled, '92 107
Hollandaise Sauce, Lime, '93 121
Hollandaise Sauce, Mock, '85 49; '93 68
Hollandaise Sauce, Zesty, '04 284
Hollandaise-Shrimp Sauce, Flounder with, '86 234
Hollandaise, Tangy, '85 148
Hollandaise, Tasso, '04 67
Hollandaise, Three-Pepper, '96 52
Honey-Butter Sauce, '85 18; '98 45
Honey-Lemon Mustard Sauce, '84 275
Honey-Mustard Sauce, '85 13
Honey-Mustard Sauce, Chicken Fingers with, '05 300
Honey-Mustard Sauce, Smoked Ribs with, '92 168
Honey-Poppy Seed Sauce, '93 13
Honey Sauce, '99 210
Honey Sauce, Chicken in, '89 82
Honey Sauce, Chicken Strips with, '03 27

Horseradish Cream Sauce, Pepper-Seared Beef Tenderloin with, '01 280
Horseradish-Mustard Sauce, Creamy, '88 M177
Horseradish Sauce, '84 190; '85 224; '86 83; '87 127; '88 207, M273; '91 183; '93 215; '02 19; '05 177, 203
Horseradish Sauce and Curried Bananas, Fillets with, '85 230
Horseradish Sauce, Broccoli with, '81 2; '83 206; '84 33
Horseradish Sauce, Carrots and Broccoli with, '91 246
Horseradish Sauce, Spicy, '02 235
Horseradish Sauce, Zesty, '04 284
Horseradish Sour Cream, '86 244
Hot Diggity Dog Sauce, '93 198
Hot Sauce, '79 185; '83 74
Hot Sauce, San Antonio, '84 291
Hunter Sauce, '95 317
Italian Sauce, '80 63; '90 67
Italian Sauce, Quick, '82 230
Italian-Style Sauce, '83 250
Jalapeño-Cherry Sauce, Smoked Pork Chops with, '01 208
Jalapeño-Cranberry Sauce, '92 310
Jalapeño Dipping Sauce, Fried Green Tomatillos with, '97 143
Jalapeño Sauce, '80 193
Jalapeño Tartar Sauce, '96 69; '98 129
Jezebel Sauce, '81 29; '82 55; '93 331; '96 212; '02 219
Juniper Sauce, '93 278
Lingonberry Sauce, Turkey Tenderloins with, '97 289
Louis Sauce, '03 66
Mahogany Sauce, '91 148
Maple Brown Sauce, '96 232
Maple-Cider Sauce, '95 288
Marinara Sauce, '82 178; '89 239; '92 18
Maui Sauce, '99 310
Meat Sauce for Spaghetti, '00 256
Meat Sauce, Italian, '01 160
Meat Sauce, Spaghetti with, '02 188
Mediterranean Sauce, '94 83
Meunière Sauce, '80 57
Mexican Sauce, '80 198
Microwaving Sauces, '84 M70
Mint Sauce, '84 107; '88 M96
Mint Sauce over Vegetables, '92 104
Molasses Sauce, Grilled Pork Tenderloin with, '97 193
Mole Sauce, Burgundy, '98 174
Mushroom-Artichoke Sauce, Creamy, '05 312
Mushroom-Dill Sauce, '80 271
Mushroom Sauce, '81 90, 200; '82 46; '83 71, 205, 212; '84 M70; '85 40; '86 198; '87 36, 186, 284; '91 221; '03 255
Mushroom Sauce, Chicken with, '99 22; '04 255
Mushroom Sauce, Eggs Baked in, '93 47
Mushroom Sauce, Filet Mignon with, '94 250
Mushroom Sauce, Peppered Tuna with, '05 72
Mushroom Sauce, Savory, '96 236
Mushroom Sauce, Spicy Sherried, '89 239
Mushroom Sauce, Spinach Loaf with, '01 277
Mushroom Sauce Supreme on Vermicelli, '86 158
Mushroom-Wine Sauce, '84 84; '86 24; '00 125
Mustard Sauce, '01 102; '02 162, 245
Mustard Sauce, Special, '01 159
Natillas Sauce, '83 179
Niçoise, Sauce, '96 190
Not-So-Secret Sauce, '03 139
Olive-Butter Sauce, Broccoli with, '83 118
Onion-Balsamic Sauce, '99 44
Onion Cream Sauce, '87 232
Onion-Mushroom Sauce, '85 224; '86 84
Onion-Parsley Sauce, '85 148
Onion Sauce, '82 72; '87 248
Onion Sauce, Brussels Sprouts in, '81 308
Pancake Sauce, Cinnamon-Pecan-Honey, '88 46

Parsley-Caper Sauce, Tortellini with, '93 175
Parsley-Chive Sauce, '84 212
Parsley-Garlic Sauce, '83 138; '84 M70
Parsley Sauce, '82 248; '86 108
Peanut Basil Sauce, Thai-Style Noodles with, '98 133
Peanut Dipping Sauce, Hoisin, '99 14
Peanut Hot Sauce, '86 305
Peanut Sauce, '99 134; '02 173; '04 324
Peanut Sauce, Hot Indonesian, '93 211
Peanut Sauce, Shrimp with, '93 303
Peanut Sauce, Spicy, '96 93; '04 134
Pecan-Butter Sauce, '91 65
Pecan Pasta Sauce, '96 262
Pepper-Onion Sauce, '84 125
Pepper Sauce, '01 211; '02 106
Pesto-Clam Sauce, Pasta with, '98 17
Pesto Sauce, '89 280; '91 94; '95 267
Pesto Sauce, Racy, '97 67
Picante-Bean Sauce, '96 220
Pico de Gallo, '98 174
Pig Sauce, '98 203
Pizza Sauce, '00 314
Pizza Sauce, Traditional, '95 267
Portobello-Alfredo Sauce, Fettuccine with, '04 135
Portobello-Marsala Sauce, '05 280
Port Wine Sauce, '84 252
Pumpkin Seed Sauce, '88 246
Raisin Sauce, '83 59, 215; '84 91, 275; '87 127; '89 58; '99 19; '02 278
Raisin Sauce, Ham with, '82 M76
Red Bell Pepper Sauce, '99 267
Red Chile Sauce, '94 251; '95 17
Red Chili Sauce, '85 245
Red Hot Sauce, '93 158
Red or Green Pepper Sauce, '91 85
Red Pepper-Garlic Sauce, '98 140
Red Pepper Sauce, '98 322; '02 165
Red Pepper Sauce, Sweet-'n'-Spicy, '05 321
Red Sauce, '05 327
Red Sauce, Zippy, '91 147
Red Wine-Butter Sauce, '96 173
Red Wine Garlic Sauce, '94 250
Red Wine Sauce, '02 290; '05 332
Rémoulade, Braised Shrimp with Garlic, '98 133
Rémoulade, Citrus, '05 69
Rémoulade, Criolla, '97 227; '05 69
Rémoulade, Roasted Red Pepper, '04 144
Rémoulade Sauce, '80 58; '81 89; '82 178; '91 147; '93 280; '94 139; '99 164; '00 44; '02 134, 184; '04 66
Rémoulade Sauce, Creole, '05 69
Rémoulade Sauce, Red Pepper, '01 145
Rémoulade Sauce, Shrimp with, '91 29
Rémoulade, Watercress, '01 326
Rhubarb Sauce, Chilled, '88 94
Rib Sauce, Peach, '01 248
Roasted Pepper Sauce, Creamy, '96 183
Roasted Red Bell Pepper Sauce, '02 287
Roasted Red Pepper Sauce, '98 16; '00 58
Rosemary Sauce, '97 127
Rum Sauce, Mango-Spiced, '86 215
Sauerbraten Sauce, '93 16
Savory Sauce, '84 196
Seafood
  Cheese Sauce, Seafood, '89 240
  Clam Sauce, Linguine with, '84 124; '88 90; '89 178
  Clam Sauce, Pasta with, '84 291
  Clam Sauce, Vermicelli and Sprouts with Red, '86 143
  Clam Sauce, Vermicelli with, '85 295
  Clam Sauce with Linguine, '84 9
  Crab and Shrimp Sauce Piquante, '83 92
  Crab Marinara Sauce, Quick, '85 M151
  Delight, Seafood Sauce, '82 91
  Linguine with Seafood Sauce, '83 232

Red Seafood Sauce, '95 107
Seafood Sauce, '79 3; '82 84; '83 36; '86 304; '89 239
Shrimp-and-Almond Sauce, '87 282
Shrimp-and-Crab Sauce, Cajun, '05 206
Shrimp-and-Creamy Herb Sauce, Fettuccine with, '01 257
Shrimp Cocktail Sauce, '01 182
Shrimp Sauce, '87 138, 232; '01 182; '04 147
Shrimp Sauce, Broccoli and Cauliflower with, '84 248
Shrimp Sauce, Creamy, '03 53
Shrimp Sauce, Flounder Fillets in, '83 227
Shrimp Sauce, Flounder with Hollandaise-, '86 234
Shrimp Sauce, Grandpa Jim's, '01 182
Shrimp Sauce, Oysters in, '87 40
Stone Crab Mustard Sauce, '80 3
Stone Crab Sauce, Tangy, '80 3
Tartar Sauce, Pecan, '03 101
Seasoning Sauce, '00 110
Sesame-Ginger Sauce, '00 148
Sesame Sauce, Vegetables with, '83 112
Sesame-Soy Dipping Sauce, '02 145
Shallot-Thyme Sauce, '96 121
Sherry Sauce, '87 96
Shiitake Madeira Sauce, Filet Mignons with, '95 265
Shiitake Sauce, Pork Tenderloin with Fruit Stuffing and, '97 218
Smoky Sweet Sauce, '03 32
Sofrito, '92 158
Sour Cream-Cucumber Sauce, '05 207
Sour Cream-Dill Sauce, Mushrooms in, '84 215
Sour Cream-Horseradish Sauce, '88 4
Sour Cream, Mock, '83 71, 205
Sour Cream Sauce, '82 68; '84 132; '87 233; '93 162; '00 194; '02 169
Sour Cream Sauce, Broccoli with, '87 127
Soy Sauce, Grilled Trout with Ginger and, '85 228
Soy Sauce, Sweet, '03 248
Spaghetti Sauce, Grisanti, '94 194
Special Sauce, Morton's, '01 331
Spicy Sauce, '99 291
Spinach Pasta Sauce, '93 71
Spinach Sauce, Fettuccine with, '84 329
Spinach Sauce, Vermicelli with Fresh, '89 256
Stilton-Portobello Sauce, Beef Fillets with, '02 310
Sunshine Sauce, '87 96
Sweet-and-Sour Apple Sauce, Pork Chops with, '98 132
Sweet-and-Sour Sauce, '80 20; '85 12, 34; '86 240
Sweet 'n' Saucy Sauce, '01 210
Sweet Sauce, '01 106
Taco Sauce, '82 M283; '93 69
Tahini Sauce, '96 23; '03 183
Tarragon-Mustard Sauce, Turkey Cutlets with, '93 239
Tarragon Sauce, '83 56; '84 190; '87 229; '97 42
Tartar Sauce, '79 184; '81 134; '82 135; '86 233; '91 147; '95 107, 155; '99 174; '01 316; '02 60; '05 327
Tartar Sauce, Boiled Shrimp with Green Peppercorn, '94 144
Tartar Sauce, Bold-and-Spicy, '86 180
Tartar Sauce, Creamy, '80 164
Tartar Sauce, Lemony, '95 32
Tartar Sauce, Quick, '87 128
Tartar Sauce, Shrimp with, '00 178
Tartar Sauce, Spicy, '04 313
Tempura Sauce, Basic, '81 68
Teriyaki Sauce, '93 258
Tex-Mex Secret Sauce, '04 127
The Sauce, '95 237; '03 312
Tomatillo Sauce, '94 231; '95 206; '97 25; '04 119
Tomatillo Sauce, Grilled Jerk Shrimp with Creamy, '01 332
Tomatillo Sauce, Roasted Chiles Rellenos with, '94 203
Tomato
  Basic Tomato Sauce, '04 145
  Basil Cream, Tomato-, '99 240
  Basil Sauce, Tomato, '91 85
  Basil Sauce, Tomato-, '92 180; '96 220; '97 144; '02 182
  Basil-Tomato Sauce, '92 198; '93 25, 48, 65

Caper Sauce, Turkey Cutlets with Tomato-, '91 61
Chunky Tomato Sauce, '95 264
Cream Sauce, Angel Hair Pasta with Tomato, '93 292
Cream Sauce, Linguine with Tomato-, '86 158
Cream, Tomato, '94 70
Creamy Tomato Sauce, '93 71
Cucumber Sauce, Tomato-, '98 45
Dried Tomato Sauce, '96 220; '99 135
Fish in Tomato Sauce, '85 75
Fresh Tomato Sauce, '83 224; '87 171
Fresh Tomato Sauce over Basil Pasta, '93 176
Gingered Tomato Sauce, Spicy, '96 220
Greek-Style Tomato Sauce, Penne with, '05 187
Green Beans in Tomato Sauce, '01 84
Green Chiles, Tomato Sauce with, '81 196
Ground Beef-Tomato Sauce, '05 290
Herbed Fresh Tomato Sauce, '85 M151
Herbed Tomato Sauce, '86 277
Herb Sauce, Tomato-and-, '00 125
Hot Sauce, Kleberg, '94 28
Italian-Style Tomato Sauce, '87 182
Italian Tomato Sauce, '82 M68; '92 57; '03 202
Italian Tomato Sauce for Spaghetti, '81 134
Lemon Sauce, Salmon with Almonds and Tomato-, '04 23
Light Tomato Sauce, '97 246
Marinara Sauce, '89 239; '92 18; '94 64; '99 266
Meat Sauce, Italian, '83 193
Mint-and-Garlic Tomato Sauce, Spaghetti with, '05 100
Pasta Sauce, '01 53
Pasta Sauce with Meatballs, '01 55
Picante Sauce, '94 116
Picante Sauce, Homemade, '90 205
Picante Sauce, Processed, '91 257
Pico de Gallo, '79 185; '86 19; '97 141; '02 168, 306
Pizza Sauce, '80 163; '84 33; '85 285
Ranchero Sauce, '96 168
Rancheros Sauce, '88 148
Red Pepper-Tomato Sauce, '93 59
Red Sauce and Meatballs, '04 17
Refrigerator Tomato Sauce, '85 188
Roasted Garlic-Tomato Sauce, '97 46
Seasoned Tomato Sauce, '83 150
Spaghetti Meat Sauce for 4, Easy, '92 244
Spaghetti Meat Sauce for 25, Easy, '92 245
Spaghetti Sauce, Beer, '85 13
Spaghetti Sauce, Dried Tomato, '90 202
Spaghetti Sauce, Herbed, '85 13
Spaghetti Sauce, Lentil, '90 198
Spaghetti Sauce, Meat Loaves with, '03 204
Spaghetti Sauce, Sicilian, '03 62
Spaghetti Sauce, Slow-Simmered, '96 72
Spaghetti Sauce, Thick, '84 118
Spaghetti Sauce, Turkey, '85 13
Spicy Sauce, '84 77
Spicy Tomato Sauce, '84 294; '88 19
Sweet-and-Sour Tomato Sauce, Stuffed Chicken Breasts with, '01 120
Taco Sauce, '94 30
Tarragon-Tomato Sauce, '84 131
Tomato Sauce, '85 193, 244; '87 249; '88 116; '97 96, 269; '99 270; '04 43
Vermicelli with Tomato Sauce, '83 164
Zesty Tomato Sauce, '98 176
Turkey Mole, '03 18
Tzatziki Sauce, '04 108; '05 82
Vanilla Wine Sauce, Pan-Fried Grouper with, '94 241
Vegetable Sauce, '89 98
Vegetable Sauce, Greek Fish with, '82 72
Vegetable Sauce, Pasta with, '83 163
Vegetable Sauce, Tangy, '89 280
Vegetable Sauce, Vermicelli with Chunky, '04 180
Velouté Sauce, '84 22
Venison Reduction Sauce, '94 303

Verde Sauce, '93 275; '00 241
Vermouth-Cream Sauce, Scallops in, '96 49
Vidalia Onion Sauce, '99 52
Vinaigrette, Versatile, '93 141
Vinegar Basting Sauce, '91 205
Walnut Cream Sauce, '93 275; '01 229
Walnut-Parmesan Pesto Sauce, '96 251
Walnut Sauce, Linguine with Green Beans and, '04 128
Walnut Sauce, Spaghetti with Parsley and, '80 30
Watercress Sauce, '91 85
Whiskey Sauce, '80 58
White Butter Sauce, '92 107
White Clam Sauce, Linguine with, '05 49
White Dipping Sauce, '00 167
White Sauce, '82 269; '83 138, 245; '87 166
White Sauce, Asparagus, '80 147
White Sauce, Basic, '79 M156; '81 89
White Sauce, Low-Calorie, Medium, '87 26
White Sauce, Medium, '93 48
White Sauce, Thick, '82 42
Wine Reduction Sauce, '94 270; '00 321
Wine Sauce, Beef Cubes in, '79 264
Wine Sauce, Beef Tenderloin in, '02 136
Wine Sauce, Broccoli with, '84 187
Wine Sauce, Chicken in, '80 8
Wine Sauce, Creamy, '01 81; '02 109
Wine Sauce, Marsala, '81 77
Wine Sauce, Mushrooms with, '85 292
Wine Sauce, Red Snapper in, '85 138
Wine Sauce, Shrimp and, '98 50
Wine Sauce, Skillet Steak in Red, '85 21
Wine Sauce, Veal and Carrots in, '86 M139
Wine Sauce, White, '84 132; '89 24; '92 41; '93 49
Yellow Pepper Sauce, '02 165
Yellow Pepper Sauce, Poached Salmon with, '98 230
Yogurt-Cucumber Sauce, '04 216
Yogurt-Cucumber Sauce, London Broil Sandwiches with, '01 162
Yogurt-Horseradish Sauce, '85 66
Yogurt Sauce, '89 283; '05 321
Yogurt Sauce, Creamy, '91 238; '92 28
Yogurt Sauce, Lamb Meatballs with, '85 132
Zesty Sauce, '94 82; '97 312
Zippy Sauce, '86 44
Zucchini-Mushroom Sauce, '93 71
Zucchini Sauce, Spaghetti with, '81 38

SAUERKRAUT
Bratwurst and Sauerkraut, '84 250
Bratwurst Dinner, Krause's Café, '87 238
Cake, Sauerkraut, '94 254
Franks, Beany Kraut and, '79 64
Homemade Sauerkraut, '81 216
Meatballs, Sauerkraut, '86 257
Pork Chops and Sauerkraut, '88 98
Relish, Kraut, '91 232
Relish, Sauerkraut, '85 136
Reuben Casserole, Chicken, '03 69
Reuben Pizza, '03 69
Reuben Puffs, '98 231
Reuben Rolls, Snappy, '02 58
Reuben Sandwiches, '80 M201
Reuben Sandwiches, Broiled, '81 240; '83 69
Reuben Sandwiches, Cripsy, '85 299
Reuben Sandwiches, Grilled, '81 206
Reuben Sandwiches, Open-Face, '91 199
Reuben Sandwich, Rolled, '99 219
Reubens, Oven-Grilled, '97 304
Reubens, Party, '90 61
Reuben Turnovers, '94 253
Salad, Crunchy Sauerkraut, '87 9
Salad, Sauerkraut, '80 178; '97 195
Sandwich, Beef-and-Kraut, '91 167
Sausage and Kraut, '83 11
Sausage-Apple Kraut Dinner, '02 234

SAUSAGE
Acorn Squash, Sausage-Stuffed, '81 231; '83 296; '84 285
Acorn Squash with Sausage, '85 9
Andouille, '92 242
Andouille Alfredo Sauce Over Pasta, Cajun Shrimp and, '05 57
Andouille Grits, Grilled, '04 165
Andouille Gumbo, Chicken-, '98 14
Andouille Sausage, Apple, and Pecan Dressing, '02 249
Appetizers. *See also* **APPETIZERS/Meatballs.**
Balls in Cheese Pastry, Sausage, '80 248
Balls, Sausage, '98 93
Balls, Sausage-Apple, '90 85
Balls, Venison Sausage, '80 42
Basil-Pepper Appetizers, '98 133
Bites, Bourbon-Mustard Glazed Sausage, '05 305
Bites, Spicy Chipotle-Barbecue Sausage, '05 305
Bites, Sweet-and-Sour Sausage, '05 305
Cheese Queso, Chunky, '99 279
Chile con Queso Supreme, '80 265
Cocktail Sausages, Saucy, '87 173
Cocktail Smoky Links, '90 168
Dip, Braunschweiger-and-Beer, '85 69
Dip, Chili con Queso, '86 81
Dumplings, Make-Ahead Pork, '03 64
Egg Rolls, Golden Sausage, '03 284
Kielbasa, Sweet-and-Sour, '89 327
Monster Eyes, '02 222
Mushrooms, Italian Sausage-Stuffed, '83 127
Mushrooms, Sausage-Stuffed, '80 248; '91 164; '05 300
Pepperoni Pie hors d'Oeuvres, '98 251
Phyllo Bites, Sausage-Mushroom-, '89 284
Pizza Snacks, '01 231
Pizza Snacks, Tasty Little, '79 248
Puffs, Cajun Hot, '94 277
Quesadillas, Sausage, '90 118
Rolls with Sweet-and-Sour Sauce, Sausage, '83 74
Rye Appetizers, Party, '86 262
Ryes, Sausage Party, '89 315
Salami Rollups, '90 226
Smoked Sausages with Mustard Sauce, '81 56
Squares, Chile-Sausage, '86 297
Sticks, Beef, '93 331
Sweet-and-Sour Sausage, '88 296
Turkey Sausage Turnovers, '95 239
Baked Peaches and Sausage, '82 50
Baked Sausage Patties, '90 82
Bake, Sausage Egg, '81 225
Barbecued Sausage, '86 153
Basic Sausage, '88 104
Beans, and Rice, Texas Sausage, '84 296
Beans, Spicy-Hot, '89 17
Bean Supper, Sausage-and-, '02 233
Black-Eyed Peas, Creole, '98 22
Black-Eyed Peas, Easy, '99 204
Black-Eyed Peas Mexicano, '79 10
Black-Eyed Peas with Sausage, '86 7
Boudin, Old-Fashioned, '85 250
Bourbon Sausage Dogs, '02 57
Bratwurst and Sauerkraut, '84 250
Bratwurst Dinner, Krause's Café, '87 238
Bratwurst, Grilled, '94 253; '01 159
Breads. *See also* **BISCUITS.**
Biscuit Bites, Sausage, '84 95
Biscuits with Sausage, Angel Heart, '87 156
Biscuits with Sausage, Best, '99 103
Black-Eyed Pea Bread, '02 224
Muffins, Cheesy Sausage, '92 252; '93 144
Muffins, Sausage, '88 52; '95 49
Muffins, Sausage-Cheese, '86 213
Pig-in-a-Blanket Bread, '99 134
Rolls, Ground-Pepperoni, '83 244
Waffles, Sausage, '83 50
Breakfast Delight, '93 195

SAUSAGE
(continued)

Burritos, Breakfast, '84 57; '90 192; '05 204
Cabbage, Italian Stuffed, '84 294
Cabbage Rolls, Hot-and-Spicy, '84 249
Cabbage, Sausage-Sauced, '81 271
Cabbage, Stuffed, '84 282
Cabbage with Polish Sausage, '83 104
Calzones with Pasta Sauce, '01 54
Casseroles
Beefy Sausage Dinner, '80 M9
Breakfast Casserole, '91 285; '99 273; '01 130, 243
Breakfast Casserole, Brie-and-Sausage, '00 284; '03 36
Breakfast Casserole, Sausage, '81 270
Breakfast Casserole, Sausage-Ham, '01 54; '04 332
Breakfast Casserole, Sausage-Hash Brown, '03 218
Breakfast Casserole, Sausage-Mushroom, '86 95
Breakfast Dish, Sausage-Apricot, '82 10
Breakfast, Mexican, '00 194
Breakfast Strata, Southwest, '05 136
Broccoli Casserole, Sausage and, '80 33
Brunch Casserole, '82 124
Brunch Casserole, Italian, '03 29
Brunch for a Bunch, '88 57
Cajun Casserole, Ragin', '02 199
Cheese Bake, Sausage-, '88 58
Cheesy Sausage Casserole, '82 124
Chicken Sausage and Shiitake Mushrooms, Cheese
    Grits with, '03 254
Chile Rellenos Casserole, Sausage-, '88 52
Chiles Rellenos Casserole, '98 48
Country Sausage Casserole, '79 192
Creole Sausage-and-Rice Bake, '88 58
Crunchy Sausage Casserole, '81 288
Easy Sausage Casserole, '87 M189
Egg Casserole, Sausage-, '86 M12
Egg Casserole, Sausage-and-, '94 284
Eggplant Main Dish, Sausage-, '80 211
Eggplant Parmesan, '86 53
Eggplant-Sausage Bake, '85 221
Eggplant-Sausage Casserole, '84 215
Eggplant-Sausage-Pasta Casserole, Freezer, '95 197
Enchiladas, Breakfast, '04 281; '05 333
Grits-Sausage Casserole, '84 75; '86 241
Ground Beef and Sausage Casserole, '80 260
Hawaiian Sausage Casserole, '85 42
Hominy-Sausage Bake, '88 51
Italian Casserole, '90 238
Italian Sausage Brunch, '88 57
Jambalaya Casserole, Sausage, '82 M203
Lasagna Florentine, Creamy, '91 94
Lasagna, Gourmet White, '96 225
Lasagna, Italian Sausage, '96 225
Lasagna Maria, '90 191
Lasagna, Mexican, '01 282
Lasagna Rollups, Sausage-, '80 236
Lasagna, Sausage, '83 288
Lasagna Sausage Pinwheels, '79 6
Lasagna, Speedy, '05 M252
Macaroni and Cheese, Tex-Mex, '00 92
Manicotti, Cheesy Sausage-and-Tomato, '03 257
Manicotti, Meaty Cheese, '05 34
Manicotti, Meaty Stuffed, '00 19
Manicotti, Saucy Stuffed, '83 288
Mostaccioli Casserole, '04 316
Noodle Bake, Sausage-, '81 92
Noodle Casserole, Sausage and, '82 123
Noodle Casserole, Sausage-and-, '95 255
Paella Casserole, '95 254
Pizza Casserole, Upside-Down, '03 284
Potato Casserole, Sausage-, '86 217
Rice Casserole, Oriental Sausage and, '82 M123

Rice Casserole, Sausage-, '82 50; '83 75
Salami-Corn Casserole, '80 209
Sausage Casserole, '81 112; '82 12
Shells, Sausage-Stuffed, '96 102
Skillet Sausage Casserole, '99 123
Smoked Sausage-Egg Bake, '85 248
Spanish Rice Casserole, '79 192
Spud Bake, Sunday Night Spicy Cheesy Sausage-,
    '03 331
Strata, Christmas Morning, '95 282
Swiss Sausage Casserole, '80 209
Turkey-and-Sausage Wild Rice Casserole,
    '03 239
Venison-Vegetable Bake, '87 304
Wild Rice and Sausage, '86 268
Wild Rice Casserole, Sausage-, '84 250
Wild Rice Casserole, Sausage and, '83 196
Zucchini and Sausages, Baked, '80 300
Cassoulet, '96 328
Cassoulet, Easy Herb Crust, '01 311
Cassoulet, Sausage-and-Chicken, '05 237
Chicken Rolls Elégante, '80 210
Chicken Sausage with Fennel, '98 312
Chicken, Stuffed Alfredo, '04 56
Chicken with Tomatoes and Sausage, '97 266
Chili, Beefy Sausage, '82 11
Chili, Company, '82 311
Chili con Carne, Beef and Sausage, '83 284
Chili Goes Southwest, Basic, '93 326
Chili, Hearty Kielbasa, '91 28
Chili, Hotto Lotto, '89 316
Chili-I-Cious, '89 315
Chili, Lolly's Pop, '89 316
Chili, Now, Thatsa, '95 16
Chili, Sausage-Beef, '86 232
Chili, Texas-Style, '82 311; '83 30
Chorizo, '92 241
Chorizo and Egg Tortillas, '81 193
Chorizo, Black Bean, and Corn Quesadillas, '00 148
Chorizo, Breakfast, '91 77
Chorizo Carbonara, '94 230
Chorizo Grits with Red Bean Salsa, Shrimp-Manchego-,
    '97 227
Chorizo (Spicy Spanish Sausage), '81 193
Chorizo, Spoonbread with Simple, '04 207
Chorizo Substitute, '87 238
Chowder, Clam-and-Sausage, '94 104
Chowder, Sausage-Bean, '83 20
Cobbler, Turkey-Vegetable-Sausage, '04 325
Corn Boil, Monroe County, '96 167
Corn Maque Choux, Cajun, '01 284
Country Sausage, '88 104; '92 242
Country Sausage, Spiced, '88 104
Crêpes, Apple Breakfast, '97 331
Crêpes, Cheesy Sausage, '82 240; '83 71
Crêpes, Sausage, '88 295
Crêpes, Sausage-Filled, '79 39; '98 266; '99 25
Dinner, Sausage-and-Bean, '95 108
Dinner, Sausage-Vegetable, '84 250
Dressing, Cajun, '82 307
Dressing, Cornbread-and-Sausage, '83 213
Dressing, Cornbread-Sausage, '82 307; '85 280
Dressing, Cornbread, Sausage, and Pecan, '99 257
Dressing, Fruited Turkey, '99 257
Dressing, Harvest Sausage, '88 254
Dressing, Louise's Cornbread, '03 251
Dressing, Rice, '01 222
Dressing, Sausage, '86 280
Dressing, Sausage-Apple, '93 305; '94 296
Dressing, Sausage-Cornbread, '95 289
Dressing, Southern Rice, '99 256
Dressing, Turkey with Sausage-Cornbread, '83 287
Eggplant, Sausage Stuffed, '81 204
Eggplant, Sausage-Stuffed, '91 211

Egg Rolls with Creamy Cilantro Dipping Sauce,
    Tex-Mex, '03 327
Eggs, Armadillo, '97 270; '05 139
Eggs Creole, '92 86
Eggs, Scotch, '79 261; '83 289; '98 101
Empanadas, Meaty, '05 138
Filling, Omelet with Sausage, '81 43
Fondue, Beer-and-Cheddar, '03 223
Garlic Sausage, '88 104
Gravy, Sausage, '92 271; '94 20; '97 243; '03 67
Gravy, Sawmill, '03 67; '05 110
Grilled Pork, Cheddar, and Jalapeño Sausage, '98 311
Grits and Sausage, Country, '83 54
Grits Italiano, '92 43
Grits, Nassau, '99 214
Grits, Sausage, '86 92
Grits, Sausage-Cheese, '90 238
Grits with Sausage, '99 233
Gumbo, Chicken-and-Sausage, '89 275; '90 256;
    '94 20; '00 221; '01 324; '03 313; '04 213
Gumbo, Dove and Sausage, '81 199
Gumbo, Duck, Oyster, and Sausage, '79 226
Gumbo, The Gullah House, '92 237
Gumbo with Smoked Sausage, Chicken, '81 199
Gumbo Ya Ya, '87 210
Gumbo z'Herbes, '94 239
Homemade Sausage, Spicy, '84 320
Hominy-Sausage Skillet, '81 29
Italian Meat Sauce, '83 193
Italian Sauce with Noodles, '84 250
Italian Sausage, '88 104; '92 242
Italian Sausage and Peppers, '84 9
Italian Sausage and Rice, '86 53
Italian Sausage Dinner, '91 218
Italian Sausage Quiche, '81 200
Italian Sausage Soup, '84 235
Italian Sausage Soup with Tortellini, '88 46
Italian Sausage Supper, '88 164
Italian Sausage-Zucchini Soup, '84 4
Italian Turkey Sausage, Marinara Sauce with, '89 239
Jalapeños, Hot Stuffed, '99 123
Jambalaya, '03 144; '04 288
Jambalaya, Chicken-and-Sausage, '88 200; '91 216;
    '01 278; '02 36; '03 201
Jambalaya, Creole, '81 51; '03 83
Jambalaya de Covington, '87 211
Jambalaya, Northshore, '87 45
Jambalaya, 1-2-3, '97 301
Jambalaya, Oven, '84 44
Jambalaya, Sausage, '80 210; '84 249
Jambalaya, Smoked Sausage, '79 42
Jambalaya, Smoky Cajun, '96 62
Jambalaya, Trail, '93 179
Kielbasa, '92 242
Kielbasa and Cabbage, '85 67; '89 M196
Kielbasa, Cabbage, '87 42
Kielbasa-Vegetable Dinner, '91 274
Kielbasa with Beans, Easy Cheesy, '01 28
Kraut Dinner, Sausage-Apple, '02 234
Kraut, Sausage and, '83 11
Linguine with Sausage and Peppers, '03 170
Loaf, Hawaiian Ham, '79 71
Loaf, Skillet Liver, '80 11
Log, Phyllo Sausage, '84 294
Log, Stuffed Beef, '79 71
Meatballs and Sausage, Spicy, '79 163
Meat Loaf, French Market, '02 33
Meat Loaf, Herb-and-Veggie, '05 161
Meat Loaf, Mozzarella-Layered, '79 71
Meat Loaf, Sweet 'n' Saucy, '01 210
Mexican Luncheon, '87 192
Minestrone, Cheesy, '99 17
Muffins, Breakfast, '04 209
Muffins, Sausage-and-Cheese, '03 81

Omelet, Puffy Sausage, '80 M268
Omelet with Fresh Avocado Salsa, Spanish, '02 247
Onions, Baked Stuffed, '83 135
Paella, '97 328
Paella, Shortcut, '01 309
Pancake-Sausage Wedges, '93 196
Pasta, Three Pepper-Sausage, '02 122
Pasta with Broccoli and Sausage, '87 109; '97 266
Pasta with Collards and Sausage, '94 230
Pasta with Sausage and Bell Peppers, '02 63
Pasta with Sausage and Kale, '03 279
Pasta with Sausage and Mixed Vegetables, '84 249
Patties, Apples on Sausage, '82 120
Pepperoni-and-Broccoli Salad, '83 216
Pepperoni Pasta, '83 105
Pepperoni Pinwheels, '96 247
Pepperoni Soup, Italian-Style Beef-and-, '00 316
Pepperoni-Squash Toss, '84 127
Peppers, Sausage and, '95 165
Peppers with Parmesan Cheese Grits, Sausage and, '02 233
Pie, Breakfast, '86 242
Pie, Cornbread-Sausage-Apple, '87 171
Pie, Sausage-and-Cornbread, '90 25
Pie, Tumbleweed, '98 205
Pie, Turkey-Sausage, '01 297
Pigs in a Blanket, '03 167
Pilau, Sausage, '99 184
Pintos and Sausage, Hearty, '88 296
Pinwheels, Sausage, '80 209; '93 238
Pizza, Breakfast, '85 44; '88 288
Pizza, Deep-Dish, '01 29
Pizza, Double Cheesy Beef-and-Sausage, '86 77
Pizza Luncheon Pie, Deep-Dish, '80 286
Pizza, Mexican, '02 72
Pizza Peppers, '83 135
Pizza Pie, Link-Sausage, '85 33
Pizza, Sausage-and-Scrambled Egg, '05 88
Pizza, Sausage-Potato, '01 199
Pizza, Speedy, '81 214
Pizza, Spicy Sausage-Pepperoni, '83 226
Pizza, The King Henry, '95 267
Pizza, Thick 'n' Crusty Pepperoni, '85 244
Polenta with Sausage, '93 32
Polish Sausage, Cabbage with, '83 104
Pork Rib Roast, Sausage Stuffed, '94 240
Pork Sausage, '81 55; '97 243
Pork Sausage Ring, '80 49
Pork Tenderloin, Stuffed, '00 213
Potato-and-Sausage Salad, Warm, '96 25
Potatoes, Mexican-Topped, '83 3
Potatoes, Sausage-Vegetable-Topped, '98 29
Potatoes with Eggs and Meat, '91 311; '92 25
Potato Salad with Smoked Sausage, Warm, '97 267
Quesadillas, Breakfast Sausage, '04 183
Quiche, Crustless Sausage-Apple, '87 70
Quiche, Crustless Veggie Sausage, '03 175
Quiche Cups, Mexican, '02 72
Quiche, Easy Sausage, '79 261
Quiche, Pizza, '86 53
Quiche, Sausage-Cheddar, '79 26
Quiche, South-of-the-Border, '93 321
Quiche, Spicy Sausage, '80 M108
Quiche with Avocado Topping, Mexicali, '93 309; '94 96
Quiche, Zucchini-Sausage, '83 122
Ratatouille, Sausage, '89 248
Red Beans and Rice, '02 35
Red Beans and Rice, Delta, '98 146
Red Beans and Rice, New Orleans, '97 235
Red Beans and Rice, Spicy, '02 56
Red Rice, '00 289
Rice, Cajun Dirty, '04 288
Rice, Pork Sausage-Seasoned, '00 236
Rice, Shrimp and Sausage, '79 64
Rice with Sausage, Fried, '83 12

Rigatoni with Sausage and Bell Peppers, '05 215
Risotto, Redneck, '98 107
Rollups, Pancake-Sausage, '83 246; '84 42
Rollups, Sausage-Bacon, '88 51
Roll-Ups, Spicy Egg, '90 140
Salad, Bean-and-Sausage, '91 313
Salad, Warm Potato-and-Sausage, '96 25
Salisbury Steak, Tex-Mex, '05 204

Sandwiches
Breakfast Pita Pockets, '89 M21
Breakfast Sandwiches, '80 52
Bun, Sausage in a, '89 M22
Burgers, All-American Pizza, '92 148
Burgers, Sausage, '83 212; '96 102
Calzone, '85 94
Calzones, Beef-and-Pepperoni, '03 202
Cheese Muffin Sandwiches, Sausage-, '92 M212
Italian Sausage and Pepper Loaves, '83 11
Italian Sausage Sandwich, '80 92
Italian Sausage Sloppy Joes, '86 160
Loaf, Sausage-Stuffed French, '90 19
Loaves, Sausage-Cheese, '88 235
Muffuletta Loaf, '97 86
Mustard Sauce, Sausage Sandwiches with, '84 250
Pepperoni and Cheese Loaf, '82 32
Pizza Sandwich, Giant, '80 93
Salami Sandwiches, Open-Faced, '87 279
Sleeping Bag, Sausage in a, '98 206
Sauce, Sicilian Spaghetti, '03 62
Shrimp and Sausage over Creamy Grits with Tasso Gravy, Spicy, '92 236
Shrimp Sausage, '97 164
Skillet Dinner, Sausage, '83 29
Skillet Express, Sausage, '83 117
Skillet, Mexican-Style, '83 12
Skillet Sausage and Cabbage, '01 28
Skillet Sausage and Pasta, '97 267
Skillet Supper, Chicken-and-Sausage, '03 49
Skillet Supper, Sausage, '85 293
Smoked Sausage, '86 154
Smoked Sausage, Chicken Gumbo with, '81 199
Smoked Sausage Jambalaya, '79 42
Smoked Sausage Pilau, Chicken-and-, '04 204
Smoked Sausage Stew, '82 231
Soup, Easy Potato-Sausage, '98 315
Soup, Peasant, '01 54
Soup, Polish Sausage, '99 317
Soup, Sausage and Okra, '80 209
Soup, Sausage-Bean, '85 88
Soup, Sausage-Potato, '80 25
Soup, Sausage, Spinach, and Bean, '99 311
Soup, Sausage-Tortellini, '99 20
Soup, Spicy Sausage-Bean, '83 229
Soup, Sweet Potato-and-Sausage, '95 23
Spaghetti Dinner, Sausage, '79 194
Spaghetti, Italian, '81 38
Spaghetti, Italian Zucchini, '85 2
Spaghetti, Real Italian, '81 233
Spaghetti, Sausage, '83 160
Spicy Sausage, Dieters', '85 49
Squares, Chile-Sausage, '86 297
Squares, Sausage-Onion, '83 112
Squash, Harvest, '80 214
Squash, Sausage-Stuffed, '81 183
Stew, Frogmore, '92 236; '00 174, 336; '03 181; '05 111
Stew, Mirliton, '02 57
Stew, Oyster-Sausage, '89 242
Stew, Venison Sausage, '87 238
Stir-Fry, Sausage, '82 236; '98 156
Stir-Fry Sausage and Vegetables, '86 213; '87 82
Strata, Sausage, '83 243; '84 101
Stuffing, Chicken Breasts with Pecan-Sausage, '94 212
Stuffing, Crown Roast of Pork with Cranberry-Sausage, '88 49

Stuffing, Sausage, '99 293; '00 292; '03 255
Stuffing, Sausage-and-Wild Mushroom, '96 267
Summer Sausage, '99 85
Supper, Cabbage, '89 314
Supper, Sausage, '01 28
Supper, Sausage-Bean, '86 52
Surprise, Sausage, '83 245; '84 42
Sweet Peppery Sausage, '95 69
Tacos, Breakfast, '80 43; '95 340
Tacos, Sausage-Egg Soft, '05 26
Tamales, Breakfast, '00 122
Taquitos, Breakfast, '87 237
Tarts, Sausage 'n' Cheese, '88 51
Tasso Bread Pudding, Rosemary-, '00 104
Tomatoes, Italian-Style, '97 169
Tomatoes, Sausage-Stuffed, '80 47
Tortilla Campesina, '89 85
Tortillas, Egg-and-Sausage, '83 246; '84 42
Turban Squash, Sausage-Stuffed, '80 214
Turkey Sausage Patties, Breakfast, '05 169
Turnovers, Sausage-Cheese, '88 231; '89 22
Vegetables and Sausage, Spicy, '80 82
Vegetable Skillet, Sausage-, '96 102
Veggie Sausage Pizzas, '00 294
Waffle Stack, Hoppin' John, '04 19
Wild Rice, Sausage and, '85 65
Ziti with Sausage and Broccoli, '95 340
Zucchini and Sausage, Sautéed, '83 289

SCALLOPS
Angel Hair Pasta, Scallops and, '99 176
Appetizer, Scallop, '86 155
Appetizers, Flaky Scallop, '86 327
Artichokes Stuffed with Shrimp and Scallops, '84 174
Bacon-Wrapped Scallops, '87 94
Bacon-Wrapped Scallops with Orange-Honey Sauce, '97 236
Baked Gruyère Scallops, '92 57
Bay Scallops, Linguine with, '97 201
Broiled Scallops, '91 170
Broiled Scallops with Tartar Sauce, '80 164
Broth with Black Beans and Cilantro, Southwestern Scallop, '87 123
Cakes, Crab-and-Scallop, '02 165
Casserole, Creamy Shrimp-and-Scallops, '01 256
Casserole, Scallop, '79 228
Ceviche (Marinated Raw Fish), '82 220
Champagne-Saffron Sauce, Scallops with, '93 177
Cheese Scallops, Chip and, '80 301
Coquilles Saint Cyrano, '86 90
Coquilles St. Jacques, '97 201
Creamy Scallops and Mushrooms, '83 144
Crêpes, Coquilles St. Jacques, '83 13
en Brochette with Vegetables, Scallops, '80 163
Fettuccine, Scallop-Mushroom, '96 198
Ginger Scallops, '99 177
Grilled Orange Scallops with Cilantro-Lime Vinaigrette, '94 77
Grilled Scallops, Marinated, '84 171
Grilled Sweet-and-Sour Scallops, '01 92
Kebabs, Grilled Scallop, '83 101
Kebabs, Grilled Shrimp-and-Scallop, '92 210
Kebabs, Scallop-Bacon, '81 111
Kebabs, Sea Scallop, '82 162
Maple Scallops, '99 176
Mornay, Scallops, '80 164
Mornay, Shrimp and Scallops, '97 238
Mustard Sauce, Scallops with, '84 163
Pasta, Fresh Scallops and, '83 164
Provençal, Scallops, '85 66
Rumaki, Scallop, '98 M173
Salad, Thai-Rific Orange Scallop, '04 317
Sautéed Scallops with Cranberry Relish, '83 144
Sauté, Scallop, '88 28
Sauté, Shrimp-and-Scallop, '85 103
Sauté with Pecan Rice, Shrimp-and-Scallop, '90 317

SCALLOPS

(continued)

Savannah, Scallops, '79 145
Seared Scallops with Tomato-Mango Salsa, '95 122
Seared Sea Scallops with Tomato Puree, '97 201
Sesame-Crusted Scallops with Orange-Ginger Sauce, '97 125
Sherried Scallops, '83 281
Stir-Fry, Scallop, '94 32
Supreme, Seafood, '82 284
Tostada, Grilled Scallops, '87 120
Vegetable Nests, Scallops in, '91 70
Vegetables, Bay Scallops with, '84 233
Vermicelli, Scallop-Vegetable, '87 143
Vermouth-Cream Sauce, Scallops in, '96 49
Véronique, Scallops, '83 144
Wild Rice, Scallops and, '90 129
Wine, Scallops in, '91 48

SCONES. *See* **BREADS.**

SEAFOOD. *See also* **CASSEROLES; CLAMS; CRAB; CRAWFISH; FISH; GUMBOS/Seafood; LOBSTER; OYSTERS; SALMON; SCALLOPS; SHRIMP; TUNA.**

Appetizer, Layered Seafood, '88 2
Bisque, Seafood, '86 66
Boil, Low Country Seafood, '80 119
Boil, Southern Shellfish, '93 258
Bouchées aux Fruits de Mer, '98 267
Bouillabaisse, Florida, '79 158
Brochette, Seafood, '87 96
Broiled Shellfish, Quick, '79 228
Butter, Seafood, '97 306
Cakes with Jalapeño Tartar Sauce, Seafood, '98 129
Calamari, Fried, '00 283
Casserole, Seafood, '87 109; '89 63
Chowder, Curried Seafood, '94 103
Chowder, Seafood, '85 9; '92 122
Chowder, So-Quick Seafood, '01 18
Chowder, Southern Seafood, '83 20
Cioppino, Gulf Coast, '94 102
Crêpes in Wine-Cheese Sauce, Shellfish, '00 310
Delight, Seafood, '86 208
Dip, Hot Artichoke-Seafood, '80 241
Dip, Hot Artichoke Seafood, '85 M212
Dip, Hot Cheesy Seafood, '84 221
Dip, Seafood, '79 3
Dip, Super Seafood, '90 292
Eggplant, Seafood Stuffed, '79 187
Hot Brown, Seafood, '88 158
Imperials, Individual Seafood, '84 162
Jambalaya, Three-Seafood, '82 126
Linguine, Seafood, '79 227
Manicotti, Seafood, '94 195
Mayonnaise, Seafood with Dill, '86 234
Mold, Chilled Seafood, '86 70
Mornay, Seafood, '83 67
Mussels Linguine, '90 M112
Mussels Marinara, '00 283
Mussel Soup, '93 259
Oriental Marinade, Seafood in, '98 128
Paella, Chicken-Seafood, '88 68
Paella, Party, '88 M189
Paella, Seafood, '82 245
Papillote, Ocean, '84 M287
Parmesan, Savannah Seafood, '99 312
Pasta, Herbed Seafood, '04 255
Pasta, Seafood and, '90 234
Pie, Hot Seafood, '80 32
Pizza, Seafood Alfredo, '03 236
Po' Boy, Grilled Seafood, '96 244
Potatoes, Seafood-Stuffed, '95 M192
Prawns with Winter Cabbage Salad, '98 284
Risotto, Seafood, '95 280

Risotto with Shellfish and Peas, '96 131
Robert, Seafood, '97 106
Salads
  Baked Seafood Salad, '86 10
  Hot Seafood Salad, '79 117; '80 164
  Paella Salad, '86 207
  Pasta Salad, Seafood, '90 62
  Polynesian Seafood Salad, '79 57
  Seafood Salad, '90 88
  Seaside Salad, '86 183
  Sewee Preserve's Seafood Salad, '05 173
  Slaw, Seafood, '79 56
  Smoky Seafood Salad, '84 46
  Sussex Shores, Seafood Salad, '93 98
Sandwiches, Caribbean Seafood, '98 105
Sauce Delight, Seafood, '82 91
Sauce, Linguine with Seafood, '83 232
Sauce, Red Seafood, '95 107
Sauce, Seafood, '79 3; '82 48; '86 304; '89 239
Sauce, Seafood Cheese, '89 240
Sautéed Seafood Platter, '83 89
Seasoning Blend, Bay Seafood, '92 121
Seasoning Blend, Fish-and-Seafood, '88 28
Seasoning Rub, Seafood, '93 101
Soup, Seafood-Tortellini, '97 324
Spread, Grandma Reed's Seafood, '98 268
Spread, Seafood, '86 M58; '87 146
Spread, Seafood Sandwich, '82 87
Stew, Seafood, '84 280
Stir-Fry with Noodle Pancake, Szechuan Ginger, '97 292
Stock, Seafood, '94 238
Supreme, Seafood, '82 284
Tartlets, Seafood, '87 247
Tempura, Basic, '81 68
Tempura, Cornmeal, '81 68
Terrine with Dill Sauce, Asparagus-Seafood, '98 157

SEASONINGS. *See also* **MARINADES, OILS, SPICE.**

Adobo, '92 158
Barbecue Rub, '03 130; '04 104; '05 166
Barbecue Rub, All-Purpose, '03 130; '04 104
Barbecue Rub, Master Class, '98 244
Basil Puree, '03 208
Bay Seafood Seasoning Blend, '92 121
Better-Than-Potpourri Brew, '95 271
Blend, Seasoning, '92 296
Chipotle Rub, '04 87
Court-Bouillon, '98 229
Creole Rub, '93 101
Creole Seasoning Blend, '92 121
Creole Seasoning, Crescent City Grill, '04 289
Dry Rub, Biltmore, '99 231; '00 20
Essence, Emeril's, '99 198
Fish-and-Seafood Seasoning Blend, '88 28
Fish Herb Mix, '98 51
Five-Spice Powder Blend, '92 121
Garlic, Herbed Roasted, '94 177
Garlic Puree, Roasted, '92 55
Garlic, Roasted, '94 177; '96 304
Ginger Rub, '04 87
Greek Seasoning Blend, '92 121
Gremolata, '95 280; '05 319
Gremolata, Citrus-Mint, '04 108
Ground Seasoning Blend, '92 121
Herb Mix, Italian Parmesan, '05 284
Herb Rub, '93 102
Herb Seasoning, '99 63
Herbs Seasoning Blend, '92 121
Hoisin Mixture, '99 125
Italian Breadcrumb Mix, '99 265
Jamaican Jerk Rub, '00 88
Jerk Rub, '93 101
Lemon-Mint Sugar, '95 32
Lemon Squeezers, '95 32
Marinade, Italian, '03 180

Marinade, Zesty Chicken, '03 180
Meat Seasoning, '98 62
Meat Seasoning Blend, '88 29
Mexican Rub, '93 102
Mix, GOPPS Seasoning, '92 305
Mix, Melvyn's Seasoning, '04 132
Mix, Seasoning, '91 64; '00 322
Mix, Weaver D's Seasoning, '96 248
Moroccan Spice Rub, '95 231
Olive Oil, Basil-Infused, '95 231
Olive Oil, Lemon-Infused, '95 231
Poultry Seasoning Blend, '88 28
Roux, '03 111
Rub, Brisket, '03 188
Rub, Caribbean Spice, '02 144
Rub, Mediterranean, '03 180
Rub, Paul's Chicken, '05 174
Rub, Paul's Pork Ribs, '05 174
Rub, Spice, '05 259
Salt, Dragon, '03 236
Salt, Gourmet Seasoning, '82 297; '97 254
Sauce, Seasoning, '00 110
Sazon, '92 157
Seafood Seasoning Rub, '93 101
Southwest Seasoning, '95 266
Spice Blend, Southwestern, '03 180
Sweet Spice Blend, '05 274
Taco Seasoning Blend, '96 159
Vanilla Extract, '94 243; '97 288
Vanilla Sugar, '94 243
Vegetable Seasoning Blend, '88 29

SHERBETS. *See also* **ICE CREAMS.**

Ambrosia Cups, Sherbet, '82 159
Apricot Sherbet, '81 177; '92 164
Avocado Sherbet, '83 162
Banana-Orange Sherbet, '83 162
Beverages
  Float, Pineapple Sherbet, '79 148
  Punch, Double Sherbet, '79 232
  Punch, Orange Sherbet Party, '83 142
  Punch, Pineapple Sherbet, '95 141
  Punch, Raspberry Sherbet, '95 141
  Smoothie, Citrus, '99 196
  Smoothie, Orange-Banana, '97 173
  Smoothie, Pineapple, '97 172
Blackberry-Buttermilk Sherbet, '05 133
Blackberry Sherbet, 1-2-3, '99 130; '00 21
Blackberry Sherbet, Three-Ingredient, '01 105
Blueberry-Buttermilk Sherbet, '05 133
Blueberry Sherbet, '04 283
Buttermilk Sherbet, '84 184; '99 99
Cantaloupe Sherbet, '88 183
Cantaloupe Sherbet, Frosty, '82 144
Cranberry Sherbet, '88 280
Dessert, Layered Sherbet, '87 109
Dessert, Macaroon-Sherbet Frozen, '79 212
Fruit Punch Sherbet, '86 129
Fruit Sherbet, Freezer, '86 334
Fruit Sherbet, Frozen, '79 155
Fruit Sherbet, Instant, '85 158
Jalapeño-Mint Sherbet, '98 202
Lemon Cream Sherbet, '79 114
Lemon-Pineapple Sherbet, '96 330
Lemon Sherbet, '91 309
Lemon Sherbet, Refreshing, '05 133
Lime Sherbet, '82 159; '89 202
Lime Sherbet, Creamy, '84 165
Lime Sherbet, Refreshing, '05 133
Mexican Sherbet, '79 155
Mint Sherbet, Fresh, '88 23
Nectarine Sherbet, '89 199
Orange Sherbet, '79 155
Orange Sherbet Salad, '81 154
Orange Sherbet, Three-Ingredient, '01 105

Orange Sherbet with Blackberry Sauce, '94 232
Peach Sherbet, '90 179
Peach Sherbet, Three-Ingredient, '01 105
Pineapple Sherbet, '81 177; '84 83; '89 199
Pineapple Sherbet, Creamy, '79 155
Pineapple Sherbet, Easy, '92 199
Raspberry-Buttermilk Sherbet, '05 133
Raspberry Sherbet, '83 162
Strawberry Sherbet, '82 112, 160
Strawberry Sherbet, Three-Ingredient, '01 105
Watermelon Sherbet, '79 155; '92 124
Watermelon Sherbet, Light, '81 147

SHRIMP

Appetizers. *See also* **APPETIZERS/Shrimp.**
Artichoke-and-Shrimp Appetizer, '93 271
Ball, Curried Shrimp Cheese, '86 135
Ball, Shrimp-Cheese, '85 208
Boiled Shrimp, '79 3
Boil, Southern Shellfish, '93 258
Butter, Shrimp, '92 91
Cajun Shrimp, '89 283
Canapés, Shrimp, '84 116
Canapés, Shrimp-and-Cucumber, '93 164
Cheesecake, Shrimp-and-Gruyère, '92 57
Cheese, Shrimp with Herbed Jalapeño, '87 112
Dip, Chunky Shrimp, '96 214
Dip, Hot Shrimp, '87 190
Dip, Monterey Shrimp, '99 65
Dip, Quick Shrimp, '79 153
Dip, Shrimp, '86 84; '88 M261; '98 67; '01 194
Dip, Zesty Shrimp, '80 150
Egg Rolls, '86 81
Eggrolls, Shrimp and Pork, '82 240; '83 18
Filling, Shrimp, '89 320
Fried Marinated Shrimp with Mango Slaw, '93 31
Garlic-and-Rosemary Shrimp, '01 101; '04 52
Grilled Jerk Shrimp with Creamy Tomatillo Sauce, '01 332
Grilled Zucchini-Wrapped Shrimp, '98 200
Jalapeños, Shrimp-Stuffed, '88 115
Lemon Shrimp, Luscious, '88 150
Mousse, Shrimp, '79 57; '87 196, 251
Pâté on Crostini, Shrimp, '98 316
Pâté with Dill Sauce, Shrimp, '85 39
Pickled Shrimp, Charleston Harbor, '99 275
Pickled Shrimp, New Orleans, '79 145
Puffs, Gouda-Shrimp, '79 234
Puffs, Shrimp, '96 211; '98 316
Rémoulade, Shrimp, '83 173; '90 255; '03 146
Soufflé Roll, Shrimp, '89 320
Spread, Chunky Shrimp, '85 300; '86 18
Spread, Curried Shrimp, '87 158
Spread, Shrimp, '81 306; '85 135; '87 111; '93 205; '96 104
Spread, Shrimp-Cucumber, '79 81
Spread, Tempting Shrimp, '79 57
Spread, Zippy Shrimp, '90 36
Spring Rolls with Sweet Chili Sauce, Shanghai, '01 236
Steamed Shrimp, '03 206
Tree, Shrimp, '83 320; '84 288; '85 318
Zucchini-Shrimp Appetizers, '89 311
Ariosto, Shrimp and Chicken, '79 31
Artichokes, Shrimp-Stuffed, '84 67; '87 55
Artichokes, Shrimp Stuffed, '94 62
Artichokes Stuffed with Shrimp and Scallops, '84 174
au Gratin, Crab, Shrimp, and Artichoke, '90 240
au Gratin, Shrimp, '85 79
Avocados, Shrimp-Filled, '83 2
Baked Shrimp, '87 35
Baked Shrimp, Spicy, '97 324
Barbecued Shrimp, '82 74; '84 93; '90 28
Barbecued Shrimp and Cornbread-Stuffed Peppers, '97 261
Barbecued Shrimp, Cajun, '87 95
Barbecue Shrimp, Hickory-Smoked, '00 89

Barbecue Shrimp, New Orleans, '02 201
Boats, Shrimp, '79 57
Boiled Shrimp, '79 3; '04 147
Boiled Shrimp, Ray Kidd's, '84 87
Boiled Shrimp, Special, '83 36
Boiled Shrimp Supper, '94 200
Boiled Shrimp with Green Peppercorn Tartar Sauce, '94 144
Bourbon, Shrimp, '00 125
Breakfast Shrimp, Classic Charleston, '93 60
Broiled Shrimp, Beer-, '87 142
Broiled Shrimp, Garlic-, '83 193
Broiled Shrimp, Lemon-Garlic, '82 29; '86 182
Broiled Shrimp Supreme, '79 3
Burgers, Shrimp, '03 110
Cabbage, Asian Shrimp and, '00 105
Cajun Shrimp, Fiery, '91 218
Cakes with Watercress Rémoulade, Shrimp, '01 326
Cashew Shrimp Supreme, '83 29
Casserole, Cajun Shrimp, '05 237
Casserole, Chayotes and Shrimp, '80 230
Casserole, Cheesy Shrimp-and-Grits, '03 28
Casserole, Crab-and-Shrimp, '84 71
Casserole, Creamy Shrimp-and-Scallops, '01 256
Casserole, Miss Hannah's, '92 236
Casserole, Shrimp, '85 240
Casserole, Shrimp-and-Chicken, '91 102
Casserole, Shrimp-and-Noodle, '90 240
Casserole, Shrimp and Rice, '79 228
Casserole, Shrimp-and-Rice, '94 328
Casserole, Spicy Shrimp, '96 62
Casserole, Turkey-and-Shrimp Florentine, '92 122
Catfish, Crown Room's Shrimp-Stuffed, '84 182
C'est Bon, Shrimp, '94 195
Chicken Breasts, Stuffed, '88 50
Chowder, Quick Shrimp, '04 27
Chow Mein, Shrimp, '82 30
Coconut-Pecan Shrimp with Orange Dipping Sauce, '03 212
Coconut Shrimp, '00 175
Creamed Shrimp on Pecan-Cornmeal Rounds, '95 99
Cream Sauce, Shrimp in, '84 M286
Creole, Easy Shrimp, '95 68
Creole in a Rice Ring, Shrimp, '86 222
Creole, Shrimp, '86 256; '87 18; '90 M220; '93 282; '96 210; '03 109
Creole, Special Shrimp, '87 172
Creole, Spicy Shrimp, '79 181
Creole, Wild Rice-and-Shrimp, '84 292
Croquettes, Nannie's Shrimp, '98 316

Curry
Charleston-Style Shrimp Curry, '84 109
Creamy Shrimp Curry, '90 145
Curried Shrimp, '84 110
Eggs, Saucy Shrimp-Curried, '84 143
Ginger Shrimp, Curry-, '00 316
Hot Red Curry Shrimp, '02 125
Polynesian Shrimp Curry, '89 23
Quick Curried Shrimp, '84 M198
Rice and Shrimp, Curried, '83 231
Salad, Curried Shrimp, '00 217
Sauce, Hawaiian Shrimp with Curry, '94 54
Shrimp Curry, '99 91
Shrimp Malai Curry, '84 110
Sour Cream and Shrimp Curry, '81 10
Sour Cream Shrimp Curry, '80 83
West Indian Curried Shrimp, '79 227
Daufuskie Shrimp, '00 174
Dee-Lish, Shrimp, '90 216
de Jonghe, Shrimp, '79 228
Delight, English Muffin, '82 45
Delight, Shrimp, '79 192
Destin, Shrimp, '82 29; '03 314
Dijonnaise, Shrimp, '87 91
Dilled Sauced Shrimp, '86 88
Dinner, Jollof Rice, '91 230; '92 325

di Santo, Shrimp, '99 265
Egg Foo Yong, '80 19; '86 232
Egg Foo Yong, Shrimp, '83 22
Eggplant à la Creole, '96 177
Eggplant-Shrimp Medley, '79 188
Eggplant, Shrimp-Stuffed, '92 99
Eggrolls, Shrimp and Pork, '82 240; '83 18
Egg Rolls, Vietnamese, '96 101
Eggs Benedict, Shrimp-and-Grits, '03 53
Eggs, Shrimp and Crab Scrambled, '79 261
Eggs, Shrimp-Stuffed, '00 70
Élégante, Shrimp, '83 48
Enchiladas in Tomatillo Sauce, Shrimp, '95 310
Enchiladas, Poblano-Shrimp, '00 311
Enchiladas, Shrimp, '01 104
en Papillote, Shrimp Cancun, '91 136
en Papillote, Shrimp with Asparagus, '86 145
Étouffée, Crab-and-Shrimp, '89 96
Étouffée, Shrimp, '79 4; '90 229
Feta Cheese, Shrimp with, '00 221
Filling, Shrimp and Dill, '97 171
Firecracker Shrimp, '03 144
Fire-Roasted Shrimp with Orzo, '99 42
Fish with Shrimp, Veracruz, '86 130
Flambé, Prawns, '89 24
Florentine, Chicken-and-Shrimp, '89 64
Flounder Stuffed with Shrimp, '88 51
Fondue, Shrimp, '86 244
French-Fried Shrimp, '79 4
French Shrimp, '80 85
Fresh Shrimp, Preparing, '82 127
Fried Marinated Shrimp with Mango Slaw, '93 31
Fried Noodles with Shrimp, '02 174
Fried Rice, Spicy Shrimp-and-Pineapple, '03 285
Fried Shrimp, '03 109
Fried Shrimp, Coconut, '96 248
Fried Shrimp, Cracker-Breaded, '04 122
Fried Shrimp, Golden, '82 29
Fried Shrimp, Gulf Coast, '91 29
Fried Shrimp, Puffy, '79 4
Fried Shrimp, Texas Best, '05 327
Fried Shrimp with Apricot Sauce, '87 172
Fritters, Shrimp, '00 238
Garlic-Buttered Shrimp, '86 M226
Garlic-Chili Shrimp and Grits, '00 23
Garlic Shrimp, '79 268; '80 14
Garlic Shrimp and Grits, '03 246; '05 111
Gin and Ginger, Shrimp with, '95 205
Grilled Garlic Shrimp, '99 178
Grilled Margarita-Marinated Shrimp, '97 167
Grilled Parsleyed Shrimp and Vegetables, '04 256
Grilled Shrimp, '85 103
Grilled Shrimp with Bacon and Jalapeños, '05 M200
Grilled Shrimp with Citrus Salsa, '97 141
Grilled Shrimp with Smoky Sweet Sauce, Mexican-, '03 32
Grilled Shrimp with Tropical Fruit Sauce, '01 195
Grilled Sweet-and-Sour Shrimp, '97 100
Grits, Crook's Corner Shrimp and, '04 102
Grits, Shrimp and, '01 258
Grits with Red Bean Salsa, Shrimp-Manchego-Chorizo, '97 227
Gumbo, Shrimp-Crab, '03 111
Gyros with Herbed Yogurt Spread, Grilled-Shrimp, '02 169
Hoisin Shrimp, '99 237
Honeyed Shrimp, Tangy, '94 32
Jambalaya with Shrimp, Chicken-and-Ham, '04 99
Kebabs, Grilled Shrimp-and-Scallop, '92 210
Kebabs, Marinated Shrimp, '84 276; '85 158
Kebabs, Shrimp, '80 150, 184
Kebabs, Steak-and-Shrimp, '80 184; '00 124
Lamb Chops with Shrimp, '88 58
Lemon Butter, Shrimp in, '84 163
Lemon Garlic Sauce, Shrimp in, '83 67
Lemon Shrimp, Luscious, '88 150

SHRIMP
(continued)

Marinara, Shrimp, '84 233
Marinated and Grilled Shrimp, '87 141
Marinated Shrimp, '98 317; '02 254
Marinated Shrimp, Grilled, '87 173
Marinated Shrimp, Grilled Margarita-, '97 167
Marinated Shrimp with Capers, '00 279
Marinated Shrimp with Louis Sauce, Citrus-, '03 66
Marinated Shrimp, Zesty, '87 173
Martinis with Napa Cabbage Slaw, Shrimp, '02 280
Mediterranean Shrimp Bowl, '80 174
Melba, Shrimp, '84 86
Mirlitons, Shrimp-and-Ham Stuffed, '03 251
Mirlitons, Stuffed, '97 263; '00 246
Mornay, Shrimp and Scallops, '97 238
Mustard-Vinegar Sauce, Shrimp with, '93 240
Noodles, Sesame, '01 188
Omelet, Shrimp-and-Cheddar, '84 57
Omelet, Shrimp-and-Cheese, '94 31
Omelet, Shrimp-and-Vegetable Oven, '99 286
Orange Sauce, Shrimp in, '99 292; '00 292
Oriental, Shrimp, '01 36
Oven Shrimp, Vic's, '95 215
Pad Thai, '97 202
Paella, '97 328
Paella Casserole, '95 254
Paella, Chicken-Pork-Shrimp, '82 245
Paella, Party, '88 M189
Paella, Shortcut, '01 309
Paella, Shrimp-and-Chicken, '94 168
Paella, Spanish, '85 26
Paella Valenciana, '82 246
Palermo, Shrimp, '04 241
Pasta. *See also* **SHRIMP/Salads.**
  Angel Hair Pasta, Shrimp and Mushrooms with, '92 34
  Angel Hair Pasta with Shrimp and Asparagus, '92 100
  Angel Hair Pasta with Veal and Shrimp, '04 223
  Asian Shrimp with Pasta, '04 128
  Asparagus, Tomatoes, and Shrimp, Garlicky Pasta with, '95 82
  Cajun Shrimp and Andouille Alfredo Sauce Over Pasta, '05 57
  Cheeses, Shrimp and Pasta with Two, '98 49
  Cream Sauce, Shrimp and Pasta with, '98 295
  Creole Cream Sauce, Shrimp and Pasta with, '05 49
  Fettuccine and Shrimp with Dried Tomato Pesto, '94 249
  Fettuccine, Dilled Shrimp with, '99 141
  Fettuccine, Shrimp, '94 84; '96 210
  Fettuccine, Shrimp-Herb, '01 308
  Fettuccine with Shrimp-and-Creamy Herb Sauce, '01 257
  Fettuccine with Shrimp and Tomatoes, '96 198
  Garlic-and-Rosemary Shrimp, '01 101
  Garlic Shrimp-and-Goat Cheese Pasta, '00 174
  Green Pasta with Shrimp-Mushroom Italienne, '79 170
  Herbed Shrimp and Pasta, '92 329; '97 228
  Lemon Shrimp and Pasta, '96 124
  Linguine, Artichoke and Shrimp, '95 210
  Linguine, Spicy Shrimp and, '92 34
  Manicotti, Shrimp, '97 96
  Mediterranean Shrimp and Pasta, '95 286
  Medley, Shrimp-Pasta, '88 302
  Noodles, Creamy Shrimp and, '92 100
  Noodles with Shrimp, Hoisin, '98 233
  Pasta with Shrimp, '01 164
  Primavera, Shrimp with Pasta, '93 168
  Roasted Red Pepper Cream, Shrimp with, '03 97
  Rotelle, Shrimp, '85 165
  Salad, Pasta-and-Shrimp, '83 163
  Sautéed Shrimp and Pasta, '96 288
  Scampi, Pasta with Shrimp, '01 83
  Scampi, Shrimp, '95 209

Shrimp and Pasta, '91 207
Spaghetti, Shrimp-and-Vegetable, '91 170
Spaghetti with Black Olives, Shrimp, '85 13
Spicy Pasta and Shrimp, '97 67
Spinach Pasta, Creamy Shrimp-and-, '05 239
Spinach Pasta, Shrimp-and-, '01 258
Tomato Pasta, Shrimp-, '98 172
Tortellini, Shrimp and, '92 34
Vermicelli Salad, Shrimp, '88 139
Vermicelli, Shrimp and Feta Cheese on, '87 108
Paste, Shrimp, '05 98
Patties, Shrimp, '92 128
Peanut Sauce, Shrimp with, '93 303
Peppers, Shrimp-Stuffed, '80 162; '86 131, 197; '97 268
Peppers, Spicy Stuffed, '98 243
Pesto Shrimp Over Rice, Texas, '03 327
Pickled Shrimp, '79 3; '94 182; '05 158
Pilaf, Shrimp, '82 246
Pilau, Shrimp, '99 184
Pitas, Shrimp, '05 188
Pizza, Shrimp-and-Dried Tomato, '97 49
Pizza, The Best of the Bayou, '95 268
Platter with Béarnaise Sauce, Artichoke and Shrimp, '96 132
Po' Boys, Shrimp, '97 312
Po'boys, Shrimp, '02 184
Polynesian Shrimp, '79 3
Potatoes, Broccoli-Shrimp Stuffed, '92 M228
Potatoes, Creamy Shrimp-Stuffed, '80 36
Potatoes, Shrimp-and-Mushroom Stuffed, '99 308
Potatoes, Shrimp-Sauced, '81 M61
Puff, Shrimp-Crab, '79 57
Puffs, Luncheon Shrimp, '85 72
Puppies, Hot-to-Trot Shrimp, '97 84
Quesadillas, Shrimp-and-Roasted Pepper, '00 215
Quesadillas with Shrimp and Brie, '94 173
Quiche, Shrimp, '83 50
Quiche, Shrimp-and-Artichoke, '03 196
Redfish with Shrimp and Crab, Coastal Bend, '01 281
Rellenos, Shrimp, '00 174
Rémoulade Sauce, Shrimp with, '91 29
Rice, Oriental Shrimp and, '90 183
Rice, Shrimp and Refried, '89 176
Rice, Shrimp and Sausage, '79 64
Rice, Shrimp with, '03 219
Risotto, Shrimp, '00 95; '02 124
Risotto with Shrimp and Asparagus, '03 86
Risotto with Shrimp, Pumpkin, '98 240
Rock Shrimp Tails, Batter-Fried, '80 2
Rock Shrimp Tails, Broiled, '80 3
Rock Shrimp Tails, Sweet-and-Sour, '80 3
Rolls, Shrimp, '03 162; '05 188
Rolls, Shrimp-and-Romaine, '97 197
Rollups, Shrimp-Stuffed, '82 234
Sailor Shrimp for Two, '82 276
Salads
  Aloha Shrimp Salad, '95 46
  Artichoke Salad, Shrimp-and-, '04 50
  Aspic, Shrimp-Coleslaw, '79 88
  Aspic, Shrimp-Cucumber, '83 108
  Aspic with Shrimp, Tomato, '79 241
  Avocado Salad, Shrimp and, '80 266
  Avocado Stuffed with Shrimp Salad, '82 207
  Black Bean Salad, Caribbean Shrimp-and-, '93 143
  Coastal Shrimp Salad, '00 17
  Couscous Salad, Shrimp-and-, '96 157
  Crabmeat-Shrimp Pasta Salad, '86 208
  Creamy Shrimp Salad, '79 56
  Croissants, Shrimp Salad on, '96 175
  Curried Shrimp Salad, '00 217
  Egg Salad Club, Shrimp-, '02 203
  Egg Salad Sandwiches, Shrimp-and-, '94 182
  Endive Salad, Shrimp-, '85 73
  Filling, Shrimp Salad, '87 106

Fleur-de-lis Salad, '99 164
Fruited Shrimp Salad, '86 156
Grapefruit-and-Shrimp Salad, '88 5
Greek Salad, Dawn's World-Famous, '98 276
Green Salad with Shrimp, '88 49
Grilled Shrimp, Orange, and Watermelon Salad with Peppered Peanuts in a Zesty Citrus Dressing, '04 308
Half Shell, Shrimp Salad on the, '86 73
Individual Shrimp Salads, '83 146
Layered Shrimp Salad, '88 100
Macaroni Salad, Shrimp, '79 220
Macaroni Salad, Shrimp-, '85 219
Macaroni-Shrimp Salad, '85 121
Macaroni-Shrimp Salad, Festive, '85 165
Marinated Shrimp Salad, '85 82; '93 321; '99 169
Melon and Shrimp Curry Salad, '97 129
Old Bay Shrimp Salad, '05 188
Orange, and Olive Salad with Sherry Vinaigrette, Shrimp, '93 177
Orange Rice Salad, Zesty Shrimp-and-, '87 155
Orange-Shrimp Salad, '84 197
Oriental Shrimp Salad, '91 313
Orzo Salad, Peppers Stuffed with Shrimp-and-, '91 203
Orzo Salad, Shrimp-and-, '99 182
Pasta-and-Shrimp Salad, '83 163
Pasta Salad with Green Goddess Dressing, Shrimp, '02 139
Pastry, Shrimp Salad in, '86 105
Picnic Shrimp Salad, '95 182
Potato Salad, Shrimp-and-, '96 211
Rice-and-Shrimp Salad, '83 82
Rice Salad, Baked Shrimp-, '83 22
Rice Salad, Shrimp and, '80 231; '82 207
Rice Salad, Shrimp-and-, '92 307
Rice Salad, Tangy Shrimp-, '84 66
Rice-Shrimp Salad, '79 270; '92 142
Sandwiches, Shrimp Salad, '90 178
Sea Slaw, Tomatoes Stuffed with, '89 96
Shrimp Salad, '81 94; '84 221; '86 186; '93 238; '98 333; '04 147; '05 65, 95
Spinach Salad with Grilled Shrimp, Tropical, '04 51
Super Shrimp Salad, '81 37
Tossed Shrimp-Egg Salad, '80 4
Vegetable-Shrimp Salad, '79 190
Vermicelli Salad, Shrimp, '88 139
Walnut Salad, Shrimp-, '86 182
Wild Rice-and-Shrimp Salad, '02 109
Wild Rice-Shrimp Salad, '99 55
Sandwiches, Open-Faced Shrimp-Cornbread, '02 141
Sandwiches, Shrimp-Cheese, '85 242
Sauce, Broccoli and Cauliflower with Shrimp, '84 248
Sauce, Cajun Shrimp-and-Crab, '05 206
Sauce, Creamy Shrimp, '03 53
Sauce, Flounder Fillets in Shrimp, '83 227
Sauce, Flounder with Hollandaise-Shrimp, '86 234
Sauce, Grandpa Jim's Shrimp, '01 182
Sauce, Oysters in Shrimp, '87 40
Sauce Piquante, Crab and Shrimp, '83 92
Sauce, Shrimp, '87 138, 232; '01 182; '04 147
Sauce, Shrimp-and-Almond, '87 282
Sauce, Shrimp Cocktail, '01 182
Sausage over Creamy Grits with Tasso Gravy, Spicy Shrimp and, '92 236
Sausage, Shrimp, '97 164
Sauté, Confetti Shrimp, '97 104
Sautéed Shrimp, '79 3
Sautéed Shrimp and Thai Coconut Broth with Noodles, '98 295
Sautéed Shrimp with Country Ham and Capers, '04 241
Sautéed Shrimp with Cranberry-Citrus Salsa, '97 290
Sauté, Shrimp-and-Grouper, '87 91
Sauté, Shrimp-and-Scallop, '85 103
Sauté with Pecan Rice, Shrimp-and-Scallop, '90 317

Scampi, Easy, '84 291
Scampi, Orange, '85 303
Scampi, Quick, '88 301
Scampi, Shrimp, '84 230; '92 117; '93 70; '00 283
Scampi, Speedy, '02 161
Shells, Creamy Shrimp, '79 4
Sirloin Supreme, Shrimp and, '81 131
Skewers with Vegetable Salsa, Shrimp, '98 32, 223
Skillet, Quick Shrimp, '87 50
Smoked Shrimp, Citrus-Marinated, '95 114
Snow Pea-Shrimp Combo, '79 57
Snow Peas, Shrimp with, '85 75
Soups
   Bisque, Curried Butternut-Shrimp, '01 248
   Bisque, Okra-and-Shrimp, '97 156
   Bisque, Seafarer's, '97 67
   Bisque, Shrimp, '95 19
   Bisque, Shrimp-Chile, '94 272
   Bisque, Shrimp-Cucumber, '79 172
   Bisque, Shrimp-Vegetable, '82 313; '83 66
   Bisque, Tomato-Shrimp, '86 66
   Bouillabaisse, Marcelle's, '99 200
   Cheese Soup, Shrimp-, '01 145
   Chowder, Artichoke-Shrimp, '03 91
   Chowder, Shrimp, '89 218
   Chowder, Shrimp and Corn, '79 199
   Corn Soup, Shrimp-and-, '84 88
   Corn Soup with Shiitakes and Shrimp, Sweet,
     '99 168
   Enchilada Soup, Shrimp, '94 103
   Gazpacho, Shrimp-Cream Cheese, '94 137
   Gumbo, '01 160
   Gumbo, Crab and Shrimp, '81 200
   Gumbo, Old-Style Shrimp, '98 97
   Gumbo, Quick Shrimp, '86 71
   Gumbo, Shrimp, '81 199
   Gumbo, Shrimp-Crab, '98 15
   Jambalaya, Creole Shrimp, '92 99
   Mushroom Soup, Shrimp-, '85 87
   Okra-and-Shrimp Soup, '94 323
   Stock, Shrimp, '93 60
Spicy Shrimp and Grits, '04 176
Spread, Shrimp, '81 306; '85 135; '87 111; '93 205;
   '96 104
Spread, Shrimp-Cucumber, '79 81
Squash, Stuffed, '01 223
Steak and Shrimp, '88 123
Stew and Grits, Shrimp, '80 118
Stewed Shrimp with Dumplings, '79 31
Stew, Frogmore, '92 236; '00 174, 336; '03 181;
   '05 111
Stew over Grits, Shrimp, '88 126; '89 47
Stew, Shrimp, '83 4
Stir-Fry, Beef-and-Shrimp, '93 32
Stir-Fry, Cajun Shrimp, '92 127
Stir-Fry Shrimp, '96 129; '01 95
Stir-Fry, Shrimp, '01 258
Stir-Fry, Shrimp-and-Vegetable Medley, '99 205
Stir-Fry Shrimp and Vegetables, '87 91
Stroganoff, Oven-Baked Shrimp, '81 297
Stroganoff, Shrimp, '79 81
Stroganoff, Strolling-Through-the-Holidays,
   '01 282
Stuffed Jumbo Shrimp, '05 124
Stuffed Shrimp Bundles, Crab-, '81 176
Stuffed Shrimp, Crab-, '84 259
Stuffed Shrimp, Parmesan-, '85 103
Stuffed Shrimp with Hollandaise Sauce, '95 86
Sweet-and-Sour Shrimp, '83 278; '90 M112
Sweet-and-Sour Shrimp and Chicken, '87 267;
   '88 103; '89 66
Sweet-and-Sour Shrimp with Onion and Red Pepper,
   '02 84
Szechuan Shrimp, '86 173

Tacos, Shrimp-and-Pepper Soft, '95 339
Tacos with Spicy Cream Sauce, Shrimp, '01 170
Tartar Sauce, Shrimp with, '00 178
Tart, Shrimp, '87 70
Tarts, Shrimp 'n' Grits, '03 254
Tempura "Shrimps," French-Fried, '97 128
Tempura Udon, '00 93
Topping, Shrimp, '93 291
Tostadas, Shrimp-and-Black Bean, '93 204
Vegetables, Shrimp and, '82 6
Versailles, Shrimp, '90 233
Wine Sauce, Shrimp and, '98 50
Yellow Squash, Shrimp-Stuffed, '84 194
Yogurt-Cucumber Sauce, Shrimp with, '04 216
SLAWS
Apple-Bacon Coleslaw, '04 181
Apple-Carrot Slaw, '92 243
Apple Coleslaw, '89 315
Apple-Pineapple Slaw, '79 241
Apple Slaw, Fresh, '81 63
Apple Slaw, Nutty, '88 216
Asian Slaw, '99 108
Asian Slaw, Crispy, '97 180; '01 195
Aspic, Shrimp-Coleslaw, '79 88
Bacon Coleslaw, '83 58
Banana-Nut Slaw, '86 250
Barbecue Coleslaw, '97 139
Barbecue Coleslaw, Best, '97 214; '04 100
Blue Cheese-Bacon Slaw, '05 91
Blue Cheese Coleslaw, '89 13; '95 270
Broccoli Slaw, '01 49; '05 278
Broccoli Slaw, Sweet, '96 20; '98 332
Broccoli Slaw, Zesty, '93 246
Broccoli-Squash Slaw, '05 170
Buttermilk Dressing Coleslaw, '04 24
Cabbage-Orange Slaw, '79 135
Cabbage-Pineapple Slaw, '92 182
Cabbage Slaw, Chinese, '89 312; '01 36
Cabbage Slaw, Crunchy, '02 95
Cabbage Slaw, Fresh, '85 139
Cabbage Slaw, Nutty, '88 218
Cabbage Slaw, Sweet, '79 76
Carolina Coleslaw, Creamy, '05 167
Cauliflower Slaw, '92 167
Celery Root-and-Carrot Slaw, Shredded, '98 293
Chicken Coleslaw, '84 2
Chili Coleslaw, '80 178
Cilantro Slaw, '05 324
Coleslaw, '79 152; '82 135; '02 57; '03 252
Colorful Coleslaw, '88 166
Confetti Slaw, '89 48
Cooked Dressing, Aunt Beulah's Coleslaw with, '99 82
Corn and Cabbage Slaw, '79 135
Cottage Coleslaw, '80 64
Country-Style Coleslaw, '83 59
Creamy-and-Sweet Coleslaw, '05 125
Creamy Coleslaw, '83 170; '98 244; '02 167
Creamy Sweet Coleslaw, '01 148; '03 105
Crunchy Coleslaw, '86 295
Cucumber Slaw, Creamy, '89 49
Cumin-Celery-Scented Coleslaw, '02 51
Curried Coleslaw, '85 139
Danny's Slaw, '00 275
Dill Slaw, Creamy, '01 143
Dressing, Sweet Slaw, '98 184
Fiesta Coleslaw, '04 275
Freezer Coleslaw, '89 49
Freezer Slaw, '81 279; '82 24; '83 154; '99 260; '03 106
Frozen Coleslaw, '82 102
Fruit Coleslaw, Three-, '86 250
Fruited Coleslaw, '83 209; '85 139
German Cabbage Slaw, '00 105
Ginger Slaw, Tangy, '01 92
Grape-Poppy Seed Slaw, '86 225

Grapes and Almonds, Coleslaw with, '83 59
Green Bean Slaw, '95 108
Guacamole Mexican Coleslaw, '82 302
Ham Coleslaw, '84 195
Healthy Slaw, '92 183
Hot-and-Creamy Dutch Slaw, '87 127
Hot-and-Sour Chinese Slaw, '85 139
Hot Slaw, '89 49
Jalapeño Coleslaw, '97 26
Jose Falcón's Slaw, '04 207
Kentucky Coleslaw, '81 216
Layered Coleslaw, '86 180
Layered Slaw, '93 214
Lemon-Apple Coleslaw, '05 44
Lemon-Yogurt Coleslaw, Grilled Chicken Breasts with,
   '98 148
Light and Creamy Coleslaw, '93 318
Make-Ahead Coleslaw, '81 155
Mango Slaw, '93 31; '94 71
Marinated Coleslaw, '79 135
Marinated Slaw, '91 229
Memphis Slaw, '91 28
Memphis-Style Coleslaw, '98 104
Mexicali Coleslaw, '84 18
Mexican Coleslaw, '89 48
Mustard Slaw, Texas, '88 172
Napa Cabbage Slaw, '02 280
Old-Fashioned Coleslaw, '80 120; '82 225; '99 235
Old-Fashioned Slaw, '84 149
Old-Fashioned Sweet Coleslaw, '93 128
Overnight Cabbage Slaw, '81 88; '82 7
Overnight Coleslaw, '79 135
Overnight Slaw, '79 5; '92 280; '05 208
Peach Slaw, Party, '86 250
Peanut Slaw, '85 139
Peanut Slaw, Chinese, '93 212
Pear Slaw, Peanutty-, '86 250
Peppery Hot Coleslaw, '98 159
Pineapple-Almond Slaw, '92 171
Pineapple Coleslaw, Curried, '88 172
Pineapple Slaw, '94 49; '99 26
Pineapple Slaw, Colorful, '86 250
Polka Dot Slaw, '83 59
Rainbow Slaw, '01 259
Red Bean Slaw, '79 247
Red Cabbage-and-Apple Slaw, '87 31; '91 309
Red Cabbage Coleslaw, Sweet-and-Tart, '05 125
Red Cabbage Slaw, '95 153
Seafood Slaw, '79 56
Sea Slaw, Tomatoes Stuffed with, '89 96
Sesame Slaw, '02 206
Silks, '93 236
Sour Cream Coleslaw, '99 220
Sour Cream Slaw, '87 10
Soy Slaw and Dipping Sauce, Grilled Chicken with
   Sweet, '04 123
Soy Slaw and Dipping Sauce, Grilled Salmon with
   Sweet, '04 123
Swedish Slaw, '79 135
Sweet and Crunchy Slaw, '79 104
Sweet-and-Sour Hot Slaw, '92 63
Sweet-and-Sour Slaw, '81 237
Sweet-and-Sour Slaw, Confetti, '98 89
Sweet-and-Spicy Slaw, '05 17
Sweet-and-Tangy Slaw, '04 199
Sweet Onion Slaw, '98 171
Sweet Potato-Currant Slaw, '93 246
Sweet Slaw, Creamy, '00 172; '01 322
Tangy Coleslaw, '83 59
Tangy Slaw, '02 215
"Think Pink" Slaw, '94 247
Tomatoes, Coleslaw with, '80 34
Turnip Slaw, '89 245
Vegetables, Coleslaw with Garden, '01 57

SLAWS

(continued)

Vegetable Slaw, '81 280; '00 42
Vinegar Coleslaw, Zesty, '05 125
Wraps, Chicken-and-Bean Slaw, '04 163
Zesty Slaw, '82 127; '97 324
Zucchini Coleslaw, Fiesta, '91 168

SLOW COOKER

Appetizers

Cheese Queso, Chunky, '99 279
Meatballs, Bourbon-Mustard Glazed, '05 305
Meatballs, Spicy Chipotle-Barbecue, '05 305
Meatballs, Sweet-and-Sour, '05 305
Sausage Bites, Bourbon-Mustard Glazed, '05 305
Sausage Bites, Spicy Chipotle-Barbecue, '05 305
Sausage Bites, Sweet-and-Sour, '05 305
Bean Bake, Slow Cooker Three-, '99 88
Beans, Hearty Baked, '01 259
Beans, Slow Cooker Barbecue, '05 180
Black-Eyed Peas, Hot-and-Spicy, '99 235
Butter, Slow Cooker Apple, '97 235

Desserts

Apples 'n' Pears, Saucy, '96 72
Pie, Caramel, '96 72
Dressing, Slow-Cooker Cornbread, '05 270

Main Dishes

Barbecue, Chuck Roast, '96 71
Beef Barbecue, Slow-Cooker, '02 299
Burritos, Easy, '04 32
Chalupa Dinner Bowl, '05 238
Eye of Round, Slow Cooker Spicy Marinated, '99 291
Fajitas, Slow Cooker, '02 43
Fajitas, Turkey, '01 108
Ham, Pinto Beans with, '97 210
Kielbasa with Beans, Easy Cheesy, '01 28
Pork and Vegetables, Apple Cider, '97 210
Pork Chops and Gravy, '96 71
Pork Chops, Farm-Style, '02 42
Potatoes with Ham, Scalloped, '02 42
Pot Roast, Cowboy, '05 35
Pot Roast, Italian, '05 34
Red Beans and Rice, New Orleans, '97 235
Ribs and Beans, Spicy Sweet, '02 299
Ribs and Beans, Spicy-Sweet, '03 314
Ribs, Barbecued Baby Back, '97 234
Ribs, Slow-Cooker Barbecue, '03 160
Roast Beef, Slow Cooker, '01 86
Roast, Pumpernickel, '97 234
Roast, Savory Chuck, '00 18
Roast, Slow Cooker Chuck, '98 32
Oatmeal in a Slow Cooker with Ice Cream, '99 193

Sandwiches

Adobo Pork Sandwiches with Rosemary-Garlic Mayonnaise, '01 322
Barbecue Beef Sandwiches, Slow-Cooker, '05 64
Barbecue Sandwiches, Debate, '97 234
French Dip Sandwiches, '97 211
Pork Dip Sandwiches, Easy Spanish, '04 312
Sauce, Slow-Simmered Spaghetti, '96 72

Soups and Stews

Beef Stew, Slow-Cooker, '05 235
Black Bean Soup, '98 291
Brunswick Stew, Easy, '99 235
Camp Stew, '02 42
Chicken Brunswick Stew, '97 234
Chili Bean Soup, '96 71
Chili, Big-Batch, '04 242
Chili, Easy, '02 299
Chili, Slow Cooker Cincinnati-Style, '00 34
Chili, Slow-Cooker Red Bean, '02 20
French Onion Soup, Caramelized, '00 218

Peasant Soup, '01 54
Potato Soup, Hearty, '98 292
Steak Soup, '99 260
Texas Stew, '97 211
Tortilla Soup, '98 291
Vegetable Soup, '98 32, 291

Vegetables

Onions, Caramelized, '00 218
Sweet Potatoes, Easy-Does-It Mashed, '05 250

SOUFFLÉS

Blue Cheese Soufflé, '91 244
Cheddar Cheese Soufflé, '98 24
Cheese Soufflé, '79 72, 261; '94 116
Cheese Soufflé for Two, '81 226
Cheese Soufflé, Rolled, '89 13
Cheese Soufflés, Three-, '96 219
Cheese Soufflé, Three-Egg, '87 234
Chicken-Chestnut Soufflé, '79 107
Chile-Cheese Soufflés, '96 219
Cornbread, Soufflé, '96 34
Crab Soufflé Spread, '85 4
Cups, Hot Soufflé, '85 284

Dessert

Apricot Soufflé, Baked, '88 267
au Chocolat Cointreau, Soufflé, '94 56
Banana Daiquiri Soufflé, '84 317
Blintz Soufflé, '88 155
Brandy Alexander Soufflé, '82 173; '83 M114
Bread Pudding Soufflé, Creole, '92 87
Chocolate Mint Soufflé, '81 16
Chocolate Soufflé, '84 317; '94 46
Chocolate Soufflé, Light, '83 278
Chocolate Soufflé with White Chocolate Mousse, '98 57
Coconut Soufflé, '79 73; '85 212
Cranberry-Topped Holiday Soufflé, '84 306
Cream Cheese Soufflé, '88 11
Daiquiri Soufflé, Elegant, '80 69
Devonshire Soufflé, Chilled, '88 279
Gingerbread Soufflés with Lemon Cream, '04 300
Grand Marnier Soufflé, '79 281
Grand Marnier Soufflés, '89 290; '03 318
Grasshopper Soufflé, '81 248; '86 188
Kahlúa Soufflé, '82 173
Lemon-Lime Soufflé, Cold, '84 24
Lemon Sauce Soufflés, Quick, '88 43
Lemon Soufflé, '82 170, 252; '94 199
Lemon Soufflé, Tart, '85 82
Lemon Soufflé with Raspberry-Amaretto Sauce, Frozen, '88 130
Orange Dessert Soufflé, '83 206
Orange Soufflé, Chilled, '84 317; '86 189
Orange Soufflé, Frozen, '79 211
Pineapple Dessert Soufflé, '80 153
Raspberry Soufflé, '86 188
Raspberry-Topped Soufflé, '85 317
Spiced Soufflés with Lemon Whipped Cream, '05 255
Vanilla Soufflé, Frozen, '79 230; '82 173
Vanilla Soufflés with Vanilla Crème Sauce, '94 242; '96 155
Egg Soufflé Casserole, '83 55
Egg Soufflés, Little, '83 57
Frozen Soufflés, Individual, '80 52
Grits Soufflé, '80 30
Grits Soufflé, Garlic-Cheese, '99 18
Grits Soufflé, Mexican, '79 55
Ham Breakfast Soufflé, Virginia, '93 121
Ham Soufflé with Cucumber Sauce, '92 41
Individual Soufflés, '80 190
Parmesan Soufflés, '97 280
Pizzaola Soufflé, Italian, '98 232
Pizzaola Soufflé, Mexican, '98 232
Rice-Cheese Soufflé, '79 270
Roll, Shrimp Soufflé, '89 320
Roll, Southwestern Soufflé, '97 171

Salmon Soufflé, Fresh, '81 182
Souffleeta, '05 326
Sour Cream Soufflé, '80 43
Turkey Soufflé, '80 271

Vegetable

Asparagus Soufflé, '79 66; '83 265; '89 89
Broccoli Soufflé, '81 24
Broccoli Soufflé, Golden, '84 283
Broccoli Soufflés, '96 218
Butternut Soufflé, '83 266
Butternut Squash Soufflé, '97 270
Carrot Puff, '89 89
Carrot Soufflé, '79 73; '83 265; '98 231; '99 25; '01 84, 284; '05 66
Carrot Soufflés, '96 309
Cauliflower Soufflé, '82 76; '89 279; '90 17
Corn-and-Cheese Soufflé, '88 122
Mushroom Soufflés, '87 282
Onion Soufflé, '79 247
Parsnip Soufflé, Golden, '83 266
Potatoes, Soufflé, '84 295; '85 196; '90 14
Potato Soufflé, Cheesy, '89 332
Rutabaga Soufflé, '01 213
Spinach Soufflé, '79 73; '81 304; '84 78; '85 248; '86 108; '05 66
Spinach Soufflé, Cheese-and-, '98 235
Spinach Soufflé, Cheesy, '81 53
Spinach Soufflé Deluxe, '79 8
Spinach Soufflé Roll, '80 215
Squash Soufflé, '95 215
Squash Soufflé, Cheesy, '82 146
Sweet Potato Soufflé, '82 286; '86 121; '93 325; '96 247; '00 273; '05 110
Turnip Soufflé, '79 254
Vidalia Onion Soufflé, '04 167
Yellow Squash Soufflé, '89 89
Zucchini-and-Corn Soufflé, '83 265
Zucchini-Corn Soufflés, '97 203
Zucchini Soufflé, '79 157

SOUPS. *See also* **BEANS/Soups; CHILI; CHOWDERS; GUMBOS; JAMBALAYAS; RAGOÛTS; STEWS.**

Acorn-Butternut Soup, Creamy, '96 216
Acorn Squash-and-Apple Soup, Curried, '03 221
Acorn Squash Soup, '91 294
Acorn Squash Soup, Cream of, '94 268
Acorn Squash-Thyme Soup, '99 252
Almond Soup, '79 48
Artichoke Cream Soup, '94 62
Artichoke Soup, '89 269
Artichoke Soup, Cream of, '82 232
Asparagus Soup, '84 67; '98 290; '00 84
Asparagus Soup, Cream of, '84 111
Asparagus Soup, Creamy, '94 225
Bacon, Lettuce, and Tomato Soup, '91 207

Bean

Bacon Soup, Bean and, '83 26
Barley Soup, Hearty Bean-and-, '86 304
"Bean Counter" Soup, '92 80
Beanolla Soup, '94 248
Bean Soup, '80 25
Black Beans and Cilantro, Southwestern Scallop Broth with, '87 123
Black Bean Soup, '88 30, 266; '89 28; '93 231; '98 291; '02 121; '03 219
Black Bean Soup, Carolina, '92 139
Black Bean Soup, Marge Clyde's, '96 29
Cabbage-Bean Soup, '97 301
Capitol Hill Bean Soup, '80 222
Chicken Soup, Bean-, '99 283
Chili Bean Soup, '96 71
Chill-Chaser Soup, '87 282
Drunken Bean Soup, '87 283
French Market Soup, '85 277; '92 49; '94 317
Green Bean Soup, Cream of, '84 111

Ham-and-Bean Soup, '84 4
Ham-and-Bean Soup, Spicy, '94 322
Ham Soup, Bean-and-, '04 325
Hominy Soup, Bean-and-, '95 23
Leafy Bean Soup, '86 223
Minestra, '97 246
Mix, Bean Soup, '99 283
Mix, French Market Soup, '85 277; '94 317
Navy Bean Soup, '84 280; '96 19
Navy Bean Soup, Chunky, '83 291
Navy Bean Soup, Savory, '87 282
Pasta Soup, Bean and, '94 220
Quick Bean Soup, '99 97
Red Bean Soup with Walnuts, '96 243
Refried Bean Soup, '96 136
Sausage-Bean Soup, '85 88
Sausage-Bean Soup, Spicy, '83 229
Three-Bean Soup, '89 17
Three-Bean Squash Soup, Spicy, '91 28
Turkey Soup, Bean-and-, '93 319
White Bean Pot, '86 194
White Bean Soup, '83 229; '90 201
White Bean Soup, Spicy, '94 225
Beef-and-Pepperoni Soup, Italian-Style, '00 316
Bell Pepper Soup, '89 103
Bisques
Banana-Raspberry Bisque, '93 161
Butternut-Shrimp Bisque, Curried, '01 248
Butternut Squash Bisque, Roasted, '03 230
Chicken Bisque, Curried, '00 144
Clam Bisque, '86 228
Crab-and-Corn Bisque, '87 137
Crab-and-Leek Bisque, '94 104
Crab-and-Spinach Bisque, '97 241
Crab Bisque, '88 251
Mushroom Bisque, Brisk, '81 190
Okra-and-Shrimp Bisque, '97 156
Oyster Bisque, '83 252; '96 276; '99 320
Pumpkin Bisque, Spicy, '86 67
Seafarer's Bisque, '97 67
Seafood Bisque, '86 66
Shrimp Bisque, '95 19
Shrimp-Chile Bisque, '94 272
Shrimp-Cucumber Bisque, '79 172
Shrimp-Vegetable Bisque, '82 313; '83 66
Smoked Salmon-Whiskey Bisque, '00 65
Spinach-Potato Bisque, '86 66
Squash Bisque, '84 280; '98 290
Stone Crab Bisque, '96 86
Sweet Potato-and-Pear Bisque, '00 317
Tomato-Basil Bisque, '00 49; '02 230
Tomato-Basil Bisque, Make-Ahead, '93 322
Tomato-Shrimp Bisque, '86 66
Tuna Bisque, '79 76
Black-Eyed Pea Soup, '97 213
Black-Eyed Soup, Beefy, '85 6
Black, White, and Red All Over Soup, '95 126
Borscht, Crawfish, '92 84
Borscht, Ruby Red, '83 176
Bouillabaisse, Florida, '79 158
Bouillon, Court-, '98 229
Bouillon, Redfish Court, '83 290; '84 93
Bouillon, Tomato, '83 8
Bourbon with Molasses Sauce, Burned, '95 17
Bread Bowls, Italian, '98 292
Broccoli
Broccoli Soup, '86 161, M194; '87 288
Cheese-and-Broccoli Soup, '89 276
Cheesy-Broccoli Soup, '86 258
Chicken Soup, Broccoli-and-, '90 202
Creamed Broccoli Soup, '85 24
Cream of Broccoli Soup, '79 130; '80 188, M225;
    '82 314; '83 66; '86 259
Cream-of-Broccoli Soup, '88 56

Cream of Broccoli Soup, Light, '93 17
Cream of Broccoli Soup, Mock, '85 288
Creamy Broccoli Soup, '81 75; '82 13; '83 99; '91 307
Easy Broccoli Soup, '81 307
Fresh Broccoli Soup, '91 86
Hot Broccoli Soup, '81 235; '83 44
Swiss Soup, Broccoli-, '86 6
Butternut-and-Apple Soup, Creamed, '88 228
Butternut Soup, '02 68
Butternut Soup, Creamy, '96 216
Butternut Squash-Lime Soup, '03 236
Butternut Squash-Parsnip Soup, '05 36
Butternut Squash Soup, '95 62; '03 276
Butternut Squash Soup, Curried, '05 234
Butternut Squash Soup, Saffron, '04 187
Cabbage Soup, '83 291; '85 88
Cabbage Soup, Sweet-and-Sour, '89 314
Carrot
Butternut Squash Soup with Parslied Croutons,
    Carrot-and-, '97 217
Carrot Soup, '80 88; '89 146; '98 123
Cheesy Carrot Soup, '81 262
Chilled Carrot-Mint Soup, '90 M168
Cream of Carrot Soup, '81 307; '88 46; '91 69
Cream Soup, Carrot, '90 210
Creamy Carrot Soup, '92 218
Curried Carrot Soup, '82 157
Leek Soup, Carrot-, '86 34
Leek Soup, Carrot-and-, '02 260
Orange Soup, Carrot-, '79 172
Parsnip Soup, Gingered Carrot-and-, '03 221
Savory Carrot Soup, '84 107
Tomato Soup, Cream of Carrot-and-, '94 176
Cauliflower and Caraway Soup, '82 264
Cauliflower and Watercress Soup, Cream of, '83 126
Cauliflower Soup, '90 211; '99 318
Cauliflower Soup, Cream of, '87 M7; '88 12; '96 277
Cauliflower Soup, Creamy, '82 76
Cauliflower Soup, Fresh, '84 279
Celery Soup, Burnet-, '84 107
Celery Soup, Cream of, '79 71; '90 210
Celery Soup, Light Cream-of-, '82 279
Cheese. *See also* **SOUPS/Onion, Vegetable.**
Anytime Soup, Cheesy, '81 307; '82 314; '83 66
Bacon-Beer Cheese Soup, '87 M7
Bacon-Topped Cheese Soup, '80 M224
Beer-Cheese Soup, '84 246
Blue Satin Soup, '98 248
Broccoli Soup, Cheese-and-, '89 276
Cheddar-Potato Soup, '03 M283
Chunky Cheese Soup, '98 31
Cream Cheese Soup, Austrian, '98 M85
Cream of Cheese Soup, '83 99
Favorite Cheese Soup, Uncle Ed's, '94 228
Gazebo Cheese Soup, '90 158
Hearty Cheese Soup, '84 4
Herbed Cheese Soup, '96 219
Hot Brown Soup, '00 318
Macaroni and Cheese Soup, '95 264
Mexican Cheese Soup, '97 268
Minestrone, Cheesy, '99 17
Monterey Jack Cheese Soup, '81 112; '85 M211
Pimiento Cheese Soup, Creamy, '05 254
Pimiento "Mac and Cheese" Soup, '97 M325
Rice Soup, Wildest, '01 66
Shrimp-Cheese Soup, '01 145
Velvet Soup, Cheese, '80 74; '92 193
Vichyssoise, Velvety Roquefort, '83 223
Cheeseburger Soup, '04 298
Chicken. *See* **SOUPS/Poultry.**
Chocolate Soup, Mexican, '96 277
Cilantro Soup, Cream of, '00 249
Cilantro Soup with Black Bean Salsa, Cream of, '97 226
Citrus Soup, Fiesta, '01 176

Collard Greens Soup, '00 293
Consommé aux Champignons, '79 48
Consommé, Brown Rice, '98 288
Corn-and-Bourbon Soup, '92 194
Corned Beef Soup, '83 16
Corn Soup, '80 56; '85 243; '87 156
Corn Soup, Cream of, '90 210
Corn Soup, Favorite, '85 155
Corn Soup, Grilled, '87 121
Corn Soup, Pimiento-, '89 126
Corn Soup with Crab, Sweet, '02 159
Corn Soup with Shiitakes and Shrimp, Sweet, '99 168
Cucumber-Buttermilk Soup, Chilled, '95 134
Cucumber-Dill Soup, '01 176
Cucumber Soup, Chilled, '79 144
Cucumber Soup, Cold, '79 130; '81 130
Cucumber Soup, Cold Minted, '86 34
Cucumber Soup, Cream of, '81 98
Cucumber Soup, Creamy, '80 171
Cucumber Soup, Dilled, '90 M167
Cucumber Soup with Dill Cream, '00 130
Cucumber-Yogurt Soup, '82 157; '83 205
Curried Soup, '81 130
Dill Soup, Cold, '84 107
Egg Drop Soup, '83 21; '86 16
Egg-Drop Soup, '85 M12
Egg Drop Soup, Lemon-, '93 81
Egg Drop Soup, Spinach, '03 65
Egg Flower Soup, '81 307; '82 313; '83 65
Egg-Lemon Soup, '96 88
Eggplant Soup, Herbed, '90 173
Eggplant Supper Soup, '85 221
English Pea Soup, '96 56
Fish Soup with Garlic Mayonnaise, Rich, '92 56
French Soup Maigre, '98 125
Fruit. *See also* **SOUPS/Gazpacho.**
Apple Soup, Creamed Butternut-and-, '88 228
Avocado-Banana-Yogurt Soup, '80 78
Avocado-Mushroom Soup, Creamy, '85 25
Avocado, '88 160; '05 159, 200
Avocado Soup, Chilled, '81 34; '87 37; '93 108
Avocado Soup, Creamy, '79 107; '01 176
Avocado Soup, Sherried, '84 181
Blueberry Soup, Chilled, '05 178
Cantaloupe Soup, '83 120; '88 160
Cantaloupe Soup, Chilled, '81 156; '97 148
Cantaloupe Soup, Fresh, '84 190
Chestnut Soup, '02 272
Chilled Fresh Fruit Soup, '88 160
Cold Fresh Fruit Soup, '87 157
Dessert, Fruit Soup, '79 172
Dried Fruit Soup, '79 23
Egg-Lemon Soup, '96 88
Fruit Soup, '87 98
Fruit Soup, Fresh, '98 196
Lemon-Egg Drop Soup, '93 81
Lemon Soup, '85 94
Lime Soup, '88 31; '02 168
Mango-Cantaloupe Soup, Chilled, '96 205
Melon Soup, '80 182
Melon Soup, Swirled, '87 162
Orange Soup, Carrot-, '79 172
Peach-Plum Soup, '87 157
Peach Soup, '83 120, 180
Peach Soup, Chilled, '97 159
Peach Soup, Cream of, '99 207
Pear Soup, Pumpkin-, '92 234
Plum-and-Wine Soup, '00 144
Plum Soup, '85 107
Plum Soup, Chilled, '03 161
Plum Soup, Chilled Purple, '79 162
Raspberry Soup, '00 144
Raspberry Soup, Chilled, '81 130
Sherry-Berry Dessert Soup, '91 180

SOUPS, Fruit
(continued)

Strawberry-Banana Soup, '86 181
Strawberry Soup, '88 160
Strawberry Soup, Cold, '82 157
Strawberry Soup Supreme, '81 M144
Swedish Fruit Soup, '82 313; '83 65
Watermelon Soup, Chilled, '03 168
Yogurt Fruit Soup, '86 176

Gazpacho
Berry Gazpacho, '97 181
Blanco, Gazpacho, '01 177
Blender Gazpacho, '85 93
Chilled Gazpacho, '84 138
Citrus Gazpacho, '96 70
Classy Gazpacho, '89 220
Cool Gazpacho, '83 140
Crab Gazpacho, '97 181
Gazpacho, '79 172; '80 266; '81 98; '82 73; '84 112;
   '85 164; '91 94; '92 64; '93 215; '00 118;
   '01 157; '02 130
Grilled Gazpacho, Southwestern, '00 84
Herbed Gazpacho, '95 175
Instant Gazpacho, '00 144
Pineapple Gazpacho, '01 85
Saucy Gazpacho, '82 157
Secret Gazpacho, '93 161
Shrimp-Cream Cheese Gazpacho, '94 137
Spring Gazpacho, '81 112
Summer Gazpacho, '84 181
Tomato-Avocado-Corn Gazpacho, '97 182
Tomato Gazpacho, Classic, '99 172
Tropical Gazpacho, '95 204
Vegetable Gazpacho, Grilled, '97 181
Vegetable Gazpacho, Smoked, '93 156
White Gazpacho, '97 181
Yellow Tomato Gazpacho, '04 158
Green Pepper Soup, '88 250
Green Soup, '98 23
Greens Soup, Cream with, '94 277
Guadalajara Soup, '88 30
Ham-and-Bean Soup, '05 45
Ham-and-Bean Soup, Spicy, '94 322
Hamburger Soup, '80 263
Ham Soup, Hearty, '82 4
Harvest Soup, '79 101
Homemade Soup, '79 198
Hot-and-Sour Soup, '83 68; '91 50
Italian Soup, Chunky, '99 20
Kale Soup, Creamy, '96 203
Lamb Soup with Spring Vegetables, '04 108
Leek Soup, Cream of, '99 276
Lentil Soup, '83 292; '86 304; '91 28; '97 304; '98 19
Lentil Soup, Beefy, '87 282
Lentil Soup, Spanish-Style, '96 239
Mardi Gras Soup, '96 56
Meatball Soup, Mexican, '98 315
Minestrone, '82 4
Minestrone, Dixie, '94 230
Minestrone, Mama's Mexican, '05 254
Minestrone, Meatball, '00 242
Minestrone Soup, '84 202; '86 144; '91 258
Minestrone Soup Mix, '91 258
Mushroom-and-Leek Soup, Cream of, '01 312
Mushroom-Onion Soup, '80 25
Mushroom-Rice Soup, '90 32
Mushroom Soup, '82 286; '86 M73; '94 54
Mushroom Soup, Chunky, '88 12
Mushroom Soup, Cream of, '84 5; '85 93, 261
Mushroom Soup, Creamy, '79 243; '81 307
Mushroom Soup, Curried, '84 M89
Mushroom Soup, Elegant, '83 99

Mushroom Soup, Fresh, '81 109; '90 190
Mushroom Soup, Sherried, '96 104
Mushroom Soup, Shrimp-, '85 87
Mushroom Soup, Wild, '98 281; '04 203
Mustard Green Soup, Cream of, '93 280
New Year's Day Soup, '00 25
Okra Soup, '05 98
Okra Soup, Charleston, '87 156
Okra Soup with Fou-Fou, '96 325
Onion
Beefy Vidalia Onion Soup, '97 212
Caramelized French Onion Soup, '00 218
Caramelized Onion Soup with Goat Cheese-and-
   Chive Croutons, '01 312
Cheese Soup, Onion-, '87 81
Classic Onion Soup, '84 65
Creamy Onion Soup, '90 211
Double-Cheese Onion Soup, '85 227
Double Cheese-Topped Onion Soup, '79 49
Easy Onion Soup, '85 226
French Onion-Beef Soup, '87 54
French Onion Soup, '79 49; '80 188; '83 126;
   '85 226; '86 M212; '90 31; '93 246; '04 243
French Onion Soup, Shortcut, '85 M328
French Onion Soup, Toasty, '81 306
Green Onion Soup, '84 112
Green Onion Soup, Creamed, '83 82
Mexican Onion Soup, '04 243
Mushroom-Onion Soup, '80 25
Onion Soup, '99 96
Oven-Browned Onion Soup, '79 49
Potato Soup, Creamy Onion-and-, '92 51; '97 304
Rich Onion Soup, '85 226
Superb Onion Soup, '81 86
Three-Onion Soup, '96 217
Tomato-Onion Soup, '04 243
Oyster Soup, '02 102
Pea-and-Watercress Soup, '93 162
Peanut Butter Soup, '89 28
Peanut Butter Soup, Cream of, '84 29
Peanut Soup, '87 184; '00 325
Peanut Soup, Chilled, '79 130
Peanut Soup, Cream of, '92 193; '93 288
Peanut Soup, Cream of Curried, '02 242
Peanut Soup, Creamy, '79 50
Peasant Soup, '01 54
Pea Soup, '99 67
Pea Soup, Chilled, '84 181
Pea Soup, Cold Curried, '91 120
Pea Soup, Country-Style, '86 267
Pea Soup, Cream, '90 211
Pea Soup Elégante, '79 53
Pea Soup, Fresh, '86 181
Pea Soup, Peppery, '82 271
Pea Soup, Potato-, '94 90
Pea Soup, Spring, '88 M96
Pepper Soup, Spicy, '93 98
Pepper Soup, Sweet, '93 277
Pimiento Soup, Cream of, '96 45; '01 72
Pork Rind Soup, '03 33
Potato
Asparagus-Potato Soup, '85 23
Bacon Soup, Potato-, '84 M38
Baked Potato Soup, '91 311; '92 26; '03 29
Beet Soup, Potato-, '88 156
Carrot Soup, Potato-, '88 297
Celery-and-Potato Soup, '84 279
Chilled Cucumber-Potato Soup, '85 93
Cold Potato-Cucumber Soup, '88 160
Cream of Potato Soup, '80 M224; '82 21
Cream of Potato Soup, Golden, '86 302
Creamy Potato Soup, '81 19, 98; '84 112
Easy Potato Soup, '92 17
Garlic-and-Potato Soup, Golden, '04 214

Hearty Potato Soup, '98 292
Holiday Potato Soup, '79 236
Irish Potato Soup, '99 54
Leek-and-Potato Soup, '84 112
Onion-and-Potato Soup, Creamy, '97 304
Pea Soup, Potato-, '94 90
Potato Soup, '82 278; '83 292; '92 263
Sausage-Potato Soup, '80 25
Sausage Soup, Easy Potato-, '98 315
Special Potato Soup, '82 3
Subtle Potato Potage, '80 78
Sweet Potato-and-Sausage Soup, '95 23
Sweet Potato Soup, '88 250; '02 221
Sweet Potato Soup, Southern, '00 233
Sweet Potato Soup with Rum Cream, '98 271
Sweet Potato Velouté, '94 238
Three-Potato Soup, '86 16
Wild Rice Soup, Cheesy Potato-and-, '89 16
Yogurt Soup, Potato-, '92 217
Pot-of-Gold Soup, '86 259
Poultry
Chicken-Almond Cream Soup, '92 21
Chicken-and-Black Bean Soup, '05 102
Chicken-and-Buttermilk Soup, Country, '02 144
Chicken-and-Rice Soup, '88 236
Chicken-and-Wild Rice Soup, '04 26
Chicken-and-Wild Rice Soup, Creamy, '98 M334
Chicken, Artichoke, and Mushroom Soup, '92 324
Chicken Broth, Easy Microwave, '90 M167
Chicken-Corn Soup, Cheesy, '97 158
Chicken Enchilada Soup, '86 22
Chicken, Ham, and Oyster Soup, '79 198
Chicken Noodle Soup, '80 264; '95 45; '98 30
Chicken-Noodle Soup, Chunky, '88 12
Chicken Noodle Soup, Creamy, '99 20
Chicken Soup, '81 98
Chicken Soup, Bean-, '99 283
Chicken Soup, Cheesy Mac 'n', '05 292
Chicken Soup, Cream of, '85 243
Chicken Soup, Creamy Asparagus-and-, '95 82
Chicken Soup, Curried, '86 34
Chicken Soup, Fiesta, '04 323
Chicken Soup, Homemade, '82 34
Chicken Soup, Mexican, '84 234; '00 336; '03 63
Chicken Soup, Quick, '86 M72
Chicken Soup, Roasted Pepper-and-, '90 58
Chicken Soup, Spicy, '97 268
Chicken Soup, Witches' Brew, '01 205
Chicken Stock, '95 18
Chicken-Vegetable Soup, '88 18; '99 60
Chicken-Vegetable Soup, Spicy, '02 168
Stock, Light Poultry, '90 31
Tortilla Soup, '00 98, 110
Tortilla Soup, Supereasy, '00 199
Turkey-Barley Soup, '91 312
Turkey Carcass Soup, '86 284
Turkey-Noodle Soup, '91 312
Turkey-Noodle Soup Mix, '89 330
Turkey-Rice Soup, '90 89
Turkey Soup, Curried, '86 332
Turkey Soup, Tempting, '98 314
Turkey Soup, Williamsburg, '90 287
Turkey Soup with Cornbread Dressing Dumplings,
   '03 239
Turkey Soup with Green Chile Biscuits, Fiesta, '04 233
Turkey-Vegetable Soup, '84 4; '88 264; '91 312
Pumpkin-Corn Soup with Ginger-Lime Cream, '95 227
Pumpkin-Pear Soup, '92 234
Pumpkin Soup, '79 48
Pumpkin Soup, Cream of, '93 234
Pumpkin Soup, Creamy Southwestern, '03 221
Pumpkin Soup, Curried, '96 242
Pumpkin Soup with Sweet Croutons, '00 296
Red Bell Pepper Soup, '98 104

Red Pepper Soup, Chilled Sweet, '93 69
Reuben Soup, Cream of, '97 26
Roasted Red Pepper Soup, '96 245; '05 72
Roasted Yellow Bell Pepper Soup, '96 56
Sausage and Okra Soup, '80 209
Sausage Soup, Italian, '84 235
Sausage Soup, Polish, '99 317
Sausage Soup with Tortellini, Italian, '88 46
Sausage, Spinach, and Bean Soup, '99 311
Sausage-Tortellini Soup, '99 20
Sausage-Zucchini Soup, Italian, '84 4
Seafood
    Bouillabaisse, Marcelle's, '99 200
    Cioppino, Gulf Coast, '94 102
    Clam Florentine Soup, '85 23
    Crabmeat Soup, '84 123
    Crab Soup, Beaufort, '92 238
    Crab Soup, Cream of, '88 302
    Crab Soup, Creamy, '80 M224
    Crab Soup, Elegant, '80 188
    Crab Soup, Fresh Corn-and-, '92 183
    Crab Soup, Old-Fashioned, '90 71
    Crab Soup, Plantation, '92 237
    Crab Soup, Quick, '84 279
    Crab Soup, Steamboat's Cream of, '81 127
    Crab, Sweet Corn Soup with, '02 159
    Lobster Soup, Spicy Thai, '94 102
    Mussel Soup, '93 259
    Oyster-and-Artichoke Soup, '97 21
    Oyster-and-Artichoke Soup, Louisiana, '92 81
    Oyster-and-Mushroom Soup, '87 39
    Oyster-Cheese Soup, '84 213
    Oyster Soup, '79 228; '83 211
    Oyster-Turnip Soup, '94 328
    Scallop Broth with Black Beans and Cilantro,
        Southwestern, '87 123
    She-Crab Soup, '03 137; '05 98
    She-Crab Soup with Marigold, '79 32
    Shrimp-and-Corn Soup, '84 88
    Shrimp-Cheese Soup, '01 145
    Shrimp Enchilada Soup, '94 103
    Shrimp Soup, Okra-and-, '94 323
    Shrimp, Sweet Corn Soup with Shiitakes and, '99 168
    Stock, Seafood, '94 238
    Tortellini Soup, Seafood-, '97 324
Shiitake Soup, Cream of, '95 265
Sopa de Lima, '79 211
Southwest Soup, '86 255
Spinach Soup, Cream of, '82 38; '90 211
Spinach Soup, Hot Cream of, '84 29
Spinach Soup, Oriental, '83 151
Spinach Soup with Meatballs, Italian, '92 331
Spinach-Tortellini Soup, '99 317
Split Pea and Frankfurter Soup, '79 64
Split Pea-and-Lentil Soup, Oven-Baked, '00 316
Split Pea Soup, '88 235; '89 17; '94 322
Squash and Leek Soup, Cream of, '04 42
Squash Soup, '94 134
Squash Soup, Chilled, '92 173
Squash Soup, Cold Cream of, '81 130
Squash Soup, Cream of, '81 246
Squash Soup, Perky, '85 20
Steak Soup, '99 260
Stock, Beef, '95 17
Stock, Brown Meat, '90 31
Stock, Chicken, '95 18
Stock, Fish, '95 19; '00 65
Stock, Homemade Fish, '92 237
Stock, Light Poultry, '90 31
Stock, Pumpkin Soup, '00 296
Stock, Quick Full-Bodied, '95 17
Stock, Seafood, '94 238
Stock, Vegetable, '90 31
Stock, Venison, '94 302

Summer Soup, Dilled, '99 182
Summer Squash Soup, '83 99; '84 193; '85 136
Sweet Potato-Peanut Soup, '05 104
Sweet Red Pepper Soup, Cream of Roasted, '95 65
Taco Soup, '94 225; '99 36
Tamale Soup, '95 213
Tomatillo Soup with Crunchy Jícama, '92 245; '97 143
Tomato
    Appetizer Tomato Soup, '86 258
    Bell Pepper 'n' Tomato Soup, Creamy, '05 293
    Celery Soup, Tomato-, '83 M58
    Chilled Roasted Pepper and Tomato Soup, '01 128
    Chilled Tomato Soup, '82 155
    Cioppino, Gulf Coast, '94 102
    Cold Tomato Soup, '88 160
    Consommé, Tomato, '88 250
    Cream of Tomato Soup with Lemon Basil, '96 124
    Cream of Tomato Soup with Parmesan Cheese, '86 161
    Cream Soup, Refreshing Tomato, '79 172
    Cream Soup, Tomato-Basil, '97 198
    Creamy Tomato Soup, '83 267; '86 258
    Creamy Tomato Soup with Crispy Croutons, '05 207
    Dried Tomato-Cream Soup, '90 203
    Easy Tomato Soup, '84 14
    Fire Water, '80 188
    Fresh Tomato Soup, '83 140
    Herbed Yogurt and Parmesan Toasts, Tomato Soup
        with, '96 66
    Hot Tomato Juice Soup, '86 302
    Iced Tomato Soup, '79 170
    Mexican Tomato Soup, Icy-Spicy, '90 155
    Onion Soup, Tomato-, '04 243
    Plus, Tomato Soup, '88 170
    Pumpkin-Tomato Soup, '86 291
    Rice Soup, Tomato-and-, '85 24
    Roasted Garlic-and-Basil Tomato Soup, '01 17
    Savory Tomato Soup, '94 91
    Sour Cream-Topped Tomato Soup, '80 246
    Summer Tomato Soup, '79 130
    Tomato Potage, '79 250
    Tomato Soup, '81 236; '83 44; '89 217
    Tortilla Soup, '00 110
    Vegetable Soup, Tomato-, '81 M177; '86 9
Tomato-Beef-Wild Rice Soup, '04 42
Tortellini Soup, '98 68; '00 14
Tortellini Soup, Japanese, '96 330
Tortilla Soup, '88 31, 245; '90 201; '93 197, 274;
        '94 136; '98 291; '99 310; '00 98, 110; '04 26
Tortilla Soup, Spicy, '90 32; '93 108
Turkey. See **SOUPS/Poultry.**
Turnip Soup, '92 217
Turnip Soup, Creamy, '84 279
Turtle Soup, '92 92
Turtle Soup au Sherry, '80 56
Veal-Vermicelli Soup with Quenelles, '94 14
Vegetable
    Bean Soup, Vegetable-, '83 317
    Beef-and-Barley Vegetable Soup, '89 31
    Beef and Vegetable Soup, Quick Italian, '96 235
    Beef Soup, Hearty Vegetable-, '84 102
    Beef Soup, Spicy Vegetable-, '88 11
    Beef Soup, Vegetable-, '88 296; '99 219
    Beefy Vegetable Soup, '79 113; '84 M38
    Beefy Vegetable Soup, Quick, '80 25
    Broth, Savory Vegetable, '81 230
    Burger Soup, Vegetable-, '82 6
    Cheese Soup, Creamy Vegetable-, '81 244
    Cheese Soup, Creamy Vegetable, '83 230
    Cheese Soup, Vegetable-, '89 15
    Cheesy Vegetable Soup, '80 73; '97 241
    Chicken-Vegetable Soup, '99 60
    Chicken-Vegetable Soup, Spicy, '02 168
    Chili Vegetable Soup, '94 120
    Chunky Vegetable Soup, '89 M283

    Clear Vegetable Soup, '79 130
    Cold Garden Vegetable Soup, '84 197
    Down-Home Vegetable Soup, '90 32
    Garden Harvest Soup, Italian, '90 M167
    Garden Soup, '85 241
    Garden Vegetable Soup, '83 140; '86 160
    Hearty Vegetable Soup, '80 26
    Leek-Vegetable Soup, '86 304
    Lemongrass-and-Petits Pois Soup, '01 328
    Light Vegetable Soup, '84 280
    Marvelous Vegetable Soup, '82 3
    Mix, Vegetable Soup, '84 148
    Old-Fashioned Vegetable Soup, '86 304
    Peasant Soup, '01 54
    Pot Liquor Soup, '98 273; '01 290
    Quick Vegetable Soup, '79 190; '85 24, 32
    Quick Veggie Soup, '91 31
    Southwestern Vegetable Soup, '97 268
    Spanish Fiesta Soup, '01 66
    Spicy Vegetable Soup, '79 198; '93 293; '99 337
    Stock, Vegetable, '90 31
    Vegetable Soup, '80 128; '84 148; '85 106; '86 187;
        '87 83, 123; '88 266; '93 157; '98 32, 291
    Winter Vegetable Soup, Puree of, '00 322
Venison Soup, '82 216
Vichyssoise, '86 181
Vichyssoise, Cucumber, '94 90
Vichyssoise, Velvety Roquefort, '83 223
Vichyssoise with Mint Cream, Cucumber, '98 246
Watercress-and-Leek Soup, '86 161
Watercress Soup, '79 82; '88 104; '01 176
Watercress Soup, Cream of, '96 66
Zucchini Soup, '82 104; '84 181; '86 181; '89 14
Zucchini Soup, Chilled, '87 90
Zucchini Soup, Cold, '85 265; '92 64; '99 164
Zucchini Soup, Cream of, '83 99
Zucchini Soup, Creamy, '83 140
Zucchini Soup, Dilled, '90 88
Zucchini Soup, Watercress-, '91 72
Zucchini Soup with Cilantro, '93 130
Zucchini Soup with Fresh Vegetable Salsa, Chilled, '98 194
SPAETZLE
Spaetzle, '99 242
SPAGHETTI
All-in-One Spaghetti, '98 295
Bacon Spaghetti, '86 213; '87 82
Barbecue Spaghetti, '02 121
Black Bean Spaghetti, '92 217
Black-Eyed Pea Spaghetti, '81 7
Bowl, Sweet-Hot Asian Noodle, '05 187
Carbonara, Chorizo, '94 230
Carbonara, Salmon, '83 43
Carbonara, Spaghetti, '85 34; '87 167; '03 123
Carbonara, Spaghetti alla, '81 38
Casseroles
    Asparagus-Spaghetti Casserole, '80 77
    Beef Casserole, Spaghetti and, '79 129
    Casserole Spaghetti, '95 132
    Chicken-Spaghetti Casserole, '84 15
    Chicken Spaghetti, Spicy, '02 327
    Florentine Bake, Cheesy, '95 131
    Ham-and-Turkey Spaghetti, '95 19
    Italian Casserole, '90 238
    Low-Fat Spaghetti Casserole, '99 215
    Pork Spaghetti Bake, '81 11
    Spaghetti Casserole, '84 241
    Spinach Casserole, Spaghetti-and-, '02 199
    Tetrazzini, Chicken, '79 268; '80 75; '83 288; '99 61
    Tetrazzini, Ham, '82 77; '84 241; '03 174
    Tetrazzini, Herbed Turkey, '86 47
    Tetrazzini, Turkey, '03 257
Cheese Spaghetti, Three-, '83 105
Chicken Spaghetti, '83 105; '87 221; '98 329
Chicken-Vegetable Spaghetti, '92 281; '98 296

SPAGHETTI
(continued)

Chili, Cincinnati, **'96** 18
Chili-Spaghetti, Herbed, **'84** 222
Clam Sauce, Pasta with, **'84** 291
Country-Style Spaghetti, **'02** 25
Crawfish Spaghetti, **'85** 104
Easy Spaghetti, **'83** M317; **'84** 72; **'92** 66
Etcetera, Spaghetti, **'83** 105
Ham Spaghetti Skillet, **'83** 283
Herbal Dressing, Spaghetti with, **'86** 158
Hot Dog and Spaghetti Skillet, **'83** 144
Italian Spaghetti, **'81** 38
Italian Spaghetti, Real, **'81** 233
Lemon-Garlic Pasta, **'95** 181
Marzetti's Spaghetti, **'99** 85
Meatballs, Spaghetti-and-Herb, **'84** 75
Meatballs, Spaghetti with, **'81** 38
Meaty Spaghetti, **'82** 19
Mushroom Pasta 1-2-3, **'97** 102
Mushrooms, Spicy Spaghetti with, **'85** 2
One-Pot Spaghetti, **'00** 58
Onions, Spaghetti with Smothered, **'97** 229
Parmesan Noodles, Cheesy, **'83** M7
Parsley and Walnut Sauce, Spaghetti with, **'80** 30
Parsley, Spaghetti with, **'80** 236
Peanut Sauce, Pasta with, **'95** 252
Pepperoni Pasta, **'83** 105
Pepperoni Spaghetti, Quick, **'88** 40
Pie, Spaghetti, **'81** M32
Pie, Spaghetti-Ham, **'93** 19
Pie, Weeknight Spaghetti, **'95** 312
Pizzazz, Spaghetti with, **'80** 85
Pork and Peppers, Spaghetti with, **'98** 131
Pot Roast with Spaghetti, **'80** 59
Red Wine-Tomato Pasta, **'05** 140
Salad, Asian Peanut-and-Pasta, **'03** 127
Salad, Chicken-and-Veggie Spaghetti, **'04** 129
Salad, Chicken-Spaghetti, **'90** 146
Salad, Mediterranean, **'95** 132
Salad, Spaghetti, **'82** 277; **'84** 205
Salad, Spaghetti-Vegetable, **'97** 196
Salsa Spaghetti, **'00** 58
Sauces
Beer Spaghetti Sauce, **'85** 13
Grisanti Spaghetti Sauce, **'94** 194
Herbed Spaghetti Sauce, **'85** 13
Italian Tomato Sauce for Spaghetti, **'81** 134
Meat Sauce for Spaghetti, **'00** 256
Meat Sauce, Quick Spaghetti and, **'94** 64
Meat Sauce, Spaghetti with, **'02** 188
Mint-and-Garlic Tomato Sauce, Spaghetti with, **'05** 100
Sicilian Spaghetti Sauce, **'03** 62
Slow-Simmered Spaghetti Sauce, **'96** 72
Thick Spaghetti Sauce, **'84** 118
Tomato Sauce, Spaghetti with Fresh, **'96** 135
Turkey Spaghetti Sauce, **'85** 13
Vegetable Sauce, Pasta with, **'83** 163
Zucchini Sauce, Spaghetti with, **'81** 38
Sausage Spaghetti, **'83** 160
Sausage Spaghetti Dinner, **'79** 194
Shrimp and Pasta, **'91** 207
Shrimp-and-Vegetable Spaghetti, **'91** 170
Shrimp, Pasta with, **'01** 164
Shrimp Spaghetti with Black Olives, **'85** 13
Soup, Creamy Chicken Noodle, **'99** 20
Szechuan Noodle Toss, **'91** 30
Thick-and-Spicy Spaghetti, **'83** 287
Tomatoes and Garlic, Spaghetti with, **'91** 47
Tomato Pasta, Italian, **'93** 201

Veal Spaghetti, **'84** 276
Vegetable Sauce, Pasta with, **'83** 163
Vegetables, Spaghetti with, **'85** 67
Vegetables with Spaghetti, Fresh, **'86** 257
Vegetables with Spaghetti, Sautéed, **'81** 89
White Spaghetti and Meatballs, **'03** 34
White Wine-Tomato-and-Clam Pasta, **'05** 140
Zucchini Spaghetti, **'83** 160
Zucchini Spaghetti, Italian, **'85** 2
SPICE. *See also* **SEASONINGS.**
Balls, Decorative Ribbon-Spice, **'84** 325
Blend, Five-Spice Powder, **'92** 121
Dry Spices, **'90** 120; **'01** 106
Mix, Mulled Wine Spice, **'85** 266
Mix, Tex-Mex Spice, **'94** 135; **'01** 247
Mixture, Moroccan Spice, **'01** 230
Rub, Moroccan Spice, **'95** 231
SPINACH
Appetizers
Bread, Spinach, **'83** 121
Cheese Bites, Spinach-, **'94** 23
Cheesecake, Savory Spinach Appetizer, **'02** M207
Cheesecake, Spinach-Herb, **'99** 139
Cheesecake, Spinach-Mushroom, **'92** 326
Cheesecake, Spinach Pesto, **'90** 175
con Queso, Easy Spinach, **'88** 101
Crostini, Spinach, **'01** 283
Crostini, Spinach-Red Pepper, **'03** 34
Cups, Cottage Cheese-Spinach, **'87** 190
Dip, Beef-and-Spinach, **'99** 65
Dip, Cheesy Spinach, **'82** 59
Dip, Clam, **'01** 194
Dip, Creamy Spinach, **'88** 132
Dip, Florentine Artichoke, **'96** 274
Dip, Hot Spinach, **'80** 249
Dip, Hot Spinach-Cheese, **'89** 48
Dip in Cabbage, Spinach, **'82** 155
Dip in Sourdough Round, Spinach, **'98** 173
Dip, Pine Nut-Spinach, **'99** 138
Dip, Spinach, **'80** 86; **'86** 159; **'87** 25, 214; **'93** 324
Dip, Spinach-Artichoke, **'00** 26
Eggs, Double Stuffed Spinach-and-Bacon, **'00** M333
Filling, Spinach, **'95** 316
Loaf, Four-Layer Cheese, **'99** 222
Madeleine in Chafing Dish, Spinach, **'85** 319
Mushrooms, Spinach-Stuffed, **'86** 81; **'88** 131, M261; **'89** M133
Pastries, Greek Spinach-and-Cheese, **'96** 76
Pâté with Spinach and Cream, Pork, **'83** 224
Phyllo-Spinach Triangles, **'87** 53
Phyllo Triangles, Spinach-Filled, **'84** 52
Phyllo Triangles, Spinach-Ricotta, **'88** 212
Pinwheels, Spinach-Tenderloin, **'89** M118
Puff Pastry, Spinach and Artichokes in, **'00** 277
Puffs, Cheese-and-Spinach, **'87** 246
Puffs, Spinach, **'95** 316
Puffs, Spinach-Artichoke-Tomato, **'95** 284
Quichelets, Spinach, **'87** 67
Quiche, No-Crust Spinach, **'90** 142
Quiches, Miniature Spinach, **'82** 38
Quiches, Spinach, **'01** 241
Rollups, Southwestern, **'01** 135
Rollups, Spinach, **'98** 251
Sauce, Herbed Spinach, **'86** 244
Spanakopita, **'96** 233
Spread, Parmesan-Spinach, **'93** 55
Spread, Savory Spinach, **'82** 180
Spread, Spinach, **'88** 132
Spread, Spinach-Bacon, **'92** M310
Squares, Spinach, **'88** 131
Squash, Spinach-Stuffed, **'02** 165
Strudels, Spinach, **'93** 249
Supreme, Layered Spinach, **'82** 38
Tarts, Spinach, **'82** 249

Terrine, Layered Salmon-and-Spinach, **'84** 132
Wontons, Spinach, **'83** 74
Apples, Onions, and Pears over Spinach, Sautéed, **'94** 212
Baby Spinach with Pine Nuts, **'03** 64
Baked Spinach, Gourmet, **'82** 180
Biscuits and Ham, Green Elf, **'02** 277
Bisque, Crab-and-Spinach, **'97** 241
Bisque, Spinach-Potato, **'86** 66
Bread, Spinach, **'83** 121; **'87** 144
Burgers, Spinach, **'00** 26
Burgers, Spinach-Feta, **'99** 135
Calzones, Spinach-and-Cheese, **'95** 310
Calzones with Italian Tomato Sauce, **'03** 202
Casseroles
Artichoke Bake, Spinach-, **'95** 48
Artichoke Casserole, Spicy Spinach-, **'01** 49
Artichoke Casserole, Spinach-, **'88** 252; **'93** 44; **'00** 254; **'01** 49
Artichoke Casserole, Spinach and, **'81** 103
Beef Casserole, Spinach and, **'79** 192
Beef-Macaroni Casserole, Spinach-, **'83** 313
Cannelloni, **'85** 60; **'92** 17
Celery Casserole, Spinach-and-, **'84** 294
Cheese Bake, Spinach-, **'88** 10
Cheese Casserole, Spinach-, **'83** 216; **'89** 64
Cheesy Florentine Bake, **'95** 131
Cheesy Spinach Casserole, **'81** 263
Chicken, Orzo, and Spinach Casserole, **'02** 124
Company Spinach, **'89** 280
Cottage Cheese-and-Spinach Casserole, **'84** 77
Crab and Spinach Casserole, Creamy, **'80** 3
Creamy Spinach Bake, **'89** 68
Creamy Spinach Casserole, **'86** 111
Delight, Spinach, **'84** M144
Egg Casserole, Spinach and, **'82** 270
Eggplant-Spinach Casserole, **'99** 217
Enchiladas, Black Bean-Chicken-Spinach, **'05** 95
Enchiladas, Black Bean 'n' Spinach, **'05** 95
Enchiladas, Chicken-and-Spinach, **'91** 222
Enchiladas, Spinach, **'83** 60; **'84** 14
Florentine Casserole, Turkey-and-Shrimp, **'92** 122
Florentine, Chicken-and-Shrimp, **'89** 64
Florentine, Chicken Lasagna, **'95** 158; **'02** 232
Florentine, Jumbo Seashells, **'79** 6
Florentine, Lasagna, **'88** 196
Florentine, Layered Pasta, **'00** 56
Florentine, Pasta Shells, **'00** 326
Florentine, Salmon, **'83** 43
Florentine, Turkey, **'88** 264
Lasagna, Cheesy Spinach, **'80** 32; **'83** 204; **'01** 196
Lasagna Florentine, Chicken, **'95** 158; **'02** 232
Lasagna Florentine, Creamy, **'91** 94
Lasagna, Spinach, **'79** 25; **'81** 243
Lasagna, Spinach-Bean, **'92** 96
Lasagna, Spinach-Black Bean, **'02** 44
Manicotti, Spinach, **'82** 199
Manicotti, Spinach-Stuffed, **'88** 255
Oyster-and-Spinach Casserole, **'83** 34; **'84** 44
Parmesan Casserole, Spinach-, **'82** 281; **'83** 32
Parmesan, Spinach, **'93** 72
Puff, Spinach-Cheese, **'84** 96
Rice Bake, Green, **'79** 43
Rice, Spinach, **'85** 146
Ricotta Bake, Spinach-, **'88** 97
Roll-Ups, Ham and Spinach, **'81** 143
Scalloped Spinach with Cheese, **'79** 8
Shells, Spinach-Stuffed, **'85** 60
Spaghetti-and-Spinach Casserole, **'02** 199
Spinach Casserole, **'79** 265; **'91** 31; **'99** 271
Supreme, Spinach, **'84** 77
Surprise, Spinach, **'82** 42
Turkey-Spinach Casserole, **'84** 71
Cheesy Topped Spinach, **'84** 85
Chicken Breasts, Fried Spinach-Stuffed, **'88** 206

Chicken, Garlic-Spinach, '92 56
Chicken in Puff Pastry, Spinach-Stuffed, '92 125
Chicken, Lemon-Spinach, '97 104
Chicken Rolls, Spinach-Stuffed, '86 248
Chinese Spinach, '79 179; '82 39
Chinese Spinach Sauté, '83 208
Cornbread, Spinach, '95 49
Couscous, Spinach-and-Onion, '98 23
Creamed Spinach, '81 54; '86 110; '96 252; '97 28
Creamed Spinach in Pastry Shells, '89 280
Creamed Spinach with Noodles, '84 29
Creamy Spinach, '85 289
Crêpe Cups, Florentine, '89 44
Crêpe Pie, Florentine, '79 34
Crêpes Florentine, '80 190
Crêpes, Spinach-Ricotta, '81 52
Crowder Peas, Spinach with, '00 159
Custards, Savory Spinach-Gorgonzola, '99 313; '02 284
Dumplings, Spinach and, '00 85
Eggplant, Spinach-and-Basil Stuffed, '02 147
Eggs Oso Grande, '98 279
Eggs Sardou, '92 93
Enchiladas, Spinach, '83 60; '84 14
Field Peas and Spinach, '99 169
Filling, Spinach, '79 34
Filling, Spinach and Feta, '97 171
Filling, Spinach-Mushroom, '80 215
Filling, Spinach-Ricotta, '81 53
Fish in a Wrap, '97 64
Florentine, Baked Eggs, '86 M12
Florentine, Cheesy Trout, '85 53
Florentine, Chicken, '93 107
Florentine Crêpe Cups, '89 44
Florentine Crêpe Pie, '79 34
Florentine, Crêpes, '80 190
Florentine, Eggs, '79 39; '83 56
Florentine, Fish, '86 35
Florentine in Parchment, Fish, '87 22
Florentine Panini, Chicken, '02 236
Florentine Quiche, Tomato, '04 332
Florentine Sauce, '93 48
Florentine, Stuffed Mushrooms, '82 270
Florentine Stuffed Onions, '05 141
Florentine-Style Eggs, '82 38
Florentine with Mushroom Sauce, Chicken, '87 250
Frittata, Spinach, '81 53
Garden, The, '83 134
Greek Sunburst, '94 245
Grits, Garlicky Ham-and-Spinach, '94 177
Holiday Spinach with Red Pepper Ribbons, '03 260
Italian Spinach, Easy, '02 235
Lemon and Pepper, Spinach with, '97 105
Lemon Spinach, Creamy, '82 302
Lemon Spinach with Feta, '85 190
Loaf with Mushroom Sauce, Spinach, '01 277
Loaves, Spinach-Oyster, '84 213
Madeleine, Spinach, '05 95
Marinara on Beds of Spinach and Orzo, '93 320
Meat Loaf, Spinach, '96 131
Meat Loaf, Spinach-Stuffed Turkey, '97 24
Mushrooms, Spinach with, '80 19
Nests, Baked Eggs in Spinach, '82 70
Noodles, Chicken and Spinach, '82 19
Omelet, Spinach, Cheddar, and Bacon, '03 204
Omelet, Spinach-Cheese, '83 119
Oysters Rockefeller, '98 222
Parmesan Spinach, Quick, '05 292
Parmesan Spinach, Savory, '85 68
Pastas. *See also* **FETTUCCINE, PASTAS.**
    Fantastic, Spinach, '93 173
    Lasagna, Crabmeat-and-Spinach, '04 292
    Lasagna, Won Ton Spinach, '04 129
    Linguine with Spinach, '91 30
    Macaroni with Spinach, Baked, '99 244

Pesto and Pasta, Spinach-Peanut, '93 212
Pie, Spinach-Pasta, '85 286
    Sauce, Spinach Pasta, '93 71
Peppers, Spinach-Stuffed, '82 180
Pesto, Orange Roughy with Spinach, '88 M192
Pesto, Squash Stuffed with Spinach, '89 M133
Pie, Greek Spinach, '85 59
Pie Pan Spinach, '94 195
Pie Parma, Spinach, '96 203
Pie, Spinach, '82 191; '88 56; '00 26
Pie, Spinach-Pasta, '85 286
Pie, Super Special Spinach, '04 60
Pie with Cranberry-Pecan Crusts, Turkey Pot, '02 198
Pie with Muenster Crust, Spinach, '95 48
Pinwheels, Flank Steak-and-Spinach, '95 56
Pita Pockets, Chicken-Spinach, '01 66
Pitas, Spinach-Walnut, '87 202; '88 43
Pork Loin, Tuscan, '05 296
Pork, Spinach-and-Herb Stuffed, '89 193
Pork Tenderloin, Spinach-and-Bacon Stuffed, '94 81
Potatoes, Black-Eyed Pea-Spinach-Stuffed, '95 22
Quesadillas, Greek, '03 61
Quesadillas, Spinach, Mushroom, and Cilantro, '00 148
Quiche, Cheesy Spinach, '81 228
Quiche, Crustless Spinach, '84 235
Quiche, Greek Spinach, '86 10
Quiche, Mushroom-Spinach-Swiss, '03 59
Quiche, No-Crust Spinach, '90 142
Quiches, Individual Spinach, '86 38
Quiche, Spinach, '81 44; '85 49; '91 204
Quiche, Spinach-and-Bacon, '00 240
Quiche, Spinach-Mushroom, '81 M74
Quiches, Triple-Cheese Spinach, '00 220
Ring au Fromage, Spinach, '79 8
Roll, Feta Cheese-Spinach, '91 22
Rolls, Spinach-Ham, '88 78
Rollups, Chicken and Spinach, '80 90; '82 M68
Roll-Ups, Ham and Spinach, '81 143
Rollups, Spinach-and-Ham, '86 84
Rollups, Turkey-Spinach, '00 178
Salad Dressing, Spinach, '83 181; '93 250
Salads
    Apple-Onion Vinaigrette, Spinach Salad with, '94 276
    Apple Salad, Spinach-, '90 89; '92 13; '97 308; '02 230
    Apple Salad with Cinnamon Vinaigrette, Fresh
        Spinach-and-, '05 44
    Apple-Spinach Salad, '97 14; '99 222
    Apricot Salad, Spinach-, '94 63
    Apricot Vinaigrette, Spinach Salad with, '02 120
    Arranged Spinach Salad, '91 210; '92 160
    Bacon Dressing, Spinach Salad with Hot, '82 211
    Bacon Salad, Spinach and, '81 143
    Beet Salad, Spinach-, '83 227
    Blue Cheese Dressing, Spinach Salad with Zesty, '02 121
    Blue Cheese Salad, Spinach-, '82 166
    Blues, Spinach Salad with the, '95 66
    Cantaloupe-Spinach Salad with Pistachio-Lime
        Vinaigrette, '97 148
    Chicken-and-Spinach Tossed Salad, '83 157
    Chicken-Spinach-Strawberry Salad, '97 92
    Chili-Lime Dressing, Spinach Salad with, '94 63
    Citrus Dressing, Spinach Salad with, '88 133
    Citrus Spinach Salad, '90 59
    Combination Spinach Salad, '85 327; '86 22
    Cranberry Salad with Warm Chutney Dressing,
        Spinach-and-, '97 242
    Creamy Spinach Salad, '83 60
    Crisp Spinach Salad with Creamy Dressing, '83 81
    Crunchy Spinach Salad, '80 147; '81 225
    Curry Spinach Salad, '80 242
    Dijon Spinach Salad, '89 282
    Dried Tomato Vinaigrette, Spinach Salad with, '93 272
    Easy Spinach Salad, '91 249
    Endive Salad with Warm Vinaigrette, Spinach-, '05 291

Enoki Salad, Spinach-, '89 62
Festive Spinach Salad, '80 247
French Spinach Salad, '79 8
Fresh Spinach Salad, '82 73; '83 240; '84 15, 77; '86 130
Fresh Spinach Salad Delight, '80 146
Fresh Spinach-Sprout Salad, '82 281; '83 42
Fresh Spinach with Spicy Dressing, '80 55
Garlic-Ginger Vinaigrette Dressing, Spinach Salad
    with, '92 195
Green Spinach Salad, '79 142
Grits-Spinach Salad, Stacked, '98 66
Honey Dressing, Spinach Salad with, '90 16
Hot Citrus Dressing, Spinach Salad with, '00 108
Hot Spiked Spinach, '97 195
Kiwifruit Salad, Spinach-, '87 305
Lamb Salad, Spinach-, '85 58
Layered Salad, Make-Ahead, '81 296
Layered Spinach-Lettuce Salad, '84 266
Layered Spinach Salad, '80 5; '89 163
Mandarin Spinach Salad, '85 163
Minted Spinach Salad, '94 63
Mushroom Salad, Spinach and, '80 112
Onion Salad Bowl, Spinach-and-, '81 157
Orange Dressing, Spinach Salad with, '87 187
Orange Salad, Spinach-and-, '86 15
Orange Salad, Warm Spinach-, '00 112
Orange-Spinach Salad, '83 316; '84 16
Oriental Spinach Salad, '82 23
Oysters and Red Wine Vinaigrette, Spinach Salad
    with, '94 327
Parsley Dressing, Spinach Salad with Sweet, '02 120
Pear, and Blue Cheese Salad, Easy Spinach, '05 41
Pears, Spinach Salad with Sautéed, '94 237
Pecan Salad, Spinach-, '89 128; '01 284
Pickled Spinach, '81 69
Poppy Seed Dressing, Spinach Salad with, '91 210;
    '92 160
Pork-and-Spinach Salad, Mandarin, '88 M126
Raspberry Cream Dressing, Spinach Salad with, '94 321
Rice Salad, Spinach-, '94 63
Romaine-Spinach Salad, '89 123
Russian Dressing, Spinach Salad with, '79 144
Salmon-Spinach Salad, '87 145
Sesame Salad, Spinach-, '91 211; '92 160
Sesame Spinach Salad, '90 292
Southern Spinach Salad, '80 55
Southern Spinach Salad with Cheese Grits Croutons
    and Vidalia Onion-Balsamic Vinaigrette, '04 316
Special Spinach Salad, '80 78
Spinach Salad, '82 102; '86 302; '87 62; '88 299;
    '92 281, 341; '93 46, 65; '03 246
Springtime Spinach Salad, '81 114
Steak-and-Spinach Salad with Hot Pan Dressing, '05 19
Strawberry Salad, Spinach-and-, '05 55
Strawberry Salad with Tart Poppy Seed Dressing,
    Spinach-and-, '03 241
Strawberry-Spinach Salad, '91 169; '93 168
Sun-Dried Tomato Salad, Spinach and, '93 250
Supreme, Spinach Salad, '79 243
Sweet-Sour Spinach Salad, '85 M112
Tangy Spinach Salad, '00 24
Tossed Spinach Salad, '01 159
Tropical Spinach Salad, '90 231
Tropical Spinach Salad with Grilled Chicken, '04 51
Tropical Spinach Salad with Grilled Pork Tenderloin,
    '04 51
Tropical Spinach Salad with Grilled Shrimp, '04 51
Turkish Salad, '96 137
Twist, Spinach-Mustard, '86 209
Vinaigrette Spinach, '79 8
Wilted Spinach Salad, '81 M4; '89 123; '91 210;
    '92 160; '93 125
Zesty Spinach Salad, '79 88
Sandwiches, Fresh Spinach, '85 59

SPINACH

(continued)

Sandwiches, Grilled Spinach Fondue, '99 337
Sandwich, Grilled Spinach Fondue, '94 171
Sauce, Emerald, '90 63
Sauce, Fettuccine with Spinach, '84 329
Sauce, Herbed Green, '86 244
Sauce, Spinach Pesto, '93 59
Sautéed Spinach, '93 250
Sauté, Fresh Spinach, '93 55; '04 285
Sauté, Tomato-Spinach, '04 23
Sesame Spinach, '98 24
Skillet Spinach, '96 19
Soufflé, Cheese-and-Spinach, '98 235
Soufflé, Cheesy Spinach, '81 53
Soufflé Deluxe, Spinach, '79 8
Soufflé Roll, Spinach, '80 215
Soufflé, Spinach, '79 73; '81 304; '84 78; '85 248;
    '86 108; '05 66
Soup, Cream of Spinach, '82 38; '90 211
Soup, Cream with Greens, '94 277
Soup, Green, '98 23
Soup, Hot Cream of Spinach, '84 29
Soup, Oriental Spinach, '83 151
Soup, Sausage, Spinach, and Bean, '99 311
Soup, Spinach Egg Drop, '03 65
Soup, Spinach-Tortellini, '99 317
Soup with Meatballs, Italian Spinach, '92 331
Spanakopita, '86 58; '96 233
Squares, Spinach, '95 49
Squash, Spinach-Stuffed, '82 4; '91 14; '97 119
Stir-Fry Spinach, '81 182
Strudels, Spinach, '93 249
Supreme, Layered Spinach, '82 38
Tart Milan, '87 70
Tart, Rutabaga-Spinach, '98 274
Tenderloin, Spinach-Stuffed, '89 311
Tenderloin, Stuffed Tuscany, '99 269
Terrine, Layered Salmon-and-Spinach, '84 132
Timbales, Green Rice, '97 62
Timbales, Spinach, '84 29
Timbales, Spinach-Rice, '88 271
Tomatoes, Baked Spinach, '90 92
Tomatoes, Spinach-Feta Stuffed, '04 285
Tomatoes, Spinach-Stuffed, '89 203; '93 281
Tomatoes, Spinach-Stuffed Baked, '86 14
Tomatoes, Spinach-Topped, '88 265; '94 321
Tomatoes, Veracruz, '97 169
Turnovers, Salmon-Spinach, '83 44
Wrap, Mediterranean, '03 168
Zucchini Boats with Spinach, '82 252

SPREADS. *See also* **APPETIZERS/Spreads.**
Aioli, Shortcut, '93 157
Ambrosia Spread, '92 50
Apple-Date Spread, '91 231; '92 67
Beef Spread, Hot, '83 50
Beet-and-Pecan Sandwich Spread, '99 274
Braunschweiger-Onion Spread, '79 82
Bread Spread, Party, '82 161
Caraway Spread, '85 276
Caviar Spread, Creamy, '92 58
Cheese
    Almond Cheese Spread, '87 292
    Aloha Spread, '83 93
    Avocado-Cheese Spread, Herbed, '98 335
    Bacon-Cheese Spread, '83 241
    Bacon-Olive Cream Cheese, '04 196
    Basil-Cheese Roulade, '05 143
    Basil-Cheese Spread, Fresh, '97 108
    Beer Cheese Spread, '81 69; '94 123
    Beer-Cheese Spread, '85 69
    Beer Spread, Cheesy, '87 196

Blue Cheese Spread, '95 79; '97 240
Boursin Cheese Spread, Buttery, '94 301
Boursin Cheese Spread, Garlic, '94 301
Brie Spread, Apricot, '86 275
Cheddar-Swiss Spread, '99 106
Cheese Spread, '86 135; '96 122; '99 24
Chicken-Artichoke-Cheese Spread Gift Box, '00 328
Chile-Cheese Spread, '86 297; '99 336; '02 205
Chili Cheese Spread, '93 242
Chocolate Cheese Spread, '87 292
Chocolate Chip Cheese Loaves, '91 299; '92 264
Coconut-Cranberry Cheese Spread, '92 328
Confetti Cheese Spread, '84 256
Cottage Cheese Spread, '87 107
Cream Cheese-and-Olive Pimiento Cheese, '01 169;
    '03 315
Cream Cheese-Olive Spread, '82 35
Cream Cheese Spread, Apricot-, '82 161; '87 158
Cream Cheese Spread, Caviar-, '84 256
Cream Cheese Spread, Cucumber and, '82 140
Cream Cheese Spread, Deviled, '81 235
Cream Cheese Spread, Herb-, '83 24
Cream Cheese Spread, Nutty, '89 327
Cream Cheese Spread, Peachy, '90 M215
Cream Cheese Spread, Pear-, '93 80
Cream Cheese Spread, Pineapple-, '82 35
Cream Cheese Spread, Tri-Flavored, '98 134
Curry-Almond Cheese Spread, '01 238
Edam-Sherry Spread, '84 257
Feta-and-Apple Spread, '99 106
Feta Spread, Herbed, '00 135
Four-Cheese Spread, '99 106
Fruit and Cheese Spread, '81 245
Fruit-and-Cheese Spread, Nutty, '87 246
Garlic-and-Dill Feta Cheese Spread, '04 238
German Cheese Spread, '79 82
Goat Cheese Spread, '02 198
Goat Cheese Torta, '04 186
Gouda Cheese Spread, '90 36
Green Onion-Cheese Spread, '92 24
Gruyère-Apple Spread, '81 160
Hawaiian Cheese Spread, '87 158
Herb-Cheese Spread, '91 124
Herbed Cheese, '88 152
Herbed Cheese Spread, '87 247
Herbed Goat Cheese, '01 310
Horseradish Spread, '03 139
Horseradish Spread, Cheese-, '84 222
Italian Spread, '85 135
Jalapeño-Cheese Spread, '82 248
Jalapeño Pimiento Cheese, '01 169
Make-Ahead Cheese Spread, '93 324
Mexican Cheese Spread, '90 119
Olive Spread, Cheese-, '79 82
Orange Cheese Spread, '87 292
Pesto Goat Cheese, '03 110
Pesto-Goat Cheese Spread, '03 208
Pimiento Cheese, '01 169; '03 139, 315; '05 323
Pimiento Cheese, Baked, '04 291
Pimiento Cheese, Chile-, '04 325
Pimiento Cheese, Jalapeño, '03 315
Pimiento Cheese, Pecan, '01 169; '03 315
Pimiento Cheese, Peppered, '01 137
Pimiento Cheese Spread, '82 35; '83 93; '86 127;
    '99 106, 276
Pimiento Cheese Spread, Creamy, '92 159
Pimiento Cheese Spread, Garlic, '79 58
Pimiento Cheese Spread, Low-Calorie, '85 215
Pineapple-Cheese Spread, '86 126; '91 167
Raisin-Nut Spread, '95 79
Rosemary Cheese with Fig Preserves, '02 256
Sandwich Spread, Benedictine, '80 299
Sandwich Spread, Chunky, '82 140
Sombrero Spread, '87 111

Strawberry Spread, '95 79
Sweet Cheese Spread, Creamy, '79 264
Sweet 'n' Sour Spread, '86 184
Swiss Cheese Spread, '90 60
Tipsy Cheese Spread, '80 150
Tomato-Cheddar Spread, '01 321
Tomato-Cheese Spread, '81 157
Tomato-Cheese Spread, Dried, '90 204
Tomato-Cheese Spread, Fiery, '87 196
White Cheddar Pimiento Cheese, '99 106
Zesty Cheese Spread, '82 140
Zippy Cheese Spread, '85 4
Cherry Spread, '93 309
Chicken-Artichoke-Cheese Spread Gift Box, '00 328
Chicken Salad Party Spread, '88 M8
Chicken Spread, Festive, '87 158
Chicken Spread, Low-Fat, '82 290
Chicken Spread, Tasty, '84 193
Chickpea Spread, Creamy, '04 146
Chive-Mustard Spread, '91 12
Chutney Spread, Curried, '89 283
Coconut-Pineapple Spread, '93 309
Corn-and-Walnut Spread, '96 26
Corned Beef Spread, '87 196
Cranberry-Butter Spread, '99 86
Cucumber-Yogurt Spread, '00 135
Curry Spread, '93 159
Date-Orange-Nut Spread, '02 59
Date Spread, Breakfast, '84 7
Date-Walnut Spread, '87 292
Deviled Delight, '83 130
Dijon-Mayo Spread, '96 199
Egg Salad Spread, '86 127
Egg Salad Spread, Cottage-, '82 146
Egg, Sour Cream, and Caviar Spread, '85 279
Fish Spread, Smoked, '92 305
Fruit Spread, '85 135
Fruit Spread, Sugarless, '84 60
Garbanzo Bean Spread, Herbed, '99 160
Garlic-Butter Spread, '96 199
Garlic Canapés, Roasted, '96 95
Garlic Puree, Roasted, '92 55
Garlic Spread, '85 111
"Guacamole" with Cumin Crisps, Green Goddess, '02 205
Ham-and-Egg Spread, '79 59
Ham and Pimiento Spread, '80 285; '81 56
Ham Spread, '86 126
Ham Spread, Buttery, '95 93; '97 98
Ham Spread, Cold, '82 248
Ham Spread, Country, '87 8
Ham Spread, Deviled, '79 81
Ham Spread, Hawaiian, '87 106
Honey Mustard-Butter Spread, '99 86
Honey-Nut Spread, '87 157; '03 46
Honey Spread, '81 229
Horseradish-Chive Cream, '02 313
Horseradish-Ham Spread, '91 167
Horseradish, Homemade, '92 25
Horseradish Spread, '90 243; '02 53
Hummus, '96 158
Lemon-Raisin Spread, '01 48
Lentil Spread, '99 288
Lime Dressing, Creamy, '04 46
Liver Spread, '89 161
Liver Spread, Sherried, '80 86
Mustard-Horseradish Cream, '02 53
Mustard Spread, '86 105
Not-So-Secret Sauce, '03 139
Olivata, '04 159
Olive-Parsley Spread, Cream Cheese-and-Olive Biscuits
    with, '04 238
Olive Spread, Creamy, '81 290; '05 311
Olive Spread, Tomatoes with, '85 114
Orange Toast Topper, '79 36

Party Spread, Spicy, '97 240
Peanut Butter Spread, '92 21; '96 90
Pineapple Sandwich Spread, '84 166
Raisin Spread, Creamy, '90 36
Raisin Spread, Peachy-, '86 326
Relish Spread, Creamy, '93 217
Salad Dressing Spread, '82 140
Seafood. *See also* SPREADS/Trout, Tuna, Whitefish.
  Clam Spread, Creamy, '91 274
  Crabmeat-Horseradish Spread, '90 292
  Crabmeat Spread, '79 281
  Crabmeat Spread, Layered, '83 127
  Crab Soufflé Spread, '85 4
  Crab Spread, '93 167
  Crab Spread, Baked, '80 86
  Crab Spread, Hot Artichoke-, '85 81
  Crab Spread, Superb, '81 255
  Oyster Spread, Smoked, '91 64
  Salmon-and-Horseradish Spread, '87 146
  Salmon Spread, '81 149
  Salmon Spread, Smoked, '84 324
  Salmon Spread with Capers, Smoked, '98 49
  Sandwich Spread, Seafood, '82 87
  Seafood Spread, '86 M58; '87 146
  Shrimp-Cucumber Spread, '79 81
  Shrimp Paste, '05 98
  Shrimp Spread, '81 306; '85 135; '87 111; '93 205;
    '96 104
  Shrimp Spread, Chunky, '85 300
  Shrimp Spread, Curried, '87 158
  Shrimp Spread, Tempting, '79 57
  Shrimp Spread, Zippy, '90 36
  Tuna Tapenade, '95 127
Spinach-Bacon Spread, '92 M310
Spinach Spread, '88 132
Spinach Spread, Savory, '82 180
Strawberry Spread, Light, '85 55
Sweet 'n' Sour Spread, '86 184
Tapenade, '00 135; '04 194
Trout Spread, Smoked, '84 47
Tuna Spread, '83 174; '91 305
Tuna Spread, Chunky, '89 147
Turkey Party Spread, '83 282
Turkey Spread, Curried, '92 16
Vegetable
  Antipasto Spread, '81 25
  Artichoke-Crab Spread, Hot, '85 81
  Artichoke Hearts with Caviar, '79 142
  Artichoke Spread, Hot, '79 110
  Broccamoli Curry Spread, '88 55
  Carrot Spread, Nutty, '94 123
  Cucumber Spread, '79 295; '80 31; '93 158
  Eggplant Spread, '86 278
  Egg Spread, Vegetable-, '87 106
  Garden Spread, '86 135
  Green Onion-Cheese Spread, '92 24
  Green Tomato Sandwich Spread, '95 172
  Guacamole Spread, '90 119
  Hearts of Palm Spread, '90 293
  Mushroom Spread, Hot, '81 190
  Party Spread, Vegetable, '84 166
  Potato-Garlic Spread, Creamy, '02 35
  Radish Spread, Fresh, '84 166
  Roasted Pepper Spread, '94 123
  Roasted Red Bell Pepper Spread, '97 217
  Sandwich Spread, Benedictine, '80 299
  Sandwich Spread, Home-Style, '80 179
  Sandwich Spread, Vegetable, '83 174; '85 135
  Sun-dried-Tomato-and-Basil Spread, Layered, '05 275
  Sun-Dried Tomato Spread and Bacon, Cream
    Cheese-and-Olive Biscuits with, '02 313
  Tomato Spread, '94 123
  Vegetable Spread, '90 144
  Watercress Spread, '88 103

White Bean Spread, '93 30; '95 279; '96 122
White Bean Spread with Creamy Cucumber Sauce, '00 178
Whitefish Spread, Smoked, '92 58
Yogurt Spread, Herbed, '02 169
SPROUTS
  Asparagus and Bean Sprouts, '96 95
  Beans with Sprouts, Sweet-and-Sour, '86 32
  Beef and Bean Sprouts, '82 281; '83 42
  Meat Loaf, Sprout, '85 51
  Omelet, Potato-Sprout, '79 128
  Omelet, Rising Sun, '85 9
  Patties, Ham-Sprout, '85 51
  Rolls with Thai Dipping Sauce, Summer, '97 236
  Salad, Bean Sprout, '82 113
  Salad, Crunchy Sprout, '96 45
  Salad, Fresh Spinach-Sprout, '82 281; '83 42
  Salad, Spanish Sprout, '85 327; '86 22
  Salad, Sprout, '90 137
  Sandwiches, Alfalfa Pocket Bread, '82 282; '83 41
  Sandwiches, Polynesian Sprout, '85 51
SQUASH. *See also* CHAYOTES, ZUCCHINI.
  Acorn. *See also* SQUASH/Stuffed.
    Bake, Acorn Squash, '83 280
    Baked Sweet Dumpling Squash, '94 266
    Bake, Squash, '82 107
    Bowls, Acorn Squash, '96 216
    Bread, Squash, '79 210
    Butter, Acorn Squash-and-Bourbon, '94 266
    Cake, Acorn Squash, '96 216
    Cake, Winter Squash-Spice Bundt, '99 248
    Delight, Acorn Squash, '81 267
    Grilled Acorn Squash with Rosemary, '96 266
    Orange Squash Brûlée, '94 267
    Oysters in Acorn Squash, Creamed, '97 20
    Pancakes, Granola-Squash, '94 267
    Pear Stuffing, Acorn Squash with, '01 293
    Puppies, Acorn Squash, '94 268
    Puree, Basic Acorn Squash, '94 267
    Rings, Easy Glazed Acorn, '81 M231
    Rings, Glazed Acorn, '80 214
    Roasted Acorn Squash with Cranberry Relish, '05 234
    Sherried Acorn Squash, '85 9
    Soup, Acorn Squash, '91 294
    Soup, Acorn Squash-Thyme, '99 252
    Soup, Cream of Acorn Squash, '94 268
    Soup, Creamy Acorn-Butternut, '96 216
    Soup, Curried Acorn Squash-and-Apple, '03 221
    Sugar-and-Spice Acorn Squash, '03 241; '05 289
  Baby Squash, '93 118
  Basil Butter, Squash and Cherry Tomatoes in, '98 328
  Basil Summer Squash, '01 180
  Butternut. *See also* SQUASH/Stuffed.
    Bake, Butternut-Orange, '86 295
    Bake, Butternut Squash, '05 234
    Baked Butternut Squash, '85 205
    Bake, Squash and Apple, '79 210
    Bisque, Curried Butternut-Shrimp, '01 248
    Bisque, Roasted Butternut Squash, '03 230
    Bisque, Squash, '84 280
    Bread, Butternut-Raisin, '79 25
    Bread, Squash, '79 210
    Casserole, Butternut, '83 280
    Casserole, Butternut Squash, '79 210; '96 216; '01 293
    Casserole, Squash and Apple, '79 209
    Casserole, Sweet Butternut, '83 256
    Gratin, Potato-Butternut Squash-and-Gruyère, '01 43
    Pie, Butternut Squash, '80 40; '87 212
    Pie, Butternut Squash Chiffon, '83 296; '84 285
    Pie, Spicy Butternut Squash, '80 296
    Pie, Spicy Squash, '85 9
    Pudding, Butternut Squash, '89 M313; '90 M19
    Pudding, Squash, '82 277; '83 15
    Puff, Butternut Squash, '85 205
    Puff, Squash, '01 293

    Ring, Butternut Squash, '81 M232
    Roasted Butternut Squash Salad with Blue Cheese
      Vinaigrette, '05 233
    Sauté, Savory Butternut, '85 205
    Skillet Butternut and Bacon, '85 9
    Soufflé, Butternut, '83 266
    Soufflé, Butternut Squash, '97 270
    Soup, Butternut, '02 68
    Soup, Butternut Squash, '95 62; '03 276
    Soup, Butternut Squash-Lime, '03 236
    Soup, Butternut Squash-Parsnip, '05 36
    Soup, Creamed Butternut-and-Apple, '88 228
    Soup, Cream of Squash and Leek, '04 42
    Soup, Creamy Acorn-Butternut, '96 216
    Soup, Creamy Butternut, '96 216
    Soup, Curried Butternut Squash, '05 234
    Soup, Saffron Butternut Squash, '04 187
    Soup with Parslied Croutons, Carrot-and-Butternut
      Squash, '97 217
    Stir-Fry, Honey-Butternut, '93 184
    Sunshine Squash, '85 205
    Whipped Butternut Squash, '94 302
    Whipped Squash, Tasty, '82 277; '83 15
  Cajun Squash, '88 142
  Calabacitas, '95 130
  Casserole, Broccoli-and-Squash, '01 175
  Casserole, Calico Squash, '90 290
  Casserole, Southwestern Squash, '05 M217
  Casserole, Squash, '87 163; '89 159; '90 161; '92 342;
    '96 247, 252; '97 29
  Casserole, Two-Squash, '79 101
  Chile Squash, '84 77
  con Crema, Squash, '89 148
  Creole Squash, '01 180
  Delight, Squash, '90 236
  Dilled Summer Squash, '96 148
  Dressing, Squash, '83 315; '86 280; '95 290; '01 160
  Dressing, Turkey with Squash, '87 248
  Greek-Style Squash, '92 26
  Greek-Style Squashes, '96 88
  Hubbard Squash, Tart, '80 214
  Kebabs, Summery Squash-and-Pepper, '95 193
  Marinated Grilled Squash, '02 110
  Marinated Squash, '05 129
  Marinated Squash Medley, '94 126
  Medley, Carrot-Lima-Squash, '80 123
  Medley, Fresh Squash, '81 M165
  Medley, Sautéed Vegetable, '83 101
  Medley, Squash, '81 139; '84 128
  Mirliton Balls, '90 217
  Mirlitons, Shrimp-and-Ham Stuffed, '03 251
  Muffins, Squash, '91 69
  Oregano, Summer Squash, '97 165
  "Pasta," Garden-Fresh, '94 M134
  Pattypan-Zucchini Skillet, '82 103
  Pickles, Squash, '81 174; '87 150; '97 119; '99 170
  Pie, Mock Coconut, '86 200
  Pie, Savory Squash, '00 170
  Pie, Scallopini, '94 133
  Puff, Golden Squash, '82 288
  Relish, Pollock with Summer Squash, '92 200
  Roasted Winter Squash, '05 233
  Rosemary, Summer Squash with, '88 143
  Salad, Squash, '03 M184
  Sandwiches, Skillet Squash, '98 144
  Sautéed Squash and Carrots, '05 42
  Sautéed Squash and Zucchini, '05 203
  Sauté, Squash, '82 67
  Scallop, Green-and-Gold, '81 159
  Skillet Squash, '82 195
  Soup, Dilled Summer, '99 182
  South-of-the-Border Squash, '00 137
  Spaghetti Squash, '92 340
  Spaghetti Squash and Chicken Skillet Casserole, '94 134

SQUASH
(continued)

Spaghetti Squash, Asian, '94 268
Spaghetti Squash Lasagna, '84 127
Spaghetti Squash Pie, '80 186
Spaghetti Squash Salad, '99 M322
Spaghetti Squash Salad, Marinated, '94 134
Spaghetti Squash Sauté, '98 212; '05 234
Spaghetti Squash, Sautéed Vegetables with, '84 128
Spaghetti Squash with Meat Sauce, '88 M180
Spaghetti Squash with Sesame Eggplant, '92 252
Stir-Fried Squash Medley, '80 123
Stir-Fry, Squash, '80 184
Stir-Fry, Two-Squash, '86 174
Stuffed
    Acorn Squash, Apple-Stuffed, '83 296; '84 285
    Acorn Squash, Baked, '81 24
    Acorn Squash, Cranberry-Filled, '81 M231
    Acorn Squash, Custard-Filled, '86 334
    Acorn Squash, Deluxe, '80 215
    Acorn Squash, Fruited, '85 235; '90 228
    Acorn Squash, Fruit-Stuffed, '81 295
    Acorn Squash, Ham-Stuffed, '81 239; '83 66
    Acorn Squash-Mushroom Puree, '93 305
    Acorn Squash, Pineapple-Stuffed, '84 255
    Acorn Squash, Sausage-Stuffed, '81 M231; '83 296; '84 285
    Acorn Squash, Stuffed, '82 277; '83 15
    Acorn Squash with Molasses and Pecans, '85 205
    Acorn Squash with Nutmeg, '85 267
    Acorn Squash with Sausage, '85 9
    Acorn Squash with Spiced Cranberry Sauce, Gingered, '96 267
    Apple-and-Pecan-Filled Squash, '88 228
    Apple-Stuffed Squash, '85 206
    Baked Squash, Stuffed, '85 206
    Beef-Stuffed Squash, '83 134
    Butternut Squash, Apple-Stuffed, '81 232
    Chayote, Stuffed, '92 247
    Cheesy Stuffed Squash, '82 134
    Crumb-Stuffed Squash, '89 148
    Green Chiles, Stuffed Squash with, '83 148
    Harvest Squash, '80 214
    Maple-Flavored Stuffed Squash, '85 205
    Mexican, Stuffed Squash, '90 200
    Mirlitons, Stuffed, '90 217; '93 278
    Parmesan-Stuffed Squash Boats, '79 156
    Pattypan Squash, Stuffed, '82 103; '85 136; '88 142
    Plantation Squash, '79 225
    Sausage-Stuffed Squash, '81 183
    Spinach Pesto, Squash Stuffed with, '89 M133
    Spinach-Stuffed Squash, '82 4; '91 14; '97 119; '02 165
    Stuffed Squash, '98 177
    Summer Squash, Stuffed, '02 M181
    Turban Chicken Curry, '94 266
    Turban Squash, Sausage-Stuffed, '80 214
    Turban Squash, Stuffed Turks, '88 228
    Vegetable-Stuffed Squash, '84 104
    White Squash, Stuffed, '90 M201
    Yellow Squash, Garden-Stuffed, '84 106
    Yellow Squash, Italian Stuffed, '86 111
    Yellow Squash, Mushroom-Stuffed, '84 154
    Yellow Squash, Shrimp-Stuffed, '84 194
    Yellow Squash with Cheese Sauce, Stuffed, '80 162
Summer Squash, Southern, '98 207
Tart, Squash, '96 83
Tomatoes, Squash-Stuffed, '82 102
Tomato Squash, '86 111
Toss, Pepperoni-Squash, '84 127
Turban Squash, Glazed, '81 24
Yellow. *See also* **SQUASH/Stuffed.**
    à l'Orange, Squash, '85 230

Amarillo Squash, '99 M218
Bacon-Flavored Squash, '82 158
Bake, Cheddar-Squash, '84 M113, 128
Bake, Cheesy Squash, '80 183
Bake, Squash and Tomato, '95 180
Beans, and Tomatoes, Squash, '83 148
Bisque, Squash, '98 290
Bread, Spicy Squash, '83 121
Bread, Yellow Squash, '84 140
Buttered Summer Squash, '81 84
Cake, Squash, '86 200
Casserole, Baked Squash, '83 149
Casserole, Blender Squash, '81 212
Casserole, Cheesy Squash, '79 123; '82 M21
Casserole, Chicken-Squash, '95 121
Casserole, Company Squash, '81 183
Casserole, Creamy Rice and Squash, '95 26
Casserole, Crunchy Squash, '84 293
Casserole, Fresh Squash, '82 204
Casserole, Hearty Tex-Mex Squash-Chicken, '99 312; '03 107
Casserole, Jiffy Squash, '81 M144
Casserole, Squash, '87 163; '89 159; '90 161; '92 342; '96 247, 252; '97 29; '04 126; '05 277
Casserole, Squash and Egg, '80 146
Casserole, Squash-Carrot, '81 157
Casserole, Summer Squash, '81 102, 184
Casserole, Two-Cheese Squash, '04 126
Casserole, Yellow Squash, '79 179; '85 135; '88 166
Casserole, Zippy Squash, '80 183
Corn Casserole, Easy Squash-and-, '03 69
Country Club Squash, '79 158; '88 M16
Croquettes, Squash, '79 157; '83 148; '88 142; '97 118
Dip, Yellow Squash-Zucchini, '89 48
Dressing, Squash, '83 315; '86 280; '95 290; '01 160
Fiesta Squash, '82 102
Fried Yellow Squash, '86 211
Fritters, Squash, '89 68; '99 203
Fritters, Squash-Jalapeño, '98 249
Greek-Style Squash, '91 285
Grilled Corn and Squash, '02 122
Grilled Corn-and-Squash Quesadillas, '02 123
Grilled Squash and Onion, '79 150
Grilled Squash Fans, '97 118
Grilled Summer Squash and Tomatoes, '99 144
Grilled Vegetables, '84 172
Grilled Yellow Squash and Tomatoes, '00 102
Grilled Yellow Squash Halves, '04 138
Marinated Cucumbers and Squash, '86 146
Medley, Summer Garden, '84 158
Mexican Squash, '82 103
Muffins, Yellow Squash, '81 163
Nicholas, Squash, '94 236
Nosh, Squash, '90 147
Pats, Squash, '80 298; '81 25
Patties, Squash, '79 158
Patties, Summer Squash, '81 184
Pickled Yellow Squash, '93 136
Pickles, Squash, '81 174; '87 150; '97 119; '99 170
Pie, Italian Squash, '02 183
Posh Squash, '81 159
Puffs, Yellow Squash, '82 103
Puppies, Squash, '83 170; '01 179
Quiche, Squash-and-Green Chile, '88 143
Rings, Asparagus in Squash, '87 68
Savory Squash, '99 111
Skillet Squash, '92 62
Skillet Summer Squash, '82 96
Slaw, Broccoli-Squash, '05 170
Soufflé, Cheesy Squash, '82 146
Soufflé, Squash, '95 215
Soufflé, Yellow Squash, '89 89
Soup, Chilled Squash, '92 173
Soup, Cold Cream of Squash, '81 130

Soup, Cream of Squash, '81 246
Soup, Perky Squash, '85 20
Soup, Squash, '94 134
Soup, Summer Squash, '83 99; '85 136
South-of-the-Border Squash, '89 148; '96 178
Stir-Fried Squash, '97 118
Stir-Fried Squash Medley, '80 123
Stuffed Squash, '01 223
Stuffed Yellow Squash, Tomato-, '00 42
Summer Squash, '80 127; '85 105
Toss, Asparagus-Carrot-Squash, '91 45
Toss, Crisp Squash-and-Pepper, '87 M152
Toss, Simple Squash, '85 M142
Vegetable-Herb Trio, '83 172
STEWS. *See also* CHILI, CHOWDERS, GUMBOS, JAMBALAYAS, RAGOÛTS, SOUPS.
Bean Pot, White, '86 194
Beef-and-Celery Root Stew, '98 292
Beef-and-Onion Stew, '87 18
Beef and Vegetable Stew, Sweet-and-Sour, '85 87
Beef Stew, '86 51; '90 230; '96 16
Beef Stew, Burgundy, '88 234
Beef Stew, Company, '83 85; '97 198
Beef Stew, Hungarian, '03 35
Beef Stew, Oven, '79 222; '80 64
Beef Stew, Quick, '86 302; '92 71
Beef Stew, Slow-Cooker, '05 235
Beef Stew, Spicy, '86 228
Beef Stew with Dumplings, '84 3
Beef Stew with Parsley Dumplings, '81 76; '82 13; '85 M246
Black-Eyed Pea Stew with Rice, '04 19
Brown Stew, '85 239
Brunswick
    Aunt Willette's Brunswick Stew, '85 320
    Bama Brunswick Stew, '87 4
    Blakely Brunswick Stew, '87 4
    Breeden Liles's Brunswick Stew, '91 14
    Brunswick Stew, '80 264; '97 138, 315; '01 148, 219; '03 29
    Chicken Brunswick Stew, '97 234
    Chicken Stew, Brunswick, '87 4
    Dan Dickerson's Brunswick Stew, '91 16
    Easy Brunswick Stew, '92 280; '99 235; '00 138; '05 292
    Family-Size Brunswick Stew, Van Doyle's, '91 14
    Favorite Brunswick Stew, Virginia Ramsey's, '91 16
    Gay Neale's Brunswick Stew, '91 17
    Georgian Brunswick Stew, '92 35
    Jeff Daniel's Brunswick Stew, '91 16
    Pie, Brunswick Stew-Cornbread, '02 121
    Sonny Frye's Brunswick Stew, '87 4
    Virginian Brunswick Stew, '92 34
Burgoo, Five-Meat, '87 3
Burgoo, Harry Young's, '87 3
Burgoo, Kentucky, '88 235; '97 138
Burgoo, Old-Fashioned, '87 3
Burgundy Stew with Drop Dumplings, '83 125
Caldo de Rez (Mexican Beef Stew), '89 276
Camp Stew, '02 42
Catfish Stew, Cajun-Style, '88 12
Chicken-and-Vegetable Stew, '05 235
Chicken, Kale, and Chickpea Stew, '98 47
Chicken Stew, '97 26
Chicken Stew and Dumplings, '84 4
Chicken Stew, Chili-, '90 319
Chicken Stew, Greek-Style, '03 219
Chicken Stew, Santa Fe, '97 193
Chicken Stew, Speedy, '03 42
Chicken Stew, Zesty, '02 127
Chili Stew, Red, '95 226
Collard 'n' Black-Eyed Pea Stew, '04 24
Collard Stew, '02 17
Emerald Isle Stew, '95 71
Étouffée, Crawfish, '02 85

Étouffée, Okra, '98 207
Étouffée, Quick Crawfish, '05 57
Étouffée, Roasted Quail, '96 34
Étouffée, Traditional, '05 56
Fish-and-Vegetable Stew, '87 220
Fisherman's Stew, '81 98
Fricassee, White Chicken, '98 122
Frogmore Stew, '92 236; '00 174, 336; '03 181; '05 111
Game Pot Pie with Parmesan Crust, '94 304
Garbanzo Stew, Greek, '02 43
Ham-and-Black-Eyed Pea Stew, '93 20
Ham-and-Collard Stew, Hearty, '05 236
Hamburger Oven Stew, '84 4
Hungarian Stew with Noodles, '80 263
Hunter's Stew, '85 270
Irish Stew, '90 64
Lamb-and-Okra Stew, '97 156
Lamb Stew, '79 293; '88 58
Lamb Stew-in-a-Loaf, '85 37
Lamb Stew with Popovers, '94 43
Lentil-Rice Stew, '82 232
Meatball Stew, '79 198; '98 30
Mexican Stew, '82 231
Mexican Stew Olé, '86 296
Minestrone Stew, '93 184
Mirliton Stew, '02 57
Okra Stew, Old-Fashioned, '84 158
Okra Stew, Quick, '97 88
Oyster-Broccoli Stew, '89 242
Oyster-Sausage Stew, '89 242
Oyster Stew, '80 221; '05 48
Oyster Stew, Company, '80 297
Oyster Stew, Golden, '86 132
Oyster Stew, Holiday, '85 264
Oyster Stew, Potato-, '89 243
Pancho Villa Stew, '94 44
Pollo en Pipián, Mexican, '88 31
Pork Stew, Baja, '98 283
Reggae Rundown, '96 71
Rib-Tickling Stew, Campeche Bay, '89 317
Sausage Stew, Smoked, '82 231
Seafood Stew, '84 280
Shrimp Creole, '93 282; '96 210
Shrimp Creole, Spicy, '79 181
Shrimp Creole, Wild Rice-and-, '84 292
Shrimp Stew, '83 4
Shrimp Stew and Grits, '80 118
Shrimp Stew over Grits, '88 126; '89 47
Strader Stew, '89 28
Succotash with Serrano Chile Polenta, Ancho Chile, '98 104
Texas Stew, '97 211
Turkey Stew, Hearty, '79 252
Turkey-Tomato Stew, '90 279
Turnip Greens Stew, '02 17; '04 24
Tzimmes with Brisket, Mixed Fruit, '93 114
Vegetable-Beef Stew, '94 323
Vegetable-Beef Stew, Shortcut, '89 218
Vegetable Stew, '00 248
Vegetable Stew, Mixed, '84 13
Vegetable Tagine, '96 289
Venison Sausage Stew, '87 238
Venison Stew, '86 294
Venison Stew with Potato Dumplings, '87 304
White Wine Stew, '82 228
STRAWBERRIES
Almond Cream Dip with Strawberries, '92 164
Arnaud, Strawberries, '93 50
Balsamic Strawberries, '02 170
Banana-Berry Flip, '88 215; '89 20
Bars, Strawberry, '81 301
Bavarian, Raspberry-Strawberry, '89 15
Bavarian, Rhubarb-Strawberry, '86 140
Beets, Strawberry-Glazed, '83 234
Best-Dressed Berries, '96 317

Beverages. *See also* **BEVERAGES/Smoothies.**
Brandied Orange Juice, Strawberries with, '82 160
Calypso, Coco-Berry, '89 171
Cubes, Berry-Good, '95 201
Frost, Banana-Strawberry, '87 199
Frozen Strawberry Refresher, '93 213
Ice Mold, Strawberry, '91 278
Ice Ring, Strawberry, '94 176
Mimosa, Sparkling Strawberry, '88 169
Pineapple-Strawberry Slush, '94 227
Shrub, Berry, '95 29
Slush, Strawberry, '98 178; '02 185
Slush, Strawberry-Orange, '83 172
Spritzer, Strawberry, '90 14; '97 272
Spritzer, Strawberry-Kiwi-Lemonade, '03 89
Tea, Berry-Mint Iced, '98 152
Tea, Sparkling Strawberry, '94 131
Bordeaux, Beauberries, '98 18
Bread, Strawberry, '81 250; '83 140; '84 49
Bread, Strawberry Jam, '79 216
Bread, Strawberry-Nut, '79 24
Butter, Strawberry, '79 36; '81 286; '91 71; '99 44, 234
Cake, Chocolate-Strawberry Basket, '98 100
Cake, Layered Strawberry, '00 82
Cake Roll, Strawberries 'n Cream Sponge, '81 95
Cake Roll, Strawberry, '79 49; '83 129; '84 305; '85 172
Cake, Strawberry Cream, '86 61
Cake, Strawberry Crunch, '79 288; '80 35
Cake, Strawberry Delight, '85 30
Cake, Strawberry-Lemon Sheet, '04 137
Cake, Strawberry Meringue, '86 240
Cake, Strawberry-Studded White Chocolate Mousse, '99 154
Cake, Strawberry Yogurt Layer, '94 85
Cake, Triple-Decker Strawberry, '04 55
Cake with Strawberries and Chocolate Glaze, White, '87 76
Cake with Strawberries and Cream, Cream Cheese Pound, '02 104
Carousel, Strawberry, '91 247
Cheesecake, Almost Strawberry, '86 32
Cheesecake, Irish Strawberry-and-Cream, '05 273
Cheesecake, Pear-Berry, '82 M141
Cheesecake, Strawberry, '02 176, 209
Cheesecake, Strawberry-Lemon, '04 237
Cheese Horseshoe, Strawberry-, '00 106
Cheese Ring, Strawberry-, '86 14
Cherry-Berry on a Cloud, '79 94
Chocolate Combo, Strawberry-, '85 96
Christmas Strawberries, '87 293; '94 331
Citrus Twist, Berry-, '95 100
Cobbler, Fresh Strawberry, '96 84
Cobbler, Rosy Strawberry-Rhubarb, '79 154
Cobbler, Strawberry-Rhubarb, '88 93
Coffee Cake, Strawberry, '85 46
Compote, Peach-Berry, '89 112
Cookie Tarts, Strawberry, '89 112
Cream, Chocolate Baskets with Berry, '92 118
Cream Dip, Fresh Strawberries with, '90 86
Cream in Vanilla Lace Cups, Strawberry, '98 93
Cream Puffs, Strawberry, '81 95
Cream Puffs, Strawberry-Lemon, '87 75
Cream, Strawberries and, '82 100; '92 132
Cream, Strawberries in, '89 88
Cream, Strawberries 'n', '90 30
Cream, Strawberries 'n Lemon, '85 112
Cream, Strawberries with Chocolate, '85 81
Cream, Strawberries with French, '83 191
Cream, Strawberries with Lemon, '90 170
Cream, Strawberries with Strawberry, '84 108
Cream, Strawberry, '88 153
Cream with Fresh Strawberries, Almond, '87 93
Crêpes, Nutritious Brunch, '80 44
Crêpes, Strawberry Dessert, '83 122
Crisp, Strawberry-Rhubarb, '95 119
Croissants, Strawberry or Apricot, '96 303

Deep-Fried Strawberries, '84 109
Delight, Frozen Strawberry, '82 112, 174
Delight, Strawberry, '81 85
Delight, Strawberry Cheese, '79 50
Delight, Strawberry Yogurt, '85 77
Dessert, Chilled Strawberry, '84 164
Dessert, Glazed Strawberry, '84 33
Dessert, Honeydew-Berry, '83 120
Dessert, Strawberry, '83 123
Dessert, Strawberry-Cream Cheese, '83 123
Dessert, Strawberry-Lemon, '86 162
Dessert, Strawberry-Yogurt, '90 295
Dessert, Summer Strawberry, '92 143
Dessert, Sweet-and-Sour Strawberry, '92 54
Dip, Apple-Berry, '01 109
Dipped in White Chocolate, Strawberries, '90 83
Dipped Strawberries, '94 17
Dipped Strawberries, Chocolate-, '98 M100
Dip, Strawberries with Brown Sugar-and-Sour Cream, '03 93
Dip, Strawberries with Fluffy Cream Cheese, '03 93
Dip, Strawberries with Mint Yogurt, '03 93
Dip, Strawberries with Vanilla Pudding, '03 93
Dip, Strawberry, '01 109
Divinity, Strawberry, '91 272
Dressing, Creamy Strawberry, '84 161
Éclairs, Strawberry Cream, '01 45
Filling, Strawberry-Lemon, '04 137
Freeze, Strawberry, '04 141
French Toast Sandwiches, Strawberry-, '91 160
Frosting, Strawberry, '89 184
Frosting, Strawberry Buttercream, '04 55
Frost, Strawberry, '81 279; '82 24; '83 154
Frozen Strawberry Cups, '91 173
Fudge Balls, Strawberry, '93 80
Gazpacho, Berry, '97 181
Glaze, Strawberry, '80 35; '83 142
Ham, Strawberry-Glazed, '91 84
Ice Cream Crêpes, Strawberry, '87 290; '88 135
Ice Cream, Fresh Strawberry, '89 111
Ice Cream, Homemade Strawberry, '84 184
Ice Cream, No-Cook Strawberry, '04 179
Ice Cream, Old-Fashioned Strawberry, '79 94
Ice Cream Roll, Strawberry, '84 105
Ice Cream, Straw-Ba-Nut, '80 177
Ice Cream, Strawberry, '80 177; '98 221
Ice Cream, Strawberry-Banana-Nut, '88 203
Ice Cream Torte, Chocolate-Strawberry, '79 7
Ice Cream, Very Strawberry, '81 155
Ice Milk, Fresh Strawberry, '92 94
Ice, Strawberry, '84 175; '85 108
Ice, Strawberry-Orange, '86 196
Jamaica, Strawberries, '85 161; '93 239
Jam, Christmas, '88 288
Jam, Strawberry, '89 138
Jam, Strawberry Freezer, '84 M182
Jam, Strawberry-Port, '03 134
Jellyroll, Easy, '82 176
Jelly, Strawberry, '81 147
Juliet, Strawberries, '84 82
Ladyfingers, Creamy Berry, '05 36
Marinated Strawberries with Balsamic-Strawberry Syrup, '02 146
Marmalade, Strawberry-Pineapple, '85 130
Marsala, Strawberries, '88 171
Melon, Berry-Filled, '86 93
Meringues, Strawberry, '84 188
Mousse, Fresh Strawberry, '82 72
Mousse, Strawberry, '81 95
Mousse, Strawberry-Lemon, '82 128
Muffins, Strawberry, '99 234
Napoleons, Strawberry, '81 126
Nests, Strawberry Coconut, '88 136
Omelet, Puffy Dessert, '00 35
Omelet, Strawberry-Sour Cream, '89 229

STRAWBERRIES
(continued)

Oranges and Strawberries, Grand, '03 119
Pancakes, Strawberry, '84 219
Parfait, Crunchy Strawberry-Yogurt, '79 124
Parfaits, Frosty Strawberry, '85 213
Parfaits, Strawberry-Lemon, '84 198
Parfaits, Strawberry Meringue, '02 62
Parfaits, Super Fast Strawberry Shortcake, '05 196
Parfait, Strawberry, '79 99
Parfait, Surprise Strawberry, '86 151

Pies
Angel Pie, Strawberry, '88 136
Banana Glazed Pie, Strawberry-, '81 181
Bumbleberry Pie, '97 163
Chilled Strawberry Pie, '82 112
Chocolate-Berry Pie, Heavenly, '85 102
Chocolate Truffle Pie, Strawberry-, '89 112
Custard Pie, Strawberry, '00 81
Easy Strawberry Pie, '02 146
Fried Strawberry Pies, '02 147
Glazed Strawberry Pie, '82 M142
Glaze Pie, Strawberry-, '81 141
Ice-Cream Pie, Spiked Strawberry-Lime, '05 89
Ice-Cream Pie, Strawberry-Lime, '05 89
Ice-Cream Pie, Strawberry Smoothie, '05 89
Lemon-Strawberry Pie, '88 127
Red, White, and Blueberry Pie, '98 162
Rhubarb Pie, Strawberry-, '98 99; '05 132
Yogurt Pie, Strawberry, '80 232
Yogurt Pie, Strawberry-, '85 122; '86 124

Pizza, Kiwi-Berry, '86 198; '87 55
Pizza, Strawberry, '79 94
Popsicles, Smoothie Strawberry, '82 112
Pops, Strawberry, '04 141
Pops, Strawberry-Cinnamon, '99 132
Pops, Strawberry-Orange, '03 179
Pound Cake with Mint Berries and Cream, Lemon, '99 183
Preserves Deluxe, Strawberry, '82 150
Preserves, Freezer Strawberry, '82 112
Preserves, Hanukkah Doughnuts with Strawberry,
'01 M275
Preserves, Quick Strawberry-Fig, '96 194
Preserves, Strawberry, '79 120; '81 96
Pudding, Summer, '98 217
Puff, Strawberry, '82 5
Raspberry Custard Sauce, Fresh Berries with, '88 163
Rock Cream with Strawberries, Old-Fashioned, '90 125
Roll, Heavenly Strawberry, '82 176
Roll, Strawberry, '82 120
Romanoff, Strawberries, '84 108; '88 95; '91 126; '94 68
Romanoff, Strawberry-Almond, '98 99
Ruby Strawberries, '82 100
Sabayon, Strawberries, '79 94
Salad, Baby Blue, '00 81
Salad, Chicken-and-Strawberry, '05 132
Salad, Chicken-Spinach-Strawberry, '97 92
Salad, Citrus-Strawberry, '04 249
Salad, Cranberry-Strawberry-Jicama, '02 300
Salad, Frozen Strawberry, '94 119
Salad, Hidden Treasure Strawberry, '79 11
Salad, Mimosa, '98 310
Salad Mold, Strawberry-Wine, '83 261
Salad, Spinach-and-Strawberry, '05 55
Salad, Strawberry-Chicken, '84 50
Salad, Strawberry-Citrus Chicken, '05 84
Salad, Strawberry-Cranberry-Orange, '05 249
Salad, Strawberry-Nut, '94 132
Salad, Strawberry-Pretzel, '03 290
Salad, Strawberry-Spinach, '91 169; '93 168
Salad, Strawberry Yogurt, '80 232
Salad with Cinnamon Vinaigrette, Strawberry, '05 133

Salad with Orange-Curd Dressing, Orange-Strawberry,
'93 22
Salad with Tart Poppy Seed Dressing, Spinach-and-
Strawberry, '03 241

Sauces
Amaretto-Strawberry Sauce, '87 M165
Arnaud Sauce, Strawberries, '93 50
Banana Sauce, Strawberry-, '81 41
Berry Sauce, '87 290; '88 135; '95 103
Brandied Strawberry Sauce, '88 196
Butter Sauce, Strawberry-, '81 41
Crunchy Topping, Strawberry Sauce with, '81 170
Dumplings, Strawberry Sauce with, '84 314
French Toast with Strawberry Sauce, Make-Ahead,
'02 131
Fresh Strawberry Sauce, '82 177
Melon Wedges with Berry Sauce, '86 178
Mimosa Sauce, Berry, '90 315
Old-Fashioned Strawberry Sauce, '94 130
Orange Sauce, Strawberry-, '96 95
Peaches with Strawberry Sauce, '85 8
Peach Sauce, Strawberry-, '92 154
Salsa, Balsamic Strawberry, '02 86
Strawberry Sauce, '84 144; '87 93, 198; '92 85;
'94 121; '03 55

Sherbet, Strawberry, '82 112, 160
Sherbet, Three-Ingredient Strawberry, '01 105
Shortcake, A Favorite Strawberry, '88 136
Shortcake, Chocolate-Strawberry, '89 216
Shortcake, Elegant Strawberry, '88 37
Shortcake Jubilee, Strawberry, '88 209
Shortcake, Orange-Strawberry, '95 100
Shortcake Shells, Strawberry, '88 196
Shortcake Shortcut, '02 105
Shortcakes, Party-Perfect Strawberry, '02 105
Shortcake Squares, Strawberry, '85 122; '86 124
Shortcakes, Round, '02 105
Shortcakes, Strawberry Crispy, '93 42
Shortcake, Strawberry, '81 96; '83 122; '92 184;
'94 162
Shortcake, Strawberry-Brown Sugar, '00 82
Shortcake, Strawberry Pinwheel, '89 112
Shortcakes with Mint Cream, Strawberry, '97 144
Skewered Pineapple and Strawberries, '84 251
Sorbet, Strawberry, '88 117; '93 153; '03 171
Sorbet, Strawberry-Champagne, '83 162; '95 20
Sorbet, Strawberry Margarita, '89 111
Sorbet, Strawberry-Passion Fruit, '98 180
Sorbet, Very Berry, '90 85
Soup, Cold Strawberry, '82 157
Soup, Sherry-Berry Dessert, '91 180
Soup, Strawberry, '88 160
Soup, Strawberry-Banana, '86 181
Soup Supreme, Strawberry, '81 M144
Spiked Strawberries, '97 58
Splendid Strawberries, '05 215
Spread, Light Strawberry, '85 55
Spread, Strawberry, '95 79
Spumoni and Berries, '91 204
Stuffed Strawberries, '98 155
Stuffed Strawberries with Walnuts, '85 122; '86 124
Sundaes, Hot Strawberry, '81 M5
Supreme, Banana-Berry, '81 205
Swirl, Strawberry, '84 108
Syrup, Fresh Strawberry, '05 132
Syrup, Strawberry, '02 104
Tartlets, Fresh Berry, '91 98
Tarts, Berry Good Lemon, '91 119
Tarts, Strawberry, '80 70
Tart, Strawberry, '84 138; '89 272; '00 82; '01 71
Tart, Strawberry Dream, '92 118
Tart, Strawberry-Lemon, '89 111
Tart, Strawberry-Mascarpone, '02 146
Tea Cakes and Fresh Strawberries, Telia's, '98 110

Topping, Pound Cake with Strawberry-Banana, '89 200
Topping, Strawberry, '86 32; '90 142
Topping, Strawberry-Banana, '87 125
Torte, Spring, '91 57
Torte, Strawberry Meringue, '88 136
Treasure, Berried, '89 124
Trifle, Easy Strawberry, '88 201
Trifle, Strawberry-Sugar Biscuit, '03 84
Vinaigrette, Strawberry-Balsamic, '05 84
Whip, Strawberry, '89 198
Zabaglione, Strawberries, '81 95

STROGANOFF
Beef Burgundy Stroganoff, '85 31
Beef Stroganoff, '79 163; '81 179; '91 134; '93 18;
'03 23
Beef Stroganoff, Creamy, '02 124
Beef Stroganoff, Ground, '84 71
Beef Stroganoff, Light, '86 36
Beef Stroganoff, Quick, '92 20; '99 327
Casserole, Stroganoff, '98 48
Chicken Livers Stroganoff, '80 200; '81 57
Chicken Livers Supreme, '81 298
Chicken Stroganoff, '99 41
Crab Stroganoff, '79 116
Crawfish Stroganoff, '91 89
Hamburger Stroganoff, '82 108, 110
Hamburger Stroganoff, Easy, '79 208
Ham Stroganoff, '82 40
Ham Stroganoff on Cheesy Onion Biscuits, '95 98
Liver Stroganoff, '79 54
Meatballs, European Veal, '85 30
Meatballs Paprikash with Rice, '85 31
Meatball Stroganoff, '81 297; '02 50
Mushroom-Meatball Stroganoff, '85 85
Mushroom Stroganoff, '81 298
Quail Stroganoff, '99 41
Quickie Stroganoff, '81 200
Shrimp Stroganoff, '79 81
Shrimp Stroganoff, Oven-Baked, '81 297
Sirloin Stroganoff, '81 297
Steak Stroganoff Sandwiches, '85 110
Steak Stroganoff with Parslied Noodles, '85 31
Strolling-Through-the-Holidays Stroganoff, '01 282
Tofu, Stroganoff, '84 202
Turkey Stroganoff, '91 61
Veal Stroganoff, '79 108

STUFFINGS. *See also* DRESSINGS.
Apple-Almond Stuffing, '01 184
Apple-Crumb Stuffing, '81 234; '82 26; '83 39
Apple-Walnut Stuffing, '95 289
Barley-Mushroom Stuffing, Cornish Hens with, '97 242
Cornbread-Apple Stuffing, Pork Chops with, '99 14
Cornbread Stuffing, '94 305
Crabmeat Stuffing, '94 68
Crabmeat Stuffing, Chicken Breasts with, '85 302
Crab Stuffing, Tropical Orange Roughy with, '99 122
Cranberry-Orange-Pecan Stuffing, '01 249
Cranberry-Pecan Stuffing, '96 309
Cranberry-Sausage Stuffing, Crown Roast of Pork with,
'88 49
Cranberry Stuffing, '04 246
Fruited Stuffing, Cornish Hens with, '90 191
Fruited Stuffing Mix, '89 331
Fruit Stuffing and Shiitake Sauce, Pork Tenderloin with,
'97 218
Grits Stuffing, '96 270
Hopping John Stuffing, Pork Roast with, '01 25
Low-Sodium Stuffing, '82 66
Mincemeat Stuffing, '00 319
Mushroom Stuffing, Grilled Rainbow Trout with, '97 162
Oyster Stuffing, Roast Turkey with, '80 251
Pear Stuffing, Acorn Squash with, '01 293
Pecan-Cornbread Stuffing, Spicy, '01 207
Pecan-Sausage Stuffing, Chicken Breasts with, '94 212

Pecan Stuffing, '79 292; '80 32
Pecan Stuffing, Wild Duck with, '85 269
Piglet's Stuffing, '04 270
Rice-and-Onion Stuffing, '88 246
Rice Stuffing, '95 290
Sausage-and-Wild Mushroom Stuffing, '96 267
Sausage Stuffing, '99 293; '00 292; '03 255
Tangerine Stuffing, '90 16
Vegetable Stuffing, '01 84
Walnut-Rice Stuffing, Tomatoes with, '91 102
Wild Rice Stuffing, Cornish Hens with, '79 222; '80 64;
    '82 136

SWEET-AND-SOUR
Beets, Sweet-and-Sour, '81 167; '82 22; '89 314
Black-Eyed Peas, Sweet-and-Sour, '85 290
Burgers, Sweet-and-Sour, '90 128
Cabbage, Sweet-and-Sour, '86 295; '87 189
Cabbage, Sweet-Sour Red, '79 5
Carrots, Sweet-and-Sour, '82 137
Chicken and Rice, Sweet-and-Sour, '03 97
Chicken Nuggets, Sweet-and-Sour, '90 168
Chicken Stir-Fry, Sweet-and-Sour, '98 204
Chicken, Sweet-and-Sour, '79 106; '86 217, 240;
    '90 161; '91 202; '97 325
Chicken, Sweet-and-Sour Lemon, '84 93
Chicken, Sweet 'n' Sour, '04 311
Chicken Wings, Sweet-and-Sour, '90 206; '96 110
Dessert, Sweet-and-Sour Strawberry, '92 54
Dressing, Citrus Salad with Sweet-and-Sour, '01 104
Dressing, Sweet-and-Sour, '80 247; '84 70, 161;
    '85 163; '87 305; '89 62; '91 126; '94 281;
    '02 24; '03 28
Dressing, Sweet-and-Sour Fruit, '84 125
Dressing, Sweet-Sour, '80 246
Fish, Sweet-and-Sour, '80 M54
Green Beans and Carrots, Sweet-and-Sour, '83 6
Green Beans, Sweet-and-Sour, '79 184; '81 158; '82 90;
    '91 250
Ham, Sweet-and-Sour Glazed, '88 M15
Ham, Sweet-Sour Glazed, '83 311
Kale, Sweet-and-Sour, '80 298
Kielbasa, Sweet-and-Sour, '89 327
Liver, Sweet-and-Sour, '81 277
Marinade, Sweet-and-Sour, '86 113; '87 115
Meatballs, Spicy Sweet-and-Sour, '03 186
Meatballs, Sweet-and-Sour, '82 233, 247; '86 240;
    '99 325; '05 305
Meatballs, Sweet-and-Sour Party, '79 233
Onions, Sweet-and-Sour Baked, '90 34
Pearl Onions, Sweet-and-Sour, '96 216
Peas, Sweet-and-Sour, '88 3
Pork Chops, Sweet-and-Sour, '83 160
Pork, Pineapple Sweet-and-Sour, '82 120
Pork Stir-Fry, Sweet-and-Sour, '03 92
Pork, Sweet-and-Sour, '79 42; '80 72, 227; '81 26, 104,
    111; '82 12; '84 218; '85 34, 194; '86 241;
    '90 317; '92 219; '00 110
Potatoes, Sweet-and-Sour-Topped, '83 4
Pot Roast, Sweet-and-Sour, '83 8; '99 291
Red Cabbage and Apples, Sweet-and-Sour, '00 62
Riblets, Sweet-and-Sour, '85 276
Ribs, Sweet-and-Sour, '89 M84
Ribs, Sweet-and-Sour Baby Back, '04 87
Ribs, Sweet-and-Sour Grilled, '98 331
Salads
    Asparagus, Sweet-and-Sour, '89 159
    Bean Salad, Sweet-and-Sour, '85 198; '86 147
    Beans, Sweet-and-Sour, '87 197
    Beans with Sprouts, Sweet-and-Sour, '86 32
    Carrot Salad, Sweet-and-Sour, '98 211
    Cauliflower Salad, Sweet-and-Sour, '81 2
    Fruit Salad, Sweet-and-Sour, '80 13; '84 125
    Green Salad, Sweet-and-Sour, '94 281
    Macaroni Salad, Sweet-and-Sour, '85 166

Potato Salad, Sweet and Sour, '80 152
Potato Salad, Sweet-and-Sour, '92 106
Slaw, Confetti Sweet-and-Sour, '98 89
Slaw, Sweet-and-Sour, '81 237
Slaw, Sweet-and-Sour Hot, '92 63
Spinach Salad, Sweet-Sour, '85 M112
Vegetable Salad, Sweet-and-Sour, '81 25
Sauce, Pork Chops with Sweet-and-Sour Apple, '98 132
Sauce, Sausage Rolls with Sweet-and-Sour, '83 74
Sauce, Stuffed Chicken Breasts with Sweet-and-Sour
    Tomato, '01 120
Sauce, Sweet-and-Sour, '80 20; '85 12, 34; '86 240
Sauce, Sweet-and-Sour 'Cue, '04 87
Sauce, Sweet-and-Sour Pineapple, '85 66
Sausage Bites, Sweet-and-Sour, '05 305
Sausage, Sweet-and-Sour, '88 296
Scallops, Grilled Sweet-and-Sour, '01 92
Shrimp and Chicken, Sweet-and-Sour, '87 267; '88 103;
    '89 66
Shrimp, Grilled Sweet-and-Sour, '97 100
Shrimp, Sweet-and-Sour, '83 278; '90 M112
Shrimp Tails, Sweet-and-Sour Rock, '80 3
Shrimp with Onion and Red Pepper, Sweet-and-Sour, '02 84
Snap Beans, Sweet-and-Sour, '89 173
Soup, Sweet-and-Sour Cabbage, '89 314
Spareribs, Sweet-and-Sour, '83 21
Spread, Sweet 'n' Sour, '86 184
Steaks, Sweet-and-Sour Marinated, '83 110
Stew, Sweet-and-Sour Beef and Vegetable, '85 87
Turkey, Sweet-and-Sour, '79 252
Turnips, Sweet-and-Sour, '81 274
Vegetables, Sweet-and-Sour Marinated, '83 266
Vinaigrette, Sweet-and-Sour Balsamic, '97 146

SWEET POTATOES
Apple Shells, Sweet Potatoes in, '85 206
Apples, Sweet Potato-Stuffed, '97 216; '00 232
Apple-Stuffed Sweet Potatoes, '88 207
Baked Whole Sweet Potatoes, '05 108
Bake, Southern Sweet Potato, '85 229
Bake, Sweet Potato-Apricot, '85 206
Balls, Sweet Potato, '86 312
Bisque, Sweet Potato-and-Pear, '00 317
Boats, Sweet Potato, '80 287
Bourbon-Sweet Potato Stacks, '04 246
Brandied Sweet Potatoes, '97 248
Breads
    Biscuits, Sweet Potato, '80 287; '84 140; '89 210;
        '98 222; '00 232; '01 250; '05 22
    Biscuits, Sweet Potato Angel, '93 312; '01 42
    Cornbread, Sweet Potato, '05 252
    Muffins, Sweet Potato, '81 224; '85 6; '87 280; '92 31
    Muffins, Yam, '79 7
    Rolls, Golden Yams, '86 299
    Rolls, Sweet Potato, '93 172; '97 107
Broiled Sweet Potatoes, Coconut-, '84 231
Butter, Sweet Potato, '95 M290
Candied Sweet Potatoes, '79 9, 251; '86 111; '88 207;
    '97 312; '01 49
Candied Sweet Potatoes, Nannie's, '95 306
Casseroles
    Apple Bake, Sweet Potato-, '83 25; '86 282
    Apple Casserole, Sweet Potato-and-, '94 280
    Apple Casserole, Sweet Potatoes-and-, '90 228
    Applesauce Sweet Potatoes, '91 292; '92 256
    Apples, Sweet Potatoes and, '97 249
    Apricot Casserole, Sweet Potato, '82 228
    Bake, Sweet Potato, '80 287
    Banana Casserole, Sweet Potato-, '86 276
    Bell's Sweet Potato Casserole, '04 271
    Berries Casserole, Sweet Potatoes-and-, '84 231
    Bourbon Sweet Potatoes, '86 324; '87 280
    Candied Sweet Potatoes, '88 207
    Coconut-Orange Sweet Potatoes, '84 252
    Delight, Sweet Potato, '86 335; '87 83

Eggnog Casserole, Sweet Potato-, '95 291
Festive Sweet Potatoes, '80 244
Glazed Sweet Potato Casserole, '90 250
Glazed Sweet Potatoes, Tropical, '83 226
Gratin, Smoky Potato, '00 233
Holiday Sweet Potato Bake, '90 291
Maple-Sweet Potato Casserole, '05 245
Mashed Sweet Potatoes, '98 269
Mashed Sweet Potatoes, Orange-Spice, '02 34
Orange Bake, Sweet Potato-, '83 226
Peaches, Sweet Potatoes and, '86 11
Pear-Sweet Potato Casserole, '86 280
Pineapple-Orange Sweet Potatoes, '96 46
Pones, Sweet Potato, '96 270
Praline-Topped Sweet Potatoes, '98 96
Puree, Carrot-and-Sweet Potato, '94 56
Royale, Sweet Potatoes, '91 250
Rum Casserole, Sweet Potato-, '84 231
Scallop, Yam-and-Apple, '91 199
Sherry and Walnuts, Sweet Potatoes with, '86 286
Surprise, Holiday Sweet Potato, '84 254
Surprise, Sweet Potato, '81 267; '97 139
Sweet Potato Casserole, '79 289; '80 26; '85 256;
    '89 279; '02 292; '03 M24
Swirled Mashed-Potato Bake, '02 98
Yams, Cornwallis, '79 276
Chips, Boniato, '92 247
Chips, Sweet Potato, '91 138; '93 332; '95 M203; '97 63
Chips with Blue Cheese, Sweet Potato, '93 290
Chowder, Asian Sweet Potato, '97 213
Chutney, Sweet Potato, '99 45
Cinnamon-Apple Sweet Potatoes, '95 M23
Croquettes, Sweet Potato, '81 223; '96 238
Cups, Sunshine Sweet Potato, '82 195
Desserts
    Buñuelos, '05 295
    Cakes, Sweet Potato, '01 105
    Cake, Sweet Potato, '79 207; '89 295
    Cake, Sweet Potato Loaf, '81 224
    Cake, Sweet Potato Pound, '83 85
    Cake, Sweet Potato Surprise, '80 287
    Cake with Citrus Filling, Sweet Potato, '02 221
    Cake with Coconut Filling and Caramel Frosting,
        Sweet Potato, '03 329
    Cheesecake, Sweet Potato, '80 287; '96 312
    Cheesecake, Yam, '81 224
    Cobbler, Sweet Potato, '99 255; '01 214
    Cobbler, Sweet Potato-Apple, '04 M232
    Crème Brûlée, Sweet Potato, '02 275
    Flan, Sweet Potato, '95 291
    Pie, Carolina Sweet Potato, '89 295
    Pie, Louisiana Yam, '81 223
    Pie, No-Crust Sweet Potato, '84 236
    Pie, Old-Fashioned Sweet Potato, '79 9
    Pie, Southern Sweet Potato Cream, '87 260
    Pie, Speedy Sweet Potato, '90 219
    Pie, Sweet Potato, '79 207; '85 255, 275; '86 269;
        '89 289; '96 131, 326; '00 232; '01 243; '04 331
    Pie, Sweet Potato Meringue, '81 126; '83 225
    Pie, Sweet Potato-Orange, '88 207
    Pie, Sweet Potato-Pecan, '83 90
    Pie, Sweet Potato Pone, '80 288
    Pudding, Sweet Potato, '80 228; '86 52
    Pudding, Sweet Potato Bread, '94 241
    Roll, Sweet Potato Log, '82 227
    Torte, Caramel-Sweet Potato, '96 312
French-Fried Sweet Potatoes, '81 223
Fried Sweet Potatoes, '83 226
Fried Sweet Potato Strips, '94 238
Fritters, Golden Sweet Potato, '79 9
Fritters, Sweet Potato, '88 44
Glazed Sweet Potatoes, '85 206; '89 274
Glazed Sweet Potatoes, Apple-, '82 303
Glazed Sweet Potatoes, Apricot-, '81 295

SWEET POTATOES
(continued)

Glazed Sweet Potatoes, Orange-, '81 223; '83 280
Glaze, Sweet Potatoes with Apricot, '89 331
Gravy, Roast Duck with Sweet Potato-Eggplant, '83 90
Grilled Sweet Potatoes, '93 213
Hash Browns, Cheesy Sweet Potato, '02 248
Hash Browns, Rosemary-Garlic, '02 248
Hash Browns, Sweet Potato, '02 248
Hash, Sweet Potato, '92 337
Latkes, Sweet Potato, '01 275
Lime Sweet Potatoes, '02 307
Maple-Ginger Cream, Sweet Potatoes with, '97 27
Mashed-Potato Bake, Swirled, '03 293
Mashed Potatoes, Golden Buttermilk, '05 298
Mashed Sweet Potatoes, '85 25
Mashed Sweet Potatoes, Easy-Does-It, '05 250
Mashed Sweet Potatoes, Southwest, '05 271
Mashed Sweet Potatoes with Cumin, '99 244
Orange-Baked Sweet Potatoes, '88 M294
Orange Cups, Sweet Potatoes in, '82 272
Orange Cups, Sweet Potato-Stuffed, '81 223
Orange Sweet Potatoes, '86 279
Oven-Fried Sweet Potatoes with Chutney, '93 241
Oven-Roasted Sweet Potatoes and Onions, '00 24
Pancakes, Quick Sweet Potato-Chive, '04 248
Pancakes, Sweet Potato, '87 280
Pancakes with Goat Cheese, Sweet Potato, '96 271
Peaks, Sweet Potato, '95 291
Peanut Crust, Sweet Potatoes with, '93 212
Pones, Sweet Potato, '96 270
Pork Chops with Sweet Potatoes, '96 269
Pork Dinner, Saucy, '97 26
Praline Sweet Potatoes and Apples, '03 260
Pudding, Sweet Potato, '79 244; '80 228; '86 52
Puffs, Peach Sweet Potato, '87 280
Puffs, Sweet Potato, '87 253
Puff, Sweet Potato, '85 235
Puree, Carrot-Sweet Potato, '92 90; '00 M32; '02 M285
Puree, Sweet Potato, '92 306
Raspberry Sweet Potatoes, '87 280
Roasted Gingered Sweet Potatoes, '01 92
Roasted Potatoes, Two-Color Rosemary, '05 18
Roasted Potato Trio, '00 311; '02 310
Roasted Sweet Potatoes and Onions, '01 234
Sage Vinaigrette, Sweet Potatoes with, '97 270
Salad, Black-Eyed Pea-and-Sweet Potato, '01 198
Salad, Fresh Sweet Potato, '86 226
Salad, Hawaiian Ham-Sweet Potato, '82 232
Salad, Sweet Potato, '05 171
Salad, Sweet Potato-Apple, '96 240
Salad, Sweet Potato Fruit, '00 325
Salad with Rosemary-Honey Vinaigrette, Sweet Potato, '98 243
Scalloped Root Vegetables, '98 310
Scalloped Sweet Potatoes with Apples, '00 253
Slaw, Sweet Potato-Currant, '93 246
Soufflé, Sweet Potato, '82 286; '86 121; '93 325; '96 247; '00 273; '05 110
Soup, Southern Sweet Potato, '00 233
Soup, Sweet Potato, '88 250; '02 221
Soup, Sweet Potato-and-Sausage, '95 23
Soup, Sweet Potato-Peanut, '05 104
Soup with Rum Cream, Sweet Potato, '98 271
Spicy Island Sweet Potatoes, Caribbean Catfish with, '04 310
Spicy Sweet Potatoes, '02 207
Stacked Sweet Potato Blues, '95 290
Stuffed Baked Sweet Potatoes, '79 207; '84 231
Stuffed Sweet Potatoes, '86 224
Stuffed Sweet Potatoes, Bacon-, '86 224
Stuffed Sweet Potatoes, Coconut-, '82 204
Stuffed Sweet Potatoes, Fluffy, '79 9
Stuffed with Apples, Sweet Potatoes, '82 228
Supreme, Sweet Potato, '94 196
Tzimmes, '95 102
Tzimmes, Sweet Potato-Beef, '92 234
Velouté, Sweet Potato, '94 238
Waffles, Sweet Potato, '88 208
Waffles with Orange Butter, Sweet Potato, '90 323
Yams, Bourbon, '90 232
Yams, Brandied, '94 273
Yams Cointreau, '92 192
Yams, Rosemary-Garlic, '93 174
Yam Tartlets, Zamaani's Nutty, '02 21

SWISS CHARD
Bundles, Swiss Chard, '94 48
Buttered Chard, '83 36
Creamy Chard and Potatoes, '98 250
Green and Gold, '00 91
Sautéed Chard with Onion and Apple, '98 48
Tomatoes, Swiss Chard with, '83 36

SYRUPS
Almond Syrup, '82 47
Anise Sugar Syrup, '86 248
Apple Syrup, Spiced, '79 114
Apricot Fruit Syrup, '82 10
Barbecue Sauce, Maple Syrup, '94 154
Berry Syrup, '96 161
Blackberry Syrup, '99 131
Bourbon Syrup, '98 277; '03 233
Caramel Syrup, '82 43
Caramel Syrup, Citrus Compote with, '98 313
Caramel Syrup, The Ultimate No-Bake Cheesecake Banana Pudding with, '05 326
Cherry-Lemonade Syrup, '86 214
Cinnamon Syrup, '91 315
Citrus Syrup, Sweet, '86 270
Coffee Syrup, '01 64
Fruit Syrup, '86 176
Ginger Syrup, '96 161
Honey Syrup, '96 21
Kirsch Syrup, '80 280
Lime Syrup, Fresh Fruit with, '05 220
Madeira Syrup, '98 247
Maple-Banana Syrup, '03 47
Maple-Honey-Cinnamon Syrup, '85 19
Maple-Nut Syrup, '80 228
Maple Syrup, '81 120; '82 23; '93 16
Maple Syrup, Homemade, '79 114
Mint Simple Syrup, '03 129
Mint Sugar Syrup, Fresh, '03 89
Mint Syrup, '90 89; '96 161; '97 120
Mocha Latte Syrup, '96 161
Orange-Ginger Syrup, '03 167
Orange Marmalade Syrup, '96 27
Orange Syrup, '80 228; '89 254; '96 161, 164; '97 32; '02 295; '05 240
Peanut Butter and Jelly Syrups, Banana Pancakes with, '01 24
Pecan Syrup, Chunky, '85 278
Pomegranate Syrup, '96 241
Rum Syrup, '95 313; '05 279
Simple Syrup, '99 161; '05 135
Strawberry Syrup, '02 104
Strawberry Syrup, Fresh, '05 132
Sugar Syrup, '93 29; '96 161; '02 161; '03 224

Tabbouleh
Appetizers, Endive with Arugula Tabbouleh, '98 67
Couscous, Tabbouleh, '96 251; '02 200
Endive with Arugula Tabbouleh, '98 67
Pitas, Tabbouleh, '98 105
Salad), Boot Scoot Tabbouli (Tabbouleh, '96 159
Salad, Southwestern Tabbouleh, '01 216
Salad, Tabbouleh, '92 212; '94 174
Tabbouleh, '93 70; '99 175

TACOS
al Carbón, Tacos, '86 19
al Carbón, Tailgate Tacos, '79 185
Appetizer, Layered Taco, '84 206
Bake, Taco, '97 326
Bake, Taco Beef-Noodle, '81 141
Basic Tacos, '83 199
Beef Tacos, Soft, '91 88
Biscuit Bites, Taco, '91 89
Breakfast Tacos, '80 43; '91 316; '95 340
Burgers, Taco, '98 224
Casserole, Taco, '80 33
Catfish Tacos, Baja-Style Fried, '04 311
Cheesecake, Taco, '00 56
Chicken-and-Bean Tacos, '93 293
Chicken Skewers, Taco-, '99 119
Chicken Tacos, Pizza-Flavored, '95 340
Corn Chip Tacos, '81 67
Deep-Dish Taco Squares, '91 88
Dessert Tacos, '97 141
Dip, Hot Taco, '93 238
Dogs, Taco, '02 M57
Easy Tacos, '96 159
Egg Salad Tacos, Mexican, '94 181
Fish Taco Appetizers, '04 324
Fish Tacos, Barbecued, '95 339
Fish Tacos, Southern-Style, '05 327
Jiffy Tacos, '83 M318
Joes, Taco, '91 167
Lentil Tacos, '88 197
Lobster Taco with Yellow Tomato Salsa and Jicama Salad, Warm, '87 122
Margarita Tacos, '97 167
Microwave Tacos, '88 M213
Navajo Tacos, '84 246
Pasta, Easy Taco, '03 124
Peppers, Taco, '81 86
Pepper Tacos, Grilled, '95 340
Pie, Crescent Taco, '80 80
Pie, Double-Crust Taco, '88 272; '89 180
Pies, Individual Taco, '82 M282
Pie, Taco, '88 256
Pitas, Taco, '83 31
Pizza, Taco, '89 M177; '98 176; '00 293
Pork Tacos with Cucumber-Radish Salsa, Adobo Grilled, '01 186
Pork Tacos with Pineapple Salsa, '03 128
Potatoes, Taco-Topped, '93 M18
Rolls, Chinese Taco, '95 339
Salad, Beefy Taco, '03 128
Salad, Chicken Taco, '94 M136
Salad Cups, Taco, '85 M29
Salad, Meatless Taco, '81 204
Salad, Party Taco, '97 19
Salad, Spicy Taco, '87 287
Salad, Taco, '79 56; '83 145; '85 84; '89 332; '90 20; '02 188
Salad, Taco Macaroni, '85 165
Salad, Tuna-Taco, '87 145
Sauce, Taco, '82 M283; '93 69; '94 30
Sausage-Egg Soft Tacos, '05 26
Seasoning Blend, Taco, '96 159
Shrimp-and-Pepper Soft Tacos, '95 339
Shrimp Tacos with Spicy Cream Sauce, '01 170
Skillet Tacos, Easy, '04 180
Soup, Taco, '94 225; '99 36
Stacks, Soft Taco, '02 54
Steak Tacos, Jerk, '01 170
Tacos, '80 196
Tassies, Taco, '95 339
Teasers, Taco, '01 134
Tilapia Tacos, Shredded Grilled, '05 16

Veggie Tacos, Loaded, '00 294
Veggie Tacos, Skillet, '01 170
Waffle Taco Sundaes, '05 M62
Wrapidos, Tacos, '03 172
TAMALES
Bake, Cornbread Tamale, '79 163
Breakfast Tamales, '00 122
Casserole, Quick Tamale, '94 255
Chicken Tamales, '88 151
Dessert Tamales, Mango, '94 190
Dressing, Corny Cornbread, '99 258
Helena Tamales, '05 112
Hot Tamales, '83 51
Meatballs, Tamale, '80 194
Miniature Tamales, '85 154
Mozzarella Tamale, '95 70
Pie, Chili-Tamale, '82 9; '83 68
Pie, Cornbread-Tamale, '92 123
Soup, Tamale, '95 213
Sweet Tamales, '83 52
Tamales, '80 195
TASTE OF THE SOUTH
Ambrosia, '04 233
Ambrosia, Kitchen Express, '04 233
Applesauce, Sweet Onion, '02 319
Beverages
Eggnog, Aunt Kat's Creamy, '01 287
Lemonade, Sweet-Tart, '02 160
Mint Julep, Classic, '03 129
Syrup, Mint Simple, '03 129
Tea, Southern Sweet, '02 107
Tea, Southern Sweetened, '00 70
Breads
Beignets, '01 59
Cornbread, Bacon-Cheddar Hot-Water, '01 29; '02 107
Cornbread, Baked Hot-Water, '01 29; '02 107
Cornbread, Country Ham Hot-Water, '01 29; '02 107
Cornbread, Hot-Water, '01 29; '02 107
Cornbread, Skillet, '00 22
Cornbread, Southwestern Hot-Water, '01 29; '02 107
Hush Puppies, '05 99
Hush Puppies, Jalapeño, '05 99
Rolls, Icebox, '04 70
Sally Lunn Bread, '03 27
Spoonbread, '04 58
Spoonbread, Memmie's, '04 57
Brisket Rub, '03 188
Butter, Blackberry, '03 27
Butter, Oven Apple, '00 237
Butter, Spiced Oven Apple, '00 237
Cheese, Cream Cheese-and-Olive Pimiento, '01 169
Cheese, Jalapeño Pimiento, '01 169
Cheese, Pecan Pimiento, '01 169
Cheese, Pimiento, '01 169
Desserts
Brittle, Cooktop, '02 223
Cake, Coca-Cola, '02 181
Cake, Express Pineapple Upside-Down, '03 65
Cake, Skillet Pineapple Upside-Down, '03 65
Cake, Two-Step Pound, '00 36
Cheesecake, Pecan Pie, '02 318
Divinity, Mrs. Floyd's, '00 315
Frosting, Coca-Cola, '02 181
Peanut Brittle, Chocolate-Dipped, '02 M223
Peanut Brittle, Classic, '02 M223
Peanut Brittle, Popcorn, '02 M223
Pecan Brittle, '02 M223
Pie, Chocolate-Bourbon Pecan, '05 134
Pie, Chocolate-Pecan Chess, '00 60; '02 107
Pie, Chocolate-Walnut, '05 134
Pie, Classic Chess, '00 60; '02 107
Pie, Coconut Chess, '00 60; '02 107
Pie, Key Lime, '00 120
Pie, Lemon Chess, '00 60; '02 107

Pralines, '01 201
Tea Cakes, '02 161
Dressing, Andouille Sausage, Apple, and Pecan, '02 249
Dressing, Cornbread, '02 249
Eggs, Basic Deviled, '03 88
Gravy, Tomato, '00 216
Grits, Creamy, '00 215
Grits, Garlic-Cheese, '00 215
Grits, Smoked Gouda, '02 319
Hoppin' John, '05 21
Macaroni and Cheese, Baked, '02 26
Macaroni and Cheese, Creamy, '02 26
Main Dishes
Brisket, Traditional, '03 188
Catfish, Classic Fried, '01 135
Catfish, Fried Lemon-Rosemary, '02 319
Chicken and Dumplings, '01 231
Chicken, Our Best Southern Fried, '00 142
Country Ham, '00 298
Country Ham with Redeye Gravy, '00 216
Crab Cakes, Faidley's, '01 97
Fried Chicken, Our Best Southern, '02 106
Oysters Rockefeller, '03 272
Oysters, Southwest Fried, '03 45
Pork on Smoked Gouda Grits with Sweet Onion Applesauce, Maple-Chipotle, '02 319
Red Beans and Rice, Spicy, '02 56
Ribs, Baby Loin Back, '01 106
Shrimp, New Orleans Barbecue, '02 201
Steak, Chicken-Fried, '01 47
Preserves, Fig, '00 175
Salads
Olive Salad, '04 27
Potato Salad, Fipps Family, '02 138
Potato Salad, Light, '02 138
Potato Salad, Red, '02 138
Potato Salad with Onion and Celery, '02 138
Potato Salad with Sweet Pickle, '02 138
Sandwiches
Hot Browns, Biscuit, '02 94
Hot Browns, Kentucky, '02 94
Hot Browns, Southwestern, '02 94
Hot Browns with Fried Cheese Grits, '02 94
Muffuletta, '04 27
Sauces
Barbecue Sauce, White, '05 196
Basting Sauce, '01 106
Brisket Mopping Sauce, '03 188
Brisket Red Sauce, '03 188
Cheese Sauce, '02 94
Pepper Sauce, '02 106
Rémoulade, Criolla, '05 69
Rémoulade Sauce, Creole, '05 69
Sweet Sauce, '01 106
Soups and Stews
Brunswick Stew, '01 219
Chili, Chunky Beef, '05 235
Frogmore Stew, '03 181
Gumbo, Chicken-and-Sausage, '04 213
She-Crab Soup, '03 137
Spices, Dry, '01 106
Syrup, Sugar, '02 161
Vegetables
Black-Eyed Peas, Hearty, '00 22; '02 107
Corn Pudding, Southwestern, '01 165
Corn Pudding, Tee's, '01 165
Okra, Fried, '00 205
Okra Pods, Fried, '00 205
Onion Rings, Buttermilk Batter-Fried, '02 131
Squash Casserole, '04 126
Squash Casserole, Two-Cheese, '04 126
Sweet Potato Casserole, '02 309
Tomatoes, Fried Green, '03 173

Turnip Greens and Ham Hocks, Southern, '03 220
Turnip Greens, Simple, '02 106
TEA
Cake, Tea Pound, '99 90
Cake, Vanilla-Jasmine-Sour Cream Tea, '05 135
Chicken, Tea-Thyme Grilled, '05 M52
Granita, Ginger Tea, '98 334
Granita, Mint Tea, '88 117
Granita, Wild Raspberry Tea, '99 89
Hot
Almond Tea, '85 43; '86 329
Apple-Cinnamon Tea, Hot, '87 57
Apple Tea, '05 24
Apricot Tea, Hot Spiced, '88 248
Brew, Quilter's, '85 43
Cider Tea, '98 241; '99 335
Citrus Tea, Hot, '83 275
Cranberry Tea, Mulled, '01 240
Fruit Tea, Christmas, '83 275
Fruit Tea, Hot Spiced, '87 242
Grape Tea, Spiced, '79 174
Hawaiian Tea, '87 57
Honey Tea, '81 105
Johnny Appleseed Tea, '85 23
Marmalade Tea, '98 330
Minted Tea, '86 101
Mint Tea, Moroccan, '98 211
Mix, Deluxe Spiced Tea, '88 257
Mix, Friendship Tea, '83 283
Mix, Spiced Tea, '86 32
Mix, Sugar-Free Spiced Tea, '91 258
Punch, Cran-Grape-Tea, '92 209
Punch, Spiked Tea, '86 101
Russian Tea, Hot, '97 274
Spiced Tea, Hot, '83 244
Strawberry Tea, '88 248
Verla's Hot Tea, '05 257
Yaupon Tea, '79 31
Ice Cream, Orange Pekoe-Chocolate, '99 90
Iced
Almond-Lemonade Tea, '86 229; '99 207
Almond Tea, '89 212; '97 226; '01 93
Apple Tea, '05 24
Apple Tea, Iced, '98 84
Berry-Mint Iced Tea, '98 332
Blackberry Iced Tea, '04 158
Bubbly Iced Tea, '81 168
Cider Tea, '98 241
Citrus Iced Tea, '00 139
Citrus-Mint Tea Cooler, '92 105
Citrus Tea, Iced, '85 162
Cranberry-Apple Tea, '88 169
Cranberry-Raspberry Herb Tea, '05 61
Cranberry Tea, '94 131; '97 121, 160; '04 63
Cranberry Tea Cooler, '01 322
Cranberry Tea, Holiday, '03 233
Cranberry Tea, Mulled, '01 240
Cubes, Frozen Tea, '85 161
Fruit-and-Mint Iced Tea, '98 84
Fruited Tea Cooler, '94 131
Fruit Tea, Christmas, '01 240
Fruit Tea, Refreshing, '97 122
Ginger-Almond Tea, '94 131
Ginger Tea, '81 100; '96 100
Grapefruit Tea, '92 67
Grape Tea, Spiced, '79 174
Green Tea, Iced, '05 196
Hawaiian Tea, '87 57
Hibiscus Tea, Iced, '04 72
Juleps, Tea, '99 90
Lemon Iced Tea, Minted, '00 131
Lemon-Mint Tea, '85 162
Lemon Tea, '82 156
Lemon Tea Tingler, '95 200

TEA, Iced
(continued)

Lime-Mint Tea, '97 122
Lime Tea, '98 198
Long Island Iced Tea, Southern, '90 207
Marian's Iced Tea, '05 135
Minted Tea, '88 163; '92 54
Mint Tea, '87 107; '90 89
Mint Tea, Easy, '91 187
Mint Tea, Fresh, '95 88
Mint Tea, Frosted, '84 161
Mint Tea, Fruited, '88 79; '91 81
Mint Tea, Fruity, '04 143
Mint Tea, Iced, '83 170
Mint Tea, Moroccan, '98 211
Orange Tea Cooler, '05 216
Passion Tea, '04 63
Peach Iced Tea, '02 181
Pineapple-Orange Herb Tea, '05 61
Pineapple Tea, '93 165
Punch, Apple-Tea, '85 82
Punch, Bourbon-Tea, '87 57
Punch, Citrus-Tea, '85 116
Punch, Cran-Grape-Tea, '92 209
Punch, Minted Tea, '00 164
Punch, Mint Tea, '04 63
Punch, Southern Fresh Fruit, '99 70
Punch, Tea, '90 143, 207
Rasp-Berry Good Tea, '95 200
Red Tea, Iced, '04 143
Sangría, Mock Tea, '99 336
Sangría Tea, '94 131
Sangría, Teaberry, '87 147
Sangría Tea, Pink, '95 200
Sparkling Summer Tea, '96 172
Spiced Iced Tea, '91 209; '97 121
Spiced Tea Cooler, '83 55
Strawberry Tea Slush, '04 63
Strawberry Tea, Sparkling, '94 131
Summer Tea, '85 162
Summertime Tea, '81 167
Sun Tea, Southern, '81 168
Sweetened Tea, Southern, '00 70
Sweet Tea, '98 84
Sweet Tea, Southern, '02 107; '04 107
Thai Iced Tea, '02 174
Tropical Tea-Ser, '95 200
White Grape Iced Tea, '98 84
White Grape Juice Tea, '87 57
Yaupon Tea, '79 31
Jelly, Red Zinger, '99 89
Salad, Lapsang-Poached Chicken, '05 135
Sauce, Tea-Berry, '94 130; '99 334
Vinaigrette, Salad Greens with Herbed Earl Grey, '99 89
TEMPURA
Basic Tempura, '81 68
Chicken Tempura Delight, '85 66
Cornmeal Tempura, '81 68
Green Onions, Tempura-Battered, '96 93
Sauce, Basic Tempura, '81 68
Sauce, Mustard-Sour Cream, '81 68
"Shrimps," French-Fried Tempura, '97 128
Vegetable Tempura, '79 112
TERRINES
Asparagus-Seafood Terrine with Dill Sauce, '98 157
Banana Split Terrine, '96 164
Black Bean Terrine with Fresh Tomato Coulis and
    Jalapeño Sauce, '93 230
Black Bean Terrine with Goat Cheese, '87 120
Blue Cheese Terrine with Tomato-Basil Vinaigrette,
    '99 288
Cheese Terrine, Basil-, '96 322

Cheese Terrine, Italian, '93 64
Chicken-Leek Terrine, Cold, '92 145
Chicken Terrine Ring, '84 132
Chicken-Vegetable Terrine, '84 131
Fruit Terrine with Raspberry Sauce, '98 157
Pork and Veal, Terrine of, '93 287
Pork Terrine, Jeweled, '84 130
Salmon-and-Spinach Terrine, Layered, '84 132
Veal Terrine with Mustard Sauce, '93 118
Vegetable-Chicken Terrine, '83 224
TIMBALES
Cheesy Mexicali Appetizer, '82 108
Chicken Chutney Salad, '82 108
Corn-and-Zucchini Timbales, '92 100
Green Rice Timbales, '97 62
Grits Timbales, '88 223
Grits Timbales, Chives-, '90 172
Hamburger Stroganoff, '82 108
Peach Almond Cream, '82 108
Rice Timbales, '94 32
Shells, Timbale, '82 108
Shrimp Sauté, Confetti, '97 104
Spinach-Rice Timbales, '88 271
Spinach Timbales, '84 29
TOFU
Cheesecake, Tropical Tofu, '00 204
Dip, Tofu, '86 109
Drink, Tofruitti Breakfast, '88 26
Lasagna, Tofu, '83 312
Rice with Tofu, Spanish, '88 26
Salad, Tofu, '88 27
Sandwiches, Open-Face Tofu-Veggie, '86 5
Stroganoff Tofu, '84 202
TOMATILLOS
Beef Saltillo (Beef with Tomatillos), '82 219
Enchiladas Verde, Chicken, '00 M240
Fillets Tomatillo, '94 135
Green Tomatillos with Jalapeño Dipping Sauce, Fried,
    '97 143
Pudding, Green Tomato-Tomatillo-Corn, '04 103
Relish, Black Bean-Tomatillo, '87 121
Salsa, Fresh Tomatillo, '97 143
Salsa, Grilled Chicken with Tomatillo, '02 123
Salsa, Roasted Tomatillo, '95 64
Salsa, Tomatillo, '92 245; '02 123
Salsa Verde, '96 160
Sandwiches, Open-Faced Tomatillo, '92 246
Sauce, Avocado-Tomatillo, '95 206
Sauce, Drunken, '03 33
Sauce, Green Barbecue, '02 183
Sauce, Grilled Jerk Shrimp with Creamy Tomatillo,
    '01 332
Sauce, Roasted Chiles Rellenos with Tomatillo, '94 203
Sauce, Shrimp Enchiladas in Tomatillo, '95 310
Sauce, Tomatillo, '94 231; '95 206; '97 25; '04 119
Sauce, Verde, '00 241
Soup with Crunchy Jícama, Tomatillo, '92 245; '97 143
Stacks, Fried Green Tomato, '02 184
Vinaigrette, Poblano, '99 71
Zucchini, Southwestern Stuffed, '03 M127
TOMATOES
Appetizers, Oven-Baked Tomato, '95 172
au Gratin, Zucchini and Tomato, '82 208
Bake, Chicken-Tomato, '83 35
Baked Cheddar Tomatoes, '85 43
Baked Ranch Tomatoes, '94 72
Baked Tomatoes, '83 53; '87 197
Baked Tomatoes, Honey-, '02 166
Baked Tomato Halves, Zippy, '81 182
Bake, Ham-Rice-Tomato, '87 78
Bake, Okra-and-Tomato, '89 173
Bake, Okra-Tomato, '80 298; '81 26
Bake, Potato-Tomato, '86 17
Bake, Tomato-and-Artichoke Heart, '85 81

Bake, Tomato-and-Okra, '03 158
Bake, Zucchini and Tomato, '82 158
Basil, and Cheese, Tomato, '95 165
Basil, Zucchini and Tomatoes, '89 147
Bean-and-Tomato Skillet, '90 316
Beans and Tomatoes, Basil, '83 172
Beans, Texas, '97 139
Beans with Tomatoes, Great Northern, '05 23
Beef with Tomatoes and Artichokes, '92 282
Biscuit Bites, Savory Tomato-Bacon, '03 196
Biscuit Cakes, Tomato-Eggplant, '95 170
Biscuits, Fresh Tomato, '04 138
Biscuits, Tomato, '86 72
Biscuits, Tomato-Herb, '94 215
BLT, Caramelized Onion, '03 90
Bowl, Tomato, '81 69
Braised with Tomatoes, Lamb Shanks, '03 87
Breaded Tomatoes, '95 180
Bread, Grilled, '00 88
Bread, Herbed Tomato-Cheese, '88 143
Bread, Sun-dried Tomato-Herb, '05 252
Bread, Tomato-Black Olive Grits, '05 83
Bread, Tomato-Cheese, '98 172; '99 M157
Broiled Parmesan Tomatoes, '04 322
Broiled Tomatoes, '80 152
Broiled Tomatoes, Quick, '79 153
Broiled Tomatoes, Romano, '80 42
Broiled Tomatoes with Dill Sauce, '80 161
Broiled Tomatoes with Mushroom Sauce, '81 103
Broil, Tomato-English Pea, '83 192
Bruschetta, Caper-and-Olive, '00 276
Bruschetta, Roasted Pepper-Tomato, '02 213
Burgers, Stuffed Southwestern-Style, '99 201
Butterbeans, Bacon, and Tomatoes, '96 36; '00 184
Butter, Tomato, '86 128
Butter, Tomato-Curry-Orange, '93 159
Cabbage and Tomatoes, '83 104
Cabbage and Tomatoes, Tasty, '86 72
Cabbage, Creole, '00 105
Cacciatore, Chicken, '86 42
Cacciatore, Hearty Chicken, '02 269
Canned Flavored Tomatoes, '95 217
Canning Tomatoes, '80 128; '85 106
Caponata, '98 50
Caponata alla Siciliana, '02 269
Casserole, Corn and Tomato, '81 127
Casserole, Corn-and-Tomato, '84 145
Casserole, Eggplant-and-Tomato, '83 187
Casserole, Light Italian, '03 198
Casserole, Saucy Potato-Tomato, '79 46
Casserole, Scalloped Tomato, '88 144
Casserole, Tomato, '05 22
Casserole, Zucchini-and-Tomato, '88 265
Catsup, Spicy Tomato, '83 182
Cauliflower au Gratin, '99 59
Cheese Herbed-Topped Tomatoes, '86 108
Cheese Sauce over Toast, Tomatoes with, '88 159
Cheese-Topped Tomatoes, '81 160
Cheesy Puff-Top Tomatoes, '86 187
Cherry. *See also* **TOMATOES/Dried.**
    Basil Butter, Squash and Cherry Tomatoes in, '98 328
    Bites, Tomato, '84 80
    Brown Butter Sauce, Cherry Tomatoes in, '81 168
    Caviar Tomatoes, '91 12
    Cheesy Cherry Tomatoes, '83 135
    Green Beans with Cherry Tomatoes, '86 177
    Herbed Cherry Tomatoes, '82 128
    Pasta, Herbed Cherry Tomatoes over, '95 229
    Roasted Cherry Tomatoes, Rosemary-, '05 257
    Rockefeller, Tomatoes, '97 169
    Rum, Cherry Tomatoes with, '83 192
    Salad, Cherry Tomato, '87 156
    Salad, Cherry Tomato-Caper, '00 140; '02 32
    Sautéed Roma Tomatoes, '92 338

Stuffed Cherry Tomatoes, '84 160; '88 95, 212; '92 25
Stuffed Cherry Tomatoes, Crab-, '82 289; '88 78
Stuffed Cherry Tomatoes, Cucumber-, '88 262
Stuffed Cherry Tomatoes, Tuna-, '89 214
Chicken, Creamy Tomato-Stuffed, '04 16
Chicken Mediterranean, '01 17
Chicken, Tomato-Baked, '81 281; '82 30
Chicken with Tomatoes and Sausage, '97 266
Chili, Chilly Night, '99 317
Chili, Chunky Beef 'n' Tomato, '05 20
Chili in a Biscuit Bowl, '98 224
Chutney, Chicken Bites with Sweet-Hot Tomato, '00 309
Chutney, Tomato, '99 143
Chutney, Tomato-Apple, '84 180
Cocktail, Tomato, '83 M203
Cocktail, Tomato-Clam, '87 252
Cocktail, Tomato Juice, '79 212; '83 230; '90 12
Cocktail, Tomato-Orange Juice, '83 169
Cocktail, Zesty Tomato Juice, '83 289
Couscous, Tabbouleh, '97 103; '02 200
Crackers, Tomato-Blue Cheese, '02 213
Cream, Tomato, '94 70
Creole, Okra, '02 234
Creole-Style Tomatoes-and-Corn, '84 142
Crêpes, Southwestern Cornbread, '98 42
Croissants, BLT, '93 158
Crostini, Festive, '99 M325
Crostini, Feta-Tomato, '92 159
Crostini, Tomato, '99 230
Crostini, Tomato-and-Goat Cheese, '04 168
Delight, Tomato-Pea, '84 196
Dip, Bacon-and-Tomato, '90 147
Dip, Fiesta, '96 212
Dip, Steamed Asparagus with Tomato-Basil, '00 69; '04 53
Dip, Tomato-Basil, '05 219
Dressing, Fresh Tomato, '00 182
Dressing, Fresh Tomato Salad, '83 193
Dressing, Garden Salad with Tomato-Cream Cheese, '79 173
Dressing, Spicy Tomato, '03 143
Dressing, Tomato-Honey French, '81 105
Dried
  Cheese Balls with Sun-Dried Tomatoes, '94 317
  Cheesecake, Sun-Dried Tomato, '03 118
  Cherry Tomatoes, Marinated Dried, '93 23
  Chicken, Undercover, '97 64
  Dip, Cottage Cheese Sun-Dried Tomato, '93 13
  Elephant Ears Provençale, Baby, '00 87
  Fettuccine, Chicken and Dried Tomatoes over, '98 233
  Focaccia, Dried Tomato, '94 65
  Focaccia, Fast Rosemary-Dried Tomato, '98 53
  Goat Cheese, Dried Tomato Mock, '97 105
  Goat Cheese with Sun-Dried Tomatoes and Rosemary, '93 175
  Hummus, Creamy Dried Tomato, '95 284
  Mayonnaise, Dried Tomato, '98 144
  Meat Loaf with Sun-Dried Tomatoes and Herbs, '92 192
  Pesto, Dried Tomato, '90 204; '94 249; '01 62
  Pesto, Dried Tomato-Basil, '04 101
  Pizza, Shrimp-and-Dried Tomato, '97 49
  Salad, Spinach and Sun-Dried Tomato, '93 250
  Sandwiches, Dried Tomato-and-Basil, '99 274
  Sauce, Dried Tomato, '99 135
  Sauce, Dried Tomato Spaghetti, '90 202
  Soup, Dried Tomato-Cream, '90 203
  Spread and Bacon, Cream Cheese-and-Olive Biscuits with Sun-Dried Tomato, '02 313
  Spread, Dried Tomato-Cheese, '90 204
  Spread, Layered Sun-dried-Tomato-and-Basil, '05 275
  Spread, Tri-Flavored Cream Cheese, '98 134
  Tart, Dried Tomato-Cheese, '90 203
  Torte, Tomato-Cheese, '97 49; '00 72
  Vinaigrette, Couscous Salad with Dried Tomato, '96 244
  Vinaigrette, Dried Tomato, '93 272

Dumplings, Tomato, '88 144; '97 209
Eggplant Parmigiana, '01 310
Eggs Benedict, Bacon-and-Tomato, '87 195
Eggs, Layered, '96 97
Eggs Oso Grande, '98 279
Enchiladas, Enticing, '99 57
Enchiladas, Healthy Chicken, '02 19
Fettuccine with Shrimp and Tomatoes, '96 198
Fire-and-Ice Tomatoes, '87 92; '03 183
Flank Steak, Tomato-Stuffed, '97 49
Fried Herb Tomatoes, '83 160
Fried Red Tomatoes, '81 102
Fried Ripe Tomatoes, '81 168
Fried Ripe Tomatoes with Gravy, '82 180
Fried Tomatoes, Pan-, '02 67
Fried Tomatoes with Bacon, Saucy, '81 210
Fried Tomatoes with Gravy, '86 211
Gazpacho-Stuffed Endive, '95 287
Gnocchi with Olive Oil, Tomato, and Parmesan, '04 47
Grape Tomatoes, Green Beans with, '03 231
Gratin, Tomato-Zucchini, '95 171
Gravy, Green Chile-Tomato, '05 42
Gravy, Southwestern, '99 34
Gravy, Spicy Tomato, '95 172
Gravy, Tomato, '93 18; '99 35; '00 216, 330; '02 17, 33
Gravy, Tomato-and-Crabmeat Cream, '04 165
Greek Tomatoes, '98 173
Green
  Baked Green Tomatoes, Herb-, '85 214
  Chutney, Green Tomato-Cranberry, '00 140
  Curried Green Tomatoes, '93 138
  Fried Green Tomato Casserole, Stuffed, '04 145
  Fried Green Tomato Cheeseburgers, '94 138
  Fried Green Tomatoes, '79 123; '80 178; '81 210; '85 214
  "Fried" Green Tomatoes, '89 174
  Fried Green Tomatoes, '95 171; '98 172; '03 173
  Fried Green Tomatoes, Blue Willow, '99 143
  Fried Green Tomatoes, Kentucky Bibb Salad with, '01 121
  Fried Green Tomatoes with Roasted Red Pepper Rémoulade and Goat Cheese, '04 144
  Fried Green Tomato Napoleons, '99 230
  Fried Green Tomato Po' Boys, '05 330
  Fried Green Tomato Sandwiches, '04 145
  Fried Green Tomato Stacks, '02 184
  Fried Okra and Green Tomatoes, '93 160; '01 325
  Grilled Summer Squash and Tomatoes, '99 144
  Gumbo, Green Tomato, '04 314
  Hot Tomatoes, '93 138
  Italian-Sauced Green Tomatoes, '85 214
  Jam, Green Tomato, '79 121
  Jam, Green Tomato-Blueberry, '01 140
  Marinated Green Tomatoes, '03 139
  Marmalade, Green Tomato, '01 140
  Okra and Green Tomatoes, '79 160
  Oven-Fried Green Tomatoes, '82 107; '91 122
  Pickled Green Tomatoes, '99 143
  Pickles, Green Tomato, '87 134; '01 141
  Pie Filling, Green Tomato, '01 141
  Pie, Green Tomato, '79 195; '91 141
  Pudding, Green Tomato-Tomatillo-Corn, '04 103
  Relish, Green Tomato, '96 168; '98 124
  Relish, Green Tomato Sweet, '93 136
  Salsa, Peachy Green Tomato, '99 143
  Spread, Green Tomato Sandwich, '95 172
Green Beans, Tomato-Feta, '99 59
Green Beans with Tomatoes, '85 137
Grilled Okra and Tomatoes, '98 124
Grilled Tomatoes, '85 158; '99 173
Grilled Tomatoes, Cheesy, '79 150
Grilled Tomatoes with Basil Vinaigrette, '97 168
Grilled Yellow Squash and Tomatoes, '00 102
Grits, Hot Tomato, '95 171; '01 131
Grits, Tomato, '03 199

Grits Wedges, Southwestern, '04 332
Grouper, Guadalajara, '98 17
Guacamole, Margarita, '97 167
"Guacamole" with Cumin Crisps, Green Goddess, '02 205
Herbed Tomatoes, '81 102; '82 49; '83 173
Herbed Tomato Slices, '89 173
Hoppin' John Waffle Stack, '04 19
Hush Puppies, Creole, '98 43
Hush Puppies, Green Onion-Tomato, '97 84
Hush Puppies, Tomato-Onion, '91 201
Italian Tomatoes, Cold, '99 173
Journey Cakes, Tomato, Parmesan, and Kalamata Olive, '04 99
Juice, Homemade Tomato, '81 50
Juice, Spicy Tomato, '85 189
Kale with Tomato and Onion, '92 244
Kale with Tomatoes, Spicy, '99 243
Lentils, Tex-Mex, '99 288
Lima and Tomato Combo, Hot, '83 219
Macaroni and Cheese, Spicy Tomato, '03 68
Mahimahi, Middle Eastern, '96 92
Marinade, Bright Tomato, '88 176
Marinara Vinaigrette, '94 64
Marinated Green Beans with Tomatoes, Olives, and Feta, '03 163
Marinated Tomatoes with Basil and Balsamic Vinegar, '04 140
Marmalade, Tomato, '00 170
Mayonnaise, Tomato-Basil, '00 136; '05 180
Medley, Okra-Corn-Tomato, '81 159
Medley, Tomato, '81 159
Melts, Tomato-Cheese-Bacon, '99 72
Mexicorn, '96 189
Muffins, Tomato Corn, '81 137
Mussels Marinara, '00 283
Mustard, Green Beans and Tomatoes with, '87 83
Mustard Tomatoes, Zippy, '86 M226
Okra and Tomatoes, '80 185; '81 139; '92 215; '98 286
Okra and Tomatoes, Fresh, '81 M165; '87 89
Okra Caponata, '97 157
Okra, Corn, and Tomatoes, '95 203
Okra-Tomato Combo, '83 157
Okra, Tomatoes and, '86 170; '87 164; '00 182
Okra, Tomatoes with, '85 106
Omelet, Farmer's Oven-Baked, '03 204
Onions, Baked Sweet, '98 130
Paella, Shortcut, '01 309
Parmesan Tomatoes, '80 161
Parsleyed Tomatoes, Broiled Mahi-Mahi with, '05 130
Pastas. *See also* **TOMATOES/Sauces.**
  Asparagus, Tomatoes, and Shrimp, Garlicky Pasta with, '95 82
  Basil Pasta, Tomato-, '94 204
  Caribbean Tomato Pasta, '93 201
  Fettuccine, Chicken-and-Tomatoes over, '90 204
  Fresh Tomatoes and Basil, Pasta with, '98 233
  Garlic Pasta, Tomato-, '94 177
  Herb-and-Tomato Pasta, '96 122
  Italian Pasta, Weeknight, '03 48
  Italian Tomato Pasta, '93 201
  Late-Night Pasta Chez Frank, '95 228
  Linguine, Two Tomato, '05 187
  Macaroni, Cheese, and Tomatoes, '95 213
  Manicotti, Cheesy Sausage-and-Tomato, '03 257
  Manicotti, Ground Beef-and-Tomato, '03 257
  Penne with Pancetta, '00 51
  Primavera, Tomato-Pasta, '86 209
  Quick Pasta and Tomatoes, '92 180
  Red Wine-Tomato-and-Steak Pasta, '05 140
  Red Wine-Tomato Pasta, '05 140
  Rotelle, Chicken and Tomato with, '87 108
  Shrimp-Tomato Pasta, '98 172
  Southwestern Tomato Pasta, '93 201
  Spaghetti, All-in-One, '98 295

TOMATOES, Pastas
(continued)

Spaghetti with Tomatoes and Garlic, '91 47
Summer Pasta, '04 223
Tortellini, Creamy Tomato Pesto Dip with, '00 196
Toss, Tomato-Olive Pasta, '86 209
White Wine-Tomato-and-Clam Pasta, '05 140
Pesto, Bow-Tie, '94 231
Pesto, Tomatoes, '86 150
Pie, Tomato, '88 198; '97 249; '02 172
Pita Pockets, BLT in, '93 158
Pizza, Breakfast, '00 193
Pizza, Greek Eggplant, Tomato, and Feta, '01 312
Pizza, Nutty Pesto, '97 267
Pizza, Sicilian, '01 125
Pizzas, Roasted Potato, '99 16
Pork Chops and Rice, Savannah, '00 236
Pork Loin, Marinated, '01 331
Potato Boats, Southwestern, '96 33
Preserves, Tomato, '98 214
Provençal, Tomatoes, '82 181
Puffs, Spinach-Artichoke-Tomato, '95 284
Puree, Seared Sea Scallops with Tomato, '97 201
Puree, Seasoned Tomato, '83 182
Quesadillas, Bacon-Jalapeño-Tomato, '95 240
Quesadillas with Chipotle Salsa, Chicken-and-Brie, '99 311
Quiche, Asparagus-Tomato, '88 198
Quiche, Tomato Florentine, '04 332
Red Beans and Couscous, '99 22
Red Rice, '00 289
Red Rice and Ham, '00 289
Refresher, Tomato, '81 94; '83 318
Refried Beans, Easy, '99 57
Relish, Easy Tomato, '80 126
Relish, End-of-the-Garden, '80 179
Relish, Flank Steak with Tomato-Olive, '03 210
Relish, Hot, '01 123
Relish, Sweet White Corn-and-Tomato, '00 130
Relish, Tomato, '85 188
Relish, Tomato, Basil and Corn, '05 321
Rice, Blended, '96 68
Rice, Charleston, '97 310
Rice, Red, '92 235; '97 138
Rice, Tomato, '02 169
Rice with Tomatoes and Basil, '95 232
Risotto, Tomato-Basil, '95 269
Rollups, Mediterranean, '00 277
Roma Tomatoes, Sautéed, '92 338
Ropa Vieja, '98 20
Rose, Tomato, '82 51; '85 338
Salads
Artichoke-Stuffed Tomato Salad, '82 101
Artichoke-Tomato Salad, '82 239
Asparagus and Tomatoes, Fresh, '94 162
Asparagus and Tomatoes with Herb Vinaigrette, '99 56
Asparagus Salad, Tomato-, '92 79
Aspic, Bloody Mary-Tomato, '81 77
Aspic, Chicken in Tomato, '84 190
Aspic, Chili Sauce Tomato, '85 252
Aspic, Classic Tomato, '91 229
Aspic, Gazpacho, '96 65
Aspic, Herbed Tomato, '81 73
Aspic, Layered Tomato, '90 99
Aspic, Light Tomato, '85 83
Aspic, Ranch Tomato, '83 218
Aspic, Raspberry-Tomato, '05 65
Aspic, Spicy Tomato, '81 40; '89 288
Aspic, Tangy Tomato, '83 124
Aspic, Tomato-Artichoke, '84 320; '86 92
Aspic, Tomato-Crab, '85 287
Aspic with Shrimp, Tomato, '79 241
Avocado Salad, Tomato-, '86 74

Bacon-Lettuce-Mozzarella-and-Tomato Salad, '98 209
Basil-and-Tomato Couscous Salad, '94 175
Basil-Mozzarella Salad, Tomato-, '95 171
BLT Salad, Layered, '01 96
Bread Salad, Italian BLT, '03 90
Charred Tomato Salad, '01 158
Chile-Tomato Salad, Spicy, '88 121
Citrus Marinade, Summer Salad with, '92 133
Coleslaw with Tomatoes, '80 34
Congealed Lemon-Tomato Salad, '89 178
Cottage Cheese Salad in Tomatoes, '86 208
Cottage-Tomato Salad, '85 163
Crab-Stuffed Tomato Salad, '80 148
Cucumber-and-Tomato Salad, '01 127
Cucumber and Tomato Salad, Dilled, '81 153
Cucumber-Onion Salad, Tomato-, '81 239
Cucumber on Tomatoes, Dilled, '84 142
Cucumber Salad, Tomato-, '86 218; '92 199
Cucumber Salad, Tomato-and-, '05 69
Cucumber Salad with Yogurt-Herb Dressing, Tomato-, '92 96
Cucumber Summer Salad, Tomato-and-, '93 141
Cucumber-Tomato Salad, '90 144
Endive-Tomato Starburst Salad, '93 323
Feta Salad, Tomato-, '81 246; '91 168; '05 207
Flower Salad, Tomato, '89 128
Frozen Tomato Salad, '84 52
Grape Tomatoes with Capers, '01 329
Green Bean Salad, Tomato-and-, '97 162
Grilled Tomato, Bell Pepper, and Portobello Salad, '98 211
Gruyère-Basil Salad, Tomato-, '99 172
Guacamole-Tomato Salad, '81 302
Herbed Pasta-and-Tomato Salad, '92 144
Herbed Tomatoes, '83 173
Herb Salad, Tomato-, '89 220
Hot Tomato Salad, '05 129
Italian Dressing, Tomato, Onion, and Cucumber in, '81 83
Italiano, Tomatoes, '88 29
Italian Tomato Salad, '01 124
Layered Salad, Tex-Mex, '03 201
Lemon Dressing, Tomato Slices with, '87 167
Lettuce Salad, Tomato-Feta, '05 207
Lima Bean-Tomato Salad, '85 137
Marinated Cucumber-Tomato Salad, '02 167
Marinated Salad, '83 170
Marinated Salsa Tomatoes, '82 164
Marinated Sliced Tomatoes, '92 173
Marinated Tomato and Brie Salad, '95 95
Marinated Tomato-and-Cucumber Salad, '92 216
Marinated Tomatoes, '85 156, 163; '89 174, 202
Marinated Tomato Slices, '82 134; '83 193
Mexican Dinner Salad, '98 330
Mold, Tangy Tomato, '79 74
Mozzarella, Avocado, and Tomato Salad, '05 41
Mozzarella Salad, Tomato-, '89 220
Mozzarella-Tomato-Basil Salad, Fresh, '93 131
Mozzarella-Tomato Basil Salad, Fresh, '02 110
Napoleon, Tomato, '00 182
Olive Spread, Tomatoes with, '85 114
Onion Salad, Tomato-and-, '05 167
Onion Salad, Tomato-and-Sweet, '05 141
Oregano Tomatoes, '83 145
Pasta Salad, Tomato-, '97 M160
Petal Salad, Tomato, '79 88
Potato Salad with Cucumbers and Tomatoes, '03 92
Red Onion Salad, Tomato-, '04 181
Red, White, and Green Salad, '90 18
Relish Salad, Tomato, '83 111
Ring, Tangy Tomato, '84 164
Ring, Tomato-Vegetable, '81 302
Roasted Tomato-and-Pepper Salad, '01 196
Ruby-and-Emerald Salad, '85 79

Stuffed Tomato Salad, Oriental-, '82 101
Summer Tomato Salad, '94 201
Summer Tomato Treat, '79 143
Trout-and-Tomato Salad with Black Pepper Vinaigrette, '98 284
Tuna with Warm Tomato Salad, '97 179
Vidalia-Tomato Salad, '84 65
Vinaigrette, Marinara, '94 64
Vinaigrette, Okra-Corn-and-Tomato, '90 173
Vinaigrette, Tomato-Basil, '87 89
Vinaigrette, Tomatoes, '84 106
Watercress-Tomato Salad, '85 132
Salsas
Artichoke-Tomato Salsa, '96 182
Avocado Salsa, Tomato-, '94 83
Basil Salsa, Pan-Fried Roughy with Tomato-, '99 123
Black Bean Salsa, Chunky, '03 25
Chunky Salsa, '86 130; '90 206
Corn, Pepper, and Tomato Salsa, Yellowfin Tuna with, '94 164
Fresh Salsa, '95 42; '00 59; '04 274
Fresh Tomato Salsa, '91 182; '95 181; '01 249
Homemade Salsa, '05 59
Hot Salsa, '98 135
Mango Salsa, '98 232
Mango Salsa, Seared Scallops with Tomato-, '95 122
One-Minute Salsa, '95 93
Party Salsa, Quick, '03 292
Peachy Green Tomato Salsa, '99 143
Picante, Salsa, '04 41
Quick Party Salsa, '04 146
Red Salsa, '90 172
Roasted Tomato Salsa, '95 64
Salsa, '88 147; '97 171; '01 273; '03 95
Santa Fe Salsa, Zesty, '03 198
Simple Salsa, '01 60
Strawberry Salsa, Balsamic, '02 86
Summer Salsa, '98 172
Texas Salsa, '96 160
Three Tomato Salsa, '93 138
Tomato Salsa, '87 120; '96 15; '02 118
Warm-and-Spicy Salsa, '99 279
Yellow Tomato Salsa, '87 122
Sandwiches, Bacon, Cheese, and Tomato, '84 14
Sandwiches, Curried BLT, '93 158
Sandwiches, Eggplant, Tomato, and Feta, '98 106
Sandwiches, Grilled Bacon, Cheese, and Tomato, '97 170
Sandwiches, Italian BLT, '02 230
Sandwiches, Miniature Tomato, '00 130
Sandwiches, Open-Face Crab Tomato, '81 29
Sandwiches, Super Open-Faced, '97 52
Sandwiches, Tomato, Swiss, and Bacon, '04 140
Sandwich, Floyd's Favorite Tomato, '95 172; '00 182
Sandwich with Tomato, Avocado, and Bacon, Grilled Four-Cheese, '00 199
Sauces
Asparagus with Tomato Sauce, '83 46
Barbecue Sauce, Green, '02 183
Basic Tomato Sauce, '04 145
Basil Cream, Tomato-, '99 240
Basil Sauce, Tomato, '91 85
Basil Sauce, Tomato-, '92 180; '96 220; '97 144; '02 182
Basil-Tomato Sauce, '92 198; '93 25, 48, 65
Caper Sauce, Turkey Cutlets with Tomato-, '91 61
Chili Sauce, '94 287
Chunky Tomato Sauce, '95 264
Cocktail Sauce, Southwestern, '98 46
Coulis, Fresh Tomato, '93 230
Cream Sauce, Angel Hair Pasta with Tomato, '93 292
Cream Sauce, Linguine with Tomato-, '86 158
Cream, Tomato, '94 70
Creamy Tomato Sauce, '93 71
Creole Sauce, '98 98
Cucumber Sauce, Tomato-, '98 45

Dried Tomato Sauce, '96 220
Fish in Tomato Sauce, '85 75
Fresh Tomato Sauce, '83 224; '87 171
Fresh Tomato Sauce over Basil Pasta, '93 176
Fresh Tomato Sauce, Spaghetti with, '96 135
Fresh Tomato Sauce with Linguine, '02 213
Gingered Tomato Sauce, Spicy, '96 220
Greek-Style Tomato Sauce, Penne with, '05 187
Green Beans in Tomato Sauce, '01 84
Green Chiles, Tomato Sauce with, '81 196
Ground Beef-Tomato Sauce, '05 290
Hamburgers with Tomato Sauce, '81 73
Herbed Fresh Tomato Sauce, '85 M151
Herb Sauce, Tomato-and-, '00 125
Hot Sauce, Kleberg, '94 28
Italian-Style Tomato Sauce, '87 182
Italian Tomato Sauce, '82 M68; '92 57; '03 202
Italian Tomato Sauce for Spaghetti, '81 134
Lemon Sauce, Salmon with Almonds and Tomato-,
    '04 23
Light Tomato Sauce, '97 246
Marinara Sauce, '94 64; '99 266
Meat Sauce, Italian, '01 160
Mint-and-Garlic Tomato Sauce, Spaghetti with, '05 100
Pesto, Bow-Tie, '94 231
Pesto, Tomatoes, '86 150
Pico de Gallo, '96 227; '97 141; '98 87; '02 168,
    306; '04 32, 61, 89, 311
Pintos, Texas Souper, '98 51
Pizza Sauce, Traditional, '95 267
Ranchero Sauce, '96 168
Red Pepper-Tomato Sauce, '93 59
Red Sauce and Meatballs, '04 17
Refrigerator Tomato Sauce, '85 188
Roasted Garlic-Tomato Sauce, '97 46
Seasoned Tomato Sauce, '83 150
Spicy Tomato Sauce, '84 294; '88 19
Spinach Tortellini with Tomato Sauce, '88 302
Sweet-and-Sour Tomato Sauce, Stuffed Chicken
    Breasts with, '01 120
Tarragon-Tomato Sauce, '84 131
Tomato Sauce, '85 193, 244; '87 249; '88 116;
    '97 96, 269; '99 270; '04 43
Vegetable-Tomato Sauce, Turkey Patties in, '87 18
Vermicelli with Tomato Sauce, '83 164
Zesty Tomato Sauce, '98 176
Sautéed Tomato with Fresh Mozzarella, '00 163
Sauté, Spicy Okra-Tomato-Corn, '04 327
Sauté, Tomato-Pepper, '84 142
Sauté, Tomato-Spinach, '04 23
Scalloped Tomatoes, '84 142; '00 183
Scalloped Tomato Slices, '81 168
Scallops, Ginger, '99 177
Sesame Tomatoes, '84 142
Shrimp Creole, '03 109
Shrimp, Daufuskie, '00 174
Shrimp with Feta Cheese, '00 221
Sipper, Peppy Tomato, '94 227
Sipper, Spicy Tomato, '86 229
Skillet, Cabbage-and-Tomato, '86 110
Skillet Tomatoes, '81 108
Skillet, Zucchini-Tomato, '93 206
Sloppy Joe Cups, '98 204
Snow Peas and Tomatoes, '83 111
Snow Peas and Tomatoes, Basil, '88 M185
Soufflé, Italian Pizzaola, '98 232
Soups
    Appetizer Tomato Soup, '86 258
    Bacon, Lettuce, and Tomato Soup, '91 207
    Beef-Wild Rice Soup, Tomato-, '04 42
    Bell Pepper 'n' Tomato Soup, Creamy, '05 293
    Bisque, Make-Ahead Tomato-Basil, '93 322
    Bisque, Tomato-Basil, '00 49; '02 230
    Bisque, Tomato-Shrimp, '86 66

Black, White, and Red All Over Soup, '95 126
Bouillon, New Year's Tomato, '94 24
Bouillon, Tomato, '83 8
Carrot-and-Tomato Soup, Cream of, '94 176
Celery Soup, Tomato-, '83 M58
Chilled Roasted Pepper and Tomato Soup, '01 128
Chilled Tomato Soup, '82 155
Chowder, Tomato-Clam, '84 251
Cioppino, Gulf Coast, '94 102
Cold Tomato Soup, '88 160
Consommé, Tomato, '88 250
Cream of Tomato Soup with Lemon Basil, '96 124
Cream of Tomato Soup with Parmesan Cheese, '86 161
Cream Soup, Refreshing Tomato, '79 172
Cream Soup, Tomato-Basil, '97 198
Creamy Tomato Soup, '83 267; '86 258
Creamy Tomato Soup with Crispy Croutons, '05 207
Easy Tomato Soup, '84 14
French Market Soup, '94 317
Fresh Tomato Soup, '83 140
Gazpacho, '00 118; '01 157; '02 130
Gazpacho, Classic Tomato, '99 172
Gazpacho, Tomato-Avocado-Corn, '97 182
Gazpacho, Yellow Tomato, '04 158
Herbed Yogurt and Parmesan Toasts, Tomato Soup
    with, '96 66
Hot Tomato Juice Soup, '86 302
Iced Tomato Soup, '79 170
Italian Soup, Chunky, '99 20
Mexican Tomato Soup, Icy-Spicy, '90 155
New Year's Day Soup, '00 25
Onion Soup, Tomato-, '04 243
Plus, Tomato Soup, '88 170
Pork Rind Soup, '03 33
Potage, Tomato, '79 250
Pumpkin-Tomato Soup, '86 291
Rice Soup, Tomato-and-, '85 24
Roasted Garlic-and-Basil Tomato Soup, '01 17
Sausage-Tortellini Soup, '99 20
Savory Tomato Soup, '94 91
Sour Cream-Topped Tomato Soup, '80 246
Summer Tomato Soup, '79 130
Tomato Soup, '81 236; '83 44; '89 217
Tortellini Soup, '98 68; '00 14
Tortilla Soup, '98 291; '00 98, 110
Vegetable Soup, Tomato-, '81 M177; '86 9
Spaghetti, Country-Style, '02 25
Spicy Tomato Warm-Up, '95 328
Spinach-Topped Tomatoes, '88 265; '94 321
Spread, Fiery Tomato-Cheese, '87 196
Spread, Home-Style Sandwich, '80 179
Spread, Peppered Cheese, '01 123
Spread, Tomato, '99 123
Spread, Tomato-Cheddar, '01 321
Spread, Tomato-Cheese, '81 157
Squash and Tomato Bake, '95 180
Squash, Beans, and Tomatoes, '83 148
Squash, Tomato, '86 111
Stack-Ups, Jiffy Tomato, '80 161
Stewed Tomatoes, '83 182; '00 183
Stewed Tomatoes and Greens, '95 234
Stew, Greek Garbanzo, '02 43
Stew, Turkey-Tomato, '90 279
Stir-Fried Sweet Peppers with Tomatoes, '93 207
Stir-Fry, Italian, '92 126
Stir-Fry, Tomato-Zucchini, '80 158
Stir-Fry, Zucchini-and-Tomato, '85 108
Strata, Tomato-Bacon, '03 100
Strata, Tomato-Cheese, '81 209
Stuffed
    Avocado-Stuffed Tomatoes, '82 101
    Bacon-and-Egg-Stuffed Tomatoes, '80 162
    Baked Spinach Tomatoes, '90 92
    Baked Stuffed Tomatoes, '88 162

Baked Tangy Tomatoes, '81 168
Baked Tomatoes with Corn, '80 161
Bean-Stuffed Tomatoes, '84 34
Broccoli-Stuffed Tomatoes, '83 136; '93 216
Buffet Tomatoes, '82 180
Cheese-Stuffed Tomatoes, '91 69
Cheesy Stuffed Tomatoes, '80 161
Chile-Cheese Stuffed Tomatoes, '94 141
Cold Stuffed Tomatoes, '80 100
Cornbread-Stuffed Tomatoes, '97 169
Corn-Stuffed Tomatoes, '82 270
Crab-and-Avocado Stuffed Tomatoes, '94 141
Cups, Turkey-Tomato, '84 119
Curry Sauce, Stuffed Tomatoes with, '97 170
Delights, Tomato, '81 140
Easy Stuffed Tomatoes, '82 264
Eggs-and-Tomato Slices, Stuffed, '84 152
Feta-Stuffed Tomatoes, '05 148
Green Bean Salad in Tomatoes, '01 181
Herbed Tomatoes, '82 49
Homestead Tomatoes, Stuffed, '96 87
Hot Tomatoes, '93 138
Italian-Style Tomatoes, '97 169
Maque Chou-Stuffed Tomatoes, '87 89
Mushroom-Stuffed Tomatoes, '86 218; '96 106
Parmesan-Stuffed Tomatoes, '92 182
Provençal Tomatoes, '98 267
Puffs, Tomato Cheese, '81 48
Sausage-Stuffed Tomatoes, '80 47
Scalloped Tomatoes, Stuffed, '90 29
Sea Slaw, Tomatoes Stuffed with, '89 96
Spinach-Feta Stuffed Tomatoes, '04 285
Spinach-Stuffed Baked Tomatoes, '86 14
Spinach-Stuffed Tomatoes, '89 203; '93 281
Squash-Stuffed Tomatoes, '82 102
Stuffed Tomatoes, '83 252; '96 82
Tuna-Mac in Tomatoes, '87 188
Tuna Pasta, Stuffed Tomato with, '88 54
Turkey Stuffed Tomatoes, '94 140
Vegetable Stuffed Tomatoes, '94 141
Veracruz Tomatoes, '97 169
Walnut-Rice Stuffing, Tomatoes with, '91 102
Swiss Chard with Tomatoes, '83 36
Swiss Steak Monterey, '99 23
Tabbouleh, '99 175
Tapas, Two-Tomato, '00 308
Tart, Fresh Tomato, '95 170
Tart, Herbed Tomato, '96 94
Tarts, Mini Tomato-Pesto, '02 108
Tart, Tomato, '03 158
Tart, Tomato-Basil, '98 132
Tart, Tomato-Leek-Bacon, '03 325
Tart, Tomato-Pesto, '00 195; '02 108
Tenderloin, Stuffed Tuscany, '99 269
Toasts, Tomato-Basil, '01 254
Topping, Tomato-Basil, '04 327
Venison and Tomatoes, '85 270
Vinaigrette, Tomato-Basil, '99 288
Vinegar, Tomato-Herb, '94 200
Welsh Rarebit with Tomatoes and Bacon, '92 M159
Yellow Squash, Tomato-Stuffed, '00 42
Zippy 'Maters, '99 172
Zucchini and Tomato with Herbs, '92 182
TOPPINGS. See also FROSTINGS, GLAZES, PESTOS,
    RELISHES, SALSAS, SAUCES, SYRUPS.
Savory
    Almond-Garlic Streusel, '95 159
    Almonds, Sweet-and-Spicy, '96 274; '01 42
    Apricot Vinaigrette, '05 M312
    Asian Dressing, '00 93
    Avocado Topping, '93 309; '94 96
    Biscuit Topping, '86 157, 265
    Black Pepper-Pineapple Vinaigrette, '97 181
    Blueberry-Ginger Topping, Baked Brie with, '05 179

TOPPINGS, Savory
(continued)

Blue Cheese Burger Topping, '93 218
Blue Pecan Confetti, Maple-Mustard-Glazed
    Balsamic Steaks with, '05 330
Breadcrumb Topping, '02 233
Butter-Pecan Topping, '95 158
Catsup Topping, '81 170
Cereal Topping, Crunchy, '96 216
Cheese Topping, '86 233
Chestnuts, Braised, '02 272
Chili Topping, '94 22
Chipotle-Lime Cream, '05 329
Cilantro-Lime Cream, '98 129
Citrus-Herb Dressing, '04 182
Cornbread Topping, '01 215. 298
Crabmeat Topping, '91 64
Crumble Mix, Asian, '96 327
Eggs and Cheese, '95 165
Garlic Cream, Asparagus with, '00 71
Garlic-Lime Mojo, Yuca with, '05 294
Ginger-Lime Cream, '95 227
Grecian Skillet Rib Eyes, '96 234
Guacamole, '96 170
Guacamole Aioli, '04 314
Guac, Baine's, '98 88
Horseradish Cream, '90 96; '00 277; '05 309
Jalapeño-Cilantro Dressing, Creamy, '04 311
Ketchup, Christmas, '97 254
Ketchup, Hoisin, '94 138
Ketchup, Sweet-Hot, '03 139; '04 178
Lemon Cream, '03 213
Lime Sour Cream, '04 324
Marmalade Cream, '03 230
Miso-Ginger Dressing, Creamy, '02 144
Mushrooms, Garlic and, '95 165
Nutmeg-Molasses Cream, '05 104
Nutty Topping, '86 16
Olive Salad, '00 335
Olive Salad, Doodles, '94 35
Olive Salad, Italian, '94 35
Orange Dressing, '97 129
Parmesan Crisps, '03 142
Parmesan Topping, Buttery, '05 277
Peach Ketchup, '95 306
Peach Ketchup, Spicy, '03 139
Peach Topping, '94 22
Pecans, Smoky, '01 168
Pecans, Spicy, '02 304
Pecans, Sweet-and-Spicy, '00 81; '03 178
Pecan Topping, '94 36
Pepper Topping, Rainbow, '90 117
Pico de Gallo, '96 227; '97 141; '98 87; '04 32, 61, 89, 311
Pico de Gallo, Mango, '04 318
Pimiento Topping, '83 93
Potato Topping, Mashed, '89 243
Red Chile Paste, '05 118
Red Curry-Coconut Cream, '00 197
Red Pepper Puree, '93 275; '00 241
Roasted Pepper Vinaigrette, '04 142
Roasted Red Bell Pepper Spread, '97 217
Roquefort Firecrackers, '97 19
Rum Cream, '98 271
Salad Mix, Muffy, '94 34
Salad Topping, Curry, '96 326
Sausage and Peppers, '95 165
Shrimp Topping, '93 291
Sour Cream Topping, Spicy, '95 15
Southwestern Dressing, '91 195
Sweet Potato Chips, '97 63
Tomato, Basil, and Cheese, '95 165
Tomato-Basil Topping, '04 327

Tomatoes, Marinated Green, '03 139
Top-Notch Toppings, '03 139
Tortilla Strips, '04 243
Turkey Mole, '03 18
Turkey-Vegetable Topping, '94 22
Vegetable Dip, Quick Creamy, '00 34
Vegetable Topping, '79 79
Vinaigrette, Warm Garlic, '00 324
Yogurt-Cheese Topping, '88 55

Sweet
Almond Topping, '85 152; '86 200
Apple-Nut Topping, '93 162
Apples 'n' Pears, Saucy, '96 72
Apple Topping, '89 107
Apricot Flambé Topping, '98 127
Bananas, Brown Sugar, '05 45
Bananas Hawaiian, '89 94
Blackberries Chantilly, '99 130
Blackberry Syrup, '99 131
Bourbon Whipped Cream, '04 232
Brown Sugar Topping, '81 162
Candied Cream, '04 300
Caramel Drizzle, '86 247
Chantilly Cream, '83 91
Chocolate Cream, '94 57
Chocolate Ganache, '97 282; '00 M72; '03 M286
Chocolate Ganache, Simple, '03 M212
Chocolate-Peanut Topping, '79 222
Cinnamon Crème, Apple Pie with Warm, '99 337
Cinnamon-Pecan Topping, '85 277
Coconut-Pecan Topping, '04 41
Cream Topping, Spicy, '85 177
Crème Anglaise, '05 239
Crème Chantilly, '91 297
Crème Chantilly, Gingered, '96 163
Crème Patissière, '83 225
Crumb Topping, '83 183; '88 216
Devonshire Cream, Mock, '81 288; '99 275
Firewater Cream, '00 161
Fruit Dressing, Nutty, '88 68
Fruit Fluff, Tropical, '88 68
Fruit Topping, '81 42; '87 225; '89 50; '03 145
Fruity Dessert Topping, '82 167
Ginger-Almond Topping, '01 215
Ginger Cream Topping, '84 312
Ginger-Molasses Whipped Cream, '03 297
Hazelnut Whipped Cream, '94 16
Honey Topping, '83 154
Hot Fudge Ice Cream Topping, '98 317
Hot Fudge Ice-Cream Topping, '02 109
Kahlúa Cream, '91 197
Key Lime Curd, '96 126
Lemon-Blueberry Cream, '92 153
Lemon Cream, '82 237; '04 300
Lemon Curd, '87 139; '94 315
Lemon-Pineapple Topping, '86 60
Lemon Whipped Cream, '05 255
Lime-Rum Cream, '93 169
Macadamia-Fudge Topping, '01 278
Maple-Mint Cream, '04 33
Maple-Pecan Ice Cream Topping, '98 317
Mocha Cream, '94 47
Mocha Ganache, '04 M260
Nutty Topping, '85 256
Oat Crunch Topping, '89 108
Oatmeal Cookie Topping, '95 291
Orange-Mallow Cream, '94 295
Oranges in Grand Marnier, '95 142
Oranges, Italian Caramelized, '05 101
Orange Topping, Whipped, '80 254
Orange Whipped Cream, '02 315
Paint, Egg Yolk, '86 322
Papaya Topping, '86 181
Peaches, Stewed Yard, '05 23

Pears, Sautéed, '03 195
Pear Whip, '89 94
Pecan Halves, Glazed, '02 295
Pineapple Topping, '86 239
Powdered Sugar Paints, '97 286
Praline Cream, '01 272
Raspberries, Spirited, '95 142
Raspberry Topping, '85 317
Rum Cream, '88 154
Rum Cream Topping, '80 255
Rumtopf, '95 142
Sour Cream Topping, '85 298; '86 120
Sticky Bun Toast Topper, '99 M72
Strawberries, Splendid, '05 215
Strawberry Cream, '88 153
Strawberry Topping, '86 32; '90 142
Streusel, '85 326
Streusel Topping, '88 154, M275; '94 280; '96 216;
    '01 214; '02 324; '03 195; '04 194
Sugar, Colored, '99 179
Sugared Almonds, '04 105
Sugars, Colored, '90 21; '00 61
Vanilla Cream, '81 248
Vanilla Cream Topping, '02 252
Walnuts, Candied, '05 60
Walnuts, Sugared Curried, '05 281
Whipped Cream, '05 269
Whipped Cream, Sweetened, '05 132
Whipped Cream Topping, '87 264; '89 154; '01 285;
    '03 320
Whipped Topping, Reduced-Calorie, '85 55
Wild Blueberry-and-Peach Topping, '05 326

TOP-RATED MENU RECIPES
Appetizers
Almonds, Sweet-and-Spicy, '01 42
Asparagus with Garlic Cream, '00 71
Blue Cheese Logs, '04 53
Chile-Cheese Logs, '05 64
Cranberry-Cheese Box, '03 238
Cucumber-Dill Rounds, '05 96
Dip, Quick Creamy Vegetable, '05 20
Eggs, Armadillo, '05 139
Hot Browns, Baby, '03 238
Parmesan Cheese Bites, '00 20
Pecans, Sweet-and-Spicy, '01 20
Pork Tenderloin with Mustard Sauce, '03 238
Shrimp Cocktail, Cinco de Mayo, '05 138
Shrimp, Garlic-and-Rosemary, '04 52
Shrimp Tartlets, '00 71
Tapenade, '04 194
Tomato-Cheese Torte, '00 72
Wings, Buffalo, '05 64
Apples, Minted, '00 21
Apples, Spiced, '03 36
Beverages
Bellinis, Apricot, '05 96
Cider, Mulled Pomegranate, '05 309
Coffee, Maple, '01 130
Cranberry Drink, Mulled, '03 36
Hot Chocolate Deluxe, '00 33
Slush, Lemon-Rum, '04 240
Breads
Biscuits, Blue Cheese, '05 309
Biscuits, Quick Whipping Cream, '03 238
Biscuits, Sweet Potato Angel, '01 42
Breadsticks, Parmesan Cheese, '05 20
Crescent Twists, Pecan, '03 36
Focaccia with Roasted Pepper Vinaigrette, Stuffed, '04 142
Muffins, Blueberry-Streusel, '01 131
Parmesan Bread, '00 54
Rolls, Homemade Butter, '01 21
Rolls, Sour Cream Yeast, '00 33
Scones, Orange-Pecan, '01 72
Waffles, Cornbread, '03 205

Butter, Jalapeño-Pecan-Mustard, '03 205
Cream, Horseradish, '05 309

Desserts
Brownies, Amaretto-Walnut, '04 142
Cake, Best Carrot Sheet, '03 55
Cake, Ginger Pound, '02 97
Cheesecake with Strawberry Sauce, Key Lime, '03 55
Cobbler, Apple-Gingerbread, '04 218
Cookies, Ginger-Oatmeal Sorghum, '02 230
Flan, Almond-Orange, '04 241
Freeze, Grapefruit, '00 241
Frosting, Cream Cheese, '03 55
Ganache, Chocolate, '00 M72
Glaze, Buttermilk, '03 55
Ice Cream, Lemon, '00 55
Ice Cream-Toffee Dessert, '04 82
Ice Cream, Vanilla-Cinnamon, '01 195
Layered Dessert, Lemon-Blueberry, '05 206
Petits Fours, Chocolate-Almond, '00 72
Pie, Applesauce, '01 213
Pie, Lemon Chess, '03 217
Pie, Tiramisù Toffee Trifle, '04 195
Pineapple with Vanilla-Cinnamon Ice Cream, Grilled, '01 195
Pudding, Rich Black-and-White, '01 111
Sauce, Strawberry, '03 55
Sherbet, 1-2-3 Blackberry, '00 21
Shortbread, Mocha-Chocolate, '04 173
Shortbread, Raspberry, '02 33
Tarts, Blackberry Pudding, '00 147
Dressing, Honey-Mustard, '00 54
Granola, Mixed Fruit, '05 240
Grits, Chile-Blue Cheese, '04 240
Grits, Hot Tomato, '01 131
Grits, Margaret's Creamy, '00 21
Grits, Smoked Gouda, '04 173
Grits, Stackable, '02 204

Main Dishes
Beef Fillets with Stilton-Portobello Sauce, '02 310
Beef Tenderloin, Chutneyed, '00 320
Beef Tenderloin with Henry Bain Sauce, '01 20; '04 52
Beef Tenderloin with Horseradish Cream, '05 309
Burgers, Barbara's Big Juicy, '04 M178
Casserole, Breakfast, '01 130
Casserole, Brie-and-Sausage Breakfast, '03 36
Chicken and Dumplings, '00 111
Chicken, Buttermilk Baked, '01 212
Chicken Cakes with Creole Sauce, '02 32
Chicken, Glazed Roasted, '03 217
Chicken Strips and Vegetables, Marinated, '00 54
Chicken Strips, Honey-Pecan, '05 188
Empanadas, Meaty, '05 138
Enchiladas Verde, Chicken, '00 M240
Ham-and-Swiss Breakfast Pie, Savory, '05 240
Ham with Bourbon Glaze, Baked, '01 M42
Lamb Chops with Chipotle and Cilantro Oils, Grilled, '02 96
Lamb Chops with Minted Apples, '00 20
Lasagna, Ground Sirloin, '03 143
Lasagna, Meatball, '03 142
Omelet, Farmer's Oven-Baked, '03 204
Omelet, Spinach, Cheddar, and Bacon, '03 204
Pork Chops on Smoked Gouda Grits, Grilled Maple Chipotle, '04 172
Pork Chops, Stuffed, '02 204
Pork Chops with Apples, Balsamic, '03 204
Pork Chops with Minted Apples, '00 21
Pork, Honey-Roasted, '02 282
Pork Medaillons in Mustard Sauce, '00 32
Pork Tenderloins with Rosemary Pesto, Grilled, '04 82
Quail, Chipotle-Marinated, '04 240
Rib Roast, Rosemary-Thyme, '05 248
Roast, Festive Pork, '05 46
Shrimp-and-Crab Sauce, Cajun, '05 206

Shrimp with Tropical Fruit Sauce, Grilled, '01 195
Steak-and-Vegetable Kebabs, '04 218
Steak, Chicken-Fried, '03 72
Steaks, Peppered Rib-Eye, '00 146
Tetrazzini, Smoked Turkey, '05 96
Tetrazzini with Artichokes and Red Bell Peppers, Smoked Turkey, '05 97
Trout Amandine, Classic, '01 110
Vegetables with Penne Pasta, Spicy, '04 195
Oil, Chipotle, '02 97
Oil, Cilantro, '02 97
Oranges, Grand, '01 131
Parmesan Crisps, '03 142
Pinto Beans, Mexican, '00 241
Rice, Orphan's, '04 218
Rice Pilaf, Lemon, '04 82
Risotto, Onion, '02 97
Risotto, Sweet Onion, '03 217
Rub, Biltmore Dry, '00 20

Salads and Salad Dressings
Almond-Citrus Salad, '01 42
Apple-Spinach Salad, '02 230
Asparagus, Roasted-Beet, and Goat Cheese Salad, '02 96
Asparagus Salad with Orange Vinaigrette, Grilled, '01 110
Baby Blue Salad, '01 20
Blue Cheese Dressing, '03 72
Cherry Tomato-Caper Salad, '02 32
Chicken-and-Fruit Salad, '01 178
Goat Cheese Salad, Warm, '01 179
Green Bean-Potato Salad, '04 142
Green Bean, Walnut, and Feta Salad, '00 321
Lettuce Wedges with Blue Cheese Dressing, Iceberg, '03 72
Potato Salad, Bacon 'n' Onion, '05 188
Potato Salad, Lemon-Basil, '01 178
Roasted Onion Salad, '03 142
Shrimp Salad, Old Bay, '05 188
Slaw, Crispy Asian, '01 195
Strawberry-Cranberry-Orange Salad, '05 249
Vegetable Salad, Grilled, '00 146
Vinaigrette, Balsamic, '01 20
Vinaigrette, Garlic, '03 142
Vinaigrette, Orange-Raspberry, '01 178
Vinaigrette, Sesame-Soy, '01 195
Wild Rice-Chicken Salad, '01 72

Sandwiches
Barbecue Beef Sandwiches, Slow-Cooker, '05 64
BLT Sandwiches, Italian, '02 230
Pitas, Shrimp, '05 188
Shrimp Rolls, '05 188

Sauces
Cream Sauce, '05 248
Creole Sauce, '02 32
Mustard Sauce, '00 32
Verde Sauce, '00 241
Wine Reduction Sauce, '00 321

Soups and Stews
Chili, Chunky Beef 'n' Tomato, '05 20
Cream of Pimiento Soup, '01 72
Tomato-Basil Bisque, '02 230
Tortilla Soup, '00 110
Syrup, Orange, '05 240

Vegetables
Butterbeans, Bacon, and Tomatoes, '00 184
Carrot-Pecan Casserole, '02 282
Carrots, Apricot-Glazed, '01 212
Carrot-Sweet Potato Puree, '00 32
Corn, Buttermilk Fried, '00 184
Corn, Skillet Creamed, '02 204
Corn with Jalapeño-Lime Butter, Grilled, '04 178
Green Beans, Sautéed, '05 206
Green Beans with Caramelized Onion, '00 33
Green Beans with Pimiento, Tangy, '01 21

Greens, Edna's, '00 184
Onion Pudding, Sweet, '02 310
Potato-and-Gruyère Casserole, '05 248
Potato Bake, Smoky Mashed, '01 21
Potato Casserole, Three-Cheese Mashed, '03 72
Potatoes, Roasted Garlic-Parmesan Mashed, '00 146
Potatoes, Whipped Celery, '01 212
Potato Trio, Roasted, '02 310
Red Pepper Puree, '00 241
Roasted Baby Vegetables, '05 47
Roasted Vegetables, '00 321
Steamed Asparagus with Tomato-Basil Dip, '04 53
Sugar Snap Peas, Lemon-Scented, '02 282
Tomatoes, Grilled, '04 178
Vinaigrette, Roasted Pepper, '04 142

TORTES. *See* **CAKES/Tortes.**
TORTILLAS. *See also* **BURRITOS, ENCHILADAS, FAJITAS, QUESADILLAS, TAMALES.**
Appetizers, Tex-Mex Tortilla, '86 297
Bake, Chicken Tortilla, '82 89
Bake, Texas Tortilla, '94 285
Baskets, Tortilla, '94 97
Bites, Tortilla, '95 42
Bites with Sesame-Soy Dipping Sauce, Tortilla, '02 145
Buñuelos, '80 199
Buñuelos, King-Size, '86 5
Burgers, Tortilla, '94 138
Campesina, Tortilla, '89 85
Casserole, Cabin Mexican, '97 95
Casserole, Chicken Tortilla, '81 166
Casserole, El Dorado, '81 140
Casserole, Hearty Tex-Mex Squash-Chicken, '03 107
Casserole, King Ranch Chicken, '00 280
Casserole, Light King Ranch Chicken, '04 57
Casserole, Mexican, '00 280
Casserole, Mexican Chicken, '82 143
Chalupas, Bean, '83 313
Chalupas, Chicken, '79 185
Chalupas, Chicken-Olive, '81 227
Chalupas, Texas Turkey, '80 196
Cheese Tortilla Snack, Two-, '90 119
Cheesy Tortillas, '81 62
Chicken Acapulco, '84 32
Chicken, King Ranch, '99 330
Chicken-Tortilla Stack, Cheesy, '86 3
Chicken Tostadas, '93 204
Chilaquiles, '82 220
Chilaquiles con Pollo, '81 66
Chimichangas, '86 114; '05 290
Chimichangas, Apple, '95 43
Chimichangas, Baked Spicy Beef, '97 319
Chimichangas, Bean-and-Cheese, '01 16
Chimichangas, Chicken, '98 95
Chimichangas, Oven-Fried Beef, '92 124
Chimichangas, Pineapple Dessert, '86 4
Chimichangas, Traditional Spicy Beef, '97 319
Chips, Corn Tortilla, '91 17
Chips, Light Tortilla, '90 278; '91 257
Chips, Tortilla, '91 137
Chorizo and Egg Tortillas, '81 193
Cinnamon Crisps, South Seas Ice Cream with Sweet Heat Salsa and, '04 315
Crackers, Bone, '01 204
Crackers, Tortilla-Lime, '99 17
Crisps, Fruit Salsa with Cinnamon, '01 108
Dinner, Quick Mexican, '98 224
Dippers, Rolled Tortilla, '86 4
Dumplings, Chicken and Tortilla, '99 327
Egg-and-Sausage Tortillas, '83 246; '84 42
Eggs Benedict, Southwest, '03 53
Eggs Sonora, '80 196
Espanola, Tortilla, '92 175
Fillet, Acapulco, '98 174
Flautas, '83 199; '00 293

TORTILLAS

(continued)

Flautas, Rancho Ramillete, '96 M125
Flautas with Guacamole, Chicken, '89 226
Flour Tortillas, '81 303; '95 44
Flour Tortillas, Never-Fail, '80 198
Franks, Mexican, '93 78
Garlic Crisps, '99 60
Ham Appetillas, '93 63
Huevos con Queso, '00 123
Huevos Rancheros, '82 197; '91 77; '02 72
Huevos Rancheros, Spicy, '05 221
Jumpin' Jack Tortillas, '02 54
Lasagna, Mexican, '98 283
Lasagna, Southwestern Chicken, '03 173
Lasagna, Texas, '98 52
Migas, '94 26; '98 312
Philly Firecrackers, '01 142
Picadillo, '84 118
Pie, Mexican Cheese, '82 9; '83 69
Pie, Montezuma Tortilla, '83 199
Pie, Tortilla, '85 M211; '96 135
Pie with Snappy Mango Salsa, Cuban Pulled Pork
    Tortilla, '05 329
Pigs in a Blanket, Mexican, '00 199
Pizza, Mexican, '99 119
Pizza, Southwestern, '03 146
Potato Tortilla, '00 85
Rolls, Shrimp, '05 188
Rollups, Cream Cheese, '98 134
Rollups, Mediterranean, '00 277
Rollups, Mexican, '98 134
Roll-Ups, Mexican Beef, '90 176
Rollups, Parmesan-Turkey-Ranch, '01 177
Rollups, Pizza, '99 197
Rollups, Roasted Red Pepper, '98 285
Rollups, Southwestern, '01 135
Rollups, Spinach, '98 251
Rollups, Tortilla, '89 87
Rollups, Vegetable, '98 134
Rollup, Veggie, '01 109
Salad in a Shell, Mexican, '86 4
Salads, Mexican Chicken Tortilla, '95 129
Salad, Southwestern Spiral, '98 66
Sandwiches, Caribbean Seafood, '98 105
Sandwiches, Guacamole, '82 9; '83 68
Sandwiches, Tuna Roll, '96 199
Sandwich, Tex-Mex Ham-and-Cheese, '86 4
Savory Triangles, '02 54
Snacks, Pesto Tortilla, '89 19
Soft Taco Stacks, '02 54
Soup, Spicy Tortilla, '90 32; '93 108
Soup, Supereasy Tortilla, '00 199
Soup, Tortilla, '88 31, 245; '90 201; '93 197, 274;
    '94 136; '98 291; '99 310; '00 98, 110; '04 26
Spinach and Dumplings, '00 85
Spirals, Southwestern Chicken Salad, '02 58
Stack-Ups, Tortilla, '92 196
Steak, Matt's Chicken-Fried, '97 25
Stew, Baja Pork, '98 283
Strata, Southwest Breakfast, '05 136
Strips, Tortilla, '04 243
Sweet Tortilla Triangles with Fruit Salsa, '02 54
Tacoritos, '90 133
Taquitos with Pork Picadillo, '04 206
Tostada Compuestas, '81 194
Tostadas, Chicken, '95 122
Tostadas, Chickpea-Chipotle, '01 54; '03 181
Tostadas, Crab, '93 203
Tostadas, Crispy, '83 2
Tostadas, Party, '98 M33
Tostadas, Quick Chicken, '99 159
Tostadas, Rice-and-Black Bean, '97 65
Tostadas, Shrimp-and-Black Bean, '93 204
Tostadas, Super, '83 199
Triangles, Tortilla, '94 107
Wrap, BLT, '04 298
Wrapidos, Tacos, '03 172
Wrap, Mediterranean, '03 168
Wraps, Black Bean, '00 211
Wraps, Cheese-Steak, '00 M335
Wraps, Chicken-and-Bean Slaw, '04 163
Wraps, Chicken-Cranberry, '01 34
Wraps, Club, '01 23
Wraps, Lemon-Basil Chicken Salad, '00 216
Wrap, Southwest BLT, '03 90
Wraps, Smoked Turkey, '01 61
Wraps, Thai Chicken-Avocado, '02 206
Wraps, Turkey, '00 318
Wraps, Western, '99 194

TRUFFLES. *See* **CANDIES/Truffles.**

TUNA

Amandine, Tuna, '02 165

Appetizers

Ball, Tuna-Pecan, '87 94
Cherry Tomatoes, Tuna-Stuffed, '89 214
Dip, Low-Cal Tuna, '87 25
Dip, Tasty Tuna, '96 190
Dip, Tuna-Curry, '84 31
Mold, Creamy Tuna-Cheese, '81 135
Mound, Tuna, '80 276
Mousse, Tuna, '80 275
Nachos, Tuna, '96 201
Spread, Chunky Tuna, '89 147
Spread, Tuna, '83 174; '91 305
Baked Tuna and Peas in Wine Sauce, '83 196
Bake, Shoestring Potato Tuna, '82 211
Barbecued Tuna, '80 275
Bisque, Tuna, '79 76
Broiled Tuna with Rosemary, '93 127
Burgers, Tuna, '95 128; '96 139
Burgers, Zippy Tuna, '81 135
Casserole, Biscuit-Topped Tuna, '79 113
Casserole, Easy Tuna, '82 M203
Casserole, Fabulous Tuna-Noodle, '02 63
Casserole, Nippy Tuna, '84 241
Casserole, Tangy Tuna-Broccoli, '83 75
Casserole, Tuna, '82 119; '96 103
Casserole, Tuna Vegetable, '81 135
Casserole with Cheese Swirls, Tuna, '88 256
Cheesies, Tuna, '82 191
Chopsticks, Tuna, '94 255
Creamed Chipped Tuna, '95 127
Croquettes, Tuna-Egg, '80 275
Croquettes with Parsley Sauce, Tuna, '86 108
Grilled Florida Tuna, '93 128
Grilled Tuna, Inland, '96 197
Grilled Tuna with Poblano Salsa, '91 135
Jambalaya, Tuna, '83 44
Lasagna, Tuna, '83 44; '84 123
Lemon and Capers, Tuna with, '97 180
Loaf, Mediterranean Picnic, '96 156
Macaroni Treat, Tuna-, '82 131
Melts, Curried Tuna, '95 46
Melts, Hot Tuna, '95 126; '96 201
Melt, Southwestern Tuna, '96 201
Melts, Tempting Tuna, '88 158
Melts, Tuna, '02 60
Mustard Sauce, Tuna with Tangy, '92 201
Nachos, Tuna, '95 127
Patties, Tuna, '00 247
Peppered Tuna with Crowder Peas, '00 159
Peppered Tuna with Mushroom Sauce, '05 72
Pie, Tuna-Rice, '84 123
Pie with Cheese Roll Crust, Tuna, '80 286
Pita Pocket, Tuna-in-a-, '87 202
Pita, Tuna-Veggie Stuffed, '01 216
Pockets, Tuna, '88 139
Potatoes, Tuna-Stuffed, '79 210

Salads

Almond Salad, Crunchy Tuna-and-, '04 72
Best Tuna Salad, My, '05 328
Cannellini Bean Salad, Tuna-and-, '86 143
Cheese-Sauced Tuna Salad, '87 M124
Chef Salad, Tuna, '82 78
Company Tuna Salad, '87 201
Confetti Salad, '80 4
Congealed Tuna Salad, '84 163
Creamy Tuna Salad, '82 87, 208
Crunchy Tuna Salad, '87 201
Cucumber Tuna Boats, '83 136
Curried Tuna Salad, '86 208
Curried Tuna Salad with Grapes, '87 201
Egg Salad, Tuna-, '81 135
Eggs, Tuna-Stuffed, '83 83
Favorite Tuna Salad, '82 208
Flavorful Tuna Salad, '81 37
Greens and Tuna Salad, Fresh, '80 55
Hot Tuna Salad Rolls, '84 281
Layered Tuna Salad, '84 221
Luncheon Tuna Salad, '81 135
Macaroni Salad, Tuna, '83 44, 145
Macaroni Salad, Tuna-, '84 66
Macaroni-Tuna Salad, Whole Wheat, '84 193
Meal-in-One Salad, '82 232
Niçoise, Salad, '03 35
Pasta Salad, Tuna-, '91 43; '92 141; '00 247
Pasta Salad, Tuna, '92 108
Pasta, Stuffed Tomato with Tuna, '88 54
Potato Salad, Tuna-, '84 289
Red Pepper Salad, Tuna-and-, '93 143
Rice Salad, Tuna-, '87 202
Ring, Creamy Tuna, '80 275
Sandwiches, White Bean-and-Tuna Salad, '02 31
Swiss Tuna Salad, '86 186
Taco Salad, Tuna-, '87 145
Tomatoes, Tuna-Mac in, '87 188
Tomato Salad, Tuna with Warm, '97 179
White Bean-and-Tuna Salad, '01 35
White Bean Salad, Tuna-and-, '98 209
White Bean-Tuna Salad, '98 208
Wild Tuna Salad, '95 243
Sandwich Boats, Tuna, '91 166
Sandwiches, Curried Tuna-Apple, '00 247
Sandwiches, French Toasted Tuna, '80 275
Sandwiches, Grilled-Tuna, '02 173
Sandwiches, Hot Tuna, '85 299; '86 M194
Sandwiches, Tuna Club, '83 134
Sandwiches, Tuna Roll, '96 199
Seared Tuna with Olive-Rosemary Pesto, '01 317
Southwestern Tuna Melts, '95 127
Steaks, Grilled Tuna, '90 129
Steaks on Mixed Greens with Lemon-Basil Vinaigrette,
    Seared Tuna, '94 205
Steaks with Cucumber Sauce, Tuna, '97 180
Steaks with Tarragon Butter, Tuna, '92 328
Tapenade, Tuna, '95 127; '96 201
Vegetables, Tuna with Sautéed, '98 222
Waffle-Wich, Hot Tuna, '88 272; '89 181
Yellowfin Tuna with Corn, Pepper, and Tomato Salsa, '94 164

TURKEY

à la King, Turkey, '04 232
Appetizers, Turkey, '91 314
Apple Brandy Turkey, '03 230
Baked Turkey, Cider, '83 263
Baked Turkey Tenders, '01 81
Bake, Layered Ham and Turkey, '79 252
Bake, Next-Day Turkey Dinner, '05 246
Barbecue, Turkey, '90 158
Black-Eyed Peas, Creole, '98 22

Bourbon Turkey, Hickory-Smoked, '02 270
Bread Rollups, Pizza, '04 M35
Breast and Gravy, Savory Seasoned Turkey, '89 M309
Breast, Apple-Rosemary Turkey, '99 253
Breast, Braised Turkey, '84 260
Breast, Citrus-Marinated Turkey, '94 272
Breast, Citrus-Rosemary Turkey, '02 270
Breast, Herb Butter-Basted Turkey, '86 285
Breast, Herbed Turkey, '92 266
Breast, Maple-Plum Glazed Turkey, '00 285
Breast, Smoky Turkey, '89 323
Breast, Spicy-Sweet Smoked Turkey, '03 250
Breast with Orange-Raspberry Glaze, Turkey, '91 253
Buffet Turkey, '80 29
Cabbage Rolls, Stuffed, '88 18
Casserole, Crunchy Turkey, '89 M282
Casserole, Day-After-the-Holiday, '96 276
Casserole, Golden Turkey, '80 271
Casserole, Stuffed Turkey, '88 246
Casserole, Turkey, '84 327; '96 302
Casserole, Turkey-and-Broccoli, '86 332
Casserole, Turkey-and-Sausage Wild Rice, '03 239
Casserole, Turkey-and-Shrimp Florentine, '92 122
Casserole, Turkey-Asparagus, '86 284
Casserole, Turkey-Olive, '87 268
Casserole, Turkey-Spinach, '84 71
Casserole, Turkey-Swiss, '86 283
Chalupas, Texas Turkey, '80 196
Chili, Southwestern, '91 284
Chili Topping, '84 246
Chili, Turkey-Bean, '88 M213
Chowder, Turkey, '85 10; '91 312
Chowder, Turkey-Corn, '81 98; '96 279
Citrus-and-Herb Turkey, '01 254
Cobbler, Turkey-Vegetable-Sausage, '04 325
Cornbread Crust, Turkey and Peppers in, '95 312
Creamed Turkey, Southern, '80 272
Crêpes, Elegant Turkey, '83 282
Crêpes, Turkey, '92 41
Cups, Turkey-Tomato, '84 119
Curried Cream Sauce, Turkey Slices with, '91 60
Cutlets, Oven-Fried Turkey, '91 121
Cutlets, Parmesan Turkey, '01 81
Cutlets, Pecan-Crusted Turkey, '94 282
Cutlets with Pepper Salsa, Spicy Turkey, '88 26
Cutlets with Sage Gravy, Turkey, '96 268
Cutlets with Tarragon-Mustard Sauce, Turkey, '93 239
Cutlets with Tomato-Caper Sauce, Turkey, '91 61
Deep-Fried Turkey, '92 339; '00 252
Dijon with Garden Vegetables, Turkey, '01 102
Divan, Creamy Turkey, '90 M34
Divan, Quick Turkey, '89 178
Divan, Turkey, '82 268
Dressing, Easy Turkey and, '79 296
Dressing, Fruited Turkey, '99 257
Dressing, Turkey, '85 298
Drumsticks, Grilled Turkey, '89 168
Empanadas, Easy Turkey, '96 63
Fajitas, Turkey, '01 108
Fast-and-Savory Turkey, '87 306
Florentine, Turkey, '88 264
"Fried" Rice, Turkey, '00 97
Galantine of Turkey, '85 150
Giblet Dressing and Turkey Gravy, Turkey with, '91 254
Glazed Turkey Breast, Molasses-Coffee, '03 119
Gravy, Quick Herbed Turkey, '05 270
Gravy, Savory Turkey and, '94 326
Gravy, Turkey, '91 255; '94 306
Grilled Turkey Breast with Cranberry Salsa, '95 252
Gumbo, Turkey, '82 268; '85 258
Hash, Turkey, '95 262
Herbed Turkey-in-a-Bag, '91 253
Herbed Turkey Strips with Roasted Peppers and Beans, '04 282

Indian Turkey, '85 302
Italiano, Turkey, '91 62
Jambalaya de Covington, '87 211
Jerk Turkey Tenderloin with Raspberry-Chipotle Sauce, '05 M194
Kebabs, Turkey-and-Fruit, '88 140
Lazy Day Turkey, '93 93
Loaf, Cranberry-Glazed Turkey, '86 171
Loaf, Ground Turkey, '86 171
Loaf, Herb-and-Veggie Turkey, '05 161
Loaf, Turkey, '92 33
Marinated Turkey, Benny Sauce, '98 306
Marinated Turkey with Peppery Milk Gravy, Buttermilk-, '98 311
Meatballs, Turkey, '89 237
Meat Loaf, Spinach-Stuffed Turkey, '97 24
Meat Mixture, Basic, '92 241
Mignons, Sesame-Crusted Turkey, '01 81
Mignons with Creamy Wine Sauce, Sesame-Crusted Turkey, '02 109
Mix, Ground Meat, '89 143
Molasses-Coffee Turkey Breast, '05 M289
Mole, Turkey, '03 18
Nachos, Turkey, '90 118
New Year's Turkey, '97 255
Oriental Turkey, '82 268
Parmesan, Turkey, '82 268
Parmigiana, Turkey, '87 193
Pasta
  Basil Pasta, Creamy Turkey-, '89 216
  Lasagna, Easy, '92 M197; '93 24
  Lasagna, Lean, '86 37
  Lasagna, Turkey, '83 239; '91 130
  Lasagna, Turkey-Picante, '97 93
  Noodle Bake, Turkey, '93 243
  Noodle-Poppyseed Casserole, Turkey-, '90 239
  Noodle Soup Mix, Turkey-, '89 330
  Noodle Soup, Turkey-, '91 312
  Pie, Broccoli-and-Turkey Pasta, '88 269
  Primavera, Smoked Turkey Pasta, '90 84
  Salad, Ranch-Style Turkey 'n' Pasta, '94 184
  Scaloppine, Turkey, '04 321
  Spaghetti, Ham-and-Turkey, '95 19
  Spaghetti Sauce, Turkey, '85 13
  Stroganoff, Turkey, '91 61
  Tetrazzini, Herbed Turkey, '86 47
  Tetrazzini, Smoked Turkey, '02 286; '05 96
  Tetrazzini, Turkey, '00 318; '03 257
  Tetrazzini with Artichokes and Red Bell Peppers, Smoked Turkey, '05 97
Pâté in Pastry, Turkey-Mushroom, '92 327
Patties in Vegetable-Tomato Sauce, Turkey, '87 18
Patties, Stuffed Ground Turkey, '86 171
Peppers, Turkey with, '92 182
Piccata, Turkey, '91 137
Piccata, Turkey-Basil, '96 49
Piccata with Caper Sauce, Turkey, '98 49
Pie, Crumb-Crust Curried Turkey, '86 265
Pie, Golden Turkey, '79 253
Pie, Italian Meat, '89 109
Pie, Lattice-Topped Turkey, '81 277; '82 7
Pie, Potato-Topped Turkey, '86 265
Pie, Turkey, '80 285
Pie, Turkey-and-Dressing, '84 326
Pie, Turkey-and-Oyster, '82 267
Pie, Turkey-Cheese, '88 264
Pie, Turkey Pot, '86 265; '90 24; '93 45
Pie, Turkey-Sausage, '01 297
Pie with Biscuit Crust, Turkey Pot, '98 296
Pie with Cranberry-Pecan Crusts, Turkey Pot, '02 198
Pilaf, Turkey-Asparagus, '88 200
Pilaf, Turkey-Rice, '86 284
Pizza, Turkey-Vegetable, '90 139
Puffs, Turkey-Cheese, '87 301

Rice, Herbed Turkey and, '97 327
Rice, Turkey Fried, '83 282
Roasted Turkey, '05 244
Roasted Turkey, Apple-Rosemary, '99 252
Roasted Turkey Breasts, Jackie's, '98 269
Roasted Turkey, Rosemary, '99 312
Roasted Turkey with Gravy, Old-Fashioned, '04 270
Roasted Turkey with Sausage-and-Wild Mushroom Stuffing, '96 266
Roast Turkey, '79 250; '80 262; '86 47; '88 253; '90 321
Roast Turkey and Cornbread Dressing, '89 324
Roast Turkey and Giblet Gravy, '94 308
Roast Turkey Breast and Gravy, '88 303
Roast Turkey Breast with Special Gravy, '86 282
Roast Turkey, How to, '83 286
Roast Turkey with Grandmother's Dressing, Madeira, '91 254
Roast Turkey with Herbs, '95 305
Roast Turkey with Oyster Stuffing, '80 251
Roast Turkey with Peanut Dressing, '79 283
Roast Turkey with Rice Dressing, '82 286
Roast Turkey with Sage and Thyme, '04 230
Rollups, Turkey, '86 198
Rollups, Turkey-Spinach, '00 178
Salads
  Apple Salad, Turkey-, '88 123; '90 181
  Bake, Turkey Salad, '79 253
  Caesar Salad, Turkey, '93 320
  Carrot Salad, Turkey-, '86 283
  Cobb Salad, Southern-Style Turkey, '05 214
  Curried Turkey Salad, '88 140
  Curried Turkey Salad, Chutney, '98 314
  Fruit-and-Spice Turkey Salad, '94 325
  Fruit-and-Turkey Salad, '89 176
  Fruitful Turkey Salad, '84 197
  Fruit Salad, Turkey-, '79 56
  Fruit Salad, Turkey, '83 233; '84 244
  Holiday Turkey Salad, '84 320
  Honey-Mustard Turkey Salad, '92 309; '01 230
  Hot Bacon Dressing, Turkey Salad with, '87 285
  Hot Turkey Salad, '86 10, 297; '87 176
  Layered Cornbread-and-Turkey Salad, '02 141; '05 147
  Layered Salad, Old-Fashioned, '01 96
  Layered Southwest Cornbread-and-Turkey Salad, '05 147
  Layered Turkey Salad, '86 332; '92 220
  Macaroni Salad, Turkey, '83 282
  Main Dish Turkey Salad with Cranberry Vinaigrette and Garlic Croutons, '05 246
  Meal-in-One Salad, '86 43
  Orange Salad, Turkey-in-the-, '93 21
  Pasta Salad, Ranch-Style Turkey 'n', '94 184
  Polynesian Turkey Salad, '87 285
  Sandwiches, Turkey Salad Pita, '87 202; '88 43
  Sautéed Walnuts, Turkey Salad with, '86 117
  Smoked Turkey Salad, '96 184
  Southwestern Turkey Salad, '91 313
  Stir-Fry Salad, Chilled Turkey-and-Pepper, '88 140
  Straw Salad, Turkey-in-the-, '96 286
  Taco Salad, Turkey, '95 25
  Turkey Salad, '90 318
  Waldorf Salad with Yogurt Dressing, Turkey, '88 53
  Walnut Salad, Turkey-, '03 239
  Zucchini Salad, Turkey-, '85 74
Sandwiches
  Asparagus Sandwiches, Turkey-, '96 74
  Bacon, and Havarti Sandwich, Turkey, '05 92
  Burgers, All-American Pizza, '92 148
  Burgers, Garlic Turkey, '99 135
  Burgers, Grilled Turkey, '91 61
  Burgers, Pizza, '89 165
  Burgers, Toasted Pecan, Cranberry, and Gorgonzola Turkey, '05 320
  Burgers, Turkey, '98 22
  Cheese Dogs, Turkey-, '97 203
  Club Sandwiches, Double-Decker, '91 231; '92 68

TURKEY, Sandwiches
(continued)

Clubs, Cobb, '01 22
Cranberry Salsa, Turkey Sandwiches with, '00 269
Croissant, Turkey-Cranberry, '96 320
Focaccia Sandwich, Pesto, '05 131
Ham-and-Turkey Specials, Cheesy, '84 14
Ham Pine-Berry Sandwiches, Turkey and, '00 59
Hero Sandwiches, Turkey, '92 196
Hero with Garlic Sauce, Turkey, '90 145
Hot Browns, '98 287
Hot Brown Sandwiches, '80 M202
Hot Browns, Baby, '00 107; '03 238
Hot Browns, Biscuit, '02 94
Hot Browns, Kentucky, '02 94
Hot Browns, Southwestern, '02 94
Hot Browns with Fried Cheese Grits, '02 94
Hot Turkey Sandwich, '93 306
Mayflower Sandwiches, '96 287
Meal-in-One Sandwiches, '80 218
Melt, Loaded Turkey, '05 159
Melts, Oven-Grilled Loaded Turkey, '05 159
Melts, Pineapple-Turkey, '03 159
Monte Cristo Sandwiches, '83 134; '97 319
Monte Cristo Sandwiches, Open-Faced, '01 171; '05 222
Mozzarella Rounds, Turkey-, '82 3
Open-Faced Sandwiches, '79 214
Open-Facers, Turkey, '82 190
Pineapple-Turkey Sandwich, '01 85
Rollups, Parmesan-Turkey-Ranch, '01 177
Schoolwich Sandwiches, Turkey, '00 198
Slaw Sandwich, Turkey-in-the-, '90 177
Sloppy Toms, '91 51
Smoked Turkey, Mozzarella, and Blackberry
    Sandwiches, '99 220
Smoked Turkey-Roasted Pepper Sandwiches, '94 66
Stuffed Sandwich, Deli, '98 287
Sweet Smoky Sandwiches, '97 219
Tea Sandwiches, Turkey, '99 86
Turnovers, Mexican Turkey, '02 245
Waffle-Grilled Turkey Sandwich, '94 170
Wraps, Club, '01 23
Wraps, Smoked Turkey, '01 61
Wraps, Turkey, '00 318
Wrap, Turkey, '03 168
Sausage-Cornbread Dressing, Turkey with, '83 287
Sausage, Marinara Sauce with Italian Turkey, '89 239
Sausage Patties, Breakfast Turkey, '05 169
Sauté, Creamy Turkey, '93 19
Sautéed Turkey Tenders, '01 81
Sauté, Turkey, '89 105
Scaloppine, Easy Turkey, '95 M192
Scaloppine with Angel Hair Pasta, Turkey, '02 44
Schnitzel, Turkey, '84 230
Skillet, Oriental Turkey-Orange, '86 284
Skillet Turkey Dinner, '91 61
Slices, Orange-Turkey, '90 53
Smoked Turkey, '79 293; '84 160; '85 258; '90 249
Smoked Turkey Breast, '88 169; '01 129
Smoked Turkey Medley, '90 128
Smoked Turkey, Seasoned, '97 85
Soufflé, Turkey, '80 271
Soup, Bean-and-Turkey, '93 319
Soup, Curried Turkey, '86 332
Soup, Hot Brown, '00 318
Soup Mix, Turkey-Noodle, '89 330
Soup, Tempting Turkey, '98 314
Soup, Tortilla, '00 98
Soup, Turkey-Barley, '91 312
Soup, Turkey Carcass, '86 284
Soup, Turkey-Noodle, '91 312
Soup, Turkey-Rice, '90 89

Soup, Turkey-Vegetable, '84 4; '88 264; '91 312
Soup, Williamsburg Turkey, '90 287
Soup with Cornbread Dressing Dumplings, Turkey, '03 239
Soup with Green Chile Biscuits, Fiesta Turkey, '04 233
Spread, Curried Turkey, '92 16
Spread, Turkey Party, '83 282
Squash Dressing, Turkey with, '87 248
Steaks, Grilled Marinated Turkey, '93 170
Stew, Hearty Turkey, '79 252
Stew, Turkey-Tomato, '90 279
Stir-Fry, Italian, '92 126
Stir-Fry, Turkey-Broccoli, '91 62
Stock, Light Poultry, '90 31
Strata, Turkey-Cheddar-Broccoli, '03 100
Stuffed Turkey Breast, '87 270; '89 322
Stuffed Turkey Breast, Wild Rice-, '97 281
Stuffed Turkey Breast with Seasoned Dressing, '83 320;
    '84 128
Sugar-and-Spice Cured Turkey, '02 243
Sweet-and-Sour Turkey, '79 252
Tarragon Cream, Turkey with, '91 60
Tenderloin Scaloppine, Turkey, '02 137
Tenderloins, Lime-Buttered Turkey, '92 127
Tenderloins, Maple-Plum Glazed Turkey, '00 285
Tenderloins with Lingonberry Sauce, Turkey, '97 289
Tomatoes, Turkey Stuffed, '94 140
Topping, Turkey-Vegetable, '94 22
Treats, Turkey, '93 256
Turnovers, Home-Style Turkey, '94 325
Turnovers, Turkey Sausage, '95 239
Wild Turkey, Country-Fried, '94 306
Wraps, Crispy Ginger-and-Garlic Asian Turkey Lettuce,
    '05 325

TURNIP GREENS. *See* **GREENS.**
TURNIPS
au Gratin, Turnip, '79 289
au Gratin, Turnips, '84 229; '88 229; '89 244
Boiled Turnips, '83 242
Braised Turnips, '91 219
Casserole, Baked Turnip, '82 274
Casserole, Turnip, '83 242; '84 229; '04 213
Cheese Sauce, Turnips in, '84 229
Creamy Cooked Turnips, '86 224
Dip, Turnip Green, '91 13
Fried Turnips, Shoestring, '81 274
Gingered Turnips, '82 274
Glazed Turnips, '81 274
Greens and Ham Hock, Southern Turnip, '80 119
Greens, Fresh Turnip, '92 339
Greens, Old-Fashioned Turnip, '85 255
Greens Stew, Turnip, '02 17
Greens, Turnip, '90 13, 232; '95 306
Greens, Turnip-and-Collard, '92 215
Greens with Turnips, Turnip, '84 230; '01 211
Hash Brown Turnips, '79 254
Julienne, Turnips and Carrots, '86 295
Onions, Turnips and, '83 242
Orange Carrots and Turnips, Sunset, '94 213
Parsleyed Turnips and Carrots, '79 253
Party Turnips, '84 230
Potatoes, Turnips and, '79 254
Pudding, Turnip, '94 213
Salad, Irish Turnip, '94 178
Salad, Turnip, '85 235
Salad, Turnip-and-Carrot, '91 212
Saucy Turnips, '85 289
Sauté, Carrot-Turnip, '93 241
Scalloped Potatoes and Turnips, '85 235
Scalloped Turnips, '79 254
Skillet Turnips, Sweet, '04 212
Slaw, Turnip, '89 245
Soufflé, Turnip, '79 254
Soup, Creamy Turnip, '84 279
Soup, Oyster-Turnip, '94 328

Soup, Turnip, '92 217
Southern Turnips, '87 190
Stir-Fry, Turnip-and-Carrot, '96 36
Supreme, Turnip, '79 254
Sweet-and-Sour Turnips, '81 274
Turnovers, Turnip, '04 212
Turnovers, Turnip-Bacon, '04 213
Whipped Turnip Puff, '00 254
TURTLE
Fried Cooter (Soft-Shell Turtle), '80 99
Soup au Sherry, Turtle, '80 56
Soup, Turtle, '92 92
TZIMMES
Fruit Tzimmes with Brisket, Mixed, '93 114
Sweet Potato-Beef Tzimmes, '92 234
Tzimmes, '95 102

VANILLA
Almond Crunch, Vanilla, '93 243
Beach, The, '95 168
Breakfast Ring, Almond-Vanilla, '04 M249
Cakes, Spring's Little, '01 M91
Cake, Vanilla Chiffon, '79 266
Cake, Vanilla-Jasmine-Sour Cream Tea, '05 135
Cheesecake, Creamy Vanilla, '89 93
Cookies 'n' Cream Dessert, Gold-Dusted, '94 271
Cookies, Vanilla Meringue, '01 197
Cookies, Vanilla Slice-and-Bake, '85 171
Cream, Vanilla, '81 248; '83 M115; '97 272; '00 27
Crescents, Vanilla, '82 307
Cupcakes, Golden Vanilla, '85 121
Cupcakes, Vanilla, '92 14
Cups, Vanilla Lace, '98 M93
Custard, Baked Vanilla, '82 129
Custard, Pecan Pie with Chilled Vanilla, '00 331
Custard, Vanilla, '99 27
Dessert, Glorified Vanilla Sherry, '81 85
Dip, Strawberries with Vanilla Pudding, '03 93
Éclairs, Vanilla Cream-Filled, '01 45
Extract, Home-Brewed Vanilla, '83 228
Extract, Homemade Vanilla, '83 228
Extract, Vanilla, '94 243; '97 288
Finger Painting Never Tasted So Good, '95 167
Fondant, Faux, '98 M154
Frosting, Easy Microwave, '05 M63
Frosting, Vanilla, '84 36; '85 236; '92 14, 274
Frosting, Vanilla Buttercream, '92 239; '94 99; '96 229;
    '97 111; '99 117; '03 286
Frosting, Vanilla-Rum, '85 324
Frosty, French Vanilla, '79 148
Fruit Cup, Vanilla, '80 183
Glaze, Vanilla, '85 M89; '89 211; '04 M84; '05 287
Ice Cream, Basic Vanilla, '88 202
Ice Cream, Country Vanilla, '82 143
Ice Cream) Helado, Caramel-Vanilla (Caramel-Vanilla, '81 67
Ice Cream, Honey-Vanilla, '95 178
Ice Cream, Kick-the-Can, '00 171
Ice Cream, No-Cook Vanilla, '04 179
Ice Cream, Old-Fashioned Vanilla, '97 166
Ice Cream Pumpkin, '96 255
Ice Cream Spectacular, Vanilla, '82 166
Ice Cream, Vanilla, '80 176; '86 129; '91 174; '04 275
Ice Cream, Vanilla-Cinnamon, '00 127; '01 195
Ice Cream, Vanilla Custard, '92 148; '96 145; '98 221;
    '00 143
Oil, Vanilla, '94 243
Parfait, Bodacious Peanut, '95 167
Parfaits, Hooray, '96 229
Pastry Cream, Vanilla, '01 45
Pears, Vanilla Poached, '90 57
Pie, Fruit-Topped Vanilla Cream, '84 49
Pralines, Vanilla, '92 313; '93 51
Pudding, Creamy Vanilla, '83 227

Pudding, French Vanilla Latte, '03 M282
Pudding, Vanilla, '88 32
Punch, Vanilla-Nut Coffee, '03 282
Salad, Vanilla-Scented Fruit, '05 209
Sauce, Almond-Vanilla Custard, '88 M177
Sauce, Lemon-Vanilla, '02 231
Sauce, Pan-Fried Grouper with Vanilla Wine, '94 241
Sauce, Vanilla, '97 M15
Sauce, Vanilla Cream, '05 260
Sauce, Vanilla Crème, '94 243; '96 155
Sauce, Vanilla Custard, '99 27
Sauce, Vanilla-Nutmeg, '02 208
Shortbread, Scottish, '94 242
S'mores, Indoor, '01 33
Soufflé, Frozen Vanilla, '79 230; '82 173
Soufflés with Vanilla Crème Sauce, Vanilla, '94 242; '96 155
Spooky Ghosts, '98 M256
Sugar, Vanilla, '94 243
Topping, Vanilla Cream, '02 252
Torte, Chocolate-Vanilla Holiday, '01 252
Vinaigrette, Vanilla, '94 242
Zabaglione with Fruit, Champagne Vanilla, '00 31

VEAL
Amaretto-Lime Veal, '93 54
Amelio, Veal, '86 142
au Madeira, Veal, '81 131
Birds, Veal, '84 260
Burgoo, Five-Meat, '87 3
Casserole, Veal and Wild Rice, '79 180
Casserole, Veal Cutlet, '79 109
Chops, Apple Veal, '87 220
Chops, Herb-Peppered Veal, '98 60
Chops Mediterranean, Veal, '79 108
Company Veal and Carrots, '85 22
Cordon Bleu, Veal, '87 219
Cutlets, Stuffed Veal, '92 329
Cutlets with Leeks and Zinfandel Cream, Veal, '96 237
Delight, Veal, '79 109
Grilled Pork Chops, '98 246
Herbed Veal and Onions, '79 108
Herbed Veal with Wine, '86 193
Italian Style, Veal, '82 M68
Lemon Veal, '93 35
Lemon Veal with Artichoke Hearts, '87 219
Marsala, Veal, '91 218, 310
Marsala, Veal-and-Mushrooms, '89 44
Meatballs, European Veal, '85 30
Meat Loaf, Italian, '79 187
Meat Loaf, Savory, '87 216
Meat Loaf, Triple, '79 186
Meat Loaf, Veal, '93 292
New Orleans Veal with Crabmeat, '86 94
Osso Buco, '98 260
Paprika, Veal, '88 113
Parmigiana, Veal, '81 227
Pasta with Veal and Shrimp, Angel Hair, '04 223
Peppercorns, Veal with Green, '87 220
Picante, Veal, '87 31
Piccata, Lemon Veal, '86 118
Piccata, Veal, '92 181
Piccata with Capers, Veal, '87 142
Ragoût, Veal-and-Artichoke, '94 43
Roast, Best Baked Veal, '87 219
Roast with Vegetables, Veal, '89 71
Sauce, Noodles with Veal, '80 236
Sauté, Veal-Cepe, '89 62
Savory Veal, '83 281
Scallopini à la Marsala, Veal, '79 109
Scallopini Marsala, Veal, '85 295
Scallopini of Veal al Sorriso, '79 85
Scallopini, Veal, '83 8, 125
Scallopini with Shiitakes, Veal, '99 232
Scaloppine in Lemon Sauce, Veal, '00 166
Schnitzel, Swiss, '80 189

Skillet Veal, '83 200
Soup with Quenelles, Veal-Vermicelli, '94 14
Spaghetti, Veal, '84 276
Spaghetti with Veal and Peppers, '81 201; '82 14
Steak, Veal, '82 276
Stock, Brown Meat, '90 31
Stroganoff, Veal, '79 108
Supreme, Veal, '85 109
Sweetbreads, Creamed, '90 82
Swirls, Veal-and-Smithfield Ham, '86 253
Terrine of Pork and Veal, '93 287
Terrine with Mustard Sauce, Veal, '93 118
Turkey, New Year's, '97 255
Wine Sauce, Veal and Carrots in, '81 31; '86 M139

VEGETABLES. *See also* specific types and **CASSEROLES.**
à la Grill, Vegetables, '88 130
Antipasto Skillet Dinner, '97 327

Appetizers
Antipasto, Easy, '92 24
Antipasto, Grandpa's, '98 183
Antipasto, Lemon-Vinaigrette Marinated, '04 256
Antipasto, Vegetable, '85 263
Bites, Veggie, '91 171
Canapés, Vegetable, '91 252
Caviar, Texas, '99 84; '01 160, 257
Cheesecake, Roasted Vegetable, '99 140
Cheesecake, Vegetable, '96 110
Cocktail, Fresh Vegetable, '82 165
Cream Cheese-Vegetable Squares, '04 293
Dip and Vegetable Platter, Curry, '89 327
Dip, Creamy Vegetable, '83 180; '03 25
Dip, Cucumber-Cheese Vegetable, '83 128
Dip, Fresh Vegetable, '80 249
Dip, Herb Vegetable, '89 269
Dip, Quick Creamy Vegetable, '00 34; '05 20
Dip, Starburst Vegetable, '82 248
Dip, Tangy Vegetable, '87 196
Dip, Vegetable, '79 52; '82 161; '02 18
Dip, Vegetable Garden, '85 215
Dip, Zippy Vegetable, '84 256
Egg Rolls, Tex-Mex, '01 328
Egg Rolls, Vegetarian, '86 148
Fresh Vegetables, Parsley-Dill Dip with, '85 79
Fried Veggies, '96 19
Hot Vegetable Juice Appetizer, '93 324
Marinated Vegetable Medley, '85 319; '95 91
Marinated Vegetables, '94 183; '96 213
Marinated Vegetables Italian, '90 242
Mushroom Caps, Vegetable, '81 246
Nachos, Vegetable, '91 17
Pâté, Vegetable-Chicken, '86 66
Platter with Creamy Honey-Herb Dip, Vegetable, '98 135
Relish Tree, Christmas, '84 257
Rice with Spring Vegetables, '96 132
Rollups, Vegetable, '98 134
Rollup, Veggie, '01 109
Salsa, Greek Vegetable, '98 32
Salsa, Shrimp Skewers with Vegetable, '98 32
Shrimp-and-Vegetable Appetizer, '97 161
Spread, Garden, '86 135
Spread, Garden Vegetable, '93 184
Spread, Vegetable, '90 144
Spread, Vegetable Party, '84 166
Tarragon Vegetable Appetizer, '83 277
Terrine, Chicken-Vegetable, '84 131
Terrine, Vegetable-Chicken, '83 224
Tortilla Bites with Sesame-Soy Dipping Sauce, '02 145
Tray, Fresh Vegetable Party, '82 122
Apple Cider Pork and Vegetables, '97 210
Baked Vegetables, Rosemary, '05 313
Bake, Winter, '99 273
Bake with Sweet Bacon Dressing, Vegetable-Chicken, '93 108
Barbecue Hobo Supper, '99 108

Barley and Vegetables, '91 81
Beef and Vegetables, '01 86
Beef and Vegetables, Company, '88 234
Beef and Vegetables, Savory, '79 163
Beef Brisket with Fall Vegetables, '02 237
Benne Veggies, '01 327
Black-Eyed Peas, Marinated, '01 30
Blanching Chart, Microwave, '80 M181
Bolognese, Vegetable, '00 326
Bratwurst, Grilled, '01 159
Bread Bowl, Veggie, '01 132
Bread, Breakaway Vegetable, '82 74
Bread, Herb-Vegetable-Cheese, '88 172
Broth, Vegetables with Arugula, '02 281
Brunswick Stew, Easy, '00 138
Bundles, Vegetable, '93 181
Buñuelos, '93 29
Burgers, Beef-and-Vegetable, '84 125
Burgers, Beefy Vegetable, '98 143
Burgers, Vegetable, '89 164
Burgoo, Kentucky, '97 138
Burritos, Tony's Veggie, '96 289
Burritos, Vegetable, '80 197; '90 134; '92 138
Burritos, Vegetarian, '93 319
Burritos with Avocado Sauce, Vegetable, '83 200
Buttermilk Sauce, Vegetables with, '84 6
Cabbage Rolls, Vegetarian, '91 86
Calabacitas, '95 130

Casseroles
Beef and Vegetable Chow Mein Casserole, '83 313
Beefy Vegetable Casserole, '79 248
Brunch Casserole, Italian, '03 29
Cajun Casserole, Ragin', '02 199
Cashew Casserole, '95 166
Cheesy Vegetable Casserole, '81 103
Creamy Vegetable Casserole, '98 96
Curry Casserole, Vegetable-, '91 286; '92 27
Enchiladas, Meatless, '93 106
Fresh Vegetable Casserole, '82 225
Garden Casserole, '82 168; '88 122
Garden Medley, '98 236
Gratin, Summer Vegetable, '03 159
Ham Casserole, Vegetable-and-, '84 91
King Ranch Casserole, '02 210
Lasagna, Avocado-Vegetable, '01 310
Lasagna Casserole, Vegetable, '92 198; '93 25
Lasagna, Cheesy Vegetable, '79 84
Lasagna, Colorful Vegetable, '87 19
Lasagna, Garden, '83 119
Lasagna, Roasted Vegetable-Meat, '99 M332
Lasagna, Saucy Cheese-Vegetable, '01 306
Lasagna, Vegetable, '84 201; '93 320; '95 211; '96 47; '99 97
Layered Vegetable Casserole, '91 286; '92 27
Macaroni Primavera, '96 73
Medley Bake, Vegetable, '81 268
Medley, Green Vegetable, '79 287; '80 34
Medley, Vegetable-Cheese, '99 M287
Mexican Vegetarian Casserole, '96 276
Mixed Vegetable Casserole, '83 208, 256; '86 327
Mixed-Vegetable Casserole, '87 154
Noodle Casserole, Vegetable, '91 30
Pork Combo, Vegetable-, '85 113
Rotini, Baked, '01 185
Scalloped Mixed Vegetables, '83 5
Squares, Checkerboard Vegetable, '96 178
Strata, Vegetable-Cheese, '98 98
Swiss Steak, Pizza, '02 36
Swiss Vegetable Medley, '95 26
Tuna Vegetable Casserole, '81 135
Vegetarian Casserole, '96 302
Veggies Casserole, '88 123
Wine Sauce Casserole, Vegetables in, '95 133
Winter Root Vegetable Casserole, '98 265

Cassoulet, Vegetarian, '96 329
Catfish with Vegetables and Basil Cream, Spicy, '03 56
Cheesecake, Layered Vegetable, '91 62; '92 51
Chicken and Dumplings with Vegetables, '85 M56
Chicken-and-Vegetable Platter, '88 M52
Chicken and Vegetables, '88 165
Chicken and Vegetables, Creamed, '91 90
Chicken and Vegetables, Ginger-Poached, '98 229
Chicken and Vegetables, Grilled, '99 200
Chicken and Vegetables, Jim's, '99 237
Chicken and Vegetables, Roast, '81 3
Chicken and Vegetables Vermouth, '87 M37
Chicken and Vegetables with Ginger-Soy Sauce, '91 32
Chicken, Beer-Smothered, '01 107
Chicken Breast with Turned Vegetables and Chive
    Sauce, Poached, '94 309
Chicken Cacciatore, '99 213
Chicken Chow Mein, '98 283
Chicken, Foil-Wrapped, '99 108
Chicken, Roasted Stuffed, '98 109
Chicken Sausage with Fennel, '98 312
Chicken Skillet, Confetti, '97 327
Chicken Strips and Vegetables, Marinated, '90 110
Chicken, Vegetable-Stuffed, '89 M65
Chicken, Whole Poached, '98 229
Chicken with Fresh Herbs and Vegetables, '02 91
Chicken with Vegetables, Roasted, '98 108
Chicken with Vegetables Vinaigrette, Grilled, '91 26
Chicken with Wine-Soaked Vegetables, Baked, '84 277
Chili, Bodacious, '95 14
Chili, Full-of-Veggies, '00 294
Chili, Mom's, '93 292
Chili, Vegetable, '91 28; '97 179
Chili, Vegetarian, '84 280, 327; '91 284
Chops with Vegetables, Glazed, '98 132
Chops with Vegetables, Golden, '89 218
Chowchow, '00 158
Chowchow, Nannie's, '95 250
Clubs, Cobb, '01 22
Cobbler, Autumn Vegetable, '01 215
Cobbler, Turkey-Vegetable-Sausage, '04 325
con Queso, Chile, '97 25
Cornbread-Vegetable Supper, '97 319
Cornish Hens with Vegetables, Tarragon Roasted, '94 79
Couscous, Vegetables and, '96 136
Crabs, Fried Stuffed Soft-Shell, '98 140
Crackers, Vegetable, '96 105
Crawfish Delicacy, '99 M23
Creamed Spring Vegetables, '87 127
Crêpes, Chicken-Vegetable, '83 70
Crêpes, Vegetable-Filled Bran, '86 44
Croutons, Vegetable-Flavored, '84 148
Crunchy Vegetables, '99 43
Curried Vegetables with Couscous, '04 328
Curry, Vegetable, '99 91; '04 217
Dilled Vegetable Sticks, '88 179
Dinner, Jollof Rice, '91 230; '92 325
Dinner, Pork Skillet, '00 335
Egg Rolls, Vegetarian, '86 148
Enchiladas, Meatless, '93 106
Enchiladas, Vegetable-Cheese, '94 42
en Papillote, Chicken and Vegetables, '86 145
Étouffée, Roasted Quail, '96 34
Fajitas, Slow Cooker, '02 43
Fajitas, Tex-Mex, '01 188
Fall Vegetables, '03 260
Fennel, Braised, '88 46
Fennel, Italian-Style Braised, '93 56
Fennel with Garlic Butter, Steamed, '93 56
Fish-and-Vegetable Dinner, '91 196

Fish and Vegetables, Cheesy, '94 254
Fish and Vegetables, Grilled, '89 179
Fish Rolls, Vegetable-Filled, '86 M251
Fish with Vegetables, Poached, '89 332; '90 18
Flounder Rolls, Vegetable-Stuffed, '87 6
Flounder-Vegetable Medley, '85 217
Freezing Chart, Vegetable, '85 185
Fresh Vegetable Potpourri, '79 208
"Fried" Vegetables, Garlicky, '05 177
Fries, Mixed Vegetable, '96 140
Frittata, Fresh Vegetable, '93 140
Frittata, Vegetable, '92 48; '93 183
Garbanzo-Black Bean Medley, '99 236
Garden Combo, '86 172
Garden Harvest, '85 M142
Garden Surprise, '83 112
Garnishes, '82 280; '85 338, 339
Glazed Fall Vegetables, '00 230
Glazed Vegetables, '97 105
Greens, Super-Charged, '01 211
Grilled Marinated Vegetables, '00 137; '04 133
Grilled Parsleyed Shrimp and Vegetables, '04 256
Grilled Vegetable Medley, '98 158
Grilled Vegetables, '84 172; '92 124, 231; '96 123, 173
Grilled Vegetables, Italian-Style, '92 143
Grilled Vegetable Skewers, '94 160
Grilled Vegetables, Marinated, '95 162; '00 126
Grilled Vegetables with Cilantro Butter, '98 182
Grilled Vegetables with Herbs, '00 220
Grilled Veggies, Easy, '05 194
Grouper with Confetti Vegetables, '88 M189
Ham-and-Vegetables, Skillet, '84 90
Hash, Vegetable, '95 262
Herbed-Smoked Vegetables, '85 145
Heroes, Vegetable Garden, '84 14
Honey-Dijon Vegetables, '98 311
Juice Delight, Vegetable, '84 58
Julienne Vegetables, '93 31
Julienne Vegetables with Walnuts, '86 M251
Kebabs, Beef-and-Vegetable, '91 148
Kebabs, Beef Tenderloin Shish, '00 200
Kebabs, Chicken-Vegetable, '03 95
Kebabs, Easy Vegetable, '02 142
Kebabs, Fresh Vegetable, '81 158; '92 101
Kebabs, Grilled Vegetable, '93 170
Kebabs, Marinated Vegetable, '83 M195
Kebabs, Tangy Marinated Vegetable, '88 142
Kebabs, Vegetable, '87 116; '01 132
Kebabs with Vegetables, Beef, '90 148
Kebabs with Vegetables, Marinated Beef, '99 292
Kebabs, Steak-and-Vegetable, '04 218
Kielbasa-Vegetable Dinner, '91 274
Kugel, Vegetable-Noodle, '96 228
Lamb Chops, Easy Baked, '02 66
Lamb with Vegetables, Fillets of, '85 36
Lamb with Vegetables, Roasted, '98 266
Lemon Vegetables, '93 83
Lentils and Vegetables, Savory, '98 29
Limping Susan, '90 155
Liver with Vegetables, Calf's, '85 219
Loaf, Beef-Vegetable, '79 164
Loaf, Herb-and-Veggie Turkey, '05 161
Loaf, Pureed Vegetable-Cheese, '85 297
Loaf, Vegetable Meat, '85 M29
Lo Mein, Sesame-Vegetable, '03 91
Marinade, Fresh Vegetable, '83 209
Marinade, Vegetable, '92 231
Marinated Vegetable Medley, '85 319; '89 14; '95 91
Marinated Vegetables, '79 146; '81 239; '85 67;
    '86 286; '88 4, 170; '96 176; '98 178; '99 36, 105
Marinated Vegetables, Honey-Mustard, '93 236
Marinated Vegetables, Sweet-and-Sour, '83 266
Meatballs and Vegetables with Horseradish Dressing, '91 32
Meat Loaf, Herb-and-Veggie, '05 161

Meat Loaf, Summer, '01 162
Medley, Baked Vegetable, '81 75
Medley, Barley, Vegetable, and Fruit, '05 127
Medley, Crunchy Vegetable, '84 254
Medley, Day-by-Day Vegetable, '03 219
Medley, Fresh Vegetable, '85 155
Medley, Garden Vegetable, '91 45
Medley, Herbed Vegetable, '99 46; '00 138
Medley, Italian Vegetable, '88 143
Medley, Masala Vegetable, '94 56
Medley, Mixed Vegetable, '82 126
Medley, Root Vegetable, '03 260
Medley, Sautéed Vegetable, '83 101
Medley, Skillet Vegetable, '81 134
Medley, Spring Vegetable, '86 115
Medley, Summer Garden, '84 158
Medley, Summer Vegetable, '83 208
Medley, Vegetable, '79 102; '83 112; '86 327; '89 M129
Microwaving Fresh Vegetables, '82 M138
Migas, '98 312
Mint Sauce over Vegetables, '92 104
Mirlitons, Stuffed, '97 263
Mixed Vegetables, '83 M195
Mixed Vegetables, Tangy, '96 273
Mosaic of Vegetables, '98 280
Mushroom Caps, Vegetable, '81 246
Nests, Scallops in Vegetable, '91 70
Olive Butter, Vegetables Tossed in, '91 295
Omelet, Beefy Vegetable, '83 188
Omelet, Cheddar-Vegetable, '83 205
Omelet, Cheesy Vegetable, '85 49
Omelet, Creamy Veggie, '02 248
Omelet, Fresh Vegetable, '84 211
Omelet, Garden, '99 174
Omelet, Golden Vegetable, '82 123
Omelet Primavera, '87 71
Omelet, Puffy Vegetable, '83 188
Omelet, Shrimp-and-Vegetable Oven, '99 286
Omelet, Spanish, '00 35
Omelet, Vegetable-Pasta Oven, '99 286
Omelet, Vegetarian, '84 114
Open-Faced Vegetarian Melt, '87 106
Orange Roughy, Vegetable-Topped, '93 67
Orange Roughy with Vegetables, Basil-, '92 98
Osso Buco, '98 260
Packets, Vegetable, '97 64
Paella, '97 328
Paella, Garden, '82 245
Paella, Spanish, '85 26
Pancakes, Vegetable, '88 297; '98 236
Pancakes, Vegetable-Rice, '93 43
Pancakes, Veggie, '00 85
Parmesan Vegetables, '97 147
Pasta. See also VEGETABLES/Casseroles.
    Beans and Pasta, '99 35
    Bow Ties with Crab and Vegetables, '98 233
    Fennel, Pasta with, '98 46
    Fettuccine and Vegetables, '97 178
    Fettuccine Primavera, '89 238; '94 85
    Fettuccine, Ranch House, '03 123
    Fettuccine, Vegetable, '83 312
    Fettuccini Primavera, '04 64
    Garden Pasta, '82 199
    Garden Vegetables, Pasta and, '87 192
    Grilled Vegetable Pasta, '97 142
    Italiano, Pasta, '01 41
    Linguine with Roasted Vegetables, Traveling, '93 178
    Lo Mein, Sesame-Vegetable, '03 91
    Mac-and-Cheese, Veggie, '01 111
    Mediterranean Pasta, '95 341
    Mixed Vegetables, Pasta with Sausage and, '84 249
    Noodle Bowl, Sweet-Hot Asian, '05 187
    Noodle Ring, Beef and Vegetables in a, '85 285
    Noodles with Spring Vegetables, '02 125

Orzo Primavera, '92 192
Penne, Fresh Vegetable, '05 101
Penne, Garden Sauté with, '98 207
Penne Pasta, Spicy Vegetables with, '04 195
Potpourri, Pasta, '94 33
Primavera, Almost Pasta, '86 38
Primavera, Chicken-Pasta, '91 72
Primavera, Creamy Pasta, '95 167
Primavera, Garden Spiral, '91 30
Primavera, Pasta, '85 86; '89 105; '93 168; '97 228
Primavera, Peppery Pasta, '02 161
Primavera, Smoked Turkey Pasta, '90 84
Roasted Vegetables and Pasta, '93 184
Sauce, Pasta with Vegetable, '83 163
Spaghetti, Chicken-Vegetable, '92 281; '98 296
Spaghetti, Fresh Vegetables with, '86 257
Spaghetti, Sautéed Vegetables with, '81 89
Spaghetti, Shrimp-and-Vegetable, '91 170
Spaghetti with Vegetables, '85 67
Stir-Fry Pasta, Vegetable, '96 29
Toss, Garden Pasta, '00 57
Vermicelli, Chicken, '01 237
Vermicelli, Scallop-Vegetable, '87 143
Vermicelli with Chunky Vegetable Sauce, '04 180
Peperonata, '97 291
Pepper Cups, Hot Vegetable, '88 M188
Peppers, Spicy Stuffed, '98 243
Pesto Primavera, '96 170
Picadillo, Lettuce-Wrapped, '03 193
Pickled Confetti Vegetables, '00 133
Pie, Chicken-Vegetable Pot, '81 281; '82 30
Pie Filling, Pot, '03 247
Pie, Savory Summer, '99 159; '03 182
Pie, Shortcut Greek Shepherd's, '05 238
Pies, Maque Choux, '02 182
Pies, Vegetable-Beef, '80 286
Pie with Biscuit Crust, Turkey Pot, '98 296
Pilaf, Barley-Vegetable, '91 33
Pilaf, Chicken-Vegetable, '97 51
Pilaf, Fruit-and-Vegetable Rice, '84 196
Pilau, Chicken, '99 184
Pilau, Shrimp, '99 184
Pitas, Garbanzo-Vegetable, '00 58
Pizza, Blazing Sunset, '95 267
Pizza, Deep-Dish Vegetarian, '85 243
Pizza, Garden, '89 108
Pizza, Grilled Vegetable, '98 176
Pizza, Quick 3-Cheese, '00 94
Pizza, Roasted Vegetable-and-Goat Cheese, '05 176
Pizzas, Grilled Vegetable, '97 323
Pizzas, Individual, '03 219
Pizza, Southwestern Veggie, '95 126
Pizzas, Veggie, '99 97
Pizzas, Veggie Sausage, '00 294
Pizza, Turkey-Vegetable, '90 139
Pizza, Vegetable, '89 64; '94 218
Pizza, Vegetarian Processor, '89 225
Pizza, Veggie, '94 78
Platter, Fresh Vegetable, '92 60
Platter, Vegetable, '88 M187
Pockets, Vegetable, '85 215
Pork Chops and Garden Vegetables, '88 297
Pork Chops, Skillet Vegetable, '85 179
Pork Skillet Dinner, '98 131
Pork Tenderloin with Vegetables, '01 122
Pork with Vegetables, Medaillons of, '88 223
Potatoes, Sausage-Vegetable-Topped, '98 29
Potatoes, Vegetable-Topped Stuffed, '85 235
Pot Roast, '00 65
Pot Roast, Italian, '02 88
Pot Roast Medley, Vegetable-, '83 319
Pot Roast of Beef with Vegetables, '98 65
Pot Roast with Vegetables, '80 59; '81 M208; '00 18
Pot Roast with Vegetables, Marinated, '88 M52

Primavera, Rice, '98 237
Punch, Hot Vegetable, '93 12
Puree, Smoked Vegetable, '93 156
Quesadillas, Vegetable, '97 65
Quesadilla with Roasted Salsa, Northern New Mexican
    Vegetable, '95 130
Quiche, Cheese-Vegetable, '81 228
Quiche, Ham-and-Vegetable, '84 326
Quiche, Light Vegetable, '97 332
Quiche, Vegetable, '87 M219
Ragoût of Summer Vegetables, '98 119
Ragoût, Salmon-and-Vegetable, '96 45
Ragoût, Vegetable, '89 172; '98 181
Ratatouille, '84 105, 243; '85 92; '89 174
Ratatouille-Bran Stuffed Eggplant, '86 44
Ratatouille, Eggplant-Zucchini, '81 205
Ratatouille, Microwave, '95 M232
Ratatouille Niçoise, '81 22
Ratatouille Pie, '88 198
Ratatouille, Quick-and-Easy, '80 212
Ratatouille, Sausage, '89 248
Ratatouille-Stuffed Eggplant, '83 187
Ratatouille-Stuffed Onions, '96 91
Ratatouille Supreme, '86 172
Reggae Rundown, '96 71
Relish, Eight-Vegetable, '84 179
Relish, Garden, '83 259
Relish, Vegetable, '90 147
Rib-Eyes, Italian, '98 215
Ribs, Braised Short, '98 44
Rice, Garden, '92 12
Rice Jardin, '01 106
Rice, Picadillo, '98 237
Rice Pilaf, White, '97 238
Rice, Spicy, '99 214
Rice Toss, Vegetable-, '91 309
Rice, Vegetables and, '93 91
Rice with Spring Vegetables, '96 132
Rice with Vegetables, '79 64; '85 83
Risotto, Microwave, '97 M213
Risotto Primavera, '95 163; '00 138
Risotto with Vegetables, '98 193
Roast, Easy Banquet, '99 291
Roasted Baby Vegetables, '98 61; '05 47
Roasted Fall Vegetables, '05 217
Roasted Fall Vegetables, Honey-Glazed, '99 244
Roasted Glazed Vegetables, '01 277
Roasted Root Vegetables, '00 259; '03 243
Roasted Root Vegetables, Rosemary, '01 255
Roasted Summer Vegetables, '98 213
Roasted Vegetable Medley, '01 298, 331
Roasted-Vegetable Paella, '04 89
Roasted Vegetable Quesadillas, '04 322
Roasted Vegetables, '95 64; '99 143; '00 321; '04 47
Roasted Vegetables and Pork, Oven-, '99 259
Roasted Vegetables, Bill's, '00 276
Roasted Vegetables, Fried Pork Chops with, '98 153
Roasted Vegetables, Honey-, '97 29
Roasted Vegetables with Fresh Sage, '00 125
Roasted Winter Vegetables, '97 281
Rolls with Thai Dipping Sauce, Summer, '97 236
Salads
Antipasto, Salad, '96 161
Antipasto Salad Platter, Mediterranean, '05 220
Aspic, Cheesy Vegetable, '81 73
Aspic with Horseradish Dressing, Crisp Vegetable, '87 152
Bean-and-Veggie Salad, Sweet-and-Hot, '04 184
Bean Salad, Veggie-, '04 328
Boats, Salad, '80 93
Brown Rice-and-Vegetable Salad, '84 202
Calico Salad, '82 35
Cauliflower-Vegetable Salad, '85 158
Chef's Salad, '98 209
Chicken-and-Veggie Spaghetti Salad, '04 129

Chicken Salad, Lively Lemon-, '00 16
Chicken Salad, Vegetable-, '91 287
Chicken Salad, Vegetable Patch, '04 92
Chicken Salad with Veggies, Spicy, '04 177
Chicken Strips and Vegetables, Marinated, '00 54
Chicken-Vegetable Salad, Basil-, '92 162
Chicken Vinaigrette Salad, Vegetable-, '86 135
Chilled Vegetable Salad, '00 285
Chinese Salad, '80 4
Coleslaw with Garden Vegetables, '01 57
Colorful Vegetable Salad, '04 34
Composée, Salad, '79 171
Composé, Salad, '93 126
Congealed Fresh Vegetable Salad, '82 240
Congealed Salad, Cheesy-Vegetable, '86 199
Congealed Salad, Fresh Vegetable, '91 229
Congealed Salad, Lemon-Vegetable, '85 22
Congealed Vegetable Salad, '79 276
Corned Beef Salad, Vegetable-, '80 148
Corn Salad, Colorful, '00 139
Creamy Vegetable Salad, '79 47
Creole Salad, '79 147
Crunchy Vegetable Salad, '79 11; '80 217; '83 216
Different Vegetable Salad, '82 143
Easy Vegetable Salad, '83 316; '84 16
Eight-Layer Salad, '99 107
Fennel Salad, Marinated, '93 56
Freezer Salad, '94 118
Garden Medley Salad, '80 122
Garden Salad, '87 62
Garden Salad Bowl, '82 239
Greek Salad, '93 208
Greek Salad, Dawn's World-Famous, '98 276
Greek Salad, Garden, '86 173
Greek Salad, Quick, '02 24
Greek Vegetable Salad, '99 202
Green-and-White Vegetable Salad, '79 286
Green Salad, Rich, '99 203
Greens and Veggies with Fried Okra Croutons, Salad,
    '96 178
Green Vegetable and Egg Salad, '79 191
Green Vegetable Salad, Overnight, '80 5
Grilled Marinated Vegetable Salad, '01 143
Grilled Vegetable Salad, '94 203; '00 146
Healthy Salad, '95 133
Hoppin' John Salad, '01 250
Horseradish Dressing, Vegetable Salad with, '92 85
Italian Garden Salad, '99 203
Italian Vegetable Salad, '81 253; '82 19
Layered Salad, Mexican, '02 65
Layered Vegetable Salad with Parmesan Dressing,
    '01 96
Loaded Veggie Salad, '03 58
Luncheon Salad, '84 232
Macaroni-Vegetable Salad, '86 209
Marinade, Garden, '81 23
Marinade, Medley, '79 20
Marinade, Tossed Vegetable, '84 266
Marinated Combo Salad, '82 267
Marinated Garden Salad, '00 178
Marinated Garden Vegetables, '87 252
Marinated Mixed Vegetables, '89 276; '92 106
Marinated Salad, '91 186
Marinated Salad, Eight-Vegetable, '80 218
Marinated Summer Salad, '81 153
Marinated Vegetable-Bacon Bowl, '79 191
Marinated Vegetable Medley, '95 91
Marinated Vegetable Patch Salad, '84 232
Marinated Vegetables, '85 67; '86 286; '88 4, 170
Marinated Vegetable Salad, '79 106, 143; '81 280;
    '82 163; '83 260; '84 13; '87 243; '92 64, 91;
    '97 219; '02 211; '05 129
Marinated Vegetable Salad, Crispy, '84 193
Marinated Vegetable Salad, Fresh, '86 173

VEGETABLES, Salads
(continued)

Marinated Vegetables, Creole-, '02 69
Marinated Vegetables, Honey-Mustard, '93 236
Marinated Vegetables, Zesty, '82 272
Marinated Vegetable Toss, '82 113
Marinated Veggies, '91 46; '01 127
Marinate, Fresh Vegetable, '80 33; '81 230
Meal in a Bowl, '96 138
Meal-in-One Salad, '82 232
Mediterranean Salad, '95 132
Medley Salad, Vegetable, '88 86
Mexican Salad, '81 113
Minted Vegetable Salad, '88 23; '98 158
Mixed Vegetable Salad, '80 115; '81 302; '82 239;
   '83 317; '84 16; '86 136
Next-Day Vegetable Salad, '83 81
Niçoise, Beef Salad, '99 159
Olive Salad, '98 184
Oriental Salad, Make-Ahead, '82 163
Oriental Vegetable Salad, '84 290
Overnight Salad, '98 18
Overnight Vegetable Salad, '90 33
Panzanella, '00 62
Pasta and Vegetables, '89 255
Pasta Salad, Ratatouille, '90 74
Pasta Salad, Vegetable, '89 256; '91 143
Pasta Salad, Vegetable-, '92 167
Pasta Salad with Peppered Cheese Crisps, Roasted
   Onion, '98 107
Pasta-Vegetable Salad, '95 238
Pasta-Veggie Salad, '96 106
Pebble Salad, '91 27
Pita Bread Salad, '95 86
Potato Salad, Vegetable, '03 136
Primavera Salad, '93 140
Quick Summer Italian Salad, '92 79
Radish-Vegetable Salad with Parmesan Dressing, '01 101
Rainbow Salad, '02 18
Rainbow Vegetable Salad, '83 111
Refrigerated Vegetable Salad, '84 120
Relish Salad, Vegetable, '82 267
Rice-and-Vegetable Salad, '86 42
Rice Primavera Salad, '00 131
Rice Salad, Vegetable-, '80 148; '83 198; '85 87
Ring, Tomato-Vegetable, '81 302
Riviera, Salade, '89 12
Roasted Vegetable Salad with Dried Peach
   Vinaigrette, '97 265
Rolls, Vegetable Salad, '82 278
Senator's Salad, '79 191
Seven-Layer Vegetable Salad, '79 88
Shrimp Salad, Vegetable-, '79 190
Slaw, Confetti Sweet-and-Sour, '98 89
Slaw, Layered, '93 214
Slaw, Rainbow, '01 259
Slaw, Vegetable, '81 280; '00 42
Spaghetti-Vegetable Salad, '97 196
Spinach Salad with Apricot Vinaigrette, '02 120
Spring Vegetable Salad, '88 48
Sprout Salad, Crunchy, '98 52
Summertime Salad, '79 143
Summer Vegetable-and-Orzo Salad, '00 165
Suzie or Steven Salad, '98 204
Swedish Vegetable Salad, '82 23
Sweet-and-Sour Vegetable Salad, '81 25
Tangy Vegetable Toss, '79 144
Tarragon-Vegetable Salad, '85 288
Tortellini Salad, Garden, '91 44
Tortellini Salad, Terrific, '96 134
Tossed Salad, Lively Lemon, '00 16
Variety Salad, '79 113

Vegetable Salad, '98 92; '00 136
Vinaigrette, Vegetables, '82 225, 290
Walnuts, Vegetable Salad with, '86 118
Warm Vegetable Salad, '95 174
Wild Rice-and-Roasted Vegetable Salad, '99 316
Winter Salad, '97 304
Winter Vegetable Salad, '86 42
Winter Vegetable Salad, Baked, '04 45
Salmon Scaloppine with Vegetable Confetti and Pernod
   Sauce, '94 172
Salsa, Cha-Cha, '97 160; '98 333
Salsa, Colorful, '99 119
Salsa, Fresh Vegetable, '98 194
Salsa, Garden, '91 182
Salsa, Greek Vegetable, '98 32
Salsa, Hill Country, '97 123
Salsa, Shrimp Skewers with Vegetable, '98 32, 223
Salsa, Tropical, '96 14
Salsa, Vegetable, '96 208, 220
Salsa with Citrus Dressing, Black Bean, '01 60
Sandwich, Big Veggie, '92 196
Sandwiches, Creamy Vegetable, '97 122
Sandwiches, Focaccia, '98 53
Sandwiches, Grilled Garden, '98 315
Sandwiches, Grilled Vegetable, '01 310
Sandwiches, Open-Faced Summer, '01 171
Sandwiches, Open-Face Tofu-Veggie, '86 5
Sandwiches, Summer Open-Faced, '99 201
Sandwiches, Vegetable Pita, '96 199
Sandwiches, Vegetarian Pita, '84 193
Sandwich, Vegetable Puff, '85 51
Sauce, Cheesy Vegetable, '92 M134
Sauce, Creole, '98 98
Sauce, Crescent City Grill Creole, '04 289
Sauce, Greek Fish with Vegetable, '82 72
Sauce, Tangy Vegetable, '89 280
Sauce, Turkey Patties in Vegetable-Tomato, '87 18
Sauce, Vegetable, '89 98
Sauce, Vegetable Butter, '86 174
Sauce, Vegetable-Cheese, '85 M152
Sausage, Spicy Vegetables and, '80 82
Sausage Supper, '01 28
Sausage Vegetable Dinner, '84 250
Sausage-Vegetable Skillet, '96 102
Sauté, Cajun Vegetable, '92 62
Sautéed Vegetables, Grouper with, '90 M233
Sautéed Vegetables, Tuna with, '98 222
Sautéed Vegetables with Spaghetti Squash, '84 128
Sauté, Garden, '87 90
Sautéing Fresh Vegetables, '82 138
Sauté, Tossed Vegetable, '92 138
Sauté, Vegetable-Egg, '96 204
Sauté, Vegetarian, '95 69
Scalloped Root Vegetables, '98 310
Scallops en Brochette with Vegetables, '80 163
Scallops with Vegetables, Bay, '84 233
Scramble, Veggie, '01 288
Seafood Robert, '97 106
Seasoning Blend, Vegetable, '88 29
Sesame Sauce, Vegetables with, '83 112
Shrimp and Vegetables, '82 6
Shrimp with Rice, '03 219
Skillet Dinner, Fresh Vegetable, '95 229
Skillet, Potato-Vegetable, '92 61
Skillet, Summer Vegetable, '00 138
Skillet, Vegetable-Beef, '86 172
Skillet Zucchini Combo, '96 178
Soufflé Roll, Southwestern, '97 171
Soups
   Bean Soup, Vegetable-, '83 317
   Beef-and-Barley Vegetable Soup, '89 31
   Beef and Vegetable Soup, Quick Italian, '96 235
   Beef Soup, Hearty Vegetable-, '84 102
   Beef Soup, Spicy Vegetable-, '88 11

Beef Soup, Vegetable-, '88 296; '99 219
Beefy Vegetable Soup, '79 113; '84 M38
Beefy Vegetable Soup, Quick, '80 25
Bisque, Shrimp-Vegetable, '82 313; '83 66
Black Bean Soup, '03 219
Bouillabaisse, Marcelle's, '99 200
Broth, Savory Vegetable, '81 230
Burger Soup, Vegetable-, '82 6
Cheese Soup, Creamy Vegetable-, '81 244
Cheese Soup, Creamy Vegetable, '83 230
Cheese Soup, Vegetable-, '89 15
Cheesy Vegetable Soup, '80 73; '97 241
Chicken-Vegetable Soup, '88 18; '99 60
Chicken-Vegetable Soup, Spicy, '02 168
Chili Vegetable Soup, '94 120
Chocolate Soup, Mexican, '96 277
Chowder, Cheese-Vegetable, '02 305
Chowder, Cheesy Vegetable, '80 25; '83 20; '00 272;
   '01 18
Chowder, Chicken-and-Roasted Vegetable, '97 21
Chowder, Chicken-Vegetable, '04 326
Chowder, Creamy Chicken-Vegetable, '92 20
Chowder, Easy Vegetable, '97 304
Chowder, Fiesta, '02 305
Chowder, Harvest, '83 317
Chowder, Hearty Vegetable, '88 56
Chowder, Mixed Greens, '97 262
Chowder, Oven-Roasted Vegetable, '95 229
Chowder, Potato-Vegetable, '98 335
Chunky Vegetable Soup, '89 M283
Clear Vegetable Soup, '79 130
Down-Home Vegetable Soup, '90 32
French Soup Maigre, '98 125
Garden Soup, '85 241
Garden Vegetable Soup, '83 140; '86 160
Garden Vegetable Soup, Cold, '84 197
Gazpacho, '84 112; '85 164; '01 157
Gazpacho, Chilled, '84 138
Gazpacho, Cool, '83 140
Gazpacho, Grilled Vegetable, '97 181
Gazpacho, Instant, '00 144
Gazpacho, Smoked Vegetable, '93 156
Gazpacho, Southwestern Grilled, '00 84
Gazpacho, Spring, '81 112
Gazpacho, Summer, '84 181
Harvest Soup, '79 101
Hearty Vegetable Soup, '80 26
Homemade Soup, '79 198
Leek-Vegetable Soup, '86 304
Lemongrass-and-Petits Pois Soup, '01 328
Light Vegetable Soup, '84 280
Marvelous Vegetable Soup, '82 3
Meatball Soup, Mexican, '98 315
Minestrone, Cheesy, '99 17
Minestrone, Mama's Mexican, '05 254
Mix, Vegetable Soup, '84 148
Old-Fashioned Vegetable Soup, '86 304
Pot Liquor Soup, '98 273; '01 290
Quick Vegetable Soup, '79 190; '85 24, 32
Quick Veggie Soup, '91 31
Southwestern Vegetable Soup, '97 268
Spanish Fiesta Soup, '01 66
Spicy Vegetable Soup, '79 198; '93 293; '99 337
Spring Vegetables, Lamb Soup with, '04 108
Stock, Pumpkin Soup, '00 296
Stock, Vegetable, '90 31
Tomato-Vegetable Soup, '81 177; '86 9
Turkey Soup, Tempting, '98 314
Turkey-Vegetable Soup, '84 4; '88 264; '91 312
Vegetable Soup, '80 128; '84 148; '85 106; '86 187;
   '87 83, 123; '88 266; '93 157; '98 32, 291
Watercress Soup, '01 176
Winter Vegetable Soup, Puree of, '00 322
Spicy Fruit and Veggies with Lime, '04 141

Spread, Vegetable-Egg, '87 106
Spread, Vegetable Sandwich, '83 174; '85 135
Spring Rolls, '99 238
Squash, Stuffed, '98 177
Squash, Vegetable-Stuffed, '84 104
Steak, Festive Cajun Pepper, '03 23
Steak with Pasta and Sesame-Ginger Butter, '99 142
Steak with Vegetables, Skewered, '81 124
Steak with Vegetables, Swiss, '81 273
Steamed and Minted Garden Toss, '83 173
Steamed Dinner, Easy, '83 M314
Steamed Fish and Vegetables, '91 32
Steamed Garden Vegetables, '93 155
Steamed Herbed Vegetables, '93 M303
Steamed Vegetable Medley, '86 50; '90 29
Steamed Vegetables with Garlic-Ginger Butter Sauce, '94 89
Steamed Vegetables with Mustard Sauce, '83 208
Steaming Fresh Vegetables, '82 138, 183
Stew, Brunswick, '01 148, 219; '03 29
Stew, Camp, '02 42
Stew, Chicken-and-Vegetable, '05 235
Stew, Easy Brunswick, '99 235; '05 292
Stew, Fish-and-Vegetable, '87 220
Stew, Frogmore, '00 174, 336; '03 181
Stew, Greek-Style Chicken, '03 219
Stew, Hungarian Beef, '03 35
Stew, Minestrone, '93 184
Stew, Mixed Vegetable, '84 13
Stew, Shortcut Vegetable-Beef, '89 218
Stew, Sweet-and-Sour Beef and Vegetable, '85 87
Stew, Texas, '97 211
Stew, Vegetable, '00 248
Stew, Vegetable-Beef, '94 323
Stew, Zesty Chicken, '02 127
Stir-Fry
Almond-Vegetable Stir-Fry, '86 222
Beef and Vegetables, Stir-Fried, '88 301
Beef-and-Vegetables, Stir-Fry, '84 141
Beef-and-Vegetable Stir-Fry, '81 211; '87 22; '99 204
Beef with Chinese Vegetables, '81 211
Beef with Oriental Vegetables, '84 140
Chicken and Vegetables, Almond, '86 21
Chicken and Vegetables, Chinese, '81 212
Chicken and Vegetables, Lemon, '88 118
Chicken-and-Vegetables, Stir-Fry, '86 68
Chicken and Vegetables, Stir-Fry, '86 249
Chicken and Vegetable Stir-Fry, '82 237
Chicken-and-Vegetable Stir-Fry, '96 19
Chicken and Vegetables, Walnut, '85 194
Chicken Stir-Fry, Sweet-and-Sour, '98 204
Chicken, Stir-Fry Vegetables with, '84 195
Chicken-Vegetable Stir-Fry, '83 151; '84 13, 141; '01 175
Chicken Vegetable Stir-Fry, '00 245
Chicken with Vegetables, Stir-Fry, '96 128
Chinese Vegetable Pouches, '94 34
Convenient Vegetable Stir-Fry, '95 157
Curried Vegetables, '89 219
Curry, Stir-Fried Vegetables with, '87 51
Fresh Stir-Fry, '97 179
Glazed Stir-Fry Vegetables, '99 205
Glazed Stir-Fry Vegetables and Chicken, '99 205
Lo Mein, Vegetable, '97 321
Medley, Chinese Vegetable, '84 33
Medley, Stir-Fry, '88 156
Medley Stir-Fry, Vegetable, '85 109; '99 205
Mixed Vegetable Stir-Fry, '79 268; '80 14
Mixed Veggie-and-Pork Stir-Fry, '99 206
Mixed Veggie Stir-Fry, '99 206
Orange Roughy-and-Vegetable Stir-Fry, '91 50
Orange Roughy Stir-Fry, '98 50
Oriental Vegetables, '84 26; '85 108
Salmon with Stir-Fried Vegetables, Glazed, '02 69
Sausage and Vegetables, Stir-Fry, '86 213; '87 82
Sausage Stir-Fry, '98 156

Shrimp-and-Vegetable Medley Stir-Fry, '99 205
Shrimp and Vegetables, Stir-Fry, '87 91
Shrimp Stir-Fry, '01 258
Skillet-Fried Vegetables, '88 156
Steak-and-Vegetable Stir-Fry, '84 8
Stir-Fried Vegetables, '79 217; '83 193; '90 136
Stir-Frying Fresh Vegetables, '82 138
Three-Vegetable Stir-Fry, '86 174
Vegetable Stir-Fry, '79 214; '82 M172, 208; '84 104;
   '98 156; '99 204
Stuffing, Piglet's, '04 270
Stuffing, Vegetable, '01 84
Succotash, '85 106; '98 177
Succotash, Easy, '80 165
Succotash, Garden, '04 160
Succotash, Quick, '97 302
Succotash, Summer, '86 170
Succotash with Serrano Chile Polenta, Ancho Chile, '98 104
Summer Vegetables, '91 136
Supper, Beef-and-Vegetable, '03 219
Supper, Vegetarian, '86 222
Tacos, Loaded Veggie, '00 294
Tacos, Skillet Veggie, '01 170
Tagine, Vegetable, '96 289
Tangy Vegetable Toss, '97 306
Tempura, Basic, '81 68
Tempura, Cornmeal, '81 68
Tempura Udon, '00 93
Tempura, Vegetable, '79 112
Tempura Vegetables, '00 15
Terrine, Chicken-Vegetable, '84 131
Terrine, Vegetable-Chicken, '83 224
Tomatoes, Vegetable Stuffed, '94 141
Topper, Vegetable-Cheese Potato, '86 6
Topping, Turkey-Vegetable, '94 22
Topping, Vegetable, '79 79
Torta, Mediterranean, '98 23
Torte, Layered Vegetable, '84 52
Trio, Vegetable-Herb, '83 172
Trout, Cornmeal-Crusted, '99 52
Turkey Breasts, Jackie's Roasted, '98 269
Turkey Dijon with Garden Vegetables, '01 102
Turnovers, Vegetable, '86 24
Tzimmes, '95 102
Veal Roast with Vegetables, '89 71
Vegewiches, '99 86
Venison-Vegetable Bake, '87 304
Wild Rice, Veggie, '00 141
Wrap, Garden, '03 168
Yataklete Kilkil, '95 71
Yuca Con Mojo, '93 29
Yuca with Garlic-Lime Mojo, '05 294
VENISON. *See* **GAME.**
VINEGARS
Basil Vinegar, '93 218
Cranberry Vinegar, '91 288
Dill-and-Chive Vinegar, '84 300
Garlic-Basil Vinegar, '85 124
Herb Vinegar, Five-, '85 124
Herb Vinegar, Homemade, '79 100
Herb Vinegar, Mixed, '84 107
Lemon-Mint Vinegar, '85 124
Lemon Vinegar, '95 31; '96 124
Mango-Cilantro Vinegar, '95 190
Mint Vinegar, '92 104
Orange Vinegar, '95 31
Oregano-Lemon Vinegar, Spicy, '85 124
Peach-Mint Vinegar, '95 190
Raspberry-Lemon Vinegar, '87 134
Raspberry-Thyme Vinegar, '95 190
Raspberry Vinegar, '97 146
Rosemary-Red Wine Vinegar, '97 62
Shallot-Tarragon-Garlic Vinegar, '93 191
Southwest Vinegar, '94 200

Tarragon-Dill Vinegar, '85 124
Tarragon Vinegar, '84 107; '89 194; '94 201; '97 165
Tomato-Herb Vinegar, '94 200

WAFFLES
Banana-Ginger Waffles, '86 96
Banana-Oatmeal Waffles, '94 206
Banana Split Waffles, '89 205
Belgian Waffles, '94 206
Brunch Waffles, Crunchy, '81 41
Chocolate Waffles with Strawberry Cream, '88 153
Club Soda Waffles, '94 206
Cornbread Waffles, '03 205
Cornmeal Waffles, '85 201; '94 22
Corn Waffles, '01 24
Corn Waffles with Cilantro-Lime Butter, '02 109
Crispy Waffles, '00 243
French Toast, Waffled, '82 47
French Waffles, '86 138
Fudge Waffles, '94 205
Gingerbread Waffles, '91 68
Gingerbread Waffles with Apples and Caramel, '98 M237
Light Waffles, '91 139
Oat Bran Waffles, '92 139
Oatmeal-Nut Waffles, '83 96
Oatmeal Waffles, '89 107
Peanut Butter Waffles, Honey-Buttered, '94 M206
Pecan Waffles, '87 225
Pumpkin-Nut Waffles, '86 96
Pumpkin Waffles, '95 282
Pumpkin Waffles with Mandarin Orange Sauce, Dessert,
   '89 204
Quick Bread Mix, '81 90
Quick Mix Waffles, '86 9
Refrigerator Waffles, Best Ever, '87 225
Savory
Chicken-Pecan Waffles, Southern, '82 231
Cornbread Waffles, '79 265; '91 90; '98 42
Corn-Chile Waffles, '94 206
Ham Waffles, '80 44
Rice Waffles, '98 124
Sausage Waffles, '83 50
Tuna Waffle-Wich, Hot, '88 272; '89 181
Sorghum-Ginger Waffles, '85 239
Southern Waffles, '87 225
Stack, Hoppin' John Waffle, '04 19
Sundae, Breakfast, '98 206
Sweet Potato Waffles, '88 208
Sweet Potato Waffles with Orange Butter, '90 323
Wacky Waffles, '93 195
Waffles, '81 90; '01 24
Walnut Waffles, Crunchy, '85 48
Whole Wheat Dessert Waffle, '79 92
Whole Wheat Waffles, '84 228
WALNUTS
Apple-Date-Nut Ring, '90 212
Bars, Magic Cookie, '02 253
Bars, Walnut-Date, '02 287; '03 272
Bonbons, Coconut-Black Walnut, '82 307
Breads
Apple-Nut Bread, '79 12
Apple-Nut Bread, Fresh, '87 256
Applesauce-Honey Nut Bread, '87 300
Apricot-Nut Bread, '79 24
Banana-Nut Bread, '01 239
Boule, Walnut-Raisin Pumpernickel, '02 259
Carrot-Walnut Bread, '88 284
Cherry Nut Bread, '81 306; '82 36
Chocolate Date-Nut Bread, '81 284
Cinnamon-Nut Bubble Bread, '80 22
Cranberry-Orange Nut Bread, '80 288
Date-Nut Bread, '85 306
Honey-Walnut Swirl, '80 21

Loaf, Apricot-Nut, '81 8
Loaf, Blue Ribbon Date-Walnut, '80 15
Loaf, Nutty Wheat, '90 65
Muffins, Carrot-Date-Nut, '86 262
Muffins, Holiday Pumpkin, '03 281
Muffins, Nutty Pumpkin, '86 291
Nut Bread, '04 281
Pumpkin Bread, Holiday, '03 281
Rolls, Dried Cherry-Walnut Sweet, '03 235
Scones, Merry Cranberry-Nut Yeast, '99 274
Tea Bread, Lemon-Walnut, '05 59
Twists, Fruit-Nut, '82 253
Walnut Bread, '93 77
Wine-Date Nut Bread, '82 253
Brie, Walnut-Baked, '93 241
Brie, Walnut-Fried, '86 244
Broccoli and Walnut Sauté, '95 52
Broccoli, English Walnut, '89 68
Brownies, Amaretto-Walnut, '99 311; '04 142
Brownies, Chocolate, '02 M207
Brownies, Chocolate-Walnut, '89 325
Brownies Deluxe, '03 330
Brownies for Passover, '99 56
Brownies, Walnut-Cream Cheese, '84 240
Burgers, Nutty, '87 185
Burgers, Walnut, '89 163
Butter, Spaghettini with Green Beans and Walnut
    Brown, '03 170
Cake, Apple-Nut, '87 76; '96 268
Cake, Apple-Walnut, '94 242
Cake, Black Walnut, '80 253; '84 316; '90 308
Cake, Black Walnut Pound, '92 16
Cake, Maryland Black Walnut, '05 106
Cake, Orange Nut, '80 70
Cake, Orange-Nut Butter, '80 254
Cake Roll, Date-Nut, '89 94
Cake, Saucy Pudding, '98 196
Cakes, Mini-Mincemeat Nut, '88 257
Cake, Yogurt-Lemon-Nut, '89 169
Candied Nuts, '81 261
Candied Walnuts, '05 60
Carrots with Walnuts, Julienne, '84 188
Cheese, Crostini with Walnut-Blue, '01 321
Cheese Logs, Port Wine, '02 279
Cheese Logs, Spicy Monterey Jack, '02 279
Cheese, Nutty Date Dessert, '87 299
Chicken and Vegetables, Walnut, '85 194
Chicken Breasts, Walnut-Stuffed, '85 293
Chicken, Crispy Walnut, '90 89
Chicken, Deep-Fried Walnut, '87 175
Chicken, Walnut, '85 126
Chocolate Chubbies, '01 144
Chocolate-Nut Chews, '81 92
Chutney, Cranberry-Ginger, '00 253
Citrus and Greens, Holiday, '03 280
Cobbler, Apple-Walnut, '79 154; '81 248
Coffee Cake, Cranberry-Nut, '81 250
Coffee Cake, Sour Cream-Walnut, '79 209
Coffee Cake, Walnut, '93 124
Cookies, Apple-Nut, '80 228
Cookies, Cran-bear-y Bread, '02 254
Cookies, Date Pinwheel, '02 93
Cookies, Frosted Pumpkin-Walnut, '82 217
Cookies, Ginger-Oatmeal Sorghum, '02 230
Cookies, Nutty Oatmeal, '81 130
Cookies, Rich Date-Nut Chocolate Chip, '92 207
Cookies, Simply Walnut, '91 236
Cookies, Walnut, '81 301; '97 275; '98 35
Crunch, Apple-Blueberry, '02 128
Cupcakes, Apple-Nut, '82 279

Cups, Chocolate-Walnut, '85 213
Dainties, Choco-Nut, '04 M124
Date Drops, Stuffed, '97 247
Date Moons, '01 295
Dressing, Green Beans with Walnut, '94 279
Dressing, Honey-Walnut, '93 107
Dressing, Walnut, '99 125
Eggplant with Walnuts, Georgian, '01 87
Figs with Prosciutto, Walnuts, and Cream, '96 194
Fillets, Blue Cheese-Walnut Stuffed, '95 327
Filling, Honey-Walnut, '80 21
Finikia, '96 21
Fried Walnuts, Chinese, '81 254
Frosting, Chocolate, '99 271
Frosting, Nutty Coconut, '86 8
Fruit, Cheese, and Nuts, '93 324
Fudge, Buttermilk, '97 317
Fudge, Nutty White, '81 253
Fudge, Orange-Walnut, '92 288
Green Beans, Lemon-Walnut, '93 304
Green Beans with Roquefort Cheese and Walnuts, '02 255
Greens with Raspberries and Walnuts, Mixed, '98 194
Greens with Walnuts, Mixed, '99 107
Hamburgers, Meatless Walnut, '96 243
Ice Cream Balls, Nutty, '89 72
Macaroni with Blue Cheese and Walnuts, '02 M208
Mandel Bread, '99 57
Meatballs, Mock, '81 243
Mousse, Coffee-Nut, '86 319
Panzanella, '00 62
Parmesan Walnuts, Mixed Greens with, '95 301
Pears Blue, '99 246
Pesto, Littleneck Clams with Cilantro-Black Walnut, '97 164
Phyllo Baskets, Walnut-, '93 210
Pie, Black-and-White Fudge, '99 249
Pie, Black Walnut, '97 275; '98 35
Pie, Chocolate-Walnut, '05 134
Pie, Elegant Pumpkin-Walnut Layered, '02 244
Pie, Sweetheart Fudge, '03 319
Pie, Walnut-Cranberry, '87 259
Pitas, Spinach-Walnut, '87 202; '88 43
Pudding, Fig-Walnut, '03 244
Romaine Toss, Crunchy, '00 30
Salad, Asian Chicken, '99 124
Salad, Beet, Apple, and Walnut, '98 269
Salad, Bluegrass, '02 255
Salad, Gorgonzola-Walnut, '96 170
Salad, Green Bean, Walnut, and Feta, '96 273; '00 321
Salad, Okra-Walnut, '04 291
Salad, Orange Walnut, '80 246
Salad, Ramen Noodle, '02 24
Salad, Raspberry-Walnut, '94 158
Salad, Shrimp-Walnut, '86 182
Salad, Sunburst Chicken-and-Walnut, '93 91
Salad, Turkey-Walnut, '03 239
Salad, Tuscan Fennel, '02 170
Salad, Walnut-Chicken, '89 14; '96 243
Salad with Orange Vinaigrette, Roasted Beet-and-
    Sugared Walnut, '97 229
Salad with Sautéed Walnuts, Turkey, '86 117
Salad with Walnuts, Vegetable, '86 118
Sandwich, Date-Nut Lettuce, '94 202
Sandwiches, Nutty Cream Cheese Party, '00 119
Sauce, Apricot-Walnut Hard, '88 153
Sauce, Linguine with Green Beans and Walnut, '04 128
Sauce, Spaghetti with Parsley and Walnut, '80 30
Sauce, Walnut Cream, '93 275; '01 229
Sauce, Walnut-Parmesan Pesto, '96 251; '97 104
Sherry-Orange Nuts, '86 M289
Shortbread, Blue Cheese-Walnut, '03 108
Slaw, Nutty Apple, '88 216
Snowcaps, Smoky Mountain, '00 288
Soup with Walnuts, Red Bean, '96 243
Spice Kisses, Walnut, '89 295

Spread, Corn-and-Walnut, '96 26
Spread, Date-Orange-Nut, '02 59
Spread, Date-Walnut, '87 292
Spread, Date-Walnut-Cheese, '96 322
Spread, Honey-Nut, '03 46
Spread, Nutty Fruit-and-Cheese, '87 246; '02 164
Spread with Walnuts, Buttery Blue Cheese, '00 329
Strawberries with Walnuts, Stuffed, '85 122; '86 124
Stuffing, Apple-Walnut, '95 289
Stuffing, Sausage, '00 292
Stuffing, Tomatoes with Walnut-Rice, '91 102
Sugared Curried Walnuts, '05 281
Sweet Potatoes with Sherry and Walnuts, '86 286
Swirls, Cranberry-Walnut, '00 290
Syrup, Maple-Nut, '80 228
Tart, Apricot-Nut, '99 249
Toffee, '01 218
Topping, Nutty, '86 16
Vegetables with Walnuts, Julienne, '86 M251
Vinaigrette, Maple-Walnut, '04 45
Wafers, Blue Cheese-Walnut, '00 56
Wafers, Spicy Cheese-Walnut, '03 61
Waffles, Crunchy Walnut, '85 48
Zucchini with Walnuts, '84 213
WATERMELON. *See* **MELONS.**
WHAT'S FOR SUPPER?
Appetizers
    Cherry Pepper Appetizers, Fiery Stuffed, '97 269
    Dip, Quick Creamy Vegetable, '00 34
    Dip, Quick Hummus, '05 206
Beans, Hearty Baked, '01 259
Breads
    Biscuits, Easy Pan, '05 26
    Biscuits, Fresh Tomato, '04 138
    Breadsticks, Parmesan-Garlic, '99 46
    Cheddar-Nut Bread, '03 42
    Cornbread, Buttermilk, '99 235
    Cornbread, Cheese-and-Onion, '05 35
    Knots, Cajun Bread, '03 63
    Knots, Italian Bread, '03 63
    Knots, Southwestern, '03 63
    Rolls, Hurry-Up Crescent, '97 50
    Toast, Lemon-Garlic, '05 171
Cheese Crisps, Peppered, '98 107
Chutney, Cranberry-and-Apricot, '02 286
Couscous, Lemon, '00 99
Croutons, Garlic, '05 247
Desserts
    Apple Bundles, Quick, '04 242
    Cobbler, Warm Blueberry, '98 153
    Cookies, Candy Wrap, '04 139
    Cookies, Peanut Butter-Kiss, '03 42
    Doughnut Stacks, Mini-, '05 58
    Pizza, Apple-Pineapple Dessert, '00 313
    Sundaes, Chocolate Mint, '03 M120
    Turtle Dessert, '04 127
Fried Rice, Cashew, '99 171
Grits, Chili-Cheese, '01 86
Grits, Parmesan Cheese, '02 233
Grits Squares, Chili-Cheese, '01 86
Lemonade, Pink, '01 163
Mac-and-Cheese, Veggie, '01 111
Macaroni-Mushroom Bake, '97 96
Main Dishes
    Barbecue Hobo Supper, '99 108
    Beef à la Beer, '98 64
    Beef à la Mode, '98 122
    Beef and Macaroni, Easy, '02 188
    Beef and Vegetables, '01 86
    Beef-and-Vegetable Supper, '03 219
    Beef Barbecue, Slow-Cooker, '02 299
    Beef Filets, Spicy, '00 121
    Beef Patties, Marmalade-Glazed, '01 136
    Beef Stroganoff, '03 23

Beef Stroganoff, Quick, '99 327
Brisket, Oven Barbecue, '01 259
Brisket, Smoky Barbecue, '03 160
Buffalo Hot Wings, '03 184
Buffalo Tenders, '03 184
Burgers, Stuffed Border, '04 127
Burgers, Taco, '98 224
Burgers with Caramelized Onions, Pepper, '00 218
Casserole, Beef, Cheese, and Noodle, '99 58
Casserole, Chiles Rellenos, '98 48
Casserole, Creamy Chicken-Rice, '99 21
Casserole, Fajita, '97 96
Casserole, Ham, '98 314
Casserole, Stroganoff, '98 48
Catfish Parmesan, '99 91
Catfish, Quick Pan-fried, '05 170
Chicken and Pasta, Mediterranean, '03 63
Chicken and Pears, Glazed, '99 21
Chicken-and-Rice Bake, Herbed, '02 215
Chicken and Vegetables, Grilled, '99 200
Chicken, Baked Pecan, '05 312
Chicken Bundles, Southwestern, '02 215
Chicken, Cashew, '01 188
Chicken-Cashew Fried Rice, '99 171
Chicken Casserole D'Iberville, '04 182
Chicken Curry, Indian-Style, '97 119
Chicken Cutlets, Oven-Fried, '04 81
Chicken, Dijon, '99 21
Chicken Fettuccine Alfredo, '00 57
Chicken, Foil-Wrapped, '99 108
Chicken in Foil, Barbecued, '04 222
Chicken, Lime-Grilled, '02 142
Chicken, Marmalade Baked, '99 286
Chicken, Mom's Fried, '01 163
Chicken Olé Foil Supper, '04 222
Chicken Oriental, '01 36
Chicken, Oven-Baked Barbecue, '03 160
Chicken Parmigiana, Zesty, '00 19
Chicken Penne, Cheesy, '00 289
Chicken Penne, Spicy Cheesy, '00 289
Chicken, Pinot Noir Risotto with Rosemary, '97 214
Chicken Quarters, Marinated, '02 142
Chicken Tenders, Lemon, '03 184
Chicken Thighs, Herb-Roasted, '02 127
Chicken Thighs, Honey-Pecan, '02 127
Chicken, Undercover, '97 64
Chops, Easy Scalloped Potatoes and, '00 289
Corn Puppies, '97 140
Dinner, Quick Mexican, '98 224
Drumsticks, Tangy, '97 120
Eggs, Armadillo, '97 270
Eggs, Cream Cheese Scrambled, '05 26
Enchiladas, Enticing, '99 57
Enchiladas, Green Chile, '02 188
Fajitas, Tex-Mex, '01 188
Fillets, Crispy Baked, '99 90
Fish, Baked, '98 122
Fish, Caribbean, '99 109
Fish in a Wrap, '97 64
Flank Steak, Easy Greek, '05 207
Flank Steak, Soy-Ginger, '02 90
Flank Steaks with Mushrooms, '00 121
Flounder with Lemon Couscous, Creole, '00 99
Hamburger-Corn Bake, '99 58
Hamburger-Rice Skillet, '00 236
Hamburger Steaks, Smothered, '00 289
Ham, Sweet Orange-Glazed, '02 286
Hot Dog Deluxe, '97 140
Kebabs, Pineapple-Pork, '99 144
Kielbasa with Beans, Easy Cheesy, '01 28
Lasagna, Fiesta Taco, '05 140
Loaves, Mini Teriyaki, '98 224
Manicotti, Cheesy Sausage-and-Tomato, '03 257
Manicotti, Meaty Stuffed, '00 19

Meatball Packets, Italian, '04 222
Meatballs, Marmalade-Glazed, '01 136
Meat Loaf, Alabama, '04 188
Meat Loaf, Cheeseburger, '03 204
Meat Loaf, Easy, '97 24
Meat Loaf, Spinach-Stuffed Turkey, '97 24
Meat Loaf, Sweet Ketchup-and-Bacon-Topped, '03 203
Meat Loaf, Sweet 'n' Saucy, '01 210
Meat Loaf, Teriyaki, '98 224
Meat Loaf with Feta Cheese, Lamb, '97 24
Meat Loaves, Mini Alabama, '04 188
Meat Loaves, Mini Mexican, '02 90
Meat Loaves with Spaghetti Sauce, '03 204
Noodles, Sesame, '01 188
Omelet, Shrimp-and-Vegetable Oven, '99 286
Omelet, Vegetable-Pasta Oven, '99 286
Pasta, Red Wine-Tomato-and-Steak, '05 140
Pasta Toss, Garden, '00 57
Pasta, White Wine-Tomato-and-Clam, '05 140
Peppers, Shrimp-Stuffed, '97 268
Pie, Beef-and-Onion Cornbread, '01 298
Pie, Italian Meat, '01 297
Pie, Turkey-Sausage, '01 297
Pizza Bake, Upside-Down, '98 224
Pizza, Cheesy Mexican, '00 314
Pizza, Chicken Parmesan, '00 134
Pizza, Deep-Dish, '01 29
Pizza Dogs, Grilled, '97 139
Pizzas, Individual, '03 219
Poblanos, Corn-Stuffed, '97 269
Poblanos Stuffed with Pork and Fruit, '97 269
Pork Chops and Rice, Savannah, '00 236
Pork Chops, Bourbon-Glazed, '04 44
Pork Chops, Flavorful Crusted, '04 44
Pork Chops, Greek-Style Baked, '04 44
Pork Chops in Onion Gravy, '99 222
Pork Chops, Mexican, '99 108
Pork Chops with Orange Slices, Saucy, '05 197
Pork Chops with Roasted Vegetables, Fried, '98 153
Pork Loin, Marinated, '01 331
Pork Sausage-Seasoned Rice, '00 236
Pork Stir-Fry, Sweet-and-Sour, '03 92
Pork Tenderloin, Apple Butter, '99 145
Pork Tenderloin, Grilled Balsamic, '05 241
Pork Tenderloins, Coriander-Pepper, '99 145
Pork Tenderloin with Gingered Jezebel Sauce,
    Grilled, '04 138
Pork Tenderloin with Mustard Sauce, '99 145
Potatoes, Cheddar, Broccoli, and Ham Stuffed,
    '04 26
Pot Roast, Cowboy, '05 35
Pot Roast, Italian, '05 34
Pot Roast, Mexican, '98 64
Pot Roast of Beef with Vegetables, '98 65
Pot Roast, Old-Fashioned, '98 64
Pot Roast with Dumplings, '98 245
Pot Roast with Mushroom Gravy, '02 90
Red Rice, '00 289
Red Rice and Ham, '00 289
Ribs and Beans, Spicy-Sweet, '02 299
Ribs, Slow-Cooker Barbecue, '03 160
Risotto, Redneck, '98 107
Roast, Barbecue, '98 245
Roast Beef, Mary's, '01 86
Roast Beef, Pressure Cooker, '01 86
Roast Beef, Slow Cooker, '01 86
Roast Beef, Sunday, '99 327
Sausage-and-Bean Supper, '02 233
Sausage and Cabbage, Skillet, '01 28
Sausage and Peppers with Parmesan Cheese Grits,
    '02 233
Sausage-Apple Kraut Dinner, '02 234
Sausage Supper, '01 28
Shrimp and Pasta with Cream Sauce, '98 295

Shrimp Manicotti, '97 96
Shrimp Oriental, '01 36
Shrimp with Rice, '03 219
Shrimp with Tartar Sauce, '00 178
Spaghetti, All-in-One, '98 295
Spaghetti, Chicken-Vegetable, '98 296
Spaghetti, One-Pot, '00 58
Spaghetti, Salsa, '00 58
Spaghetti with Meat Sauce, '02 188
Spinach Shells, '97 50
Spuds with Black Bean Salsa, Chicken Fajita, '04 25
Steak, Festive Cajun Pepper, '03 23
Steak, Hamburger, '99 45
Steaks, Italian Sirloin, '04 61
Steaks, Stately, '00 121
Tacos, Sausage-Egg Soft, '05 26
Tetrazzini, Turkey, '03 257
Thighs, Grilled Tarragon-Dijon, '97 120
Tuna Steaks with Cucumber Sauce, '97 180
Tuna with Lemon and Capers, '97 180
Tuna with Warm Tomato Salad, '97 179
Turkey Dinner Bake, Next-Day, '05 246
Turkey-Spinach Rollups, '00 178
Vegetable Lo Mein, Sesame-, '03 91
Mayonnaise, Caramelized Onion, '00 218
Meat Base, Savory, '02 188
Pasta, Red Wine-Tomato, '05 140
Penne, Garden Sauté with, '98 207
Pico de Gallo, '04 61
Refried Beans, Easy, '99 57
Rice Pilaf, Basil, '05 M197
Rice Pilaf, Lemon, '01 36
Risotto, Lemon-Lime, '97 213
Risotto, Microwave, '97 M213

Salads and Salad Dressings
Apple Salad, Lemony, '05 241
Apple-Spinach Salad, '99 222
Bacon Dressing, Jeweled Hot, '97 196
Black Bean Salad, '97 196; '98 208
Broccoli-Grape Salad, '01 163
Buffalo Tenders Salad, '03 184
Cabbage Salad, Tangy, '05 162
Caesar Salad, '00 19
Chicken on Greens, Grilled, '99 201
Chicken Salad, Gazpacho-, '00 203
Chili-Corn Chip Stack-Up Salad, '04 242
Coleslaw, Old-Fashioned, '99 235
Corn Salad, '02 234
Corn Salad, Roasted, '97 196
Cucumber-Radish Dressing, '00 99
Fiesta Salad, '05 58
Fried Chicken Salad, Fiesta, '03 120
Fruit-Jícama Salad, '00 203
Fruit Salad, '03 42
Garden Salad, Marinated, '00 178
Greens with Raspberry Dressing, Mixed, '97 50
Noodle Chicken Salad, '03 143
Pasta Salad, Bayou, '00 203
Pasta Salad with Peppered Cheese Crisps, Roasted
    Onion, '98 107
Pork-and-Rice Salad with Spicy Tomato Dressing,
    '03 143
Potato Salad, '01 163
Potato Salad, Charletta's, '98 153
Potato Salad, German, '97 195
Slaw, Broccoli-Squash, '05 170
Slaw, Chinese Cabbage, '01 36
Slaw, Rainbow, '01 259
Slaw, Tangy, '02 215
Spaghetti-Vegetable Salad, '97 196
Taco Salad, '02 188
Tomato Dressing, Spicy, '03 143
Tomato-Feta Lettuce Salad, '05 207
Tomato-Feta Salad, '05 207

WHAT'S FOR SUPPER? Salads and Salad Dressings *(continued)*

Turkey Salad, Chutney Curried, '98 314
Turkey Salad with Cranberry Vinaigrette and Garlic Croutons, Main Dish, '05 246
Vinaigrette, Cranberry, '05 247

Sandwiches

Barbecue Beef Sandwiches, '99 327; '01 136
Beef-and-Artichoke Open-Faced Italian Sandwich, '98 22
Burgers, Garden Herb, '01 136
Chicken Salad Melts, Open-Faced Cheesy, '00 134
Crab Melts, Open-Faced, '01 171
Fish Po'boys, Zesty, '03 120
Focaccia with Roasted Pepper Vinaigrette, Stuffed, '00 134
Grilled Cheese Meat Loaf Sandwiches, '04 188
Ham Sandwiches, Holiday, '02 286
Meat Loaf Sandwich, '01 210
Meat Loaf Sandwiches, Barbecue, '04 188
Monte Cristo Sandwiches, Open-Faced, '01 171
Open-Faced Sandwiches, Summer, '99 201
Open-Faced Summer Sandwiches, '01 171
Reubens, Summer, '00 134
Roast Beef Wraps, Tangy-and-Sweet, '05 92
Sloppy Joes, '02 188
Spread with Creamy Cucumber Sauce, White Bean, '00 178
Torta, Mediterranean, '98 23
Turkey, Bacon, and Havarti Sandwich, '05 92

Sauces

Black Bean Salsa, '04 25
Jezebel Sauce, Gingered, '04 M138
Mushroom-Artichoke Sauce, Creamy, '05 312
Pizza Sauce, '00 314
Sour Cream-Cucumber Sauce, '05 207
Special Sauce, Morton's, '01 331
Sweet 'n' Saucy Sauce, '01 210
Tex-Mex Secret Sauce, '04 127
Tomato Sauce, '97 96, 269

Soups and Stews

Black Bean Soup, '03 219
Brunswick Stew, Easy, '99 235
Chicken Soup, Mexican, '03 63
Chicken Stew, Greek-Style, '03 219
Chicken Stew, Speedy, '03 42
Chicken Stew, Zesty, '02 127
Chili, Big-Batch, '04 242
Chili, Cincinnati-Style, '00 34
Chili, Easy, '02 299
Chili in a Biscuit Bowl, '98 224
Chili, Slow Cooker Cincinnati-Style, '00 34
Chili, Three-Bean, '00 34
Étouffée, Okra, '98 207
French Onion Soup, Caramelized, '00 218
Fricassee, White Chicken, '98 122
Turkey Soup, Tempting, '98 314
Topping, Breadcrumb, '02 233
Topping, Cornbread, '01 298
Tortellini, Creamy, '99 171

Vegetables

Asparagus, Grilled, '05 197
Baked Vegetables, Rosemary, '05 313
Black-Eyed Peas, Hot-and-Spicy, '99 235
Broccoli, Garlic, '99 46
Broccoli, Lemon Pepper Steamed, '02 215
Broccoli, Stir-Fried, '00 99
Carrots and Green Beans, Dilled, '99 223
Celery, Nutty Stuffed, '03 184
Corn Fritters, '98 207
Corn on the Cob with Garlic-Chive Butter, '01 331
Eggplant Italian Style, '01 111

French Fries, Ranch-Seasoned, '05 93
Fries, Seasoned Steak, '04 127
Green Beans, Garlic, '01 111
Green Beans, Speedy Rosemary, '05 241
Kebabs, Easy Vegetable, '02 142
Mashed Potatoes, Speedy Garlic, '04 M81
Medley, Day-by-Day Vegetable, '03 219
Medley, Vegetable-Cheese, '99 M287
Onions, Caramelized, '00 218
Packets, Vegetable, '97 64
Potato Casserole, Mashed, '99 223
Potatoes, Double-Stuffed Barbecue, '05 162
Potatoes, Simple Seasoned, '01 259
Potatoes, Whipped Celery, '99 45
Roasted Vegetable Medley, '01 331
Spinach, Hot Spiked, '97 195
Squash, Southern Summer, '98 207
Vinaigrette, Apricot, '05 M312
Vinaigrette, Roasted Pepper, '00 134

WHEAT GERM

Biscuits, Wheat Germ, '86 261
Bread, Banana Wheat, '81 14
Cookies, Breakfast, '97 52
Crackers, Oatmeal-Wheat Germ, '84 236
Crisps, Sesame Wheat, '81 106
Muffins, Carrot-Wheat, '88 9
Muffins, Wheat Germ-Prune, '81 106
Pancakes, Wheat Germ, '86 242
Pancakes, Wheat Germ-Banana, '79 114
Squares, Spicy Wheat Germ, '80 44

WILD RICE. *See* **RICE/Wild Rice.**

WOK COOKING

Beef

Asparagus, Stir-Fry Beef and, '91 124
Broccoli and Beef, Stir-Fry, '83 110
Broccoli, Quick Beef and, '91 123
Broccoli, Stir-Fry Beef and, '79 47
Broccoli Stir-Fry, Beef-and-, '91 46
Carrot Stir-Fry, Beef-and-, '98 335
Chinese Beef Stir-Fry, '83 151
Chinese-Style Beef, '87 50
Chinese Vegetables, Beef with, '81 211
Coconut-Beef Stir-Fry, '97 18
Curried Beef Stir-Fry, '01 162
Hungarian Stir-Fry, '93 64
Indian Stir-Fry, '92 126
Italian Beef Stir-Fry, '99 35
Lime-Ginger Beef Stir-Fry, '92 65
Meatballs, Sweet-and-Sour, '86 240
Mongolian Beef, '85 2, 75; '01 94
Mongolian Beef Stir-Fry, '89 25
Oriental Beef, '85 20
Oriental Vegetables, Beef with, '84 140
Peanutty Beef Stir-Fry, '95 157
Pea Pods, Stir-Fry Beef and, '80 19
Shredded Beef over Rice Noodles, '85 74
Shrimp Stir-Fry, Beef-and-, '93 32
Snow Peas, Oriental Beef and, '79 105
Snow Peas, Stir-Fry Beef and, '83 22
Snow Pea Stir-Fry, Beef and, '82 98
Steak, Chinese Pepper, '82 236
Steak, Fast-and-Easy Stir-Fried, '87 50
Steak, Pepper Stir-Fry, '81 240
Steak Sukiyaki, Flank, '88 233
Stew, Beef, '86 51
Stir-Fried Beef, '84 26
Teriyaki Stir-Fry, '83 110
Thai Lemon Beef, '97 292
Vegetables, Stir-Fried Beef and, '88 301
Vegetables, Stir-Fry Beef-and-, '84 141
Vegetable Stir-Fry, Beef-and-, '81 211; '87 22; '99 204
Wontons, Tex-Mex, '87 196

Catfish Stir, '84 184
Cheese Wontons with Hot Sauce, '83 74

Chicken

Almond Chicken and Vegetables, '86 21
à l'Orange, Stir-Fry Chicken, '83 82
Braised Bourbon Chicken, '86 51
Broccoli Stir-Fry, Chicken-, '82 33
Cashew Chicken, '79 255; '83 21; '01 188
Cashews, Chicken with, '79 207
Cashews, Szechwan Chicken with, '81 212
Chinese, Chicken, '94 33
Chinese Chicken and Vegetables, '81 212
Chinese Chicken Stir-Fry, '90 100
Chinese-Style Dinner, '84 26
Curry, Stir-Fried Chicken, '87 51
Easy Chicken Stir-Fry, '91 124
Garden, Chicken-in-a-, '80 18
Herb-Chicken Stir-Fry, '89 177
Hurry-Up Chicken Stir-Fry, '91 124
Italian Stir-Fry, '92 126
Lemon Chicken, '86 173
Mexican Stir-Fry, '92 126
Orange-Chicken Stir-Fry, '84 68
Orange-Chicken Stir-Fry, Kyoto, '87 96
Oriental, Chicken, '01 36
Oriental Chicken with Peanuts, '82 236
Oriental Chicken with Pineapple, '86 42
Pineapple-Chicken Stir-Fry, '89 176
Plum Sauce, Chicken with, '82 236
Princess Chicken, '86 122
Shiitake-Chicken Stir-Fry, '89 61
Snow Pea Stir-Fry, Chicken and, '95 157
Soy and Wine, Chicken in, '84 26
Sweet-and-Sour Chicken, '86 240
Szechuan Chicken, '98 155
Szechwan Chicken, '83 85
Tempura Delight, Chicken, '85 66
Thai Chicken Stir-Fry, '00 23
Vegetables and Chicken, Glazed Stir-Fry, '99 205
Vegetables, Jim's, Chicken and, '99 237
Vegetables, Stir-Fry Chicken with, '96 128
Vegetable Stir-Fry, Chicken-, '83 151; '84 13, 141
Vegetable Stir-Fry, Chicken, '00 245
Vegetable Stir-Fry, Chicken-and-, '82 237; '86 68; '96 19
Vegetables with Chicken, Stir-Fry, '84 195
Walnut Chicken, '85 126
Walnut Chicken and Vegetables, '85 194
Zesty Stir-Fried Chicken, '83 82
Zucchini Stir-Fry, Chicken-, '84 50

Egg Rolls, '86 81
Egg Rolls, Scrumptious, '96 101
Indian Stir-Fry, '92 126
Orange Roughy-and-Vegetable Stir-Fry, '91 50
Orange Roughy Stir-Fry, '98 50
Pasta Potpourri, '94 33
Pear Fritters, Ol' Timey, '86 51

Pork

Cashews, Stir-Fry Pork and, '01 16
Curried Pork Tenderloin, '86 76
Eggrolls, Shrimp and Pork, '82 240; '83 18
Garlic Sauce, Stir-Fried Pork in, '84 141
Ham and Zucchini Stir-Fry, '79 47
Ham Stir-Fry, Easy, '86 332
Hot-and-Spicy Pork, '81 228
Kung Pao Pork, '96 49
Mixed Veggie-and-Pork Stir-Fry, '99 206
Moo Shu Pork, '99 237
Onions with Bean Sauce, Pork-and-, '85 76
Oriental, Pork, '81 212
Sausage, Fried Rice with, '83 12
Sausage Rolls with Sweet-and-Sour Sauce, '83 74
Sausage Stir-Fry, '82 236; '98 156
Stir-Fried Pork, '87 51
Sweet-and-Sour Pork, '79 42; '80 227; '81 26; '85 34, 194
Sweet-and-Sour Pork Stir-Fry, '03 92

Rice, Easy Fried, '84 76
Rice, Egg Fried, '80 19
Rice, Fried, '00 273
Rice Special, Fried, '80 56
Rice with Sausage, Fried, '83 12
Scallop Stir-Fry, '94 32
Shrimp and Refried Rice, '89 176
Shrimp and Sirloin Supreme, '81 131
Shrimp-and-Vegetable Medley Stir-Fry, '99 205
Shrimp and Vegetables, Stir-Fry, '87 91
Shrimp, Hoisin, '99 237
Shrimp Oriental, '01 36
Shrimp Skillet, Quick, '87 50
Shrimp, Stir-Fry, '96 129; '01 95
Shrimp Stir-Fry, Cajun, '92 127
Shrimp, Szechuan, '86 173
Shrimp, Tangy Honeyed, '94 32
Shrimp with Snow Peas, '85 75
Sugar Flips, '83 74
Swordfish Stir-Fry, '96 128
Szechuan Ginger Stir-Fry with Noodle Pancake,
    '97 292

Turkey
Broccoli Stir-Fry, Turkey-, '91 62
Rice, Turkey , '00 97
Spring Rolls, '99 238

Vegetables
Asparagus and Mushrooms, '85 108
Asparagus, Stir-Fried, '87 52
Bok Choy-Broccoli Stir-Fry, '84 2
Bok Choy, Stir-Fried, '97 105
Broccoli, Jade-Green, '80 12
Broccoli, Stir-Fried, '83 227
Broccoli, Stir-Fry, '80 19
Broccoli with Sesame, '80 13
Broccoli with Sesame Seeds, '82 34; '02 45
Brussels Sprouts Stir-Fry, '81 308
Cabbage, Lemon-Butter, '88 156
Cabbage, Stir-Fried, '81 75, 271; '85 109
Chinese Vegetable Medley, '84 33
Chinese Vegetable Pouches, '94 34
Convenient Vegetable Stir-Fry, '95 157
Curry, Stir-Fried Vegetables with, '87 51
Egg Rolls, Vegetarian, '86 148
Fresh Stir-Fry, '97 179
Glazed Stir-Fry Vegetables, '99 205
Green Bean Medley, '85 108
Green Beans, Stir-Fried, '85 148
Greens, Stir-Fried, '94 33; '97 270
Lo Mein, Sesame-Vegetable, '03 91
Medley, Stir-Fry, '88 156
Medley Stir-Fry, Vegetable, '85 109; '99 205
Mixed Vegetable Stir-Fry, '79 268; '80 14
Mixed Veggie Stir-Fry, '99 206
Mushrooms with Bacon, Stir-Fried, '80 123
Onion-Asparagus Stir-Fry, Sweet, '98 135
Oriental Vegetables, '84 26; '85 108
Pasta Potpourri, '94 33
Pasta, Vegetable Stir-Fry, '96 29
Peas and Peppers, Stir-Fried, '87 51
Potato-Snow Pea Stir-Fry, '86 173
Skillet-Fried Vegetables, '88 156
Spinach, Chinese, '79 179
Spinach, Stir-Fry, '81 182
Spinach with Mushrooms, '80 19
Spinach Wontons, '83 74
Squash Medley, '84 128
Squash Medley, Stir-Fried, '80 123
Squash, Stir-Fried, '97 118
Squash Stir-Fry, '80 184
Squash Stir-Fry, Two-, '86 174
Sweet Potato Pudding, '86 52
Three-Vegetable Stir-Fry, '86 174
Tomato-Zucchini Stir-Fry, '80 158

Turnip-and-Carrot Stir-Fry, '96 36
Vegetables, Stir-Fried, '79 217; '83 193; '90 136
Vegetable Stir-Fry, '82 208; '84 104; '99 204
Zucchini-and-Tomato Stir-Fry, '85 108
Zucchini, Italian-Style, '80 123
Zucchini Pesto, '84 194
Zucchini Toss, Stir-Fry, '88 156

WONTONS
Bowls, Wonton Wrapper, '95 58
Cheese Wontons with Hot Sauce, '83 74
Chicken Wontons, '92 284
Chicken Wontons with Hoisin Peanut Dipping Sauce,
    '99 14
Chips, Baked Wonton, '91 138
Chips, Cinnamon-and-Sugar Wonton, '91 138
Chips, Garlic Wonton, '91 138
Chips, Lemon-and-Herb Wonton, '91 138
Chips, Parmesan Cheese Wonton, '91 138
Fried Wonton Envelopes, '95 96
Fried Wontons, Crispy, '83 21
Fruit-Filled Wontons, '85 287
Lasagna, Won Ton Spinach, '04 129
Lobster Scallion Shooters, '00 197
Moroccan Triangles, Crispy, '03 60
Nibbles, Wonton, '85 287
Pork on Mixed Greens, Hot Sesame, '97 19
Preparation Techniques, '83 74
Sausage Rolls with Sweet-and-Sour Sauce, '83 74
Sesame Dumplings, Steamed, '97 208
Sesame Wontons, Spicy Crab-and-Ginger Salsa with, '01 283
Spinach Wontons, '83 74
Sugar Flips, '83 74
Taco Teasers, '01 134
Tex-Mex Wontons, '87 196

YOGURT
Apples, Honey-Yogurt, '92 46
Bread, Yogurt, '97 130
Breakfast-in-a-Bowl, '89 87
Carambola-Yogurt Calypso, '90 169
Cheese Appetizer, Yogurt, '04 217
Cheese, Yogurt, '04 217
Chicken, Grilled Yogurt-Lemon, '81 111
Chicken, Savory Yogurt, '91 238; '92 28
Chicken, Yogurt-Sesame, '90 216
Coffee Freeze, Amaretto-, '99 161
Coleslaw, Grilled Chicken Breasts with Lemon-Yogurt,
    '98 148

Desserts
Bars, Lemon Yogurt Wheat, '79 93
Cake, Strawberry Yogurt Layer, '94 85
Cake, Yogurt-Lemon-Nut, '89 169
Cake, Yogurt Pound, '84 10
Chocolate Yogurt, Mocha Sauce with, '92 243
Dip, Strawberries with Mint Yogurt, '03 93
Ice, Apricot Yogurt, '81 177
Ice Milk, Banana Yogurt, '89 199
Ice, Peach-Yogurt, '84 83
Lemon-Chiffon Frozen Yogurt, '85 54
Nectarines Royale, '85 132
Parfait, Crunchy Strawberry-Yogurt, '79 124
Peach Yogurt, Frozen Fresh, '90 139
Pie, Strawberry Yogurt, '80 232
Pie, Strawberry-Yogurt, '85 122; '86 124
Pie, Yogurt-Apricot, '85 132
Pie, Yogurt-Cheese, '82 121
Pops, Pineapple-Yogurt, '91 173
Sauce, Honey-Yogurt, '92 307
Strawberry Yogurt Delight, '85 77
Strawberry-Yogurt Dessert, '90 295
Tortoni, Apricot-Yogurt, '95 124
Vanilla Frozen Yogurt, '87 125
Dip, Cucumber-Yogurt, '99 93

Dip, Curry, '85 132
Dip, Fruited Yogurt, '84 171
Dip, Yogurt, '94 21
Dip, Yogurt Herring, '80 232
Dressing, Asparagus with Yogurt, '79 66
Dressing, Ginger-Yogurt, '81 302
Dressing, Honey-Yogurt, '93 172
Dressing, Lemon-Yogurt, '93 17
Dressing, Low-Cal Dilled Yogurt, '05 128
Dressing, Orange-Yogurt, '85 304
Dressing, Sweet-Hot Yogurt, '86 40
Dressing, Turkey Waldorf Salad with Yogurt, '88 53
Dressing, Yogurt, '85 59, 215; '88 27
Dressing, Yogurt-Herb, '92 96
Dressing, Yogurt-Honey Poppy Seed, '83 177
Dressing, Yogurt Salad, '79 69
Filling, Fresh Raspberry Crêpes with Yogurt, '93 123
Fruit Medley, Yogurt-Granola, '91 58
Herbed Yogurt, '96 66
Honey Yogurt, Orange Slices with, '91 68
Lima Beans, Minted, '98 86
Malt, Chocolate-Yogurt, '01 173
Muffins, Yogurt, '88 55
Muffins, Yogurt-Muesli, '90 215
Omelet, Yogurt-Avocado, '81 33
Pancakes, Orange-Yogurt, '87 225
Peach Yogurt Refresher, '03 166
Pineapple-Yogurt Whirl, '91 132
Pork Tenderloin with Yogurt and Lime, Grilled,
    '04 216
Potatoes, Yogurt-Stuffed, '88 24
Rolls, Yogurt Crescent, '91 123
Salad, Crème de Menthe, '82 122
Salad, Cucumber-Yogurt, '87 33
Salad, Frozen Yogurt, '92 303
Salad, Strawberry Yogurt, '80 232
Salad, Yogurt-Cucumber, '82 122
Salad, Yogurt Fruit, '81 114; '96 247
Sauce, Creamy Yogurt, '91 238; '92 28
Sauce, Cucumber-and-Yogurt Dipping, '02 172
Sauce, Cucumber-Yogurt, '03 44
Sauce, Lamb Meatballs with Yogurt, '85 132
Sauce, London Broil Sandwiches with Yogurt-
    Cucumber, '01 162
Sauce, Yogurt, '89 283; '05 321
Sauce, Yogurt-Cucumber, '04 216
Sauce, Yogurt-Horseradish, '85 66
Shake, Light Double Strawberry-Banana, '01 173
Shake, Strawberry-Yogurt, '87 199
Shake, Three-Fruit Yogurt, '01 173
Slaw or Salad Dressing, Lemon-Yogurt, '88 54
Smoothie, Fruited Honey-Yogurt, '88 231; '89 23
Smoothie, Honey-Yogurt, '97 326
Smoothie, Strawberry, '97 173
Smoothie, Yogurt-Fruit, '03 25
Snack, Yogurt, '88 55
Soup, Avocado-Banana-Yogurt, '80 78
Soup, Cucumber-Yogurt, '82 157; '83 205
Soup, Potato-Yogurt, '92 217
Soup, Yogurt Fruit, '86 176
Spread, Cucumber-Yogurt, '00 135
Spread, Herbed Yogurt, '02 169
Sundae, Breakfast, '98 206
Tangy Yogurt, '02 258
Topping, Yogurt-Cheese, '88 55

YUCA
Buñuelos, '05 295
Con Mojo, Yuca, '93 29
Garlic-Lime Mojo, Yuca with, '05 294

ZUCCHINI
Appetizers
Caviar, Zucchini, '88 212

ZUCCHINI, Appetizers
(continued)

Crab-Zucchini Bites, '84 M216
Dip, Yellow Squash-Zucchini, '89 48
French Fried Zucchini with Cocktail Sauce,
 '86 146
French Fries, Zucchini, '82 78
Fries, Zucchini, '90 147
Hors d'Oeuvres, Zucchini, '80 151
Pizzas, Zucchini, '88 212
Scalloped Zucchini Bites, '91 165
Shrimp Appetizers, Zucchini-, '89 311
Baked Zucchini, '83 209
Baked Zucchini Fans, '87 243
Bars, Zucchini, '85 77
Basil, Zucchini and Tomatoes, '89 147
Boats with Spinach, Zucchini, '82 252
Boats, Zucchini, '85 M143
Breads
Apple Bread, Zucchini-, '87 255
Banana-Zucchini Bread, '85 326
Carrot Bread, Zucchini-, '83 190
Chocolate-Zucchini Bread, '93 308
Fritters, Cheesy Zucchini, '88 44
Fritters, Zucchini, '81 163
Honey Bread, Zucchini-, '89 143
Loaves, Zucchini, '96 130
Muffins, Carrot-Zucchini, '01 200
Muffins, Zucchini, '83 121; '86 146
Spiced Zucchini Bread, '79 161; '86 162
Spicy Zucchini Bread, '81 305; '82 36
Squares, Zucchini, '82 103
Zucchini Bread, '85 111; '86 93
Broiled Zucchini, Quick-and-Easy, '86 169
Buttered Zucchini and Carrots, '83 252
Cajun Squash, '88 142
Cake, Chocolate-Zucchini, '85 156; '02 181
Cake, Zucchini, '79 24
Cake, Zucchini-Carrot, '93 20
Cake, Zucchini-Pineapple, '95 160
Calabaza Guisada con Puerco (Pumpkin Cooked
 with Pork), '80 193
Carrots and Zucchini, '84 262
Carrots, Zucchini with Baby, '88 24
Casseroles
au Gratin, Potatoes-and-Zucchini, '84 5
au Gratin, Zucchini and Tomato, '82 208
Bacon, Zucchini, and Cornbread Bake, '99 123
Beef Bake, Zucchini-, '86 146
Calabaza Mexicana (Mexican Squash), '81 196
Carrot and Zucchini Casserole, '83 256
Carrot Casserole, Zucchini-, '99 61
Cheese-Egg-Zucchini Casserole, '84 114
Cheesy Zucchini Casserole, '82 168; '84 145
Corn-Zucchini Bake, '79 178
Egg Casserole, Zucchini-, '84 M113
Eggplant and Zucchini, Italian-Style, '79 289;
 '80 26
Italian Squash, '79 158
Italian Zucchini Casserole, '85 59
Jack Casserole, Zucchini-, '85 296
Lasagna, Garden, '83 119
Lasagna, Zucchini, '85 194
Manicotti, Zucchini, '84 194
Mexican Squash, '83 31
Parmesan, Zucchini, '81 108
Parmesan Zucchini, '81 234
Rice Casserole Italiano, Zucchini-, '89 146
Sausages Baked Zucchini and, '80 300
Scallop, Green-and-Gold, '81 159
Squash Bake, '82 107
Squash Casserole, '96 252

Stuffed Zucchini with Pasta, '97 101
Tomato Bake, Zucchini and, '82 158
Tomato Casserole, Zucchini-and-, '88 265
Zucchini Casserole, '79 157; '87 154
Chicken, Moroccan Garlic, '99 15
Citrus-Herb Dressing, Zucchini with,
 '04 182
Coleslaw, Fiesta Zucchini, '91 168
Cookies, Spicy Zucchini, '97 273
Corn and Zucchini, '83 190
Corn Combo, Zucchini-, '86 218
Corn, Zucchini and, '86 177
Crab Cakes, Mock, '95 159
Crêpes, Zucchini, '79 157
Crispies, Zucchini, '95 179
Delight, Zucchini-Basil, '85 267
Dilled Fresh Zucchini, '81 174
Dilled Summer Squash, '96 148
Dilled Zucchini and Corn, '83 173
Dressing, Zucchini, '86 282
Easy Zucchini, '87 167
Eggplant and Squash, '83 187
Eggplant and Zucchini, Sautéed, '82 96
Fans, Baked Zucchini, '88 246
Fans, Herb Butter Zucchini, '90 201
Fans, Zucchini, '91 33
Fried Zucchini Strips, '81 184
Fries, Parmesan-Zucchini, '95 129
Frittata, Corn-and-Squash, '89 144
Frittata, Zucchini, '86 103
Fruitcake, Zucchini, '88 284
Fry, Zucchini, '81 102
Gratin, Tomato-Zucchini, '95 171
Green Beans with Zucchini, '84 128; '02 251
Grilled Zucchini Fans, '89 200
Grilled Zucchini with Feta, Greek, '95 190
Herbed Zucchini, '84 104
Italiano, Zucchini, '81 183
Italian Squash, '79 158
Italian-Style Zucchini, '80 123
Italian Zucchini, '83 M147
Jam, Zucchini, '00 168
Julienne Zucchini and Carrots, '90 M14
Lemon-Garlic Zucchini, '89 226
Marinated Squash Medley, '94 126
Marinated Zucchini, '80 33; '89 102
Medley, Zucchini-and-Corn, '80 298; '81 25
Mexican Style, Zucchini, '80 184
Omelet, Zucchini, '81 99
Oven-Fried Zucchini, '86 211
Oven-Fried Zucchini Spears, '91 121
Pancakes, Zucchini, '93 43
Parmesan, Zucchini, '81 108; '82 103
Pecans, Zucchini with, '87 31
Pesto, Zucchini, '84 194
Pie, Cheesy Zucchini, '82 103
Pie, Italian-Style Zucchini, '83 43
Pie, Zucchini, '98 236
Pie, Zucchini-Ham-Cheese, '80 272
Pollo con Calabacita (Mexican Chicken with
 Zucchini), '82 219
Provençal, Zucchini, '86 146
Quiche, Cheesy Zucchini, '83 312
Quiche, Swiss-Zucchini, '82 49
Quiche, Zucchini-Mushroom, '79 127
Quiche, Zucchini-Sausage, '83 122
Ratatouille, Eggplant-Zucchini, '81 205
Relish, Pollock with Summer Squash, '92 200
Relish, Sweet Zucchini, '95 159
Relish, Zucchini, '87 200
Roasted Zucchini, '02 89
Rosemary, Summer Squash with, '88 143
Salad, Apple-and-Zucchini, '97 216
Salad, Carrot-and-Zucchini, '83 240

Salad, Creamy Avocado and Zucchini, '79 208
Salad, Marinated Zucchini, '82 164; '90 32
Salad, Mushroom-Zucchini, '85 8
Salad, Summer Zucchini, '95 229
Salad, Turkey-Zucchini, '85 74
Salad, Zucchini, '82 104; '87 103; '89 128
Salad, Zucchini-Artichoke, '91 229
Salad, Zucchini Chef's, '83 143
Salad, Zucchini-Corn Marinated, '98 236
Salsa, Zucchini-Carrot, '05 298
Sandwiches, Open-Faced Zucchini, '88 159
Sandwiches, Skillet Squash, '98 144
Sauce, Spaghetti with Zucchini, '81 38
Sauce, Zucchini-Mushroom, '93 71
Sautéed Squash and Carrots, '05 42
Sautéed Squash and Zucchini, '05 203
Sautéed with Fresh Mint, Zucchini, '03 87
Sautéed Zucchini, '83 86; '92 60
Sautéed Zucchini and Carrots, '92 62, 99
Sautéed Zucchini and Sausage, '83 289
Sautéed Zucchini with Mushrooms, '94 135
Sauté, Zucchini, '81 183; '84 35
Scramble, Zucchini-Basil, '87 34
Shrimp, Grilled Zucchini-Wrapped, '98 200
Skillet, Pattypan-Zucchini, '82 103
Skillet, Squash, '82 195
Skillet, Zippy Zucchini, '82 158
Skillet, Zucchini-and-Corn, '01 137
Skillet Zucchini Combo, '96 178
Skillet, Zucchini-Tomato, '93 206
Soufflés, Zucchini-Corn, '97 203
Soufflé, Zucchini, '79 157
Soufflé, Zucchini-and-Corn, '83 265
Soups
Chilled Zucchini Soup, '87 90
Chilled Zucchini Soup with Fresh Vegetable
 Salsa, '98 194
Cilantro, Zucchini Soup with, '93 130
Cold Zucchini Soup, '85 265; '92 64;
 '99 164
Cream of Zucchini Soup, '83 99
Creamy Zucchini Soup, '83 140
Dilled Summer Soup, '99 182
Dilled Zucchini Soup, '90 88
Green Soup, '98 23
Italian Sausage-Zucchini Soup, '84 4
Summer Squash Soup, '84 193
Watercress-Zucchini Soup, '91 72
Zucchini Soup, '82 104; '84 181; '86 181;
 '89 14
South-of-the-Border Zucchini, '85 135
Spaghetti, Italian Zucchini, '85 2
Spaghetti, Zucchini, '83 160
Stir-Fried Squash Medley, '80 123
Stir-Fry, Chicken-Zucchini, '84 50
Stir-Fry, Ham and Zucchini, '79 47
Stir-Fry, Squash, '80 184
Stir-Fry, Tomato-Zucchini, '80 158
Stir-Fry, Two-Squash, '86 174
Stir-Fry, Zucchini-and-Tomato, '85 108
Stir-Fry Zucchini Toss, '88 156
Stuffed Zucchini, '86 54, 187; '89 M133
Stuffed Zucchini, Beef-, '86 M139
Stuffed Zucchini, Ham and Cheese, '79 157
Stuffed Zucchini, Italian, '84 119
Stuffed Zucchini Main Dish, '79 215
Stuffed Zucchini, Savory, '80 161
Stuffed Zucchini, Southwestern, '03 M127
Stuffed Zucchini Supreme, '83 136
Stuffing, Haddock Fillets with Zucchini,
 '88 M191
Timbales, Corn-and-Zucchini, '92 100
Tomatoes with Herbs, Zucchini and, '92 182
Toss, Zucchini, '91 292